P9-CSB-870

John Dewey Library
Johnson State College
Johnson, Vermont 0565

PSYCHOANALYSIS
THE MAJOR CONCEPTS

PSYCHOANALYSIS
THE MAJOR CONCEPTS

EDITED BY

BURNESS E. MOORE, M.D.

AND BERNARD D. FINE, M.D.

EDITORIAL BOARD

ALVIN FRANK, M.D.

JULES GLENN, M.D.

LEO GOLDBERGER, PH.D.

EUGENE HALPERT, M.D.

OTTO F. KERNBERG, M.D.

SELMA KRAMER, M.D.

SYDNEY E. PULVER, M.D.

RALPH E. ROUGHTON, M.D.

VANN SPRUIELL, M.D.

PHYLLIS TYSON, PH.D.

EDWARD M. WEINSHEL, M.D.

GEORGE H. WIEDEMAN, M.D.

CONSULTANTS

JACOB A. ARLOW, M.D.

HAROLD P. BLUM, M.D.

DALE BOESKY, M.D.

GEORGE H. KLUMPNER, M.D.

YALE UNIVERSITY PRESS
NEW HAVEN & LONDON

616.8917
M781p

FE 28 '97

Copyright © 1995 by Yale University. All rights reserved.
This book may not be reproduced, in whole or in part,
including illustrations, in any form (beyond that copying
permitted by Sections 107 and 108 of the U.S. Copyright
Law and except by reviewers for the public press), without
written permission from the publishers.

Portions of chapter 12, "Freud on Dreams and Dreaming,"
by Harry Trosman, are reprinted from Dr. Trosman's
article "Freud's Dream Theory" in ENCYCLOPEDIA OF
SLEEP AND DREAMING, Mary A. Carskadon, Editor in
Chief, pp. 251–254. Copyright © 1993 by Macmillan
Publishing Company. Used by permission of Simon &
Schuster Macmillan.

Printed in the United States of America by BookCrafters,
Inc., Chelsea, Michigan.

Library of Congress Cataloging-in-Publication Data
Psychoanalysis : the major concepts / edited by Burness E.
Moore and Bernard D. Fine ; editorial board, Alvin Frank
. . . [et al.] ; consultants, Jacob A. Arlow . . . [et al.].
   p.   cm.
   Companion v. to: Psychoanalytic terms and concepts.
© 1990.
   Includes bibliographical references and index.
   ISBN 0–300–06329–6 (alk. paper)
   1. Psychoanalysis. I. Moore, Burness E. II. Fine,
Bernard D., 1917–1992. III. Psychoanalytic terms and
concepts.
[DNLM: 1. Psychoanalysis. 2. Psychoanalytic
Therapy. 3. Psychoanalytic Interpretation.
WM 460 P97447 1995]
RC504.P754   1995
616.89'17—dc20
DNLM/DLC
for Library of Congress   95-173
                                           CIP

A catalogue record for this book is available from the
British Library.

The paper in this book meets the guidelines for perma-
nence and durability of the Committee on Production
Guidelines for Book Longevity of the Council on Library
Resources.

10   9   8   7   6   5   4   3   2   1

CONTENTS

SECTION II THEORETICAL CONCEPTS

PART IV FACTORS AFFECTING NORMALITY AND PATHOLOGY

PART V INSTINCT THEORY, SEXUALITY, AND AFFECTS

PART VI DEVELOPMENT, SELF, OBJECTS, AND IDENTIFICATION

ALPHABETICAL LIST OF CHAPTER TOPICS

PREFACE

Slightly more than a century has passed since the founding of psychoanalysis by Sigmund Freud, and the fiftieth anniversary of his death was marked in 1988. We are, in a sense, at a midway point, as his successors have had equal time to elaborate and modify his theories. This seems an appropriate time, therefore, to survey the field of psychoanalysis, specify the areas of human behavior to which it has been applied, reexamine its scientific underpinnings, review the progress made, and assess the results.

Such an undertaking is a virtually impossible task, however, and any approach to it must necessarily be sharply delimited. Our effort in this volume is presented for the most part from the perspective of traditional mainstream American psychoanalysis. At a time when there is more pluralism in psychoanalysis than ever before, our choice of a single theoretical orientation is dictated by pragmatic and personal considerations rather than value judgments. To attempt to represent all the divergent theories in psychoanalysis would require many volumes and a greatly expanded, international effort; and the variability in scope, style, perspective, and quality of the chapters evident in this volume would be so magnified as to prevent a balanced overview of concepts, our primary objective. Ego psychology or modern structural theory, with some admixture of object relations theory and Mahler's developmental theory, has been the background of most of our editorial board and authors, and their preference has been to stay within their area of expertise.

This volume is the second work compiled by the same editors and editorial board, whose first project was to revise the *Glossary of Psychoanalytic Terms and Concepts,* first published by the American Psychoanalytic Association in 1967. The resulting third edition, published as *Psychoanalytic Terms and Concepts* by the Association and Yale University Press in 1990, was a greatly expanded work, approaching a mini-encyclopedia in scope, and covering most of the working terminology of psychoanalysis. Its primary purpose was definition, with some integration of each term with other psychoanalytic theory, but the essays were necessarily brief in order for the work to be all-inclusive. However, not all the terms and concepts are of equal importance; some barely deserve mention, while others are monolithic theoretical structures with a host of subsidiary terms. All require positioning in the context of a very complex body of knowledge, theory, and practice that has been developing, expanding, and changing for over a century. For the major concepts more explication was needed for comprehension than was possible in that essentially definitional volume. Recognizing this, the board planned this second book to provide a more comprehensive discussion of subjects of central importance in psychoanalysis, including its applications, technical aspects, clinical phenomena, and more general theoretical concepts.

Following Waelder's (1962) delineation of the various levels of psychoanalytic theoretical conceptualization, increasing attention has been given to the separation of theory derived from more directly observable clinical phenomena and theory at higher levels of abstraction. This is an appealing idea, and we have attempted to follow it in separating this volume into two sections, one devoted primarily to clinical psychoanalysis, the other to more abstract theories, including Freud's metapsychology. But the separation is not perfect, nor are all the subjects included concepts in a strict definitional sense; so we have subdivided the sections into parts to reflect the differences. Many of the major concepts, clinical and abstract, have been grouped together in a topical table of contents to facilitate integration and exposition. Ultimately, however, each chapter stands alone, and for that reason an alphabetical list of chapter topics is appended. While Part I, for example, deals with the therapeutic applications of psychoanalysis, each chapter has a different objective. The first, by Sydney E. Pulver, presents a modern-day, flexible view of technique as employed in psychoanalysis proper. The second, by A. Scott Dowling and Joanne Naegele, places the field of child and adolescent psychoanalysis on an equal footing with that of adult analysis and informs the reader of important research work in this field that has altered for the better society's attitude toward the care of children. The third chapter, by Beth J. Seelig, discusses the difference between psychoanalytically-oriented individual psychotherapy and psychoanalysis proper and presents several illustrative case reports. The fourth chapter, by Ramon Ganzarain, presents aspects of the psychology of groups and illustrations of group psychotherapy. Similarly, Part VIII in Section II abandons the subject of concepts and deals with the preparation of the psychoanalyst for analytic work—current trends in education and training, the application of psychoanalytic research to the understanding of human behavior and mental

phenomena and the study of art and literature, and the correlation between psychoanalysis and recent findings in brain physiology, an early interest of Freud.

Joseph Sandler (1983) has observed that there is an expectation that psychoanalytic theory should constitute a body of ideas that is essentially complete and organized, with each part fully integrated with every other. In practice, however, concepts become stretched to encompass new insights and new ideas and often have multiple meanings, which vary according to the context in which a particular term is used, so that their developmental-historical dimension needs to be emphasized (p. 35). Psychoanalytic educators have long recognized this fact—that the student needs to know how the theory developed in order to master it. The literature is now so massive that this is not feasible without some scholarly assistance. To meet this need, the editors and editorial board asked the authors selected for the major concepts to present a broad overview of their subjects. The general guidelines given to contributors were that each chapter should define its subject, trace its historical development within psychoanalysis, describe its present status, discuss criticisms and controversies with regard to it, and point out emerging trends. Whenever possible, emphasis was to be placed on developmental issues, and an objective rather than a partisan approach to controversy was recommended. Clinical examples were requested when feasible, and a representative, but not necessarily comprehensive, bibliography was to be supplied.

Together with *Psychoanalytic Terms and Concepts,* with its focus on definition, this book is intended to serve as an introduction to modern-day psychoanalysis for beginning students and as a review and updating of the fundamental theories of psychoanalysis for the more sophisticated. In addition to this educational purpose, however, it is hoped that this comprehensive view of mainstream psychoanalysis will provide experts with a systematic consensus regarding the scientific basis of psychoanalysis that will raise questions for future research. A critical overview of our entire theoretical infrastructure is a necessary preliminary to revision. No single effort of this nature can be wholly successful, or sufficient even if successful, but we believe it is a step in the right direction.

Though this book has been overseen by the same editorial board as *Psychoanalytic Terms and Concepts,* which was a project of the American Psychoanalytic Association and was published under its imprimatur, it is being published independently. The detailed exposition of theory contained herein inevitably reflects the views of the editors, editorial board, and contributors; the American Psychoanalytic Association, on the other hand, has within its membership a varied spectrum of theoretical orientations. Removal of this work from the aegis of the Association avoids putting the Association in the position of appearing officially to endorse a particular viewpoint.

REFERENCES

Sandler, J. (1983). Reflections on some relations between psychoanalytic concepts and psychoanalytic practice. *Int. J. Psychoanal.*, 64:35–45.

Waelder, R. (1962). Psychoanalysis, scientific method and philosophy. In *Psychoanalysis: Observation, Theory, and Application*, pp. 248–274. New York: Int. Univ. Press, 1976.

ACKNOWLEDGMENTS

The contributions of colleagues in the American Psychoanalytic Association to *Psychoanalytic Terms and Concepts,* a revision of an earlier *Glossary,* provided the inspiration for this book. Their devotion to clarifying the terms and concepts of psychoanalysis was contagious—all the more so because that objective is so difficult to achieve. Our continuing effort was committed to a survey of the field of psychoanalysis and its applications and an examination in greater depth of some of the major theoretical constructs only briefly presented in that volume. Albert J. Solnit was consulted for advice at the beginning of the project, and we greatly appreciate the enthusiasm with which he greeted the prospect of the undertaking and the impetus he gave to the start of the work.

Similar devotion to the task has been manifested by the Editorial Board, which has steadfastly supported and contributed to the work over a period of many years. Its members have given freely of their time in advising about the selection of topics and authors, in evaluating and making suggestions about chapters submitted, and in contributions of chapters of their own. We are grateful for their confidence in the outcome and encouragement and support through many vicissitudes. Though all, including our consultants, have played a significant role in the production of both books, several deserve special mention for their helpfulness: Alvin Frank, Jules Glenn, Selma Kramer, Sydney E. Pulver, Ralph E. Roughton, and Vann Spruiell.

Aside from the Editorial Board we are indebted for authoritative opinions on subjects within their areas of expertise to Charles Brenner, Kenneth T. Calder, Aaron H. Esman, John Frosch, Lawrence B. Inderbitzin, Mark Kanzer, Steven T. Levy, Bernard C. Meyer, Morton F. Reiser, Calvin F. Settlage, and Robert L. Tyson.

Edward M. Weinshel made a unique contribution by organizing a small study group of analysts to determine how the field of psychoanalysis might be best presented. The initial formulations of this group were valuable and were given serious consideration, but a lag in the project's production schedule interfered with continuation of the group's joint efforts to put the material in final form. Ultimately, however, four of the group assumed responsibility for important chapters in the volume. We are grateful to them, to Edward Weinshel, and to all who participated: Victor Calef, Phyllis J. Cath, Scott Dowling, Charles Hanly, Samuel Hoch, Lester Isenstadt, Ronald F. Krasner, Elizabeth Lloyd Mayer, and Owen Renik.

It is not possible to thank the contributors of the chapters adequately for their careful research, revisions in response to suggestions, and patience with the delays of editing and production. They have been unfailingly kind, courteous, and tolerant, rewarding our editorial efforts with chapters that are mutually satisfying.

Lottie M. Newman, whose distinguished work over many years as an editor of psychoanalytic publications won for her a Distinguished Contributor Award from the American Psychoanalytic Association in 1984, was the unanimous choice of the Editorial Board for the professional editing of *Psychoanalytic Terms and Concepts* and this book. Her encyclopedic knowledge of psychoanalysis was a tremendous help to the editors, and her untimely death in February 1993 was a great loss to us and to the psychoanalytic community. We were fortunate, however, in the fact that Gladys Topkis, senior editor at Yale University Press, had been active in promoting the works from the beginning and has remained involved throughout their production. For this book in particular her assistance has been invaluable.

In a work of this nature, which necessarily goes on for a long while, losses by death must be expected. Unfortunately, my co-editor, Bernard D. Fine, died in July 1992, so was deprived of the pleasure of seeing the completion of a project for which he had tremendous enthusiasm, dating back to the beginning of our collaboration on the Glossary in 1966. His friendship, as well as his participation in our work, has been greatly missed. George H. Wiedeman, another loyal friend and long-time collaborator, died in December 1991, and Peter H. Knapp in April 1992. Wiedeman contributed the chapter on sexuality and Knapp the one on somatization, both reflecting their authors' profound knowledge of the subjects on which they had been recognized experts for many years.

Burness E. Moore

CONTRIBUTORS

Sander M. Abend, M.D.
Training and Supervising Analyst and former President, New York Psychoanalytic Institute; former Secretary, American Psychoanalytic Association; former Editor-in-Chief, *Psychoanalytic Quarterly.*

Salman Akhtar, M.D.
Training and Supervising Analyst, Philadelphia Psychoanalytic Institute; Professor of Psychiatry, Jefferson Medical College.

Jacob A. Arlow, M.D.
Training and Supervising Analyst, New York Psychoanalytic Institute; former President and Chairman of the Board on Professional Standards of the American Psychoanalytic Association; former Editor-in-Chief, *Psychoanalytic Quarterly;* Clinical Professor of Psychiatry at New York University College of Medicine.

Francis D. Baudry, M.D.
Training and Supervising Analyst, New York Psychoanalytic Institute; Associate Professor of Clinical Psychiatry, Albert Einstein College of Medicine; Fellow, American Psychiatric Association.

David Beres, M.D.
Training and Supervising Analyst and former President, New York Psychoanalytic Institute; former President, American Psychoanalytic Association; former member, Editorial Board, *Psychoanalytic Quarterly.*

Isidor Bernstein, M.D.
Training and Supervising Analyst for Adult, Child, and Adolescent Analysis, New York Psychoanalytic Institute; Training and Supervising Analyst for Child and Adolescent Analysis, Psychoanalytic Institute, New York University Medical Center; Clinical Associate Professor of Psychiatry, New York University Medical Center.

Harold P. Blum, M.D.
Clinical Professor of Psychiatry and Training and Supervising Analyst, Psychoanalytic Institute, New York University Medical Center; Executive Director, Sigmund Freud Archives; former Editor, *Journal of the American Psychoanalytic Association.*

Dale Boesky, M.D.
Training and Supervising Analyst, Michigan Psychoanalytic Institute; former Editor-in-Chief, *Psychoanalytic Quarterly.*

Donald J. Cohen, M.D.
Director of Child Study Center and Irving B. Harris Professor of Child Psychiatry, Pediatrics, and Psychology, Yale University School of Medicine; Child Psychiatrist and Psychoanalyst with research and clinical interests in normal development and developmental psychopathology; President, International Association for Child and Adolescent Psychiatry and Allied Professions (IACAPAP).

Allan Compton, M.D.
Training and Supervising Analyst, Los Angeles Psychoanalytic Institute; Clinical Professor of Psychiatry, University of California, Los Angeles; Editorial Board, *Journal of the American Psychoanalytic Association;* Editorial Board, *Psychoanalytic Quarterly;* Board, Fund for Psychoanalytic Research.

A. Scott Dowling, M.D.
Training and Supervising Analyst, Cleveland Psychoanalytic Institute; Clinical Associate Professor, Case Western Reserve University; Editor, *The Psychoanalytic Study of the Child;* Editor, Workshop Series of the American Psychoanalytic Association.

Alvin Frank, M.D.
Training and Supervising Analyst, St. Louis Psychoanalytic Institute; Professor of Clinical Psychiatry, St. Louis University; Chairman, Committee on Scientific Activities, American Psychoanalytic Association; member, Psychoanalytic Research and Development Fund; Participant, Center for Advanced Psychoanalytic Studies.

Sidney S. Furst, M.D.
Training and Supervising Analyst, New York Psychoanalytic Institute; Professional Director, Psychoanalytic Research and Development Fund.

Ramon Ganzarain, M.D.
Clinical Associate Professor of Psychiatry, Emory University School of Medicine; Training and Supervising Analyst, Emory University Psychoanalytic Institute; member, Board of Directors, American Group Psychotherapy Association, 1993–96. Formerly Training Analyst, Topeka Psychoanalytic Institute, and Director of Group Psychotherapy at the Menninger Clinic.

Jules Glenn, M.D.
Clinical Professor of Psychiatry and Training and Supervising Analyst, Psychoanalytic Institute, New York University Medical Center; former President of the Association for Child Psychoanalysis.

Leo Goldberger, Ph.D.
Professor of Psychology, New York University; graduate, New York Psychoanalytic Institute; Editor-in-Chief, *Psychoanalysis and Contemporary Thought;* Editorial Board, *Psychoanalytic Terms and Concepts;* Editorial Board, *Psychological Issues;* Series Editor, *Psychoanalytic Crosscurrents.*

Warren H. Goodman, M.D.
Faculty, Departments of Psychiatry, Cornell University Medical College, Albert Einstein College of Medicine of Yeshiva University, and New York University Medical Center.

Alexander Grinstein, M.D.
Training and Supervising Analyst, Michigan Psychoanalytic Institute; Clinical Professor of Psychiatry, Wayne State University School of Medicine, Detroit; private psychoanalytic practice, Birmingham, Michigan.

Lee Grossman, M.D.
Training and Supervising Analyst, San Francisco Psychoanalytic Institute; Assistant Clinical Professor of Psychiatry, University of California, San Francisco; former member, Editorial Board, *Journal of the American Psychoanalytic Association;* private practice of psychoanalysis, Berkeley, California.

Charles M. T. Hanly, Ph.D.
Training Analyst, Toronto Psychoanalytic Institute; Vice-President, International Psychoanalytic Association; Professor of Philosophy, University of Toronto; private psychoanalytic practice.

Roberta K. Jaeger, M.D.
Training and Supervising Analyst, Columbia University Center for Psychoanalytic Training and Research; Assistant Professor of Clinical Psychiatry, College of Physicians and Surgeons, Columbia University.

Otto F. Kernberg, M.D.
Associate Chairman and Medical Director, New York Hospital–Cornell Medical Center, Westchester Division; Professor of Psychiatry, Cornell University Medical College; Training and Supervising Analyst, Columbia University Center for Psychoanalytic Training and Research; Vice-President, International Psychoanalytic Association.

Peter H. Knapp, M.D. (died 7 April 1992)
Formerly Professor of Psychiatry and Associate
Chairman and Director of Education Programs in
Psychiatry, Boston University School of Medicine;
Training and Supervising Analyst, Boston Psycho-
analytic Society and Institute; member, Committee
on Research Training and Committee on Scientific
Affairs, American Psychoanalytic Association; Pres-
ident, American Psychosomatic Society; Fellow,
Center for Advanced Study in the Behavioral Sci-
ences; Editorial Boards, *Psychosomatic Medicine,
Journal of Nervous and Mental Disease,* and *Inter-
national Journal of Psychiatry.*

Fred M. Levin, M.D.
Training and Supervising Analyst, Chicago Institute
for Psychoanalysis; Assistant Professor of Clinical
Psychiatry, Northwestern University School of
Medicine; Medical Director, Mendac Program, Mt.
Sinai Medical Center.

Elizabeth Lloyd Mayer, Ph.D.
Training and Supervising Analyst, San Francisco
Psychoanalytic Institute; Clinical Professor of Psy-
chiatry, University of California, San Francisco;
Clinical Professor of Psychology, University of
California, Berkeley; member, Editorial Board,
Journal of the American Psychoanalytic Association
and *Psychoanalytic Quarterly.*

Linda C. Mayes, M.D.
Arnold Gesell Associate Professor of Child Development, Pediatrics, and Psychology in the Yale Child
Study Center; candidate, Western New England Institute for Psychoanalysis.

James T. McLaughlin, M.D.
Training and Supervising Analyst and former Direc-
tor, Pittsburgh Psychoanalytic Institute; former Sec-
retary, Board on Professional Standards, American
Psychoanalytic Association; Clinical Associate Pro-
fessor of Psychiatry Emeritus, School of Medicine,
University of Pittsburgh; member, Editorial Board,
Psychoanalytic Quarterly; former member, Editorial
Board, *Journal of the American Psychoanalytic
Association,* and North American Editorial Board,
International Journal of Psychoanalysis.

Jon K. Meyer, M.D.
Training and Supervising Analyst, Chicago Institute
for Psychoanalysis; Professor of Psychiatry, Psychoanalysis, and Family Medicine and Vice-Chairman,
Department of Psychiatry and Mental Health Sci-

ences, Medical College of Wisconsin; Director, Psy-
chotherapy Center, Columbia Hospital, Milwaukee,
Wisconsin; Erik H. Erikson Scholar-in-Residence,
Austin Riggs Center, 1991–92.

Robert Michels, M.D.
Provost for Medical Affairs, Cornell University;
Stephen and Suzanne Weiss Dean and Barklie
McKee Henry Professor of Psychiatry, Cornell Uni-
versity Medical College; Training and Supervising
Analyst, Columbia University Center for Psycho-
analytic Training and Research.

Burness E. Moore, M.D.
Training and Supervising Analyst Emeritus, Emory
University Psychoanalytic Institute; Clinical Professor of Psychiatry, Emory University School of
Medicine; former President, American Psychoanalytic Association; former President, New York Psychoanalytic Institute; former Treasurer, International
Psychoanalytic Association; former member, Editorial Board, *Journal of the American Psychoanalytic
Association;* Chairman of Editorial Board and Editor, *Psychoanalytic Terms and Concepts.*

Joanne Naegele, M.A.
Instructor, Cleveland Psychoanalytic Institute; Faculty, Cleveland Center for Research in Child Development; private practice of child analysis.

Shelley Orgel, M.D.
Clinical Professor of Psychiatry, Training and Su-
pervising Analyst and former Director, Psycho-
analytic Institute, New York University Medical
Center; former Chairman, Board of Professional
Standards, American Psychoanalytic Association.

Michael S. Porder, M.D.
Training and Supervising Analyst, New York Psy-
choanalytic Institute; Associate Clinical Professor of
Psychiatry, Mt. Sinai School of Medicine.

Sydney E. Pulver, M.D.
Training and Supervising Analyst, Philadelphia
Psychoanalytic Institute; Clinical Professor of Psy-
chiatry, University of Pennsylvania Medical School;
Senior Attending Staff, Institute of Pennsylvania
Hospital.

Leo Rangell, M.D.
Former President, American Psychoanalytic Association; former President, International Psychoanalytical Association; Clinical Professor, University of
California, Los Angeles, and University of California, San Francisco.

Owen D. Renik, M.D.
Training and Supervising Analyst, San Francisco
Psychoanalytic Institute; Secretary, Board on Profes-
sional Standards, American Psychoanalytic Associ-
ation; Editor-in-Chief, *Psychoanalytic Quarterly;*
Associate Editor, *Journal of the American Psycho-
analytic Association;* North American Editorial
Board, *International Journal of Psycho-Analysis/
International Review of Psycho-Analysis;* Associate
Chief, Department of Psychiatry, Mount Zion Hos-
pital; Associate Clinical Professor, Department of
Psychiatry, University of California, San Francisco.

Samuel Ritvo, M.D.
Clinical Professor of Psychiatry, Yale University
Child Study Center; Training and Supervising Ana-
lyst, Western New England Institute for Psycho-
analysis; former President of the Association for
Child Psychoanalysis; former President, American
Psychoanalytic Association.

Ralph E. Roughton, M.D.
Training and Supervising Analyst, Emory University
Psychoanalytic Institute; Clinical Professor of Psy-
chiatry, Emory University School of Medicine;
former member, Editorial Board, *Journal of the
American Psychoanalytic Association.*

Jean Schimek, Ph.D.
Associate Professor of Psychology, New York University; Training Analyst, Institute for Psychoanalytic Training and Research (IPTAR); member,
International Psychoanalytic Association.

Beth J. Seelig, M.D.
Training and Supervising Analyst, Emory University
Psychoanalytic Institute; Assistant Professor of Psy-
chiatry, Emory University School of Medicine.

Albert J. Solnit, M.D.
Sterling Professor Emeritus, Pediatrics and Psychi-
atry, and Senior Research Scientist, Yale University
Child Study Center; Training and Supervising Ana-
lyst, Western New England Institute for Psycho-
analysis; Commissioner, Department of Mental
Health, State of Connecticut; Editor, *Psychoanalytic
Study of the Child.*

Vann Spruiell, M.D.
Training and Supervising Analyst, New Orleans
Psychoanalytic Institute; Clinical Professor of Psy-
chiatry, Louisiana State University Medical School;
Clinical Professor of Psychiatry, Tulane Medical

School; North American Editor, *International Journal of Psycho-Analysis;* Editorial Board, *Psychoanalytic Quarterly.*

Leo Stone, M.D.
Training and Supervising Analyst, former Director
of the Treatment Center, and former President of the
New York Psychoanalytic Institute; former President, New York Psychoanalytic Society; Training
Analyst, Columbia University Center for Psychoanalytic Training and Research.

Harry Trosman, M.D.
Training and Supervising Analyst, Chicago Institute
for Psychoanalysis; Professor of Psychiatry, University of Chicago.

Phyllis Tyson, Ph.D.
Child and Adult Training and Supervising Analyst,
San Diego Psychoanalytic Society and Institute;
Geographic Child Supervising Analyst, Denver Psy-
choanalytic Institute.

Robert L. Tyson, M.D.
Training and Supervising Analyst (Adult and Child),
San Diego Psychoanalytic Institute; Geographic
Child Supervising Analyst, Denver Psychoanalytic
Institute; Clinical Professor of Psychiatry, Univer-
sity of California, San Diego; former President, As-
sociation for Child Psychoanalysis.

Robert S. Wallerstein, M.D.
Emeritus Professor of Psychiatry, University of Cal-
ifornia, San Francisco, School of Medicine; former
President, International Psychoanalytic Association;
former President, American Psychoanalytic
Association.

**George H. Wiedeman, M.D. (died 27 December
1991)**
Formerly Training and Supervising Analyst, Psychoanalytic Institute, New York University Medical
Center; Marion Kenworthy Professor of Psychiatry,
School of Social Work, Columbia University,
1962–80.

Martin S. Willick, M.D.
Training and Supervising Analyst, New York Psychoanalytic Institute; Lecturer in Psychiatry, College
of Physicians and Surgeons, Columbia University;
former member, Editorial Board, *Psychoanalytic
Quarterly.*

CLINICAL PSYCHOANALYSIS

PART I

THERAPEUTIC APPLICATIONS

1

THE TECHNIQUE OF PSYCHOANALYSIS PROPER

INTRODUCTION

Current psychoanalytic technique, as it has evolved from its original form, is the subject of this chapter. When such technique is used with appropriate patients, a process follows and changes occur; they will be the topic of Chapter 5. Psychoanalytic technique differs throughout the world; here I will describe the technique that I believe is used by the majority of experienced analysts in the United States. When my own practices differ from those of the majority, I will try to say as much. I will focus most strongly on those aspects of technique not covered elsewhere in this volume: the consultative process, the respective roles of patient and analyst, their relationship, the analyst's attitude, and the principles he follows.[1] Such crucial aspects of technique as resistance, transference, countertransference, the handling of acting out, and techniques with specific types of patients such as those with narcissistic and sadomasochistic disorders have been dealt with by others in separate chapters, and I will merely touch on them here.

---

1. Since English unfortunately does not have a pronoun that refers to both sexes, in this chapter I follow the not infrequent practice of using the pronoun which is the same as the sex of the author. "He" should thus be understood as referring to either sex and is used merely to avoid the awkwardness of "he or she," "his or her," and so on.

As in any healthy science, controversies abound. These are particularly charged when it comes to matters of technique. Some analysts, for example, feel that interpretation is the hallmark of psychoanalytic technique with all patients and that any major departure from interpretation renders the therapy something other than psychoanalysis. Others (and I am one) feel that different patients require different technical approaches and that these are all psychoanalysis as long as the therapist's main intent throughout the therapy is to effect change through understanding. This position holds that there are many psychoanalytic techniques and that we are just beginning to understand when, how, and with whom to apply these technical variations. To clarify this and other controversies, I will begin with a brief history.

SOME MAJOR TRENDS IN THE HISTORY OF PSYCHOANALYTIC TECHNIQUE

Freud (1914a) himself provides the best brief discussion of the evolution of his technique. Early in his career as a neurologist, Freud dealt with his neurotic patients using the standard supportive approaches of the time. When his friend and teacher Joseph Breuer told him in 1882 of his treatment of Anna O. by abreaction of her trauma while she was hypnotized (the "cathartic method"), Freud was deeply impressed. His interest in hypnosis intensified during his winter with Charcot in 1885–86. Though he used it in an exploratory manner for some time afterwards, it was not until 1888 (or 1889—the date is uncertain) that he first treated a patient, Frau Emmy von N., exclusively by the cathartic method.

During the next ten years a remarkable evolution occurred. Disappointed because many of his patients were not deeply hypnotizable, Freud found in 1892 (with Fraulein Elisabeth von R.) that hypnosis was not necessary to achieve recall of trauma. Simple insistence, at first accompanied by the pressure of his hand on the patient's forehead, sufficed. By 1896, Freud had developed the technique of free association, in which he simply asked the patients to say everything without exception that came to his or her mind.

Early on, Freud became aware that patients did not always willingly cooperate in therapy; the idea of "resistance" as an important part of uncovering therapy had become explicit by 1892. Freud (1905) had recognized transference (the repetition in the analytic relationship of fantasies, feelings, and behavior displaced from relationships with earlier significant persons) in the Dora case. By 1914 most of the important principles of psychoanalytic technique had been worked out and described in the famous "Papers on Technique" (Freud, 1911, 1912a, 1912b, 1913, 1914a, 1915). (See Ellman, 1991, for an excellent discussion of these papers.)

During this period, the goals of therapy had changed dramatically. Reliving traumatic experiences was no longer primary. Conflict between intrapsychic motivations and the intrapsychic forces that opposed them was recognized, as were the various ways in which patients kept these motivations out of consciousness. By 1919, Freud had conceptualized therapy as the attempt to help patients understand their unconscious wish-fulfilling fantasies, the reasons these fantasies were felt to be unacceptable, the ways they protected themselves against becoming aware of these unacceptable fantasies (their defenses), and the manifestations of these defenses in analysis (resistance). The aim of therapy was always understanding (insight). The main object of understanding at that time was the material that was unconscious; the resistances were thought of as something to be overcome more than understood. Bringing this unconscious material to awareness was considered necessary to enable the patient to change.

In 1923, with the publication of *The Ego and the Id,* Freud introduced the structural theory (q.v.). The Early Period of psychoanalytic technique was over, and the Classical Period had begun. Emphasis shifted from a preoccupation with the recovery of id material to include a deeper exploration of the ego defenses. This period, which continued into the mid-1950s, was characterized by a specific theory of neurosogenesis: that is, that neuroses arose from oedipal conflict. Pre-oedipal factors were thought of by mainstream psychoanalysts as regressions away from oedipal anxieties. Interpretation remained the primary mode of analytic activity.

By the mid-1950s, the Contemporary Period of psychoanalytic technique had begun. It was characterized, first, by a gradual shift from the emphasis on oedipal conflict as the basis of all psychopathology to a recognition of the importance of pre-oedipal factors, including developmental deficits (de Jonghe et al., 1991) and, second, by a gradual shift away from Freud's original view of the analyst as an impartial observer objectively examining his patient's distortions of reality and informing the patient of them. Analysts increasingly recognized that the analytic situation is best viewed as a relationship in which each of the participants is shaping the subjective experience of the other. Neither has an exclusive view of what is and what is not reality, and both are working together to try to discover a mutual reality (Greenberg, 1993).

All these developments have been complex and, to say the least, controversial. In fact, almost all of them were foreshadowed by Freud and his colleagues. Descriptions of pre-oedipal factors as primary in psychopathology, the importance of the analyst–analysand relationship, and almost everything that has been advanced as good psychoanalytic technique can be found early in the history of psychoanalysis.

My hope in this brief survey has been to give the reader a feel for the background of the trends that have taken place. I turn now to some of the specifics of contemporary technique itself. Perhaps the best place to begin is with the consultative process and the events leading to the actual beginning of analysis. While not strictly an integral part of analysis, these events may have a crucial impact upon it.

THE INITIAL CONSULTATION

Analytic patients are not as plentiful today as they once were, and this makes the consultative process particularly important. Occasionally a patient comes specifically for analysis and needs little prior evaluation. He may have already been evaluated by a colleague whose clinical judgment the analyst trusts or be an analytic candidate or be continuing an interrupted analysis with a colleague in another city or not need evaluation for some other reason with which the analyst is comfortable. Usually, however, a preliminary evaluation is essential. From the very beginning, the consultant should make it clear that this is indeed a consultation—that is, a short series of interviews to determine what kind of treatment might be most useful for the patient and who might be the best person to carry it out. During this evaluation, the analyst will be able to get an idea of whether he can work with the patient. Just as important, the patient will get at least some feeling about whether he can work with the analyst, a crucial factor in making a decision about a therapist. The analyst should discuss all this with the patient. During the consultation, the analyst will consider the patient's analyzability (Moore and Fine, 1990), motivation, and many other factors.

Making such an evaluation is familiar to all clinicians and need not be discussed here. I will remind you only that its purpose is not simply to reach a conclusion about the proper treatment for the patient but to establish sufficient rapport that the patient feels understood and is willing to take the consultant's recommendations seriously.

At some point, usually in two to four sessions, when the consultant feels that he has enough information and that there is enough rapport, he presents the treatment options to the patient. I say "options" because there is usually more than one type of treatment that might be useful, and it is the clinician's responsibility to give the patient all reasonable choices, telling him what can and cannot be expected from each. The clinician should have no hesitation about forcefully recommending analysis if he feels that is best for the patient, but only rarely will it be the only choice. If the patient decides upon some form of treatment that the analyst does not wish to undertake or chooses analysis but does not feel able to work with that particular consultant, it is the latter's responsibility to help the patient find proper treatment. When referral is necessary, for clinical, financial, or other reasons, it is not enough just to give the patient a list of names of possible therapists. Coping with the refusals that often occur and the approaches and personalities of the therapists that are likely to be encountered from such a list tends to be too much for the average patient, particularly when he or she is in emotional difficulty. Instead, the consultant should contact the potential therapist, explain the clinical and financial situation, and see if the therapist has time and is willing to see the patient, at least for a preliminary evaluation. The patient should then be told that Dr. Jones is willing to explore the possibility of therapy with him, and that the initial session or two will be an opportunity not only for Dr. Jones to see if he agrees with the consultant's recommendation but for the patient to see if he can work with Dr. Jones. I always explain that, while it is not necessary for the patient to be en-

raptured by Dr. Jones at first sight, he should at least have the feeling that this is someone he can work with. If the patient is immediately repelled, he should simply tell Dr. Jones he would like to consider things further and then contact me for another recommendation. If a clinic referral is necessary, we often cannot make specific recommendations, but we can tell the patient how to handle the situation if he gets a therapist with whom he is not comfortable. We are much more familiar with the mental health system than our patients are, and part of the consultant's duty is to help the patient negotiate that system.

PRACTICAL ARRANGEMENTS AND THE ANALYTIC SETTING

If the patient decides on analysis, the analyst and patient next discuss the practical arrangements. It is of the utmost importance that they come to an agreement in detail before the analysis begins and that the patient truly understands everything he is agreeing to. In the negotiations that are about to take place, the patient is at a disadvantage in being the one who needs help. Transference factors are already operative, and he may not be able to appreciate at a deep level all the implications of the time, money, and emotional demands that will ensue once the analysis gets under way. Furthermore, patients may agree to the practical arrangements but nevertheless have unconscious reservations about this agreement that may or may not be analyzable and that may threaten the analysis. Since much of the inevitable struggle between analyst and patient often takes place on the battleground of these practical arrangements, it is important that the patient understand them precisely, at least cognitively. It is very difficult to help the patient see the emotional implications of the struggle if the realistic arrangements have not been negotiated fairly and clearly.

Among the major elements of the practical arrangements are the frequency and length of sessions and the monetary arrangements (often called the "frame" of the analysis: see Spruiell, 1983). Because these form a significant part of the setting in which the analysis takes place, they have a major impact on the psychoanalytic process. Let us look at each of them in some detail.

Frequency of Sessions
Continuity of treatment is of the essence in establishing and maintaining the psychoanalytic process. This means that daily sessions are optimal. In practice, however, seven sessions a week are impractical, and it has become generally accepted by

psychoanalysts and their organizations that five sessions per week are desirable and four the minimum number to constitute a psychoanalysis. Daily sessions are important because a major part of the psychoanalytic process, one that helps differentiate it from psychotherapy, is the intensity of the transference that evolves. Daily sessions lead to a more intense relationship and thus to more intense transference. While there seems to be no question that a few people are able to establish an analytic process at a frequency of three or even fewer times per week, most people require at least four.

The Length of the Session

Freud's sessions were originally one hour in length. He himself says nothing about how he arrived at that amount of time, and we must assume that he determined it empirically. External pressures (perhaps the widespread use of the telephone?) led early in psychoanalytic history to the adoption of the fifty-minute session ("the fifty-minute hour"). Shortly after World War II, the tremendous demand for analysis led many analysts to decrease their sessions to forty-five minutes, enabling them to see an additional patient a day. Current practice seems evenly divided between forty-five and fifty minutes. Some experimentation has taken place with shorter sessions (Muller, 1990), but, as with frequencies of less than four times per week, less than forty-five minutes is usually insufficient. Longer sessions have been tried and were even recommended for some patients by Freud but are rarely implemented today.

The Schedule

There seems to be no reason why a patient's appointment should be at the same time every day, nor does there seem to be a problem with changing appointment times if desired by either analyst or patient, as long as such changes are mutually convenient. For practical reasons, such as when the patient is coming from a long distance, attempts have been made to schedule two sessions per day for two days to fit in four per week, but experience seems to indicate that this is not usually sufficient for the development of an analytic process. The important point in scheduling is that the times agreed upon are not deeply inconvenient for either the patient or the analyst. As in any aspect of setting up the practical arrangements, neither the analyst nor the patient should feel exploited. Masochistic patients may accept or even insist on manifestly unfair or excessively burdensome practical arrangements, and masochistic analysts may do the same. The analyst must do his best in the initial negotiations to prevent this from happening.

Fees

Mutual agreement about all aspects of paying the analyst is particularly important since enactments around money are so common during an analysis. While some analysts have a usual fee from which they will not depart, setting the fee is frequently a matter of negotiation. Analysts wish to do analysis, and many patients have limited resources. In such a situation, when the analyst quotes the usual fee and the patient indicates a difficulty in paying it, the analyst, depending on the state of his practice and finances, will often indicate a willingness to accept a lower fee, and a negotiation begins. Again, the crucial consideration is that the outcome of this negotiation be satisfactory to both parties. As part of the arrangements, the analyst should also specify how he will let the patient know what is owed and when the money should be paid. Common practice is for the analyst to send a monthly statement and to expect payment at some time during the following month. It is particularly important for the analyst to describe clearly his policy about charging for missed appointments and for vacations. Many analysts follow Freud's recommendation to charge for all scheduled appointments whether kept or not, regardless of the reason, including vacations that do not coincide with the analyst's vacation. However, many other arrangements are possible and in use, and no specific approach seems inherently superior. What is clear is that a variety of arrangements may be workable as long as both patient and analyst clearly understand the arrangement they have made and agree to it.

Miscellaneous

Patient and analyst should understand the preferred mode of emergency communication with each other. Patients often prefer not to be called at certain times or locations, and the analyst should respect this. Likewise, the analyst will have his own preferences about contact outside the session, and these should be made clear to the patient at the beginning.

PSYCHOANALYSIS AS A RELATIONSHIP

Since the psychoanalytic situation consists of two people working together, by definition a relationship exists. This obvious fact did not escape Freud. All his clinical works emphasize one aspect or another of the relationship, at times from the viewpoint of either the patient or the analyst, at other times from the aspect of the relationship itself. However, Freud's major theoretical interest was what was happening intrapsychically, within the patient. This, plus the scientific zeitgeist of the time, led him to view the relationship as one in which an objective observer interacted from a distance with someone who was being observed. This stance had powerful effects on the nature of the relationship. It led the analyst to think that what was happening in the relationship arose predominantly from within the patient. This was particularly true when "what was happening" was that the analysand was having thoughts and feelings about the analyst that seemed distorted— that is, that did not seem to the analyst to conform to the way he really was. This was called "transference" and was assumed to originate in the patient's thoughts and feelings about earlier important emotional objects that were now displaced onto the analyst. This in turn had important effects on technique. The analyst generally interpreted transference as displaced feelings, with the implication that he had little or no role in its development aside from interpreting the patient's resistance to recognizing it. Concomitantly, "inappropriate" feelings that the analyst had toward the patient were assumed to arise in a similar manner and were called "countertransference." Countertransference was felt to interfere with the objective observation of the patient. It was therefore seen as something that should not occur and, if it did, should be rapidly done away with. The analyst attempted more and more to be the objective, observing scientist who did not participate in the relationship but merely watched and interpreted it.

The focus on the relationship between patient and analyst rather than on each as individuals began early in the history of analysis. Sullivan in the late 1920s (Perry & Gawell, 1953) founded the interpersonalist school. At about the same time Melanie Klein (1948) began the work that evolved into the various object relations schools. These did not immediately have a major impact on the post-Freudian ego psychology that formed the mainstream of psychoanalytic thought in the United States. That school continued to view the analytic situation in the same way as Freud. Its main interest was the individuality of the patient and, to a much lesser degree, the analyst. It was not until the 1950s that the focus of the mainstream began to turn to the relationship, catalyzed by three important developments: the introduction of the concept of the therapeutic or working alliance by Zetzel (1956), Loewald's (1970) presentation of an interactional view of the psychoanalytic relationship, and Kohut's (1971) development of self psychology.

The Therapeutic Alliance

Although "the collaborative aspects of the relationship between patient and analyst have been recog-

nized from the earliest stages of psychoanalysis" (Curtis, 1979), most analysts, with a few important exceptions such as Sterba (1934) and Bibring (1937), focused on transference. It was not until Zetzel gave those collaborative aspects a name, the "therapeutic alliance," that real attention began to be paid to that aspect of the relationship. Although there has been some controversy about this since then (Brenner, 1979; Curtis, 1979), most analysts now agree that part of the relationship entails patient and analyst working together in a relatively mature, realistic way so as to bring about a better understanding of the patient. The importance of this idea is twofold. The first point, a theoretical one, has to do with the dynamics of the collaboration. Freud (1912a) considered it built upon the "unobjectionable positive transference." This led many to think of it as an unconscious infantile displacement that needed analyzing, *pace* Freud's feeling that it was unobjectionable. Recently, however, Ellman (1991) and others have pointed out that Freud's position was a holdover from the time when the aim of analysis was to uncover repressed traumatic memories. The positive transference was considered the means by which this could be done and, as such, was considered "unobjectionable." Today, if the positive transference represents important unconscious motivations, we want to understand them.

The second point is more practical. It now seems clear that there is a relatively mature part of the patient such that, for nonconflicted, realistic reasons, he recognizes that it is in his best interest to work with the analyst. If this does not exist to some significant degree, analysis cannot take place. I am not implying that a therapeutic alliance exists at every moment but that, if it is impaired for any significant length of time, an impasse will develop. If the analyst thinks about the state of the therapeutic alliance from time to time, he will be more likely to recognize when a patient who seems to be working constructively is actually being compliant, collaborating for the sake of seduction or enacting some other unconscious transference configuration. Helping the patient see this is not always easy, but if it is not done, the analysis will not progress (Meissner, 1992).

The Real Relationship

The therapeutic alliance is one part of a broader aspect of the collaboration, the "real relationship." This term highlights the fact that the analyst is perceived and reacted to as a real person as well as a transference object. At any moment of the interaction, of course, neither the transference, the therapeutic alliance, nor the real relationship can be seen in pure culture. To some degree, the relationship is always determined by both real and transference factors, and their relative dominance depends on the situation. If, for example, the analyst takes a five-minute telephone call (not a recommended procedure!) in the midst of a session, the patient's irritation will be due to both "realistic" factors (no one likes to be interrupted in the midst of an intimate conversation) and transference factors (the patient's mother used to lure him into a discussion of something important and then betray her underlying indifference by devoting much of her attention to a sibling). An important technical principle arises out of this: not everything is transference. It is important to analyze the patient's reaction to anything that occurs in the analytic situation, whether that occurrence relates primarily to the patient, the analyst, or both. By "analyzing" something, I mean attempting to enlist the patient's collaboration in understanding its meaning as fully as possible. In the work of analysis, the concept of the real relationship helps the analyst to recognize and acknowledge that at least some of the patient's reaction is due to realistic factors.

Changing Views on the Psychoanalytic Relationship

If early psychoanalysts recognized that psychoanalysis took place within a relationship, what is the difference between the relationship of old and the relationship as it is currently seen? Although many complexities exist, the difference can, without too much distortion, be reduced to differing perceptions of the amount and kind of influence each participant has on the other. Mainstream psychoanalysis until the mid-1950s tended to view the analyst as having relatively firm boundaries and being relatively uninfluenced in the relationship. The analyst maintained his equilibrium and equanimity. When disturbed or influenced beyond the usual boundaries, he recognized the experience as countertransference and tried to understand and master it. Of course, many analysts realized that they were involved with the patient beyond what was considered ideal. From early analytic times, people like Melanie Klein were writing about projective identification and describing clinical situations in which the analyst was deeply involved emotionally. However, it was not until Loewald (1970), Sandler (1976), and others pointed out the very powerful mutual influence of analyst and patient on each other's experience of the analytic situation that an accurate picture emerged.

The degree and type of mutual influence are still open to discussion. Loewald's contribution focused on the role of the analyst as a new object in producing therapeutic change. Sandler pointed out that,

contrary to the common belief that the analyst reacts for the most part realistically to what is going on, more often than not, and perhaps inevitably, he is caught up in the role that has been assigned by the patient. Many analyses, he felt, progressed by periods of transference–countertransference enactments that were understood and interpreted, and then neutrality was reestablished until the process inevitably recurred. Perhaps the most extreme of these positions is what Hoffman (1992) called "social constructivism," which holds that the analyst and the patient are constantly contributing to each other's subjective view of the analytic situation. "The patient's subjective experience of the analyst is open to, and to a large extent shaped by, the actual interactions with the analyst" (Mitchell, 1988).

This shift in view has had a major impact on mainstream analytic technique in the last ten years (Pulver, 1991). The basic question in the mind of the analyst exploring the transference used to be "How is the patient seeing me in a distorted way, influenced by self-projections and displacements from old object relationships?" Now, analysts explore the relationship, not just the transference, and their basic question is "How do the patient and I experience what is going on, and how are the experiences of each of us influenced by the other, as well as by ourselves?" Interpretations of displacements from the past are still frequently made, but they often include the analyst's contribution to the patient's experience, if he can become aware of it, and sometimes the analyst's experience itself. This apparently small change in the analyst's attitude has led to a dramatic shift in analytic technique and in the nature of the analytic experience for both analyst and patient. Idealization of the analyst has tended to diminish. Patients feel more genuinely understood and as a result understand themselves better. While no objective data are available about this, the clinical impression of analysts who have lived through this shift is that their analyses are much more effective today than in the past.

THE ANALYSIS ITSELF: THE ROLE OF THE PATIENT

Having settled the practical arrangements, the analysis is about to begin. What will take place is an interaction between two people. We begin with the patient, who, if the analysis is to succeed, will have to do a significant amount of the analytic work. He will have to do his best to cooperate in the joint attempt to understand him by adhering to the practical arrangements, revealing himself to the analyst by lying on the couch and free-associating and attempting to express and understand all aspects of himself as best he can. This will include such things as early memories, dreams, bodily sensations, traumas, motivations, fantasies, thoughts, imagery, and characterological ways of behaving, particularly those designed to protect him against unpleasant affect. He will particularly try to note all these as they arise in the psychoanalytic situation and in relation to the analyst. Simply free-associating and listening to interpretations will not be enough. He will have to listen critically to the analyst, weigh what the analyst says, try to fit it into his own knowledge of himself, and actively work on obtaining insight. Furthermore, although insight is essential, it, too, is not enough. In addition, the patient will need to mourn lost objects and fantasies, abreact traumas, and consciously attempt to change. Of course, the analyst cannot possibly explain all this to the patient, but he can explain the way analysis works and the two tools the patient can use to facilitate it, the couch and free association.

Explaining how analysis works. The way analysis works is still a matter of deep controversy, and the analyst does not attempt to go into the complex theoretical details involved; he simply tries to ensure that the patient has an understanding of how the two of them are trying to work together. To the uninitiated, analysis is a mystifying procedure. All too often analysts have permitted this mystification to flourish. The patient needs to be given an initial explanation of how and why they are doing what they are doing. I explain to my patients that they have countless thoughts and feelings of which they are unaware, that these have important effects on the way they think and feel, and are an important cause of their symptoms. Our mutual job is to try to understand them, so that the patient may then have an opportunity to try to change them. I may give an illustration of how difficult it is to change a feeling if you do not know you are feeling it. I ask the patient if he or she has any questions about the matter and then try to clarify as much as possible. Although all this registers mainly on an intellectual level, it is important to demystify what we are doing as much as we can.

The use of the couch. The couch seems initially to have been an outgrowth of Freud's use of hypnosis. Certainly he used it at the time he was developing his "pressure" technique, and it became an accepted part of psychoanalysis from the beginning. Freud gave personal reasons for using this procedure (he did not like being stared at) as well as theoretical reasons (it helped the patient relax and say whatever came to mind). It seems clear from its almost universal adoption by analysts that the couch facilitates

the analytic process, probably by lending itself to an altered state of consciousness through the recumbent position, the relaxation, and the relative sensory deprivation the procedure involves. This does not, however, mean that an analysis cannot be carried out if the patient, because of anxiety or other reasons, is unable to lie on the couch. While it is true that one focus of the subsequent analysis will be on understanding this anxiety, such understanding may never be complete enough for the patient to be able to use the couch. Nevertheless, an analytic process may evolve to such a degree that most observers would say that an analysis had taken place. In brief, the use of the couch is usually but not always helpful, and it certainly is not an absolute prerequisite for analysis. It is explained to the patient simply as part of a method that seems to be most helpful in allowing a patient to relax and free-associate.

Free association. Probably the last thing the analyst does before the actual analysis begins is to explain free association, the "fundamental rule" of analysis, to the patient. The latter is told that to achieve optimal understanding he must lie on the couch and say absolutely everything that comes to his mind: not only his thoughts, but his feelings, his bodily sensations, his fantasies, his dreams, and anything else that may occur to him. He is alerted to the fact that, while this may seem easy, in fact it will turn out to be difficult. Inevitably he will feel that some things are irrelevant or embarrassing or trivial and will be tempted not to talk about them. He should do his best to talk about them anyway but should also realize that free association, while it is called the fundamental rule, is not in any way a moral imperative. It is simply the best way to begin in the attempt to get the job done. In fact, the patient should be told that no one is able to free-associate continually and constantly. Everyone, usually sooner rather than later, avoids saying what comes to mind. An understanding of the ways he avoids doing so and the reasons for that avoidance is as important a part of the analysis as the content of the thought itself. In practice, the extent to which all this is explained to the patient varies greatly. Many analysts feel that, in view of the powerful emotional factors that are about to come into play, cognitive understanding has little import. Some simply tell the patient to say whatever he wishes. Most, however, want the patient to understand as fully as possible and may go into even further detail. They may explain why and how free association works: that whatever is in the patient's mind that he is unaware of at the moment is bound to have an effect on what he is thinking and that the analyst will be listening for this. When the analyst feels that he understands something that will be useful to the patient, he will tell the patient about it. He will ask the patient if he has any questions about what they are about to undertake and will try to answer these questions clearly. Whatever the controversies about how extensively one should explain free association to the patient, the usefulness of some explanation is generally accepted.

THE ANALYSIS ITSELF: THE ROLE OF THE ANALYST

As the patient lies on the couch for the first time, the analyst sits back in his chair, out of the patient's line of vision, and prepares to play his part in the relationship. That part has many aspects. First, the analyst will have a specific aim in mind and will pursue this aim with a certain set of attitudes and use a particular and unique mode of thought. Furthermore, in pursuing this aim, he will engage in certain actions, such as making interpretations, and in doing so (and, in fact, in all his behavior), will follow certain principles. Finally, the analyst will inevitably react emotionally to the patient in many different ways.

The aim of the analyst. I think it is fair to say that the primary, foremost, overriding aim of every analyst, regardless of the analytic school of thought he upholds or his theory of the mechanism of therapeutic change, is to help the patient understand as much about himself as possible. He will do this mainly by conveying as much about the relationship between himself and his patient as he can. He will, that is, hope to help his patient attain insight. A secondary but closely related aim will be to help his patient use that insight in an adaptive way. Although Freud was right in pointing out the danger of too much therapeutic zeal, most analysts nevertheless hope that their patients will be relieved of their symptoms and maladaptive character traits. They hope that their quality of life at the end of the analysis will be better than it was at the beginning. The analyst may not believe that insight alone is enough to enable the patient to make these changes (Rangell, 1981) or that it is the only agent at work. He may, for instance, feel that the patient must experience the analyst as a new object or repair empathic failures or identify with his own more benign superego. He may believe that he must do many things along with interpretation to ultimately arrive at understanding: that he must provide an atmosphere of safety or that he must soothe, confront, or point out reality. Whatever his beliefs, however, he will be carrying them out with the predominant intent of helping the patient to understand. I would submit that if his intent is to effect change in any other way, he is not doing analysis.

Helping the patient to understand himself and deal more efficiently with his multiple and often conflicting feelings and ideas is a very broad aim. Every analyst will have a large subset of subsidiary aims, all consistent with the major aim of understanding and better functioning. Analysts may think of their aims in theoretical terms ("Where id was, let ego be"); in terms of subsidiary steps leading to greater understanding, such as the expansion of freedom of association (Kris, 1982) or the reduction of resistance (Gray, 1987); or, at any particular moment in the analysis, in terms of a specific task that will ultimately lead to greater understanding, such as helping the patient become aware of the transference (Gill, 1982) or exploring an empathic failure (Kohut, 1971). In the end, however, better functioning through deeper understanding is the goal.

The Analytic Attitude

By the analytic attitude, we refer to the feelings, opinions, and values the analyst maintains in the analytic situation and those relatively settled and consistent ways in which he expresses them to his patients. Analysts always have a number of attitudes which, in the aggregate, are thought of as "the" analytic attitude. Among them are the following:

Flexibility, in the sense of open-mindedness to various analytic theories and, more important, to new impressions about what his patient might be thinking and experiencing and what might be the best way at any particular time to help him understand. Flexibility, of course, has its limits. Bion's (1977) idea that the analyst should enter each session as if he had never met the patient before is impossible. He will inevitably have preconceptions based on his knowledge of the patient, his theories, his personality, and other factors. Nevertheless, he should always strive to be open to change.

Valuing insight, a steady adherence to the primary analytic aim: the search for understanding.

Humility, the realization that the analyst is fallible and will not infrequently make mistakes. Closely allied to this is the ability to tolerate uncertainty. While he strives to understand, much of his working time will be spent in puzzlement and nonunderstanding. He needs to know that this is the norm and that he must not yield to premature closure.

Recognition of the joint responsibility for therapeutic results. The analyst must avoid excessive therapeutic zeal by combining the paradoxical qualities of caring about the patient, in the sense that the patient's well-being and the work they are doing really matters, and at the same time realizing that the patient's improvement is a joint responsibility. The ultimate way the analyst can help is by trying to understand the patient. If he does his best in that regard, he is doing as much as he can do.

Empathy, the ability to place oneself in another's place and sense what the other is feeling as deeply as possible and on all levels, conscious, preconscious, and unconscious.

Consistency and reliability.

Respect for the patient as an individual whose autonomy is to be fostered.

An appreciation of the patient—that is, the ability to recognize and communicate to the patient his achievements as well as his conflicts and deficits.

Spontaneity. While guided by experience and technical principles, the analyst must be himself. We are different people in different situations, but we should strive to be the way we are naturally, rather than distant, withdrawn, rule-bound, or artificial. Closely related to this is the attitude of being available as a partner in an intense relationship and being willing to accept all the feelings such a relationship arouses.

How the Analyst Thinks: Free-floating Attention

The way in which the analyst thinks has commanded analytic interest ever since Freud recommended free-floating (evenly suspended, hovering) attention. Although recommending a similar mental attitude in *The Interpretation of Dreams* (1900), he did not specifically name and describe it until 1912. By *gleichschwebende Aufmerksamkeit* Freud meant the suspension of all efforts on the part of the analyst to direct his attention, listening to the patient without trying to focus on any particular aspect of what he says, soaking in what he says as a sponge, one might say. Any other attitude, Freud felt, would inevitably lead the analyst to introduce his own meanings, based on theoretical and personal preconceptions and preferences, into his understanding of what the patient was saying. Furthermore, such free-floating attention permitted the analyst's own mind to associate to the patient's associations and was much more likely to lead to real understanding than were attempts at cognitive deciphering.

While free-floating attention is undoubtedly an important aspect of the analyst's thinking, it takes very little introspection to recognize that a great deal more goes on in the analyst's mind. He knows something about the patient, and it is impossible and undesirable not to try from time to time to fit his immediate impressions with those he has had from the past. Furthermore, he has had a wealth of experience with other patients and a large store of theoretical knowledge, and these also inform his attempts to understand. In addition to listening, he is observing the patient's nonverbal communications. He is often attempting to put himself in the patient's place (that is, forming trial identifications, empathizing) and imagining how he would feel in the situation the patient is describing. He is observing his own reactions to the patient and using those reactions as a guide to what is happening in the relationship. Finally, he is forming conjectures about all this and making judgments about which of these conjectures might be useful to impart to the patient and when. And, of course, he is keeping track of the time and doing other things that are necessary to maintain the structure of the session. It is probably best to characterize the analyst's average, day-to-day thinking as a mélange of free-floating attention and purposeful cognitive and affective activities, each of which contains a number of different processes. All of these are ultimately designed to help the analyst understand what is going on in the patient's mind and in the relationship and to help him communicate this usefully to the patient.

Basic Principles Followed by the Analyst

In carrying out his part of the analytic task, the analyst is guided by several general principles. Most of these were first described in Freud's technique papers, where he advanced them only as guidelines: "I must, however, make it clear that what I am asserting is that this technique is the only one suited to my individuality; I do not venture to deny that a physician quite differently constituted might find himself driven to adopt a different attitude to his patients and to the task before him" (1912b, p. 111). He cautioned against adopting these principles as rigid rules defining the only way in which psychoanalysis might be practiced: "I think I am well-advised, however, to call these rules 'recommendations' and not to claim any unconditional acceptance for them. The extraordinary diversity of the psychical constellations concerned, the plasticity of all mental processes and the wealth of determining factors oppose any mechanization of technique: and they bring it about that a course of action that is as a rule justified may at times prove ineffective, whilst one that is usually mistaken may once in a while lead to the desired end" (1913, p. 123). Freud's fears that these guidelines would become rigid rules were justified. During the Classical Period, his recommendations were often looked upon as a set of commandments that had to be followed to the letter. This led all too frequently to the distant, uninvolved analyst who sat behind the patient impassively and occasionally made an interpretation, a caricature of the good analyst. Fortunately, our current, more flexible interpretation of Freud's principles, which are useful with many but not all patients in many but not all circumstances, has prevailed. The uninvolved analyst is now uncommon. With this in mind, let us turn to the principles themselves.

Neutrality. Considering that neutrality is perhaps the most important principle of psychoanalytic technique, the confusion that has grown up around the term is mind-boggling. At least some of this stems from the fact that Freud never defined *Indifferenz* (translated as "indifference" by Riviere and "neutrality" by Strachey) and used the term in different ways in different contexts. For instance, his first use of it (1915, p. 164) was followed in the next paragraph by the term translated *abstinence,* but which clearly meant the same thing. Anna Freud (1937) appeared to be speaking of neutrality when she wrote about equidistance from the id, the ego, and the superego, but she never used the word. It was not until the early 1950s (Glover, 1955) that neutrality was actually discussed as a principle in the psychoanalytic literature. Without going too deeply into the controversy about definition, it would seem that the term should represent something that guides the analyst in an important way in his technique, that does not overlap with other principles such as abstinence and anonymity, and that has more than a passing resemblance to the meaning of neutrality in ordinary English. "Not taking sides" would seem to fulfill all these requirements. The principle of neutrality might best be stated as follows: The analyst does not take sides with any aspect of his patient's personality. From the standpoint of id, ego, and superego, he does not support nor oppose his patient's desires to be sexual or aggressive, to deal with reality in whatever way he chooses, to strive for any ambition or yield to any prohibition. He maintains a neutral attitude toward all these, toward every aspect of his patient's desires, fantasies, cognition, and affect.

This definition captures a crucial attitude of the analyst, but, as Levy and Inderbitzin (1992) point out, it is flawed in one major respect: in fact, analysts do and, indeed, must take sides quite frequently. When their actual practice is examined, it appears that analysts take sides whenever it is necessary to do so to facilitate the psychoanalytic process. If we add to the above definition the phrase "except when necessary to help the patient achieve the ultimate aim of understanding and integrating," we satisfy that objection and have a statement of the principle that will persuade everyone.

The definition offered above is almost the same as saying that neutrality means that the analyst respects the autonomy of the patient. When we say that he does not take sides, we obviously do not mean that

the analyst has no opinions, values, or beliefs of his own. We do mean that the analyst undertakes to keep those beliefs to himself and, as far as possible, not to impose them on the patient or let them influence his feelings about the patient or any aspect of what the patient is feeling. As with all principles, exceptions exist. The analyst believes strongly that it will be useful if the patient can come to understand his unconscious fantasies as clearly as possible. He conveys this belief to the patient and consistently behaves in accordance with it. But even here, the neutral analyst tries not to impose this belief on the patient through emotional pressure. As strongly as he feels that understanding will help, he recognizes that the patient has a right and often many good reasons not to understand. While he will try to point these out to the patient, he will not think any the less of him if he is unwilling or unable to understand himself.

Here we are talking about patients who do not adopt the analyst's goals and values. But what about patients who have radically different values, of sorts that collide head-on with those the analyst holds dear? In this situation the analyst's neutrality is rarely tested unless the patient puts these values into action. Let us suppose that we are treating a young parent who feels that severe physical punishment is required to rear a well-disciplined child. As long as this is only a feeling, most analysts would be aware of their own contrary views and able to set them aside so as to enable the patient to explore his feelings to the greatest extent possible. Most analysts have become aware, through their own analysis and training, of the infinite variety of human fantasy and desire and are deeply imbued with the philosophy that there are always reasons for beliefs and fantasies, if only they can be discovered. If, however, our hypothetical patient were to carry out on his children what the analyst saw as abuse, then the analyst (legal considerations aside) might have a great deal of difficulty in maintaining his neutrality. Although this kind of value conflict has not been discussed very much, at least some analysts (Greenson, 1967) feel that if the analyst cannot resolve it in his own mind, he is not likely to be able to conduct the analysis successfully.

Our definition needs to be elaborated upon slightly. Neutrality means not taking sides, but with what? Certainly the analyst does not take sides with any intrapsychic aspect of the patient. Furthermore, he does not take sides with the patient in any interpersonal encounters he may have, including those with the analyst himself. If the patient is involved in a marital conflict, the analyst attempts to keep his mind open to the role played in the conflict by both the patient and the spouse. He attempts to have no ambitions for the patient except therapeutic ones, and even these are not fanatical. "No ambitions" has to be qualified: the analyst and the patient are in an intense relationship, and the analyst certainly has ambitions for his patient, including the wish that he get well. But as much as possible, he recognizes his narcissistic investment in these wishes and keeps them to a minimum. I may hope that the candidate I am analyzing will finish his analysis and his training successfully, but if he ends analysis with different ambitions and becomes (God forbid!) a behavior therapist, I do not take it as a personal insult, and my feelings for him remain very much the same as before his new career decision.

Finally, neutrality means that the analyst does not take sides with the patient in his struggles with reality. The patient may be about to make a major decision that I do not feel is a wise one, but I realize that my greatest contribution to his well-being will be to help him understand all his motivations, as he and I have contracted to do in the beginning. I may abandon neutrality to preserve his life and health, but otherwise my neutrality extends to his dealings with the external world as well as the internal.

Abstinence. The principle of abstinence has been the center of an important psychoanalytic controversy since Freud (1915) introduced it: "I have already let it be understood that analytic technique requires of the physician that he should deny to the patient who is craving for love the satisfaction that she demands. The treatment must be carried out in abstinence" (p. 165). Although Freud was referring here to romantic love, he clearly felt that the analyst should abstain from the gratification of other wishes as well. At the same time, he recognized that complete absence of gratification within the treatment situation was undesirable and, in fact, impossible: "Some concessions must of course be made to him [the patient], greater or less, according to the case and the patient's individuality. But it is not good to let them get too great" (Freud, 1919, p. 164). Since setting the boundaries of these gratifications, both in type and amount, has been a significant factor in the development of different lines of psychoanalytic therapy, it will be useful to trace some of Freud's reasoning in detail and see how this applies to contemporary psychoanalysis.

Freud's theoretical reasons for advocating abstinence were clear. He felt that the patient's illness was caused by his inability to obtain libidinal satisfaction, for psychological reasons originating in his childhood. The patient's desire for treatment was based on the suffering attendant upon this privation.

Providing libidinal gratification within the treatment or permitting him to achieve substitute gratification outside the treatment would relieve the suffering and decrease his motivation. More practical reasons lay in Freud's recognition of the tremendous temptation that transference love presents to the analyst, particularly the inexperienced one, and the opportunity for exploitation it offers to unscrupulous practitioners. Freud's rule of abstinence was advanced at least partly to help the first and warn the second. Finally, Freud found himself confronted with the technical experimentation of his friend Ferenczi, some of which consisted of "activity" designed to gratify wishes of the patient in an attempt to make up for what the patient had missed as a child. Freud's initial support for Ferenczi's work, based partly on friendship and partly on his own practice (he had no hesitation about giving the Rat Man food, for example), was obviously mixed with reservations. Later these reservations became paramount (Gay, 1988).

As with so many of his recommendations, Freud's advice on abstinence was extrapolated by his students to the absurd point of refusing to gratify any wish of the patient, regardless of its motivation or its realistic nature. We have gradually come to see that many things the patient desires—for example, a change of schedule—are reasonable and can be discussed reasonably. We always wonder about their unconscious motivations, but sometimes these can be explored only after the reality has been dealt with. Taken in the sense of abstinence from the gratification of unconscious, often infantile wishes, only one of Freud's points on abstinence is no longer a part of current psychoanalytic practice. Analysis now lasts so long and our understanding of pathogenesis and motivation for treatment is so different from Freud's that we no longer expect our patients to refrain from gratifications outside the treatment situation, except when those gratifications have such a destructive impact on the patient as to make treatment impossible. Patients are no longer advised to postpone important decisions or action until analysis is over. They are advised instead to try to understand their behavior as deeply as possible before taking action. When their behavior seems to be designed to gratify wishes displaced from the transference, we are particularly concerned to help the patient understand this, but we do not forbid it.

Freud's position on abstinence within the treatment, however, is still followed, although some points remain controversial. Note that the abstinence involved is incurred by the patient but imposed by the analyst, who does or does not refrain from gratifying the patient's wishes. In general, the principle holds that most unconscious wishes of the patient are to be understood, not gratified. It is clear, however, that certain exceptions to this, some temporary and some permanent, are crucial. The very aim of psychoanalysis, understanding, involves the gratification of a wish. All our patients wish to be understood, some consciously and some unconsciously, and some more urgently than others. In addition, the maintenance by the analyst of an attitude of sufficient genuineness, cordiality, and caring to enable the patient to continue the relationship inevitably involves the gratification of unconscious wishes for attention and affection. Finally, situations sometimes arise in which the frustration of an unconscious wish would provoke such intolerable anxiety and rage as to cause the patient to break off therapy. In these situations the analyst may have to gratify the wish temporarily until he and the patient are able to understand it. One patient, for example, had been subjected to intense abuse by his mother, who at the same time acted as if she were not in any way angry. My initial attempts to explore his inquiries about whether he was making me angry implied that I was *not* angry, though he was sure that I was. This was an intolerable repetition of the situation with his mother, and simply interpreting it was not sufficient. It was necessary for me to keep him overtly appraised of the state of my feelings when he was dealing with things he felt would antagonize me until we finally could understand what was going on.

Part of the controversial trend toward greater flexibility around the principle of abstinence arises from the ongoing debate about the degree to which insight and the relationship with a new object are responsible for therapeutic change. This will be discussed at greater length in Chapter 5. In brief, the spectrum ranges from those who feel that insight alone is responsible (probably a minority) to those who feel that the relationship with a new object is equally or even more important. Those holding the former opinion tend to adhere more strictly to abstinence in the hope of ultimately understanding every wish the patient wants gratified. Those holding the latter opinion tend to feel that many gratifications inevitably take place and that understanding all of them is not only unnecessary but at times counterproductive. Most analysts maintain a position somewhere in the middle, but a great deal of work has yet to be done on the topic.

Anonymity. The principle of the analyst's anonymity —or, as it is sometimes called, impersonality— states that the patient should know as little about the analyst as possible. Freud enunciated it very clearly: "It might be expected that it would be quite allow-able and indeed useful . . . for the doctor to afford him [the patient] a glimpse of his own mental defects and conflicts and, by giving him intimate information about his own life, enable him to put himself on an equal footing. . . . [But] experience does not speak in favor of an affective technique of this kind. . . . I have no hesitation, therefore, in condemning this kind of technique as incorrect. The doctor should be opaque to his patients and, like a mirror, should show them nothing but what is shown to him" (1912b, p. 117). Since then, the principle, though widely accepted, has received very little specific attention. Although the mirror metaphor has often been referred to in other contexts, remarkably few papers with the words *anonymity* or *impersonality* in their title exist in the major analytic literature (see Paul, 1978, for one example).

While anonymity is related in some ways to neutrality and abstinence, it is sufficiently different to be thought of as a principle in itself. Its relationship to neutrality is apparent: if the analyst takes sides, he is revealing something about himself. As for abstinence, the temptation to reveal something about oneself often arises in response to a desire of the patient, and the actual revelation, therefore, may be the gratification of a wish of the patient. However, Freud implied (and the word *anonymity* has come to mean), "In psychoanalysis, personal facts about the analyst should remain unknown to the analysand" (Moore & Fine, 1990, p. 23). The principle, therefore, is clearly different from neutrality or abstinence.

Freud gave three reasons for not telling the patient personal facts: (1) telling "makes him even more incapable of overcoming his deeper resistances" (Freud does not say why); (2) it may encourage the patient to be insatiable in his curiosity; (3) it makes resolution of the transference more difficult. The usual explanation of this is that the patient is then no longer able to recognize the unreality of his transference distortions, since he now has realistic information about the analyst which supports his feeling that his distortions are accurate. An additional reason often given for anonymity is that the less the patient knows about the analyst, the more easily he is able to fantasize about him. If, for example, a patient knows I am married, he is less easily able to fantasize that I am living with a homosexual lover. Finally, anonymity can be viewed as facilitating the basic focus of the therapy on the patient, not the analyst.

I have grave doubts about the value of anonymity as applied in the strict manner that Freud advised and most analysts follow (though Freud himself certainly did not). As a broad guideline holding that the analyst should, in general, not spontaneously volunteer personal information without having a reason for doing so, the principle is useful. The focus of the treatment, after all, is the patient. However, when anonymity is thought of as a strict injunction that personal information about the analyst is always detrimental and should be scrupulously avoided, the trend of the literature would seem to disagree. Interestingly, when analytic principles are discussed, the recommendation that the analyst remain anonymous is usually repeated *ex cathedra,* without discussion of the reasons behind it. I can find no convincing evidence that having information about the analyst makes it more difficult to fantasize about him or to resolve the transference. There is, in fact, considerable evidence to the contrary. In addition, there is a growing literature to the effect that the emergence of some information about the analyst may be beneficial, not harmful, to the analysis. I will briefly summarize some of my reasons for advocating a more liberal application of the principle of abstinence.

First, it is obvious that strict anonymity is impossible. Patients meet us, see us, interact with us, visit our offices, note how we decorate them, what books we read, what hours we keep, whether we are shy, warm, or argumentative. In short, they obtain a great deal of personal information about our character and our lives from the very contact that is the essence of analysis. No one has suggested that any attempt be made to restrict this. To do so would create an artificiality that would undoubtedly interfere with a genuine relationship.

Second, medical ethics as well as medicolegal considerations require that we enable patients to make well-informed decisions about their choice of therapist. As a result, it has become standard practice for analysts to answer basic questions about their qualifications: where they went to medical school, how much experience they have had, and so on. These questions almost always have unconscious as well as realistic bases, but in the consultative process we answer them first and explore them only when appropriate. Furthermore, in many institutes candidates are required for medicolegal reasons to inform their patients that they are students and will be receiving supervision. While this certainly has an impact on the analysis, experience indicates that the impact is idiosyncratic, unpredictable, almost always "grist for the mill" and usually beneficial rather than detrimental to the analysis.

Third, extra-analytic contacts of various kinds (meetings in the elevator, at professional meetings, at cocktail parties) are frequent in ordinary analyses and inevitable in training analyses. The many papers that have been written about this almost all cite the facilitating effect such contacts have on the analysis, usually by stimulating transference fantasies, often in unexpected and productive directions. Reports of negative effects of such contact are rare. Levy and Inderbitzin (personal communication) feel that the reality arising from such interactions can be used defensively, and this is certainly true, as can any reality. This defensive use of reality, however, would seem to be better handled by analyzing it than by avoiding it. It should be emphasized that planned personal contact amounting to socializing is an entirely different matter. It changes the nature of the analytic relationship, which, by agreement, is devoted solely to understanding. It is usually guarded against when it is likely to occur, as in training analyses, by an initial agreement that when the analyst and patient meet outside the analytic situation, they behave cordially to each other and keep the contact to a minimum.

Fourth, self-disclosure by the analyst in the analytic situation is more controversial than knowledge about the analyst gained in other ways. Such self-disclosure takes many forms and cannot be dealt with at length here. Perhaps the only generally agreed-upon principle is that when the patient detects a clear-cut manifestation of countertransference, it is incumbent on the analyst to take responsibility for his behavior ("My forgetting about that appointment clearly means that I am feeling something that I am not aware of, and I'll have to try to understand it. In the meantime, how did you feel when I didn't show up?"). Other instances of the analyst disclosing his thoughts, feelings, fantasies, and images are increasingly common in the literature. The general view seems to be that this is very useful in certain situations, but these have yet to be carefully delineated.

In brief, the principle of anonymity as Freud originally described it—that is, analysts refraining from "bringing their own individuality freely into the discussion" (Freud, 1912b, p. 117)—continues to be an important principle of technique, although when and how the analyst should disclose his own thoughts and feelings needs further investigation. Broadening the principle to the idea that "personal facts about the analyst should remain unknown to the analysand" not only is unwarranted but encourages an artificial withholding on the part of the analyst that impedes the analytic process.

Confidentiality. The principle that everything the patient says during the analytic sessions—indeed, everything the analyst knows about the patient, including the very fact that he is a patient—is utterly confidential dates from the time of Hippocrates and is well-nigh sacred. The reason for confidentiality is obvious. We are asking the patient to withhold nothing, to bring out his deepest secrets, including all those thoughts and feelings of which he may be most ashamed and may most wish to conceal. To expect anyone to engage in such revelation without a guarantee that what he discloses will remain absolutely confidential is clearly unreasonable, and analysts from the beginning have afforded such a guarantee. The principle is one that is adhered to not just in the letter but in the spirit. One may tell one's spouse about almost everything, but one does not tell her about one's analytic patients. Analysts do not gossip about patients, nor do they discuss them in public, such as on the evening's train ride home with a colleague, no matter how well disguised they feel the identity of the patient may be.

I have presented the principle of confidentiality with such conviction that I must also discuss certain departures from the principle, which, unfortunately, seem absolutely necessary. In the first place, we are not immune to legal requirements, and, if subpoenaed, we may be forced to produce notes or testify. We do so with reluctance, even if our patient gives permission. Third parties contributing to the cost of analysis are increasingly requiring more and more detailed reporting, and analysts, with the permission of the patient, are reluctantly complying. My own practice when doing so is to first let the patient read everything I am submitting to the insurance company. If the patient requests changes, I will comply with the request as long as it does not alter the basic truth of the report.

A different kind of violation of confidentiality arises from the needs of the analyst, who may wish to discuss the analysis with colleagues for educational or consultative purposes or to use clinical material in writing scientific articles. Some analysts feel that simply disguising the patient's identity is sufficient in such situations. I feel that it is necessary in addition to get the patient's permission when possible and show him the content of what is to be revealed. This obviously introduces complications when done in the midst of an analysis, but I have so far not encountered a situation in which the patient's reaction cannot be understood, sometimes even profitably. I do not doubt that the effects of such a procedure can be adverse, however. When I suspect that this might be so, I simply do not introduce the subject or use the material.

Apropos educational needs, candidates at the Philadelphia Psychoanalytic Institute are required to inform patients before the analysis starts that they are in training, that the case will be discussed periodically with a supervisor and may be discussed for educational purposes in front of groups of other candidates, and that all possible measures will be taken to protect the patient's identity. If patients object, their cases are not presented before other students, although supervision cannot be waived. In brief, confidentiality is one of our most important principles, and we adhere to it with the fewest possible exceptions.

WHAT THE ANALYST ACTUALLY DOES: INTERPRETATION

I come now to what most people think of when they think of analytic technique: what the analyst actually does. I have already said that he listens, and one might think that all he does aside from that is explain to the patient what the patient does not already know—that is, interpret. Indeed, if we gave credence to common caricatures, one might think that the analyst interprets only rarely. As we shall see, however, he does a great deal more than that. The analyst who sits silently through sessions and once or twice makes an interpretation is almost extinct, if he ever existed at all. Certainly, from the diaries Freud's patients kept about their analyses with him, Freud was never like that, and I doubt that any good analyst ever has been. Still, since analysis was once defined as an activity in which the analyst only makes interpretations (Eissler, 1953), and interpretation is still considered "the central therapeutic activity of the analyst during treatment" (Moore & Fine, 1990, p. 103), it seems a good place to begin. In discussing it, we will unavoidably encounter phenomena such as transference, resistance, and countertransference. These are perhaps better thought of as part of the psychoanalytic process and are discussed further in other chapters of the book.

A definition of interpretation that seems to capture its essence is that of Loewenstein (1951): "In psychoanalysis this term [interpretation] is applied to those explanations, given to patients by the analyst, which add to their knowledge about themselves" (pp. 3–4). Perhaps it would be wise to amend that to "which are intended to add to their knowledge about themselves," since we all know that interpretations often fall on deaf ears. As we shall see, this is a very broad definition that encompasses many different kinds of interpretation. To illustrate them, I will discuss Mr. B., a fictitious young man who, let us pretend, has now been in analysis with me for three and a half years. As I explore what I might interpret to him, you will come to know him a lot better. For the moment, let me simply say that his initial shyness has changed. He is now full of ebullience and a mild, usually good-natured, but somewhat arrogant intrusiveness. Nevertheless, he continues to have flare-ups of the work inhibition for which he sought analysis. His mother was a rather passive and clinging woman, and he was the apple of her eye. She had a depressive episode when he was two years old which resulted in her hospitalization for six months. His father was a hard-working, distant man of whom he had always been terrified. He started this session by telling me a dream: "A young child was crying because he had fallen and hurt his knee. A woman with glasses came over to help him, but as she was about to pick him up, someone called her away. A man gave him some ice cream after she left, so he wouldn't cry. I was just watching." He then began to associate, but we will stop for a moment to look at the types of interpretation that might arise in a session beginning like this. Obviously, the interpretations I make and when I make them will depend on many more factors than can be discussed here, but at least some of the major issues in the area of interpretation can be touched upon.

Types of Interpretations

Transference versus extra-transference interpretations. If this session occurred shortly before I was leaving on a vacation, I would have to consider whether Mr. B. was reacting to my leaving in the way he reacted to his mother's leaving when he was a child. If I felt this was probable and interpreted it thus to him, I would be making a transference interpretation. This is in contrast to an extra-transference interpretation, which is not about the patient's relationship to the analyst.

Several years ago, a controversy raged about this point. A number of analysts felt that only transference interpretations should be made: "I wonder if you are feeling abandoned by me because I am leaving on vacation?" (Parenthetically, whether this in itself constitutes a transference interpretation is an interesting point.) Some insisted that it should be combined with an interpretation that refers to the genesis of the feeling, in order for it to be complete: "Perhaps you are sad today because I am leaving on vacation, just as you were sad when your mother left you as a two-year-old." Some held that extra-transference interpretations—"You seem to be sad today because your wife is going on a trip and you are going to miss her"—might be made, but that only transference interpretations produced significant change. Still others held that both types of interpretation were important and contributed to psychoanalytic change. Today, this last is the prevailing opinion.

Among the different kinds of interpretation, some

of which may be made in the transference, others not, are the following.

Reconstructions. If the patient did not remember and had never been told that his mother had left, and if sufficient evidence existed (a sine qua non for all interpretations), traumatic events and interactional patterns from childhood might be reconstructed: "You have had a series of dreams about older women crying and leaving you. I wonder if your mother got depressed and left when you were a child? Maybe she went to the hospital or to a relative's house."

Character interpretations. Character traits often enter into conflict and need to be interpreted. Working with them follows a special course (Fenichel, 1941). First, one must avoid the temptation to interpret them as if they were transference. Mr. B., in spite of his shyness, was mildly arrogant from the time of his first visit to me. However, to have pointed out that he was treating me the way he treated his father would have been inaccurate and counterproductive. He was, in fact, treating me the way he treated everyone. To understand his arrogance usefully, Mr. B. would first have to become aware that it was a pattern—that is, a character trait. He would then have to recognize that it caused him significant trouble. Only after he had begun to dislike it and wonder about it would he be motivated to look into it and understand it. All this takes place over a long period of time. Just when to begin the analysis of a character trait is something that I find is mainly a matter of intuition. There must be some principles to guide one in this area, but I have been unable to discover them.

Resistance interpretations. As Glover (1955) pointed out, telling a patient that he is resisting is like telling a man in a sandstorm that his conjunctival reflex is working and will he please stop blinking. Patients "resist" for unconscious reasons, and telling them they are doing so is not only fruitless but accusatory. Nevertheless, resistance is an important part of behavior in analysis, and it must be understood. Ordinarily, interpretations of resistance are made in the context of how and why the resistance is taking place: "Remember the man in the dream who didn't seem to want you to cry? I think you may be staying away from your sadness right now because it feels as if I don't want you to cry." Resistance interpretation was first emphasized by Kaiser (1934) and recently has been focused upon by Gray (1987), who recommends pointing out manifestations of it as they appear in the thought processes (not the contents) of the sessions: "Did you notice that as you told me your thoughts about the dream, you came to the glasses the woman wore, and your mind then went blank?" This may include pointing out shifts in affect, abrupt changes of content, or any other indications of some impediment to the flow of associations.

Oedipal versus pre-oedipal interpretations. Many years ago, all conflict was considered to have arisen, or at least to have been primarily organized, in the oedipal period. When evidence of pre-oedipal conflict was found, it was thought to constitute a regressive movement away from oedipal anxieties. Today, as the enduring effect of pre-oedipal feelings and experiences has become incontrovertible, pre-oedipal material is interpreted just as freely as that from the oedipal period. One would be as concerned to help Mr. B. become aware of the sadness, helplessness, and rage arising from the trauma of his mother's leaving him at the age of two as to help him see that he is using these feelings to some extent to avoid his more positive feelings toward her and the competitive attitude toward his father that developed after his mother had returned and his relationship with her had been reestablished.

The Art of Interpreting

As the patient free-associates, the analyst carries out his two tasks of the session: trying to understand what is on the patient's mind on all levels, conscious, preconscious, and unconscious; and deciding what aspect of that might be most useful at any particular moment to impart to the patient. These tasks are rarely conscious; most analysts begin each session with a simple attitude of expectant interest and an open mind. As the session proceeds, the analyst is immersed in information from many sources: his patient's words, the way he says them, and a variety of nonverbal vocalizations and behavior, as well as his own feelings, imagery, and thoughts. Some of these are the result of associations that take place during periods of evenly hovering attention, some arise from his previous knowledge of the patient, and some derive from experience with other patients and from theory. He may interact with the patient in a variety of ways, as will be discussed in more detail below. Gradually a picture of how the patient is feeling and thinking will form in his mind, at times with relative certainty because the patient has told him clearly about those thoughts and feelings, and at other times, when his picture derives more from inferences, with less certainty. We may call those inferences "conjectures" or "hypotheses."

At some point we will wish to communicate some aspect of this picture to the patient, and certain principles lie behind our decision of what to impart and when to do so—that is, of content and timing. Like the more general principles related to the analyst's attitude, these principles of interpretation are no more than flexible guidelines. Experienced analysts rarely think about them consciously. The more experience one gets, the freer one feels to do what seems useful whether it follows the guidelines or not, provided only that it is in the service of understanding. As Fenichel (1941) says: "Anything is permissible if you only know why." Nevertheless, there *are* guidelines, and they can be useful. A few follow; many others exist.

First, interpretations are generally made "from the surface" (Kris, 1951). By that I mean that we try to interpret what a patient is almost aware of, what is preconscious. We want him to be able to understand, and he is much more likely to understand something that he is already close to understanding than something that is deeply unconscious. Much of our work, in fact, will consist in helping the patient get near a feeling or a fantasy, of preparing for an interpretation, rather than formally interpreting. If I am fairly certain that Mr. B. feels I do not want him to cry, I might ask him at various times in the session how he feels, whether he has had any feelings about my vacation, what his picture of my attitude is at the moment, whether he notices the sadness in what he is saying, and similar things. All this will let me judge whether or not he is ready to hear what one might think of as the interpretation proper, that he feels I do not want him to cry. Again, I must emphasize the flexibility in all this. At times I will make an interpretation beyond what Mr. B. is ready for, in the hope of gradually furthering his readiness by giving him something to think about, but this is not usual.

Second, we are guided by the predominant affect in the session. If Mr. B. is sad throughout the session, I am likely to try to connect his sadness with my vacation even if he has made it clear that he is also, at a deeper level, angry. His rage can wait until he is nearer to feeling it. Whether we make a content interpretation of his affect, thoughts, or fantasies or a resistance interpretation, or whether we combine them, is a matter of our sense of what he will be able to hear.

Third, we prefer a transference interpretation, but only if we sense that the transference is the main issue of the session and that there is at least a chance that he will recognize it. We try not to be fooled by how clear the transference is to ourselves: we almost always see it more clearly than the patient.

Fourth, when we interpret (at the beginning, middle, or end of the session) is (or should be) utterly unpredictable. A patient who was irritated yesterday may walk in and casually remark, "Did you know your tie doesn't match your socks?" and that may be enough for us to point out that he still seems to be irritated. We do our best to walk the tightrope between too little evidence and absolute certainty. Usually, we need to wait for the evidence. Our conjectures always carry a greater or lesser sense of inner conviction, and we try not to jump to conclusions.

Fifth, spontaneity is important. We recognize that our timing depends not a little on our mood. Those of us who are labile will interpret sooner when we are happy and later when we are a bit low. One might think that an analyst should be alert to such mood swings and correct for them, and to some degree he should. But spontaneity is so important that it should be given great reign. The analytic relationship is an affective one. Good analysts usually do not think very much about what they are going to say before they say it; calculated interpretations usually have less emotional impact. Interpretive routines are to be frowned on. One of my supervisors used to insist that his supervisees listen for at least thirty-five minutes before making an interpretation. Aside from my personal inability to engage in such restraint, the routine took the life out of the analysis.

The concept of the relationship and interpretations. The growing recognition of the importance of the relationship in psychoanalysis has had a deep impact upon the way transference is interpreted. I apologize here for my use of a straw man to make a point. I know full well that neither Freud nor any good analyst since his time has looked upon himself as a detached, objective observer in the actual analytic situation. But our focus on the transference and the whole tenor of some of our principles of technique have led us to a tendency toward detachment, toward assuming the position of arbiter of reality who points out the patient's distortions. We continue rightly to make classical transference interpretations ("I wonder if you felt I wasn't interested in what you were saying about the way your boss harassed you, because you were seeing me as your mother, who didn't seem to be interested in the way your father mistreated you?"). But we are now much less inclined to take the patient's observations about us as distortions and more likely to wonder how we participated in the interaction in question. As a result, we are more likely to recognize the ubiquitous transference–countertransference enactments that take place in all good analyses. We are more likely to explore them and, by exploring them, to expand our own and our patient's understanding of the impact we have on each other. As a result, instead of the interpretation I gave above, I might now say such things as: "Tell me more about how I seemed

disinterested," or "What was it I did or didn't do that gave you that feeling?" or "Just when did you notice it?" or "You know, in a certain way I think you were right when you noticed a kind of disinterest. I think the tone of your voice dropped a little, and you told me about the fight with relatively little feeling, and I recall now that I began thinking about something else you had been talking about, which I realize now wasn't really pertinent." To which the patient might say, "You know, when I started talking about that, I really didn't expect you to be interested." And either of us might say, using the proper pronouns: "It sounds like the way your mother was when your father was beating on you. She just wasn't interested. So when you started talking about your boss doing the same thing, you didn't expect me to be interested, and you began withdrawing and talking in a way that caused me actually to lose interest." Exchanges of this sort seem to lead to a deeper kind of insight without the tendency to idealize the analyst, which the more classical transference interpretation may promote.

Interpretive styles. Perhaps the most important thing that can be said about interpretive style is that one should be oneself. Analysis is based upon honesty and the search for truth, and trying to be something one is not can only undermine that search. There is, of course, an "analytic self," a way one learns to be over the years, in order to understand and interpret most effectively. Certain stylistic principles have been recommended, and these can be useful, but only if they fit the analyst's own individuality. Among these are brevity, affective nontechnical language, humor when appropriate, spontaneity, an open-minded genuine inquisitiveness, an affirmative approach of the type advocated by Schafer (1983), and a kind of tentativeness—that is, a readiness to be wrong. It is well to note that one's style will vary significantly from patient to patient and to wonder about that variation from time to time; it may be a clue to something special going on between the two of you. Finally, one is well advised to note the consistent elements in one's style. They will be reflective of the way you are and may lead you to make discoveries about yourself, something that is always welcome.

Is an interpretation "correct"? It is probably apparent that "correct" in this context means "useful in advancing the psychoanalytic process." The content of an interpretation may be accurate, but any number of factors (timing, level, the state of the transference, and so forth) may make it of no use to the patient, and in that sense it is incorrect. Paradoxically, interpretations that are inaccurate may advance the psychoanalytic process in that the exploration of the reasons for and the impact of their inaccuracy may lead to further understanding. In general, analysts use a number of criteria to judge clinically whether an interpretation has been useful. Simple agreement by the patient is not one of them, nor, as Glover (1931) has shown, is therapeutic effect, which may occur after inexact or completely inaccurate interpretations. While Freud (1925) pointed out that disagreement cannot reliably be taken as evidence that one did not get it right, in fact the analyst can usually sense whether the disagreement is a defensive maneuver or is really on target. Simply put, the analyst looks for some indicator of advancement of the analytic process: new memories (accompanied or not by the "aha" feeling), new lines of association, deepening of the transference or revelation of some new transference attitude, abreaction, the appearance of confirmatory somatic feelings, and similar things.

Strategy in interpretation. As Levy (1987) pointed out, there is a paradox inherent in two principles of psychoanalytic technique. On the one hand, we are urged to approach each session afresh, with no preconceptions as to what is going to happen or what the patient will be feeling, and to listen without bias. This implies that psychoanalysis has no strategy except for the simple one of following the patient and helping him to understand. On the other hand, it is clear (if explicitly stated in the literature only infrequently) that psychoanalysts do indeed have a strategy, probably with every patient. They know a lot about their patients and expect that analyses will go in certain specific ways. They know about typical defenses, that certain sequences of interpretation are usually necessary, that narcissistic defenses will usually need to be interpreted before oedipal conflicts can be reached, and many other things that influence what they encourage the patient to focus upon and what they interpret. They know that typical therapeutic problems and situations arise with certain kinds of patients. Whole books have been written about the analysis of specific character types. Some (Glover, 1955, for example) even feel that analyses of different kinds of problems will proceed in very predictable ways and that these ways can be categorized and described. A great deal of the literature of psychoanalytic technique is of this nature, and the very quantity of it indicates that it is a valuable body of knowledge that analysts use constantly. It would appear, then, that analysts do have a strategy that influences their expectations and the way they analyze.

The resolution of the paradox is not difficult. One of course brings all one's experience and knowledge to bear on one's work, and this involves the formulation of both a strategy and, at times, specific technical tactics. But these are formed and utilized in a particular way: in the back of one's mind, without dogmatic expectations, with a readiness to be surprised, to be uncertain, and to be wrong. They form a background against which current hypotheses are more actively formulated. At the beginning of a session with a hysterical patient who has made a flirtatious remark on leaving the previous day, one knows that one is likely to encounter repression and is somewhat more than usually alert for evidences of coquetry and repressive defenses against it. At the same time, one is attempting to be as open to everything else as possible. In short, analytic technique has numerous strategies. These are probably not taught or used nearly as extensively as they should be. In the immediate analytic situation, however, the analyst consciously sets his strategy aside and is open to whatever may appear.

WHAT THE ANALYST ACTUALLY DOES: OTHER INTERVENTIONS

The idea that the analyst only interprets, as formalized by Eissler (1953) with his concept of "parameters," is now passé. The analyst does many things beside interpret. I have already mentioned a number of them under preparation for interpretation and implied others elsewhere. The word *interventions* has come to be used for all the ways in which the analyst participates in the analytic relationship aside from interpretation. It is not a very good way to designate these activities since it connotes intrusion rather than participation, but it is hard to think of a better way to talk about them without being clumsy.

Bibring (1937), in a classical paper, has described four interventions used by the analyst in addition to interpretation—clarification, suggestion, manipulation, and abreaction—but this hardly does justice to the analyst's activity; nor does Bibring use these words in quite the way we do nowadays. Good technique requires that the analyst do a variety of things that advance the psychoanalytic process. If the analyst conceives of his goals mainly in terms of insight, he will do whatever he feels is needed to help advance his patient's understanding. If the analyst conceives of his goal as also including the promotion of development which has been arrested, his activity may include a good deal more. Of the almost infinite variety of the analyst's interventions, I will describe some of the more common types encountered among analysts who emphasize insight.

Confrontation. Confrontation is the act of drawing the patient's attention to some aspect of his behavior or of reality that he has either been genuinely unaware of or has denied. Confrontations can be more or less gentle. If I ask Mr. B., "Are you aware that there are tears in your eyes?" the question may be a gentle but necessary preliminary to exploring what he is feeling. If I say to him, "You deny drinking before our sessions, but I smell alcohol on your breath right at this moment," my confrontation is less gentle but may be equally necessary.

Education. Freud (1937) was quite aware of the educational function of the analyst. At one point, he included education as part of the process by which psychoanalysis works. Currently, education is ubiquitous in analyses, but it is almost always education in the service of promoting insight. For instance, even before analysis begins, I educate my patient about the fundamental rule and give him at least a basic idea of what he and I will be doing together, how we will be proceeding, and how our procedure works. I make every effort throughout the analysis to demystify what is happening. I am on the alert, that is, for evidence that my patient either has no idea or a confused idea about what he and I are doing. While I carefully search for unconscious sources of that confusion, I also explain my own vision of what we are both trying to do. I not infrequently educate my patients about themselves and other aspects of reality not directly connected with the analytic process. For example, if it became clear that Mr. B. genuinely believed that he was the only man ever to feel like crying, I might tell him about Winston Churchill and Alexander the Great's frequent tears and inform him that in my experience all men more or less often feel like crying.

Maintaining the integrity of the psychoanalytic situation. Since the analysis obviously cannot proceed if a therapeutic alliance is not maintained, if the patient does not attend the sessions or is in real danger of harming himself, we do a number of noninterpretive things when and if they become necessary to preserve the psychoanalysis or the patient. If a patient is suicidal, we take whatever measures are necessary to prevent suicide. If a patient becomes too anxious or depressed, we may use reassurance, support, or medication to allay the anxiety or depression. If regression appears to be getting out of control, we may take anti-regressive measures: asking the patient to sit up, for example. Needless to say, we attempt to handle all these things by understanding them first; but if this is not enough, we use other, noninterpretive measures.

Promoting development. While many analysts today feel that the task of analysis with many patients involves helping the patient to resume arrested development as well as to cope with conflicts through insight, discussions of the modes of accomplishing this are remarkably few (de Jonghe et al., 1991; Myerson, 1991; Killingmo, 1989). Perhaps the most comprehensive approach to this problem (unfortunately, too complex to summarize here) is the remarkable work of Gedo, who, in a series of publications (1979, 1984, 1986, 1988) has developed a detailed and systematic description of patients in a wide range of dynamic diagnostic categories and has described the theories and technical approaches necessary to work with them. Undoubtedly, this will be an important area in the study of psychoanalytic technique in the future.

Miscellaneous. Analysis is full of activities by the analyst which are noninterpretive: expressions of his humanity, such as affective and verbal reactions which express surprise, delight, interest, and other reactions; apologies for egregious countertransference behavior as an important part of getting to understand its effects on the patient; even physical contact in rare instances (Casement, 1982). The list could go on.

In closing, I must emphasize that analysts are as acutely aware of the potential unconscious meanings of their interventions in noninterpretive modes as they are when they are interpreting. When confronting, for example, they are aware of the potentiality of being seen as dictators; when educating, as longed-for teachers; when preserving the psychoanalytic situation, as rescuers. This must be understood in the same way as anything else that arises in the relationship. At the same time, analysts are aware that it is not possible to understand everything, and that whether or not the therapy can be considered analysis depends on whether a psychoanalytic process has taken place, not on whether absolutely everything that has taken place has been completely understood.

CONCLUSION

Psychoanalytic technique is both an art and a science. This chapter has given a very brief synopsis of both aspects. Some of what has been omitted will be covered in Chapter 5 on the psychoanalytic process and mechanisms of therapeutic change, and some elsewhere in the book. If the beginner, to whom this chapter is primarily addressed, is unsettled because he does not yet feel like the Compleat Analyst, he should take comfort in the realization that a comprehensive coverage would take volumes, that life is short and the art long, and that, while his technical skills will gradually improve over the years, he will be of immense help to his patients from the very beginning if he simply adheres to the basic psychoanalytic value: a genuine interest in his patient and in their mutual search for truth.

REFERENCES

Bibring, E. (1937). Theory of the therapeutic results of psychoanalysis symposium. *Int. J. Psychoanal.*, 18:170.

Bion, W. R. (1977). *Seven Servants.* New York: Aronson.

Brenner, C. (1979). Working alliance, therapeutic alliance, and transference. *J. Amer. Psychoanal. Assn.*, 27:137–157.

Casement, P. J. (1982). Some pressures on the analyst for physical contact during the reliving of an early trauma. *Int. Rev. Psychoanal.*, 2:279–286.

Curtis, H. C. (1979). The concept of therapeutic alliance. *J. Amer. Psychoanal. Assn.*, 27 (suppl.): 159–192.

De Jonghe, F., Rijnierse, P., & Janssen, R. (1991). Aspects of the analytic relationship. *Int. J. Psychoanal.*, 72:693–707.

Eissler, K. R. (1953). Effect of the structure of the ego on psychoanalytic technique. *J. Amer. Psychoanal. Assn.*, 1:104–143.

Ellman, S. J. (1991). *Freud's Technique Papers.* New York: Aronson.

Fenichel, O. (1941). *Problems of Psychoanalytic Technique.* Albany, N.Y.: Psychoanalytic Quarterly Inc.

Freud, A. (1937). *Writings of Anna Freud,* Vol. 2: *The Ego and Mechanisms of Defense.* New York: Int. Univ. Press, 1966.

Freud, S. (1900). *The Interpretation of Dreams. SE,* 4 and 5.

———. (1905). Fragment of an analysis of a case of hysteria. *SE,* 7:3–124.

———. (1911). The handling of dream interpretation in psychoanalysis. *SE,* 12:89–96.

———. (1912a). The dynamics of the transference. *SE,* 12:97–108.

———. (1912b). Recommendations to physicians practicing psychoanalysis. *SE,* 12:109–120.

———. (1913). On beginning the treatment. *SE,* 12:121–144.

———. (1914a). Remembering, repeating and working through. *SE,* 12:145–156.

———. (1914b). On the history of the psychoanalytic movement. *SE,* 14:3–66.

———. (1915). Observations on transference-love. *SE,* 12:157–174.

———. (1919). Lines of advance in psycho-analytic therapy. *SE,* 17:157–168.

———. (1923). *The Ego and the Id. SE,* 19:3–68.

———. (1925). Negation. *SE,* 19:235–242.

———. (1937). Analysis terminable and interminable. *SE,* 23:209–254.

Gay, P. (1988). *Freud: A Life for our Time.* New York & London: Norton.

Gedo, J. (1979). *Beyond Interpretation.* New York: Int. Univ. Press.

———. (1984). *Psychoanalysis and Its Discontents.* New York & London: Guilford Press.

———. (1986). *Conceptual Issues in Psychoanalysis.* Hillsdale, N.J.: Analytic Press.

———. (1988). *The Mind in Disorder.* Hillsdale, N.J.: Analytic Press.

Gill, M. M. (1982). *Analysis of Transference,* Vol. 1: *Theory and Technique.* New York: Int. Univ. Press.

Glover, E. (1931). The therapeutic effect of inexact interpretation. *Int. J. Psychoanal.*, 12:397.

———. (1955). *The Technique of Psycho-Analysis.* New York: Int. Univ. Press.

Gray, P. (1987). On the technique of analysis of the superego. *Psychoanal. Q.,* 56:130–154.

Greenberg, J. R. (1993). Psychoanalytic interaction. *Psychoanal. Inq.* (in press).

Greenson, R. R. (1967). *The Technique and Practice of Psychoanalysis.* New York: Int. Univ. Press.

Hoffman, I. (1992). Some practical implications of a social-constructivist view of the psychoanalytic situation. *Psychoanal. Dialogues,* vol. 312:287–304.

Kaiser, H. (1934). Probleme der technik. *Jahrbuch für psychoanalytische Forschungen,* 20.

Killingmo, B. (1989). Conflict and deficit. *Int. J. Psychoanal.*, 71:113–130.

Klein, M. (1948). *Contributions to Psycho-Analysis 1921–1945.* London: Hogarth Press.

Kohut, H. (1971). *The Analysis of the Self.* New York: Int. Univ. Press.

Kris, A. (1982). *Free Association.* New Haven & London: Yale Univ. Press.

Kris, E. (1951). Ego psychology and interpretation in psychoanalytic therapy. *Psychoanal. Q.,* 20: 15–30.

Levy, S. T. (1987). Therapeutic strategy and psychoanalytic technique. *J. Amer. Psychoanal. Assn.*, 35:447–466.

Levy, S. T., & Inderbitzin, L. B. (1992). Neutrality, interpretation, and therapeutic intent. *J. Amer. Psychoanal. Assn.*, 40:989–1011.

Loewald, H. (1970). Psychoanalytic theory and the psychoanalytic process. *Psychoanal. Study Child,* 25:45–68.

Loewenstein, R. (1951). The problem of interpretation. *Psychoanal. Q.,* 20:1–14.

Meissner, W. W. (1992). The concept of the therapeutic alliance. *J. Amer. Psychoanal. Assn.*, 40: 1059–1087.

Mitchell, S. A. (1988). The intrapsychic and the interpersonal. *Psychoanal. Inq.*, 8:472–496.

Moore, B., & Fine, B., eds. (1990). *Psychoanalytic Terms and Concepts*. New Haven & London: Amer. Psychoanal. Assn. & Yale Univ. Press.

Muller, J. P. (1990). How theory shapes technique. *Psychoanal. Inq.*, 10:567.

Myerson, P. G. (1991). *Childhood Dialogues and the Lifting of Repression*. New Haven & London: Yale Univ. Press.

Paul, I. H. (1978). *The Form and Technique of Psychotherapy*. Chicago & London: Univ. Chicago Press.

Perry, H. S., & Gawell, M. L. (1953). *The Collected Works of Harry Stack Sullivan*. New York: Norton.

Pulver, S. E. (1991). Psychoanalytic technique. *Psychoanal. Inq.*, 11:65–87.

Rangell, L. (1981). From insight to change. *J. Amer. Psychoanal. Assn.*, 29:119–142.

Sandler, J. (1976). Countertransference and role-responsiveness. *Int. Rev. Psychoanal.*, 3:43–48.

Schafer, R. (1983). *The Analytic Attitude*. New York: Basic Books.

Spruiell, V. (1983). Rules and frames of the psychoanalytic situation. *Psychoanal. Q.*, 52:1–33.

Sterba, R. (1934). The fate of the ego in analytic therapy. *Int. J. Psychoanal.*, 15:117–126.

Zetzel, E. (1956). Current concepts of transference. *Int. J. Psychoanal.*, 37:369–376.

A. Scott Dowling, M.D.,

and Joanne Naegele

2

CHILD AND ADOLESCENT
PSYCHOANALYSIS

Analysis seeks to undo the interfering results of intrapsychic conflict. If successful, it permits the individual, of whatever age, to take advantage of his or her psychological potential for relationships, learning, and emotional responsiveness. There is no fixed technique by which this is accomplished; overall principles are modified by the developmental and individual characteristics of each patient, adult or child. It is, however, unique to child psychoanalysis that it takes place within the crucible of the unfolding development of an immature personality. For this reason, child analysis, from an external viewpoint, is dramatically different from adult analysis. Rather than being contained in verbalization, the child's impulses and fantasies are frequently expressed in drawings, play, or action. There may be no free association. It is only with some adolescents that the couch is used as it is with adults. The transference neurosis, in the sense of a near-exclusive focusing of neurotic responses in the analytic relationship, is transitory or absent. The analyst has both a real relationship and an analytic relationship with the child and is often in regular contact with members of the child's family. These obvious differences and others are dictated by the psychological characteristics of childhood; they result in the modifications of technique discussed below. The special centrality of developmental considerations is responsible for other unique problems and solutions to those problems. Issues of verification, research

methodology, and applied analysis are of particular interest and will be described in the following pages.

THE GENESIS AND EVOLUTION
OF CHILD PSYCHOANALYSIS

Child and adult analysis have evolved along different, though interacting, paths. The evolution of both has been complex and replete with controversy, and, as with any growing science, there continue to be widely varying views about many of the topics described in this chapter. Some of the liveliest controversy surrounds such issues as whether analytic work can be done with preschool children, the intensity and type of work with the parents of children in analysis, the nature of the transference and of the transference neurosis in child analysis at different ages, what sorts of play material to have available for children of different ages, the degree and kinds of gratification to be allowed within the analytic setting, and the indications and forms of limit setting. The list could be extended, an indication that virtually all aspects of the theory and technique of child analysis continue to be open for discussion and revision.

Child analysis began, inauspiciously, as an "application" of adult analysis, part of the "widening scope" which included the study of psychotics, criminals, and delinquents. The way had been amply prepared by Freud's (1909) case study of Hans, a

5-year-old boy with a severe phobia of horses. Hans was treated by his physician father under Freud's direction. The findings confirmed Freud's reconstruction of infantile sexuality from his self-analysis and from his therapeutic analyses of adults. But Freud doubted the general applicability of this "treatment by the father"; furthermore, the possibility of direct analysis of children was not even mentioned in his report. However, Freud continued to be interested in observations that revealed the psychology of young children and published a number of observations of his own; the best known are his description of his daughter Anna's wishful dream for strawberries (1900) and his grandson's separation game (1920).

The first statement of child analytic technique was made by Hug-Hellmuth (1921). In addition to the more specifically analytic aspects of the work, she also emphasized educational instruction of the child and the instillation of morals. The complexity of defense and resistance and the potential for understanding and integration by the young ego were not recognized.

> The curative and educative work of analysis does not consist only in freeing the young creature from his sufferings, it must also furnish him with moral and aesthetic values. The object of such curative and educative treatment is not the mature man . . . but the child, the adolescent, that is human beings who are still in the developing stage, who have to be strengthened through the educative guidance of the analyst, in order to become human beings with strong wills and definite aims. [Hug-Hellmuth, 1921, p. 287]

As the child might not understand the function of the analyst, Hug-Hellmuth suggested that he or she could be told that the analyst was a friend of the parents, a speech teacher, or whatever. In these manipulative suggestions, the innocence of the child, no longer ascribed to his or her sexuality, was mistakenly attributed to his or her ego's capacity for awareness and integration.

By contrast with the educative-analytic technique of Hug-Hellmuth, Melanie Klein, working under the direct influence of Ferenczi and Abraham, presented a noneducative view of child analysis (1921). She stressed the availability of analytically meaningful verbalizations and activities by the child and advocated that the analyst establish an interpretive relationship from the beginning.

Anna Freud, trained as a nursery school and kindergarten teacher, presented her early views on child analytic technique in 1927. Like Hug-Hellmuth, she stressed an initial educational phase, designed to assure the positive transference that she felt was essential to the establishment of an analytic relationship. In the midst of these developments, Sigmund Freud (1926b) wrote again of the theoretical value of child analysis, referring to the "unambiguous information" it gave on "problems which remained unsolved in the analysis of adults" and of the protection child analysis offered the adult analyst from "errors that might have momentous consequences for him" (p. 215).

In the ongoing debate between Melanie Klein and Anna Freud, the weight of opinion was strongly in favor of the noneducative techniques of Melanie Klein et al. (1927). In Vienna, a number of creative investigators joined Anna Freud in conducting child analyses and in case seminars. These early pioneers included August Aichhorn, Anny Angel (Katan), S. Bernstein, Berta Bornstein, Edith Buxbaum, Jenny Waelder-Hall, Willi Hoffer, Marianne Kris, A. Poerth, and Editha Sterba. Their case reports and theoretical contributions pointed the way to a far more flexible and effective analytic technique. The most important change in technique occurred as a result of the brilliant insight of Berta Bornstein (1945) that the introductory educative phase of child analysis could be effectively replaced by analysis of the child's defensive responses to anxiety-provoking affects. This technique continues to be a cornerstone of the early phase of child analysis. Defensively prohibited affects can often be inferred; effective interpretation provides the child with greater contact with his or her emotional inner life and the beginning of an understanding of the nature of the analytic process.

The theoretical and clinical harvest of the early child analytic investigations appeared in 1936 in Anna Freud's *The Ego and the Mechanisms of Defense,* a landmark advance in psychoanalytic technique. Drawing on her experiences with children, Anna Freud detailed the analytic recognition of and response to the defensive activity of the ego—a keystone of later psychoanalytic advances.

Her book ignited an intense study of the place of the ego in clinical technique and stimulated a broadening of emphasis from analysis of the id to a balanced analysis of all components of the personality. The unique theoretical contributions from clinical child analysis are especially important in specifying the details of normal human development. Infantile life, which, in the adult, can be perceived only from afar and after the remodeling and influences of intervening periods of development, is directly accessible in child analytic material. In particular, successfully resolved childhood issues which cannot be perceived in adult analysis are opened to analytic understanding.

The later theoretical and clinical positions of both

Anna Freud and Melanie Klein present marked changes from their earlier statements. Anna Freud set aside the educative approach when she recognized the power of defense interpretation in establishing the analysis. Her later investigations extend to all aspects of psychoanalysis; her contributions are considered by many to be second only to those of her father.

Many of Melanie Klein's ideas have become influential in psychoanalysis—for example, the accessibility of the young child to modified but basically noneducative psychoanalytic technique, the importance of enactments and play activity as expressions of unconscious conflict and fantasies, and the psychological complexity of preverbal infancy. However, in her later works, the specific formulations in each of these areas became increasingly reductionist, with all issues seen as originating in hypothesized, innately determined psychodynamics of the first year. She also emphasized primitive defenses such as splitting, introjection, and projection, conceptualizations that sprang from theoretical convictions rather than clinical observation. These later formulations have been widely criticized (see, for example, Glover, 1945) and have had little direct influence in North American psychoanalysis, though they are a powerful influence in Europe and South America. In the United States her influence has been largely through the writing of others—for example, Winnicott, Kernberg, and Bion.

Child analysis has contributed to a new understanding of reconstructed traumatic events. Just as screen memories are multiply determined, so the reconstructed traumatic event has often been shown to be a series of related events which become condensed in a remembered or reconstructed single trauma.

Three landmark contributions of Anna Freud's later work were creative efforts to integrate analytic developmental findings concerning drive, ego, and superego development in ways that can be of immediate use in clinical work. The first of these contributions is the diagnostic profile (A. Freud, 1962; Nagera, 1963), a method of ordering historical and diagnostic data obtained from interviews with parents and child. The profile includes syncretic organizations of data such as "progressive forces versus regressive tendencies," "over-all attitude to anxiety," and "sublimation potential." The second contribution is the concept of developmental lines (A. Freud, 1963; see also Neubauer, 1984), an effort to specify the ways in which sexual and aggressive drives (id), conscience and self-evaluation (superego), and organizing and reality interests (ego) are expressed in specific areas at successive levels of development.

Other clinicians have made wide use of this concept to organize and conceptualize the developmental process, for example, with regard to gender development (Tyson, 1982). The third clinical contribution was her diagnostic scheme of childhood disturbances, utilizing psychoanalytic concepts to formulate a nomenclature with both etiological and treatment consequences (A. Freud, 1965). Subsequent developments will be discussed in the last section of this chapter.

INDICATIONS FOR CHILD ANALYSIS–MAKING AN ASSESSMENT

Child analysis may be considered whenever mental disturbance has resulted in a significant interruption of the forward thrust of psychological development. All analysts would agree that child analysis is indicated when there is a structured neurosis or when there are severe developmental disturbances or interferences that do not resolve, so impeding the developmental process (Nagera, 1966). In a *structured neurosis,* stable drive regression to previously established fixation points leads to secondary id–ego–superego conflict, the return of the repressed, and symptom formation. *Developmental disturbance* refers to the inevitable, but sometimes disabling, intrapsychic and external conflicts and psychological distress that accompany the forward movement of development and are usually temporary. The infantile neurosis of the oedipal phase, with its varying intensity and uncertain ultimate significance, is the best known and most important of the developmental disturbances. In some instances, a developmental disturbance does not resolve without analytic assistance. A *developmental interference* is a similar disequilibrium but one due to an adventitious circumstance. Hospitalization, loss of a caretaker, physical illness, and other environmental and emotional disruptions may precipitate a developmental interference. Analytic concern for children experiencing developmental disturbances and interferences encompasses the child's immediate difficulties; but of even greater significance, it focuses on the possibility of long-term skewed or disordered development.

A more controversial indication for child analysis is the presence of an atypical or borderline disturbance. Atypical children suffer from a variety of ego deficiencies and from the effects of uneven development. For them, analytic treatment may depart from the more classical methods by placing greater emphasis on provision of direct developmental assistance than on the resolution of intrapsychic conflict. Examples of developmental assistance include frequent reality orientation, the strengthening and support of adaptive defenses, verbalization of affects (Katan, 1961), and careful modulation of instinctual expression.

A child analytic assessment includes detailed consideration of the child's present and past functioning and of the interpersonal environment in which he or she lives. Id, ego, and superego functioning are individually assessed and are also viewed in terms of their balance and interactions with the physical and interpersonal environment.

The child's progress through the psychosexual stages of development, from oral to anal to phallic-oedipal to latency to preadolescence to adolescence to young adulthood, is assessed not only in terms of the movement from one stage to the next but also in terms of the extent of phase dominance. The child analyst considers ego functions such as motility, use of speech, intellectual functioning, differentiating and integrating capacities and repertoire, and mode of defenses. The child's superego—that is, his or her developing moral sense—is examined for the extent of its internalization and its capacity to be both firm and loving.

The balance and interaction of the separate components of the personality with each other and with reality are judged through examination of a number of developmental lines (A. Freud, 1963). In this analytic assessment the analyst is looking for manifestations of persistent obstacles to a child's development —intrapsychic conflicts or inhibitions that are not transient or phase-bound. Conflicts between the different agencies of the mind divert energy needed for the tasks of life. Inefficient defenses impose excessive restrictions on the ego; for example, they may prevent learning, limit motility, or block emotional expression. Unresolved concerns or curiosities with associated anxiety may interfere with ego functioning. Fixations may reverse more mature expressions of sexuality or aggression or may lead to regression of ego or superego functioning. There may be attempts totally to repress aggressive or sexual impulses, limiting productive activity.

The quality of the child's suffering is an important consideration in assessing whether an analysis will succeed. In adult analysis, the patient brings him- or herself to the analyst; he or she is suffering and wishes to change. With children, we carefully assess who is suffering and why. Sometimes the parent wishes a change, not the child. If it is the child who suffers from his or her symptoms, this bodes well for the child's later ability to work in the analysis. This ability to work in analysis is not the same as the child's expressed wish to be rid of his or her symptoms, which often involves a wish for the real-

ization of an unconscious fantasy. These conscious and unconscious wishes regarding what the analysis will do constitute a resistance and must eventually be analyzed. If a child can be helped to look at an internalized conflict, if he or she wishes help in dealing with the difficulty within him- or herself and can feel that his or her anxiety gets in the way of living an adequate life, these will be positive forces in promoting the analysis.

POOR PROGNOSTIC SIGNS FOR CHILD ANALYSIS

There are a variety of circumstances that make it difficult for a child to respond to analytic therapy: a low threshold of tolerance for the frustration of instinctual wishes, which makes the taming of instincts more difficult; a low threshold of tolerance for anxiety, with less flexible defense activity, more active symptom formation, and less tolerance for the inevitable anxiety that accompanies analytic treatment; a low sublimation potential, with restriction of alternate sources of gratification; and a preponderance of regressive tendencies over progressive ones. Child analysis is particularly difficult when parental pathology promotes regression or prevents sublimation.

Parental motivation is an important consideration in assessing whether analysis is feasible for a child or a teenager. The parents must be emotionally able to support an analysis—that is, to tolerate the child's examination of him- or herself and the environment and to tolerate changes within the child. For example, during analysis a child may change from being quiet, passive, and inhibited to being more independent and outspoken, with opinions that diverge from those of the parents—a change some parents are unable to deal with. Likewise, parents may have an unconscious need for their child to remain ill. Parents with such needs often remove the child from analysis when he or she is beginning to get better. For other parents, a child's pathology masks a family secret; and when the family secret becomes known to the child's analyst, the child may be taken away.

One such child came to analysis at age ten with an intense learning difficulty. After fifteen months of analysis she was able to tell the analyst about a recent incident that was representative of many past incidents. She told of her father becoming upset and going into a rage, smashing and breaking things. She watched the destruction, convinced that she was about to be killed. The father's rages were a carefully guarded secret, which family members were not permitted to discuss among themselves and outsiders were not permitted to know. Shortly after the incident was divulged, the parents terminated the analysis, stating that the child had made such improvements in learning that the analyst's services were no longer needed. In fact, the child had not done better in school; the parents had stopped the analysis simply because they could not tolerate having their secret exposed.

For child analysis to provide its greatest benefits, it is necessary for the child's parents to have reached sufficient maturity that they can recognize the child as an individual and are able to place the child's interests at the same or a higher level than their own (Rosenbaum, 1992).

CHILD AND ADULT ANALYSIS

Similarities. The basic similarity of adult and child analysis rests on the use of the same therapeutic tool, interpretation, directed to the same therapeutic goal, the resolution of unconscious conflict. The process of interpretation follows certain general principles. Surface content is interpreted before deeper unconscious material. Defenses are interpreted before unconscious, drive-oriented wishes. Comments are often directed toward the patient's affect. As the analysis proceeds, the conflicts between drives and ego or superego attitudes become more clearly delineated; both analyst and analysand are more aware of the details of the child's conflicts, setting the stage for the analyst's interpretations. The patient understands better how he or she has dealt with forbidden urges. With reduction of inhibitions and resolution of conflicts, the child or adult functions more adaptively, crippling defenses are altered, and the superego is modified. More drive gratification is allowed. As partial fixation points are better understood and reworked, the tendency to regress to such points decreases. Inhibitions and neurotic symptom formation are overcome. Sublimations are free to develop. Ego functions are strengthened, and the area of the mind over which the ego can exert influence is widened (Freud, 1933, p. 80).

Differences. Though the goals and basic technique are similar, however, child analysis is strikingly different from adult analysis (Panel, 1974). Children have less capacity for insight and are less tolerant of distress and anxiety than most adults. Child analysis depends on the parents' interest and willingness to extend themselves for the child's welfare. The child is dependent on them for emotional support during times of resistance, during flights into health, and during exacerbations of the illness. Parents must pay for the analysis and are often responsible for transporting the child to and from the daily analytic sessions.

The usual child analytic patient is not expected to lie on the couch. He or she may move around the room or play while talking. Objects brought from home or supplies provided by the analyst are used to dramatize or express his or her thoughts and feelings. The analyst provides items for self-expression, such as crayons, pencils, paper, clay, dolls, blocks, and cars, and participates in their use. Play and physical activity, as well as verbal communication, are the means through which the child brings his or her inner life to the analysis.

Toys are used in child analysis, and motor expression is allowed, because they are often a child's necessary means of self-expression. But toys and motor expression are not the main "tools of the trade." It is the verbalization between patient and analyst that establishes the content of interpretation, and it is the therapeutic relationship with the analyst that most actively facilitates self-expression.

> Just as in adult analysis it is left up to the patient to decide what particular mixture of reality, fantasy and transference he will bring in, so in child analysis it is left up to the child how fully to express his thoughts, fantasies and wishes directly toward the person of the therapist, how much to use the medium of toys, and how far to account verbally for experiences at school and at home. [Sandler et al., 1980, p. 39]

CHILD ANALYTIC TECHNIQUE

How a child selects and uses a medium for expression is illustrated by the example of Joey. An eight-year-old of slight build, Joey entered analysis with an uncertainty about his masculinity that manifested itself in bed-wetting and occasional dressing up in his sister's high heels and clothes. A significant event in his history was the traumatic death of a significant male relative prior to his birth. During the first year of analysis, Joey expressed his intense castration anxiety by repeatedly getting hurt, either by tripping over things or in bicycle accidents. In the analysis he built structures out of blocks, repeatedly staging scenes of the traumatic accident that led to the death of his relative. These performances usually contained magical rescues or surprises. For example, a person who was thought to be dead was later discovered to be alive, or a person might look terribly injured, but the injury would later be revealed to be a mere disguise.

Insisting on daily block building, Joey revealed his thoughts and feelings in play. In the analysis he talked about the sadistic fantasies expressed in the play, and his analyst interpreted how these fantasies warded off unhappiness in his real life. Thus, although the play was a flight into fantasy, where Joey could reign supreme as ruler of the universe, torturing and maiming those he wished to hurt, defensiveness was not its only importance; in the fantasy Joey also revealed his intrapsychic life, which he had been unable to describe in words initially.

Another major contrast with adult analysis is the absence of free association—that is, uncensored expression during self-observation. Until adolescence, many children, especially younger ones, are cognitively unable comfortably to effect this combination of expression and self-observation. If asked to say whatever comes to mind, the child may refuse, not necessarily out of uncooperativeness but because of a limited cognitive capacity consciously to direct his or her speech in this way. Furthermore, it is developmentally appropriate for the child patient to be afraid to regress when, like all children, he or she is struggling to be mature and to control his or her thoughts. It is evident that there are a number of reasons why the capacity for sustained free association with self-observation is limited, particularly in the younger child.

When children bring dreams, as they often do, it is usually without free associations, though their spontaneous thoughts often have the significance of free associations. For this reason, links between the manifest dream content and the latent dream thoughts may be difficult to establish. On the other hand, many children's dreams can be understood as thinly disguised statements of wish and fantasy. As in adult analysis, dreams become easier to interpret as the analyst comes to know the child and his or her conflicts. Some dreams, even of young children, may be complex and well disguised. Though these dreams often remain uninterpreted, the alert analyst may find links to latent meaning in associated comments, in the child's play, or in fantasy material.

Without free association as the main avenue to the unconscious, the child analyst must rely on the various derivatives of the child's unconscious being communicated in other ways—in conversation with the analyst, in daydreams, in imaginary play, in drawings, in slips, and in transference phenomena.

All analytic patients respond to their analysts in ways they originally responded to important persons in their past; understanding these transference reactions is a central issue in all analyses. In addition, a focusing of conflicts on the relationship with the analyst, a transference neurosis, will develop with most adult patients, sometimes transiently, sometimes for longer periods of time (Bird, 1972). During periods of transference neurosis, the patient's symptoms may fade or disappear outside the analysis, but a more intense and conflictual quality is evident in the analysis itself.

Understanding transference phenomena is more complex in child analysis than adult analysis. The child's original love objects, the parents, are still very much part of his or her life. As real love objects, they alter and confuse the clarity of transference phenomena. To a child, the analyst will be (1) a new, unique person to whom he or she is relating, (2) a person who is similar to the parents as they are currently, and (3) a person with whom he or she repeats relationships and responses from the past. It is often impossible to differentiate these different meanings of the analyst. The analyst will be the recipient of the child's love and hate feelings as a real person, as a parentlike adult, and as an object of transference. Despite these technical difficulties, transference phenomena can, in many instances, be understood and interpreted, leading to reconstructions—formulations of past events, actions, and psychological states, including wishes, feelings, and defenses, that are helpful in understanding subsequent events, actions, and psychological states.

Most, though not all, child analysts agree that the development of a transference neurosis is rare in children. It has been documented in some cases (Harley, 1971; Chused, 1988; Fraiberg, 1951, 1966). It is often stated that a sine qua non of adult analysis is that a transference neurosis develop and be resolved. When this does not occur in adult analysis, some analysts doubt that there has been a truly analytic experience. The absence of a transference neurosis in adults is often due to intense resistance, other ego attributes that limit the patient's psychological accessibility, or errors of analytic technique. In child analysis, the absence or transitory nature of a transference neurosis is a function of the immaturity of the child; it does not necessarily reflect severity of psychopathology or analytic error. In spite of the various limitations on the formation and recognition of transference, analytic work with children does take place, in great part, by way of transference reactions.

Another distinctive feature of psychoanalytic process in child analysis is the variety and complexity of forms of communication, particularly nonverbal communication in action. This is again in keeping with the developmental characteristics of children. It becomes an essential part of the process that communication in action achieve verbal representation, a task that is usually less pressing in adult analysis.

Child analysis makes special demands on the analyst. Because a child's instinctual expression is not always limited to speech, and because a child's conflicts are a potent stimulus to anger, excitement, and regression, the analyst is, at times, confronted with an out-of-control child who will hit, kick, bite, and spit. It may be necessary to hold the child to prevent harm to him- or herself, the analyst, or the surroundings. On other occasions, the child analyst may encounter a patient who runs out of the office, soils him- or herself, gets excited in the bathroom by throwing wads of wet toilet paper to the ceiling, or who suddenly undresses in the office as a way of expressing sexual concerns and excitement.

Because of the rigors of such work, child analysts must be in good physical condition, must know themselves well, must be in tune with their own feelings about each stage of their own childhood development, and must be aware of their defensive responses to the child. The regressive pull on the child analyst is a constant pressure. The analyst must empathize with regressed states of the patient while avoiding his or her own tendency to regress.

These factors make child analysts particularly susceptible to unconsciously determined responses to a child. Countertransference is further complicated by the relationship with the child's parents. Unconscious tendencies to blame or submit to the parents or to rescue or punish the child may be stimulated by the attitudes of the parents as well as by the patient. As in adult analysis, self-analysis of countertransference responses is a necessary and ongoing process. The directness of instinctual expression, the pressure to regress, the analyst's role in the child's life as a real person, and the danger of identification with child or parent put analytic neutrality in near-constant jeopardy.

CHILD ANALYSIS AT DIFFERING DEVELOPMENTAL STAGES

Child analysis is a lengthy and time-consuming procedure. Children are seen four or five times a week for forty-five to fifty minutes, usually for several years. Because communication between child and analyst relies on speech, analysis is rarely considered before age three.

Those who undertake treatment with the youngest of child analytic patients, the pre-latency three- to five-year-olds, do so primarily because the child is experiencing either an arrest in development at a very early stage or because a partial fixation at the oral or anal level is of such magnitude that later development will be severely crippled.

With the active pre-latency child, the analyst cannot sit back in his or her chair, speaking only at carefully chosen moments. The child initiates and directs play with the analyst, an important avenue to understanding the child's conflicts. Primary-process

fantasies of birth and impregnation are more vividly and visibly expressed at this stage than in any subsequent phase. Although the child's ego is not yet fully formed, superego precursors influence behavior and attitudes. Repression is not yet an active defense; thus, the child may have almost total recall of his or her past. Impulses such as sucking, biting, hurting, cutting, kicking, and loving are grist for the analytic mill and at times are acted out in play. Omnipotent wishes, which often peak at age three and are developmentally appropriate for a child of that age, complicate the process of sorting out events for which the child feels acutely responsible—for example, illness of a sibling, birth of a baby, or death of a pet.

The parents are very real, necessary objects to the child. For this reason, the parent of the young child may remain in the room, especially during the first few weeks of treatment. The analyst of a young patient sees the child's parents regularly and must be keenly sensitive to their feelings, especially feelings of responsibility for the child's problems, of shame or guilt for not being able to cure the child themselves, or feelings of being left out of the analysis.

There are several published reports of analytic work with two- to four-year-olds which include discussions of technique (Bornstein, 1935; Fraiberg, 1951; Harley, 1951; Kestenberg, 1969; Kolansky, 1960; Neubauer, 1972; R. L. Tyson, 1978). Jules Glenn's report (1978) of the analysis of three-and-a-half-year-old Betty conveys the flavor of the analytic experience. We paraphrase and condense his report in the following paragraphs.

Betty entered analysis after seven months of withholding feces for as long as nine days at a time. After a period of withholding, she would produce stools the size of a baseball. She would then avoid sitting on the toilet, instead soiling her pants for several days before retaining once more. In addition, she wet her bed at night.

Mrs. G., Betty's mother, became pregnant with Betty's brother, Phil, when Betty was two years, two months. Her constipation started in the last trimester of her mother's pregnancy, not long after Mrs. G. announced that she had a baby in her "stomach."

Betty's constipation was an identification with her pregnant mother, whom she feared losing. The stool within her symbolized the baby she wished to keep within. It also represented the penis she wished to possess. She envied her younger brother's favored position in the family.

In the analysis Betty played games which expressed her wishes, defenses, and conflicts. She let the analyst know that she wanted to have bowel movements like other people, and the analyst's agreement with this goal helped to establish a therapeutic alliance.

Betty's feelings around the birth of her younger brother were reconstructed in the analysis when a new cousin was born. Betty wished to throw out the new baby and his mother. In an undisguised expression of penis envy, she first struck Dr. Glenn in the genitals and then broke the penis off a clay figure. She agreed when the analyst interpreted what she had done as showing that she had wished to be Mommy and Daddy's only child. Betty remembered that her mother's abdomen had been big when her brother had been in it. She then stated that her stools made her abdomen big; she too could have a baby inside her.

Betty invented the story of Captain Jack and Bosco Bear, the Captain's servant and assistant. Captain Jack, representing her mother, was played by Betty, while Bosco Bear, representing Betty, was played by the analyst. In an early version of the game, Bosco Bear fed Captain Jack chocolate. Then the pair went hunting for a baby or a nose. Captain Jack became ill and was examined by a doctor (played by the analyst). The illness was a pregnancy. The doctor removed the BM babies from Captain Jack's anus. Later in the analysis, after Betty was firmly entrenched in the phallic phase, the doctor again delivered babies, this time from Captain Jack's genitals.

Fantasies of oral conception, anal birth, and penis envy, as well as her many toileting conflicts, all appeared in play during analysis as Betty expressed and tried to understand her feelings of envy about her mother's pregnancy, her wish to be like her mother, her resentment of toilet training, and her own feelings of being broken. Other issues which emerged were her feelings of being forced, her belief that adults do not have BMs, her identification of BMs with penises, and the fantasy that her mother had castrated her and taken her penis.

With the onset of genital masturbation, Betty relinquished her withholding symptom and began to make regular use of the toilet for bowel movements. She had progressed from an anal fixation to the phallic-oedipal stage.

This piece of analytic work took about one year of daily sessions. At this point, her parents felt that Betty's development was satisfactory and insisted on planning for termination; the analyst would have preferred a more thorough working through to stabilize the therapeutic benefits. Five years later, the parents described her as a happy, asymptomatic girl who had not regressed to soiling or wetting.

In contrast to direct analysis of children under five years, some analysts prefer to provide "treatment via the parent" (E. Furman, 1957; R. Furman & A. Katan, eds., 1969), in which the parent and child analyst meet regularly; here it is the parent who helps the child resolve his or her conflicts. When working in this manner, it is helpful for the child analyst regularly to observe the young child—for example, in the setting of a nursery school. When "treatment via the parent" does not help sufficiently, the child may then be taken into analysis. (See also Kennedy & Moran, 1991.)

The developmental period of latency, roughly the time following the oedipal phase prior to the upsurge of adolescent drives, is considered an ideal time for analysis; many children begin analytic treatment during this period (Bornstein, 1949; Brody, 1961; Buxbaum, 1954; Sarnoff, 1976). The psychic structure is now more completely formed, and there has been an attempt to resolve oedipal feelings. The latency child has a functioning superego and can use repression as well as a variety of other defense mechanisms in dealing with instinctual urges. As the child enters the world of school, internalized conflicts are more visible to parents and to people outside the family. Achievement in academic subjects is expected, difficulties in developing friendships will be glaring, and the child's psychic pain will be evident. The child is also more independent of parents than previously and has a growing interest in people and experiences outside his or her immediate family. Much of the work of analysis can now be done by way of transference phenomena.

In early latency the child's personality is more open to change than will be true later. At the same time, the fragility and uncompromising quality of superego attitudes during this period require special sensitivity on the part of the analyst. The child feels threatened by any temptation to regress because his or her defenses are easily overwhelmed by instinctual needs.

When external circumstances that the analyst cannot influence support or contribute to the child's neurosis, it may be best to delay treatment until late latency, when the child is more independent of the parents. By that time the child may be able to get to the analytic hour alone, by public transportation or bicycle, and be capable of selective identification with healthy aspects of adults other than parents.

Most analysts agree that analysis during adolescence is a difficult venture. The adolescent is in the process of "reorganization." Reawakened sexual feelings are strong and difficult for the child to integrate. The struggle against masturbation is intense, with the teenager seeking discharge of his or her sexual urges but fearing conscious recognition of such wishes and fantasies. Defenses that worked well in late latency and preadolescence are now inadequate; new defenses are in process of forming. It is a period well known for open hostility to parents, intellectualization, asceticism, and sexual acting out. There is an intensification of narcissism, and the teenager appears self-absorbed, preoccupied, and detached from the immediate family. A rapid succession of fluctuating moods appears, ranging from the heights of elation to the depths of despair and utter helplessness (A. Freud, 1958).

Introducing analysis in the midst of such upheaval is not easy. Reasons for undertaking analysis must outweigh the forces militating against it. It is difficult to establish a treatment alliance at a time when it is developmentally appropriate for the patient to be moving away from adults and when the structure of the superego is changing. The analyst will be caught up in the whirlwind of feelings the teenager is experiencing as the fear of old incestuous ties to the parents is transferred onto the analyst.

Analytic technique with adolescents is closer to the technique of adult analysis. The patient may be on the couch, and free association may be possible. The analysis must belong to the patient alone, and confidentiality must be assured. Thus, analysts of teenagers usually do not see the patient's parents.

Anna Freud (1958) describes the problems of adolescent analysis this way: "The analytic treatment of adolescents is a hazardous venture from beginning to end, a venture in which the analyst has to meet resistances of unusual strength and variety" (p. 261).

Peter Blos (1962, 1970) has written extensively about analytic work with preadolescents and adolescents and is encouraging about the usefulness of analysis to this age-group. Many analysts who work with teenagers also have positive feelings about its possibilities. Selma Fraiberg (1955) writes thus about work with preadolescents:

If we can overcome these initial resistances and establish a therapeutic attitude we find many factors in the pubertal situation which go to work for us. I do not need to mention all those factors in puberty which do not work for us, the rigidity of the defense, the fear of the homosexual transference, the acting out, etc. But the morbid aspects of the clinical picture in puberty are counterbalanced by the tremendous forward thrust of the drives. It is also then, a time of hope and of promise and while the clinical picture of puberty can at times be alarming and can resemble in every aspect certain morbid disturbances of later life, the impetus toward growth, fulfillment, toward the future, can work for puberty toward a favorable outcome. [pp. 285–286]

The Laufers (1978, 1982, 1984) have extended their analytic work to more severely disturbed adolescents with both good results and increased insight into the psychological events of adolescence.

A brief clinical vignette will give a feel for some of the complexities of analytic work with adolescents. Sam began analysis at age ten when, in spite of good intellectual ability, he stopped learning and began to get low grades in school. His analysis was to last eight years and spanned most of his adolescence. Sam was a boy at odds with himself, had no friends, often engaged in teasing, excited, destructive neighborhood play. As a nine-year-old he was still making oedipal overtures to his mother, exhibiting himself by running nude from his bedroom into the shower and patting his mother "on the fanny" as he passed by.

His mother had suffered psychotic depressions accompanied by suicidal gestures since Sam was three. Analysis revealed that Sam abruptly stopped learning shortly after a particularly difficult episode, which left mother hospitalized and then visibly bandaged.

After three months of analysis, Sam's neurosis became organized into an obsessional neurosis. In part, this was a result of having a safer oedipal object in the transference. He overcame most of the obsessional symptomatology in the following eighteen months, through a reworking, in the transference, of his oedipal feelings. These included the fear of his mother as an oedipal object, his worry that she might harm him as she had harmed herself, and his defensive wish to be a girl, thus eliminating the fear of castration. In the second and third years of analysis, material focused on Sam's masturbation fantasies, which took the form of "slapping and hitting a no-good woman." This seemed to be both how he felt his penis should be treated and also his idea of how a woman should be treated—as someone to be slapped, whipped, and broken. In the analysis he became aware that these ideas were a means of identifying with his mother; he also realized how this fantasy would have pleased his mother, since she was a woman who derived pleasure from hurting herself. In seventh grade, Sam engaged in intense homosexual excitement with the older junior-high boys. He provoked fights in which he sought the passive excitement of being chased, caught, and slapped by the boys, just as in the masturbation fantasy the woman was slapped. The fantasy of being a woman also stimulated his extreme fear of the older boys.

By age thirteen, Sam was fully adolescent and at about six feet towered over his female analyst. His affect became more guarded, and he was reluctant to share his feelings. For years, on entering or leaving the office, he whisked past his analyst, permitting her only a brief glimpse of his face. For much of the hour he then sat at a desk with his back toward the analyst as he pored over books or magazines.

For the next five years Sam worked toward understanding his learning difficulty. He came to recognize that he had mixed up school "production" with earlier toilet-training feelings. He had provoked an excited anal struggle in school, passively resisting when the teacher pulled the work out of him. Two reconstructions helped Sam reach the point of *wishing* to get A's and B's in school. He remembered once feeling like a "no good, messy boy," a "stinky bottom." These feelings had first occurred at age two when his mother had gone to the hospital to have a baby and arose subsequently with her psychiatric hospitalizations. The second reconstruction was of a belief that he and his siblings were to blame for their mother's departures. If only they had not been fighting, then perhaps she would not have left. The "I don't give a shit about schoolwork" feelings were later understood to be an identification with the parent who seemed to care so little for her children that she left them.

Sam began to work effectively in school, with the goal of having grades no lower than C. Yet he always had one subject that "needed to be rescued," just as his mother so often needed to be rescued, a connection Sam could understand.

Sam worked very slowly. He treated the analysis both as a "safe haven" and as an "anchor of reality," yet he felt he needed to be very cautious. He believed that if he spoke openly of his feelings, he would not be able to continue the analysis. The analyst did not pressure him for associations or make frequent interpretations; either would have felt like a seduction to Sam and would have taxed his capacity for integration. Sam struggled to "put himself together" by finding things that interested him and by talking about himself at his own pace. He formed a rock band in his basement at age fifteen and worked at becoming a drummer for several years. He carefully worked on his car, rebuilding it and polishing it and ordering the latest in fancy mufflers and tailpipes. By age seventeen, he had a girlfriend, and although he carefully guarded from the analyst what he and she did together, he did share the fact that he cared for her and believed the feeling could continue.

Thus, Sam's development had progressed by the time he ended analysis at age seventeen. He had begun to have heterosexual relationships and had achieved grades and educational objectives consistent with his talents. He was more open and was able to explore his relationships with his parents and with the analyst. He was no longer hiding his face but looked the analyst squarely in the eyes and on the last day directly and warmly said, "Thank you very much."

Even in late adolescence, which is considered a time of consolidation and stabilization of sexual identity, object relations, and ego functions, analysis remains a tenuous venture. The idea of analytic treatment may be especially threatening when the adolescent is leaving home to go to college or to live on his or her own and work. At the same time, difficulty in establishing new object relationships, concern about sexual functioning, and trouble establishing him- or herself in an independent and fulfilling work situation may prompt the late adolescent or young adult especially to value the help that can be obtained from analysis (Abend, 1974, 1987).

TRAINING OF CHILD ANALYSTS

The sometimes ambiguous status of child analysis vis-à-vis adult analysis has been reflected in continuing controversies about child analytic training. Though we have long outgrown an early bias reflected in Freud's statement "It has automatically happened that child analysis has become the domain of women analysts, and no doubt this will remain" (1933, p. 148), there continue to be questions concerning the comparable value of child and adult analytic training. Few would question Anna Freud's philosophy that just as a knowledge of adult analysis broadens the child analyst's point of view, so knowledge of child analysis enhances the adult analyst's point of view. However, some would question her statement "It does not matter as much any more at which end of the scale we initiate child training; just as child analysis can be acquired as an addition to adult training, so can adult training come in as a second period additional to child analysis" (A. Freud, 1966, pp. 53–54). In the United States child analytic training now begins when adult training is nearly completed or well under way, and it is always an addition to adult training. This sequence has been questioned, and some training analysts propose simultaneous training or beginning with analysis of children.

Long-simmering issues concerning lay analysis bubble beneath the surface of discussions of child analytic training. Whereas lay—that is, nonmedical —analysts have been important in adult analysis, their contribution to child analysis is immense. A majority of the early pioneers were nonmedical analysts; Anna Freud's preeminent position guarantees respect for lay analysis among all child analysts.

Child analytic training at the Hampstead Clinic, under Anna Freud's direction, has been a model of joint medical and nonmedical training. Similar programs providing child analytic training to nonmedical candidates have been developed both in Europe and in the United States. Graduates of these programs have joined with other child analysts to form the Association for Child Psychoanalysis, an international forum for exchange among all child analysts.

RESEARCH AND APPLIED ANALYSIS

The pioneers of child analysis not only established a rational intensive therapy for childhood psychological disturbances, they also made important contributions to the factual and theoretical foundations of psychoanalysis, to our understanding of the psychology of normal and disturbed children, and to societal awareness and provision for the psychological needs of children. Research on early development as a pathway to a more complete understanding of adult psychology has appealed both to child analysts and to adult analysts, some of whom devoted their lives to this field. Freud collected his colleagues' observations of their children as a means of substantiating his reconstructions of normal childhood. Heinz Hartmann (1950) believed that child observational research was the natural complement of clinical psychoanalysis in the development of a general psychoanalytic psychology, and Ernst Kris, with no prior professional experience with children but with a profound belief that an understanding of children was essential to the progress of psychoanalysis, became an active supporter and researcher at the Yale Child Study Center and a founder of *The Psychoanalytic Study of the Child.*

It is helpful to recognize that many of the issues and methodological discussions of research in child analysis have arisen in connection with the controversy that swirled around Anna Freud and Melanie Klein during the 1920s and 1930s and culminated in the *Freud–Klein Controversies 1941–1945* (King & Steiner, 1991). In connection with research on infancy and childhood, this controversy concerned two related issues. Melanie Klein believed that complex fantasy life takes place during the first year, based upon innately determined instinctual conflicts concerning parental objects. She saw dyadic conflicts (schizoid and depressive positions) and triadic conflicts (oedipal conflicts) as occurring during the early months of life, a belief opposed by Anna Freud, who thought that the early months were characterized by a far-reaching immaturity that gives way to object relations and fantasy formation only through a gradual and, at that time, unmapped process of matura-

tion and development. The second, related, issue concerns the place of deduction from theory versus observation and clinical analytic work in establishing the presence or absence of specific forms and types of mental content. Anna Freud studied children and wrote about them on the basis of such experience; Melanie Klein's work derives from her understanding of the requirements of instinctual theory. For example, the death instinct, as Klein understood it, *requires* object-directed, destructive aggression in the early months to prevent self-destruction; both object relatedness and destructiveness must, therefore, be present from birth. Such an assumption virtually requires postulating complex relationships such as the paranoid-schizoid and depressive positions, extensive ego splitting to deal with good and bad objects, and innately, rather than experientially, determined object representations. These a priori beliefs and their consequences are the foundation of Kleinian theory and entail a very different approach to childhood than Anna Freud's.

In the United States, the tradition established by Anna Freud, with its emphasis on a developmental perspective of epigenetic gradualism and on the importance of observation, has been far more influential than Klein's a priori immanence of function. It is interesting to note that although adherence to an extreme view of the death instinct has not been influential in American psychoanalysis, Klein's focus on the psychological complexity of early infant development has been important. An emphasis on object relations in child development, as opposed to the influence of drives, has also, paradoxically, been stimulated by Klein's work.

For many years, research by child psychoanalysts has been stimulated by the Freud–Klein controversy. In part because of Klein, the area of psychoanalytic research has been broadened to include early infancy, and the formation and evolution of relationships, especially pre-oedipal dyadic relationships, have become issues of lasting concern. These Kleinian-inspired issues have been studied by techniques advocated by Anna Freud: careful observation, both in natural and in analytic settings, attention to detail and recording, and the use of an epigenetic frame of reference in formulating conclusions.

Winnicott retained involvement with both Melanie Klein and Anna Freud but worked independently of either. He took inspiration from Klein's interest in the young infant and used his pediatrically educated eye for observing behavior and his Freudian awareness of developmental issues to craft an original and deeply evocative sense of the life of the young infant (1975). The infant's far-reaching immaturity was appreciated and articulated in ways not known before. He stressed the essential place of mothering in shaping a personality capable of confidence, self-knowledge, and creativity (1960). His insistent focus on the mother–infant relationship rather than on the infant alone has been a key contribution to infant studies by analytic and nonanalytic investigators alike and has been one of a number of reasons for the trend toward seeing the formation and quality of relationships as the central interest of psychoanalysis.

Spitz (1946) was the first analyst who carefully documented, statistically and on film, the extreme morbidity and mortality among infants who lacked the psychological "nutrition" of human interaction. His studies, like those of Anna Freud and Dorothy Burlingham during World War II (1973), moved investigators from the consulting room to family and group settings, such as infant homes or day nurseries. In a series of later studies Spitz (1965) described a normal sequence of psychosocial organizers in infancy, an approach to an understanding of development which has been influential with later investigators of infant behavior (see especially Sander, 1980).

Contemporary infant research was made possible by Peter Wolff (1959), who was the first to define *states* in infancy. These universal behavioral and physiological conditions of infant life are uniform and can be determined by verifiable observation; by conducting investigations with infants who are all in a given state, studies can be replicated, and results from different investigators can be combined or compared. The modern infancy research movement, with its many studies of infant competency, behavioral organization, and social responsiveness, was made possible by Wolff's recognition of definable, universal arousal and behavioral states. Because of the relative ease of observation, most studies documenting the competencies of infants have been done with infants in the alert inactive state. However, most of infant life is lived outside the alert inactive state, much of it in high tension, less well-organized need, or sleep; and psychological aspects of these other states remain relatively unexplored by infant researchers.

Though Winnicott, Spitz, and Wolff represent somewhat different emphases in their approaches to the study of infants, and though each has his champions among present-day researchers, none of them is the leader of a "school." Their differences lie in the degree to which systematic and repeated observations are used and in the various theoretical emphases that inform their interpretation of those observations.

Among contemporary psychoanalytic researchers, Robert Emde, an analytic and research colleague of

Spitz's, has continued and extended Spitz's studies, with an emphasis on affect development and on the organizing role of affects in infancy (Emde et al., 1976; Emde, 1983, 1990). In early Freudian theory (1900), affects were understood as discharge phenomena; later, Freud (1926a) understood them as mnemic residues of infantile experiences of discharge or as ego responses to threat which are elicited by the signal function of the ego. In the new formulations, affects are seen as innate primary motivators or reinforcers of behavior, as in Lichtenberg's theory of motivation (1989) and in the theoretical discussions by Tomkins (1962–91).

In recent years, infant research has been the most prominent research endeavor with children. Its findings have been surprising, revealing, and appealing. Once infant states were defined and the resources of modern technology were utilized to record and dissect infant behavior, infant research took on the assurance of hard science. Some of its practitioners have been vocal and provocative in applying their findings to clinical issues in both children and adults (Stern, 1985).

There is another, older tradition in psychoanalytic research with children which has, unfortunately, been eclipsed by the newer findings. The subjects of this research include infants, toddlers, and preschoolers; the methods used are largely naturalistic and descriptive and have neither the technological nor statistical sophistication of modern infancy research. On the other hand, being naturalistic, they are able to demonstrate fluctuations, sequences, interactions, and variations of psychological events over time. These studies are not limited to a single state or emotional condition of the child. They have the advantage of a breadth of observation and data gathering concerning the ordinary circumstances of toddler life, which includes transitional, integrative, conflict resolution and disintegrative processes. For example, Anna Freud and Dorothy Burlingham (1973) detailed the special characteristics and limitations of children raised, during wartime, by thoughtful, caring, but less fully committed and total caretakers than is the usual mother. More systematic studies by Provence and Lipton (1962) of infants raised in a foundling home provided further details of the limitations imposed by such conditions.

A now classic single case study in this older tradition was conducted by George Engel and Franz Reichsman (1956) with an infant born with esophageal atresia, a congenital closure of the esophagus with inability to be fed by mouth. Monica suffered from deprivation of maternal care as well as the abnormal feeding experiences necessitated by esophageal atresia. Engel documented patterns of psychological response to both familiar and strange people. These responses were one rationale for his postulation of human conservation–withdrawal reactions to stressful situations (Engel, 1962). In later studies, continued into Monica's adult life, Engel and his colleagues (1985) have shown the continued impact of infantile experience on overt behavior and attitudes. Monica fed her own infants using the same distancing body postures as were used when she was gastrostomy-fed in infancy and employed devices of social control that were typical of her own infant experience. Even more astonishing is his documentation of the fact that her children fed their dolls in the manner in which they were fed.

Margaret Mahler's studies began with severely disturbed infants (1952), but her most influential contribution has been in elucidating the normal process of separation-individuation of the infant from the mother between the ages of six and thirty-six months. On the basis of toddler observation, Mahler et al. (1975) constructed a view of the three- to six-month-old infant caught up in a symbiotic relationship with the mother which progressively gives way to a measure of separation and individuation through processes of "hatching" at six months, "practicing" at twelve to thirteen months, "rapprochement" at eighteen months, and "object constancy" at thirty to thirty-six months. Her observational studies provide detailed information organized within these postulated stages of separation-individuation.

A confusing outcome of the work of both Winnicott and Mahler is that terms coined by them have entered into the argot of psychoanalysis concerning early development with expanded and unclear meanings. Misunderstood or burdened with connotations or significance not intended by their authors, these terms have achieved something of a life of their own, often to be either praised or condemned along with their authors. "Holding environment," "good enough mother," "transitional object," and "primary maternal preoccupation" are Winnicottian terms that have sometimes been accorded this independence of their original meanings. "Symbiosis," "hatching," "rapprochement," "separation-individuation" are Mahlerian terms that are likewise sometimes used with little regard for their original meanings. These terms have come to be used to form scenarios of expected or potentially pathological childhood events in analyses of both adults and children. Even the term "development" has, for some, lost its original meaning and become a buzzword for a belief that psychopathology arises primarily from pre-oedipal issues.

Until her untimely death, Selma Fraiberg was leader of a group of investigators who not only continued the tradition of Anna Freud and René Spitz but successfully extended its scope and theoretical foundation. No one else has been as successful as Fraiberg (1959) in blending psychoanalytic ideas with Piaget's many insights into the normal infant's and child's techniques of approach and understanding of the world of objects and persons. Fraiberg's talent in combining analytic and Piagetian ideas touches on an important change in theory building concerning infant and child development. Though many of the pioneers of infant and child development research were analysts, the field has become increasingly independent of its psychoanalytic origins. Like Fraiberg, other researchers have made use of techniques and theory that are foreign to analysis, resulting in formulations geared to the field of child development but distant from an analytic understanding of adult psychology. This trend has been given further impetus by the current majority of infant and child researchers who come from academic psychology, neurophysiology, nursing, and other backgrounds. Today, child development is a separate discipline, drawing on and contributing to psychoanalysis but, in many ways, independent of it.

Normative studies of preadolescence and adolescence have been the particular province of Peter Blos, whose writings (1962, 1967, 1970) have informed several generations of analysts about this age period. His findings, together with those of Anna Freud (1958), led to a general pessimism about the effectiveness of psychoanalysis with adolescents. However, subsequent experience—for example, that of Samuel Ritvo (1971, 1976, 1984) and the Laufers (1978, 1982, 1984)—has demonstrated that a thoroughgoing analytic approach can be useful for this age-group, even for those with very disabling nonpsychotic psychological conditions.

Eric Erikson (1950, 1987) gave substance to the concept of identity formation in his elucidation of the modes of resolution of identity issues in adolescence. He did so by introducing concepts that acknowledged and detailed the influence on the individual of his interpersonal and cultural environment. Moreover, his studies extended beyond childhood and adolescence to encompass the entire span of life.

The work cited above relates primarily to the characteristics of normative development and its variations. Other, sometimes overlapping, studies have focused on the psychological impact of particular caretaking practices, the effects of the legal system on children, the psychological effects of physical disabilities, and the definition and optimal treatment of various psychological states. In the remainder of this section, we will give examples from each of these areas.

Studies, by analysts, of special problems of childhood have contributed to our understanding of both normal and disordered development; they have also been a means of developing therapeutic programs for afflicted children. This has been particularly true for infants. Perhaps the best example of this type of study was the investigation of the impact of blindness on development, both psychological and physical. Prominent contributors to these studies and to the establishment of preventive programs of developmental assistance have been Dorothy Burlingham (1972), Selma Fraiberg (1977), and David Freedman (1975). Earlier, Omwake and Solnit (1961) reported on the psychoanalytic treatment of an older blind child.

Fraiberg brought her combined psychoanalytic and Piagetian approach to her studies of blind infants and of distressed infant–mother pairs. She was the first to recognize that the blind infant and child who receives consistent loving care but is nevertheless severely limited both socially and motorically is often an infant who has never learned to negotiate sensorimotor activities across the midline. This developmental step, usually requiring vision, was blocked unless special attention was paid to helping the infant achieve these cross-midline coordinations.

Also of special importance are the pioneering studies of Fraiberg on the effects of severe deprivation in infancy and her discovery of effective methods of therapy for some infant–mother pairs. Her book *Clinical Studies in Infant Mental Health* (1980) records the studies that led to her recognition that many severely deprived infants are mistreated by their mothers because of their connection to "ghosts in the nursery," ambivalently viewed family members who become identified by the mother with herself or with her infant. Special techniques of psychological treatment, which Fraiberg details, help to break the pathological bond to the "ghosts."

More recent psychoanalytic research has been done with children whose parents have died (Furman, 1974), children exposed to life-endangering traumas (Terr, 1979, 1984), and children living with psychotic parents (Anthony, 1986).

Viewed from the perspective of the past forty years, the most societally influential of these studies have been those by René Spitz, cited above, describing the morbidity and mortality suffered by infants who receive impersonal institutional care. These investigations were extended by Provence and Lipton (1962), who highlighted many further details, and by the observational research initiated by James Robertson (1952). The Spitz studies led to the closing of most infant institutions that provided impersonal, minimal caretaking, although recent reports from

Rumania remind us again of their horrors. The Robertson studies have given rise to changes in hospitalization procedures for children, particularly in Britain and the United States.

The Robertsons documented, both in words (1989) and on film, the anguish of young children separated from their parents during hospitalization (1952, 1958) or for other reasons (1969, 1971) for periods of days or weeks. Sufficient concern was generated by their findings to result in the formation of the Platt Commission by the British government, which recommended that all hospital facilities for young children make allowance for the regular presence of parents (Central Health Services Council, 1959). A quiet revolution has subsequently occurred both in Britain and in the United States, where all major hospitals have instituted reforms of their earlier policies of infrequent visiting and inadequate supportive assistance to children and parents in children's hospitals (Bergman, 1965; Plank, 1962).

In addition to giving rise to the enriching and competing concepts of Anna Freud and Melanie Klein, child analysts and infant researchers have organized a group of observations, concepts, and research methods into a set of propositions known as "attachment theory." It is the accomplishment of John Bowlby (1969–73) with Mary Ainsworth (1973) and, more recently, Marjorie Main and D. Weston (1981) and others. Attachment theory postulates a primary inclination towards affiliation or attachment as one of several bio-behavioral systems that can be investigated in its own right, apart from other systems and issues such as feeding, safety, and aggression. Attachment theory has been inventive in its research design and creative in providing reproducible techniques for determining the nature of child–parent attachment (Main & Weston, 1981).

With changing social patterns in American society, there is interest in understanding the implications for child development of day-care (Provence et al., 1977), single-parent families, and families in which the father, not the mother, is the principal caretaker. With this has come a belated interest in defining the differences between the contributions of mothers and fathers to the development of young children (Chused, 1986; Herzog, 1980; Pruett, 1983, 1985).

Children who run foul of the law drew the attention of one of the founding fathers of child analysis, August Aichhorn. His book *Wayward Youth* (1935) has inspired others to study the juvenile offender (for example, Gardiner, 1985) and to devise modes of treatment that build on Aichhorn's central finding —namely, that it is through relationships between the child and effective adults and through an environment that provides educational, social, and aesthetic "nutriment" that antisocial behavior is best resolved (Redl, 1945; Bettelheim, 1950; Mayer & Blum, 1971; Mayer et al., 1977; Dowling, 1975).

Among Albert Solnit's many contributions has been his influence on pediatric care and the legal rights of children. With Anna Freud and Joseph Goldstein (Goldstein et al., 1973) he has made the term "the best interests of the child" a meaningful consideration in American jurisprudence. Traditionally, in legal proceedings concerning the custody of children, legal emphasis was on the rights of parents, children being considered property to be assigned to the parent with the most compelling rights of possession. "The best interests of the child" means considering the psychological well-being of the child as a valid consideration in making legal decisions. Solnit and his coauthors make a strong plea for the child's right to a loving, considerate, committed caretaker; they point out that it is what they call "the psychological parent," not the legally defined parent, who can best assist the child in reaching productive adulthood and who therefore should be given primary consideration for custody.

Child analysis has always had close ties with education, beginning with Anna Freud's early book *Four Lectures on Psychoanalysis for Teachers and Parents* (1930). Psychoanalysts have urged education that takes advantage of the developmental strengths of the child, takes account of the psychological needs of children, and teaches in an atmosphere of respect for the needs and individual characteristics of each child.

From its inception, child analysis has studied and devised therapeutic approaches to forms of childhood psychopathology other than neurosis. What in later years became known in adult psychoanalysis as the "widening scope of psychoanalysis" (Stone, 1954) was found in child analysis from the beginning. However, child analysis has been more forthright in developing variations of treatment to meet varying requirements, the most obvious example being the variations of analytic technique at different developmental levels.

The limits of the effectiveness of psychoanalytic intervention with children and the use of other modalities of help in place of or in conjunction with psychoanalysis have been fruitful areas of study. "Borderline" or "atypical" children have been the topic of much of this work; a central question is whether their psychopathology is the result of intrapsychic conflict or of deficits, either congenital or acquired. If the latter, in what ways, if at all, can psychoanalysis be helpful? The issue of conflict versus deficit remains an unsettled and highly contentious issue, discussion of which promises to further enlighten and clarify our understanding of human growth and psychopathology. Anna Freud (1970), Hansi Kennedy (1979), and Kennedy and Moran (1991) have made major contributions to these discussions.

Although there are many published descriptions of child analytic cases (see *Psychoanalytic Study of the Child* and *Bulletin of the Anna Freud Centre*), until recently there were few studies utilizing sophisticated statistical techniques. As recently as 1991, a review of outcome and follow-up studies in psychoanalysis (Bachrach et al., 1991) included no studies of child analysis.

In the single example of a comparison study until recent years, C. Heinicke (1965) compared once-weekly psychotherapy with four times per week psychoanalysis in a group of ten children with similar symptomatology and comparable defensive organizations. Six children were treated with psychotherapy, four children with analysis. Both groups benefited from therapy, but at follow-up, one year after termination, the analyzed children showed "a more balanced use of defenses, indications of more benign superego functioning, and perhaps most important, such indications of flexibility and differentiation as the ability to elaborate an idea imaginatively, the capacity to express a variety of affects, the nondefensive use of humor, and the capacity to observe their own behavior and the motives underlying it" (p. 96).

By contrast with the paucity of past efforts, the Anna Freud Centre has recently presented a series of impressive studies of the efficacy of psychoanalytic psychotherapy and psychoanalysis. Peter Fonagy and Anne-Marie Tallandini-Shallice (1993) present a thoughtful critique of psychoanalytic research, defending the importance of the case study and clinical material within the framework of the traditional requirements of scientific research. They conclude:

Science is characterized by public data and procedures open to inspection and re-analysis. With proper training and knowledge of relevant methods anyone should be able to determine if findings are replicable. Persuasion has to be restricted to methods where replication is accessible to all. Where replication and open inspection are unwelcome a community of truth-seekers cannot flourish. Psychoanalysis must retain its community of truth-seekers who share each other's discoveries and learn from each other's experience. [p. 19]

Mary Target and Hansi Kennedy (1991) reviewed the experience of the Anna Freud Centre with treatment of 143 under-fives with a wide range of disorders; 85 percent were treated with analysis. The authors found that "17% of the children referred under five were psychiatrically diagnosable at the end of treatment, compared with 75% at the beginning." Children's Global Assessment Scale scores rose "an average of 14 points, bringing the average score at termination to the lower end of the normal range."

The findings of a retrospective study of 763 children in psychoanalysis or psychoanalytic psychotherapy (Fonagy & Target, 1994; Target & Fonagy, 1994a) have been summarized (Target & Fonagy, 1994b). Younger children benefited most from the treatment and benefited more than adolescents from intensive (analytic) therapy as compared with psychoanalytic psychotherapy. Another conclusion, supporting an emphasis on developmental issues in child analysis, was that a developmental framework must be considered when examining predictors of the outcome of child therapy.

While the daily experience of developmental change and resolution of psychological conflict inspires the individual analytic practitioner, methodologically adequate, psychoanalytically informed outcome and follow-up studies are required if non-psychoanalytic investigators are to be convinced of the power of the method.

CONCLUSION

It is evident that child analysis—late in appearance and struggling still for equal status with adult analysis—has, in fact, gained and contributed to psychoanalysis generally, in part because of that struggle. At the heart of child analysis is the awareness and conviction that Freud was correct when he stated, many years ago:

> In any case it may be maintained that analysis of children's neuroses can claim to possess a specially high theoretical interest. They afford us, roughly speaking, as much help towards a proper understanding of the neuroses of adults as do children's dreams in respect to the dreams of adults. Not, indeed, that they are more perspicuous or poorer in elements; in fact, the difficulty of feeling one's way into the mental life of a child makes them set the physician a particularly difficult task. But nevertheless, so many of the later deposits are wanting in them that the essence of the neurosis springs to the eyes with unmistakable distinctness. [1918, p. 9]

Child analysis is dedicated to "feeling one's way into the mental life of a child" and presenting to others what is found when "the essence of the neurosis springs to the eyes with unmistakable distinctness."

As the richness of its applications testifies, child analysis is equally dedicated to utilizing its insights to enhance the lives of all children.

REFERENCES

Abend, S. (1974). Problems of identity. *Psychoanal. Q.,* 43:505–637.
———. (1987). Evaluating young adults for analysis. *Psychoanal. Inq.,* 7:31–38.
Aichhorn, A. (1935). *Wayward Youth.* New York: Viking.
Ainsworth, M. (1973). The development of mother–infant attachment. In *Review of Child Development Research,* vol. 3, ed. B. M. Caldwell & H. N. Ricciuti (Chicago: Univ. Chicago Press).
Anthony, E. (1980). The family and the psychoanalytic process in children. *Psychoanal. Study Child,* 35:3–34.
———. (1986). Terrorizing attacks on children by psychotic parents. *J. Amer. Acad. Child Psychiat.,* 25:326–335.
Bachrach, H., Galatzer-Levy, R., Skolnikoff, A., & Waldron, S. (1991). On the efficacy of psychoanalysis. *J. Amer. Psychoanal. Assn.,* 39:871–916.
Bergman, T. (1965). *Children in the Hospital.* New York: Int. Univ. Press.
Bettelheim, B. (1950). *Love is Not Enough.* Glencoe, Ill.: Free Press.
Bion, W. (1963). *Elements of Psychoanalysis.* New York: Basic Books.
Bird, B. (1972). Transference. *J. Amer. Psychoanal. Assn.,* 20:267–301.
Blos, P. (1962). *On Adolescence.* New York: Free Press.
———. (1967). The second individuation process of adolescence. *Psychoanal. Study Child,* 22:162–187.
———. (1970). *The Young Adolescent.* New York: Free Press.
Bornstein, B. (1935). Phobia in a two-and-a-half-year-old child. *Psychoanal. Q.,* 4:93–119.
———. (1945). Clinical notes on child analysis. *Psychoanal. Study Child,* 1:151–166.
———. (1949). The analysis of a phobic child. *Psychoanal. Study Child,* 3/4:181–226.
Bowlby, J. (1951). *Maternal Care and Mental Health.* New York: Columbia Univ. Press.
———. (1969–73). *Attachment and Loss,* 2 vols. London: Hogarth Press.
Brody, S. (1961). Some aspects of transference resistance in prepuberty. *Psychoanal. Study Child,* 16:251–275.
Burlingham, D. (1972). *Psychoanalytic Studies of the Sighted and the Blind.* New York: Int. Univ. Press.

Buxbaum, E. (1954). Technique of child therapy. *Psychoanal. Study Child,* 9:297–333.

Central Health Services Council (1959). *The Welfare of Children in Hospital.* London: H.M.S.O. (The Platt Report).

Chused, J. (1986). Consequences of paternal nurturing. *Psychoanal. Study Child,* 41:419–438.

———. (1988). The transference neurosis in child analysis. *Psychoanal. Study Child,* 43:51–81.

Dowling, S. (1975). Treatment in cottage programs for children with severe developmental disturbances. *Child Welfare,* 54:395–405.

———. (1977). Seven children with esophageal atresia. *Psychoanal. Study Child,* 32:215–236.

———. (1980). Going forth to meet the environment. *Psychosom. Med.,* 42:153–161.

Emde, R. N. (1983). The prerepresentational self and its affective core. *Psychoanal. Study Child,* 38:165–192.

———. (1990). Mobilizing fundamental modes of development. *J. Amer. Psychoanal. Assn.,* 38:881–914.

Emde, R. N., Gaensbauer, T., & Harmon, R. (1976). *Emotional Expression in Infancy.* Psychological Issues, monograph 37. New York: Int. Univ. Press.

Engel, G. L. (1962). Anxiety depression-withdrawal. *Int. J. Psychoanal.,* 43:89–97.

Engel, G. L., Reichsman, F. (1956). Spontaneous and experimentally induced depression in an infant with a gastric fistula. *J. Amer. Psychoanal. Assn.,* 4:428–452.

Engel, G. L., Reichsman, F., Harway, V., & Hess, W. (1985). Monica: infant-feeding behavior of a mother gastric fistula-fed as an infant. In *Parental Influences in Health and Disease,* ed. E. J. Anthony & G. Pollack. Boston: Little, Brown.

Erikson, E. (1950). *Childhood and Society.* New York: Norton.

———. (1987). *A Way of Looking at Things.* New York: Norton.

Fonagy, P., & Tallandini-Shallice, A.-M. (1993). On some problems of psychoanalytic research in practice. *Bull. Anna Freud Centre,* 16:5–25.

Fonagy, P., & Target, M. (1994). The efficacy of psychoanalysis for children with disruptive disorders. *J. Amer. Acad. Child Adolesc. Psychiat.,* 33:45–55.

Fraiberg, S. (1951). Clinical notes on the nature of transference in child analysis. *Psychoanal. Study Child,* 6:286–306.

———. (1952). A critical neurosis in a two-and-a-half-year-old girl. *Psychoanal. Study Child,* 7:173–215.

———. (1955). Some considerations in the introduction to therapy in puberty. *Psychoanal. Study Child,* 10:264–286.

———. (1959). *The Magic Years.* New York: Charles Scribner's.

———. (1966). Further considerations of the role of transference in latency. *Psychoanal. Study Child,* 21:213–236.

———. (1977). *Insights from the Blind.* New York: Basic Books.

———. (1980). *Clinical Studies in Infant Mental Health.* New York: Basic Books.

Freedman, D. A. (1975). Congenital and perinatal sensory deprivations. *Psychoanal. Q.,* 44:62–80.

Freud, A. (1927). Four lectures on child analysis. In *Writings of Anna Freud,* 1:3–69.

———. (1930). *Four Lectures on Psychoanalysis for Teachers and Parents.* N.Y.: Int. Univ. Press. In *Writings of Anna Freud,* 1:73–133.

———. (1936). *The Ego and the Mechanisms of Defense.* New York: Int. Univ. Press.

———. (1958). Adolescence. *Psychoanal. Study Child,* 13:255–278.

———. (1962). Assessment of childhood disturbances. *Psychoanal. Study Child,* 17:149–158.

———. (1963). The concept of developmental lines. *Psychoanal. Study Child,* 18:245–265.

———. (1965). *Normality and Pathology of Childhood.* New York: Int. Univ. Press.

———. (1966). A short history of child analysis. In *Writings of Anna Freud,* 7:48–58.

———. (1969). Adolescence as a developmental disturbance. In *Writings of Anna Freud,* 7:39–47.

———. (1970). The symptomatology of childhood. *Psychoanal. Study Child,* 25:19–41.

———. (1974). A psychoanalytic view of developmental psychopathology. *J. Philadelphia Assn. Psychoanal.,* 1:7–17.

Freud, A., & Burlingham, D. B. (1973). *Infants without Families.* In *Writings of Anna Freud,* 3:1–664.

Freud, S. (1900). *The Interpretation of Dreams. SE,* 4 & 5.

———. (1909). Analysis of a phobia in a five-year-old boy. *SE,* 10:3–149.

———. (1918). From the history of an infantile neurosis. *SE,* 17:3–123.

———. (1920). *Beyond the Pleasure Principle. SE,* 18:7–64.

———. (1926a). *Inhibitions, Symptoms and Anxiety. SE,* 20:77–175.

———. (1926b). *The Question of Lay Analysis. SE,* 20:183–258.

———. (1933). *New Introductory Lectures on Psycho-Analysis. SE,* 22:3–182.

Furman, E. (1956). An ego disturbance in a young child. *Psychoanal. Study Child,* 11:312–335.

———. (1957). Treatment of under-fives by way of their parents. *Psychoanal. Study Child,* 12:250–262.

————. (1974). *A Child's Parent Dies.* New Haven: Yale Univ. Press.

Furman, R., & Katan, A., eds. (1969). *The Therapeutic Nursery School.* New York: Int. Univ. Press.

Gardiner, M. (1985). *The Deadly Innocents.* New Haven: Yale Univ. Press.

Glenn, J., ed. (1978). *Child Analysis and Therapy.* New York: Aronson.

Glover, E. (1945). Examination of the Klein system of child psychology. *Psychoanal. Study Child,* 1:75–118.

Goldstein, J., Freud, A., & Solnit, A. J. (1973). *Beyond the Best Interests of the Child.* New York: Free Press.

Greenspan, S. I. (1981). *Psychopathology and Adaptation in Infancy and Early Childhood.* New York: Int. Univ. Press.

Hall, J. (1946). The analysis of a case of night terror. *Psychoanal. Study Child,* 2:189–227.

Harley, M. (1951). Analysis of a severely disturbed three-and-a-half-year-old boy. *Psychoanal. Study Child,* 6:206–234.

————. (1967). Transference developments in a five-year-old child. In *The Child Analyst at Work,* ed. E. R. Geleerd, pp. 115–141. New York: Int. Univ. Press.

————. (1971). The current status of transference neurosis in children. *J. Amer. Psychoanal. Assn.,* 19:26–40.

Hartmann, H. (1950). Psychoanalysis and developmental psychology. *Psychoanal. Study Child,* 5:7–17.

Heinicke, C. (1965). Frequency of psychotherapeutic session as a factor affecting the child's developmental status. *Psychoanal. Study Child,* 20:42–98.

Herzog, J. M. (1980). Sleep disturbance and father hunger in 18–28-month-old boys. *Psychoanal. Study Child,* 35:219–236.

Hoffer, W. (1949). Mouth, hand, and ego-integration. *Psychoanal. Study Child,* 3/4:49–56.

————. (1950). Development of the body ego. *Psychoanal. Study Child,* 5:18–23.

Hug-Hellmuth, H. (1920). Child psychology and education. *Int. J. Psychoanal.,* 1:316–323.

————. (1921). On the technique of child analysis. *Int. J. Psychoanal.,* 2:287–303.

Katan, A. (1961). Some thoughts about the role of verbalization in childhood. *Psychoanal. Study Child,* 16:184–188.

————. (1972). The infant's first reaction to strangers. *Int. J. Psychoanal.,* 53:501–503.

Kennedy, H. (1979). The role of insight in child analysis. *J. Amer. Psychoanal. Assn.,* 27 (suppl.): 9–28.

Kennedy, H., & Moran, G. (1991). Reflections on the aim of child analysis. *Psychoanal. Study Child,* 46: 181–198.

Kernberg, O. F. (1976). *Object Relations Theory and Clinical Psychoanalysis.* New York: Aronson.

Kestenberg, J. (1969). Problems of technique in child analysis in relation to the various developmental stages. *Psychoanal. Study Child,* 24:358–383.

King, P., & Steiner, R., eds. (1991). *The Freud–Klein Controversies 1941–1945.* London: Routledge.

Klein, M. (1921). The development of a child. *Int. J. Psychoanal.,* 4:419–474.

————. (1932). *The Psycho-Analysis of Children.* London: Hogarth Press.

————. (1964). *Contributions to Psychoanalysis: 1921–1945.* New York: McGraw-Hill.

Klein, M., Riviere, J., Searl, M., Sharpe, E., Glover, E., & Jones, E. (1927). Symposium on child-analysis. *Int. J. Psychoanal.,* 8:339–391.

Kolansky, H. (1960). Treatment of a three-year-old girl's severe neurosis. *Psychoanal. Study Child,* 15:261–285.

Kris, E. (1956). The recovery of childhood memories in psychoanalysis. *Psychoanal. Study Child,* 11:54–88.

Laufer, M. (1978). Nature of adolescent pathology and the psychoanalytic process. *Psychoanal. Study Child,* 33:307–322.

Laufer, M., & Laufer, M. E. (1984). *Adolescence and Developmental Breakdown.* New Haven: Yale Univ. Press.

Laufer, M. E. (1982). Female masturbation in adolescence and the development of relationship to the body. *Int. J. Psychoanal.,* 63:295–302.

Lebovici, S. (1974). Traumatization. *Int. Rev. Psychoanal.,* 1:117–123.

Lichtenberg, J. (1989). *Psychoanalysis and Motivation.* Hillsdale, N.J.: Analytic Press.

Mahler, M. S. (1952). On child psychosis and schizophrenia. *Psychoanal. Study Child,* 7:286–305.

Mahler, M. S., Pine, F., & Bergman, A. (1975). *The Psychological Birth of the Human Infant.* New York: Basic Books.

Main, M., & Weston, D. (1981). Security of attachment to mother and father. *Child Development,* 49:932–940.

Mayer, M., & Blum, A. (1971). *Healing through Living.* Springfield, Ill.: Thomas.

Mayer, M., Richman, L., & Balcerzak, E. (1977). *Group Care of Children.* New York: Child Welfare League of America.

Nagera, H. (1963). The developmental profile. *Psychoanal. Study Child,* 18:511–540.

———. (1966). *Early Childhood Disturbances, the Infantile Neurosis and the Adulthood Disturbances.* New York: Int. Univ. Press.

Neubauer, P. B. (1972). Psychoanalysis of the preschool child. In *Handbook of Child Psychoanalysis,* ed. B. Wolman, pp. 221–252. New York: Van Nostrand.

——— (1984). Anna Freud's concept of developmental lines. *Psychoanal. Study Child,* 39:15–28.

Omwake, E. B., & Solnit, A. J. (1961). "It isn't fair." *Psychoanal. Study Child,* 16:352–404.

Panel (1974). A comparison between adult and child analysis. C. Feigelson, reporter. *J. Amer. Psychoanal. Assn.,* 22:603–611.

Parens, H. (1979). *The Development of Aggression in Early Childhood.* New York: Aronson.

Pine, F. (1985). *Developmental Theory and Clinical Process.* New Haven: Yale Univ. Press.

Plank, E. (1962). *Working with Children in Hospitals.* Cleveland, Ohio: Press of Western Reserve University.

Provence, S., ed. (1983). *Infants and Parents.* New York: Int. Univ. Press.

Provence, S., & Lipton, R. (1962). *Infants in Institutions.* New York: Int. Univ. Press.

Provence, S., Naylor, A., & Patterson, J. (1977). *The Challenge of Daycare.* New Haven: Yale Univ. Press.

Pruett, K. D. (1983). Infants of primary nurturing fathers. *Psychoanal. Study Child,* 38:257–280.

———. (1985). Oedipal configurations in young father-raised children. *Psychoanal. Study Child,* 40:435–456.

Redl, F. (1945). Psychology of gang formation and the treatment of juvenile delinquents. *Psychoanal. Study Child,* 1:367–378.

Ritvo, S. (1971). Late adolescence. *Psychoanal. Study Child,* 26:241–263.

———. (1976). Adolescent to woman. *J. Amer. Psychoanal. Assn.,* 24:127–138.

———. (1984). the image and uses of the body in psychic conflict. *Psychoanal. Study Child,* 39: 449–470.

Robertson, James (1952). Film: *A Two-Year-Old Goes to Hospital.* London: Tavistock Child Development Research Unit; New York: New York University Film Library.

———. (1958). Film: *Going to Hospital with Mother.* London: Tavistock Child Development Research Unit; New York: New York University Film Library.

Robertson, James, & Robertson, Joyce (1969). Film: *John, 17 Months: For 9 Days in a Residential Nursery.* London: Tavistock Child Development

Research Unit; New York: New York University Film Library.

———. (1971). Film: *Thomas, 2 Years 4 Months: In Foster Care for 10 Days.* London: Tavistock Child Development Research Unit; New York: New York University Film Library.

Rosenbaum, A. (1992). The assessment of parental functioning. *Psychoanal. Q.,* 63:466–490.

Sander, L. (1962). Issues in early mother–child interaction. *J. Amer. Acad. Child Psychiat.,* 1:141–166.

———. (1980). Investigation of the infant and its caregiving environment as a biological system. In *The Course of Life,* ed. S. I. Greenspan & G. H. Pollock, vol. 1, pp. 177–201. Washington, D.C.: National Institute of Mental Health.

Sandler, J., Kennedy, H., & Tyson, R. (1980). *The Technique of Child Psychoanalysis.* Cambridge, Mass.: Harvard Univ. Press.

Sarnoff, C. (1976). *Latency.* New York: Aronson.

Spitz, R. A. (1946). Hospitalism. *Psychoanal. Study Child,* 2:113–118.

———. (1965). *The First Year of Life.* New York: Int. Univ. Press.

Steiner, R. (1985). British psychoanalytical society's controversial discussions. *Int. Rev. Psychoanal.,* 12:27–72.

Sterba, E. (1949). Analysis of psychogenic constipation in a two-year-old child. *Psychoanal. Study Child,* 3/4:227–252.

Stern, D. (1985). *The Interpersonal World of the Infant.* New York: Basic Books.

Stone, L. (1954). The widening scope of indications for psychoanalysis. *J. Amer. Psychoanal. Assn.,* 2:567–594.

Target, M., & Fonagy, P. (1994a). The efficacy of psychoanalysis for children with emotional disorders. *J. Amer. Acad. Child Adolesc. Psychiat.,* 33:361–371.

———. (1994b). The efficacy of psychoanalysis for children: prediction of outcome in a developmental context. *J. Amer. Acad. Child Adolesc. Psychiat.,* 33:1134–1144.

Target, M., & Kennedy, H. (1991). Psychoanalytic work with the under-fives. *Bull. Anna Freud Centre,* 14:5–29.

Terr, L. C. (1979). Children of Chowchilla. *Psychoanal. Study Child,* 34:547–623.

———. (1984). Time and trauma. *Psychoanal. Study Child,* 39:633–665.

Tomkins, S. (1962–91). *Affect, Imagery, Consciousness,* 3 vols. New York: Springer.

Tyson, P. (1978). Transference and developmental issues in the analysis of a prelatency child. *Psychoanal. Study Child,* 33:213–236.

———. (1982). A developmental line of gender identity, gender role, and choice of love object. *J. Amer. Psychoanal. Assn.*, 30:61–86.

Tyson, R. L. (1978). Notes on the analysis of a pre-latency boy with a dog phobia. *Psychoanal. Study Child*, 33:427–460.

Weil, A. P. (1970). The basic core. *Psychoanal. Study Child*, 25:442–460.

Winnicott, D. W. (1960). The theory of the parent–infant relationship. *Int. J. Psychoanal.*, 41:585–595.

———. (1962). The theory of the parent–infant relationship: further remarks. *Int. J. Psychoanal.*, 43:238–239.

———. (1975). *Through Paediatrics to Psychoanalysis*. New York: Basic Books.

Wolff, P. H. (1959). Observations on newborn infants. *Psychosom. Med.*, 21:110–118.

Young-Bruehl, E. (1988). *Anna Freud*. New York: Summit.

3

PSYCHOANALYTICALLY ORIENTED INDIVIDUAL PSYCHOTHERAPY

INTRODUCTION

The term "psychotherapy" encompasses a broad spectrum of therapies that have in common only the fact that they attempt to better the patient's mental and emotional condition by means of verbal communication. This chapter will not attempt to cover this extensive field but will be limited to a discussion of the therapies that have branched out from psychoanalysis proper and acknowledge the existence of a dynamic unconscious and intrapsychic conflict. The indications for and selection of treatment, as well as basic techniques that differentiate these modalities, will be discussed. Short-term (time-limited) analytically oriented psychotherapy, open-ended (long-term) psychoanalytically oriented psychotherapy, analytically informed supportive psychotherapy, and psychotherapy in preparation for subsequent psychoanalysis will be distinguished. Clinical examples illustrating different therapeutic approaches will be presented.

Psychoanalysis and the various psychoanalytically oriented psychotherapies currently being practiced have a common origin in the work of Sigmund Freud. Before becoming the first psychoanalyst, Freud was a psychotherapist. Like generations of physicians before him, he used the authority delegated to him by patients to effect change with forms of suggestion, including direct advice and manipulation of events of the patient's life (Bibring, 1954).

While this approach apparently succeeded with some hysterical patients, Freud was not satisfied with the efficacy of suggestion and hypnosis, and his continuing efforts to understand and treat formerly untreatable patients laid the foundation not only for the theory and practice of psychoanalysis but also for the subsequent evolution of psychotherapeutic approaches based on psychoanalytic principles. Freud's primary interest was in developing and refining the technique of psychoanalysis. Nevertheless, in 1919 he stated: "It is very probable too, that the large-scale application of our therapy will compel us to alloy the pure gold of analysis freely with the copper of direct suggestion; and hypnotic influence, too, might find a place in it again, as it has in the treatment of war neuroses. But, whatever form this psychotherapy for the people may take, whatever the elements out of which it is compounded, its most effective and most important ingredients will assuredly remain those borrowed from strict and untendentious psycho-analysis" (pp. 167–168). This prescient statement indicates his recognition of the enduring value of earlier techniques but also provides a precedent for regarding psychotherapy as a less valuable form of treatment than psychoanalysis.

Glover (1931) in his frequently cited paper "The therapeutic effects of inexact interpretation" advanced the thesis that all psychotherapies other than analysis were varieties of suggestion. Even though he stated that what might be poor analysis might be good suggestion, the message that suggestion is an inferior treatment technique was quite clear.

The 1950s were the heyday of psychoanalysis. Analytic treatment was applied to an ever widening range of patients. At the same time, it was becoming clear that psychoanalysis, even with modifications, was not suitable for all patients and that some form of psychotherapy would be a better choice in many situations. Stone (1951), in a paper about analytic work with patients with severe character disorders, suggested that with time "further advances or modifications of psychoanalysis may make certain of these extensions (of psychoanalysis) more secure; however, it is possible that the tide of therapeutic optimism will recede in certain areas, leaving large groups of illnesses to be better treated by techniques of 'brief psychotherapy,' 'psychoanalytic psychiatry,' or 'modified psychoanalysis,' yet to be established" (p. 217). He also suggested that in cases of relatively acute reactive neurosis or mild neurosis, less extensive methods might be adequate or more appropriate, thus pointing in the direction of a more short-term psychoanalytic psychotherapy for such patients. In his later paper "The widening scope of indications for psychoanalysis," Stone (1954) amplified his discussion of analytic treatment of patients with serious character disorders as well as borderline patients. It was his opinion that psychoanalysis, sometimes with significant parameters, offers hope of improvement to patients who cannot be helped by a less ambitious form of treatment. This differentiation of choice of treatment options on the basis of a more sophisticated psychoanalytic theoretical understanding encouraged the further development of psychotherapeutic techniques, and psychotherapy gained in respectability within the psychoanalytic community.

From the 1950s on, new schools of psychodynamic psychotherapy emerged, some of them repudiating their ancestral connection to psychoanalysis. Since then, a very extensive psychotherapy literature has evolved, much of it geared to students who do not plan to get analytic training, written by authors who are not analysts. This literature is beyond the scope of this chapter. Wallerstein in "The current state of psychotherapy: theory, practice, research" (1966) provides a thorough review and summary of the major contributions to the field of psychoanalytic psychotherapy to that date, including those of Bullard (1959), Rubenstein and Parloff (1959), Strupp (1960), Frank (1961), Strupp and Luborsky (1962), Edelson (1963), Tarachow (1963), and DeWald (1964). In a more recent article, Wallerstein (1989) also presents a scholarly perspective on the complex

and ever evolving relationship between psychoanalysis and psychotherapy.

As various forms of psychotherapy have evolved, efforts to study the efficacy of treatment have been initiated. The field of psychotherapy research has been expanding. The first major long-term longitudinal study of psychotherapy (and of psychoanalysis) was made by the Psychotherapy Research Project of the Menninger Foundation. The results of this study, which began in 1952, are published in *Forty-Two Lives in Treatment* (Wallerstein, 1986). The findings of the Menninger Project are summarized in Wallerstein's 1988 paper "Psychoanalysis and psychotherapy: relative roles reconsidered." The study found that all the treatments, including psychoanalysis, had more supportive elements than had been expected initially. Additionally, the various forms of treatment tended to converge toward a mixture of expressive-supportive techniques. Treatment outcome was found to be difficult to predict accurately.

Reder and Tyson (1980) published an extensive study of the phenomenon of patient dropout from both brief and long-term psychotherapy. One of their few consistent findings was that there is a high patient dropout rate in the early stages of all treatments. They suggest, in view of this fact, that it may be wise to see the initial stages of any psychotherapy as a "trial" period in which the suitability of the treatment for the patient and the match of therapist and patient are assessed.

Who Will Benefit from Psychotherapy? (Luborsky et al., 1988) details the results of the Penn Psychotherapy Project and also reexamines data from other psychotherapy studies, including the Chicago Psychotherapy Project. The Penn study found that benefits from treatment *can* be consistently measured. Additionally, there is a good correlation between patients' and therapists' assessment of treatment outcome. The Penn study found two-thirds of the patients to be "moderately" to "much" improved, and the gains, particularly in the most improved group, were well maintained over a seven-year follow-up period.

Efforts to identify and quantify components of psychodynamic psychotherapy so that the efficacy of various aspects of treatment can be studied more systematically have led to the development of psychotherapy manuals that can be used to teach specific quantifiable psychotherapeutic techniques. In *Principles of Psychoanalytic Psychotherapy: A Manual for Supportive-Expressive Treatment,* Luborsky (1984) details the Penn Psychotherapy Project's recommendations for a standardized, and therefore more reproducible and quantifiable, form of psychotherapy. Techniques for the treatment of severe character disorders, particularly borderline personality disorder, are being studied systematically by Kernberg's group. Their approach and initial results are described by Clarkin et al. (1992). Other psychotherapy manuals for some specialized forms of psychotherapy include *Psychotherapy in a New Key: A Guide to Time-Limited Dynamic Psychotherapy (TLDP)* by Strupp and Binder (1984), *Interpersonal Psychotherapy of Depression* (IPT) by Klerman et al. (1984), and *Cognitive Therapy of Depression* by Beck et al. (1979).

Measures that can be used to study various aspects of the treatment process, as well as diagnostic instruments, continue to be developed and refined by various groups of research workers, some of whom have also developed treatment manuals. There is currently great interest in the study of interpersonal interactions in the course of the psychotherapy; these include the therapeutic alliance and transference/countertransference manifestations, as well as significant relationship patterns outside the treatment setting. Measures of these interactions and patterns within the psychotherapy session can be found in Luborsky, 1976; Horowitz, 1979; Gill and Hoffman, 1982; Schacht et al., 1984; Maxim, 1986; Kiesler, 1987; and Perry et al., 1989.

Research in the field of psychoanalytically oriented psychotherapy continues, despite the difficulties inherent in studying treatment that is often lengthy, as well as difficult to quantify. For a recent summary of the current state of psychodynamic research efforts, the reader is referred to *Psychodynamic Treatment Research: A Handbook for Clinical Practice* by Miller et al. (1993). This useful volume includes sections on patient selection, definition of treatments, and measures used to study various psychodynamic psychotherapies.

DIFFERENCES BETWEEN PSYCHOANALYSIS AND PSYCHOTHERAPY

Debates among analysts about the essential differences and similarities between psychoanalysis and psychoanalytically oriented psychotherapy have continued to the present time. There is still controversy over the question of whether the psychoanalytic psychotherapy of neurotic patients as generally practiced is or is not something other than watered-down psychoanalysis. The fact that some authors have written about psychotherapeutic and psychoanalytic technique without clearly distinguishing between them has contributed to this confusion. Additionally, psychotherapy is frequently taught to nonpsychoanalysts utilizing psychoanalytic readings.

This can be problematic if the instructor does not clearly delineate the ways in which the psychotherapeutic technique that is being taught differs from standard psychoanalytic technique. This is not an easy task. It may be impossible unless the student of psychotherapy already has some analytic training and experience in conducting psychoanalysis with which to contrast psychotherapy.

The major theoretical constructs on which both psychoanalysis proper and psychoanalytically oriented psychotherapy are based are set forth in this volume. Chapters 1 and 5 of this book, on psychoanalytic technique and the psychoanalytic process, by Sydney E. Pulver, discuss in detail the technical procedures utilized in, and the process of, a classical analysis. A brief resumé of these subjects may be found under the headings "Psychoanalysis," "Analysis," "Analytic Technique," and "Analytic Therapy" in *Psychoanalytic Terms and Concepts* (Moore & Fine, eds., 1990). With regard to psychoanalysis proper, suffice it to say here that the patient's use of a couch, with the analyst behind him or her, diminishes external perceptual stimuli, thereby encouraging regression and the reactivation of instinctual impulses and wishes toward earlier meaningful persons in the patient's childhood, which are then displaced onto the analyst (transference). The patient is encouraged to say without reservation whatever comes to mind (free association), with the result that these loving and hating thoughts and the parental and societal influences restraining them, previously unconscious, find expression in derivative form. The analyst, utilizing his "evenly hovering attention" (Freud, 1912, p. 111) to the patient's affects and behavior, verbal productions in the form of accounts of realistic events, opinions, memories, fantasies, and dreams, processes the information in terms of his own theoretical knowledge, clinical experience, affective reaction, and fantasy. By this means he is able to observe episodes of resistance to the process on the part of the patient, explore these, deduce the intrapsychic conflicts to which they are related and the compromises whereby such conflicts are resolved (often by means of symptoms or character traits). The analyst's technical procedures are limited for the most part to interpretations: verbal efforts to facilitate the free flow of the patient's associations, explore various aspects of the patient's resistances, call attention to connections between past and present psychic phenomena and everyday behavior, clarify aspects of the transference, and reconstruct past events, especially those about which fantasies have evolved leading to current conflict. This process, conducted with a frequency of four or more sessions per week over a period of three years or more, brings about a gradual modification in the instinctual drive impulses and the severity of the superego, with a lessening of conflict and more adaptive resolutions (structural change).

Certain types of psychoanalytic psychotherapies to be described share some of these features. In contrast to the psychoanalytic technique outlined above, however, the usual procedures followed in psychotherapy minimize regression and lessen the intensity of the transference. The patient sits up with the therapist in full view, a less passive situation that stresses the reality of the current situation and the therapist as a new object with his or her own individuality. Free association is usually not encouraged, and though it may occur spontaneously, it is less directed by deeply unconscious forces. Treatment sessions are less frequent, varying from one to three per week, which also reduces the intensity of the relationship. Though the patient is given an opportunity to select the topics to be discussed, the therapist is more active, asking questions for clarification, often leading the patient to recognize connections more quickly than would be the case in analysis, and sometimes bringing up aspects of the patient's life for exploration. There is not sufficient opportunity to explore resistances at length, and they may be overcome by virtue of an idealized transference, education, and persuasion.

Perhaps it should be emphasized that systematic interpretation of the transference from a position of technical neutrality is the essential feature of psychoanalysis proper and the one that most distinguishes it from other psychotherapies, even those that are psychoanalytically oriented (Gill, 1954). By contrast with psychoanalysis proper, in the psychotherapies the transference may be left alone or utilized manipulatively. When transference is interpreted in psychotherapy, it is not a systematic interpretation of a transference neurosis. Usually such transference interpretation occurs only in psychotherapies in which sessions are frequent, the period of treatment is not limited, and the patient is especially psychologically minded. It is obvious that in such cases the psychotherapy may come close to being an analysis. It must be added, however, that the line dividing psychoanalytically oriented psychotherapy from psychoanalysis is not now as clear to all authors, even to Gill, as it was to him in 1954.

Currently, there is much discussion of the nature of the interaction between the therapist and the patient. In some cases, an interactive focus has replaced the focus on the transference. This approach is described by Oremland (1991), who prefers the term "interactive" rather than "supportive" for treatments in which the interaction between therapist and patient (rather than the patient's transference) is utilized as a vehicle for change instead of being interpreted, as it would be in psychoanalysis. Despite the current influence of the interactive approach, most psychoanalytic authors continue to view the systematic analysis of the transference (rather than the interaction) as central to analysis and consider incomplete or absent analysis of the transference to be one of the major characteristics of the psychotherapies, distinguishing them from psychoanalysis. In this context, I refer the reader to *Psychotherapy: The Analytic Approach* (Aronson & Scharfman, 1992), in which a clear distinction between the technique and goals of analysis, as contrasted with those of psychotherapy, is preserved.

Bibring (1954) enumerated and discussed the role of five groups of basic techniques utilized in both psychoanalysis and psychoanalytic psychotherapy: suggestion, abreaction, manipulation, clarification, and interpretation. By suggestion, the therapist brings about changes in the patient's behavior, thinking, and feelings through the exercise of his or her authority over the patient. This is possible because the patient delegates authoritarian power to the therapist via the transference. Except in the most supportive type of psychotherapy, to be discussed later, direct advice as to recommended changes in the patient's behavior is now seldom given. Nevertheless, it must be recognized that subtle, nonverbal indications of what the therapist wants the patient to do may be communicated to the patient, even though both may be unconscious of the fact. Changes brought about by suggestion generally require the continued presence of the transference figure and are often not lasting.

Abreaction is the discharge of previously repressed affects during the therapy session. Although technical maneuvers specifically designed to produce abreaction have fallen into disuse, except perhaps in the treatment of post-traumatic stress disorder syndromes, the phenomenon has its place in most psychotherapies. For example, the achievement of affectively meaningful insight depends on a combination of intellectual and emotional understanding brought about in part by abreaction in the course of the psychotherapy.

Manipulations of various types include the giving of direct advice, as well as other less dramatic efforts to structure the treatment and the patient's life. Bibring (1954) regarded as manipulation the therapist's use of statements that lessen resentment or other emotional obstacles to the patient's remaining within the treatment framework. Currently the term is not generally used in this way, although specific alterations in the framework of the treatment that are made to bring about changes in the patient are still considered manipulations. Such alterations include things like increasing or decreasing the number of sessions to regulate the intensity of the treatment.

Clarification includes all those efforts made by the therapist to aid in increasing the patients' awareness of his feelings, attitudes, and fantasies. Clarification is used as preparation for subsequent interpretation. It is also extensively employed in various forms of psychotherapy without subsequent interpretation. It is, for example, a clarification to point out that a patient's clenched fist or raised voice is indicative of anger when he or she is talking about something that elicits that emotion without conscious awareness of it.

Interpretation is the central technique of psychoanalysis and psychoanalytic psychotherapy. Interpretation brings together the present conscious wishes, fantasies, and feelings of the patient with their unconscious counterparts, linking both with their origins in the past and their current transferential manifestations.

To these techniques might be added education. However, the effectiveness of education as a technique is limited by its cognitive, rather than affective, nature.

CATEGORIES OF PSYCHOTHERAPY

Robert Knight (1949), following Freud, divided psychotherapy into two types: expressive (exploratory), as contrasted with suppressive (supportive), a division that is still generally accepted. In the expressive types of psychotherapy, the aim is to resolve conflict through uncovering, investigative, exploratory, and ventilating techniques. Psychoanalysis is the paradigmatic expressive psychotherapy. In the suppressive treatments the aim is primarily to strengthen defenses. Conflicts are therefore not brought to the surface; symptoms are ameliorated by explanation, education, and reassurance; and maladaptive behavior is dealt with by inspiration, counseling, persuasion, control by personnel other than the therapist, as well as environmental change.

Psychotherapies can be further differentiated from each other by the time frame within which the treatment is conducted. They may be time-limited and narrowly focused by design or open-ended. Though time-limited treatment is generally quite focused, open-ended psychotherapy can be short for special reasons. There are significant differences between these forms of treatment. In the time-limited so-called focal psychotherapies, the therapist concentrates on a specific area of the patient's personality rather than conducting a more global exploration. In

addition, he addresses issues of termination from the very beginning of the work.

Evaluation of the Patient

Before a course of treatment is suggested to a patient, a thorough evaluation should be performed. If there is a psychiatric emergency, such as serious suicidal risk, dealing with the emergency takes precedence. It is essential to rule out organic causes of the patient's difficulties and to determine if the patient is suffering from a psychosis or major affective disorder. After the initial psychiatric evaluation, the form of treatment may be considered. Psychotherapy may well be indicated for patients with organic mental syndromes and/or psychotic disorders, but the appropriate medical and neurological evaluation and, if indicated, treatment with psychopharmacological agents takes precedence. If substance abuse is present, treatment for this problem is generally indicated prior to any other form of psychotherapy.

Different approaches are used to evaluate patients seeking psychotherapy. I have found Otto Kernberg's (1975, 1984) approach very helpful, both in evaluating patients and in deciding on a recommendation for treatment. Kernberg divides patients into neurotic, borderline, and psychotic categories based on a "structural interview" which evaluates the predominant defenses utilized by the patient. Borderline patients rely on the primitive defenses of splitting, various forms of projection, in particular projective identification, primitive idealization, denial, omnipotence, and devaluation. In Kernberg's terminology, structurally psychotic patients (these include overtly psychotic patients and some descriptively borderline), unlike other borderline and neurotic individuals, have an underlying deficit in reality testing that can be demonstrated in the course of an interview. In response to carefully conducted repeated sequences of clarification, confrontation, and interpretation during Kernberg's structural interview, these patients either become worse, exhibiting frankly impaired reality testing, which may manifest as delusions or thought disorder, or they rigidify their (primitive) defenses. In contrast, borderline patients improve when their primitive defenses are confronted and interpreted in the here and now of the interview setting. Neurotic patients do not rely primarily on the more primitive defenses but utilize predominantly higher-level defenses such as repression, reaction formation, isolation, undoing, rationalization, and intellectualization.

Selection of Treatment

After the diagnostic evaluation, the choice of treatment for the patient at that particular time must be determined. In addition to the nature of the manifest psychopathology, factors to be weighed in reaching a decision are the life stage of the patient, the difficulties he or she is experiencing, questions of motivation and initial resistances, as well as issues of external reality.

Neurotic patients and some higher-level borderline patients—that is, those who have access to higher-level defenses and do not exclusively rely on the primitive mechanisms of projective identification and splitting—may be treated in psychoanalysis or psychotherapy. If the neurotic difficulties are serious and appear to infiltrate most areas of the patient's life, analysis will generally be the treatment of choice. In this context, it should be stressed that the fact that a patient appears to be analyzable does not necessarily mean that analysis is the most suitable treatment for the patient. Tyson and Sandler (1971) state:

> The selection of a patient for treatment depends far more on the assessment of criteria of suitability than on the symptomatic picture which he presents. . . . indications for psychoanalytic treatment might be present, but the patient [may be] unsuitable for analysis. Similarly, a patient might present with a symptom which is known not to respond well to psychoanalysis (e.g., stammering or a tic), but is assessed, on the basis of other criteria, as being a suitable person to undergo psychoanalysis and who would benefit from it, although his original symptoms might remain. [p. 215]

If analysis appears to be the treatment of choice and the therapist making the evaluation is not an analyst, the patient should be referred to an analyst. If such a patient cannot afford analysis, referral to a psychoanalytic institute as a control case is often possible.

Patients who should be treated in psychoanalytically oriented psychotherapy include those whose neurotic difficulties appear to be relatively circumscribed, acute, or mild. Another group is composed of those with limitations on the frequency with which they can come for treatment or the length of time they will be in the same geographic area as the analyst. When considering these "reality" reasons for choosing a form of psychotherapy, rather than psychoanalysis, it is essential to be aware of how reality is often employed in the service of resistance. If the patient appears to be analyzable and has significant ongoing neurotic difficulties, the external factors may not be immutable. Often a psychotherapy can be converted into an analysis when the resistance aspects of these external factors have been adequately explored. Dealing with such initial resis-

tances can be the focus of a preparatory psychotherapy.

Patients with significant ongoing problems who are not suitable for psychoanalysis at the time that they are seen for evaluation can be divided into those who might reasonably benefit from exploratory psychotherapy and those for whom an uncovering approach is contraindicated. The second subgroup includes overtly psychotic as well as severe borderline (often structurally psychotic) individuals. For such patients, supportive psychotherapy, often in conjunction with pharmacotherapy, will be the treatment(s) of choice. There are exceptions. Certain motivated, psychologically minded psychotic patients can benefit greatly from psychoanalytic psychotherapy with an admixture of supportive techniques.

VARIOUS FORMS OF PSYCHOANALYTIC PSYCHOTHERAPY

Expressive Psychoanalytic Psychotherapy

Time-limited focal psychotherapy. All Freud's initial treatments were brief, and some of his later ones were as well. As psychoanalysis and psychotherapies have evolved, analyses and psychoanalytic psychotherapies have lengthened and become progressively more expensive. This has led to efforts to develop techniques of brief treatment that are less costly in terms of both time and money but still helpful to a large group of patients seeking psychotherapy.

In the early 1960s various researchers began to publish on the topic of brief dynamic psychotherapy. Malan (1963) and Balint et al. (1972) were early contributors to this subject. The literature on techniques of psychodynamically oriented, brief psychotherapy continued to grow in the seventies (Mann, 1973; Malan, 1976; Davaloo, 1978; Sifneos, 1979). In these so-called focal approaches, an area of conflict causing neurotic symptomatology is identified, and the treatment is focused on that conflictual area. An essential feature of this approach is that the length of the treatment is set at the beginning, in marked contrast to open-ended forms of psychotherapy. The therapist is very active and directive with the patient, who is instructed to associate about selected issues.

Weissberg (1984) summarizes the orientation of the psychoanalyst conducting short-term dynamic psychotherapy thus: "He is very active by traditional standards, and confrontational, rather than reflective and contemplative. His attitude is one of relentless vigilance, rather than of hovering expectant attention. . . . Regression and detours around the therapeutic focus are vigorously discouraged. The therapist concentrates on the active pursuit of repressed affect. He then ties it to cognitive process through interpretation" (p. 109). In these treatments the initial evaluation defines the focus of the work. Although a psychodynamic understanding of the patient is central to this form of treatment, the process is drastically different from analysis and from the more open-ended and less directive psychoanalytically oriented psychotherapies, whether short- or long-term. The fact that the end of the treatment is set at the beginning insures that issues of termination are central from the start.

The field of brief dynamic psychotherapy has continued to expand. Recent contributions to the literature have been made by Gustafson (1986) and Horowitz et al. (1984). The following vignette illustrates the treatment of an adolescent in short-term, psychoanalytically oriented psychotherapy.

Amy was an eighteen-year-old college freshman. She had come home from school for vacation and felt too miserable to go back. The acute cause of her misery was that her boyfriend had borrowed several hundred dollars and her car and had disappeared. She felt "crushed" and too humiliated and depressed to return to college and sought psychotherapy.

Amy said that her life up until then had been very happy, except for a terrible family tragedy. When she was eight years old, her two-year-old brother had been run over by a truck and crushed. He had been playing in the front yard of the family house, which was on a street with very little traffic, but had run out into the road at exactly the wrong time. The driver of the truck had not been able to stop. She had not actually seen the accident, as she had been playing in the back of the house, but when she heard her mother's screams, she ran up and saw her brother lying under the wheels of the truck. After the accident, Amy said that she and her father had handled the tragedy better than her mother, who had needed psychotherapy to help her deal with her grief and severe feelings of guilt. Although she said that she was sure that it was no one's fault, she also said that she had the thought that maybe the incident would not have happened if she had invited her brother to play with her in the backyard.

Amy agreed to the recommendation of intensive (three times a week) therapy. She planned to return to school the next semester, and that gave us a time frame of four months.

Amy was psychologically minded, bright, and did not have borderline features. I was concerned that getting involved in painful relationships might prove to be a neurotic pattern that would not be easily treated in a brief format. However, I felt that she was at a point in her development such that it was important for her to get back on track and finish the tasks of her adolescence (see Blos, 1979). If brief, intensive treatment could help her do this, it seemed worth the attempt, even if it was likely that more extensive work, perhaps psychoanalysis, might be indicated later. Of course, it is always important for our patients to get back on track, and our awareness of this fact can contribute to us complying with a patient's desire to finish treatment quickly, especially when there are reality issues that make ongoing treatment too onerous. There is always a resistance aspect to these issues of reality (Inderbitzin and Levy, 1994), and in the initial evaluation a decision needs to be made as to whether to attempt to help a patient overcome resistance to a more extensive psychotherapeutic effort. There is always the potential for a countertransferential component in choosing which of the patient's "realities" to leave unchallenged and which to attempt to analyze. Whenever a focal treatment is attempted, there is an implicit agreement not to deal with major areas of the patient's personality, hence the potential for unrecognized countertransferential collusion with the patient's resistance to address neurotic problems is magnified.

Early in the course of the treatment, Amy, whose depression had evaporated in the warm glow of the positive transference, developed the fantasy that I was irritated with her for "toying" with the feelings of a young man whom she had begun to date. She enjoyed her power over this youth, and she projected her disapproval of herself onto me. She was afraid that she had the power (and desire) to "crush" him. I told her that her feeling that I was irritated with her reflected her inner conviction (which was also a wish) that I would punish her for her pleasurable exercise of power over him. It was she who wished to be crushed (by me) before she had a chance to crush him. The next time she came for a session, she reported the following dream: "I saw myself lying on the ground, on the driveway in front of my house. There were tire tracks on my back. I heard my little brother's voice say 'It doesn't hurt.' I woke up feeling relieved, it really hadn't hurt."

Her associations went directly from the fact that in the dream it was she, rather than her brother, who was crushed to her childhood fear that it had hurt him terribly and her wish that it had not. She felt vividly her previously unconscious guilt over his death. In her associations she recalled the fact that at times she had seen him as a real pest and had wished him gone. Unconsciously she had felt that his death was a fulfillment of her wish. Amy's insight into the significance of the dream did not extend to an awareness of the fact that she had unconsciously felt that, having been able to destroy her sibling rival, meant that she could also destroy her mother (her oedipal rival) or even her father. However, despite the incompleteness of the work that she was able to do in therapy as compared to what might have been achieved in an analysis, her need to find a boyfriend who would both control and also punish her became less pressing. The next young man whom she dated, who soon became her new boyfriend, was a tackle on a local college football team (she had met him at the bookstore in which she was working). Amy's compromise formation (Brenner, 1982) had shifted somewhat as a result of the psychotherapy. She was still attracted to a man who *could* crush her (like her father or the truck), but this man directed most of his aggression at male peers (brother figures) rather than at her. She remained unaware of the unconscious significance of her choice of the tackle-truck boyfriend, and I decided against interpreting it. Amy returned to college as planned.

Open-ended, short-term psychoanalytic psychotherapy. Short-term analytically oriented psychotherapy is the treatment of choice for mildly neurotic patients whose problems seem to be fairly circumscribed. This form of treatment can help the patient overcome the (relatively minor) neurotic problem, although further treatment later on in life may be needed. Often, problems that are amenable to a short-term treatment will manifest in response to a life crisis. The degree of painful affect that is felt by the patient may well be intense, but the problem is acute and circumscribed. Generally, short-term treatment is not suitable for chronic pervasive characterological difficulties, even though such a patient may have less subjective sense of distress than one suffering from a more acute problem, for whom short-term treatment is considered suitable. On the other hand, if the acute problem is embedded in a seriously neurotic matrix, it is unlikely that a short-term approach will be adequate, although it may be attempted in some circumstances with the understanding that the goals must be limited at this point and that a more extensive treatment may be called for later on.

The following vignette will illustrate the sort of patient for whom brief analytically oriented psychotherapy is preferable. Mrs. N., a thirty-year-old musician, sought psychotherapy in an acutely anxious, depressed state after her husband, a thirty-four-year-old lawyer, had a mild myocardial infarction. There was a history of familial hyperlipidemia. The illness of her husband was a major shock to Mrs. N. She loved him and wanted children, but since his hospi-

talization she had become painfully obsessed with the fear that any child of his would inherit his illness and most likely die young. She became anxious and depressed and sought treatment to help her deal with her painful and confusing feelings. She had never previously had such symptoms and had always functioned well and been a rather happy person, with many good friends and a satisfying marriage. She was structurally neurotic. The severe stress had overtaxed her defenses, causing her to become symptomatic.

Twice-weekly psychotherapy was recommended and agreed to by the patient. The treatment was conducted in an exploratory manner, and no time limit was imposed at the beginning of the treatment.

Mrs. N. very shortly began to become aware of her previously unconscious impulses to leave her husband before he died of another infarction and find another man who would be free of this "genetic taint." She had not allowed herself to consider this possibility, as such a thought would have been unacceptably disloyal. In the safe environment of the psychotherapy session, she *felt* a strong desire to leave and cried bitterly over both her disloyalty to her husband, whom she greatly loved, and her feeling that it was totally unfair that she should be burdened by this problem. I pointed out to her that she was feeling guilty about the fantasy of leaving. She was reacting as if having such a thought was the same as doing it. I further invited her to ask herself if she thought this it was unusual for someone in her situation to imagine various ways of getting out of the predicament, including getting rid of the problem by getting rid of the husband. In response, she talked about the fact that she had very high standards for herself and that when she did not live up to them she felt very guilty. She went on to say that in even thinking about leaving her husband, she felt she was being like her mother. She described a time when she was five years old and her mother had left her father, taking her too. The couple had later reconciled, but the episode had made a lasting impression. Mrs. N. had always severely condemned her mother's act and been convinced that *she herself* would never have done such a thing. However, at the same time as she had condemned her mother, Mrs. N., who had always prided herself on being a good girl, had felt that somehow if she had only been good enough she might have been able to prevent the marital rupture. Mrs. N.'s anxiety and depression began to diminish. As we continued the work together, her fearful fantasy that if she had a child by her husband, the child would necessarily inherit the problem and die young came to be seen as the talion punishment for her unacceptable aggressive hostile impulses towards her husband. The obsessive thoughts vanished. Mrs. N. initiated discussions with her husband about their situation, now that she was no longer so terrified of her fantasies. To her pleasant surprise, she found that her husband was relieved that she was able to talk so realistically about the situation. He had felt unable to discuss it with her, as it seemed to him that it hurt her even to think about it. The couple began to feel closer and decided to seek further medical advice as well as genetic counseling so that they could deal with their situation with as much information as possible.

The major way in which this psychotherapy was different from the early phase of an analysis was in the consistently maintained focus on an exploration of the acute crisis situation and the psychodynamic issues involved, as contrasted with the fostering of full free association. Additionally, the patient was seen twice a week sitting up, and I was more active than I would generally be in an analysis. The fact that transference was not a focus of this work does not differentiate it particularly from the early phases of an analysis in which the material is unfolding and the transference has not yet evolved sufficiently to become the primary area of work. The psychotherapy was focal and brief (it lasted for five months) but was open-ended rather than time-limited. This differentiates it from the time-limited forms of brief treatment in which the termination date is set at the beginning. In the psychotherapy of Mrs. N., the decision to terminate was arrived at after four months of treatment. Mrs. N. had achieved the symptomatic relief she sought and it was she who brought up the idea of ending the treatment. Termination took place a month later.

Psychotherapy prior to analysis ("preparatory psychotherapy"). Frequently patients arrive seeking psychotherapy for whom careful evaluation indicates that analysis is the treatment of choice; however, such a patient may be initially reluctant to accept the recommendation of analysis. Work on the neurotic difficulties which brought the patient to treatment may make it possible to begin to analyze the initial resistances to analytic treatment, including the use of external reality in the service of resistance. With such patients it is useful to think of the psychotherapy as being the first stage of an analysis, essentially a parameter of technique (Eissler, 1953) that must be employed in the initial period of the work but which can be analyzed later. Such patients are often able to work analytically in a displaced framework, and the insights they derive in the psychotherapy fuel their interest in further self-exploration. Mrs. F., whose psychotherapy I will describe below, was

such a patient. She was able to achieve partial awareness of some of the origins of her neurotic difficulties with both her daughter and her husband. However, a deeper, affectively meaningful understanding, linking these partial insights with her instinctual impulses and unconscious fantasies, could not have been achieved without analysis of their manifestations in the transference during subsequent psychoanalysis.

In the course of the psychotherapy the patient will usually become eager for more intensive work and will become frustrated by the limitations imposed by the infrequent sessions. When this occurs, the recommendation of an increase in frequency to four or five times a week can be made, and the use of the couch can be introduced. The transition to an unmodified analysis with the same analyst can often be made very smoothly. The need for the initial period of psychotherapy can be analyzed during the subsequent unmodified analysis. The use of supportive techniques, such as suggestion, manipulation, and direct giving of advice should be avoided. The period of time required for this sort of preparatory psychotherapy is variable but is generally less than one year.

Mrs. F. was a thirty-eight-year-old woman who was referred to me by her husband's analyst because of her inability to have an orgasm during intercourse. She came to treatment reluctantly, feeling that this was not a problem for her, as she was perfectly capable of having orgasms when masturbating. However, she accepted the referral to keep peace in the house and also because she thought that it might be helpful to talk about some of her difficulties with her two-year-old daughter.

Mrs. F. was the eldest of four children, with a sister two years and twin brothers twelve years younger than herself. Her parents were owners of a small retail business, and she grew up as her mother's "built-in baby sitter," caring for her little brothers. She resented this to some extent, as it interfered with her own social life with peers, but she felt proud of the good job she did and even felt that she was a better mother to her brothers than their mother was. Mother was a controlling woman, always the decision-maker in the family. Mrs. F. loved her quiet father and resented the way that Mother dominated him. Mother's controlling extended to reshaping her daughter's body. She had Mrs. F.'s nose, teeth, and skin "fixed" and, in the process of attempting to make her beautiful, convinced the girl that she had started out extremely ugly.

Mrs. F. rebelled against her mother in late adolescence. She experimented with alcohol and sex and saw herself as a very sexy and attractive woman.

The fact that she never had an orgasm in intercourse did not consciously bother her, and she prided herself on her sexual technique.

In her late twenties, Mrs. F. met and married her husband after a tempestuous courtship. He began psychotherapy to deal with his own anxiety symptoms and eventually confronted his wife with his dissatisfaction about her never having an orgasm with him, which led to the referral for treatment.

Psychoanalysis was the treatment of choice for Mrs. F., as her neurotic difficulties were long-standing and she had significant character pathology. However, her initial resistances were such that she was reluctant to commit herself even to psychotherapy. Realizing this, I did not initially recommend analysis to her. It seemed highly likely that she would have fled treatment altogether if presented with such a suggestion. Instead, I explored with her the area that she herself was troubled about, her difficulties with her two-year-old daughter, who was running Mrs. F. ragged with her demandingness and misbehavior. She was motivated to work on this problem and accepted the recommendation for twice-weekly psychotherapy, although she protested that it was very time-consuming and that it would be very expensive.

Mrs. F. gained some insight into the roots of her difficulty in setting any limits at all with her daughter (she was afraid of stifling her spirit as she herself had previously felt stifled and controlled by her own mother). As a result, she was able to change her mothering style somewhat, and the little girl's behavior improved. Finding that self-exploration could actually help her feel better and make some changes in her life, Mrs. F. became more willing to examine herself in a psychotherapeutic setting. She gradually began to explore some of the reasons why it had previously been so important to her to maintain the facade of everything being "just fine" in her sexual life, despite her inability to achieve orgasm with her husband. She had been afraid that to acknowledge that there was any problem at all would mean that she was a total mess. She started to have some sense of the intensity of her fear of the power of her impulses which contributed to her "freezing" in bed, as well as in other circumstances that represented sexual or aggressive temptation. Her symptom expressed her unconscious hostility toward her husband; her inability to have an orgasm deprived him of feeling fully potent with her, defended her from awareness of her unconscious hostility and castrative wishes, and also punished her for those unacceptable wishes. In psychotherapy, although these dynamics were far from evident to Mrs. F. herself, she became aware of anger with her husband for numerous failings. Her lack of orgasm with him took on the meaning that she was withholding her orgasm from him in retaliation. She knew that she did not want to be like her pushy mother. She began to actually *feel* that if she did not hold herself in check, she might be able to totally dominate him as she felt Mother had dominated Father. She now could see that much of her previous inability to set appropriate limits with her daughter had been based on her fear that she would try to control her the way that she had been controlled by her own mother. This insight helped her to realize that fear of her power to harm others contributed significantly to her difficulty in allowing herself to function effectively in multiple areas of life. These preliminary and incomplete insights decreased the severe anxiety surrounding self-exploration and made Mrs. F. eager to learn more about herself. She became dissatisfied with the amount that could be accomplished in the twice-weekly setting. One year after beginning psychotherapy, she accepted the recommendation of psychoanalysis and began her analysis on the couch four times a week. She proved to be an excellent analytic patient.

Long-term psychoanalytically oriented psychotherapy. Psychoanalytically oriented psychotherapy is the treatment of choice for patients who have sufficient strength to be likely to benefit from explorative treatment but who also have areas of ego weakness such that analysis is not indicated. Such patients generally fall in the higher-level borderline or severely neurotic, generally with borderline features, range of psychopathology. Many narcissistic patients fall into this category. Treatment of such patients is generally long. This is the form of psychotherapy that is most like psychoanalysis, both in technique and in results, since structural change can be brought about in the course of such psychotherapy. Generally, the technique of psychoanalytically oriented psychotherapy differs from that of psychoanalysis in that the area of exploration, while not focal as in short-term treatments, is not as broad as in psychoanalysis. The therapist is more active than is generally the case in analysis. Development of a transference neurosis that will be systematically analyzed is not fostered in this type of psychotherapy, although patients often have intense transference manifestations, interpretation of which forms an important part of the work. Also, while negative transference is interpreted vigorously, positive transference is generally left alone unless it becomes an impediment to further work.

Mr. H. was a graduate student who was referred for treatment because he was in danger of being expelled from school. His intellectual ability was not in question, but he was continually in trouble due to his remarkably abrasive manner and his failure to complete his work in a timely manner.

Mr. H. felt that he was being badly treated by his professors but did not recognize his own role in the genesis of his difficulties. He admitted that he got into arguments with teachers, but he viewed the arguments as having been their fault. These difficulties were the most recent manifestation of a lifelong pattern. Mr. H. had always felt unjustly and abusively treated.

The first of Mr. H.'s persecutors was his mother. He described his mother as having a terrible temper. She was devoutly religious, and when she was enraged with him, which was a frequent occurrence throughout his childhood, she would scream at him that he was "worse than the Devil." She accused him of making her life hell, and he, as he grew up, would accuse her of doing the same thing to him. Essentially, mother and son agreed that life at home was hell; what they disagreed on, in their frequent verbal battles, was which of them was the Devil. Mr. H. described his father, by contrast, as passive and fearful of the rageful outbursts. He was a quiet figure who retreated into his work; but he would sometimes comfort his little boy by cuddling him.

Mr. H. suffered greatly in all areas of his life. No areas seemed conflict-free. When evaluated initially, he had little capacity for self-reflection and insight. He steadfastly maintained that all his problems resulted from external misfortune. He had a capacity for intense relationships with others, but his relationships were sadomasochistic re-editions of his relationship with his mother. In this sort of rigid character pathology, change is very difficult, but only an exploratory approach offers the possibility of helping the patient recognize his own role in his misfortunes and eventually change the maladaptive behavior.

Sadomasochistic transference manifestations became a major focus very early in the treatment. This early appearance of intense transference manifestations is quite typical of severe neurotic and character-disorder patients who have significant borderline features. As could be anticipated for a patient with Mr. H.'s degree of pathology with its sadomasochistic features (Kernberg, 1988), Mr. H. developed a negative therapeutic reaction. He experienced interpretations as attacks. Each new insight was a fresh source of misery. He began to accuse me of making him worse rather than better.

Mr. H. was enacting a transference fantasy. He was recreating his role of victim, but now I was cast in the role of sadistic abuser. I interpreted this and told him that it also seemed to me that he had the fantasy that he could destroy me by failing. I inquired whether he felt it would be worth it to make himself a failure so that I would be a partial failure, acknowledging that he could, in fact, cause me to fail in my efforts to treat him effectively. Such interventions, by consistently interpreting the pathological object relationship when it was activated in the transference, helped Mr. H. begin to moderate his self-destructiveness. Over time, he came to see that he provoked people, including me and his professors, into becoming his persecutors in an effort to unmask them as being "really" horrible under their facade of goodness. He became somewhat more aware of the pleasure he felt in "exposing the shits," as he put it, everywhere.

Years of psychotherapy enabled Mr. H. to decrease his masochistic provocations of authority figures and improved his capacity for relationships that were less sadomasochistic. Even his relationship with his mother improved somewhat. He no longer needed to cling to the conviction that his problems were entirely due to external reality. He acquired the ability to reflect and be introspective. His tendency to enact his conflicts moderated, and he was generally able to stop himself from acting out his most self-destructive impulses.

Mr. H. is an example of the sort of patient with major character pathology, requiring lengthy intensive psychoanalytically oriented psychotherapy, for whom analysis would not be indicated. The regressive aspects of standard analytic technique would have been intolerable for Mr. H., but he was able to benefit greatly from an exploratory psychotherapy and achieved significant structural change.

Analytically Informed Supportive Psychotherapy

Psychoanalytically informed supportive psychotherapy has a scanty literature by comparison with other forms of psychotherapy. This form of treatment has its origins in attempts by analysts to modify psychoanalytic treatment so as to make it applicable to cases of severe psychopathology. Knight (1949) pointed out that in general the decision to use supportive (suppressive) techniques is based on negative indicators for expressive treatment, such as a patient's fragility, inflexibility, or too strongly defensive nature. This recommendation still holds in general, especially with regard to supportive treatments that do not utilize an admixture of expressive techniques.

Supportive psychotherapy in its pure form does not use interpretation as do expressive forms of psychotherapy. However, as Werman (1984) points out, at times one may interpret upwards (giving higher-level significance to overtly primitive material), to avoid regression and to foster higher-level defenses such as intellectualization. Rockland (1989) goes further; he advocates deliberate use of the inexact interpretation, as described by Glover (1931), to strengthen defenses and improve adaptation. For example, he writes: "A borderline patient is expressing derision toward several people, including the therapist. Her manner is one of haughty arrogance, and she seems totally pleased with herself. The therapist ignores the devaluation and says, 'I wonder if you're not frightened of getting too close to me,' or 'you seem to be getting more comfortable expressing your aggression!'" (p. 96). In this example, the narcissistic devaluation in the transference is sidestepped rather than interpreted, and the patient is given an acceptable and comfortable but not strictly accurate rationalization for her behavior that helps her to avoid having to recognize and deal with her aggression toward the therapist and others. The aggression is defused, and the patient is subtly encouraged to idealize and identify with the therapist. Kernberg (1984) defines supportive psychotherapy by saying that it "does not use interpretation, partially uses clarification and abreaction, and mostly uses suggestion and (what he calls) environmental intervention" (p. 150).

The presence or absence of neutrality on the part of the therapist conducting the psychotherapy further differentiates psychotherapies. In this context it must be stressed that neutrality does not mean indifference or lack of engagement. According to Levy and Inderbitzin (1992), in psychoanalysis and psychoanalytic psychotherapy, neutrality is optimally manifested in the consistent fostering of a process in the course of which "the analysand . . . recognize(s) how conflicts and the affects they generate are managed within the analytic setting, and particularly in relation to the analyst as transference figure" (p. 1009). By contrast, the therapist giving supportive treatment aligns himself strongly with the demands of reality and makes efforts to strengthen the ego. Efforts are made to help the patient avoid or "seal over" conflict, in contrast to attempting full exploration to its infantile roots. There is general concurrence that supportive treatment involves attempts to strengthen higher-level defenses, such as intellectualization, and to undermine the more primitive defenses of splitting and projective identification. Manipulation of the patient's environment, the giving of advice, and various forms of suggestion all have their place in supportive psychotherapy. Supportive psychotherapy depends to a great extent on the maintenance of a positive idealizing transference, the vehicle of successful suggestion.

However, intensification of this positive transference can also cause difficulties, and it is advisable to attempt to minimize transference intensity if possible.

John, a twenty-two-year-old recent college graduate who had been unable to find a job and was living at home, arrived at my office in an agitated and depressed state. He had vegetative signs of depression, including sleep disturbance, anorexia with a fifteen-pound weight loss, and poor concentration. He was preoccupied with fantasies of throwing himself in front of a train and mentioned that the train tracks were only a block from his home. He was unable to sit still for any length of time and was fidgety during the consultation. Despite his agitated depression and suicidal thoughts, John had not attempted suicide and stated that he felt he could control his impulse to do so. As the family was able and willing to provide twenty-four-hour supervision, I agreed to treat him as an outpatient so long as this external structure could be provided during the initial period of our work together. John and his parents agreed to this contract, and John additionally contracted to call me if he felt he could not control his suicidal impulses.

The depression responded to antidepressant medication, and the issues that precipitated the depression became clear. John had always had trouble socially. He had been an awkward child and had felt like a "geek" as an adolescent. His sense of difference had been painful and pervasive. Things had been better in college, where he had made several friends and had done reasonably well. Once he was home again, however, his social awkwardness greatly impeded his job search. As we worked together after he was no longer depressed, I took an exploratory approach. John was unable to tolerate this. In the context of telling me that he thought that his mother had wanted him to be a girl and that maybe his trouble finding a girlfriend was due to his not being masculine enough, he began to exhibit difficulty with reality testing, telling me that he had noticed that all the homosexuals on television were named John and that this was a message to him. When it became clear that he was beginning to become delusional, I changed my approach. I attempted reassurance by pointing out that this idea was a fantasy that he had because he was worried about his difficulty in getting a job and a girlfriend. I also told him that perhaps some of the characters named John *were* homosexual but that this was a coincidence. I said that his idea was a symptom of anxiety and suggested that perhaps he was working too intensively on his psychotherapy. He replied that he had been spending a lot of time alone trying to free-associate and write down his thoughts. I suggested that he stop doing this and asked if there were anything else he could do to occupy his mind. He talked about playing the guitar, and I encouraged him to do that instead of brooding about his difficulties. I also decreased the number of sessions per week from two to one. From that time on, we continued in a supportive mode focusing on external reality. John did much better, eventually finding work, which helped him greatly with his self-esteem. Thereafter he also began to go out with groups of friends and finally to date. He did not again show any psychotic features.

My purpose in describing the case of John is to illustrate how a switch from exploratory to supportive treatment can be quite effective when the diagnosis of an underlying psychotic structure becomes evident. John did not require phenothiazines, nor did I have to hospitalize him. The positive transference was sufficient to allow him to accept my suggestions and to bolster his ability to distinguish fantasy from reality. I was aware of the fact that he was dealing with the primitive wish/fear of merger with me in the transference and that this contributed to his wish/fear of becoming a female—not a male—homosexual; this conflict had been reflected in his talk about his mother. It is also likely that emerging oedipal transference strivings contributed to the severe regression; however, material that might have confirmed this speculation was not elicited and could not be without the likelihood of worsening the psychotic regression. Interpretation of the transference was totally avoided; instead, I helped him to differentiate himself from me and seal over his emerging conflicts by suggesting less frequent sessions, by discouraging free association, and by promoting concentration on other activities.

CONCLUSION

Many factors contribute to the decision to embark on a particular course of psychotherapy with a given patient. The issues and core dynamic struggles may be similar in two patients, but the therapeutic approach chosen will vary according to the severity and nature of the psychopathology, the time frame available for treatment, and the patient's inclination, often influenced by resistance. Goals of treatment can range from focal symptom relief to structural change of the personality through intensive psychotherapy or psychoanalysis. If a short-term treatment seems sufficient to meet the goals, it should be attempted prior to undertaking a more extensive one. However, the question should always be raised, "sufficient for what therapeutic goals, and to or for whom?"

The patient's goals in coming for therapy are of central concern. However, these will be significantly influenced by psychopathology, as in the case of Mrs. F., whose character pathology prevented her from wanting relief from her neurotic symptom of frigidity. The therapist must steer a careful course between the Scylla of taking the condescending attitude that, since the patient is sick, his or her choices should not be considered, and the Charybdis of accepting all the patient's life decisions at face value. The responsible course is to evaluate the patient fully and present the various options available for treatment but also to recommend the one that the therapist believes optimal in the clinical situation. In this process a consistently respectful and inquiring attitude is essential.

If there is significant neurotic difficulty and character pathology, the optimal treatment remains psychoanalysis, provided the patient can reasonably be expected to be able to tolerate the regression and the intensification of the transference that is part of analytic treatment. Psychoanalytically oriented psychotherapy is the treatment of choice either if the extent of neurotic difficulty is circumscribed, relatively mild, or acute or when the extent of the psychopathology makes it unlikely that analysis will be tolerable. Supportive analytically informed psychotherapy is the treatment of choice when the patient is psychotic or has the clear potential of becoming psychotic if uncovering techniques are employed. In intermediate situations, admixtures of supportive and expressive techniques may be utilized.

It is important to reassess periodically our clinical decisions in the light of new information, so that we can modify our treatment approach if indicated. My clinical examples have illustrated the ongoing process of selecting and conducting psychotherapies appropriate to each individual's situation.

REFERENCES

Alexander, F., French, T. M., et al. (1946). *Psychoanalytic Therapy.* New York: Ronald Press.

Aronson, M. J., & Scharfman, M. A., eds. (1992). *Psychotherapy: The Analytic Approach.* Northvale, N.J.: Aronson.

Balint, M., Ornstein, P. H., & Balint, E. (1972). *Focal Psychotherapy.* London: Tavistock.

Beck, A. T., Rush, J. A., Shaw, B. F., & Emery, G. (1979). *Cognitive Therapy of Depression.* New York: Guilford Press.

Bibring, E. (1954). Psychoanalysis and the dynamic psychotherapies. *J. Amer. Psychoanal. Assn.,* 2:745–770.

Blos, P. (1979). *The Adolescent Passage*. New York: Int. Univ. Press.

Brenner, C. (1982). *The Mind in Conflict*. Madison, Conn.: Int. Univ. Press.

Bullard, D. M., ed. (1959). *Psychoanalysis and Psychotherapy: Selected Papers of Frieda Fromm-Reichmann*. Chicago: Univ. Chicago Press.

Clarkin, J. F., et al. (1992). Psychodynamic psychotherapy of the borderline patient. In *Borderline Personality Disorder*, ed. J. F. Clarkin, E. Marziali & H. Munroe-Blum, pp. 268–287. New York: Guilford Press.

Davanloo, H. (1978). *Basic Principles and Techniques in Short-Term Dynamic Psychotherapy*. New York: Spectrum Publishers.

Dewald, P. A. (1964). *Psychotherapy: A Dynamic Approach*. New York: Basic Books.

Edelson, M. (1963). *The Termination of Intensive Psychotherapy*. Springfield, Ill.: Thomas.

Eissler, K. R. (1953). The effect of the structure of the ego on psychoanalytic technique. *J. Amer. Psychoanal. Assn.*, 1:104–143.

Frank, J. D. (1961). *Persuasion and Healing*. Baltimore: Johns Hopkins Univ. Press.

Freud, S. (1893). *Studies on Hysteria. SE*, 2.

———. (1912). Recommendations to physicians practising psychoanalysis. *SE*, 12:111–120.

———. (1919). Lines of advance in psycho-analytic therapy. *SE*, 17:159–168.

Gill, M. (1954). Psychoanalysis and exploratory psychotherapy. *J. Amer. Psychoanal. Assn.*, 2:771–797.

Gill, M., & Hoffman, I. (1982). A method for studying the analysis of aspects of the patient's experience of the relationship in psychoanalysis and psychotherapy. *J. Amer. Psychoanal. Assn.*, 30:137–167.

Glover, E. (1931). The therapeutic effect of inexact interpretation. *Int. J. Psychoanal.*, 12:397–411.

Gustafson, J. P. (1986). *The Complex Secret of Brief Psychotherapy*. New York: Norton.

Horowitz, M. J. (1979). *States of Mind*. New York: Plenum. 2d ed., 1987.

Horowitz, M. J., Marmor, C., Krupnuk, J., Wilner, N., & Wallerstein, R. (1984). *Personality Styles and Brief Psychotherapy*. New York: Basic Books.

Inderbitzin, L., & Levy, S. T. (1994). On grist for the mill: External reality as defense. *Am. J. Psychoanal.*, 42:763–788.

Kernberg, O. (1975). *Borderline Conditions and Pathological Narcissism*. New York: Aronson.

———. (1984). *Severe Personality Disorders*. New Haven: Yale Univ. Press.

———. (1988). Clinical dimensions of masochism. *Am. J. Psychoanal.*, 36:1005–1029.

Kiesler, D. J. (1987). *Check List of Psychotherapy Transactions—Revised (CLOPT-R) and Check List of Interpersonal Transactions—Revised (CLOIT-R)*. Richmond, Va.: Virginia Commonwealth Univ.

Klerman, G., Weissman, M., Rounsaville, B., & Chevron, E. (1984). *Interpersonal Psychotherapy of Depression*. New York: Guilford Press.

Knight, R. P. (1949). Psychoanalytically oriented psychotherapy. *Bull. Am. Psychoanal. Assn.*, 4/3:36.

Levy, S. T., & Inderbitzin, L. B. (1992). Neutrality, interpretation, and therapeutic intent. *J. Amer. Psychoanal. Assn.*, 40:989–1011.

Luborsky, L. (1976). Helping alliances in psychotherapy. In *Successful Psychotherapy*, ed. J. L. Claghorn, pp. 92–116. New York: Brunner/Mazel.

———. (1984). *Principles of Psychoanalytic Psychotherapy*. New York: Basic Books.

Luborsky, L., Crits-Christoph, P., Mintz, J., & Auerbach, A. (1988). *Who Will Benefit from Psychotherapy?* New York: Basic Books.

Malan, D. (1963). *A Study of Brief Psychotherapy*. London: Tavistock.

———. (1976). *The Frontier of Brief Psychotherapy*. New York: Plenum.

Mann, J. (1973). *Time-Limited Psychotherapy*. Cambridge, Mass.: Harvard Univ. Press.

Maxim, P. (1986). *The Seattle Psychotherapy Language Analysis Schema*. Seattle: Univ. Washington Press.

Moore, B., & Fine, B., eds. (1990). *Psychoanalytic Terms and Concepts*. New Haven: Yale Univ. Press.

Oremland, J. D. (1991). *Interpretation and Interaction*. Hillsdale, N.J.: Analytic Press.

Perry, J. C., Augusto, F., & Cooper, S. H. (1989). Assessing psychodynamic conflicts, 1. *Psychiatry*, 52:289–301.

Reder, P., & Tyson, R. L. (1980). Patient dropout from individual psychotherapy. *Bull. Menninger Clinic*, 44:229–252.

Rockland, L. H. (1989). *Supportive Therapy*. New York: Basic Books.

Rubenstein, E. A., & Parloff, M. B., eds. (1959). *Research in Psychotherapy*, vol. 1. Washington, D.C.: Amer. Psychol. Assn.

Schacht, T. B., Binder, J., & Strupp, H. (1984). The dynamic focus. In Strupp & Binder, pp. 65–109.

Sifneos, P. (1979). *Short Term Dynamic Psychotherapy*. New York: Plenum.

Stone, L. (1951). Psychoanalysis and brief psychotherapy. *Psychoanal. Q.*, 20:215–236.

———. (1954). The widening scope of indications

for psychoanalysis. *J. Amer. Psychoanal. Assn.,* 2:567–594.

———. (1984). *Transference and its Context.* New York: Aronson.

Strupp, H. H. (1960). *Psychotherapists in Action.* New York: Grune & Stratton.

Strupp, H. H., & Binder, J. (1984). *Psychotherapy in a New Key.* New York: Basic Books.

Strupp, H. H., & Luborsky, L., eds. (1962). *Research in Psychotherapy,* vol. 2. Washington, D.C.: American Psychological Association.

Tarachow, S. (1963). *An Introduction to Psychotherapy.* New York: Int. Univ. Press.

Tyson, R. L., & Sandler, J. (1971). Problems in the selection of patients for psychoanalysis. *Brit. J. Med. Psychol.,* 44:211–228.

Wallerstein, R. S. (1966). The current state of psychotherapy. *J. Amer. Psychoanal. Assn.,* 14:183–225.

———. (1986). *Forty-Two Lives in Treatment.* New York: Guilford Press.

———. (1988). Psychoanalysis and psychotherapy: relative roles reconsidered. *Annu. Psychoanal.,* 16:129–151.

———. (1989). Psychoanalysis and psychotherapy: an historical perspective. *Int. J. Psychoanal.,* 70:563–591.

Weissberg, J. H. (1984). Short-term dynamic psychotherapy. *J. Amer. Acad. Psychoanal.,* 12:101–113.

Werman, D. S. (1984). *The Practice of Supportive Psychotherapy.* New York: Brunner/Mazel.

4

PSYCHOLOGY AND PSYCHOTHERAPY OF GROUPS

Psychoanalysis has shifted from a unipersonal psychology, with the ego as an organ of biological adaptation mastering id drives in an average predictable environment (Hartmann, 1964), to a bi-personal or multipersonal psychology, in which "environment" no longer means nature in general but, for the infant, mother in particular and, for the grown-up, the society of fellow human beings (Guntrip, 1971). Adaptation, strictly speaking, has only a one-sided reference—to the individual's changes to fit the environment. Personal relations involve instead mutual self-fulfillment in the communication and shared experience of two or more people. The concept of adaptation should therefore be supplemented by a higher concept of meaningful relationships that are a matter of caring and concern. The psychoanalytic view of groups was born almost simultaneously with the so-called structural theory, in which the superego's social nature and functions were first described in relational terms as the area of the mind where the child's earliest "whole-object" relationships are enshrined by identification and introjection (Guntrip, 1967, p. 220). The acknowledgment of humans' social nature, beyond mere biology, was based upon discovering the intrinsic and inescapable presence of others as "internalized" representations within the human mind. The therapeutic goal of psychoanalysis—as of group therapy—is predicated upon the ability of the human mind to grow and develop within relationships. There, ego identifications can be reviewed and become modifiable, and the self can develop further.

In this paper I plan to describe psychoanalytic group psychology, some sociopsychological studies of groups, group psychotherapy, some controversial issues regarding those topics, and some new trends emerging in the field.

PSYCHOANALYTIC GROUP PSYCHOLOGY

Psychoanalytic group psychology has evolved from attempts to understand the "masses" to studies of small groups, from viewing groups as replicas of the father-centered primal oedipal horde to a pre-oedipal view of mother-centered group features; from the analogical comprehension of the group's mental life as comparable to that of the psychoneuroses to comparing group psychology with the mentality of psychoses. There have also been developments in social-psychological studies of small groups— namely, in research about leadership and different group roles, as well as in new theories. I shall briefly examine these developments.

From the "Masses" to Small Groups
Sigmund Freud's study of group psychology (1921), elaborating on Le Bon's observations (1897), was

indeed about the "masses" or large groups.[1] Freud's theoretical considerations were an extrapolation from his clinical observations on melancholic-introjective identification mechanisms during mourning, understood as an overinvestment in the relationship with a lost object. Freud's application to group psychology of his concept regarding the ego's identification with the loved object was an important psychoanalytic contribution to a better understanding of group psychology. Based on the introjection of a shared loved object, such identification modifies each group member's ego, creating new special bonds among the group members, insofar as they now find themselves being alike, in imitation of their group leader.

The psychological characteristics of groups vary according to their size, in spite of there being elements common to all of them. A "crowd" is a gathering of 300 persons or more (Anzieu, 1975). Le Bon described crowd behavior before smaller groups were studied. He characterized it by (1) the emotional contagion among members; (2) a weakening of their reality testing; (3) an alternation between apathy and paroxysmal expressions of impulses; and (4) their dependency on a leader. A "large group" is formed by twenty-five to sixty participants (Anzieu, 1975, p. 80). Gatherings of up to twenty persons allow each member quickly to identify each group-mate and to establish numerous relationships of sympathy and antipathy. Large groups are characterized, by contrast, by a difficulty in differentiating the personal identity of each participant, which triggers anxieties about losing one's own identity. Hence, being a member of a large group becomes like "a transient experience of depersonalization" (ibid., p. 86). The absence of social feedback evokes feelings of loss of maternal protection. Each individual is confronted with the typical archaic unconscious defense mechanisms of splitting of the objects, projection of destructive impulses, and desperate search for links, mobilized by primitive psychotic anxieties. Often large group participants describe feeling like a "fracture" of their personality. "Facing a great number of anonymous individuals threatens with the realization of one's own anonymity" (Turquet, 1975). Those who dare to speak, talk to themselves in a loud voice, or address the empty space; often they criticize or attack those who spoke immediately before.

1. Gay (1988, p. 384) commented on the "infelicitous translation" of Freud's German *Massenpsychologie* as "group" psychology and elaborated that the editors of the *Standard Edition* preferred the term "group" for *Masse* in spite of Freud's English reference to this work as the "psychology of the mass."

The "group relations conferences" organized by the A. K. Rice Institute to learn experientially about group behavior and leadership usually schedule alternating small and large group meetings. Hence, transference is split, with the positive one concentrated in the small group, the negative transference obvious in the large group. The collective negative transference is initially expressed through fantasies of self-destruction but soon becomes open hostility toward the instructors; sometimes it is displaced onto a participant, one unconsciously designated by the large group as a victim at risk of mental decompensation (Anzieu, 1975, p. 97).

Human beings are emotionally involved in small groups every day, whether at home, school, work, or in leisure activities, but only occasionally take part in large group gatherings like mass meetings, apart from the contemporary immersion in the mass media that nowadays influence us all from a distance by bringing current events into our living rooms. In spite of Freud's limited observations about groups, which focused only on the masses, he was accurate in his assessment of how the individual is basically affected by participating in a group. Group members share a common identification with the group leader, which holds them together, and each regresses to a more primitive emotional level of responses.

But it was left to the other analysts to observe and reflect more specifically on small groups. Among them, Bion (1961) carried out his "experiences with groups" by utilizing a psychoanalytic method of observation and applying Melanie Klein's concepts of primitive defense mechanisms (namely, projective identification and splitting) and the early psychoticlike anxieties (melancholic and schizoparanoid) to the psychology of small groups.

From Father-Centered to Mother-Focused

In *Totem and Taboo* Freud wove together "speculations from anthropology, ethnography, biology, the history of religion, and psychoanalysis" (Gay, 1988, pp. 328–329). He interpreted the totem animal as representing the father and reconstructed the fears of the jealous father who dominated the primal horde and kept the women for himself, driving away his sons as soon as they grew up. "One day the brothers who had been driven out came together, killed and devoured their father and so made an end of the patriarchal horde. . . . The violent primal father had doubtless been the feared and envied model of each one of the company of brothers: and in the act of devouring him they accomplished their identification with him" (Freud, 1913, pp. 141–142).

Freud attempted to attribute the foundation of religion to the oedipus complex, while searching for the origin of guilt feelings. As Peter Gay (p. 335) comments: "It is telling that in his reconstruction Freud said virtually nothing about the mother, even though the ethnographic material pointing to the fantasy of devouring the mother is richer than that for devouring the father." Anyway, according to Freud's line of thought, ambivalence toward and identification with the father, together with guilt feelings for shared murderous wishes against him, put groups together around the father. By contrast, "the authoritarian father seems now almost gone. The new tyranny is that of the mother who like the goddess Kali presents a dual face: the source of love and life and the rival for love and life" (Hearst, 1981, p. 25).

In her clinical observations during the psychoanalysis of children, Melanie Klein (1932) discovered the individual developmental origin of guilt feelings in the ambivalence toward the primary object of love: the mother. What Freud presented as speculations regarding mankind's early historical development, Melanie Klein observed clinically in children's fantasies of devouring mother's breast or her body contents, as expressions of their ambivalence regarding the mother. Guilt is at the center of Klein's "depressive position," which is a major milestone in her developmental theory about the infant's emotional growth. Mother as a source of nurturance, care, and support becomes the "good" object whose loss is extremely painful. But mother's power to choose between giving and withholding nurturance and care triggers envy and fear of her, of her power. Hence the infant fantasizes doing away with such differences in power, by devouring her and incorporating or stealing her possessions, or, alternatively, he or she may "spoil" her goods through fantasized anal-like attacks on her, using projective identification to dump on mother or on mother's breast.

Some group therapists (Scheidlinger, 1974; Hearst, 1981) have described the group itself as a good mother for its members insofar as it is (1) "life-giving," by making each member come alive to social existence through "belonging" to that group; (2) "confirming," by acknowledging each member's worth in terms of the group's values; and (3) "sustaining," by offering support and care when a member is in distress. I have elsewhere described the "bad" mother group on the basis of fantasies depicting the group as (1) "overdemanding," in imposing the group's values on the individual; (2) "devouring," in taking away the member's credit and possessions; (3) "intruding," by inquiring with hostile curiosity into members' secret, private affairs and attempting to influence them; and (4) "lacking in reciprocity," to the extent that the group can survive socially without any given member (Ganzarain, 1991, p. 158). "Good" and "bad" mother-group fantasies express members' ambivalence regarding the group as an object that has become a mother surrogate.

Bion (1961) applied to group psychology Klein's concepts of primitive defense mechanisms (namely, projective identification and splitting) to protect the self from psychoticlike anxieties (schizoparanoid and depressive). He compared members' regressive struggles against psychotic anxieties reactivated upon becoming members of a group to the infant's experience of negotiating the relationship with the mother's breast. He viewed the group as a fantasied "breast surrogate." Bion confirmed Freud's view regarding the individual's experience of regression when participating in the emotional life of a group and elaborated on the nature of returning to very early pre-oedipal, mainly "oral" fantasies about such relationships. He expanded Freud's view concerning the role of identification in group psychology by adding projective identification.

From Oedipal to Pre-oedipal Features

Group psychology is currently conceived psychoanalytically as comparable to a dyadic relationship between each individual and the internal representation of the group, perceived as a mother surrogate in a pre-oedipal fashion. Oedipal triadic issues, although also present, are less pressing than issues of nurturance/hunger; power/sadism; survival/extinction. Intense, primitive aggression seems stronger than libido. Anxieties about the survival of the self and/or of the object prevail over castration anxiety. The dominant defense mechanisms are splitting, projective identification, introjection, denial, and projection, rather than simply repression. As Kauff (1991, p. 189) says, "The group can simultaneously be a stimulus for pre-oedipal material and an effective therapeutic tool providing a salutary setting to handle such repressive resistances"—hence its considerable psychotherapeutic value. Glatzer (1985) described the pre-oedipal "witch-mother" fantasy:

> The mother is at once the object of the child's projected aggression and the object of reactive rage against her real or fantasied offenses. At the end, the child is faced with a malevolent excessively powerful figure, largely of the child's creation . . . the child feels locked into a life-or-death struggle. Thus, the internal world can become all-but impervious to reality. . . . The part played by denial of the negatively experienced parts of the self also contributes to its intransigence. . . . Once projected to the powerful mother

imago, unacceptable feelings and fantasies become safely non-self. As a result, the "bad" mother is at once a dangerous persecutor and simultaneously a protection against the child's most undesirable aspects of itself. [Quoted by Kauff, 1991, pp. 177–178]

Characterological masochism (Glatzer, 1985) is a tenacious source of resistance:

In his attempt to minimize the power of the "bad" mother and his feelings of being victimized by her, and in order to regain lost control and recapture the fantasies of omnipotence, the masochistic patient will find ways to provoke his own deprivation. He will, in effect, become his own "bad parent" repeatedly looking for water from stones and blackwashing whatever is gratifying in life. . . . It often will provoke rage in those from whom he ostensibly seeks love and care, unconsciously reproducing the interaction with the "bad" mother, but with a new twist: now the patient *controls* the deprivation. The patient is repeatedly reassured that the "bad" is located outside the patient's self. [Quoted by Kauff, 1991, pp. 178–179]

As well as describing pre-oedipal character pathology as a powerful resistance to psychotherapy and a self-perpetrating source of mental misery, analytically oriented group therapists have used the salutary setting of the group to resolve such resistances and to help patients learn to enjoy their lives and thus progress beyond their early fixations to masochistically determined pyrrhic victories in dealing with their internal objects (Glatzer, 1969; Ganzarain, 1983, 1989).

From Neurotic to Psychotic Anxieties

Group psychology pushes each member to regress to early levels of mental functioning, so that primitive defenses and psychoticlike anxieties again dominate collective mental life. But group psychology simultaneously enables each member to retain the combined adaptive reality-oriented ego resources available among all group members, thus providing a salutary setting potentially allowing members to face extremely threatening situations in an effectively creative way. In other words, paradoxically, a group can sometimes hate reality and avoid or distort it as in a full-fledged psychosis, while later on that same group can mobilize adaptive ego resources to resolve and overcome their previous psychotic fears creatively. When I taught psychiatry at the University of Chile, the medical students were offered the option of being psychotherapy patients in groups formed exclusively of those students who were interested (Ganzarain, 1989). I was the therapist of one of those groups. Once I had to miss one of their weekly sessions. We agreed that they would meet without me but in the presence, as in every session, of an observer-recorder. When I returned, some changes were immediately apparent. For instance, no one helped me bring the extra chairs always needed, in clear contrast to their previous polite helpfulness. When I arrived at the office to start the meeting, I found my "official seat" occupied and also had difficulty finding a place for the last chair, my own. I commented that their nonverbal behavior suggested that they did not want me back, and I speculated that perhaps they felt that I had abandoned them the previous week.

The student occupying my official seat, wishing to please me with their good work, inquired whether the observer-recorder had briefed me on the excellent session they had had in my absence. I told them the recorder had informed me about the preceding session. But, I added, I could now hear the message: "We don't need you to have a good session." There was a tense silence. The student occupying my seat pointed out after a while, "You see, this is what happens when you are present. Your comments produce these silences, and we don't feel at ease." I responded, "Maybe my absence irritated you. You wanted to show me that you do not need me. Today, you probably felt I might hear about your good previous session as if it were an attack on me. Hence, you expressed your fear of me by not letting me enter the room nor allow me to occupy my so-called 'official seat.'" Tense, even more prolonged silence followed. Someone said, "You see what you are doing. We cannot have a good session with you." I responded, "You are hearing me as if I were criticizing you, or even spoiling your ability to have a good session."

By then, the student occupying my seat had started covering his eyes with his right hand and repeatedly looked through a nearby window. He said, "You repeat the same words in a monotonous voice, as if you were trying to hypnotize me, also glancing at me. I started to feel sleepy, as if about to fall into a hypnotic trance. I also felt an intense headache, which I thought you intended to give me. I needed to protect myself from your glances by looking outside and covering my eyes." Anxiety and surprise spread throughout the room after these comments. Another member immediately said, "I felt something similar. I was convinced you wanted to cause me the intense stomachache I am having."

I elaborated on their conviction that I wanted to cause them pain, to attack their leader's head, and make them fearful of me, as if I were returning their fantasied assaults against me. I reflected that the two who felt they were targets of my assumed revenge were precisely those who led the group in my absence; one was now sitting in my official seat. The group members looked surprised, having shared an intense emotional experience, now mixed with some relief after understanding what had been going on. Time was up, and we adjourned in the midst of relieved laughter. There were comments of amazement at what we had just experienced together.

Two members experienced a paranoidlike "delusion of influence." More remarkable was how such delusional belief was quickly dismissed by interpreting its unconscious meaning and the underlying psychoticlike, paranoid anxieties. No psychotic behavior, thoughts, or feelings remained. They had evaporated after the emotionally shared understanding. None of these students was clinically psychotic before or after the session. But the intensity of their anxiety during the session was considerable, especially in its nonverbal expressions: glances, hands covering eyes, avoidance of eye contact, tense prolonged silence, squirming on chairs, and so on. The next meeting allowed the group to reflect and to gain some even deeper understanding of the previous week's experiences.

Group mentation is comparable to that of dreams (Anzieu, 1975), insofar as both allow human beings to plunge into the wilderness of psychoticlike emotional experiences or sometimes engage in effective problem solving. Delusions and creativity are neighbors in our unconscious life, and we can experience both in our groups and in our dreams. Object relations psychoanalytic group theory and therapy focus their attention on the internal fantasied world of psychic reality, on the exchanges between the self and its internal objects. "Internal objects" are the mental representations of external persons who have left in our minds residual impressions of previous relationships between them and ourselves. Our mind works simultaneously in an external, objective reality and in an internal, subjective reality and also in a series of transitional phenomena between the two worlds. Object relations psychoanalytic therapy makes specific use of the characteristic psychoticlike style of group mentation by focusing on the early anxieties aroused by aggressive fantasies that distort the exchanges between the self and its objects, misrepresenting them as a threat either of annihilation of the self (schizoparanoid anxiety) or of destruction of the loved objects (depressive anxiety).

Group members fantasize the existence of a "group-as-an-entity," as an "internal object" different from the collection of individuals in the room. This illusory entity replaces the "real" group as a vaguely shared fantasy in the members' minds. The group as an internal object can take various forms; Bion coined the term "basic assumptions group" to describe this common fantasy. As a consequence of the group members' use of projective identification to defend themselves from psychotic anxieties, each member disowns the shared common basic assumptions, claiming no personal participation in them, perceiving them as alien or "not mine." The same individual simultaneously believes that those assumptions are a malevolent, powerful component of "his" or "her" group and hence also perceives them as "mine" or part of "me." In other words, the group as an internal object is "neither self, nor other, but both." It is like a transitional object a la Winnicott, like a collective creation of the group members, situated in Winnicott's "area of illusion" or "psychological space" that is both self and other but neither. The action of object relations psychoanalytic group therapy takes place at the core of group psychology, on these vaguely shared fantasies about a common internal object situated in the "area of illusion" (Winnicott, 1967) of the members' minds, as a mother surrogate. Several psychoanalysts—Tolpin (1972), Volkan (1976), Rizzuto (1979), and Modell (1984)—have described the human need, beyond childhood, "for relating to each other, specially collectively, through shared representations of objects which are neither self, nor other but both" (Jacobson, 1989, p. 480). According to Winnicott (1967, p. 117), such images allow us to keep the potential vitality of "the interplay between separateness and union."

The group entity is not an abstract concept but has a vivid psychic reality; since it is experienced as real, it influences the interactions among groupmates. "It is arrived at by a process of (unspoken) negotiations in which members try to make the group-entity what they want it to be, and try to convince others that that is what it is. In this process, everyone's negotiating strength is limited by the need to belong to the group-entity, whatever it is" (Jacobson, 1989, p. 483). The group entity ends up mentally representing the objective external group as the members wish it to be, as a mother surrogate. However, since certain wishes are unacceptable, they can become the disowned, rejected, and projected parts of the individuals. The basic assumptions group becomes the sum of those disowned parts of the members. Hence, no group member wants to own those assumptions. There is a kind of conspiracy of anonymity. By virtue of being anonymous, the basic assumptions can function quite ruthlessly, which is why those assumptions are intensely feared. The group members' wishes also express the need to protect the self and the loved objects from the destruction predicted and expected by the early psychoticlike anxieties resulting from aggressive fantasies. The primitive defense mechanisms of splitting, projective identification, projection, omnipotent denial, and introjection are the basic ego's early resources for protecting the endangered self and the loved object from such destruction.

The group's extensive use of projective identification as a defense mechanism leads to the development of transitional phenomena that simultaneously acknowledge and deny the objective external reality of separation/loss of the object. Such transitional phenomena avoid the subjective internal reality, because what was projected is no longer seen as "not me"; however, since there is or still remains an ongoing diffuse identification (projective identification), what was projected can be retrieved and reintrojected, thus becoming again "mine," a "recovered" part of "me." Even the distinction between external and internal realities becomes blurred, since by definition a transitional phenomenon is self and other without being either. The resultant "area of illusion" alternately denies and states both objective and subjective realities.

CONTRIBUTIONS FROM SOCIAL PSYCHOLOGY

I shall now briefly examine how social psychology has studied and conceptualized groups. Social psychology is an admixture of sociology and psychology. I can address here only some social-psychological theories that have significantly influenced contemporary views on groups—namely, K. Lewin's (1952) field theory and von Bertalanffy's (1968) general systems theory, as well as so-called role theories. All three have been relevant to group psychotherapy.

Field Theory

Lewin (1952) tried to elevate the scientific methodology for research in social psychology to a level comparable to that in mathematics and physics. He moved from the empirical and intuitive to the abstract and formal. He insisted that the determinants of human behavior can be presented in rigorous mathematical terms. He borrowed from physics terms such as "field," which evokes the magnetic field, and "feedback," or "group dynamics," to imply "forces" active in groups. Lewin's fundamental construct is that of "field." He conceived all behavior as entailing a change in some state of a field in a given unit of time $(dx)/(dt)$. The field is the "life space" of an individual or group. The scientist's task is to develop constructs and techniques of observa-

tion and measurement adequate to characterize the properties of any given life space at any given time and to state the laws governing changes in these properties. It is a basic assertion of field theory (inspired by Koestler's Gestalt psychology) that the various parts of a given life space are to some degree interdependent (like foreground and background in visual perception). A set of interdependent facts can be adequately handled only conceptually, with the mathematical notion of space and the dynamic ideas of tension and force. For Lewin, contemporaneity was essential. At a given time, the determinants are the properties of the field present at the same time. Lewin did not consider the subjective phenomena of human psychology, such as fantasies and dreams. His emphasis on the contemporaneity of properties within the field as the only relevant causes of effects on such a field promoted an ahistorical view of psychology, focused *only* on the here and now. He treated the time dimension in a way that seems to deny the importance of early emotional developments. In proposing a nonsubjective and ahistorical psychology, field theory seems opposed to matters essential in psychoanalysis.

Nevertheless, the Sullivanian school of interpersonal psychiatry applied Lewin's field theory to psychopathology and therapy. Sullivan's (1953) ideas inspired the interpersonal or interactional approach to group psychotherapy, represented in the United States mainly by I. Yalom (1975). Field theory also provided Foulkes (Foulkes, 1948; Foulkes & Anthony, 1957) and his London followers with their notions about group dynamics.

General Systems Theory

GST is a method of analysis that lists the essential components of a system and describes their reciprocal influence within such a totality. It is an abstract formulation applicable to many topics, from astronomy and physics to biology and psychology. Hence, it needs to be filled with specific descriptions of the concrete subject matter being studied. So, to apply GST to group psychotherapy, it is necessary to fill out the general schemas with specific group theories. A combination of general systems and some group theories can become like the "metatheory" that integrates various analytic concepts about groups. Elsewhere I have proposed combining GST with object relations theories as a useful approach in group psychotherapy (Ganzarain, 1977, 1989). In 1989 I wrote:

> G.S.T. concepts can help us to better understand the interplay between individual and group mental process. For example, "isomorphism" (the basic

structural similarity among subsystems, and between them and a global system which encompasses them), can enrich the comparison between
ego and group, regarding their shared fluctuations
between the opposite states of integration and
fragmentation. A split, noncohesive, schizoid ego
state is comparable to a similarly unintegrated
group, while the well-integrated ego states reached,
after working through the depressive position, are
comparable to the times when the cohesive therapeutic work-group is focused on the task of insight, integration, and reparation. [p. 40]
[G.S.T. emphasizes] how boundaries are constantly crossed, from the inside and the outside of the
living systems, in a dynamic, holistic interaction.
Hence, G.S.T. may add a new understanding of
how groups and self-boundaries are extended—
through projection and introjection—beyond the
more obvious ones of space and time; with the
here-and-now blending with the there-and-then
through displacement. [p. 64]

Role Theory

As in the theater a role is a part played by an actor,
so too in group psychology members are collectively
assigned to perform the group's various functions;
each person may choose and negotiate with other
members which functions to assume. Those who
choose—and are accepted—to deliver some group
functions will occupy specific positions that are collectively recognized. Roles are like social expectations, sanctioned and agreed upon, that suggest how
individual members should behave so as to perform
together adequately the group functions required to
meet the needs of the social conglomerate at any
given moment. Roles, then, are collective manifestations of social needs figuratively handed down as
scripts to group members. Individuals can choose
how they are cast, provided their collective needs
are fulfilled. Roles and actors are different, separate
aspects of an unspoken social negotiation as to who
will play which part. Individuals can be interchanged in playing a given part, hence each person
can leave the scene; but someone else must replace
the person who has left and perform the abandoned
function, since each role needs to be present on the
group stage.

Clinically, object relations theory conceives roles
as composite manifestations of group and individual
psychologies, whereby collective expectations may
be the result of each member's projections searching
for some specific person who can be "pushed" to
perform necessary group functions; those functions
can also be described as "roles" fitting the person-

ality characteristics of certain individuals. For instance, the "hatchet" role may be handed over to
someone with significant sadistic characterological
traits, so that the group can utilize the hatchet man
to eliminate some undesirable member through a
symbolic execution; or a masochistic personality
may seem predestined to become the group's "scapegoat," so that the group can reinforce social norms
by condemning/punishing a given rebellious member. Many roles are not linked to group members'
unconscious defenses but are instead expressions of
collective functions or group needs (for instance,
gate-keeping or time-keeping roles).

There have been many experimental studies on
the social psychology of small groups concerning
topics such as leadership, membership, boundaries,
norms, power, communications, different sizes of
groups, various leadership styles, and so on (see
Cartwright & Zander, 1968).

PSYCHOANALYTIC CONTRIBUTIONS
TO SOCIAL PSYCHOLOGY

British analysts' interests in society and its institutions converged during World War II with those of
social scientists who valued psychoanalytic insights.
This powerful partnership has continued and spread
from England to continental Europe and the United
States.

Bion (1961) and Foulkes (1948) started to build
connections between psychoanalysis and social psychology. Other analysts who contributed are Jacques
(1976, 1982), Menzies (1988), Anzieu (1975), Mitscherlich (1969), and Zalesnik et al. (1975); some
noteworthy scientists in this field are A. K. Rice
(1963) and H. Levinson (1980). Many developed
"institutional consultancy" in ways derivative or parallel to psychoanalytic practice, likewise "oriented
to facilitating change for the benefit of the client"
(Menzies, 1988, p. 285). "Institutions can be helped
to change, so that they become better places to be,
more able to act effectively and constructively,"
consequently more productively. But to achieve
such healthy functioning, it is necessary to overcome "the basic difficulties human beings have in
co-operating effectively together, the anxieties these
arouse and the defenses mobilized against them"
(p. 297), among them the dynamics of power abuse
in leadership.

In the United States, Levinson (1980) developed
criteria based on psychoanalytic concepts to assess
who would make successful leaders in organizations. He asked such questions as (1) How does a
person handle aggression, affection (the need for
closeness), or dependency? (2) What values will this

person use to measure effectiveness? He also applied analytic notions on adult development to the various transitions in the life of executives.

GROUP PSYCHOTHERAPY

The field of group psychotherapy has grown so fast and in so many directions that it has become very difficult to agree on a definition of it. Contingent upon the practitioner's theoretical persuasion, certain concepts and techniques are preferred over others. Efforts have been made "to reach some operational definition of a 'standard' model of group psychotherapy." Scheidlinger (1982) attempted "the strictest possible delineation between the spectrum of group modalities and traditional psychotherapy" (p. 6). Hence, he distinguished four major categories of people-helping groups: (1) psychotherapy groups, (2) therapeutic groups for clients in mental health settings, (3) training and human development groups, and (4) self-help and mutual help groups. He defined group psychotherapy as a specific field of clinical practice within the realm of the psychotherapies, a psychosocial process wherein an expert psychotherapist "with a special additional group process training utilizes the emotional interaction in small carefully planned groups to 'repair' mental ill health, i.e., to effect amelioration of personality dysfunctions in individuals specifically selected for this purpose" (p. 7). He included under "therapeutic" groups "all other approaches utilized by human services personnel (not necessarily trained professionals), in outpatient or inpatient clinical facilities. Often they are auxiliary modalities to a primary treatment of psychiatric patients. The training groups can be distinguished from the other categories insofar as the aim of training groups is more in the realm of affective and cognitive education than psychotherapy" (p. 8). Included here are so-called T-groups (NTL), self-analytic groups, and the Tavistock study groups. Finally, there are the self-help groups dealing with problem-solving objectives, such as AA (Alcoholics Anonymous) or some other healing groups where mutual aid is put at the service of accomplishing a special purpose.

Various Types of Psychoanalytic Group Therapy

Abse (1974) underscored that the criterion distinguishing psychoanalytic group psychotherapy from nonanalytic modalities is that the former entails a working through of the transference, which is at the core of the therapeutic process and therefore involves a long-term approach. The analysis of resistances focused on the transference requires the exploration and working through of the ego's un-

conscious defenses against unrecognized conflicts. Some therapists require for psychoanalytic group therapy a frequency of at least twice a week of seventy-five- to ninety-minute group sessions. Whereas some practitioners aim for a "purely" analytic model, others accept combinations of psychoanalytic group therapy with various supplementary modalities. Psychopharmacological medications, individual psychotherapy (even with another therapist), or concomitant participation in marital/family therapy or in supportive mutual help groups may be permitted, provided the risks of splitting the transference can be counteracted by frequent, meaningful collaborative consultations among the various therapists.

Parloff (1968) distinguished, within psychoanalytic group psychotherapies, three types of technical focuses.

First, the *intrapsychic modality* treats individuals in a group and aims at exploring the unconscious conflicts within each individual. It is somehow comparable to doing individual psychoanalysis with a number of patients in the same room, each taking a turn to talk in the group about their emotional problems. Some New York analysts (e.g., Wolf & Schwartz, 1962) practiced this modality by placing their individual psychoanalytic patients in a group that they themselves also treated, so that each person attended individual and group sessions with the same therapist.

Second, the *interpersonal approach* is a modality that focuses primarily on the interactions between members. It has theoretical connections with Sullivan's interpersonal school of psychiatry, with Berne's (1966) transactional analysis, or TA, and with Perls's (1969) gestalt therapy (or with a combination of these last two). Yalom's approach (1975) also belongs in this category. However, Yalom utilizes the interaction among members more than do the others just mentioned, the latter preferring to focus on the therapist's exchanges with one member at a time (Goulding, 1972). The TA tasks are to diagnose the different ego states (parent, child, or adult) characteristic of the patient's interactions, to identify the specific "game" being played and the unconscious "life plan"—or "script"—that each patient may have learned or chosen early in life. The purpose is to help the patient become able to shift deliberately from one ego state to another.

The intrapsychic and interpersonal modalities do not focus on psychoticlike group phenomena; that is to say, these approaches do not use Kleinian/Bionian concepts about primitive anxieties and defenses but mainly some modified Freudian notions, focused on neurotic conflicts.

Third, the *group-centered*, holistic, or integralist

psychoanalytic approach studies group forces or group dynamics, ever present in the background, while also focusing on the foreground interactions among individuals. This school promotes therapy *of* the group or *by* the group. Bion (1961) and Ezriel (1950) represent this orientation in England, Whitaker and Lieberman (1964) and Horwitz (1983) among others in the United States. Foulkes (1948) and Foulkes with Anthony (1957) developed group analysis in England. They borrowed concepts from Lewin's (1952) field theory to understand the dynamics of the here and now as dependent on current group forces rather than on the individual's past experiences. According to Lewin's "principle of contemporaneity," the group's "childhood is contained in the present" (Whiteley & Gordon, 1979, p. 19). Foulkes's technique was not therapist-centered; hence he preferred the leader to take a covert role, "behind the scenes" as a "conductor." "He's both a part yet apart from the group. He is the servant of the group" (p. 21). Foulkes's approach is a mixture of an interpersonal with an occasional group-centered focus on what he called the group "matrix," meaning the total network of communications in the group, which form the background for interpersonal exchanges.

Each group member's expressions, interactions among all the persons in the room, and the general group atmosphere all happen simultaneously. Hence, the situation of the group psychotherapist can be compared with that of an overloaded computer, with an excess of input. The therapist will frequently be perplexed, wondering which among the many group phenomena to address first. Ezriel's concept of "common group tension" can help to diagnose, on a verbal level, where the meaningful emotional action is at a given moment. But observing the predominant affect within the group, expressed mainly in nonverbal ways, is more meaningful than paying attention to the words. Actually, learning to observe and read the nonverbal communications in the group is the paramount skill that group psychotherapists need to cultivate, since as Bion (1961) wrote: "Groups communicate basically through nonverbal exchanges which express the primitive preverbal layers of the mind" (p. 185).

The group-centered or integralist psychoanalytic approach is the only group psychotherapy modality that attempts to focus on specific group phenomena beyond the extrapolation of concepts borrowed from the individual psychoanalytic setting. In fact, most group psychotherapy modalities are essentially transpositions of individual treatment concepts to the group situation, applying basic Freudian psychoanalytic concepts. Although many analytic terms, such as regression, identification, conflict, defenses, self, object, transference and countertransference, acting out, working through, and so forth, can be applied or adapted to group psychotherapy, in addition we are required to postulate group-specific theoretical notions that may capture what is unique to group psychology. A combination of general systems and object relations theories may bring together and predict many of the puzzling, often chaotic, complex combinations of contradictory behavior in groups: adaptive behavior coexists with regressive moments (tasks may be performed adequately but alternating with inefficient group performances influenced by basic assumptions); anxiety can sometimes escalate to unbearable intensity, while at other times fears are soothed and alleviated. Many familial and societal issues are replicated in groups and are dealt with as in these microcosms, where social reality is intertwined with the individuals' early anxieties. Envy can sometimes become unbearable or at other times promote imaginative "equalizing" policies that smooth over the harshness of dealing with human differences. Both poles of extreme ambivalence can flip-flop; boundaries are required but are also potentially permeable so that the self can be formed, supported, stimulated, or sometimes annihilated; the whole system may resonate and respond intensely to an individual's needs or—just the opposite—ignore the person. Finally, the ultimate paradox is that all of the above have the potential to become psychotherapeutically useful.

Object relations group psychotherapy technique is centered at the core of group psychology, which is formed by shared fantasies about a common internal object: the group entity situated in the "area of illusion," in the members' minds, as a mother surrogate. Object relations group technique focuses especially on the primitive defense mechanisms that also shape that group-entity image, resulting from the "me/not me" fluctuating transitions between each member's self and the group. The early defenses promote fantasies of altering either the self, the objects (including the group), or both through various identifications, denial, splitting, or projection. Psychotherapeutic change is fueled by the need to resolve depressive anxiety (feelings of guilt for having damaged the loved objects), through fostering the ability to make reparation for the damages fantasized as done to the loved objects, while promoting the self's responsibility in the exchanges with its objects. Such vital growth of the proactive self, in Stern's (1985) sense, may expand its capacity for self-reliance, concern for others, sublimation, and creativity. Object relations group psychotherapy is the only technical modality that applies Kleinian/Bionian psychoanalytic concepts to clinical practice, with some occasional Winnicottian additions.

Clinical Vignettes of Object Relations Group-Centered Therapy

I shall illustrate (1) the exploration of group patients' unconscious ego defenses; (2) some detailed working through done in groups; (3) transference in group psychotherapy; and (4) projective identification.

Exploring unconscious defenses. In the third session of an outpatient group formed of eight married persons, one of the four men, Jack, spoke of his doubts as to whether he would continue to attend group meetings. This group had been formed by adding four new patients to four members of a former group. Jack attended only one session of the former group because his wife forbade his continuing to participate. A year later he applied for another group. But in this third meeting he reported that his wife was threatening him with divorce if he kept coming.

When Jack first sought therapy, he had just learned that his wife was having an affair with another man. He was feeling rejected, jealous, and anxious. His wife apparently felt that Jack's participation in the group was revenge for her extramarital affair.

Jack had an infantile personality. He was also extremely anxious. He was the youngest child of a family of four. His mother, a widow, lived by herself with her two younger children on a farm in the Kansas countryside. Jack's immediately older brother was mentally retarded. When Jack was eight years old, his mother decided to place her retarded child in an institution. Jack did not dare to ask about the decision. He was left with fantasies that his mother had kicked his brother out of the home because of the brother's "badness." Because he was extremely dependent upon his mother, he did not dare to challenge her because of his fear of also being kicked out of the household. He was fearful of repeating with the group psychotherapist the relationship he had had with his mother. He unconsciously sided with his wife's reluctance to accept his entering group therapy and let her speak for him in voicing his own fears and doubts. This matter was discussed in the session I am reporting. He went on to give a long-winded explanation of his relationship with his wife, apparently misusing the group's time. Some of the members began raising the question: "Why are we discussing Jack's wife? Since she is not a member of the group, why should he be talking about her?" The group had diagnosed that Jack was under his wife's thumb and that she was afraid

of possible changes in Jack's personality that would lead him to oppose her domination.

Significant psychological exchanges were happening on the boundary between two systems: the psychotherapeutic group and the marital couple. Jack's wife had become the "container," through projection, of two fears shared by the group members: the fear of becoming "hooked" on the therapeutic relationship and the fear of change. Just as they sensed Jack's wife's fear of change, so also each member was fearful of the possible risks involved if they themselves were to change.

I interpreted such projection onto an "outsider." The group had permitted the information about exchanges between Jack and his wife to enter the group but had attempted to keep this issue outside the group system, handling it as if it were a matter foreign to the group. The therapist's help consisted of interpreting the projection.

The group also performed another boundary function by encouraging Jack to stay. Members were really concerned about possible attrition of the group; hence Jack's threat of quitting increased the activities designed to hold him. Jack was simultaneously doing to the group what his wife had done to him; he was threatening the group with losing him, just as his wife had threatened him with the possibility of losing her to another man. From a general systems point of view, Jack's interactions with his wife became in effect an extension of the group system through projection. It can also be said that through Jack's introjection of his wife's attitudes, she was figuratively present through Jack.

In general, through these very complex ways, the boundaries of the psychotherapy group are extended to the different personages surrounding each member outside the group—spouses, parents, siblings, bosses, workmates, and others. Introjection and projection blur the current space boundaries of the group almost in the same way that the timelessness of the unconscious blurs the time boundaries of the group; thus, we may witness a live reproduction of the patterns of interaction between any of the members and his or her objects, both of the members' current or of their past lives.

The question of what to include within the group and what to leave out of the group's attention is illustrated by this clinical example. Jack's wife ended up being the container for several elements of the psychic life of the group members, and she became like a satellite member of the group, perceived as the container of Jack's basic fears of the group together with the comparable fears of other members. Interpreting the projection brought back into the group system the contents that were being expelled and excluded from the group. The group's reaction was of some initial resistance, but gradually they began working mainly on the fear of possible changes.

The role of the group therapist has been described as fundamentally to keep the boundary controls oriented toward the primary task—namely, therapy. He or she performs this function by preventing the exclusion of contents that are being avoided. In the case cited, the therapist decided to increase the system's boundary permeability both within Jack's self and within the group. He accomplished it by interpreting the projection onto Jack's wife of what was going on in both systems. By helping both Jack and the group realize their childish anxieties vis-à-vis old introjects of "bad" mother, the therapist opened the patients' minds to new possibilities, so that they no longer needed to repeat their previous behavior based on past archaic fears. Now they could examine their situation in a different way. Jack began conceiving of a new, more assertive, self-presentation, stronger and less fearful. He stayed in the group, faced the risk of divorce, and indeed chose to get divorced later on. The therapist, with his concerned understanding, made the group boundary permeable to further the analysis of the situation. The members could now realize they were not really threatened by planning to change. The system analysis clarified the fact that Jack was a component of two systems: the therapy group and the marital couple. He was at the boundary between the two systems, with a part of himself in each one.

Working through in psychoanalytic group therapy. Daniel was forty years old when he started his treatment with me. He had been married for twelve years and had been in another group for ten months. He and three other old-timers formed a new group with four additional members. Daniel's personality was described by his previous therapist as masochistic. He had become the scapegoat of her group. She described him as going downhill. When I saw Daniel before starting the group, I tried to dissuade him from continuing treatment. However, he wanted to accomplish something he had not yet achieved and insisted on being included, and I finally agreed.

In the sixth session Daniel reported that he had been impotent since puberty, being able only occasionally to achieve orgasm. He related his lack of ejaculation to his fear of impregnating his partner. In addition, he had suffered from lack of erection since his vasectomy three years earlier. He had hoped he could stop fearing impregnating his partner and become sexually freer. To his dismay, however, he had lost his erections.

The other three male group members had also had vasectomies; however, none of them had suffered from impotence afterward. Daniel was thus confronted with the fact that his lack of erection was not an anatomical consequence of the vasectomy and that his impotence was instead psychological. A female group member reported that her husband had also suffered from impotence after a vasectomy. Lucy had insisted that he see a urologist, and her husband had recovered his potency shortly thereafter. Lucy's report stirred up in Daniel the wish to be taken care of by his wife, by a similar action on her part demonstrating her interest in his sexual potency. The group confronted him with his overdependent stance and suggested that he himself could make an appointment with a urologist.

Daniel had regressed to a dependent attitude, adopting a depressive pining for his wife as a lost sexual partner and developing a paranoid view of her. He felt that she did not love him any longer; he suspected that she had married him for his apparent wealth. The group confronted Daniel with his conflicting wishes to be taken care of by his wife while deeply mistrusting her.

In the sixteenth session Daniel reported in a self-effacing way that he had been to a urologist and had been able to perform sexually with his wife. He apologized for being so dependent upon his wife. He reported their satisfactory sexual intercourse almost as if he were displaying a sign of weakness—needing to be loved by his wife. He had actually been extremely tentative and indirect in stating his sexual needs to her. In the following sessions Daniel was happy and boastful about his restored masculine capacity.

Between sessions 17 and 50 we reviewed his shame at depending on women. He was his mother's favorite, but now he never took the initiative of writing or calling her. He waited for her to take the initiative. There was a conflict between his relish in being mother's favorite and his grandiose self-image as a tough he-man who did not need anyone. The old-group patients remembered that Daniel had had a peculiar reaction when their former female therapist had announced that she was leaving town. Daniel had stopped coming to the group, missing the last two months of meetings. He stated, "I had a pretext," intending to say, "I had a good reason." He meant that his son was playing Little League baseball at the same time that the group met. He added that he did not mind at all whether that doctor was going to stay in town or leave. He tried to name her, but he had forgotten her name! He then realized that he was denying his previous doctor's emotional importance for him while angrily wiping her out of his memory. He had denied his wishes to depend on women, reacting with anger to them and distancing himself from them, frustrated by both his wife and the female therapist. Daniel denied the emotional importance for him of female therapist, wife, and mother and tried to delete them from his life. The depressive reaction caused by the loss of an important woman was hypomanically denied, together with his internal psychic reality of needing and missing her. He perpetuated the psychic reality of such a loss by denying it. Daniel turned away from his woman therapist and from his wife, feeling omnipotently above the weakness of needing them. He was convinced he could regulate how emotionally important they were for him and had felt triumphant over them through devaluing them. The denial of mourning for the losses (feared or real, past or future) of important women prevented him from facing, dealing with, or elaborating those mournings. Coming to terms with them, accepting those women's emotional value for him, and accepting also his denied wishes to restore his relationships with them, all needed the specific working through that allowed Daniel to start repairing his relations with his wife. Daniel did learn and succeed in practicing new behavior after elaborating a pathological mourning for his wife and for his woman group therapist. The presence of two other members of his first group created a bridge between the current group and the previous one.

Daniel bribed his superego by offering his impotence as self-punishment for his wishes to be sexually promiscuous while remaining emotionally uninvolved with his sexual partners. He planned his vasectomy to enjoy a free sexual life, with the paradoxical result that the vasectomy "caused" his impotence. Daniel was a stubborn, masochistic personality, who displayed help-rejecting complaining patterns. He provoked, devalued, and mistrusted significant persons in his life, including the group therapists; he presented himself as a pitiful victim of fate or of somebody else's wrongdoings; he occasionally dragged me, with his provocations, into potential power battles within the group. Then other group members gave me a respite in which to regain my objectivity without getting involved in a transference/countertransference sadomasochistic tug of war.

Separation anxiety is an important aspect of working through. It stimulates a progression to resolve the depressive position or the regression to schizoparanoid and manic defenses (as illustrated by Daniel's response to his former therapist's departure). If the depressive position is solved successfully, the capacity for reparation allows loving concern to prevail over hate for the patients' objects.

Transference. Advances in psychoanalytic theory have led to the discovery of new aspects of transference. For instance, the study of object relations promoted the view that the analytic situation is also a repetition of the early mother–child relationship. Research on ego psychology increased the importance attributed to the defensive processes an individual uses to avoid anxiety. Other new aspects of transference were revealed as psychoanalytic therapy was used for different types of patients such as children and adults suffering from psychotic or narcissistic personality disorders.

Whether transference requires well-integrated, mature ego functions and whether psychoanalytic psychotherapy can occur in the absence of a mature ego are related questions that have occasioned strong polemics. As intense regressions occur in group psychotherapy, we should ask ourselves whether regression is only a resistance (Zetzel, 1956) or whether it also allows a deeper exploration of early anxieties, thus broadening the understanding of transference.

When applied to psychoanalytic group therapy, the concept of transference requires further examination, most notably because the transference targets are multiple: therapists (one or two), other members, and the group as an entity. The presence of various targets raises the question of transference "dilution" as well as the issue of whether a complete transference neurosis can develop in the group setting, regardless of a defusion or decrease in the intensity of transference.

The group as a whole can become the site of a displacement of feelings toward the family of origin, as happened when a patient said, "We were eight at home as we are here in this group"; or when a group of incest victims, treated by female and male cotherapists, perceived their group as a replica of their chaotic families of origin and considered leaving our outpatient clinic together in order to go to another agency, thus repeating the wish to leave home that each one of them experienced while growing up.

The group entity can also become like a "bad" mother, as was perceived by a patient who said, "This group only gives me cuts but no recognition at all, just like my mother." But the group entity can also provide a maternal holding environment as a "good" mother that loves the patients and lets them know that they are worthy of being loved. It can also provide company, encouragement, and support when a member is in need. In one particular case, during a Thanksgiving evening, a victim of father/daughter incest, raised by a psychotic mother, felt alone and depressed, realizing she had missed in life the usual family experiences associated with special holidays;

she longed then for her mother and wished to call her. She decided not to call mother, however, but instead phoned another group member in a clear displacement from needing mother to gratifying the wishes for mother's loving care by talking with a groupmate.

The therapist and other group members can be cast in a wide variety of transference roles: as parents, siblings, spouses, lovers, persecutors, and so on. For instance, both Jack and Daniel transferred some of their feelings for their mothers to their group therapists.

Bion (1961) described the emotional life of the individual in a group as comparable to the infant's experience of early psychoticlike anxieties when first dealing with the breast. He thus postulated a part-object transference from the breast to an internal object, the group entity. He also described how primitive defense mechanisms, such as projective identification and splitting, prevail as defensive operations in groups. Regarding projective identification, Bion's disciple Ezriel (1950) stated: "When several people meet in a group, each member projects his own unconscious fantasy-objects upon various other group members and then tries to manipulate them accordingly" (p. 62).

Thus, according to Ezriel, each patient is also the recipient of multiple projective identifications from other group members, so that each one is pushed into assuming certain roles or is coerced by the group's "role suction" (Redl, 1963) into adopting characteristic patterns. Specific behaviors automatically invite complementary responses or roles. For instance, a member's exhibitionistic behavior is an invitation to the others to look, or masochistic needs become an invitation for others to injure, dominate, or abuse (Ganzarain & Buchele, 1988). Several comparable pairs of reciprocal, complementary roles can be described. Reversal from a specific role to the reciprocal but opposite one produces the effect of using projective identification as a defense. Shifting from one role to another can happen repeatedly back and forth, creating confusion. For instance, victims of abuse can become like their torturers, just as incest victims often become perpetrators of the same abuse.

Projective identification. Projective identification is both an intrapsychic defense mechanism (Klein, 1952, pp. 300–301) and a vehicle for interpersonal communication (Bion, 1962, pp. 36–37). As a defense, projective identification can be used by the anxious self (after or following splitting and projection) to protect against annihilation fears, through fantasies of entering the objects and omnipotently

controlling them. Klein labeled this aspect of projective identification an "intrusive identification fantasy of defense," which also elaborates wishes to get rid of and evacuate unacceptable mental contents onto the objects. A group scapegoating a member operates in the same way. But in reality the self can influence its objects only to a limited extent when resorting to projective identification. When projective identification becomes a "fantasy aimed at communication" (Bion, 1962), it operates through "implementing the nonlexical (or nonverbal) language" (Meltzer et al., 1982, p. 202). Nonverbal messages are extensively used in small groups. For instance, after a session when I announced to the group that in three months I was planning to leave Topeka for good, the patients abruptly left the room while I was talking and saying that I was going to be absent two weeks from then but present in the following session. Group members did not pay attention to me and turned their backs on me, leaving without listening and without looking at me. They were nonverbally getting back at me, doing to me what they felt I was doing to them. They succeeded in making me feel deserted and guilty, and I actually became confused, stating that I would also be absent from the next meeting (meaning the subsequent one). I was unconsciously taking my turn at getting back at them by saying—in a Freudian slip!—that I would not attend the next session. When I needed to correct my mistake, I became even more confused. I was nonverbally expecting to keep the patients in the room, to counteract my feeling deserted by them. Role reversals took place, with the identification as deserter and desertee flip-flopping back and forth between myself and the group members. All these exchanges happened nonverbally while I was using words as a smoke screen to hide the intense nonverbal dialogue.

Nonverbal communications among persons are multiple, complex, and often unconscious. Our general appearance, posture, grooming, facial expressions, tone of voice, and so on convey multiple images that recipients decode according to their perceptions of us. Messages sent through projective identification "activate internal experiences (or internal objects) in the recipients" (Torras de Beas, 1989). In group psychotherapy, each patient will interact with the therapist and the other groupmates along the same lines. In each member there will also occur an "activation of internal experiences" (or internal objects). There will ensue a dialogue between the sender's messages and each groupmate. The other members resonate with the interacting patients. In addition, they have learned—by imitation—to act as co-therapists. Redl's role suction (1963) is mediated by projective identification. However, we need to clarify the fact that such mediation does not mean that a specific mental content—for instance, a person's anger—is removed from his mind and transplanted into someone else's mind. The mediation is rather an unconscious perception or nonverbal communication of the sender's prevailing affect, which is then induced and resonates in the recipient's mind (Ogden, 1979), but reversing the process. What was first projected can again be reintrojected, and a new role reversal will occur. The recipient's calmed solution of the self's previous acute anxiety may also be assimilated, incorporated by the self. "The end result, when successful, is the transformation of a defensive projective identification, into a communicative projective identification" (Torras de Beas, 1989, p. 266). According to Bion (1962), mother's reverie, while caring for an infant, can contain her infant's anxiety by processing or metabolizing it and can offer in return to her infant a calmed state of mind through such communicative projective identification.

DISCUSSION

I shall briefly examine here some technical and theoretical controversial issues. Some debatable technical questions are: (1) Is group psychotherapy really "psychoanalytic"? (2) Do psychotherapeutic groups provide merely a social network of support, or can they really promote the emotional growth of their members? (3) What are the relationships between, object relations groups and the neighboring psychotherapies such as psychodrama, transactional analysis, and gestalt?

Psychoanalysis?

Since group psychotherapy can be focused on the analysis of the patients' defensive resistances to explore and uncover the unconscious patterns and conflicts repeated in the transference, it can properly be called "psychoanalytic," provided the resistances in the transference are explored and overcome (as with Jack). However, some analysts and group practitioners alike may disagree that group psychotherapy can be regarded as psychoanalytic. Analysts like Anthony (1971) have questioned whether patients can regress enough in groups and whether transference neuroses can actually occur in the group setting. And distinguished practitioners of group treatment, like Yalom, claim that while groups offer opportunities for interpersonal learning that are effective in improving patients' mental health, they do not explore the unconscious.

Just as there is a range of expressive-supportive individual psychotherapy modalities, so there are group treatments that mix in various proportions the uncovering of the unconscious and supportive, defense-reinforcing psychotherapeutic elements. In addition, there are different combinations of concurrent individual and group modalities, ranging from having the same therapist for both to having a different one for each modality. However, a clinical evaluation, prior to starting treatment, can assess a patient's capacity to work in and benefit from an expressive/uncovering approach. Scheidlinger's (1982) four types of groups that help people are relevant here, reaffirming his point that there is a category of group psychotherapists who are specialists (specifically trained in psychoanalysis and group dynamic techniques) in utilizing the emotional interactions that take place in small groups and the subsequent reflections about them to "repair mental ill health."

What Prevails: Support or Growth?

Self-help groups of mutual support have become increasingly popular, at least in the United States, where the Alcoholics Anonymous movement began and spread. When the general population has been affected by a significant collective event, as occurred in the United States during the recent Gulf War, or by a catastrophe, such as the devastating earthquake that occurred not too long ago in Mexico City, self-help support groups have been used to alleviate the pain and the fears experienced by those affected. Such support groups do not prevent or stop each individual's further emotional growth; they merely demonstrate the temporary need to have a group of peers with whom to share a common problem. Psychotherapeutic groups may encourage further personal growth in addition to offering some emotional gratification of dependency needs.

Neighboring Group Therapies

Psychodrama (Moreno, 1951), transactional analysis (Berne, 1966), and gestalt therapy have some important psychoanalytic roots and connections. Drama promotes spontaneity in acting, like a free-association surrogate. TA and gestalt group therapy help the individual to examine different ego states that are poorly or not at all integrated into the person's global personality. Different parts (or "roles") of the protagonist are examined: either the unintegrated split selves or the child, parental, or adult roles. Characteristic styles ("scripts") and preferred adaptive behavior ("games") are also examined. Sometimes these modalities are offered in weekend workshops (called "marathons") or as brief experiences with no time available for detailed working through of the emotional conflicts examined. Hence, these modalities are not psychoanalytic.

In these neighboring group therapies, group-as-a-whole phenomena are not conceived as related to the group entity or to the group as internal object. Instead, each patient waits for his or her turn to perform in front of the others as an audience, whose activity is like that of a Greek chorus in classic theater.

I shall finally address the theoretical issue: Is it possible to integrate the various psychoanalytic theories about groups, or is pluralism unavoidable?

Integration or Pluralism?

The dramatic growth of group psychotherapy in the 1960s and 1970s was accompanied by much theoretical disagreement and professional "provincialism" or "chauvinism." For instance, for Wolf and Schwartz (1962), the "emphasis on group dynamics is anti-analytic." They believe that such a view is a mystique, because it claims to heal by group cohesion or atmosphere rather than through the expert intervention of an analyst (p. 79). "During the last decade, however, the ideological controversy has yielded to pluralism [meaning the belief that no single explanatory system can account for all the phenomena of a discipline] in theory, and eclectism [meaning the choosing of what appears to be the best for diverse techniques] in practice" (Scheidlinger, 1991, p. 217).

Hence, "the most recent group psychotherapy literature abandoned theoretical monism in favor of pluralism and integration," writes Scheidlinger (1991, p. 222), "with the hope that links would lead to the eventual development of a general theory of group psychotherapy." Here group psychotherapy again coincides with the recent trend in psychoanalysis, indicated when Wallerstein (1988) took the topic "One psychoanalysis or many?" for his presidential address to the International Psychoanalytic Association's Montreal Congress. His ideas stimulated a search for the common ground of different analytic schools. They evoked warnings as well against carrying integration too far, thereby losing the stimulant effect of differences and "conflicts that made us both wiser and creative" and leading us instead to the "blindness of conformism" (Schafer, 1990, p. 52). Some (Curtis, 1993) reacted against this "ecumenical" new look of psychoanalysis, defending instead the traditional American psychoanalytic viewpoint. Raquel Goldstein (1991) in her contribution to the Buenos Aires International Congress of Training Analysts proposes a third alternative to the dilemma between the chaos of ideological confusion and the ossification of rigid orthodoxy.

Her solution is to learn from ambiguity and its concomitant anxiety while realizing that adherence to a given ideology serves mainly a reassuring, defensively comforting purpose—to deny the unbearable complexities of the ambiguous reality of the human mind. Learning to tolerate such essential confusion and ambiguity, responding creatively in understanding without the "sacralization" of any theory, becomes the major psychoanalytic lesson, which our students may learn from their training analyses and teachers. No orthodoxy, but pluralism, is what she therefore proposes. Strupp (1989) welcomed integrated (eclectic) psychotherapists, because they gear their techniques to the specific needs of their patients under specific conditions rather than deriving them from the therapist's "bible." Scheidlinger (1991, p. 223) underscores, in this context, the relevance of the conclusions arrived at by Smith et al. (1980) following their study of the benefits of psychotherapy. In the absence of evidence that would testify to the superiority of any one clinical practice model, they advocated a pluralistic stance in which each therapist learns and practices one model well, while acknowledging that "that model does not represent the one and only true path." The American Group Psychotherapy Association and the American Psychoanalytic Association seem both committed now to pluralism, while the International Psychoanalytic Association is also moving in this direction. It is both fascinating and confusing that everybody seems to be asserting that the patient/therapist relationship is what counts in psychotherapy, regardless of the theory by which their dialogue is conducted.

EMERGING TRENDS

In Theory

There is a growing tendency to integrate Kleinian concepts with those of Winnicott. For instance, Klein's projective identification seems to me to be the mediator of Winnicott's "transitional phenomena," whereby those situations or areas which are "neither self nor other, but both" help the developing self to overcome separation anxieties, while the definition of the self becomes possible. Kohut's (1971) notion of the selfobject seems an extension of Winnicott's transitional phenomena. Hence, some contributions of Kohut's self psychology seem complementary to those of the British authors Klein, Bion, and Winnicott.

There is also a trend toward theoretical expansion, by acknowledging the phenomenology of "chaos" as applicable to the human mind. Mental phenomena are isomorphically expressed—like those of any system—in chaotic interactions among the integrating parts that form such systems, so that some "bangs" (minor when compared to the big one that happened to the universe!) can happen; our intuition can grasp such new organizing synthesis, provided we learn how to tolerate the ambiguity of unstructured mental chaos. Contemporary theory in psychoanalysis is beginning to be influenced by the so-called chaos theory (Spruiell, 1991). As transitional phenomena and projective identification open our minds to better understand how the boundaries between self and object can be blurred to promote growth and to alleviate mental tension, in spite of the conceptual confusion introduced, it is possible that further deepening of our comprehension of chaos may enrich our understanding of the human mind in its social context.

In Practical Applications of Group Psychology

The supplementary use of couple, family, and group psychotherapeutic techniques enhances the patients' benefits from such professional help. Skinner (1976) in the United Kingdom and many practitioners in the United States combine these various interventions.

Institutional/administrative psychology has applied to human organizations psychoanalytic ideas about group psychology. The A. K. Rice (1965) Institute with branches in Britain and the United States has been teaching and applying these ideas over many years; so have the National Training Laboratories for group development, subdivided into many branches. New studies on the psychology of large groups have also been carried out by some A. K. Rice consultants.

Group psychotherapy (like other group techniques to help patients with psychological problems) is becoming a subspecialty of medical or clinical psychology, while institutional/administrative psychology has become a section of social psychology. Both have multiple meaningful practical applications.

As we have seen, the understanding of group psychology has incorporated important contributions from psychoanalysis, with the result that some modalities are part of psychoanalysis. Group psychology has also expanded into different, more specific domains of theory and practice.

REFERENCES

Abse, W. D. (1974). *Clinical Notes on Group Analytic Psychotherapy.* Charlottesville: Univ. Press, Virginia.

Anthony, E. J. (1971). Comparison between individual and group psychotherapy. In *Comprehensive Group Psychotherapy,* ed. H. I. Kaplan & B. J.

Sadock, pp. 104–117. Baltimore: Williams & Wilkins.

Anzieu, D. (1975). *The Group and the Unconscious.* London: Routledge & Kegan Paul, 1984.

Berne, E. (1966). *Principles of Group Treatment.* New York: Grove Press.

Bion, W. R. (1961). *Experiences in Groups.* London: Tavistock.

———. (1962). *Learning from Experience.* London: Heinemann.

Cartwright, D., & Zander, A. (1968). *Group Dynamics Research and Theory,* 3d ed. New York & London: Harper & Row.

Curtis, H. (1993). Psychoanalytic ecumenism and varieties of psychoanalytic experience. Presidential address. *J. Amer. Psychoanal. Assn.,* 40:643–663.

Ezriel, H. (1950). A psychoanalytic approach in group treatment. *Brit. J. Med. Psychol.,* 23:59–74.

Foulkes, S. H. (1948). *Introduction to Group Analytic Psychotherapy.* London: Heinemann.

———. (1964). *Group Analytic Psychotherapy.* London: Gordon & Breach.

Foulkes, S. H., & Anthony, E. J. (1957). *Group Psychotherapy.* Harmondsworth: Penguin.

Freud, S. (1913). *Totem and Taboo. SE,* 13:1–161.

———. (1921). *Group Psychology and the Analysis of the Ego. SE,* 18:69–143.

Ganzarain, R. (1977). General systems and object relations theories. *Int. J. Group Psychother.,* 27:441–456.

———. (1983). Working through in analytic group psychotherapy. *Int. J. Group Psychother.,* 33:281–296.

———. (1985). Primitive defenses and psychotic-like anxieties. *Issues in Ego Psychology,* 3(2): 42–48.

———. (1989). General systems and object relations theories. In *Object Relations Group Psychotherapy.* Madison, Conn.: Int. Univ. Press.

———. (1991). The "bad" mother-group. In *Psychoanalytic Group Theory and Practice,* ed. S. Tuttman. Madison, Conn.: Int. Univ. Press.

Ganzarain, R., & Buchele, B. (1988). *Fugitives of Incest.* Madison, Conn.: Int. Univ. Press.

Gay, P. (1988). *Freud: A Life for Our Time.* New York: Norton.

Glatzer, H. T. (1969). Working through in analytic group psychotherapy. *Int. J. Group Psychother.,* 29:292–306.

———. (1985). Early mother–child relationships. *Psychodynam. Psychother.,* 3:27–37.

Gleick, J. (1987). *Chaos.* New York: Viking.

Goldstein, R. (1991). Chaos, ossification or what? Precirculated paper of the Fifth IPA Conference of Training Analysts, Buenos Aires.

Goulding, R. (1972). New directions in transactional analysis. In *Progress in Group and Family Therapy*, ed. C. J. Sager & H. S. Kaplan, pp. 105–134. New York: Brunner/Mazel.

Guntrip, H. (1967). Discussion of H. Segal's paper "M. Klein's technique." *Psychoanal. Forum*, 2:212–227.

———. (1971). *Psychoanalytic Theory, Therapy and the Self*. London: Hogarth Press.

Hartmann, H. (1964). *Ego Psychology and the Problem of Adaptation*. New York: Int. Univ. Press.

Hearst, L. (1981). The emergence of the mother group. *Group Analysis*, 14:25–33.

Horwitz, L. (1983). Projective identification in dyads and groups. *Int. J. Group Psychother.*, 33:259–279.

Jacobson, L. (1989). The group as an object in the cultural field. *Int. J. Group Psychother.*, 39:475–497.

Jacques, E. (1955). Social systems as defense against persecutory and depressive anxieties. In *New Directions*, ed. M. Klein, P. Heimann, & R. Money-Kyrle, pp. 478–498. London: Tavistock.

———. (1976). *A General Theory of Bureaucracy*. New York: Halstead Press.

———. (1982). *The Form of Time*. New York: Crane & Russak.

Kauff, P. F. (1991). The unique contribution of analytic group psychotherapy to the treatment of pre-oedipal character pathology. In *Psychoanalytic Group Theory and Practice*, ed. S. Tuttman, pp. 175–190. Madison, Conn.: Int. Univ. Press.

Klein, M. (1932). *The Psychoanalysis of Children*. New York: Grove Press, 1960.

———. (1946). Notes on some schizoid mechanisms. Rpt. in *Developments in Psycho-analysis*, pp. 292–320. London: Hogarth Press, 1952.

Kohut, H. (1971). *The Analysis of the Self*. New York: Int. Univ. Press.

Le Bon, G. (1897). *The Crowd*. London: Fisher Unwin, 1920.

Levinson, H. (1980). Criteria for choosing chief executives. *Harvard Business Rev.*, 58(4):113–120.

———. (1981). *Executive*. Cambridge, Mass.: Harvard Univ. Press.

Lewin, K. (1952). *Field Theory in Social Sciences*. London: Tavistock.

Meltzer, D., et al. (1982). The conceptual distinction between projective identification (Klein) and container/contained (Bion). *J. Child Psychother.*, 8:195–202.

Menzies, I. E. P. (1988). A psycho-analytic perspective on social institutions. In *Melanie Klein Today*, ed. E. B. Spillius, vol. 2, pp. 284–299. London & New York: Routledge.

Mitscherlich, A. (1969). *Society without Father*. New York: Harcourt, Brace & World.

Modell, A. (1984). *Psychoanalysis in a New Context*. New York: Int. Univ. Press.

Moreno, J. L. (1951). *Sociometry*. New York: Beacon House.

Ogden, T. H. (1979). On projective identification. *Int. J. Psychoanal.*, 60:357–373.

Parloff, M. (1968). Analytic group psychotherapy. In *Modern Psychoanalysis*, ed. J. Marmor, pp. 492–531. New York: Basic Books.

Perls, F. (1969). *Gestalt Therapy Verbatim*. Lafayette, Ind.: Real People Press.

Redl, F. (1963). Psychoanalysis and group psychotherapy. *Amer. J. Orthopsychiat.*, 33:135–147.

Rice, A. K. (1963). *The Enterprise and Its Environment*. London: Tavistock.

———. (1965). *Learning for Leadership*. London: Tavistock.

———. (1969). Individual, group and inter-group processes. *Human Relations*, 22:562.

Rizzuto, A. M. (1979). *The Birth of a Living God*. Chicago: Univ. Chicago Press.

Rosenfeld, H. (1979). Transference psychoses in the borderline patient. In *Advances in Psychotherapy of the Borderline Patient*, ed. J. Le Boit & A. Capponi, pp. 485–510. New York: Aronson.

Scheidlinger, S. (1974). On the concept of the "Mother-Group." *Int. J. Group Psychother.*, 24:417–428. Rpt. in Scheidlinger, 1982.

———. (1982). *Focus on Group Psychotherapy*. Madison, Conn.: Int. Univ. Press.

———. (1991). Conceptual pluralism. *Int. J. Group Psychother.*, 41:217–226.

Schafer, R. (1990). The search for the common ground. *Int. J. Psychoanal.*, 41:49–52.

Skinner, R. (1976). *One Flesh, Separate Persons*. London: Constable.

Smith, M. L., Glass, C. G., & Miller, J. J. (1980). *The Benefits of Psychotherapy*. Baltimore: Johns Hopkins Univ. Press.

Spruiell, V. (1991). Being a psychoanalyst. Paper read at the annual meeting of the American Psychoanalytic Association.

Stern, D. N. (1985). *The Interpersonal World of the Infant*. New York: Basic Books.

Strupp, H. H. (1989). Psychotherapy. *Amer. Psychol.*, 44:717–724.

Sullivan, H. S. (1953). *The Interpersonal Theory of Psychiatry*. New York: Norton.

Tolpin, M. (1972). On the beginnings of the cohesive self. *Psychoanal. Study Child*, 26:316–352.

Torras de Beas, E. (1989). Projective identification and differentiation. *Int. J. Psychoanal.*, 70:265–274.

Turquet, P. M. (1975). Threats to identity in the large group. In *The Large Group*, ed. L. Kreeger. London: Constable.

Volkan, V. (1976). *Primitive Internalized Object Relations*. New York: Int. Univ. Press.

Von Bertalanffy, L. (1968). *General Systems Theory*. New York: Braziller.

Wallerstein, R. (1988). One psychoanalysis or many? *Int. J. Psychoanal.*, 69:5–21.

Whitaker, D., & Lieberman, M. (1964). *Psychotherapy through the Group Process*. New York: Atherton.

Whiteley, J. S., & Gordon, J. (1979). *Group Approaches in Psychiatry*. London: Routledge & Kegan Paul.

Winnicott, D. W. (1967). The location of cultural experiences. In *Playing and Reality*, pp. 112–121. Harmondsworth: Penguin.

Wolf, A., & Schwartz, E. K. (1962). *Psychoanalysis in Groups*. New York: Grune & Stratton.

Yalom, I. (1975). *The Theory and Practice of Group Psychotherapy*. New York: Int. Univ. Press.

Zalesnik, A., & Kets de Vries, M. F. R. (1975). *Power and the Corporate Mind*. Boston: Houghton Mifflin.

Zetzel, E. R. (1956). Current concepts of transference. *Int. J. Psychoanal.*, 37:369–376.

PART II

TECHNICAL ISSUES

5

THE PSYCHOANALYTIC PROCESS AND MECHANISMS OF THERAPEUTIC CHANGE

It is not difficult to understand why attempts to describe the psychoanalytic process are so fraught with difficulty. The subject is so complex that authors inevitably get lost unless they comprehend exactly what they are describing and have some idea of the problems involved in the attempt. In the hope of staying at least somewhat oriented, I will begin this chapter by defining "process" and clarifying (or at least describing) some of these problems.

I have defined "process" in some detail elsewhere (Pulver, 1988). According to the *Oxford English Dictionary,* it means: "a continuous action or succession of actions, taking place or carried on in a definite manner, and leading to the accomplishment of some result; a continuous operation or series of operations." A description of the psychoanalytic process, then, must at the very least include an account of the actions that take place, the participants (the analyst and the analysand), the analytic situation, the order and manner in which those actions occur, and, finally, the result.

Before examining those elements in more detail, I would like to clear up two common misconceptions. First, psychoanalysis and the psychoanalytic process are not the same thing. "Psychoanalysis" is a comprehensive term referring to a discipline developed by Freud. It includes a treatment method, a set of theories about the human mind, and a mode of investigating it. The term "psychoanalytic process" refers to what goes on during the treatment itself.

Second, psychoanalytic process is not the same thing as psychoanalytic technique. It is easy to see how the two might be confused (Arlow & Brenner, 1990), because psychoanalytic technique deals with what the analyst does and how he decides to do it. The psychoanalytic process certainly includes many elements of technique. But it also includes a great deal about what the patient does and what happens in the minds of both patient and analyst and in the relationship between them. Psychoanalytic technique concerns the way the analyst conducts the analysis, whereas the psychoanalytic process is a description of what happens when the analysis is properly conducted. Some aspects of technique will inevitably be considered in this chapter on process, but they will be discussed from the standpoint of the effects they have on the process and how those effects come about. Conversely, many aspects of what is properly the psychoanalytic process are also important in technique (the psychoanalytic situation, for example) and have been described in Chapter 1. In spite of this overlap, technique and process are different things. Each needs its own description.

PROBLEMS IN DESCRIBING THE PSYCHOANALYTIC PROCESS

Now to tackle some of the descriptive problems. The first is the problem of complexity. Freud's early descriptions of psychoanalysis implied that the process was fairly well understood and could be described rather easily. Unfortunately, the opposite is true. We have a great deal of difficulty describing biological processes, and psychological processes, even within a single individual, are still more abstruse. Psychological processes taking place between two or more individuals almost always defy more than the most superficial description (Boesky, 1990). For example, the simple act of formulating an interpretation, one small part of the psychoanalytic process, is itself comprised of an intricate network of complicated subprocesses. Yet we glibly talk about the psychoanalytic process as if any intelligent psychoanalyst ought to know what it is and be able to describe it.

This leads to a related problem: what depth of detail is appropriate or even possible in a description of the psychoanalytic process? A process is a series of changes. It is relatively easy to describe these changes in broad brush strokes but much harder to describe their details, the combinations of small changes that produce these major changes. We can, for example, say that the patient begins to regress as part of the psychoanalytic process. Describing the process of regression, however, is far more problematic. What changes are involved in regression? In what sequence do they occur, and is the sequence invariable? If one of the changes is a shift in the patient's sexual motivations toward those characteristic of earlier phases of development, just how does this happen? How much of his sexuality is involved? When we attempt to describe the psychoanalytic process, therefore, we must make a decision about the depth of detail we are going to aim for. Since we know more about some parts of the process than others, these decisions are very complex and are usually not spelled out. As a result, authors who appear to disagree about some aspect of the process may be simply describing different degrees of detail without realizing it.

A third problem, that of viewpoint, is also a thorny one. The changes inherent in any process can be seen from a number of viewpoints, in a way analogous to the viewpoints of metapsychology. For example, they can be described chronologically, according to the locale (analyst, patient, relationship) in which they occur, in terms of certain typical phenomena that arise during psychoanalysis, such as transference and resistance, or, on a more abstract level, according to the changes that take place in the id, ego, and superego. It is clearly desirable in undertaking such a description to specify one's viewpoint. Here, I have enough space to make only a rather feeble attempt at such specification. Ideally, a

complete description of the psychoanalytic process would include every viewpoint, but we are a long way from accomplishing such a goal. For the most part, I will be adopting an amalgam of viewpoints.

Several other questions are related to the concept of viewpoint. Should the psychoanalytic process be viewed from the vantage point of the patient alone or from that of the patient–analyst combination? Freud's early attitudes set the precedent for viewing the process as something occurring mainly in the psyche of the patient. The analyst perhaps had some influence on it but did not seem to play an essential part in its form or shape. Today we recognize the deep interaction that takes place between the analysand and the analyst, and much of our focus is on their relationship. Nevertheless, one still finds the psychoanalytic process being described in terms of the patient's psyche alone. The argument has come to be expressed in terms of the use of a "one-person" versus a "two-person" psychology in describing the process. Many analysts today use a two-person psychology, although the patient often continues to be the focus in actual descriptions of the process.

Closely related to this is the question of whether the psychoanalytic process occurs automatically. A few analysts (Menninger, 1958) seem to view it that way, and they are supported by Freud: "The analyst . . . sets in motion a process, that of the resolving of existing repressions. He can supervise this process, further it, remove obstacles in its way, and he can undoubtedly vitiate much of it. But on the whole, once begun, it goes its own way and does not allow either the direction it takes or the order in which it picks up its points to be prescribed for it" (Freud, 1912, p. 130). If this point of view is correct—if the process is determined by the nature of things—it would seem that there is little for the analyst to do except to stay out of the way. Most analysts today would disagree, however. They would feel that both patient and analyst play a role in creating the process; their argument would be about the degree. My own feeling is that for most patients, the process would probably be similar regardless of the particular analyst. With some patients, however, the personality and technique of the analyst are likely to have a much stronger impact on the process; whereas others seem to be remarkably impervious to the reality of the analyst. Furthermore, some analysts are likely to have more and others less impact on the process that takes place in their analyses. In short, a great deal of variation exists, and we should probably look upon the psychoanalytic process as being only somewhat innate. It is almost always influenced in its details, and often in its broader pattern, by the relationship between the patient and the analyst.

One final, vexing question must be considered: Is there one psychoanalytic process or many? This question is crucial. One might argue that there is an infinity of processes, since each patient–analyst pair is different. But we are talking about a broader, more general psychoanalytic process, abstracted from the many details of many individual analyses. It seems unquestionable that there are marked differences in the process of analyzing very different patients, such as, let us say, a borderline and a phobic. It also seems clear that varying constellations of dynamics, character traits, and techniques have important effects on the process. However, whether one can describe a general overall process common to all psychoanalyses or whether a number of different processes will ultimately be delineated is still obscure. I lean toward the latter view. Here, I will try to describe a psychoanalytic process which, while it may not be the only one, will be recognizable to most analysts as occurring in many, perhaps most, of their patients, particularly those with neuroses.

In spite of these difficulties, we must try to explore the psychoanalytic process as best we can. As Abrams (1987) points out, our attempts to delineate the psychoanalytic process draw our attention to "what is fundamental about the methods as well as the facts and theories of our discipline" (p. 441). Furthermore, a true understanding of the psychoanalytic process would go a long way toward resolving the dispute about just how psychoanalysis differs from psychoanalytic psychotherapy. It would be an immense practical help in assessing the progress of our patients. It would certainly solve innumerable issues of technique, since it seems reasonable to define good technique as anything that advances the psychoanalytic process.

THE PSYCHOANALYTIC PROCESS DESCRIBED

As Arlow and Brenner (1990) and others have pointed out, one's view of the psychoanalytic process depends heavily on one's view of the nature of pathogenesis. If, for example, the analyst feels that most of his patients have symptoms resulting from psychic conflict, he will tend to see the process in terms of the resolution of such conflict.[1] If, on the other hand, he sees the problems of his patients as due to deficits in ego development, self-structures,

or other areas, he will tend to see the process in terms of the repair of such deficits. Instead of trying to summarize the myriad ways others have thought about this,[2] I will give a relatively brief description of my view of the process that is likely to occur during the analysis of a patient whose problems are predominantly due to conflict and are manifested as either symptoms or character traits. The patient is probably relatively analyzable and in analysis is in a fairly standard analytic situation (lying on a couch and free-associating in sessions that take place four or five times weekly). He is with an analyst who is typical of the average American analyst of this day and age—that is, one who has been trained rather classically in an ego-psychological approach but is flexible enough to embrace aspects of other schools that he has found useful (Pulver, 1993). I will refer to some other theories of pathogenesis in this discussion, but my emphasis throughout will be on conflict. I would guess that the process I am describing often takes place with other types of patients in other types of analysis, but I am not making that claim here. I will try to include those aspects of the process upon which there is general agreement, such as what the patient and the analyst do, how they interact with each other, and what happens intrapsychically in each of them. Where these matters have already been described elsewhere in this volume, I will only touch on them here. I will discuss some of the more important facets of the process, such as regression, transference, and the mechanism of psychic change, in more detail, and certain subprocesses such as resolution of the transference neurosis and working through in lesser detail. My essential aim is to present a view of the psychoanalytic process as seen by the average American analyst, an eclectic view rather than a perfectly consistent and unified one. The latter, I fear, must be left for the future.

THE OVERALL PROCESS

1. *The pathogenic conflicts consist of drive and other motivations and the prohibitions against these motivations. They usually have their origin early in life. The analytic setting and procedure encourage the emergence of these infantile conflicts in the form of their later derivatives.* When the patient lies down on the couch and talks about whatever is on his mind, what he talks about will be influenced by a combination of conscious, preconscious, and uncon-

---

1. As in Ch. 1, "he," "his," "him," are to be understood as referring to either sex.

2. Interested readers will find a good collection of articles on the topic in the *Psychoanalytic Quarterly,* 59(4) (1990).

scious motivations. (When I speak of motivation in this chapter, I am referring to all motivations, not just to drives and drive derivatives. Motivations of any sort may be involved in conflict, and I thus use the term in its broadest sense.) The patient may, for example, begin telling the analyst the story of his traumatic childhood, with the conscious intent of giving the analyst as much information as possible about himself. Preconsciously he may have determined to approach the analysis in an orderly fashion, and unconsciously he may be hoping that the analyst will feel sorry for him.

2. *Because these conflicts arouse painful feelings, the patient tries to keep them out of consciousness. The methods he uses to keep mental content from awareness are called defenses. When manifested in the treatment as either subtle or overt oppositional behavior, these defenses are called resistances.* From the beginning, some of what comes to the patient's mind will arise from motivations about which he is conflicted. The patient will therefore withhold it, distract himself from it, or in one way or another protect himself against feeling or revealing it. The analyst will point out the manifestations and causes of this resistance as tactfully as possible. These interpretations will gradually help the patient see and accept what he has previously been afraid to see, and to understand how he has avoided seeing it.

3. *Under the continuing influence of the setting and procedure, regression occurs.* The patient gradually begins functioning psychically at an earlier level than he does when he is not in the session. With this regression, earlier conflictual motivations become activated.

4. *As the relationship intensifies and the derivatives of the conflict become more infantile, they become increasingly focused on the analyst (the transference). As this focus increases in intensity, a transference neurosis is said to have developed.* As the analysis proceeds, the feelings of the patient and the analyst about each other become stronger. Some of those feelings in the patient will be based on feelings he had toward earlier important people in his life; this is called the "transference." Their counterpart in the analyst is called the "countertransference." The transference gradually intensifies until it reaches a point at which the analyst can be considered one of the most important people in the patient's life. At that time we say a transference neurosis has developed.

5. *During all this, the analyst interprets aspects of the conflict as it seems useful to do so, and the patient works to understand the interpretation. Gradual understanding leads toward increasing access to the stronger and more primitive aspects of the*

conflict and toward more effective and adaptive methods of handling it. After the development of the transference neurosis, the conflicts reappear in a multitude of derivative forms and are interpreted and further understood, a period called "working through." This period is one in which various aspects of the patient's conflicts in more or less regressed form manifest themselves in many different ways. They are expressed most frequently as they occur in the transference, but at other times as they occur in the patient's everyday life and as they occurred in childhood. As they are interpreted in their many guises, the patient gradually becomes aware of and accepts them.

6. *When working through has progressed sufficiently, the analyst and the patient agree on a date for ending the analysis, and the termination stage begins. This stimulates further working through, particularly of conflicts connected with separation. This working through continues until the end of the analysis.* More adaptive ways are found to handle the motivations that had previously been unacceptable. The analyst is gradually seen in more realistic as well as transference terms ("the resolution of the transference neurosis"), symptoms abate, undesirable character traits are changed, and finally patient and analyst agree that ending the analysis ("termination") is feasible. During this termination stage, analysis proceeds as usual, with focus both on old issues and on new issues stirred up by the prospect of termination. It is negotiated, and the analysis is over.

The psychoanalytic process outlined above focuses on conflict. The description is both oversimplified and idealized, but I hope that it gives enough of an overview that, as each of the major subprocesses is discussed in more detail, a relatively clear picture of the psychoanalytic process will emerge.

IMPORTANT SUBPROCESSES OF THE PSYCHOANALYTIC PROCESS[3]

Resistance
When the patient first lies down on the couch, he has some idea, more or less sophisticated, of what he and the analyst are attempting to do. His part in their joint endeavor has been explained to him: he is to say everything that comes into his mind. However, he has had no experience of analysis and thus has no real notion of how he is supposed to participate or

3. The next three topics—resistance, transference, and countertransference—are covered in detail in Chapters 6–8. I will mention only a few points here which seem particularly pertinent to the psychoanalytic process.

just where to begin. He is usually beset with anxieties, worrying consciously about trying to accomplish he knows not what and unconsciously about any number of fearful eventualities. Nevertheless, under the impact of his own desire to get better and with some reassurance, a bit of education, and occasional interpretation from the analyst, the patient begins to free-associate. He does this in his own way: coherently, fragmentedly, volubly, laconically. There are as many styles of free association as there are individual patients. All, however, are characterized by a paradoxical phenomenon. While the patient consciously wishes to work with the analyst to get the job done and is more or less determined to say everything that comes to mind, sooner or later he will find that he is no longer able or willing to do so. The patient, sometimes knowingly but more often not, will begin "resisting" the fundamental rule. Noncompliance of patients is familiar to all physicians: patients do not take their medicine, they do not do their exercise. But only in psychoanalysis is resistance a ubiquitous and necessary phenomenon. The explanation is perhaps obvious. We have asked the patient to free-associate in order to discover those feelings that are causing his emotional problems. But he is unaware of these feelings, precisely because they cause him so much distress, and because he does not want to be aware of them. From the beginning, then, free association is an impossible task. At the same time that the patient is working with us, he is resisting us.[4]

The timing of this resistance and the way it manifests itself are quite idiosyncratic. Some patients will be unable to utter a word from the moment they lie down on the couch. Others free-associate rather well until certain topics are touched upon. Entire sessions may go by with little evidence of resistance, or there may be an ebb and flow of resistance within an individual session. Resistances may be quite overt ("I know how important it is to say everything that comes to mind, but I think I should warn you that there is one thing about me which I am never under any circumstance going to tell you"). They may be covert but obvious ("I came late today because I simply had to finish my exercises"). Or—and these are usually the most difficult to deal with—they may be almost silent, as with the compliant patient who productively and affectively free-associates for months but does so for the purpose of pleasing the analyst, with no impact whatsoever on the analytic process. Perhaps the most important resistances are

4. I have given only one of the many reasons for resistance. Freud (1926) lists a number of others, and in Chapter 6 McLaughlin describes them in some detail.

the transference resistances, which are described more fully below.

All of the above implies that resistance is undesirable. And when the aim of psychoanalysis was to discover unconscious content, resistance *was* undesirable. Freud, even after giving up hypnosis, tried to overcome resistance when he encountered it by using the prestige and authority of the analyst. Not until the Classical Period was well under way did it become clear that resistance is both a valuable and an essential part of the analytic process. It is the patient's way of dealing with distressing feelings, thoughts, and fantasies in a relationship. It is just as important for him to understand these aspects of himself as it is for him to understand what he is protecting himself from. His ability to continue his ongoing task of self-analysis after the formal analysis is finished depends on this. Realizing this, the experienced analyst has a different attitude toward manifestations of resistance from the beginner, who invariably frets about the "interference" with the analysis that the resistance seems to be causing. With more experience, the analyst will still feel a surge of annoyance, as is natural when any working relationship turns oppositional. But he will feel far more intensely a surge of interest. A new development is being heralded: here is another opportunity to deepen the relationship and further the analytic process.

In a sense, understanding resistance can be considered even more important than understanding unconscious content. Failure to understand a particular unconscious fantasy will lead to unresolved conflict in what might be considered a quite successful analysis when taken in its entirety. Failure to understand an important resistance, on the other hand, may lead to impasse. Note the emphasis on understanding. The idea of "handling" or "managing" resistance is a holdover from the era of the analyst as the objective, authoritarian therapist. Nowadays we think in terms of helping the patient understand the resistance. While there are many ways of doing this (some have been discussed in Chapter 1 on technique), the overall principle is that the analyst helps the patient recognize the particular manner in which he is resisting, the context in which the resistance first appeared, how that helps him remain unaware of some important feelings, and what those feelings may be. Further steps, such as the giving up of identifications or the relinquishment of infantile longings and objects, are often part of resistance analysis, but the essential steps are all aimed at understanding.

The fate of resistance in the analysis is an important aspect of the psychoanalytic process. Resistance, it must be remembered, is the behavioral equivalent of defense. Resistances may change according to the particular conflict being dealt with. It is not unusual, for example, to see a patient who volubly tries to distract the analyst when he is dealing with hostile wishes but falls silent when sexual material comes up. Neither resistance nor defenses disappear with analysis. For the most part, the patient retains his characteristic style of defense but becomes familiar with it and with the kind of conflict it usually relates to and better able to note and understand what is bothering him. Furthermore, as the conflictual motivations are more accepted, the need to resist them diminishes. In general, one might say that the amount of resistance tends to diminish as the patient understands himself better. However, defenses, and thus resistance, are ready to be mobilized whenever unacceptable impulses arise, and an ebb and flow of resistance is characteristic not just of an analysis throughout its duration but in life before and after analysis as well.

Transference and the Transference Neurosis

If any single thing characterizes the psychoanalytic process, it is the development of an intense transference. The classical definition of transference is a narrow one (Moore & Fine, eds., 1990): "The displacement of patterns of feelings, thoughts, and behavior, originally experienced in relation to significant figures during childhood, onto a person involved in a current interpersonal relationship." In the case of analysis, the "person" is the analyst. Transference thus defined is a reaction to the analyst which is inappropriate, emotionally intense, always consciously or unconsciously ambivalent, sometimes capricious, and tenacious (Greenson, 1967). However, other reactions of the patient to the analyst also have these characteristics. Among them are characterological reactions, which are general modes of interpersonal behavior rather than specific displacements to the analyst, and, perhaps even more strikingly, projections of aspects of the patient's self that he finds intolerable. This has led to a looser use of the term "transference" to refer to all the patient's emotional reactions to the analyst, particularly if they appear to be inappropriate. Furthermore, in recent years, still other behaviors of the patient to the analyst have been called transference (Kohut, 1971; Fourcher, 1979). These, while not strictly fitting the definitions above, nevertheless shape the patient–analyst relationship in ways that are vital for us to understand. For instance, as De Jonghe et al. (1991) have pointed out, displacement implies the existence of thoughts and feelings toward a separate object. The classical definition of transference centers around displacement and therefore neglects those aspects of relationships that took place in the early

years, before complete self–object differentiation takes place. Yet those aspects are often replicated in the patient–analyst relationship and have profound effects on it in the form of what are now commonly called the narcissistic, separation-individuation, and other pre-oedipal transferences. It would seem most useful to use the word *transference* broadly to include all aspects of the patient's emotional relationship to the analyst that arise predominantly from within the patient. These may not all be displacements from early objects.

Nothing in the foregoing should be taken to support the old view of the analyst as an objective observer rather than as a participant in a relationship. Currently we recognize that little if any of the patient's experience of the analyst, which includes the transference, arises solely from within the patient. To varying degrees, the patient is not only repeating the past in his experience with the analyst but is also eliciting behavior from the analyst which confirms that experience. Even constructivists, who emphasize the impact of the actual relationship on the experience, would, I think, allow that at certain times the patient's experience arises more from a repetition of the past (the transference) than from the analyst's confirmatory behavior. The same, of course, can be said about the experience of the patient by the analyst (countertransference).

The transference neurosis is a concept currently in debate. Freud (1917) held early on that during all analyses a development arose in which "the whole of [the patient's] illness's new production is concentrated upon a single point—his relation to the doctor. . . . We are no longer concerned with the patient's earlier illness but with a newly created and transformed neurosis which has taken the former's place. All of the patient's symptoms have abandoned their original meaning and have taken on a new sense which lies in a relation to the transference" (p. 444). Few would now hold that this happens in all analyses, or that the infantile neurosis is revived *in toto* surrounding the person of the analyst. Opinions range from those who wish to abandon the concept altogether, viewing the phenomena as merely intense transference (Cooper, 1987), to those who feel that some transference structure beyond mere intense transference arises and that such a structure should be recognized and named, even if Freud's description is not necessarily applicable. Current opinion would seem to favor the former view (Panel, 1993).

Countertransference

Just as patients develop transference to their analysts, so analysts develop transference to their patients. From the narrow meaning of specific transference feelings, conscious or unconscious, toward a patient, the term has been broadened by some to refer to any feeling that an analyst has toward his patient. Some of these have been mentioned in the chapter on technique under the analyst's attitude (Chapter 1). Awareness of these feelings, an understanding of their origins, particularly their intrapsychic versus interactional aspects, and an appreciation of their value in helping to understand the patient are all of extreme importance and current interest. Since Blum and Goodman deal with these aspects in Chapter 8, I will not describe them further here; but the reader should not be misled by the brevity of this paragraph, which is in inverse proportion to the importance of the topic for psychoanalytic technique, especially in view of our increasing awareness of the part played by the analyst in the relationship. This is particularly relevant to the question of enactment of the countertransference, which I will elaborate upon when discussing the mechanism of therapeutic change below.

Regression

Regression is one of the major subprocesses of the psychoanalytic process. Freud's early topographic use of the term was soon replaced by two other, closely related concepts: temporal regression and formal regression. Temporal regression is said to occur when things that the individual would ordinarily think about in his more mature moments ("later psychic content") are replaced by things which he thought about in earlier states of development. Formal regression occurs when the way in which the individual thinks, the form of his thinking, shifts from a form characteristic of later development (more secondary process, for example) to a form characteristic of earlier psychic development (for example, primary process). Currently, the two concepts are conflated, and regression is thought of simply as "a return to a more developmentally immature level of mental functioning" (Moore & Fine, eds., 1990). Any type of mental functioning, on any level of abstraction, may be said to have regressed. Thus, all of the following would be called regression: (1) a toddler who had rather easily achieved bowel and bladder control lost control after his baby sister was brought home from the hospital; (2) a skier who had learned parallel skiing quite well and was taking the intermediate slopes with ease ventured onto a rather steep slope and immediately began snowplowing; (3) an analytic patient (Mr. B. in Chapter 1), who had been separated from his mother as a young child for an extended period of time, began crying uncontrollably as he lay on the couch and remembered an operation he had when she was away.

Arlow and Brenner (1964) note that "(1) Regression is a universal tendency of mental functioning. (2) Primitive forms of mental activity are persistent and may exist side by side with more mature forms of mental functioning. (3) Many forms of regression, perhaps most, are transient and reversible. (4) As a rule regression is neither global, nor uniform. It usually affects particular aspects of the instinctual life, or of ego or superego functioning, rather than the whole of either, and what functions it does affect, are affected to different degrees" (pp. 71–72).

Regression can be a normal as well as a pathological psychoanalytic process. It can be voluntarily as well as involuntarily induced. As I came to the point in writing this chapter at which I needed some examples of regression, I did not search my memory in an organized, secondary process manner. Instead, I let my mind wander and began having images of the toddler, the skier, and Mr. B. For the moment I had intentionally regressed, a phenomenon that Kris (1951) called "regression in the service of the ego." A similarly useful regression occurs in psychoanalysis, facilitated by a number of factors, some derived from the illness, some from the psychoanalytic situation itself. Most of the factors are related to the reproduction of some aspect of a childlike state, although some are due to interference with the everyday stimuli the ego needs to continue functioning at a mature level. Among these factors are:

(1) The illness itself causes some regression. Pain, suffering, fatigue, and strong affect all tend to interfere with more recently developed psychic functioning. Our patients are suffering and are thus regressed.

(2) Psychoanalysis entails the frustration of many wishes (even though others are gratified), and this frustration, like the pain and suffering mentioned above, leads to regression.

(3) In psychoanalysis the patient has come to an analyst for help. Feeling the need for help and the very act of turning to someone for help promote regression.

(4) The analytic situation itself contains powerful regressive forces. The patient reclines in what is often felt to be an infantile position. His restricted visual field and auditory input, and particularly the relative lack of input from the analyst, entail a form of sensory deprivation, which promotes regression. Macalpine (1950) discusses this aspect of the treatment in some detail, although, interestingly, she does not use the word *regression*.

(5) The natural self-preoccupation of the analytic task detracts from the patient's ordinary interest and interaction with the environment, which promote everyday psychic functioning.

(6) Finally, the fundamental method of the treatment (free association and the intense relationship with the analyst) interferes with ordinary mental functioning and promotes regression.

There are those who think that insight alone is the major mechanism of psychoanalytic change, and others who feel that the promotion of development is also important, but all agree that regression plays a vital role in the process. Many of the unconscious memories and fantasies involved in pathological conflict arose during periods of earlier mental functioning. Regression activates these feelings and tends to bring them into the transference and make them topics for analysis. Furthermore, many of these conflicts are cognitively and memorially organized in more primitive ways. This, and the fact that certain defenses are weakened during periods of regression, make this material more easily accessible in regressed states.

Regression, it should be noted, can be a two- (or perhaps three-) edged sword. A certain amount of regression is desirable in analysis, but the patient must be able to control it in order for it to be useful. There are patients who are unable to permit themselves to regress, and others in whom the regression gets out of hand, becomes "malignant" (Balint, 1968), and needs special management, if it can be managed at all. The topic is an important one, but it is more a matter of technique than process, and I will not deal with it here.[5]

The Resolution of the Transference Neurosis

By the end of the analysis, a rather dramatic change has happened within the transference. Over a period of several years, the patient slowly begins to see more and more of the reality of the analyst, to see him unidealized, to see him as an individual with kindly intent but with the same idiosyncrasies as any other human. Unrealistic feelings, fantasies, desires, and fears from the past persist. Often, when they are stirred up by events or mistakes, they persist with frightening intensity. But they gradually become fewer, less profound, and more easily understood and handled. This shift has come to be known as the "resolution of the transference." The term is perhaps unfortunate, since it implies the complete disappearance of transference feelings. However, the phenomenon itself is a crucial accompaniment of change in other areas of the patient's psyche and one of the heralds of the period of termination.

5. For more details, interested readers can refer to *Psychoanalytic Inquiry,* 1(1) (1981).

THE MECHANISMS OF PSYCHOANALYTIC CHANGE

How does psychoanalysis actually cause change? Cooper (1989) described the situation well: "Analysts differ in their views of the therapeutic power assigned to these diverse aspects of the analytic process. It seems clear that, depending on the analyst's theoretical persuasion, different combinations of the new cognitions, internalizations, insights, experiences . . . will lead to therapeutic change in the form of a resumption of interrupted development, establishment of a meaningful and coherent internal history, changed internal structures and representations, new feelings of safety, and altered defensive postures, belief systems, wishes, and relationships." Clearly, multiple factors are at work and need to be discussed.

First, however, let us consider what "psychoanalytic change" actually means. For the past forty years, "structural change" has been the shibboleth used to designate such change, particularly to differentiate it from the change that takes place in psychoanalytic psychotherapy. Structural change is a theoretical term that denotes change taking place within the psychic structures of id, ego, and superego and in the relationships between them. Werman (1989) and Abend (1990) have pointed out the many problems the term engenders, including the implication that changes in psychic structures occur only in psychoanalysis and an inherent ambiguity as to just what these changes are. Another problem is that analysts of different theoretical persuasions emphasize aspects of change in abstract terms that they find germane to their theories. As Meissner (1991) points out:

Ego psychologists emphasize the alteration of psychic structure on the basis of conflict resolution and internalization; self psychologists also emphasize changes in structure, but see it more in terms of transmuting internalizations resulting in renewed psychic growth; hermeneuticists focus on the more comprehensive and coherent narrative of the self; the object relations view stresses the modifications of the inner representational world and the correspondingly more adaptive relations with external objects; and the information-processing approach envisions change of false belief systems and other cognitive apprehensions.

At first glance, this disparity of ideas seems dismaying. How can we talk about the mechanisms of change when psychoanalysts seem to have so many different theories about what change actually takes place? On reflection, much of this difficulty probably arises from trying to describe goals and change in theoretical terms. It is understandable, then, that currently there is a growing tendency to look at psychological change in more clinical terms while still adhering to one's own theoretical constructs. When change is spelled out phenomenologically, I suspect that the goals of most psychoanalysts will turn out to be very similar. Resolution of conflict will turn out to be accompanied by renewed psychic growth, a coherent narrative of the self, modifications of the internal representational world, and the changing of false belief systems. This kind of comparative morphology of the goals of the various psychoanalytic schools badly needs to be carried out in detail.

The specific phenomenological changes we can expect from psychoanalysis obviously depend on the individual patient and his unique interaction with his particular analyst. For purposes of discussion, let us simply look at some very broad changes that we expect to occur in a successful analysis. The patient's symptoms will decrease or disappear. He will feel better about himself in a very profound way, and his internal picture of others as well as his relations with them will improve. He will be more aware and more tolerant of his feelings, which he will feel more deeply and with more pleasure than he did previously.

How do these and similar changes occur? Here again I must begin with some general principles. Paramount is the realization that a search for "the way" psychoanalysis works is as foolish as a quest for "the right interpretation." A very intricate system is in operation, and change comes from all parts of the system. In certain patients, some modes of change are more important than others, and we do not yet have more than an inkling of which modes are important in whom. Almost all specific attempts to describe the mechanism of cure ("the relationship," the "holding environment," "resolution of conflict," "abreaction") emphasize one aspect of the system at the expense of others.

A second point is that in each of the major "mechanisms" of change subprocesses play an important role. Furthermore, these subprocesses are often the same, or at least overlapping, in supposedly different mechanisms, even when apparently differing techniques characteristic of different psychoanalytic schools are used. For example, internalization, the process of taking some aspect of another person into oneself and in some way becoming like that person, is regarded as important by those who feel that insight is the main road to cure and by those who feel that the experience with the analyst predominates. Learning, conditioning, and mourning are other subprocesses.

Learning takes place in a number of ways during a psychoanalysis, yet psychoanalysis does not have a good learning theory. To explain its mechanism of cure, it must develop one or must adopt the best features of the theories of others. The false cognitive belief theory of pathogenesis of Weiss and Sampson and their colleagues (1986) is an example of a theory that highlights the role of learning as a mechanism of therapeutic change, but it is not a comprehensive learning theory.

There are several kinds of conditioning, and they operate in different ways at different times with different patients and analysts. There have been very few attempts to integrate what psychology knows about conditioning into standard psychoanalytic theory.

The relinquishment of old self and object ties involves mourning, a complex subprocess that is rarely discussed as a part of therapeutic change.

Even these few subprocesses are complex. Many others could be named, and a good theory of the mechanism of therapeutic change will require an extensive description of all of them. Here, I have space only to focus on some of the major processes related to change.

Abreaction. Historically, the emotional upheaval that accompanies the recovery of repressed memories was considered the major mechanism of therapeutic results. Under an archaic name (catharsis) and an even more archaic theory (dammed-up affects got "discharged"), abreaction was considered to be *the* way psychoanalysis worked. It still plays an important role in many psychoanalyses, but our theory about the way it works has become more complex. It is clear that reliving a traumatic event, with its full affect, in the presence of someone who is seen as ensuring the patient's safety reduces the experience of helplessness that originally caused the event to be traumatic. Through a gradual process of conditioning, the patient feels less and less helpless during the experience, is able to bring his previously paralyzed cognitive faculties to bear, and develops a sense that in the same situation he would now know how to handle himself. He has, that is to say, "mastered the trauma." This is never the entire content of a psychoanalysis, but it often plays a role. The deep emotion that is felt during these moments and during the entire transference experience has been seen by some (Pine, 1993) to have a therapeutic effect by "destabilizing" the conflictual structure and giving the patient an opportunity to restabilize it in a different and more adaptive pattern.

Insight. All explanations of the mechanism of change in psychoanalysis include insight as an important factor. This is in keeping with the universal emphasis on attaining understanding as the prime task of both participants in the analytic relationship. By insight, of course, we refer to "emotional insight," a deep affective understanding, not to the purely cognitive comprehension the word may connote in ordinary usage. Emotional insight *includes* the cognitive understanding of an event or dynamics or interaction but is accompanied by the ability to experience all the feelings surrounding the situation, as well as by the capacity to make and utilize connections between what is now understood and other aspects of one's behavior. From the prehistory of psychoanalysis, when Breuer and Freud were attempting to help their patients recall buried memories connected with present symptoms, the role of insight was implicit. They wanted their patients not only to recall and relive traumatic experiences but also to understand their connection with current symptoms. As psychoanalysis developed, through each of its theoretical shifts, a mutual endeavor to achieve insight remained the hallmark of psychoanalytic technique. The acquisition of insight remains the sine qua non of psychoanalytic change today.

Insight works in manifold ways. Awareness is of crucial importance in the higher-order evaluative, affective, judgmental, and synthesizing processes that are involved in our feelings, decisions, and behavior. If I know I am feeling sad because my children are no longer as interested in me as they used to be, I can plan to reinvolve myself with them, or find other sources of love, or do something else to ease the pain. If I know I am angry because I was insulted, I can plan the best course of action to handle the insult. If I know that the reason I feel my wife doesn't love me is that she doesn't care for me in quite the same way as my mother did, I can attempt to change my expectations and relieve the hurt I feel. Without insight, without knowing what I am feeling and believing, I am helpless to make plans and take action to deal with unconscious feelings that distress me.

But the ways of insight are not quite so simple. Let us look at another example. If I become deeply aware that I hate my father and know all the reasons, realize that I feel guilty about hating him and grasp all the reasons, and recognize that I keep my hate out of awareness and comprehend all the ways in which I do that, then I can change in ways that go beyond making plans and taking action. I may realize that the reasons for my hate are not warranted, and the hate may diminish. I may come to understand some of the reasons he was the way he was and to forgive him. I may realize that in fact he did not take my mother away, or perhaps see that he did but come to know that I can get my own woman. I

may recognize my wish for a better father and be set free to mourn the fact that I did not and will never have one. Insofar as the hate has to do with my own feelings of inferiority, as I see my father in a more realistic and less omnipotent light and feel better about myself, the hate may diminish. Furthermore, as the hate diminishes, I feel less guilty, since much of my guilt was due to baleful fantasies I had about him. Inasmuch as the hate had a realistic basis, I feel more justified and, therefore, less guilty. Inasmuch as the guilt arose from my acceptance of my father's values or those of others ("Thou shalt honor thy father and mother"), I can adopt my own values and feel less guilty. Inasmuch as my defenses are based on identifications, I can see the needs behind the identifications and modify them. Inasmuch as the hate and guilt are less and my ability to tolerate affects improves, I need defend less against my anger, and I can express it in more appropriate ways. And finally, I am more familiar with all my feelings and the way I handle them. I know why I get symptoms, can trace them to current stimuli and their past origins, and I feel better. And all the above is basically due to greater emotional understanding—that is, to insight. Insight does not automatically change things (Rangell, 1981), but it puts change within the patient's power.

Historical versus narrative truth. Insight often implies historical truth—that is, an understanding of something that really happened, something that, with enough effort, could probably be confirmed by others. We recognize these days that history to a large degree takes place in the eyes of the historian. Our perception and understanding of events are deeply influenced by the way our own thinking has been shaped in the past and by the views and opinions of others. Nevertheless, one's perception, however influenced by internal factors, also depends more or less on external events, independent of the observer. The concept of insight, inasmuch as it has to do with the patient's emotional knowledge of his reaction to events and people in his life, implies that those events really happened, that they contain historical truth (Spence, 1982; Schafer, 1983). I have described the therapeutic effects of understanding the emotionally important historical events in one's life. Recently, as part of the hermeneutic approach to psychoanalysis, the impact of our own contribution to our perception of the world has been emphasized. The claim has been made that the therapeutic action of psychoanalysis resides primarily in the construction of a narrative about the patient's life and feelings that is deeply believed by both the patient and the analyst. It may not be historically true, but it contains narrative truth. It helps the patient by giving a sense of organization and meaning to his life that he did not have previously. Furthermore, he has the sense of being believed and supported in this world view by someone he trusts and values, his analyst. Most analysts, although they realize that there is some validity to this viewpoint, disagree with it in essence. They know that some of what they and the patient end up believing may not correspond exactly to historical reality, but they feel that by and large it reflects the patient's real experience as determined to a significant degree by his actual experiences.

The role of a new relationship. Insight has for years been seen as the most significant, if not the only, mechanism of therapeutic change in psychoanalysis. However, many analysts today feel that other factors also play a role: identification with the analyst, empathy, the experience of safety, the provision of a holding environment, a new relationship with an appropriate selfobject, and nonspecific support by the analyst, to name just a few. Almost all these can be subsumed under the idea of the effect of the relationship with the analyst as a new object. Which is most important, insight or the relationship with a new object? Or, perhaps a better question, what is the relative importance of each? I sense that most analysts now regard the experience of the analyst as a new object at least on a par with insight. Writing from a Kleinian perspective, Strachey (1934) described the patient's introjection of the analyst's more benign superego. This description highlights the difference between insight and the analyst as a new object. The patient, whose superego is telling him, "Your sexual feelings are bad," enters into an intense relationship with the analyst, who, unlike his old objects, implies that his sexual feelings are not bad but are feelings to be understood, just like all other feelings. Gradually, Strachey says, the patient introjects the analyst's values. While insight is crucial in this mechanism, it is not enough. The patient must experience that the analyst, like his father, feels that his sexual feelings are bad and gradually come to recognize that this experience is just not so. The role that insight plays in this recognition of and identification with the analyst's values is highly variable. The patient may come to realize that he is seeing the analyst as he saw his father, or he may simply recognize that his picture of the analyst does not quite correspond with reality. In all this, the role of insight into the transference as well as the new experience with the analyst is crucial. Were the analyst simply to reassure the patient from the beginning that his sexual feelings were not bad, the patient might change superficially, but it would be at best a temporary cure by suggestion. Conversely, were the patient to read before his analysis a psychological evaluation written by the analyst indicating that he felt his sexual feelings were bad because he identified with his father, it is unlikely that his feelings would change in the same way they would through the combination of insight and identification with the analyst, even if he were to appreciate the psychological evaluation in a deeply emotional way.

Interestingly, Strachey's rather revolutionary emphasis on the role of a new object was accepted with little controversy. Nevertheless, the role of insight as the single crucial factor remained the mainstream view. Those who thought of the analyst as a new object either remained within the American mainstream, with their views on this point relatively disregarded (Ferenczi and his followers), or became relative outcasts (Klein and her followers, Rado, and Horney). It was not until Loewald (1960) advocated the importance of the analyst as a new object that the mainstream began to change. Loewald emphasized the promotion of development by both the analyst and the analytic situation:

> We know from analytic as well as from life experience that new spurts of self-development may be intimately connected with such 'regressive' rediscoveries of oneself as may occur through the establishment of new object-relationships, and this means: new discovery of 'objects.' I say new discovery of objects, and not discovery of new objects, because the essence of such new object-relationships is the opportunity they offer for rediscovery of the early paths of the development of object-relations, leading to a new way of relating to objects as well as of being and relating to oneself. [p. 18]

This change was undoubtedly facilitated by the growing influence of Klein and the neo-Kleinians, of Kohut (1984), and of respected analysts such as Stone (1961) and Modell (1978), all of whom emphasized the importance of the new relationship, particularly for sicker patients.

Transference–countertransference enactments. Another controversy related to the mechanism of therapeutic change involves the degree to which the enactment of unconscious conflicts (transference–countertransference enactments) occurs between the patient and the analyst, and whether or not this is desirable. Many analysts feel that the neutrality of the analyst, his ability to resist becoming involved in transference–countertransference enactments, is the essential factor that moves the process forward (Pine, 1993). These analysts feel that such enactments, while they often occur, are usually destructive to the psychoanalytic process or, at the very least, inessential. The analyst should be constantly alert for them and avoid them as much as possible. Others feel that appropriate involvement by the analyst in the relationship always leads to transference–countertransference enactments and that the analysis of such enactments actually propels the psychoanalytic process (Sandler, 1976).

I believe these two viewpoints are not incompatible. In many analyses, the analyst will maintain sufficient neutrality to enable the patient to continue his analytic work in spite of the occurrence of transference–countertransference enactments. Analyses of that sort will not focus on the enactments but will proceed essentially as Pine describes. In many instances, however, analysis of the ubiquitous transference–countertransference enactments will be more or less the focus of interpretation. This will happen when the patient's narcissistic sensitivity is so great that the analyst's attempt to interpret as transference a patient's conjectures about the way the analyst is feeling, without acknowledging the possibility that such a feeling may in fact exist, is seen by the patient as denial or criticism; and when the transference–countertransference enactment is of such proportions (blatant countertransference acting out, for example) that even a reasonably trusting patient is unable to make allowances for them. Other factors undoubtedly are part of what to me is the obvious clinical observation that in some analyses there is a major focus on such enactments, while in others they seem to play a relatively minor role.

Empathy. The actual mechanism by which the patient's relationship with the analyst as a new object produces changes deserves further elaboration. A brief description of the role of empathy, one aspect of the process, may be helpful in clarifying it.

Empathy means many things to many people. I use it here in its self-psychological sense of signifying "a fitting and appropriate perception of and response to the patient's feelings and needs" (Moore & Fine, eds., 1990, p. 67). In the regression that leads to the transference neurosis, the patient is in an intense emotional relationship, which he unconsciously feels will be the same in all emotional particulars as the relationship he had with his parents. As the analyst, maintaining his neutral but empathic and compassionately interested stance, interprets, the patient gains insight into many of his feelings and fantasies from earlier times. At the same time, he is experiencing and introjecting a picture of himself in an affective connection with the analyst and his attitude of warmth, interest, and a desire to help. This is

very different from the affective connection he experienced with his parents. As he takes the new picture in, his image of himself changes, as does his picture of his objects. He is no longer only a bad little boy with bad sexual fantasies about an angry mother. He is also a person with understandable and even good and enjoyable fantasies toward an accepting person. In the working through, this more positive self-representation begins to predominate, and his attitudes and behavior change.

But this is only one aspect of the importance of empathy. As the self psychologists emphasize, no analyst is perfectly empathically attuned. All analysts make mistakes. The analyst is constantly aware of the possibility of his empathic failure and is looking for responses to it by the patient. When he finds them, he admits his role in the empathic disruption and explores the patient's reaction to it. This is in sharp contrast to the patient's previous experience, in which the important people in his life denied their imperfections and failed to empathize with his reactions to them. It is the exploration of the relationship in this safe emotional context that permits the patient to internalize it, to gain real understanding of what has happened, and to put that understanding to use. Note that insight remains crucial. Were the analyst not consistently trying to understand and point out the displacements from the bad mother, he would quickly be endowed with these characteristics, and the patient would have no sense of his acceptance and warmth. If, on the other hand, he did not just as consistently look for his own empathic failures and "analyze" (admit and explore) them, the patient would feel his own view of reality disavowed and depreciated. In both cases, the patient would not feel understood and would experience all the hostility and distance that such misunderstanding engenders.

The role of empathy in producing therapeutic change is certainly more complex than I have described. Furthermore, there are many other things transpiring between patient and analyst that support the importance of the therapeutic role of the new object experience. A consistent search for insight into his own and his patient's perceptions and misperceptions and a willingness to bring them into the analysis are crucial on the part of the analyst. Such an attitude results in change in the patient, some of which is due to the insight itself and some to processes relating to the relationship. Usually, neither the patient nor the analyst is aware of or understands those processes when they are happening, but they can often be described later. The importance of further exploration of these mechanisms is obvious.

The patient's inherent drive toward integration. All the above mechanisms have focused on the analyst or the analyst–patient interaction. This is important, but it might be seen as giving short shrift to factors within the patient that in their own right lead to change. As Moore has pointed out (1994), the patient as well as the analyst listens to his free associations and processes them on all levels of consciousness. He links past and present, dreams, fantasy, thoughts, and behavior. Using symbol and metaphor and the synthetic function of the ego, as well as the analyst's interpretations and his experience of the interaction, he achieves via his own mental processes the insight and integration needed to relieve his conflicts and dysphoria. The analytic process is indeed the product of a joint endeavor, in which the patient is an active integrator, not just the recipient of the analyst's insights.

CONCLUSION

Freud once defined psychoanalysis as any therapy that dealt with the transference and resistance. Clearly, that definition will no longer do. I myself think of psychoanalysis as any therapy in which the analyst's intent is to facilitate as deep a relationship as possible with the patient for the purpose of working together to achieve maximum understanding of the patient's thoughts, feelings, and behavior. Given that definition, I believe that many different psychoanalytic processes and mechanisms of change occur with different patients and different analysts. Some common characteristics emerge in many of them, and at some time in the future we may be able to delineate certain categories of those processes and mechanisms and even predict, knowing the analyst and the patient, which are more likely to occur. We are at the beginning of that delineation. Our work is more like that of Schliemann than like that of modern archaeologists. However, our trench has at least laid bare the existence of many Troys, and there is good hope that our younger colleagues can build upon our first crude efforts. The work is both fascinating and worthwhile. What more could one ask?

REFERENCES

Abend, S. M. (1990). Psychoanalytic process. *Psychoanal. Q.*, 59(4):532–549.

Abrams, S. (1987). The psychoanalytic process. *Int. J. Psychoanal.*, 68(4):441–452.

Arlow, J., & Brenner, C. (1964). *Psychoanalytic Concepts and the Structural Theory*. New York: Int. Univ. Press.

———. (1990). The psychoanalytic process. *Psychoanal. Q.*, 59(4):678–692.

Balint, M. (1968). *The Basic Fault*. London: Tavistock.

Boesky, D. (1990). The psychoanalytic process and its components. *Psychoanal. Q.*, 59(4):550–584.

Cooper, A. M. (1987). The transference neurosis. *Psychoanal. Inq.*, 7(4):569–586.

———. (1989). Concepts of therapeutic effectiveness in psychoanalysis. *Psychoanal. Inq.*, 9:4–25.

De Jonghe, F., et al. (1991). Aspects of the analytic relationship. *Int. J. Psychoanal.*, 72(4):693–708.

Fourcher, B. I. (1979). The relevance of Mahler's research to psychoanalytic clinical theory. *Bull. Menninger Clinic*, 43(3):201–216.

Freud, S. (1912). On beginning the treatment (Further recommendations on the technique of Psychoanalysis). *SE*, 12:121–144.

———. (1917). *Introductory Lectures on Psycho-Analysis*, Part III. *SE*, 16:243–463.

———. (1926). *Inhibitions, Symptoms and Anxiety*. *SE*, 20:77–178.

Greenson, R. (1967). *The Technique and Practice of Psychoanalysis*, vol. 1. New York: Int. Univ. Press.

Kohut, H. (1971). *The Analysis of the Self*. New York: Int. Univ. Press.

———. (1984). *How Does Analysis Cure?* Edited by A. Goldberg. Chicago & London: Univ. Chicago Press.

Kris, E. (1951). Ego psychology and interpretation in psychoanalytic therapy. *Psychoanal. Q.*, 20(1):15–30.

Loewald, H. (1960). On the therapeutic action of psychoanalysis. *Int. J. Psychoanal.*, 41(1):16–33.

Macalpine, I. (1950). The development of the transference. *Psychoanal. Q.*, 19:501–539.

Meissner, W. W. (1991). *What is Effective in Psychoanalytic Therapy*. Northvale, N.J.: Aronson.

Menninger, K. (1958). *Theory of Psychoanalytic Technique*. New York: Basic Books.

Modell, A. H. (1978). Conceptualization of the therapeutic action of psychoanalysis. *Bull. Menninger Clinic*, 42(6):493–504.

Moore, B. E. (1994). Personal communication.

Moore, B. E., & Fine, B. D., eds. (1990). *Psychoanalytic Terms and Concepts*. New Haven: Yale Univ. Press.

Panel (1993). Current controversies about transference. Presented at the Fall meeting of the American Psychoanalytic Association, 18 December 1993.

Pine, F. (1993). Analysis of the psychoanalytic process. *Psychoanal. Q.*, 62(2):185–205.

Pulver, S. E. (1988). Psychic structure, function, process, and content. *J. Amer. Psychoanal. Assn.*, 36 (suppl.):165–190.

————. (1993). The eclectic analyst, or the many roads to insight and change. *J. Amer. Psychoanal. Assn.*, 41(2):339–358.

Rangell, L. (1981). From insight to change. *J. Amer. Psychoanal. Assn.*, 29(1):119–142.

Sandler, J. (1976). Countertransference and role-responsiveness. *Int. Rev. Psychoanal.*, 3(1):43–48.

Schafer, R. (1983). Construction of the psychoanalytic narrative. *Psychoanal. Contemp. Thought*, 6(3):403–404.

Spence, D. (1982). *Narrative Truth and Historical Truth*. New York: Norton.

Stone, L. (1961). *The Psychoanalytic Situation*. New York: Int. Univ. Press.

Strachey, J. (1934). The nature of the therapeutic action of psychoanalysis. *Int. J. Psychoanal.*, 15:127–159.

Weiss, J., Sampson, H., & The Mount Zion Research Group (1986). *The Psychoanalytic Process*. New York: Guilford Press.

Werman, D. S. (1989). The idealization of structural change. *Psychoanal. Inq.*, 9(1):119–139.

James T. McLaughlin, M.D.

6

RESISTANCE

Resistance as term and concept has had a durable place in Freudian psychoanalysis, despite ongoing disagreement over its value in theory and its significance for technique. In this respect it is not different from other propositions in psychoanalysis such as transference and repetition compulsion, with whose shifting meanings and significance the unfolding complexity of resistance is historically entwined.

This chapter provides, first, a historical overview of the concept in terms of what has been considered to be essential to the phenomenon designated resistance; second, an overview of some of the current shifts and shadings in the contesting viewpoints regarding resistance; and third, some perspectives on the technical consequences of these differing perspectives.

A standard dictionary definition of resistance in the 1950s—"Psychoanalysis: Opposition displayed by the patient to attempts of the analyst to penetrate the unconscious" (*Webster's,* 1952)—captures the specifically psychoanalytic context and meaning that still prevail, essentially unchanged from Freud's noting its significance in the case of Anna O. in 1893 (Breuer & Freud, 1893–95). Freud himself never wavered in stressing the organizing and explanatory significance of resistance, a term referring to clinically observable indicators from which he drew his theoretical inferences about intrapsychic events. Indeed, in his autobiographical study Freud (1925) identified resistance as a key constituent of his ana-

lytic theory. The term, of course, had prior and general meaning, as in war, physics, and mechanics: any opposing force, a force tending to prevent motion (*Webster's,* 1952). As a generalization about force and power, the concept lent itself well to the abstractions of Freud's later metapsychology, as well as to the reifying and impersonalizing tendencies for which Freudian psychoanalysis has been criticized.

Freud made resistance pivotal to the rationale of his technique for reasons that are still valid. The term designates clinically observable phenomena and is thus closer to actual experience and stands at a lower level of abstraction than such other indispensable constituents of his theory as repression, the unconscious, and infantile sexuality (Freud, 1925, p. 40). Here is one way to account for the enduring clinical utility of the term. Yet it is important to acknowledge its inherent liability: "resistance" entails an inference drawn by the analyst regarding the meaning of the behavior of the one whom he or she[1] is observing; it does not necessarily reflect the experience of the behaving other. Here is a major controversy around which we have circled for a very long

1. The use of "he/she" in all its variations throughout this work would be socially desirable, but it makes for stilted and awkward exposition. I ask that the reader accept the use of "he" and its variants as generic and inclusive, intended to ease reading rather than assert bias.

time: from whose vantage point are the patient's behaviors best understood, the analyst's or the patient's? Whose knowing, whose truth, is crucial to the analytic search?

HISTORICAL REVIEW

Freud made much of what he saw as a paradox, that the patient would strenuously ward off the efforts of the analyst to bring about the cure the patient sought. He became convinced that "the resistance with which she repeatedly met the reproduction of scenes which operated traumatically corresponded in fact to the energy with which the incompatible idea had been forced out of her associations" (Breuer & Freud, 1893–95, p. 157). Here is an assumption central to Freud's most basic conception of mental functioning: what is being experienced as an interpersonal tension is identical with an intrapsychic force (repression). This schema, of an intrapsychic tendency manifesting itself in an external relationship, Freud would later employ to account for the phenomenon of transference.

Freud had early recognized this relational significance in his patients' symptoms and the memories being retrieved. As early as 1895, in a letter to Fliess, he ascribed the hysterical behaviors of his patients to wishes and impulses aimed at a prehistoric person, not simply as discharges of affect-laden memory (Masson, 1984, pp. 212–239). Yet in evolving his theoretical formulations regarding resistance and transference, he gradually subordinated the relational dimensions to an emphasis upon the working of internal forces operative in the mind.

From this relational perspective Freud construed those behaviors of his patients that he was coming to recognize as transference as being in the service of resistance to the recovery of memories. Thus, in "The future prospects of psycho-analytic therapy" (1910), he linked this resistance in his male patients to attitudes of fear and defiance based on their earlier relations to the father; and in his basic technique papers a few years later he found a similar father-transference in the passionate intensities of his female patients (Freud, 1915b). However, Freud chose to regard such transference attitudes abstractly as action repetitions, driven by inner instinctual forces that defended against and screened off the analytically desired retrieval of memories to be recovered and verbalized. He saw the enactment of these obstructive attitudes in the analytic relationship as inevitable and informative, and made their exploration and eventual verbal elucidation as forms of resistance indispensable to the therapeutic process. Their resistance function remained in the foreground of his

theory building, which was centered in a one-person psychology based upon the interplay of biologically determined instinctual forces between structures in the mind. Thus the ego became the executive mental agency for coping with internal mental life by bringing about repression, the paradigm of resistance, as it mediates the counterforces of id and superego (Freud, 1924). In this model the ego became the source of the resistance to be overcome in the analysis as well as providing the counterforce whereby the repressed is held out of consciousness.

Freud added further complexities to his account of resistance in the last major revision of his theory of anxiety, *Inhibitions, Symptoms and Anxiety* (1926). Resistance became the clinically observable evidence of an anticathexis, defined as the expenditure of repressive energy continuously required of the ego out of its need to secure the repression of an instinctual drive incessantly seeking discharge (p. 27). He then listed five sources of resistance. The first three, *repression, transference,* and the *compulsion to repeat,* he attributed to the workings of the ego. These were the earliest to be identified analytically and are inferences about internal processes drawn from observable behaviors in the clinical situation. The last two are very different. Freud invokes his powerful theoretical constructs of the repetition compulsion to account for *id resistances,* presumed to derive from the necessity to repeat old ways, ascribable to the inherent conservatism of instinct. *Superego resistance,* manifesting as a repudiation of easement or cure out of a need to suffer or self-destruct, reflected the workings of the death instinct.

The overriding biological emphasis evident in these last two categories of resistance and their formulation in high-level abstractions are reinforced in "Analysis terminable and interminable," a product of Freud's last years, when his interests had largely turned to philosophical matters (1937). There he dwelled on the protracted nature of the analytic endeavor and the limited efficacy of the analytic method. This paper holds perennial significance for its pessimism and resignation. It is especially important to our topic in its pointing to implacable and/or unreachable sources of resistance that lie in the biological givens of instinct and constitution.

Freud based this perspective on an economic approach to the constitutional strength of the instincts versus the capacities of the ego (1937, pp. 224–230). The intolerance of the psychic apparatus for unpleasure, for which anxiety is the prototypic signal of ultimate disaster, forces the ego to repression or to character-shaping alterations of its own capacities through defensive mechanisms that permanently impair its perception of both its own inner drive states and the nature of external reality (pp. 237–238). He was referring to the "mechanisms of defense" detailed by his daughter (A. Freud, 1937), primitive copings necessary to the immature ego for warding off danger situations but anachronisms deforming to the ego when relied upon in adult life. These primitive ways were what the ego would bring to bear against the whole thrust of the analysis in order to balk the analyst's efforts to identify and decipher these defenses. Hence the concept of "resistance against the uncovering of resistances" (Freud, 1937, p. 239) as an allusion to habitual behaviors based upon layerings of ego alterations expressed as character.

He acknowledged the shaping power of heredity in laying down the lines of development of the individual ego, now to be seen as precipitates in the id of archaic heritage (ibid., p. 240). One of these id resistances he designated "adhesiveness of the libido," the innate reluctance to give up an older libidinal tie for the sake of a later attachment. Its opposite was the "mobile cathexis" to be found in those individuals ever ready to move on to new emotional investments. Yet another variant was the "psychic inertia" of those too rigidly fixed, or exhausted in receptivity (p. 242).

The most formidable roots of the ego's powers to resist, reaching into all parts of the mental apparatus, lay in the nature of the id, the repository of the two primal instincts, particularly the unneutralized aggression of the death instinct. A clinical manifestation of this instinctual force was the id resistance latent in superego pressure upon the ego to respond with guilt and the need for punishment. More subtle and pervasive manifestations of this same instinctual aggression lay in the clinical obscurities of masochism, the negative therapeutic reaction, and the irreconcilability of one's bisexuality (pp. 242–246).

In closing this portentous paper, Freud chose to dwell on the distinctly different basic resistances that he identified in the two sexes, stated in terms of the castration complex: penis envy in the female, and in the male the abhorrence of a feminine attitude toward another man. The therapeutic limits of analytic persuasion he attributed to the overriding obduracy of these basic resistances. "The decisive thing remains that resistance prevents any change from taking place—that everything stays as it was. We often have the impression that with the wish for a penis and the masculine protest we have penetrated through all the psychological strata and have reached bedrock, and that thus our activities are at an end. This is probably true, since, for the psychical field, the biological field does in fact play the part of the underlying bedrock" (p. 252).

A notable feature of this paper is that the topic of transference is touched upon just twice, and only at the close of the work; and the term is used only to describe a particular form of resistance.

It is evident that Freud, here ending his lifework, did not fully recognize, or at least continue to acknowledge, the profound significance of transference as the *psychological* source and shaper of resistance. Instead, his mounting emphasis on the biologically determined sources of resistance had effects that persist to this day. Max Schur (1966) noted that Freud's linkage of id resistance to the repetition compulsion and the death instinct created a fatalistic attitude in the analyst.

Freud's shift of interest from the immediacies of clinical psychoanalysis to the abstract and philosophical aspects of his science formed the background for the emerging differences and shadings of clinical and theoretical perspectives among his followers during the 1920s and 1930s. He left the clinical field open for others to assert their special contentions in ways that inevitably led to the polyphony of analytic voices we hear sixty years later.

Only a sampling of this oft-told history will be attempted here, confined to the intertwining of resistance with defense and transference, as these essential concepts became variously conceptualized. There are differences in the relative importance assigned to the views and values of analyst and patient which guide and determine the analytic exploration and in how to blend these. From this fundamental concern emerge other important weightings which are endlessly nuanced.

Some chose to follow and extend Freud's structural perspective in its application to observable clinical phenomena. Abraham in 1919 provided still valid portrayals of resistance behaviors anchored in the narcissism of the obsessional character and derived from pregenital oral and anal developmental experience. Others used the terms of Freud's new instinct theory to conceptualize the analytic task as combat with an entrenched enemy whose resistances are driven by a primitive superego.

Alexander (1925) saw the aim of analysis as the elimination of the superego through the active provision of opportunity for identification with the more enlightened and benign authority of the analyst. Reich concurrently brought out a series of influential works on the analytic battle against resistance (Reich, 1931, 1933). More than any other analyst of his time, he pointed to character manifesting as resistance. The individual's habitual ways of adapting, his prevailing and ego-syntonic modes of defense against both unwanted internal pressures from the id and superego and those from the external world, were enduring characterological precipitates from and markers of childhood neurosis. These habitual ways would be lived out in the analytic relationship as the character armor, perceived by the analyst as resistance and addressed by him in a methodical, aggressive campaign intended to shatter this armor and reveal the childhood neurosis.

Evolving at the same time, but in quite a different direction, was the perspective advanced by Ferenczi. He and Rank (1923) insisted that it was essential to the analytic work for the patient to live out all the nuances of the transference in the relationship with the analyst. This shift of emphasis away from the accustomed pursuit of memories stressed that resistances were indeed defenses of the ego against analytic uncovering. But their relevance lay in their being the necessary and valid behaviors whereby the patient had learned to contain anxiety and guilt rooted in early development, behaviors intended to ward off the tendency to fall once again into early traumatic states of narcissistic wounding and loss of self-esteem. When such guilt and anxiety had been reduced through sufficient analytic work, the patient would dare to allow full expression of his infantile wishes and fears of their consequences, now in relation to the analyst. For Ferenczi, whose personal views shaped the clinical perspectives of this work, this experiential dimension, with its affective intensities, was what would convince the patient of the concurrent reality of past and present, to an extent not attainable by remembering alone or by the persuasiveness of the analyst's interpretations. He considered this living out of transference to be a manifestation of a special instinct or human desire (ibid., p. 7).

The technical consequences of Ferenczi's shift of emphasis will be described more fully later in this chapter. For now, suffice it to note that his primary focus was upon the interplay between patient and analyst, with theoretical inferences other than transference kept in the background. Thus the analyst's experience of the patient as being too resistant or his transference as too violent was viewed as a function of the analyst's ignorance or defense against his own narcissistic wounding. This same narcissism could lead the analyst to overlook the patient's resistance hidden behind the positive transference and to fall into the error of regarding the castration and masculinity complexes as setting limits to analytic solution (p. 42).

Ferenczi alluded to most of the theoretical differences and divisive controversies that soon emerged, some of them still unresolved. From a historical viewpoint it is unfortunate that some of Ferenczi's shifts of emphasis, while initially receiving Freud's cautious endorsement, came in the temporal context of Rank's defection, made manifest in the publication of *The Trauma of Birth* (1923). Most of Freud's Committee were outraged by what they saw as radical deviations from Freud. And they felt preempted by Ferenczi of ideas they thought common to their group, on a topic all were to discuss at the Salzburg Congress later that same year. Freud gradually concurred in their insistence upon repudiation of Ferenczi's viewpoint (Jones, 1957, vol. 3, pp. 56–61). The ensuing alienation became deep and permanent, with lines of cleavage that are still evident.

It is a sad aspect of the history of psychoanalysis that such polarization of perspectives interfered with the assimilation and possible synthesis of what later turned out to be complementarities. With Ferenczi, a strong case can be made that those who saw themselves as heirs to Freud pulled back from a full exploration of the experiential and relational dimensions of the analytic encounter in their repudiation of Ferenczi (Alexander, 1925; Sachs, 1925; Fenichel, 1941). It would fall to others to extend the line of interest of which Ferenczi was the exemplar and take years for assimilation to occur.

An example was the prevailing conceptual stance in German psychoanalysis, later translocated to the United States in the 1930s, which became that of instinct theory expressed in structural metaphor (Sterba, 1953). Analysis of resistances became the central task of analysis, requiring of the analyst painstaking, systematic exploration and attack of the defenses latent in the character of the adversarial patient (Reich, 1933).

Meanwhile, a different perspective was being advocated by a few Germanic voices and a swelling chorus in England. Reflecting the viewpoint of Ferenczi and later of Melanie Klein (1932), these kept a more clinically descriptive focus, emphasizing the transferring of early personal relations into the nuances of relating between the analytic pair and the crucial contributions of the analyst, for better and worse, in the nature of that relationship.

Theodor Reik (1924) in Vienna described the subtle nuances of resistance in every aspect of the analytic relationship and the "counterresistances" of the analyst's largely unconscious defensiveness toward what the patient stirred in him. Edward Glover's lectures to the "London school" in 1927–28 anticipated most current trends in our analytic world in giving primacy to early developmental experiences. Though continuing to emphasize oedipal issues, he acknowledged the inescapably two-party psychology of analytic work and put the personal defenses of the analyst on a par with those of the patient. He insisted that the subtleties inherent in such an idiosyncratic field were chartable by the theoretical givens of his Teutonic colleagues (Glover, 1955). For Glover there was no part of the mind's functions that could not serve to defend and hence give rise to resistance. The most important of these defensive operations were those outside conscious awareness except insofar as they provoked in the analyst states of confusion and burden as a signal of the patient's profound resistiveness. These resistances were transference attitudes from past experience that could best be understood not in terms of resistance but as the recognizable restatement of formative early relations with significant others. Glover took quiet exception to Freud's pessimism regarding the intractability of the newly identified id resistances, urging that the designation be made only after seeking sources of resistance in the reality of the patient, including the oversights and behaviors of the analyst.

Strachey (1934) remained within structural theory in seeing the superego, as heir to the outcome of oedipal-level conflicts, as the central, punitive source of resistance. He added Klein's emphasis upon the pre-oedipal years of infantile development and its primitive identificatory processes as primary to the shaping of the personality and its defenses. He stressed the analytic relationship as the crucible of change, in which introjection of the analyst and identification with his or her beneficent attitudes were essential to overcoming resistances and attaining intrapsychic change.

Anna Freud, in Vienna and later in London, took sharp issue with Reich's adversarial views of the guile and deception of the resistive patient, insisting that resistance was the only way the patient's ego had of giving expression to the unconscious distorted defensive measures set in place during its early development (see Sterba, 1953).

The impact of this major shift from id analysis to ego analysis, which she and other Germanic analysts championed in England and the United States, reshaped the analytic enterprise, particularly in the United States. Resistance was to be conceptualized as a general designation for primarily internal defense mechanisms which, secondarily, would be externally manifested. In common usage this distinction became blurred and the two terms interchangeable. Thus Fenichel's (1945) encyclopedic amalgamation of prevailing European psychoanalytic theory devotes little more than a page to the topic of resistance per se, defining it as "everything that prevents the patient from producing material derived from the unconscious" (pp. 27–29).

In 1955 Zetzel presented to an international congress on transference a survey of contemporary views regarding the intertwined concepts of resistance, transference, and defense, explicitly designed to convey a clamor of differing views no longer clearly distinguishable. She acknowledged the general agreement that a successful analysis required the revival and repetition in the analytic situation of struggles from the primitive stages of development. However, she noted that those who emphasized defense analysis tended to regard regression in the analytic work as a manifestation of resistance, as a primitive defense mechanism of the ego arising during the transference neurosis. By contrast, those who stressed the significance of the revival in the analysis of the early child–mother relationship looked upon regression as an indication of a diminution rather than an increase in the resistances and as a necessity for true analytic progress (Zetzel, 1956).

As an example of durability of the first position, Menninger's authoritative text on analytic technique (1973) made resistance the central issue of the analytic endeavor. He defined resistance as the trend of forces in the patient that oppose not the analyst himself but the process of ameliorative change. Transference resistance he regarded as the resurrection of old relationships to shape "revenge resistance" in retaliation for the analyst's abstinence (p. 108).

One opposing voice, that of Winnicott, turned the concepts of resistance and transference in a remarkably different direction, in the context of his insights into the dynamics of the false self. He attributed crucial significance to the analyst's errors as the precipitant of resistance and transference (Winnicott, 1956). What would otherwise be looked upon as resistance always indicates a lapse or mistake on the part of the analyst. The resistance persists until the analyst has found the error and tried to account for it (p. 387).

CONTEMPORARY HISTORY

In the ensuing years, in keeping with the pervasive shift of interest to developmental theory and the psychology of both parties in the analytic dyad and the lessened importance accorded to the abstractions of structural theory, the concept of resistance has lost even more of its central place. Yet it remains pertinent as a clinical designation of basic phenomena. In a most encompassing critique, Roy Schafer (1973) attacked the "mechanistic language of force, structure and mechanism that constitute Freud's metapsychology" (p. 284). He characterized resistance as a hotbed of concealed hostility, the analysis of which was crucial but most arduous in that it provoked much negative countertransference. But the term itself, he insisted, had been irretrievably reified by traditional views of a mental apparatus at work. He chose to redefine resistance as a self-deceiving action contrary to the analysand's own intention. The analysand contradicted himself while countering the power of both the oedipal father and, more crucially, the archaic mother. Schafer stressed the adaptive and maturational significance of such resistances as defiance and negativism (p. 280). Later he argued for discarding the concept of resistance altogether, dismissing it as a reflection of Freud's countertransference (Panel, 1990).

A less extreme point of view, persistent in more conservative and mainstream North American psychoanalysis, is conveyed in current definitions of basic psychoanalytic concepts as set forth in Moore and Fine's *Psychoanalytic Terms and Concepts* (1990), hereafter referred to as the *PTC* definition. The term will be used both to convey this middle-ground perspective and to indicate how some of the abiding areas of dispute have been dealt with.

The *PTC* definition of resistance begins: "A paradoxical phenomenon regularly encountered in the course of insight-oriented psychotherapy, particularly psychoanalysis. The patient, who has sought professional help to uncover neurotic problems, opposes the process in a variety of ways that would serve to defeat the objective of change" (p. 168). Here are echoes of the early Freud as he struggled with what he saw as the conscious recalcitrance of Anna O. and Frau Elizabeth to his insistence that they remember the past (Freud, 1893). He dubbed their refractory behaviors "resistance," to be forcibly countered by physicianly persuasion.

A later portion of the *PTC* definition conveys the evolving appreciation, by Freud and all analysts who have followed him, of what were found to be the crucial unconscious factors: "Though often evidenced by an avoidance of free association, resistance in a broader sense encompasses all of a patient's defensive efforts to avoid self-knowledge. . . . Resistance is a special instance of the ego's defensive efforts. Analysis threatens to bring into awareness (through free association) unacceptable childhood wishes, fantasies, and impulses that would produce painful affect; the ego defends against this possibility by opposing the analysis itself" (p. 168).

This condensation reflects major theoretical and technical advances that are still central to contemporary analysis. The technical focus on free association made this process central to the analytic task for both patient and analyst. This objectifying vantage point gave the analyst a sanction for his role as guardian of the process and the opportunity to claim the relative comfort of the detached observer watching the patient battle with the process, not with him. This sidestep in following the patient's inevitable

failures and defaultings in the prescribed task made it easier for the analyst to be dispassionate in experiencing the patient's transferences, to be detached as the patient turned his hostile or erotic attention to the behaviors and person of the analyst. The patient's behaviors were to be seen as defensive or resistive, his recalcitrance as serving to impede the discovery and reworking of the traumatic past through the associative process.

Advances in analytic knowledge provided a more sophisticated analytic application of the tripartite structure of the unconscious mental apparatus. Resistances became not merely contentious and undesirable obstacles to the progress of self-understanding but also clinically useful reflections of the unconscious defensive operations habitual to the ego as it tries to effect workable compromises between id and superego in adapting to the external world (Freud, 1924).

The *PTC* definition attributes special importance to "the resistances that emerge in the sphere of the transference, that is, *transference resistance* [italics in the original to indicate that the term is listed as a type of resistance]. . . . The transference itself may be thought of as a resistance, since the patient endeavors thereby to gratify his or her narcissistic, erotic, or aggressive wishes in the present rather than to remember their origins in past object relationships" (p. 168).

This contemporary position is faithful to Freud's unswerving view of resistance as a primary defensive function of the mind, except that he went further, regarding transference as a function of resistance (Freud, 1924). The *PTC* definition of transference does not accept this subordination but instead puts the influence of transference at the heart of all object relationships. Transference is seen as a ubiquitous phenomenon, which may at times be used as resistance, but whose significance is centered in the "displacement of patterns of feelings, thoughts, and behavior, originally experienced in relation to significant figures during childhood, onto a person involved in a current interpersonal relationship. . . . Transference is a type of object relationship, and insofar as every object relationship is a reediting of the first childhood attachments, transference is ubiquitous" (p. 196). Its intense occurrence in the analytic relationship is attributed to growing tolerance of childhood derivatives as analysis proceeds, along with the enhancements of frustration-induced regression in the analytic situation that lead to the development of the childhood neurosis.

These currently held definitions can be seen as attributing different dynamic importance to resistance and transference and providing still conflicting assessments of the relations between them. These differences reflect the persistence of years of struggle, for Freud and all who have come after him, to align and reconcile these two crucial, clinically based concepts with each other and with the theory and technique they support.

These essentially dialectic issues are highlighted when put in the context of yet other crucial questions about analytic work, phrased in a polar fashion suggestive of old debates.

First, is the transference better understood as an impediment to analytic work, as resistance invoked by biologically impelled intrapsychic forces that oppose the emergence in the analysis of unwanted instinctual impulses? Or rather, is resistance better perceived as an expression of transference indispensable to the analytic venture in that it reveals those specifically human-relational modes whereby we learned to defend and adapt in handling the needs and fears of our formative years?

Second, is psychoanalysis a one- or two-party psychology? Is the analyst a detached observer of the self-initiating behaviors of the patient or an involved participant who brings his or her own transferences to the shaping of a real relationship?

Third, are resistance and transference to be understood from the vantage point of the observing analyst or the experiencing patient? Whose knowing guides the analytic discovery: that of the analyst acquired through theory and experience or that of the patient in whom the personal past resides?

Fourth, what provides the therapeutic potential of the analytic effort: the orally conveyed understanding of the nature of the patient's resistance and defenses and the historical necessity inherent in their purpose and meaning, or the affective-experiential components of the analytic relationship in which the effort to understand takes place?

The polarity of these questions highlights old controversies and uncertainties, some posed originally by Freud (1911, 1914), others by those who came after. The polyphony of contemporary psychoanalysis reflects their still-unsettled blending.

In the remainder of this chapter I will scan some of these differences and blendings. The baseline throughout will continue to be that of mainstream American psychoanalysis as reflected in the *PTC* definitions. Alternative or competing views will be brought in as counterpoint and to provide historical context.

THE NATURE AND MANIFESTATIONS OF RESISTANCE

It is currently and generally assumed that resistance is rooted in fundamental biological drives and adaptive capacities that cannot be observed and known

directly yet are manifested in all those expressions of human behavior that *can* be observed. Various theoretical inferences and abstract mappings can be made about the former from the latter. These can be encapsulated in formulations such as those expressed in the idiom of drives and capacities. Clinically, however, it is generally agreed that investigation and understanding of the human expression of basic drives is best achieved through sustained attention to the detailed and specific human experience of both parties in the analytic dyad, and to articulating these in the idiom of human discourse.

Thus the interpersonal manifestations of resistance, as expressed and reacted to by both parties, remain primary in exploring the intrapsychic dimensions of both participants. As stated in *PTC*, "Resistance is pervasive in every analysis. It varies in form and intensity from patient to patient and in the same patient at different stages in the analysis. . . . Resistance may take the form of attitudes, verbalizations, and actions that prevent awareness of a perception, idea, memory, feeling, or a complex of such elements that might establish a connection with earlier experiences or contribute insight into the nature of unconscious conflicts" (p. 168). In short, any and every psychic activity may serve as resistance.

The early emphasis of Ferenczi and Glover on the importance of the analyst's reactions and defenses in a two-party psychological field is reflected in yet another part of the *PTC* definition: "Resistance in the analytic situation does not emanate exclusively from the patient; it may also reflect the state of the analytic dyad, which is profoundly affected by the analyst's style, personality, and countertransference problems" (p. 169). Close study of the psychology of the analyst and its contribution to the analytic experience has become a major preoccupation of North American psychoanalysis of the past forty years.

THE CATEGORIES OF RESISTANCE

The categorizing of resistance no longer occupies the foreground of analytic attention, for it has long been obvious that, since resistance phenomena can be found anywhere, such listings throw more light on the preferred perspective and special clinical interests of the enumerator than on resistance (Panel, 1957). Yet Freud's delineation of the five resistances in *Inhibitions, Symptoms and Anxiety* (1926) and his reiteration of them in "Analysis terminable and interminable" (1937) had an impact upon us that is discernible to this day.

Some, as we have seen, used the abstractions of Freud's new instinct theory to conceptualize the analytic task as an assault upon an entrenched enemy, embodied in the primitive superego. Analysis of character-deforming resistances was now the central task of analysis (rather than symptom analysis of a presumably intact enough person). This clinical perspective emphasized the active role of the knowing analyst dealing with a patient deficient in psychosexual development and hampered by characterological deformations. Traces of this position still retain a place and influence in our technical approaches.

Many of these pioneers retained Freud's abstract concepts as their organizing background while insisting upon paying close clinical attention to the analytic relationship and its transference implications as the basis for therapeutic change. Many stressed mutative identification of patient with analyst as the instrument of therapeutic change (Abraham, 1919; Sachs, 1925; Sterba, 1929; Strachey, 1934). In these early shifts can be seen an emerging acknowledgment of the involvement of the analyst, of his liabilities and assets, arriving at a contemporary consensus that analysis be seen as a two-party process embedded in a personal relationship.

The current *PTC* definition of resistance stresses the necessity to repeat old patterns of human relating without the need to conceptualize in terms of the conservatism or adhesiveness of instinctual sources (see Frank, 1983, for a provocative exception). In particular, the death instinct is no longer generally invoked to account for the superego resistances of unconscious guilt, the need for punishment, the negative therapeutic reaction, or masochism (Kleinian theory remains an imposing exception). Instead, these resistances are thought of categorically as superego resistance but are dealt with clinically in terms of child–parent relations, from which the superego functions are presumed to have taken shape.

Freud's categories of ego resistance have retained clinical value, with *repression* by now a generic term for, and ingredient of, all the defensive devices whereby the ego strives "tactically" to ward off full ideational/affective awareness of unwanted fear, guilt, and shame over infantile strivings. Meanwhile the patient seeks "strategically" to satisfy these same fantasies and wishes in all his relationships, now specifically that with the analyst (see Dewald, 1980 and 1982, for full explication of these categories). Since Freud, these tactical resistances had been considered "resistances against the uncovering of resistances" (Freud, 1937, p. 239) involving habitual behaviors based upon layerings of ego alterations expressed as character.

A brief sketch of analytic work with a neurotic patient may give clinical substance to these categories and to the theoretical issues embedded in them.

Clinical Example

Mr. T., a young man lovingly close to and residing with his parents, suffered repeated depressions that since his college days had denied him the full realization of the fruits of his considerable talents. He cooperated assiduously in the analytic task for the first two years, making repeated surges of progress in the acquisition of insights that allowed him to make promising starts and advances in his work and intimate relating. But each time he soon faltered, lost momentum, and sank into a state of shame and self-blaming.

We saw this repetition initially as a consequence of his strong reluctance to give up his closeness to his mother. (This could be described as a sticky resistance of the id; it was more understandable as the consequence of all that went into the special closeness between his mother and himself as her last-born son). As the analysis went on, he was able to realize genuine achievements in work and love that brought him jubilation and satisfaction. But each time he fell abruptly into a depressed state similar to those that had brought him to treatment.

We worked our way through several of these episodes, coming upon heretofore unconscious fantasies that his succeeding was an unforgivable disloyalty to his mother that could bring illness or death to both parents; it would be an unacceptable acknowledgment of and submission to the power of his father's (my) wishes for him to be a success. Falling into a depression that stopped him in his tracks was the necessary consequence of the realization of the patient's wishes.

These episodes could be explained in terms of a negative therapeutic reaction occasioned by superego-induced guilt over the aggression implicit in his obvious ambivalence toward both parents and the consequent need for punishment. But eventually we came to understand them better in terms of the web of conflicted relating to parents and to me that we would have to work through in the patient's transferences and identifications.

These strands included his feeling that his wishes to outdo and displace his father in his mother's esteem were so awful because the father's impotence as husband and provider gave the patient no safe counter to these aggressive yearnings. Yet, if he fell back to pleasing his father by succeeding, he felt shamefully like his mother, to whom he was deeply attached and whom he painfully scorned and resented for always trying to gratify the father. We had to live out and experience between us the rage and loving yearnings toward both parents before he could make peace with these early shapings.

Some of Mr. T.'s resistances are quite evident, beginning with his initial industrious compliance with what he felt the analysis and I demanded of him. These could be thought of as *character resistances,* in that they were habitual behaviors reflecting his reliable traits of goodness and mature acceptance of responsibility. In the idiom of current mainstream analysis (Dewald, 1982), these "tactical" resistances denied his unconscious "strategic" intentions to cling to me as he was doing to his parents and kept repressed his shameful wishes to cling to mother or remain identified with her femininity.

Mr. T. also demonstrated aspects of *secondary gain resistance.* This designation continues to be applied to any and all of the ways whereby some additional and compensatory satisfaction can be found to offset the limitations of the neurotic compromise the ego has devised to handle the conflict between strong wish (id) and constraining environment (internalized as superego).

Mr. T.'s neurotic compromise solution lay in the repetition of his crime of trying, the punishing defeat of failing, and the suffering of falling back in enforced dependence on home and parents as a depressed failure. This last component provided some direct satisfaction of his infantile dependency wishes to hold onto his parents even as he was punishing them and himself by falling short.

Secondary gains for Mr. T. emerged in his tenacious hold on his symptoms and later in the analytic relationship. His parents paid for all but a fraction of the fee that was the patient's to pay. We discovered behind the cover of his shame over his slow progress his grim satisfaction in making his parents pay, his wish that I not charge him his portion, and his revenge in making me endure the disappointment of failing to achieve an analytic success.

This *negative therapeutic reaction* that plagues most analytic endeavors emerged powerfully in the intransigence of Mr. T.'s repeatedly falling back into failure even after much analytic work had been accomplished. These relapses could be described in terms of the adhesiveness of the libido, the conservatism of instinct, the punitive pressures of the superego, and the self-directed aggression of the death instinct. But such behavior becomes more open to analytic inquiry when captured in the idiom of personal relating. Here, as in the phenomena of secondary gain, are dynamic complexities of human relating that abstract terms cannot adequately address. These crucial details must be discerned and grasped through the medium of transference.

RESISTANCE AND TRANSFERENCE

In 1927 Glover italicized an eminently wise operational statement about the analyst-centered meaning of resistance and, implicitly, its oneness with transference: *"When we stand back from the analysis we can visualize the defensive function of resistance; but when we are actually engaged in analysis the outstanding fact is that the patient's own personality is the mouthpiece through which these defenses are expressed"* (rpt. in Glover, 1955, p. 80). As an early voice speaking for the primacy of transference in shaping patient and analyst behaviors, Glover captured the gist of what later analysts have worked hard to expand: "it would be entirely misleading and indeed inaccurate to suggest that transferences are merely resistances. . . . they provide us with a recognizable outline of the kernel complex of infancy and childhood, namely the Oedipus situation with all its facets" (ibid., p. 68).

Later analysts, among them Heiman (1956) and Winnicott (1956) in England, along with Stone (1973) and Loewald (1951, 1960) in the United States, extended this major shift of emphasis, giving dynamic primacy to transference as the motivator of resistance. Heiman highlighted from a Kleinian position the central role of infantile fantasies, and the transferences these reflect, in shaping defense and resistance. She advanced the useful bridging concept that such transference-driven fantasies could be looked upon as the mental correlates, the psychic representatives, of instinct (Heiman, 1956, p. 305).

Such bridging between the abstractions of instinctual drives and structural theory and the vicissitudes of early object relations has been greatly extended by recent and contemporary analysis, notably Stone and Loewald. In consequence, resistance has become the analyst's process designation for any and all of the ways whereby the patient's behaviors, shaped by transference, assert in the analytic relationship his needs to protect against what he fears while attempting to gain satisfaction for libidinal and narcissistic wishes.

From this broader perspective of transference, these ways of resisting are inherent in the adaptive processes by which we live, ready to be played out in, and highlighted by, the special context of the analytic situation. They are a part of the neurotic patient's opening compliance. Once into the analysis, the patient's resistances range across repudiation of conscious awareness that he has depths of feeling about the analyst through resistance to the full elaboration of these feelings in his attachment to the analyst to resistance against working through and relinquishing both the gratifications of that attachment and the symptomatic justifications for its continuance (Stone, 1973).

Mr. T.'s case can be aligned with this schema. His initially loving compliance set the stage for repetitious behaviors whose ending in defeat played out interpersonal dynamics of alliance and subversion in relation to the analyst as parental surrogate. Internal forces of conscience pressed him to shape defeats that undid his acts of oedipally perceived aggressive accomplishment and kept him in the guilt-driven safety of shameful dependence upon both analyst and parents. In the added dimensions of infantile relating elucidated by Mahler and other observers of infant development, Mr. T.'s repetitions can also be seen as reflecting unresolved pregenital issues involving separation and individuation (Mahler et al., 1975).

The *PTC* definition accounts for the repetitive persistence of resistances encountered in the analytic work with Mr. T. thus: "Once the patient's unconscious conflicts have been uncovered and some insight obtained, resistance may lead to delay or even failure to progress, reflecting an unconsciously determined reluctance to give up inappropriate childhood wishes and their maladaptive, defensively distorted expressions in symptoms, character, or behavior. Moreover, the relief or mental equilibrium that the neurotic symptoms achieved for the individual is hard to give up" (p. 169).

Narcissistic resistances, those directed toward preserving self-esteem and found to a variable extent in all patients, are less well depicted in Mr. T.'s behaviors. His habitual modes of protecting his equilibrium, including the unconscious purposefulness of his symptom pattern, can be construed as serving essential narcissistic aims (Stone, 1973, p. 67). Mr. T.'s narcissistically driven resistances became most evident when he saw me as wanting his analysis to end successfully in order to satisfy my own needs. He felt the outrage of an exploited child, and his anger and disillusionment were part of an utterly ego-syntonic reality view of me that justified his protective and punitive withdrawal in the analytic hours. For several months he lived out his lofty disparagement of the analysis and mistrust of me as a deceiver who would abandon him once my needs were met. This resistance state descriptively accords with the defensive behaviors of the true narcissist and can be expected to appear at least transiently in the storms of negative transference that beset the average neurotic. Such regression activates transferences set in place by the inevitable hurts and disappointments of early parenting and resolves with further analysis, provided it is met with good-enough analytic responsiveness (Winnicott, 1979).

The obdurate resistances of the true narcissistic personality disorder have been recognized as the narcissistic transference since Abraham's description in 1919. Abraham saw the narcissist as eager to be analyzed, but only on his terms. With the envy and anal-sadistic aggression characteristic of the severe obsessional, the patient rejects the paternal authority of the analyst and constantly guards against any challenge to his self-love. Narcissistic resistance typically manifests in the patient's brooking no interruption or intervention not to his liking, in a readiness to withdraw libido at a hint of the analyst's failing him, and in a desire to instruct, surpass, and depreciate the analyst (Abraham, 1919).

In more current terms, Kernberg conceptualizes these forms of narcissistic transference resistance as emerging from personality configurations characterized by the lack of an integrated self-concept, with self-esteem oscillating between grandiosity and worthlessness. In his shallow personal relationships the narcissist demands total fulfillment of archaic expectations for perfection from self and other, responding defensively with isolation, depression, and narcissistic rage when inevitable disappointments injure his self-esteem. This configuration is attributed to the carry-over into adulthood of primary narcissistic and aggressive drives whose insufficient modulation prevents the development of sufficiently stable and loving self and object representations (Kernberg, 1974, 1975).

A different perspective on the nature of narcissistic resistances has been provided by Kohut's self psychology (Kohut, 1971). Both a complement and an alternative to mainstream structural perspectives, this viewpoint perceives the narcissistic transference as reflecting the primary need of the individual to achieve a state of cohesive self in relation to sustaining others and to defend against whatever threatens to disturb this equilibrium. These behaviors, which seem overbearing and affronting to the other, are for the narcissist the necessary ways by which he perceives and controls that other as a part-object whose obligation is to reflect, twin with, and affirm his omnipotence. His desperate claims derive not from intrapsychic conflict between libidinal and aggressive drives and resulting superego-driven guilt but from a psyche whose structure has been stunted or weakened by damage inflicted by nonempathic responses from the original self-objects of infancy and childhood.

From the Kohutian perspective on narcissism, the major defensive processes and resistance patterns are deployed not to cope with guilt-centered states but rather to ward off inadequacy states ranging from humiliation to fragmentation, states set off by the failures of the affirmation of others or the threat of being overwhelmed by one's own grandiose expectations. These defenses reflect problems of early psychic development rather than oedipal-level concerns and involve two forms of splitting. Vertical splitting uses denial and disavowal of internal and external reality, whereby the opposites of omnipotence and helplessness can be consciously experienced without felt contradiction. Horizontal splitting, comparable to repression in its absolute sense, involves barring from consciousness unacceptable selfobject needs and concerns (Kohut, 1971).

THE TECHNICAL HANDLING OF RESISTANCE

It is in the clinical management of resistance that the differing stances outlined above are most sharply contrasted. The role and significance of transference become paramount to how resistance per se is regarded. Here the theoretical preferences of the individual analyst, how analysts view themselves and the patient in relation to their work, their world, and each other, become persuasive.

Freud's few technical papers set forth for the generic analyst technical prescriptions and constraints whose influence can still be noted (Freud, 1911, 1915b). He chose to emphasize the identity of the analyst as the authority and possessor of a superior knowing. The analyst was to view himself as a detached and objective observer who would work in dispassionate abstinence, using the accumulated truths of his science to provide a truer reality view for the patient whose infantilisms had impaired his perception of the actual world. Yet in these same papers Freud also set forth a counterbalancing picture: the analyst, in order to keep his own perspective from blinding him to what he cannot yet know, must put aside theory and personal views in order to attune his unconscious to that of the patient and to find the hidden paths to the patient's truths. The balancing of these essentially irreconcilable ways of seeing, of knowing versus seeking, of applied theory versus open inquiry, became a dialectic that has characterized our field ever since (Panel, 1990).

Freud's emphasis on the detached analyst-scientist determined for many years the prevailing technical stance of the analyst in North America (Fenichel, 1945). As the knowing tactician with a superior grasp of reality, the analyst was methodically to demolish, first, the resistance and then the entrenched character defenses of an adversary driven by unmanageable libidinal and aggressive forces (Reich, 1933). He was to identify the significant meaning in each analytic hour and utilize this knowledge to provide interventions that would actively influence the patient's transference (Alexander, 1925). As late as the mid-1970s these views were propounded by some American analysts who advocated the technical strategy of confronting the patient with the irrationality of his views and persuading him of the inappropriate nature of his resistant behaviors (Menninger, 1973). The patient's hidden gratifications in the analytic relationship were to be searched out and removed, by temporary suspension of the analysis if necessary, in order to produce the therapeutic frustration deemed essential to effective analytic work (Sloane, cited by Segal, 1968). In like vein, management of resistance was to be considered central to the analysis and to be dealt with through the formalism of a "psychoanalytic contract" intended to protect the enterprise from uncontrolled transferences on the part of both participants (Menninger, 1973).

Quite different technical recommendations gradually became influential on the American scene during these same years, in part due to analysts trained in the British object relations perspective (Glover, Strachey, and Winnicott) as influenced by Melanie Klein (1948), by some followers of Ferenczi (Balint, 1968), and by still others in the United States and England who took issue with Reich (A. Freud, 1937; Jones, 1957; Sterba, 1953; Fliess, 1942). A further, often unacknowledged source was the interpersonal psychology of Sullivan (1953). Common to these various perspectives were a greater acceptance of the patient's ways and a commitment to exploring them, plus a keen attention to the analyst's role in augmenting or mitigating the patient's resistive behaviors. These approaches tended to place the analyst squarely within the field of action and to require that he not function from a position of superior knowing. The contrast between Winnicott's ways of dealing with the resistiveness of his patients and those of Reich epitomize old differences still being reconciled.

Mainstream analysts in the United States have largely established their position somewhere between these extremes (Brenner, 1981; Arlow, 1975; Rangell, 1983; Greenson, 1967), thus coming closer to blending Freud's two components into a working binocularity. Most of us have joined them in seeing the analyst as a full participant in the analytic endeavor, using developed capacities that allow him to shift between empathic sampling of the unknowns in the patient's experience and an objectifying assessment by which he will shape his interventions. Some of us accept that analysts bring their own liabilities and assets to this task and that their contributions, their internal resonances as well as their interventions, must be subject to the same scrutiny as those of their patients. This more even-handed approach has allowed a fuller appreciation of the communicative richness of all the behaviors of both parties and of the therapeutic yield to be found in both experiencing and exploring the actualized transferences enacted between them (Jacobs, 1991; Poland, 1975; McLaughlin, 1988).

Contemporary Nuances in Addressing Resistance

Large differences continue in what we choose to do with the yield that the different blendings of theoretical preferences and empathic inquiry have brought us—differences in how we listen, what we look for, how we organize what we see, how we convey our understanding to the patient. Such differences involve issues that go beyond the limits of the topic of resistance and now exist in a profusion that cannot be adequately addressed here. The one possibly tenable generalization might be that no two of us hold identical views about our task as psychoanalyst. What can be attempted is a crude sampling of some representative technical modes of dealing with resistance, with apologies to the reader for oversimplification, to colleagues for valued contributions gone unmentioned, and to the adherents of preferred theory for straw men rudely stacked.

First, a mainstream analyst, from his chosen position of benevolent and authoritative detachment, oriented by a structural model powered by instinctual drives, thinks of the technical handling of resistances first by identifying them in the behavior patterns of the patient. He sees resistance as integral to compromise formations embodying unconscious ego adaptations steered by superego responses to instinctual drive expressions (Dewald, 1982). In such a context he might eventually characterize as resistance both the compliance and the cooperation of a patient like Mr. T. Similarly, the analyst's reluctance to face the barrage of emotion in the transference when the resistance is understood or to activate the pain or distress in the patient that sound analytic technique might require would be understood as countertransference (Dewald, 1982, pp. 51–52). The analyst intervenes repeatedly to confront, clarify, interpret, and help the patient work through the consequences of this process (p. 53). He selects first those noncrucial resistances that are most ego-alien and impede the establishment of an optimal analytic relationship. The analyst does so in order to test the therapeutic alliance that must be in place before he can tackle strategic and characterological resistances. The analyst's nonjudgmental steadiness and interested neutrality, repeated in different contexts in the face of the patient's perturbations, serve as models for the necessary identification with the analyst (pp. 54–55).

This analyst is constantly watching for hidden resistances and evaluating the patient's responses in order to judge whether the patient is ready for further interventive steps (pp. 55–56). If repetition of the usual sequence of interventions fails to remove a resistance, the analyst needs to resort to such parameters as suggesting the postponement of a compulsive ritual or urging the relinquishment of an abusive relationship as an aid to analytic progress (p. 60). It seems fair to say that this analyst is counting upon the leverage of the quiet voice of reason, conveyed over time through considerately articulated verbal interventions, to influence the patient to join him in seeing matters as they really are.[2]

Another mainstream analyst, working within essentially the same structural framework, sees these resistance-directed strategies advocated by Freud, and now Dewald, as symptom suppression, as manipulation by suggestion (Gray, 1982). He prefers to work with resistance by engaging and optimizing the patient's self-observational powers and other aspects of the executive ego. He does this by teaching the patient to follow his own associative processes prompted in the immediacy of the analyst–patient engagement (Gray, 1973). This analyst has come to a specific focus on the workings of the superego, and his appeal is to the autonomous ego functions that will allow the patient to draw back from the affect and imagery of the associative process to a more rational alliance that will help him to consider what the analyst has noted. This juncture is crucial: the analyst points out how the patient's spontaneous flow was stopped or deflected at that moment because some fantasied risk in telling the analyst arose in the mind of the patient. In other words, this analyst wishes to educate the patient's observing ego to recognize that, at that moment, it has been preempted by the infantile defensive measures called forth by the superego. The bit-by-bit analysis of these moments of felt danger gradually reduces the patient's automatic need to restrict his freedom to express his particular hierarchy of aggression-driven transference fantasies about which the superego gave warning. In particular, this approach brings to light the habitual deflection of aggression away from the object (the analyst) onto the self, a defense that the analyst finds typical of superego-driven conflict solutions (Gray, 1973). It is fair to say that this approach allows the analyst to position himself alongside and somewhat removed from a patient who has been directed and taught to attend to the vagaries of his associating mind. From that vantage point the analyst can bring himself actively into the patient's field, both in his intervening generally and specifically in linking himself to the danger of aggression that prompted associative deflection.

2. Freud in 1919 defined the analyst's task as "to bring to the patient's knowledge the unconscious, repressed impulses existing in him, and, for that purpose, to uncover the resistances that oppose this extension of his knowledge about himself. Does the uncovering of these resistances guarantee that they will also be overcome? Certainly not always; but our hope is to achieve this by exploiting the patient's transference to the person of the physician, so as to induce him to adopt our conviction of the inexpediency of the repressive process established in childhood and of the impossibility of conducting life on the pleasure principle" (Freud, 1919, p. 159).

Yet another contemporary analyst will choose to tackle resistance from a strongly held position utilizing a dual-drive theory. His views of the patient's intrapsychic conflicts emphasize the importance of aggression and its modulation by the counter of libidinal drives (Kernberg, 1974). This model and idiom suggest those of Melanie Klein but are articulated in the metaphor of object relations and the vicissitudes of Mahler's separation-individuation phases. The multistage nature of this perspective permits the analyst a flexible stance toward the different forms and qualities of resistance encountered through a wide range of psychopathologies. Regardless of these differences, direct interpretation from a position of analytic abstinence is the mode by which unconscious transference motives are identified in the here and now of the relationship to the analyst, with close attention to the affective states of envy, competitiveness, and other forms of aggressive drive derivatives that are central to this perspective. When the resistive behaviors of the patient are of the dimensions found in severe narcissistic and borderline states, the analyst must be firm in setting limits and clear in enunciating his differences of perception and outlook to counter the patient's questionable view. The experiencing and working through of the aggression that gets evoked and focused on the analyst becomes crucial to further analytic progress (Kernberg, 1975).

An analyst based in self psychology will be similarly attentive to resistances in the patient yet will respond to these differently on the grounds of his theory. Resistance to the work of analysis is the ego's way of warding off any disturbance to the narcissistic relationship to the archaic selfobject, within which he feels safe and good (Kohut, 1971, p. 90). The patient resists any deepening involvement until he can feel safely within an idealizing transference state of union with the analyst or can experience the analyst as an extension of his own grandiose self. Any disruption of these states results in regressively defensive ways (resistances) that are pathognomic for the particular selfobject configurations of the disrupted state. These behaviors do not reflect structured defenses against instinctual forces and are not touched by interventions aimed at intrapsychic conflicts around aggressive and sexual drives. Instead, the reparative task involves empathic working through of the patient's reaction to the loss of the narcissistically experienced object (pp. 94–96). Implicit in this perspective, and made explicit in the analyst's interventive idiom, are theories accepted by self-psychologists: that the etiological factors lie not in intrapsychic conflict but in defective parenting experiences of childhood and that the precipitating factors for unwanted regression in the analysis lie in the behaviors of the analyst.

A different perspective on resistance is taken by the analyst who seeks to analyze with minimal imposition of his theoretical or preferred knowing (Schwaber, 1983; McLaughlin, 1981). The patient's psychic reality—that is, his conscious and unconscious perceptions of himself and the world—is sought and its logic perceived. The immediacies of the analytic moment, particularly shifts in the patient's affect states and experience of the interaction with the analyst, are explored and acknowledged. These are clues to the meaning of the patient's resistant behaviors, clues about some affective-cognitive change whose significance the analyst does not presume to know but seeks to learn through active inquiry and affirmation. The term "resistance" carries no loading of acquired significance beyond the supposition that something of significance has been set off in the patient. Thorough inquiry into, and shared understanding of, what has been activated provide the essential resolution of the resistance and free the patient to find his own access to the past that has shaped his view.

The samplings just scanned lack the clinical detail that would bring these approaches to life and might show their many technical likenesses along with their divergences. What they do make evident is the extent to which theory guides technical preference, clearly most evident for those espousing self psychology as well as for those who prefer the traditional linkage of resistance, instinct theory, and the structural model. Analysts like those cited above, who hold to more relativistic, transference-centered positions, look upon the analytic relationship as a continuing struggle to attain times of true collaboration in which to shape an "analytic instrument" embodying the analytic ideal of two minds meeting together (Balter et al., 1980). All share at least a more tolerant sense of resistances as important sources of information concerning the standing operating procedures of the ego (Waelder, 1936). They accept as inevitable that both parties will "resist" the transference conflicts that the intimacy of the analytic dyad inevitably stirs. These phenomena in both are to be regarded simply as transference states shielding yet other levels of transference, to be dealt with by attending to the shifts and turnings of the compromise formations inherent in all transference (Boesky, 1983; Brenner, 1981).

From perspectives grounded in attention to the inner and outer experiences of both patient and analyst, the analyst-assigned significance of resistance has proved inadequate. As term and concept, resistance has clearly lost its ordinal position in analytic theory building. Yet it is likely to continue to be valued by many as a familiar designation for ubiquitous clinical phenomena now quite variously perceived. Despite some advocacy for its abandonment, it seems unlikely that, in the immediate future, we will be faced with either mourning its demise or cheering its departure from the analytic scene.

REFERENCES

Abraham, K. (1919). A particular form of neurotic resistance against the analytic method. In *Selected Papers on Psychoanalysis*, ed. Ernest Jones. London: Hogarth Press, 1948.

Alexander, F. (1925). A metapsychological description of the process of cure. *Int. J. Psychoanal.*, 6:13–34.

Arlow, J. (1975). The structural hypothesis. *Psychoanal. Q.*, 44:509–525.

Arlow, J., & Brenner, C. (1964). *Psychoanalytic Concepts and the Structural Theory*. J. Amer. Psychoanal. Assn., monograph 3. New York: Int. Univ. Press.

Balint, M. (1968). *The Basic Fault*. London: Tavistock.

Balter, L., with Lothane, Z., & Spencer, J. (1980). On the analyzing instrument. *Psychoanal. Q.*, 49:474–504.

Boesky, D. (1983). Resistance and character theory. *J. Amer. Psychoanal. Assn.*, 31 (suppl.):227–246.

Brenner, C. (1981). Defense and defense mechanisms. *Psychoanal. Q.*, 50:557–569.

Breuer, J., & Freud, S. (1893–95). *Studies on Hysteria*. *SE*, 2.

Dewald, P. (1980). The handling of resistances in adult psychoanalysis. *Int. J. Psychoanal.*, 61:61–69.

———. (1982). Psychoanalytic perspectives on resistance. In *Resistance, Psychodynamics, and Behavioral Approaches*, ed. P. Wachtel, pp. 25–68. New York: Plenum.

Fenichel, O. (1941). *Problems of Technique*. Albany, N.Y.: Psychoanalytic Press.

———. (1945). *The Psychoanalytic Theory of the Neuroses*. New York: Norton.

Ferenczi, S., & Rank, O. (1923). *The Development of Psychoanalysis*, ed. G. Pollock. Classics in Psychoanalysis, monograph 4. Madison, Conn.: Int. Univ. Press.

Fliess, R. (1942). The metapsychology of the analyst. *Psychoanal. Q.*, 11:211–227.

Frank, A. (1983). Id resistance and instinct strength. *J. Amer. Psychoanal. Assn.*, 31(suppl.):375–404.

Freud, A. (1937). *The Ego and the Mechanisms of Defense*. London: Hogarth Press.

Freud, S. (1910). The future prospects of psychoanalytic therapy. *SE*, 11:141–151.

———. (1911). The handling of dream interpretation in psycho-analysis. *SE*, 12:89–96.

———. (1912a). The dynamics of transference. *SE*, 12:99–108.

———. (1912b). Recommendations to physicians practising psycho-analysis. *SE*, 12:111–120.

———. (1913). On beginning the treatment. *SE*, 12:123–144.

———. (1914). Remembering, repeating and working through. *SE*, 12:147–156.

———. (1915a). Instincts and their vicissitudes. *SE*, 14:117–140.

———. (1915b). Observations on transference-love. *SE*, 12:159–171.

———. (1916–17). *Introductory Lectures on Psycho-Analysis*. *SE*, 15 & 16.

———. (1919). Lines of advance in psycho-analytic therapy. *SE*, 17:159–168.

———. (1924). A short account of psycho-analysis. *SE*, 19.

———. (1925). *An Autobiographical Study*. *SE*, 20:7–74.

———. (1926). *Inhibitions, Symptoms and Anxiety*. *SE*, 20:77–172.

———. (1937). Analysis terminable and interminable. *SE*, 23:216–253.

Glover, E. (1927). Lectures on technique in psychoanalysis. *Int. J. Psychoanal.*, 8:311–328.

———. (1928). Lectures on psychoanalytic technique. *Int. J. Psychoanal.*, 9:7–46, 181–218.

———. (1955). *The Technique of Psychoanalysis*. New York: Int. Univ. Press.

Gray, P. (1973). Psychoanalytic technique and the ego's capacity for viewing intrapsychic activity. *J. Amer. Psychoanal. Assn.*, 21:474–494.

———. (1982). Developmental lag in the evolution of psychoanalytic technique. *J. Amer. Psychoanal. Assn.*, 30:621–655.

Greenson, R. (1967). *The Technique and Practice of Psychoanalysis*. New York: Int. Univ. Press.

Heiman, P. (1956). Dynamics of transference interpretations. *Int. J. Psychoanal.*, 37:303–310.

Jacobs, T. (1991). *The Uses of the Self*. Merion, Conn.: Int. Univ. Press.

Jones, E. (1957). *The Life and Work of Sigmund Freud*. New York: Basic Books.

Kernberg, O. (1974). Further contributions to the treatment of narcissistic personalities. *Int. J. Psychoanal.*, 55:215–240.

———. (1975). *Borderline Conditions and Pathological Narcissism*. New York: Aronson.

———. (1980). Character structure and analyzability. *Bull. Assn. Psychoanal. Med.*, 19:87–96.

Klein, M. (1932). *Psychoanalysis of Children*. London: Int. Psychoanal. Assn.

———. (1948). *Contributions to Psychoanalysis: 1921–1945*. Edited by E. Jones. London: Hogarth Press.

Kohut, H. (1959). Introspection and empathy. *J. Amer. Psychoanal. Assn.,* 7:459–483.

———. (1971). *The Analysis of the Self.* New York: Int. Univ. Press.

Loewald, H. (1951). Ego and reality. *Int. J. Psychoanal.,* 32:10–18.

———. (1960). On the therapeutic action of psychoanalysis. *Int. J. Psychoanal.,* 41:16–33.

———. (1981). Regression. *Psychoanal. Q.,* 50:22–43.

Mahler, M., with Pine, F., & Bergman, A. (1975). *Psychological Birth of the Human Infant.* New York: Basic Books.

Masson, J. (1984). *The Assault on Truth.* New York: Farrar, Straus & Giroux.

McLaughlin, J. (1981). Transference, psychic reality and countertransference. *Psychoanal. Q.,* 50:639–664.

———. (1988). The analyst's insights. *Psychoanal. Q.,* 47:370–389.

Menninger, C., with Holzman, P. (1973). *Theory of Psychoanalytic Technique,* 2d ed. New York: Basic Books.

Moore, B., & Fine, B., eds. (1990). *Psychoanalytic Terms and Concepts.* New Haven: Yale Univ. Press.

Panel (1957). Clinical and theoretical aspects of resistance. H. Kohut, reporter. *J. Amer. Psychoanal. Assn.,* 5:548–555.

———. (1990). Classics revisited. Freud's papers on technique. B. Burris, reporter. Presented at meeting of the Amer. Psychoanal. Assn., Dec. 1990.

Poland, W. (1975). Tact as a psychoanalytic function. *Int. J. Psychoanal.,* 56:155–162.

Rangell, L. (1983). Defense and resistance in psychoanalysis and life. *J. Amer. Psychoanal. Assn.,* 31:147–174.

Rank, O. (1923). *The Trauma of Birth.* New York: Brunner.

Reich, W. (1931). Character formation and the phobias of childhood. *Int. J. Psychoanal.,* 12:219–232.

———. (1933). *Character Analysis.* New York: Orgone Press, 1949.

Reik, T. (1924). Some remarks on the study of resistances. *Int. J. Psychoanal.,* 5:141–154.

Sachs, H. (1925). Metapsychological points of view on technique and theory. *Int. J. Psychoanal.,* 6:5–12.

Schafer, R. (1973). The idea of resistance. *Int. J. Psychoanal.,* 54:259–285.

———. (1990). The resistance and Freud's countertransference. Panel on Classics revisited: Freud's papers on technique, presented at meeting of the Amer. Psychoanal. Assn., Dec. 1990.

Schur, M. (1966). *The Id and the Regulatory Principles of Mental Functioning.* New York: Int. Univ. Press.

Schwaber, E. (1983). Psychoanalytic listening and psychic reality. *Int. Rev. Psychoanal.,* 10:379–392.

———. (1986). Reconstruction and perceptual experience. *J. Amer. Psychoanal. Assn.,* 34:911–932.

Segal, N. (1968). Narcissistic resistances. *J. Amer. Psychoanal. Assn.,* 17:941–954.

Sterba, R. (1929). The dynamics of the dissolution of the transference resistance. *Psychoanal. Q.,* 9 (1940).

———. (1953). Clinical and therapeutic aspects of character resistance. *Psychoanal. Q.,* 22:1–20.

Stone, L. (1973). On resistance in the psychoanalytic process. In *Psychoanalysis and Contemporary Science,* ed. B. Rubinstein, vol. 2, pp. 42–73. New York: Macmillan.

Strachey, J. (1934). The nature of the therapeutic action of psychoanalysis. *Int. J. Psychoanal.,* 15:127–159.

Sullivan, H. (1953). *The Interpersonal Theory of Psychiatry.* New York: Norton.

Waelder, R. (1936). The principle of multiple function. *Psychoanal. Q.,* 5:45–62.

Webster's New International Dictionary. (1952). Edited by W. H. Neilson. Springfield, Mass.: G. & C. Merriam.

Winnicott, D. (1956). On transference. *Int. J. Psychoanal.,* 37:386–388.

———. (1979). *Maturational Processes and the Facilitating Environment.* New York: Int. Univ. Press.

Zetzel, E. (1956). Current concepts of transference. *Int. J. Psychoanal.,* 37:369–376.

Leo Stone, M.D.

7

TRANSFERENCE

DEFINITION AND GENERAL FEATURES

Transference, an exceedingly complicated concept in depth, is best defined, for practical purposes, in terms of its clinical and everyday phenomenology. It is the tendency to repeat, in a current setting, attitudes, feelings, impulses, and desires experienced or generated in early life in relation to important figures in the individual's development. These original figures are primarily the parents but may include other family members or even persons outside the family who have assumed important functional roles in actuality. Sometimes the last may have been invoked for substitutive or defensive reasons; at other times because of their unique actual significance to the subject. While the transference phenomena may retain their original dynamic thrust—that is, as "unfulfilled"—they more often appear as *faits accomplis*—for example, *being* loved or *being* rejected—or *finding* specific traits in the analyst, even including occasional physical misperceptions or distortions. The early underlying experiences may not necessarily have been conscious as such in early years, or only in evanescent fragments, especially in their ego-dystonic elements, but may nonetheless be susceptible to convincing reconstruction. This may indeed be true of the erotic thrust of the oedipus complex, as of less formidable drive conflicts.

The transference may exist as an important element in the personal relationships of an individual's daily life—in relation to parental or sibling substitutes—in education, religious involvements, medical contacts, work, and idiosyncratic personal attachments, sometimes contributing a facilitating, sometimes an impeding or destructive, element to such situations, or an alternating biphasic effect, as in their prototypic background. (A common example would be the succession of attachment, disappointment, and then hostility.) In general, in most mature individuals, transferences may color and influence relationships; but only in uniquely significant instances to which the individual is vulnerable, do they exercise an effect beyond the subject's self-preservative or reality-testing functions or capacity for self-control. No doubt, in poorly organized individuals, certain destructive personal passions or irrational group or leadership adherences (the latter facilitated by the mechanisms of group psychology) are strongly rooted in the dynamics of transference. In Freud's view (1927) of monotheistic religion, one may infer a benign variant of mass transference of enormous power.

EVERYDAY CONTRASTED TO CLINICAL TRANSFERENCES

In general, the transferences of everyday life are distinguished from clinical transferences by certain important dynamic features which are present in varying degree. First, persuasion, action, and mobility as to object and, in many instances, direct gratification are intrinsically available, or at least potentially available, to the subject even if gratification is limited to sublimated spheres. For example, in a visit to a physician, the patient is examined physically, receives a prescription for drugs or some health regimen and usually advice and/or reassurance. From lawyer, teacher, or clergyman, there may be analogous although noncorporeal gratifications. Second, there is no rule prescribing the object's responses in any sphere (cognitive, affective, or physical) beyond the usual restrictions and amenities of the general social and professional codes. If a person's physician (or lawyer) is not sufficiently interested or attentive or not responsive enough as a love object, he or she can, at least in principle, move on to another relationship or, short of that, make effective (sometimes mutative) protest. A consequence of these differences is that the intensity of the transference aspects of such relationships and their regressive elaborations is usually less than in the clinical situation. Unless the subject has a potentially pathological organization, the ego-dystonic, usually repressed elements of the transference tend to remain in abeyance—in repression or in their character integrations—relative to the essential reality content of the relationship and its permissible overtones and variations. Where literal erotic or hostile breakthroughs of transference origin occur, the situation is obviously extremely complicated, with the outcome dependent on personal and professional ethical codes and individual character structures. However, such (nonanalytic) situations are seldom conditioned by the same type and degree of built-in restrictions and abstinence, rationally as well as morally supported, as in the psychoanalytic situation, where even sublimated gratifications are largely denied the patient except in the treatment modalities as such.

The classically construed psychoanalytic situation is a uniquely specific and delimited form of human relationship, which has been described often, beginning with Freud and at some length, more recently, by me (1961). Its formal characteristics are well known: prescribed free association as the patient's principal mode of communication; the recumbent posture of the patient, in a position where he or she cannot see the analyst; confinement of the analyst's communications (with rare exceptions) to essentially clarifying or interpretive interventions; and cognate to the last, the absence of all other forms of gratifying response on the part of the analyst, whether in the form of reassurance, encouragement, statement of personal interest or esteem, or other of the myriad forms of response that might be expected from an interested, caretaking individual. Also, all self-revealing information from the analyst is interdicted. Outside the realm of verbal exchange, the prohibitions are even more severe: unequivocally, no sexual contact; no other physical contact (beyond a possible handshake on occasion); no physical examination (except in a specific medical emergency); and no intentional social contact. Taken together, these prohibitions amount to the "rule of abstinence" that Freud (1919) felt was crucial in relation to the patient's transference wishes.

It is clear that this situation is dynamically different from that of any of the relationships of everyday life. It favors the patient's regressive adaptive effort to cope psychologically with the enigmatic object to whom he or she is attached by dependent need. One important aspect of this regression, which in a sense parallels the frequent precipitation of clinical neurosis by frustration, is the manifest emergence of the hitherto latent transference, previously invested in original object images, in repression. It was Macalpine's (1950) important contribution to emphasize this regressive adaptive aspect of transference. In the analytic context of "abstinence," the transferences thus have greater intensity and persistence, a stronger thrust toward regression, and heightened resistiveness to change. The tendency to move toward a transference neurosis is correspondingly augmented. The development of a transference neurosis and its interpretive reduction in the analytic situation have long been regarded as major components of genuine psychoanalytic work. Allowing for liberal construction of the concept and the occurrence of exceptions, I still adhere to this view, but there have been demurrals in recent years which should be noted. Brenner, for spectacular example (1982), argues that the concept is "anachronistic and tautologous" (p. 202). While I am aware that the current terminology can be confusing, I believe that the concept (Freud, 1916–17) remains sound, fundamental, and useful. I do not accept either the process or the extreme conclusion of Brenner's critique.

SOME HISTORICAL NOTES ABOUT THE CONCEPT

Reference to the history of the transference concept must be brief, lest its complexities overrun the limits of this compact chapter. Transference, in common with most of our fundamental concepts, was discovered by Freud. He noted the phenomenon very early (for example, Breuer & Freud, 1893–95, pp. 302–303), calling it a "false connection." Another early contributor was Ferenczi (1909), who also noted one of its more general meanings, that of object love replacing autoerotism. Freud employed the term in a clinically cognate sense to distinguish "transference neuroses" from "narcissistic neuroses" (equivalent to "psychoses" in current usage). Loewald (1960) invoked a more recondite usage of Freud (1900)—the transference from unconscious ideas to preconscious material (typically in relation to the day residue in dreams).

For an extended period, in keeping with his original view of therapeutic process, Freud viewed the transference largely as a "resistance" to recovery of the past. However, he became increasingly aware of its positive dynamic role in the psychoanalytic process. In 1912, supporting his thesis with dramatic metaphor, Freud placed the analysis of the transference at the center of psychoanalytic work. He emphasized the sense of affective reality that found expression only in this phenomenon. Freud regarded the transference neurosis as an "artificial neurosis" replacing the clinical neurosis (Freud, 1914, pp. 154–155; 1916–17; Blum, 1971; Greenson, 1967). The transference neurosis brought the essential conflicts into the context of the treatment situation,[1] making them directly accessible to analytic work.

This central position of the transference neurosis has remained a keystone in the structure of modern psychoanalysis. Allowing for developmental changes —and environmental intrusions—its broad outlines are essentially determined by the original infantile neurosis. Its nature, position, and management have been subject to elaborations and variations in emphasis which can only be mentioned sketchily. In 1924 Ferenczi and Rank proposed an extreme form of emphasis on affective experience (albeit with ultimate, if much delayed, reconstruction of the past), as the most effective element in the psychoanalytic process. Interpretation was delayed in favor of mounting emotional tension. Later, Alexander (1956) thought of his "corrective emotional experience," although oriented in a much more specifically didactic direction, as a further development of Ferenczi's and Rank's ideas. More recently, an extreme emphasis on the "here and now" has been argued by Gill and his co-workers (1976, 1979, 1982). The uniquely and exclusively "mutative" significance of transference interpretation, originally proposed by Strachey (1934), has had a remarkably continuing impact on the development of psychoanalytic technique. A recent proponent of a related (although not congruent) view, from a special orientation, is Gray (1982), who focuses on the immediacy of material within the session, nuances of ego activity (especially its capacity for self-observation), and the preeminent importance of resistance analysis within the transference itself. In a panel (1984) in which Gray participated, the continuing importance of nontransference interpretation was strongly argued by others, without denying the special—even unique—importance of transference interpretation.

While the special significance of transference interpretation must be recognized, there are areas of critical experience that cannot be thus encompassed, and the failure to assign them significance or, when indicated, to interpret them may result in a considerable deficit (sometimes of major importance) in the analytic work. As a pithy example, a patient's defiant altercation with a bad-tempered policeman, because of its reality implications, is very different from an outburst directed at the analyst. This is important, even though an ultimate core relationship between the two may be demonstrated. Where there is a genuine "acting out,"[2] this is of course a specific problem involving the ego, apart from the drive and fantasy content. But even when this well-recognized element is not conspicuous, a large and significant area of ego and superego function in relation to danger, official authority, and obvious real fear is clearly presented for consideration.

Some Closely Related Concepts

Before continuing the discussion of transference, some closely related concepts require mention. The "therapeutic alliance" and "working alliance" are practically equivalent concepts which were emphasized by Zetzel (1956) and Greenson (1965). Whereas Freud regarded the essential nonconflictive, personally binding element of the process to be subsumed in the positive transference (the "unobjectionable" fraction), many have thought it best to sequester conceptually the adult sphere of conscious, committed agreement between patient and analyst from the point of view of the healthy portion of the patient's ego and its realistic wish for professional help. With this comes the intention to cooperate with the analyst despite the expected occurrence of disturbing vicissitudes. Such a commitment, separate from transference, is included in the alliance con-

---

1. Even Freud's views on this subject have been questioned (as to their meaning and consistency). That Freud's verbal usages varied over his long career is well known, and I cannot trace these variations here. I simply follow what I think represent Freud's essential and most enduring views, pragmatically considered (i.e., in their impact on the professional community).

2. "Acting out," in its strict sense, is intimately related to the transference. This complex phenomenon is dealt with in Chapter 9, so it will not be elaborated here.

cept(s) under discussion.[3] The essential "alliance" concept, as distinct from strictly construed transference, has been challenged by Brenner (1979, 1982). However, it is widely accepted among analysts, regardless of terminology.

"Countertransference," in its essential nature, is the same phenomenon as transference. The prefix simply indicates its different direction—namely, from analyst to patient. It has been additionally specified (Gitelson, 1952) as a response to the patient's transference rather than to him or her as an object. (The latter would be a "transference to the patient.") However, this distinction is usually ignored in current usage. While a certain portion of the analyst's potential countertransference (a conflict-free expression of parental or physicianly interest) may be regarded as "unobjectionable," like the corresponding fraction of the patient's transference, it can, if overdone, cause difficulties in its own right. This is always true, of course, if the analyst's attitudes are fraught with conflict based on erotic or aggressive content. Sibling (or other) rivalries, incestuous urges, envies, old hatreds, and so on of great variety may be revived in the analyst by a patient or patients in relation to whom he or she is especially vulnerable. When such attitudes remain unconscious but influence the analyst's general feeling and interpretive orientation toward the patient, the situation can be grossly destructive. The same would be true (and worse) if impulses were acted out, beyond insight or control. It is therefore exceedingly important that the practicing analyst's self-analysis remain an ongoing part of his or her professional commitment. Obviously, if the analyst finds that he or she is in deep waters, he or she should turn to a colleague for help. If the situation threatens to overturn his or her efforts, the patient should be transferred to another analyst. In more benign situations, where the conscientious analyst becomes aware of strong or aberrant feelings or impulses toward a patient, he or she will immediately engage in augmented self-analysis or, if this is ineffective, turn to someone else for help. That emotional involvements of varying types and degrees of complexity (a "countertransference neurosis") may occur with every patient was suggested pointedly by Tower (1956). Forms of countertransference have been described and classified (see, for example, Racker, 1957; Reich, 1960; among others).

TYPES OF TRANSFERENCE

Transferences as such have been broadly classified in everyday usage as "positive" and "negative." The former usually include a broad range of affectionate and also specifically erotic wishes and fantasies. "Erotic" wishes may, of course, include seductive attitudes with concealed castrative impulses or related wishes to reduce or humiliate the analyst. The positive transference includes the "unobjectionable" (nonconflictive, ego-syntonic) fraction described by Freud, which may contribute strongly to the therapeutic (or working) alliance.

Various forms of transference can serve resistance functions (just as they may also function as rigidly maintained forms of defense in the adult character). Defenses originating in early childhood may appear as highly developed in the analytic process as they do in daily life. Note the concept of "defense transference" (A. Freud, 1936). A frequent example would be the presentation of persistent, defiant, and belligerent attitudes in place of underlying passive submissive demands for love, frequently but not exclusively homosexual in nature. Or instead of a genuine mother transference to a male analyst, this important potentiality may remain in the foreground of a woman's analysis, in avoidance of the more confronting heterosexual incestuous urge. To the well-known erotic and hostile forms of transference (as resistance) mentioned above in passing, Stein (1981) has added, as part of the repertory of potential resistances, the "unobjectionable form" of positive transference. One assumes that this is differentiated from more blatant and easily recognized resistance phenomena, such as the overcompliant "good student" reaction.

That the more subtle "positive" reaction may operate as a concealed and formidable resistance in certain instances is not to be questioned. However, this important fact should not be construed as disestablishing the fundamental—indeed indispensable—role of the genuine phenomenon, as originally elaborated by Freud (1912). One may assume that this form of "positive transference" has been importantly present as a sustaining dynamic factor in many "good analytic hours" in which the prevailing instinctual transference has been "negative," whether the indispensable sustaining element is emphasized or not

---

3. With regard to ego-dystonic or conflictive transference, this distinction is usually clearly demonstrable. With regard to the "unobjectionable" positive transference, the purity of concept must often give way to empirical fact. This infantile thrust toward the parent, a true "transference" in neutralized terms, tends to support, to fuse with, and to lend added power to the adult commitment to the therapeutic (or working) alliance. I have presented a similar point of view with regard to the concept of "mature transference" (Stone, 1961).

(although this chapter's essential thrust does not concern this issue; see Kris, 1956).

While the conventional usage ("positive" and "negative" transference) is strongly entrenched in our language, it is not without certain confused or confusing elements—for example, the inclusion of sometimes ambiguous (or latently ambivalent) erotic elements in the "positive transference" or defensive pseudo-hostile reactions in the "negative." The suggestion of Lagache (1953) that whatever transference furthers progress in analysis be regarded as "positive," whatever impedes it as "negative," while not simple as regards classification, may be thought to further more careful descriptive usage. The term "erotized transference" has been used for transference attitudes that present persistently erotic manifestations regardless of their fundamental or latent content. When such transferences are not genuinely erotic in ultimate underlying substance, the phenomenon must be regarded as a special form of resistance manifestation or a mask for more severe pathology, to be dealt with as such (see Greenson, 1967; Blum, 1973).

THE ROLE OF TRANSFERENCE IN THERAPY

The transference plays a critical role in all forms of therapy, whether or not it is manifested or dealt with as such. In instances where it is ignored, either through inadvertence or purposively, the "positive transference" may yield "transference cures," so long as the relationship with the physician is maintained or, exceptionally, even for long periods and at a distance by way of a persisting and gratifying unconscious fantasy elaborated on the basis of the original contact. Such cures are of course vulnerable to intrinsic negative dynamics or external impacts. More unfortunate are the instances of spontaneously emerging hostile transference, delayed and unanalyzed, that may strikingly invalidate previous work, even at a later date. See Freud's classic example in "Analysis terminable and interminable" (1937). And as Freud learned relatively early (1905), an analysis may fail or be aborted because the negative transference is not recognized and interpreted.

In psychoanalytically oriented psychotherapy, the transference is recognized in its major contribution to the process. However, its evolution may be thought to differ in important respects from that in analysis, depending on the degree of modification of the usually recommended psychoanalytic practice of abstinence. Important differences in technique are contingent on the modifications. The variations in evolution and management of the transference, due to circumstances, have served me as bases for defining differences in method (Stone, 1981). (See other chapters in this volume for different views.)

Even when a therapy is remote from the interpretive framework, as with behavior therapy, the reaction of the patient to the authoritative suggestions or instructions of the therapist gains a certain unique power from the nonrational sphere—that is, from the transference. Awareness of this phenomenon (including possible intrusions of the negative transference) must surely enrich the work of superior practitioners in this field of therapy, as in other forms of noninterpretive psychotherapy.

THE TRANSFERENCE IN NORMALITY AND PSYCHOPATHOLOGY

As suggested earlier, we can assume that transferences are latent, incorporated in the adult personality, and invested in the images of major archaic objects. They are, of course, present in healthy as well as neurotic personalities, the differences being in large part quantitative. In the former, we assume a much lower degree of residual (unneutralized) drive investment in archaic images, a larger quotient of sublimated ego-syntonic attitudes toward equivalent current objects, and a corresponding minimization of conflictual elements generating anxiety and/or guilt. Thus, the corresponding latent transferences find expression in the "normal" phenomenon of dreaming, in creative activities, and in sublimated human relationships. They are, in short, part of the adult character structure. They are susceptible to upset by situational stresses or stimulations of unusual import to the given individual. One such "stress" would be the psychoanalytic situation, leading to a transference neurosis, if such a fortunate (i.e., healthy) individual should succeed in involving himself genuinely in a psychoanalytic process. In that rare instance, one might predict a most favorable outcome. (We know, however, that clinical "normality" is very often "more apparent than real," and that it can constitute a most formidable defense and character resistance to severe conflicts. For a more general clinical overview, see Reider, 1950.)

In the neurotic patient too, we may assume that transferences are latent in the adult character, often affecting mostly personal relationships, with or without manifest sexual content. However, if a clinical neurosis is present, one may assume that the original archaic drive investments have also been reactivated, threatening the corresponding defensive structures, and thus have sought expression in the compromise formation of symptoms. Because of their remarkable economic condensation of gratification and suffering, these become an enduring and formidable component of resistance structure, always subject to "renewal" through well-worn channels.

The first contact with the analyst, except in certain borderline or psychotic patients, is on a characterological level, in which true transference is only part of a complicated integration. The traits that characterize the individual in most major relationships will dominate the earliest phase of analysis. Trustfulness, suspiciousness, hypersensitiveness, friendliness, "standoffishness," hypercritical attitudes, and a tremendous range of other traits and nuances will have to be dealt with or accepted as such in the initial analytic contacts.

THE EFFECT OF PSYCHOANALYTIC TECHNIQUE ON TRANSFERENCE

Under the influence of the psychoanalytic situation, including the rule of abstinence and the affirmative atmosphere of relatively total tolerance and acceptance of verbal and affective expression, the development of more discrete transference (or transferences) tends to occur. This is strongly facilitated by the imposition of abstinence and the "basic rule" and its reductive impact on defensive structures. One transference group, the nonconflictive true positive transference (the "unobjectionable" form), which Freud regarded as essential even for the initial acceptance of interpretations, reproduces the trusting, dependent, benignly expectant, and largely affectionate attitude toward parents of early development. Where it has been—and is—minimal or fragile, its growth in relation to a new object (probably compounded from fragments of reality and fantasies of longing of early years) will be a critical development. It finds important support, and often merges with, the adult elements in the therapeutic alliance: the adult wish for clinical cure, adult understanding and cooperativeness, adult capacity to sustain discomfort for a valued if relatively remote goal, and allied phenomena. In varying temporal relationships to this development, the conflictive, primarily ego-dystonic elements of transference will begin to appear, sometimes discretely, sometimes in complex groupings or alternations, as direct conscious experiences or indirectly manifested in dreams and parapraxes or indirect associative allusions. These include the entire gamut of rejected, unacceptable, or mutually incompatible attitudes toward parents (or siblings)—erotic, hostile, competitive, passive-submissive, masochistic, clinging, and many others. Where these are manifest and well established, the tendency (among analysts of classical orientation) is, with due regard for the distinction between defen-

sive and substantive trends, to institute the interpretive reduction of these elements to their genetic origins to the degree possible. This is usually more effective in the context of the transference neurosis than in relation to discrete transference fragments. In this process (including "working through"), as in other spheres, the basic, tenacious "transference resistance" is encountered. Where the analytic evidences of transference are highly developed and the patient's awareness is slight or nonexistent, the preliminary goal is the overcoming of the "resistance to the awareness of transference."[4] This should include the analysis of the superego-stimulated defenses (see A. Freud, 1936; Gray, 1982). The questions of timing, method, the economic factor, and other considerations have engendered varying, sometimes conflicting, responses in the literature (see, for example, Gill, 1979; Panel, 1984; Stone, 1981).

With continuance of the psychoanalytic process, the relatively discrete transferences tend to become included in the transference neurosis, in which the relation of one to the other, against the background of structural conflict and commingling with the latter, begins to assume a centrally integrated form. This follows the general structure of the infantile neurosis, as represented in a current context. Although the term "transference neurosis" is often used, its meaning is seldom spelled out. Actually, the term "neurosis" is not often applicable in its literal sense, although validated by everyday usage. It is applicable in a literal sense only when the lag in process occasions new symptom formations, even if temporary. More often, what happens is the transference repetition of the dynamic constellations and central conflicts that underlie the clinical neurosis, which indeed generated the infantile neurosis of the past. It is this complex phenomenon that is most frequently referred to as "the transference neurosis." If inadequately analyzed (or tenaciously resistant to analysis), this constellation can lead to new symptom formations or relapse into the current clinical neurosis. Even without such clinical developments, the working through of original dynamic conflicts may occasion briefly fluctuating symptomatic reactions—for example, fluctuations in sexual function. The expression of the transference neurosis in analy-

---

4. The term "transference interpretation" is often loosely used, even by scholarly colleagues. The preliminary step (making the patient aware that he is reacting to the person of the analyst, whatever he represents to the patient) is often so used, without qualification. Actually, the final (in fact, actual) "interpretation of transference" is the establishment of its genetic prototype(s) against the formidable "transference resistance." The earlier encounter is with the "resistance to the awareness of transference."

sis, since the analyst can usually be perceived effectively only as one person at a time, most often involves the relevant and adjacent "dramatis personae": the patient's own family, the analyst's other patients, the analyst's perceived or imagined family, employers, colleagues, and similarly important individuals. Insofar as they are inevitably invested with transferences radiating from the analytic situation, elements of love, hostility, guilt, and incipient neurotic conflict solutions may present themselves for interpretation *in statu nascendi*. The transference neurosis in its intense integration and condensation of powerful tendencies and its utilization of preformed pathways of conflict solution presents, in seeming paradox, the climactic form of resistance and the most effective potential avenue for resolution or reduction of conflicts. In this extremely condensed expression of the core content of a given analysis, the transference neurosis also offers the only sound, if not unassailably reliable, outline of the basic analytic work to be done, by contrast with the inevitable massing of diversionary resistance detail with which the analyst must also deal.

In most individuals of relatively mature psychosexual development, the transference neurosis assumes a largely phallic-oedipal framework, although showing, inevitably and significantly, the precursive influences of the major pregenital spheres, sometimes as archaic character formations. These originally gave specific quality to the individual's oedipal experience and must also be analyzed. I am convinced that predominantly pregenital transference neuroses can also occur, although there are colleagues who disagree with this. Sometimes it is a question of definition or other semantic-conceptual aspects.

THE ULTIMATE FATE OF THE TRANSFERENCE

Assuming expectable adequacy of the analytic work, what happens to the transference depends on the original depth of the illness, on the soundness of the original separation and individuation, and on the individual's capacity, intellectual and emotional, for the development of substitute sublimated interests in the world at large. In individuals with profound early disturbances of separation—I speak in broad generalities—most of life and its interpersonal relationships consist of transferences, including an unrenounced, although ambivalent, seeking for the primal object. In such instances the analytic situation is unique, yet one of various transference relationships is often preferred both because of its avoidance of the psychologically profound dangers sensed

in "real" confrontations and its general, insulating protectiveness from the harsh impingements of life on a lonely frightened individual. The painful or threatening content of the transferences may be reproduced in the analytic situation in attenuated, relatively tolerable form—with a play-acting ("as if") quality, with its built-in ultimate frustrations accepted, *faute de mieux*. While cognitive acceptance of reductive interpretations may occur, the affective motivations can persist indefinitely; and the "interminable analysis" may become or approximate a clinical reality, even if a species of (interrupted) termination is effected.

In an individual of viable neurotic pathology, the essential conflictive elements of transference can usually be analyzed, reduced to the point where the individual can separate from the analyst, and can function adequately in the essential spheres of life. That all elements of the transference bond or the possibility of its potential renewal are thereby totally extinguished is open to doubt, on the basis of empirical observation. Even from a theoretical point of view, this seems improbable—in the sense that thoroughly adequate parenting leaves transference potentialities even in the healthy individual. Such transference renewal, with due regard to influential current realities, may appear in relation to the original analyst or even materialize in relation to a subsequent analyst (see, for example, Pfeffer, 1963).

One component of transference is, in general, minimally affected by analytic work. That is the concealed or disguised universal craving for an omnipotent, omniscient, protective, and guiding parent. Its forms of expression may be altered, and its adaptive potentialities augmented, but the underlying dynamic remains essentially the same. Freud made wistful passing reference to it in his correspondence (1909–39) with Pastor Pfister (1963), envying the final religious solution that the pastor could offer. For the vast majority of humankind, this need seems best met by religion. For others, passionate devotion to political leaders or to various ideologies present more satisfactory substitutes, according to individual temperamental and intellectual bent. Science itself is not without this type of adherence. And I have previously stated (Stone, 1975) that psychoanalysis too, which views all other intense human attitudes and preoccupations with critical understanding, is sometimes unwittingly conscripted to the same end.

PROBLEMS OF THE GENESIS OF TRANSFERENCE

Some factors influencing the integration of transference in adult character or its discrete separation and its modes of emergence have already been noted.

The question of its archaic genesis has not often been the subject of inquiry. Most often it is taken for granted, viewed as a phenomenon *sui generis*. However, there have been efforts to penetrate origins from early on in analytic history—for example, Ferenczi's paper (1909). The view of transference as a relatively fixed reenactment of the past has been associated with the repetition compulsion (Freud, 1914). Silverberg's (1948) interpretation is excessively harsh and not empirically valid in my view. However, a dynamic thrust toward the future, a better adaptation of drive to reality, stimulated by the presence of a new object, have attracted increasing attention (Nunberg, 1951; Loewald, 1960). Lagache (1953) emphasized the importance of the dynamism arising from unfinished or interrupted processes, citing the Zeigarnik phenomenon. I pointed out the importance of a reasonable degree of "resemblance" for the elicitation of transference in the nonpsychotic subject (Stone, 1954). I also sought to explain the pervasive ubiquitous phenomenon of transference as a reaction to archaic separation from the primal object (Stone, 1961, 1967). On this view, the insistent urge to reunion was expressed in the "primordial transference" varying in focal emphasis with the respective psychosexual phases and finding expression in such relatively adaptive channels. In the "mature transference," physical separation is accepted, with speech and ancillary modalities as the preponderant bridge to the mother. The analytic situation is seen in its primary unconscious impact, as one of "separation-in-intimacy," the analyst as the "mother of separation." The latter is conceptually in contrast to the usual (somatic) physician, who represents to the unconscious the primary mother, the mother of intimate bodily care. It should be noted that while there are significant conceptual differences, other writers have previously offered seminal interpretations of the unconscious infantile impact on the patient of the total psychoanalytic situation (see Spitz, 1956, and Greenacre, 1954, in this connection).

The interaction between the actualities of the analytic personal relationship and the transference, discretely and literally considered, constitutes a problem of complex and subtle importance, too complicated for multidimensional consideration here. It is, however, important to mention that while there may be blurring, actual merging, and overlapping, the two phenomena remain conceptually separate and, not seldom, objectively (and demonstrably) separable in clinical phenomenology. Again, not all agree (see Brenner, 1979, 1982). While noted in the 1950s (A. Freud, 1954; Stone, 1954), it was Greenson in his later writings who elaborated the importance of the "real" (nontransference) relationship (1967). Szasz (1963), taking an extreme position, has tended to regard transference, as often invoked by analysts, as a sort of defense or counterresistance to the perception and acceptance of the patient's actual attitudes toward him or her. There is no doubt that such error may occur. However, that such occasional error should lead to the devaluation or disestablishment of a profoundly important system of facts (and operational principle) is not to be considered seriously.

VARIATIONS IN VIEWS OF TRANSFERENCE

In Relation to General Theoretical Position

The foregoing account is based on an essentially classical theoretical orientation. It would be impractical to try to deal with wide deviations from this general position in this condensed chapter—for example, those of Horney (1939) or Sullivan (1953). Writers on severe narcissistic or borderline disorders stress special characteristics of the transference in such cases, its mode of emergence, and special features of technical management (Kernberg, 1979, 1982; Modell, 1976, 1979). Kohut (1977), in developing his own view of a separate line of narcissistic development and thus his special emphasis on self psychology, evolved a new phenomenology and nomenclature for transference (for example, mirror, idealizing, grandiose transferences). With these classificatory concepts came greatly augmented importance assigned to the patient's extended acceptance of transferences and the empathic introspective mode of understanding, as compared with the interpretation of objectively perceived data. Early developmental deficits then received greater emphasis than conflict. While Kohut's views are, in general, not offered as supplanting those derived from the classical framework, they are offered as major additions to psychopathology and technique, which are felt, in some instances, to outweigh in importance the older psychology of conflict (see, for example, Kohut, 1979). Others are critical or skeptical in response to this position. I see the contributions of Kohut and his followers as important additions to the resources of the analyst, elective or imperative, but in no sense devaluing or displacing the classical technical framework or psychopathology.

In Relation to Psychopathology

Overall, the concept of transference has been broadened, deepened, and complicated since its introduction by Freud. For example, the distinction between narcissistic and transference neuroses can no longer be sustained in its original literal and radical sense, even though it retains general and useful empirical validity. The distinction does not really lie in a narcissistic lack of capacity for transference in an ultimate sense. It lies rather in the patient's profound fear of such transferences on account of their overwhelming intensities, the violent reaction to disappointment, and their potential destructiveness. The problem is if and how they can be mobilized; and, if mobilized, how they can be managed and interpretively reduced. There is no question that some individuals with severe borderline pathology, who lack other compensating personality resources, should not be exposed to the demands of the psychoanalytic situation, except in an extensively modified form (for example, after preparatory psychotherapy, and/or the maintenance of ongoing "flexibilities" of attitude and technique that do not compromise ultimate analytic goals). That others with superior resources may be helped more directly by treatments that adhere more closely to the classical analytic model is not to be excluded, however (Stone, 1954). Apparently, the borderline patients in the Kris Study Group (1983) were found suitable for relatively unmodified analytic work. Several other authors have found this the generally desirable approach. Kernberg's work has covered a range from more accessible cases to those requiring active structuring of the environment and/or ancillary professional help. There is little doubt in my mind that these differences are due in great part to the types of case material available to the practitioners.

Since this chapter is about transference, it would be inappropriate to pursue further the general subject of borderline and narcissistic disorders. In recent years, this field has evoked its own extensive literature; see the numerous writings of Kernberg (for example, 1975, 1982); Modell (1976); and Monograph 7 of the Kris Study Group of the New York Psychoanalytic Institute (1983), among others. All present strong positions regarding pathology, technical methodology, and sometimes nosology. Certainly, special features of transference (quality, mode of emergence, and the question of transference neurosis) have been stressed (for example, by Kernberg and Modell).

While I appreciate and respect the importance of these and other contributions, I remain, in keeping with my basic views, convinced of the principle that the entrance key to such treatments lies in the management (in a direct personal sense) of the actually or potentially violent transferences or transference demands of such patients. First, there must be recognition of the patient's special potential for transference regression, in response to the emotional and perceptual vacuum between him or her and the analyst; correspondingly, the willingness and ability to "titrate" the situation of abstinence in nonseductive spheres, so that regressions are more likely to occur gradually, and within reach of effective interpretation, against the background of a developing trusting bond. Second, the analyst must have the ability to accept and withstand such transferences, without responsive countertransference distortions, including the rage of frustration or despair about the total effort. In my view, these are in the realm of the *sine qua non*. In light of them, the many cogent observations and recommendations of recent years could achieve their full potential value in augmenting effective work, including the subtle interpretive sphere.

Analysts of a much earlier generation sometimes referred to the "keeping of a positive transference" with very ill patients (especially psychotics). This is not what I have in mind. Obviously, hostile transferences must appear and be interpreted if analytic work is to be effective. The principle of active avoidance or suppression of any type of material by the analyst (Knight, 1953) does not recommend itself to me. The creation of a safe and protective ambience is another matter.

It remains true that borderline conditions (or the borderline personality) do not constitute a coherent, unitary nosological or pathological entity any more than was the case in early approaches to the problem (for example, Stern, 1938; Knight, 1953; Stone, 1954). The actual or potential severity, the difficulties of treatment, and the immediate or potential narcissistic regressions remain quite frequent in this heterogeneous group. As the designation implies, such patients may be (crudely) conceived of as suspended midway between the transference and the narcissistic neuroses (or psychoses)—hence the particular and crucial position of transference management. That this midway or oscillatory position can sometimes be tenaciously maintained (or even dramatically concretized) is substantiated by the occasional occurrence of a "transference psychosis" while the extratherapeutic bond with reality is maintained (Stone, 1954; Greenson, 1967; Kernberg, 1975).

SUMMARY

This chapter has offered a broadly inclusive but not detailed overview of its large general subject, beginning with its clinical phenomenology as traditionally considered. This has been extended to a broader and deeper consideration of certain theoretical positions regarding transference and the factors influencing its course and fate in treatment. Its dual role as essential propulsive power and ultimate resistance in the analytic process was considered. The basic connection between the analytic rule of abstinence and the evolution of the analytic transference was emphasized. My own views regarding the archaic origins of transference and related ideas were presented briefly for consideration but were not offered as generally accepted or established in the analytic community. The transference neurosis and its importance have been emphasized. There was a very brief discussion of countertransference (the topic of the next chapter). There were also brief comments regarding the interaction between the transference and the "real" (nontransference) relationship with the analyst. While demurral was noted, it has been my position that these are clearly separate conceptually, and that the difference usually becomes demonstrable and clinically important in treatment. Brief reference to borderline states was made, because of the special significance of the transference in their management.

REFERENCES

Abend, S., Porder, M. S., & Willick, M. S. (1983). *Borderline Patients*. New York: Int. Univ. Press.

Alexander, F. (1956). *Psychoanalysis and Psychotherapy*. New York: Norton.

Blum, H. P. (1971). On the conception and development of the transference neurosis. *J. Amer. Psychoanal. Assn.*, 19:41–53.

———. (1973). The concept of erotized transferences. *J. Amer. Psychoanal. Assn.*, 21:69–76.

Brenner, C. (1979). Working alliance, therapeutic alliance, and transference. *J. Amer. Psychoanal. Assn.*, 27 (suppl.):137–157.

———. (1982). *The Mind in Conflict*. New York: Int. Univ. Press.

Breuer, J., & Freud, S. (1893–95). *Studies on Hysteria. SE*, 2:3–305.

Ferenczi, S. (1909). Introjection and transference. In *Sex in Psychoanalysis*, pp. 35–93. New York: Basic Books, 1950.

Ferenczi, S., & Rank, O. (1924). *The Development of Psychoanalysis*. New York: Nervous & Mental Disease Publication Co., 1925.

Freud, A. (1936). *The Ego and the Mechanisms of Defense*. New York: Int. Univ. Press.

———. (1954). The widening scope of indications for psychoanalysis. *J. Amer. Psychoanal. Assn.*, 2:607–620.

Freud, S. (1900). *The Interpretation of Dreams. SE*, 4 & 5.

———. (1905). Fragment of an analysis of a case of hysteria. *SE*, 7:7–122.

———. (1912). The dynamics of transference. *SE*, 12:99–108.

———. (1914). Remembering, repeating and working through. *SE*, 12:147–156.

———. (1916–17). *Introductory Lectures on Psycho-Analysis*, Part III. *SE*, 16:431–447.

———. (1919). Lines of advance in psycho-analytic therapy. *SE*, 17:159–168.

———. (1927). *The Future of an Illusion. SE*, 21:5–56.

———. (1937). Analysis terminable and interminable. *SE*, 23:216–253.

Freud, S., & Pfister, O. (1963). *On Psychoanalysis and Faith*. Edited by H. Meng & E. L. Freud. New York: Basic Books, pp. 39–40, 63.

Gill, M. M. (1979). The analysis of the transference. *J. Amer. Psychoanal. Assn.* 27 (suppl.):263–268.

Gill, M. M., & Hoffman, I. Z. (1982). *Analysis of Transference*. Vol. 1: *Theory and Technique*. Vol. 2: *Nine Audio-Recorded Psychoanalytic Sessions*. Psychological Issues, monograph 53. New York: Int. Univ. Press.

Gill, M. M., & Muslin, H. L. (1976). Early interpretation of transference. *J. Amer. Psychoanal. Assn.*, 24:779–794.

Gitelson, M. (1952). The emotional position of the analyst in the psycho-analytic situation. *Int. J. Psychoanal.*, 33:1–10.

Gray, P. (1982). "Developmental lag" in the evolution of technique for psychoanalysis of neurotic conflict. *J. Amer. Psychoanal. Assn.*, 30:621–655. (See also Panel, 1984.)

Greenacre, P. (1954). The role of transference. *J. Amer. Psychoanal. Assn.*, 2:671–684.

Greenson, R. R. (1965). The working alliance and the transference neurosis. *Psychoanal. Q.*, 34:155–181.

———. (1967). *The Technique and Practice of Psychoanalysis*, vol. 1. New York: Int. Univ. Press.

Horney, K. (1939). *New Ways in Psychoanalysis*. New York: Norton.

Kernberg, O. F. (1975). *Borderline Conditions and Pathological Narcissism*. New York: Aronson.

———. (1979). Character structure and analyzability. *Bull. Assn. Psychoanal. Med.*, 19:87–96.

———. (1982). To teach or not to teach psychotherapy techniques in psychoanalytic education. In *Psychotherapy: Impact on Psychoanalytic Training*, ed. E. D. Joseph & R. S. Wallerstein, IPA Monograph 1, pp. 1–37.

Knight, R. P. (1953). Borderline states. *Bull. Menninger Clinic*, 17:1–12.

Kohut, H. (1977). *The Restoration of the Self*. New York: Int. Univ. Press.

———. (1979). The two analyses of Mr. Z. *Int. J. Psychoanal.*, 60:3–27.

Kris, E. (1956). On some vicissitudes of insight in psycho-analysis. *Int. J. Psychoanal.*, 37:445–455.

Kris Study Group of the New York Psychoanalytic Institute (1983). *Borderline Patients*. Monograph 7. New York: Int. Univ. Press.

Lagache, D. (1953). Some aspects of transference. *Int. J. Psychoanal.*, 34:1–10.

Loewald, H. W. (1960). On the therapeutic action of psycho-analysis. *Int. J. Psychoanal.*, 41:1–18.

Macalpine, I. (1950). The development of transference. *Psychoanal. Q.*, 19:501–539.

Modell, A. H. (1976). "The holding environment" and the therapeutic action of psychoanalysis. *J. Amer. Psychoanal. Assn.*, 24:285–307.

———. (1979). Character structure and analyzability. *Bull. Assn. Psychoanal. Med.*, 19:97–103.

Nunberg, H. (1951). Transference and reality. *Int. J. Psychoanal.*, 32:1–9.

Panel (1984). The value of extra-transference interpretation. E. Halpert, reporter. *J. Amer. Psychoanal. Assn.*, 32:137–146.

Pfeffer, A. Z. (1963). The meaning of the analyst after analysis. *J. Amer. Psychoanal. Assn.*, 11:229–244.

Racker, H. (1957). The meanings and uses of countertransference. *Psychoanal. Q.*, 26:303–357.

Reich, A. (1960). Further remarks on countertransference. *Int. J. Psychoanal.*, 41:389–395.

Reider, N. (1950). The concept of normality. *Psychoanal. Q.* 19:43–51.

Silverberg, W. V. (1948). The concept of transference. *Psychoanal. Q.*, 17:303–321.

Spitz, R. A. (1956). Transference. *Int. J. Psychoanal.*, 37:380–385.

Stein, M. (1981). The unobjectionable part of the transference. *J. Amer. Psychoanal. Assn.*, 29:869–892.

Stern, A. (1938). Psychoanalytic investigation of and therapy in the borderline group of neuroses. *Psychoanal. Q.*, 7:467–489.

Stone, L. (1954). The widening scope of indications for psychoanalysis. *J. Amer. Psychoanal. Assn.*, 2:567–594.

———. (1961). *The Psychoanalytic Situation*. New York: Int. Univ. Press.

———. (1967). The psychoanalytic situation and transference. *J. Amer. Psychoanal. Assn.*, 15:3–58.

———. (1975). Some problems and potentialities of present-day psychoanalysis. *Psychoanal. Q.*, 44:331–370.

———. (1981). Some thoughts on the "here and now" in psychoanalytic technique and process. *Psychoanal. Q.*, 50:709–733.

Strachey, J. (1934). The nature of the therapeutic action of psycho-analysis. *Int. J. Psychoanal.*, 15:127–159.

Sullivan, H. S. (1953). *The Interpersonal Theory of Psychiatry*. New York: Norton.

Szasz, T. (1963). The concept of transference. *Int. J. Psychoanal.*, 44:432–443.

Tower, L. E. (1956). Countertransference. *J. Amer. Psychoanal. Assn.*, 4:224–255.

Zetzel, E. R. (1956). Current concepts of transference. *Int. J. Psychoanal.*, 37:369–376.

Harold P. Blum, M.D., and

Warren H. Goodman, M.D.

8

COUNTERTRANSFERENCE

The phenomenon of countertransference and the issue of what to do about it have been with psychoanalysis since its inception. When Joseph Breuer, Freud's mentor and collaborator in his early *Studies on Hysteria* (1895), abandoned the treatment of Anna O., a seductive female patient, it was presumably because he had become overly engrossed in her treatment. His guilt has been related to the conscious recognition that he had been responding to the patient's unconscious sexual wishes, clearly indicated by a fantasied pregnancy. So strong was his need to protect himself from such dangerous influences from patients that he took flight from the fledgling science (Jones, 1953). The breach of professional boundaries by having a sexual, social, or business relationship with a patient is understood today in terms of transference–countertransference enactment. The departure from usual analytic procedure, abstinence, and neutrality is indicative of a special responsiveness to some aspect of the patient.

Analysis of such experiences reveals the essence of the countertransference phenomenon, which has been defined in different ways that variously assign to it either a narrow or a broad purview. Obviously, it refers to only partly conscious attitudes and feelings, and sometimes actions, of the analyst toward the patient. These reflect unconscious conflicts that may affect his or her understanding and therapeutic handling of the patient. Countertransference then represents a displacement onto the patient of attitudes and feelings derived from earlier situations in the analyst's own life in response to the patient's behavior toward the analyst. In this sense, it is analogous to transference. Hence, as the term itself indicates, countertransference can be defined in a narrow sense as a specific reaction to the patient's transference or more generally as a neurotic reaction of the analyst to the patient. Some authors, however, "include all of the analyst's emotional reactions to the patient, conscious and unconscious, rational and irrational, especially those that interfere with analytic understanding and technique. This broad purview might be better designated *counterreaction*" (Moore & Fine, 1990, p. 47).

Laplanche and Pontalis (1973) equated countertransference with "the whole of the analyst's unconscious reactions to the individual analysand— especially to the analysand's own transference" (p. 92). Others make the definition even broader and bilateral and include the mutual reaction of analyst and analysand to each other's transference. Obviously the situation can be very complicated. Just as the patient develops a transference to the analyst and the analyst develops a countertransference to the patient's transference, so also the analyst has transferential reactions to the patient, and the patient in turn may have transference reactions to the analyst's countertransference. In addition, the patient will react to the analyst's character (for example, whether he or she is flexible, dogmatic, angry, or cheerfully disposed). Similarly, the analyst reacts to the character of the patient, and there can be a countertransference to some element common to several or many patients. If such a reaction occurs in the analyst with all patients, it undoubtedly reflects the intrusion of his or her own conflicts or character problems into the analytic work.

Basically countertransference is a species of transference, and the narrow definition has the advantage of demarcating it more precisely as inappropriate response to the patient's transference. The broader definition confuses the unconscious reactions of the analyst, for example, to a very tall or very short patient, with unconscious irrational reactions to the patient's transference conflicts. On the other hand, it has the advantage of encompassing the great variety of irrational reactions on the part of the analyst that he or she may or may not be aware of or recognize as inappropriate.

Freud (1910) first noted countertransference as follows:

We have become aware of the "counter-transference," which arises in him [the analyst] as a result of the patient's influence on his unconscious feeling, and we are almost inclined to insist that he shall recognize this counter-transference in himself and overcome it. Now that a considerable number of people are practising psycho-analysis and exchanging their observations with one another, we have noticed that no psycho-analyst goes further than his own complexes and internal resistances permit; and we consequently require that he shall begin his activity with a self-analysis and continually carry it deeper while he is making his observations on his patients. [pp. 144–145]

Freud (1912) warned about the resistances in the analyst "which hold back from his consciousness what has been perceived by his unconscious" (p. 116). Additional roots of the concept may be inferred from Freud's remark (1913) that "everyone possesses in his own unconscious an instrument with which he can interpret the utterances of the unconscious in other people" (p. 320). Earlier he had said:

It may be insisted, rather, that he [the analyst] should have undergone a psycho-analytic purification and have become aware of those complexes of his own which would be apt to interfere with his grasp of what the patient tells him. . . . [Ultimately, Freud advocated that] everyone who wishes to carry out analyses on other people shall first himself undergo an analysis by someone with expert knowledge. . . . [He admonishes that those who refrain from this course] will easily fall into the temptation of projecting outwards some of the

peculiarities of his own personality . . . into the field of science, as a theory having universal validity; he will bring the psycho-analytic method into discredit. [1912, pp. 116–117]

Freud commented on additional aspects of countertransference in various allusions to the subject at different times. His predominant viewpoint was that countertransference may be attributed specifically to a reaction to the patient's transference; and throughout his discussions there is the clear implication that it is an impediment that may interfere with neutrality, empathy, and understanding and therefore must be held in check. There are, however, hints of a more positive view of countertransference in his recognition that it could serve as a valuable source of enlightenment—that is, as a signal alerting the analyst to the need to address a possible loss of neutrality and self-control.

For the doctor the phenomenon [the patient falling in love with the doctor] signifies a valuable piece of enlightenment and a useful warning against any tendency to a counter-transference which may be present in his own mind.

[But Freud also warns,] Our control over ourselves is not so complete that we may not suddenly one day go further than we had intended. In my opinion, therefore, we ought not to give up the neutrality towards the patient, which we have acquired through keeping the counter-transference in check. [1915, pp. 160, 164]

After Freud's initial contributions between 1910 and 1915, the knotty issue of countertransference continued to engage the attention of analysts through the years. In the period between 1915 and the early 1950s, the literature (reviewed by Orr in 1954) reflected Freud's view that countertransference was an impediment to analysis. But there was also a group of analysts, largely members of the British school, who saw countertransference as potentially a very positive, powerful diagnostic and therapeutic tool. Some even took the position that countertransference is a primary therapeutic issue in treatment. In the 1920s, classical analysts (those adhering most closely to Freud's position) viewed it as having the same origin as does transference in the patient—that is, in repressed infantile sources. It could therefore manifest itself in any form that transference does but could also be limited by the analyst's previous training and knowledge. In contrast to the prior concentration on the intrapsychic manifestations of the patient's transfer from the past to the present, British analysts showed an early interest in object relations and interpersonal interactions. That interest extended to interrelationships and reciprocal reactions in the analytic situation, and with this focus upon the immediacy of the present as opposed to the influence of the past, countertransference came more to the center of attention. This interest was probably intensified by efforts to apply analytic treatment to psychotic and borderline patients, with whom countertransference issues tend to be particularly powerful.

Those who defined the concept of countertransference more broadly on the basis of the experiences described above (A. Balint & M. Balint, 1939) noted that the analyst impresses himself upon the patient in myriad ways—for example, by the arrangement of his office, by his personality, technique of working, and through the impact of the analytic situation. As a result of more complex considerations of mutual transference and countertransference reactions between patient and analyst, a serious questioning of the universal applicability of the "mirror model" took place (A. Balint & M. Balint, 1939), though it was conceded that a patient may be analyzed by a variety of individual techniques. There was general consensus among workers in the field, however, that the fundamental task of the patient remains to learn his or her own unconscious mind, not that of the analyst. However, countertransference could not only impede analysis, but could be used to facilitate analysis in this emergent view.

In 1951 Annie Reich provided a definition of countertransference that had been a touchstone for the prevailing point of view over many years. She described it as comprising "the effects of the analyst's own unconscious needs and conflicts on his understanding or technique." She observed that "whenever the activity of analysing has an unconscious meaning for the analyst" (p. 26), then his or her acting out can be seen as a form of countertransference. In that circumstance, patients do not represent real objects to the analyst but tools by means of which the needs of the analyst, which can include allaying anxiety or masking guilt, are gratified.

Even if there is conscious awareness of countertransference, its sources may nevertheless be unconscious. Annie Reich suggested that if there is no libidinal investment (for example, manifestations of underlying voyeurism, albeit desexualized and sublimated) on the part of the analyst and therefore no countertransference, then the analysis will not progress. Nevertheless, she stressed that this "voyeurism" must be sublimated to allow for smooth working in the analytic situation. The common factor operative in the analyst's countertransference responses is anxiety, whether the analyst is aware of it or not. This anxiety may result from psychosocial factors such as the need for success in intercurrent

events in the analyst's life, from unresolved neurotic problems of the analyst, or from communication of the patient's anxiety.

Reich made a distinction between countertransference and counteridentification (perhaps equivalent to overidentification). Countertransference could be useful if controlled and understood. Counteridentification, on the other hand, was described as a mutual response—that is, a response of the analyst to the patient's identifying with him or her. It is an aberrant miscarriage of analytic empathy. What should be a transient identification with the patient persists and intrudes upon the analyst's objective observing ego. Counteridentification is a mutual regressive response on the part of both patient and analyst; in both it may be seen as a phenomenon in which early identificatory processes are repeated. It should be noted that Reich was, nevertheless, a proponent of the view that countertransference could be a useful analytic tool.

In the mid-1950s, as a result of the influence of British psychoanalysts, countertransference came to be seen in a more positive light. Conscious and unconscious, as well as normal and neurotic, reactions on the analyst's part were distinguished in its definition. A distinction was also made between those aspects of countertransference that have a positive effect and those that have a negative effect on the analysis of the patient. Thus the patient's association to conflict kept repressed by the analyst might induce in the analyst a pathological interference, whereas certain identifications of the analyst and personal experiences affecting development might provide a countertransference favorable to analytic work. Those studying the phenomenon also noted that countertransference reactions should be distinguished from the reactions of the analyst to his or her more or less objective observations of the total personality and behavior of the patient. Fenichel (1940) had already expressed concern that fear of countertransference on the part of the analyst might lead him or her to suppress all human freedom in reacting to the patient. This could lead to the undesirable outcome of the patient feeling that the analyst was a special being not permitted to be human. These considerations led to a more flexible, humanistic view by contrast with the prevailing view of the mid-1930s typified in the following statement: "Overt pity, sympathy, criticism, intolerance, affection, etc., are best kept out of the attitude of the psychotherapist. His role is to skillfully and tactfully mirror the emotions and conflicts in such a way that the patient will see their origin and the futility of endless repetition" (Orr, 1954, p. 661, quoting English & Pearson, 1937, p. 303).

In the 1940s and 1950s there was a very active controversy between so-called mirror model advocates (those who believed the analyst should reflect only the patient's psychic image to him or her) and those who viewed the analyst as a human being and a participant observer. The former contended that countertransference might cause the analyst to attenuate or manipulate the transference rather than limit him- or herself to interpreting it. However, there emerged a consensus that countertransferences are ubiquitous and not necessarily undesirable, and that the analyst can and should use his or her emotional responses to enlarge understanding of the patient's unconscious. Recognition of the ubiquity of countertransference reduced its previously pejorative connotations.

This history shows that countertransference has always been a subject of interest to psychoanalysts, but it attracts even greater interest today. This is in large measure due to the larger focus on the total functioning (not just malfunctioning) of the analyst, as well as contemporary interest in how the analyst formulates the case and intervenes. Some analysts believed that it was necessary to obtain deeply unconscious satisfactions from their work in addition to the conscious ones derived from effecting cures, conducting research, and earning a living. Only in this way, they thought, could analysis thrive and interference by countertransference be avoided. Today professional and analytic satisfactions remain important but are considered peripheral to the identification, clarification, and ongoing analysis of countertransference.

There is now a tendency toward microscopic evaluation of how analytic goals are reached, as well as an emphasis on empathy as it relates to the analytic process. Originally, Freud (1912) implied that gross countertransference arose only from time to time in an analysis. Now it is felt that there is always a two-person field and that the analyst is a participant observer with his or her own subjective reactions. Transference/countertransference manifestations are ubiquitous between patient and analyst, although countertransferences are usually well modulated, sublimated, and under ego control. More attention is paid to breaches in the "frame" of the analysis, such as schedules and fee payments. Nevertheless, while breaches in these areas may be the result of eruptions from the analyst's unconscious, it is also true that flexibility or inexperience is sometimes a factor.

Racker (1968) speaks of a countertransference neurosis, paralleling the transference neurosis. This represents a minority view, which depicts analysis itself as an erotic relationship. It applies only to persistent, recurrent, intrusive manifestations of a sort that do not characterize most countertransference reactions and are symptomatic of significant psychopathology in the analyst.

Racker made many important contributions to the understanding of the concept of countertransference and influenced psychoanalytic countertransference theory and technique. He differentiated between direct and indirect countertransference and between concordant and complementary countertransference reactions. Direct countertransference refers only to the analyst's countertransference to patients, whereas indirect countertransference may refer to a colleague or a supervisor. Thus, a candidate may have a direct countertransference to a patient and an indirect countertransference to a supervisor. Concordant countertransference refers to identification with a patient's internal psychic agency, such as the ego or the id; that is (from an experiential point of view) an empathic identification with the patient's thoughts and feelings. Racker, following Helena Deutsch (1926), defines complementary countertransference as referring to the analyst's identification with the patient's infantile object representations, which in Racker's terminology are described in terms of internalized object relations. The patient regards the analyst in terms of a transference fantasy in which the analyst represents an infantile love object such as a parent or a sibling. Racker pointed out that the analyst might actually feel him- or herself to be in the position of the patient's infantile object representations. He used the concept of projective identification, deriving from Klein, in which the patient splits off and projects unwanted parts of his or her own personality onto the analyst and then succeeds in inducing in the analyst corresponding affective reactions. For example, the patient may induce the analyst to feel guilty toward the patient as a result of a projective identification. The analyst may defend against, express, or enact the unanalyzed projective identification.

Optimally the analyst will analyze his or her countertransference response and clarify and interpret the patient's projective identification, thereby facilitating the analytic process. Just as the transference may act as resistance in analysis, so too, countertransference, when intense and unanalyzed, will impede analytic work as a resistance. The term "projective identification" has often followed Racker's usage, but it has simultaneously and subsequently been used to refer to diverse transference–countertransference phenomena. Racker further recommended the use of countertransference as an aid to formulating correct interpretations. He tended to elevate the countertransference as a most reliable guide to appropriate interpretation. In his contemporary formulation, the analyst is a participant observer with emotional responses and inevitable, expectable countertransferences.

Even when it occurs to a lesser degree, however, many authors still believe that countertransference is an impediment to analysis, with the potential to interfere with neutrality. Recent writers (see Tyson, 1986) have commented upon the expansions of the concept of countertransference and shifts in its definition in the past couple of decades. In particular, the narrow focus on how the analyst's unconscious is affected by the analytic relationship has been expanded to a more encompassing view, which includes not only the unconscious but also the conscious feelings of the analyst. And a shift has occurred from defining countertransference only in terms of the analyst's reaction to the patient's transference to including all neurotically determined reactions to the patient. A more comprehensive view is one in which the patient's and the analyst's transferences are considered central. These shifts have been stimulated by theoretical change and by the widening scope of psychoanalytic treatment to embrace grossly disturbed narcissistic, borderline, and developmentally deficient and deviant patients. A number of analysts who published in the 1960s and 1970s (for example, Kernberg, 1965; Loewald, 1986) contributed to the thrust toward the broadened interpretation by highlighting their difficulties in treating such provocative, highly unstable patients. Their experience attests to the fact that countertransference on whatever definition is of singular importance in dealing with severely disturbed patients. Indeed, as Blum (1983) and others have pointed out, even subtle and relatively silent manifestations of countertransference are of importance in dealing with *all* patients. Countertransference involves not only "blind spots," but the influence of the analyst's sensitivities, preferences, value judgments, attitudes, and so on.

Current events in the analyst's life influence conflicts and thus change compromise formations (Brenner, 1985). These shifts in compromise formations change the attitudes and actions of the analyst, his or her interest in the work and understanding of his or her patients. Being an analyst may involve sublimated sexual curiosity or the wish to see another suffer. Such sublimations may be regressively drawn into conflict, interfering with analytic work.

The contemporary focus seems to be on the analytic situation as a two-person relationship with all the nuances this implies. Each party attempts to evoke or impose an intrapsychically determined role relationship on the other (Sandler, 1976). The patient unconsciously attempts in the transference to experience this relationship as a means of obtaining gratification for a spectrum of wishes. The analyst needs, therefore, to be able to monitor his or her responsiveness and increase the access to so-called useful countertransference—that is, a conscious awareness of how the analyst's own conflicts affect his or her unconscious reaction to the patient's associations and behavior. Loewald (1986) views controlled regression in the analyst in a developmental framework as parallel to parenting functions. Fine distinctions about what is helpful as opposed to what may be detrimental are difficult to make, however, since, as Arlow points out, "one man's empathy is another man's countertransference" (1985, p. 166).

The previously mentioned complexities encountered in trying to understand countertransference have led to a variety of suggestions for dealing with the phenomenon. It is important to determine whether a behavioral phenomenon in the analytic situation represents a specific countertransference toward the patient or a manifestation of pervasive characterological behavior on the part of the analyst. There are, after all, angry analysts, sad analysts, overly active or overly passive analysts, and so forth. An analyst may be sleepy with a particular patient or insufficiently attentive with all patients. Behaviors from the analytic side may reflect symptoms or characterological traits rather than specific responses to elements in the patient's presentation or unconscious.

There is general agreement that it is optimal for the analyst to become aware of manifestations of countertransference as soon as possible. Unconscious countertransference, whether negative or positive or both in alternation, is the factor on the analyst's side that is most likely to impede analytic work. It is an infantile reaction and has the capacity, as long as it remains unconscious, to blind the analyst to various aspects of the patient's transference. Persistent unconscious countertransference will tend to compromise analytic neutrality and objectivity. Manifestations of countertransference are protean, varying from those affecting the framework of analysis to matters of attention, the focus of interpretation, misunderstanding of content, disturbances of empathy, affective and cognitive disturbances in the analyst, values and judgments, preference and prejudice, and verbal and physical acting out of a sexual or aggressive nature. Countertransference can be detected through a heightened vigilance to its subtle manifestations, such as nuances of preferential attention or lack of interest, the presence of silent collusions, or the selective interpretation of only certain areas of conflict or development. For example, pre-oedipal conflicts may receive more attention than oedipal or vice versa, and maternal or other phases of transference may be neglected or even whole stages of development, such as adolescence, passed over.

Interference with any aspect of the analytic process may occur. The analyst may show too much therapeutic interest or ambition or too little. Countertransference may also affect the framework of the analytic treatment, such as issues of time, payment, or constancy. Lateness of the analyst, inadvertent early admission of the patient to the consulting room, canceling a session, forgetting a session, forgetting a bill, or submitting an incorrect bill are some of the occurrences that may signal countertransference. The analyst may thus become alerted to his or her own overreaction or avoidance, facilitating a focus upon what he or she is responding to in the patient. The patient may induce a response or seduce the analyst into action that, though inappropriate, is gratifying and meets infantile needs of one or both. Through such covert or overt rewards to both partners, countertransference fosters collusive avoidance and resistance. A minor and transient avoidance—for example, tuning the patient out through a lapse of attention—may indeed be the most common manifestation of countertransference. Such breaks in attention or concentration may be very subtle or extreme, varying from the analyst's sleepiness to falling asleep or premature termination or extension of a session because of loss of the sense of time.

The manifestations of countertransference may relate to other major issues and fine points in the course of an analysis. Examples that may be detected by self-scrutiny include misinterpretation, failure to give an interpretation, or ill-timed or tactless interpretations. Mood changes in the analyst such as depression, various parapraxes, or the appearance of the patient in the analyst's fantasies or dreams may be other indications. The analyst might also pay attention to the way he or she listens to the patient, the nature of his or her silences and special interests, the emphasis he or she places upon technical variations, or aspects of his or her extra-analytic behavior, such as the excessive recounting of details of an analysis to others. We can conclude that the very nature of psychoanalytic work potentiates the emergence of countertransference reactions. Ironically, the analyst who deems him- or herself immune to countertransference may well be the most vulnerable. Subjective responses and countertransference reactions are inevitable and universal. Unrecognized reactions may be subtle and well rationalized but nevertheless impede efforts to help the patient. Even though the source of the countertransference may remain unconscious, derivative reactions, such as annoyance or anxiety, may be conscious and observable. If he or she has been sufficiently analyzed, the analyst will not be afraid to recognize signs in him- or herself indicating anger, embarrassment, or a host of other uncomfortable affects that may accompany an emerging countertransference.

The analyst's personal analysis, by bringing to awareness his or her own conflicts, may serve to keep them from distorting the therapeutic work. This is one of the cardinal purposes of the analyst's own analysis during training (Moore & Fine, eds., 1990). Afterward, continuing self-scrutiny of countertransference derivatives frequently provides correct clues to the meaning of a patient's behavior, and the insights thus afforded can facilitate more prompt perception of the patient's unconscious. But the patient's observations must be considered as well. Little (1951) noted, for example, that the patient may interpret the countertransference before the analyst. While that interpretation may be distorted in turn by the patient's transference, it may also accurately reflect a perception of analytic countertransference before the analyst is aware of it. A patient's criticism of the analyst may be appropriate rather than simply a manifestation of negative transference. This is not an instance of the patient analyzing the analyst, but the patient's observations should certainly promote self-analysis by the analyst, which will help him or her to understand his or her own reactions.

Analysts are encouraged to reduce countertransference manifestations as much as possible through training analyses, self-analysis, and reanalysis. The long training of analysts enables them to apply their special knowledge and understanding to the psychoanalytic situation. Nevertheless, it is generally acknowledged that the analyst's conflict-free sphere, especially the "work ego" and analyzing functions, are subject to interference by defenses and regression. The completely neutral, totally objective analyst is a myth. And a new myth of analytic omniscience may be evolving from the idealization of the beneficial value of the countertransference. Analytic vigilance to emerging countertransference is honed in the process of analytic training, as the neophyte analyst encounters not only his or her own countertransference to patients but also that of his or her analyst and supervisors. Ultimately, self-analytic scrutiny is a requirement for the termination of training analyses.

Self-analysis may uncover and resolve difficulties that did not surface in the analyst's training analysis. Very fine empathic attunement to the patient, emerging in the most subtle interactions in the therapeutic relationship, has been highlighted in recent communications (Blum, 1986a, 1986b; Jacobs, 1984, 1986; Racker, 1968). Chronic postures, stances, or attitudes, unilaterally expressed or shared by analyst and patient, are now the focus of intense scrutiny. Much attention has been paid to the "autoanalytic function" (Tyson, 1986), but this has been accompanied by healthy skepticism about the capacity to analyze one's self and respect for the limitations of self-analysis. This capacity is thought to be an unconscious ego function over which one has little conscious control. Hence, consciously inspired self-analytic efforts not infrequently run into formidable resistances. Current analytic contributions emphasize that mastery of such resistances facilitates progress in analysis, converting scotomatizing countertransference to useful countertransference, thus exploiting the phenomenon in a controlled fashion to gain a deeper grasp of the patient's transference and so to promote the work of analysis. While many see countertransference, at this point, as making a creative and useful contribution to the analyst's understanding of the dynamic equilibrium of the psychoanalytic process, the degree to which awareness of it and insight as to its meaning can be conveyed to the patient remains extremely controversial. The mainstream consensual view (Kernberg, 1965) seems to be that one should attempt to use one's countertransference responses to further the analytic process. In educational efforts to promote this objective, however, it may be noted that analysts have preferred to depict countertransference in the supervision of students, in reanalysis, and in discussions of reported cases rather than in presenting their own cases. No doubt there is fear of personal exposure which may be too self-revealing.

If self-analysis proves inadequate, consultation may be sought, or the analyst may return to analysis with a colleague. A number of important considerations must be kept in mind in analyzing countertransferences. The analyst's vulnerability to countertransference is increased by life stress and personal difficulty. That vulnerability is tested by the unique transference/countertransference disposition to which each analytic dyad is subject, determined by the characters, temperaments, styles, ages, and sex of both analyst and patient. In fact, the entire gamut of conscious and unconscious emotional reactions that analysts have to patients needs to be taken into account, though not all such reactions constitute countertransference. Much can be learned from the patient's transference reaction to the analyst's countertransference. If the analyst is sleepy, it will provoke in any given patient his own particular trans-

ference reactions; these vary widely and can include overt anger, withholding of associations, denial, and so forth. Countertransference in the analyst may remain an unconscious fantasy, be acted out in various forms, or be defended against by avoidance or other behavior. Modifications in technique may be valid parameters in a given analysis or rationalizations and expressions of countertransference. There is a spectrum of countertransference reactions from the subtle, such as the subjective experience of anxiety, to the more blatant, such as not listening or blind spots, and finally very dramatic demonstrations in the form of acting out. Ideally, countertransference serves as a signal alerting the analyst to some significant conflict operative in the analysis. When gross erotic and/or aggressive feelings are involved, situations may arise, such as serious breaches of confidentiality or sexual acting out, that render further analysis impossible.

An important distinction is that between countertransference to a patient's transference and the analyst's transference to the patient. For example, an analyst might have a countertransference to a depressed, pregnant patient's transference and his own transference reaction to her pregnancy. Moreover, the patient's transference may even be anchored in the realities of the analytic situation. A masochistic patient, for instance, who accuses the analyst of mistreatment and exploitation, elicits criticism or silent inattention from the analyst, who may actually become sleepy. The complaints and accusations of hostile mistreatment are then validated in the analyst's countertransference sleepiness. This last example points to the need to correct the simplistic notion that the patient's transference is determined by the analyst and that the analyst's countertransference is a creation of the patient. The analyst's countertransference is codetermined by his or her own unconscious conflicts and is not simply induced by the patient. At the other extreme, it is also erroneous to equate countertransference with empathy or rapport.

Analysis of countertransference has, as its goal, the restoration of neutrality, empathy, correct understanding, and appropriate interpretive intervention. The patient's conflicts must not be confused with the analyst's conflicts, a situation that would occur if the analyst were to assume that his or her irrational reactions are identical to those of the patient or to those of a significant object in the patient's life. Most Freudian analysts believe that the countertransference should be analyzed without direct patient participation or communication concerning the analyst's unconscious conflicts. In point of fact, Loewald (1986) has noted that analysts do differ from patients in the scope and depth of their understanding of unconscious motivation and dynamics. The majority of authors discourage the communication of countertransference feelings to the patient. Some (Heimann, 1950) feel that to do so constitutes a confession that can be a burden to the patient. An extremist group of analysts advocates actual interpretation of the analyst's own countertransference to the patient, believing that even the origin of the analyst's technical difficulties in his or her unconscious conflicts can be explained to advantage (Little, 1951; Winnicott, 1949). The latter view is based in part on the belief that admitting mistakes to the patient will allow the patient to express his or her anger and thus get at the negative transference. Other authors (Gitelson, 1952), taking a more measured approach, advocate revealing as much of oneself as needed to foster and support the patient's discovery of the reality of the actual interpersonal situation as contrasted with a transference/countertransference situation. There has been general agreement, however, that one cannot analyze the patient by analyzing oneself or one's countertransference alone. The communication of self-analysis by the analyst, in place of analysis of the patient, confuses self and object and constitutes a flight away from analyzing the patient's transference; it is therefore a narcissistically oriented process.

There is a context of transference/countertransference interplay in all human relations, but it is especially important in all forms of psychotherapy. One caveat of importance is that the analyst, in an attempt to be rational, may tend to repress the resonances within him- or herself and the responses induced by the patient that are significant for treatment —those that give the deepest as well as the most unsettling understanding of him- or herself and the patient. Analyst and patient need to be deeply engaged in the analytic process. Analysts may be unfamiliar and ill at ease, for example, with problems stemming directly from the earliest developmental levels in patients whose conflicts involve archaic object relations. Analyzed countertransference can provide valuable clues to the attitudes, feelings, and reactions of objects internalized by the patient during childhood, interaction with whom contributed to the development and shaping of the patient's psychic life. The very deficiencies in subject/object differentiation, ego integration, and control of acting-out tendencies in such patients tend to overstrain the analyst's "work ego." There is a consequent threat of severe regression in ego organization, with blurring of boundaries and rigid defenses that compromise neutrality. The analyst is not immune to narcissistic countertransference, which may be manifest in a variety of ways, such as displays of cleverness that serve his or her self-aggrandizement. The patient observes and studies the analyst just as the analyst observes and studies him or her. For instance, the patient may be silent, forcing the analyst to intervene, which enables the patient to intuit what fantasies have been evoked in the analyst. In addition, the analyst may share unconscious wishes and defenses with the patient in other ways. Contemporary psychoanalysis has attempted to sort out and process the contributions of each party to the analytic situation, including their shared fantasies.

In summary, countertransference, broadly defined, may exist in relation to one particular patient, to a type of patient, to an aspect of psychopathology, to significant objects and figures in the patient's life, to tangential and adventitious aspects of the patient's real life situation (such as pregnancy, illness, or a death in the family, Holocaust survival, and so on), his or her history (of success or failure, for example), or personality attributes. An analyst's neurotic behavior with all patients may be either symptomatic or characterological, but it is not a specific countertransference. Countertransference may be sudden and acute, chronic and protracted, partly conscious and under the ego control of the analyst or totally unconscious; it may be defended against (as with Breuer's fleeing from Anna O.) or acted out. It is influenced by the unconscious infantile conflicts of both patient and analyst. Ubiquitous in all psychotherapy as well as analysis, it must be mastered to further the goals of treatment (Freud, 1910, 1914). Countertransference is a major source of the trials and tribulations of the analytic encounter, with the potential for both destructive regression and constructive progress in understanding.

REFERENCES

Abend, S. (1982). Serious illness in the analyst. *J. Amer. Psychoanal. Assn.,* 30:365–380.

Arlow, J. A. (1985). Some technical problems of countertransference. *Psychoanal. Q.,* 54:164–174.

Balint, A., & Balint, M. (1939). On transference and counter-transference. *Int. J. Psychoanal.,* 20:223–230.

Beres, D., & Arlow, J. A. (1974). Fantasy and identification in empathy. *Psychoanal. Q.,* 43:26–50.

Berman, L. (1949). Countertransferences and attitudes of the analyst in the therapeutic process. *Psychiatry,* 12:159–166.

Bernstein, I., & Glenn, J. (1978). The child analyst's emotional reactions to his patients. In *Child Analysis and Therapy,* ed. J. Glenn, pp. 375–392. New York: Aronson.

Blum, H. P. (1983). The position and value of extra-transference interpretation. *J. Amer. Psychoanal. Assn.*, 31:587–618.

———. (1986a). Countertransference and the theory of technique. *J. Amer. Psychoanal. Assn.*, 34:309–328.

———. (1986b). Countertransference: concepts and controversies. In *Psychoanalysis*, ed. A. Richards & M. Willick. New York: Analytic Press.

Brenner, L. (1982). *The Mind in Conflict.* New York: Int. Univ. Press.

———. (1985). Countertransference as compromise formation. *Psychoanal. Q.*, 54:155–163.

Breuer, J., & Freud, S. (1893–95). *Studies on Hysteria. SE*, 2.

Calder, K. T. (1980). An analyst's self-analysis. *J. Amer. Psychoanal. Assn.*, 28:5–20.

Cohen, M. B. (1952). Countertransference and anxiety. *Psychiatry*, 15:231–243.

Deutsch, H. (1926). Occult processes during psycho-analysis. Rpt. in *Psychoanalysis and the Occult*, ed. G. Devereaux, pp. 133–146. New York: Int. Univ. Press, 1953.

Dewald, P. (1982). Serious illness in the analyst. *J. Amer. Psychoanal. Assn.*, 30:347–364.

English, D., & Person, G. (1937). *Common Neuroses of Children and Adults.* New York: Norton.

Fenichel, O. (1940). *Problems of Psychoanalytic Technique.* Albany, NY: Psychoanalytic Quarterly Inc.

Fliess, R. (1953). Countertransference and counter-identification. *J. Amer. Psychoanal. Assn.*, 1:268–284.

Freud, S. (1910). The future prospects of psycho-analytic therapy. *SE*, 11:139–151.

———. (1912). Recommendations to physicians practising psycho-analysis. *SE*, 12:109–120.

———. (1913). The disposition to obsessional neurosis: A contribution to the choice of neurosis. *SE*, 12:317–326.

———. (1915). Observations on transference-love. *SE*, 12:157–171.

Fromm-Reichmann, F. (1950). *Principles of Intensive Psychotherapy.* Chicago: Univ. Chicago Press.

Gill, M. M. (1982). *Analysis of Transference*, vol. 1. New York: Int. Univ. Press.

Gitelson, M. (1952). The emotional position of the analyst in the psycho-analytic situation. *Int. J. Psychoanal.*, 33:1–10.

Glover, E. (1924). Lectures on techniques in psycho-analysis. *Int. J. Psychoanal.*, 5:269–311.

Grinberg, L. (1962). On a specific aspect of counter-transference due to the patient's projective identification. *Int. J. Psychoanal.*, 43:436–440.

Heimann, P. (1950). On counter-transference. *Int. J. Psychoanal.*, 31:81–84.

Jacobs, T. (1984). The analyst and the patient's object-world. *J. Amer. Psychoanal. Assn.*, 31:619–642.

———. (1986). On countertransference enactments. *J. Amer. Psychoanal. Assn.*, 34:289–307.

Jones, E. (1953). *The Life and Work of Sigmund Freud*, vol. 1. New York: Basic Books.

Kernberg, O. F. (1965). Notes on countertransference. *J. Amer. Psychoanal. Assn.*, 13:38–56.

Laplanche, J., & Pontalis, J.-B., eds. (1973). *The Language of Psychoanalysis.* New York: Norton.

Little, M. (1951). Counter-transference and the patient's response to it. *Int. J. Psychoanal.*, 32:32–40.

Loewald, H. W. (1986). Transference-counter-transference. *J. Amer. Psychoanal. Assn.*, 34:275–287.

Meissner, W. W. (1980). A note on projective identification. *J. Amer. Psychoanal. Assn.*, 28:43–68.

Moore, B. E., & Fine, B. D., eds. (1990). *Psychoanalytic Terms and Concepts.* New Haven: Yale Univ. Press.

Orr, D. W. (1954). Transference and countertransference. *J. Amer. Psychoanal. Assn.*, 2:621–670.

Racker, H. (1968). *Transference and Countertransference.* New York: Int. Univ. Press.

Reich, A. (1951). On counter-transference. *Int. J. Psychoanal.*, 32:25–31.

Sandler, J. (1976). Countertransference and role-responsiveness. *Int. Rev. Psychoanal.*, 3:43–47.

Silverman, M. A. (1985). Countertransference and the myth of the perfectly analyzed analyst. *Psychoanal. Q.*, 54:175–199.

Tyson, R. L. (1986). Countertransference, evolution in theory and practice. *J. Amer. Psychoanal. Assn.*, 34:251–274.

Winnicott, D. W. (1949). Hate in the counter-transference. *Int. J. Psychoanal.*, 30:69–75.

9

ACTION AND
ACTING OUT

THE ROLE OF ACTION IN PSYCHOANALYSIS

Action is ubiquitous in human life, and acting out occurs in every psychoanalysis. Yet, from the very beginning of "the talking cure," there has been a strong tendency to exclude action, both in fact and in theory, from this mostly verbal process and to consider it a troublesome interference. As a result, there is no consensus on a psychoanalytic theory of action, and conceptualizing about acting out has become ever more diffuse and lacking in definitional clarity.

In one sense, the limiting of action is necessary in order to create and to safeguard the analytic situation. Analysands are asked to assume a passive position, to turn their attention inward, and to report to the analyst, in words, all that they experience. They are asked to communicate verbally their hatreds and desires, their fantasies and memories and, at the same time, to forego action and gratification in order to explore the origins and the meanings of these internal experiences.

Just as the paralysis of sleep allows the dreamer's forbidden impulses to emerge without risk of being carried over into action (Freud, 1900), so the psychoanalytic method promises that anything can be said with impunity because action has been set aside (Freud, 1915; Schwartz, 1984). The analysand will not carry out the sexual or murderous fantasies that emerge; nor will the analyst retaliate, humiliate, or

be seduced. This shift from action to reflection is the implicit pact that makes it safe to loosen control of repressions and to regress. When the mind, rather than the behavior, of the analysand is the focus of the analytic work, then thinking and speaking need have no limitations (Gray, 1973).

Limitations occur, however. Various resistances to freely associative verbalization may result in memories, desires, attitudes, or conflicts being reproduced in some other form of action. This we call acting out. These actions may occur in the analytic session itself, or they may be displaced outside. The actions of acting out may be as varied as being silent on the couch, being late for the session, or refusing to perform a desirable action; behaving seductively toward the analyst or, instead, starting an affair with the boss; reliving the intense affect of a childhood trauma without remembering the event; or behaving in a subtle way that induces the unsuspecting analyst to talk more than usual.

The criterion that defines such actions as acting out is the nature of the link to the analytic process, especially to the transference. Acting out is not defined by the type or degree of activity of the behavior, nor by how pathological or socially unacceptable it is, nor by where the action takes place. The point is simply that some conflicted analytic material is discharged or expressed through an action other than verbalization.

By opposing or substituting for verbal understanding, acting out serves as a resistance to the psychoanalytic process. However, it may also represent an inability to put something into words and, as such, may be the only way that the analysand has of reproducing or expressing what cannot be said. In this sense, acting out has a potential communicative function and can further the analytic process. In fact, people communicate constantly through actions as well as in words. This is minimized but not eliminated in the psychoanalytic situation. Freud (1905) recognized this early, in his observations of Dora playing with her reticule, and he wrote that "no mortal can keep a secret. If his lips are silent, he chatters with his finger-tips; betrayal oozes out of him at every pore" (pp. 77–78).

Not all actions that occur in connection with the psychoanalytic process are acting out. The realities of life necessitate missing some analytic sessions, for example. Behavioral changes that result from resolution of conflicts may lead to new patterns of action. Symptoms and character traits that analysands bring with them to analysis often have action components as a manifestation of the psychopathology. Their enactment will necessarily become part of the analysis (Zetzel, in Panel, 1970), but they are considered acting out only when the action is exacerbated in response to the analytic process or the transference.

The repeated, unresponded-to calls for a psychoanalytic theory of action (Hartmann, 1947; Rangell, 1968; Boesky, 1982) attest to the lack of clarity in our conceptualizing. Despite the lack of theoretical precision, however, there is an extensive, clinically useful literature on the relationship of action to the psychoanalytic process, although "acting out" is usually the central focus (Rangell, 1968). Lacking a coherent theory of action, contributors to this literature have written about what is clinically troublesome, ordinarily identified as acting out. Unfortunately, with "acting out" rather than "action" at the center, other action components have tended to become inappropriately subsumed under "acting out," thereby broadening the concept beyond the point of usefulness (Blos, 1963).

In this chapter I will shift the perspective and consider action: first, as an aspect of the general psychology of human development and behavior; second, as a manifestation of psychic conflict and psychopathology; and third, as a major component of the psychoanalytic process encompassing both the resistive and the communicative aspects of acting out. The latter will receive the greatest attention, because these aspects are the forms of action that relate dynamically and creatively to the analytic process.

ACTION IN HUMAN DEVELOPMENT AND NORMAL BEHAVIOR

Action is motivated behavior.[1] Unlike simple physiological or reflex processes, action implies intention, purpose, and meaning (Moore & Fine, eds., 1990). The intention may be a conscious and deliberate choice, or it may be an unconscious compulsion. Action need not be observable or involve motor activity. It may simply be an intention carried out; and we call it an action whether the result is murdering the boss or sitting quietly in the sun. Inhibiting an impulse is an action. Even thinking, remembering, and speaking are all actions in the broadest sense.

Such a logically consistent and inclusive definition is useful for philosophical inquiry into action and intention (Brand, 1984) and for a general psychology of psychic functioning. Here the questions are about *how* actions are initiated and carried out—that is, the mechanisms of psychic processes. Psychoanalysts' questions, by contrast, are about *what* actions are carried out and *why*—that is, they concern the motivations, conflicts, and interactions of lived lives. The difficulties of using the same sparse, overworked action terminology in such diverse ways will become apparent in later sections.

This first section, however, will focus on "normal" action: that is, action as a factor in psychic function, in human development, and in mastery.

Mechanism of Action in Psychic Functioning

Relatively few psychoanalysts have followed Freud's early interest in delineating the psychic pathways of action as part of a general psychology of mental functioning. Freud (1895, 1900, 1911) postulated that, once the infant's developing ego gains control over motility, the aim of reducing excitations shifts to attempt to alter reality and is thus "converted into *action*" (1911, p. 221). A delay could now be interposed between a need and an action. The ego samples the external and the inner realities, anticipates the degree of pleasure or unpleasure, utilizing the affects as signals, and acts accordingly either to allow the action to be carried out, to postpone gratification, or to suppress the impulse as dangerous

1. The meanings of *behavior* and *action* overlap, and there is a large area in which they are used interchangeably, as they will be here. There are nuances, however. The word *behavior* is more likely to be used when the action is observable, complex or patterned, has duration, and is likely to be repeated (Moore & Fine, eds., 1990); whereas *action* is more likely to be used when the behavior is discrete or internal. *Behavior* is more concrete and part of everyday descriptive language; *action* is more abstract and explanatory.

(Freud, 1940). This formulation, along with his concept of thinking as experimental action using only small amounts of energy (1933), is as close as Freud came to a general theory of action.

Rapaport (1950) expanded Freud's idea of thinking as trial action; and Hartmann (1939, 1947) made new contributions to the theory of action, giving greater recognition to reality in the organization and regulation of action. He distinguished rational and irrational actions on motivational grounds rather than on the nature of the behavior itself, and he warned against a simplified dichotomy that would label "irrational" those actions that gratify instinctual drives and "rational" those actions under ego control.

Freud did comment on decision making: "Judging is the intellectual action which decides the choice of motor action, which puts an end to the postponement due to thought and which leads over from thinking to acting" (1925, p. 238). Rangell (1969a, 1969b, 1971, 1989) expanded Freud's ideas of the intrapsychic process to include an unconscious decision-making function of the ego. This intrapsychic process involves "intended instinctual discharge, the scanning for signal anxiety, choice of defense or other intermediate psychic formations, thought as experimental action, and decision as to final psychic outcome" (1989, p. 189). The final psychic outcome may result in thought, affect, fantasy, instinctual gratification, or the great variety of clinical psychopathologies; or the sequence may be directed outward into normal or abnormal action. Rangell emphasizes the role of an active though unconscious ego in exercising intention, will, and decision: "the ego chooses, directs and acts. In fact, it must choose. If it elects not to, that is also a choice" (ibid., p. 193). This intrapsychic process, with the ego as decisive and directive agent and with the entire process firmly anchored within structural theory, Rangell has now offered as a "cohesive and operative psychoanalytic theory of action" (ibid., p. 200).

By contrast, Schafer in his work on action language (1973, 1976, 1983) advocated replacing the mechanistic and spatial language of metapsychology with a new language of action which relentlessly focuses attention on the fact that persons are the active agents of their behavior. For example, the inhibition of an impulse is seen as "one action through which a person has succeeded in stopping another [action]," although it may be carried out in still a third action, as fantasy (1973, p. 184). Action is "all behavior performed in a personally meaningful, purposive, or goal-directed fashion and includes all the forms of thinking and feeling as well" (1983, p. 101). Schafer reformulated psychoanalysis as the study of human action, with particular emphasis on the identification of disclaimed actions. Schafer's work was seen by many as a radical attack on psychoanalysis, and it prompted vigorous criticisms on theoretical, logical, and clinical grounds.

Schwartz (1984) also addressed responsibility for one's actions but distinguished between mere agency and deliberate behavior. Schwartz defined "intentional action" (the general case of purposeful, goal-directed behavior) and "deliberate action" (the special case of intentional action that includes conscious choice among options). Free association, although consciously carried out, approaches nondeliberate intentional action, for which the analysand is not held ethically responsible. As the result of insight gained in analysis, behavior will become more the result of an expanded range of understanding, options, and choice. In that sense, psychoanalysis shifts the balance away from nondeliberate to deliberate action and toward an increased ethical responsibility for one's actions.

The Role of Action in Development

Whereas the previous section on action and psychic functioning dealt primarily with an intrapsychic action sequence, the role of action in development is mainly seen as one of action as activity.

Freud (1915) postulated that very young infants begin to differentiate inside world from outside world when they discover that certain external stimuli can be avoided by muscular action, whereas other stimuli arising within their own bodies cannot be avoided this way. For Piaget motor activity also was essential in differentiating inside and outside worlds. During the third stage of sensorimotor development (fifth to eighth month), the infant's attention shifts from his own body action to the effect that this action has on the outside world. This leads, in subsequent stages, to awareness of means–ends relationships, intentional motor exploration, and the internalization of motor activity in the form of anticipatory thought patterns (Piaget, 1936; Wolff, 1960, pp. 37–38).

Stern's infant observational research (1985) has greatly expanded our knowledge of the newborn's capacities for active communication and of the infant's ability to exercise intention and control within the first few months of life. Mahler et al.'s observational studies of young children (1975) assign great importance to the role of upright locomotion in emotional development and identity formation. Mahler (1981) and McDevitt (1983) both report that aggression promotes self–object differentiation in children and may be utilized for the maintenance of individual identity later on. An extensive literature on children's play deals with the role of action in the normal developmental process (Piaget, 1951; Winnicott, 1953; Kestenberg, 1968; Fast, 1970; Mahon, 1990; Mayes & Cohen, 1993; among others).

Blos (1963) regards "the dire need for action which is so typical of the adolescent process" (p. 173) as being as phase-specific for adolescents as is play for children and verbal communication for adults. Action serves to regulate tensions caused by the increased instinctual pressures of puberty and to resist the regressive pull of passive wishes in the conflict over disengagement from internalized parental objects. Action may be used to protect the ego from the sense of loss until new objects are found and to promote ego synthesis and consolidation of identity.

The Role of Action in Mastery

Action is the natural mode of expression in children, up to adolescence (Holder, 1970; Busch, 1989). Although language becomes the major mode of communication for adults, action continues to occupy an important place in adaptation. Adaptive action also has a special role in the psychoanalytic process, in the working through of insight into change and mastery.

Prior to the 1970s, little had been written about the place of action as a positive, adaptive force in relation to psychoanalysis. One notable exception was Wheelis's (1950) discussion of new modes of action in real life as part of the working-through process that brings about personality change. These new modes of action are opposed by the patient's well-established neurotic modes and must not be ignored or, worse, labeled as acting out by an unaware analyst. Valenstein (1962, 1983) also discussed the necessity for working through in relation to changes in action patterns.

Rangell (1981) summarized a unitary view of action. "Analysis moves from the neurotic actions or inhibitions of action for which the patient seeks analysis, through injunctions against acting out during the process, to a point in treatment where positive actions become desirable if not necessary both in the analysis and in life" (p. 130). Change does not follow automatically from insight. Results depend on actions being carried out. Hartmann (1947) and Abrams (1980) have discussed similar views of insight, action, and change. Poland (1977) elaborated a stepwise interdigitation of action and insight in describing the adaptive role of action in mastering conflict and assimilating identifications.

Discussion

This brief review of the literature on "normal" aspects of action, as well as the initial pages of this chapter, point up the conceptual problem. The word *action* is used in too many different, and sometimes contradictory, ways. Analysands are asked to forgo action yet are asked to talk about what they are experiencing on the couch. But talking is an action. Broadly defined, action includes thinking, remembering, and fantasying; yet we embrace them as the proper actions of the analytic process and frown on other actions that interfere with those functions.

Action looked at from the standpoint of psychic functioning is essentially an intrapsychic sequence, necessarily somewhat abstract, in which the focus is on the proximal end of the sequence: intention, thinking, decision making, agency, responsibility. On the other hand, when looked at from the standpoint of development and mastery, the focus is on the distal end of the action sequence: activity, concrete and observable behavior, and change. Yet our one word *action* encompasses the entire sequence. It becomes even more conceptually complex when we include nonactive, nonobservable behavior (for example, fantasy) at the distal end as an outcome of an action sequence.

Rangell's theory of action solves the problem of bringing intention, will, and decision into the language and theory of metapsychology. It has some explanatory power when applied to the concept of action in psychic functioning, as do his ideas about insight, working through, and change at the other end of the sequence. Rangell has given us a theory of action; yet it does not seem to have helped resolve the confusion in the way we think about problems relevant to the psychoanalytic process. Perhaps that is too much to ask of a single, unitary theory.

Schafer's theory (1976), on the other hand, is closer to experience in its language. As an exercise in thinking about responsibility and disclaimed actions, it provides an important corrective to our careless concepts and practices, and it imposes a rigorous discipline on thinking about intention and resistance. In clinical practice, however, it tends to fall under the weight of its cumbersome mode of expressing everything in terms of action.

Some would say that the theory of action is a conceptual problem, some a semantic problem, and some would declare it an insoluble problem.

ACTION IN PSYCHIC CONFLICT AND PSYCHOPATHOLOGY

We have considered action as a normal, adaptive aspect of development and change. Now the focus will shift to action as an expression of unconscious conflict and psychopathology.

One of Freud's early discoveries was that symptomatic, chance actions (forgetting, slips of the tongue, bungled actions) revealed an unconscious conflict in motivation. At times the analysis of such actions, which Freud called *parapraxes* (1901), may be as fruitful for insight as is the analysis of more serious symptoms. Such episodic symptomatic acts usually convey a discrete message about a specific conflict, and they often rather easily yield a hidden message.

Neurotic action or *pathological action* implies a more enduring pattern of symptomatic behavior in the form of observable actions occurring widely in the various forms of psychopathology. Behaviors tend to be stereotyped, dominated by drive demands and rigid defenses, symbolizing and repeating traumatic events, and evoking painful affects and disturbed relationships. Such a broad definition of action would encompass all symptoms, but that is beyond the scope of this chapter. This section will focus in a general way on neurotic and character pathology in which active behavior and/or lack of impulse control are the prominent symptoms. This literature is interwoven with that of *acting out* insofar as many writers do not make a distinction between the action of pathology and the action of the treatment process, which may, but may not, represent pathology. The attempt to present them as separate subjects, however, will help to clarify the important distinction.

Psychic and behavioral manifestations of psychopathology are interwoven inextricably. Observable actions may express a wish or a defense or both. At other times, action may serve not a specific defense but a general defensiveness; or it may function as an attempt to restore psychic equilibrium or to maintain the integrity of the self-structure.

Some actions, like dreams, represent a condensation of the unconscious conflict itself. In hysterics the conflict often appears in one symptom and one action. In the obsessive-compulsive, the conflict may give rise to two different actions, one expressing the wish, the other the defense (Freud, 1907, 1909; Hartmann, 1944).

In contrast to those actions arising from wish, defense, or compromise, some individuals commit crimes (Feud, 1916) or act out (Naiman, 1966) in order to deal with prior guilt or a felt need for punishment. Coen (1985) has reviewed the work of a number of authors from the perspective of perverse behavior as a solution to intrapsychic conflict, and Stolorow & Lachmann (1980) have discussed the function of sexual activity in restoring or maintaining the structural cohesion of self in narcissistic patients.

Others have described active behavior as a coping device rather than a breakthrough of impulses (Tooley, 1974). In borderline patients it may represent a defense against loss of identity (Angel, 1965)

or the repetitive behavior pattern expressing unconscious conflict, especially pre-oedipal aggressive drives (Kernberg, 1975, 1984). Kernberg also shows that these patients have a particular way of using language as action to control the interpersonal situation. Segel (1969) described a syndrome of acting out that represents an effort at active mastery of an earlier, passively experienced trauma. Stein (1973) describes acting out as a character trait in some patients whose behavior patterns are predictable, not chaotic. Analysis may reveal an unconscious fantasy that is repetitively enacted.

A different form of pathological, active behavior is seen in disorders of impulse control, in which there is a nonspecific lack of impulse control and an intolerance of delay in response to anxiety or tension. There is no repetitively enacted content, no organized fantasy, and usually no symbolism in the actions (Frosch, 1977).

Discussion

It is clear that patients who tend to externalize their inner conflicts and who utilize active behavior as symptoms present a different problem for the therapist or analyst. But is their symptomatology conceptually different from that of those who minimize active behavior? In the broadest definition of action (motivated behavior), there is no categorical difference at the proximal end of the action sequence between a motivation that will lead to a fantasy of kicking and one that will lead to the act of kicking.

This does not solve the conceptual dilemma about action and active behavior, however. What begins as an intrapsychic action sequence ends with an act, which may be active or passive, aggressive behavior or fantasy. The consequences of kicking and of thinking about kicking are different. Action of this sort attempts to have an effect on the external world. The ensuing difference in consequences and its effect on the individual inner experience would have to be taken into account in any comprehensive theory of action.

ACTING OUT

Action is part of the psychoanalytic process in the intrapsychic processes of all motivated mental activity; in the actions of development, normal behavior, change, and mastery; and in the varied forms of active behavior that may arise as expressions of psychopathology. None of these is specific to the psychoanalytic process, however. In this section, the focus is on the forms of action that are most specific for psychoanalysis or other transference-mediated forms of therapy. I will briefly consider nonverbal communication, which occurs in everyday life as well as in analysis and then more extensively review and discuss acting out.

Nonverbal Communication

Although F. Deutsch (1947, 1952) was the first to record systematically his observations of the body movements of his analysands and to correlate their postures with certain themes in the material they presented, Freud made similar use of his own observations. The Rat Man, he noted, had a peculiar expression on his face suggesting pleasure as he described the horrors of his obsessive fear (1909). W. Reich (1933), in his work on character analysis, considered the patient's behavior in the session, as well as the manner of presentation of the material, to be more important than the content of the material.

Nonverbal communication includes postures, gestures, movements, and bodily rumblings in the analytic session, as well as the infinite qualifiers of the verbal message contained in tone, pressure, syntax, rhythm, and the timing and quality of silences. McLaughlin (1987) finds that such data may reveal links between early object relations and conflicts that have become an integral part of character. Jacobs (1973) has likewise described the analyst's bodily movements during the act of listening. Observation of his or her own nonverbal behavior may provide useful clues to the analyst's unconscious response to the patient's material and may assist his or her interpretive function.

Zeligs (1957) introduced the term *acting in* to describe postural attitudes and body movements during the analytic hour, which he saw as occupying the middle ground on a continuum of acting out without verbalized memory at one end and remembering verbally without action at the other. In common usage, however, his term has come to mean acting out with*in* the analytic hour in distinction to the acting *out* that is displaced outside.

Nonverbal messages are present in all human interactions and may be considered part of normal communication. Nonverbal behavior takes on special significance in the psychoanalytic situation, however, and may be brought under the broad umbrella of acting out.

Manifestations of Acting Out

The term *acting out* is used in a precise technical way, in a loose descriptive way, and in a colloquial pejorative way. Even in psychoanalytic discourse, there is lack of agreement on its precise technical use. Here I have narrowly defined it in relation to analytic or other transference-rich therapeutic settings and have differentiated it from behaviors that result from preexisting psychopathology.

Freud's first mention of the concept and the term *acting out* was in his postscript to the Dora case. As he later came to understand it, Dora ended the analysis prematurely because of his failure to interpret correctly the source of her transference to him. "Thus she *acted out* an essential part of her recollections and phantasies instead of reproducing it in the treatment" (Freud, 1905, p. 119). There is the implication here that acting out opposes psychoanalytic treatment. Freud later shifted the emphasis from resistance to repeating as a way of remembering in his seminal paper, "Remembering, repeating and working through" (1914):

. . . we may say that the patient does not *remember* anything of what he has forgotten and repressed, but *acts* it out. He reproduced it not as a memory but as an action; he *repeats* it, without, of course, knowing that he is repeating it.

For instance, the patient does not say that he remembers that he used to be defiant and critical towards his parents' authority; instead, he behaves in that way to the doctor. . . . As long as the patient is in the treatment he cannot escape from this compulsion to repeat; and in the end we understand that this is his way of remembering. [p. 150]

Acting out as repetition had now become an inevitable part of the analysis; in fact, Freud identified the transference itself as only a piece of repetition. The compulsion to repeat (in the transference) replaces the attempt to remember; the greater the resistance, the more will acting out replace remembering. Whereas remembering under hypnosis had the quality of a laboratory experiment, repetition in the transference gives the flavor of real life, not only in repeating the past but in stirring deeper instinctual impulses that had not been previously felt. Freud recognized the risks involved for the patient or the treatment if repeating in action is not kept within limits. He continues:

The main instrument, however, for curbing the patient's compulsion to repeat and for turning it into a motive for remembering lies in the handling of the transference. We render the compulsion harmless, and indeed useful, by giving it the right to assert itself in a definite field. We admit it to the transference as a playground in which it is allowed to expand in almost complete freedom and in which it is expected to display to us everything in the way of pathogenic instincts that is hidden in the patient's mind. Provided only that the patient shows compliance enough to respect the necessary conditions of the analysis, we regularly succeed in giving all the symptoms of the illness a new transference meaning and in replacing his ordinary neurosis by a "transference-neurosis" of which he can be cured by the therapeutic work. [1914, p. 154]

As pointed out by Laplanche and Pontalis (1973), "The term 'acting out' enshrines an ambiguity that is actually intrinsic to Freud's thinking here: he fails to distinguish the element of *actualization* in the transference from the resort to *motor action*—which the transference does not necessarily entail" (p. 4). Both elements arise from a repetition of the past, but the behavioral results may be quite different; for example, an impulsively manipulated job transfer that "necessitates" an abrupt termination of the analysis or, by contrast, the gradual unfolding in an aggressive businessman of tender feelings of being cared for by his analyst, allowing him eventually to recall early memories of a warm relationship with his father prior to the onset of the father's alcoholism. It is confusing at best to use *acting out* for both. One repeats by running away to avoid the transference, while the other repeats a feeling experience in the transference and eventually remembers with insight the context in which he had felt it before.

Boesky (1982, 1989) has recently clarified this conceptual ambiguity. Freud defined acting out during the era of the topographic theory, which offered only two alternatives: remembering or repeating in action. Remembering was preferred; if repeating was necessary in order to remember, it should be minimal. Freud left his explanation of acting out essentially unchanged when he supplanted the topographic theory with his more complex structural theory. But, as Boesky points out, acting out could now be seen as a compromise formation, with defense as only one of its components.

Whether one regards acting out as opposition to the analysis or an essential ingredient or both, this view still links acting out to transference in a treatment relationship. The widest divergence from Freud's original concept has occurred where this criterion has been dropped and the term has been used, not just carelessly but in some reasoned psychoanalytic writings, to include almost any behavior that seems to express some pressing unconscious need, especially when the behavior is inappropriate or disruptive. Thus, neurotic activity, perversions, addictions, impulsive and antisocial behaviors, and much ordinary adolescent activity have all been called acting out, in and of themselves, whether in the context of treatment or not. With such expanded and imprecise usage, the term loses all dynamic meaning as a specific issue in treatment.

The preferred, narrow definition of acting out requires (1) that it arise in a transference-mediated treatment process rather than being the patient's habitual pattern of behavior; (2) that verbalization be replaced by some other mode of expression or that the act of speaking itself carry resistive or communicative meaning; and (3) that it have the potential for remembering and communicating as well as for obstructing analytic progress.

The history of the concept of acting out is an interesting one to follow. In her 1936 book Anna Freud broadened the theoretical discussion of acting out under the structural theory, emphasizing the contributions from ego, id, and superego. She spoke not of "acting out" but of "acting in the transference" and listed it as one of three forms of transference, along with transferences of libidinal impulses and of defense.

Weiss (1942) took issue with the idea of acting out as opposition to remembering, pointing out that patients often act out something which they have already remembered, although it may not have been fully remembered with appropriate affect. In a little-known paper that is remarkable for the author's early recognition of the working-through aspect of a pattern of acting out, Emch (1944) described patients who as children had had a persistently "unknowable" parent due to extreme inconsistency or a devious life pattern. Their acting out took the form of repetitive caricatures of the parental behavior, which Emch understood as an expression of the need to know. She saw it as an attempt through identificatory reenactments to find the elusive parent. Once the truth of previously unknown situations could be assimilated, the patients no longer needed the enactments.

In discussing "Neurotic acting out" (1945), Fenichel began to loosen Freud's link between acting out and transference. Transference may be a "mere emotional attitude" toward a definite person, whereas acting out involves "real action" that "has to be done regardless of toward whom" (p. 297). Although he acknowledged some ways in which transference and acting out are similar, he saw acting out as stemming from a pathological predisposition in the patient more than as a response to transference and treatment. Those who were prone to "spontaneous acting out" prior to treatment were more likely to continue it during treatment. Fenichel was discussing in particular those patients whose pathology is expressed in action, who will of course be prone to the same actions once treatment has been established. But he put acting out and neurotic action together because of similar observable behavior, rather than acting out and transference together because of similar repetition in the treatment. Even though his observations may be accurate for patients with a certain kind of pathology, Fenichel nevertheless blurred an important conceptual distinction and set a course for those who think of acting out as a description of oppositional behavior rather than a major component of the analytic process.

In the 1950s and 1960s, acting out continued to be a subject that challenged and puzzled psychoanalysts. Publications, panels, and symposia were numerous and reflected the loss of direction of the concept.[2] More and more the theoretical interest took one of two directions: the link with pathological action or the search for definitional consensus.

The clinical attitude typical of that era was that acting out occurred as an undesirable resistance when the analyst had failed to interpret the transference appropriately. The emphasis was on prevention through proper transference interpretation, although some analysts actually prohibited acting-out behavior.

Bieber (1965) broadened the term to include "any behavior deemed to be antisocial or self-destructive" (p. 142); and Bellak (1965) included "criminological aspects" and discussed "correctional measures" (pp. 12–13). In sharp contrast, however, was Ekstein's (1965) concept:

Acting out is neither good nor bad; it is usable or it is not usable. . . . In classical analysis, the patient is to tell us freely what occurs to him, and he is not to censor his thoughts or withhold. If he is to "tell us freely," he must well choose to tell us in the way that he can. . . . Sometimes he will act them out. . . . We "listen" to all these forms of communication and interpret them, and as we are impartial toward the *content* we must also learn to be impartial toward the *mode of communication*. [pp. 169–171]

Greenacre's series of papers on acting out (1950, 1963, 1968) reflect her interest in understanding the increased tendency to act out in a group of more seriously disturbed patients, whose sometimes massive and disruptive acting out presents serious technical problems in analysis. In these atypical patients she

2. In addition to numerous individual papers there were Panels in 1957, 1969, 1970; an entire issue of the *Journal of the American Psychoanalytic Association* (1957, pp. 581–705); two books (Abt & Weissman, eds., 1965; Rexford, ed., 1978; Symposium, 1968; and a Kris Study Group (Moore, 1967).

postulated "a distortion in the relation of action to speech and verbalized thought, arising most often from severe disturbances in the second year" (1950, p. 458). In such patients, speech and verbal thought tend to be inhibited and motility to be overly developed; in later life, they regress to preverbal forms of communication. Greenacre's contributions, like those of Fenichel, emphasize the link between acting out and pathological action rather than the link with transference.

With a similar orientation, one Kris Study Group studied acting-out behavior over a two-year period in a wide variety of patients; the behavior ranged from brief, circumscribed acts to repetitive, significant events that constituted a whole way of life. At the end of the study they still were unable to establish criteria that could distinguish acting out, neurotic behavior, impulsive action, and perversions in all cases; but a consensus was reached on a broad statement of the essential feature: "behavior, in or outside analysis, which is revealed to represent the translation of an unconscious fantasy into current activity" (Moore, 1967, p. 14). Expression in action allows for some drive discharge, modified by defensive and superego elements. A strong, poorly integrated aggressive drive and a history of repeated primal scene exposure were frequently found in patients who acted out most severely. In them, acting out often replaced denial when it failed as a defense.

The Twenty-Fifth International Psycho-Analytic Congress (Symposium, 1968) was devoted to the subject of acting out, and it was a time of taking stock of the concept. Anna Freud (1968) gave the opening paper, reminding the audience that fostering the emergence of drive derivatives into consciousness and interpreting them at just the point where they threaten to erupt into action so as to keep this from happening is still the ideal course of analysis. In this way, id impulses enter the conscious ego and become part of its synthetic function. However, she recognized that not all repressed psychic content is capable of becoming conscious in this way.

The "forgotten past" may be unobtainable except in the form of being re-lived. If this is the case, the analyst provides for its token satisfaction in the transference. . . but it is supposed to stop short of motor action. . . acting out is at a minimum, i.e. nipped in the bud, so far as the technical devices of free association and dream interpretation are concerned. It is allowed latitude, within the limits of the analytic rules, in the transference and for the sake of transference interpretation. And it endangers the progress of analytic treatment where it cannot be confined either within the psychical sphere (short of motor action) or within the analytic setting (i.e. within the transference). [pp. 166–167]

Anna Freud observed that as analytic interest has broadened to include patients with serious pre-oedipal pathology, less of the "forgotten past" can be recovered in memory, and it can only be relived or acted out (see also Frank, 1969). She drew distinctions between transference acting out and the habitual acting out of delinquents, addicts, and psychotics, whose impulsive behavior belongs to their pathology and not to the curative process.

Both in 1936 and in 1968, Anna Freud represented the classical position, clearly defined with careful attention to the balance between ego, id, and superego components in the compromise formations determining behavior. In her later discussion, she noted a shift in analytic interest toward reliving and repeating in the transference and away from recovery of the past through free association and interpretation of dreams. She recognized the wider use of the term *acting out* to include a variety of pathological behavior, but she cautioned against such obscuring of the concept.

Rangell (1968) emphasized the need "to establish the role of acting out within the larger realm of human *action* and to distinguish it particularly from neurotic action" (p. 195). While retaining the concept of acting out as linked to the analytic process, Rangell broadened the definition within that context. Whereas Freud saw acting out as opposed to the recovery of memories, and Anna Freud and Fenichel saw it as opposed to the emergence of repressed instinctual impulses and their derivatives, Rangell saw it as "a specific type of neurotic action, directed towards interrupting the process of achieving effective insight, therefore seen mostly in the course of psychoanalysis but also elsewhere" (p. 197).

Grinberg (1968) stressed that acting out is a process that develops in an object relationship, often originating in inadequate mourning of an early object loss and carried out in the present with the analyst, with projective identification playing a paramount role.

Moore's symposium paper (1968) made several points. Acting out is almost invariably related to communication, either serving it or designed to avoid it. His case vignette illustrated how a pattern of neurotic behavior preexisting analysis came to be regarded as acting out only after the analyst as a transference figure became involved in the conflict expressed in the action. Action in the form of motor activity is predominant over thought and speech in

the separation-individuation period, according to Moore, and locomotion is the means both of independence from and of reunion with mother. This becomes an important factor in the individual's later resort to action to protect either the object or self representations in the face of overly intense libidinal or aggressive impulses.

In a 1970 Panel, Zetzel characterized the symptomatic act (forgetting to sign the check) as a communication to the analyst that can lead to insight, in contrast to those forms of acting out that represent organized resistance to recollection. Neurotic action, which must necessarily be brought into the analysis, is distinguished from acting out not on the nature of the act but on whether it is a response to the analysis itself. Acting out differs from adaptive action in lacking the delay that allows for introspection, consideration of internal and external reality, and a decision-making process. Acting out in analysis bypasses this process and interferes with the patients' ability to know their inner life.

The 1970s and 1980s saw a major expansion in understanding patients with more primitive pathology. Although the distinction between pathological behavior patterns and acting out was better understood and could be maintained theoretically, Kernberg (1984) emphasized how easily the boundary becomes blurred clinically when patients, immediately on beginning treatment, mobilize chronic pathological behavior patterns in the transference. The topic that seems to have captured the psychoanalytic interest of the last decade, however, is the positive aspect of acting out within the psychoanalytic process itself: enactments, reliving, and actualizations as ways of remembering and communicating, and their relationship to transference and countertransference.[3]

Schafer's refreshing reminder that "the concept of acting out . . . may be used to designate acts of kindness, pseudostupidity, and conscientiousness as well as acts that are directly provocative and disruptive" (1983, p. 73) seems to exemplify the shift in tone away from mainly the oppositional and disagreeable in patients' behavior to the communicative and useful action components. Along with this shift has been a greater awareness and focus on analysts' contributions through their own enactments, coun-

3. Jacobs, 1973, 1986, 1990, 1994; Blum, 1976; Sandler, 1976a, 1976b, 1976c; Mahl, 1977; Gedo, 1979, 1984; McLaughlin, 1981, 1987, 1989, 1991; Boesky, 1982, 1989; Casement, 1982; Schafer, 1983; Erard, 1983; Fox, 1984; Loewald, 1980, 1986; Stein, 1986; Inderbitzin, 1988; Panel, 1989; Busch, 1989; Chused, 1991; Kantrowitz, 1992, 1993; Roughton, 1993, 1994; Mayes & Cohen, 1993; Ogden, 1994.

tertransferences, and participation in unconscious role responsiveness.

In a comprehensive review article, Blum (1976) includes the analyst's contribution to acting out. Incorrect interpretations or lack of timely ones tend to stimulate acting out, although it may also occur as a reaction to a correct interpretation. In addition, analysts may unwittingly foster acting out by their own behavior, either in style of intervention or through specific countertransference responses (see Kantrowitz, 1992).

Sandler's concept of transference (1976a, 1976b, 1976c) includes the patient's attempt to manipulate or otherwise bring about with the analyst a situation that is a concealed repetition of some earlier experience or relationship or, conversely, a defense against such a repetition. In this way the patient tries to "actualize" a transference wish through subtle manipulation of the "role responsiveness" of the analyst, which includes his or her thoughts and feelings as well as overt responses. Such actualization may take place outside the awareness of either patient or analyst, either due to a countertransference blind spot or because of the subtlety of the interaction imposed by the patient and accepted unwittingly by the analyst.

Boesky (1982), building on the earlier discussions of "actualization" by Laplanche & Pontalis (1973) and by Sandler (1976a, 1976b, 1976c), proposes considering acting out as two different components: "an unconscious transference fantasy and some related action or behavior" (p. 42). The action may carry out the transference fantasy, or it may block it defensively in order to avoid the painful affects that would ensue from further actualization of the fantasy. *Actualization* can mean the subjective experience of an unconscious fantasy seeming to approach fulfillment, albeit without direct gratification in action as we ordinarily think of it.

Boesky comes closer here than do most other writers to retaining Freud's 1914 equating of acting out with transference, and he emphasizes that the "actualization of the transference" aspect is just as "real" as the objectively observable motoric behavior that is more easily recognized as "acting out." For example, a patient experiencing anxiety over emerging homosexual transference fantasies embarked on a heterosexual affair, trying by doing something "real" to deny the reality of the about-to-be actualized feelings about the analyst. Thus, action was used to defend against actualization, both being manifestations of acting out in Boesky's conception. Many analysts would agree with the common current usage that would call the homosexual fantasies "transference" and the heterosexual activity "acting

out." A careful reading of Freud supports Boesky's position that Freud's original definition was ambiguous and allows for the conclusions he draws. Boesky proposes that those related phenomena in patients who characteristically express their conflicts in action can be understood in the context of a psychology of action, retaining acting out and actualization as concepts related to unconscious fantasies evoked by the transference in the psychoanalytic relationship.

If there is indeed a difference in the feedback effect of fantasy and enactment out there in the interactive world, then that should be taken into account in theorizing about action and acting out. This subject has been addressed sporadically, beginning with Freud (1928), who once commented: "Now it is a dangerous thing if reality fulfils such repressed wishes. The phantasy has become reality and all defensive measures are thereupon reinforced" (p. 186). In a 1985 Panel, I called attention to the actualizing effect of enacting an unconscious fantasy, especially when others participate as unwitting role-players. "The unconscious fantasy is reinforced by an 'actual' happening 'out there.' In a sense, the unconscious fantasy becomes external reality" (p. 656). This actualizing effect is similar to the effect of verbalized speech (Loewenstein, 1956) and of acting out (H. Deutsch, 1959) in making inner experiences more real.

Acting out in the psychoanalytic situation is not limited to patients. Countertransference may be expressed by inappropriate action, by refraining from appropriate action, or by more subtle attitudes or blind spots. All these would be considered the analyst's acting out by Annie Reich (1951), who also considered it appropriate to speak of acting out "whenever the activity of analyzing has an unconscious meaning for the analyst" (p. 139). Jacobs (1986) has focused on those subtle enactments of the analyst's countertransference that blend easily into standard analytic technique, not unlike the actualization of the patient's transference. Because they are often overlooked or rationalized, these enactments may have a greater impact on the analysis than those that are more easily recognized and corrected.

Factors Contributing to Acting Out
Some patients have so little capacity for delaying action that psychoanalysis is not a suitable treatment for them. At the other extreme are people whose acting out in treatment is either minimal or essentially useful in furthering the process. There is, however, a middle group who are action-oriented as part of their psychopathology, who also act out very disruptively in analysis. These patients exhibit both pre-treatment

pathological action and newly stimulated patterns of acting out. What is brought into treatment as pathological action may simply continue. This is not acting out. It may *become* acting out when exacerbated in the transference, however, especially when there has been a diminution of the original active behavior, only to recur at a point of tension in the analysis.

Among factors contributing to the expression of pathology in action are an intolerance of tension and frustration, a high level of oral or narcissistic needs, primitive defensive organization utilizing splitting, a history of childhood trauma, a special tendency to visualization and dramatization, and a largely unconscious belief in the magic of action.

Blum (1986) summarized the specific factors in the analytic situation that contribute to acting out. Some are inherent in the analytic situation itself: promotion of regression, lifting of repression, mobilization of strong affects, curtailment of motor behavior, encouragement to experience and to remember, lack of prohibition, and frustration of transference wishes. Other factors are unintended: failure to interpret or mistakes in content or timing, departure from neutrality, countertransference, or an excessively remote or seductive analyst. Acting out is especially likely to occur when the analyst's ordinary, unwitting behavior matches too closely that of a pathogenic object relation in the patient's childhood (Boesky, 1982).

Thus, an individual patient in analysis is more likely to act out when transference is intense and resistance to the transference is strong, and when the analyst has failed to make a needed interpretation or has failed in some other way to maintain a neutral, appropriate analytic stance. Patients who are characteristically action-oriented will act out with little or none of these provocations beyond those inherent in the analytic process.

Management of Acting Out

As long as the acting out took place within the "necessary conditions" for the analysis, Freud (1914) allowed almost complete freedom within the transference for the repetition of pathogenic instincts. He regarded acting out in the transference as material for analysis and the handling of the transference as "the main instrument" for the therapeutic work.

Fenichel (1945) focused primarily on acting out as resistance. A well-timed interpretation of the transference was the method of choice; but difficulties may arise when the patient does not acknowledge the resistance or when the action is outside the analysis and carries the transference away from the analysis. Rangell (1968) and Brenner (1969)

regarded acting out as analytic material, like any other, to be analyzed according to defensive aspects and underlying instinctual gratification.

Psychoanalysts who attempt to work analytically with more seriously disturbed patients, however, are confronted with massive, repetitive, and disruptive acting out in patients who have little capacity to utilize interpretations during stormy episodes. Greenacre (1950) advised that interpretations be aimed at strengthening the ego first, avoiding too early interpretation of early trauma. With certain borderline patients, Kernberg (1984) arranges for structuring parameters in the patient's life outside sessions in order to control acting out. The analyst is then freer to work interpretively at integrating here-and-now experiences with underlying primitive internalized object relations as activated in the transference.

Beyond the obvious manifestations of acting out, as either resistance or communication or progress, are subtle actualizations in the transference (Sandler, 1976a, 1976b, 1976c; Boesky, 1982; Roughton, 1993, 1994). What sets these apart and makes for difficulty in management is the failure to recognize that they are in fact taking place. For example, a patient secretly feels special and experiences gratification of a powerful transference yearning when the analyst unknowingly begins to talk more in response to the patient's subtle seductiveness. This may serve as a silent resistance, which goes unnoticed because nothing out of the ordinary is happening. But gratification has replaced analysis, even though the analyst does not know anything has transpired. Countertransference responses are important in this connection, because analysands are uncannily adept at sensing and using the analyst's vulnerabilities and blind spots in just such ways.

In general, acting out that seems primarily to serve resistance is handled by most analysts through appropriately timed interpretation, preceded by confrontation if necessary. Prohibition is used, if at all, as a last resort in order to prevent the destruction of the analysis itself. Acting out as communication, as reliving of trauma, or as experiencing of newly freed capacities needs no special technique. But we would do well to remember Ekstein's (1965) statement that "as we are impartial toward the *content* we must also learn to be impartial toward the *mode of communication*" (p. 171).

Discussion

Acting out has been traced through a colorful history, from Freud's original conception encompassing both opposition to and actualization in the transference, through periods in which acting out was thought of by some analysts as troublesome interference with the real work of analysis, to the current revival of interest in the useful aspects of enactments, reliving, and actualization (Roughton, 1993, 1994). Other difficulties with the concept have sprung largely from the tendency to blur the boundary between pathological action and acting out, although with some patients this boundary is thin and fleeting (Kernberg, 1984).

Acting out bears the same relationship to action as does pathological action. Both arise, as does any action, from similar intrapsychic processes involving compromise formations, expressed inwardly as affects, fantasies, or thought and outwardly as speech or other activities involving somatic musculature. The point is that, as defined, action underlies all motivated behavior, and so this definition does not help in distinguishing various types of activity, or even in distinguishing activity from passivity.

CONCLUSIONS

Action is ubiquitous. As such, it joins thinking and feeling as subjects of vital, but poorly defined, interest to psychoanalysts. The repeated calls for a psychoanalytic theory of action imply that formulating such is a task that is elusive and difficult. Another possibility is that we are ignoring the answer in its simplicity: perhaps *action* is not a psychoanalytically meaningful term. However, different types of actions and *interactions,* both intrapsychical and interpersonal, are of immense importance and can be dealt with in our psychologies of conflict, object relations, and deficit.

If we define action as all motivated behavior, including thinking and feeling and talking, then it becomes awkward to try to contrast thinking and feeling and talking with other forms of action. And much of psychoanalytic discourse depends on that dichotomy. On the other hand, it is difficult to defend a general definition of action that makes talking a categorically different experience from walking. Both are motivated behaviors, both the final common pathway of a complex, multidetermined intrapsychic process.

Action should be left in the province of a general psychology. To the degree that psychoanalysis can be considered a general psychology, action might be defined according to its physiological and psychological mechanisms to answer *how* questions, as has been attempted, divergently, by Rangell and Schafer. By contrast, the discourse of clinical psychoanalysis as a science of intrapsychic conflict or as the study of self–object relatedness or as a hermeneutic discipline will be concerned with questions about *which* actions and *why*—about motives and conflicts and

relationships and meanings. Rangell and Schafer, and many others, have also addressed this problem.

The ubiquity of action, defined to include any motivated behavior, results in action *qua* action being ignored except where it causes difficulty—that is, where it replaces verbalized free association in the psychoanalytic process and where psychopathology is manifested in inappropriate and disruptive behavior. These are the entities that have been called acting out, the former as a careful formulation of clinical observations, the latter as an inevitable spread of usage and dilution of original meaning.

There is merit in defining action as a general category of human experience in which the experiencing individual is the agent of behavior that has intention, purpose, and meaning. Action, thus broadly defined, by itself has no clinical psychoanalytic significance, just as the chemistry of an artist's paints is vital to his or her work but has nothing to do with the choice of subject or the experience of the viewer. The interplay of various actions, both intrapsychic and interpersonal ones, however, *is* the field of psychoanalytic investigation and treatment.

For further clarification, summaries that define the subsets of action having relevance for the psychoanalytic process will be given. *Acting out* is narrowly defined to include those actions that arise in response to a transference-mediated treatment process and that replace verbalization as the mode of expression, even though the action may be a step that leads to verbalization. As a compromise formation, acting out is multiply determined; it includes impulses as well as defenses and therefore is potentially capable of yielding information as well as concealing it. At times, it may be the only way that the patient can express something that cannot be verbalized. Acting out is to be distinguished from similar behavior arising from the patient's psychopathology. Acting out does not necessarily imply activity, and it may occur either in or outside the analyst's consulting room.

There is merit in Boesky's (1982) proposal that acting out be thought of as consisting of two components: an unconscious transference fantasy and a related action. Other terms are increasingly being used for various components of the original meaning of acting out, so bypassing some of the conceptual problems as well as the accretions of misuse attached to the term. They do not represent discrete, mutually exclusive categories but rather highlight different aspects of repetition in the analytic process.

Enactment means simply expressing in behavior what one is experiencing internally, without the pejorative connotation that adheres to acting out. A more specific meaning is evolving, however, that limits the term to an interactive experience between patient and analyst having either defensive or actualizing intent (Panel, 1989; Boesky, 1989; McLaughlin, 1991; Roughton, 1993, 1994). Chused (1991) makes this distinction: in acting out the analyst is an observer; in enactment, he is a participant.

Reliving is a special form of enactment, a reenactment of an earlier experience, particularly a traumatic one. The reexperience of affect may precede conscious memory and may lead to the recovery of memories.

Actualization of the transference occurs when the patient experiences the analyst's attitude or behavior as fulfilling a wishful fantasy. This often occurs without the conscious awareness of either person. It may result from some concrete action, from the inherent gratifications of the analytic situation, or from subtle interpersonal manipulations. Because of their subtle nature, actualizations are often overlooked as a source of stalemate in analysis (Kantrowitz, 1993; Roughton, 1993, 1994).

Symptomatic acts are circumscribed, often trivial-seeming behaviors, such as habitual gestures, odd avoidances, forgettings, or mistakes that in themselves carry no great weight in the person's life, but that, if analyzed, often yield new insights. A symptomatic act may be acting out if it arises in response to the analytic process, or it may be unrelated or a habitual aspect of the person's behavior.

Neurotic action or *pathological action* is a broad category of behavior including any maladaptive behavior arising from unconscious conflict, such as a compulsive ritual or a self-defeating behavior pattern. These actions are manifestations of psychopathology and are called acting out only if they occur in response to, or are exacerbated by, the psychoanalytic process.

Impulse action is a term describing behavior in persons who have disorders of impulse control. Like neurotic action, the behavior is a manifestation of psychopathology; but it differs in that the behavior is usually consonant with the impulse, in contrast to neurotic action, which is often a symbolic and distorted expression of an impulse.

Adaptive action results from a balanced consideration of inner needs and limitations imposed by the external world, including relationships with other people. It implies behavior that results from effective ego functioning, with drive derivatives and superego restrictions held to an optimal level of influence, and leading to compromise formations that allow relative internal harmony, mature decisions, and the ability to negotiate the best possible outcome within the given limits.

A broad view of action as all motivated behavior, or as an intention carried out, has been presented. With relevance for a general psychology of mental functioning, it nevertheless has little importance for psychoanalytic discourse. Common usage of the word *action* carries so many diverse and contradictory meanings that a theory of action ultimately can have little meaning. Perhaps a theory of pathological action, along with a theory of acting out, would encompass and differentiate those forms of behavior that are dynamically meaningful in psychoanalysis.

The history of the concept of acting out has been reviewed, once again showing that the seeds of later discoveries can usually be found in Freud's early writings. Though there have been developments and refinements, the current concepts of enactments and actualization in the transference, as well as resistance, have their genesis in Freud's 1914 paper.

There is a growing awareness among psychoanalysts of the infinite subtleties and complexities of the interchange between analyst and analysand, so much so that it now seems simplistic to call it "the talking cure." The words themselves carry in metacommunicative form far more than their manifest lexical messages (Poland, 1986). And the interactions subtly disguised in enactments and actualizations account for far more of the analytic process than was previously recognized. Freud introduced his psychoanalytic method in a world where treatment of mental illness was active; something was done to patients. His innovation was to listen and take seriously what was conveyed in patients' spoken communication. Now we must learn to listen to other actions as well.

REFERENCES

Abrams, S. (1980). Therapeutic action and ways of knowing. *J. Amer. Psychoanal. Assn.,* 28:291–307.

Abt, L., & Weissman, S., eds. (1965). *Acting Out.* New York: Grune & Stratton.

Angel, K. (1965). Loss of identity and acting out. *J. Amer. Psychoanal. Assn.,* 13:79–84.

Bellak, L. (1965). The concept of acting out. In Abt & Weissman, eds., pp. 3–19.

Bieber, T. (1965). Acting out in homosexuality. In Abt & Weissman, eds., pp. 142–151.

Blos, P. (1963). The concept of acting out in relation to the adolescent process. Rpt. in Rexford, ed., 1978, pp. 153–175.

Blum, H. P. (1976). Acting out, the psychoanalytic process, and interpretation. *Annu. Psychoanal.,* 4:163–184.

―――. (1986). Personal communication. Workshop: The management of acting out in psychoanalysis; H. Blum, chairman. Meeting of the American Psychoanalytic Association, Washington, D.C.

Boesky, D. (1982). Acting out. *Int. J. Psychoanal.*, 63:39–55.

―――. (1989). Enactment, acting out, and considerations of reality. Presented to the American Psychoanalytic Association, San Francisco.

Brand, M. (1984). *Intending and Acting.* Cambridge, Mass.: MIT Press.

Brenner, C. (1969). Some comments on technical precepts in psychoanalysis. *J. Amer. Psychoanal. Assn.*, 17:333–352.

Busch, F. (1989). The compulsion to repeat in action. *Int. J. Psychoanal.*, 70:535–544.

Casement, P. (1982). Some pressures on the analyst for physical contact during the re-living of an early trauma. *Int. Rev. Psychoanal.*, 9:279–286.

Chused, J. (1991). The evocative power of enactments. *J. Amer. Psychoanal. Assn.*, 39:615–639.

Coen, S. (1985). Perversion as a solution to intrapsychic conflict. *J. Amer. Psychoanal. Assn.*, 33:17–57.

Deutsch, F. (1947). Analysis of postural behaviors. *Psychoanal. Q.*, 16:195–213.

―――. (1952). Analytic posturology. *Psychoanal. Q.*, 21:196–214.

Deutsch, H. (1959). Psychoanalytic therapy in the light of follow-up. *J. Amer. Psychoanal. Assn.*, 7:445–458.

Ekstein, R. (1965). A general treatment philosophy concerning acting out. In Abt & Weissman, eds., pp. 162–172.

Emch, M. (1944). On the "need to know" as related to identification and acting out. *Int. J. Psychoanal.*, 25:13–19.

Erard, R. (1983). New wine in old skins: a reappraisal of the concept "acting out." *Int. Rev. Psychoanal.*, 10:63–73.

Fast, I. (1970). A function of action in the early development of identity. *Int. J. Psychoanal.*, 51:471–478.

Fenichel, O. (1945). Neurotic acting out. Rpt. in *The Collected Papers of Otto Fenichel*, 2d ser., pp. 296–304. New York: Norton, 1954.

Fox, R. (1984). The principle of abstinence reconsidered. *Int. Rev. Psychoanal.*, 11:227–236.

Frank, A. (1969). The unrememberable and the unforgettable. *Psychoanal. Study Child*, 24:48–77.

Freud, A. (1936). *The Ego and the Mechanisms of Defense.* Rev. ed. New York: Int. Univ. Press, 1966.

―――. (1968). Acting out. *Int. J. Psychoanal.*, 49:165–170.

Freud, S. (1895). Project for a scientific psychology. *SE*, 1:283–397.

―――. (1900). *The Interpretation of Dreams. SE*, 4 & 5.

―――. (1901). *The Psychopathology of Everyday Life. SE*, 6.

―――. (1905). Fragment of an analysis of a case of hysteria. *SE*, 7:3–122.

―――. (1907). Obsessive actions and religious practices. *SE*, 9:115–127.

―――. (1909). Notes upon a case of obsessional neurosis. *SE*, 10:153–320.

―――. (1911). Formulations on the two principles of mental functioning. *SE*, 12:213–226.

―――. (1914). Remembering, repeating and working through. *SE*, 12:145–156.

―――. (1915). Observations on transference-love. *SE*, 12:157–171.

―――. (1916). Some character-types met with in psycho-analytic work. *SE*, 14:309–333.

―――. (1925). Negation. *SE*, 19:233–239.

―――. (1928). Dostoevsky and parricide. *SE*, 21:173–196.

―――. (1933). *New Introductory Lectures on Psycho-Analysis. SE*, 22:1–182.

―――. (1940). *An Outline of Psycho-Analysis. SE*, 23:139–207.

Frosch, J. (1977). The relation between acting out and disorders of impulse control. *Psychiatry*, 40:295–314.

Gedo, J. (1979). *Beyond Interpretation.* New York: Int. Univ. Press.

―――. (1984). *Psychoanalysis and Its Discontents.* New York: Guilford Press.

Gray, P. (1973). Psychoanalytic technique and the ego's capacity for viewing intrapsychic activity. *J. Amer. Psychoanal. Assn.*, 21:474–494.

Greenacre, P. (1950). General problems of acting out. *Psychoanal. Q.*, 19:455–467.

―――. (1963). Problems of acting out in the transference relationship. Rpt. in Rexford, ed., 1978, pp. 215–234.

―――. (1968). The psychoanalytic process, transference, and acting out. *Int. J. Psychoanal.*, 49:211–218.

Grinberg, L. (1968). On acting out and its role in the psycho-analytic process. *Int. J. Psychoanal.*, 49:171–178.

Hartmann, H. (1939). *Ego Psychology and the Problem of Adaptation.* New York: Int. Univ. Press, 1958.

―――. (1944). Psychoanalysis and sociology. In

Essays on Ego Psychology, pp. 19–36. New York: Int. Univ. Press, 1964.

———. (1947). On rational and irrational action. In *Essays on Ego Psychology,* pp. 37–68. New York: Int. Univ. Press, 1964.

Holder, A. (1970). Conceptual problems of acting out in children. *J. Child Psychother.,* 2:5–22.

Inderbitzin, L. (1988). Patient's sleep on the analytic couch. *J. Amer. Psychoanal. Assn.,* 36:673–695.

Jacobs, T. (1973). Posture, gesture, and movement in the analyst. *J. Amer. Psychoanal. Assn.,* 21:77–92.

———. (1986). On countertransference enactments. *J. Amer. Psychoanal. Assn.,* 34:289–307.

———. (1990). The interplay of enactments. H. Lee Hall Memorial Lecture, Emory University Psychoanalytic Institute, Atlanta, Georgia.

———. (1994). Nonverbal communications. *J. Amer. Psychoanal. Assn.,* 42:741–762.

Kantrowitz, J. (1992). The analyst's style and its impact on the analytic process. *J. Amer. Psychoanal. Assn.,* 40:169–194.

———. (1993). Impasses in psychoanalysis. *J. Amer. Psychoanal. Assn.,* 41:1021–1050.

Kernberg, O. F. (1975). *Borderline Conditions and Pathological Narcissism.* New York: Aronson.

———. (1984). *Severe Personality Disorders.* New Haven: Yale Univ. Press.

Kestenberg, J. S. (1968). Acting out in the analysis of children and adults. *Int. J. Psychoanal.,* 49:341–346.

Laplanche, J., & Pontalis, J.-B. (1973). *The Language of Psychoanalysis.* New York: Norton.

Loewald, H. W. (1980). Some considerations on repetition and repetition compulsion. In *Papers on Psychoanalysis,* pp. 87–101. New Haven: Yale Univ. Press.

———. (1986). Transference-countertransference. *J. Amer. Psychoanal. Assn.,* 34:275–287.

Loewenstein, R. M. (1956). Some remarks on the role of speech in psychoanalytic technique. *Int. J. Psychoanal.,* 37:460–468.

Mahl, G. F. (1977). Body movement, ideation and verbalization during psychoanalysis. In *Communicative Structures and Psychic Structures,* ed. N. Freedman & S. Grand, pp. 291–310. New York: Plenum.

Mahler, M. S. (1981). Aggression in the service of separation-individuation. *Psychoanal. Q.,* 50:625–638.

Mahler, M. S., Pine, F., & Bergman, A. (1975). *The Psychological Birth of the Human Infant.* New York: Basic Books.

Mahon, E. (1990). Play, pleasure, reality. In *Pleasure Beyond the Pleasure Principle,* ed. R. Glick & S. Bone, pp. 26–37. New Haven: Yale Univ. Press.

Mayes, L., & Cohen, D. (1993). Playing and therapeutic action in child analysis. *Int. J. Psychoanal.,* 74:1235–1244.

McDevitt, J. (1983). The emergence of hostile aggression and its defensive and adaptive modifications during the separation-individuation process. *J. Amer. Psychoanal. Assn.,* 31 (suppl.):273–300.

McLaughlin, J. (1981). Transference, psychic reality, and countertransference. *Psychoanal. Q.,* 50:639–664.

———. (1987). The play of transference. *J. Amer. Psychoanal. Assn.,* 35:557–582.

———. (1991). Clinical and theoretical aspects of enactment. *J. Amer. Psychoanal. Assn.,* 39:595–614.

Moore, B. E. (1967). Acting out. Unpublished report of a Kris Study Group.

———. (1968). Contribution to symposium on acting out. *Int. J. Psychoanal.,* 49:182–184.

Moore, B. E., & Fine, B. D., eds. (1990). *Psychoanalytic Terms and Concepts.* New Haven: Yale Univ. Press.

Naiman, J. (1966). The role of the superego in certain forms of acting out. *Int. J. Psychoanal.,* 47:286–292.

Ogden, T. (1994). The concept of interpretive action. *Psychoanal. Q.,* 63:219–245.

Panel (1957). Acting out and its relation to impulse disorders. M. Kanzer, reporter. *J. Amer. Psychoanal. Assn.,* 5:136–145.

———. (1969). Nonverbal communication in the analysis of adults. A. Suslick, reporter. *J. Amer. Psychoanal. Assn.,* 17:955–967.

———. (1970). Action, acting out, and the symptomatic act. N. Atkins, reporter. *J. Amer. Psychoanal. Assn.,* 18:631–643.

———. (1980). Technical consequences of object relations theory. A. Richards, reporter. *J. Amer. Psychoanal. Assn.,* 28:623–636.

———. (1985). Perspectives on the nature of psychic reality. R. Roughton, reporter. *J. Amer. Psychoanal. Assn.,* 33:645–659.

———. (1989). Enactments in psychoanalysis. Meeting of the American Psychoanalytic Association, San Francisco.

Piaget, J. (1936). *The Origins of Intelligence in Children.* 2d ed. New York: Int. Univ. Press, 1952.

———. (1951). *Play, Dreams and Imitation in Childhood.* New York: Norton, 1962.

Poland, W. (1977). Pilgrimage: action and tradition in self-analysis. *J. Amer. Psychoanal. Assn.,* 25:399–416.

———. (1986). The analyst's words. *Psychoanal. Q.*, 57:341–369.

Rangell, L. (1968). A point of view on acting out. *Int. J. Psychoanal.*, 49:195–201.

———. (1969a). Choice-conflict and the decision-making function of the ego. *Int. J. Psychoanal.*, 50:599–602.

———. (1969b). The intrapsychic process and its analysis. *Int. J. Psychoanal.*, 50:65–77.

———. (1971). The decision-making process. *Psychoanal. Study Child*, 26:425–452.

———. (1981). From insight to change. *J. Amer. Psychoanal. Assn.*, 29:119–141.

———. (1989). Action theory within the structural view. *Int. J. Psychoanal.*, 70:189–203.

Rapaport, D. (1950). On the psychoanalytic theory of thinking. Rpt. in *The Collected Papers of David Rapaport*, ed. M. M. Gill, pp. 313–328. New York: Basic Books, 1967.

Reich, A. (1951). On countertransference. Rpt. in *Psychoanalytic Contributions*, pp. 136–154. New York: Int. Univ. Press, 1973.

Reich, W. (1933). *Character Analysis*. 3d ed. New York: Farrar, Straus & Giroux, 1949.

Rexford, E., ed. (1978). *A Developmental Approach to Problems of Acting Out*. Rev. ed. New York: Int. Univ. Press.

Roughton, R. (1993). Useful aspects of acting out. *J. Amer. Psychoanal. Assn.*, 41:443–472.

———. (1994). Repetition and interaction in the analytic process. *Annu. Psychoanal.*, 22:275–290.

Sandler, J. (1976a). Actualization and object relationships. *J. Philadelphia Assn. Psychoanal.*, 3:59–70.

———. (1976b). Countertransference and role-responsiveness. *Int. Rev. Psychoanal.*, 3:43–47.

———. (1976c). Dreams, unconscious fantasies and "identity of perception." *Int. Rev. Psychoanal.*, 3:33–42.

Schafer, R. (1973). Action: its place in psychoanalytic interpretation and theory. *Annu. Psychoanal.*, 1:159–196.

———. (1976). *A New Language for Psychoanalysis*. New Haven: Yale Univ. Press.

———. (1983). *The Analytic Attitude*. New York: Basic Books.

Schwartz, W. (1984). The two concepts of action and responsibility in psychoanalysis. *J. Amer. Psychoanal. Assn.*, 32:557–572.

Segel, N. (1969). Repetition compulsion, acting out, and identification with the doer. *J. Amer. Psychoanal. Assn.*, 17:474–488.

Stein, M. (1973). Acting out as a character trait. *Psychoanal. Study Child*, 28:347–364.

———. (1986). Acting out—transference and countertransference. In *Between Analyst and Patient*, ed. H. Meyers, pp. 63–74. Hillsdale, N.J.: Analytic Press.

Stern, D. (1985). *The Interpersonal World of the Infant*. New York: Basic Books.

Stolorow, R., & Lachmann, F. (1980). *Psychoanalysis of Developmental Arrests*. New York: Int. Univ. Press.

Symposium (1968). Acting out. *Int. J. Psychoanal.*, 49:165–253.

Tooley, K. (1974). Words, actions and "acting out." *Int. Rev. Psychoanal.*, 1:341–351.

Valenstein, A. (1962). The psycho-analytic situation. *Int. J. Psychoanal.*, 43:315–324.

———. (1983). Working through and resistance to change. *J. Amer. Psychoanal. Assn.*, 31 (suppl.):353–374.

Weiss, E. (1942). Emotional memories and acting out. *Psychoanal. Q.*, 11:477–492.

Wheelis, A. (1950). The place of action in personality change. *Psychiatry*, 13:135–148.

Winnicott, D. W. (1953). Transitional objects and transitional phenomena. *Int. J. Psychoanal.*, 34:89–97.

Wolff, P. H. (1960). *The Developmental Psychologies of Jean Piaget and Psychoanalysis*. Psychological Issues, monograph 5. New York: Int. Univ. Press.

Zeligs, M. (1957). Acting in. *J. Amer. Psychoanal. Assn.*, 5:685–705.

PART III

OTHER CLINICAL PHENOMENA

Harold P. Blum, M.D.

10

SYMBOLISM

Symbolism was a subject of interest and investigation in academic psychology and in linguistics and other related disciplines even before the advent of psychoanalysis. It was recognized that symbolic processes were uniquely human developments which have contributed, in turn, to the capacities for representational thought, language, and culture. Representational capacity through symbolic expression was seen as one of the most important evolutionary achievements of humans, leading to extraordinary differences in other areas of development as well. So it may be stated that not only have humans developed symbolic processes but that these processes have also shaped human psychological and cultural development.

TYPES OF SYMBOLISM

There are different symbolic processes, each with its own mode of symbol formation and its own type of symbolic expression and communication. The symbolism encountered in analytic work—for example, in dreams, fantasies, associations, and symptoms, as well as in folklore, legend, literature, and wit—differs in many respects from what is designated by the same term in other disciplines, which may have conscious denotations or have primarily abstract meaning (for example, language). Although there are commonalities between the various types of symbolic processes and products, the differences are sufficient to warrant careful delineation. In discussing the differences, for the sake of succinctness, I shall refer to the first type as "psychoanalytic symbolism" or simply "symbolism," without implying that the symbolism observed and interpreted in psychoanalysis is unique to that process or that psychoanalysis is not also interested in other symbolic processes. Freud, beginning with his studies of aphasia, was interested in all forms of symbolism and contributed to the understanding of language and abstract symbols as well as to the specific type of symbolism designated here as "psychoanalytic." However, paradoxically, symbolism has received "infrequent, direct, systematic treatment" despite its early recognition "as one of the irrefutable hallmarks of unconscious mental activity" (Donadeo, 1974, p. 77).

All forms of symbolism depend upon thought, perception, memory, and experience and constitute indirect means of representation. Some symbolic expressions are also referred to as symbols in the sense of ordinary linguistic usage; for example, the flag may represent the country; the crown may represent the king's authority; and scales may represent justice. The cross is another abstract symbol, one with religious significance. Emblems and signs would be other examples of such "symbols" in a non-psychoanalytic sense. (A sign as in the Morse code has directly equivalent meaning, whereas a symbol represents rather than presents meaning.) In all these cases, what is referred to as the manifest symbol and its underlying meaning depend upon individual and group social awareness. Many forms of sign and symbol can also be described as pictorial metaphor. In topographic terms, the relationship between the signifier and its referent, or what is signified, is readily understood in conscious thought and in accord with social convention. An important function of these forms of symbolism is therefore communication.

CHARACTERISTICS OF PSYCHOANALYTIC SYMBOLISM

By contrast, it may well be questioned whether what I have called "psychoanalytic symbolism" has a primary communicative function; it may be so disguised, both from the individual and from others, that it may not serve any conscious or intended internal or external communicative purpose. In contradistinction to other types of symbolism, its significant meaning lies outside conscious awareness, a meaning that is relatively independent of social, cultural, and historical settings. Yet it is a ubiquitous and universal process with a characteristic symbol system and typical expressions. Symbolism is unlearned and appears spontaneously in the course of human phylogeny and ontogeny. Because of the universality of this form of symbolism, it was first thought to be based upon inherited and innate schemas. Further considerations and the development of psychoanalytic theory emphasize the commonality of disposition and experience in early childhood and the interaction of the drives, defenses, and ego apparatuses with the developmental experience of the infant and young child. The symbols usually encountered in psychoanalytic work are, therefore, infantile products of archaic processes. They take on additional meanings with accretions from later phases of development, but, basically, these universal symbols do not undergo developmental transformation, and they have a different structure and function from abstract symbols such as language. Nevertheless, psychoanalytic symbolism emerges in conjunction with the "body ego" and object relations (for example, symbols of penis and parents). Many words also have body-image roots with possible phylogenetic contributions to language (Werner & Kaplan, 1963), indicating perhaps some common developmental determinants with symbolism.

While the unconscious aspects of symbols were first elaborated in relation to dreams, they may be found in daydreams, myths, legends, and in the play and art of all cultures of all times. Because of the influence of psychoanalysis on our own culture, the nonanalytic layperson may now know that a train can represent a penis and a tunnel a vagina. Cave or cat are words that also may have the symbolic meaning of the female genital, even though the word for the latter is different in different languages. The unconscious meaning of the symbolism identified here as psychoanalytic may be stated to be a function of archaic, primary-process thought and is the result of the same mechanisms of condensation and displacement typical of the primary process. At the same time, condensation and displacement may favor such symbol formation. On the other hand, the symbolic expression that is formed and utilized for purposes of coherent or rational communication is associated with secondary-process organization and regulation.

Symbols in the psychoanalytic setting, as delineated by Freud (1900), always indirectly represent disguised ideas and associated affects. The symbol belongs to the category of compromise formation, in which forbidden representations are disguised as a result of defenses while simultaneously being allowed token "symbolic" expression. Because of its closeness to primary-process mechanisms, symbol formation is favored by regression and reactivation of infantile conflicts, interests, and modes of thought and expression.

SYMBOLIC REPRESENTATION IN RELATION TO REPRESSION

Developing Freud's pioneering findings, Jones (1916) emphasized the derivation of psychoanalytic symbols from unconscious instinctual conflicts, so that the symbols become a special form of drive derivative. The drives with their forbidden wishes have been repressed, whereas what is not repressed does not need to be represented symbolically. Psychoanalytic symbols, therefore, are related to repression and to a return of the repressed in a form that is still disguised. These symbols always refer to infantile instinctual aims and objects, erogenous zones and functions, and the body ego. The symbol is formed by displacement from the body or primary object to a more neutral and less emotionally charged object of perception. The most common contents of psychoanalytic symbols are, therefore, body parts and functions connected with infantile instinctual conflicts. Symbolic representations of birth and death and castration are superimposed upon, and developed in relation to, the body ego and the primary object world of family members.

The basic unconscious reference may be represented or signified by an infinite number of different symbols. The penis, for example, can be represented by snakes and sticks, towers and rockets, guns and swords, and so on. The female genitals may be represented by a house, a box, a tunnel, flowers, a cave, and so on. A spider may symbolize the pre-oedipal mother. Though psychoanalytic symbolism was first thought to be connected primarily with the sexual drive and with memory experiences of instinctual gratification, symbolic expression of aggressive drive derivatives has also been noted. The (unconscious) sexual and aggressive meanings of symbols are repressed, and their connection with the libidinal phases of development is neither consciously understood nor readily accepted if pointed out to the individual. The more frequent symbols are probably those of the male and female genitals, a fact that is consistent with the extensive repression of human sexuality. Symbols, however, can be found with primary meanings deriving from every phase of early development, including the oral and anal phases as well as the phallic-libidinal phase. There are oral symbols referring to the mouth, tongue, teeth, and breast (Almansi, 1960; Arlow, 1955); anal symbols in which feces may be represented by money, gifts, or the power behind and on the throne; and phallic symbols in which a mailbox may represent bisexuality and in which a mantle may serve as a phallic representation but also as an illusory female penis and infantile fetish. Contrary to Jones's early schematic formulations, psychoanalytic symbols are often overdetermined as in the bisexual and biparental symbolism of animal phobias. They tend to retain their universal meaning even when they take on additional individual or idiosyncratic meanings and reference.

PERCEPTUAL ROOTS IN PSYCHOANALYTIC SYMBOLISM AND LANGUAGE

Psychoanalytic symbols have perceptual and sensory roots which differ from the more ego-autonomous forms of symbolism utilized by other than primary-process modes of mental activity. In psychoanalytic symbolism, the repressed is symbolized by the general and the abstract, which represent the unconscious idea and affect disposition. Yet, there is a perceptual similarity which can be found between the manifest psychoanalytic symbol and its latent unconscious reference, so that, in effect, a perceptual association exists between the conscious signifier and that which it unconsciously signifies and disguises. This perceptual association is readily discerned in the example of sticks representing the penis, stones the testicles, and boxes and rooms the female genitals.

This perceptual association, which is usually visual in the case of psychoanalytic symbols, is generally absent in the case of the crucial human symbolic system of language. As distinct from psychoanalytic symbols, language is based upon common intercommunication with arbitrarily assigned conventional and consensual meanings. In the case of auditory-vocal language, there is usually no perceptual similarity between the linguistic signifier and what it signifies. Further, verbal symbols are both learned and taught in ever-increasing complexity and additional vocabulary, while psychoanalytic symbols are not only restricted in meaning but are neither learned nor taught nor bound to a particular culture (Blum, 1978).

Conscious verbal and nonverbal communication may also have unconscious symbolic meaning, so that multiple levels of meaning can be inferred, and different types of symbolic processes and forms of symbolic expression appear together. The depiction of a train going through a tunnel, a ship sailing into harbor, a pit and a pendulum are different images conveying a range of different conscious meanings; but they all have the same unconscious meaning of sexual intercourse and the primal scene. The overall nature of the symbolic expression also conveys something of the derivative conflict, the primary libidinal/aggressive investment, and even overtones of the infantile danger situation. To the psychoanalyst, it is quite different if the ship sails smoothly into a safe harbor or if the train is derailed and jumps track inside the tunnel.

INTERRELATIONSHIP OF FORMS OF SYMBOLISM

Some analysts (Kubie, 1953; Rycroft, 1956) have proposed that symbol formation is not an exclusive primary-process function—and is not always unconscious—but a general tendency of the human mind. They considered symbols to be indirect forms of representation, but in their view the overall concept of symbolism simultaneously embraced abstract and conceptual symbols, metaphorical and allegorical expression, and psychoanalytic unconscious symbolism. While it is true that the primary and secondary processes, as well as conscious and unconscious mental activity, may be understood to be on a continuum, one of Freud's great discoveries was the differentiation of primary- and secondary-process modes of mental organization and function. Unconscious symbolism, linked to the body image and the primary objects and derived from unconscious instinctual conflict, should not be confused with other forms of symbolism and with other systems of symbolic representation and expression. It is a moot question whether primitive, primary-process forms of symbolism are precursors of later, more advanced types of symbolic processes, or whether human symbolic capacity evolved from a basic undifferentiated function along relatively different developmental lines—for example, one developmental line becoming psychoanalytic symbolism, another becoming receptive and expressive language. While there is evidence to suggest that such diverse symbolic processes may have originated from a common undifferentiated matrix of human symbolic capacity and be related to oral hunger-drive expression, there were probably early mutual influences as they then followed different evolutionary and developmental lines (Blum, 1978).

In mental activity, these processes are interwoven and are not always separable; but the differences are highlighted here to indicate the unique character of psychoanalytic symbolism in contrast to vocal language. The presumed commonality of origin in the undifferentiated phase is related to Freud's supposition that present-day symbolic connections were probably linked in prehistoric periods by a linguistic identity. The distinction between unconscious symbolism and language maintains the differentiation of primary from secondary processes but also recognizes the swings of regression and progressive movement and the interpenetration of primary- and secondary-process organization of mental activity. The symbol in the psychoanalytic sense is unconsciously formed and utilizes primary-process modes of thought which both ontogenetically and phylogenetically belong to the earliest phases of development. The primitive, archaic symbolic process just described also provides for an evolutionary basis of psychoanalytic symbolism, the relatively constant cross-cultural and historical meanings of such symbols, the relative constriction in meaning, and the relative independence of the individual experience of later life. The archaic, unconscious thought processes involved in psychoanalytic symbolism also account for the tendency for symbols to be concrete and to utilize sensory imagery, retaining an association of similarity in which some slight perceptual quality is found in both the symbol and what is symbolized.

For symbolic expression to be possible, the infant must be able to perceive similarities, which may then lead to psychological links. Displacement would then occur along linkages established by the perception of such similarities. This suggests a rudimentary association of percept and memory. The roots of symbol formation probably lie in the beginnings of development, related to the primary-process mechanisms of condensation and displacement, the

incipient development of delay and detour of drive discharge, and the effects of repression. Various conceptualizations see the symbolic process as linking the "I" and the "non-I," the inner and outer worlds, in which lost narcissistic and part objects are linked to the body image and body ego. These and other theories have not been validated for the formation of psychoanalytic symbolism. They may apply to the development of such symbolism in conjunction with instinctual conflict, or they may be more closely connected with the development of other symbolic processes in which absent objects can be represented and manipulated in thought.

Piaget (1951) and others have studied the developmental sequences in the formation of a semiotic function and have postulated that the maturational sequence in the cognitive process leads to the capacity for abstract thought utilizing abstract symbolism.

COMPLEXITIES OF SYMBOLIC MEANING

So-called abstract, anagogic, or functional symbolism, described by Silberer (1914), has been repeatedly assumed to be the same as psychoanalytic symbolism, thereby confusing unconscious symbolism with other forms of indirect representation, especially with metaphor. Silberer's "anagogic" symbolism aims at a progressive goal or ideal that achieves symbolic but not yet real expression. Thus, climbing a staircase in a fairy tale or dream does not necessarily disguise mounting sexual excitement but is primarily representative of ambition or even of being close to attaining high aspirations or ideals. The metaphorical, conscious meaning of ascending the staircase or of climbing the mountain may coexist with the symbolic unconscious meaning, and both meanings should be taken on board rather than attributing to the metaphorical meaning either exclusive or prime importance. Many idiomatic metaphors have a core of psychoanalytic symbolism. For example, "to make a big splash" usually conveys the conscious or preconscious meaning of exhibitionistic display and ostentatious seeking of attention, but it also symbolically expresses unconscious urethral exhibitionism. The metaphor conveys both preconscious and unconscious communications (Moore, 1976). Thus, the form and content of metaphor may be analyzed for access to unconscious conflicts and their symbolic expression (Arlow, 1979). This may be an example of the accretion of meanings during development and the elaboration of more complex forms of symbolic expression. Symbols may acquire conscious meaning and intent, even though they were originally formed in the infantile unconscious (Donadeo, 1974).

Referring to water dreams as representing birth and symbolically expressing both urinary and erotic stimuli, Freud (1900, p. 402) observed, "The stratification of meaning in these dreams corresponds to a change that has come over the meaning of the symbol since infancy." Psychoanalysis takes into account the various symbolic and metaphorical meanings that appear in the patient's associations and even notes threshold symbolism. Threshold symbolism, a variant of Silberer's "functional symbolism," represents a change in the state of consciousness. The patient may be more awake or more asleep during free association, and the dream of ascending from the depths to the surface may refer variously to the level of interpretation, to accessibility to consciousness, to waking up from the depths of sleep, and so on.

The multiple, stratified meanings of a psychoanalytic symbol can also derive from different developmental phases. The "pit and the pendulum" symbolically represent the vagina and the penis in phallic-phase conflicts, but the pit may also represent the mouth, and the pendulum the tongue with oral-phase derivation (Schmiedeberg, 1948). This overdetermination of symbols also pertains to the accretion of social and cultural meanings that some symbols acquire, with an evolution of less instinctual superimposed determinants. The original instinctual idea and related affect have been displaced onto noninstinctual presentations, which may acquire great conscious personal or cultural interest.

An example of a psychoanalytic symbol that has evolved into an abstract symbol with multiple and powerful metaphorical investment can be seen in the Hindu worship of the god Shiva as a *lingam*. The lingam is a symbol of an erect phallus, and its ritual significance implies unconscious phallic worship. At the same time Shiva's manifestation as a lingam carries the religious representation of Shiva as the pillar of the universe, the line of resplendent light, the creator and preserver of life, the pillar of destruction and regeneration, and so forth. The highly complex, multifaceted cultural and religious meanings of the lingam are variously further and further removed from unconscious phallic conflict. The religious meaning probably evolved in part as a defense against the forbidden instinctual impulses, but ego and superego interests and adaptive considerations are also represented.

SYMBOLISM IN SYMPTOMS

In common parlance, just as signs and emblems such as the swastika were confused with symbols, so were psychological symptoms. Many symptoms often have a symbolic meaning. Thus, eating fads and vomiting may be representative of a pregnancy fantasy or pseudocyesis. Hysterical paralysis of the finger may simultaneously symbolize both impotence and erection. In Freud's Rat Man case (1909), the rat language was actually a form of symbolic expression. The rat was an overdetermined symbol that was discovered to mean penis, feces, money, baby, and greed. Symbols and symptoms have certain compromise features in common, but at the same time they are vastly different psychological products; moreover, symbols are to be considered normal and usually adaptive phenomena. Displacement and symbolization may constitute one of the pathways toward substitute activity instead of direct drive discharge and toward eventual sublimation. Psychoanalytic symbolism may, therefore, have an adaptive function, a function that is consistent with the regular appearance of unconscious symbolism in art, literature, and play. Unconscious symbolism is more likely to appear in regressive states, but it is also utilized by the ego for adaptive and progressive solutions to conflicts. Although psychoanalytic unconscious symbolism probably had no communicative function in its formation in close association with the primary process, it may be utilized in the service of unconscious and preconscious communication. This is characteristic of art and wit, and such symbolic communication can be observed in the analytic process. In effecting an apparent change of function, the ego has adapted unconscious symbolism to its own purposes, and the symbolic meaning may be significant in intrapsychic processes, object relations, and sublimation. Psychoanalytic symbolism has been loosely compared to an archaic language that expresses itself in wit, jokes, and idiomatic and imaginative expression. Such symbols are incorporated in the protean character of language without themselves having the true characteristics of language.

INTERPRETATION OF SYMBOLS

The full appreciation of the extent and significance of unconscious symbolism developed gradually and in association with the psychoanalytic interpretation of symbols. A symbol may need to be interpreted in terms of its manifest conscious meaning in addition to, or sometimes instead of, its symbolic significance. Individual experience and preference may determine the choice of a particular symbol among typically available symbols, and in turn the typical symbol may also have an idiosyncratic as well as a universal meaning. In ancient times, arbitrary meanings were assigned to symbols, and a decoding process was then applied to dreams as if dream interpretation were equivalent to symbol interpretation. This may be appropriate in the case of some dreams or dream elements, especially because there may be no direct associations to dream symbols. Psychoanalytic knowledge of the unconscious meaning of symbols permits such interpretation without the participation of the dreamer or an awareness of the dreamer's associations. However, purely symbolic interpretation of dreams and associations is simplistic and reductionistic and is used cautiously in a psychoanalytic process that engages the entire range of the patient's associations (Freud, 1917). Symbolic representation is best understood in the context of the analytic process and the overall area and level of exploration and interpretation.

The usual technique of psychoanalysis should not be obviated in favor of a unilateral emphasis upon symbol interpretation. The psychoanalytic understanding of unconscious symbolism is part of a much larger psychoanalytic contribution to the understanding of symbolic processes and products and the role of different types of symbol systems in development and in personality disorder. For reasons that still require further research, in severe regressive states, abstract symbolism like that entailed by language may be subjected to primary-process reorganization with condensation and displacement of word representations and with words taking on concrete, unconscious meanings, as may other objects that are used as signifiers of what is symbolized.

Disorders in symbolic processes and systems may lead to bizarre symbolic products and aberrant utilization of various symbolic forms. Regression, as in dreams and symptoms, favors the emergence of symbolic expression the unconscious meaning of which may then be uncovered and explained by psychoanalysis. Further research is needed to clarify the origins of unconscious symbolism, and its relationship to nondefensive, developmental, and adaptive trends. Symbols undergo a possible change of function when utilized in conjunction with relatively autonomous ego activities.

REFERENCES

Almansi, R. (1960). The face–breast equation. *J. Amer. Psychoanal. Assn.,* 8:43–70.

Arlow, J. A. (1955). Notes on oral symbolism. *Psychoanal. Q.,* 24:63–74.

———. (1979). Metaphor and the psychoanalytic situation. *Psychoanal. Q.,* 48:363–385.

Blum, H. P. (1978). Symbolic processes and symbol formation. *Int. J. Psychoanal.,* 59:455–471.

Donadeo, J., reporter (1974). Symbolism. In *Trauma and Symbolism.* Kris Study Group. Monograph Series. New York: Int. Univ. Press.

Freud, S. (1900). *The Interpretation of Dreams. SE,* 4 & 5.

———. (1909). Notes upon a case of obsessional neurosis. *SE,* 10:153–320.

———. (1917). *Introductory Lectures on Psycho-Analysis. SE,* 15 & 16.

Jones, E. (1916). The theory of symbolism. In *Papers on Psychoanalysis.* Boston: Beacon Press, 1961.

Kubie, L. S. (1953). The distortion of the symbolic process in neurosis and psychosis. *J. Amer. Psychoanal. Assn.,* 1:59–86.

Moore, B. E. (1976). The problem of definition in psychoanalysis. Paper read at the Institute for Psychoanalysis, Chicago, 31 Mar. 1976; Long Island Psychoanalytic Society, 28 Feb. 1977.

Piaget, J. (1951). *Play, Dreams, and Imitation in Childhood.* New York: Norton.

Rycroft, E. (1956). Symbolism and its relation to the primary and secondary process. *Int. J. Psychoanal.,* 37:137–146.

Schmiedeberg, M. (1948). A note on claustrophobia. *Psychoanal. Rev.,* 35:309–311.

Silberer, H. (1914). *Probleme der Mystik und ihrer Symbolik.* Vienna: Heller.

Werner, H., & Kaplan, B. (1963). *Symbol Formation.* New York: Wiley.

Jacob A. Arlow, M.D.

11

UNCONSCIOUS FANTASY

Unconscious fantasy is a major conceptual instrument in psychoanalysis. In specific and concrete terms, it articulates the form and nature of the dynamic unconscious conflicts that mold the individual's life. It is a mental process that represents a variation of the function of daydreaming. Concerning the latter, Freud (1911) said, "With the introduction of the reality principle one species of thought-activity was split off; it was kept free from reality-testing and remained subordinated to the pleasure principle alone. This activity is *phantasying,* which begins already in children's play, and later, continued as *day-dreaming,* abandons dependence on real objects" (p. 222). Freud went on to liken the world of daydreams to a national park preserve, the original state of nature kept in its pristine form. Daydreaming is a universal activity, and fantasies are vehicles for the instinctual drives.

From the very beginning of his researches, Freud recognized that symptoms (Breuer & Freud, 1893–95), dreams (Freud, 1900), moods (1908b), and character traits (1919) represent derivative expressions of unconscious fantasies. In his early writings, Freud emphasized the role of unconscious fantasies primarily as vehicles for the discharge of the instinctual cathexes of the system Ucs. (as he designated it). This seemed at first to be evident from the very nature of the instinctual wishes conveyed in the unconscious fantasies. In contrast to the type of wishes typical of conscious daydreams, the wishes involved

in unconscious fantasies tended to be more primitive, bizarre, and in fundamental opposition to morality and reality.

Further study demonstrated that this was not true of all unconscious fantasies. When encountered in the clinical setting, unconscious fantasies were found to include elements of defense, adaptation, and considerations of moral judgment, as well as fear of punishment. These observations led Freud to the conclusion that

Among the derivatives of the *Ucs.* instinctual impulses . . . there are some which unite in themselves characters of an opposite kind. On the one hand, they are highly organized, free from self-contradiction, have made use of every acquisition of the system *Cs.,* and would hardly be distinguished in our judgement from the formations of that system. On the other hand, they are unconscious and are incapable of becoming conscious. Thus *qualitatively* they belong to the system *Pcs.,* but *factually* to the *Ucs.* . . . Of such a nature are those phantasies of normal people as well as of neurotics which we have recognized as preliminary stages in the formation both of dreams and of symptoms and which, in spite of their high degree of organization, remain repressed and therefore cannot become conscious. [1915, pp. 190–191]

These observations, together with the phenomena of self-directed aggression and evidence of the existence of unconscious *anti*-instinctual forces led Freud (1923) to reconceptualize the nature of the forces involved in intrapsychic conflict in terms of what is currently referred to as "the structural theory" (Arlow, 1956). In this new theory, the concept of unconscious fantasy came to play an even more important role, both in regard to theories of pathogenesis and in practical matters of technique. Anna Freud (1936), for example, used the concept of unconscious fantasy to explicate the defense mechanism of identification with the aggressor and denial in fantasy. She also demonstrated how repressed masturbation fantasies can interfere with the operation of certain ego functions and lead to a distortion of the individual's object relations (1949).

The nature of a person's fantasy life is peculiar to that individual. It is idiosyncratic, representing the specific compromise formations effected in response to conflicts growing out of childhood experience—that is, out of the nature of the object relations, traumatic events, unfulfilled wishes, and so forth. These decisive forces of the individual's life are organized into a number of leading unconscious fantasies that persist throughout life. They form a stream of organized mental representations and wishes which act as a constant source of inner stimulation to the mind. Furthermore, they create a mental set against which sensations are perceived, interpreted, and responded to. The influence they exert on the mind varies with several factors to be discussed presently (Arlow, 1969b).

An individual's fantasy life is hierarchically organized; that is to say, fantasies are grouped around certain basic, instinctual drive wishes, and each group is composed of different versions or editions of the fantasy. Each version corresponds to a different "psychic moment" in the history of the individual's development. The form of the unconscious fantasy develops and grows in time, expressing the forces at play at the particular time in the person's life and the level of functioning and maturity of the ego as it attempts at different stages to integrate the demands of wishes in keeping with the ego's growing adaptive and defensive responsibilities.

The organization of these fantasies takes shape early in life, probably in connection with the resolution of the oedipus complex. In one form or another, they persist throughout life. To borrow an analogy from literature, one could say that the plot line of the fantasy remains the same, although the characters and the situations may vary. It is the persistent influence of unconscious fantasy that lends cohesiveness to the story of a person's life and, accord-

ingly, renders his identity understandable during psychoanalytic work. Freud's description of the repetitive reenactment of certain basic themes in the individual's life led some of his early critics to say that his case histories sounded more like novels than scientific reports.[1] How the ego integrates the various elements in conflict may lead to different fantasy versions of the compromise, some closer to the primitive expression of the instinctual drives and therefore more likely to engender pathogenic conflict, others more removed from conflict, more adaptive, or sublimated (Hartmann, 1939). (For the transformation of unconscious, incestuous, and parricidal fantasies into the sublimatory choice of a healing profession, see Arlow et al., 1972.)

The evidence is clear that the influence of unconscious fantasy is a constant feature of mental life, operating all the time we are awake and some of the time we are asleep. In parapraxes, illusions, misperceptions, neurotic symptoms, and certain altered ego states, such as *déjà vu* (Arlow, 1959) and depersonalization (Arlow, 1966b), it is possible to demonstrate a quick and facile interaction between external events and unconscious fantasy. Freud (1900) said the same concerning dream formation. Commenting on the rapid organization of a dream in response to an external stimulus experienced during sleep, he said that there must be preformed, readily available unconscious fantasies, which can be woven instantaneously into the structure of a dream. There are, in addition, intrusive fantasies that make their appearance in conscious thought, as if out of the blue—brief and fleeting thoughts and images, often unpleasant in content and experienced as contrary to the individual's ordinary thinking and wishing.

UNCONSCIOUS FANTASY AND SYMPTOM FORMATION

The ability of instinctual wishes to evoke derivatives of unconscious fantasies varies in intensity, depending upon a number of factors that act in unison. Foremost among these is the intensity of the conflict over the instinctual drive. An extreme example may be seen in severe cases of obsessive-compulsive neurosis bordering on psychosis, cases in which the patient is so overwhelmed by his or her wishes to kill with gas and feces that he or she can perceive nothing but dangerous poisons in everything in the environment. A simpler but equally clear illustration can be seen in the experience of a man who was vio-

1. Freud agreed, countering that the great novelists had perceived intuitively what he could grasp only after laborious effort (Breuer & Freud, 1893–95).

lently furious with his employer. Thinking about his most recent quarrel with his employer, the patient passed a sign that he had seen regularly on his visits to his analyst. He was familiar with the sign, and he knew that it read the name of the owner of the shop, "Maeder." This time when he passed the sign, he mistakenly perceived it as "Murder."

A second set of factors governing the evocation of derivatives of unconscious fantasy concerns the nature of the current experience, particularly the data of perception. Current experience and data of perception that are consonant or congruent with the content of the individual's persistent unconscious fantasy stimulate the emergence of derivatives of the unconscious fantasy. This is a constant feature of mental life, which can be observed in both normal and pathological contexts. Neurotic illness that begins after adolescence is often precipitated by some event or set of circumstances congruent with or reminiscent of a persistent unconscious fantasy or set of fantasies built around a corresponding traumatic event. Such situations play a role in precipitating illness similar to that played by the day residue in the stimulation of dreams at night. In a previous paper (Arlow, 1969a), I pointed out that "Day residues are selected for inclusion in dreams not so much because of their neutral, inconspicuous nature as for the fact that they are congruent with or reminiscent of certain important fantasies or memory schemata" (p. 41).

The influence, however, does not operate in only one direction. The mental set created by the persistent unconscious fantasies leads the individual to perceive unconscious stimuli selectively and to respond to them in a similar way. Thus, there is a reciprocal interplay of influence between fantasy and reality, selective perception on one side, cathectic intensification on the other. The psychoanalytic situation dramatizes this dynamic interplay. What the patient does in the transference represents an attempt to foist upon the analyst a role that the analysand has for him or her in an unconsciously prepared scenario. The events of the analysis and the analyst's interpretations, on the other hand, function to evoke clearer and clearer derivatives of the unconscious fantasy activity.

Finally, mention should be made of the state of the ego's functioning, which, in effect, mediates between the conflicting intrapsychic forces and attempts to integrate them adaptively. Fenichel (1950) elucidated some of the factors, such as fatigue, alterations of states of consciousness, influence of drugs, illness, and so forth, which interfere with the ego's capacity for adaptive integration. Under unfavorable circumstances, there emerges a tendency for regres-

sive alteration of function, leading to the emergence of more primitive and, accordingly, more conflictual derivative expressions in the hierarchy of the unconscious fantasies (Arlow & Brenner, 1964).

From the foregoing, it should be clear that the nature and power of the unconscious fantasy influence the process of perception and thereby play a role in reality testing. The wish-fulfilling aspects of unconscious fantasy press for gratification of the sort that Freud (1911) characterized as tending toward an identity of perception. Derivatives of fantasies may influence ego functioning, interfering, for example, with the "neutral" process of registering, apperceiving, and checking the raw data of perception (Hartmann, 1950). The ego is thereby oriented to scan the data of perception and to select discriminatively elements demonstrating correspondence with the latent preformed fantasies (Linn, 1954). Under appropriate conditions this may eventuate in illusions, misconceptions, and parapraxes.[2] Hallucinations, fugue states, and certain transient confusional episodes may eventuate under certain special conditions of conflict as a result of the intrusion of unconscious fantasy derivatives (Arlow, 1969b). Finally, situations of perceptual ambiguity facilitate the foisting of elements of unconscious fantasy upon the data of perception. This plays an important role in such experimental situations as the Rorschach test and subliminal sensory stimulation (Fisher, 1954). Kris and Kaplan (1952), for example, emphasized how ambiguity in aesthetic expression stimulates a wider range of unconscious fantasy activity and thus broadens the appeal of a work of art.

The effect of unconscious fantasy on mental activity is not limited to the gratification of the instinctual drives. As mentioned above, the form of the unconscious fantasy we infer comprises elements reflecting the contributions of id, ego, and superego. Among these, the defense function of the ego may assume the predominant role in the organization of the fantasy. A case in point is fetishism. Fetishism may be regarded as an example of denial in fantasy (A. Freud, 1936). It is a special form of denial in a fantasy that is unconscious. The unconscious conceptualization of the woman with a phallus is an illustration of the ego function of fending off anxiety. For the fetishist, this fantasy is the essential condition for sexual gratification, since it serves to fend off the anxiety associated with the fear of castration. The degree to which this defensive maneuver succeeds varies from patient to patient. For some

2. Freud (1901) described this relationship from a slightly different point of view in *The Psychopathology of Everyday Life.*

individuals who are not fetishists, an unconscious fantasy of a woman with a phallus seems to fend off castration anxieties. For the fetishist, however, it becomes necessary to actualize in one way or another a derivative of this unconscious fantasy. Such people are compelled to think, see, smell, or hold in their hands a symbolic representation of the female phallus of their unconscious fantasy. The use of unconscious fantasies of denial to ward off anxiety, as well as to ward off reproaches from the superego, is probably much more widespread than has been appreciated.

There are other defenses representing enactments of specific unconscious fantasies. One example is the defensive use of identification with the aggressor (Aichhorn, 1925; A. Freud, 1936). In this instance, the individual overcomes his or her fear by fantasying that he or she is the aggressor rather than the victim. This set of conditions could eventuate in the fixed character trait of being a bully, signaling the effect of a persistent unconscious fantasy in identifying with the original tormentor. A related, though somewhat different, split in identity may occur in some cases of depersonalization. The characteristic way of mastering feelings of humiliation by a patient whom I described (Arlow, 1966b) was to identify herself in fantasy with her tormentors. As a child, whenever she felt humiliated, she would imagine that she was one of the group who were laughing at her. In her adult neurosis, in which one of the presenting symptoms was depersonalization, she would unconsciously resort to this mechanism: under circumstances that ordinarily would have aroused anxiety or humiliation, she would become depersonalized. The analysis of these attacks demonstrated the influence of an unconscious fantasy, in which once again she defensively split her self representation into two parts. One self-representation was an observer and retained the quality of selfness. The other was the object of observation and was seen as involved in some painful situation. From this second self-representation, the patient felt detached and alienated. In this connection, Jacobson (1959) has written of conflicts of identity within the ego which form the basis of certain disturbances of the sense of self. Conflicts between different identities are mediated through unconscious fantasies derived from specific experiences in the individual's life and tend to influence conscious experience simultaneously or alternately.

Essentially, what the analyst does during treatment is to infer from the patient's free associations the nature of the unconscious fantasy and to demonstrate how its derivatives influence the patient's thought and behavior. In this respect, the analysis of the transference is especially helpful. It makes it possible to demonstrate to the analysand how he or she has cast the analyst in an unconscious scenario of his or her creating, a scenario that originated in the patient's conflicts during childhood. The transference represents an attempt at actualization of this scenario. In interpreting the influence of this unconscious fantasy, the analyst helps the patient distinguish between transference and reality, past and present, fact and fantasy. The same holds true for the analysis of symptoms. When a phobia is analyzed, the patient comes to understand that he or she has been responding to a specific stimulus or situation in a manner appropriate to the content of his or her unconscious fantasy. For example, an impotent male patient with a tunnel phobia discovered that he was reacting to a tunnel as if it were a vagina in which there lurked a dangerous rival intent upon destroying him.

UNCONSCIOUS FANTASY AND CHARACTER TRAITS

The same may be said about the analysis of certain character traits. A masochistic character, Freud (1919) noted, may represent the repetitive translation into action of a persistent unconscious fantasy with a relatively fixed mental content—namely, the fantasy of being beaten. He said: "People who harbour phantasies of this kind develop a special sensitiveness and irritability towards anyone whom they can include in the class of fathers. They are easily offended by a person of this kind, and in that way (to their own sorrow and cost) bring about the realization of the imagined situation of being beaten by their father" (p. 195).

As demonstrated earlier, both symptoms and character traits develop out of the common matrix of unconscious fantasy. Accordingly, unconscious fantasy is the link uniting symptom neurosis and character neurosis. In some individuals, the conflicts stimulated by the unconscious fantasies eventuate in symptoms and/or neurotic character traits. A neurotic character trait may come to replace a preexisting symptom, or the two—that is, symptom and character trait—may exist side by side.

This can be illustrated from the experience of a patient who may be said to suffer from a character neurosis of the claustrophobic type. Problems arose immediately concerning whether she could adapt her schedule to the conditions of treatment. She had arranged her life so that her hours of employment would be flexible. She liked to be free to work either at the office or at her home. She avoided being tied down to any one place or apartment. On several occasions, she had picked herself up with ease and moved to another country. The thought of not being able to move freely from job to job, house to house, and country to country gave her a hemmed-in feeling. If she contemplated this situation for any length of time, she began to feel short of breath. The same inability to commit herself characterized her relationships to people, especially men. For example, when a man proposed marriage to her, she experienced the same hemmed-in feeling and refused the offer.

The clue to the understanding of this character trait came up in connection with her attitude toward children. As it turned out, she had a fear of children and a fear of pregnancy. The analysis of this material, in turn, led to her childhood neurosis, the main symptom of which was claustrophobia. In a closed room, she would feel suffocated, the same sensation she had when getting her head under water while bathing. Her childhood neurosis centered around conflicts connected with being an only child. As a child, she imagined that she had destroyed the unborn children in her mother's body in order to have no rivals. Within any enclosure, literal or figurative, she had a fantasy of being in the claustrum, where she would suffer retaliation from those unborn children she imagined she had destroyed. In every aspect of her life, therefore, it was essential to keep open an avenue of escape (Arlow, 1966a). In this patient, the childhood neurosis of claustrophobia did not give rise to symptom neurosis in adult life. What resulted instead was a special type of character formation—a claustrophobic character neurosis.

A similar set of factors operates in certain patients demonstrating character traits that have replaced antecedent perverse practices or perverse fantasies. Among those exhibiting these traits, which I have called "character perversions," are certain unrealistic characters, petty liars, practical jokers, and swindlers (Arlow, 1972). What these male patients have in common is the defensive use of specific unconscious fantasies of a perverse nature for the purpose of warding off extreme castration anxiety. In the case of the practical joker, he derives pleasure from arousing anxiety in others and then demonstrating to them that the situation that frightened them was unreal and never should have caused them anxiety in the first place. Earlier in life, he used to play-act being his mother, using her facial cream and eyelash curlers, as well as some of her ski clothes and snow boots. In connection with the latter, he said, "Those things are about the same for a man as for a woman." In his early adolescence, he would play a game of putting his penis between his thighs to simulate a vulva. He would then separate his legs and would be amused and reassured at the sight of his penis popping out. For him, this type of play constituted a reassurance against the danger of castration. In ef-

fect, he was saying to himself (and to any future observer), "It looks as if there were no penis there, as if the penis might have been cut off, but there is really nothing to fear. Once I relieve the pressure on my thighs, you can see the penis was there all the time." Thus, he shared with certain types of transvestite perverts the need to act out a denial of what he took to be the woman's castrated state. A special derivative of the psychopathology of perversion is the compulsion to act out a derivative expression of an unconscious fantasy that in one way or another wards off castration anxiety by endowing the woman with a fantasied penis. In the case of character perversion, what is acted out is a desexualized derivative representation of the unconscious fantasy.

UNCONSCIOUS FANTASY AND TECHNIQUE

Through its influence on language, unconscious fantasy comes to play a very important role in the therapeutic process. Sharpe (1935, 1940) wrote:

> When dynamic thought and emotional experiences of the forgotten past find the appropriate verbal image in the pre-conscious, language is as pre-determined as a slip of the tongue or a trick of behaviour. Metaphor, then, is personal and individual even though the words and phrases used are not of the speaker's coinage. The verbal imagery corresponding to the repressed ideas and emotions, sometimes found even in a single word, will yield to the investigator a wealth of knowledge. [1940, p. 159]

In a previous paper (Arlow, 1979b), I demonstrated how the examination of metaphor reveals it to be a concrete representation of an unconscious fantasy. In many instances, it is technically advantageous to treat the metaphor literally and to elicit the patient's associations. For example, in the case of a young man who was trying to face his fear of making a sexual advance to a woman, the analysis of a specific metaphor brought to light the source of his anxiety. A young woman was clearly interested in him and invited him to dinner at her home on several occasions. On each occasion, the patient carefully avoided any opportunity of being alone with her. When this pattern of behavior was called to the patient's attention, he said, "Do you think I was going to go into that lion's pit?" He was surprised by this characterization, for the woman in question was not a frightening or intimidating person. The analysis of the metaphor revealed an unconscious fantasy of a dentate vagina.

Metaphorical expressions may be said to relate to each other as the syntax of unconscious fantasy. Accordingly, large segments of an analysis often center on the understanding of one or two leading meta-phors, because the manifold metaphorical expres-sions of the basic theme regularly lead to the dis-covery of some conflictual unconscious fantasy. The differing variations of the basic metaphor take on special and clearer meaning as they become related to each other in the patient's productions in time, context, and contiguity. In a similar vein, Kris (1956) showed how unconscious fantasy may influ-ence the analysand's attitude in the process of gain-ing insight. For example, some patients strive very hard to interpret material on their own. According to Kris, this often derives from an unconscious fantasy of presenting the analyst with a gift. On the other hand, the same kind of activity, which in some re-spects is highly beneficial to the progress of the analysis, may represent in fantasy an unconscious competing with the analyst.

In many respects, interpretations may be regarded as metaphorical apprehensions of the patient's un-conscious fantasy. Sometimes they actually occur in the analyst's mind in the form of a visual metaphor. For example, a male patient could not perform ade-quately unless he entertained a fantasy of spanking a woman. His relationship with his wife was stormy, characterized by frequent quarrels, which seemed to him to have the character of a power struggle. In time, he came to recognize that he was afraid of his wife, because he was afraid of the female genital. He had always regarded it as unpleasant, distasteful, and dangerous. He related his fear of the female genital to his beating fantasy. He said, "When I turn the woman over, I don't see her genital. When I spank her, I know that I am in charge." At the fol-lowing session the patient reported that he had had very successful and satisfying intercourse with his wife. Two incidents had preceded this successful ex-perience. His wife had asked him if she could buy a very expensive item of clothing, and for the first time, the patient had refused to accede to her re-quest. When their daughter had called late one eve-ning, when they were already in bed and preparing to make love, the patient had answered the phone, spoken briefly to his daughter, and, overriding his wife's gestures of protestation, had handed her the telephone and told her how to manage the problem the daughter had raised. He was aware that he was treating his wife as if she had to take orders from him. Yet, it was after these two incidents that he had the successful intercourse. Listening to him, I had the vision of a lion-tamer in the cage at the circus cracking his whip at the lions. The interpretation was clear. By taking charge and being authoritative, he could overcome his fear of being devoured and have intercourse successfully.

Similarly, there are motor metaphors which repre-sent derivative expressions of unconscious fantasies. In the course of the analytic session, nonverbal com-munication by way of motor activity may reflect un-conscious fantasy activity in precisely the same manner as verbal communication does. Hand ges-tures, in particular, should be observed as possible derivatives of unconscious fantasy activity. Among these, one can recognize the reassuring fingering of the tie or the nose, the defensive rubbing or covering of the eyes, or hostile, mocking finger pointing. A patient who had repressed, hostile, competitive feel-ings toward me covered them in a reactive manner by a conscious attitude of admiration. In one ses-sion, while he was singing my praises, he quite un-wittingly passed his thumb from one side of his neck across to the other in a gesture of cutting the throat. Thus, while in reality he was singing my praises, in fantasy he was cutting my throat.

UNCONSCIOUS FANTASY AND EMPATHY

Unconscious fantasy plays a significant role in the all-important function of empathy. In large measure, the ability of the analyst to understand the patient depends upon his or her capacity to effect a transient unconscious identification with the patient. In this way, the analyst experiences vicariously what the patient has been going through. Specifically, and more important, the nature and form of the patient's associations evoke in the analyst derivatives of an unconscious fantasy that corresponds to the patient's unconscious fantasy. The derivatives of the uncon-scious fantasy that the patient's fantasy has evoked in the analyst's mind constitute inner communica-tions to the analyst of an emerging interpretation (Arlow, 1979a). The analyst becomes aware of this inner communication through the process of intro-spection. It is at this point that the analyst breaks off his or her identification with the patient. Instead of thinking with the patient, he or she begins to think about the patient (Brierley, 1943). The cognitive dis-ciplining of these derivatives leads to the appropriate interpretation (Arlow, 1979b). Frequently, during the conduct of an analysis, the analyst observes how previous memories, phrases, dreams, or fantasies of the patient occur to him or her almost at the same instant that the patient mentions them or even before the patient articulates them. On other occasions, what come to the analyst's mind are memories, dreams, and fantasies of his or her own that are con-gruent or identical in spirit with those of the patient. At such moments, patient and analyst share a fanta-sy in common (Beres & Arlow, 1974).

A major aspect of the capacity of one individual to empathize with another derives from the ability to share unconscious fantasies. While it is true that the world of daydreams is individual and largely idiosyncratic, there is nonetheless a certain commonality of elements in the fantasy life of individuals. This results from the fact that all human beings go through the experience of being helpless infants, depending upon the love and protection of powerful adults. It is impossible to grow up without at some time having felt small, inferior, insignificant, defeated, unloved, and disappointed, as well as treasured, idealized, and favored. The vicissitudes of development evolve along certain average, expectable lines during the early and crucial years of every individual's life, establishing a roughly comparable base of experience out of which unconscious fantasies evolve. Commonality of fantasy life is more pronounced among members of the same cultural or social group or of any group of individuals whose early childhood experiences have been patterned more or less in the same way and who share a common tradition. There are other factors, of course, that influence the analyst's capacity for empathy, but, throughout all, an inexorable component resides in the capacity to identify with the analysand to the extent that a comparable unconscious fantasy can be stimulated in the analyst.

Sharing the patient's unconscious fantasy is only the first step in empathy. A second and crucial step is necessary: namely, for the analyst to break off the identification and demonstrate to the patient how derivatives of the unconscious fantasy have been influencing his or her life. It is at this point that countertransference difficulties may arise. If the nature of the patient's unconscious fantasy evokes a corresponding fantasy wish in the analyst that he or she has not mastered in his or her own analysis, the analyst may linger in the identification with the patient's fantasy. Accordingly, it is not unusual during supervision to observe how the analyst's interventions unconsciously serve the purpose of distracting both the analysand and him- or herself from dealing with the conflictual fantasy. In effect, the analyst does not want to permit the patient's conflicts to bring to mind his or her own similar conflicts.

UNCONSCIOUS FANTASY AND ART

In almost every analysis, the patient will relate how some fairy tale, novel, myth, movie, or play from earlier in life produced an abiding effect on him or her. Some current experience with a comparable work of art may also stir the patient profoundly. In either case, analysis will reveal how the patient perceived the work as a derivative of an unconscious fantasy, the meaning of which he had intuited. In effect, such phenomena demonstrate the influence of a shared unconscious fantasy. The patient borrows the artist's creation as a vehicle for his or her own repressed fantasy wishes. This mechanism illustrates one of the fundamental social functions of the artist. He or she is the daydreamer for the community. Out of his or her own daydreams and conflicts, the artist creates a work capable of evoking unconscious fantasy activity in members of the audience (Freud, 1908a; Sachs, 1942).

UNCONSCIOUS FANTASY AND POLITICS

Shared unconscious fantasy is an important element in group formation. Myth reflects the nature of the unconscious fantasy common to members of a group. By identifying with the central figure of the group mythology, the individual becomes integrated into society, emulating the ideal qualities that the central figure of the myth represents (Arlow, 1961). In this way, the character structure of the members of the younger generation is molded in keeping with the standards and traditions of the group. For example, one of the central myths of Christianity revolves about the Madonna's impregnation by God (Jones, 1914; Arlow, 1965). The image of the Madonna represents the ideal qualities of gentleness, purity, and self-sacrifice, qualities that young girls are encouraged to emulate by way of identification. The dynamic thrust facilitating this identification comes from the gratification connected with an unconscious fantasy of incestuous relations with the God-Father figure. In the same way, prophets and political leaders intuitively play upon the latent unconscious fantasies of the masses, galvanizing them into action under their leadership. When harnessed to the dynamic force of shared unconscious fantasies, myth making may become a powerful instrument for historical change (Arlow, 1982).

The power of unconscious fantasy is ubiquitous. Through its influence on people, as individuals and in the mass, it is an ever-present force in shaping not only individual destiny but human destiny overall.

REFERENCES

Aichhorn, A. (1925). *Wayward Youth.* New York: Viking.

Arlow, J. A. (1956). *The Legacy of Sigmund Freud.* New York: Int. Univ. Press.

———. (1959). The structure of the *déjà vu* experience. *J. Amer. Psychoanal. Assn.,* 7:611–631.

————. (1961). Ego psychology and the study of mythology. *J. Amer. Psychoanal. Assn.*, 9:371–393.

————. (1965). The Madonna's conception through the eyes. *Psychoanal. Study Soc.*, 3:9–25.

————. (1966a). Character and conflict. *J. Hillside Hosp.*, 15:139–151.

————. (1966b). Depersonalization and derealization. In *Psychoanalysis—A General Psychology*, ed. R. M. Loewenstein et al., pp. 456–478. New York: Int. Univ. Press.

————. (1969a). Fantasy, memory and reality testing. *Psychoanal. Q.*, 38:28–51.

————. (1969b). Unconscious fantasy and disturbances of mental experience. *Psychoanal. Q.*, 38:1–27.

————. (1972). Character perversions. In *Currents in Psychoanalysis*, ed. I. M. Marcus, pp. 317–336. New York: Int. Univ. Press.

————. (1979a). The genesis of interpretation. *J. Amer. Psychoanal. Assn.*, 27 (suppl.):193–206.

————. (1979b). Metaphor and the psychoanalytic situation. *Psychoanal. Q.*, 48:363–385.

————. (1982). Unconscious fantasy and political movements. In *Judaism and Psychoanalysis*, ed. M. Ostow, pp. 267–282. New York: KTAV Publishing House.

Arlow, J. A., & Brenner, C. (1964). *Psychoanalytic Concepts and the Structural Theory*. New York: Int. Univ. Press.

Arlow, J. A., with M. Ostow, M. J. Blumenthal, & P. B. Neubauer. (1972). The Jewishness of Jewish young people. *Amer. J. Psychiat.*, 129:553–561.

Beres, D., & Arlow, J. A. (1974). Fantasy and identification in empathy. *Psychoanal. Q.*, 43:26–50.

Breuer, J., & Freud, S. (1893–95). *Studies on Hysteria. SE*, 2.

Brierley, M. (1943). Theory, practice and public relations. *Int. J. Psycho-anal.*, 24:119–125.

Fenichel, O. (1950). *The Psychoanalytic Theory of Neurosis*. New York: Norton.

Fisher, C. (1954). Dreams and perceptions. *J. Amer. Psychoanal. Assn.*, 2:389–445.

Freud, A. (1936). *The Ego and the Mechanisms of Defense*. New York: Int. Univ. Press, 1966.

————. (1949). Certain types and stages of social maladjustment. In *Searchlights on Delinquency*, ed. K. R. Eissler, pp. 205–215. New York: Int. Univ. Press.

Freud, S. (1900). *The Interpretation of Dreams. SE*, 4 & 5.

————. (1901). *The Psychopathology of Everyday Life. SE*, 6.

————. (1908a). Creative writers and day-dreaming. *SE*, 9:141–153.

————. (1908b). Hysterical fantasies and their relation to bisexuality. *SE*, 9:155–166.

————. (1911). Formulations on the two principles of mental functioning. *SE*, 12:213–226.

————. (1915). The unconscious. *SE*, 14:166–215.

————. (1919). "A child is being beaten." *SE*, 17:175–204.

————. (1923). *The Ego and the Id. SE*, 19:3–66.

Hartmann, H. (1939). *Ego Psychology and the Problem of Adaptation*. New York: Int. Univ. Press, 1958.

————. (1950). Comments on the psychoanalytic theory of the ego. *Psychoanal. Study Child*, 5:74–96.

Jacobson, E. (1959). Depersonalization. *J. Amer. Psychoanal. Assn.*, 7:581–610.

Jones, E. (1914). The Madonna's conception through the ear. Rpt. in *Essays on Applied Psycho-Analysis*, vol. 2, pp. 266–357. London: Hogarth Press, 1951.

Kris, E. (1956). On some vicissitudes of insight in psychoanalysis. *Int. J. Psychoanal.*, 37:445–455.

Kris, E., & Kaplan, A. (1952). Aesthetic ambiguity. In *Psychoanalytic Explorations in Art*, pp. 243–264. New York: Int. Univ. Press.

Linn, L. (1954). The discriminating function of the ego. *Psychoanal. Q.*, 23:38–47.

Sachs, H. (1942). The community of daydreams. In *The Creative Unconscious*. Cambridge: Sci-Art Publishers.

Sharpe, E. F. (1935). Similar and divergent unconscious determinants underlying the sublimations of pure art and pure science. *Int. J. Psychoanal.*, 16:186–202.

————. (1940). Psychophysical problems revealed in language. Rpt. in *Collected Papers on Psycho-Analysis*, pp. 155–169. London: Hogarth Press, 1950.

12

FREUD ON DREAMS
AND DREAMING

It is generally unrecognized that Sigmund Freud's contribution to the scientific understanding of dreams derived from a radical reorientation to the dream experience. During the nineteenth century, prior to the publication of *The Interpretation of Dreams,* dreaming was considered by the scientific community to be fundamentally a manifestation of mental activity during sleep. The state of sleep was given prominence as a factor accounting for the seeming lack of organization and meaning to the dream experience. Thus, earlier investigators viewed the nature of the dream from the standpoint of sleep, a relatively nonpsychological state. Freud, by contrast, recognized that dreams—as myth, folklore, and common sense had long understood—were linked with the psychology of waking life. This shift in orientation has proved essential for our modern view of dreams and dreaming. Dreams are no longer dismissed as senseless notes on a piano hit at random by an untrained player. Instead, they are now recognized as psychologically significant and meaningful expressions of the life of the dreamer, albeit expressed in disguised and concealed forms.

CONTEMPORARY DREAM RESEARCH

During the past quarter century, there has been an increasing scientific interest in the process of dreaming (Fischer, 1965). It has been discovered that there is a regular sleep–wakefulness cycle, and that if ex-

perimental subjects are awakened during periods of rapid eye movement (REM periods), they will frequently report dreams. In a typical night, four or five dreams occur during REM periods, accompanied by other signs of physiological activation, such as increased respiratory and heart rate and penile or clitoral erection. Dreams usually last for the duration of the period of eye movements—from about 10 to 25 minutes—and the eye movements tend to follow the direction of movement in the dream. If subjects are deprived of opportunities for dreaming by frequent awakenings under experimental conditions, psychological disturbances in the form of anxiety, irritability, and an increase in oral behavior occur during the subsequent waking state. Normally, a subject after a period of REM sleep and dreaming returns to a period of deeper sleep, in which he or she is less likely to respond to stimuli that produce wakefulness. It should also be stated that although dreaming usually occurs in such regular cycles, it may occur at other times during sleep as well as during hypnagogic or hypnapompic states, when REMs are not present.

The above findings are discoveries made since the monumental work of Freud reported in *The Interpretation of Dreams* (1900). Although they are of great interest vis-à-vis the study of the mind–body problem, they have only a peripheral bearing on the central concerns of the psychoanalyst—namely, the psychology of dream formation, the meaning of dream content, the dream as an approach to a deeper understanding of the psychic apparatus, and the use of the dream in psychoanalytic treatment.

In this chapter I will discuss these subjects only briefly, concentrating mainly on the seminal ideas of Freud. Dreams have, however, received continuing interest and attention throughout the history of psychoanalysis. I shall indicate the ways in which Freud's basic observations and theories have been elaborated in many books and papers.

RUDIMENTS OF THE DREAM

In his initial psychological work, Freud was led to the dream via his interest in neurotic symptoms. In his attempt to understand the meaning of symptoms, he asked his patients to associate freely, and in doing so they began to report dreams. He then treated the dream much like a symptom, amenable to the formation of associational links and susceptible to interpretation. Freud asked patients to report freely what came to mind in response to specific elements of a dream. The method of free association required curtailment of the tendency of the mind to judge, evaluate, and criticize and so block the natural flow of association.

This method, which is also the method used by the patient to reveal his thoughts and feelings in psychoanalytic treatment, led to clarification of the meaning of the dream. The dream as reported is called "the manifest dream" and is the dream as consciously perceived and subsequently remembered. Freud discovered, however, that behind the manifest dream the psychoanalyst could uncover the presence of numerous latent thoughts, which, by a process of dream work, were transformed into the manifest dream. When the manifest dream was analyzed by the method of free association, it was discovered that the dream representation could be understood as an attempt at the fulfillment of wishes of which the dreamer was not consciously aware.

On the surface, this proposition seemed even more radical than the view that the seemingly senseless and chaotic dream is an understandable feature of psychological life. Yet there is evidence to support such a proposition. In support of the wish-fulfillment theory, one can point to the fact that a small number of dreams, albeit not many, are clearly wish-fulfilling even in their manifest content. Explorers deprived of food and drink dream of huge banquets and luscious, clear, thirst-quenching mountain streams. Some children's dreams are also manifestly wish-fulfilling. A medical student who must report to the hospital early in the morning to make rounds dreams of himself lying in a hospital bed and continues to sleep, comforted in the thought that he is already in the hospital. Such a dream is called a dream of convenience. The wish fulfilled is the universal desire to continue to sleep.

Such easily decipherable dreams are the exception, however. Most dreams do not readily present wishes as fulfilled in the manifest content. Instead, the manifest dream is the end product of a process of disguise and distortion. In order to account for the masking of the wish, it is necessary to understand that the difficulty the dreamer experiences in recognizing the wishes underlying the dream is that they are unacceptable to his or her ego and superego. The wishes may be objectionable on moral grounds or unacceptable because they lower self-esteem or produce anxiety, guilt, shame, disgust, or embarrassment. Thus they remain unconscious, and the thoughts and feelings connected with them are subjected to a censorship that interferes with the wishes attaining ready access to awareness. Many dreams that occur during a night's sleep are forgotten or fade away with awakening. Dream censorship also affects the retention of dream content. Thus one may forget a dream because of the presence of a repressive force, and similar defensive forces adopt a variety of psychological techniques in order to distort representations of clear wish fulfillment. As an example of distortion, an unconscious hostile wish directed toward a loved one on the previous day may be re-presented in a dream by the dreamer's attempt to rescue the loved one from a dangerous and painful situation invented by the dream representation.

Psychoanalysis is interested in the varied sources which go into the formation of a dream. If we simply examine the dream on a manifest level, we note that it is made up of a large number of elements. The images of the dream may consist of previously experienced real events, waking thoughts, feelings, and ideas. Somatic sensations, memories from the previous day, or memories of experiences from the distant and even infantile past may find a place in the manifest dream. The immediate and proximal source of the dream is some psychological remnant such as a longing, worry, or concern—some incomplete task from the previous day that has not been resolved and laid to rest.

In *The Interpretation of Dreams* Freud offers several examples of such day residues serving as precipitants of the imagery of dreams. Freud had a dream of turning over a colored plate in a monograph on a plant that he had written. The immediate source was the sight of a new book on the plant that he had seen in a window the previous day. But the dream was also instigated by a conversation Freud had had on the previous day on a topic related to the book. The second instigator, the conversation, was much more emotionally meaningful to Freud than the sight of the book per se. It is common for dreams to use indifferent recent memories to conceal other situations that stir intrapsychic emotion and conflict. It is also common for thoughts about the current life of the dreamer to evoke related memories from the past with which the immediate experiences resonate.

DREAM WORK

The latent dream thoughts, stirred by the day residues, seek some form of expression. The vehicle for this expression, the means by which the latent dream thoughts are transformed into manifest dream content, is known as dream work. Before embarking on a description of it, I should point out that latent dream thoughts, when they are revealed through dream interpretation, follow the ordinary laws of logic and everyday speech. They are understandable as forms of expression in the optative mood; thus, "If only it were true that . . . ," or "Given such and such a condition, I would wish that . . . ," and other such ordinary means of expressing a desire.

Dream work is the vehicle and language available to the dreamer for expressing thought. The language resembles a rebus or pictographic puzzle more than a written language in which words bear a clear symbolic relation to a referent. The mechanisms of dream work are four in number: condensation, displacement, plastic representation, and secondary revision (also known in older psychoanalytic literature as "secondary elaboration"). The first three are archaic, prelogical modes of thinking. The last, secondary revision, is a component of rational, logical thought.

Condensation refers to the tendency to combine a number of latent dream thoughts into a more succinct element. Thus, in the well-known dream of Irma's injection which Freud discussed at length in the second chapter of *The Interpretation of Dreams,* the figure of Irma in the manifest content stands for at least seven women, including herself. A number of latent thoughts about women are condensed into a single manifest element. *Displacement* is a mechanism that allows the dreamer to shift the psychic intensity from one dream thought to another. Freud maintained that there is never any doubt about the psychic value of latent dream thoughts. We know their value on the basis of our direct judgment, our shared humanity, empathy, and introspection. In the formation of the dream, however, the accent is shifted; the psychologically important is treated casually, and the seemingly innocuous in the manifest content may stand for the emotionally intense. Displacement is facilitated by dream censorship and re-

sistance, as well as by defensive needs to conceal conflicted thoughts from the dreamer's ego and superego. Freud was fond of illustrating dream displacement by the tale of a town in which a tailor had committed a capital crime punishable by execution. Since the town had only one tailor but three butchers, it was decided to execute a butcher instead. In Freud's dream of the botanical monograph, referred to above, the trivial day residue concealed and displaced a more intensely cathected stimulus.

The means used in the construction of the dream also reveal the contents of latent dream thoughts. Since primary process mechanisms are inadequate to express relations between dream thoughts, such relations may be expressed in the formal means available to the dreamer. A close connection between two events or people may be expressed by simultaneity in time or juxtaposition of figures in the manifest dream. A causal relation in latent thoughts may be represented by a short dream that introduces another dream. A contradiction may be expressed by a reversal. Various qualities in the dreamer's perception of the dream may represent components of latent dream thoughts. The sensory quality of the dream may stand for ideas about clarity or vagueness, which are components of the latent dream thoughts; thus the analysand may have a "vague" dream that expresses his or her view of the psychoanalyst's interpretation of the previous day, it, too, having been vague.

Dream work may also make use of a universal tendency to depict a psychically important person, body part, or experience by a repertoire of common symbols. A father or the analyst may be represented by a king or president, a penis by a knife, a vagina by a cave, birth by water. However, these symbols are traps for the unwary. In the absence of confirming associations, the analyst will not be taken in by the facile glibness such symbols offer but will explore via associations of the patient the meaning of such dream elements.

The third mechanism of dream work is the capacity to form *plastic representations* of dream thoughts. The dreamer tends to form visual images rather than express formal relations among thoughts in conceptual terms. Occasionally the images are in other sensory modalities besides the visual; thus, auditory, kinesthetic, and olfactory modes are also used. Some dreams lack all sensory qualities and are present only as thoughts, isolated ideas, feeling states, or single words.

The fourth factor responsible for the work of constructing a dream is *secondary revision*. This mechanism strives to make the confusion and seeming chaos of primary process ideation coherent and intelligible. The organized narrative and storylike quality of some dreams is attributable to this factor. Occasionally the dreamer will fit the dream contents to an available daydream from waking life, much as a Renaissance painter may choose to express personal infantile wishes for maternal care by making use of conventional Nativity iconography.

ANXIETY DREAMS

Thus far, I have described some of the basic mechanisms that characterize the psychoanalytic approach to the clinical use of dreams. I shall shortly describe the conceptual scheme underlying this approach, but before doing so, I shall discuss the phenomenon of anxiety dreams to tie up some loose ends. If dreams are indeed wish-fulfilling, how does one explain the fact that some dreams are anything but pleasurable? Indeed, some dreams are accompanied by much anxiety, even of nightmarish proportions. It is important to establish that although dreams aim at wish fulfillment, they do not always succeed. The wishes striving for fulfillment may be overwhelming, unacceptable, and reprehensible to the ego or the superego, and thus the conflict that ensues strains the ego's resources and is unmanageable. The dreamer's defenses break down, and the only recourse is to wake and thereby interrupt the dream. Insofar as the dream serves a guardian function in striving to maintain sleep, the dream then admits failure.

We must also consider an alternative possibility: namely, that the presence of psychic displeasure, pain, or anxiety is what the dream paradoxically strives for. In other words, masochistic or guilt-ridden dreamers who feel in need of punishment are indeed fulfilling a wish by experiencing anxiety; thus the presence of anxiety, rather than contradicting the wish-fulfilling hypothesis, can be demonstrated as offering further support for its importance.

There is a class of anxiety dreams that stands outside wish fulfillment, however. Individuals who have been exposed to extreme and stressful external situations, such as military combat or natural disasters, or individuals who experience states of great tension when overwhelmed by instinctual demands may have anxiety dreams that are simply a form of discharge. Such individuals have a need to repeat the traumatic event and may even derive benefit from such repetition—perhaps the repetition is an attempt at mastery. There are some resemblances between such psychological experiences and the work of mourning, in that a period of time in which to work through the trauma must be permitted. The drive toward mastery of a trauma differs from the usual definition of a psychological wish in that it is

not specific, conflict-laden, or accompanied by the experience of pleasurable drive satisfaction.

There are also some dreams, particularly in narcissistic individuals or those preoccupied with internal psychic processes, in which the dream content simply reflects the state of the mental apparatus. In such dreams, in which the state of the dreamer is represented, the wish-fulfilling aspect may also be relatively minor. The dreamer merely represents a perception of his endopsychic state, such as varying levels of sleepiness and wakefulness (the functional phenomena of Silberer) or a sense of narcissistic vulnerability, emptiness, or grandeur. A related notion is the dream screen experience (proposed by Lewin, 1950), which may simply consist of a sense of a dream projected upon a background, perhaps a symbolic representative of the infantile state that follows a feeding at the maternal breast. The screen is the background upon which the dream image is projected, the background upon which the dream image of a well-visualized dream is depicted. Such formal framing devices as the dream screen are a further indication of the latent dream thoughts.

THEORETICAL EXPLANATION OF THE DREAM PROCESS

The psychology of the dream process was first worked out following the topographic model of the psychic apparatus. And although it is possible to add to our understanding by using structural concepts, the topographic model continues to have potent explanatory power, particularly from a clinical point of view. The mental apparatus can be viewed as a reflex arc; excitations have a direction and flow from a perceptual-receptive periphery toward a motor discharge end. In the state of sleep, there is relative motor paralysis, and thus discharge of excitation in the form of ego-instigated action cannot take place. Since the sluices leading to motility are closed, the excitations move in a regressive rather than progressive manner. The concept of regression is essential in understanding the uniqueness of the dream experience, and three different types of regression are at work. The reflex-arc vector is reversed so that, instead of excitations moving from perceptions toward the motoric end, they move backwards toward the perceptual end. In doing so, they activate stored thoughts and feelings, particularly memories of earlier perceptions. This backward path also activates childhood longings and wishes stored as memory traces. The repressive and regulatory controls that ordinarily keep such longings out of consciousness during waking life are less operative during sleep because of a general lowering of defense in the absence of capacity for action.

A second regression also occurs, from logical to illogical forms of thinking, from secondary to primary process modes of deploying excitation, and toward the use of the mechanisms of dream work described above. Third, as a result of the regressive movement, buried unconscious wishes become activated during sleep and find a means of expression through attachment to preconscious ideas stirred by the day residues. It may in fact be the case that unconscious wishes, which are powered by strong energic drives, have the capacity to give form to the dream and produce its reality-like, peremptory quality. Although the excitations that accompany infantile wishes may indeed provide the capital for dream formations, it is usually the derivatives of such primitive wishes that are transferred to the latent dream thoughts. There is thus a variable relationship between the preconscious day residue and unconscious infantile wishes. At times, recent experience stimulates unconscious wishes because of a similarity in the two states. At other times, unconscious wishes may attach themselves to an insignificant day residue and so find expression for repressed and activated wishes that strive for satisfaction.

Early theory of dream formation stressed the view that unconscious wishes seek expression by obtaining a preconscious attachment. This view is still the basis for our understanding of transference in the clinical context. Later theoretical refinements in psychoanalysis permit us to view the dream not only as a disguised expression of unconscious wishes but, in addition, as a resolution of conflict by means of a compromise formation. After all, ego and superego factors also play a role in the formation of dreams, and defensive operations are represented as well as the wishes they attempt to conceal and restrain. An example of the latter is the experience of the dreamer who during a dream becomes aware that he or she is dreaming—the dream within the dream. A judgment by the ego is thus brought into play. One often finds that the dream within the dream occurs when the manifest content of the dream resembles too closely the state of affairs that the dreamer knows to be the actuality of a real situation with which he or she is confronted in waking life. The dreamer dissociates him- or herself from knowledge he or she does not wish to face by claiming, "It is only a dream." In the clinical situation it is possible to use dreams to heighten one's understanding of defensive and adaptive mechanisms, as well as the unconscious wishes that seek expression.

Finally, what is the current status of the wish-fulfilling theory in view of recent dream-research findings and the accumulation of clinical psychoanalytic activity since the publication of *The Interpretation of Dreams*? The establishment of the periodicity of the dream cycle during sleep neither adds nor subtracts from the psychoanalytic theory of dream interpretation. The discovery of REM periods and other signs of physiological activation during sleep merely provides the stage, as it were, upon which the drama of the dream can be played. It may even be the case that Freud's early notion of the process of dreaming as fulfilling a sleep-preserving function now finds a partial confirmation. Dreaming takes place during phases of sleep from which the dreamer is more easily aroused to wakefulness, and following the dream a deeper level of sleep ensues. The central position of the unconscious wish as dream instigator is also supported by current research. The REM cycles themselves bear a relationship to activated drive states, periods of heightened instinctualization as evident in accompanying periods of penile or clitoral erection. Thus dreaming itself may be one manifestation of an activated biological rhythm that surfaces during sleep.

The primary interest of the psychoanalyst continues to be in the meaning of dream content, and the continued special position of dreams in clinical work warrants the familiar rubric of the dream as "the royal road to the unconscious." The dream is unique because of its ability to reestablish temporarily an experience in which perceptual identities with previous satisfactions can be represented. The dream, like the symptom or parapraxis, is indeed a compromise formation, and thus reveals hidden psychological components aside from wishes. However, the nature of the dream itself, the link with drive and the capacity to represent drive derivatives in perceptual reality, continues to provide the psychoanalyst with a unique opportunity to view unconscious processes more directly and relatively unconcealed by impenetrable defense and resistance.

THE TECHNIQUE OF DREAM INTERPRETATION

The psychoanalyst, confronted by a report of a dream of a patient in analysis, can resort to a variety of approaches in order to understand the dream. Fundamentally, the analyst is interested in associational material that will allow connections to be made between manifest and latent content. The context of the appearance of the dream during the session, links between dream content and previous and subsequent thoughts, ideas and feelings of the hour are noted. The analyst may ask the patient to begin by associating to the elements of the dream in chronological order and may choose to direct the patient's attention to elements of sensory or affective intensity. The analyst may ask for connections between the dream and events on the previous day, or he or she may leave it to the patient to start the associational process (Freud, 1923).

If the patient proves resistant to interpretation of particular dreams, this may be due to defensiveness and anxiety about the latent content. At such times, the analyst may simply make use of the manifest dream content to stimulate other connections in the patient's thoughts and not focus specifically on interpreting the dream. Although the dream enjoys a special place among the associations of an analytic session because of the relative freedom from defensiveness, there may continue to be obstacles to interpretation that prove impenetrable. Some dreams, referred to as dreams from above, are largely preconscious ruminations, a replay of thoughts or intentions from the previous day, and the connection to unconscious wishes may be barely discernible on the basis of association.

Initial dreams of an analysis are often of value in highlighting trends that are likely to follow as the analysis proceeds. Like screen memories, they may also represent crucial areas of intrapsychic conflict in the life of the analysand. As the analysis proceeds, the analyst finds that dreams concern the analysis itself and the patient's relationship with the analyst and that the dream is often an elaboration of stimuli from a previous analytic session. Thus, a dream may be an important clue to the patient's response to an intervention of the analyst. That activity may be an intentional interpretation or adventitious, such as an apparent change in the analyst's manner of greeting the patient at the beginning of an hour.

Overt anxiety dreams or nightmares are an indication of the strength of the conflict of the dreamer. Either there is an increase in intensity of unacceptable wishes that demand fulfillment in representation, or the means of defense, leading to successful disguise and concealment, are inadequate. In any case, such dreams highlight the fact that the tendency toward wish fulfillment may be more precisely stated as an *attempt* in the direction of fulfillment, an attempt that at times may not succeed. It may also be the case that the purpose of the dream is not to represent a wish connected with a drive but instead a punishment or a painful experience. If the latter is the case, the instigator of the dream may be a pressure from the superego rather than the id. In any case, the view of the dream as a compromise, a result of stirrings that have their origins in the intrapsychic structures of the mind, alerts the analyst to the relative weight to attach to the forces at any given time.

REFERENCES

Fischer, C. (1965). Psychoanalytic implications of recent research on sleep and dreaming. *J. Amer. Psychoanal. Assn.*, 13:197–303.

Freud, S. (1900). *The Interpretation of Dreams. SE*, 4 & 5.

———. (1901). On dreams. *SE*, 5:633–686.

———. (1911). The handling of dream-interpretation in psycho-analysis. *SE*, 12:91–96.

———. (1917). A metapsychological supplement to the theory of dreams. *SE*, 14:219–235.

———. (1920). Supplements to the theory of dreams. *SE*, 18:4–5.

———. (1923). Remarks upon the theory and practice of dream-interpretation. *SE*, 19:109–121.

———. (1925). Some additional notes on dream-interpretation as a whole. *SE*, 19:125–138.

Lewin, B. D. (1950). *The Psychoanalysis of Elation.* New York: Norton.

13

THE DREAM
AFTER FREUD

The hallmark of greatness of any discovery is its impact, the degree to which it initiates or influences further progress. The history of science provides innumerable examples of such great discoveries. Freud's discovery of the meaning of dreams and how they are to be interpreted in a scientific way was such a discovery. He realized this himself, when in the preface to the third English edition of *The Interpretation of Dreams* (15 March 1931), he wrote: "Insight such as this falls to one's lot but once in a lifetime."

Freud's discovery gave tremendous impetus to the development of a science of the mind, enhancing the understanding of patients in clinical practice as well as expanding the application of psychoanalysis to such fields as history, anthropology, art, literature, and biography.

Specific studies of the dream after Freud's initial discoveries flowed in a number of different directions. The main thrust of the literature was largely clinical and concerned with close scrutiny of the manifest content of dreams and associations to them. Numerous examples confirming or elaborating Freud's observations and their applications dominated the writings on dreams.

Other studies, rather than delving into questions about the specific content and meaning of dreams, pursued investigations along neurophysiological lines. This area of research utilized data gleaned from studies of sleep by means of the electroen-

cephalograph and the recording of rapid eye movements. In addition to this development in scientific interest, various studies of dreams have been made in an attempt to devise and elaborate a theory of the mind based on Freud's formulations. In yet other studies, his principles have been abandoned completely.

DREAMS IN CLINICAL PRACTICE

Over the years an extensive literature on dreams in clinical practice has evolved. One of the better books summarizing this literature is that edited by Natterson (1980). After discussing the clinical theory of dreams, it considers the dream in various psychopathological states, in special therapeutic situations, and in various psychotherapeutic modalities. Out of this extensive literature I have arbitrarily selected some aspects on which to report.

Dreams as a Diagnostic or Prognostic Indicator

Freud distinguished between the manifest dream (the dream that is remembered) and the latent dream thoughts that lay behind the various elements of the manifest dream. By collecting the associations to the various elements of the manifest dream, he was then able to look for the common thread in the latent dream thoughts that would lead to an understanding of the wish fulfilled in or by the dream. While Freud did not ignore the manifest dream, his primary emphasis was on the latent dream thoughts and the unconscious strivings behind them.

Many investigators since Freud's time have concentrated their attention on the manifest dream, in an effort to see what meaning could be derived from it. They have sought answers to the basic question of whether the manifest content of certain types of dreams could be diagnostic of psychopathology or predictive of analyzability or of the patient's prognosis in general. Some analysts, recognizing that dream analysis is related to the general problem of analyzability, doubt whether a patient who *never* dreams can even be analyzed (Blum, 1976) and regard the absence of dreams as an indication of some "faulty working in the psychic apparatus" (Sharpe, 1937, p. 197).

Initial dreams in which there is a good deal of fragmentation, intense vividness of color, chaos, or disintegration, in which various things seem to be falling apart or blowing up, in which there are indications of severe storms, conflagrations, or other types of destruction, seem to indicate that the individual's ego is in a precarious state and that the individual may be on the verge of a major psychic break or psychosis. Frankly homicidal dreams early in therapy or cannibalistic or orally aggressive dreams may alert the therapist to a possibly unanalyzable major psychopathology. While it is true that neither a diagnosis nor a prognosis can or should be made on the basis of dreams alone, the presence of such dreams should warn the therapist to look closely into the possibility of a severe disturbance (Noble, 1951; Richardson & Moore, 1963; Bonime & Bonime, 1980).

Long, involved, torturous dreams occupying the major portion of a therapeutic session so that neither therapist nor patient can do much with them may also have diagnostic or prognostic significance. If these dreams occur at the onset of therapy and persist over a lengthy period of time, the reasons behind them rather than their content must be examined. Various possibilities have been recognized: a major resistance to therapy, the emergence of dangerous transference manifestations, the wish to continue sleeping (Lewin, 1953), a verbal expression of a urinary spray, an anal barrage, or diarrhea, and so on. In addition, the possibility of a severe ego disturbance must also be considered.

Apart from the consideration of dreams as diagnostic and prognostic tools, various investigators have attempted to discern whether dreams may be used to predict a patient's behavior. In a dream of the night before, a patient may anticipate a canceled appointment, an accident, or some acting out, whether in an analytic session or outside the therapy (Sterba,

1946). The question then is to what extent an understanding of the individual's dreams enables the therapist to predict a patient's behavior on a much larger scale. Such information is especially valuable in those instances in which one suspects that a patient may be on the verge of doing something destructive or self-destructive (for example, committing suicide) or may be heading for a psychotic break.

An extension of this interest in the predictability aspect of dreams is Freud's (1917) observation that "In dreams, incipient physical disease is often detected earlier and more clearly than in waking life, and all the current bodily sensations assume gigantic proportions" (p. 223). The extent to which this is true is a subject of considerable concern, especially among therapists interested in psychosomatic illnesses. As in so many instances, problems on the interface between the psychic and the somatic have not been resolved.

Initial Dreams

In recent years a number of publications have explored the significance—for analyzability, diagnosis, or prognosis—of the *undisguised appearance of the analyst* in the manifest content of initial or early dreams (Rapaport, 1959; Harris, 1962; Yazmajian, 1964; Rosenbaum, 1965; Savitt, 1969; Fleming, 1972; Bradlow & Coen, 1975). The significance of this type of dream may be "partially related to the patient's intense mistrust of the analyst because of his fear that the analyst would be like the parental transference figures" and that there is "an attempted denial of [the patient's] intense fear and mistrust in the service of a more powerful wish for gratification from the analyst" (Bradlow & Coen, 1975, pp. 423, 422). Some writers have suggested that patients reporting such dreams may be responding to countertransference reactions on the part of the analyst. While the ultimate significance of this type of dream has not been settled, therapists are urged to be especially on the lookout for determinants arising from some change in the transference–countertransference interaction.

Color in Dreams

Generally when people relate their dreams, they do not specify if the dream itself or any elements in the dream are in color. When they do, the color is to be considered an element just like any other element in the manifest dream content and hence subject to exploration. Sometimes the choice of a particular color occurs because a number of thoughts have converged upon it or because the color itself has special significance.

Color in dreams has been the subject of many papers. Some investigators have considered parallels between color in dreams and the color response to Rorschach cards. Calef (1954) suggested that in addition to the specific choice of color perhaps being related to experiences during the dream day, the latent content may refer "to the scoptophilic-exhibitionistic impulses of the [dream and its relation to] primal scene material" (p. 459).

In some dreams, color is not confined to one or a few disparate elements but is pervasive throughout the dream as in so-called technicolor dreams. Whereas color may be present in the dreams of people who are artistic or who are trained in the use of color, its continual presence in the dreams of some people may indicate severe disturbances.

Kohut (1971) wrote that technicolor dreams "often appear to signify the intrusion of unmodified material into the ego in the guise of realism, and the ego's inability to integrate it completely. One might say that the technicolor expresses the ego's subliminally experienced anxious hypomanic excitement over certain intrusions of the grandiosity and the exhibitionism of the grandiose self" (p. 172). He added, "The fact that the dream was in color (especially in the unnatural technicolor . . .) is an expression of the fact that the dreamer's ego was unable to achieve the complete integration of the new experiences; that it was able fully to absorb neither the intensity nor the content of the drive demands" (p. 322).

Typical Dreams

In *The Interpretation of Dreams* Freud mentions a number of typical dreams. He distinguishes between those with a constant meaning and those with a variety of meanings. As in the case of some of his other observations, various investigators have attempted to amplify and elaborate his remarks.

In a very comprehensive study of dental dreams, for example, Lorand and Feldman (1955) demonstrated, on the basis of clinical material as well as myths and folklore, that dreams of teeth may allude to all stages of libidinal development. As references to the oral stage, they may allude to any loss, separation, or deprivation. "The deep oral regression gratifies the wish for primitive narcissism—being back at the mother's breast" (p. 160). Their observations and the results of their research go well beyond Freud's categorical statement that in males, dreams with a dental stimulus are from "the masturbatory desires of the pubertal period" (1900, p. 385) and "the dreaded punishment for it" (1916–17, p. 190) and his subsequent addition to the effect that dreams "with a dental stimulus occurring in women have the

meaning of birth dreams." Freud notes: "The element in common between [the castration and birth interpretations] . . . lies in the fact that in both cases . . . what is in question is the separation of a part of the body from the whole" (1900, pp. 387–388). Lorand and Feldman (1955) suggest that the removal of teeth in some dreams can easily represent the loss of the nursing nipple. Dreams of teeth not only have phallic and childbirth significance but may also refer to the vagina dentata, abortion, death, and psychosis. The toothless state of both the infant and the aged are also important considerations. Moreover, dreams of teeth may refer directly to aggression, to biting or chewing. Such references are particularly significant in the case of depressed patients who have a good deal of oral aggression.

The *examination dream* mentioned by Freud as a typical dream has been the subject of a good deal of discussion. At times, the examination in such a dream is a physical or anatomical examination. In such instances, the individual may have actively participated in such examinations, as in the doctor game in childhood or in medical or physical examinations. Clinical material often reveals that the individual dreads that the doctor will discover that the patient has masturbated, will divine his particular fantasies, and will punish him severely by castration, humiliation, rejection, or abandonment. In therapy, these dreams often have transferential significance (Sterba, 1928; Arlow, 1951; Kavka, 1979; Renik, 1981; Grinstein, 1983).

Initially Freud classified *dreams of "flying* through the air to the accompaniment of agreeable feelings or falling with feelings of anxiety" as typical dreams that always have the same meaning (1900, p. 271). Yet, in 1909, he added that he viewed these dreams as meaning "something different in every instance; it is only the raw material of sensations contained in them which is always derived from the same source" (p. 393).

Freud believed that these dreams essentially had two determinants. The first is the reproduction of sensations experienced during childhood games of movement (as well as during play on swings and seesaws) or when being tossed about by fond adults. He observed, moreover, that "it not uncommonly happens that these games of movement, though innocent in themselves, give rise to sexual feelings" (1900, p. 393). The association of these games with such sensations led Freud to mention Federn's theory that "a good number of these flying dreams are dreams of erection" and Mourly Vold's observation that frequently such dreams are "connected with erections or emission" (1900, p. 394). By the same token, Freud went on to say that, in women, flying dreams indicate the conscious or unconscious wish to be a man (1916–17, p. 155).

Kohut (1971) considered "the flying fantasy [or dream] to be a frequent feature of unmodified infantile grandiosity. Its early stages are common to both sexes and are probably reinforced by ecstatic sensations while the small child is being carried by the omnipotent idealized self-object" (p. 144). He described "the unmodified grandiose self" as urging "the ego to jump into the void in order to soar or sail through space" (p. 145).

Other determinants of flying dreams are actual experiences of aircraft or aviation—flights taken or planned (Bond, 1952). Sometimes such dreams are to be viewed metaphorically as dealing with separation anxiety (that is, the fear that someone may fly away) or as an expression of such ego wishes as the wish for freedom or for increased or expanded ego boundaries. Ambition, "flying high," mania or hypomanic excitement, exhilaration, ecstasy, soaring "like a bird," may all be determinants of this type of dream.

Another element in the manifest dream content that has received some attention since Freud concerns dreams in which an individual is looking at, him- or herself in a mirror (Myers, 1973; Shengold, 1974; Berman, 1985). Such dreams may refer to the individual's recognition that analysis is a way of looking at him- or herself and his or her conflicts (Miller, 1948). Eisnitz (1980) states that *mirror dreams* "usually are reactions to a narcissistic crisis in the life of the patient, often induced by the emergence of an unacceptable wish (often a transference wish) during the analysis. In practically every instance the self-scanning activity, which is represented by the mirror in the dream, is closely connected to superego qualities" (p. 378). But mirror dreams may have another significance. Kohut (1971) wrote that "there also occur dreams during the analysis which portray a relationship (of the self) with someone who is seen as through a mirror (the analyst as the reflector of the grandiose self)"; these dreams occur "in cases in which a major part of the instinctual investment of the grandiose self was in the process of becoming mobilized in relationship to the therapist" (p. 116).

Other writers have suggested that the mirror in the manifest content of such dreams may refer to the mother's face (Silver, 1985). Rear-view mirror dreams may refer to anality, the analyst, or looking back at the past (Berman, 1985).

While Freud did not include *observation dreams* in either of his two categories of typical dreams, his detailed analysis of a dream of the Wolf Man is a clear example of a typical dream referring to primal scene observation (1918). Such dreams regularly contain certain specific elements. The dreamer finds him- or herself in a locale (for example, an auditorium) in which an observation can be made. He or she views (or hears) some activity. Frequently, there are indications of an interruption of the activity and references to the dreamer's reaction to the observation, either in the dream itself or later in an association to it. These may include anxiety, anger, frustration, a feeling of being left out, rejected, or abandoned, a flooding of the ego with sexual excitement, an identification with one or the other parent in an active or passive position, or some gross visceral or physiological response (Grinstein, 1983).

Izner (1959) pointed out that often a series of dreams with primal scene content occurs when a separation between analyst and patient is anticipated, as when the analyst has announced plans for a vacation or trip. Dreams influenced by such circumstances may occur early in an analysis; unlike primal scene dreams brought in after a good deal of analytic work has been done, these seem almost totally unrelated to the general thrust of the material. Dreams with primal scene content often occur during the termination phase of an analysis.

Not all observation dreams typically refer to primal scene observations. They may also refer to the observation during childhood of the genitals of a playmate, a sibling, or of an adult, usually of the opposite sex.

Self State and Manifest Perverse Dreams

While some elements of the dream are to be understood as a result of structural conflict and are "resolvable through the analysis of free associations that gradually lead toward formerly hidden wishes and impulses" (Kohut, 1977, p. 111), others contain "elements (often the total setting of the dream, its atmosphere) [which] portray aspects of the archaic self that have emerged" (ibid., pp. 110–111). He described a type of dream that attempts "with the aid of verbalizable dream-imagery, to bind the nonverbal tensions of traumatic states (the dread of overstimulation, or of the disintegration of the self [psychosis])" (p. 109). He writes:

Dreams of this . . . type portray the dreamer's dread vis-à-vis some uncontrollable tension-increase or his dread of the dissolution of the self. The very act of portraying these vicissitudes in the dream constitutes an attempt to deal with the psychological danger by covering frightening nameless processes with nameable visual imagery. . . . In [this] type of dream . . . free associations do not lead to unconscious hidden layers of the mind; at best they provide us with further imagery which remains on the same level as the manifest content of the dream. The scrutiny of the manifest content of the dream and of the associative elaborations of the manifest content will then allow us to recognize that the healthy sectors of the patient's psyche are reacting with anxiety to a disturbing change in the condition of the self— manic overstimulation or a serious depressive drop in self-esteem—or to the threat of the dissolution of the self. [p. 109]

Socarides (1980) considered that "manifest perverse dreams are similar to the 'self-state' dreams" that Kohut described. He states that these dreams do not

> express in visual imagery the content of drives or wishes in an attempted solution to a conflict represented by the manifest content, but [help] the narcissist to reintegrate himself by pressing into service primitive modes of adaptation which have proved useful and necessary in the earliest years of life. Sexualization has played and continues to play a major role to this end. A sexualization of narcissistic needs promotes a discharge of narcissistic tension: seeking a penis; incorporating the body of the male partner in homosexuality; wearing the clothes of the opposite sex in transvestitism; the libidinization of aggression in a spanking perversion, etc., are all attempts at achieving internalization and structure formation. [p. 250]

Recurrent and Traumatic Dreams

With his understanding of the concept of repetition compulsion, Freud (1920) indicated that "dreams occurring in traumatic neuroses have the characteristic of repeatedly bringing the patient back into the situation of his accident, a situation from which he wakes up in another fright" (p. 13). "These dreams," he continued, "are endeavouring to master the stimulus retrospectively, by developing the anxiety whose omission was the cause of the traumatic neurosis" (p. 32).

Unfortunately, as Levitan (1980) has pointed out, mastery of a traumatic event is not always accomplished through its repetition in dreams. "The repetition in dreams while serving to bind the trauma may in and of itself by the very virtue of the repetition be traumatic" (p. 280).

A variant of recurrent traumatic dreams are the so-called catastrophic dreams reported by Kardiner (1932) and Levitan (1967, 1976–77). Such dreams are rare and represent a waking-life trauma (for example, a flare-up of chronic dermatomyositis or a

grand mal seizure). The patient experiences the condition as a "body-shattering experience." The memory of the experience (for example, of a convulsion) is then represented in the manifest content of the dream (Levitan, 1980, p. 274).

Children's Dreams

Over the years, as psychoanalysis has developed, and with the work of Anna Freud and others, there has been a burgeoning of literature regarding the psychological development of the individual from birth. In addition to clinical studies, various types of direct observations as well as diverse experimental studies have been carried out. Children's dreams have been investigated with an eye toward understanding them in terms of child development in such areas as separation and individuation and the relationship between the child and his or her parents, as well as attempting to assess the development of the child's concept of self.

Various observers have indicated that at two years of age children who have developed some mastery of language begin to give verbal accounts of their dreams. The developmental stresses of childhood become woven into the dreams of children. Tomkins (1962–63), Serog (1964), Izard and Tomkins (1966), and others have studied facial expressions in children as a way of understanding their affect and have tried to relate these to affect in children's dreams.

Originally, Freud believed that children's dreams were essentially quite simple and expressed an obvious wish fulfillment. Later he modified this view, however, because he realized that as a child developed, his dreams increased in complexity and sophistication. Anna Freud (1927) put it this way:

> [When it comes to] dream interpretation, . . . we can apply unchanged to children the methods of analysis of adults. During analysis the child dreams neither less nor more than the grown-up, the transparency or obscurity of the dream content conforms as in the case of adults to the strength of the resistance. Children's dreams are certainly easier to interpret, if indeed they are not always so simple as the examples given in *The Interpretation of Dreams*. We find in them every such distortion of wish-fulfillment as corresponds to the complicated neurotic organisation of the childish patient. [pp. 18–19]

She emphasized, moreover, that besides wish fulfillment, children's dreams reflect their repertoire of defensive mechanisms (1936, 1965). While dreams are useful in child analysis and in psychoanalytic psychotherapy of children, there is a problem inasmuch as children cannot associate to their dreams in the way adults do, and the use of play technique as a substitute for free association is open to some question. She wrote:

> Play with toys, drawings, painting, staging of fantasy games, acting in the transference have been introduced and accepted in place of free association and, *faute de mieux,* child analysts have tried to convince themselves that they are valid substitutes for it. In truth, they are nothing of the kind. It is one disadvantage that some of these modes of behavior produce mainly symbolic material and that this introduces into child analysis the element of doubt, uncertainty, arbitrariness which are inseparable from symbolic interpretation in general. [1965, pp. 29–30]

Ablon and Mack (1980) suggest, however, that "the potential arbitrariness of an interpretation can be balanced by a child's subsequent play and verbal response, which may or may not provide confirmation that the analyst is following a fruitful avenue" (p. 205).

In her analysis of a severely disturbed boy, Furman (1962) related that dreams played a significant role. She emphasized that, "When his ego becomes strong enough to give up, in reality, a pathological behavior pattern which serves defensive purposes, the underlying conflict appears in intense dream activity." She observed that when reality became less threatening and her patient felt in a better position to cope with it, "his ego allows certain of its own normal functions to appear first in dreams at a time when it still wards them off in waking life" (p. 269).

Other analysts, such as Harley (1962), for example, reported that dreams were useful in understanding what was happening in the child psychologically whether or not the dream was interpreted to the child. Grolnick (1978) postulated the intriguing notion that in children symbols in dreams may serve as a bridge between past and present, as well as between fantasy and reality.

DREAM NEUROPHYSIOLOGY

Probably the greatest advance in the study of dreams since Freud's original publications has come from the experimental investigations of sleep and dreams. The discovery of various types of sleep and dreaming, with the correlation of EEG and REM studies, has opened new vistas of exploration. While they have not provided an increase in the specific understanding of the content of individual dreams, such as one needs in psychotherapy, the insights that they are providing will undoubtedly be fruitful in the future.

A good many of these studies have entailed comparisons of REM and non-REM sleep. In summarizing the findings along these lines, Ablon and Mack (1980) indicated that premature infants have the largest amount of REM sleep (approximately 80 percent of their total sleep). "By the second half of the first year," they write, "REM sleep comprises about 30 percent of total sleep. In normal young adults, 20 to 25 percent of sleep is REM sleep" (p. 201). The situation is different with stage 4 sleep, which is the deepest level of sleep and is non-REM sleep. It "comprises 20 to 25 percent of sleep in children from age 1 year to young adulthood, approximately 10 percent in young adults, and is minimal to absent in people over 65 years of age" (ibid.).

The prevailing notion is that REM and non-REM sleep may actually represent two different types of sleep. Of considerable interest is the finding that when subjects are awakened during REM sleep, they are able to recall elaborate dreams; whereas when they are awakened during stage 4 sleep, they are able to report only single vivid images.

Recent evidence suggests that a clear-cut distinction must be made between the usual so-called *nightmares* and *night terrors* (which Mack, Hartmann, Fisher, and others refer to as *pavor nocturnus*). Nightmares generally occur in the second half of the night or sleep period during REM or D (desynchronized, or dreaming) sleep. They are frightening dreams that awaken the sleeper and are clearly remembered as "a very detailed, vivid, and intense dream experience" (Fisher et al., 1968, in Hartmann, 1984, p. 19). Night terrors, or *pavor nocturnus,* on the other hand, are not experienced or recalled as dreams. Hartmann (1984) believes that night terrors are not really dreams but are sudden arousals from stage 3 or 4 sleep that occur *early* in the night or sleep period (p. 20). They are characterized by "marked fear, frequently screaming, autonomic arousal, and often body movement with little or no dream recall or recollection of the experience" (p. 12). Hartmann indicates that "Either [the sleepers] recall nothing at all and are only aware of the episode because they are told of it, or they are aware of a single frightening image—'something is sitting on me.' 'I am choking.' 'something is closing in on me'" (p. 18). (See also Fisher et al., 1973, 1974; Broughton, 1968.)

In one study of a group of people, Hartmann (1984) reported that whereas people who had night terrors included individuals with no specific psychopathology or artistic tendencies, nightmare-sufferers had "some features of schizophrenia or a vulnerability to schizophrenia; they had artistic tendencies and a kind of openness and sensitivity" (p. 23). (See also

Fisher et al., 1970; Gastaut & Broughton, 1964; Hartmann, 1967, 1984; Mack, 1970.)

THEORETICAL DEVELOPMENTS

At the outset I said that the importance of any discovery was the degree to which it initiated or influenced further progress. Once Freud's insight was gained—namely, that dreams have a meaning that can be understood by pursuing a specific method of investigation—dreams became objects of respectable scientific inquiry. With every advance in other disciplines, researchers have attempted to integrate the discoveries with what was already known about dreams and the functioning of the mind by postulating new theories.

Thus, in an effort to understand the significance of sleep disturbances and nightmares, Hartmann (1984, chap. 6) has postulated various types of "boundaries within the mind." He attempted to understand some of the characteristics of dream thought as related to the functioning of the brain during sleep. In 1973 he wrote: "primary process in dreaming— primitive connections, large discharges of energy, opposites occurring together—shall be seen as characteristics of a 'reconnecting' process in which daytime residues are reconnected to large, old, and thus 'primitive' pathways or brain storage systems." A vivid dream "may indicate a nodal point representing interconnections between multiple brain pathways which somehow achieve enough prominence to be noticed by dreaming consciousness" (p. 133). We may compare this new concept with some of Freud's original ideas about *nodal points* (see Breuer & Freud, 1893–95, pp. 289–290, 294–295; Freud, 1896, pp. 198–199; 1905, p. 96).

Some years ago, McCarley and Hobson (1975) published new findings about neurophysiology and REM sleep. They see their findings as necessitating a revision of neurobiologically derived psychoanalytic concepts, particularly those pertaining to dream theory. A detailed discussion of these matters may be found in an article by Wasserman (1984).

Other investigators (Ablon & Mack, 1980; Jessner et al., 1952; Levy, 1945) have endeavored to explore the adaptive function of dreams, the mastery of important or traumatic material from the dream day and its integration by the ego.

Palombo (1978) attempted to combine the classical psychoanalytic view of dreams with the newer information-processing models. He described "an autonomous mechanism of nonconscious, adaptive ego functioning called 'the memory cycle.'" He wrote:

The memory cycle is a sequence of processes through which new experiential information is introduced into adaptively suitable locations in the permanent memory structure. The most striking hypothesis of the memory cycle model is that the critical step in the sequence—the step which matches representations of the new experiences with the representations of closely related experiences of the past—takes place during dreaming. [p. 13]

Palombo further discussed the therapeutic effects of psychoanalytic dream interpretation as resulting from a "synergistic collaboration between the analyst's interpretive activity and the adaptive functioning of dreaming in the memory cycle. It is distinct from, but complementary to, the role played by dreams in providing new data from that part of the patient's memory structure which is ordinarily inaccessible to consciousness" (p. 14).

Jacques Lacan, leader of a French school of psychoanalysis, viewed the unconscious as structured like a language (1978, p. 20). Writing about dreams, he said: "What concerns us is the tissue that envelops these messages" (p. 45). He suggested that "a child's dreams may be the first primal linguistic expression of the unconscious" (in Ablon & Mack, p. 194).

Other structuralists such as Claude Lévi-Strauss and Jean Piaget have attempted to describe and understand dreams along similar lines. Linguists have also contributed to a theoretical understanding of dreams.

In summary, while the basic techniques for dream interpretation in clinical practice have remained essentially the same as those espoused by Freud, the understanding and utilization of dreams since his discoveries have both widened and deepened. This is evidenced by the literature on dreams. What has changed distinctly, due to the remarkable advances of the neurosciences, is the investigation of dreams as neurophysiological phenomena. Whether this research, by bringing about a greater comprehension of how the mind works (a goal Freud himself pursued), will lead to a further understanding of the meaning of dreams and will alter our utilization of them remains to be seen.

REFERENCES

Ablon, S. L., & Mack, J. E. (1980). Children's dreams reconsidered. *Psychoanal. Study Child*, 35:179–217.

Arlow, J. A. (1951). A psychoanalytic study of a religious initiation rite. *Psychoanal. Study Child*, 6:353–374.

Berman, L. E. A. (1985). Rear view mirror dreams. *Psychoanal. Inq.*, 5:257–269.

Blum, H. P. (1976). The changing use of dreams in psychoanalytic practice. *Int. J. Psychoanal.*, 57: 315–324.

Bond, D. D. (1952). *The Love and Fear of Flying.* New York: Int. Univ. Press.

Bonime, W., & Bonime, F. (1980). The dream in the depressive personality. In Natterson, ed., 1980, pp. 131–147.

Bradlow, P. A., & Coen, S. J. (1975). The analyst undisguised in the initial dream in psychoanalysis. *Int. J. Psychoanal.*, 56:415–425.

Breuer, J., & Freud, S. (1893–95). *Studies on Hysteria. SE*, 2.

Broughton, R. (1968). Sleep disorders. *Science*, 159:1070–1078.

Calef, V. (1954). Color in dreams. *J. Amer. Psychoanal. Assn.*, 2:453–461.

Eisnitz, A. J. (1980). The organization of the self-representation and its influence on pathology. *Psychoanal. Q.*, 49:361–392.

Fisher, C., Byrne, J. V., & Edwards, A. (1968). NREM and REM nightmares. *Psychophysiology*, 5:221–222.

Fisher, C., Byrne, J. V., Edwards, A., & Kahn, E. (1970). A psychophysiological study of nightmares. *J. Amer. Psychoanal. Assn.*, 18:747–782.

Fisher, C., Kahn, E., Edwards, A. & Davis, D. M. (1973). A psychophysiological study of nightmares and night terrors: I. *J. Nerv. Ment. Dis.*, 15:75–97.

Fisher, C., Kahn, E., Edwards, A., Davis, D. M., & Fine, J. (1974). A psychophysiological study of nightmares and night terrors: III. *J. Nerv. Ment. Dis.*, 15:174–189.

Fleming, J. (1972). Early object deprivation and transference phenomena. *Psychoanal. Q.*, 41:23–49.

Freud, A. (1927). *The Psycho-Analytical Treatment of Children.* London: Imago Publishing Co., 1946.

———. (1936). *The Ego and the Mechanisms of Defence.* New York: Int. Univ. Press, 1966.

———. (1965). *Normality and Pathology in Childhood.* In *Writings of Anna Freud*, vol. 6. New York: Int. Univ. Press.

Freud, S. (1896). The aetiology of hysteria. *SE*, 3: 191–221.

———. (1900). *The Interpretation of Dreams. SE*, 4 & 5.

———. (1905). Fragment of an analysis of a case of hysteria. *SE*, 7:7–122.

———. (1916–17). *Introductory Lectures on Psycho-Analysis*, Part II. *SE*, 15:83–239.

———. (1917). A metapsychological supplement to the theory of dreams. *SE*, 14:222–235.

———. (1918). From the history of an infantile neurosis. *SE*, 17:7–122.

———. (1920). *Beyond the Pleasure Principle. SE*, 18:7–64.

Furman, E. (1962). Some features of the dream function of a severely disturbed young child. *J. Amer. Psychoanal. Assn.*, 10:258–270.

Gastaut, H., & Broughton, R. (1964). A clinical and polygraphic study of episodic phenomena during sleep. *Recent Advances in Biological Psychiatry*, 7:197–221.

Grinstein, A. (1983). *Freud's Rules of Dream Interpretation.* New York: Int. Univ. Press.

Grolnick, A. (1978). Dreams and dreaming as transitional phenomena. In *Between Reality and Fantasy*, ed. S. A. Grolnick, I. Barkin, & W. Muensterberger, pp. 213–231. New York: Aronson.

Harley, M. (1962). The role of the dream in the analysis of a latency child. *J. Amer. Psychoanal. Assn.*, 10:271–288.

Harris, I. D. (1962). Typical anxiety dreams and object relations. *Int. J. Psychoanal.*, 41:604–611.

Hartmann, E. (1967). *The Biology of Dreaming.* Springfield, Ill.: Thomas.

———. (1973). *The Functions of Sleep.* New Haven: Yale Univ. Press.

———. (1984). *The Nightmare.* New York: Basic Books.

Izard, C. E., & Tomkins, S. S. (1966). Anxiety as a negative affect. In *Anxiety and Behavior*, ed. C. D. Spielberger, pp. 81–125. New York & London: Academic Press.

Izner, S. (1959). On the appearance of primal scene content in dreams. *J. Amer. Psychoanal. Assn.*, 7:317–328.

Jessner, L., Blom, G. E., & Waldfogel, S. (1952). Emotional implications of tonsillectomy and adenoidectomy on children. *Psychoanal. Study Child*, 7:126–169.

Kardiner, A. (1932). The bio-analysis of the epileptic reaction. *Psychoanal. Q.*, 1:375–483.

Kavka, J. (1979). On examination dreams. *Psychoanal. Q.*, 48:426–427.

Kohut, H. (1971). *The Analysis of the Self.* New York: Int. Univ. Press.

———. (1977). *The Restoration of the Self.* New York: Int. Univ. Press.

Lacan, J. (1968). *The Language of the Self.* Baltimore: Johns Hopkins Univ. Press.

———. (1978). *The Four Fundamental Concepts of Psychoanalysis.* New York: Norton.

Levitan, H. (1967). Depersonalization and the dream. *Psychoanal. Q.*, 36:157–171.

———. (1976–77). Observations on certain catastrophic dreams. *Psychotherapy and Psychosomatics*, 27:1–7.

———. (1980). The dream in traumatic states. In Natterson, ed., 1980, pp. 271–281.

Levy, D. (1945). Psychic trauma of operations in children. *Amer. J. Dis. Child.*, 59:7–25.

Lewin, B. D. (1953). The forgetting of dreams. In *Drives, Affects, Behavior*, vol. 1, ed. R. M. Loewenstein, pp. 191–202. New York: Int. Univ. Press.

Lorand, S., & Feldman, S. (1955). The symbolism of teeth in dreams. *Int. J. Psychoanal.*, 36:145–161.

Mack, J. E. (1970). *Nightmares and Human Conflict*. Boston: Little, Brown.

McCarley, R., & Hobson, J. A. (1975). Neuronal excitability modulation over the sleep cycle. *Science*, 189:58.

Miller, M. L. (1948). Ego functioning in two types of dreams. *Psychoanal. Q.*, 17:346–355.

Myers, W. A. (1973). Split self-representation and the primal scene. *Psychoanal. Q.*, 42:525–538.

Natterson, J. M., ed. (1980). *The Dream in Clinical Practice*. New York: Aronson.

Noble, D. (1951). The study of dreams in schizophrenia and allied states. *Amer. J. Psychiat.*, 107:612–616.

Palombo, S. R. (1978). *Dreaming and Memory*. New York: Basic Books.

Rapaport, E. A. (1959). The first dream in an erotized transference. *Int. J. Psychoanal.*, 40:240–245.

Renik, O. (1981). Typical examination dreams, "superego dreams," and traumatic dreams. *Psychoanal. Q.*, 50:159–189.

Richardson, G. A., & Moore, R. A. (1963). On the manifest dream in schizophrenia. *J. Amer. Psychoanal. Assn.*, 11:281–302.

Rosenbaum, M. (1965). Dreams in which the analyst appears undisguised. *Int. J. Psychoanal.*, 46:429–437.

Savitt, R. A. (1969). Transference somatization and symbiotic need. *J. Amer. Psychoanal. Assn.*, 17:1030–1054.

Serog, M. (1964). The dream, its phenomenology, its theory and its interpretation. In *Problems of Sleep and Dreams in Children*, ed. E. Harms, pp. 47–59. New York: Macmillan.

Sharpe, E. F. (1937). *Dream Analysis*. 2d ed. London: Hogarth Press, 1949.

Shengold, L. (1974). The metaphor of the mirror. *J. Amer. Psychoanal. Assn.*, 22:97–115.

Silver, D. (1985). Mirror in dreams. *Psychoanal. Inq.*, 5:253–256.

Socarides, C. W. (1980). Perverse symptoms and the manifest dream of perversion. In Natterson, ed., pp. 237–256.

Sterba, R. (1928). An examination dream. *Int. J. Psychoanal.*, 9:353–354.

———. (1946). Dreams and acting out. *Psychoanal. Q.*, 15:175–179.

Tomkins, S. S. (1962–63). *Affect, Imagery, Consciousness*, 2 vols. New York: Springer.

Wasserman, M. D. (1984). Psychoanalytic dream theory and recent neurobiological findings about REM sleep. *J. Amer. Psychoanal. Assn.*, 32:831–846.

Yazmajian, R. V. (1964). First dreams directly representing the analyst. *Psychoanal. Q.*, 33:536–551.

Owen D. Renik, M.D., and

Lee Grossman, M.D.

14

WORKING WITH DREAMS

We will consider the role played by dreams in clinical psychoanalysis. Work with dreams has always
been a conspicuous feature of psychoanalytic technique, although the way analysts work with dreams
has changed considerably over the years. Erikson
(1954) lamented that the art and ritual of exhaustive
dream analysis had all but vanished. He emphasized
that there is much to be learned from formal, systematic study of a dreamer's associations to every
element of the manifest content of his or her reported dream, and suggested that attending to selected aspects of a dream constitutes an advanced
technique—something an analyst learns by virtue of
accumulated experience in conducting thorough investigations of his or her patients' dreams.

Most contemporary analysts would not consider it
clinically advantageous to procure copious associations to every element of every dream a patient reports. Today our approach to a dream is likely to
vary according to the context of its appearance in
the analysis. Selection of material for interpretation
is guided by the analyst's accumulated knowledge of
the patient and the current state of the treatment. At
any given moment, the emphasis may be on a particular conflict, on the relationship with the analyst,
on a specific defensive strategy, or on an attitude
toward internal or external reality. Any of these
may be demonstrated in the manifest content of the
dream, in the patient's associations, or in the patient's approach to the dream and dreaming. In the
examples that follow, we will try to show how attention to selected elements of a dream and its presentation can provide important information about all
these aspects of the patient's mental life.

In recent years, there has been some controversy
about whether a dream reported in analysis provides
a unique opportunity for furthering the work. Some
analysts feel that there is nothing special about
dreams and that many other mental products are
equally useful (for example, Waldhorn, 1967). By
contrast, there are those who argue that dreams have
an exceptional place in clinical work because they
represent a form of mentation unapproached in waking life (for example, Greenson, 1970). Clearly, an
analyst's view of dreams and dream analysis will be
shaped by his or her general theoretical orientation.
Some see dreams as compromise formations, no different in that respect from other multiply determined
mental phenomena (Brenner, 1976). Others regard
certain dreams as self-state reports that provide
unique, crucial data (Slap & Trunnell, 1987).

Our view is that the thinking process involved in
dreams is the same kind of thinking as takes place in
a waking state, but that the circumstances during
sleep (notably, limited sensory stimulation and the
inhibition of motor systems) influence the outcome,
allowing a relative neglect of reality testing and producing a timeless, internal focus with diminished
use of verbal residues. As a consequence, the primary process underlying all mentation is revealed. A

dreamlike state is approached in waking life when a person restricts sensory input, makes a voluntary effort to suspend reality testing, and rules out motor action—for example, when he or she attempts to free-associate in the psychoanalytic situation.

Thus, we regard dreams as essentially providing a concentrate of our usual fare (see Panel, 1984) rather than a qualitatively different text for analysis. The important question for us, then, is not whether dreams are unique analytic opportunities—since every analytic opportunity is unique in some ways and not in others—but rather, how dreams can be approached to best advantage clinically.

Whatever the contemporary controversies concerning use of dreams in analysis, and however modern views may differ from the one Freud held when he wrote *The Interpretation of Dreams,* analysts can still agree to a certain fundamental validity in the premise that dreams constitute "the royal road to a knowledge of the unconscious activities of the mind" (1900, p. 608). Dreams do indicate thoughts that the dreamer is holding outside conscious awareness in the waking state. They also permit investigation of the particular manner in which the dreamer holds a thought outside conscious awareness and of the motivations for doing so. A patient's dreams can be used to help the patient see what he or she is trying not to think about and how and why he or she is trying not to think about it.

What is being warded off can be a sensory perception, an observation the patient has made which he or she wants to avoid thinking about because of the observation's emotional significance. For example, it is quite common for a woman in analysis not to mention that she is menstruating while at the same time reporting dreams containing images of rivers flowing or the color red or themes of periodic change or something of the sort. The defensive maneuver by which mention of menstruation is avoided is conscious withholding or frank denial; and the analyst, if he or she is inspired by the suggestive dream imagery to inquire about menstruation, may learn that feelings of embarrassment lead the patient to wish not to discuss such an intimate physical matter. Beneath such feelings of embarrassment there are likely to be other, more obscure and threatening concerns.

Denial and conscious withholding are not the only ways to keep the emotional charge connected with an intimate physical event out of conscious awareness. Dreams can be very instructive in bringing various subtle defensive maneuvers to light. Here is another example related to the menstrual cycle. One morning, a woman in analysis reported a dream in which she was being chased by a man brandishing a long knife. The dream ended as he caught her and stabbed her in the abdomen, and she awoke feeling the pain of being stabbed. In her associations, she stated that she sometimes had nightmares of being chased by a man with a knife, but this was the first time he had actually caught her. She was impressed with how real the pain seemed.

She went on to say that, of course, the dream could be viewed as a symbolization of sexual intercourse. Perhaps it even represented a wish to have sex with her analyst—or her father. But so what? Yes, she sometimes had the thought that she might be able to seduce her analyst if she really tried, that she might have been able to seduce her father, but all that was theory and fantasy and had nothing to do with anything real. She was adamant in this conviction.

On the subject of reality, the analyst asked her what thoughts she had about the real pain she had felt upon awakening. It turned out that she had wondered whether she had a stomach flu. She even thought of appendicitis, but the pain was on the wrong side. In any event, it had soon gone away. Where was she in her menstrual cycle? the analyst asked. It wasn't cramps, she answered quickly—she was not having her period; in fact, she was right in the middle. Did she ever have physical sensations when she ovulated? the analyst asked. She paused for a moment, greatly embarrassed. Of course that was what it was, she said. She felt *Mittelschmerz* during most of her cycles and knew what it was. She was puzzled and humiliated at having pushed the knowledge that she was ovulating out of her mind.

Here the defensive maneuver involved was neither conscious withholding nor frank denial, but rather disavowal. The pain associated with ovulation insisted itself upon the patient's awareness to the degree that she could not deny it or keep it out of her reported thoughts. She could not avoid being consciously aware of the pain. However, she had been able to dismiss her perception of the pain by regarding it as merely part of a dream fantasy. She discounted the pain as unreal, and this permitted her not to have to take account of its real meaning.

One of the values of analytic work with dreams is that what is discovered usually applies widely to the dreamer's way of operating in waking life, and the insight gained extends beyond the matter immediately at hand. This patient, for example, realized in the course of continuing analytic work that she made use of disavowal in many situations. She had feelings of sexual attraction to her analyst, as well as thoughts that he might be attracted to her, all of which disturbed her greatly; but she reassured herself that such notions were only "transference," part of analysis, not life! She discounted her sexual thoughts and feelings as unreal fantasies, in the same way as she had discounted her Mittelschmerz as only a dream image. At the time of her dream, her sexual interest in the analyst had reached the point at which her wish to be impregnated by him made ovulation an especially exciting and anxiety-provoking event; therefore, she both thought about it and had to disavow her wishful interest in it while she slept.

It should not surprise us that the events of a woman's menstrual cycle are experienced in a highly charged way and become embroiled in conflict, since their connection to sex, pregnancy, and other psychologically loaded matters is obvious. However, there are times when a patient takes the trouble to keep what one would expect to be a trivial perception out of conscious awareness, and discovery of this fact through the analysis of a dream reveals emotional meanings whose exploration proves quite useful.

One such instance involved a man who for many years had been troubled by intermittent psychogenic urinary frequency and groin pain. As a boy, he had felt that in order to spare his mother from feeling inferior, he had to hide his masculinity except when she could use it vicariously. When he began to have wet dreams, he quickly learned to prevent them by pinching his penis. A mighty struggle with masturbation ensued in adolescence, later to be replaced by obsessional rituals. Eventually his confining sexual conflicts and psychosomatic symptoms caused him to enter treatment. The following incident took place while he was in analysis.

In the city where the patient lived, torrential rain had been falling without stop for weeks. The rain had been on everyone's minds, since it was causing floods and traffic accidents, soaking clothes, and generally creating a great deal of inconvenience, not to say danger. The patient mentioned not a word about the rain. It remained out of his conscious awareness most of the time. But he did have a dream about it, in which he was living with his mother and sister in a valley where it rained all the time. He was climbing to the top of one of the hills that surrounded the valley when he saw a huge tidal wave approaching from the distance. Instead of warning his mother and sister, and thereby risking his life, he simply climbed to safety. He felt stricken by remorse. Later in the dream, his mother and sister reappeared unhurt, knowing nothing of any tidal wave.

The patient's associations to this dream led him to recognize that he had confused his sexual and urinary functions in his mind. Masturbation was like submitting his sexuality to his mother's regulation,

since he masturbated only on the toilet and made sure the mess was disposed of. It meant renouncing the spontaneity and passive pleasure of messy wet dreams, which he remembered idyllically and longed for. The dream portrayed his repressed urges to overwhelm women with his bodily fluids and his conflicts about those urges, as well as their childhood origins. In waking life, he had applied the lessons learned during toilet training, particularly in achieving bladder control, to orgasm: always do it in the right place and at the right time, and don't wet your bed.

The association between rain and urination, and by extension masturbation and orgasm, was so strong and anxiety-provoking for this man that he had to deny the rain in his waking thoughts. However, it intruded into his conscious awareness while he slept, and exploration of the conflicts evoked by perception of it was a crucial part of the analytic work and resulted in marked symptomatic relief. Dream analysis revealed the important meanings that had become attached to what otherwise might have seemed a psychologically insignificant circumstance.

Just as analytic work on a dream can reveal how the dreamer holds current perceptions outside consciousness, so too it can reveal how threatening memories are handled by the dreamer. It was Freud's observation (1914) that people often dream of traumatic events from long ago that they do not recall when they are awake.

When analysis is able to elucidate a recurring dream, it almost always turns out to represent, at least in part, the memory of a past traumatic event. For example, a patient had many dreams in which he would be gazing at a stormy sea. It would make him frightened and strangely sad to look at the water. As he watched, he felt drawn to the turbulence and had to caution himself not to go closer. The meaning of this patient's recurring dream of being simultaneously attracted and repelled by a storm remained elusive until other analytic work allowed him to remember that he had been told that when he was two years old his mother had delivered a stillborn child and become very depressed. Following this, the patient had another dream that was in a way a prototype for the recurrent ones and explicated their meaning in terms of his traumatic history.

In the new dream, his mother was squatting and had a miserable, dejected expression. Something was terribly wrong. A long lip of bleeding flesh drooped from between her legs. He had a strong urge to go toward her to help, but at the same time he dreaded touching her.

The dream portrayed what the dreamer's childhood experience of his mother's post-partum depression had been—the memory of awful feelings and conflicts that he had been struggling to keep out of conscious awareness. When he had been very young, fantasies about the stillbirth, his mother's genitalia, and the loss of body products by excretion had all become confused and condensed in his mind into an impression that his mother was depressed because she had lost something important. This impression resulted in a conflict: he wished to substitute himself for what was missing, in order to make his mother once more loving and lovable, but he feared having to sacrifice himself to restore her loss. He had been expressing this same conflict in his reports of recurring dreams in which he would be irresistibly drawn toward a boiling sea or into the eye of a dangerous storm. The dreams presented disguised versions of a traumatic memory that was being kept out of conscious awareness in the waking state.

Note that the woman mentioned before who disavowed her Mittelschmerz, telling herself it was only a dream, had a recurrent nightmare of being chased by a man with a knife. That recurrent nightmare, too, turned out to describe a traumatic event from the dreamer's past. When she was a little girl, she had once sat on her father's lap and felt that he had an erection. This both excited and disturbed her. Subsequently, she was at various times moved to bring up the pleasurable but conflicted memory. She did this in disguised form in her recurrent nightmare. Analysis of her contemporary conflicts regarding her wish to get pregnant and her thoughts that she and her analyst could be mutually sexually attracted permitted her consciously to recall the traumatic childhood event. The threatening, stimulating phallic figure in her dream, the man with the knife, referred to both her fantasy of her analyst with an erection and her memory of her father with one. Analysis of the dream helped her deal with a father transference and led to greater freedom in her thinking about both present and past.

Dreams are often very useful as indicators of the current state of the treatment relationship and of the transference elements that may be involved in it, as in the following case. For a variety of reasons, a young man in analysis was exquisitely sensitive to any feelings of attachment to his analyst. His foremost method of denying them was to experience the analytic relationship entirely in terms of rivalry and struggle. If the analyst canceled an hour, the patient did the same in short order. If the patient had fantasies of the analyst enjoying himself over a weekend —something the patient would never disclose but which the analyst could sometimes infer—the patient began the week by regaling the analyst with tales of his recent adventures. Any suggestion that the patient's competitive view of the treatment relationship might have a defensive function he dismissed as a hackneyed theory of the analyst's, an attempt to brainwash him into becoming a typical dependent and submissive analytic patient.

Not long after the analyst announced the dates of an impending summer vacation, the patient had a dream in which he was back in college, meeting a group of students in the auditorium. It was fall, and the professor was reading aloud from a list of names. Those students who were mentioned would not be allowed to enroll again because they had received "incompletes" in certain necessary courses. The patient knew that his name was to be called. He could remember no more about the dream except a vague feeling of discomfort.

Undoubtedly, the dream had something to do with the upcoming vacation and with the question of whether the patient would continue his analysis in the fall, although he volunteered no concern about the analyst terminating the analysis. As a matter of fact, he made it very clear that he was looking forward to the break and that he was nonchalant about beginning again the following month. He had no associations to his feeling of discomfort and was skeptical that this aspect of the dream had anything to do with the analyst or his vacation. He expected the analyst to assume that he was upset because they were not going to be meeting.

However, while the patient could insist on his conscious indifference to the vacation and the question of resumption of analysis in the fall, there was no denying that the dream was his; and the analyst was able to use the patient's dream to help him further investigate what was going on beneath the surface of his current preoccupations. Some questions seemed pertinent to the dream's manifest content. Had the patient ever, in fact, been prevented from registering in college? The answer was no. Had he ever received an "incomplete"? Again, no. Yet his dream indicated that there must have been some reason why being readmitted in the fall had been a concern for him during his college years. Could he think of why?

The patient responded readily. In order to devote a good part of their time to working on the school newspaper, he and a group of his friends had reduced their course loads during the regular academic season, making up for it by scheduling courses in the summer session. When summer came, the temptation to play was too strong for some of his friends, who had received "incompletes" and, as a result, had not been allowed to continue the next year. The patient himself had been sufficiently disciplined, but just barely, to get by.

Now the dream could be understood in terms of the transference relationship and the analyst's vacation. The patient's dream indicated his belief that he had obligations he must attend to over the summer if he wished to ensure the continuation of his analysis in the fall. He was afraid that the temptation to play might be too strong for him this time.

The analyst pointed out a parallel between the patient's college experience and what could be concerning him about the approaching summer break in the analysis. The analyst reminded the patient of the glee he usually felt about "one-upping" the analyst and suggested to the patient that he might be afraid that he would do things over the summer that he would not be able to talk about when analytic sessions began again. This brought a rueful chuckle. The patient admitted that he expected the analyst to think of him as pining away, whereas he had no such intention. Furthermore, since the analyst was so straight, the patient could never be sure how what he liked to do would be regarded.

It will come as no surprise to learn that it now came to light that the patient had for some time been avoiding mention of his occasional homosexual activity. Another aspect of the current state of the transference relationship that was expressed through the dream and the college memories—namely, the patient's wish that he might be the sole survivor in the analyst's case load, an only child as it were— was not revealed until further on in the analysis.

Not only the dream report itself but the patient's associations to the dream report make up the text that is used in what we are referring to when we speak of analyzing a dream. The example just given illustrates how helping the patient pursue his or her associations to a dream is a crucial part of the work. So does the next vignette, in which analysis of a dream allowed a patient to realize that her conscious feelings of guilty responsibility were obscuring another important attitude that she held out of conscious awareness—a feeling of narcissistic justification, about which she had some misgivings.

A graduate student was having trouble writing her dissertation. This conscientious young woman was plagued by an unjustified fear that she would be accused of plagiarism. She would have to copy work already done, she felt, because she was incapable of being sufficiently original. In the midst of this struggle she had a dream in which she stole a bicycle and was caught and humiliated for it. In her associations she had no difficulty connecting the bicycle with her dissertation, which she also felt she could produce only through theft. The preceding day she had been thinking about how much time she wasted riding her bicycle instead of working on her dissertation.

From preceding work, patient and analyst had a great deal to draw upon in understanding the dream. For example, successful completion of her disserta-tion meant to the patient following in the footsteps of her academically prominent father, something she equated with theft because of its connection with her fantasies of oedipal triumph and competition with her younger brother. Also, much attention had been given to the significance of producing something and to originality. Bicycle riding was, no doubt, an overdetermined metaphor, referring in part to sexual impulses about which she was concerned. These and similar ideas marked well-traveled interpretive paths that were no less valid for their being familiar but seemed stale and yielded little of value in connection with the dream.

Among her associations to the particular bicycle portrayed in the dream, the patient mentioned the details she could recall—a headlight, a dented fender, a wire basket on the back—and realized that she was describing the bicycle she currently owned. Thus the patient's actual bicycle had appeared in the manifest content of her dream, and the discovery of this piece of reality necessitated that the dream be understood in an entirely new way. Instead of simply expressing a confession of guilt and a need for punishment, the dream now appeared to contain a complaint about being unjustly accused and attacked for a blameless activity: taking possession of her own bicycle. Following the patient's association of the bicycle with her dissertation, the dream expressed her objection that she had a right to complete her degree and go on in her career without feeling guilty of theft. Analysis of the dream brought to light a narcissistic attitude of entitlement of which the patient had not been consciously aware.

This sequence of clinical events also gives us the chance to consider what we look for to determine the validity of analytic work done in connection with a dream. Since dreams are nocturnal continuations of preconscious waking thoughts from the preceding day, the aptness of a dream interpretation can be confirmed if it permits these thoughts to be recalled. This young woman had already mentioned having wondered the day before why she spent so much time riding her bicycle instead of working on her dissertation. After she had unveiled the aspect of her dream that was a complaint and a protest of innocence, she remembered a fleeting idea from the day before—something like, "I ought to be able to feel as free and enthusiastic working on my dissertation as I feel now riding my bicycle."

We have already mentioned that analysis of a dream can unveil aspects of a patient's defensive style that apply widely to his or her functioning in various aspects of waking life. Thorough investigation also frequently unearths something about the historical roots of the particular defensive maneuver in question. For instance, the young woman who dreamed of stealing her own bicycle used a specific method of falsifying a pleasurable, conflict-producing image. The method had traceable roots.

She had been cared for in childhood by a warm, kindly maid, whose attentions she had sometimes interpreted as openly seductive. When her parents went away, she pretended to herself that the maid was her mother. This game would be conveniently put out of the child's mind when the parents returned. It was one childhood version of the disavowal and omission of a feeling of righteous possessiveness that occurred in her dream.

In addition to a dream itself and subsequent associations to it, a patient's way of presenting a dream and the attitudes he or she takes toward it can be very informative. For instance, remarks made to introduce a dream report can be considered associations produced in advance. Here is an example.

Early in her analysis, a woman mentioned that she had had a dream and upon awakening had felt disappointed by it. She judged that the dream was not good enough for analysis, and therefore she promptly forgot it. Her analyst pointed out to her that calling the dream inadequate permitted her to conceal it. In response to this interpretation, the patient had an intrusive thought of performing very well at her job. She became excited, but she dismissed the thought as an avoidance of her dream. Her analyst asked how she could be sure that the thought was an avoidance rather than an association to the dream. The patient now recognized that she had dismissed her exciting train of thought as unfit for analysis in order not to pursue it—just as she had done with her dream.

The patient's way of talking about her dream—or of not talking about it—turned out to be a useful matter for analytic investigation. It opened up the whole topic of her defensive use of her sense of inadequacy and her fear of inciting envy in others. Thus, a useful piece of analytic work was accomplished, despite the fact that the patient never did bring to mind what she had dreamed.

Another patient, a therapist himself, had just begun to talk about constrictions in his sex life when he announced that he had "another dream about water." He repeated a formula that he had learned from his reading: that water signifies the unconscious. In the dream, he was in a pool filled with people. The ones facing him wore shorts; the ones with their backs to him were naked. He thought about other dreams involving water. Eventually, his analyst commented that the patient seemed to treat his dreams about water as if they were all the same and not to notice the differences between them. Turning then to his current dream, the patient noted that the shorts the people were wearing obscured differences among

them—for example, the differences between men and women. From behind, everyone looked the same. It turned out that the patient's preferred position in intercourse was to enter his wife from behind. He did not like to see her naked from the front. Investigation of his wish to regard different dreams as if they were the same revealed his wish to eliminate the anatomical differences between men and women.

The way a patient presents a dream can enact a fantasy about his or her relationship with the analyst. One very common fantasy of this kind is illustrated by a woman who told her analyst, "I have a dream for you." Her analyst suggested that she consider how the dream was for him. It developed that the patient intended the dream as a gift, which she expected her analyst to appreciate. Subsequent work revealed her fantasy of what she expected in return.

Sometimes the same way of introducing dreams will have different meanings at different times in the analysis. Early in analysis, a patient introduced her dream reports by saying that she remembered only fragments, the important parts of her dreams having been forgotten. Efforts made to understand her dreams would leave her unimpressed. She was always ready to point out how she and her analyst had not seemed to have gotten very far.

After a time, her analyst commented on the fact that she emphasized her feeling that there was more to her dreams than had been revealed. This made her think of "showing a little skin." She was aware of wanting to lure the analyst into a fatal misstep. The presentation of dream fragments was a tease, an invitation for the analyst to show off, and an opportunity for him to fall short.

Later in the treatment, the patient began to sense again that she was recalling only fragments of her dreams. By now, she seemed to take pleasure in the work she and her analyst were doing together and in the analyst's ability to make something whole out of the fragments she presented. She saw their collaboration on dreams as confirming her wishful fantasy that the analyst would supply her with something she was lacking—in particular, that their analytic interactions produced a result in the same way that a man and a woman having sex together produces a baby.

Still later, the patient introduced a dream fragment consisting of the single image of a falling handkerchief. Her associations brought back the idea of "showing a little skin." However, this time it was linked to the Victorian conceit of dropping a handkerchief in front of a gentleman. She realized that she was teasing again, but in a playful, flirtatious manner that she enjoyed and hoped her analyst would enjoy as well.

Reporting a dream can be a way of introducing a topic that the patient is reluctant to talk about with the analyst directly. A woman who was apparently very pleased with the progress she had made in analysis began to consider termination. She was very grateful to her analyst for many successes, particularly in her work life. Although she was vaguely dissatisfied with what her boyfriend had to offer, on balance she considered her life happy and rewarding.

She then had a dream in which she was having a problem delivering a baby. The doctor was no help. He was preoccupied with a bunch of fawning nurses who flattered him. So she delivered the baby herself.

The patient was startled at the portrayal of the doctor in her dream, whom she immediately associated with her analyst. She had never doubted her analyst and had felt that he had been extremely helpful. The analyst remarked that it seemed very important for the patient to make sure that he knew how helpful she thought he was. As she began to wonder about her need to make a point of her gratitude, she reluctantly started admitting some disappointment with the analysis, a sense of "Is that all I get out of this?" Her thoughts went to her relationship with her boyfriend, which was still in its early stages. She had hoped to be married with a baby by the time she finished analysis.

These complaints frightened the patient as she became aware of them. She realized that she had the idea that her analyst demanded complete gratitude as the price of his good will. Her fantasy was that he might take away any gift that was not sufficiently appreciated. Bringing in the dream was the patient's indirect way of expressing a complaint about her analyst.

A patient's attitude toward dreams and dreaming in general may suggest an interpretive approach to a particular dream report. One man described a dream for the first time in analysis, making clear his conviction that dreams "don't mean anything." It was his view that dreams simply reflect mundane, realistic concerns.

The dream he told portrayed how he had enjoyed his visit to his mother on Halloween. He insisted that there was nothing further to understand about the dream: he had, in fact, enjoyed his visit. He chided his analyst for always trying to read into everything.

The analyst pointed out that the visit described in the patient's ostensibly realistic dream had actually taken place on Thanksgiving, not Halloween. The patient was taken aback and began to explore the horror stirred up by his contact with his mother that had made his time with her seem like Halloween.

He recognized that his need to be "realistic" was to prove that there was nothing going on behind the scenes. His dealings with his mother had been anything but mundane. The visit had taken place in a hospital. The patient had tried to believe his mother's serious chronic illness was nothing grave, that it "didn't mean anything."

Some patients never report dreams because they are afraid of what might be revealed about their secret wishes and fears. Other patients bring in a dream or two every session, feeling much more comfortable discussing what they regard as thoughts for which they cannot be held responsible than those they have while awake. Either extreme, of course, is worth noting and investigating.

Though work with dreams remains an invaluable part of analysis, the clinical handling of dreams has evolved significantly. Freud's original technique of formal, systematic, exhaustive pursuit of associations to each manifest dream element has given way to a more selective approach, governed by the same principles of technique that apply to the analysis of other material. What we have tried to show are the special opportunities provided by dreams reported in analysis.

Work with dreams can involve, among other things, consideration of a particular dream report, of a patient's associations to a dream, of his or her manner of presenting the dream and associations, of his or her attitude toward dreams and dreaming in general, or of recurring patterns in dream life.

We have tried to demonstrate how dreams reveal not only what is being kept out of consciousness in the waking state but also how and why. Frank denial or subtle disavowal of sensory perceptions can be revealed through work with dreams. Defensive maneuvers discovered in dream analysis can be seen to be operative in waking life as well. Attitudes toward reality, toward unconscious processes, and toward the analyst may be most accessible through work with dreams. Work with dreams can clarify the dreamer's transferences, and traumatic memories may be discovered in disguised form in dreams, particularly in recurrent dreams.

Our examples are commonplace ones. They indicate that while work with dreams makes use of principles and techniques no different from those used in the rest of clinical analysis, the yield from the work is often especially rich.

REFERENCES

Brenner, C. (1976). *Psychoanalytic Technique and Psychic Conflict*. New York: Int. Univ. Press.

Erikson, E. H. (1954). The dream specimen of psychoanalysis. *J. Amer. Psychoanal. Assn.*, 2:5–56.

Freud, S. (1900). *The Interpretation of Dreams. SE*, 4 & 5.

———. (1914). Remembering, repeating and working through. *SE*, 12:145–156.

Greenson, R. R. (1970). The exceptional position of the dream in psychoanalytic practice. *Psychoanal. Q.*, 39:519–549.

Panel (1984). The clinical use of the manifest dream.

O. Renik, reporter. *J. Amer. Psychoanal. Assn.*, 32:157–162.

Slap, J. W. & Trunnell, E. E. (1987). Reflections on the self state dream. *Psychoanal. Q.*, 56:251–262.

Waldhorn, H. F. (1967). The place of the dream in clinical psychoanalysis. In The Kris Study Group of the New York Psychoanalytic Institute, monograph 2, ed. E. D. Joseph. New York: Int. Univ. Press.

Sydney E. Pulver, M.D.

15

SYMPTOMATOLOGY

With the exception of Anna Freud's classical article on symptomatology in childhood (1970), there are no comprehensive discussions of symptomatology in the psychoanalytic literature. Yet symptoms are of both theoretical and practical importance in psychoanalysis. Behind symptoms are a "whole range of possible derivations, causations, and developmental affiliations" (A. Freud, 1970, p. 38). It is to these forces that analysts devote their primary attention. Like the manifest dream, symptoms are overt manifestations of underlying conflicts. Understanding their meaning and the mechanism of their formation can be of major help in clarifying the dynamics of an emotional illness. If for no other reason, a study of symptoms is worthwhile.

The differences between symptoms, character traits, and inhibitions need to be emphasized. Originally, no distinction was made between a symptom and a sign of an illness. Any manifestation of an illness was considered a symptom. Later, in medicine, symptoms came to be distinguished from signs as complaints by the patient rather than abnormalities observable to the physician. The psychoanalytic aspects of this narrower definition ("A symptom is a mental phenomenon of which an individual complains") are elaborated in Moore and Fine, eds. (1990). General psychiatry still does not pay much attention to the difference between signs and symptoms, but in psychoanalysis the distinction is important. The fact that the patient complains indicates

that the symptom is ego-dystonic, and this is an important consideration in understanding the mechanism of symptom formation. The narrow definition, therefore, is the accepted one.[1]

Ego-dystonic means, literally, "not in harmony with the ego." The term is currently used to describe a mental phenomenon that is either uncomfortable or painful or not integrated with one's usual way of functioning or one's sense of oneself. "The symptom is generally regarded by the ego as an alien, inimical element which has intruded itself into its domain and which is not subject to its control" (Arlow, 1953, pp. 47–48). However, not all manifestations of an illness are ego-dystonic. Certain character traits and various forms of acting out are ego-syntonic (acceptable to the ego), and inhibitions may be either syntonic or dystonic. I shall discuss each of these.

Character is "the enduring, patterned functioning of an individual . . . the person's habitual way of thinking, feeling, acting . . . the person's habitual mode of reconciling intrapsychic conflicts" (Moore & Fine, eds., 1990). Character traits are less global, more specific patterns of perceiving and relating to the environment and oneself. Character disorders are

---

1. Freud's use of the term is congruent with this definition (1917, p. 358; 1926b, pp. 185–187). It is true that Freud used the word *symptom* to refer to delusions (1911b, p. 66), but this would appear to be simply loose usage.

constellations of character traits that are maladaptive to the individual and/or to those individuals with whom he interacts.[2]

Although their psychodynamics are identical, symptoms and character traits differ from each other in three ways.

First, character traits are ego-syntonic, whereas symptoms are ego-dystonic. Character traits are generally not unpleasant, although one may come to dislike certain aspects of one's character; whereas symptoms are almost always uncomfortable. Character traits are always felt to be part of the self, whereas symptoms are often felt to be alien.

Second, a person is always aware of symptoms and, indeed, must be aware of them for them to be unpleasant. Character traits, on the other hand, are often outside of awareness, although this, of course, is not absolute.

Third, character traits by definition are enduring parts of the personality, whereas symptoms are more transitory. Again, this is not without exceptions. Some manifestations of illness do not fit neatly into any category. Elation or grandiosity, for example, may not be enduring parts of the personality, in which case they cannot be considered to be character traits. They are ego-syntonic, however, and thus not properly called symptoms.

The difference between character traits and symptoms is illustrated by the case of a thirty-three-year-old woman who entered analysis complaining of a hand-washing compulsion which had begun three years previously. Before the onset of her symptoms, many aspects of her behavior related to the issue of cleanliness. She dressed immaculately and kept herself and her possessions neat and tidy. She prided herself on taking two showers daily and had a very precise schedule for cleaning her house. All these characteristics had been part of her personality for almost as long as she could remember; they were enduring. They were a source of pride to her (they were ego-syntonic) and were second nature; she was not aware of them on a day-by-day basis. They were, in short, character traits. Her neurosis began with a compulsion to wash her hands more frequently than was natural for her, reaching at its height a frequency of thirty to forty times a day. This hand-washing behavior was a source of distress; it was ego-dystonic. It was transitory in the sense of waxing and waning under various stresses, although at all times she was aware of it and plagued by it. It was, in short, a symptom.

Inhibitions can be either symptoms or character

2. "He," "him," and so on, are to be taken as referring to either sex.

traits. Freud (1926a) defined and illustrated them: "Linguistic usage, then, employs the word *inhibition* when there is a simple lowering of function, and *symptom* when a function has undergone some unusual change or when a new phenomenon has arisen out of it" (p. 87). Using Little Hans, who had an infantile hysterical phobia of animals, as an example, Freud distinguished between his unaccountable fear of a horse biting him, a symptom, and his refusal to go out into the street, "an inhibition, a restriction which his ego had imposed on itself so as not to arouse the anxiety-symptom" (p. 101).

The terms *symptomatic act, acting out,* and *neurotic action* all refer to patterns of action arising out of conflict. A symptomatic act is a discrete act that expresses an unconscious conflict and in structure is exactly like a symptom (Freud, 1901, pp. 191–216). When such behavior is broader in scope but is still relatively delimited, it is called "acting out." When the action is so generalized as to be a character trait, it may be called "neurotic action." Thus, if, in response to an aggressive act that makes him feel guilty, an individual injures his hand in a car door, that is a symptomatic act. If he provokes punishment for his guilt by a more elaborate series of behaviors leading to the failure of an important project, he would be said to be "acting out," particularly if the behavior occurred as a resistance during therapy. And if he habitually caused himself to fail in that kind of way, so that failure out of a sense of guilt constituted one of his character traits, that would be called "neurotic action." The distinction between these terms is a quantitative rather than a qualitative one.

SYMPTOM FORMATION

Even separating symptoms from character traits leaves a rather extensive and heterogeneous group of behaviors. To understand the way symptoms form, a further classification will be useful. In undertaking this, Anna Freud's caution (1970) against doing so purely on a phenomenological basis must be heeded. Using only the surface characteristics of symptoms would be misleading, since, as will be seen, any single symptom, and very often any constellation of symptoms, can have many different underlying dynamics.

The first group to be considered is that of the *classic neurotic symptom.* This is the type of symptom that Freud first investigated; it remains the type about which we have the most understanding. Broadly speaking, the group consists of those symptoms found in the hysterical and obsessive-compulsive neuroses. According to the "standard formula"[3] for the development of this type of symptom, instinctual drives or their derivatives threaten to emerge into consciousness, are perceived by the ego as dangerous, and are defended against. If the defense is not entirely successful, they emerge in the form of compromise formations which contain either a disguised gratification of the drive, the defense against the drive, and/or a gratification of the superego prohibition against the drive. They emerge, that is, in the distorted form known as symptoms (Freud, 1905b, p. 164). The history of the development of Freud's understanding is fascinating but outside the scope of this chapter. Those interested in further details should see Arlow, 1963, or Waelder, 1967.

To illustrate this mechanism in detail, I will follow Freud's description of symptom formation in Little Hans (1926a, pp. 101–110). As we have seen, Little Hans refused to go out into the street because he was afraid of horses, and this refusal was an inhibition that protected him against the anxiety aroused by encountering a horse. His fear of horses was, in fact, a very specific fear of being bitten by a horse; but it was expressed in a more general way to further distance Little Hans from his instinctual wish, which was more closely connected with "being bitten." Put another way, "being bitten by a horse" was a drive derivative, and the more general "fear of horses" was a more disguised drive derivative. Little Hans was immersed in a typical oedipal situation. He wished to have his mother for himself and thus wished that his father was out of the way. More specifically, he wished that he himself could cause his father to "fall down and hurt himself" and die of convulsions. At the same time, since he loved his father as well as hated him, he wished that he could be tenderly close to his father in the same way that his mother was. These wishes were perceived as dangerous and led to anxiety. To protect himself against that anxiety, Little Hans used a variety of defensive maneuvers (predominantly displacement and regression) to keep his wishes out of awareness.

The essence of the formula might be stated as follows: "If I want to injure my father and be sexually close to my mother, my father will want to injure me, and that scares me. Specifically, I am afraid that my father will castrate me. But I love my father, so I cannot want to harm him, nor he me. It is not him I am afraid of; I am afraid of horses [a displacement to a symbolic representative of father]. And it is not genital things I am afraid of, it is oral dangers: I am afraid a horse will bite me [a regression to oral rather than genital wishes]." Freud points out that it is not possible to say whether the actual drive has regressed ("I wish to eat and be eaten by father") or whether the displacement is merely expressed in oral terms. Whichever it is, the symptom is a compromise which expresses at least four components: the hostile wish toward his father, the libidinal wish to be passively involved with him, the punishment that might be meted out for entertaining those wishes, and the anxiety which that punishment gives rise to.

To help understand why the standard formula does not apply to all symptoms, let me consider a variety of the factors involved in symptom formation in more detail.

Drives. Freud's standard formula for symptom formation postulates that instinctual drives or their derivatives are the items of mental content that threaten to emerge into consciousness. As the psychoanalytic theory of motivation has developed, this position has given rise to considerable controversy. In a discussion of symptom formation, Arlow (1963) supports Freud's position. But Loewenstein (1964) and others argue convincingly that there are many other sources of danger (and hence anxiety) that the ego defends against, and this point of view is probably the predominant one. It now appears that almost any motivational state, including some only loosely if at all connected to drives, may be considered dangerous, may be repressed, and may subsequently threaten to emerge from repression. In addition, certain ego states such as depersonalization or fragmentation may provoke anxiety, as may traumatic states of helplessness.

Anxiety. As we have seen, Freud's position was that anxiety was the only affect to engender symptom formation, a statement he reaffirmed over the course of the years (1933, pp. 83–85). But this seemed to contradict clinical data and soon came to be questioned. Zetzel (1964) described "depression, its equivalents, or its denial as a major determinant of symptom and character formation" (p. 153). This view was supported by Bibring (1953), Brenner (1975), and many others. It would appear that *any* dysphoric affect—including, for example, shame, guilt, and disgust—may act as a motivator of repression. For a good survey of this literature, see Thoma and Kachele, 1987, pp. 106–112.

Conflict. A basic aspect of neurotic symptoms, upon which there is general agreement, is their origin in psychic conflict, the struggle between two or more opposing forces or tendencies in the mind. The nature of that conflict, however, has given rise to two questions. The first is whether the conflict is always intersystemic—that is, whether it arises from a clash

---

3. A term coined by Strachey; see Freud, 1950, p. 222, n. 2.

between major psychic systems such as the id and the superego—or whether it may also be intra-systemic. Some theoreticians (for example, Arlow, 1963) think that the conflict underlying a neurotic symptom is always intersystemic. Most, however, acknowledge that intrasystemic conflicts (arising, for example, entirely within the ego) may also lead to symptoms. Note that this question is a variant of the one discussed above under "Drives."

A second major controversy is whether the conflict is always oedipal in origin (Arlow, 1963, pp. 14, 17, 19), or whether it may also be pre-oedipal. Evidence for the frequent participation of pre-oedipal factors would seem to be overwhelming (A. Freud, 1970, pp. 165–166).

Defense. An essential step in symptom formation is the ego's effort to protect itself against the experience of dysphoric affects by casting offending impulses out of consciousness. This effort is called "defense," and the specific steps taken by the ego are called "defense mechanisms." Defense, of course, is a universal phenomenon and not necessarily pathological. When it is successful, no symptoms occur. However, defense is never completely successful; symptoms are present in everyone. Whether the symptoms are of sufficient intensity to be called a neurosis is purely a quantitative matter. Repression, the simple removal of psychic content from consciousness, may be thought of as the primary defense; but the ego uses a variety of other defense mechanisms to facilitate repression, and these are discussed elsewhere in this volume. Those characteristically associated with specific symptom complexes will be discussed in more detail under "meaning" below.

Compromise formation. Freud described three different mechanisms of symptom formation: substitution formation, reaction formation, and compromise formation (1913b, p. 208). *Substitution formation* is simply the replacement of a repressed impulse by a symbolic substitute. *Reaction formation* is its replacement by something opposite in meaning to the impulse, a reaction against it. *Compromise formation* is the symptomatic expression in disguised form of both a repressed impulse and the repressing force. Freud used the terms "compromise" and "compromise formation" in several different senses, and this has led to some confusion. He first formulated the idea of symptoms as compromises in a draft of a paper sent to Fliess on 1 January 1896. By "compromise" here, he meant that the symptom is a compromise with truth: "[the symptom is] . . . correct as regards affect and category but false owing to chronological displacement and substitution by analogy" (Freud, 1950, p. 224). In later works, he used "compromise" to refer broadly to the outcome of a conflict between any of a number of motivational factors. The compromise in the fetishist is between his wish that the woman have a penis and his realistic knowledge that she does not, and it is represented by the idea that she has something just as exciting: the fetish (Freud, 1927). The dream is a compromise between the wish to sleep and a repressed instinctual impulse (Freud, 1933, p. 19).

In its broad sense, then, Freud used the expression "compromise formation" to refer to psychic phenomena resulting from a conflict between two or more emotional forces. At first, particularly in his work on hysteria, Freud saw symptoms not only as the result of conflicting forces but also as the expression or representation of both sides of the conflict in the symptom itself. This narrower use of the term first appeared in 1896 (p. 170), in a paper in which he described symptoms as a compromise between contradictory pairs of wish fulfillments—namely, the repressed material and the repressing thoughts. As psychoanalytic theory developed, "the repressed material" gradually came to be spelled out as sexual (Freud, 1908b, p. 164), aggressive (Freud, 1920), traumatic (Freud, 1939, p. 78), and, in fact, anything ego-dystonic enough to have been subject to repression. The "repressing thoughts" evolved from self-reproaches about sexual ideas (Freud, 1896, p. 163) into aspects of the ego and the superego (Freud, 1928, p. 185).

Freud's broad use of the term "compromise" has led some authors to take the position that all symptoms are compromise formations in the sense that they express both sides of the conflict and even to hold that all psychic acts are compromise formations (Brenner, 1976, pp. 22, 192). While this is consistent with Waelder's principle of multiple functioning (1936), it is correct only in the sense that all the systems are involved in psychic functioning and must be taken into consideration. Freud certainly did not intend to imply that all symptoms express or represent both sides of the conflict from which they emerge. This is indicated by his explicit description of other mechanisms of symptom formation, such as substitute and reaction formation. Symptoms may represent both sides of the compromise, but they may not. By the time of the Rat Man, Freud (1909) had realized that isolated symptoms in obsessive-compulsive neurosis might represent only the repressing force, and that often there was a biphasic quality, with the first symptom representing the repressing force and the second the underlying impulse. At times he simply meant by "compromise" that the distorted expression of the id wish is accepted by the ego (Freud, 1924, p. 150; 1925, pp. 30, 65; 1940, p. 167) or that the impulse is blotted out completely (Freud, 1933, p. 15). In brief, all symptoms are compromise formations in the sense that they are the result of a compromise between conflicting psychic forces, but only some symptoms are compromise formations in the sense of expressing or representing both sides of the conflict in the symptom itself.

Trauma. One cause of the dysphoric affects that lead to symptom formation is the threatened emergence of repressed instinctual impulses. Because there is a tendency to view this as the only cause (Arlow, 1963), the role of repressed trauma needs to be emphasized. The mechanism by which trauma causes symptoms is the same as that associated with the emergence of unacceptable motivations. Trauma, by definition, is any event that the ego is unable to master and that thereby creates a state of helplessness. The experience of the traumatic event is repressed but remains active and presses toward consciousness. The threatened emergence of the experience creates anxiety, and, if defenses against it are unsuccessful, symptoms result. Freud, of course, very early recognized the importance of trauma; his original theory concerning the etiology of hysteria was based on the repression of memories of early traumatic events (Freud, 1888, pp. 51, 56). As is well known, he later expanded his theory to include defense against intrapsychic wishes and fantasies in addition to "actual" trauma, but he never abandoned his recognition of the importance of trauma itself (Freud, 1939, p. 74). That importance continues to be recognized by most authors.

Freud dealt mainly with the formation of the classic neurotic symptom. Subsequent advances in knowledge have shed light on the formation of symptoms in cases other than those of the classic neuroses, and these will now be discussed. In what follows, the term "symptom" will be used in the broad sense as any manifestation of a disorder, whether or not the patient complains about it.

Symptoms resulting from a persisting dysphoric affective state. Symptoms resulting from intrapsychic conflict may be manifestations of the underlying impulse, of attempts to defend against the impulse, of the prohibitions against the impulse, or of some combination of all these. However, another possibility exists: that repression is successful enough to prevent the emergence of any of these but is not successful enough to eliminate the dysphoric affect (anxiety, shame, disgust, or depression) that is the ego's response to the unwelcome impulse. These affects are obviously ego-dystonic, and, if they per-

sist for any length of time, they are properly called symptoms. Occasionally, relatively pure affective symptom states (panic attacks devoid of conscious ideation, for example) occur, although a combination with other symptoms is the more usual state of affairs. Since affective reactions are at least partially neurophysiological responses, the psychological factors activating them may be operating in the presence of an underlying hypo- or hyperreactive neurophysiological affective response system. In other words, affects have a physiological component, and affective symptoms may have such a component as well. Psychological factors, however, are always present. Specific affective states have specific psychological causes only in the broadest sense: anxiety as a reaction to danger, depression to loss, and shame to inadequacy. But danger can arise from a wide variety of psychic causes, and anxiety may therefore be due to psychic conflict on almost any level. The same applies to other affective symptomatic states.

Psychosomatic symptoms. This term is very loosely used to describe any somatic symptom the etiology of which includes significant emotional factors. The complexity of the mechanism of formation of these symptoms was already apparent in the early debate between Freud and Adler about "organ inferiority" and "somatic compliance" (Nunberg & Federn, 1967, pp. 320–321, 525). At least two broad categories of psychosomatic symptoms can be delineated: those in which the somatic symptom is the symbolic representation of an unconscious fantasy along the lines of the conversion symptom in hysteria (see Bressler et al., 1958, for an example); and those in which the symptom is the physiological concomitant of an affective state that has been defended against. The structure of the latter type has been discussed in some detail by Benedetti (1983). Historically, there have been valiant attempts to assign specific emotional constellations to specific psychosomatic symptoms. Although this effort produced valuable data, our current understanding of the complexities of the mind–brain–body interrelationship indicates that such simple linear correlations are not likely to be accurate (Reiser, 1990).

Symptoms resulting from the irruption of direct primary process thinking or direct drive behavior into the ego. In certain states, usually of a psychotic nature, the ego is unable to maintain its usual separation from the id. Compromise formation does not occur; rather, unconscious material intrudes directly into everyday rational behavior. This appears manifestly in disturbances of thought and language, misidentifications, delusions, and the undefended acting out of drive derivatives (A. Freud, 1970, pp. 166–167). The individual experiences this as a catastrophe and attempts to recover by a process that results in additional symptoms (Freud, 1911b, p. 71; Pao, 1977).

Symptoms due to developmental arrest. From infancy onward, the personality evolves, and the development of any aspect of the personality may be interfered with and thus not progress in the usual manner. The result is a developmental arrest, and from such an arrest symptoms may emerge. For example, a child may, because of severe anal preoccupations or because of a lack of environmental stimulation, fail to develop the cognitive capacity to do well in school. The intellectual failure in such a situation (a symptom in the broad sense of the term) is due primarily to developmental arrest and not to inhibition of the neurotic type. This is not to say that emotional conflict is not present in such a child; it invariably is. From this simple fact an extensive controversy has burgeoned in psychoanalytic thinking, the argument over "conflict versus deficit." Some authors believe that all symptoms arise primarily from conflict, the appearance of developmental arrest or deficit being a surface manifestation of the conflict, usually defensive in nature. Prevailing opinion, however, holds that developmental arrest arising from factors other than psychic conflict does in fact occur and often bears primary responsibility for the symptomatic picture.

Symptoms arising from attempts to cope with organic deficit. In many organic disorders—such as, for example, mild learning disorders or minimal brain damage—compensatory techniques appear as symptoms, particularly when the deficit is not recognized. For example, one patient struggled for years in analysis with compulsive traits: a certain rigidity of thinking, an inability to complete tasks, poorly organized work habits, and an inordinate need to check his work and set up repetitive protocols to avoid errors. Finally, neuropsychological testing revealed a specific brain lesion that made certain tasks inordinately difficult. The compulsive traits had developed as an attempt to cope with this difficulty.

Understanding symptom formation is made more complex by the fact that the initial appearance of primary symptoms is often only the beginning of a long process. The painful nature of the primary symptoms provokes a struggle which in turn produces secondary symptoms, and then tertiary symptoms, and so on. Such secondary symptoms are not characteristic of all symptom complexes (Freud, 1926a, p. 112), but they are more likely than not to be present and to complicate the symptomatic pic-

ture. An illustration is seen in the case of a thirty-four-year-old man who entered analysis complaining of being unable to relax. He periodically found himself engaging in bouts of almost frenetic activity, often accomplishing a great deal but driven in a way that he disliked intensely. As the analysis progressed, it became clear that a primary conflict involved his mother, a critical and distant woman who aroused in him strong feelings of anger. The anger was intolerable, and he repressed it, but the resultant conflict generated deep feelings of depression and abandonment. These feelings constituted the primary symptoms of his illness. They were so painful, however, that he struggled against experiencing them by immersing himself in frenzied activity. This entire process was unconscious, and he was aware only of his compulsion to be active, a secondary symptom.

THE MEANING OF SYMPTOMS

The meaning of symptoms has been a major concern of psychoanalysis from its beginning. The attempt to understand symptoms was one of the factors that led Freud to his monumental work on dream interpretation (1900). From early on, he saw symptom formation as analogous or identical with dream and fantasy formation (Freud, 1914, p. 20). Like the meaning of manifest dreams, that of symptoms is not always obvious from superficial examination, and care must be taken to distinguish between manifest and latent content. Symptoms, like dreams and many other psychic phenomena, are overdetermined. They may express several simultaneous meanings as well as several meanings in succession (Freud, 1905a, p. 53). And, like dreams, the complexities of symptoms often cannot be unraveled until the end of a complete analysis (Freud, 1911a, p. 93). All these injunctions notwithstanding, we can understand a great deal from the symptom alone. Again, the analogy with dreams holds. Just as something about the dreamer can be learned from the manifest dream, so something can be learned from the manifest symptom (Pulver, 1987). When this is possible, it is very much like our understanding of typical dreams (Freud, 1917, p. 270). Insight into the meaning of manifest symptoms is usually based on the affect present in the symptom, the defense used in the formation of the symptom, or the mode of symbolization of the underlying conscious fantasy. I will explore each of these.

The affective content of the symptom. Many symptoms are connected with, or even consist solely of, a specific dysphoric affect; often the ideational content in which the affect is embedded indicates something about its source. Let us take anxiety as an example. Although anxiety may be expressed in an infinite variety of ways, there is a tendency for fear about certain things to be connected with specific kinds of anxiety. Patients who consciously fear starvation, loneliness, or helplessness, for example, frequently have an underlying fear of separation from important objects. Similar connections can be made for any of the dysphoric affects such as shame or guilt. (See A. Freud, 1970, p. 176, for a more detailed list of these connections pertaining to anxiety.)

Association of specific symptoms and specific defenses. From early on, the relationship of defense mechanisms to the symptoms resulting from them have been of interest, and a number of correlations are now well accepted. For instance, the major defenses found in phobias are displacement and avoidance. Typically, displacement of the drive onto an external object occurs. Because contact with the object tends to stir up the drive and thus threatens the repression of the original drive–object relationship, anxiety is aroused. The patient uses avoidance to stay away from the external object and thus to stay away from anxiety, as was the case with Little Hans. Note that displacement is not always the primary defense in phobias, although in every phobia there is some threat to repression brought on by an external object. Another instance is the association of the defense mechanism of projection with the symptom of paranoia. Invariably, an individual who feels that he is being persecuted by external agents will be found to be disowning certain attacking, violent parts of himself, sensing that they are present instead in the external world. Similar linkages can be found between other symptom complexes and defenses typically used in their formation. A good survey of these for all nosological groups is found in Fenichel, 1945.

Symptoms as expressions of fantasies. The formation of repressed unconscious fantasies representing compromise formations arising out of conflict is a ubiquitous phenomenon (Freud, 1901; 1908a, p. 148; 1908b). Many symptoms are symbolic expressions of these fantasies (Arlow, 1963). Although fantasies arising from any motivational source may play a role in symptom formation, those relating to the primal scene, seduction by an adult, and castration are among the most frequent (Freud, 1917, p. 369). The following examples are illustrative of the wealth of literature attempting to link specific dynamics to specific symptoms on the basis of such symbolism.

Occasionally the problem is approached from the standpoint of the type of fantasy involved and the various symptoms it may lead to, as in discussions of masturbation (Arlow, 1953), the primal scene (Niederland, 1958), or pregnancy fantasies (Bressler et al., 1958). More frequently, the approach is from the standpoint of the symptom itself. Spider phobias, for example, have been described as symbolic of fantasies about the oral incorporative or the phallic mother. A common fantasy in claustrophobia is of being disturbed by parental coitus while a fetus in the mother's body. Agoraphobia may be a displacement of anxiety about incestuous fantasies. *Globus hystericus* may represent the wish to cry or fellatio fantasies. Hypochondriasis has been described as the symbolic expression of torture fantasies. Conversions may represent fantasies of symbolic union with a lost object, in which the object is symbolized as part of the body. Obsessions may represent parodies of superego commands, while compulsions are sometimes symbolic travesties of appropriate responses to those commands. This is but a smattering of the information in the literature on the appearance of fantasies in symptoms.

THE ETIOLOGY OF SYMPTOMS

Although some experimental work has been done on the etiology of individual symptoms (Luborsky & Auerbach, 1969), most of the literature on this topic deals with the onset of a neurosis. Freud divided the factors contributing to the start of a neurosis into two main groups: those starting from reality—that is, from factors originating in the current frustrations in the individual's life (1917, pp. 349–350)—and those starting from the infantile neurosis, the older fixation point (1918, p. 54). Another way of looking at the problem is from the viewpoint of the structural theory. As has been described, symptoms arise when, for one reason or another, the individual is unable to maintain a successful defense against unacceptable motivations. In the case of the classical neurotic symptom, this means an inability to defend against repressed feelings and thoughts—the "return of the repressed." The predisposing and precipitating factors leading to a return of the repressed can be categorized on the basis of the structural theory.

1. Id factors. Drives that are too intense resist repression and also interfere with the ability of the ego to defend against them.

2. Ego factors. The ego's ability successfully to resolve conflicts may be impaired congenitally or on an acquired basis (Freud, 1937, p. 235).

3. Superego factors. Faulty development of the superego, resulting in a superego that is too harsh, inflexible, or inconsistent, makes conflict resolution difficult and may predispose toward symptoms.

4. Environmental factors. The situation in which the individual finds himself at any particular time may interact with any or all of the above and stimulate the production of conflicts that cannot be resolved successfully.

Relief of symptoms occurs in an inverse manner. When, for instance, psychoanalysis leads to an easing of superego rigidity, with a corresponding increase in the ability to get drive satisfaction, less repression is necessary. The ego is better able to defend itself, and symptoms remit. Sometimes, however, even in the face of internal or external circumstances that one would expect to lead to the disappearance of symptoms, they in fact persist. An understanding of the difference between primary and secondary gain (Freud, 1905a, p. 43; 1917, pp. 378–391; Katz, 1964) often helps to explain this. The function of symptoms in resolving conflict through compromise formation and in the other ways described above is called "the primary gain." It is the principal reason why symptoms develop. It can be divided into two components, the internal or intrapsychic gains from the symptom and the external gains—that is, the gains derived from the immediate effect on the environment. For instance, a high-level executive developed a phobia of flying in response to the arrival of a new company president, a man who turned out to be extremely critical and abrasive. In analysis, it was discovered that his phobia was a compromise formation designed to help him avoid the intrapsychic submissiveness and accompanying homosexual fantasies with which he responded to his new boss, which were stirred up during the long plane trips they took together. In addition, it enabled him to avoid the demands and criticisms leveled at him by the boss during those trips. The primary gain of the symptom, then, was the relief it provided from both internal and external conflicts. Once the symptom develops, however, the individual sometimes finds that it is useful in gaining other ends. The phobic man described above discovered that his anxious state resulted in a great deal of attention from his wife, something he valued highly. This reward from symptoms, one that did not enter into their primary motivation and that could not reasonably have been foreseen or anticipated at the time of symptom formation, arose secondarily, and is thus called "secondary gain." When it is present, it is often a major obstacle to symptom cure.

At this point the question of symptom choice may be considered. Why, for example, do some individuals with a particular conflict become phobic, while others, with apparently the same conflict, become victims of a peptic ulcer? In Freud's early explanations, he attempted to fix the responsibility for the choice of symptoms on certain aspects of libido, such as the degree of activity versus passivity. This proved unsatisfactory, and he moved on to other hypotheses. By the time he advanced the thesis that it was the point of libidinal fixation that was of crucial importance, he realized that the complexity of the subject was such that a simple answer would not be possible. It is now clear that a variety of factors contribute to symptom choice.

1. The nature of the motivations that have to be warded off. This is determined at least in part by the type and degree of fixation, and thus the type and degree of regression.

2. Vicissitudes of trauma. Of importance is the time of the trauma, which will influence the form of drive expression and the type of defense mechanism selected. The content and intensity of the frustrations are also important. The nature of the frustrating factors, particularly the personalities of the frustrating parent and of other caretakers, is of particular significance because of identification with the aggressor, which plays such an important part in the choice of defense mechanisms.

3. The suitability of the defensive operation in the child's environment—in other words, adaptive features of the defense.

4. Cultural factors. The response of the culture to specific symptoms has a significant effect upon which symptoms are selected.

5. Constitutional predispositions to use certain defense mechanisms and coping behaviors.

In addition to producing good case reports (for example, Gann, 1984), which are always of value, the past few decades have seen increasing interest in more formal research in this area. Luborsky and Auerbach (1969) have studied symptom formation in the psychotherapeutic situation, using an approach they call "the symptom–context method." In this method, transcripts of material before and after the appearance of a symptom in the therapeutic session are evaluated in a number of ways. The study of momentary forgetting, episodic stomach pain, and migraine headaches using this method led to the identification of specific conditions for symptom formation immediately preceding the symptoms and in the larger context of the session. Silverman et al. (1976), using subliminal stimulation to activate unconscious fantasies, were able not only to support experimentally the general hypothesis that libidinal and aggressive wishes are linked to psychopathology but more specifically to connect homosexuality with incestuous wishes, stuttering with anal wishes, and thought disorder with aggressive wishes. The Hampstead Psychoanalytic Index, a card-file system of compiling data obtained during the psychoanalytic treatment of children, has proved a gold mine of information about symptom formation in children (Bolland & Sandler, 1965). It seems likely that experimental work of this nature will join with clinical investigation in continuing to expand our knowledge of symptoms and their complexities.

REFERENCES

Arlow, J. A. (1953). Masturbation and symptom formation. *J. Amer. Psychoanal. Assn.,* 1:45–58.
———. (1963). Conflict, regression, and symptom formation. *Int. J. Psychoanal.,* 44:12–22.
Benedetti, G. (1983). The structure of psychosomatic symptoms. *Amer. J. Psychoanal.,* 43:57–70.
Bibring, E. (1953). The mechanism of depression. In *Affective Disorders,* ed. P. Greenacre, pp. 13–48. New York: Int. Univ. Press.
Bolland, J., & Sandler, J. (1965). *The Hampstead Psychoanalytic Index.* New York: Int. Univ. Press.
Brenner, C. (1975). Affects and psychic conflict. *Psychoanal. Q.,* 44:5–28.
———. (1976). *Psychoanalytic Technique and Psychic Conflict.* New York: Int. Univ. Press.
Bressler, B., Nyhus, P., & Magnussen, F. (1958). Pregnancy fantasies in psychosomatic illness and symptom formation. *Psychosom. Med.,* 20:187–202.
Fenichel, O. (1945). *The Psychoanalytic Theory of Neurosis.* New York: Norton.
Freud, A. (1970). The symptomatology of childhood. *Psychoanal. Study Child,* 25:19–41.
Freud, S. (1888). Hysteria. *SE,* 1:39–59.
———. (1896). Further remarks on the neuropsychoses of defence. *SE,* 3:157–185.
———. (1900). *The Interpretation of Dreams. SE,* 4 & 5.
———. (1901). *The Psychopathology of Everyday Life. SE,* 6.
———. (1905a). Fragment of an analysis of a case of hysteria. *SE,* 7:3–122.
———. (1905b). *Three Essays on the Theory of Sexuality. SE,* 7:125–245.
———. (1908a). Creative writers and day-dreaming. *SE,* 9:141–153.
———. (1908b). Hysterical phantasies and their relation to bisexuality. *SE,* 9:155–166.
———. (1909). Notes upon a case of obsessional neurosis. *SE,* 10:153–320.
———. (1911a). The handling of dream-interpretation in psycho-analysis. *SE,* 12:89–96.
———. (1911b). Psycho-analytic notes on an autobiographical account of a case of paranoia (dementia paranoides). *SE,* 12:3–82.
———. (1913a). The disposition to obsessional neurosis. *SE,* 12:311–326.
———. (1913b). On psycho-analysis. *SE,* 12:205–211.
———. (1914). On the history of the psychoanalytic movement. *SE,* 14:7–66.
———. (1917). *Introductory Lectures on Psycho-Analysis,* Part III. *SE,* 16.
———. (1918). From the history of an infantile neurosis. *SE,* 17:3–123.
———. (1920). *Beyond the Pleasure Principle. SE,* 18:7–64.
———. (1924). Neurosis and psychosis. *SE,* 19: 149–153.
———. (1925). *An Autobiographical Study. SE,* 20:3–74.
———. (1926a). *Inhibitions, Symptoms and Anxiety. SE,* 20:77–175.
———. (1926b). *The Question of Lay Analysis. SE,* 20:179–258.
———. (1927). Fetishism. *SE,* 21:149–157.
———. (1928). Dostoevsky and parricide. *SE,* 21: 175–196.
———. (1933). *New Introductory Lectures on Psycho-Analysis. SE,* 22:5–182.
———. (1937). Analysis terminable and interminable. *SE,* 23:209–253.
———. (1939). *Moses and Monotheism. SE,* 23:3–137.
———. (1940). *An Outline of Psycho-Analysis. SE,* 23:141–207.
———. (1950). Extracts from the Fliess papers. *SE,* 1:175–279.
Gann, E. (1984). Some theoretical and technical considerations concerning the emergence of a symptom of the transference neurosis. *J. Amer. Psychoanal. Assn.,* 32:797–829.
Katz, J. (1964). On primary and secondary gain. *Psychoanal. Study Child,* 18:9–50.
Loewenstein, R. M. (1964). Symptom formation and character formation. *Int. J. Psychoanal.,* 45:155–157.
Luborsky, L., & Auerbach, A. (1969). The symptom-context method. *J. Amer. Psychoanal. Assn.,* 17:68–99.
Moore, B. E., & Fine, B. D., eds. (1990). *Psychoanalytic Terms and Concepts.* New Haven: Yale Univ. Press.
Niederland, W. G. (1958). Early experiences, beating fantasies, and the primal scene. *Psychoanal. Study Child,* 13:471–504.
Nunberg, H., & Federn, E. (1967). *Minutes of the Vienna Psychoanalytic Society,* vol. 2. New York: Int. Univ. Press.
Panel (1959). Phobias and their vicissitudes. H. Wein-

stock, reporter. *J. Amer. Psychoanal. Assn.*, 7: 182–192.

———. (1963). Symptom formation. H. Nierenberg, reporter. *J. Amer. Psychoanal. Assn.*, 11:161–172.

Pao, P. (1977). On the formation of schizophrenic symptoms. *Int. J. Psychoanal.*, 58:389–410.

Pulver, S. (1987). The manifest dream in psychoanalysis. *J. Amer. Psychoanal. Assn.*, 35:99–118.

Reiser, M. F. (1990). *Memory in Mind and Brain.* New York: Basic Books.

Ritvo, S. (1981). Anxiety, symptom formation, and ego autonomy. *Psychoanal. Study Child,* 36:339–364.

Rubinfine, D. (1973). Notes toward a theory of con-

sciousness. *Int. J. Psychoanal. Psychother.,* 2:391–410.

Silverman, L., Bronstein, A., & Mendelsohn, E. (1976). The further use of the subliminal psychodynamic activation method for the experimental study of the clinical theory of psychoanalysis. *Psychotherapy: Theory, Research and Practice,* 13:2–16.

Thoma, H., & Kachele, H. (1987). *Psychoanalytic Practice.* Heidelberg: Springer.

Waelder, R. (1936). The principle of multiple function. *Psychoanal. Q.,* 5:45–62.

———. (1967). Inhibitions, symptoms and anxiety: forty years later. *Psychoanal. Q.,* 36:1–36.

Zetzel, E. R. (1964). Symptom formation and character formation. *Int. J. Psychoanal.,* 45:151–154.

Francis D. Baudry, M.D.

16

CHARACTER

The term "character" has a long history in lay language. Its analytic usage is more restrictive, shedding the implication of moral sturdiness commonly associated with its origins. Also deleted is the idea that a character need be notable or conspicuous, as in the colloquial expression "He is a character." In psychiatry the term "character" is closely related to, and often used interchangeably with, "personality"; but personality refers to the totality of physical, emotional, intellectual, behavioral, and social attributes, whereas character is more limited, denoting consistent attitudes and behaviors of a person as observed by others. While both character and symptoms are the result of conflict resolution by means of compromise formation, the attributes that make up character are experienced as an acceptable part of the self to a greater degree than are symptoms; that is, character is ego-syntonic, whereas symptoms are ego-dystonic. Consideration of character is a means whereby we group these ego-syntonic aspects of functioning; its assessment is crucial for the determination of analyzability, and attitudinal or character changes are one way of evaluating the progress of an analysis.[1]

After the pioneer contribution of Wilhelm Reich (1949), the concept of character was relatively neglected for a long time. During the last two decades, however, the concept and its clinical and theoretical significance have assumed an increasingly central role in psychoanalytic thought and technique. This may be due in part to the fact that the majority of patients now coming for analysis do not complain of symptoms. Their major psychopathology lies in the sphere of character.

The term "character" is used in psychoanalysis on two levels: a clinical one, close to the level of observation, and an abstract one, describing a conceptual organization of the psyche. Clinically it consists of a constellation of relatively stable patterns of attitudes and behavior specific to a given individual, usually referred to as "character traits." There is no person without a character, and character itself is an individual's typical way of functioning, implying neither health nor pathology. Character traits may be either adaptive or maladaptive; attempts to develop clinical criteria that distinguish normality from abnormality are only moderately successful. (For a more extended definition, see Moore & Fine, eds., 1990.)

---

1. Sections of an early draft of an overview of the concept of character were expanded and published separately in three papers in the *Journal of the American Psychoanalytic Association* (Baudry, 1983, 1984, 1989). Some of the content of those publications has been incorporated relatively unchanged in this chapter in an attempt to present the subject as an integrated whole.

HISTORY

Freud (1908) laid the foundation for the psychoanalytic concept of character in his paper entitled "Character and anal erotism." It was a first attempt to delineate a common clinical picture involving three outstanding character traits (parsimony, obstinacy, and orderliness) dynamically related to one another as derivatives of a stage of the libidinal drive. The truly novel aspect of this new concept of character was not its description of the traits themselves, which could be found in many different personality organizations, but the establishment of a relationship between traits close to the data of observation and an unconscious structural component. It is not sufficiently emphasized that in the history of psychoanalysis, character as a structural organization originated fifteen years before the structural theory. Unfortunately, it has not been possible to delineate other character organizations that are as closely and recurrently related to other stages of the libido as the obsessional character is to anal libido. Following Freud's pioneering attempts to define character in a libidinal framework, others (Abraham, 1921, 1924, 1925; Jones, 1918) spelled out in greater detail the variety of traits that could be clearly derived from other libidinal stages.

Freud's 1908 formulation, that character traits were either a perpetuation of original impulses in modified form, reaction formations, or sublimations, gave way to more sophisticated formulations with the introduction of the structural theory. Freud had already initiated the study of the relation of character to the analysis of resistances (1916). This focus on resistances was most acutely pursued in the work of Wilhelm Reich (1949). The emergence of the structural point of view allowed for the development of a theory of mind based on such concepts as internalization, introjection, and identification and on timetables of structure formation (of ego, superego, and ego ideal). Anna Freud's (1936) description of mechanisms of defense and the development and refinement of the workings of the ego expanded her father's ideas about the intimate connection between modes of defense and certain illnesses. The most exhaustive study of character is still the chapter in Fenichel's (1945) classic textbook. In addition to developing the most ambitious attempt at classification, Fenichel broadened our understanding of character formation by utilizing Waelder's (1930) principle of multiple function. Character reflects the ego's attempt to synthesize and integrate the demands of id, superego, reality, and the repetition compulsion.

Subsequently, interest shifted to the sphere of adaptation, introduced by Hartmann (1939), and to his concepts of primary and secondary autonomy. In discussions of styles (Rosen, 1961; Stein, 1969), the contributions of cognition and perception were also elaborated. Erikson's work (1956) describing stages of development, each with its specialized developmental task, stimulated interest in the developmental phases (modes) and the challenges posed by them in the investigation of the significant interplay between libidinal phases, ego apparatuses, parental influences, and societal demands. There has also been concern with broader phenomena of a person's functioning related to certain more general concepts such as identity and self, but the articulation of these ideas with current analytic theory remains problematic. In addition, the careful dissection of the early developmental phases of separation-individuation by Mahler and her co-workers (1979) has sharpened our appreciation of some of the early stages in character formation, particularly as related to object relations.

CHARACTER TRAITS AND CHARACTER

Recognition of the traits that collectively make up the character of a person requires identification of individual patterns of behavior that are recurrent, including attitudes, which Jacobson (1964) defined as "characteristic features which become manifest in the most general way in all mental areas; in a person's ideals and ideas, his feelings, and his behavior" (p. 97). But a character trait is not exactly identical with behavior; rather, it is inferred from observable, stable, repetitive behavior patterns, and it requires some consideration of the subject's inner experience. Consider, for example, an individual who presents him- or herself as a generous person. He or she may truly care about others and wish to share with them or alternatively may have learned that the appearance of generosity will gain approval from others and thus help him or her deny greed, covetousness, or anger. To further complicate matters, a particular behavior may be the expression of many different character traits.

The range of data from which one can infer such traits is very great indeed—body language, mannerisms of speech, the entire range of expressive movements, posture, gait, dress, and so forth. Other data more specific to the clinical situation, and therefore directly observable by the analyst, include the way the patient reacts to interpretations and the way he or she handles the external aspects of the treatment (time, money, and the rest).

While descriptively based on data of observation, a character trait is an abstraction dependent on the inferences of an observer and subject to his or her value judgments, prejudices, and bias. Observers may differ in their sensitivity to aggression or depression. Sociocultural factors also have to be considered in evaluating pathology. Certain cultures may tolerate or encourage behavior that would be considered deviant in other settings. Since the superego is often very much involved in the development of character, there is a strong tendency to moralize about character traits, to regard them as "good" or "bad," desirable or undesirable. However, character traits represent complex admixtures not only of superego influences but also of drive derivatives and defenses. By contrast with character, symptoms are ego-alien and a definitive sign of pathology. While there is some advantage in stressing these differences, they are not always clear-cut. Thus, developing a symptom, such as anxiety, in a particular setting may be characteristic of an individual; thus the symptom is similar to a character trait, especially if it is part of a chronic state of being on guard. Moreover, character traits are sometimes ego-alien: "I am this way and I am very unhappy about it. I suffer from it and wish I were different but cannot change." Certain symptoms, especially those of a compulsive nature, may be rationalized with the utmost tenacity and emerge only late in an analysis.

The breadth of what is included under the rubric "character" is enormous—in fact, the whole of the individual's stable functioning. Character traits describe ways of relating to people or reacting to situations or ways of being. A trait will include, or be significantly influenced by, defenses but is obviously more than a defense. It will bring together references to the person's moral system (whether dishonest, a cheat, or a liar), to his or her instinctual makeup (impulsive), basic temperament (cheerful, optimistic, or pessimistic), complex ego functions (humorous, perceptive, brilliant, or superstitious), and basic attitudes toward the world (kind, trustful, or skeptical) and him- or herself (hesitant). Whether to include affects, especially moods, in the concept of character is debatable. Moods are "generalized modifications of [affective] discharge patterns lend[ing] to our thoughts, actions, and above all our feelings a characteristic color" (Jacobson, 1964, p. 133). They resemble character traits in often being recurrent, stable, and chronic, however, and certainly may be an outstanding feature of the personality, particularly during certain developmental phases (for example, the typical moodiness or anger of the adolescent). Although certain traits will be more directly determined by one specific factor than others, most character traits represent an amalgam—a synthesis that expresses a combination of drive derivatives, defenses, identifications, and superego aspects.

CLASSIFICATION

The attempt to organize behavior patterns into character types on a descriptive level leaves much to be desired; there is considerable heterogeneity within each group. Character typologies are determined by the theoretical point of view of the observer. There are several vantage points from which to evaluate character: descriptive, dynamic, functional, adaptational, and structural. The task is rendered difficult, however, by the fact that, as previously mentioned, character does not occupy a well-defined place on the continuum between health and pathology. However, since both psychiatry and psychoanalysis focus on the abnormal, classification has tended to evolve from work with character disorders. These are made up of groupings of chronic maladaptive patterns that are inflexible in nature and without subjective discomfort. Yet abnormality may not be correlated with successful adaptation; narcissistic traits reflecting severe pathology may not interfere with achievement, whereas shyness or feelings of inferiority associated with higher-level conflicts may be extremely crippling. The sociocultural setting in which a given behavior occurs will also influence whether it is judged to be abnormal; but both internal and external factors must be considered, since internal strength and autonomy may lead to rebellion rather than conforming behavior.

It is also typical of character disorders that complaints may arise that are secondary to the consequences of pathological behavior rather than due to the character traits themselves. The pathological behavior is often diffused through everyday life and so heavily rationalized that an observer is misled about the unconscious dynamic elements. These factors add to the difficulty of arriving at a satisfactory classification.

Fenichel (1945) devised several approaches but was clearly dissatisfied with his efforts. He first divided traits into those that are all-pervasive versus those that arise only in certain situations. Second, he distinguished those traits that express an attitude of avoidance (phobic) versus those that oppose an original impulse (reaction formations). Finally, he distinguished pathological behavior resulting from the ego's conflict with the id, with the superego, and reality. Of these three approaches to classification, the first is based on a descriptive level of observation, the second on inferences about defensive mechanisms (a dynamic viewpoint), and the third on structural concepts. The multiple points of view contributing to the psychoanalytic study of character are reflected in the confused nomenclature found in the literature. There are libidinal types (for example, oral and anal characters), types based on modes of relating to objects (passive-feminine character), and those named after the type of neurotic or psychotic organization (phobic, hysterical; borderline, schizoid, psychotic).

Some terms are derived from the partial instincts and perversions: the histrionic, exhibitionistic, sadistic, and masochistic. Study of the superego has led indirectly to a description of certain types albeit with no attempt at formal classification: for example, "exceptions" or "those wrecked by success" (Alexander's "fate neurosis"). Likewise, interest in affects and object relations has led to other types, such as the depressive and "as-if" characters. Clearly not all these types are on the same level of abstraction. Waelder (1958) coined the term "character neuroses" to describe character disorders that are similar in organization to neuroses. This designation reflects the fact that whereas neurosis is characterized by discrete symptoms, in character disorders the entire personality is involved in the neurotic conflict, including those ego functions determining tolerance of frustration, drive regulation, affective responses, and object relationships. But the compromise formations resolving conflict are often so integrated as to be adaptive and only vaguely disturbing, so that there is little motivation for change. Hence in some instances "character neurosis" refers to what is essentially an asymptomatic neurosis. For a more detailed description of the various types, listed separately, see Moore and Fine, eds., 1990.

CHARACTER, FANTASY, AND OBJECT RELATIONS

Since character is a global, all-inclusive concept, its component parts provide many different ways of describing it. Determinants include defenses, instincts, identifications, and reactions to trauma. While each of these can be viewed as a relevant component, a more comprehensive, all-inclusive approach to understanding character is possible by considering it in relation to object relations and fantasy. Fantasies are compromise formations that, once formed, become part of the mental organization affecting a wide variety of behaviors and determining the form they take. A particular fantasy can influence more than one trait—in fact, it can color an entire character. Conversely, a particular trait may be the outcome of more than one unconscious fantasy. In an earlier pa-

per (1984) I suggested that many character traits or attitudes can be seen as the enactment of certain unconscious expectations the person has about him- or herself, the world at large (objects), and how he or she should be treated. These fantasies, often involving a self representation and an object representation, are the dramatization of a scenario relating to some past crucial relationship. The superego is a prime example of the internalization of a very specialized relation to the parents' values and expectations, one that contributes to the formation of sublimatory character traits.

A number of character traits have as one of their aims the evocation of a complementary response from others. Sometimes the wished-for interaction is a way of maintaining an object tie with an infantile object—occasionally the only way out of a particular dilemma confronting a child, even though the trait in question appears maladaptive or undesirable. Thus, nagging might be the only way to maintain a link with an emotionally unavailable mother. As will be clarified in the section on development, however, one of the major tasks facing the child is how to adapt to the demands of external objects more powerful than him- or herself without sacrificing any more than necessary of his or her own wishes and goals. One of the most powerful ways to solve it is through a process of identification with positive attributes of the parents, which plays a central role in fostering development of the nondefensive aspects of character.

A considerable part of an analysis is devoted to the understanding of the child's evolving identifications with aspects of his parents' behaviors and attitudes. We carefully try to reconstruct both the experience of the child at the time and the meaning of the parental attitude as a function of the child's conflicts and developmental stage. The shifting and combining of these identifications, which internalize an object relations scenario of varying complexity, is predominantly the work of the ego. According to Kernberg (1976), character is a manifestation of the organization of basic units, which he sees as including affective state, object representation, and self representation. It is the outcome of identificatory processes leading to internalized object relations. These are then stabilized and become character patterns. Thus, in Kernberg's view, character can be seen as structured object relations.

THE CONCEPT OF CHARACTER ORGANIZATION

From observable behavior, we isolate recurrent stable modes of reaction and attitudes, from which we deduce character traits. These are found in individuals in recurrent clusters, with a degree of consistency suggesting that some underlying principles govern the selection, ordering, and relations of traits to one another. When recurrent clusters of character traits have been identified, they form the basis for a classification of character types, which may then be examined to arrive at general principles that account for the origins, existence, and structure of character as a whole. These principles may be referred to as "character organization."

For character to become a psychoanalytic concept, it is necessary to bring in our traditional metapsychological points of view (dynamic, structural, economic, adaptive, and genetic). We also need to relate character to the traditional concepts of our theory: the drives, conflict, defense, resistance, the dynamic unconscious, and the principle of multiple function (Baudry, 1989). The metapsychological points of view are so interrelated, however, that it is difficult, if not impossible, to discuss them separately. The subheadings below, therefore, do not reflect absolute distinctions but rather the ways in which these points of view about character organization have come to be associated in my flow of thought.

Structural and Economical Considerations

To begin with, our grouping of stable behaviors and attitudes (character traits) into character types appears purely descriptive. The constellation is clearly not a structure or an agency like, for instance, the ego; that is, it does not have energy at its disposal and does not influence or control anything. One cannot ascribe causal effects to it; nor does it have explanatory value as such. The ego, by contrast, was defined by Freud (1923) as a cohesive organization whose function it is to synthesize the demands of the id, the superego, and reality. While outlining the process of character formation is one way of describing how that synthesis takes place, it is certainly not the only way. And character is not the means of the synthesis but rather the resultant of many ego functions. If this distinction is not made, functions ascribed to the ego may be inappropriately attributed to character.

It is true, however, that the formation of a character trait is an attempt to solve the multiple problems confronting the ego—how to reconcile the conflicting demands of the instincts, the superego, and the outside world. Through character development, intersystemic balance is established. The concept of structure implies stability. The stability of character may be thought of along the axes of rigidity/flexibility or autonomy. Rigidity refers to a person's inability to alter his or her behavior even when

circumstances would make a change appropriate or adaptive. It may be related to stubbornness and should be differentiated from persistence, though such a distinction has to include a subjective element.

The anal character, historically the earliest described and also the simplest and most clearly defined, is useful in demonstrating how a relatively simple organization of three traits grew in complexity and came to include many of the core concepts in analysis related to character—instinct, defense, identification, aggression, superego, perception, memory, autonomous functions, narcissism, and trauma. Freud's 1908 paper also included the basic elements of a theory of the mind, including aspects of development, etiology, mental mechanisms (dynamics), and economics. It established a relationship between the behavioral traits of parsimony, obstinacy, and orderliness and the anal instinctual phase. Freud (1926) also showed that the behavioral attitudes from which the typical defense mechanisms in anal characters (isolation, reaction formation, undoing) are inferred also include drive manifestations. In addition, the cognitive style of patients of this type (memory, attention to detail) will be consonant with the interplay of drive and defense. We may also anticipate an unusually harsh superego functioning and difficulties (chiefly inhibitions) with direct expression of aggression. These widely divergent aspects of functioning are dynamically related to one another. In the case of obstinacy, the basic ingredients include vicissitudes of aggression toward an object resolved via the internalization of an early childhood object relationship and the incorporation of both drive and defense aspects. On this level, then, character is a convenient and appropriate way of grouping many different attributes under one label.

It is said that character itself binds, unifies, and saves cathectic energy by achieving a once-and-for-all solution to a conflict that then becomes frozen. This statement attributes to character an energic aspect that properly belongs to the ego, however; character cannot both effect a synthesis and be the result of the synthesis at the same time. The secondary autonomy of character, which can also be described in terms of relative stability or instability, refers both to the end stage of a developmental process leading to relative independence from conflict and to the protection of character against instinctualization and regression; but these processes are reciprocal. Once established, the formation of character makes repression less necessary, particularly in instances in which the conflict is no longer active. The latter may result from the person deciding to abandon certain pursuits. For example, a man with a passive-feminine character may resign himself to not trying to establish a relationship with a woman. The energy of the warded-off instinctual impulses is used in the maintenance of the anticathexis—the defense that becomes rigidified in the character trait. Character is another way we have of talking about fixation. An individual may be forced to make choices because of who he or she is and what he or she is like; in that sense, character is a limitation on the selection of options by the ego. These qualities of character give it an indirect, dynamic, organizing influence, even though we do not conceptualize it as having an energy of its own.

The protection against destabilization afforded by character formation is relative, not absolute. Some patients have a tendency to regress considerably under states of stress, fatigue, or illness. I prefer to view such regression as a behavior change reflecting certain aspects of the character makeup rather than a true character change based on a modification of some deeper structure.

Dynamic Point of View: Character, Symptom, Conflict, and Defense

Frustration and conflict, whether intrasystemic, intersystemic, or with an external agent, make major contributions to the formation of both symptoms and character. Although conflict influences the content, quality, and nature of the end result, the process of character formation itself is a normal outcome of maturation and development. Jacobson (1964) has described the resolution of the oedipal struggle and its effects on the ego and budding superego identifications. She points out that this process succeeds in excluding a considerable sector of memories from the preconscious and conscious mind. Consequently, the object and self representations that emerge as the infantile psychosexual conflicts subside bear the imprint of the exclusion as well as of the counter-cathectic ego formations that safeguard the results of infantile repression. It is quite likely that character formation plays a particularly important role in this development, since it allows for and often promotes a nonsymptomatic mode of conflict resolution, depending on ego and superego identifications. Clinical experience certainly suggests that the conflicts which are resolved through the formation of character traits are for the most part totally outside the realm of consciousness. It could be said that character depends on the development of interpersonal strategies for avoiding or minimizing internal conflict, both inter- and intrasystemic, a fact of considerable adaptive value.

Once formed, a character trait may influence many other traits or contribute to symptoms as the ego struggles with it. A person who is stingy will, if called upon to be generous, develop anger or anxiety or will rationalize and flee from the situation altogether. Except in rare circumstances, he or she will not be able to avoid acting out his or her customary beliefs and attitudes. If not, he or she will be said to be acting "out of character," exhibiting behavior that requires explanation, since character implies a degree of predictability of behavior. It is possible that the person may at some point be ashamed of his or her stinginess and attempt to hide it through reactive generosity, or he or she may develop guilty reactions or self-punitive attitudes or even a compulsive symptom.

How do character and symptom differ economically from one another? It is often said that the former is a fixed, relatively frozen attitude that, once established, does not require renewed expenditure of psychic energy to maintain. Yet character is not necessarily a "once-and-for-all resolution." To add to the complexity, the differences between character and symptom are not always distinct: certain traits may be structurally similar to symptoms; that is, they perform similar functions and, most important, are less pervasive of the entire mental apparatus than is true of other character traits. Excessive cleanliness, for example, is closer to neurosis in that it is anchored in similar fixation points and serves to ward off more limited conflicts than such traits as frankness or smugness, which seem to pervade the entire mental apparatus—something described less clumsily in character terms than in id, ego, and superego terms.

Traits such as shyness and withdrawal from competitive situations are closer to symptoms or inhibitions. Based on their stability and repetitiveness, such traits would seem to belong to character. They are a result of exhibitionistic conflicts that remain unresolved, painfully experienced, and dynamically active in the present. It would follow that not all character traits minimize the conflict they were meant to resolve. When this conflict is still active in the person, unhappiness or other symptoms may follow.

The contribution of pregenitality to character was overemphasized in the early days of analysis, in contrast to the emphasis on regression from oedipal conflicts in the case of symptoms. Freud originally thought that sublimation and reaction formation acted primarily against pregenital drives, especially sadism and anality. Initially, he regarded a symptom as a relatively simple structure —a compromise between a drive and a defense; likewise, character traits were oversimplified as a particular type of transformation of a drive vicissitude. The principle of multiple function has obviously broadened our outlook on the many influences that play a significant role in relation to every product of mental functioning.

The relation between character and defense is a particularly close one, both descriptively and genetically. Traditionally, we are accustomed to thinking of anxiety as the main stimulus to defense, but as Brenner (1982) has pointed out, other painful affects such as anger and depression also play a role. More recently, much attention has been devoted to so-called narcissistic defenses around issues of shame, embarrassment, and the maintenance of self-esteem. The coping styles adopted by the child to deal with these distressing affects significantly influences his or her evolving sense of self and character formation. From a descriptive point of view, the structuralization of defense patterns is a major determinant of the emerging character trait. For example, a patient who relies heavily on the mechanism of projection can develop several behavior patterns, allowing one to infer different character traits. His or her readiness to blame the other person may lead him or her to be paranoid, suspicious, pugnacious, hostile, vindictive, or inquisitive, analytic, or curious, depending on many factors, including the underlying fantasy that is expressed and the fate of the aggressive drive, including its degree of neutralization.

In regard to the last-named factor, the lack of an adequate developmental theory of aggression limits our understanding of the role of this drive in early character formation. Normal and pathological identifications may be intensified by fear of object loss due to an aggressive conflict. Certain character traits relate specifically to vicissitudes of aggression; masochistic character receives its stamp from a turning of aggression back onto the self, often in part as a solution to conflicts involving guilt. The more severe character disorders involve vicissitudes of aggression to a greater extent than the benign disorders. Finally, aggression, like sexuality, has to be understood as a manifest content; it may serve a variety of aims, some nonaggressive—for example, the screening out of sexual derivatives. Hence, behavioral manifestations of aggression should not necessarily be equated with the aggressive drive.

The Genetic Point of View and the Development of Character

When does character formation begin? This is largely a matter of definition. The newborn infant shows patterns of behavior that clearly differentiate him or her from other newborns, but its organization is primitive, and its intent and meaning cannot be evaluated. The behavioral schema are prestructural. Instead of viewing character formation as beginning at birth or even *in utero* and developing in very slow increments, I believe that it is more useful to say that character formation is a specific developmental step which has its onset some time during latency and, under normal circumstances, is more or less completed in late adolescence. It would add clarity to our conceptualization if we were to regard the earlier phenomena as "prestages," analogous to the well-recognized prestages of superego formation. Clinical evidence suggests that a considerable level of ego development, including the capacity for neutralization, identification, internalization, self–object differentiation, and ideal formation, is necessary before one can consider a stable, well-defined character to be formed. The establishment and integration of these capacities does not occur before the resolution of the oedipal complex in early latency, and a final reworking of character development takes place during adolescence. Ordinarily, character formation hinges on a felicitous resolution of the oedipal complex, while departure from ideal resolution can lead to a whole gamut of pathology—symptoms, abnormal character traits, and perversions. There are notable exceptions to this chronology, however, in instances in which the ego is confronted by early fixations in the pregenital phase. In these cases, very stable reaction formations may occur and become an integral part of character, leading to rigid character traits and attitudes that are resistant to the pressures of later developmental stages. Yet, while certain rigid obsessional adults develop from fearful, rigid, obsessional children, some do not, and few children with obsessional symptoms go on to develop obsessional character as adults. Apparently diametrically opposite to this rigid patterning, other individuals develop unstable, shifting, or chaotic characters, but with a certain degree of predictability in their impulsivity or lack of reliability. Yet these outcomes are not inevitable.

The time of completion of the process of character formation is uncertain, but there is general agreement that character formation cannot be said to be completed before the conflict resolution of the adolescent period. The steps in such resolution have been described only incompletely thus far (Blos, 1968). There seems little doubt, too, that subsequent life experiences, both good and bad, contribute to change of lesser degree in some aspects of character structure, though the core manifestations remain stable.

In his summary of the genesis of character, Arlow (1960) describes a substrate including the biological endowments (inborn tendencies) and the infant's earliest experiences of gratification of instinctual needs. These influence the ways in which the child learns to master his or her primitive sexual and aggressive impulses, as well as the tempering effects of experiences, especially of sorrow (including loss) and humiliation. Innate factors influencing the outcome, such as constitution, strength of drives, and stimulus barrier, have to be inferred. Temperament and other natural endowments such as anatomy, sex, appearance (including height), beauty, race, and the like may play a more obvious role, but the only feature that has predictive value seems to be the amount of activity (Fries et al., 1935). There are hardly any character traits that are not influenced by the instincts, and Emde's (1988) work shows that patterns of emotionality remain fairly stable from early on, although influenced of course by the environment.

The developmental factors include the normal unfolding of maturational sequences, along with possible developmental lags or out-of-phase advances (for example, precocious intellectual development in obsessional characters). They also include fixations and regression. The compulsion to repeat, characteristic of the transference, the play of children, traumatic dreams, and the fate neurosis, may have a constitutional basis or may result from influences in the very early stages of development. In either event this repetition compulsion imposes certain limitations on the range of possible character types and the content of certain basic attitudes. These attitudes (for example, aloofness) are often preconflictual and may be beyond analytic resolution. On the other hand, Hartmann (1952) explores in detail the nonconflictual, autonomous factors that play a role in shaping the outcome of conflict and the development of certain defense mechanisms. As he points out, certain character traits may develop independently of conflicts or be influenced by them only minimally. Mahler (1979) has given support to this view by delineating phases in the separation-individuation process from a perspective outside the domain of conflict.

Although the role of environmental factors is the special purview of psychoanalysis, the analytic approach has tended to favor investigation of the one-to-one relationship and has lagged behind in studying the relevance and detailed influence of family (group) processes on character formation. Because of his or her immaturity and normal dependency needs, the child is easily cast in the role of scapegoat or as the carrier of the parents' unconscious inferiority feelings. The effect on the child's character depends on whether he or she accepts the role as-signed, rebels against it, or is able to form alliances with one parent against the other. Another approach to understanding the influence of the family has been to study the family's general or preferred mode of conflict resolution, which becomes a model for the child. There may be a dissociative type of family interaction in which one part of the family remains strong as long as another part is weak or sickly. Denial, masochistic or paranoid formations, and phobic mechanisms may also characterize defensive styles of families. The child's defensive style is determined by the compromises he or she effects as conflicting identifications are reconciled under the pressure of the group and its individual members. Among the methods the ego utilizes to achieve conflict resolution, identification plays a central role, including identification with the aggressor, and turning passivity into activity may become the child's means of coping with his or her relative smallness and helplessness.

There are obviously many other motives for identification, not all of them necessarily pathological, although it would be difficult to find one that is not in some way involved with conflict. The other basic principle of character (or, for that matter, symptom) formation is the principle of multiple function. There is a tendency within the mind to find the most adaptive solution among those available. Each new phase of development presents the ego with a series of challenges that need to be mastered. The challenges multiply in complexity as the child matures and are understood and colored by the libidinal phase active at the time. Erikson has built one possible model; to take an example, he points out the importance of the acquisition of locomotion in the middle of the anal phase and of speech in the oral phase. For identification to occur, there are certain prerequisites: the development of an ego apparatus separate enough from its object, with appropriate inner/outer boundaries to perceive (not necessarily consciously) the qualities of the other.

In attempting to depict the genesis of specific traits, analytic work may enable us to describe retrospectively the meanings of the choice of a particular solution by tracing the history of the transformation of the drive processes, the defenses chosen, and the principal existing identifications and traumas being dealt with at the time of the emergence of the trait in question. Nevertheless, it is not easy to explain why a person chooses to identify with certain traits of the parents and not others. To understand the process of such identifications, the meaning of the behaviors of the parent at the time the identification took place has to be reconstructed. Superficially, similar traits will have different functions and meanings in parent and child; certain meanings, however, may be shared. A given trait—for example, being overly willing to do one's share of work—may be ideally suited to handling guilty feelings or discharging aggression on the self, for both parent and child. At other times, the child's efforts may be directed to not being like the parent.

The process of character formation, the backbone of the theory, remains incompletely understood. We can describe certain mechanisms (for example, ego and superego identifications, reaction formations, and sublimations) as well as certain requirements, antecedents, and influences that will modify the end result—constitution, trauma, early experiences with the mother (for example, the way a misfit between mother and child will warp or influence the budding processes). However, we still lack a basic organizational scheme and timetable except as an extrapolation from the abnormal.

CHARACTER AND INFANTILE NEUROSIS

The relation between character development and infantile neurosis is complicated. Examined from a metapsychological standpoint, the adaptive resolution of the infantile neurosis is followed by the formation of a stable ego ideal and superego, which ultimately leads to stabilization of character traits. But this statement does not explain how a neurotic character emerges as a solution to a childhood neurosis or the relation between the neurotic symptoms and character in the adult. After two or three years of age, the immature ego of the child will attempt to take certain defensive measures against anxiety. If the immediate response fails, a symptom may develop. Should a chronically stressful situation persist (for example, the child being confronted with incompatible demands over long periods of time), the resultant permanent ego deformation will result in a compromise formation of a different order. It may be that ongoing developmental processes of maturation will then be devoted to overcoming the neurotic symptoms and the conflicts that gave rise to them. The unconscious fantasy that earlier gave rise to a symptom now finds expression in a character trait. As an example, a boy's fear of his father and the related castration anxiety may be dealt with first by an animal phobia and later by the development of a submissive/masochistic attitude to authority figures with the accompanying fantasy: "There is no need to castrate me; I will behave as though I am already castrated." Other responses (solutions), involving either different character traits or psychopathology such as acting out, are possible outcomes. In this de-

velopmental schema, character trait formation is an attempt to deal with a conflict that was inadequately resolved through symptom formation. Conversely, a symptom may represent the inability of a character structure to master a particular conflict. An example is the case of a student with a character trait that demanded that she do everything perfectly, based in part on competition with her outwardly more successful siblings and in part on a wish to replace her mother with her father. Her guilt over these wishes was manifested in self-destructive behavior, and her lack of success in her social life led to considerable turmoil and an inability to concentrate on her work. Allegedly to help her study better, she began to recopy her class notes, an occupation that began to take over her life, consuming many hours and taking up time she needed to study for tests.

We have limited knowledge about the conditions that favor the emergence of symptoms rather than character traits. Loewald (1978) has suggested that if a behavior pattern of a child meets parental disapproval, it is more likely to give rise to a symptom. If conflicts in a family are brought out into the open and confronted, symptoms are more likely to emerge than in situations in which the resolution is nonverbal, the latter instance favoring the development of character traits. It is also true that certain defense mechanisms, such as reaction formation, predispose to the development of character traits.

The relation between character and symptomatology in the adult is complex. Either one can be a defense against the other. Arlow (1960) cites the example of a character change undertaken in order to avoid a phobia. In other instances, as noted above, symptoms may express the inability of a character structure to master or resolve a particular conflict. The presence of symptoms is not necessarily indicative of a poor prognosis, however. In fact, quite the opposite may be the case (Glover, 1926). Analysis of a character trait may lead to anxiety, to some other affect, or to symptom formation, suggesting that these are alternative and alternating means of attempting to deal with conflict.

CHARACTER AND ADAPTATION

Descriptively, character traits are stable attitudes typical of a particular individual and generally related to a modification within the ego—not infrequently an impairment or restriction of its flexibility. As demonstrated in the preceding discussion, these impairments are in the nature of compromise formations—attempts by the ego to come to terms longitudinally with multiple developmental challenges and cross-sectionally with drive elements, repetition compulsion, and the demands of external reality and of the superego. Most, though not all, are the outcome of psychic conflict. As such, they are in the service of adaptation, since they achieve a stability that contributes to our sense of continuity in time and to our sense of identity. Character formation serves other positive adaptive functions as well. It is the means whereby the ego incorporates and integrates elements of infantile sexuality that have been excluded, for one reason or another, from gratification or expression and are not otherwise dealt with by sublimation or repressed. In the process a limited gratification is achieved.

The concept of adaptation also involves the person's relation to external reality. A given character trait often represents the best possible solution in a particular situation. A submissive attitude may, for example, serve the purpose of maintaining an otherwise jeopardized object relationship with a controlling parent. Character participates in broad areas of a person's functioning, relating to both internal and external factors, including the qualities of masculinity and femininity, choices of life-style, and even gender identity. Qualities such as persistence, hard work, optimism, warmth, and openness are in part derived from identification with related traits in parents but contribute significantly to occupational goals and the achievements of a relatively happy and contented life.

CHARACTER RESISTANCE AND CHARACTER ANALYSIS

Most of the daily work of the analyst involves some analysis of character, but few guidelines have been advanced as to how and when to explore and interpret character traits. Glover (1926) remarked that subjecting the seemingly banal routine of everyday life to detailed scrutiny is the surest way of conducting an analysis of character. It is hard to improve on this simple principle enunciated more than fifty years ago. Often, however, the patient experiences such attempts as a confrontation and feels criticized, derogated, even humiliated. Character has narcissistic value for the patient—"This is me"—and is something to be proud of and carefully guarded. It should not be surprising, therefore, that our efforts to analyze ego-syntonic character traits meet with a remarkable degree of resistance.

Reich (1949) introduced the term "character resistance" to refer to certain stereotypic, formal aspects of general behavior, "the manner of talking, of the gait, facial expression and typical attitudes such as

smiling, deriding haughtiness, overcorrectness, the manner of the politeness or of the aggression. [These resistances] remain the same no matter what the material is against which it is directed" (p. 47). While it is true that character resistances also arise in reaction to earlier experiences with significant persons, by contrast with transference resistances they are general, diffuse responses to people at large and to dangers emanating from the patient's inner world of conflict. People are treated indiscriminately, as though they are all the same. These stubborn character resistances represent static residues of conflict, though some may still be active.

By character analysis, Reich had in mind the single-minded pursuit of the hidden characterologically-based resistances of the patient, always of a negative nature, which had to be mercilessly rooted out and aggressively confronted early in treatment in order to avoid stalemated or affectless analysis. Reich used as a point of entry the bodily manifestations of such hidden attitudes—postural rigidities and speech mannerisms or patterns, making up what he termed the "character armor." His merciless focus on aggression appears one-sided and excessive. Analysis of character traits often leads to states of anxiety and transient symptom formation as the rigid conflict is remobilized. There is considerable uncertainty as to when and how these attitudes should be tackled. Art as well as science is required, and each practitioner must develop his or her own personal style and approach.

The relation of character to analyzability is complicated. It is possible, of course, to describe the more obvious obstacles to analysis in terms of either traits (impulsivity, tendency to act out, inability to tolerate frustration, unreliability, excessive passivity, dishonesty) or various ego and superego functions. Traits are closer to clinical observation and hence easier to evaluate. Certain global qualities facilitating analysis, such as psychological-mindedness or motivation, depend in part on the presence of certain character traits (curiosity, willingness to wait, tolerance). There are also certain attitudes such as the inability to tolerate shame, embarrassment, or criticism which vastly complicate our task. The most difficult character traits to deal with are related to the hidden or latent resistances described by Glover (1955). The patient will very subtly distort the analytic process, or the analyst will become numbed to the destructive effect of certain chronic attitudes. A patient may seemingly accept interpretations while maintaining inner doubt and skepticism. The flexibility of his or her character has been seriously impaired, limiting the development of nondefensive self-observation. The more disturbed the patient, the more careful and detailed the initial evaluation must be in order to rule out unsuitable patients and to avoid exposing the person to a traumatic situation that he or she will not be able to handle.

What promotes the emergence of a particular character response in a patient? Clearly some aspect of the conflict to which the character is a solution must be touched upon at the moment. The character of the analyst (his or her attitudes and behavior) and the major transference paradigms will also play a role in determining which traits are used as resistances at any particular moment. In turn, the unfolding of the transference will be influenced by the patient's character structure. There is general agreement that for analytic work to be productive, character resistances must be changed into transference resistances. The readiness to share one's private thoughts, the dread of closeness, the capacity to trust, and the fear of letting go are all basic attitudes profoundly affecting the course of treatment and its feasibility.

What is the relationship between character and the transference neurosis? Although historically the latter concept was developed to describe the substitution or creation *de novo* in the analysis of an entity replacing the original neurosis, some of the more recent writings do not stress this replacement aspect. This is understandable for neurosis, since a new symptom or a new edition of an old one (for example, temporary impotence), may be a sign of an emerging transference neurosis. But I believe that neurosis does not exist apart from a corresponding character structure, and the transference "character disorder" is a reenactment with the analyst of certain neurotic character traits. Which specific traits become reactivated in the transference neurosis is a complex question. The patient is no longer struggling with his or her parents but with a person who adopts and presents certain attitudes for therapeutic purposes, refusing to be drawn into reenactments of the patient's wishes or fears. This refusal facilitates the emergence of certain attitudes and fantasies. The transference neurosis, then, is a compromise formation, involving the patient's reaction to the multiple aspects, both positive and negative, of the analyst's behavior and its intrapsychic meanings for the patient in the present.

There is disagreement in the literature about the timing of the emergence of the transference neurosis and what promotes its appearance. Some patients with character disorders may undergo a successful analysis without dramatic manifestations of a classical transference neurosis.

If we accept character as the behavioral expres-sion of certain unconscious fantasies, then for true character change to occur, a different attitude toward some of these fantasies must emerge within the patient, and the fantasies must lose some of their pathogenic influence. An individual in a typical danger situation that provokes some characteristic pathological response must be able at some point to halt, step back, and choose some more appropriate response. But the change need not be total, and it is often of a quantitative rather than a qualitative nature. An obsessional patient in analysis will never become a hysteric, no matter how long he or she is treated. However, such a patient will become less rigid, better able to enjoy him- or herself, more giving, less worrisome, and so on. Such quantitative change may make the difference between being a miserable human being and a relatively happy one.

Implied in the above, however, is the idea that some types of traits remain relatively impervious to analysis. It seems to me that those traits that are more firmly rooted in the person's constitution or basic instinctual makeup—that is, those belonging to a preconflict period—are more resistant to change than those based on identifications with early parental figures. Freud observed that the prognosis for masochistic character was better when the masochism was the result of an identification with a masochistic parent. Characteristics related to a person's temperament are probably more fixed than those which are the outcome of conflicts. A slow-to-warm-up child may turn into a somewhat distant, aloof adult with limited capacity to change this basic orientation. Pathology rooted in earlier conflicts and trauma is generally considered more resistant to structural change. Certain character types are more flexible than others; rigidity is more commonly encountered in obsessional than in hysterical characters. A trait that arises in reaction to a specific situation is more likely to be flexible and amenable to change than one that encompasses broader issues. Conflicts around ambition are often difficult to resolve. Certain oral character traits related to the need to be needed often respond well to analysis, better than certain anally-rooted traits, thus contradicting the hypothesis that traits deriving from earlier life phases are more stubbornly rooted and therefore more resistant to change.

SUMMARY AND CONCLUSIONS

I have discussed character on two levels: descriptively, as a clinical concept close to the data of observation, and abstractly, as the stable psychic organization achieved as a result of compromise formation in conflict resolution. The traits that collectively constitute character are patterns of attitudes and behavior that are consistent and specific for a given individual; as typical ways of functioning, they imply neither health nor pathology but may be adaptive or maladaptive. Classification of types has tended primarily to categorize behavior judged by an observer in a particular sociocultural setting to be pathological.

If one were to attempt to list the sequence of developmental challenges in relation to character formation, the list would have to include all the vicissitudes of drive formation and all the well-known mechanisms of defense, but a special role would have to be allotted to identification. Character traits can be viewed as the enactment of unconscious expectations the person has about him- or herself, objects, and how he or she should be treated. They often represent the internalization of a very specialized relation to parents and others, accomplished by means of complex identifications. The integrative process of character organization is not completed until the major ego and superego identifications are established, and this does not occur until the resolution of the adolescent phase. When such stabilization does not occur, severely chaotic character traits appear.

In an earlier paper (1983) I listed the major determinants of character as developed by Freud. These comprise character as (1) derivative of libidinal drives (we would now add aggressive drives as well); (2) reflecting the influence on behavior of certain unconscious fantasies, often the product of masturbation (for example, a child is being beaten); (3) identification with significant adults; (4) the outgrowth of solutions to critical complexes (castration and the oedipus complex); (5) influenced by constitution and (6) defense, through certain mechanisms of mental functioning (denial, projection, reaction formation, introjection, displacement); (7) reaction to traumas (positive and negative); (8) conflicts subsequent to superego formation and (9) conflicts resulting from attempts to deal with an infantile neurosis or an early ego distortion. The latter factors are generally more inclusive than the earlier ones listed and are a testimony to the growing complexity of psychoanalytic theory.

In the same paper I attempted to order the above list sequentially. Clearly, constitution and the drives are the bedrock. These are influenced by interaction with significant adults largely (but not entirely) through mechanisms of identification. This interaction can be described along several different axes, such as the organizing effect of unconscious fantasies. Another, implying a developmental thrust, would be the resolution of the major complexes

(castration and the oedipus complex), relying on certain preferred mechanisms for defense. The most advanced factor developmentally is the superego. Trauma combines both accidental factors and an economic point of view. Finally, as preferred solutions lead to neurosis or ego distortions, character formation must integrate these disturbances.

On a more abstract level, character organization represents the way individual traits are amalgamated into a complex structure. Clearly it is difficult to predict the outcome of a complex interaction of ego functioning—defensive, adaptive, and integrative. It is easier to study the component roots of discrete character traits. The inclusive concept of character as a whole may be studied from several different angles, however, and I have suggested object relations as a particularly useful one, since identificatory processes lead to internalized object relations and, stabilized, these become character traits. Character has also been described along various metapsychological axes, but we still lack a comprehensive developmental theory of character.

The explanatory value of the more abstract concept of character as an organization is limited, perhaps primarily because of its breadth. Since it includes almost all aspects of a person's stable functioning, its specific potential usefulness in analysis is diminished. Nevertheless, it does allow for a relation to be established between something close to behavior and a more abstract concept—a drive or a defense, to cite common examples. The clinical concept has several worthwhile applications. It is a key concept in our daily work, particularly in the areas of assessment of analyzability, diagnosis, and the understanding and working through of difficult resistances. As character traits are classified, analyzed, and understood, the patient becomes increasingly aware of his behavior patterns and is better able to control the obvious interferences and obstructions that have previously hampered his performance. Because of its capacity to effect significant modification in psychic structure, character analysis is a valuable conceptual tool for further theoretical and therapeutic work.

REFERENCES

Abraham, K. (1921). Contributions to the theory of the anal character. Rpt. In *Selected Papers of Karl Abraham,* pp. 370–392. London: Hogarth Press, 1948.

———. (1924). The influence of oral erotism on character-formation. Rpt. in *Selected Papers of Karl Abraham,* pp. 393–406. London: Hogarth Press, 1948.

———. (1925). Character-formation on the genital level of the libido. Rpt. in *Selected Papers of Karl Abraham*, pp. 407–417. London: Hogarth Press, 1948.

Arlow, J. A. (1960). Character and conflict. *J. Hillside Hosp.*, 15:140–150.

Baudry, F. D. (1983). The evolution of the concept of character in Freud's work. *J. Amer. Psychoanal. Assn.*, 31:3–32.

———. (1984). Character: a concept in search of an identity. *J. Amer. Psychoanal. Assn.*, 32:455–478.

———. (1989). Character, character type, and character organization. *J. Amer. Psychoanal. Assn.*, 37:655–686.

Blos, P. (1968). Character formation in adolescence. *Psychoanal. Study Child*, 23:245–263.

Brenner, C. (1982). *The Mind in Conflict*. New York: Int. Univ. Press.

Emde, R. N. (1988). Development terminable and interminable: I. *Int. J. Psychoanal.*, 69:23–42.

Erikson, E. H. (1956). The problem of ego identity. *J. Amer. Psychoanal. Assn.*, 4:56–121.

Fenichel, O. (1945). *The Psychoanalytic Theory of Neurosis*. New York: Norton.

Freud, A. (1936). *The Ego and the Mechanisms of Defense*. In *Writings of Anna Freud*, vol. 2. Rev. ed. New York: Int. Univ. Press, 1966.

Freud, S. (1908). Character and anal erotism. *SE*, 9:167–175.

———. (1916). Some character-types met with in psycho-analytic work. *SE*, 14:309–336.

———. (1923). *The Ego and the Id. SE*, 19:3–66.

———. (1926). *Inhibitions, Symptoms and Anxiety. SE*, 20:77–175.

Fries, M. E., Brokaw, K., & Murray, V. F. (1935). The formation of character as observed in the well baby clinic. *Amer. J. Dis. Child.*, 49:28–42.

Frosch, J. (1969). The psychotic character. *Psychiat. Rev.*, 38:81–96.

Glover, E. (1926). The neurotic character. *Int. J. Psychoanal.*, 1:11–20.

———. (1955). *The Technique of Psychoanalysis*. New York: Int. Univ. Press.

Greenson, R. R. (1967). *Technique and Practice of Psychoanalysis*. New York: Int. Univ. Press.

Hartmann, H. (1939). *Ego Psychology and the Problem of Adaptation*. New York: Int. Univ. Press.

———. (1952). The mutual influences in the development of the ego and the id. In *Essays on Ego Psychology*, pp. 155–181. New York: Int. Univ. Press, 1964.

Jacobson, E. (1964). *The Self and the Object World*. New York: Int. Univ. Press.

Jones, E. (1918). Anal-erotic character traits. Rpt. in *Papers on Psychoanalysis*, pp. 413–437. London: Baillière, Tindall and Cox, 1948.

Kernberg, O. F. (1976). *Object Relations Theory and Clinical Psychoanalysis*. New York: Aronson.

Laughlin, H. (1956). *The Neuroses in Clinical Practice*. Philadelphia: W. B. Saunders.

Loewald, H. W. (1978). Instinct theory, object relations, and psychic structure formation. *J. Amer. Psychoanal. Assn.*, 26:493–506.

Lustman, S. (1962). Defense, symptom and character. *Psychoanal. Study Child*, 17:216–244.

Mahler, M. S. (1979). *Selected Papers*, vol. 2. New York: Aronson.

Moore, B. E., & Fine, B. D., eds. (1990). *Psychoanalytic Terms and Concepts*. New Haven: Yale Univ. Press.

Reich, W. (1949). *Character Analysis*. New York: Orgone Institute Press.

Rosen, V. H. (1961). The relevance of "style" to certain aspects of defence and the synthetic function of the ego. *Int. J. Psychoanal.*, 42:447–457.

Stein, M. H. (1969). The problem of character theory. *J. Amer. Psychoanal. Assn.*, 17:675–701.

Thomas, A., & Chess, S. (1977). *Temperament and Development*. New York: Brunner/Mazel.

Waelder, R. (1930). The principle of multiple function. Rpt. in *Psychoanalysis: Observation, Theory, Application*, ed. S. A. Guttman, pp. 68–83. New York: Int. Univ. Press, 1976.

———. (1958). Neurotic ego distortion. *Int. J. Psychoanal.*, 39:243–244.

Zetzel, E. R. (1968). The so-called good hysteric. *Int. J. Psychoanal.*, 49:216–260.

Jean Schimek and
Leo Goldberger

17

THOUGHT

Any specific definition of thinking implies a particular theory of thinking and a philosophical position about the nature of human knowledge. In a broad sense, thinking can encompass all mental activities —from perception to memory and concept formation—through which the individual constructs his or her experience of the world, of external and internal reality. It may be superfluous to observe that the concept of thinking is at the very center of any study of the nature of humanity, be it from a philosophical perspective with its focus on mind, a psychological perspective with its traditional emphasis on consciousness, or indeed from the standpoint of contemporary experimental analysis of behavior.

Rather than providing a capsule history of the relevant literature, which spans more than a millennium, we shall simply remind the reader of the broad currents in the writings on thinking. Fundamentally, one can discern two broad traditions or positions in the theoretical attempts to track the ultimate source of human ideas, thoughts, and images: the material-empiricist's position as contrasted with the idealist-nativist's position. These contrasting points of view have informed almost every element or aspect of any general theory of thought, such as the thinker's activity versus passivity, the degree of veridicality of the thoughts, and the related question of reason versus passion.

Flowing fairly directly from these contrasting positions is the distinction that has recurred and persisted since the days of Aristotle—namely, between a type of thinking under voluntary control, directed by the thinker's conscious purposes and intentions, and another type that is seemingly random, meaningless, and beyond the person's volitional control. It is in relation to this distinction that Freud's theory of primary- and secondary-process thought is situated, and it is on this issue that the theory has made its momentous impact, not only among psychoanalysts but far beyond the borders of the discipline. His novel explication of the traditional distinction between two modes of thought—the emphasis that Freud put on unconscious thinking processes and his thoroughgoing determinism (within which even the most insignificant-seeming, fleeting thought has meaning)—may be rightly viewed as the very hallmark of the Freudian revolution in the study of humanity.

Especially from a psychoanalytic point of view, a definition of thinking cannot be restricted to a consideration of logical reasoning and the manipulation of abstract symbols. Psychoanalysis focuses on thinking in its more subjective, irrational aspects and uses symptoms, fantasies, dreams, and memories as its primary data. Psychoanalysis is primarily interested in drives, desires, and conflicts as the unconscious regulators and organizers of thought. What for traditional approaches is falsehood and distortion is for psychoanalysis the "royal road to the unconscious," to psychic reality, to some of the basic

209

motives, goals, and organizing forces of the individual.

FREUD

The core concepts of Freud's theory of thinking are part of the theoretical model of the quantitative, mechanistic functioning of a mental apparatus. This model was presented in 1900, in chapter 7 of *The Interpretation of Dreams,* but had already been spelled out in greater detail in the never published "Project for a Scientific Psychology" (1895) at a time when most of Freud's clinical discoveries and formulations were yet to come. Freud's concepts reflect two specific influences. The first is his clinical investigations of the 1890s, which led to the interpretation and explanation of neurotic symptoms and dreams as disguised, transformed expressions of repressed memories from the past. The second involves many aspects of Freud's intellectual and cultural background, ranging from the neurological approach of Helmholz and Brücke, with its goal of explaining mental processes in terms of physical forces and energies (see Amacher, 1965) to association psychology, as well as the philosophies of Schopenhauer and Nietzsche, with their emphasis on the irrational "will" of sexual and power drives as organizers of thought.

The essential elements of Freud's theory of thinking as presented in 1900 remained basically unchanged in his later writings. Thus his views on thinking remained relatively unintegrated with the changes he made in other aspects of his theory, particularly the new tripartite model of the mental apparatus and its relation to the conscious–unconscious distinction and the increasing emphasis on universal unconscious fantasies as basic organizers of thought (for a later attempt at integration, see Arlow & Brenner, 1964).

On the issue of the relation between mind and brain, between a psychological and a neurological framework, Freud maintained a position of psychophysical parallelism, at least in principle. Referring to the relation in his last writing on the subject (1940), he said: "Everything that lies between is unknown to us, and the data do not include any direct relation between these two terminal points of our knowledge. If it existed, it would at the most afford an exact localization of the processes of consciousness and would give us no help towards understanding them" (pp. 144–145). Yet in many of Freud's formulations, from the *Interpretation of Dreams* to the *Outline of Psycho-Analysis,* we find neurological concepts (innervations, memory traces, nervous energy) intermingled with psychological ones.

THE PRIMARY PROCESS: HALLUCINATORY WISH FULFILLMENT, CONDENSATION, AND DISPLACEMENT

In Freud's basic model, thinking is originally in the service of the pleasure principle, the tendency of the apparatus to discharge stimulation or tension in the quickest way possible. In principle, the quickest path toward such discharge is through the repetition of a previous experience of satisfaction by refinding the object that made the experience possible. The easiest and fastest way to insure such a repetition is to hallucinate the memory of the previous object of satisfaction. Thus, hallucinatory wish fulfillment is the theoretical model of thought in its most primitive form. Freud speculated that this involves a primary process of discharge of energy in a free, mobile state. Thinking is regulated by drive tension and unsatisfied wishes. It is first and foremost wishful thinking, taking our wishes for realities (dreams, fantasies, delusions, and so on) and remodeling our experience of reality in terms of our wishes. Freud derived these concepts primarily from the study of dream work, the transformation of the latent dream thoughts into the manifest content. This comes about through two mechanisms: condensation and displacement. Condensation is "an inclination to form fresh unities out of elements which in our waking thought we should certainly have kept separate" (Freud, 1940, p. 167). Displacement refers to a complete transfer of cathexis (interest, investment, and affect) from one content to another. These two mechanisms are closely linked; they are both in the service of the quickest possible road to discharge but operate under the constraints of censorship (defense), which forces disguise and substitute expressions. What does the economic concept of discharge refer to in psychological terms? Essentially, to the repetitive tendency of repressed infantile wishes to keep expressing themselves by any means available, regardless of reality constraints (pleasure principle and repetition compulsion).

Insofar as thinking involves ordering, abstracting, and synthesis between concrete aspects of experience, some form of condensation and displacement is always involved. What is specific to the primary process is that it operates not on rational or realistic principles but on the basis of quite insignificant similarities between elements and what Freud calls "external and superficial" links, often based on "assonance, verbal ambiguity, temporal coincidence without connection in meaning, or by any association of the kind that we allow in jokes or in play upon words" (1900, p. 530).

It is specifically with reference to such loose and irrational displacements that Freud speculated about an unbound, or free, primary state of psychic energy. But such seemingly arbitrary and bizarre thought connections are guided by an underlying purposive idea—namely, to provide a disguised expression to some unconscious wish or fantasy. Such an assumption is fundamental to the very rationale of interpretation in psychoanalysis.

Condensation and displacement express the selective influence, or transfer, of unconscious wishes and conflicts on ongoing experience and behavior. They are a fundamental part of the formation of dreams, fantasies, parapraxes, myths, and, last but not least, symptoms. Psychoanalysis assumes that the repressed unconscious influences all our thinking to some degree, if only by giving "a special meaning and a secret significance" (Freud, 1924, p. 187) to some aspects of our reality. The expression "primary-process thinking" has been used somewhat broadly and loosely in the post-Freudian literature to refer to any aspect of thought that departs from rationality and objectivity, in content and/or organization. This would encompass any thought dominated by subjective context, affectivity, imagery, metaphor, and so on. One would, of course, have to specify further when and why such aspects reflect regression, pathology, immaturity or creativity, compelling intrusion or open playfulness.

We should also note the central role of linguistic usage in primary-process transformations. This is not surprising, since the data from which the analyst infers primary-process transformation (for example, manifest dream, fantasy, symptom) consist primarily of verbal communications. Associations via assonance and verbal ambiguity constitute an idiosyncratic, context-dependent use of language—itself a socially shared system of symbolic representation—presumably in the service of primary-process transformations and disguise. Thus the primary process makes use of, and is often equated with, the pictorial and concrete level of linguistic representation, similes and metaphors resembling those of poetic speech, language on a connotative and evocative level. Among these "archaic means of expression and representation," Freud increasingly (but only to a very limited extent in the original edition of the *Interpretation of Dreams*) singled out symbolism as a universal semantic system for the representation of a limited number of bodily libidinal states and functions and their primary objects. Symbolism is not

created by condensation and displacement; while often used for defensive purposes, it cannot be accounted for by individual drive–defense dynamics. Symbolism, for Freud, represents the remnants of a universal archaic language. Though symbolism is usually listed in the analytic literature as one of the defining characteristics of the primary process, it is not on a par with condensation and displacement, either historically or conceptually. The role of symbolism, as involving universal categories of meaning, in Freud's theory can be seen in the context of his increasing emphasis on the innate and universal aspects of unconscious fantasies as primary organizers of thought rather than on specific contingent environmental gratifications, frustrations, and traumas.

SECONDARY PROCESS, HYPERCATHEXIS, AND HIGHER MENTAL ORGANIZATION

The secondary process progressively tames and inhibits the effects of the primary process. It is ruled by the reality principle, as a modification of the pleasure principle, in the service of adaptation and survival. This involves delay of motor discharge and the inhibition of affect to the level at which it functions as a signal, rather than automatically controlling access of memories to consciousness and judgments of their correspondence with external reality. As Freud (1911, p. 219) indicated, "what was presented in the mind was no longer what was agreeable but what was real, even if it happened to be disagreeable." In economic terms, this involves the "binding" of drive energy through some unspecified "raising of the level of the whole cathectic process." Through the inhibiting effects of the secondary process, the mental apparatus can keep the contents of perceptions and memories undistorted and use them to guide purposeful action. Anticipation and planning become possible through thinking as experimental action with small quantities of energy.

But the secondary process involves more than inhibition of primary-process distortion of memories. Thinking becomes "hypercathected," desexualized, and no longer under the control of drive fluctuations. An essential aspect of hypercathexis involves the acquisition of speech, seen as the learned associations of concrete memory contents (thing representations), with the memory of words (word representations), thus allowing a higher level of preconscious mental organization. Thinking is then no longer limited to "pictures" and "concrete subject matter" as a very incomplete form of becoming conscious (Freud, 1923, p. 21); instead it can deal with patterns and relations between various experiences, which requires a higher level of abstraction. Through language, "internal thought processes are made into perceptions"; thoughts become objectified and externalized, thus allowing for self-reflective awareness as a higher level of consciousness. It is this level of consciousness that is prevented by repression, as the unavailability, through countercathexis, of word representations.

The role of verbalization and language is a crucial but undeveloped aspect of Freud's theory of thinking and consciousness (see below). It implies different levels of consciousness, from the compelling emergence of drive-cathected memories, passively experienced with affective and sensory concreteness and vividness (characteristic of primary-process ideation), to the active, selective manipulation of ideas, the capacity for reflective, self-observing awareness and conceptual thought. This suggests that making the unconscious conscious is more than the retrieval of specific memories from repression but involves "a higher stage of psychical organization" (Freud, 1915, p. 192), a new synthesis through a process in which verbalization plays a central role.

Issues and Comments

It should be clear that primary process is an economic concept, referring to the "primary," uninhibited mode of drive discharge. To the extent that mental representations are subjected to the primary process, they will be experienced as real (hallucinatory wish fulfillment) and/or be distorted through the mechanisms of condensation and displacement. Thus primary-process mechanisms are largely responsible for transformations between the latent and the manifest content of displacement and lead to "superficial and external associations" that are dependent on specific individual context; but such associations are dominated by an unconscious "purposive idea" or wish that expresses itself in multiple and variable surface manifestations.

The term "primary process" is often used in a descriptive sense to refer to the directly observable features of certain thought products—for example, dreams, fantasies, and delusions. Insofar as they are unrealistic, bizarre, subjective, illogical, or dominated by primitive and crude drive expression, they reveal fairly directly the influence of the primary process and the pleasure principle.

The theory of the primary process is an essential part of the fundamental psychoanalytic assumption that any manifest thought product can have multiple hidden meanings and is, in varying degrees, the expression of unconscious conflicted wishes.

Freud's theory of thinking also incorporates much of the association psychology of his time. Discrete

perceptions of specific external objects and their copies in memory form the basic elemental units of cognition, from the start of development. Freud assumed that a memory can exist at different levels of organization and have several "transcriptions" (1895, 1900, 1915). The lower levels will be more concrete, subjective, and drive-organized, and the higher ones more objective, conceptual, and secondary process. Because of repression, a memory content may not be able to reach the higher levels of organization and become integrated into a broader context. But conversely, a memory or datum can be known at a higher intellectual level without making contact with the lower ones or lifting the effects of repression. Separate memory images become linked in terms of contiguity and similarity provided by further experiences. Of course, Freud specifically focused on the role of internal experiences of pleasure and unpleasure in ruling the course of associations. The primary process distorts the original objective content of memories; the main contribution of the secondary process is to limit the effects of this distortion and allow objective knowledge to guide actions. The very concepts of condensation and displacement assume prior, separate, differentiated units which then get condensed or between which displacements can occur.

Such a model is hard to reconcile with the assumptions of diffuse, undifferentiated experiences (lack of self–object differentiation and constancy) in contemporary developmental theory. Freud's theory was based on the hypothesis of *actual* experiences of satisfaction with the perception and memory of an external object. It is probably no coincidence that this theory was formulated during the years when his clinical theory of the etiology of neuroses was based on the assumption of the role of repressed memories of actual traumatic *events* (that is, the seduction theory). With the gradual shift to the central role of psychic reality and unconscious fantasies, "the firm ground of reality was gone" (Freud, 1914, p. 17). This meant not only that the claims for an environmental causal etiology of neuroses were weakened but also that much of the cognitive theory formulated in 1895 and 1900 became shaky, since it rested on the cathectic dynamics of the contents—perceptions of memories of actual experiences. Yet Freud never explicitly revised it, except through the increasing emphasis on universal primal fantasies, as innate unconscious organizers of thought.

Freud always stressed the fixed, timeless aspects of the contents and motivating power of our core unconscious fantasies. Such fantasies are partly derived from memories of actual experiences, transformed through condensation, displacement, and symbolization. But Freud did not think that the modified memories of accidental events of individual history could account for the power, persistence, and universal aspects of basic unconscious fantasies. He gave increasing emphasis to universal primal fantasies which, like Kantian categories, are concerned with "placing" the impressions derived from actual experience. The issue is too complex to pursue here. The main point is that Freud came to assign increasing importance to inborn organizers of experience, in contrast to his early, primarily empiricist associationist views. And one may add (without accepting his speculation about inherited memory contents) that the general concept of inherited organizers of cognition and language, while controversial, is present in many areas of contemporary thought, particularly among the so-called structuralists in linguistics (Chomsky), anthropology (Lévi-Strauss), and, in a modified form, in developmental psychology (Piaget). In any case, the clinical theory of psychoanalysis and the technique of interpretation rely very much on the assumption of the central role of a limited number of recurrent unconscious fantasies— an assumption for which Freud's dominant cognitive theory, as reviewed earlier, provides an inadequate basis (which may have contributed to its becoming divorced from clinical formulations).

Even without the assumption of unconscious fantasies, it is clear that any manifestation of primary-process thought requires an organization of cognitive contents, reflecting the combined influence of drive, defense, and some inputs from external and somatic reality. Primary-process thought makes use of "archaic modes of representation," as socially shared symbolic and linguistic systems, and therefore is not purely subjective, idiosyncratic, and improvised. As Freud stressed in many places, primary-process manifestation can be seen in art, religion, myths, social beliefs, and rituals—all essential and shared aspects of an individual's "reality." On one occasion, Freud referred explicitly to "an intellectual function in us which demands unity, connection and intelligibility from any material, whether of perception or thought, that comes within its grasp; and if, as a result of special circumstances, it is unable to establish a true connection, it does not hesitate to fabricate a false one. Systems constructed in this way are known to us not only from dreams, but also from phobias, from obsessive thinking and from delusions" (1913, p. 95), as well as the animistic systems of so-called primitives. Freud saw such systems as mostly defensive rationalizations, covering the true unconscious motives, and the demand for unity is conceptually most clearly connected with the secondary process and with the ego as a coherent organization. Yet empirically it is described as an intrinsic aspect of phenomena which, in their unrealistic and drive-dominated contents (phobias, delusions, and so on), can certainly be labeled as primary process. And are not basic unconscious fantasies, such as the complete oedipus constellation with its multiple identifications, already complex and persistent systems of this kind, however unrealistic and conflicted?

EGO PSYCHOLOGY AND THE AUTONOMY OF THOUGHT

The expansion of ego psychology in the 1950s was accompanied by a renewed interest in Freud's theory of thinking. There were numerous attempts to systematize and extend Freud's formulations, particularly in relation to the concept of secondary process and the adaptive functions of thought (Hartmann, 1964; Rapaport, 1951, 1960, 1967). The emphasis was on the ego as man's organ of adaptation to reality. The ego psychologists were intent on developing psychoanalytic theory into a general psychology with more of a focus on "conflict-free" aspects of human functioning. In relation to the theory of thinking, some of the main questions they addressed concerned the origins and development of the secondary process and the nature of the stable, organized aspects of thought (Holt, 1967). Freud had defined the secondary process in terms of its drive-restraining function, but he had not specified when and how such a process develops.

Hartmann and Rapaport stressed that one had to assume that the secondary process was present from the beginning of development and had its roots in the biological preadaptedness of the human organism to its "average expectable environment," an environment that is intrinsically social as well as physical (Hartmann, 1950). This preadaptedness is grounded on ego apparatuses of "primary autonomy" (motility, perception, memory, and so on), which are part of the earliest, undifferentiated ego–id matrix and which, after differentiation, through the combined influence of maturation and external reality, become the ego's major control and executive functions. Thus secondary-process thinking is not simply derived from the primary-process "drive organization of memories" but includes "intrinsic maturational restraining and integrating factors." While stressing the maturational and environmental determinants of thought organization, the ego psychologists also kept Freud's economic explanation in terms of changes in the nature of cathexes; binding, hypercathexis, and neutralization were supposed to provide autonomous energies for the higher, stable, and structured levels of secondary-process thinking.

Rapaport called attention to the organized, synthesizing, and socially shared aspects of primary-process systems, from fantasies to myths and cosmologies; conversely, he and other authors (for example, Noy, 1969) also stressed the personalized subjective and pictorial components of adaptive, realistic secondary-process thought, particularly in their creative aspects. Rapaport concluded that "all thought forms involve both primary and secondary processes, but differ from each other in the kind of synthetic function they involve; that is to say, they differ in the degree of dominance the secondary process achieves over the primary process" (1967, p. 843). The main implications are that it is difficult to maintain a sharp distinction between primary and secondary process (for example, to attribute anything uniquely to either of them) or to account for the origins, organization, and persistence of different levels of thought organization solely in terms of fluctuating shifts in drive–defense dynamics.

To the extent that Hartmann and Rapaport dealt mostly with Freud's dominant economic, dynamic view of thinking—with the id as a "seething cauldron"—they may have underestimated the primary autonomy of perception and the fixed, organized, persistent aspects of unconscious wishes and fantasy systems that were also an integral part of Freud's formulations, especially in their more clinical aspects.

One of Rapaport's most original and potentially fruitful clinical contributions may have been his elaboration of the concept of a hierarchy of normal and pathological ego states (including dreaming and alert wakefulness but also anxiety, depressive, and psychotic states). Each state is characterized by a specific, patterned, recurrent organization and balance of primary and secondary process, of integration of thought and affect contents, and a particular kind of self experience, reflective awareness, and subject–object differentiation.

Issues and Comments

Historically, the identification of normal thought with the secondary process (reality principle, *Cs.*, or ego) and pathological thought with regression to the primary process (pleasure principle, *Ucs.*, or id) was rather neat and elegant; however, with the advent of ego psychology, a far more complex theoretical scaffold has been erected, the main components of which we will briefly underscore.

We have already touched on some of the relevant concepts and ideas—such as the notion of the ego's relative autonomy from both the id and the environment, a notion that is applicable to all aspects of cognition, including the ego functions of perception, memory, and thought. The concept of neutralization is an energic term that plays an important role in "fueling" the ego functions, in addition to the ego's inherent source of energy. That there is a "conflict-free sphere," to use Hartmann's term, further emphasizes the notion of an autonomous ego, conceptualized as only relatively dependent on vicissitudes of the drives and conflict, against the backdrop of certain basic, preadaptive ego apparatuses that make cognition possible at all.

Although it was mentioned in passing, it should be stressed that another important concept in psychoanalytic ego psychology is the assumption of hierarchically organized and layered levels of functioning, a structural conception that also emphasizes a continuum of ego states, each state, layer, or level being defined in terms of a complex configuration of wish–defense balance, ego–id–superego relations, as well as internal relations among ego processes. Within this larger conception is embedded the hypothesis of a continuous, graded admixture in the mode of thought, a continuum extending from the primitive, drive-dominated, and unrealistic primary-process mode (with only the most rudimentary secondary-process accompaniment) through intermediary stages—where primary and secondary processes liberally coexist—to a mode characterized by a dominance of secondary process, though presumably with some minor influx of the primary process. Such a conception quite clearly assumes, as did Freud, the persistence of the primary process throughout life. Its presence is not simply a mark of immaturity or pathology. In fact, the *absence* of primary-process indications in a patient's presentation is to be carefully assessed, as it may indicate severe pathology, in the form of a reliance on too rigid a defense structure (see also McDougall, 1980).

It should also be noted that as Kris, via his popular notion of "regression in the service of the ego" (1952), and others with various modifications (for example, Noy, 1969) have emphasized, the primary process is centrally engaged in facilitating creativity and aesthetic appreciation, providing, as it were, the "imaginative basis" by contrast with the "rational basis" for life (Rycroft, 1975). Freud, and most insistently Kubie (1954), maintained that, hidden behind each instance of thought, even one that appears most like secondary process, there lie associative threads to concomitant preconscious primary-process ideation (a notion that is compatible with "parallel processing" in modern information-processing theory).

THE DEVELOPMENT OF THOUGHT
AND MODES OF REPRESENTATION

In his formulation of the different levels of thought organization and their autonomous maturational aspects, Rapaport was substantially influenced by contemporary developmental psychologies, particularly those of Werner and Piaget. In part through the medium of psychoanalytic ego psychology, these authors have had a lasting influence on many aspects of the contemporary psychoanalytic views of the development of thought and symbolization. We can only give a brief summary of these developmental theories, highlighting their relevance to psychoanalytic issues. These theories distinguish three main stages or levels in development of cognitive activity and the symbolic representation and construction of the individual's outer and inner reality.

1. The first stage is the sensorimotor one and involves the formation and integration of action patterns or sensorimotor schemes. Such schemas (looking, grasping, sucking), originally based on inborn reflex patterns, are repeated and generalized; they become progressively modified by interaction with the environment and integrated with each other. There is no assumption of a clear differentiation between separate objects, between object and self, or between external sensorimotor stimulation and internal visceral affective reactions. The subjective, affective, and motivational meaning of the experience of an object is an intrinsic, inseparable aspect of immediate perception, not something added on to a prior objective perceptual registration. "The earliest forms of thought *are* sensorimotor actions . . . the sensory event and the motor response constitute one integral unit" (Wolff, 1967, p. 324). During the first year of life, one can observe a growing capacity to differentiate the action pattern from the object, to recognize familiar objects, and to use them as clues or anticipatory signals within specific action sequences (being fed, held, and so forth). The influence of the past is carried on through the repetition of patterns of action, not through the persistence of memory images of absent objects.

There is no room for such a stage within Freud's developmental model starting with hallucinatory wish fulfillment. This pre-representational world of "things of action" and the progressive differentiation and integration of action patterns are assumed by Piaget and Werner to form the basis of intentional, goal-directed behavior and to be the source of later internalized patterns of thought in the adult. This level remains as a substrate, a bodily anchoring and referent (as diffuse affective reactions, gestures, and so on) for later experience, organized around im-

ages, words, and concepts. However, Piaget's theory gives no priority to special objects, such as the mother, or to particular body zones and functions as organizers of the earliest sensorimotor patterns. Werner and Kaplan (1963), however, stress that the child's exploration of his or her environment is largely shared, shaped, and mediated by the prime caretaker, a point developed within psychoanalysis by Loewald (1960) among others.

2. The second stage includes the beginnings of true representation, the capacity for the symbolic evocation of absent objects through the construction of memory images and fantasies. This level of representation tends to be "iconic," based on some concrete similarity between the representation and what is represented, a similarity often derived from the specific prior experience and personal frame of reference of the individual. Such a representation may function as an evocative, affective substitute "presence" for the absent object and lead to various degrees of felt equivalence between signifier and signified, the thought and the deed (magical thinking, omnipotence of thought, and so on).

3. At the third stage, that of logical conceptual thought, a representation (for example, a word) has no concrete similarity to what is represented; the relationship is "arbitrary"—that is, based on a learned, socially shared system of relationships and rules of transformation (languages and other semiotic systems). Representations as signifiers refer to concepts and categories rather than to specific concrete experiences and imply the construction of invariant structures as systems of stable relationships with various changing contents (as part of a *Gestalt* or as variables in an equation). Natural language, indispensable at the conceptual level of representation but probably not at the iconic level, can and does frequently function at both levels—being impersonal and general as well as context-bound, evocative, and personal. Hence the ambiguity, multiple connotations, and allusions that characterize most communicative speech and thereby allow, if not require, multiple interpretations.

Such a developmental model has been accepted by many contemporary psychoanalytic writers since Rapaport, but its implications, particularly its incompatibility with some of Freud's basic assumptions, have been considered only in a very piecemeal fashion (Schimek, 1975). We briefly summarize these implications.

(a) The individual's experience of reality, in its subjective and objective, private and consensual aspects, is an active, selective *construction,* not the passive registration of what is objectively given (albeit subject to distortion by wishes and conflicts). This construction involves the building of invariant features as stable and differentiated attributes of the subject and the object, from an originally fluctuating and global level of experience.

(b) Perception is not a copy of the external event, and this is even more true for the construction of memory images—a capacity that is likely to develop only during the second year of life.

(c) The descriptive aspects of primary-process thought would correspond to the early iconic, concrete level of representation, with its own system of organization and classification, its own logic and construction of reality. These forms of thought, insofar as they characterize the child's experience, are not limited to thoughts pertaining to instinctual drive objects or to states of tension and conflict. They can be seen as adapted to the child's world and level of knowledge (see Freud's discussion of the sexual theories of children and the animistic, magical systems of "primitives"), a stage beyond the level of sensorimotor reactions and a necessary precursor (rather than distortion of regression) to the more impersonal and conceptual construction of reality.

In the shift and interpretations from one mode to another, condensation and displacement are bound to be involved, in the sense that there can be no exact point-to-point translation or correspondence between their contents. (One might think of the limitations of a prose version of a poem or the verbal description of a painting.) Freud had already stated that symbolism and the many levels of linguistic usage were not created by the primary process but were broad, "primitive modes of expression and representation," which could serve the purposes of disguise and defense. This point of view can and should be extended to all mechanisms of the primary process, including condensation and displacement. One could say that drive–defense dynamics make use of different levels of thought organization and regulate their relative predominance, integration, or dissociation, especially in the adult, but do not fully account for them as developmental stages (for a further elaboration, see Wolff, 1967). The distinction between different levels of representation and meaning may allow a sharper specification of the global descriptive distinction between primary and secondary process. It also allows for a more differentiated view of the dimensions of regression (not simply the reinstatement of an earlier developmental stage) and warns us against a simple equation of the pictorial, the concrete, and the primitive without consideration of the context of the interacting levels of

thought and the ego state of the individual (Horowitz, 1972).

There have been many attempts to compare and integrate Piaget with psychoanalytic views of development. One of the most comprehensive is that of Greenspan (1979), which includes a detailed review of previous literature on the subject. Most of these attempts appear as essentially descriptive comparisons of stages, using the vocabulary of both theories, stressing the similarities rather than the incompatibilities, and providing little by way of specific integration. The main problem is that Piaget focuses on the stages of the autonomous development of intelligence, whereas psychoanalysis is primarily concerned with the motivational and conflictual dynamics of the interaction and fluctuations of the different coexisting levels of thought, not just with the highest, most rational level achieved. Piaget considers a particular stage only as a step toward a higher one, whereas for psychoanalysts the persistence of the lower stages and their influence and interaction with the higher ones remain the central issue. In this context, and with similar reservations as to their ultimate contribution, we might also mention various interesting attempts to apply information-processing concepts (encoding, decoding, feedback loops) to psychoanalytic issues of thinking, defense, and motivation (Klein, 1970; Peterfreund, 1971; Rosenblatt & Thickstun, 1977; Horowitz, 1988) and to understanding the role of imagery.

On the more clinical side, the developmental-cognitive issues of the progressive construction of self and object representations, in terms of self–object boundaries and object and self constancy, have become central in many diverse contemporary psychoanalytic approaches (those of Jacobson, Mahler, and Kernberg, among others). But these approaches, unlike those of Piaget and developmental cognitive psychology, stress the interpersonal and dynamic aspects of the formation, functioning, or impairment of such basic cognitive structures. Impairment in the capacity for self–object differentiation and constancy is seen as a major component of severe pathology and structural ego deficits. These clinical theories stress the role of actual interactions of the child with parental objects as providing or hindering consistency and differentiation of the child's experience. These interactions, through identification and internalization, become the basis of enduring cognitive structures and of the individual's construction of his or her inner reality. From this point of view, object relations, as environmental factors, seem to have mostly taken the place assigned by Freud to drives and conflicts as organizers of cognition. There also seems to be a trend toward an environmental view of the causation of pathology, of structural deficits resulting from environmental, parental deficits—as a kind of cumulative trauma, reminiscent of Freud's early trauma theory of neurosis.

While a minimum of environmental support and preorganized stimulation (the right dosage and timing being described as "good enough mothering") is necessary for the development of cognitive functions, this does not mean that such development is simply a reflection of environmental input, a passive internalization of actual parental behavior and speech. One must remember that the child does not internalize the object as defined in objective adult terms; he or she internalizes his or her own experience of the object, which not only includes drive and affect components but is a selective construction dependent on the cognitive structures that the child has available at a particular stage of development. In turn, the partly autonomous development of cognitive capacities is a necessary condition for further changes in object relations (greater tolerance for separation and delay, libidinal object constancy).

Interpretation and insight into unconscious meaning can be formulated as an ongoing (re)establishment of the links and integration between the more immediate, concrete and the more abstract, relational meanings of experience—links that were absent or disrupted because of conflicts and defensive processes (Rosen, 1969). Finally, words can refer to concepts, evoke images, and serve as signals, often all three at once—which brings us back to the central role of speech and language for thought in general and psychoanalysis in particular.

THINKING AND LANGUAGE

The primary data of clinical psychoanalysis are verbal communications. Freud frequently made the analogy between interpretation and a process of translating or decoding a different language "whose characters and syntactic laws it is our business to discover by comparing the original and the translation" (1900, p. 277). (But how can we discover them if we do not have the original, which is accessible only through the decoding or interpreting of the manifest translation?) We have already seen how for Freud the dream work makes use of "similes, metaphors and images resembling those of poetic speech." Condensation and displacement, while involving motility of drive cathexes, are also described more specifically as "compression" of meaning—one term alludes to many others—and

displacement as "a change in the verbal expression of thoughts."

Freud's general formulation of the acquisition of language as the association of the memory of specific sounds (word representations) with the images of concrete objects (thing representations) is rather limited and outdated relative to contemporary linguistic approaches. It ignores the syntactic aspects of language and the fact that signifiers acquire their meaning by being part of a semantic system of relationships and categories, not simply through their association with a concrete object referent.

There is of course no unified, agreed-upon linguistic theory available. Edelson (1975) used Chomsky's transformational grammar as a model for psychoanalytic interpretation, spelling out the analogy between the transformations of deep to surface syntactic structures and those between latent and manifest content. Edelson's approach highlights the need to clarify the linguistic and semantic principles involved in psychoanalytic interpretations and inferences—including attention to the syntactic style, not just the content, of the patient's speech, as well as the occurrence of sudden shifts and "deviance" from linguistic rules and usage (maybe as mini-parapraxes) as key starting points for interpretations. But a specific application of this model to clinical data still remains a promissory note.

Many contemporary linguistic approaches are limited in their relevance to psychoanalysis by the fact that they consider language as a closed system of signifiers, with little reference to the signified as an extra-linguistic reality (the meaning of a word is another word). This is reflected in Lacan's theories (1977), which seem to view the "symbolic" as a self-contained system of rules, with individual speech as an endless sliding and substitution of signifiers, a game of metaphors, puns, and allusions, all as illusory approximations for a signified that can never be reached ("the lack of being"). Whatever its merits, complexities, and obscurities, the Lacanian approach reminds us of the importance of linguistic and socially shared rules in the organization of primary-process thought (the unconscious as the "other" and "structured as a language"). The emphasis, however one-sided, is clearly on the central role of psychic reality and unconscious fantasy for the psychoanalytic level of discourse—in contrast to the environmentalist bio-social orientation manifest in ego psychology and developmental object relations theories.

The prominent linguist Roman Jakobson is mentioned not only by Lacan but by several psychoanalytic writers, including Rosen and Edelson.

Jakobson and Halle (1956) spell out different functions of language—not only cognitive-referential but also expressive-affective, conative (giving orders, making demands), pathic (making verbal noise to keep in contact with the other), and poetic (attention to the sound of words). Usually speech makes use of all these functions simultaneously, with a shifting dominance of one or another. These functions are obviously directly relevant to how the analyst listens to the analysand and how the latter hears the analyst's interventions. Another central concept of Jakobson is that meaning in discourse is generated by the interaction of two axes, or frames of references—the principles of combination and selection. Combination involves the order and context of words, sentences, and topics within the immediate contiguity of narrative speech; whereas selection involves choice and substitution of words within a more permanent code or vocabulary, as a system of similarities and equivalences. This may be a useful model for describing and specifying the process of interpretation in psychoanalysis: combination as the choice and use of the immediate context and sequence (free associations, the specifics of the analytic situation, and interaction), and selection as substitutions and translations in terms of a system of equivalences based on a limited number of basic meanings and interpretative categories ("symbolism," unconscious fantasies). Specific interpretations and the interpretive method of a particular analyst might be looked at in terms of the relative predominance or integration of these two axes.

PRIMARY PROCESS AND THE PATHOLOGY OF THOUGHT

The emergence of primary-process ideation is a function not only of internal factors, such as organismic state (level of arousal, toxicity, fever), in addition to the ego–id–superego balance and relations among ego functions, but also of external situational demands and reality constraints or unusual circumstances. Unusual environments, such as entail sensory deprivation, for example (Goldberger, 1961; Goldberger & Holt, 1958), have been found to facilitate primary-process ideation without pathology being implied. Whereas it may be considered acceptable, albeit within certain limits, for a patient in analysis to experience primary-process breakthroughs, the same phenomena during an initial assessment interview might be viewed with alarm, perhaps heralding a borderline or psychotic disorder. In other words, manifestations of the primary process —be it in the form of a fleeting train of thought, a hallucinatory image, blatant drive material, slips of the tongue—in consciousness (or verbalization) does not in and of itself have pathological implications. A comprehensive assessment of the total situation, the context, the person's characteristic, defensive makeup, cognitive style, and organismic state is called for.

This, of course, is one of the essential functions of the psychiatric interview and the focus of psychological testing. In the area of psychological diagnostic testing, the application of psychoanalytic theory has been significant (Rapaport et al., 1946; Schafer, 1948, 1954). A manual that operationally and systematically attempts to identify formal and content aspects of the primary process (along with degree and modes of control) in the Rorschach test was developed by Holt and Havel (1960). For an overview of the various difficulties encountered in the attempt to "pin down" in operational terms Freud's concept of the primary and secondary process, see Holt, 1967.

In making a comprehensive assessment of the nature of a patient's thought process, we must pay attention to all aspects of cognition, such as perception, concentration, attention, judgment, reality testing, and sense of reality, as well as the patient's characteristic controls, most saliently the defenses, and the effectiveness or decompensation of these control structures must be gauged. We pointed out earlier that primary-process manifestations are always a compromise between instinctual wishes and defenses. In this compromise, the relative weight will vary as a joint function of the intensity of the wish and the strength of the defenses.

In the neuroses, where the defenses are commonly fairly sturdy and stable over time, the characteristics of thought that one finds clinically tend to be quite far removed from the drives and instinctual wishes. The primary-process derivatives, the significance of which go undetected by the conscious part of the ego, are discernible nevertheless. Thus, in the obsessive-compulsive disorders, with their heavy reliance on such defenses as isolation, reaction formation, and intellectualization, one finds thinking that is circumstantial, pedantic, rigid, ambivalent, indecisive, peremptory, and under certain conditions temporarily even blocked. In hysteria, the defense of repression mediates thought that is characteristically global, diffuse, egocentric, unreflective, affect-laden, and cliché-ridden. In *Neurotic Styles* (1965), Shapiro has systematically described the thinking and cognitive styles of paranoid and impulsive characters, in addition to the obsessive-compulsive and the hysteric. He suggests, moreover, that the difference between a *style* and a *defense* is more a matter of the special conditions of tension and conflict (that is, of intensity) than any fundamental difference in their function, which is to control drive stimulation and drive derivatives.

When we turn, finally, to schizophrenia, we are faced with the historical and continuing debate about the nature and etiology of its most salient symptom, a gross disorder in thinking. There have been numerous attempts to pinpoint the nature of the thought disorder, from Bleuler (1911), who assigned it a central role (and whose associationistic leanings were similar to Freud's, by whom he was also influenced), to more current writers (see, for example, Johnston & Holzman, 1979; Frosch, 1982). Rather than go over this highly specialized domain, with its numerous theoretical variations in both the biological and psychological-functional sphere, we will confine ourselves to a summary statement regarding some of the psychoanalytic ideas that have been advanced in relation to schizophrenia.

According to what is probably the earliest and most classical formulation, schizophrenic phenomena are regressive and may be regarded as reinstatements of the primary process in thought and language. In Fenichel's view, for example, schizophrenic thinking is "identical with primitive, magical thinking, that is, with a form of thinking that also is found in the unconscious of neurotics, in small children, in normal persons under conditions of fatigue, as 'antecedents' of thought, . . . and in primitive man" (1945, p. 421)—a rather broad, overinclusive formulation! Freud himself spoke of the analogy of the schizophrenic's waking life with the dream, thus identifying the salience of primary-process breakthroughs into conscious awareness, while pointing to the more formal aspects of the primary-process manifestations, rather than their direct drive contents.

It is at times difficult to separate formal (that is, process) aspects of the primary process from blatantly inappropriate drive contents in consciousness (and verbalization), which presumably also serve a direct discharge function and thus qualify as "primary process" phenomena (Holt, 1967; Gill, 1967). However, in the thought disorder of the schizophrenic it is clearly the *formal* aspects of the primary process that are pathognomonic. Thus one finds such manifestations of the primary process as distant associations, clang associations, phrase completions, magical and autistic logic, total blocking— all clear and dramatic exemplification of a profound disorganization of conceptual and associative processes. The regressive pull toward drive-dominated thinking and the use of primitive modes of thought were originally viewed as being a consequence of developmentally early, libidinal, or aggressive core conflicts. In more recent years, other psychoanalytic formulations have emphasized developmental features, such as defective barriers in relation to drive and environmental stimulation (Hartmann et al., 1964), failure to develop adequate self–other boundaries (Blatt & Wild, 1976), and specific as well as generalized ego defects, as causal links to schizophrenia (for example, Bellak, 1984), rather than simply invoking "regression." But elaboration of these formulations lies beyond the scope of the present chapter. In summary, it should be emphasized that the core notion and singular contribution of the psychoanalytic perspective on schizophrenic thinking is the insistence on its inherent psychological meaningfulness as an expression of the patient's wishes, conflicts, and defenses, his or her "inner life."

REFERENCES

Amacher, P. (1965). *Freud's Neurological Education and Its Influence on Psychoanalytic Theory.* Psychological Issues, monograph 16. New York: Int. Univ. Press.

Arlow, J. A., & Brenner, C. (1964). *Psychoanalytic Concepts and the Structural Theory.* New York: Int. Univ. Press.

Bellak, L. (1984). Basic aspects of ego function assessment. In *The Broad Scope of Ego Function Assessment,* ed. L. Bellak & L. A. Goldsmith, pp. 6–19. New York: Wiley.

Blatt, S., & Wild, C. (1976). *Schizophrenia.* New York: Academic Press.

Bleuler, E. (1911). *Dementia Praecox or the Group of Schizophrenias.* Rpt. New York: Int. Univ. Press, 1950.

Edelson, M. (1975). *Language and Interpretation in Psychoanalysis.* New Haven: Yale Univ. Press.

Fenichel, O. (1945). *The Psychoanalytic Theory of Neurosis.* New York: Norton.

Freud, S. (1895). Project for a scientific psychology. *SE,* 1:283–397.

———. (1900). *The Interpretation of Dreams. SE,* 4 & 5.

———. (1911). Formulations on the two principles of mental functioning. *SE,* 12:213–226.

———. (1913). *Totem and Taboo. SE,* 13:1–162.

———. (1914). On the history of the psychoanalytic movement. *SE,* 14:3–66.

———. (1915). The unconscious. *SE,* 14:159–215.

———. (1923). *The Ego and the Id. SE,* 19:3–66.

———. (1924). The loss of reality in neurosis and psychosis. *SE,* 19:182–187.

———. (1940). *An Outline of Psycho-Analysis. SE,* 23:141–207.

Frosch, J. (1982). *The Psychotic Process.* New York: Int. Univ. Press.

Gill, M. M. (1967). The primary process. In *Motives and Thought,* Psychological Issues, monograph 18/19, ed. R. R. Holt, pp. 259–298. New York: Int. Univ. Press.

Goldberger, L. (1961). Reactions to perceptual isolation and Rorschach manifestations of the primary process. *J. Proj. Techniques,* 25:287–302.

Goldberger, L., & Holt, R. R. (1958). Experimental interference with reality contact (perceptual isolation). *J. Nerv. Ment. Dis.,* 127:99–112.

Greenspan, S. I. (1979). *Intelligence and Adaption.* Psychological Issues, monograph 47/48. New York: Int. Univ. Press.

Hartmann, H. (1950). Comments on the psychoanalytic theory of the ego. *Psychoanal. Study Child,* 5:74–97.

———. (1964). *Essays on Ego Psychology.* New York: Int. Univ. Press.

Hartmann, H., Kris, E., & Loewenstein, R. M. (1964). *Papers on Psychoanalytic Psychology.* Psychological Issues, monograph 14. New York: Int. Univ. Press.

Holt, R. R. (1967). The development of the primary process. In *Motives and Thought,* Psychological Issues, monograph 18/19, ed. Holt, pp. 344–383. New York: Int. Univ. Press.

Holt, R. R., & Havel, J. (1960). A method for assessing primary and secondary processes in the Rorschach. In *Rorschach Psychology,* ed. M. A. Rickers-Ovsiankina. New York: Wiley.

Horowitz, M. J. (1972). Modes of representation of thought. *J. Amer. Psychoanal. Assn.,* 20:793–819.

———. (1988). *Introduction to Psychodynamics.* New York: Basic Books.

Jakobson, R. & Halle, M. (1956). *Fundamentals of Language.* The Hague: Mouton.

Johnston, M., & Holzman, P. (1979). *Assessing Schizophrenic Thinking.* San Francisco: Jossey-Bass.

Klein, G. S. (1970). *Perception, Motives and Personality.* New York: Knopf.

Kris, E. (1952). *Psychoanalytic Exploration in Art.* New York: Int. Univ. Press.

Kubie, L. S. (1954). The fundamental nature of the distinction between normality and neurosis. *Psychoanal. Q.,* 23:167–204.

Lacan, J. (1977). *Ecrits.* New York: Norton.

Loewald, H. W. (1960). On the therapeutic action of psycho-analysis. *Int. J. Psychoanal.* 41:16–33.

McDougall, J. (1980). *Plea for a Measure of Abnormality.* New York: Int. Univ. Press.

Noy, P. (1969). A revision of the psycho-analytic theory of the primary process. *Int. J. Psychoanal.* 50:155–178.

Peterfreund, E. (1971). *Information Systems and Psychoanalysis.* Psychological Issues, monograph 25/26. New York: Int. Univ. Press.

Rapaport, D., ed. (1951). *Organization and Pathology of Thought.* New York: Columbia Univ. Press.

———. (1960). *The Structure of Psychoanalytic Theory.* Psychological Issues, monograph 6. New York: Int. Univ. Press.

———. (1967). *The Collected Papers of David Rapaport,* ed. M. M. Gill. New York: Basic Books.

Rapaport, D., Gill, M. M., & Schafer, R. (1946). *Diagnostic Psychological Testing.* Chicago: Year Book Publishers.

Rosen, V. H. (1969). Sign phenomena and their relationship to unconscious meaning. *Int. J. Psychoanal.,* 50:197–202.

Rosenblatt, A. D., & Thickstun, J. T. (1977). *Modern Psychoanalytic Concepts in a General Psychology.* Psychological Issues, monograph 42/43. New York: Int. Univ. Press.

Rycroft, C. (1975). Freud and the imagination. *New York Review,* 3 Apr., pp. 26–30.

Schafer, R. (1948). *Clinical Applications of Psychological Tests.* New York: Int. Univ. Press.

———. (1954). *Psychoanalytic Interpretation in Rorschach Testing.* New York: Grune & Stratton.

Schimek, J. G. (1975). A critical re-examination of Freud's concept of unconscious mental representation. *Int. Rev. Psychoanal.,* 2:171–187.

Shapiro, D. (1965). *Neurotic Styles.* New York: Basic Books.

Werner, H., & Kaplan, B. (1963). *Symbol Formation.* New York: Wiley.

Wolff, P. H. (1967). Cognitive considerations for a psychoanalytic theory of language acquisition. In *Motives and Thought,* Psychological Issues, monograph 18/19, ed. R. R. Holt, pp. 299–343. New York: Int. Univ. Press.

Peter H. Knapp, M.D.

18

SOMATIZATION

Somatization bears a curious conceptual relationship to psychoanalysis. Germinating in the ambience surrounding Freud's first discoveries, which bore a heavy medical and neurological stamp, it emerged, fully born, in the third and fourth decades of this century, as a subdivision of medical science. Formally christened "psychosomatic medicine," it was strongly—though not exclusively—influenced by psychoanalytic pioneers, notably Franz Alexander and Felix Deutsch, who from different perspectives looked beneath the surface of a variety of medical disorders and saw hidden psychodynamic mechanisms.

Yet, as the interdisciplinary study of psychosomatic processes proceeded, psychoanalytic insight and psychoanalytic practitioners played a diminishing role. The recent comprehensive monograph of Weiner, *Psychobiology and Human Disease* (1977), contains nearly 3,000 bibliographic references, only a handful of which are psychoanalytic in orientation. L. Deutsch, in a recent review (1980), laments this fact, while pointing out the richness of potential continued psychoanalytic contributions to the topic of somatization.

PSYCHOSOMATIC MODELS

Freud's early observations reveal two threads. Both had to do with postulated energy changes, or cathexis, connected with emotion. If not discharged,

presumably in a healthy manner, emotion might lead to generalized pathological changes, attributable to some sort of accumulation in the body, resulting in what Freud (1895) called "actual neurosis." On the other hand, it might be symbolically shaped and locally bound, resulting in hysterical symptoms that unconsciously enacted a conflictual fantasy. Both kinds of disorders represented an equilibrium between psychological factors (in the case of hysteria, shaped by memory—that is, learned patterns) and varying degrees of bodily compliance (1909). Thus, a complementary series of states existed, characterized by lesser or greater symbolic versus constitutional contributions.

In Freud's own thought, these two possibilities—generalized emotional perturbation and symbolic expression—led to theories of affect and to his views on the quasi-linguistic organization of conscious memories and meanings and their translation into a wide variety of psychopathological phenomena. Each strand also contributed to subsequent thought about somatization by his successors.

Some of Freud's early followers pointed to relatively fixed personality aspects of bodily dysfunction. Abraham (1927) emphasized characterological features stemming from the oral, anal, and urethral instinctual phases. W. Reich (1933) contributed brilliant observations about bodily and postural features, which formed a kind of character shell or armor for the individual. Later, these were elaborated on the

221

basis of Paul Schilder's observations (1936) concerning the creation and perpetuation of a neuropsychological body image which could be distorted by either somatic or psychological damage.

Increasing attention centered on a number of medical disorders of uncertain etiology. Dunbar (1938) surveyed a vast literature in her monumental monograph *Emotions and Bodily Changes*. She reported an extensive anecdotal literature suggesting a psychologically meaningful context for many episodes of disease. More specifically, picking up the familiar theme of constitution, Dunbar suggested that different diseases might occur in individuals of differing personality types. Her survey was interdisciplinary, and so was the group stimulated by it, which in 1939 founded the American Psychosomatic Society and, under her editorship, started the journal *Psychosomatic Medicine*. Prominent among the psychoanalysts in this group were Franz Alexander and his colleagues in Chicago, particularly T. French, M. Gerard, G. Ham, A. Johnson, M. Miller, and G. Pollock.

Homeostatic Disruption

Somatization, as conceived by this group under Alexander's leadership, was seen in some ways as an updated version of Freud's actual neurosis. Alexander drew on the psychophysiology of Walter Cannon, involving the autonomic nervous system, subdivided into the sympathetic and parasympathetic nervous systems. Together they regulate vital physiological processes which, integrated with the emotions, maintain an optimal balance of bodily functions, called "homeostasis." Alexander argued that the autonomic nervous system, along with closely related parts of the endocrine system, was directly implicated in a number of chronic diseases of unknown origin (1950). Specifically, his group studied seven such disorders: bronchial asthma, neurodermatitis, peptic ulcer, ulcerative colitis, rheumatoid arthritis, essential hypertension, and thyrotoxicosis. The detailed hypotheses surrounding each disorder were partially verified by an experiment in blind diagnosis carried out by Alexander et al. (1968).

The important consideration here is mechanism. These "classical seven" disorders were all seen principally as manifestations of blocked emotion—that is, emotion mobilized but achieving only distorted, inhibited, partial expression. Asthma, for example, represented a "suppressed cry" of anguish for, or anger toward, a mother; peptic ulcer, a disguised oral longing; hypertension was rage on the verge of open expression. In 1950 Alexander proposed a circular-cyclic model; in this, emotional constellations were mobilized sequentially, replacing one another: asser-

tive aggression, replaced by fear; passive longing, by shame. In some individuals aggressive strivings predominated, in others passive longings. Each was presumably abetted by unknown constitutional or "X factors," resulting in disease manifestations.

The theory left open the question of what role this kind of model might play in a large number of other disorders. Alexander himself argued that such vegetative neuroses, or "true" psychosomatic disease, represented involuntary nervous system manifestations and should be sharply distinguished from conversion hysteria, which stemmed from symbolic processes influencing the voluntary nervous system. His theory was elegant, powerful, and of great heuristic value. It remains a central model of somatization, which we may call, in its most general form, the model of *homeostatic disruption*.

Learned Dysfunction

A different set of observations, and ultimately a second model, can be traced to the other early thread in Freud. A symbolic, hysteroid basis for a wide range of somatic symptoms was proposed by Georg Groddeck (1916) and elaborated by Felix Deutsch (1939). Both men were internists-turned-psychoanalysts, and both had a keen eye for bodily expression and the way in which a somatic illness appeared to have meaning and serve to resolve conflict. Rather than holding to the view that vegetative and endocrine manifestations were automatic, obligatory concomitants of emotion, conceived as a stereotyped "discharge" process, they argued that such manifestations could be the outgrowth of primitive fantasy and represent "pregenital conversion," the term applied to them by Fenichel (1945).

For example, Engel (1968) stated: "We have seen Raynaud's phenomenon appear first in the index finger of a woman about to dial the phone and 'tell off' her mother; and rheumatoid arthritis first in the ankle of a man upon the impulse to kick down the door of a rejecting girl friend."

A patient in his late thirties, suffering from angioedema, came in for a session immediately after discovering that his wife had become pregnant. In the twenty-four hours after learning this news, he had developed a huge, localized patch of edema covering his entire upper abdomen. After this same patient's mother died, a wheal appeared on his left cheek. As he reflected on this, he recalled with intense sadness that it was in the very spot where she always used to kiss him goodnight. Another patient with urticaria, who was beginning psychotherapy, quarreled with her husband, insisting for the first time that she was going to learn to drive, so that she could come to this new experience on her own.

In spite of his violent resistance, she "put her foot down"; but by the next day she had developed a large wheal across the sole of her right foot.

The symbolic element in urticaria was also suggested in clinical observations by Sperling (1949, 1953), who proposed that symbolism might be a factor in other disorders. She felt that mother–child interaction was an area where such symbolism might be instilled. Some of her observations concerned mother–child pairs and suggested that reinforcement within the family might serve as a potent contributing factor to ulcerative colitis. Felix Deutsch theorized that there was early fusion in bodily experience between self and other key persons and that subsequent loss might result in an effort to retain or regain the lost person by fantasy activity in which he or she was personified in their bodily symptom. This view was elaborated by Mushatt (1975). Engel (1968) argued along different theoretical lines that conversion processes, resulting in somatic change, might be explained by generalized responses to sensory stimuli that had become associated with some traumatic or noxious experience.

One of Engel's patients was a twenty-four-year-old single woman suffering from many conversion symptoms. Since age ten she had suffered from recurrent eczematoid dermatitis, which usually occurred after contact with metal, to which she was allegedly sensitive. Her first lesions were around the neck and shoulder, which had been in contact with the metal chain of a crucifix presented to her by her aunt on the occasion of her confirmation. At that time she had been preoccupied with sin. Subsequent eruptions developed when she graduated from high school and was given a watch by her father, later when she was a court stenographer recording testimony in a case of rape, and in an instance reported from her current life when she misinterpreted a question from her mother to be an accusation about her sexual activity. Engel postulated that sensations from the original chain and crucifix had become associated with sexualized fantasies against which fantasies of punishment were mobilized, leading to a biological defensive reaction mediated by normal anti-inflammatory neuronal mechanisms. Later there was generalization: other fantasies became associated with and activated the same sequence, in a manner analogous to classical, or respondent, conditioning. Such evidence contributed to a second model, which may be called symptom formation as a result of *selectively learned dysfunction*.

Psychophysiological Regression
Both these models—homeostatic disruption and learned dysfunction—imply psychophysiological

processes having their roots in early phases of development. This consideration led to a third model. It postulated some form of *psychophysiological regression*. It was proposed by Hendrick (1953) and elaborated by Margolin (1953), who suggested that psychosomatic illness represented a regression to early modes of functioning, along with massive uncontrolled affective responses and badly integrated physiological manifestations. Margolin argued that treatment might try to permit such regression to take place, so that patients could relive the earliest levels of dependence, which he called "anaclitic" (meaning "leaning upon"), presumably antedating the period in which the pathological responses originated; thus, a more appropriate and healthy development might be reenacted in the therapeutic setting. The formulation proved to be oversimple; but the concept of regression remained viable. Schur (1955) gave it its most elegant formulation. He postulated a phase of "desomatization," which took place as the labile, poorly controlled, psychophysiological reactions of infancy became "tamed" and reduced to traces or signals under relative control of cognitive processes. Later, a situation of conflict might bring about "resomatization" and the pathophysiological excesses characteristic of psychosomatic malfunction.

Such a model not only involves regression; it also logically entails a prior progression. It is developmental. Many implications follow from this; here I note only that it is far from antithetical to the earlier models of homeostatic disruption and selective dysfunction. Homeostatic regulation evolves slowly through the various phases of development. Learning of many kinds is essential to its evolution. The developmental dimension can be seen as amplifying and extending the other models of somatization.

Science follows the slow drift of theory but also the winds of fact. These have their own empirical logic; they go where previous facts have shown the way and where precision seems obtainable, even at the cost of oversimplification. In the case of somatization, one result has been that investigators have been attracted to physiologically-oriented work and the use of animal experimentation.

MORE RECENT DEVELOPMENTS REGARDING UNDERLYING MECHANISMS

Attempts to Deal with Psychosomatic Complexity
Homeostasis, both its disruption and its maintenance, has been enormously elaborated. Much if not most of physiology can be seen as a complex balance of responses that maintains relative constancy but also promotes adaptation. Cannon's simple du-

ality of responses was amplified by Selye (1975) to include endocrine components of the "stress response." Both the sympathetic and parasympathetic nervous systems have been found to be complex, with important subdivisions, and related to neuroendocrine and enzymatic systems, running from the central nervous system to intracellular regulatory messengers. The endocrine nervous system has proved to be equally complex. Its relationships to a host of behavioral processes continue to be discovered. Their importance to psychosomatic medicine has been summarized in a series of related articles by Mason (1968) and his colleagues. At the same time, components of the central nervous system that control behavior have been elaborated. MacLean (1973), in particular, has opened the way to the study of the so-called limbic system of the brain as a central set of anatomical and physiological components responsible for emotional behavior, not only concerned with regulation of peripheral emotional responses but implicated in central processes of major importance for understanding psychotic status. Neuroendocrine activity extends to a wide range of bodily functions, including recently discovered relationships between the central nervous and immunological systems (Ader, 1981).

Concepts of disease have also grown in complexity. Boundaries between disease and health and between different disease syndromes have proved to be less clear than was once thought. The "classical" disorders first studied from a psychosomatic and psychoanalytic viewpoint are far from being as homogeneous as they seemed originally. There may, for instance, be multiple types of hypertension or bronchial asthma, characterized by differing contributions from genetic, social, and intrapersonal factors.

The explosion of knowledge in contemporary physiology, pathophysiology, and psychophysiology, gave rise to an ironic development in the psychological sciences. To keep pace with quantitative disciplines and to facilitate experimentation, reliance was placed upon increasingly simple psychological models. "Stress" is an example. The term became a catchword for psychosocial perturbations of many sorts. "Life events" became a similarly oversimplified metric, which attempted to assign uniform weight to a variety of changes to which individuals are subject.

Some investigators have continued to use psychoanalytic concepts, insisting upon their relevance to the complex phenomena of human behavior. Weiner and his colleagues (1957), for example, used Alexander's formulation of oral frustration, in conjunction with somatic liability—the latter being gauged by serum pepsinogen levels—to make predictions about more than two thousand Army recruits exposed to the rigors of basic training. The investigators were able to identify, on a blind basis, those who developed peptic ulcers. The impact of environmental precipitants, interacting with depression, served to predict variations in endocrine function in different groups of subjects, both normal (Wolff et al., 1964) and depressed (Sachar et al., 1968). The need to look not only at emotion but at the defensive maneuvers that accompanied it, was stressed by these authors and also by Knapp et al. (1970).

In 1954 Engel called for "a new physiology" that would look at reactions other than those outlined by Cannon and Selye. He and his colleagues examined reactions to loss and developed the notion of a "giving up—given up" response, of helplessness and hopelessness, which they felt was a precursor to a wide variety of illnesses. Schmale and Iker (1966), guided by this hypothesis, performed an experiment in blind prediction with women coming for cone biopsy, some of whom proved to have cancer, some of whom had benign cervical disease. Without any knowledge of the pathology report, they were able to identify the two groups with statistically significant success. Observations such as these have led to speculations about the possible, important role of emotional dislocation, depression, or other psychological factors in the development of malignant disease, possibly acting by way of impairment of immunological surveillance.

Types of Learning Affecting Homeostasis
Learning is an intrinsic part of this emerging picture of an overall physiological homeostatic system. The outmoded concept of an organism with fixed, stereotyped responses rigidly preshaped by fixed genetic patterns and automatically set off by outside forces, has proved inadequate. It has yielded to a view of the organism in continuous transactional relationship with the environment. Its responses and, indeed, its structure are molded by prior experience in all places and at all levels, down to the intracellular, as the elegant work of Kandel and Spencer (1968), among others, has shown. And prior experience is not merely endured passively; rather, the organism actively seeks it and shapes it. Put in the familiar language of conditioning, respondent learning, in which environmental stimuli lead to predictable responses, becomes powerfully augmented by operant learning, in which the organism operates on the environment to obtain desired reinforcements.

The degree to which learning of both these types —as well as gradations and mixtures of the two— plays a role in the somatization syndromes with which clinicians have been concerned is still a matter of debate. Again, animal work has provided some evidence, such as the demonstration by Gantt (1958) of long-standing, respondent (or "classical") conditioning of cardiovascular and fear responses in dogs or the demonstration by Brady (1974) of operant conditioning capable of inducing sustained elevations of blood pressure in baboons.

Experimental induction of symptoms is seldom possible in human research. Interest here has centered in part on naturalistic observations of symptom onset, recurrence, maintenance, and cessation, as in some of the vignettes already mentioned. The psychoanalytic situation offers opportunities for observations of this kind, which have by no means been exhausted.

More extensive investigation has centered on quasi-experimental attempts to relieve symptoms. Again, the initial search has been for simple models. In consequence, a new movement developed in the 1970s, calling itself "behavioral medicine." It subscribed to many of the tenets proposed by psychosomatic investigators, such as the importance of interdisciplinary collaboration and the need to think of multifactorial etiologic theories; but it endeavored to attack psychophysiological disease states with direct interventions devoid of psychological complexity. It relied heavily on theories of conditioned learning. Two of the most prominent techniques have been systematic relaxation and biofeedback. The latter is actually a variant of operant learning, in which a biological response, ordinarily not under voluntary control, is displayed to an individual, who is reinforced in "learning" to alter it in a desired direction.

The efficacy of such interventions, in conditions like hypertension, bronchial asthma, migraine, and other forms of headache, various types of pain, eating and addictive disorders, still remains to be settled by physiological and psychotherapeutic research. Of crucial importance is the question of mechanism. If symptomatic change occurs, is it the result of the behavioral intervention carried out or of more subtle interpersonal factors in the treatment relationship? Evaluation of the latter aspect can scarcely avoid psychoanalytic knowledge about suggestion and transference.

Maternal and Social Relationships as External Psychobiological Regulators

In the area of the third model, that of psychophysiological progression and "regression" (or relative failure and "fixation"), equally important evidence has accumulated. Research in this area has focused on

attachment and bonding, the influence of maternal caregiving on maturation and physiological functioning, and the consequences of disrupted bonds. For example, meticulous studies by Hofer and Reiser (1969) of infant rats have shown that maternal milk, maternal odors, tactile contact, and visual presence, although differing in importance during different phases, have intricate and interlocking effects on infant heart and respiratory rates, temperature regulation, vocal and motor behavior, and metabolic activities. As Weiner (1982), one of Hofer's associates, puts it in reviewing this work:

> The mother, acting as the external psychobiological regulator of the infant's behavior and physiology, is crucial for the maturation and development of her infant. At some point in the life of the infant (e.g., at the time of weaning), the mother is no longer essential to the infant's complete psychobiological functioning. Behavior and bodily functioning then become self-regulating. Internal autonomic mechanisms presumably take over to regulate the heart rate. But what if they did not? What if the proper functioning of organ systems and behavior continue to depend on social relationships? Does disease begin at the point of their disruption? . . . Is that what "dependency" means? Is that why so many patients, psychologically fixated (or arrested) in their development as they are, fall ill because their total functioning —their psychobiological adaptation—depends on another person?

These questions go well beyond animal models to the heart of human clinical problems. With some extension, they could be worded to apply to the whole emergence of the self to psychic as well as somatic autonomy, as posited by Benedek (1952) and later by Mahler and McDevitt (1982). Psychoanalytically-informed investigation of human development is of direct relevance to this aspect of somatization.

CURRENT STATUS OF PSYCHOSOMATIC MODELS

Psychosomatic advances have modified but far from vitiated—indeed, at points have revitalized—early psychoanalytic models of somatization. The converse is no less apparent; psychoanalytic advances have made a coordinated contribution to psychosomatics. This reciprocal interaction can be illustrated by a few examples.

Homeostasis and Emotion

Concepts of homeostasis, both its maintenance and disruption, bear a direct relationship to psychoanalytic theories of emotion. Though central to psychoanalysis, emotion has never been fully encompassed by psychoanalytic theory, as Rapaport (1953) pointed out some years ago.

It is necessary to use the term "emotion" broadly. It involves the whole range of affective experience, with all the subtle gradations and mixtures that one encounters in the fully expressive clinical situation, particularly at intense and meaningful moments in the psychoanalytic encounter. It is also related to instinctive behaviors and their neuroanatomical substrates. Moreover, one cannot consider emotion, along with its instinctual roots, without placing it in context and considering the defensive organization that either contains, liberates, or at times is disrupted by it. All these factors exist in an equilibrium that is adaptive, tends to persevere, yet is not immutable. A psychoanalytic perspective is ideally suited to investigating both the complex surface of emotion and its elaborate underpinnings, which exist out of awareness.

Recent attention has focused on the character pattern marked by an inability to name, identify, and presumably to experience emotions. This has been named alexithymia (literally, "no words for mood") by Sifneos (1973). Following his French predecessors Marty and de M'Uzan, he postulated that this syndrome is particularly characteristic of patients with psychosomatic disease—indeed, that such patients may have some innate constitutional inability to experience emotion and fantasy. Others question the extent to which this syndrome characterizes psychosomatic patients and wonder whether, if it does occur, it may not be more related to primitive defenses, such as denial, avoidance, and, of course, the intricate process known as conversion.

What we do need to do is to specify the levels of actual and potential emotion we see in individuals. Enormous advances have been made in characterizing visual and kinesthetic expression of emotion (Ekman et al., 1972); but it is equally important to look beneath the surface. Hidden affective currents play a role in determining illness. For instance, Loewald (1972) states: "The patient for whom suffering, inner conflict, sickness, misfortune in whatever form, is a necessity does not understand when we talk to him of a sense of guilt. We may have a measure of success if we can transform his 'unbound' death instinct into a sense of guilt, i.e., into a higher mental form which is potentially accessible to mental therapy, to reason, which can help in a novel way to alter the balance of forces."

Questions about How Learning Occurs

Learning represents a further, equally challenging frontier for psychoanalysis, one also pointed out by Rapaport (1953). What goes into the learning of our deeply ingrained patterns, their unlearning, and relearning remains a central area of inquiry. Questions become even more challenging when we consider the somatic sphere. How can symbolic activity shape bodily processes that appear totally beyond the reach of volition? The simplistic models of respondent and operant learning (or conditioning) provide at best only a beginning. When we think of symbolic punishment inflicted via a specific organ dysfunction or postulate a fantasy of fusion expressed through another type of organic reaction or envision an individual partly "becoming" a totally different person by mobilizing in him- or herself the other's disabling processes—those phenomena all call for more complex, "higher" types of learning, learning that may take place in a single "trial," which may be based upon cognitive match or "feedforward" plans.

It is important to recall that the ego was originally a body ego—in Freud's dictum—and also that the self was originally an otherself, indistinctly separated from key other persons. Moreover, among the earliest responses of the developing infant are those involving imitation, documented so clearly by Piaget (1951). Imitation and its gradual transformation into highly selective and far-reaching types of identification constitute a terrain yet to be fully explored. In particular, we need to inquire about the extent to which identification, with or without genetic priming, can influence somatic function.

Looking Ahead to Studies of Regression

Finally, we come to the third model, that of progression and regression. Already, we have indicated the general relevance of developmental psychology to the organization of somatic patterns. Psychoanalytically-informed observations and reconstructions—the two interacting with each other—must be used in conjunction with physiological data to address questions about the nature, intensity, and permanence of early emotions and the hierarchical sequencing of phases in the development of ego mechanisms and stability of the self. What are the somatic consequences of maternal or familial anxiety, aggression, defects in empathy? What is the role of timing, of failure to negotiate one or another critical period, on later capacities? Clinical data suggest that somatization, often involving multiple organ systems, tends to occur in families. To what extent does this represent some generalized genetic disturbance? To what extent—as Reiser (1966) suggested—does it indicate intense, unmodulated, unmastered emotional turmoil, overflowing along involuntary pathways? To what extent, on the other hand, do more specifically "learned" forms of behavior aimed at defending and mastering become involved in the establishment of pathological patterns?

CONCLUSION

These questions have important implications for therapy, which, in turn, offers some answers, though they are clinical and preliminary. Clinical wisdom suggests that patients with serious somatization are similar in many ways to patients with severe narcissistic or borderline personality organization, though the psychological disturbance is often localized and masked by areas of apparently intact functioning. The early suggestions of Lindemann (1945) regarding the need to begin psychological treatment of ulcerative colitis with a sensitive, empathic, non-probing, supportive approach, respecting the patient's incomplete psychic structure, typically enmeshed with that of other, key persons, foreshadows much of what Kohut, two decades later, laid down as necessary for work with narcissistic patients (1971). Bruch (1982) has pointed to the limitations of unmodified psychoanalytic approaches for patients with anorexia nervosa, whose sense of identity and feeling of autonomy are fragile, and the need to alter the pathogenic family structure. It remains a matter for future investigation whether such caution places permanent constraints on psychoanalytic therapy or whether, as some authors believe, after a preliminary period of support and the establishment of a solid attachment, one can—indeed, should—move toward interpretation and insight, which may lead to profound psychic and also somatic change. Regardless, psychoanalysis continues to have an important theoretical and practical role in disorders involving somatization.

REFERENCES

Abraham, K. (1927). A short study of the development of the libido, viewed in the light of mental disorders. In *Selected Papers on Psycho-Analysis*, pp. 418–501. London: Hogarth Press.

Ader, R., ed. (1981). *Psychoimmunology*. New York: Academic Press.

Alexander, F. (1950). *Psychosomatic Medicine*. New York: Norton.

Alexander, F., French, T. M., & Pollock, G. H., eds. (1968). *Psychosomatic Specificity*. Chicago: Univ. Chicago Press.

Benedek, T. (1952). The psychosomatic implications of the primary unit: mother–child. Rpt. in *Psychosexual Functions in Women*, pp. 419–423. New York: Ronald Press.

Brady, J. V. (1974). Learning to have high blood pressure. *Med. World News*, Oct.

Bruch, H. (1982). Anorexia nervosa. *Amer. J. Psychiat.*, 139:1531–1538.

Deutsch, F. (1939). The choice of organ in organ neurosis. *Int. J. Psychoanal.*, 20:252–262.

Deutsch, L. (1980). Psychosomatic medicine from a psychoanalytic viewpoint. *J. Amer. Psychoanal. Assn.*, 28:651–702.

Dunbar, H. F. (1938). *Emotions and Bodily Changes*. New York: Columbia Univ. Press.

Ekman, P., Freisen, W. V., & Ellsworth, P. (1972). *Emotion in the Human Face*. New York: Pergamon.

Engel, G. L. (1954). Selection of clinical material in psychosomatic medicine. *Psychosom. Med.*, 16:368–373.

———. (1968). A reconsideration of the role of conversion in somatic disease. *Comprehensive Psychiat.*, 9:316–326.

Fenichel, O. (1945). *The Psychoanalytic Theory of Neurosis*. New York: Norton.

Freud, S. (1895). On the grounds for detaching a particular syndrome from neuroasthenia under the description "anxiety neurosis." *SE*, 3:87–117.

———. (1909). Some general remarks on hysterical attacks. *SE*, 9:227–234.

Gantt, W. H., ed. (1958). *Physiologic Bases of Psychiatry*. Springfield, Ill.: Thomas.

Groddeck, G. (1916). *The Book of the "It."* New York: Nervous and Mental Disease Publications, 1928.

Hendrick, I. (1953). Somatic regression and fixation. In *Psychosomatic Concept in Psychoanalysis*, ed. F. Deutsch, pp. 139–140. New York: Int. Univ. Press.

Hofer, M., & Reiser, M. F. (1969). The development of cardiac regulation in pre-weaning rats. *Psychosom. Med.*, 31:372–388.

Kandel, E. R., & Spencer, W. A. (1968). Cellular neurophysiologic approaches in the study of learning. *Physiol. Rev.*, 48:65–134.

Knapp, P. H., Mushatt, C., & Nemetz, S. J. (1970). The context of reported asthma during psychoanalysis. *Psychosom. Med.*, 32:167–187.

Kohut, H. (1971). *The Analysis of the Self*. New York: Int. Univ. Press.

Lindemann, E. (1945). Psychiatric problems in conservative treatment of ulcerative colitis. *Arch. Neurol. & Psychiat.*, 53:322.

Loewald, H. W. (1972). Freud's conception of the negative therapeutic reaction with comments on instinct theory. *J. Amer. Psychoanal. Assn.*, 20:237–245.

MacLean, P. D. (1973). A triune concept of the

brain and behavior. In *The Clarence M. Hincks Memorial Lectures,* ed. T. J. Boag & D. Campbell, pp. 4–66. Toronto: Univ. Toronto Press.

Mahler, M. S., & McDevitt, J. B. (1982). Thoughts on the emergence of the sense of self, with particular emphasis on the body self. *J. Amer. Psychoanal. Assn.,* 30:827–848.

Margolin, S. G. (1953). Genetic and dynamic psychophysiologic determinants of pathophysiologic processes. In *Psychosomatic Concept in Psychoanalysis,* ed. F. Deutsch, pp. 3–36. New York: Int. Univ. Press.

Mason, J. W. (1968). Organization of psychoendocrine mechanisms. *Psychosom. Med.,* 30:565–575. Issue 5 supplement.

Mushatt, C. (1975). Mind–body environment. *Psychoanal. Q.,* 44:81–106.

Piaget, J. (1951). *Play, Dreams and Imitation in Childhood.* New York: Norton.

Rangell, L. (1959). The nature of conversion. *J. Amer. Psychoanal. Assn.,* 7:632–662.

Rapaport, D. (1953). On the psychoanalytic theory of affects. Rpt. in *The Collected Papers of David Rapaport,* ed. M. M. Gill, pp. 476–512. New York: Basic Books, 1967.

Reich, W. (1933). *Character Analysis.* 3d ed. New York: Orgone Institute, 1949.

Reiser, M. F. (1966). Toward an integrated psychoanalytic physiologic theory of psychosomatic disorders. In *Psychoanalysis—A General Psychology,* ed. R. M. Loewenstein et al., pp. 570–582. New York: Int. Univ. Press.

Sachar, E. J., et al. (1968). Corticosteroid responses to the psychotherapy of reactive depression. *Psychosom. Med.,* 30:23–44.

Schilder, P. C. (1936). *The Image and Appearance of the Human Body.* New York: Int. Univ. Press, 1950.

Schmale, A. H., & Iker, H. (1966). The affect of hopelessness and the development of cancer. *Psychosom. Med.,* 5:714–721.

Schur, M. (1955). Comments on the metapsychology of somatization. *Psychoanal. Study Child,* 10:119–195.

Selye, H. (1975). *The Physiology and Pathology of Exposure to Stress.* Montreal: Acta.

Sifneos, P. (1973). The prevalence of "alexithymia" characteristics in psychosomatic patients. *Psychother. & Psychosom.,* 26:65–70.

Sperling, M. (1949). The role of the mother in psychosomatic disorders in children. *Psychosom. Med.,* 11:377–385.

———. (1953). Food allergies and conversion hysteria. *Psychoanal. Q.,* 22:525–538.

Weiner, H. (1977). *Psychobiology and Human Disease.* New York: Elsevier.

———. (1982). The prospects for psychosomatic disease. *Psychosom. Med.,* 44:491–518.

Weiner, H., Thaler, M. W., et al. (1957). Etiology of duodenal ulcer. *Psychosom. Med.,* 10:1–10.

Wolff, C. T., Friedman, S. B., Hofer, M. A., & Mason, J. W. (1964). Relationship between psychological defenses and mean urinary 17-hydroxycorticosteroid excretion rates. *Psychosom. Med.,* 26:576–609.

Burness E. Moore, M.D.

19

NARCISSISM

Long considered one of Freud's most seminal concepts, narcissism today occupies a preeminent position in psychoanalytic theory and practice. An enormous literature dealing with various aspects of the concept now exists as a result of the proliferation of so-called narcissistic disorders in a culture that itself has been labeled narcissistic (Lasch, 1979; Morganthau & Person, 1978; Cooper, 1986). Used first as a descriptive analogy, narcissism came to be regarded successively as an aim of the libido, a stage in development, a type of object choice, a force in its own right comparable to the drives of the id, a supraordinate agency, the glue that holds the cohesive self together, and, finally, the basis for a new school of psychoanalytic psychology. Along the way, narcissism contributed to the development of many other important concepts.

However, despite its importance and the many writings on the subject, narcissism has from the first been plagued by conceptual unclarity. A contributory reason may be that, perhaps more than with any other subject, the study of narcissism encompasses almost the whole of psychoanalytic theory. The literature covered in this overview, therefore, will be highly selective, intended to elucidate specific topics. For a fuller explication of related subjects, the reader may consult other chapters of this book. Short essays on the major concepts, as well as definitions of terms, are also available in *Psychoanalytic Terms and Concepts* (Moore & Fine, eds., 1990).

Here I shall summarize parts of my own comprehensive review of the literature of twenty years ago (Moore, 1975), deal with aspects not discussed there and more recent developments, and present a case.

FREUD'S IDEAS ABOUT NARCISSISM

The literature on narcissism before Freud's 1914 paper "On narcissism: An Introduction" has little relevance today and in any case has been summarized elsewhere (Pulver, 1970; Moore, 1975; Cooper, 1986). Freud's ideas on the subject were crystallized in the 1914 paper and underwent little change thereafter. In it he conceived of an undifferentiated psychic energy that at first cathected (invested) the ego,[1] a state he called "primary narcissism." Some of this energy was later directed to objects (object libido), but it could be drawn back to the ego ("secondary narcissism"), setting up an antithesis between ego libido and object libido, so that more of

---

1. Hartmann (1950) and Strachey (1957) pointed out that it helps understanding of this paper to recognize that Freud used the term "ego" to refer to both a person's self as a whole (including the intrapsychic representation and perhaps the body) and to a psychic system of functions that later became part of the tripartite structural theory. Although this differentiation of the ego-as-self from the ego-as-a-psychic-system appears to be generally accepted, there have been objections (see Weiss, 1957; Kardiner et al., 1959; Balint, 1960; and Chapter 31 below).

one meant less of the other. Presumably, when the primary narcissistic energy cathected an object, it became sexual energy; the term "libido," however, was applied to both forms of energy, the first designated "ego libido" (sometimes simply "narcissism"), the second "object libido."

Freud observed that "the first auto-erotic sexual satisfactions are experienced in connection with vital functions which serve the purpose of self-preservation" (p. 87). Hence, the mother, or whoever is primarily concerned with the child's care, is cathected with libido and becomes the earliest sexual object. Freud called this an "anaclitic" (leaning on) or "attachment" type of object choice, which persists into adult life in some individuals. Others—for example, some homosexuals—take themselves as models for love objects, a "narcissistic" type of object choice. Freud postulated the existence of a primary narcissism in everyone, which may dominate the object choice in some instances; but he assumed that both types of object choice were open to each individual. For those who renounced part of their own narcissism in search of object love, another person's narcissism was presumed to have a great attraction. A narcissistic woman can find her way to complete object love in a child she bears, a part of her own body, and women who had boyish proclivities before puberty may fulfill their longing for a masculine ideal in object love. In summary, Freud said that a person of the narcissistic type may love what he himself is, was, or would like to be or someone who was once part of himself; the anaclitic type may love the woman who feeds him, the man who protects him, and the succession of others who take their places. Parental love, he concluded, "is nothing but the parents' narcissism born again, which, transformed into object-love, unmistakably reveals its former nature" (p. 91).

Freud noted that not all ego libido (that is, self or narcissistic libido) passes into object cathexes. As a person matures, he can no longer retain the narcissistic illusion of omnipotence and perfection characteristic of early childhood, when he was his own ideal. Unwilling to give it up entirely, he seeks to recover it in the new form of an ego ideal, "which, like the infantile ego, finds itself possessed of every perfection that is of value" (p. 94) and is a substitute for the lost narcissism of his childhood. The new ideal, which also embodies the subject's cultural and ethical ideas, is the means whereby he measures his actual ego, and its formation provides the basis for repression of ideas inconsistent with it. At this time Freud also advanced the idea of a "special psychical agency which performs the task of seeing that narcissistic satisfaction from the ego ideal is ensured and which, with this end in view, constantly watches the actual ego and measures it by that ideal" (p. 95). He later (1921, 1923a) combined this agency and the ego ideal in the superego.

Self-regard, Freud (1914) said, is intimately dependent on narcissistic libido. Dependence on a love object that is libidinally cathected lowers self-regard, as does realization of one's inability to love. "Loving in itself, in so far as it involves longing and deprivation, lowers self-regard; whereas being loved, having one's love returned, and possessing the loved object raises it once more" (p. 99). He concluded that "One part of self-regard is primary—the residue of infantile narcissism; another part arises out of the omnipotence which is corroborated by experience [the fulfillment of the ego ideal], whilst a third part proceeds from the satisfaction of object-libido" (p. 100).

At the end of his paper, Freud suggested that the ego ideal also has a social side, for it may be the common ideal of a family, a class, or a nation, providing an important avenue for the understanding of group psychology, on which he expanded in 1921. Differences in others offend narcissistic persons, but the intolerance disappears when a group is formed on the basis of a quality common to its members, who then identify with each other. A revered leader, an idea, an abstraction, or particular aspiration may become, as elements of a shared ideal, the binding force for the cohesiveness of the group.

PROBLEMS INHERENT IN FREUD'S "ON NARCISSISM"

"On narcissism" was a landmark paper. Its importance is indicated by its selection by a Committee of the International Psychoanalytic Association to be the second volume of the series "Contemporary Freud: Turning Points and Critical Issues," in which one of Freud's classic papers is followed by essays by distinguished psychoanalysts from theoretically diverse and geographically dispersed backgrounds (Sandler et al., eds., 1991). In his chapter Kernberg (1991) remarks that only two contemporary issues concerning narcissism are missing in Freud's 1914 essay: "pathological narcissism considered as a specific type or spectrum of character pathology and narcissistic resistances as an important factor in psychoanalytic technique" (p. 131).

Nevertheless, Freud was dissatisfied with his 1914 paper, and looking back over the history of psychoanalysis, it is clear why. At this period of his life, Freud was not only undergoing emotional turmoil but was in the process of changing his theoretical conceptualizations (Waelder, 1960). "On narcissism" has a transitional quality; it is overburdened with ideas portending future developments but is formulated in terms of earlier concepts, which very soon became outdated. It is stated in terms of the libido concept and Freud's first instinct theory, though it goes beyond them. In several reviews of the development of his libido theory, Freud (1920, pp. 50ff., 61; 1923b, p. 255; 1930, pp. 117–120; 1933, pp. 132ff.) mentions the significant role that the concept of narcissism played in his gradual formulation of the second dual instinct theory (see Moore, 1975, p. 247).

Freud introduced the concept of narcissism, therefore, at what might be called an undifferentiated stage of his theoretical conceptualization in which id and ego elements were intermingled. Even so, there are statements in his 1914 paper (pp. 76, 79) and in later papers (1920, p. 57; 1930, p. 119; 1940, p. 149) that presage Hartmann's (1939) concept of the undifferentiated developmental stage in which structures and drives are not separable. But despite this evidence of Freud's recognition of the contribution made by the 1914 paper to these later advances in theory, even in the *Outline* (1940) he never brought aggression directly into relation with narcissism, and this was very largely true of his followers too, though not all (see Moore, 1975, pp. 254–257).

By not revising his ideas about narcissism, Freud failed to integrate them fully with his later structural theory. Hartmann (1950) attributed to this fact most of the difficulty in regard to understanding narcissism and attempted some clarification. A great deal of confusion also stemmed from contradictions in Freud's various statements about primary object love, primary autoerotism, and primary narcissism (Balint, 1960). Initially, he described both of the latter as an early state of the libido. Although later Freud and others attempted to distinguish between the terms (Freud, 1914, p. 77; 1915, p. 134; Bing et al., 1959; Kanzer, 1964; and Moore, 1975), Kohut's (1971) usage of the terms perpetuates and adds to the earlier confusion. With added knowledge based on observations of infant development these terms have come to mean little more than a "very early stage" and are used infrequently. Still further semantic confusion was caused by Freud's use of such terms as "narcissistic libido," "object libido," and "homosexual libido" so ambiguously as to suggest either the direction of cathexis or a qualitative difference among these types of libido. In "Instincts and their vicissitudes" (1915) Freud argued against qualitative differences in instincts; yet at the same time he referred to transformations and even spoke of the development of an instinct, as did Schur (1966). Freud was also loose in his use of the term

"narcissism" in his writings, applying it to a hypothecated energy, to self-love (its direction or attachment), and to the feeling of omnipotence and perfection in early childhood.

Perhaps the strongest objection to Freud's formulations about narcissism is based on the fact that they are part of his libido theory, an economic concept relating to the fate of instinctual energies or drives. The validity of the economic concept subsequently came under strong attack (Kardiner et al., 1959; Apfelbaum, 1965; Holt, 1967), and the elaboration of drive theory to include energic modifications such as neutralized energy and sublimation seems less acceptable today than it once was.[2] Further, Freud's essentially economic conception of narcissism as a libidinal investment of the ego (self) was so nonspecific that the term came to be applied to many different phenomena, including "clinically observable aspects and attributes of human behavior (biological as well as psychological; individual, social; normal and pathological); pathological syndromes; and abstractions—i.e., theoretical concepts of (economic), genetic, structural, dynamic, and adaptive significance" (Moore, 1975, p. 251). As Pulver (1970) points out, "A theoretical construct which can be applied to so many things is not necessarily meaningless, but its explanatory value is certainly reduced" (p. 325). Moreover, while Freud's formulations about narcissism appeared to have explanatory usefulness with regard to certain aspects of these subjects—at least in the light of knowledge at that time—both the phenomena involved and the theoretical concepts are now considered to be extremely complex and beyond comprehension on the basis of instinctual drives alone.

Attempts to Revise the Definition

At this time the most common usage of the term "narcissism" refers to the phenomenon of self-esteem and often implicitly conveys the implication that high self-esteem is the result of a positive libidinal investment of the self. But as Pulver points out, self-esteem consists of self representations linked with affective states of pleasure or unpleasure and organized into a cohesive affective picture of the self that may be conscious, preconscious, or uncon-

2. However, "The psychoanalytic concept of instinctual drive . . . transcends, at present, any definite link to physiological processes, to subjective experience, or to data obtainable from the behavioristic approach" (Hartmann et al., 1949, p. 15). Certainly, as the subsequent sections of this chapter demonstrate, drive theory has an indissoluble historical continuity with later theories and has provided a heuristically useful basis for understanding clinical phenomena, especially those relating to narcissistic disorders.

scious. In the structural theory, id, ego, and superego forces contribute to self-esteem, but so does the response of external objects (the mother in particular) as well (Dare & Holder, 1981). Thus such ego states have complex origins and many defensive and adaptive functions that cannot be explained by drives alone. The term "narcissism" is applied not only to such defensive inflations of self-regard as feelings of superiority and megalomania but also to high self-esteem existing on the basis of a realistic, nondefensive feeling, an oxymoronic use of the term; and narcissistic disorders also include individuals who consciously suffer from feelings of low self-esteem.

For these reasons and others, attempts have been made to redefine narcissism. Jacobson (1964) pointed out that "narcissism," as Freud (1914) originally postulated it, would refer to libidinal cathexis of the self representation rather than the self or system ego with its functions. Horney (1939) advocated limiting the term to situations of defensive, unrealistic self-aggrandizement. Joffe and Sandler (1967) suggested that "clinical understanding of narcissism and its disorders should be explicitly oriented towards a conceptualization in terms of a metapsychology of affects, attitudes, values and the ideational content associated with these" (p. 63) instead of the state of the drives or the hypothetical distribution of energic cathexes. They postulated that the ego functions best when it is related to an affective state of well-being, an ideal state, and that there is "mental pain" when there is "a substantial discrepancy between the mental representation of the actual self of the moment and an ideal shape of the self" (p. 65). This pain is indicated by lack of self-esteem and feelings of inferiority, unworthiness, shame, and guilt. They would define narcissistic disorder by the existence of an overt or latent state of such pain, which must be dealt with constantly by defensive and adaptive maneuvers, sometimes assuming pathological proportions. Pulver (1970), on the other hand, regarded this feeling of well-being as essentially the same as self-esteem and found it inadequate to explain such common applications of "narcissism" as "narcissistic object choice" and primitive types of mental functioning characterized by fantasies or experiences of fusion between self and object images. Pulver noted that the "common factor in all of these [so-called narcissistic phenomena] is the relationship to the self as contrasted to objects . . . [Thus,] *the unifying concept is a focus on some aspect of the self on any one of a number of levels*" (p. 337; my italics). Accordingly, he favored the definition of narcissism given in the *Glossary of Psychoanalytic Terms and Concepts* of the American Psychoanalytic Association (Moore & Fine, eds., 1968): "a concentration of psychological interest upon the self" (p. 57). Pulver

advocated that the term no longer be used to describe either a developmental stage or immature object relationships but be retained as a "broad, nonspecific concept describing a number of phenomena all in some way referring to some aspect of the self" (p. 339).

With regard to Pulver's objections to the conceptualization of Joffe and Sandler, his own definition of self-esteem, given at the beginning of this section, includes unpleasurable affective states, which cannot be equated with well-being. Moreover, Joffe and Sandler were not presenting a causal explanation but specifying the requisites for a metapsychological definition of narcissistic disorders. In my opinion, for some individuals a narcissistic object choice may be a necessary condition for a feeling of well-being, and fusion between self and object images an unconscious fantasy of a wished-for but threatening state.

Dare and Holder (1981) defined narcissism as "the positively coloured affective qualities associated with self-experience which subsequently become an integral part of the self-representation that derives from such experience" (p. 329). This would seem to apply to "healthy" or "normal" narcissism, so called, but not to the negatively colored affective qualities also referred to as "narcissism," the result of what they call "anti-narcissistic influences" and often manifested by defensive traits.

One of the most persuasive redefinitions is that of Stolorow (1975b), who states that "Mental activity is narcissistic to the degree that its function is to maintain the structural cohesiveness, temporal stability and positive affective colouring of the self-representation" (p. 180). Reviewing historically the many functions served by narcissistic disturbances, he demonstrated the clarification achieved by his functional definition of narcissism in the situations where Pulver had shown that Freud's libidinal drive explanation was unsatisfactory; these included a sexual perversion, a mode of relating to objects, a developmental stage, self-esteem, and healthy versus unhealthy narcissism. I am in agreement with his conclusion that "self-esteem regulation by means of a depersonified, abstract, fully internalized and realistically tempered superego-ego ideal system represents a highly successful exercise of the narcissistic function." An elaboration of my own views is presented in the summary and conclusions.

In my 1975 paper I commented that although we may be tempted to abandon the concept of narcissism as outmoded or to limit its application, it is still very useful in succinctly conveying a complex meaning that is usually readily recognizable in conditions that have common features despite some variability. Lichtenstein (1964) expressed the same conclusion in describing narcissism "not so much as an abstract concept, but as a kind of ideogram—i.e., a pictorial symbol or [quoting Etiemble, 1954], a 'word in its visual, not in its auditory, form, the mere tracing of which evokes the whole group of ideas or notions that it connotes'" (p. 49).

In spite of the fact that it is outmoded, another reason for retaining the concept is that for Freud narcissism evidently constituted an organizing matrix for the construction of a body of psychoanalytic theory that remains relatively intact to this day. In short, although narcissism was presented initially as an extension of his libido theory, it also contributed to the formulation of a metapsychology applied first to dreams, led to a deeper understanding of the mechanism of identification in relation to melancholia, pointed the way to the second dual instinct theory, and played a pivotal role in the development of the structural theory. The further development of the structural theory after his 1914 paper by Freud and his followers is essential for an understanding of narcissistic disorders.

NARCISSISM AND THE STRUCTURAL THEORY

The Ego, Self, and Identity

Freud's ideas about narcissism were relevant to the development of the ego as both self and system (or agency), the double implication of ego mentioned earlier. Though he did not make an explicit distinction between internal and external objects or between total and partial objects, it is implicit in his statement that as a result of the disturbance of the state of primal narcissism due to dependence on objects, the ego takes into itself, or introjects, the objects presented to it that are a source of pleasure and expels what is unpleasurable (1915, p. 136). We may assume that the result of this first of two identificatory stages posited by Freud establishes memory traces of the object, or mental representations. A second stage, which would provide energy for the psychic utilization of the mental representations, was derived from his study "Mourning and melancholia" (1917). He reasoned that the loss of a sexual object is made easier when it is installed within the ego, because a permanent alteration of the ego (self representation) occurs whereby it becomes as acceptable for loving as the object (1923a). Thus, he explained melancholia on the assumption that an object that is lost is set up again inside the ego. He also drew the conclusion that an object cathexis is replaced by an identification and thus can regress to narcissism. Further, the transformation of object libido into narcissistic libido resulting from the identification implies an "abandonment of sexual aims, a desexualization—a kind of sublimation" (p. 30). It followed that the character of the ego [self and system] could be seen to be "a precipitate of abandoned object cathexes and . . . contains the history of those object-choices" (p. 29). Hence, secondary narcissism, the cathexis attached to the precipitates of lost objects installed within the ego, would provide the ego with the energy for its development and operation.

But as Jacobson (1954, 1964) pointed out, more than narcissistic libido is involved in the buildup and strengthening of the ego. The maturation of autonomous ego functions—such as perception, memory, and the active capacity for fantasies of total incorporation of the gratifying object to reestablish psychic unity with the object after separation—must have preceded identification and cathectic interchange. In regard to sublimation, she postulated that shifts of emotional and sexual interest back and forth between self and object representations result in a diminution of the sexual quality of the interest, which is turned then to other objects and concerns. Identification with other objects brings libido (interest) back to the self, expanding the executive functions of the system ego and building up the self representations. As new ego (self) interests are developed, not only libido but also aggression are called away from the love object and, after fusion, are vested in the new objects and interests. After the passively experienced changes just described, a forerunner of true ego identification develops through active imitation, first in the affective, then in the motor sphere.

These stages are transitional but form the first primitive nucleus of the ego ideal and indicate progress from wishes for total to only partial incorporation of the love object. In the constant cathectic shifts and changes between object and self accompanying these identifications, there is a tendency to cathect one composite image unit with libido only, another with aggression, until ambivalence can be tolerated. This formulation is suggestive of the early splitting mechanisms described by Melanie Klein. Spiegel (1959) discusses another complicating factor: namely, that what is perceived, and especially what is hypercathected, tends to have object quality, whether external or part of the self. Hence, conflict may develop in distinguishing a part of the self that is intensely cathected from an outside object because of the object quality arising from the intense cathexis.

Along with Elkisch (1957), Greenacre (1958), Mahler (in Panel, 1958), and others, Lichtenstein (1964) emphasizes "the mirroring quality of the sensory responsiveness on the part of the infant to the mother's libidinal attachment . . . a reflection through touch, smell, and other primitive sensations" (p. 53), which provides a dimly emerging outline of the child's own image. Lichtenstein regarded this first, archaic mirroring experience of the child as a narcissistic primary identity, not yet a sense of identity that presupposes consciousness, but rather "a primary organizational principle without which the process of developmental differentiation could not begin" (ibid.). He believed that this primary identity was comparable to the concept of organizers of the psyche in Spitz's (1959) terminology and to Spiegel's (1959) concept of the self.

It seems apparent that the concepts of primary identity and self are therefore closely related, if not indistinguishable, in the earliest stages of development, and both are of special importance in narcissistic disorders. Like other constructs, they take on added complexity as life progresses and structural functions are differentiated. Spiegel (1959) noted that each successive libidinal stage makes its own narcissistic contribution to ego development, but the genitals receive the greatest cathexis, and there is a close connection between the constancy of the (self) frame of reference and sexuality that simultaneously contributes to intense self-feeling and threatening oscillations. Like Spiegel, Jacobson (1964) differentiates self representations from the self and defines the latter as "the whole person of an individual, including his body and body parts as well as his psychic organization and its parts" (p. 6). Kohut and Wolf (1978) defined the "self" as the core of the personality, with two major poles of constituents acquired in the interplay with persons experienced as selfobjects in the earliest childhood environment: one pole from which emanate the basic strivings for power and success, another that harbors basic idealized goals. They also described "an intermediate area of basic talents and skills that are activated by the tension-arc that establishes itself between ambitions and ideals" (p. 414). This bipolar self became a basic tenet of self psychology theory.

Erikson (1956) and Jacobson (1964), in particular, among many others, made important contributions to the concept of identity (see Chapter 35 below). The subject will not be pursued further here. Suffice it to say that the concepts of self and identity have never been clearly delineated, and I will deal with the self only in relation to the subject of this chapter (though see also Chapter 31). Teicholz (1978) has usefully enumerated the steps in the elaboration of the concepts of the self, objects, and the structures of the psyche: id, ego, and superego (pp. 833–834).

The Ego Ideal and the Superego

In *The Ego and the Id* (1923a) Freud expanded on the formation of the ego ideal and the superego. The first identifications in earliest childhood relate to the origin of the ego ideal, but they take place before there are object cathexes. Later the child assumes that the parents have the omnipotence that he or she lacks and cathects them with narcissistic as well as object libido. As their fallibility is revealed, however, the narcissistic libido is withdrawn to the self and invested in an ego ideal modeled after aspects of the objects and the self. There may be some resistance to this second influence in the formation of the ego ideal, but the effects of first identifications in earliest childhood are likely to be general and lasting, the most important being with the parent of the same sex. Freud postulated that it is only when the oedipus complex becomes strong that ambivalence toward that parent ensues, with an outcome that results in identifications with both parents and some degree of masculine and feminine sexual disposition in men and women. Freud speaks of these two identifications as forming a "precipitate" in the ego that has a special position and confronts the other contents of the ego as an ego ideal or superego.

At this stage Freud did not clearly distinguish between the ego ideal and the superego, and thereafter he dropped the term "ego ideal" altogether except for a brief reference in the *New Introductory Lectures* (1933). It is apparent, though, that he regarded both as heirs of the oedipus complex, expressions of the most powerful impulses and most important libidinal vicissitudes of the id, therefore among the transformations of narcissism. He added, however, that "the superego is more than simply a residue of the earliest object choices of the id; it also represents an energetic reaction-formation against those choices" (1923a, p. 34). It dictates to the ego not only the admonition to be like the father but also a prohibition against the admonition, since "some things are his prerogative" (ibid.). As in the case of the ego, the precipitate of these identifications endows the mental apparatus with both psychic representations and the energy for their functions.

These views of Freud constitute what is now called the "structural theory." Freud conceptualized those functions we call structures as being the result of the constant interchange of psychic energies between mental representations. This concept is comparable to the physical concept of the interchangeability of matter and energy.

Contributions to the Ego Ideal and Superego after Freud

Since Freud's time, there have been significant advances in knowledge regarding the development of the psychic structures that are relevant to narcissistic disorders, and the emphasis on libido investment has gradually diminished. Among the notable early contributors to the theory of the formation of the ego ideal and superego are A. Reich (1953, 1954, 1960), Jacobson (1954, 1964), Hartmann and Loewenstein (1962), Murray (1964), and Blos (1974). They are in general agreement with Freud that the ego ideal is an earlier, more narcissistic structure, based at first on the earliest identifications with the mother, and that the superego is a later, more reality-syntonic one, initiated by castration fears and involving identification with the father at the time of the resolution of the oedipus complex. Both structures, however, include identifications with both parents. Early phenomena related to both have a genetic connection with the later structuralization linked to the resolution of the conflicts of the oedipal phase. As Loewald (1951) says, the earliest identification with the mother provides an unconscious structural basis for reality and striving for unification and synthesis, but it is also a source of the deepest dread. The father constitutes a powerful force against the threat of maternal engulfment, a sinking back into the structureless unity from which the ego emerged. This protective force leads to an early identification of the boy child with the father, which precedes and prepares the oedipus complex and is essential for the differentiation and structuralization of the ego and reality. The boy's identification with the father after the passing of the oedipus complex thus has two components: one based on a genetically later, hostile (castration) threat, the other on an early active, positive identification with an ideal (p. 17).

Teicholz (1978) says that Kohut and Murray pay more attention than others to the role of the ego ideal in their formulations of narcissism, both suggesting that some patients with narcissistic disorders use their objects to serve the psychic functions normally carried out by the ego ideal. But she also states that "the relation between early ego ideal development and adult narcissistic pathology has not yet been fully clarified" (p. 839). Such clarification cannot come, however, without attending to the intermediary steps in the development of the ego and the ego ideal. Early identifications, expressed in imaginary wish fulfillments or masturbation fantasies or as a permanent part of the personality leading to actual change, may take place to undo a narcissistic hurt. The ego ideal has magic thought among its precursors and embodies the idealization of power before that of moral behavior. The mature ego ideal tends to function antithetically to the narcissistic entitlements of the pregenital era. Failure of its proper development in severe neuroses is therefore reflected in the persistence of pregenital characteristics. Most pregenital sexual aims are narcissistic (in the sense of being the result of incomplete structural forma-

tion), and narcissistic wounds (rejections, humiliations, and so on) and frustrations may contribute to a compensatory cathexis of the precursors of the mature ego ideal (for example, identification with images of parents and others representing power or pregenital sexual gratification) and lead to regressions involving pregenital sexual acting out of exhibitionistic or sadomasochistic nature.

Both self-idealization and idealization of the parents play a role in the development of the ego ideal, but the acquisition of ideals is not identical with ego ideal structuralization. At a special stage in its development, the ego ideal may be represented externally by an actual person who was necessary for healthy libidinal gratification (Murray, 1964). This is suggestive of Kohut's "selfobject." Hendrick (1964) regarded this stage as indicative of a prepuberty ego ideal, because displacement of love for the idealized person to other objects had not occurred, as it often does in adolescence. In the latter period, self-idealization is typical, and its narcissistic origin and function as a regulator of self-esteem are unmistakable. Formation of an abstract ideal that can survive the loss of a person who represents the ideal is a necessary step in the development of the ego ideal. This occurs as its precursors are transformed and merged with other aspects of the developing superego after the passing of the oedipal phase. Opinions vary as to whether the ego ideal is then a function of the superego or an independent structure. In any event, Jacobson, Hartmann and Loewenstein, and others agree that the degree of self-esteem reflects the harmony or discrepancy between the self representation and the wishful concept of the self represented in the ego ideal and later the distance between the ego and the superego.

More recently Phyllis and Robert Tyson (1984) have presented an excellent review of Freud's ideas as well as the relevant theories of Kohut, Kernberg, and certain ego psychologists, as background for a developmental framework for the superego and its relationship to narcissism. As they point out, the gradual evolution of the superego (including the ego ideal) "is profoundly influenced by concurrent drive activity, ego functions and emerging object relations; through the synthesizing function of the ego (Nunberg, 1931), the primitive multinuclear superego structure (Glover, 1943) is eventually unified" (p. 81). It is not possible to do justice here to the richly detailed interactions of these developmental influences presented in their paper. But since I have mentioned Loewald's views about the effect of these influences on the masculine identifications of the boy child, it seems appropriate to present the Tysons' conclusion that ego ideal formation, based on identification with the same-sex parent viewed as ideal, begins earlier for the girl than for the boy. At its core is the idealized state of the early closeness of the mother–child unit, which serves a guiding role in the establishment of gender identity and in later positive oedipal development. Discovery of the anatomical differences between the sexes may, however, compound rapprochement difficulties, particularly if the girl child feels narcissistically injured, angry, and disappointed with her mother in conjunction with the discovery. A precocious disillusionment and deidealization of the mother may follow, along with self-devaluation (p. 92).

In a paper on "Clinical aspects of the narcissistic personality," Gertrude Ticho (1972) described several types of such personalities, including one who is not conscious of his or her grandiose self-concept but needs an omnipotent, idealized object to whom he or she can be second (see also A. Reich, 1953). In discussing this paper, I suggested that there has been a greater differentiation of self and objects in this type than in others and that the main disturbance in self-esteem in such cases arose in the oedipal period. When oedipal wishes are denied and repressed, there is regression to an earlier period, in which refusion with the object represents not only defense but also a return of the repressed—the wish to replace the oedipal parent. Oedipal conflict has been solved regressively by fusion with both parental objects, but there is the threat of a structureless state, and further defenses are necessary (Moore, 1972).

The views of Chasseguet-Smirgel (1976) on the ego ideal support and expand on this hypothesis in a way that is particularly relevant to the case report that will be given later. When the child gives up his narcissistic omnipotence to the object, his first ego ideal, Chasseguet-Smirgel says that "he senses within himself a gap which he will seek to fill throughout his life . . . [and which] cannot be closed except by returning to a fusion with the primary object. This hoped for fusion may be transformed into the incestuous desire to re-enter the mother's body through genital coitus" (p. 348), leading to oedipal desire and turning the genital father into an ideal. But the child's incapacity to satisfy his oedipal wishes is the basis of the incest taboo, a taboo projected onto the father in order to safeguard the child's narcissism. Further, incest is a return to primary fusion and thus precludes separation between the ego and the ego ideal; merging eliminates development, with deleterious effect on the ego, since it prevents differentiation of the psychic systems and the different ego functions. Inadequate completion of any stage of development gives rise to tension between the ego and the ego ideal. If serious deviations in develop-

ment occur, the maturational influence of the ego ideal can become inoperative. Seeking reunion with the ego, the ego ideal may follow either the shorter route of regression or the evolutionary route leading to integration of each stage of development. Chasseguet-Smirgel emphasizes a fundamental difference between the ego ideal and the superego: namely, that the ego ideal is the inheritor of primary narcissism, initially an attempt to repossess lost omnipotence and restore illusion; whereas the superego is the inheritor of the oedipus complex, stems from the castration complex, and promotes reality. It cuts the child off from his mother, by contrast with the ego ideal, which pushes him toward fusion with her (p. 359).

CLINICAL MANIFESTATIONS OF NARCISSISM

Not all the clinical manifestations associated with narcissism can be categorized as symptoms. Some may be considered character traits, certainly ego-syntonic, and, depending on one's definition of pathology, not necessarily pathological. All the same, in spite of theoretical differences regarding the concept, there is remarkable unanimity about the clinical features characterizing pathological narcissism. In general there is an insufficient differentiation of self from object, resulting in instability of self, identity, and esteem, and poor relations with objects, based on inadequate libidinal investment of clearly distinguished mental representations; a hunger for object attention, doomed by past experience to an expectation of disappointment; a compensatory, defensive delusion of self-sufficiency (Kohut's and Kernberg's "grandiose self"); and affective lability. In such persons there have been uneven development and utilization of ego functions and failure to incorporate an idealized figure as a basis for ego ideal and superego formation (Ticho, 1972).

The most striking features of pathological narcissism are grandiosity and a sense of entitlement. Both are compensatory, the first for feelings of inferiority or inadequacy (low self-esteem), which may be unconscious or may even coexist consciously with the grandiosity but not be integrated with it; the second represents desired reparation for real or fantasied injury. "The ubiquitous attraction, almost addiction, for illusions of narcissistic perfection" in patients with this special pathology is a fundamental tenet of Rothstein's (1980a) book on the subject; he has also written papers on the ego attitude of entitlement (1977) and the fear of humiliation (1984) which, with rejection, constitutes the major narcissistic injury. Relatively minor bodily defects (Niederland, 1965) or cognitive aberrations are often present in these patients and may disturb the normal development of certain narcissistic structures of the personality. Regression of these structures may also occur in particularly stressful and degrading situations and be evident in depersonalization. Jacobson (1971) described such phenomena in Nazi prison camps and postulated that depersonalization is the result of a conflict within the ego between a part that has accepted and a part that attempts to undo identification with a degraded object image. Guilt and shame are especially frequent affects, and depression and sometimes even manic denial or projection can be observed.

There is often, particularly in borderline conditions, a painful sense of emptiness, aloneness, or isolation, but at the same time closeness may be too great a threat and may be defended against by coldness and detachment. Narcissistic individuals frequently possess considerable talent and charm and function very well in social and business settings, where relationships are relatively superficial. Their intimate private and personal relationships are more likely to suffer from their conflicts over dependency and sometimes even paranoid ideation. Sensitivity to narcissistic hurts is marked. Hypochondriasis is common, and in the borderline conditions there are occasional lapses in reality testing.

Bernstein (1957), Stolorow (1975a), and Cooper (1987) have noted the frequent, perhaps even invariable, association of masochism with narcissism. Stolorow's paper shows how sadomasochistic development can aid in maintaining a satisfactory self-image. As an example, one borderline patient told me that he was like a big sore; but his hurts made him aware that he existed. Cooper quotes Hermann (1976) to the effect that pain is a necessary concomitant of separation and aids in the differentiation of the self during the separation of mother and child. The mastery of pain is also a gratifying achievement, and rites of passage involving painful or mortifying experiences are means of assuring individual and cultural identity. Cooper believes that the child defensively restores self-esteem and reasserts control by making suffering ego-syntonic. When early narcissistic humiliation is excessive, these essentially normal mechanisms become a preferred mode, and narcissistic and masochistic distortions dominate the character. In such cases aggression derived from an excessive harshness of the superego becomes a feature of the clinical picture. These narcissistic and masochistic aspects of the character have their origin in the pre-oedipal stages of development, and the oedipal stage confirms but is unlikely to alter, their nature significantly.

Narcissistic rage is a particularly important phenomenon because of the danger it presents to others and sometimes to the affected individual. Kohut's (1972) description is unparalleled. Though it may occur in many forms and degrees, narcissistic rage "expresses the need for revenge [for narcissistic injury], for righting a wrong, for undoing a hurt by whatever means, and a deeply anchored, unrelenting compulsion in the pursuit of these aims" (p. 380). While there is an irrational disregard for reasonable limitations, reasoning capacity is often not only intact but even sharpened and totally in the service of the overriding emotion. I would add that the self-esteem of narcissistic persons is defensively maintained, but fragile and dependent on the feeling of some degree of power in relation to the external world. When injured by rejection or humiliation, aggressive action partially restores the feeling of omnipotence, though by a compromise formation in which the superego exacts punishment on the self as well.

The defensive function of many of these manifestations is readily apparent, but the reader is referred to Hanly (1992) for detailed discussion of the narcissistic defenses. These are of course reflected in the resistances to treatment, the subject of a panel discussion (1969), and a section of Chapter 6 above.

NARCISSISTIC DISORDERS

The writings of Kohut and Kernberg, the foremost theorists of narcissism, inadvertently convey the impression that narcissism exhibits itself only in the particular forms they describe, although these appear to be extremes that are less likely to be encountered by most analysts than manifestations of lesser degree that are present in a spectrum ranging from relatively normal individuals to those with neuroses and psychoses. This raises questions about the applicability of the term "narcissism" to all these manifestations, as if it refers to a single entity. When we speak of "normal" or "healthy" narcissism, we are usually referring to a person who has stable affects, good cognitive and self-critical functioning, satisfying object relationships, and a sense of pride in his or her accomplishments and their recognition, with consequent self-respect—in short, a person who has good self-esteem. This state is brought about by a harmonious integration of the functions of the psychic structures, for which both libidinal and aggressive expression must be satisfying (see Marcovitz, 1972).

But "narcissism" is also used as a sort of verbal shorthand to designate pathological traits or global disorders. Freud designated as having "narcissistic neuroses" patients with paraphrenia (schizophrenia), because he thought they were incapable of developing a transference due to the withdrawal of libido from objects to the self. This idea is no longer held to be valid, and though so-called narcissistic symptoms are undeniably present in psychotic patients, Freud's explanation of psychotic disorders on the basis of narcissism is now considered only part of a very complex etiology involving heredity, ego, and superego pathology.

Some of the pathological traits commonly present in the major narcissistic disorders (narcissistic personality disorder, borderline disorders, schizoid disorders, and psychoses) have been observed in hysterias, obsessive-compulsive disorders, manic depressive disorders, and major depressions. When encountered in the neuroses, they have sometimes been regarded as pseudo-narcissistic symptoms defending against oedipal conflicts. Freeman (1964) put forward the general view that the pathological narcissism of the neuroses and sexual deviations arises out of an advanced level of ego and instinctual development, whereas the narcissism of the psychotic reaction is part of a more primitive and undifferentiated matrix of mental functioning. Though on the behavioral level there may be a resemblance between obsessional and hysterical and narcissistic personalities, Akhtar (1989b) notes that the former do not have a history of a deeply traumatized childhood. "Unlike narcissistic characters, they display the evidence of a successful separation-individuation process, greater internalization of conflict, better superego integration, consolidation of identity, predominance of repression over splitting as the main defensive operation, and the capacity for deep object relationships" (p. 521).

Kohut, Kernberg, Cooper, and others have described the narcissistic and borderline personality disorders. From a comprehensive review of the literature, Akhtar (1989b) has put together a useful picture of their clinical features. He describes six areas of psychosocial functioning, with overt and covert manifestations in each area that he sees as underscoring the centrality of splitting and the divided self in such personalities: self-concept; interpersonal relations; social adaptation; ethics, standards, and ideals; love and sexuality; and cognitive style. Although the "overt" and "covert" designations denote seemingly contradictory phenomenological aspects of the patient's functioning in these areas, they do not necessarily imply their conscious or unconscious existence. Contradictions are not restricted to the individual's self-concept but permeate all the other areas. Thus "the individual with a narcissistic personality disorder is 'overtly' grandiose, scornful of others, successful, enthusiastic about ideologies, se-

ductive, and often strikingly articulate. However, 'covertly' he is doubt-ridden, envious, bored, incapable of genuine sublimations, unable to love, corruptible, forgetful, and impaired in the capacity for genuine learning" (pp. 520–521). Often such a person is arrogant and reacts to any offense to his vanity by cold disdain, marked ill-humor, or downright aggression. Persons with narcissistic disorders are also often promiscuous, and have a tendency toward sadistic perversions, sexual impotence, homosexuality, addictions, and superego defects. They lack tenderness and concentrate on their own sexual pleasure at the expense of their partners, to whom they are frequently unfaithful.

The borderline, schizoid, paranoid, hypomanic, antisocial, and as-if disorders are distinguished from narcissistic personality disorders by a lower level of character organization. There are important differences among these more serious conditions, which Akhtar (1989b) discusses but which cannot be taken up here. I shall focus on the similarities. All have varying degrees of identity diffusion. A major defensive operation consists of splitting or active dissociation of mutually contradictory self and object representations. In their development there is usually "a history of pre-oedipal trauma; an aborted separation-individuation process; much pregenital aggression; distorted and unresolved oedipus complex; uneven, defective, and poorly internalized superego functions; failure to establish an optimal state of latency; and a more than usually troublesome adolescence" (Akhtar, 1989b, p. 522). In spite of traumatic events during childhood, such as divorce, desertion or death, or familial alcoholism or violence, individuals suffering from these conditions were often treated as "special" because of outstanding intelligence or physical charm. The self is poorly integrated and in more danger of regressive fragmentation into psychosis-like states during stress or under the influence of addictive substances than is the case with narcissistic personality disorders. The latter also show a greater tolerance for aloneness, better impulse control, and anxiety tolerance. They have a better work record and greater social adjustment.

SOME VIEWS OF NARCISSISM SINCE FREUD

Soon after Freud's last statements about narcissism, Wilhelm Reich (1933) described a phallic-narcissistic character structure in certain patients, based on a phallic-mother identification when the father was weak or absent. Vengeance against the mother was a character defense against deeply repressed love of her which could not continue to exist in the face of frustrations. The frustrations mobilized rage, which was expressed in sadistic behavior toward women and in sexual perversions. Reich gave other clinical descriptions demonstrating differing degrees of integration of narcissistic character pathology explained in terms of regression in the context of oedipal conflict.

Annie Reich (1953) described how in both normal and neurotic women a narcissistic object choice (an object different from the self but with the qualities once desired) may be used to undo a narcissistic trauma of fantasied castration. She presented cases of dependent subservience to a man considered great and admirable and a second group of "as-if" women who have short-lived, dependent infatuations; they completely take over the man's personality, only to drop him after a short time and deify another object. These cases represent a regressive revival, following trauma, of primitive, narcissistic ego ideals featuring the paternal (or, sometimes, maternal) phallus and the subsequent externalization of this ego ideal and its fusion with a love object. In a subsequent paper (1954) on archaic elements in the superego, she also showed how "The revival or persistence of an early identification within the structure of the later superego imbues the personality with characteristics of the ego level on which the identification was originally formed, like unstable ego boundaries, confusion between ego and object, and between wish and reality. In more regressed cases, the picture is complicated by an admixture of sadistic superego forerunners as well as of crudely sexual ideals. Such superegos are marked by inadequate integration, which expresses itself in continual vacillations of self-esteem" (p. 237). In another paper she described the various pathologic forms of self-esteem regulation in such narcissistic persons (1960).

The work of Jacobson (1954, 1964) represents a transition from Freud's primarily drive theory to one embracing drives, affects, internal objects, and their integration in the functioning of psychic structures. She thus provides a bridge to the British object relations theorists while maintaining a distinctive viewpoint of her own.

Alford (1988) states that Klein and her associates rejected the proposition that primary narcissism reflects an original objectless state. "Klein replaces Freud's distinction between narcissistic and object libido with a distinction between internal and external object relationships" (p. 35). By reformulating libidinal issues in terms of the individual's relationship to internal objects, Klein helped connect narcissism to the schizoid phenomena described by Fairbairn and Guntrip. Feelings of fragmentation, diffusion, unreality, and emptiness, common in the symp-

tomatology of both narcissistic and schizoid states, were not readily explicable in terms of libido theory but could be understood as related to a splitting of the ego (fragmentation and diffusion of self representations) and its detachment from the world of external object relations. Fairbairn emphasizes that the drives, especially libido, are object-seeking, with the goal of relationships rather than pleasure. The earliest months of life are characterized not by self-absorbed primary narcissism but by the infant's merger with the mother, a state of identification with the object. Throughout life the fundamental issues are independence versus dependence, separation versus fusion, rather than the vicissitudes of the drives. Consistent with this view is the observation of Franz Cohn (1940) that in the transferences of patients with narcissistic neuroses there are serious difficulties in distinguishing between subject and object. Stone (1954) also described such transferences in which the analyst is confused with the self or is like the self in all respects, as if alternately they seem to be parts of each other. Introjection and projection of both idealizing and destructive tendencies in oral and anal terms in relation to the analyst "results from this fragmentation of the ego and the devotion of the resulting portions of the ego to their internal objects at the expense of relations with real people" (Greenberg & Mitchell, 1983, p. 165). Rosenfeld (1964) believed that confusion could be avoided if it were recognized that clinical conditions resembling Freud's description of primary narcissism are in fact primitive object relations in which omnipotence and a part object, the breast, may be incorporated and treated as the infant's possession. Defenses against recognition of separateness from the object protect against feelings of dependence and recognition of the value of the object, which would lead to envy, frustration, aggression, and anxiety. When the object is perceived as separate from the self, self-idealization is maintained by omnipotent introjective and projective identifications with good objects and their qualities, but omnipotent destructive parts of the self may be similarly idealized and directed against any positive libidinal part of the self and the desire or need for dependence on an object (Rosenfeld, 1971).

The writings of Béla Grunberger and Janine Chasseguet-Smirgel on narcissism and the ego ideal are erudite, imaginative, and even poetic contributions within the framework of classical Freudian theory, albeit with significant modifications. Grunberger (1971) views narcissism as an agency like the id, ego, and superego, calling it "le Soi," although he points out that recent Anglo-Saxon usage of the "self" (presumably by Kohut) is different, denoting the total personality. Yet, paradoxically, he believes that narcissism is "structured like an instinct, for it is present at (and even before) birth, whereas the ego is a later acquisition. It appears full-blown [though narcissistic pleasure undergoes maturation], . . . is always characterized by a certain fragility, and easily loses its cohesion and unity . . . [but] is as absolute and forceful in its demands as an instinct" (p. 105). He regards narcissism as a quasi-biological force, like libido, yet different in that it has a tonal quality of elation, "an inexpressible sense of well-being, a particularly gratifying bliss, which seems to derive primarily from an existential feeling of extending to infinity" (p. 107). This contrasts sharply with conflicted instinctual libido. Thus, though he considers them analogous, Grunberger says that narcissism and the instinctual drives are different currents which for a long time "flow separately in the same bed" (p. 173) and whose synthesis is a slow process. The child tries to invest his pregenital activities with narcissistic libido, but, because of his inadequacy vis-à-vis his narcissistic ideal, he is unsuccessful and feels worthless. By projecting his omnipotence onto his parents and merging with them in ego ideals, he can recover his narcissistic integrity. Thereafter a necessary synthesis of narcissistic and instinctual strivings can occur as each phase of psychosexual development proceeds, but narcissistic confirmation is required for this to happen. Thus, like Kohut, Grunberger sees narcissism as having a separate line of development throughout life, and integration, rather than abandonment of narcissism for object love, is the goal of maturity.

Chasseguet-Smirgel's concept of the primary narcissistic state appears to be similar to that of Mahler (1979), who defined it as the cathexis of a still merged image of self and object. She regards oedipal conflict as secondary in importance to pre-oedipal factors, but not unimportant. She believes that the child's sexual instinct becomes intensively directed toward the mother, because the oedipal wishes are carried along by the search for lost omnipotence. Thus sexuality is a vehicle or means to an object relationship in the narcissistic quest for refusion with what can make the individual whole: "the wish to penetrate one's mother also includes that of rediscovering the boundless and the absolute, the perfection of an ego whose wound, left gaping by the tearing out of its narcissism, finds itself healed at last" (1984, p. 184). But as Spruiell (1975) noted, when earlier frustrations or gratifications have been too extreme for ordinary mastery, derivatives will be repressed or organizationally split off within the ego, and the oedipal organization will become distorted.

While these French psychoanalysts are, like Kohut, less rigorous and systematic in their thinking than Kernberg, Alford (1988) finds their formulations and Kohut's especially well suited to explaining the cultural expression of narcissism. Grunberger's work, he says, shows that "narcissism may be progressive or regressive, mature or immature, and that it can support humanity's greatest achievements or its most regressive follies . . . and it confounds opposites, such as freedom and dependence" (p. 68).

Kohut, Kernberg, and Rothstein

Kohut (1966, 1968, 1971, 1977, 1978, 1979) derived his concept of the self from the study of narcissistic patients and at first attempted to fit his conceptualizations into the framework of classical drive/conflict/ego psychology, but by the time of the publication of the *Restoration of the Self* (1977), his self psychology school was already well established, and he felt he had to acknowledge his radical departures from traditional theory. He did not leave instinctual theory entirely behind but, rather, came to regard the drives as constituents of the self; aggression he considered to be normal assertiveness that has degenerated as a result of frustration. Without designating it an energy, he said that primary narcissism refers to the psychological state of the infant before differentiation from the primary object has occurred, and that, throughout life, a direct residue of the original position remains as a basic narcissistic tonus, suffusing all aspects of the personality and ultimately becoming differentiated into the "narcissistic self" (later called "grandiose self") and an "idealized parent imago." In his view, the narcissistic libido imbuing these structures has an independent line of development from object cathexis throughout life and ideally undergoes transformations that endow the individual with mature attributes such as creativity, empathy, the capacity to contemplate one's own impermanence, humor, and wisdom.

When the baby's primary narcissism is disturbed, the idealized parent imago develops as a result of investment with both narcissistic and object libido. The libido of the narcissistic cathexis thereby undergoes a transformation into idealizing libido, a unique maturational step that differentiates it from the development of object love. If deprived of instinctual gratification, the psyche changes the object imago into an introject, a structure that takes over the functions previously performed by the object. Its projected external counterpart is what Kohut called a "selfobject." During the pre-oedipal period, as a result of frustrations that amount to losses, there is normally a gradual relinquishment of the idealized parent imago and a concomitant accretion of the drive-regulating matrix of the ego; while the massive loss during the oedipal period contributes to the formation of the superego. The ego ideal is that aspect of the superego that corresponds to the phase-specific, massive introjection of the idealized qualities of the object. This formulation seems to be a restatement of the previously described stages in the development of the ego ideal and superego, but with an important difference: what were described earlier in this chapter as precursors of the ego ideal in the form of idealized images, which might progress or remain relatively unchanged but are in any event protean and fluid, have apparently been concretized into an all-encompassing, rigid, idealized parental imago.

The grandiose self does not move toward the object love that results in idealization but instead retains its narcissistic cathexis and exhibitionistic wishes, which are the predominant drive aspect. Both the idealized object and the grandiose self are considered phase-appropriate and adaptive, gradually becoming integrated into the adult personality. Premature interference with them may, however, lead to later narcissistic vulnerability. Severe narcissistic trauma may prevent the grandiose fantasy from merging into the relevant ego content and cause it to be retained in its unaltered form. Similarly, traumatic disappointment in the admired adult causes the idealized parent imago to remain unchanged and not be transformed into tension-regulating psychic structure. Instead, it remains an archaic, transitional object required for the maintenance of narcissistic homeostasis. Both become repressed and inaccessible to modifying influences. Unempathic parental care is the usual cause of such interference, which produces injury to the child's self-esteem, leading to repression of the grandiose fantasies and vacillation between an irrational overestimation of the self and feelings of inferiority and shame. Under optimal circumstances, however, small amounts of narcissistic-exhibitionistic libido are transformed into subliminal signals of narcissistic imbalance, and the ego is alerted to potential experiences of painful shame and transforms the narcissistic constellations into more highly differentiated, adaptive psychological configurations. In the treatment of narcissistic disorders, the analyst allows the gradual emergence of the patient's grandiosity and idealization of the therapist. The analyst may then empathically point out the realistic limitations of the patient and him- or herself and the childhood determinants of the patient's damaged self-esteem. An essential part of this therapeutic process is the occasional inevitable failure of empathy on the part of the analyst, which

leads to frustration and a sense of loss, followed by psychic internalization of the analyst selfobject, a phenomenon Kohut calls "transmuting internalization," the principal means whereby change is effected. (The similarity to Freud's description of the formation of the ego should be noted.) This process within the transference is essentially the same as the interchange between parents and child which, under ideal circumstances, results in a "cohesive self."

For the most part Kohut worked with narcissistic personality disorders (a term he devised) almost solely within an analytic situation. He largely ignored empirical criteria and based his diagnosis on the nature of the spontaneously developing transference. The idealized parent imago is activated in an "idealizing transference," and the grandiose self in the "mirror transference" (see Kohut, 1968, 1971). For a differently organized short essay on self psychology, see Moore and Fine, eds., 1990.

Kernberg's theory of narcissism, presented in a number of papers and books, attempts to integrate classical Freudian, Kleinian, Bionian, and object relations theories, linking drives, affects, and self and object representations into functioning units under the sway of the traditional agencies of structural theory—id, ego, ego ideal, and superego. Although he acknowledges the role of narcissism in normal development and integration, he regards its pathological syndromes as the result of abnormal mental structures, fixated in early childhood. Thus he views narcissistic disorder as a specific pathological formation rather than a type of developmental arrest. He proposes that the "grandiose self" (Kohut's term, differently formulated) is formed by a fusion of aspects of the real self, the idealized self, and an idealized object representation. While he is in accord with Kohut that such patients were often treated by their parents in a cold, detached, sometimes spiteful, but also "special" way, he does not attribute the pathology entirely to this external, unempathic treatment. Instead, he considers the mistrust, hunger, rage, and guilt about the rage (1975) induced by such treatment and emphasizes the pathognomonic condensation of oedipal and pre-oedipal conflicts under the overriding influence of pregenital aggression (1967, 1975). The inflation of the "grandiose self" is not merely reactive; Kernberg believes that a chronic envy underlies seeming scorn for others, and he considers devaluation, omnipotent control, and narcissistic withdrawal as defenses against such envy. He sees the pathology of narcissistic personality disorders and borderline personality disorders of various types as similar but of varying severity. The narcissistic personality disorder has a cohesive, even though pathological, grandiose self that hides the inner identity diffusion and aimlessness; but that disorder, as well as the borderline disorder, shows a predominance of splitting over repression as the ego's main defensive operation. Obsessional and hysterical personalities are organized around repression rather than splitting and have better organized superegos and a greater capacity for genuinely reciprocal object relations.

Rothstein's (1980) book *The Narcissistic Pursuit of Perfection* offers an excellent review of the subject, as well as his own definition, intended to avoid some of the imperfections he saw in the theories of Kernberg and Kohut. He limited the definition of narcissism to a felt quality of perfection that may be consciously perceived or unconsciously active as an affectively valent fantasy. It should, he says, "encompass the libidinal concept primary narcissism, the object-representational concept self–object duality, and Andreas-Salome's (1921) 'deep identification with the totality'" (p. 17). This narcissistic pursuit of perfection is ubiquitous but differs from person to person in its elaboration and integration by the ego. It is "felt to be part of a self that includes within it qualities of an object narcissistically perceived as perfect" (p. 18). It may be invested in parts of the body or activities. Its cognitive component is expressed in ideas of omniscience or omnipotence, and when it is felt to be a part of the self representation, the subject's positive self-esteem is experienced along a spectrum from well-being to elation (the affective component).

Rothstein's critiques of the views of Kernberg and Kohut seem to me more valid than his definition, for while the pursuit of perfection is a frequent characterological trait in narcissistic individuals and must represent a fixation on, or regression to, certain ideals that are precursors of the ego ideal and bolster self-esteem, its use to define narcissism strikes me as an attempt to explain very complex psychopathology in terms of one of its defensive manifestations. In other papers (1979a, 1979b, 1982) he has discussed the diagnostic term "narcissistic personality disorder" and the oedipal conflicts, early psychopathology, and the analyzability of such conditions. He sees narcissism as a defense against separation anxiety. As the child becomes aware of separation at the time of self–object differentiation, there is a narcissistic investment in the mother's body parts, thought processes, behavior patterns, and other ego activities, and the identification interacts with the child's own endowment as development proceeds. Functions and activities that particularly defend against separation are positively invested narcissistically, and their exercise is associated with feelings of elation and omnipotence, because it recalls the feeling of being able to maintain a primary union with the mother.

Eisnitz (1974) regards narcissistic conflict as occurring whenever the stability of the self representation is threatened. Since "consolidation of the self representation depends on oedipal identifications, the more disturbance there has been with the processes of separation and individuation and the more immature the ego organization, the less stable will be the self representation and the greater the likelihood that there will be serious instability within it" (p. 282). "If a particular aspect of the self representation is connected with forbidden unconscious wishes, the superego causes aggression to be mobilized and directed against that aspect of the self representation" (p. 281). Settlage (1977) too believes the pathogenesis of narcissism occurs as a result of traumata during the period of separation-individuation, especially the rapprochement subphase. Examples of such traumata might be the mother's withdrawal of emotional support in reaction to the child's rebellious and aggressive behavior, abandoning the child to his or her already intense impulses and affects, or an excessively strong and frightening expression of anger and assertion of control over the child's behavior. In either case, the threat of intrapsychic loss engenders a severe rapprochement crisis and lasting separation anxiety.

The various post-Freudian theories have each been subject to criticisms. I shall mention only a few of the principal ones with respect to the work of Kernberg and Kohut. But before doing so, I will focus on the positive contributions and the commonalities inherent in most of the theories. In doing so, I shall borrow freely from the reviews and critiques of Rothstein (1980), Alford (1988), and Akhtar (1989a).

All the authors agree that the cardinal manifestations of narcissism are a disturbance in self-esteem and in the relations between self and objects. The phenomenon is ubiquitous, present throughout life in varying degrees of normality and pathology. It predisposes to an intense need for fusion and separation and manifests dependence through a mask of autonomy and control. All writers stress the importance of the maternal object in determining either normal or pathological outcomes, depending on the nature, timing, and severity of frustrations and traumata. The pre-oedipal period is judged to be of paramount importance in the inception of narcissistic traits, but the oedipus complex is still considered crucial. Rothstein (1980, p. 15) stresses what is implicit in the writings of others, that both narcissism and masochism refer to felt qualities of experience. Except for Kernberg, most other theorists regard narcissism as a continuum from normal to abnormal, characteristic of the most sublime achievements or the most sadistic and heinous aspects of human behavior. That almost no author mentions consciously held low self-esteem as narcissistic seems strange, although patients with this feature are so regarded. Instead, defensive traits obviously bolstering self-esteem are labeled narcissistic, as if the observer, like the patient, is deceived into accepting them as the self-love traditionally associated with the term "narcissism."

Kohut deserves credit for encouraging a more sympathetic attitude toward the treatment of these disorders, but he has been criticized for not acknowledging the influence of the related work of others on his self psychology and for failing to give due respect to the contributions of infant observational research in his own developmental schema. He disavows an empirical approach to the recognition of narcissistic disorders, relying instead on the nature of the developing transference. His description of the narcissistic transferences is helpful, but such transferences also occur in neurotic individuals. In relying solely on the transference for diagnosis, he limits his view to patients who are deemed analyzable, perhaps thereby restricting his experience and knowledge of the gamut of narcissistic pathology. His observational methodology differs significantly from that of classical psychoanalysis, according to Balter and Spencer (1991). In their view he has consistently used introspection and empathy and virtually abandoned free association and evenly suspended attention, emphasizing the patient's conscious, introspectively available experience of his mental life and empathically comprehending and accepting the patient's viewpoint. This corresponds to the process of clarification described by Bibring (1954), but unconscious mental life and its interpretation are neglected almost entirely in Kohut's later works.

Except as a didactic exercise, Kohut's assumption of an independent line of development for narcissism does not seem useful and runs contrary to clinical data. His abandonment of traditional conflict and structural theory in his later years was foreshadowed by his failure to see the grandiose self and idealized parent imago as representational precursors in the development of the ego ideal. Instead, his "supraordinate self" took over and as a concretized internal object underwent fragmentation in the face of frustration or narcissistic trauma. His ideas thus led to a defect theory of narcissism. Nevertheless, his contribution has been significant, and I am in accord with the efforts of Basch (1981) and Wallerstein (1981) to reconcile his views with traditional psychoanalytic theory.

In my judgment and that of many others, Kernberg is more conscientious scientifically, regularly acknowledging the contributions of others that he finds useful in integrating a broad range of psychoanalytic theories previously held to be essentially incompatible. Perhaps more than any other author he has traced the peregrinations of narcissism throughout life, from early childhood to old age, in love and hate, and in solitary and group activities. As an analyst working within hospital settings, he has also had the opportunity to observe, describe, and treat the most severely pathological manifestations. My principal objection to his theory relates to what he borrowed from Kohut: "the grandiose self." Both theorists have, it seems to me, given this concept the quality of a too-concrete structure. While I would agree that what Kernberg designates as "grandiose self" has aspects of the real self, the idealized self, and the idealized object representation, there is a clinically evident fluid, inconstant, evanescent quality to the psychic representations involved.

A case report will demonstrate the complexity of disorders that exhibit so-called narcissistic phenomena. It is not presented as a complete or successful case but to demonstrate the role of conflict and classical pre-oedipal and oedipal positions in contrast to Kohut's defect theory in regard to such pathology. Only once-a-week treatment was possible. The material therefore lacks analytic depth, but it is sufficiently rich to show clearly the genetic and dynamic bases for the narcissistic disorder.

CASE REPORT

R.S., a thirty-seven-year-old internist, entered treatment with analyst A. because of obsessive preoccupation with sexual and aggressive impulses toward his wife, J., and guilt over physical abuse of his stepson, toward whom his wife was seductive. After the birth of their second son, his wife had begun to withdraw; previously very passionate, she was no longer interested in sex, suffered from constant headaches but would not seek medical attention, and frequently asked R. for controlled substances, trading sexual favors to get his agreement. R. gradually took over virtually all of her responsibilities in addition to his own very active practice. His constant preoccupation with fantasies of sex with his wife occurred in spite of twice-a-week intercourse and daily masturbation, and his approaches to her were occasionally too insistent and forceful. He also had angry thoughts of killing someone, and acted out some of his aggressive impulses, driving his car like a madman and constantly watching out for offensive behavior from other drivers. Once when another driver gave him "the finger," he chased the man and rammed his car. He was an impulsive spender, mostly on gifts for his wife, who was even more extravagant. As a result, he had no savings, was seriously in debt, and had not paid his income taxes for three years. He thought he could handle the expenses he incurred—an unconscious grandiose fantasy, since collections from his thriving practice were badly managed, and he was always short of funds.

R.S. believed that he did not get much attention at an early age from his mother, who was already depressed and exhausted from his two older siblings at the time of his birth. He thought that his depression began at the age of five, when his younger brother was born. He tried very hard to please his mother and eventually became her confidant and support in regard to his father's shortcomings. In elementary school he was known for his violent temper, and his mother, who also had a very volatile temper, regularly beat him with a belt. His father and older brother were also abusive. Throughout R.'s childhood his father played an insignificant role and was a disappointment to both R. and R.'s mother, since his attention was devoted almost entirely to the delinquent older brother.

After puberty and in a different school, R. was able to control his temper better and became popular with the teachers and other students. His mother gave birth to his younger sister when he was fourteen. Because of his closeness to his mother, he was afraid that people might think the child was his, so he turned his attention to a succession of girl friends. When there was a possibility of sex with these "good" girls, he would find a replacement, then break away from them. He learned by listening because he had a reading problem and also difficulty with mathematics and abstract concepts. In college he had to study many hours a day to maintain a grade-point average sufficient to get him into medical school. He met his first wife, S., in college and was more devoted to her than he thought she was to him. Feeling neglected, he finally divorced her, but only after meeting his second wife, J., who seemed to be much more responsive. This was an acting out; it occurred while his first psychiatrist was on vacation.

R.'s depression, sleep disturbance, and obsessive thoughts were significantly lessened by a combina-tion of paroxetine (Paxil) and clomipramine (An-afranil). Though neuropsychological tests were equivocal with regard to A.'s suspicion of attention deficit disorder, a trial of methylphenidate (Ritalin) greatly helped R.'s concentration and increased his control over aggressive impulses. R.'s problems were far from solved, but medication made the previously chaotic situation more amenable to psychotherapy, for which R. was well suited.

As R. improved, however, his wife's condition deteriorated. She became more depressed and nonfunctional and over two years made ten suicide attempts. Except briefly, after two hospitalizations, she continued to refuse to see a psychiatrist or even a neurologist for her headaches. She regressed to a childlike state, on occasion hallucinated, then developed a multiple personality disorder. Her last suicide attempt at this time seemed to restore her to some degree of normalcy, and R. decided to move out, especially since his therapist pointed out that his assumption of all her responsibilities essentially deprived her of any purpose in life.

After the separation, his wife's mental condition did indeed improve. She took over the care of the house and the children and was no longer psychotic. R. found it difficult to be alone, however, and became very dependent on his secretary and P., a woman he met at an athletic club, though without romantic or sexual involvement with either. His faithful attendance to the joint custody of the children kept him in contact with his wife. From time to time she behaved seductively, and they would end up having sex. But invariably, she would be angry with him the next day and would attack him verbally for his alleged unfaithfulness to her. Sometimes her seduction seemed to be for the purpose of obtaining drugs or getting revenge for narcissistic hurts. Once she invited him to watch a pornographic video with her, met him in a negligee, and lay down on the floor. But when he made sexual advances to her, she resisted. He left but returned to get his car keys; she had borrowed his car but denied having the keys. When she would not let him in the house, he broke down the door, whereupon she had him arrested for sexual assault.

Though this pattern of seduction followed by driving him away was repeated many times, was pointed out to him, and apparently was recognized by him as part of her serious mental disorder, R. behaved each time as if he still loved her and hoped they would be reconciled. Though they had tentatively filed for divorce, he was by no means certain that he wanted to go through with it. During one of their sexual encounters, his wife said that she wanted to "blend into him." He immediately recognized that what she said had been his wish with his first wife years earlier. When he had felt that this was not possible, he had found J., with whom he could blend, and had then been able to initiate divorce proceedings against his first wife.

His analyst interpreted the fact that they had some attributes in common (the wish to blend, for instance), possibly the reason for the initial attraction between them (a narcissistic object choice for both) and the reason why R. still loved her and desired sex with her more than with anyone else. It was also possible that she had initially withdrawn from him sexually and now had to drive him away after sex because in blending with him she would lose herself (loss of ego boundaries and psychic structure). After separation, each was again drawn to the other, but his wife provoked him by alternately seducing and then rejecting him, so that his rage made both of them victims.

After his wife's recovery from another suicide attempt, R. reluctantly decided that he must go through with a divorce and wrote to tell her. That night he dreamed that he was a patient in a nearby mental hospital, to which he associated the idea that he must be crazy to divorce his wife. After reading his letter, J. called him, was understanding of his decision, not angry, and in fact extended a sexual invitation which he accepted and enjoyed, apparently without reservation. Afterward he reported another "strange" dream. In it he was in his family's home at a party with a childhood male friend who was so big that R. had feelings toward him as if he were his father. The friend took a bath, and R. saw him nude. He pushed his friend's clothing aside and saw women's clothing that had been hidden underneath. The water in the tub was black, as if the pipes were old and dirty. His father came and cleaned up the mess and fixed the pipes. His associations included the fact that his father had always been so preoccupied with his brother's problems that he gave him little fathering. He thought the female garments in the dream were somehow connected with his sexual activities with his wife the day before. His analyst suggested that the male friend might also represent his wife, while his father's fixing the dirty pipes might refer to correcting some defect in his genitals. R. was silent for a moment, then wondered if this meant that he had homosexual tendencies. He added that his father's brother was a homosexual, a fact openly discussed within the family since he was a child. Also his older brother would often punch him and call him a faggot throughout his childhood. He eventually knew that he was attracted to girls, but he was always bothered by lingering doubt about his sexual orientation.

A. interpreted that in the absence of adequate fathering, R. must have had doubts about his own masculinity and sought to reassure himself by associating with the bigger, father-sized friend. It must have been comforting to see that they both had penises. But as time passed, he had dealt with his questions about himself in a different way. Having sex with a girl was reassuring about his masculinity, but his wish to blend with women suggests the unconscious fantasy that he could be loved by his father just as his mother was. If father loved him in such fashion, he would be receiving a penis and would be more certain of the masculinity he had always hoped to obtain from his father. As a confirmatory association R. brought up the fact that his first wife was rather boyish in appearance, and that this, as well as her work, which took her away from him a lot, interfered with his wish to blend with her, but he was never aggressive toward her. By contrast, J.'s femininity made her irresistible. He recognized that P. was also masculine in appearance; he could be good friends with her but had no desire to blend with her sexually.

Desperate to restore relations with J., R. fired his secretary and broke off all contact with P., though this moved him to tears. A. said that giving up any of these women was obviously difficult, but he wondered about the danger to R. of giving up his wife, suggested by his dream of being crazy—that is, out of control. R. mentioned that J. could control him by the offer of sex, causing him to do things he would not otherwise do. He thought next of his therapist—he was afraid to be without one—and then of his mother. A. reminded him of her whipping him with a strap when he was a child and yelling, "Don't you ever lie to me again." In response R. recalled that it was lying that had elicited his abuse of his stepson —"as if you were now mother," A. interpreted.

After an interlude, R. mentioned that he had just learned that his younger brother was "going to have a baby" soon. This made him happy, and he called J. and told her they should have another child. A. said that in view of the fact that her tubes had been ligated, it was strange that R. should be thinking of having a child with J.; it was as if he wanted to have the child himself. R. thought maybe that was true. Once during his first marriage when he had severe abdominal pains, he had had the thought that he was giving birth to himself. A. asked if his first wife was pregnant at the time. She was not; their son was then about five. This reminded R. that he was about five when his younger brother was born. A. remarked that he seemed to have identified with his mother and the child she was giving birth to. R. acknowledged that he has a great deal of maternal feeling. He had looked after his youngest sibling, and always took care of the babies in both his marriages. There were times when he had even fantasied nursing the babies. The thought occurred to him that "perhaps in having a baby the spouse will love him." A. asked "Which spouse?" and R's association was to the fact that his father paid little attention to him. It seemed apparent that his identification with his mother was unconsciously in the hope of receiving father's penis/baby/love/masculinity.

R. started another session by wondering how sick he was and whether he had been completely honest in reporting what happened between him and his wife. He said that J. was afraid of him, because he was still potentially violent despite all his years of treatment. In retrospect he felt that his first psychiatrist had not done a good job and compared him unfavorably with A.; but A. responded that he seemed to be excusing A. and even questioning his own honesty and integrity as a reason for his continued failure to improve significantly, just as small children blame themselves instead of their parents. R. then acknowledged having been somewhat angry with the analyst because he had not improved enough, and this made him wonder if perhaps he needed more frequent sessions or even analysis. He had heard that improvement came about as a result of transference, but he had not recognized any such feelings in regard to the analyst. A. pointed out that he had been reacting to the analyst as he did to his mother—idealizing A. and blaming himself to avoid recognizing angry feelings for not getting what he wanted.

Though he felt that he had improved somewhat, he also recognized that his aggressive behavior persisted to a greater degree than was acceptable. His analyst suspected that this might be due to the fear that if he improved much more or was able to separate from his wife, treatment might end, and he would again feel rejected and enraged at the analyst. The patient confirmed this by recalling thoughts he had had about what he would do if his therapist moved or died.

The insight apparently achieved by the patient in the course of treatment over four years seemed remarkable; no doubt, much of it was intellectual and served resistance. For the most part an idealizing transference was in evidence, but his stubborn persistence in behavior that he knew would be harmful to his wife and himself reflected pre-oedipal conflicts and on occasion both positive and negative

oedipal transference reactions. Nevertheless, there seemed to be some evidence of structural change and promise of further improvement.

Discussion

R. had a severe narcissistic personality disorder, and his wife, J., was definitely a borderline personality with some paranoid and psychotic features. In such cases one may conclude from the work of the authors reported in this chapter that an impaired and incompletely developed ego ideal, modified by pathological precursors, produces tension between the ego and the ego ideal and predisposes to regressive fusion with the maternal object representation (see especially the ideas of Teicholz and Chasseguet-Smirgel). Further development of the ego functions and differentiation of the psychic systems is handicapped, so that the affects are not tamed and impulsivity controlled. Object relations suffer as a consequence.

It seems clear that R.'s pathology had its inception in the pre-oedipal period, when his longing for his mother's attention was frustrated by her exhaustion and depression. Such frustration must have resulted in her psychic representation being charged with aggressive cathexis, and his identification with her led to early sadomasochistic aspects in the precursors of his ego ideal as well as gender identity confusion. R.'s wishes for his distant father to rescue him from merger with his unsatisfying mother would have predisposed him to a negative oedipal solution and contributed to the consolidation of his identification with his mother at the time of the birth of his brother. As relations with his mother improved, however, the oedipal situation took on a positive quality, so much so that it became a conscious danger by the time his younger sister was born. Displacement to secondary objects then occurred.

His marriages essentially repeated these reciprocal oedipal solutions, the first with a woman of masculine build, a good friend and companion—when she was available—with whom he could strengthen his sense of masculinity by association and partial identification, but with whom sexual gratification was not possible. The second marriage, to a physically more feminine woman, reassured him because of his tremendous sexual desire for her, but it resulted in a psychic fusion in which he took over all her female responsibilities, leaving her a structureless shell. Moreover, the frustrations he experienced with her reawakened the aggressive reactions he had experienced in relation to his mother during early childhood. Though this marriage ostensibly represented a more positive oedipal solution, it was condensed with the earlier negative one—union with mother to receive the father's masculinity. Having always felt inferior because of his attention deficit disorder, he married women of superior intelligence with whom he could identify. In both cases the object choice was a narcissistic one, with an intense desire for union alternating with the need for separation, a feature of such cases emphasized by Fairbairn. R.'s reality testing was sufficiently intact for him to recognize the undesirability of his behavior and the danger inherent in it, and superego disapproval exacted its toll in guilt and depression for his failure to live up to his more mature ego ideal.

Like many narcissistic personalities, R. had an especially close and special relationship with his mother, which helped him to achieve more than his siblings. But again like many of these personalities, he suffered from a genetic cognitive defect. R. had superior intelligence and a likable personality and was able to follow his profession with dedication and competence. He was respected by his colleagues, but he always felt inferior, isolated, and lonely. He reacted to rejection with narcissistic rage, during which there was an instantaneous regression from his mature ego ideal to primitive sadomasochistic identifications derived from the early images of his parents as modified by his own projected aggression. It also represented an active attempt to regain lost control and power, early precursors in his ego ideal. His so-called narcissistic disorder resided not in a self positively cathected with libido but in chronic dissatisfaction and unhappiness at the discrepancy between his ego (self representation and system functions) and his mature ego ideal.

SUMMARY AND CONCLUSIONS

Freud described himself as a conquistador in spirit, revealing a narcissistic fantasy that he fulfilled by opening up a new internal world for exploration. His achievement is an example of the heights to which the ego ideal may lead, but it falls short of the total conquest demanded by pathological forces. Instead his achievement, though great and unprecedented, was limited by the realities of the times, a compromise acceptable to the mature superego. The result in this instance with respect to narcissism is a scientific paradigm, in the sense of Kuhn (1970). Freud embarked on a course which he could never complete, but his direction led other psychoanalytic explorers to further discoveries.

Freud's theory of narcissism is couched almost wholly in terms of drive theory, but there are many indications of his elaboration of theory from libido only to an ever more complex instinctual concept, including the significance of object relations in the development of mental structure. Examples are his explanations of the withdrawal of object libido to the self in schizophrenic disorders, the attachment of libido to objects in fantasy in the transference neuroses, and the loss of an external object in melancholia, followed by identification with it. It is true, however, that in his writings he did not always distinguish between internal and external objects. Melanie Klein was right in claiming that she was following Freud, at least in her emphasis on a world of internal objects subject to the powerful influence of instinctual drives. So too were Fairbairn and Guntrip, who elaborated the concept of object relations, even though they almost eliminated drives from consideration. Hartmann, Jacobson, and Kernberg kept within his structural framework while making significant advances. Kohut announced his independence but remains within the psychoanalytic fold.

Our preoccupation with the attributes, functions, and conflicts of the id, ego, and superego has tended to obscure the importance of their developmental stages. Though these were described long ago, one now seldom sees reference to the precursors of the ego ideal. These are charged with partial sexual drives and unneutralized aggression attached to primitive part and whole object representations. They may be integrated with superego precursors under the synthesizing influence of the ego and become the mature ego ideal, with aspirations tempered by reality and impulses that are controlled. However, under the impact of severe frustration and traumata, that synthesis may be impaired, and regression to the earlier precursors may occur if there have been earlier fixating traumata.

Narcissism is to be understood not only from the standpoint of drives or objects but also in terms of an integration of the whole of psychoanalytic theory —some of it not yet developed. At the present time, we may consider it as involving not merely the elements mentioned but also their mutual effect on a human being with a given constitutional predisposition, leading to the development and differentiation of psychic structures and satisfying or unsatisfying relationships between self and objects and their representations within the mind. The common use of the term "narcissism" in place of "narcissistic disorder" carries the implication that all narcissism is pathological, and Kohut's and Kernberg's emphasis on narcissism in the context of special pathological syndromes has contributed to this. These unintended effects of linguistic usage also convey the idea that narcissism is an entity; rather, narcissism is a concept which necessarily includes but is not the same as narcissistic disorder.

My own viewpoint is that narcissism is an abstraction, a highly condensed metaphor referring to an ego attitude of dissatisfaction with one's self or a defensive overcompensation for such feelings. The feelings are likely to be ill-defined and may be wholly or partially unconscious. The dissatisfaction may relate to object love and behavior designed to win it or to self-regard and the requisites to achieve it in light of the individual's jealousy, envy, and early identifications. Such requisites may include power, exhibitionism or other sexual gratification, sadomasochistic behavior or even altruistic wishes, since all these may contribute to an ego ideal influenced by instinctual drives, unique talents, identification with primary objects, and the culture in which the individual lives.

The dynamic basis for this state of dissatisfaction with the self and the resulting low self-esteem can no longer be attributed wholly to vicissitudes of the libido, even if narcissism as libidinal investment of the self is a firmly entrenched idea. The idea of narcissism as self-love is an over-used metaphor that is no longer tenable. Acknowledged or disavowed low self-esteem is the consequence of a failure of reconciliation between the ego (self representation) and the ego ideal, which sets standards. Analogies are useful even if they involve much deplored anthropomorphism, and we may look upon the superego as prosecutor and judge, meting out appropriate punishment for such failure in the form of vague dissatisfaction with oneself, painful depressive self-accusations, or injury from external sources.

The discrepancy between ego (self and system) and ego ideal is ubiquitous, present to varying degrees in everyone. I believe it should be considered pathological only when, in a qualitative or a quantitative way, it seriously interferes with affective stability, reality testing, adaptation, and harmonious relations between the self and objects in particular. But if "narcissism" connotes pathology, it is confusing, I think, to regard minimal discrepancies as normal or healthy narcissism.

My conclusion is that there is no need for a new theory or terminology to understand so-called narcissistic disorders; they may be adequately explained by existing structural and developmental concepts. There is no question that "narcissism" is anachronistic and outmoded as both term and concept. Nevertheless, it will persist, because it is well established, no substitute has even been offered, and it condenses a complex of ideas into one word that, like the "ego," can be differentiated from its context.

REFERENCES

Akhtar, S. (1989a). Kohut and Kernberg. In *Self Psychology,* ed. D. W. Detrick & S. P. Detrick, pp. 329–362. Hillsdale, N.J.: Analytic Press.

———. (1989b). Narcissistic personality disorder. *Psychiat. Clinics N. Amer.,* 12:505–529.

Alford, C. F. (1988). *Narcissism: Socrates, the Frankfurt School, and Psychoanalytic Theory.* New Haven: Yale Univ. Press.

Andreas-Salome, L. (1921). The dual orientation of narcissism. Trans. and rpt. in *Psychoanal. Q.,* 31(1962):1–30.

Apfelbaum, B. (1965). Ego psychology, psychic energy, and the hazards of quantitative explanation in psycho-analytic theory. *Int. J. Psychoanal.,* 46:168–182.

Balint, M. (1960). Primary narcissism and primary love. *Psychoanal. Q.,* 29:6–43.

Balter, L., & Spencer, J. H. (1991). Observation and theory in psychoanalysis. *Psychoanal. Q.,* 50:361–395.

Basch, M. F. (1981). Selfobject disorders and psychoanalytic theory. *J. Amer. Psychoanal. Assn.,* 29:337–353.

Beres, D., & Joseph, E. D. (1970). The concept of mental representation in psychoanalysis. *Int. J. Psychoanal.,* 51:1–10.

Bernstein, I. (1957). The role of narcissism in moral masochism. *Psychoanal. Q.,* 26:358–377.

Bibring, E. (1954). Psychoanalysis and the dynamic psychotherapies. *J. Amer. Psychoanal. Assn.,* 2:745–770.

Bing, J. F., McLaughlin, F., & Marburg, R. (1959). The metapsychology of narcissism. *Psychoanal. Study Child,* 14:9–26.

Blos, P. (1974). The genealogy of the ego ideal. *Psychoanal. Study Child,* 29:43–88.

Chasseguet-Smirgel, J. (1976). Some thoughts on the ego ideal. *Psychoanal. Q.,* 45:345–373.

———. (1984). *The Ego Ideal.* New York: Norton.

Cohn, Franz. (1940). Practical approach to the problem of narcissistic neuroses. *Psychoanal. Q.,* 9:64–79.

Cooper, A. M. (1984). Narcissism in normal development. In *Character Pathology,* ed. Michael Zales, pp. 39–56. New York: Brunner/Mazel.

———. (1986). Narcissism. In *Essential Papers on Narcissism,* ed. A. P. Morrison, pp. 112–143. New York: New York Univ. Press.

———. (1987). The narcissistic-masochistic character. In *Masochism: Current Psychoanalytic Perspectives,* ed. R. A. Glick & D. Meyers, pp. 117–138. Hillsdale, N.J.: Analytic Press.

Dare, C., & Holder, A. (1981). Developmental aspects of the interaction between narcissism, self-esteem and object relations. *Int. J. Psychoanal.*, 62:323–337.

Eisnitz, A. J. (1974). On the metapsychology of narcissistic pathology. *J. Amer. Psychoanal. Assn.*, 22:279–291.

Elkisch, P. (1957). The psychological significance of the mirror. *J. Amer. Psychoanal. Assn.*, 5:235–244.

Erikson, E. H. (1956). The problem of ego identity. *J. Amer. Psychoanal. Assn.*, 4:56–121.

Etiemble, R. (1954). The new China and the Chinese language. *Int. Rev. Philosophy and Humanistic Studies*, 8:93–110.

Freeman, T. (1964). Some aspects of pathological narcissism. *J. Amer. Psychoanal. Assn.*, 12:540–561.

Freud, S. (1905). *Three Essays on the Theory of Sexuality. SE*, 7:130–243.

———. (1910). The psycho-analytic view of psychogenic disturbance of vision. *SE*, 11:211–218.

———. (1911). Psycho-analytic notes on an autobiographical account of a case of paranoia (dementia paranoides). *SE*, 12:9–82.

———. (1914). On narcissism. *SE*, 14:73–102.

———. (1915). Instincts and their vicissitudes. *SE*, 14:117–140.

———. (1916–17). *Introductory Lectures on Psycho-Analysis. SE*, 15 & 16.

———. (1917). Mourning and melancholia. *SE*, 14:243–258.

———. (1920). *Beyond the Pleasure Principle. SE*, 18:7–64.

———. (1921). *Group Psychology and the Analysis of the Ego. SE*, 18:69–143.

———. (1923a). *The Ego and the Id. SE*, 19:3–66.

———. (1923b). Two encyclopedia articles. *SE*, 18:235–259.

———. (1930). *Civilization and Its Discontents. SE*, 21:64–145.

———. (1931). Libidinal types. *SE*, 21:217–220.

———. (1933). *New Introductory Lectures on Psycho-Analysis. SE*, 22:5–182.

———. (1940). *An Outline of Psycho-Analysis. SE*, 23:144–207.

Glover, E. (1943). The concept of dissociation. *Int. J. Psychoanal.*, 24:7–13.

Greenacre, P. (1945). The biologic economy of birth. *Psychoanal. Study Child*, 1:31–51.

———. (1958). Early physical determinants in the development of the sense of identity. *J. Amer. Psychoanal. Assn.*, 6:612–627.

Greenberg, J. R., & Mitchell, S. A. (1983). *Object Relations in Psychoanalytic Theory*. Cambridge, Mass.: Harvard Univ. Press.

Grunberger, B. (1971). *Narcissism: Psychoanalytic Essays*. New York: Int. Univ. Press, 1979.

Guntrip, H. (1961). *Personality Structure and Human Interaction*. New York: Int. Univ. Press.

———. (1979). *Psychoanalytic Theory, Therapy, and the Self*. New York: Basic Books.

Hanly, Charles (1992). On narcissistic defenses. *Psychoanal. Study Child*, 47:139–158.

Hartmann, H. (1939). *Ego Psychology and the Problem of Adaptation*. New York: Int. Univ. Press, 1958.

———. (1950). Comments on the psychoanalytic theory of the ego. *Psychoanal. Study Child*, 5:74–96.

Hartmann, H., & Loewenstein, R. M. (1962). Notes on the superego. *Psychoanal. Study Child*, 17:42–81.

Hartmann, H., Kris, E., & Loewenstein, R. M. (1949). Notes on the theory of aggression. *Psychoanal. Study Child*, 3/4:9–36.

Hendrick, I. (1964). Narcissism and the prepuberty ego ideal. *J. Amer. Psychoanal. Assn.*, 12:522–528.

Hermann, I. (1976). Clinging—going-in-search. *Psychoanal. Q.*, 44:5–36.

Holt, R. R. (1967). On the insufficiency of drive as a motivational concept in the light of evidence from experimental psychology (abst.). *J. Amer. Psychoanal. Assn.*, 16:627–632.

Horney, K. (1939). *New Ways in Psychoanalysis*. New York: Norton.

Jacobson, E. (1954). The self and the object world. *Psychoanal. Study Child*, 9:75–127.

———. (1964). *The Self and the Object World*. New York: Int. Univ. Press.

———. (1971). *Depression*. New York: Int. Univ. Press.

Joffe, W. G., & Sandler, J. (1967). Some conceptual problems involved in the consideration of disorders of narcissism. *J. Child Psychother.*, 2:56–66.

Kanzer, M. (1964). Freud's uses of the terms "auto-erotism" and "narcissism." *J. Amer. Psychoanal. Assn.*, 12:529–539.

Kardiner, A., Karush, A., & Oversey, L. (1959). A methodological study of Freudian theory. *J. Nerv. Ment. Dis.*, 129:133–143.

Kernberg, O. (1967). Borderline personality organization. *J. Amer. Psychoanal. Assn.*, 15:641–685.

———. (1974). Further contributions to the treatment of the narcissistic personality. *Int. J. Psychoanal.*, 55:215–240.

———. (1975). *Borderline Conditions and Pathological Narcissism*. New York: Aronson.

———. (1978). The diagnosis of borderline conditions in adolescence. *Adolesc. Psychiat.*, 16:298–319.

———. (1980). *Internal World and External Reality*. New York: Aronson.

———. (1984). *Severe Personality Disorders*. New Haven: Yale Univ. Press.

———. (1991). A contemporary reading of "On narcissism." In Sandler et al., eds., pp. 131–148.

Kohut, H. (1966). Forms and transformations of narcissism. *J. Amer. Psychoanal. Assn.*, 14:243–272.

———. (1968). The psychoanalytic treatment of narcissistic personality disorders. *Psychoanal. Study Child*, 23:86–113.

———. (1971). *The Analysis of the Self*. New York: Int. Univ. Press.

———. (1972). Thoughts on narcissism and narcissistic rage. *Psychoanal. Study Child*, 27:360–400.

———. (1977). *The Restoration of the Self*. New York: Int. Univ. Press.

———. (1978). *The Search for the Self*, ed. P. H. Ornstein. New York: Int. Univ. Press.

———. (1979). The two analyses of Mr. Z. *Int. J. Psychoanal.*, 60:3–27.

———. (1984). *How Does Analysis Cure?* Edited by A. Goldberg with P. E. Stepansky. Chicago: Univ. Chicago Press.

Kohut, H., & Wolf, E. S. (1978). The disorders of the self and their treatment. *Int. J. Psychoanal.*, 59:413–425.

Kuhn, R. S. (1970). *The Structure of Scientific Revolutions*. Chicago: Univ. Chicago Press.

Lasch, C. (1979). *The Culture of Narcissism*. New York: Warner Books.

Lichtenstein, H. (1964). The role of narcissism in the emergence and maintenance of a primary identity. *Int. J. Psychoanal.*, 45:49–56.

Loewald, H. W. (1951). Ego and reality. *Int. J. Psychoanal.*, 32:10–18.

Mahler, M. S. (1979). On human symbiosis and the vicissitudes of individuation. In *Selected Papers*, vol. 2, pp. 77–98. New York: Aronson.

Mahler, M. S., & McDevitt, J. B. (1968). Observations on adaptation and defense *in statu nascendi*. *Psychoanal. Q.*, 37:1–21.

Marcovitz, E. (1972). Some aspects of aggression in the concept of narcissism. *Bull. Philadelphia Assn. Psychoanal.*, 22:276–283.

Moore, B. E. (1972). Discussion of paper by G. R. Ticho on "Clinical Aspects of the Narcissistic Personality," presented to the Western Regional Psychoanalytic Assn. in San Diego.

———. (1975). Toward a clarification of the concept of narcissism. *Psychoanal. Study Child*, 30:243–276.

Moore, B. E., & Fine, B. D., eds. (1968). *A Glossary of Psychoanalytic Terms and Concepts*. New York: American Psychoanalytic Assn.

———, eds. (1990). *Psychoanalytic Terms and Concepts*. New Haven: Yale Univ. Press.

Morganthau, H., & Person, E. (1978). The roots of narcissism. *Partisan Review*, 3:338–347.

Murray, J. M. (1964). Narcissism and the ego ideal. *J. Amer. Psychoanal. Assn.*, 12:477–511.

Niederland, W. G. (1965). Narcissistic ego impairment in patients with early physical malformations. *Psychoanal. Study Child*, 20:518–534.

Nunberg, H. (1931). The synthetic function of the ego. *Int. J. Psychoanal.*, 12:123–140.

Nunberg, H., & Federn, F., eds. (1962, 1967). *Minutes of the Vienna Psychoanalytic Society*, 1:118 & 2:312. New York: Int. Univ. Press.

Panel (1958). Problems of identity (abst.). M. S. Mahler, reporter. *J. Amer. Psychoanal. Assn.*, 6:136–138.

———. (1961). Narcissism. J. F. Bing & R. O. Marburg, reporters. *J. Amer. Psychoanal. Assn.*, 10(1962):593–605.

———. (1969). Narcissistic resistance. N. P. Segel, reporter. *J. Amer. Psychoanal. Assn.*, 17:941–954.

Pulver, S. E. (1970). Narcissism. *J. Amer. Psychoanal. Assn.*, 18:319–341.

Reich, A. (1953). Narcissistic object choice in women. *J. Amer. Psychoanal. Assn.*, 1:22–44.

———. (1954). Early identifications as archaic elements in the superego. *J. Amer. Psychoanal. Assn.*, 2:218–238.

———. (1960). Pathologic forms of self-esteem regulation. *Psychoanal. Study Child*, 15:215–231.

Reich, W. (1933). *Character Analysis*. New York: Orgone Institute Press.

Rosenfeld, H. (1964). On the psychopathology of narcissism. *Int. J. Psychoanal.*, 45:332–337.

———. (1971). A clinical approach to the psychoanalytic theory of the life and death instincts. *Int. J. Psychoanal.*, 52:169–178.

Rothstein, A. (1977). The ego attitude of entitlement. *Int. Rev. Psychoanal.*, 4:409–417.

———. (1979a). The diagnostic term. *J. Amer. Psychoanal. Assn.*, 27:893–912.

———. (1979b). Oedipal conflicts in narcissistic personality disorders. *Int. J. Psychoanal.*, 60:189–199.

———. (1980a). *The Narcissistic Pursuit of Perfection*. New York: Int. Univ. Press.

———. (1980b). Toward a critique of the psychology of the self. *Psychoanal. Q.*, 49:423–455.

———. (1982). The implications of early psychopathology for the analyzability of narcissistic disorders. *Int. J. Psychoanal.*, 63:177–188.

———. (1984). The fear of humiliation. *J. Amer. Psychoanal. Assn.*, 32:99–116.

Sandler, J., Person, E. S., & Fonagy, P., eds. (1991).

Freud's "On Narcissism: An Introduction." New Haven: Yale Univ. Press.

Schur, M. (1966). *The Id and the Regulatory Principles of Mental Functioning.* New York: Int. Univ. Press.

Settlage, C. (1977). The psychoanalytic understanding of narcissistic and borderline personality disorders. *J. Amer. Psychoanal. Assn.,* 25:805–834.

Spiegel, L. A. (1959). The self, the sense of self, and perception. *Psychoanal. Study Child,* 14:81–109.

Spitz, R. (1959). *A Genetic Field Theory of Ego Formation.* New York: Int. Univ. Press.

Spruiell, V. (1974). Theories of the treatment of narcissistic personalities. *J. Amer. Psychoanal. Assn.,* 22:255–278.

———. (1975). Three strands of narcissism. *Psychoanal. Q.,* 44:577–595.

Stolorow, R. D. (1975a). The narcissistic function of masochism and sadism. *Int. J. Psychoanal.,* 56:441–448.

———. (1975b). Toward a functional definition of narcissism. *Int. J. Psychoanal.,* 56:179–185.

Stone, Leo (1954). The widening scope of indications for psychoanalysis. *J. Amer. Psychoanal. Assn.,* 2:567–594.

Strachey, J. (1957). Editor's Introduction to *The Ego and the Id. SE,* 19:7–8.

Teicholz, J. G. (1978). A selective review of the psychoanalytic literature on theoretical conceptualizations of narcissism. *J. Amer. Psychoanal. Assn.,* 26:831–861.

Ticho, G. (1972). Clinical aspects of the narcissistic personality. Paper presented to the Western Regional Psychoanalytic Assn., in San Diego.

Tyson, P., & Tyson, R. L. (1984). Narcissism and superego development. *J. Amer. Psychoanal. Assn.,* 32:75–98.

Waelder, R. (1960). *Basic Theory of Psychoanalysis.* New York: Int. Univ. Press.

———. (1961). Discussion, Section III, Conference, Institute for Advanced Psychoanalytic Studies, Princeton, N.J.

Wallerstein, R. S. (1981). The bipolar self. *J. Amer. Psychoanal. Assn.,* 29:377–398.

Weiss, E. (1957). A comparative study of psychoanalytical ego concepts. *Int. J. Psychoanal.,* 38:209–222.

Jules Glenn, M.D., and

Isidor Bernstein, M.D.

20

SADOMASOCHISM

DEFINITIONS

Although the terms "masochism" and "sadism" originally connoted overt sexual perversions, their meanings, especially that of masochism, have been greatly broadened. They now include a variety of psychic phenomena in which the aggressive and libidinal drives fuse. They encompass the full breadth of the personality structure, and serve functions of defense as well as drive gratification and superego demands. Because sadism and masochism generally appear together (Freud, 1905; Blum, 1991), the word *sado-masochism* has been coined.

The term "masochism" derives from the writings of Leopold von Sacher Masoch, a novelist who described persons who derive sexual satisfaction from being treated cruelly. Krafft-Ebing (1908) defined masochism as "a peculiar perversion of the psychic *vita sexualis* in which the individual affected, in sexual feeling and thought, is controlled by the idea of being completely and unconditionally subject to the will of a person of the opposite sex, of being treated by this person as by a master, humiliated and abused. This idea is colored by sexual feeling; the masochist lives in fantasies in which he creates situations of this kind, and he often attempts to realize them" (p. 115). Many persons require beating, humiliation, or torture for sexual gratification, including orgasm, but clinical experience has demonstrated that the real or imagined partner need not be

of the opposite sex. Nor does the sexual consummation have to involve an actual partner; the partner may exist in fantasy, and the sexual act may be a masturbatory one.

The term "sadism," which likewise has a literary derivation, comes from the works of the Marquis de Sade (Donatien Alphonse François Sade), whose characters depend on inflicting cruelty on others for sexual gratification. Hinsie and Campbell (1970) define it as "a sexual perversion in which orgasm is dependent upon torturing others or inflicting pain, ill-treatment and humiliation on others" (p. 673). As with masochism, the partner may be of the same or the opposite sex, actual or fantasied, and the sexual act may be masturbatory.

Masochism and sadism have been used colloquially, and later scientifically, to designate not only undisguised perversions but also behavior in which the sexual component is unconscious. Hence, one can call "sadistic" a person who is mean or enjoys cruelty even if he or she is not aware of any sexual component to it. Similarly, a person who habitually invites punishment, psychic or physical, pain, or humiliation is often designated "masochistic."

Currently, *masochism* is defined as a "propensity to seek physical or mental suffering in order to achieve sexual arousal and gratification" (Moore & Fine, eds., 1990). This propensity may be conscious or unconscious. Similarly, *sadism* consists of the propensity to produce in others physical or mental suffering in reality or fantasy in order to achieve, consciously or unconsciously, gratification or pleasure —sexual arousal in the widest sense.

Freud (1924), while cognizant of the overlap of categories, classified masochism as erotogenic, feminine, or moral. "Erotogenic masochism" connoted the instinctual bases for masochism; "feminine masochism" referred to the fact that men (or women) may identify with women who, they imagine, by nature seek pain; in "moral masochism," the person, under the influence of his superego, seeks punishment. In addition, analysts now employ the category of "masochistic character" to include persons whose behavior is determined by masochistic mechanisms and fantasies.

Freud also observed that a degree of sadism and masochism occurs in normal childhood and adult development and that specific factors can cause it to reach pathological proportions. Further, masochism can be hidden by repression and other defenses and reappear disguised as neurosis.

Brenner (1959) emphasized that masochism, a universal phenomenon, results from compromise formation in which id, ego, and superego participate. The individual punishes him- or herself for oedipal wishes that are defended against but gratified in a disguised way. Despite a disclaimer on his part, in Brenner's clinical descriptions object relations and reality factors play important roles in determining the form and content of the unconscious conflicts involved in masochism.

Blum (1991) says that sadism and masochism "are closely related and universally found together so that it is virtually impossible to conceptualize one without the other" (p. 432). Some think, as Pulver (Panel, 1991) has stated, that the presence of conscious or unconscious sexual fantasies is essential to the diagnosis of masochism (Coen, 1988; Glenn, 1989). Others, focusing on moral masochism, assert that sexual fantasies need not be present; in their view, masochism includes a variety of self-defeating behaviors with or without a sexual base (Maleson, 1984). We believe that masochism includes a sexual component which may consist of erotized pain.

FREUD ON SADOMASOCHISM

Early on, Freud (1905) emphasized the importance of drives as determinants of masochism and sadism. He established that sadomasochism has a constitutional basis, but that environmental factors influence its development. This continues to be a fundamental psychoanalytic premise. Masochism and sadism, Freud observed, cannot be understood without noting their relation to each other; they generally coexist (p. 159). He said that the two comprise the active and passive forms of cruelty (p. 166). Which form is primary, if either is, he did not make entirely clear. In 1905 he *appeared* to believe that sadism is primary; later, in 1920, he seems to have decided that masochism was the fundamental and initial form. But even in the earlier work, he made statements that indicated an uncertainty; indeed, clinically we see that each may defend against the other.

In 1905 he said that masochism consists of sadism turned around upon the subject's own self, which thus takes the place of the sexual object. Emphasizing the instinctual basis for masochism, Freud (1905) suggested that an "erotogenic effect attaches even to intensely painful feelings, especially where the pain is toned down or kept at a distance by some accompanying condition" and that herein lies one of the main roots of the "masochistic-sadistic instinct" (p. 204). In a 1924 footnote he coined the term "erotogenic masochism" for this basic instinctual configuration. We may conclude that for Freud in 1905 sadism and masochism evolved together.

As formulated by Freud (1905), the drive determinants of sadomasochism thus include:

(1) The primary fact that all painful experiences contain within themselves the possibility of pleasurable feelings.

(2) The aggressive component of the sexual instinct, which is necessary to overcome the love object's resistance. In this sense, sadism corresponds to a component of the sexual instinct becoming independent and exaggerated and, by displacement, usurping the leading position.

(3) The instinct for mastery, which may have an anal aspect as well as a more general value.

(4) An anal component. Freud stated that all children pass through an anal-sadistic stage which includes an active and a passive aspect. An "instinct for mastery" determines the active form, which expresses itself in muscular activities. The passive sexual aim derives largely from the erotogenic mucous membrane of the anus. The "anality" may involve the skin of the buttocks. Citing Jean Jacques Rousseau's *Confessions,* Freud observed that educators have known "that the painful stimulation of the skin of the buttocks is one of the erotogenic roots of the *passive* instinct of cruelty (masochism)" (p. 193).

(5) The erotogenic importance of the skin in general and "of those components of the sexual instinct which involve pain and cruelty" (p. 169).

(6) The influence of observation of the primal scene, which the child misinterprets as sadistic.

When Freud established the somatic underpinnings for sadism and masochism, he believed that libido encompassed aggression. Later, in 1920, he developed the dual instinct theory, according to which sexual and aggressive drives exist but can fuse. Libidinal and aggressive components of various intensities appear together in what may be called a psychic amalgam. Freud's concept of a death instinct, a primary masochistic aggressive drive directed at the self, is now disavowed by a majority of analysts.

When Freud wrote his *Three Essays,* he had not fully developed the concept of defenses. He talked of active or passive aims—the drive being directed toward the self (passive) or the object (active) as characteristics of the drives, which they are. But he did not describe the defensive significance of shifting from active to passive aims, or vice versa, as carefully as later analysts have done. Nor had Freud in 1905 developed the structural theory, which did not come until 1923, and the concept of the superego. Hence he did not fully appreciate the role and interactions of the various agencies of the personality or the role of self-punishment.

In 1919, when he wrote "A child is being beaten," Freud could deal with developmental and defensive shifts more extensively, but even then he did not appreciate fully the intricacy of the conditions that analysts today recognize. Masochism or sadism in different people may be enhanced by different types of experiences and the use of different hierarchies of defenses. We will demonstrate Freud's pioneering efforts in "A child is being beaten" by commenting on his observations and theories regarding masochistic and sadistic fantasies in girls but will for brevity's sake omit his discussion of boys.

Freud describes three stages in the development of the conscious or unconscious fantasy "a child is being beaten" in girls. In the earliest version, the girl imagines that her father is beating a child, most often a brother or sister whom she hates. This initial fantasy, which may appear as a memory, signifies: my father, whom I love, does not love the other child; he loves only me. The girl thus gratifies her jealousy, with its erotic underpinnings, as well as her narcissism.

Freud observed that in the second period the fantasy, which the analyst must reconstruct, is transformed into a highly pleasurable one: "I am being beaten by my father." The child, now feeling guilty because of her wishes for the father's love, which have become incestuous and perhaps masturbatory, punishes herself by reversing the situation. The sadism expressed in the first beating fantasy is converted into masochism. At the same time, the forbidden libidinal desires appear in disguised form as an anal regressive substitute for the genital feelings

toward the father. The beating now signifies sexual activity.

In its final form, a man, such as a teacher but never the father, beats a number of children, most often boys whom the girl does not know, as the girl looks on. The achievement of this form of the fantasy is complicated indeed. The teacher is the father in disguise, and the boys being beaten stand for the patient; hence the masochistic gratification of the second stage maintains itself. Simultaneously, the girl continues to express her hatred for her rivals and for the first time gives vent to her hatred of boys, whose masculinity she envies.

Although Freud did not use the term "defense" and had not systematically categorized the different defense mechanisms in 1919, we can see the patient's use of repression, regression, displacement, identification, and reversal.

PHENOMENOLOGY AND DIAGNOSIS

Sadomasochism covers a wide variety of phenomena. Freud, as we have noted, categorized masochism as erotogenic, feminine, and moral. Symptomatically, sadism and masochism manifest themselves in behavior ranging from minor forms such as scratching or nail biting to more serious forms such as hair pulling, torturing animals, self-mutilation. In the sexual realm, sadism and masochism may appear as unconscious masturbation fantasies, conscious sexual fantasies, or overt sexual perversions. The individual may unknowingly enact masturbation fantasies in the social arena, committing crimes or provoking attacks (A. Freud, 1949). Or he or she may become inhibited or suffer from impotence or frigidity.

A degree of sadomasochism is normal, universal, and inevitable. It may appear in sublimated forms with a minimal degree of neutralization of energy (Hartmann, 1964), as in the professions of boxing, wrestling, and many contact sports, or with a great deal of neutralization as in the case of nurses, surgeons, and other medical specialists. At times, internal conflicts or external circumstances may bring about a change in psychic balance, a diminution of neutralization, and the emergence of sadism or masochism in rawer forms.

Sadomasochism appears in all diagnostic categories. In fact, any form of psychopathology may involve conscious or unconscious sadomasochism. Such disturbances include perversions, character disturbances, sexual and other inhibitions, conversion hysteria, and paranoid states. Unconscious sadism plays an important role in obsessive-compulsive neuroses in which defenses like reaction formation hide the patient's aggression by the appearance of opposite tendencies, such as extreme kindness or gentleness. Paranoid thinking (Bak, 1946; Blum, 1980) appears in paranoid personalities and in borderline and narcissistic patients. It also occurs as blatant paranoid delusions in schizophrenics and other psychotics. The fantasy that others will attack, when it plagues patients with seriously defective reality testing, will result in such delusions. Kernberg (1988, 1991) has offered a detailed differentiation of types of persons in whom masochism is a dominant trait and the developmental levels involved. He has observed that sadism and masochism can appear in persons with any form of personality structuring, from the most primitive pre-oedipal organization to the more advanced.

Sadomasochistic conditions encompass many different dynamics. Rarely if ever does one find a simple structure to sadomasochism; the principles of multiple function and overdetermination (Waelder, 1936) govern our understanding of the condition. In the sections that follow we will describe the building blocks comprising sadomasochism and will then present a case to illustrate how unconscious conflicts and their attempted resolution through compromise formation organize the components described (Brenner, 1959).

Masochism does not encompass all forms of suffering. People may be willing to endure pain as a necessary condition for achieving an ideal, a gratification, or a realistic goal. For instance, a child may accept marked discomfort to have a splinter removed, or a woman may tolerate considerable pain in order to give birth. Only when a person seeks pain as a source of pleasure can we consider it masochistic.

DRIVES, DEVELOPMENT, AND SADOMASOCHISM

From the start, analysts have observed instinctual drive aspects of sadomasochism. We have seen that initially Freud postulated a complicated "instinct of cruelty," which appears as sadism and masochism, and which results from a host of determinants. Clinical experience indicates that sadism and masochism are not isolated drives, but appear in different configurations throughout development—in the pre-oedipal and oedipal periods, latency, adolescence, and adulthood (Panel, 1985). Aggressive and libidinal drives fuse in their formation. During the oral phase, the infant's urges to bite and aggressively incorporate the mother occur in conjunction with loving wishes for mother. During the anal phase, the child's pleasure in squeezing the stool and producing anal stimulation forms another basis for sado-masochism. The stool, which may represent a part of the self, a baby, or another person, is hurt in fantasy, while the intestinal and anal mucosa are both stimulated and hurt. In addition, toilet training may involve a battle between mother and child. The mother may wish that her toddler surrender his or her stool, which the child values. The child may resist, insisting that he or she defecate or urinate at a time and place of his or her own choosing. Parent and child may become angry with each other, an anger colored by their loving relationship.

For example, Betty, aged three, consciously and intentionally withheld bowel movements for days at a time. In her analytic sessions she loved to play a game in which she toilet-trained her analyst in fantasy. In another game she instructed her analyst to pretend that he had attempted unsuccessfully to make her defecate in the pot.

As a boy's scrotum and testicles become more important to him, he may combine stimulation of them with masochistic fantasies (Glenn, 1969). Their proximity to the anus may facilitate displacement of anal pleasures to the testicular area along with associated fantasies. The penis, which the child has nonspecific urges to use to thrust and enter, often becomes associated with more aggressive feelings (Kestenberg, 1967–68), while the rest of the genitals, with their relatively slow and poorly perceived movements, become associated with passive behavior in the sense of relative inactivity. The scrotum and testicles may also become a locus of passivity in the sense that the individual imagines others doing things to him. The fact that hitting or squeezing the testicles is painful, at least after puberty, facilitates masochistic experiences connected with them. The boy may cause himself pain during masturbation by applying pressure to the testicles.

The penis may also be the source of such passive aims (Loewenstein, 1935). Being touched or stroked is pleasurable. But soon the child experiences his penis as a thrusting or penetrating organ by means of which he can enter unspecified, mysterious, confusing areas. A child in the phallic and oedipal phases does not understand fully what sexual intercourse involves, but his bodily feelings propel him to activity. The linking of the aggressive with the libidinal at the oedipal period may give rise to sadistic or, if the aggression is turned against the self, masochistic wishes.

Girls go through an active phase in the phallic and oedipal periods (Deutsch, 1944). During clitoral cathexis, the girl may also experience impulses to thrust and enter; often fantasies of lovingly and aggressively entering mother appear. Then, as the child's genital sensations change, passive aims may predominate; the girl will have vague wishes that something enter her inner bodily space (Erikson, 1951).

As the child continues to develop, he or she experiences a series of unpleasurable tension states followed by relief and pleasure. The sources of pain and gratification are, at first, localized in the various erogenous zones. Those parts of the body (mouth-lip, anus-rectum, genitals) then become valued as sources of pleasure or narcissistic gratification. The painful sensations or experiences may be projected or externalized and be perceived as an outside persecutor (Arlow, 1949), a prototype of subsequent sadomasochistic and, in more severely disturbed individuals, paranoid trends.

The child's observations of, or fantasies about, his parents' interaction influence his or her state of mind. During the oedipal and pre-oedipal periods, the child may have seen or heard his parents engage in intercourse (the primal scene) or have watched or heard them argue or fight physically. Either of these parental encounters can excite a child, who often identifies with both partners, picturing him- or herself as the attacker as well as the victim, the active as well as the passive sexual partner. He or she thus places him- or herself in both a sadistic and a masochistic position. These primal scene experiences or fantasies, when they occur before the appearance of the oedipal complex, may later be integrated with that stage. The child watching, hearing, or imagining the primal scene or related incidents that he or she interprets as such may imagine one parent castrating the other, again, perceiving what to him or her is a sadomasochistic act (Freud, 1918).

As we noted in our discussion of "A child is being beaten," the girl may be angry with boys because she envies their masculine status—their possession of a penis and their special favored position in the family and society (Horney, 1935, 1936). Her anger with males (and with the parents when they produce and favor boys) becomes part of her sadism or, when the sadism is turned against the self, her masochism. Boys, too, may harbor fantasies and fears of disfavor and deficiency, with a similar sadistic and masochistic outcome. Stoller (1975) has emphasized the importance of the hostility present in all pornography and in perversions.

The masochist may reveal his or her own sadistic inclinations as he or she attempts to humiliate, figuratively castrate, and defeat a partner viewed as sadistic and may also try to create guilt or shame in him or her. This may be done by seducing or provoking the partner and causing him to lose control (Loewenstein, 1957). This may enact a sadistic, vengeful reversal of childhood humiliations and de-

feats. These derivatives become especially apparent to the analyst when the masochistic patient tries to provoke him or her to angry, unprofessional behavior. If the patient succeeds in causing the analyst to abandon his or her analytic stance, the therapist often mentally chastises him- or herself.

During latency, sadomasochistic impulses are generally dampened along with undisguised sexual urges in general. They may appear in overt form during interruptions of latency and in covert form in games and other interchanges. During preadolescence and adolescence the drives erupt again, and sadomasochism will once more appear, sometimes as a result of regression to earlier states, sometimes as a defense against incestuous longings. Commonly, adolescents retreat from their loving feelings toward their parents by provoking and fighting with them. The parents may join their children in their defensive stance, engaging in exciting and disturbing battles.

THE OEDIPUS COMPLEX AND THE SUPEREGO

The oedipus complex is often the most important driving force behind sadomasochism. Forbidden incestuous and hostile wishes may stir castration anxiety and fears of loss of love and of the approval of the superego, which in turn press the ego to invoke defenses that accentuate sadomasochism. The defenses evoked include turning aggression toward the self; regressing to the anal-sadistic, oral, and/or narcissistic states; or becoming the passive victim or the active attacker in identification with the aggressor. Sadomasochism then becomes a compromise formation combining gratification of oedipal wishes, defenses against them, pre-oedipal pleasures and conflicts resulting from aggressive expressions, and punishment by the patient's superego. The source of punishment may be the self or others whom the person provokes, and often, but not always, pain is a prerequisite for oedipal gratification. Brenner (1959) suggests that superego function involves masochism, in that it entails aggression directed against the self.

The turning of aggression against the self may involve not only self-punishment but also defense. Children, not wishing to hurt the parents whom they love and hate, attack themselves in masochistic behavior. In another defensive maneuver the children may create and accept punishment for a crime other than the oedipal one, a lesser crime involving defiance of toilet training, for instance. In addition, children who fear loving feelings may become masochistic or sadistic in relation to the loved person in order to avoid affectionate closeness. Men may fear tenderness because they equate tenderness with femininity. Women may fear tenderness because it reminds them of their relationship with their mother and so poses a homosexual threat.

The quality of the superego may propel the individual toward moral masochism. The more primitive the superego and the more it is charged with aggression or sadism, the more punishing it will be, and the more it will favor acceptance of pain, submission, and humiliation. The setting of unrealistically high standards of conduct or achievement will diminish self-esteem and intensify the hostility of the superego toward the self (Reich, 1954). A child who is harshly treated or severely punished may establish, through identification, a harsh and punishing superego and a self representation as "bad" and deserving of punishment or mistreatment. Likewise, a child who has set high standards as a means of controlling threatening instinctual urges will be intolerant of even minor infractions. A child may also defensively set up a strict superego when the environment is overly permissive or seductive.

Masochism may be used to diminish a person's guilty feelings through suffering. For example, a ten-year-old girl's masochistic suffering served to alleviate her guilt regarding her hostility to her mother and her sexual feelings toward boys. She complained of her mother's treatment of her, claiming that the mother favored her younger brother. Similarly, she felt that her friends sided with each other against her. Nothing she did or that was done for her gave her pleasure. She was troubled by severe obsessional doubts: had she or had she not cheated in school by looking at another student's paper? Had she or had she not stolen something from a store? She tortured herself and her parents with these doubts. Her conflict about looking was also present in relation to showing. She imagined being a gymnast or a ballerina and displaying her talents. On the conscious level, she was embarrassed by the beginnings of breast development and tried to hide it. Nevertheless, she had fantasies of boys looking at her breasts and guilt-provoking wishes for boys to touch them. The doubts could be related to her ambivalent feelings toward her mother and to the struggle over her sexual wishes. The mother had recently recovered from a life-threatening illness for which she had been hospitalized for several weeks. In discussing this, the girl declared that she was not sure that she had wanted her mother to live. The guilty feelings could be alleviated by causing or imagining other people to be critical of her. Her dissatisfaction with her body and herself and her disapproval of her sexual and hostile wishes made it difficult for her to derive pleasure from anything she did or anything that was done for her and made her

feel criticized and unloved. She identified with the mother's self-demanding, self-critical attitudes. The girl continually expected criticism and failure, an externalization of her own critical, self-defeating orientation.

In cases where the suffering alleviates guilt and/ or serves as punishment for guilt, the pain has been considered a prerequisite for sexual pleasure rather than part of the sexual pleasure (Brenner, 1959). Although oedipal conflicts are often the chief motor, forming and organizing sadomasochistic patterns, there are cases in which the prime conflict is pre-oedipal. Indeed, a controversy exists as to whether and when pre-oedipal versus oedipal factors play leading roles in the formation of sadomasochism. Some contend that sadistic and masochistic perversions occur as expressions of and defenses against oedipal drives (Fenichel, 1945; Gedo, in Panel, 1984). Others, including the authors, believe that frank perversions most frequently appear in primitive personalities who are immersed in pre-oedipal conflict and often only weakly and tentatively enter the oedipal stage. The oedipal stage of many perverts is distorted under the influence of early drive and ego configurations as well as primitive superegos dominated by harsh superego precursors. In people with perversions, difficulties in reality testing interfere with proper evaluation and facilitate the capacity to get pleasure from intense fantasies that are dramatized in the sex act. An ego split may occur in which the individual at one and the same time believes in a fantastic idea (such as that women have penises) and also knows the truth (Freud, 1940). Controversy exists in efforts to explain the evolution of particular cases of overt perversion—for example, as to whether a developmental arrest initiates the perverse behavior, whether it results from regression to fixation points, or whether it grows out of distorted development. These same questions may arise in the assessment of other forms of sadomasochism as well. Brenner's (1959) view that there is a continuum between normal and pathological expressions of masochism tends to obscure the qualitative differences between the more primitive, instinctualized nature of pathological masochism in the masochistic perversion or character and the more neutralized varieties in the subtler manifestations of masochism.

OBJECT RELATIONS

Freud correctly described the relationship between object relations and drives. Through the persons around him, the child can satisfy his or her urges. Indeed, the quality and quantity of parental response may determine the nature and intensity of the child's relationships with others. The child will develop a set of inner representations of the parents and then react to others as if they are identical, a phenomenon referred to by the terms "displacement" and "transference." Object relations thus involve not only actual interactions but also fantasies about persons, which may indeed be of overriding significance.

Parents can encourage particular types of object relations through their behavior and attitudes, but they are limited in the degree to which they can produce such relations. The child's own characteristics, his or her drives and the constitutional bases for the structure of his or her ego, will play a major role. In fact, the child can provoke a parent to play a part that he or she needs.

In the child's very early dependency period, the mother is perceived as all-powerful and all-knowing. Aspects of the mother (and the world she represents) that are gratifying, protective, and nourishing are pleasurable and are perceived as loving. They constitute an idealized image of a "good" mother. Frustrating, disappointing, and painful experiences are embodied in a hating and hated "bad" mother. This split image of the mother (and world) persists until the child is able to perceive both images as related to the one mother; he or she then forms a composite, or integrated, representation of the mother. In some instances, where there has been interference with the integration (due to prolonged separation from the mother, for instance), the child may need to preserve and retain the image of the ideal mother by representing the mother as perfect and attributing all the "badness" to his or her own self representation. Thus devalued, the child deprives him- or herself of the right to be loved, to assert him- or herself, and to satisfy his or her needs, or even claim the prerogative to exist—a powerful thrust toward masochistic submission. An alternative maneuver is for the child to attribute all bad characteristics to persons other than parent and self.

It has been observed that parents with sadistic needs may encourage their children's masochism (Berliner, 1947). The child, in order to attain love, will try to please a sadistic adult by reciprocal masochistic compliance. Or a masochistic parent may successfully encourage his or her child's sadism. The child may respond to a sadistic parent not only with compliance but also by attempting symbolically to manipulate, castrate, or defeat such a parent.

The child's compliant masochistic behavior may take on particular significance and effectiveness in the oedipal period or in adolescence. In many cases the sadomasochistic interaction starts even earlier and takes the following typical form (Bernstein,

1957): a narcissistic mother who considers her child a part of herself (Freud, 1914) encourages the child who has not fully passed through the substages of separation-individuation (Mahler et al., 1975) to conform to her wishes in order to maintain a sense of symbiotic unity with the beloved mother. This interaction can continue into adulthood.

Mrs. A., a fifty-year-old woman, sought analytic treatment because she was unhappy in her marriage. She especially resented her husband's criticism of her in the presence of their friends. He would ridicule her attempts at conversation and characterize her as stupid or incompetent. She would suffer the humiliation in speechless shame and rage until the couple was alone and then burst into hysterical sobbing. The early part of the analysis demonstrated that she was trying to elicit sympathy for her sad plight as the victim of her sadistic, tyrannical husband. This was a repetition of a childhood relationship with her mother, who complained about the father to her daughter.

Mrs. A.'s masochism was in part determined by her serving as a part object, an extension of her mother's self representation, to gratify her mother's phallic narcissistic needs. Mrs. A.'s mother would tell her daughter repeatedly how beautiful, popular, and sought after the mother had been as a young woman. This was embellished by accounts of the wonderful man she could have married had she not consented to wed Mrs. A.'s father. When the mother dressed for evening parties, she would display herself in her finery and jewels to elicit the little girl's admiring response. As Mrs. A. reached adolescence, her mother would criticize her for not being attractive (for example, her mouth was too wide). The mother would try to temper this by telling her that her redeeming feature was her personality. Mrs. A. accepted her mother's view of herself, in effect idealizing the mother and devaluing herself. Her mother pressed her for detailed accounts of her dates, including physical intimacies. This vicarious participation in her daughter's desirability constituted a narcissistic extension of the mother's wished-for self-image. It required a surrender of the girl's privacy and separateness. To this masochistic submission was added humiliation when the mother would mock and caricature her daughter's suitors, thereby depreciating those physical and intellectual attributes of her daughter that attracted realistically desirable suitors. Identification with the mother as a victim in her marriage could also be related to narcissistic needs of the patient.

Either parent may use a child as an extension of him- or herself to gratify his or her own instinctual needs. This gratification may take the form of bodily stimulation, as with Mrs. A., whose mother responded to her daughter's intestinal colic by giving her enemas for a number of years. In adolescence, her father would take her out to restaurants and bars, treating and presenting her as his "date." This stimulated and gratified her sexual fantasies, but it also frightened her. She retreated defensively from an overt oedipal stance, which her father encouraged, to a sadomasochistic relationship modeled on the repeated parental fights she had witnessed.

The appearance of primitive narcissistic configurations may result from regression. As a consequence of intense conflict over forbidden oedipal feeling, the patient may attempt to resolve the conflict through the reactivation or intensification of early narcissistic stages. The child may feel one with his or her mother and in that way feel powerful and safe. For such persons pregenital involvement is safer than genital relations. Succumbing to the mother or a surrogate may, however, lead to a sadomasochistic involvement.

Because parents may be associated with pain, the child may find that through a painful relationship he or she can retain the parents in his or her imagination. Valenstein (1973) has described the effects of painful stimulation in the early pre-oedipal period before representations of self and object are clearly separated. He states: "If the affects, especially those primal and primitive affects associated with the early self and self-object experience, take a predominantly painful direction, then a set is established wherein pain, i.e., painful affect, connotes the original self-object, and more succinctly later, the self and/or object" (p. 374). The child who has experienced pain in the pre-oedipal period due to operative procedures, illness (such as mastoiditis), constipation, diarrhea, enemas, or object loss will seek pain in order illusorily to experience the object's presence or to hurt the object with whom he or she confuses him- or herself.

Children who undergo pain during the oedipal period or later will also associate their parents with pain and attempt to recreate it (Glenn, 1984a). Thus Andy, aged three, who became terribly aggrieved and tormented by painful emotions when his parents left him for ten days, developed a masochistic need for painful experiences. He later got his sister to squeeze his penis and his brother and parents to hit or scold him. The need for painful stimulation involved other factors as well. Andy learned that his father, a distant, passive man, could be aroused by annoying him until he struck his son. His mother, who had a long-standing, mutually antagonistic relationship with her own brother, found substitute aggressive gratification through fights with Andy.

Through provocation of both parents, Andy could thus attain love in a distorted form.

In addition to using pain to retain an object tie, people who have difficulty with separation-individuation may evoke pain to solidify their body-image boundaries (Asch, 1971).

MECHANISMS OF CONTROL AND MASTERY

Children who respond to early experiences of pain, trauma, or other situations in which they are passive, helpless, or overwhelmed develop defenses whereby they attempt to control the adults around them and the impulses within. These mechanisms can be used in efforts to delimit the narcissistic injury that may occur at varying stages of development. Such injuries include deflation of fantasies of omnipotence or of fusion in the pre-oedipal period. Feelings of humiliation or disappointment in the oedipal period or later may likewise mobilize such reparative defenses. Although these defenses need not lead to masochism, they may (Bergler, 1949; Eidelberg, 1954, 1968; Glenn, 1984b; Blos, 1991; Panel, 1956, 1981, 1984, 1985, 1990, 1991).

Loewenstein (1957) has described what he calls "seduction of the aggressor." He reported the behavior of a child who responded to a scolding adult in such a way as to get the grown-up to smile. If adult and child engage in games in which such a pattern is recurrent, the defenses may encourage sadomasochistic activity and pleasure. In some societies a teasing interaction is institutionalized. Balinese mothers tease their hungry babies by breastfeeding other children in their presence (Bateson & Mead, 1942). The nasty, teasing mother later becomes personified in the witch Rangda, a prominent character in Balinese mythology and dance.

Masochists often attempt to exert control through their behavior. They know how to encourage people to attack them but can "titrate" (as one of our patients put it) the degree of provocation so as to regulate the amount of pain inflicted on them. In this way they control the extent of narcissistic mortification they have learned in childhood to anticipate (Eidelberg, ed., 1968).

Some people sadistically try to provoke painful excitement in others but consciously try to avoid physical attacks by their target. Billy, at fourteen, would stimulate his teacher by misbehaving in class until her face became flushed with excitement and then anger. He usually succeeded in inhibiting himself before she became so irate as to hit him. He enjoyed watching her suffer as she fought to contain her anger.

Masochism may appear as a person attempts mastery of trauma caused by deprivation, overwhelming stimulation, or painful and frightening illnesses in childhood. It may serve to reverse states of helplessness and passivity by actually creating such experiences. Such efforts often fail and are then repeated, leading to what appears as a repetition compulsion. When masochists achieve victory through their own defeat, an aim Reik (1941) considers basic to masochism, they gratify narcissistic and aggressive wishes as well.

Attempts at control are especially clear when a patient has undergone severe trauma due to an operation in childhood. Dr. P., after terrifying surgery for a retropharyngeal abscess at five years of age, during which he became unconscious, would repeat the trauma in disguise over and over again. For instance, he would stab the heads of people in pictures, a procedure that, when libidinized, was sadistic. Or, in somewhat less disguised form, he would cruelly attack the people around him—his wife, the doctors for whom he worked, and his analyst. The attacks often contained provocations. He would get people to attack him, as he felt the surgeon had, but would control the degree to which he was hurt. Sometimes he would exert control by identifying with the aggressor (A. Freud, 1936), sometimes by seducing the aggressor, sometimes by regulating the aggressor's actions. In a bizarre masturbation fantasy he imagined placing his penis in the mouth of a worm with sharp teeth. If he attempted to withdraw his penis, the teeth would rip it. In this fantasy, as in other aspects of his life, he kept control by being both the surgeon who pierced the mouth with his penis/knife and the victim/worm/patient who was pierced but could retaliate. In another fantasy he was Prometheus, who stole fire from Zeus, and also the eagle who attacked Prometheus, the eagle representing the now powerful patient.

The sexual fantasy involved erotization (see Glenn, 1984b; Laforgue, 1930; Fenichel, 1934; Coen, 1981, 1988), another defense that contributes to both masochism and sadism. A person who fears being injured can reassure himself by sexualizing the frightening, even traumatic situation. Often this mechanism involves masturbation to dampen the feelings of fear. The erotization can be of the anxiety itself or of the situation creating the danger. The dangerous situation can be a stress trauma, a strain trauma, or something less seriously disturbing, or any situation in which the individual feels helpless.

Stoller (1989; Panel, 1991), interviewing individuals who were not patients who engaged in severe sadomasochistic sexual perversions, found that an early history of severe shock trauma was common.

Herzog and Ruttenberg (Panel, 1985) reported that children who underwent severe shock trauma frequently became masochistic. In cases of child molestation, masochism frequently appears (Levine, ed., 1990), whether the child abuse is overtly sexual or only aggressive.

Certain situations in which a child is restrained or helpless will evoke rage or submissiveness or both. Erotization will convert these feelings into sadism and masochism, especially when a cruel adult restricts with affection. A child's illness may require physical restriction, such as casts for musculoskeletal deformities or bed rest for infectious diseases. Surgical procedures may involve severe restraint, as when medical personnel hold or bind a patient. Discomfort may be compounded when one cannot relieve oneself of distressing feelings. For example, the parents of a patient who became masochistic had prohibited him from scratching himself when his eczema tortured him; his itching became intolerable, but he soon learned to find pleasure in his painful state.

Restraint may be imposed to prevent masturbation, thumb sucking, and other forms of autoerotic activity, or as an aspect of severe child-rearing practices employed by a parent. The father of Schreber, the famous jurist whose autobiography Freud (1911) analyzed, used a variety of restrictive gadgets to prevent his son from masturbating and to improve his posture and even, the father thought, his character (Niederland, 1974). Schreber's paranoid condition included many masochistic features, some clearly derived from his father's manipulations.

FEMININITY AND MASOCHISM—MASCULINITY AND SADISM

In his early formulations, Freud identified activity with masculinity and passivity with femininity, but later he discarded this idea (1931). He observed that although women may be passive insofar as they wish to be penetrated by men in the sexual act, they are also active in caring for their children, including feeding them. It is now common, in politics and business, for women to take active roles. Similarly, men need no longer be active but may wish to be catered to and cared for. Nevertheless, the idea that women are essentially passive (in the sense of both inactive and wishing to have something done to them) and men essentially active persists in many individuals and is reflected in social attitudes and customs. It plays an important role in the erroneous conception of women as inherently masochistic (Blum, 1976), by contrast with men, who are not. Indeed, men or women may engage in masochistic behavior or fantasies while imagining that they are women and are being treated as such (Freud's feminine masochism). Usually such a fantasy involves a caricature of what women are like. The attacks on them may actually be conceived of as filling them, making up for the emptiness they imagine they have as women (Reich, 1940, 1953). The fantasy here is that the male's sadism can serve to fill and complete the woman. A similar fantasy with pregenital narcissistic overtones may appear (Kohut, 1977). A person who feels incomplete except in the presence of a powerful woman, usually representing the pre-oedipal mother with whom he or she can unite, may imagine that an attack will serve to complete him or her.

Despite the fallacy of equating femininity with masochism, we should nevertheless recognize that certain societal factors encourage masochism in women (Horney, 1935, 1937; Bernstein, 1983). Parents and other significant authorities in our society generally encourage girls to be passive, to restrain their aggression. As a result, they may turn it inward. Boys are generally appreciated or valued more than girls, and men find it easier to achieve certain economic goals than women, thus providing women with a basis for anger at and sadism toward males, which again may be turned against the self. Girls, finding it more difficult to separate from the narcissistic and erotic ties to their mothers, may give in to parental sadism more easily than boys and are more prone to identify with masochistic mothers. The quality of the masochism may be different for males and females, for biological as well as social reasons. The proximity of anal-rectal and vaginal-vulval areas may serve to transfer localization of sensations in each direction. A similar phenomenon appears in men. Anatomically, the anus and the scrotal sac and testicles are in close proximity. Further, the closeness of anus and vagina, with danger of infection that parents warn against, may predispose to anal derogation and depreciation of female genitals. It may enhance a feeling of inferiority, dirtiness, and unworthiness which becomes incorporated into a masochistic self representation (Bernstein, 1983).

OVERDETERMINATION: A CLINICAL ILLUSTRATION

We have emphasized that many factors determine the functions and structure of individual cases of sadomasochism. We have discussed the importance of unconscious psychic conflict, compromise formation, and childhood experiences at various stages of development. We will now illustrate the complicated

interweaving of some of these factors in a summary of a single analytic case. Other cases could also be used to demonstrate the complexity of sadomasochism and would necessarily contain the elements we have described in different configurations.

Mrs. V.[1] entered analysis because of "panic dreams" which started when she was nineteen years old. She could prevent these dreams by taking a sedative. Mrs. V.'s sadomasochism manifested itself in provocative behavior in and out of the analysis which was unconsciously intended to hurt people and to make them angry with her. It also appeared in a repeated sexual fantasy in which she was being raped; although terrified, she was nevertheless "attracted to the idea."

Relatively early, her attacking, provocative behavior appeared in the analytic setting. She withheld payment of fees and became furious when she felt the analyst was attempting to pry the money from her. She also withheld words and thoughts, refused to say everything on her mind, again with the fantasy that the analyst would force her. After she recognized these patterns, she and the analyst were able to see their connection with early toilet-training experiences. She had suffered severe constipation—indeed, had withheld bowel movements for three days at a time—from the age of three to six years. Her withholding of money and words was a displaced repetition of her early childhood behavior. She repeated in her fantasy the battle over toileting that she and her mother had engaged in during the anal-sadistic stage and again later during the oedipal period. Memories of the events that led to her withholding behavior at three emerged. Shortly after engaging in sexual play with a teenage male baby-sitter at that time, she required a tonsillectomy. She imagined that the doctor's removal of a "kind of phallus" was a punishment for her forbidden sexual wishes and behavior. In her mind, the baby-sitter was a surrogate for her father, whom she loved and who, as appeared late in the analysis, used to argue and fight with her playfully. After the operation, Mrs. V. started retaining her stools. This served to reassure her that she would not have more removed from her, that she would avert further castration. The stool retention also involved a defensive regression from sexual to anal interests. In addition, it acted as a source of punishment for her tabooed wishes as she revived in her mind battles with her mother in which she was hurt. She both wished and feared that her analyst, whom she equated with her father, would attack her anally, a substitute and dis-

1. See Glenn, 1984b, for a more detailed description of this patient.

guise for her wishes that he would penetrate her genitally.

The panic dreams had started at age nineteen after a series of events similar to those at three. Shortly after engaging in sexual intercourse for the first time—with a man her parents disapproved of—she required an appendectomy. Again she imagined that her forbidden sexual wishes and activity were what underlay her need for surgery, which she conceived of as a castration and punishment. Her panic dreams, in which she, on a bicycle, sped dangerously down a hill backward in bright sunlight, reminded her of her surgery; she associated the bright light with the operating room lights and recalled that the hospital stood on a hill. In the dreams she repeatedly and masochistically put herself in danger and got herself injured, operated upon, and punished for superego violations, as she sexualized the surgery and enjoyed being assaulted.

Similar patterns and wishes appeared in the analysis as she provoked, withheld, and imagined attack on her person. She enjoyed feeling that she was hurting the analyst when she did not pay him or free-associate. Similarly, outside the analysis she took pleasure in withholding dues from an organization she had joined, and she had difficulty toilet training her children. She would encourage their rebellion and find fun in mutual teasing at the pot (Brenman, 1952). Regression to anality complemented the other factors in determining her sadomasochism.

Efforts at mastery of trauma were also part of the clinical picture. Mrs. V. experienced the operations as traumas that had had to be mastered through evoking mechanisms of control. Through her behavior, she induced repeated threats that reminded her of the surgery but that she could control. She became the initiator of the danger and the aggressor who attacked, rather than the victim who was attacked. She also eroticized the dangerous situation, adding a further dimension to her sadomasochism.

After several years of analysis, the significance of Mrs. V.'s regression to primitive narcissistic states in the creation of her masochism became clear. Mrs. V.'s mother had attempted with some success to foster a close relationship between her child and herself, in which they often felt like a unit. Her mother, even when Mrs. V. was an adult, tried to convince her that their thoughts were identical. For instance, she insisted that Mrs. V. preferred representational art, as mother did, even though she actually enjoyed abstract work more. Mrs. V. had married a man who resembled her mother, a man who wanted husband and wife to be one to a degree greater than with most couples. Although he could not play the violin well, he vigorously insisted that he could tell Mrs. V., a trained, skillful violinist, how to play and that together they would be great. Mrs. V. agreed, cooperated with him, but felt like his servant. We understood the wish for union with her mother and husband to be due to a regression from forbidden oedipal conflicts to primitive narcissistic states—to symbiotic states but not to the symbiotic stage—and observed that this contributed to her sadomasochism. Being one with and under the influence of a powerful domineering mother or mother surrogate, she felt like a slave. Similar feelings appeared toward the analyst in the transference.

The various facets of Mrs. V.'s sadomasochism were numerous and interlocking, but we cannot here present the whole picture. For instance, we have omitted her erotization of her fury, her turning of rage against herself—rage at her father and brother whom she envied, rage at her mother as a rival and trainer, rage when she failed to achieve impossible narcissistic wishes for perfection. Nevertheless, we hope that the reader will appreciate the complexity and numerous determinants of her sadomasochism and the compromise formation involved.

PSYCHOANALYTIC TECHNIQUE

The technique for psychoanalysis of patients with strong sadomasochistic propensities is essentially no different from that used in other analyses. The analyst gradually offers interpretations based on the patient's free associations and his or her difficulties in expressing him- or herself fully. Interpretations generally proceed from those of defenses to those of drive derivatives, with due attention paid to the superego and unconscious psychic conflicts. As a transference neurosis develops, the origins of the patient's conflicts in childhood come into focus. The hierarchy of defenses changes, with the appearance of sublimation and diminished regression, so that more mature, less conflictual, more adaptive gratification becomes possible.

The wide variety of clinical forms and manifestations of masochism preclude a uniform technical approach. However, certain issues come up repeatedly. Analysis of pre-oedipal conflicts, especially those dealing with early traumas occurring during separation-individuation, is often of great importance. Oedipal material should be analyzed both as such and as regressively energizing earlier sadomasochistic wishes and conflicts. The dominant fantasy needs to be uncovered and its defenses and derivatives demonstrated—for example, beating fantasies, prostitution fantasies, and Cinderella fantasies.

A number of difficulties generally arise. The masochist's need for omnipotence and control may propel him to fight the analyst and his or her interpretations (Novick & Novick, 1991). Sadomasochistic patients often develop negative therapeutic reactions (Asch, 1976). A negative therapeutic reaction occurs when proper, tactful, well-timed, accurate interpretations lead not to further insight and symptomatic relief but to increased disturbance. Even when the patient develops insight, his or her functioning sometimes deteriorates after a while, if not immediately. Despite interpretation of the causes of the difficulties, a stalemate may develop.

Factors connected with sadomasochism account for the negative therapeutic reaction. The patient's superego may be so severe as to prohibit relief. The patient may have such an intense need for pain, including a painful relationship with objects he loves, that he produces or continues painful symptoms despite correct interpretations. The sadistic component of the patient's personality may find gratification in defeating the analyst, even though it means defeat for the patient as well. This kind of attack through failure can be quite provocative and stir the analyst's animosity, a fact the masochist will unconsciously revel in.

One patient imagined herself to be Samson as she sought to defeat the analyst through forgetting what had been said, teasingly denying interpretations she knew were true, and misquoting him so as to make him look like a fool. Like Samson, whose hair Delilah had shorn, she felt she had been weakened by the analyst, who had placed her in a subservient position. The patient fantasied that now that her hair had grown back and she had regained her strength, she, like Samson, could pull down the columns that supported the temple, thereby destroying both the analyst and herself. Significantly, the patient's mother had died during an operation for a brain tumor, a procedure carried out after the mother's hair had been shaved off. The patient identified with her mother who had, in her fantasy, been weakened and killed by the neurosurgeon.

This patient, as is true of others as well, clung to the analyst through her sadomasochism. Because of the negative therapeutic reaction, she found it difficult to recover and end treatment. The sadomasochistic interaction in the transference replicated her relations with her mother, stepmother, and father.

The negative therapeutic reaction is but one way in which the sadomasochistic patient can provoke the analyst. Such analysands are experts at the snide attack. They find the analyst's weak spot and hurt him or her by punching it. At the same time, the masochistic aspects of the patient will find satisfaction in actual or fantasied reprisals on the part of the analyst. There is a danger that an analyst's sadistic response may appear to further an analysis. Thus, in one case, when an analyst got angry on account of a patient's stubborn resistance, the patient complied by producing oedipal material which the analyst then interpreted at face value. The patient's pleasure in submitting to the analyst was not analyzed.

The analyst's management of his or her own emotional reactions to the patient (Bernstein & Glenn, 1979) is a key to the analysis of sadomasochistic patients. Optimally, the analyst will observe his or her minimal signal reactions to the patient's attacks and provocations to alert him or her to the patient's behavior and the pathology behind it. The analyst will then make proper interpretations. This may require self-analysis as well as self-observation. Sometimes the analyst's reactions reach great intensity, and he or she may then respond with a counterattack that adversely affects the analytic process.

One possible way of dealing with a situation in which the analyst actually gets angry and attacks the patient is to use the experience to demonstrate to the patient his or her provocation and the response it evokes. This may be particularly useful if the patient lacks awareness of what is going on. The analyst may then point out the patient's use of denial as a defense. Admitting to the patient that the analyst has indeed gotten angry can clarify the difference between an actual reaction by the analyst and one that the patient merely imagines. This may throw light on the patient's reactions outside the analysis as well.

Despite the possible helpfulness of such an intervention, the analyst should be cautious in instituting it. The therapist may find that after the patient recognizes the analyst's response, the analysand feels even more justified than before in believing him- or herself attacked. If the therapist reveals personal feelings out of contrition, the patient, watching the doctor confess, may identify with the analyst's masochistic stance. Or the patient may take sadistic pleasure in the analyst's cringing behavior. Self-analysis may help the analyst determine whether telling his or her own reactions serves rational therapeutic purposes or whether in so doing he or she is enacting a countertransference or transference.

As masochistic behavior often stirs anxiety in caretakers, so too it may evoke discomfort in the analyst. This can adaptively create desires to help the patient through interpretation.

REFERENCES

Arlow, J. A. (1949). Anal sensations and feelings of persecution. *Psychoanal. Q.*, 18:79–84.

Asch, S. S. (1971). Wrist scratching as a symptom of anhedonia. *Psychoanal. Q.*, 40:603–617.

———. (1976). Varieties of negative therapeutic reaction and problems of technique. *J. Amer. Psychoanal. Assn.*, 24:383–408.

Bak, R. C. (1946). Masochism in paranoia. *Psychoanal. Q.*, 15:285–301.

Bateson, G., & Mead, M. (1942). *Balinese Character*. New York: New York Academy of Sciences.

Bergler, E. (1949). *The Basic Neurosis*. New York: Grune & Stratton.

Berliner, B. (1947). On some psychodynamics of masochism. *Psychoanal. Q.*, 16:459–471.

Bernstein, I. (1957). The role of narcissism in moral masochism. *Psychoanal. Q.*, 26:358–377.

———. (1983). Masochistic pathology and feminine development. *J. Amer. Psychoanal. Assn.*, 31:467–486.

Bernstein, I., & Glenn, J. (1978). The child analyst's emotional reactions to his patients. In *Child Analysis and Therapy*, ed. J. Glenn, pp. 375–392. New York: Aronson.

Blos, P., Jr. (1991). Sadomasochism and the defense against recall of painful affect. *J. Amer. Psychoanal. Assn.*, 39:417–430.

Blum, H. P. (1976). Masochism, the ego ideal and the psychology of women. *J. Amer. Psychoanal. Assn.*, 24(5):157–192.

———. (1980). Paranoia and beating fantasy. *J. Amer. Psychoanal. Assn.*, 28:331–362.

———. (1991). Sadomasochism in the psychoanalytic process, within and beyond the pleasure principle. *J. Amer. Psychoanal. Assn.*, 39:431–450.

Brenman, M. (1952). On teasing and being teased. *Psychoanal. Study Child*, 7:264–285.

Brenner, C. (1959). The masochistic character. *J. Amer. Psychoanal. Assn.*, 7:197–226.

Coen, S. J. (1981). Sexualization as a predominant mode of defense. *J. Amer. Psychoanal. Assn.*, 29:893–920.

———. (1988). Sadomasochistic excitement. In *Masochism*, ed. R. A. Glick & D. I. Meyers, pp. 43–59. Hillsdale, N.J.: Analytic Press.

Deutsch, H. (1944). *The Psychology of Women*, vol. 1. New York: Grune & Stratton.

Eidelberg, L. (1954). *An Outline of a Comparative Pathology of the Neuroses*. New York: Int. Univ. Press.

Eidelberg, L., ed. (1968). *Encyclopedia of Psychoanalysis*. New York: Free Press.

Erikson, E. H. (1951). Sex differences in the play configurations of pre-adolescents. *Amer. J. Orthopsychiat.*, 21:667–692.

Fenichel, O. (1934). Defense against anxiety, particularly by libidinization. Rpt. in *The Collected Papers of Otto Fenichel*, vol. 1, pp. 303–317. New York: Norton, 1953.

———. (1945). *The Psychoanalytic Theory of Neurosis*. New York: Norton.

Freud, A. (1936). *The Ego and the Mechanisms of Defense*. New York: Int. Univ. Press.

———. (1949). Certain types and stages of social maladjustment. In *Searchlights on Delinquency*, ed. K. R. Eissler, pp. 193–204. New York: Int. Univ. Press.

Freud, S. (1905). *Three Essays on the Theory of Sexuality. SE*, 7:130–243.

———. (1911). Psycho-analytic notes on an autobiographical account of a case of paranoia (dementia paranoides). *SE*, 12:9–82.

———. (1914). On narcissism. *SE*, 14:73–102.

———. (1918). From the history of an infantile neurosis. *SE*, 17:7–123.

———. (1919). "A child is being beaten." *SE*, 17:179–204.

———. (1920). *Beyond the Pleasure Principle. SE*, 18:7–64.

———. (1923). *The Ego and the Id. SE*, 19:12–66.

———. (1924). The economic problem of masochism. *SE*, 19:159–170.

———. (1931). Female sexuality. *SE*, 21:225–243.

———. (1940). Splitting of the ego in the process of defence. *SE*, 23:275–278.

Galenson, E. (1988). The precursors of masochism. In *Masochism*, ed. R. A. Glick & D. I. Meyers, pp. 189–204. Hillsdale, N.J.: Analytic Press.

Glenn, J. (1969). Testicular and scrotal masturbation. *Int. J. Psychoanal.*, 50:353–362.

———. (1984a). A note on loss, pain, and masochism in children. *J. Amer. Psychoanal. Assn.*, 32:63–75.

———. (1984b). Psychic trauma and masochism. *J. Amer. Psychoanal. Assn.*, 32:357–386.

———. (1989). From protomasochism to masochism. *Psychoanal. Study Child*, 44:73–86.

Hartmann, H. (1964). *Essays on Ego Psychology*. New York: Int. Univ. Press.

Hinsie, L. E., & Campbell, R. J. (1970). *Psychiatric Dictionary*. 4th ed. New York: Oxford Univ. Press.

Horney, K. (1935). The problem of feminine masochism. *Psychoanal. Rev.*, 22:241–257.

———. (1937). *The Neurotic Personality of Our Time*. New York: Norton.

Kernberg, O. F. (1988). Clinical dimensions of masochism. In *Masochism*, ed. R. A. Glick & D. I.

Meyers, pp. 61–79. Hillsdale, N.J.: Analytic Press.

———. (1991). Sadomasochism, sexual excitement and perversion. *J. Amer. Psychoanal. Assn.*, 39: 333–362.

Kestenberg, J. S. (1967–68). Phases of adolescence with suggestions for a correlation of psychic and hormonal organizations. *J. Amer. Acad. Child Psychiat.*, 6:426–463, 577–614, 7:108–151.

Kohut, H. (1977). *The Restoration of the Self*. New York: Int. Univ. Press.

Krafft-Ebing, R. von (1908). *Psychopathia Sexualis*. New York: Login.

Laforgue, R. (1930). On the erotization of anxiety. *Int. J. Psychoanal.*, 11:312–321.

Levine, B. B., ed. (1990). *Adult Analysis and Childhood Sexual Abuse*. Hillsdale, N.J.: Analytic Press.

Loewenstein, R. M. (1935). Phallic passivity in men. *Int. J. Psychoanal.*, 16:334–340.

———. (1957). A contribution to the psychoanalytic theory of masochism. *J. Amer. Psychoanal. Assn.*, 5:197–234.

Mahler, M. S., Pine, F., & Bergman, A. (1975). *The Psychological Birth of the Human Infant*. New York: Basic Books.

Maleson, F. G. (1984). The multiple meanings of masochism in psychoanalytic discourse. *J. Amer. Psychoanal. Assn.*, 32:325–356.

Moore, B. E., & Fine, B. D., eds. (1990). *Psychoanalytic Terms and Concepts*. New Haven: Amer. Psychoanal. Assn. and Yale Univ. Press.

Niederland, W. G. (1974). *The Schreber Case*. New York: Quadrangle/New York Times.

Novick, J., & Novick, K. K. (1991). Some comments on masochism and the delusion of omnipotence from a developmental perspective. *J. Amer. Psychoanal. Assn.*, 39:307–332.

Panel (1956). The problem of masochism in the theory and technique of psychoanalysis. M. H. Stein, reporter. *J. Amer. Psychoanal. Assn.*, 4:526–538.

———. (1981). Masochism. N. Fischer, reporter. *J. Amer. Psychoanal. Assn.*, 29:673–688.

———. (1984). The relationship between masochism and depression. J. Caston, reporter. *J. Amer. Psychoanal. Assn.*, 32:603–614.

———. (1985). Sadomasochism in children. M. H. Etezady, reporter. Presented at the American Psychoanalytic Association Meetings.

———. (1990). Sadism and masochism in neurosis and symptom formation. F. M. Levin, reporter. *J. Amer. Psychoanal. Assn.*, 38:789–804.

———. (1991). Sadomasochism in the perversions. S. Akhtar, reporter. *J. Amer. Psychoanal. Assn.*, 39:739–755.

Reich, A. (1940). A contribution to the psychoanalysis of extreme submissiveness in women. *Psychoanal. Q.*, 9:470–480.

———. (1953). Narcissistic object choice in women. *J. Amer. Psychoanal. Assn.*, 1:22–44.

———. (1954). Early identifications as archaic elements in the superego. *J. Amer. Psychoanal. Assn.*, 2:218–238.

Reik, T. (1941). *Masochism in Modern Man*. New York: Farrar & Rhinehart.

Stoller, R. J. (1975). *Perversion*. New York: Pantheon.

———. (1989). Consensual sadomasochistic perversions. In *The Psychoanalytic Core*, ed. H. P. Blum, E. M. Weinshel, & F. R. Rodman, pp. 265–282. Madison, Conn.: Int. Univ. Press.

Valenstein, A. F. (1973). On attachment to painful feelings and the negative therapeutic reaction. *Psychoanal. Study Child*, 28:365–394.

Waelder, R. (1936). The principle of multiple functions. *Psychoanal. Q.*, 5:45–62.

Section II

THEORETICAL
CONCEPTS

PART IV

**FACTORS AFFECTING
NORMALITY AND
PATHOLOGY**

Linda C. Mayes, M.D., and

Donald J. Cohen, M.D.

21

CONSTITUTION

Constitution defines that which keeps us grounded—in phylogeny, heredity, and biology. Traditionally, constitution has been seen as the biological given, the inherent, unalterable genetic endowment that determines both the foundation and the course of development. Long before Mendelian genetics and Darwinian evolutionary theory gave inheritance a scientific basis, it was popularly believed that both strength and weakness of moral character followed family bloodlines and that mental instability was passed from generation to generation. Thus Prospero judged Caliban to be "A devil, a born devil, on whose nature nurture can never stick" (*The Tempest*, IV, 1, 188–189). Historically, the fatalistic comfort available in the determinism offered by beliefs in endowment has been matched by a simultaneous struggle to secure freedom from the clutches of such fated causality. Whether the constitutionally determined outcome is good or bad, to know is surely better than not. But to be the autonomous master of one's own fate, to rise above the earthbound quality of endowment, is a cherished wish. Such a Janusian view of the psychological meaning of endowment is at the very core of psychoanalytic concepts and practice and was very much a part of Freud's evolving theories.

Indeed, psychoanalysis emerged in the midst of a nineteenth-century scientific fervor that revolved around notions of endowment, biological determinism, heredity, and evolution. Freud's most eminent

neurological colleagues were biological determinists. Krafft-Ebing, attempting to define "nervousness," wrote: "The vast majority of individuals afflicted with a nervous disposition are nervous from their earliest years, on the basis of congenital influences" (Gay, 1988, p. 120). It was in this climate that Freud presented his discoveries of the potency of reminiscences and the power of experience to alter the biologically or constitutionally determined course of individual development and genetic endowment. Any number of experiences in the course of individual development might turn the endowed developmental course in a drastically different direction. Consequently, psychoanalysis is most often viewed as a developmental theory that underscores the centrality of early experience for the emergence of mature mental structures, organization, and function.

However, from the very beginning of his medical career, Freud himself embraced the genetic/evolutionary conviction, and throughout his work he struggled to maintain a synthetic view of the complex interactions between experience and endowment in which neither was primarily causal of any given mental process: "Psycho-analysis has warned us that we must give up the unfruitful contrast between external and internal factors, between experience and constitution, and has taught us that we shall invariably find the cause of the onset of neurotic illness in a particular psychical situation which can be brought about in a variety of ways" (1912b, p. 238).

Over and over, Freud emphasized that overt, behavioral (or phenotypic) differences among individuals can arise from differences in their underlying constitution (or genotype), differences in their experiences (in the context of the same endowment or genotype), or a combination of genotypic and environmental factors—quite a modern statement. Though it is not always said explicitly, constitution, or endowment, is thus as much at the heart of psychoanalytic theory and practice as is the formative and mutative effect of early experience.

THE ROLE OF CONSTITUTION IN PSYCHOANALYTIC THEORY

Late in life, Freud wrote: "I was already alive when Charles Darwin published his work on the origin of species" (1933, p. 173). Freud referred to "the great Darwin" at least twice (1901, p. 48; 1987, p. 76) and in 1938 noted with pleasure that his signature stood with those of Darwin and Newton in the book of the Royal Society. "Good company!" he wrote to a friend (quoted in L. Ritvo, 1974, p. 190). Given Freud's lifelong admiration for the creator of the theory of evolution, an individual Freud believed stood with Copernicus as a deliverer of a mighty blow to man's narcissism, we might expect to find psychoanalytic theory heavily influenced by concepts of evolution, natural selection, and genetic endowment. As others have detailed, this is indeed so (L. Ritvo, 1965, 1974, 1990).

In medical school, Freud studied with Carl Claus and Ernst Wilhelm von Brücke, both noted Darwinians, and worked on questions of genetic differentiation in Brücke's Institute of Physiology and Meynert's Institute of Cerebral Anatomy. Some of his earliest laboratory investigations concerned the evolution of neurological adaptation in studies of the origin of posterior nerve roots in the spinal cord of the brook lamprey (Freud, 1916–17, p. 340). By the time Freud left the laboratory and came to study the treatment of hysteria, he was thoroughly steeped in the models of genetic evolution, phylogenetics, and ontogenetics. These models had served him well early in his career, and they followed him into the consulting room and into his theories of mental functioning.

Endowment in Freud's Theories
At least five concepts traceable to Darwin and other evolutionary geneticists of the time are apparent in Freud's earliest work and persist through the metapsychological papers:

1. Every detail of an organism's functioning has some meaning for adaptation and survival.

2. Development proceeds gradually along a continuum, and each developmental (or evolutionary) shift may leave its vestigial traces.

3. Evolution of the species inherently involves conflict between progressive and retrogressive forces in development and between adaptive and maladaptive changes.

4. Experiences lead to individual variations in the organism's function, which over time may result in phylogenetic shifts. These variations may be adaptive and thus contribute to survival or maladaptive and lead to extinction (e.g., natural selection).

5. Most curiously, acquired characteristics (for example, experiences) are heritable.

The first concept is apparent in Freud's interest in such phenomena as parapraxes and dreams and in the meanings associated with hysterical symptoms. Symptoms and even everyday verbal expressions are never arbitrary productions but rather reflect the individual's "genetic" history—his or her individual evolution and adaptation to experience. In *Studies on Hysteria,* Breuer and Freud wrote: "All these sensations and innervations belong to the field of [emotional expression] which . . . consists of actions which originally had a meaning and served a purpose. These may now for the most part have become . . . weakened . . . whereas in all probability the description was once meant literally" (Breuer & Freud, 1893–95, p. 181).

The second concept, of a developmental continuum and vestigial traces of developmental epochs, is contained in the psychosexual stages and in the notion of fixation points in development. Later, Freud said that "in the case of every particular sexual trend . . . some portions of it have stayed behind at earlier stages of its development, even though other portions may have reached their final goal . . . we are picturing every such trend as a current which has been continuous since the beginning of life. . . . [Further,] we propose to describe the lagging behind of a part trend at an earlier stage as a *fixation*" (1916–17, p. 340). Such fixation points represent nidi for regression from a later developmental stage—a concept reminiscent of the evolutionists' observations of surviving species that seem to represent earlier phylogenetic stages of evolution.

The evolutionary notions of conflict between progressive and retrogressive forces in development and between adaptive and maladaptive changes are equally evident in Freud's theories. He could never quite move away from conflict and, with his concept of the death instinct, gave it a darker side than

Darwin's notion of inevitable progress. It was not until 1939 that Hartmann introduced his theory of a conflict-free ego sphere. The parallel between Freud's views and the evolutionary notion of conflict underscores a central paradox; for, in a sense, Freud's theory of mental functioning was as deterministic as the prevailing ideology of the immutable determinism of biological endowment, with which he would break when he discovered the power of experience to alter mental functioning. Freud offered his theory as a road to freedom from the limiting principles of heritability, but it was a freedom within bounds, of which Freud was quite aware. The psychoanalytic version of determinism presented a mind in continuous conflict with concealed, passionate forces of a dynamic unconscious. While he later came to speak of "accidental factors" as they interacted with endowment, Freud allowed for few, if any, accidents within the mind. What on the surface appeared as random or as an act of free will was projected from within the inner mental world from a complex network of interwoven causal threads in constant, dynamic (and usually conflicted) interaction. By accepting and recognizing their own unconscious wishes and conflicts (often within the course of psychoanalytic treatment), individuals might become more or less masters of their biological endowment; but understanding one's conflicts did not provide absolute freedom from biological determinism.

The fourth evolutionary concept, the effect of experience on the expression of individual variation in biological, and, for psychoanalysis, mental functioning underlay Freud's earliest discoveries in the pathogenesis of hysteria. It was in this area that he made his first break with the biological determinists. Steeped in evolutionary theories of the gradual effect of experiences on phylogenetic shifts, he was primed to recognize the pathogenic effects of individual experiences on mental functioning in the symptoms of hysteria. These discoveries represented a divergence from Charcot's singular emphasis on hereditary factors in the pathogenesis of hysteria and other nervous disorders. In 1893, in an obituary written only a few days after his mentor's death, Freud said: "the aetiological theories supported by Charcot in his doctrine of the *'famille névropathique'* which he made the basis of his whole concept of nervous disorders, will no doubt soon require sifting and emending. So greatly did Charcot overestimate heredity as a causative agent that he left no room for the acquisition of nervous illness" (1893, p. 23).

Despite their intellectual disagreement, Freud maintained a lifelong respect for Charcot, whose ideas were influential in Freud's support of the heritability of acquired characteristics. Nevertheless, from the time of his own work on hysteria, Freud maintained more and more explicitly that endowment and experience were always in constant interaction in the pathogenesis of mental disorders and in the development of normal mental functioning. For example, he wrote: "Neurosis will always produce its greatest effects when constitution and experience work together in the same direction" (1905b, pp. 170–171). Similarly, only a short time later he affirmed emphatically that "To look for the aetiology of the neuroses exclusively in heredity or in the constitution would be just as one-sided as to attribute that aetiology solely to the accidental influences" (1906, p. 279).

It was apparently not an easy balance to maintain, particularly as the pathogenic power of early experience was a new discovery about which confirming evidence seemed to present itself almost daily. Challenged many times for his preoccupation with environment, experience, and "accidental factors," rather than "dispositions," Freud wrote: "I take this opportunity of defending myself against the mistaken charge of having denied the importance of innate (constitutional) factors because I have stressed that of infantile impressions. A charge such as this arises from the restricted nature of what men look for in the field of causation. . . . Psycho-analysis has talked a lot about the accidental factors in aetiology and little about the constitutional ones; but that is only because it was able to contribute something fresh to the former, while, to begin with, it knew no more than was commonly known about the latter" (1912a, p. 99n.).

Despite this admission, Freud pointed to at least five areas in which he felt endowment played a role in the variability of individual expression: (1) the "choice" of neurosis; (2) the tendency toward sexual perversions; (3) those seemingly bedrock differences between the sexes (for example, activity versus passivity); (4) the regulation of anxiety; and (5) the response to psychoanalytic treatment.

In attempting to understand the pathogenesis of neurotic illnesses and what predisposed any individual to one form of neurosis rather than another, Freud frequently returned to the issue of constitution or heritable dispositions. True to his medical training and the views of his teachers, he carefully outlined the details of his patients' "neuropathic" families and "hereditary taint" (1909, p. 141), such as the severe hypochondria of a brother or a mother's obsessional tidiness. Indeed, in his earliest studies, he was more cautious and explicit in detailing such histories, and only gradually did he become more vocal in his criticism of colleagues who assigned too much importance to heredity (1905a). But as early as 1896, Freud pointed out the problem of what he called "similar" and "dissimilar" heredity—that is, instances in which family members are or are not affected by the same disorder. In the case of "similar" heredity, for which he cited Huntington's chorea and "the myopathies," he fully acknowledged the primary importance of endowment and genetic transmission. With "dissimilar" heredity, he insisted that endowment might serve as a precondition—that is, it might influence in part how an individual experienced any given external situation and influence whether a given situation was experienced as traumatic or not: "the importance of hereditary disposition is proved by the fact that the same . . . [experiences] acting on a healthy individual produce no manifest pathological effect, whereas in a predisposed person their action causes the neurosis to come to light, whose development will be proportionate in intensity and extent to the degree of the hereditary precondition" (1896, p. 147).

By 1937, he was quite explicit: "The stronger the constitutional factor, the more readily will a trauma lead to a fixation and leave behind a developmental disturbance" (p. 220). Present-day models for the genetic contributions to the occurrence of schizophrenia, affective disorders, or Tourette's syndrome are compatible with Freud's notion of hereditary predispositions, the expression of which is modified by environmental conditions (Cohen, 1991; Gershon et al., 1976; Gottesman & Shields, 1982).

As the theory evolved, Freud used the notion of dispositions to indicate not only heritable factors but also the effects of experience in infancy and early childhood, the imprinted legacies of the preverbal years, and a slightly different way of expressing "genetic" contributions. In particular, such dispositions might influence the development of fixation points for later regression: "Where are we to look for the source of these dispositions? [Individuals] . . . have to undergo a long and complicated development before reaching the state characteristic of the normal adult. We can assume that these developments are not always so smoothly carried out. . . . Whenever a portion of it clings to a previous stage, what is known as a 'point of fixation' results. . . . Thus our dispositions are inhibitions in development" (1913a, pp. 317–318).

Disruptions in the normal path of development were most often the result of early sexual experiences. It was on the very issue of infantile sexuality and pregenital sexual conflicts that Freud assiduously chided his psychiatric colleagues: they were interested in their patients' remote, heritable past but avoided the personal prehistory of early childhood

sexuality. This point also leads to the second area for which Freud saw a role for constitutional factors in concert with experience—the development of sexual perversions. For example, in the development of fetishism, Freud suggested that "Some degree of [constitutional] diminution in the urge towards the normal sexual aim . . . seems to be a necessary precondition in every case" (1905b, p. 153). Such a precondition was frequently constitutionally determined, although even on this point Freud allowed for accidental factors (p. 153n.). Similarly, he suggested that constitutionally based variation in the relative strength of sexual interests accounted in part for the emergence of perversions such as voyeurism but that relatively strong sexual instincts might be sublimated into constructive efforts such as the creative work of Leonardo da Vinci (Freud, 1910). Transitions in psychosexual development were also constitutionally determined. Latency "is organically determined and fixed by heredity" (1905b, p. 177). The latter is one of Freud's few explicit statements that developmental changes themselves are genetically programmed.

Just as endowment contributed to some of the variations in sexual development and interests, so it also played a role in the differences between the sexes, an enduring topic that is only slightly more resolved now than when Freud first wrote about it (Tyson & Tyson, 1990). He pointed to constitutional factors as important in two fundamental differences between men and women: the balance between activity and passivity and the suppression of aggression. As to aggression, Freud wrote not only that "The suppression of women's aggressiveness . . . is prescribed for them constitutionally" but also that girls had "a greater need for being shown affection and on that account to be more dependent and pliant" (1933, pp. 116–117). The balance between activity and passivity relates to this greater dependency and compliance and contributes to the positive or negative cast of the girl's experience of the oedipal conflict (p. 130).

By the time Freud (1926) was working out his theories for the regulation of anxiety, "dispositions" and "constitution" referred more often, though not exclusively, to the genetic history of the preverbal years and less to heredity. In considering the problem of anxiety as a reaction to dangers that are common to all, he again stated the problem as one of understanding individual variation—what distinguishes individuals who are most subject to the effects of anxiety and have more difficulty regulating the anxious state. He looked to the moment of birth as a prototype for the first danger situation and to the infant's reaction to it as the prototype of the first experience of anxiety. Responses to subsequent danger situations were modeled on the prototypic response and were most fundamentally elicited by threats of object loss. Rank had attempted to account for varying degrees of intensity in the anxiety response as due to varying severity in the birth trauma itself, a position, Freud argued, that left "no room for the legitimate claims of hereditary constitution as an aetiological factor" (1926, p. 151). Such factors, although left unspecified, accounted for some of the variability in individuals' susceptibility to anxiety in the face of external or internal threats.

The fifth area in which Freud cited the role of constitutional factors was in response to analytic treatment; here endowment stands curiously static and immutable. Rather than presenting constitution (either heritable or resulting from preverbal experience) as dynamically interacting with experience, most of his metaphors suggest endowment as constituting the final limit of the analytic experience, beyond which no further change can occur. By 1937, speaking as a prudent, resigned clinician, he implied that cases with apparent constitutional factors presented a poorer prognosis for response to psychoanalysis than those in which no such constitutional factors were present and that endowment often stood as a barrier to an individual's coming face to face with a dynamic unconscious. But even before this, he had suggested that within the therapeutic frame, the constitutional factor "consists of something fixed and unalterable" (1905a, p. 267). This is an unfortunate legacy if it leads to overlooking those biologically based sources of individual variation that not only influence mental functioning but are rich in symbolic expression and meaning and, when acknowledged, expand the analytic field of focus.

Finally, Freud's interest in the inheritability of acquired traits and experiences represents a curious byroad in psychoanalytic history and its relation to prevailing theories of evolutionary genetics. Originally attributed to Lamarck but also endorsed in part by Darwin, it was a notion Freud returned to several times, despite its already having been discredited by many of his contemporaries. To modern ears, it is an odd idea, but, as Gay (1988) has pointed out, the status of genetic studies at the turn of the century was such that even the most varied ideas concerning heritability could be accommodated by the theory. The genetic specificity afforded by the discovery of the chromosome was several decades away. Furthermore, Mendel's work, though completed in 1865, was not known to the scientific world until 1900. Without Mendel's rules specifying the patterns of inheritance and indicating how an individual mutation could be expressed generations later, the best understanding available to Darwin and others, including Freud, was that heredity involved some blending of individual traits and experiences for the species as a whole.

Freud's concept of the heritability of experiences appeared most directly in his speculations about the primal horde, the original patricide from which all subsequent oedipal fantasies arise, and the underlying cultural heritability of rebellion against the patriarchy (1913b). But it occurs elsewhere as well. In the posthumously published metapsychological papers, *A Phylogenetic Fantasy* (1987), he suggested that the desires and anxieties of man recapitulate the course of experiences in man's distant past. And in considering the case of the Wolf Man, he proposed that "scenes of observing parental intercourse, of being seduced in childhood, and of being threatened with castration are unquestionably an inherited endowment, a phylogenetic heritage" (1918, p. 97). While Freud also went on to suggest that such scenes might just as easily be known through direct experience, he was attracted to the possibility of the heritability of memory and experience. Except for Anna Freud, who made early (1936) passing references to "phylogenetic inheritance, a kind of deposit accumulated from acts of repression practiced by many generations and merely continued, not initiated, by individuals" (p. 157), psychoanalysts have tended to view Freud's interest in the heritability of acquired characteristics as neither essential nor threatening to the larger theory and perhaps as a metaphor for the powerful, almost biological, effects of continuity of cultural experience and its cross-generational transmission.

Freud's interest in phylogenetic inheritance may also reflect another motivation that was sufficiently powerful to outweigh skepticism—his adherence to a biologically based view of mental development and functioning.[1] Even after he rejected the seduction theory as the specific physical trauma in the childhood of hysterics, he never completely abandoned the idea that mental events had a somatic basis, as evidenced at the least by the "Project" (1895). His interest in the contribution of sexual malfunction to the neuroses was in part because of the organic, endowed aspects of sexuality (Gay, 1988). And when he made his break with those who emphasized heredity to the exclusion of all else, he did not discard the view but merely assigned

---

1. Gay (1988) has also suggested that Freud's persistent interest in the heritability of acquired characteristics may have been in part a reflection of his personal concerns for the heritability of some of his own characteristics and beliefs.

to experience an equal footing. Thus, he found his way toward a view of the effects of experience that would allow for some heritability, some biological explanation. Empirically, it may have lacked a firm footing, but motivationally it served him well.

Furthermore, though the heritability of acquired characteristics sounds like a curious notion when viewed in terms of nonspecific experiences, contemporary research again raises the paradigm for investigation: parental behaviors and experiences may indeed alter or influence genetic material, and this affects the development of the offspring. A parent's chronic exposure to substances such as marijuana, opiates, or other potential teratogens may alter chromosomal material so that the effects of these parental experiences are passed on to the fetus. Similarly, changes in immunity based on previous generations' exposure to viral infections or the mutability of genetic material with certain viral agents suggest that genetic material is not necessarily impervious to the effects of the environment (Davidson, 1986).

The Concept of Endowment in the Development of Psychoanalytic Theory after Freud

Theorists since Freud have continued to struggle with the tension between endowment and experience. These struggles have not usually been explicit, and some have essentially stated, without developing the notion further, that constitution is probably active in such areas as the degree of cathexis associated with various erogenous zones or in the capacity for discharge of instinctual tension (for example, Fenichel, 1945, p. 65). However, modern psychoanalytic considerations of the role of endowment as a factor in psychological functioning have been specifically informed by the careful longitudinal observations of the development of infants and young children. Such observations were begun by analysts interested in obtaining direct data to confirm, modify, and elaborate Freud's theories of early psychological development. Observations of infants and young children have provided a clearer map of how infant capacities essential to psychic differentiation and adaptive ego development emerge in the first years. Theoretical contributions from the observational studies include the distinction between biological maturation and development, the early process of differentiation between self and other, the biological and experiential roots of early preverbal disturbances in psychological development, and the relation between impairments in early object relationships and later borderline conditions and narcissistic personality disorders (Kernberg, 1975). Also, from direct observations of infants and young children, it became clear that, however conceptualized, endow-

ment determines not only how an experience is organized but also whether the experience has any meaning for the individual. As such, endowment implies something more dynamic than simply what is present at birth as the immutable substrate for experience. Because of genetically programmed maturational forces, endowment is a viable force throughout the life span.

At least three trends in the ways in which psychoanalytic theorists weigh endowment as a factor in psychological functioning are traceable to direct observations of infants and young children. The first is a more explicit consideration of the biologically determined roots of anxiety regulation, the vicissitudes of aggression, and the capacity to regulate emotional states. The second is the acknowledgment that the infant brings to the environment a set of biologically determined organizational capacities that influence how he or she interacts with, and processes information from, the external world and, vice versa, how the external world responds to the infant. The third is the redefining of endowment as those structures that emerge from the earliest interactions between biology and infantile (first-year) experience—the "preverbal" endowment or the "basic core" (Mahler, 1974; Weil, 1970).

Observational work with infants and young children began in the 1920s and 1930s, being undertaken simultaneously in several different fields— pediatrics, psychology, and early childhood education. Interest was sparked in some areas because of essentially pragmatic needs. Arnold Gesell, the consummate observer and recorder of early infant development, began his work on early infant assessment as a way of identifying infants at risk for delayed development. As early as 1916, Gesell and his colleagues began a series of meticulous observations of infants' and preschool children's behavior at home and in the well-child clinic in order to define norms for behavior (Gesell, 1925). For psychoanalysis, these efforts to describe early childhood maturation and development were well timed, as such information provided a window on what, up to that point, had seemed relatively inaccessible through adult analysis—the preverbal years and the early genetic/ maturational basis of drive endowment and development. Moreover, Freud had outlined a number of concepts such as the stimulus barrier, the process of ego differentiation from id, and individual differences in the regulation of anxiety states, which, he implied, were processes operative from early in childhood and underlay psychic differentiation and character organization. Just as Freud's lifelong interest in evolutionary biology placed notions of endowment at the core of psychoanalysis, so the studies of early infant development placed behavioral observation at the center of child analysis.

Such observations were one of Anna Freud's goals in planning the Jackson Nursery in Vienna in the mid-1930s: "We know something about infants from developmental studies, from adults' retrospective reconstructions, and from child analysis with its microscopic view of the infant's inner life. What we need to see now are the actual experiences of the first years of life, from the outside, as they present themselves. Thorough knowledge of infancy is the goal" (quoted in Young-Bruehl, 1988, p. 218). Years later, in an obituary for Edith Jackson, Anna Freud reaffirmed that her plan had been to gather direct information about "the second year of life, which we deemed all-important for the child's essential advance from primary to secondary process functioning; for the establishment of feeding and sleeping habits; for acquiring the rudiments of superego development and impulse control; for the establishment of object ties to peers" (1978).

While the Jackson Nursery was short-lived and brought to an abrupt close by the German occupation of Vienna, it was here that Anna Freud and her colleagues began the tradition of detailed observations of children's day-to-day activities during feeding, naptime, and play that provided data about early drive derivatives, the vicissitudes of aggression, and the capacities of young children to regulate their experiences of pleasure. Both the Jackson Nursery and its successor, the Hampstead War Nursery, furnished invaluable observational data about the effects of environmental deprivation, inasmuch as many of the children in both nurseries came from poor, often broken homes marred by violence and addiction. In addition, the War Nursery provided care for a number of children whose parents were absent. Residential nurseries housing such children were natural laboratories for observing both the resiliency and vulnerability of early ego development in domains such as object relatedness and the capacity to regulate arousal and aggression. In these settings, Anna Freud and Dorothy Burlingham noted the effects of institutional upbringing at each developmental phase and carefully detailed the interweaving effects of maturation and experience: "The institutional child in the first two years has advantages in all spheres of life which are independent of the emotional side of his nature; he is at a disadvantage whenever the emotional tie to the mother or to the family is the mainspring of development" (A. Freud, 1944, p. 558).

Others were also interested in the unfolding of development in infants reared in institutions, and it was through the observations of investigators such

as Spitz and Provence that the distinction between biological maturation and psychological development in early infancy was made clear. Spitz (1945) documented the devastating, often fatal, consequences of providing children with basic nutritional and physical care divorced from interactions with a consistent, emotionally available adult. Provence and her collaborators demonstrated how infants deprived of adequate maternal care showed a number of developmental disturbances. "The apparatuses for functioning appeared according to the intrinsic maturational timetable, but [the skills] were delayed in being brought under the control of the ego" (Provence & Ritvo, 1961, p. 189).

The maturational patterns described so clearly by Gesell (1925) and Viennese psychologists such as Charlotte Bühler and H. Hetzer (1935) were present in institutionalized infants; however, with continuing deprivation, the skills acquired were not integrated into more complex behavioral patterns that could be put to use by the infant in the service of adaptation to the environment. In other words, "the maturational sequence and timetable are not disturbed, but development is retarded" (Provence and Ritvo, 1961, p. 204). Examples included the grasping patterns of the hands. When directly tested, the infant's functioning was neurologically age-appropriate, but the infant's grasping and exploring of toys were immature and often distorted; the hand functioning was not combined with visual pursuit for a successful, pleasurable exploratory venture. Similarly, while infants developed the motoric capacities for self-stimulatory activities such as thumb sucking, the activity disappeared after only a few days or weeks. Such findings spoke eloquently to the essential need for maternal investment in the child's genetically driven and determined motoric and perceptual capacities; maternal engagement was necessary for apparently autonomous ego functions (Hartmann, 1939) to come into service of the infant's developing sense of an object-related world and for the development of the body ego and sense of self.

Indeed, Anna Freud (1965) made the emergence of self her prototypic developmental line and spoke of the move "from dependency to emotional self-reliance and adult object relationships" as the line that supported many, more specific developmental tasks. Body independence, moving from egocentricity to peer relationships and partnerships, from nursing to independent or "rational" eating, or from wetting and soiling to bowel and bladder control, all examples of specific developmental lines, require the child's increasing awareness and understanding of the environment as a separate entity which responds to him or her and to which he or she can respond. Variation in "innate givens" (1974, p. 69) was one of the factors that influenced progress along the various lines and contributed to accelerated, delayed, or inhibited development. For Anna Freud, the ideal developmental situation was even, harmonious development along all developmental lines, a situation that rarely occurs, in part because of the effects of differences in endowment and in part because of how parents respond to constitutional differences.

Margaret Mahler, another Viennese emigré, also focused on the earliest aspects of self–other differentiation. Her training in pediatrics gave her a firm grounding in the details of early infant development, and she directed her investigative efforts to the separation-individuation process beginning in the second year. Like other researchers at that time, she based her observations on the maturational timetables being outlined by infant developmentalists and made the nursery school her developmental laboratory. Like Anna Freud, she studied deviations in development through her understanding of normal patterns of maturation. Her earliest thoughts about infant development and the contributions of endowment came while she was the director of a well-baby clinic in the late 1920s. Combining this experience with observations made during psychoanalytic treatment of psychotic children, she formulated the notion that "the human infant's *biological, actual birth experience* did not coincide with his 'psychological birth.'" The sensorium of the newborn and very young infant did not seem to be 'tuned in' to the outside world" (1974, p. 89). The expected course of development was for the infant to emerge in the first year of life from what Mahler termed the state of "symbiotic oneness with mother" (p. 91), a "psychological birth" (p. 93) characterized by a change in the nature of cathexis in the bodily self and a shift in approach and distancing behaviors between mother and infant. But with certain children, she believed that "genetic and structural concomitants" (p. 91) prevented this differentiation from occurring and led to disorders in self–other differentiation (for example, autism) (1968).

Mahler and others (for example, Benjamin, 1961; Weil, 1970, 1978) defined a combination of constitutional (or biological) characteristics of the infant and maternal responsiveness as the "basic core" (Weil, 1970) of the early mother–child symbiotic unit. It is this basic core that determines "every human individual's unique somatic and psychological makeup" (Mahler, 1974, p. 92). (Note the similarity to Freud's use of constitution to indicate the preverbal experience.) From the infant's standpoint, the endowed elements of such a core involve both the equipment or capacities and the range of modifiability: "The neonate's congenital equipment (genetic heritage plus irreversible paranatal influences) represents a combination of congenitally given potentials in different spheres of functioning. . . . The limits in each sphere as well as the fact and ease of modifiability are genetically given. In other words, each child has in each sphere . . . a certain span of potential developments, with the upper and lower limits constitutionally given. (Constitutional variations of this span explain why not every child responds in the same way to the same kind of care.)" (Weil, 1970, pp. 442–443).

Working with this model of the infant's contribution to the basic core of the mother–infant unit, a number of investigators described individual differences in various functions in the newborn, including differences in autonomic nervous system reactivity and the integration between central and peripheral nervous systems (Richmond & Lustman, 1955; Lustman, 1956), in the level of sensitivity and reaction to sensory stimuli (Bergman & Escalona, 1949), in the capacity to achieve rhythmic, predictable cycles of sleeping, waking, and feeding (Sander, 1962; Wolff, 1967). Several psychoanalytic investigators also described profiles of infants along such organizational spectrums as sensory sensitivity, activity level, social responsivity, neuroregulatory predictability, or the capacity to sustain attention (Bergman & Escalona, 1949; Escalona, 1968; Weil, 1956, 1983). Emde et al. (1976) combined psychobiological measures with behavioral observations to study neurological organizational shifts in the first months in sleep–wake cycles or in patterns of activity, arousal, fussing, and smiling. Such patterns of reactivity, established as part of the early basic core, were felt by some to be enduring and unique (Chess et al., 1959). Extreme patterns of reactivity in certain spheres (such as sensory sensitivity or neurological disorganization) made infants particularly vulnerable to problems in the regulation of states of arousal and anxiety.

Greenacre (1941, 1945, 1952) returned frequently to the problems of organizational impairments in the regulation and modulation of anxiety and the relation of such problems to the development of subsequent neuroses. Like Freud, she looked to the moment of birth as the prototypic anxiety-provoking situation, but she was more explicit about those innate, biological, or endowed factors that led to individual variation in the infant's early capacities to regulate anxiety. First, Greenacre suggested that the degree of tension or anxiety in any individual infant depends on the ratio between sensory stimulation and the capacity to effect some sort of motor discharge. The latter capacity in turn reflects the degree of maturation of the infant (as determined by genetic contributions) and experiential factors. Second, she saw some of these experiential factors as prenatal—that is, the effect of the intra-uterine environment on somatic differentiation and maturation. At this point she presented the amalgam between earliest experiences and biology as what we might call the "genetic–experience endowment," a concept similar to Mahler's and Weil's "basic core." Greenacre conceived of prenatal, natal, and early postnatal experiences in which unique, specific events left indelible somatic traces (and thus modified the biological substrate) but were not experienced psychologically. As she stated, "It is in fact extremely difficult to say exactly at what time the human organism develops from a biological to a psychobiological organization" (1945, p. 35). In addition, the birth experience, by eliciting a number of physiological responses such as cardiorespiratory excitation and stimulation of many body parts, organizes the anxiety pattern for that infant (as in the prototypic situation suggested by Freud).

It is from this early amalgam that individual variation in the primary regulatory organization in response to danger arises, and such individual variations are central elements in subsequent "patterning of the drive and energy distribution" (ibid.). Furthermore, it was this early amalgamated predisposition to anxiety that Greenacre saw as endowing the infant and child with a continued physiological sensitivity, "a kind of increased indelibility of reaction to experience which heightens the anxiety potential and gives greater resonance to the anxieties of later life" (1941, p. 610). Such a predisposition increases the risk of faulty ego development and drive modulation. For Greenacre, the infant's early patterns of defensive reactions to any number of situations are also primarily biologically (constitutionally) driven and serve as prototypes for later, more psychologically elaborated, defensive responses.

Hartmann and Kris (1945) also studied the emergence of early regulatory capacities that were essential for the infant's participation in the social world and for ego maturation. Hartmann's notion of the conflict-free sphere of ego development or autonomous ego functions is one of the contributions since Freud most relevant to considerations of the place of endowment within psychoanalysis. Hartmann (1939) proposed that the psychic systems that control perception, motility, and information-processing capacities develop largely outside the sphere of psychological conflict and are predominantly dependent upon biological maturation (which is genetically programmed) for their expression. Such functions may come into the service of psychic functions such as defensive reactions, but they determine the individual's biological readiness at any given point to deal with all experiences, whether painful or pleasurable. Furthermore, the maturational sequence of these autonomous ego functions influences not only the maturation of the ego but also determines the importance of a given experience for a child. The meaning that any individual experience has for a child's life depends a great deal on the maturational status of the autonomous ego functions. In this particular model, the biologically (or genetically) based functions are in constant interaction and correlation with experience and in part determine it.

In all the approaches to observational studies, there is an intricate and early interweaving of the parental contribution to adaptive development. Although Hartmann spoke of ego functions as autonomous, it is only through these functions that the child is able to experience and interpret the world and the parent to respond. In this sense, as Hartmann (1939) pointed out, it is misleading to equate biological with nonexperiential, for it is the biologically determined maturational patterns that give psychological meaning to experiences, and the constant interaction with maturing ego functions means that every experience is a biological event. For example, the changes in the patterns of interaction between a mother and her infant in the first year of life have psychological meanings for the infant that are closely interwoven with the infant's capacity to discriminate affect, to respond contingently, and to distinguish communicative signals across several perceptual channels, all of which reflect neurobiological maturation. Individual variations in infant responsiveness also determine parental activity—in that the infant's endowment influences the response of the environment in certain ways, a model that guided Escalona's longitudinal studies of individual development (1968) and the longitudinal study of the Yale Child Study Center.

Conversely, how differences in parent responsiveness and style of interacting facilitated or impaired the genetically determined unfolding of these infant capacities was also a focus of several infant observation studies. Mahler, Weil, Escalona, Hartmann, Provence, and others emphasized repeatedly how "Success or failure . . . will depend on the jibing of the infant's initial endowment and the mother's specific attunement to this infant. Some infants, because of their endowment and predisposition to disorganization, "are unable to experience an ordinary devoted mother's caretaking positively" (Weil, 1983, p. 340). For such genetically burdened infants, how well their mothers were attuned to their needs determined how successfully they passed from the symbiotic phase to the period of separation-individuation and developmental progression toward adaptive ego function and a differentiated self (Mahler, 1968; Mahler et al., 1975; Weil, 1970). Moreover, the infant's needs change with time as the genetically programmed capacities mature. The particular needs for maternal responsiveness shift with the infant's maturation, and in so doing equipment and environment are in constant interaction and change. Successful progression along any of Anna Freud's developmental lines involves a process of constant interaction between the child's capacities and the parent's understanding and responsiveness. As Mahler and McDevitt (1982) pointed out, "to try to speak of self-development separately from the development of object relations imposes an impossible strain on the data" (p. 837).

In the context of maternal responsiveness to early infant behaviors, perceptual and motor development attracted particular interest, because these were the domains that seemed most necessary for early self–other differentiation and for the infant to begin to move away from the symbiotic unit (Mahler & McDevitt, 1982). Early perceptual activity in coordination with motor activity (both genetically given) predominates in the first months, and vision and touch bring the body together as image and tactual sensation. The infant also uses perceptual capacities to experience the mother actively and passively, "to touch and be touched; to babble and hear; to look and be looked at" (Weil, 1978, p. 466). Genetically-determined differences in the speed of processing such perceptual information influence the infant's receptivity and level of adaptability to new situations. Too much sensory stimulation, particularly at a level beyond what the infant can process, is overwhelming; at this point the mother, or caregiving environment, must actively mediate the sensory experience and the infant's reaction to it. Motility capacities, emerging gradually in the first year, allow the infant first to grasp objects and mother, then to explore dimensionality and distance by reaching, and finally to move physically away from or toward the mother. Like too much sensory stimulation, premature walking before the infant is ready to separate may be overwhelming and perplexing; again, how the parent intervenes and mediates such experiences is critical (Mahler, 1971; Mahler et al., 1975).

The longitudinal study at the Yale Child Study Center was designed explicitly to study the emergence of endowed capacities in the context of evolving mother–child interactions. It began in 1949, under the direction of Ernst Kris, and was undertaken to learn about the relationship between the child's equipment and the mechanisms of adaptation preferred by the child (S. Ritvo & Solnit, 1958). The study represented an intensive effort, with both parent and child in separate analyses and with repeated developmental evaluations of the children and observations of their play and behavior while in the nursery. These observational frames provided converging data. A question implicit in the longitudinal study was how a child's early adaptations to innate, endowed predispositions and to the environment's responses to such predispositions continued to shape the child's approaches and adaptations to new developmental tasks, the basic premise being that environment and experience may either reinforce the child's endowed predisposition or equipment or work in the opposite direction (E. Kris, 1962; M. Kris, 1957). The child whose predispositions and basic equipment are reinforced by the environment will have different personality characteristics than they would if such predispositions were muted by environmental influences. While the investigators accepted the premise that certain personality characteristics, whether genetically determined or expressed as "preverbal endowment," tended to remain constant, they were interested in exploring in what ways such endowed traits express their constancy. For example, how does a child whose needs for tactile stimulation and holding are not met, because the mother feels anxious and frightened by such demands, continue to express those needs with ongoing psychic differentiation (Provence, 1983).

Finally, most of the observational studies of infants and young children were focused on the question of how the libidinal ties between infant and parent did or did not emerge and how the libidinal relationship facilitated the emergence of adaptive ego functioning. Less emphasis was placed in these studies on the role of aggression and the constitutional contributions to the strength of aggressive drives and their behavioral expression. Aggression as a separate instinctual drive plays an important role in the psychic energy necessary for growth, maturation, and development and in the differentiation of psychic structures (Hartmann et al., 1949; Solnit, 1970). Furthermore, although the earliest theory of aggression was not as clearly linked to specific bodily locations as were libidinal aims, infant observations indicate that a number of motor and perceptual capacities serve the direct expression of aggressive derivatives. For example, gaze aversion is for the infant a means of turning away from the mother and expressing frustration (Downey, 1984).

By 1949, Anna Freud recognized the role of innate aggressive urges in shaping character and defensive structures; but only later did she acknowledge Melanie Klein's emphasis on the early manifestations of aggression and hate as part of the infant's entry into the object world and the importance of part objects in the infant's early perceptions of other (M. Klein, 1937, 1957; A. Freud, 1974). Of all the theorists who worked with children in the mid-twentieth century, Melanie Klein (1937, 1957) was clearest about the constitutional basis of aggression and destructive impulses in the child's emerging tie with his parents (Tyson & Tyson, 1990). While Klein acknowledged the central importance of the infant's gradual integration of the capacity to form libidinal ties to parents, she emphasized that the infant also experienced frustration during myriad early caretaking situations such as feeding or being held. It was this frustration and individual variations in the infant's capacity to tolerate it that engendered more aggressive behaviors (for example, the protests of crying and looking away).

These individual variations in the capacity to tolerate frustration and, by implication, in the strength of aggressive impulses were in part constitutionally based. Moreover, the immature ego (or, stated in other terms, the immaturity of the infant's neurologically-based organizational capacities) contributed to a lack of perceptual cohesion so that the infant was able to accept part objects such as the division of the breast into a good and bad object. It was the latter, the bad object, toward which aggressive, destructive impulses were directed. Early development represented a struggle to integrate good and bad perceptions, hostile and loving feelings, aggressive and libidinal parts, into a whole. The constitutional contributions to the vicissitudes of aggression and the role of endowment in individual differences in the expression of aggression represent an important theoretical area requiring more observational study.

THE CONTINUING RELEVANCE OF BIOLOGICAL APPROACHES TO CONSTITUTION FOR PSYCHOANALYSIS

Throughout its history, psychoanalysis has influenced, and has been influenced by, other fields, particularly developmental psychology and neurobiology, which study the interactions between endowment and experience in any given individual and the concept of endowment as a developmental phenomenon. Just as Freud drew on the genetics, neurobiology, and developmental psychology of his era, so psychoanalysis today continues to find advances in associated fields relevant to psychoanalytic principles. Such advances facilitate the continuing development of psychoanalytic theory regarding the inter-

actions between endowment and experience and also enrich the therapeutic analytic dialogue. These advances come from fields such as behavioral genetics, neuroanatomy, neurophysiology, and developmental psychology and have developed through studies of cellular and biochemical function, animal models, and carefully controlled experimental conditions, as well as through the methods of naturalistic observation of behavior familiar to psychoanalysts.

Behavioral Genetics: Distinguishing the Contributions of Endowment and Experience-Genotype, Phenotype, and Development

Stated simply, "development is the process by which the genotype becomes phenotype" (Scarr & Kidd, 1983, p. 346), and in developmental psychology and behavioral genetics, "endowment" and "constitution" mostly refer to genotype. "Genotype" refers to the species-specific genetic material (DNA) that programmatically influences all levels of human functioning, including behavior and mental activity. Genotypic activity occurs through many complicated functions such as determine the patterns of brain structure, enzyme activity, and cellular organization and specialization within an organ. From the standpoint of behavioral science, it entails an intricate web of events (each involving different levels of analysis) from chromosomal material to overt behavioral expression. These pathways become even more complex when the factors of time and developmental change are added. It is not just that the genotypic material is active at any given time with any given psychological expression but that the sequence and rate of maturation of capacities essential to psychological development are also genetically programmed. For example, the motor milestones and puberty are genotypically timed events. Similarly, the events of aging such as menopause are also genetically programmed. Thus, the genotypic material finds expression throughout the life span.

"Phenotype" indicates the individual expression of a genotype. Different genotypes may result in a single or different phenotypes. On the other hand, several phenotypes may result from one genotype—the basic genetic observation perhaps most relevant to psychoanalysis and all other developmental theories. The "range of reaction" of a given genotype refers to the different phenotypes that can develop from that genotype under different environmental conditions (Scarr & Kidd, 1983). For instance, within a genotypic-specific range, the timing of puberty can be altered by environmental factors such as nutritional status. The range of reaction for a genotype is active throughout development but may vary according to the developmental period. For example, malnutrition early in life affects the phenotypic expression of height more severely than malnutrition later in life. Analogously, separation or abandonment is more pathogenic if it occurs early on than if it occurs later. Furthermore, the capacity for an organism to react to a given set of conditions is also in part genotypically determined. Before the advent of language, for example, infants do not have the capacity to respond to their mothers' verbal signals with a verbal response.

How genotype or endowment and environment interact to produce a phenotype at any point in development is a complex process. Certain environmental events are more discrete than others and more easily conceptualized. A severe neurological illness or traumatic injury early in life will alter the phenotypic expression of that individual's genotype for information-processing capacities. However, most developmental investigators, including psychoanalysts, are interested in far more complicated environmental events or situations, such as separations or parent–child interactions, and more complex genotypes, such as those shaping personality, affect regulation, the modulation of tension states, or vulnerability to psychiatric disorders. Studies of twins, longitudinal studies of families, and studies of adoptions are of long-standing interest to psychoanalysts in this connection (Hartmann, 1934–35; Dibble & Cohen, 1981; Neubauer & Neubauer, 1990) Such studies and the data resulting from them are often hampered by disagreement about the phenomenon in question (for example, what determines "persistence" or "lability of mood," or what diagnostic criteria define a disorder). The less clearly defined the phenomenon being studied, the more likely it is that evidence for genotypic contributions will be diluted by the multivariate nature of the study sample. Furthermore, on the environmental side of the equation (albeit an artificial distinction), complex environmental events such as affective signaling between parent and child or the effects of repeated separations or foster placements are far more difficult to quantify, because of their repetitive nature and the enormous variability possible for social interactions.

Despite these methodological difficulties, there is good evidence for genotypic contributions in the expression of certain psychiatric disorders such as schizophrenia, affective disorders, or Tourette's syndrome (Cohen, 1991; Gershon et al., 1976; Gottesman & Shields, 1982). While findings such as these confirm certain of Freud's predictions, perhaps of more interest to psychoanalysts are the data which suggest that personality traits or other mental functions governing personality and adaptive functioning are also genetically influenced. Genetic studies of

the development of behavior and personality are relatively recent; as techniques have improved, the evidence in favor of genotypic contributions has become clearer.

Studies of temperament in young children provide an illustration of the genetic approach to complex behavioral phenotypes, one that has roots both in psychoanalysis and in developmental psychology. Such studies began as an approach to understanding the inherent, genetically determined aspects of personality that were enduring and influenced normal and deviant development (Thomas & Chess, 1984). While the concept of temperament remains an imperfect one, most investigators continue to use the term to indicate characteristics that are the constitutionally based sources of variance in personality functioning (Buss & Plomin, 1975; Bornstein et al., 1986). In part, the conceptual problems are related to great variations in measurement techniques (Hubert et al., 1982). To measure temperament, children's behaviors are generally grouped into behavioral categories such as activity level, rhythmicity, threshold of responsiveness, distractibility, attention span, and persistence. Recent revisions of the approach, however, have focused less on component behaviors and more on response characteristics such as duration, intensity, or frequency (Derryberry & Rothbart, 1984). Such revisions have extended temperament conceptualizations beyond observable behaviors onto the level of physiological observations—that is, to the neuroregulation of states of arousal (Bornstein et al., 1986), a concept more relevant to analytic formulations of anxiety regulation (for example, those of Greenacre or Hartmann).

Although a number of other techniques (family and adoption studies) have also provided suggestive data regarding the constitutional basis of temperament, it is research on twins that has yielded the most supportive data (and has been of most interest to psychoanalysts, who have used direct observation of the stability of personality characteristics in twins as a way of examining the interactions between basic endowed equipment and experience (Hartmann, 1934–35; Dibble & Cohen, 1981; Neubauer & Neubauer, 1990). Given that monozygotic twins (MZ, identical) share exactly the same genotype and dizygotic twins (DZ, fraternal) on average only 50 percent of the genotype, a greater concordance of temperament profiles in identical twins would be supportive evidence for a constitutional basis for certain characteristics of temperament (Goldsmith, 1983). For example, MZ correlations are significantly greater than DZ correlations for activity level and distress at limitations (Goldsmith & Campos, 1982). Similarly, MZ concordance is higher for emotionality, sociability, and impulsivity (Buss et al., 1973) and increases with age, a finding usually interpreted as indicative of growing expression of genotypic characteristics with maturation (Stevenson & Fielding, 1985; Wilson & Matheny, 1986).

What, then, of the interactions with environment in the expression of personality traits as defined by temperament genotypes or other genotypically-related constructs? Models from the field of behavioral genetics provide ways of conceptualizing the relationship between genotypic factors and experience (Plomin et al., 1977; Plomin, 1983; Scarr & McCartney, 1983). One approach to clarifying the interactions between genotype and environment describes how individuals of different genotypes respond differently to similar environments. Examples of genotype–environment interaction include the facts that children of greater intellectual ability do better in any given educational system, that patients with better self-regulatory capacities respond better to psychotherapy, and that infants with a longer attention span are more likely to respond to adults' bids for social interaction.

An elegant demonstration of genotype–environment interaction was provided by a study of early separation experiences in three species of macaque monkeys (Sackett et al., 1981). Beginning soon after birth, monkeys of these three species were placed alone in sound-attenuated, separate rooms. Though the "rearing" conditions were similar, the three species showed very different patterns of social responsiveness after they were reunited with peers who had been reared normally. Individual differences within a species (differences that are conceptually akin to certain characteristics of temperament in human infants) have also been reported to affect the individual's response to stressful experiences. In detailed studies of the anxiety reactions of rhesus monkeys to a number of experiences (introduction of strangers, separation from parent), substantial differences in the range and nature of the reactions are evident (as measured behaviorally and by changes in blood cortisol and cerebrospinal fluid catecholamine levels and heart rate variability). When early rearing experiences are similar (that is, when the monkeys are raised in isolation), these individual differences follow sibships. Monkeys with the same parents show similar anxiety reactivity patterns (Suomi et al., 1981).

On the other hand, the genotype–environment interaction model does not allow for the possibility that endowment may lead an individual to different experiences. That notion is contained in the model of genetic–environment correlations, in which it is posited that individuals, guided by their endowment, selectively experience and shape their own environments (Buss & Plomin, 1984; Plomin et al., 1977; Scarr & McCartney, 1983). On this view, it is the genotype, both in its individual variability and its species specificity, that shapes the effects of environment on development, because the genotypic differences guide the individual's response to environmental opportunities. Such active or evocative genetic–environment correlations occur because individuals seek out the settings that fit their predilections and capacities best or because they evoke specific responses from the environments in which they find themselves. It is not just that environments and individuals come together in multi-determinant ways, but that certain endowed factors in the individual affect how he or she experiences the world and how the world experiences him or her, a model that is particularly harmonious with psychoanalytic views described earlier.

Different stages of genetic–environment correlation have been proposed. The earliest, evident in infancy, is passive and reflects the parents' genotype, which in turn governs the type of environment they select and provide for their infant. Such a passive correlation occurs relatively independently of the individual infant and is the model for interaction at least at the time of birth (and prenatally inasmuch as it influences maternal behavior). Very quickly, the correlation between endowment and environment changes to a reactive one, in that certain genotypically-determined characteristics of the infant (in terms of both maturation and individual variation) influence the parents' patterns of responsiveness. Such a reactive correlation is contained in the hypotheses of Escalona's (1968) work and of the longitudinal study of the Yale Child Study Center and in underlying notions of temperamental differences as part of the variance in measures of parent–child interactions (Plomin et al., 1988). Reactive correlations continue throughout life, influencing, for example, sociability and relationships in peer groups; that is, they continue to be particularly salient correlations for the elaboration of object relations.

The third form of genetic–environment correlation is active: individuals' genotypes lead them to seek experiences most suited to their needs. More sociable infants actively engage the adults in their world by smiling, vocalizing, or sustained attention. Similarly, more persistent infants tend to seek out novelty and to explore for longer periods of time, efforts that both encourage social interaction with those around them and facilitate exposure to the world. It is not just that these infants make better use of what is available but that they actively seek out novel opportunities and engage adults.

Neither of these two models of the relations between genotype and environment is mutually exclusive of the other. However, the genotype–environment correlation model does explain certain observations reported in longitudinal studies of personality characteristics. For example, over time, identical twins become increasingly concordant on several personality dimensions and show a greater change in concordance than fraternal twins. Similarly, identical twins reared apart in very different environments show increasing concordance on several measures of temperament (Scarr & McCartney, 1983; Plomin et al., 1988).

Neuroanatomy and Neurophysiology: Physiological Manifestations of Genetic–Environment Relations

What actually happens on a physiological level when environment and genotype come together in either the interactive or the correlative model? The present state of the art is a long way from understanding how mental events (in either a social or an individual context) are translated into neurobiological events or vice versa. Yet, there are illustrations of how environmental events may alter brain development or functioning at a neuroanatomical and neurophysiological level. Even the receptivity at a cellular or chemical level to change as a result of experience is in part genotypically determined (see the concept of range above). Consistent with the earliest psychoanalytic views, biological differences are not equivalent to nonexperience, and experience is not equivalent to nonbiological differences. There are translations of the relationships between genotype and environment at the levels of both meaning and physiology.

The now classic experiments of the effects of early sensory deprivation on subsequent perceptual development revealed that certain experiences are absolutely necessary for shaping the developing sensory and motor systems, the age-dependent, or critical-period, phenomena (Greenough et al., 1987). For example, permanent impairments in the maturation of the visual cortex occur with manipulation of early visual experiences in young animals (Hubel & Wiesel, 1970; for a review, see Movshon & van Sluyters, 1981). Irreversibility appears to arise because synapses become committed to a particular pattern of organization, and those that could have served alternative patterns are lost (Greenough et al., 1987). On the other hand, excess synapse formation and a multi-plural potential for synaptic differentiation and function are characteristic of postnatal brain development (Rakic & Goldman-Rakic, 1982).

Furthermore, it is important to distinguish between experiences that are absolutely necessary for shaping the developing sensory systems, such as those just cited, and experiences that are unique to the individual (Greenough et al., 1987). The latter do not occur in the same degree or in the same order for every individual and are perhaps closer to the "accidental factors" emphasized in psychoanalysis. Such experiences also have direct effects on brain morphology and neurophysiological functioning. Animal models used to study such effects employ variations in the physical and social complexity of the rearing environments as the experiential variable (environments that may also serve as paradigms for early deprivation experiences in human infants). Animals reared with others in environments filled with opportunities for novel exploration show increases in brain size and synaptic density when compared with animals reared in isolated conditions (Greenough & Volkmar, 1973). These differences are reported for the occipital region, the hippocampus, and the neocortical regions associated with audition and somesthesis (Greenough et al., 1987). These regions are also those apparently most involved in visual memory function and are extensively connected to the limbic and thalamic systems where arousal states are regulated (Mishkin, 1982; Spiegler & Mishkin, 1981). Moreover, some neural plasticity persists into adulthood. Adult animals housed in differing conditions show parallel changes in cortical size and dendritic surface area in both the cerebral and cerebellar cortex (Greenough et al., 1987). The degree of plasticity is in all likelihood genotypically determined, and, in contrast to earlier beliefs, it does persist throughout the life span.

Studies of gender development and the effect of sex hormones on brain development give rise to a second model for the effects of experience on biological differentiation. Core gender identity (Stoller, 1968) begins with the effects of sex hormones on the developing fetal brain. The sex steroids influence neural proliferation and differentiation in the fetal brain, particularly in the hypothalamic region (Naftolin et al., 1990). Such an effect on neurogenesis in the fetal brain determines the pattern of gonadotropin release in the mature adult (cyclic for females, tonic for males). In the first months after birth, which are times of rapid synaptogenesis and synaptic differentiation (see above), estrogen in particular induces gender-specific changes in synaptic density and postsynaptic membrane structure in key hypothalamic nuclei. Social and psychological factors do influence gender identity, and sexual assignment at birth does influence parental behaviors with the infant. However, recent evidence suggests that sex steroids continue to influence brain function at the level of synaptogenesis and synaptic remodeling throughout life (ibid.). For example, synaptic remodeling seems to accompany the pre-ovulatory estrogen surge in animal models; that is, there are demonstrable changes in brain morphology and synaptic functioning with monthly estrogen cycles. Data such as these suggest a complicated model for gender-based behavioral and psychological differences, a model that takes into account the continual effects of sex hormones on brain structure and function, as well as the influence of parental and social responses to the child.

Recent studies of memory storage furnish a third model for how experience and endowment come together at a neurophysiological level. This area is particularly relevant to psychoanalysis inasmuch as a central question is how past experiences and their accompanying memories continue to influence behavior. Contemporary models of memory suggest an intricate relation between central storage and recall mechanisms and experiential factors, with intricate systems for registering the relative intensity of an experience and for allowing that memory to be more or less active in influencing behavior (Pittman, 1989). Following an event or stimulus, there is a time-dependent sensitive period during which the storage of newly learned information can be enhanced or impaired (retrograde amnesia). A number of so-called stress-modulator hormones (for example, ACTH, norepinephrine, vasopressin) released at the time of the event modulate the storage of the memory during the time-sensitive period (McGaugh, 1985; Zager & Black, 1985). Experiences are differentially stored because of the relative strength of the hormonal response during the event, which also leads to the formation of behavioral responses that are highly resistant to modification or extinction (Pittman, 1989). An extremely stressful event overstimulates endogenous stress-responsive hormones, which in turn produce an overconsolidation or "superconditioning" (Pittman, 1988) of the memory trace.

Few data are yet available that address either individual variation in sensitivity and responsivity to stress-modulating hormones or developmental variations in activity. For example, are the memory systems of younger children more sensitive to such hormonal effects, so that early stressful experiences have more permanent effects on behavior? Furthermore, how memories are stored so that their registered intensities continue to influence behavior and affect regulation is not yet clearly understood. Studies of post-traumatic stress disorder or of animal models of inescapable shock suggest that particularly intense or stressful experiences actually lead to *chronic* alterations in the neurohormonal regulation of memory storage and recall mechanisms, as well as memory-related regulation of affect (van der Kolk et al., 1985). Implicated in these neurophysio-

logical alterations are a relatively permanent augmentation in limbic-system-mediated memory retrieval (Delaney et al., 1983) and similar relatively fixed changes in limbic system modulation of autonomic activity (Watson et al., 1988). These findings raise interesting questions for psychoanalytic study, such as whether the therapeutic effects of psychoanalysis are reflected in modification of the hormonal regulatory systems for memory storage and retrieval.

Finally, these illustrations of how genetic–environment relationships alter neurophysiological as well as psychological functioning are relevant to our earlier review of the misconception of endowment as a fixed, immutable, substrate, as the organic framework that weathers the storms of experience. Even at the level of the chromosome, genetic material is not necessarily stable and fixed throughout development. Genes turn on and off, and there are often changes of gene coding within any given individual (Davidson, 1986). The genotype is constantly developing toward a phenotype at every point in the life span; in a sense, the process is never complete and is halted only by death. An endowment that is vital, shifting, and in a constant state of change throughout the life span has implications for mental representations and symbolization.

Developmental Psychology: Perceptual Competencies and Early Endowment

The capacities of infants to perceive and to process information in the first year, described by developmental psychologists, are clearly related to the child's perceptual world, early mother–infant interaction, and the infant's emerging self-differentiation and ego maturation, as described by psychoanalysts (Stern, 1985). In the first six to nine months of life, infants exhibit rapidly emerging discriminative capacities that are uniquely suited to perceiving and interpreting social information (see Aslin et al., 1983; Banks & Salapatek, 1983; Olson & Sherman, 1983). There is thus a convergence between the models of developmental psychology and the results of psychoanalytically oriented observational studies. Researchers in both fields continue to work to define the range of basic, perceptual endowment with which the infant enters the social world.

The newborn's external world quickly becomes a social world; much of the newborn's early visual searching is directed toward social cues, such as a parent's voice or face. In the first three months after birth, a rapid reorganization of the central nervous system occurs. Infants are then able to sustain an alert state for longer periods of time, during which they are receptive to environmental stimulation and social interaction (Wolff, 1967). Concomitant with this change in the duration of alertness is a marked change in patterns of visual scanning (Haith, 1980). In the first months, infants show a preference for curved lines over straight ones, for patterns with a high contour density, and for symmetry (Olson & Sherman, 1983). Newborns and infants of one to two months old are most sensitive to changes in boundaries and contours and ignore changes within contours. Thus, their visual exploration defines the edges of objects and persons but not the individual details. By three months, infants scan details within boundaries and make more subtle discriminations of shapes and sizes (Milewski, 1976).

By four to five months, infants respond to the face as a whole; that is, they scan both the external boundaries of the face and the internal features (Haith et al., 1977). More generally, they respond to whole forms rather than individual elements, contours, or boundaries (Bertenthal et al., 1980) and show a major change in form-perception capabilities (Campos & Stenberg, 1981). By five months, infants discriminate the necessary and usual configuration of a face and detect subtle changes in internal features that they previously ignored (Caron et al., 1973). Also, in this same time period, infants come to discriminate among several different facial expressions of affective states and react differently to these different expressions when displayed by an adult (Nelson, 1987). Finally, in the second six months of life, children begin to show the capacity to appraise an object or event before acting. Before nine months of age, infants reach for familiar and unfamiliar objects with equal speed, but after nine months, they are slower to touch what is unfamiliar (Schaffer et al., 1972). Such a delay implies the capacity to stop and look to the mother or others for guidance (social referencing) or to compare the object or situation with memories before acting. Thus, by the latter half of the first year, infants are perceptually able to use information contained in their parents' affective responses and to respond discriminatingly to such information. Moreover, by this time, perception of an object is more than a mechanistic stimulus–response action (Lewis & Brooks, 1975). Rather, with the capacity to perceive greater complexity, contingency, and wholeness, perceptual events have acquired meaning. Another individual's interpretation of an event is part of the perceptual event itself. In other words, how another person reacts to a novel event, object, or individual becomes an internalized part of the infant's perceptual schema and influences the infant's immediate and subsequent responses. The shift of perception from being primarily stimulus-bound to involving construction

and meaning is addressed in more detail by work on the infant's emerging theory of mind (Bretherton et al., 1981). It is this shift that allows the infant to discriminate self from other and to begin the first moves toward autonomy and exploration described by Mahler in her observational studies.

The importance for psychoanalysis of studies such as these is how closely the experimental investigations using stimulus–response and discrimination paradigms in infants parallel the concepts and theories based on observations of infant behavior in the nursery. Infants come into the world endowed with a range of perceptual capacities uniquely suited to social interaction. The complementary data provided by developmental psychology models also support the validity and feasibility of testing many of the hypotheses generated by analytically informed observations.

THE ROLE OF ENDOWMENT IN THE PSYCHOANALYTIC PROCESS

The roots of psychoanalysis are firmly placed in notions of genetics, inheritance, and biological evolution, and psychoanalysis continues to draw on findings from relevant neurobiological and developmental sciences. But how is endowment apparent in mental representations and symbolic life? What are the therapeutic implications of keeping in mind that endowment is vital, shifting, and in a constant state of change throughout the life span? How is endowment evident in the therapeutic process? It is in addressing such questions that we can see a contrast between Freud's legacy of endowment as something that is static and not amenable to therapeutic techniques and the legacy of psychoanalytically informed observations of the developing infant and young child and the theories based on that work.

Child analysts often find themselves considering endowment and maturational shifts in the context of changes during the course of an analysis. Indeed, in child analysis, constitutional considerations are more in the forefront than is usually true in work with adults (except in special circumstances such as chronic illnesses or genetic conditions). For example, the beginning of puberty, with the associated dramatic shifts in hormonal control, body habitus, and concomitant strength of drives, changes both the content and affective tone of mental representation and symbolization. Analogous changes in mental representation and presentation occur earlier, as a child enters the so-called latency years or as a toddler enters the more complex, conflicted world of triadic relationships characterizing the oedipal conflict. Changes in the child's information-processing capacities and the sophistication of his or her abstract reasoning abilities reflected in the emergence of secondary-process thinking are events programmed in large degree by genetic factors. While our understanding of the neurobehavioral concomitants of these various developmental epochs is still rudimentary, their universality and inevitability are constant factors in child analysis. Indeed, when one is in the presence of such phenomena, it is difficult not to be impressed with the fact that endowment has taken hold and is the driving force of individual psychic development.

By contrast, in the analysis of an adult, endowment is often not as clearly in view. There are several reasons for this difference, not least of which is that developmental shifts in adulthood are not as rapid or usually as dramatic as they are in early childhood and adolescence. Furthermore, as psychoanalysis has become more focused on mental representation, the potency of symbolization, and intrapsychic narrative and meaning, the biological concomitants of mental functioning may appear extraneous to the analyst's view. This reflects several trends in adult analysis. First, as the illustrations in the previous section suggest, studies of constitutional factors now require methodological techniques from other fields besides psychoanalysis. Whereas Freud began as a neurologist and continued to be influenced by neurological ideas, and his education (as well as his endowment) made it possible for him to embrace much of the science of his day, more recent advances in the neurosciences, developmental psychology, and genetics make it far more difficult, if not impossible, for contemporary psychoanalysts to be knowledgeable in all related fields. Analysts may assume that every mental event they observe probably has some genetically determined correlate and vice versa (Smith & Ballenger, 1983), but these events and the scientific advances that define them occur outside the analyst's view.

Moreover, after its initial breathtakingly broad formulations of models of mental functioning, psychoanalysis has increasingly defined itself by a metapsychological theory that is semantically different from the more reductionist approach of other developmental sciences (Reiser, 1984). Schafer (1976) and G. Klein (1976) among others have contended that the most valuable propositions of psychoanalysis are those that give meaning to individual human experience. Ricoeur (1970) suggests that analysis is essentially an interpretive or hermeneutic activity that looks for the ways in which the symbols involved in the communications between analyst and analysand are endowed with meaning. In either case,

the biological roots and causes of communications so defined are essentially outside the purview of the analytic process. In a sense, the emphasis on individual meaning supplants the need to understand the biological roots of such meaning. Moreover, while such a metatheory is necessary, conceptually rich, and in many cases clinically useful, it does not lend itself easily to empirical validation by other techniques. The mental phenomena defined by one theory are simply in different domains from the biological phenomena underlying variation in psychic functioning (Edelson, 1984). Productive dialogue between psychoanalysis and the relevant neurosciences is increasingly difficult, even if it is such dialogue that forces analysts and their neurobiological colleagues to refine theories and interpretations of analytic data and that keeps biology and constitution in psychoanalytic view.

A third trend that keeps endowment partially out of view in the analysis of adults is the gradual change in the focus of psychoanalysis as a clinical technique. Symptoms such as the hysterical conversions with which Freud began are no longer the *raison d'être* for analysis. Rather, symptoms are only one of many symbolic phenomena encountered within the contemporary analytic frame, which is more broadly concerned with object relationships as manifest in transference phenomena and with the symbolic nature of object-related life. Yet, it was such symptoms that early on provided conceptual links to body-based processes and to questions about diagnosis that naturally invoked constitutional issues. Similarly, psychoanalysis as a clinical field is now less concerned with defining more precise diagnostic categories. Thus, inasmuch as the diagnostic process often involves etiological considerations, the dilemmas of constitutional contributions enter less often into analytic formulations.

Fourth, analysts are perhaps struggling with the legacy left by Freud in "Analysis terminable and interminable" (1937) and by scientists in other fields, that constitution or endowment stands for that which is immutable, the final bedrock of analysis. If it represents a limitation to analysis and to analytic treatment, it is a difficult issue to ponder. But the notion of endowment as something that is changing vitally and is expressed throughout the life span is most pertinent to analysis as a therapeutic technique, for it is the vital, evolving endowment that is most evident in the daily analytic process.

Where might the symbolic and functional traces of endowment issues be most evident in the course of analysis with an adult? Differences in cognitive style or intellectual level have been discussed by others (for example, Keiser, 1969) but, while relevant, this work does not address the more dynamic view of endowment that has been the focus of this chapter or those biological events and functions that will most certainly vary within the course of an analysis. Events such as pregnancy or serious illness in either analyst or analysand bring endowment and constitution into sharp relief in the analytic material. For example, pregnancy represents a highly charged, biological process in which issues of endowment are primary. The pregnant woman considers the endowment she will pass on to her child, her own endowment from her parents both as genetic material and as her capacity to be a parent, and the changes in her own body. An analyst's pregnancy may evoke a constellation of childhood wishes and fantasies in the analysand that were not readily available through other less body-bound experiences. Certain transference experiences are surely heightened or experienced more intensely than might be the case without such direct evidence of endowment (Bassen, 1988). An analyst's pregnancy is not only a special event for the analysand but may also affect how the analyst hears and experiences the preverbal material of her analysands (Lax, 1969).

Similarly, sudden or chronic illness in the analyst (or, for that matter, in the analysand) means that biological endowment cannot be denied and is a vital presence in the associative material. Several researchers have commented on how few references there are in the literature to serious illness or death of the analyst and have suggested that this paucity reflects the anxiety generally aroused when such issues are considered (Dewald, 1982; Schwartz, 1987). Just as serious or chronic illness in the analyst is a disturbing experience for the analysand, so too for the analyst. Being seriously ill activates fantasies of mutilation, abandonment, and death and shatters the wish for physical omnipotence and invulnerability. An analyst's illness not only raises technical issues about how the analyst will handle potential disruptions in the analysis but his or her reaction to the illness dramatically alters the ratio of reality to fantasy in the transferential balance (Abend, 1982). Endowment as biology is ever present in such instances and intrudes even more harshly into the analytic world of symbols and meaning in the case of death of the analyst during the course of an analysis (Lord et al., 1978).

Pregnancy or serious illness provide dramatic, notable examples of times when constitution plays a central role in the analytic process, but neither one occurs in every analysis. By contrast, other biological processes that are fundamentally part of endowment occur daily in every analysis. For example, the influence of the analyst's gender on transference

phenomena and the emergence of the transference neurosis involve complex relations with issues of endowment as represented intrapsychically (Raphling & Chused, 1988). Perceptions of gender, different expressions of sexual impulses and feelings, and differences in object-directed strivings—all fundamentally part of day-to-day analytic material—are colored by gender and are in part woven into the transferential fabric.

In some ways related to gender, but more subtle, are the various biological rhythms which influence our daily, monthly, even seasonal functioning. It is well documented, for example, that menstrual cycles influence affect regulation and have an effect on memory and recall (Altemus et al., 1989; Schmidt et al., 1990). Similarly, there are diurnal variations in cortisol levels that minimally influence levels of alertness and arousal and may more subtly effect the recall of associative memories and feelings (Wolkowitz et al., 1990). Changes in season, particularly entailing variations in the amount of daylight, are well recognized as influencing mood (Wehr & Rosenthal, 1989); but it is also likely that such changes are evident in the representations and symbols that are most salient for the analysand in that season. Similarly, variations in sensory-perceptual threshold, a biologically-based function evident even in infants, influence individuals' reactions not only to variations in light (as in seasonal changes) but also to changes in the perceptual atmosphere of the consulting room—changes in colors, textures, or the artificial lighting of lamps. Such is the stuff of endowment from very early on, the internal programming or hard-wiring that is constantly evident in the ways individuals choose to represent their perceptual world. Finally, aging likewise affects a number of psychological functions, including memory, and contributes to the analysand (and the analyst) becoming more aware of changing bodily functions.

Maturation and bodily changes—pregnancy, menopause, fluctuations in the sexual drive with age and life events—are analytic opportunities for understanding how constitution is represented in a number of complex ways. Also, illnesses, those "biological accidents" of life, are part of the dynamic view of endowment. Whether through a mild or a major illness, most individuals become more aware of bodily functions and of their biological limitations. All these phenomena are the potential or actual experiences of both analyst and analysand. Both are dealing with their own constitutions. Both are subject to the vagaries of neuroregulatory rhythms, to the affective shifts associated with seasonal changes, and certainly to the effects of aging and illness and concerns about them. Endowment is thus always in the background of any analytic hour, influencing the ebb and flow of symbolic thought. One of the tasks of analysis is to bring endowment more into the analytic frame, to allow the analysand to feel at one with his or her body and to experience all the vigorous, sometimes unanticipated changes that entails. Such work, along with the working through of unresolved conflict and losses, is part of the personal integration offered by analysis: a coming face to face with the body, the constitution granted analyst and analysand, within which and with which the psychological being of each functions.

To deny endowment or those constitutional factors that form the constant background of psychic functioning is protective, in that it limits an individual's vision of mortality and allows the analysand (and analyst) to work outside the limits of physiology—in a sense, outside the body. Endowment is what keeps individuals grounded in biology and genetics; but it is a cherished, ever present wish to be free of that grounding. In the ways of the symbolic world, the wish contains both its aim and its solution. To work within the personal endowment, as it is given and as it evolves, is to come to an integration of constitution and experience that in and of itself expands the range of psychological awareness.

REFERENCES

Abend, S. M. (1982). Serious illness in the analyst. *J. Amer. Psychoanal. Assn.*, 30:365–379.

Altemus, M., Wexler, B. E., & Boulis, M. (1989). Neuropsychological correlates of menstrual mood changes. *Psychosom. Med.*, 51:329–336.

Aslin, R. N., Pisoni, D. B., & Jusczyk, P. W. (1983). Auditory development and speech perception in infancy. In *Infancy and Developmental Psychobiology*, ed. M. Haith & J. J. Campos, vol. 2, pp. 573–688. New York: Wiley.

Banks, M. S., & Salapatek, P. (1983). Infant visual perception. In *Infancy and Developmental Psychobiology*, ed. M. Haith & J. J. Campos, vol. 2, pp. 435–572. New York: Wiley.

Bassen, C. (1988). The impact of the analyst's pregnancy on the course of analysis. *Psychoanal. Inq.*, 8:280–298.

Benjamin, J. D. (1961). Some developmental observations relating to the theory of anxiety. *J. Amer. Psychoanal. Assn.*, 9:652–668.

Bergman, P., & Escalona, S. K. (1949). Unusual sensitivities in very young children. *Psychoanal. Study Child*, 3/4:333–352.

Bertenthal, B., Campos, J. J., & Haith, M. (1980). Development of visual organization. *Child Develpm.*, 50:1072–1080.

Bornstein, M., Gaughran, J., & Homel, P. (1986). Infant temperament. In *Measuring Emotions in Infants and Children*, ed. C. E. Izard & P. B. Read, vol. 2, pp. 172–199. New York: Cambridge Univ. Press.

Bretherton, I., McNew, S., & Beeghly-Smith, M. (1981). Early person knowledge as expressed in gestural and verbal communication. In *Infant Social Cognition*, ed. M. E. Lamb & L. R. Sherrod, pp. 333–373. Hillsdale, N.J.: Erlbaum.

Breuer, J., & Freud, S. (1893–95). *Studies on Hysteria. SE*, 2.

Bühler, C., & Hetzer, H. (1935). *Testing Children's Development from Birth to School Age*. New York: Farrar & Rinehart.

Buss, A. H., & Plomin, R. (1975). *A Temperament Theory of Personality Development*. New York: Wiley.

——— (1984). *Temperament*. Hillsdale, N.J.: Erlbaum.

Buss, A. H., Plomin, R., & Willerman, L. (1973). The inheritance of temperaments. *J. Pers.*, 41:513–524.

Campos, J. & Stenberg, C. (1981). Perception, appraisal, and emotion. In *Infant Social Cognition*, ed. M. E. Lamb & L. R. Sherrod, pp. 273–314. Hillsdale, N.J.: Erlbaum.

Caron, A., Caron, R., Caldwell, R., & Weiss, S. (1973). Infant perception of the structural properties of the face. *Develpm. Psychol.*, 9:229–243.

Chess, S., Thomas, A., & Birch, H. G. (1959). Characteristics of the individual child's behavioral responses to the environment. *Amer. J. Orthopsychiat.*, 29:791–802.

Cohen, D. J. (1991). Tourette's syndrome. *Int. Rev. Psychoanal.*, 18:195–209.

Davidson, E. H. (1986). *Gene Activity in Early Development*. New York: Academic Press.

Delaney, R., Tussi, D., & Gold, P. E. (1983). Long-term potentiation as a neurophysiological analog of memory. *Pharmacol., Biochem. & Behav.*, 18: 137–139.

Derryberry, D., & Rothbart, M. K. (1984). Emotion, attention, and temperament. In *Emotions, Cognition, and Behavior*, ed. C. E. Izard, J. Kagan, & R. B. Zajonc, pp. 132–166. New York: Cambridge Univ. Press.

Dewald, P. A. (1982). Serious illness in the analyst. *J. Amer. Psychoanal. Assn.*, 30:347–363.

Dibble, E. D., & Cohen, D. J. (1981). Personality development in identical twins. *Psychoanal. Study Child*, 36:45–70.

Downey, T. W. (1984). Within the pleasure principle. *Psychoanal. Study Child*, 39:101–136.

Ritvo, L. (1965). Darwin as the source of Freud's neo-Lamarckianism. *J. Amer. Psychoanal. Assn.*, 13:499–517.

———. (1974). The impact of Darwin on Freud. *Psychoanal. Q.*, 43:177–192.

———. (1990). *Darwin's Influence on Freud*. New Haven: Yale Univ. Press.

Ritvo, S., & Solnit, A. J. (1958). Influences of early mother–child interaction on identification processes. *Psychoanal. Study Child*, 13:64–85.

Sackett, G. P., Ruppenthal, G. C., Fahrenbruch, C. E., & Holm, R. A. (1981). Social isolation rearing effects in monkeys vary with genotype. *Develpm. Psychol.*, 17:313–318.

Sander, L. W. (1962). Issues in early mother–child interaction. *J. Amer. Acad. Child Psychiat.*, 1: 141–166.

Scarr, S., & Kidd, K. K. (1983). Developmental behavioral genetics. In *Handbook of Child Psychology*, ed. M. M. Haith & J. J. Campos, vol. 2, pp. 345–433. New York: Wiley.

Scarr, S., & McCartney, K. (1983). How people make their own environments. *Child Develpm.*, 54:424–435.

Schafer, R. (1976). *A New Language for Psychoanalysis*. New Haven: Yale Univ. Press.

Schaffer, H. R., Greenwood, A., & Parry, M. H. (1972). The onset of wariness. *Child Develpm.*, 43:165–175.

Schmidt, P. J., Grover, G. N., Hoban, M. C., & Rubinow, D. R. (1990). State-dependent alterations in the perception of life events in menstrual-related mood disorders. *Amer. J. Psychiat.*, 147: 230–234.

Schwartz, H. J. (1987). Illness in the doctor. *J. Amer. Psychoanal. Process*, 35:657–692.

Smith, J. H., & Ballenger, J. C. (1983). Psychology and neurobiology. *Psychoanal. & Contemp. Thought*, 3:407–421.

Solnit, A. J. (1970). Aggression. *J. Amer. Psychoanal. Assn.*, 20:435–450.

Spiegler, B. J., & Mishkin, M. (1981). Evidence for the sequential participation of inferior temporal cortex and amygdala in the acquisition of stimulus–reward associations. *Behav. Brain Research*, 3:303–317.

Spitz, R. A. (1945). Hospitalism. *Psychoanal. Study Child*, 1:53–74.

Stern, D. N. (1985). *The Interpersonal World of the Infant*. New York: Basic Books.

Stevenson, J., & Fielding, J. (1985). Ratings of temperament in families of young twins. *Brit. J. Develpm. Psychol.*, 3:143–152.

Stoller, R. J. (1968). *Sex and Gender*. New York: Science House.

Suomi, S. J., Kraemer, G. W., Baysinger, C. M., & DeLizio, R. D. (1981). Inherited and experiential factors associated with individual differences in anxious behavior displayed by rhesus monkeys. In *Anxiety*, ed. D. F. Klein & J. Rabkin, pp. 179–201. New York: Raven Press.

Thomas, A., & Chess, S. (1984). Genesis and evolution of behavioral disorders. *Amer. J. Psychiat.*, 141:1–9.

Tyson, P., & Tyson, R. L. (1990). *Psychoanalytic Theories of Development*. New Haven: Yale Univ. Press.

van der Kolk, B., Greenberg, M., Boyd, H., & Krystal, J. (1985). Inescapable shock, neurotransmitters, and addiction to trauma. *Biol. Psychiat.*, 20:314–325.

Watson, I. P. B., Hoffman, L., & Wilson, G. V. (1988). The neuropsychiatry of post-traumatic stress disorder. *Brit. J. Psychiat.*, 152:164–173.

Wehr, T. A., & Rosenthal, N. E. (1989). Seasonality and affective illness. *Amer. J. Psychiat.*, 146:829–839.

Weil, A. P. (1956). Some evidences of deviational development in infancy and early childhood. *Psychoanal. Study Child*, 8:251–257.

———. (1970). The basic core. *Psychoanal. Study Child*, 25:442–460.

———. (1978). Maturational variations and genetic-dynamic issues. *J. Amer. Psychoanal. Assn.*, 26: 461–491.

———. (1983). Thoughts about early pathology. *J. Amer. Psychoanal. Assn.*, 33:335–352.

Wilson, R. S., & Matheny, A. P., Jr. (1986). Behavior-genetics research in infant temperament. In *The Study of Temperament*, ed. R. Plomin & J. Dunn, pp. 81–97. Hillsdale, N.J.: Erlbaum.

Wolff, P. H. (1967). The role of biological rhythms in early psychological development. *Bull. Menninger Clinic*, 31:197–218.

Wolkowitz, D. M., Reus, V. I., Weingartner, H., Thompson, K., et al. (1990). Cognitive effects of corticosteroids. *Amer. J. Psychiat.*, 147:1297–1303.

Young-Bruehl, E. (1988). *Anna Freud*. New York: Summit Books.

Zager, E. L., & Black, P. M. (1985). Neuropeptides in human memory and learning processes. *Neurosurgery*, 17:355–369.

22

REALITY

In his late major theoretical reformulations—*The Ego and the Id* (1923) and *Inhibitions, Symptoms and Anxiety* (1926)—into his metapsychological structural theory, Freud placed the ego at the crossroads where the drive demands of the id, the moral constraints of the superego, and the exigent requirements of outer reality all met and were mediated. In so doing, he implicitly made reality directly comparable to the intrapsychic instances in its role in mental life. Nonetheless, as I have stated elsewhere (Wallerstein, 1973), the full implications for our theory of this positioning of reality have never been adequately remarked or more than rudimentarily developed.

Yet, in the very earliest Freudian formulation of mental disorder, the original traumatic theory of the neuroses, it was outer reality that was deemed the central locus of the pathogenic impact, in the form of adult sexual seductions of the unformed child. And in that framework, the original conceptualization of defense was as defense against the memory and the affect of the reality experience, not against drive cathexis. It was only with Freud's embarrassing and painful discovery that the ubiquitous sexual seductions were fantasy elaborations, not facts in the real world, that analytic interest was withdrawn from the world of reality and an inner psychology of the vicissitudes of drive (and the defenses against it) came to be developed. It is this fateful turning of psychoanalysis as a psychology that both determined

its main historical developmental line as a psychology of the inner (unconscious) mental life and concomitantly led to a lessened concern with the nature or role of reality as a significant participant in psychic functioning.

THE CONCEPT OF REALITY TESTING

From the very beginning of his psychological theorizing, in the "Project for a scientific psychology" (1895), Freud recognized *reality testing,* which he defined simply as the capacity to distinguish ideas from perceptions, a fundamental concern in any theory of mental functioning. He credited this capacity to an "inhibition by the ego" (p. 326). Freud's argument was, however, a circular one. Wishful cathexes, or "psychical primary processes," do not by themselves distinguish between an idea and a perception. They require an inhibition by "psychical secondary processes," which can come into operation only when there is an "ego" with a large enough store of cathexis to provide the energy necessary to put the inhibition into effect. This will give time for the "indications of reality" (p. 327) to arrive from the perceptual apparatus. Here is the circularity of this first (metapsychological) argument.

Freud first used the actual phrase "reality testing" in "Two principles of mental functioning" (1911), in the context of describing as the "strangest characteristic" (p. 225) of unconscious mental processes their entire disregard of reality testing, their equating wishful thinking with the actual real event that is wished for. In that same paper he also carried further his concept of how the inhibition of the ego, upon which the reality-testing capacity rested, was carried out. This was said to be by way of the special function of *attention*, defined as a periodic scanning of the external world so that its data might be already familiar if an urgent internal need should arise. This deployment of attention then enables a deliberate judgment to replace an automatic repression; the decision is made by comparing the idea "with the memory-traces of reality" (p. 221).

Laplanche and Pontalis (1973) have called attention to the fact that actually two different conceptions exist in Freud's writings as to how the reality-testing function is constituted. The first, the one enunciated in the "Project" and elaborated in "Two Principles," they term "an economic explanation" (p. 383), in which the difference between the dream and the waking state is accounted for by a differing distribution of energy or cathexes among mental systems. But Freud then went on to develop what Laplanche and Pontalis describe as a "more empiricist view" (ibid.) of reality testing, which ascribed this function to the outcome of motor exploration. This explanation was first advanced in "Instincts and their vicissitudes" (1915a, p. 119). It deserves quotation in full:

> Let us imagine ourselves in the situation of an almost entirely helpless living organism, as yet unoriented in the world, which is receiving stimuli in its nervous substance. This organism will very soon be in a position to make a first distinction and a first orientation. On the one hand, it will be aware of stimuli which can be avoided by muscular action (flight); these it ascribes to an external world. On the other hand, it will also be aware of stimuli against which such action is of no avail and whose character of constant pressure persists in spite of it; these stimuli are the signs of an internal world, the evidence of instinctual needs. The perceptual substance of the living organism will thus have found in the efficacy of its muscular activity a basis for distinguishing between an "outside" and an "inside."

This "empiricist" criterion for reality testing, based on response to the effort at avoidance by muscular movement, deals with the issue of making the discriminatory judgment about reality in the first place, in a way in which the "economic" model, based on cathectic distributions that permit attention deployment, scanning, and delay, does not. Freud's satisfaction with this reformulation is underlined by

the fact of his repeating it almost verbatim two years later in "A metapsychological supplement to the theory of dreams" (1917a).

In this same essay Freud both reiterated the importance of a sound, reliable basis for reality testing and saw failures of this "contrivance" as central to explanations both in pathology (psychosis) and in normal mental functioning (dreams). He stated that reality testing was of such central psychological importance because our whole relation to the external world depended on it. He then made the observation that we can learn from pathology just how the reality-testing function can be done away with or put out of action. In psychosis, he said, the ego breaks off its relation to reality by withdrawing cathexis (or energy) from the perceptual system, thereby allowing unrepressed, conscious, wishful fantasies to flood that system, where, as hallucinations, they are "regarded as a better reality" (p. 233). This same mechanism he declared to be in operation in normal dreaming, where, again, reality testing is abandoned —on the same basis, the sleeper's withdrawal of cathexis from the perceptual system.

Clearly, by this time, Freud had made another major conceptual commitment, locating reality testing as a central function of the ego, as that institution was itself taking conceptual shape. In his paper on "The unconscious" (1915b), cast in terms of the earlier, topographic model of the mind, Freud had declared reality testing to be an attribute of the system *Preconscious*. In the "Metapsychological supplement" (1917a), while still talking the language of the topographical model, he was also employing the new language of a structured psychic apparatus, and there he included reality testing among the "major *institutions* of the ego" (p. 233). Except for a brief and confusing temporary switch which placed it in the ego ideal (or the superego) in the "Group psychology" paper of 1921, Freud thereafter continued to define reality testing as a task of the ego, as in "Mourning and melancholia" (1917b, p. 247) and *The Ego and the Id* (1923, p. 28).

Freud's last substantial statement on (and revision of) the issue of reality testing occurred in his short paper "Negation" (1925), where he spoke of reality testing not as finding but as "re-finding" an external reality "out there." In that paper he considered the function of judgment involved in reality testing as a question of whether a presentation in the ego can be rediscovered in perception (reality) as well. He called this "once more a question of *external* and *internal*. What is unreal, merely a presentation and subjective, is only internal; what is real is also there outside" (p. 237). This view is based on the assumption that *all* presentations in the ego originate from perceptions and are merely repetitions of them. The task of thinking is to bring before the mind once more something that has been perceived previously, by reproducing it first as a presentation without the need for the external object to be there. The aim of reality testing, therefore, is not to *find* an object in reality that corresponds to the internal presentation but to *refind* such an object, in order to convince oneself that it is still there.

It was this revision by Freud that prompted Laplanche and Pontalis (1973, p. 173) to emphasize that in Freud's usage the term "reality testing" confused two quite different functions: the function of discriminating between the merely represented and the actually perceived—that is, between the internal and the external world—and the function of comparing what is perceived objectively with mental representations so as to rectify possible distortions in the latter.

After Freud it was Nunberg who, in a paper on "Transference and reality" (1951), developed further the conceptualization of reality testing by exploring its operation (more specifically than Freud had) within the psychoanalytic treatment situation. His approach was by forging a conceptual link between our concept of transference as the imposition of the past upon the present and Freud's concept of the urge to establish an identity of perception. This was for Nunberg in the service of conceptualizing the role of reality testing in *analyzing the transference* —that is, undoing the tendency to "identity of perception." He described how the patient "reanimated" representations of repressed objects in the transference, thereby gaining "direct access" to childhood experiences (p. 5). As these transferences were rendered conscious, the patient *pari passu* gained the ability to assess his or her real feelings in relation to the infantile situation. This then helped the patient to distinguish between images returning from the past and perceptions of real external objects, thus improving his or her ability to test reality. Nunberg added that when the patient recognized these attempts to relive the past in the present, he or she usually gave them up, or at least modified them. In this process, the transference, which created an *artificial reality,* was unmasked.

It was Hartmann who erected the capstone to our modern-day psychoanalytic conceptualization of the meaning(s) of reality testing, as part of his considerations regarding the varying psychoanalytic perspectives on reality, in his comprehensive paper "Notes on the reality principle" (1956). He framed his considerations within his well-known penchant (shared with Freud) for philosophical dualisms. He spoke of two kinds of meaning to reality testing. "When Freud speaks about reality testing he usually means the capacity to distinguish between ideas and perceptions. In a broader sense, reality testing also refers to the ability to discern subjective and objective elements in our judgments of reality" (p. 256). Here Hartmann means not the distinction between inner (psychic) and outer reality (reality testing in Freud's sense of the distinction between fantasy and perception) but rather the distinction between two kinds of outer reality—that which corresponds to the so-called "objective" reality validated by the methods of science and what he calls "subjective" or socialized reality, the world of "more immediate experience" (p. 263) that is intersubjectively accepted. I will return to this distinction between two kinds of external reality later.

THE CONCEPT OF THE REALITY PRINCIPLE

Alongside Freud's lifelong preoccupation with the nature and essence of reality testing was a concomitant concern with another aspect of the organism's relatedness to reality, the development and operation in mental life of the *reality principle,* as a counterpoint to the original, more archaic pleasure principle. This was spelled out in explicit detail in the paper "Formulations on the two principles of mental functioning" (1911). The main theme of the paper is the distinction between the two regulatory principles (the pleasure principle and the reality principle) that respectively dominate the primary and secondary mental processes. Basically, in infantile development, in response to repeated disappointments in efforts at hallucinatory wish fulfillment, the developing psychic apparatus gradually forms a conception of the real circumstances in the external world and endeavors to make a real alteration in them. Thus, what comes to be presented to the mind is no longer what is agreeable but what is real, even if it happens to be disagreeable. This constitutes the setting up of the *reality principle,* which Freud called "a momentous step" (p. 219). To do this, of course, one has to *know* what is real and be able to *test* reality. It is in this same paper that Freud introduced the term "reality testing."

The ascendancy of the reality principle over the pleasure principle is never complete in mental life; it is always vulnerable to regressive reversal. And because of the autoerotism that enables the sexual instincts to find satisfaction in the subject's own body without the pressing need to seek object attachments in the outer world, the sexual instincts characteristically come under the sway of the reality principle much later than the ego instincts. Along this same line, no matter how firm the hegemony of the reality principle, it is never at the total expense of the pleasure principle, because in the end their aims are one. Thus Freud called the substitution of the reality principle for the pleasure principle not a deposing of the pleasure principle but only a safeguarding of it. A momentary pleasure is given up, but only in order to gain (along the new path) an assured pleasure at a later time.

The same main points are summarized in Freud's *Introductory Lectures* (1916–17) as follows: "An ego thus educated has become 'reasonable'; it no longer lets itself be governed by the pleasure principle, but obeys the *reality principle,* which also at bottom seeks to obtain pleasure, but pleasure which is assured through taking account of reality, even though it is postponed and diminished. The transition from the pleasure principle to the reality principle is one of the most important steps forward in the ego's development" (p. 357). But Freud then goes on to say that one arena, "the mental realm of phantasy," is excluded from the domination of the reality principle, and here he uses the metaphor of the nature reserve, which preserves the original state that everywhere else has been sacrificed to the encroachments of necessity. In the nature reserve, everything, including what is useless and even what is noxious, can grow and proliferate as it pleases. Freud stated that "the mental realm of phantasy" was just such a reservation, protected from the reality principle.

Freud (1920) placed the operative motor in establishing the reality principle in "the ego's instincts of self-preservation" (p. 10). After all, from the point of view of self-preservation of the organism, the pleasure principle is from the outset inefficient, not to say highly dangerous. It is therefore under the influence of the ego's instincts for self-preservation that the pleasure principle is of necessity replaced by the reality principle. Laplanche and Pontalis (1973) have succinctly summarized Freud's overall development of the reality principle as follows: "As a regulatory principle of mental functioning, the reality principle emerges secondarily, modifying the pleasure principle, which has been dominant up to this point" (p. 380). Once the hegemony of the reality principle has been established, "the search for satisfaction does not take the most direct routes but instead makes detours and postpones the attainment of its goal according to the conditions imposed by the outside world" (p. 379). Here the role of reality testing is crucial.

Again, it was Hartmann (1956) who drew out what was inherent in Freud's positions into more complex, modern-day, ego-psychological conceptualizations by teasing out (again, by dichotomization)

two distinctive psychoanalytic meanings of the term "reality principle." In his seminal paper "Notes on the reality principle" (1956), he identified two meanings that currently attach to the term "reality principle." One is the tendency to take into account in an adaptive way—in perception, thinking, and action— whatever we consider to be the "real" features of an object or a situation. The other, perhaps narrower meaning is the tendency to wrest our activities from the immediate need for discharge inherent in the pleasure principle. In this latter sense we speak of the reality principle as the natural opponent, or at least modifier, of the pleasure principle. But this poses a problem, in that one cannot say simply that reality-syntonic behavior generally curtails pleasure. That would be an unwarranted generalization, because behavior under the guidance of the reality principle is aimed at gaining, in a new way, an assured pleasure at a later stage, while giving up only a momentary pleasure.

Correlated somewhat to the distinction Hartmann has thus clarified between two meanings of the concept "reality principle," but also somewhat different, is a concomitant distinction between two meanings of the phrase "reality-syntonic": "It may mean that the thought is true in the sense that it corresponds to reality [the idea of 'knowledge of reality']. On the other hand, it may also mean that its use, in a given reality situation, leads to a successful mastery of the situation [the idea of 'acting in regard to reality']. That in a large sector of human behavior there is *no simple* correlation between the degree of objective insight and the degree of adaptiveness of the corresponding action is not in need of being proved. Objective knowledge of and practical orientation in reality do not necessarily coincide" (p. 253, my emphasis).

THE DISTINCTION BETWEEN EXTERNAL AND INTERNAL REALITY

As compared with his lifelong preoccupation with the concepts of reality testing and the reality principle and the closely intertwined relationship between them, Freud devoted far less explicit attention to defining what he meant by reality or to distinguishing between outer (or factual) reality and inner (or psychic) reality. Perhaps he took the nature of reality to be essentially self-evident, especially to a psychology that tried to exclude the problems of philosophy and epistemology from its purview, in much the same way that Hartmann (1960) said of Freud in relation to moral values that "he used to quote F. T. Vischer's 'What is *moral* is self-evident'" (p. 14.).

Freud's first, brief statement on the nature of reality goes back to the "Project" (1895), where he distinguished, without definition, between "thought-reality" and "external reality" (p. 373). In *The Interpretation of Dreams* (1900), Freud altered the former phrase to "psychical reality" (p. 613). In *Totem and Taboo* (1913), he counterposed "psychical reality" to "factual reality" (p. 159). In a subsequent edition of *The Interpretation of Dreams* (in 1919) he changed the latter term to "material reality." The final form of the sentence at issue then became: "If we look at unconscious wishes reduced to their most fundamental and truest shape, we shall have to conclude, no doubt, that *psychical* reality is a particular form of existence not to be confused with material reality" (p. 620). Laplanche and Pontalis (1973) here as elsewhere accurately summarize Freud's thinking. They define psychical reality as a "term often used by Freud to designate whatever in the subject's psyche presents a consistency and a resistance comparable to those displayed by material reality; fundamentally, what is involved here is unconscious desire and its associated phantasies," which leads naturally to, "in the world of the neuroses it is psychical reality which is the decisive kind" (p. 363).

At this point I wish to turn to a paper by Arlow, "Fantasy, memory, and reality testing" (1969), in order to delineate more recent elaborations and implications of Freud's original conceptions along this particular line of thought. Arlow's thesis has to do with the role of unconscious fantasy activity in the assessment of reality (i.e., in reality-testing) and the complex creation of our idiosyncratic psychic reality within this interplay. Arlow sets out to demonstrate that how reality is experienced depends for the most part on the interaction between one's perception of the external world and the concomitant effect of unconscious fantasy activity.

His argument begins with the observation that the most powerful influence distorting the image of the past and contributing to misperception of the present is the intrusion of unconscious fantasy thinking. In describing this ubiquitous intrusion of fantasy activity into conscious experience, he cites clinical experiences from the daily lives of analytic patients demonstrating that, while the patients were alert and vigorously involved in reality-oriented activity, their judgment of reality and their responses to it were quite completely distorted by unconscious fantasy. This kind of distortion is, of course, an essential feature of the transference as well as the neurotic process. It is just this constant intermingling of fantasy and perception that makes clear why memory is so unreliable, especially memory from childhood, be-

cause in childhood this process of intermingling perception and fantasy is present to such a high degree. Whatever the child experiences is at the very moment of experiencing it a complex intermingling of perception and fantasy. And the result of this complex intermingling is what "really" happened as far as the individual is concerned. Only through the process of inference can the analyst sometimes elucidate from the material the part of the individual's recollection that belongs to objective history, as opposed to the patient's "personal 'mythological' past" (p. 39). In summary, Arlow states: "There is . . . a reciprocal interplay between reality and fantasy, selective perception on one side, cathectic intensification on the other" (p. 41).

All this builds to Arlow's central thesis:

External perception and internal fantasy were intermingled at the time of the experience and together they formed the reality which to the patient was the record of his past. It was upon this confused fantasy thinking, which was dynamically effective in influencing so many aspects of his life, that the inner eye of the patient remained consistently focused. This is what I think is the *proper understanding of the concept "psychic reality."* It is not a fantasy that is taken for the real truth, for an actual event, but the "real" recollection of a psychic event with its mixture of fact and fantasy. . . . Subsequent events and perceptions of reality are selectively organized into memory schema consonant with inner fantasy thinking. [p. 43, my emphasis]

The individual then takes as a task the scanning of the data of perception of reality, in order to discover reassuring evidence of the validity of the solution he or she has arrived at in fantasy.

Arlow ends his article with a visual model to illustrate this interaction between fantasy thinking and reality. He compares this aspect of mental functioning to the effect that would be obtained if two motion picture projectors were to flash a continuous series of images simultaneously, but from opposite sides, onto a translucent screen. By analogy, there are two centers of perceptual input, introspection and extrospection, which supply data from the inner eye and data from the outer eye. It is the function of the ego to integrate, judge, and discard as appropriate the competing data of perceptual experience. All these factors influence the final judgment as to what is real and what is unreal. This, then, is "the connection between fantasy, memory, and reality" (p. 50)—linking to both psychic reality and external reality.

THE NATURE OF EXTERNAL REALITY

Freud nowhere undertook to define reality, not even in his paper "The loss of reality in neurosis and psychosis" (1924a). He saw reality as simply the material world "out there," even after he had introduced the concept of reality directly into his metapsychological structuring of his theoretical reformulations in *The Ego and the Id* (1923), which made reality directly comparable to the intrapsychic instances in its role in mental life. In his last systematic statement on reality, the 1925 paper on "Negation," his major thesis, that reality testing is not a finding but a refinding of an object previously perceived, rests on the assumption that reality is just what is out there, originally discovered as a presentation originating from perception, later to be rediscovered as one lives in a reality that is being continually tested.

Again, it was Hartmann who, in the same 1956 paper from which I have already presented a whole series of dualisms—two kinds of meaning to reality-testing (the distinction between inner ideas and outer perceptions; and also, the ability to discern subjective and objective elements in our judgment of outer reality); two kinds of meaning to reality principle (taking adaptive account of the "real" features of an object or situation; and also, more narrowly, the tendency to wrest our activities from the dominion of the pleasure-principle); and two kinds of meaning to reality syntonic (thought corresponding to reality, and also thought that leads to successful mastery or action in regard to reality)—also developed, at greatest length, his views on the two kinds of reality. Hartmann's main thesis sprang from his conceptualization of adaptation as a central regulatory principle of mental life mediating the phylogenetically guaranteed and biologically created coordination of the functioning human organism with the world of external reality, for each person in his or her time and place, in relation to his or her "average expectable environment" (1956). With its focus on specificity of time and place, this description of the adaptational process necessarily and immediately separates into the distinction indicated earlier in this chapter between two kinds of outer reality: the preexistent, invariant, physical environment, the reality that is validated objectively by the methods of science, and the man-made sociocultural reality, the socialized or conventional knowledge of reality that is intersubjectively accepted.

Hartmann stated that the criteria chiefly used in Freud's assessment of reality were those of science or, more correctly, those that find their clearest expression in science. Science strives for validation of its statements concerning reality; it accepts as "objective" what is verifiable by certain methods. Intersubjectivity of course plays a role in scientific validation. But "conventional," or "socialized," knowledge of reality means, in contradistinction to scientific knowledge, not so much what allows intersubjective validation but what is intersubjectively accepted, to a considerable extent without validation or even any attempt at validation. For the child, this means accepted by those closest to him or her, primarily the parents. In one sense, the reality of science is always vying with the reality outside science. Hartmann added his own conviction that the scientific conception of reality will never entirely oust the other conception except in the case of the scientist, and even then, only in his or her scientific work. He felt that it should not be forgotten that much of our "knowledge" of reality is of this socially accepted kind and the actions based on it.

Hartmann elaborated the reality outside science, "personal" reality, "our world" (p. 263), "the world of immediate experience" (p. 261), quoting Buytendijk, apparently approvingly, to the effect that "one's world . . . is no system of objective correlations, but a system of meanings and hence of values" (p. 264). Then, inconsistently, it appears, he reverted to seeing the world of immediate experience as only a way station en route to the world of science: "The cues to our actions are widely found in the world of immediate experience. There is no doubt that the evolving of this world, though it falls short of exactly reproducing or corresponding to 'objective reality,' is helpful toward developing our relations to it" (p. 263). All in all, this is evidence of an inconclusive struggle, with a nonresolution through recourse to the dualisms in thinking that always served Hartmann (and Freud) so well in theory construction in psychoanalysis.

Frosch, in his paper on the concept of reality constancy (1966), further amplified Hartmann's conceptions of the two kinds of external reality, the so-called "material objective reality," which stimulates the sense organs, which is Hartmann's objectively scientific reality, as well as "nonmaterial reality," such as conventionally accepted knowledge, which is Hartmann's intersubjectively social reality, by adding a counterpart dual *internal* reality, also divided into the "material" and the nonmaterial, or "psychic." In his view, internal psychic reality included memories, fantasies, impulses, desires, affects, thoughts, the body image, identity, self representation, and so on. However, he separated off an internal material reality, consisting of various somatic phenomena that may be derived from explicable or inexplicable processes such as pain and heart rhythm. These are generally not included in the concept of the internal world, which Frosch saw as usually construed in too limited a way as only psychic. Clearly, this represents a logical extension and amplification of Hartmann's perspective.

In fact, somewhat earlier than Hartmann, Loewald had addressed himself to this same issue of the essential nature of reality, taking a more uncompromisingly radical approach. In his provocative paper "Ego and reality" (1951), Loewald began by stating that an important implication of Freud's psychoanalytic metapsychology was that a constant tension existed in the relationship of the ego to reality. One task of the ego is adjustment or adaptation to reality, and this requires renunciation of the pleasure principle and substitution of the reality principle. This in turn creates a "fundamental antagonism" (p. 10) that needs to be bridged in order to make life in reality possible. Thus he states that "external reality has predominantly been seen in the aspect of a hostile, threatening power" (ibid.). In the evolving stages of object relatedness of the developing child, this alien outer reality comes to be represented by the father, seen as a hostile and jealous force, interfering with the intimate ties between mother and child and forcing the child into submission. On the other hand, Loewald also proposed that the developing ego, growing out of the pre-ego of primary narcissism, begins with "reality" contained within itself, only gradually detaching reality from itself as inner and outer start to crystallize as distinct, bounded domains. Loewald summarized this as, "the (primitive) ego detaches an external world from itself" (p. 14).

In this conceptualization, reality is seen as two-sided, as a precipitate detached from the ego and projected "out there," where it is then represented in its threatening, potentially hostile aspects by the figure of the father interfering with the intimacy of the primordial mother–child dyad. That is, Loewald conceptualized reality in terms of the projected and constructed precipitates of evolving object relationships. He then contrapuntally conceptualized these object relationships with regard to the primary parental figures: the father principle as an awesome, potentially hostile, threatening power, representing, via the oedipal conflict and the castration threat, the prototype of the demands of reality; and the mother principle as the tug toward maintenance of the primary tie to, and unity with, the environment. Loewald conceptualized these object attachments in their interplay as the *field of forces* within whose vicissitudes the differentiation, as well as the construction, of the child's developing sense of reality gradually takes place. In this sense, the primitive ego "detaches" the external world from itself, and

"ego and reality evolve gradually in conjunction with each other; the psychic apparatus undergoes a series of modifications, repressions, deflections of its original tendencies toward reestablishment of the primary narcissistic unity or identity with the environment (mother), under the interfering influence of the (paternal) castration threat. The resultants of this development are the structures which we call ego and reality" (pp. 14–15).

Quite aside from the degree of emphasis that we ourselves might wish to give to the primacy of the various stages of object relatedness in the young child's development of connection to reality, we have here the (epi)genetic and maturational basis for a conception of reality as created, evolved, and differentiated out of a more primordial, undifferentiated matrix, in the same way that the ego and the id separate out of such a matrix (in the mode made familiar by Hartmann). In this sense the development of reality is akin to, or at least comparable to, those gradually differentiating psychic instances themselves. Incidentally, reality itself is then comprised of at least two major organizing principles: paternal and maternal. In this construct, reality becomes an integral aspect of the psychic apparatus itself. Thus Loewald has far extended the parameters of Arlow's exposition. Arlow spoke of the creation of inner reality out of the interplay between external perception (of the real) and internal impinging and distorting fantasy, whereas Loewald has more boldly spoken of the evolution of our conception of external reality as well, out of the comparable interplay of outer experience anchored in object relationships and inner responsiveness.

It is at this point that I, building on the work of Freud, Hartmann, Loewald, and others, developed my own "Psychoanalytic perspectives on the problem of reality" (1973). I quote my own central statement at this point:

It is this way of conceptualizing reality, derived by Loewald within the fabric of psychoanalytic theory as a consequence of the ontogenetic developmental dynamic itself, that I wish to propose as the basis for the understanding, not only of our interpersonal reality (our "socialized" or our "social" reality in Hartmann's sense)—with which I think none would quarrel—but also as the basis for understanding the nature of even that other, that seeming polar opposite, which Hartmann calls the objective or the scientific reality. Because even natural science and its organizing postulates represents but a world view, guided and constrained by human-created methodological assumptions and consensually accepted values. Here

I wish to call on the distinguished physical chemist and social philosopher, Michael Polanyi, who so cogently argued in the Lindsay Memorial Lectures of 1958 the role of what he called "tacit knowledge," or "pre-articulate knowledge" or the "personal coefficient of knowledge" as essential ingredients in the creation of that world view represented by natural science.

How this world view is manifest in the very structure of science was stated by William Earle in a review of Polanyi's work in the journal *Science* (Polanyi, 1959), as follows: "How then does the personal factor manifest itself in the very structure of science? Polanyi discovers it wherever there is an act of appraisal, choice, or accreditation. Each science operates within a conceptual framework which it regards as the 'most fruitful' for those facts which it 'wishes' to study because they are 'important,' and it thereby chooses to ignore other facts which are 'unimportant,' 'misleading,' and 'of no consequence.'" That is, when we look at the assumptive or postulational bases of the thought systems of the natural sciences, we are back here, too, ultimately in the realm of belief and value systems, and of meanings, i.e., of realities created by acts of perspective and of interpretation. This Polanyi stated directly as, "The Theory of Personal Knowledge offers an interpretation of meaning. It says that no meaningful knowledge [not even, that is, in the so-called hard sciences, the physical sciences] can be acquired, except by an *act of comprehension* which consists in merging our awareness of a set of particulars into our focal awareness of their joint *significance*" (p. 44, my emphasis). That is, even the world of natural science is a man-created reality, a particular way of looking at and giving meaning to the facts of nature.

Implicit in all this is that there is not, then, one large and encompassing reality (or world of reality) that we deal with psychologically, the same and uniform for all, but rather many smaller, varyingly overlapping and varyingly congruent partial realities, man-constructed realities, to which different men in turn declare varying and differentiated allegiances. Though clearly also man does not easily abandon the quest for a single overarching reality and for ultimate cosmological answers. Through most of recorded history, religious systems have in fact traditionally fulfilled just that role; in more modern times the role has been accorded to or usurped by science, at least for the Western world. [pp. 18–19][1]

1. Subsequent to writing this chapter, I published two additional articles on this issue of external vis-à-vis inter-

THE DIMENSIONS OF EXTERNAL REALITY

As with much else in this subject, Hartmann inaugurated our modern-day understandings and yet did so in a considerably restricted way. I suggested this in my 1973 paper on reality when I spoke to the initial

> formulation, as part of the new ego psychology, of the adaptational as one of the metapsychological points of view, and within this vantage point, the conceptualization by Hartmann and his collaborators of ego apparatuses of primary autonomy that unfolded in a state of "preadaptedness," that is, not as a product of experiential vicissitude and of conflict solution, but rather as an outcome of a maturationally unfolding and a phylogenetically guaranteed coordination to *reality*. With this conceptualization of the adaptational viewpoint, Hartmann put reality and, by implication, the structuring of reality, squarely back into the center of psychoanalytic interest. But in taking this step his focus was still on the intrapsychic and on its development, and in wanting it highlighted against a clear and stable field, he left us with the concept of a varying, i.e., a variable adaptation to an unvarying, or at least a presumed relatively unvarying "average expectable environment." [p. 11]

It was Hartmann's conceptualization of the average expectable environment that I called both a "significant advance" and at the same time a "consider-

nal reality (Wallerstein, 1985, 1988). I quote here from the 1988 article in favor of the conception of a *continuum of reality,* inner and outer (as against our traditional dichotomization), through combining Arlow's (1969) conceptualization of psychic or inner reality as arising out of the interplay of external perception (of the real) and internal impinging and distorting fantasy, and my comparable conceptualization (1973) of even our experience of external reality as not invariant, but as also a man-created reality, a particular way of looking at and giving meaning to the facts of nature—that is, influenced by psychology, value judgment, tradition, and idiosyncratic history. I therefore proposed a perspectival enlargement of our frame through "the surmounting of the counterpoint between the view from within (the world of psychic reality) and the view from without (the world of material reality), in favor of a conception of the interplay of multiple perspectives, multiple versions, each its own story, each its own admixture or fusion of drive-dictated fantasy interacting with appropriately selected environmental stimuli or vicissitudes—out of the well-balanced consideration of all of which will come that filled-out rewriting of one's autobiography that we call a completed analysis" (1988, pp. 318–319). This view of a continuum of reality in no way alters—except in interpretive nuance, which *is* important—our central psychoanalytic task, conceptually and technically, of constant clarification of the inner and outer realms as they fashion our mental life through their interaction.

able restriction" on the possibilities for theory exposition and development. I will not recapitulate the reasoning I adduced to support this view—it is already implied in much of this chapter. Rather, I will turn to those few programmatic efforts within psychoanalytic theorizing to this point to specify attributes and dimensions of our constructs of reality that are directly comparable to the long-standing psychoanalytic concern with just that kind of specification of attributes and dimensions in regard to the psychic instances of Freud's tripartite structural model. Here the starting point is Rapaport's (1960) focus on issues of the ego's (relative) dependence upon, and at the same time autonomy with regard to, both the inner world (id and superego) and the outer world (environment) in maintaining its stable functioning and its functional integrity.

Rapaport began by reminding us that for a long while the role of external (environmental) stimuli had been grossly underestimated in psychoanalytic theory, although both Hartmann's adaptation theory and Erikson's psychosocial theory had contributed significantly to accounting theoretically both for an independent role for external stimulation in the determination of behavior and for the interaction of such stimulation with the instinctual drives. Rapaport took as his principal concern the extent to which external stimuli in psychoanalytic theory can be considered as causes or motives. He felt that in addition to reality relationships established by frustrations and motivations deriving from drives in consequence of frustration, we must postulate autonomous, inborn apparatuses of contact with reality and also corresponding, therefore reality-attuned, autonomous motivations. The consequence of this was his conception of balanced dependence and autonomy. In Rapaport's words, "I have attempted to demonstrate that these two ontogenetic processes of increasing relative independence of behavior [from instinctual drives via *ego autonomy* and from external stimulation via *internalization*] are interdependent, in that the relative independence of behavior from instinctual drives is contingent upon its *dependence* on external stimulation, and that the relative independence of behavior from external stimulation is contingent upon its *dependence* on instinctual drives" (p. 888).

This reasoning leads logically to Rapaport's conception of the differentiated role of the environment as providing "stimulus nutriment" (p. 893) for psychic structures, thus helping to guarantee the ego's relative autonomy from the id. All this is called the (differentiated) role of the environment (external reality) in defense maintenance and, more broadly, in structure maintenance. A variety of everyday examples are cited, including the so-called secondary gain

of illness, the advantage the patient derives in the real world from the maintenance of defensive and symptomatic behaviors. Another example is the common observation that therapeutic efforts may be of no avail if the patient is continually exposed to situations with which he or she has no other way of coping but his or her characteristic behavior—that is, situations in which the "very defenses which the work of the patient and the therapist would have to weaken and penetrate are continuously maintained and strengthened by the environment" (p. 892). Still another is the exacerbation of the passive-regressive tendencies of psychiatric patients by hospitalization, unless the hospital setting specifically combats these tendencies. Lastly, there is the increased corruptibility of the superego of a person who is removed from his or her usual setting, whose mores and standards have nourished and supported his or her superego.

It is this emphasis on the differentiated or, at least, differentiatable structure-maintaining role of various environmental forces in relation to stable ego functioning that Gould (1970) undertook to further elaborate a decade later. He began with the realities of the new American community psychiatry (community mental health) movement and the implicit intellectual demand it placed on psychoanalysis to develop a comprehensive field theory of reality forces: "I shall argue the mutual usefulness of such a [field] theory for both preventative (community) psychiatry and psychoanalysis as theory and practice" (p. 440). He stated that the writings of Rapaport, Erikson, and Hartmann "make an *implicit* demand for a systematic definition of that psychic space called reality" (p. 441, my emphasis). And he himself began at the same point, of reality conceptualized only "vaguely as the average expectable environment" (p. 441) or as an "outer world . . . deliberately focused out" (p. 442) (in order better to study the inner processes) or as merely what Gould called the container of projected elements, with the elements declared to be the valuable essentials in our work (that is, the figures), while all the rest becomes merely the ground. It is this ground, the description of reality, that is the figure for those who, like Gould, have adopted a different strategy—from the perspective, that is, of the outer reality, or "field of forces."

This perspective provides the theoretical underpinning for the strategy of the community psychiatry movement in primary prevention, which is designed to affect specific intrapsychic systems through their connection with external systems. Carrying this strategy out requires what Gould calls the capacity for a "dynamic oscillation" (p. 444) between figures and grounds of various force fields, such as empirically determining the relative importance of inner and outer variables by looking systematically at the total field of forces for any given problem at any given time. In dealing with the concept of structures in the field of forces, we are led to the corollary concept of "structuralizing forces," pro and con. That is, to Rapaport's concept of structure-maintaining forces in dynamic equilibrium with structures, Gould adds the logical counterpart of "structure-changing forces" (p. 450), of which, incidentally, formal education and psychotherapy are two major institutional forms. Within an overall spectrum of structure-maintaining forces, structure-changing forces, and a third, "reality guidance factor" (p. 455), which tunes into and responds to these forces, we have the beginnings of the unique particularization of the "average expectable environment" that Gould explicitly calls for. That is, Gould has begun the effort to develop a differentiated set of dimensions, or field of forces, in outer reality as counterpart structures to our acknowledged, highly differentiated, internal psychological organization. My own paper on reality (Wallerstein, 1973), in presenting examples under five headings (developmental considerations, psychopathological manifestations considered from the standpoint of the relationship of inner to outer, the natural history of illness and/or the phenomenon of spontaneous change, technical implications for psychoanalytic therapeutic work, and widened applications of psychoanalysis), is but an extension of the manifold implications of these conceptualizations.

REALITY CONSTANCY

Reality constancy is a concept introduced by Frosch in a paper published in 1966. He began by defining it as a psychic structure that arises in conjunction with the establishment of stabilized internal representations of the environment. Genetically, he believed it to be intimately interwoven with the development of object constancy, to a considerable extent actually evolving out of the latter. On the one hand, reality constancy was declared to be quite comparable to object constancy—for example, in its developmental unfolding—with reality constancy being just as dependent as object constancy on the processes of individuation and separation, of self and nonself discrimination. On the other hand, there are some significant differences. Frosch quoted Jacobson as referring to cases in which adequate reality constancy seemed to have developed, although object constancy was defective. Jacobson accounted for this by proposing that reality constancy rested on a somewhat different basis from object constancy, in that the mastery of reality—that is, of the inanimate

object world—allows more room for aggressive drives, ambitions, and narcissistic gratifications.

The establishment of reality constancy is facilitated by and in turn facilitates a variety of interrelated ego operations, such as anticipation, perception, predictability, and reality testing. For example, predictability, the confident expectation of finding things in the future, is completely contingent upon an established reality constancy. Conversely, defects in reality constancy clearly play a role in the development of feelings of unreality, difficulty in experiencing new and experimental situations, and the preservation of reality contacts. Centrally, reality constancy is related intimately to the capacity for reality testing. That is, "the evolution of reality constancy . . . constitutes a more reliable frame of reference for reality testing. It is clear that the more advanced the modes of reality testing are, the more firmly is reality constancy established, and vice versa" (Frosch, 1966, p. 362). From the reverse side, "When we confront a patient with reality and help him test reality and develop trust in his own perceptions, we facilitate the development of reality constancy" (ibid., p. 374).

THE BREAK WITH REALITY AND PSYCHOSIS

In "Neurosis and psychosis," Freud (1924a) used the tripartite model of the psychic apparatus that he had just introduced in *The Ego and the Id* (1923) as the basis for proposing a "simple formula" (p. 149) to define the most important difference between a neurosis and a psychosis: namely, whereas a neurosis is the result of a conflict between the ego and the id, a psychosis is the outcome of a similar disturbance in relations between the ego and the external world of reality. Freud continued this discussion in a paper written some months later, "The loss of reality in neurosis and psychosis" (1924b). There he qualified this simple formula, making of the development of neurotic and psychotic illness a two-step sequence, with an initial strain or rupture of the ego's relationship with the id or reality, followed by a reparative and restitutional phase that, in compromise fashion, represented the neurotic or psychotic illness.

Frosch, in a series of papers (1964, 1970, 1971; see also Ross, 1960), separated out various component parts of good reality functioning and their differential impairment in illnesses representing different degrees of departure from reality. He spoke specifically of the "psychotic character disorders" (a group that has been differently designated by various authors over the years, today most commonly called "borderline disorders") as distinct from the openly psychotic disorders and then assessed the functioning of these two major nosological categories along each of three elements of reality functioning: the relationship to reality, the sense of reality, and the capacity to test reality.

In a paper entitled "Psychoanalytic considerations of the psychotic character" (1970), Frosch pointedly defined the psychotic character as a stable character organization. He said that it was not a transitional phase on the way to or from symptom psychosis; nor was it a latent or larval psychosis that might become overt, any more than we would define the neurotic character as a transitional phase on the way to or from a full symptom neurosis. He saw the psychotic character, rather, as a crystallization into a character structure that reflected predictable modes of adaptation and responses to stress.

In delineating the kind of impaired relationship with reality that exists in this disorder, as distinguished from that in overt psychoses, Frosch found Freud's term "break with reality" too broad a frame of reference. With the development of psychoanalytic ego psychology, it had became possible to examine specific ego operations involved in disturbances with reality. Frosch sought to designate the specific areas of disturbance involved along the three indicated dimensions: the relationship with reality, the sense of reality, and the capacity to test reality.

Frosch defined the relationship with reality as a person's capacity to preserve the external and internal worlds and the appropriateness of his or her relationship to them. There should of course be an awareness of the limits of each of these worlds, since an important factor in a healthy relationship with reality is the existence of clearly defined ego boundaries with adequately developed differentiation of self. An impaired relationship with reality is manifested in numerous ways (described actually in each of his articles in the sequence): perceptual distortions, such as illusions and hallucinations; diffusion of ego boundaries with difficulty in distinguishing between self and nonself and between human and nonhuman objects (1970, p. 35) and a concomitant propensity under stress to dedifferentiation and to fusion with objects and with the environment; confusions in the sense of identity with feelings of separateness and "consciousness of ego splits"; proneness to (augmented) perceptual distortions under the influence of drugs, illness, fever, stress; bizarre attitudes and deviations in the expression of social amenities; and infantile, primitive, and insufficiently differentiated object relations. Common to all these manifestations is that the relationship with reality involves a person's capacity to perceive the external and internal worlds and the appropriateness of his relationship to them.

The feeling or sense of reality is differently experienced. Here one is concerned with the feelings and sensations of outer and inner reality as perceived by the patient. Pathology in this area is manifest in feelings of unreality, derealization or depersonalization, along with enhanced proneness to Isakower phenomena, hypnagogic states, oceanic feelings, and so forth.

Last of these three dimensions is the capacity to test reality and the appropriate evaluation of the reality of external and internal phenomena. This requires a basis for comparison and the ability to arrive at a logical conclusion from a series of observable phenomena. If the individual is unable to reach such a conclusion when presented with objective data, his or her capacity to test reality is impaired. Frosch adds that we must make provision for nonobjective reality within a given culture, as represented by conventional acceptance of such reality without objective validation. From this it follows that the attitudes of parents and, subsequently, of other external objects are constantly utilized in reality testing, just as they are in the early stages of psychic development. In those who are somewhat impaired, the psychotic characters, this reality testing, even when maintained, can take regressive forms, involving, for example, the use of the senses to establish direct physical contact; that is, physical presence and vivid sensory stimulation can become vital adjuvants to successful testing of reality. Overall, in assessing the individual's capacity properly to test reality, the clinical observer is basically evaluating the person's relationship to reality and sense of reality.

How, then, does Frosch utilize this tripartite division of the concept "break with reality" to distinguish the nonovertly psychotic character from the overtly psychotic? Frosch indicates that it is the degree of intactness of the capacity to test reality that is crucial in differentiating the two states. With the psychotic character, the impairment is predominantly in the first two areas, with relatively less disturbance in the third; that is, the capacity to test reality, while often quite defective, is relatively intact. Although regression takes place readily, there exists simultaneously a capacity for reversibility so that, in spite of severe disturbances, psychotic characters make in the main a syntonic adaptation to object reality. By contrast, the openly psychotic person builds a new reality that results in actual distortions of external material reality. One therefore sees in frank psychosis an ego-syntonic adaptation that is *dystonic* with reality.

Lastly, Frosch drew some implications from these distinctions for therapeutic strategy in the treatment of psychotic characters. In reviewing some of the relevant psychoanalytic contributions to this subject, he concluded that despite widespread divergence on matters of nosology, there was essential agreement on many aspects of the therapeutic approach. He stated that all contributors emphasized the wisdom of introducing reality factors, reinforcing reality testing, facilitating self–nonself differentiation, encouraging the patient to evolve an identity, and so forth. He emphasized that one of the consequences of the tenuously established reality constancy was the need for continual reinforcement by material reality of the shaky internalized reality constancy. Needless to say, it is not true that *all* psychoanalytic contributors to the literature on the treatment of borderline (and even psychotic) characters would agree on all these elements of therapeutic technique with such patients (see, for example, Kernberg, 1975, 1976).

SUMMARY

I have tried to review the nature and development of the concept of reality and its attributes from a psychoanalytic perspective. I have shown that, while after the very earliest period of psychoanalytic conceptualizing—that is, with the formulation of psychoanalysis as essentially a psychology of the drives and their vicissitudes (and of the defenses against them)—the nature and qualities of reality have not been, until recently, a central psychoanalytic preoccupation, they have nonetheless from the beginning played a role that can be traced historically and used as a context for our expanded modern-day concerns.

Along such lines, I have traced the following reality and reality-related concepts through their vicissitudes from their psychoanalytic beginnings: reality testing, the reality principle, the distinctions between external and internal reality, the nature of (the construct) reality, the dimensions of (external) reality, reality constancy, and the nature of the break with reality in borderline and overt psychotic illnesses, with differentiation under that heading of the relationship to reality, the sense of reality, and the capacity to test reality. In so doing, I have not specifically written about such other reality-related psychoanalytic constructs as depersonalization, derealization, dissociation, ego boundaries, and so on. I think, though, that the sense in which these concepts interrelate with the main constructs that have been defined and delineated in this chapter is evident from the context in which they are discussed.[2]

2. I have published a significantly expanded version of this historical review in *Int. Rev. Psychoanal.*, 10 (1983): 125–144.

REFERENCES

Arlow, J. A. (1969). Fantasy, memory, and reality testing. *Psychoanal. Q.*, 38:28–51.

Freud, S. (1895). Project for a scientific psychology. *SE*, 1:281–397.

———. (1900). *The Interpretation of Dreams. SE*, 4 & 5.

———. (1911). Formulations on the two principles of mental functioning. *SE*, 12:213–226.

———. (1913). *Totem and Taboo. SE*, 13:1–162.

———. (1915a). Instincts and their vicissitudes. *SE*, 14:109–140.

———. (1915b). The unconscious. *SE*, 14:159–215.

———. (1916–17). *Introductory Lectures on Psycho-Analysis. SE*, 16:241–496.

———. (1917a). A metapsychological supplement to the theory of dreams. *SE*, 14:217–235.

———. (1917b). Mourning and melancholia. *SE*, 14:237–258.

———. (1920). *Beyond the Pleasure Principle. SE*, 18:1–64.

———. (1921). *Group Psychology and the Analysis of the Ego. SE*, 18:65–143.

———. (1923). *The Ego and the Id. SE*, 19:1–66.

———. (1924a). Neurosis and psychosis. *SE*, 19: 147–153.

———. (1924b). The loss of reality in neurosis and psychosis. *SE*, 19:183–187.

———. (1925). Negation. *SE*, 19:233–239.

———. (1926). *Inhibitions, Symptoms and Anxiety. SE*, 20:75–175.

Frosch, J. (1964). The psychotic character. *Psychiatr. Q.*, 38:81–96.

———. (1966). A note on reality constancy. In *Psychoanalysis—A General Psychology*, ed. R. M. Loewenstein, L. M. Newman, M. Schur & A. J. Solnit, pp. 349–376. New York: Int. Univ. Press.

———. (1970). Psychoanalytic considerations of the psychotic character. *J. Amer. Psychoanal. Assn.*, 18:24–50.

———. (1971). Technique in regard to some specific ego defects in the treatment of borderline patients. *Psychiat. Q.*, 45:216–220.

Gould, R. L. (1970). Preventive psychiatry and the field theory of reality. *J. Amer. Psychoanal. Assn.*, 18:440–461.

Hartmann, H. (1956). Notes on the reality principle. Rpt. in *Essays on Ego Psychology*, pp. 241–267. New York: Int. Univ. Press, 1964.

———. (1960). *Psychoanalysis and Moral Values*. New York: Int. Univ. Press.

Kernberg, O. F. (1975). *Borderline Conditions and Pathological Narcissism*. New York: Aronson.

————. (1976). *Object Relations Theory and Clinical Psychoanalysis*. New York: Aronson.

Laplanche, J., & Pontalis, J. B. (1973). *The Language of Psychoanalysis*. New York: Norton.

Loewald, H. W. (1951). Ego and reality. *Int. J. Psychoanal.*, 32:10–18.

Nunberg, H. (1951). Transference and reality. *Int. J. Psychoanal.*, 32:1–9.

Polanyi, M. (1959). *The Study of Man*. Chicago: Univ. Chicago Press.

Rapaport, D. (1960). On the psychoanalytic theory of motivation. Rpt. in *The Collected Papers of David Rapoport*, ed. M. M. Gill, pp. 853–915. New York: Basic Books, 1967.

Ross, N. (1960). Panel report: An examination of nosology according to psychoanalytic concepts. *J. Amer. Psychoanal. Assn.*, 8:535–551.

Wallerstein, R. S. (1973). Psychoanalytic perspectives on the problem of reality. *J. Amer. Psychoanal. Assn.*, 21:5–33.

————. (1985). The concept of psychic reality. *J. Amer. Psychoanal. Assn.*, 33:555–569.

————. (1988). The continuum of reality, inner and outer. In *Fantasy, Myth and Reality*, ed. Harold P. Blum, Yale Kramer, Arlene K. Richards, & Arnold D. Richards, pp. 305–321. Madison, Conn.: Int. Univ. Press.

Sidney S. Furst, M.D.

23

TRAUMA

Psychoanalysis began with Freud's investigation of hysteria, first at Charcot's clinic in Paris, then in Vienna in collaboration with Breuer, and finally alone. Among the momentous discoveries resulting from these early studies was the fact that certain discrete childhood experiences crucially influenced the subsequent lives of his patients. These experiences, to which he gave the name "psychical traumas," first impressed him because of the central and specific role they played in the causation of illness and in the formation of symptoms.

Clearly, Freud's early theory of neurosis was centered on trauma. As a clinician, he was concerned with trauma because of its pathogenicity. In this connection he dealt with those formal and dynamic aspects of traumatic events that determined the pathological outcome. These included the *psychic conditions* under which certain experiences achieve the status of traumas, the *content* of traumatic experiences, the *consequences* of trauma, and the relationship of trauma to *symptom formation*. From this point of view, trauma could be defined only in retrospect—that is, as an experience or group of experiences that has given rise to psychopathology.

As a theoretician, Freud was concerned with the intrapsychic events and mechanisms operative in trauma at the time of its occurrence. Here his formulations centered on the concept of a *stimulus barrier*. Essentially a mechanistic or biological concept, it permitted trauma to be defined independently of its

consequences—that is, as a stimulus which causes a breach in, or an overwhelming of, a protective shield.

The duality that seemed to be implied in this conception of trauma was more apparent than real. Though the two definitions were not mutually inclusive, they were shown to be related in a specific way: the breaching of the stimulus barrier had as its consequence a sequence of intrapsychic events that disposed to psychopathology. While Freud considered trauma to be a component in the structure of all neuroses, he realized from the outset that not all traumas result in neurosis.

THE EVOLUTION OF FREUD'S VIEWS OF TRAUMA

Among Freud's early concerns was to establish why certain experiences rather than others predisposed to psychopathology. The similarity between common hysteria and the traumatic neuroses led initially to emphasis on the component of *affect,* and Freud's first definition of trauma read: "Any experience which calls up distressing affects—such as those of fright, anxiety, shame or physical pain—may operate as a trauma of this kind" (Breuer & Freud, 1893–95, p. 6). Continued clinical observations led to the delineation of several types of experiences that may operate as traumas. In contrast to the traumatic neurosis precipitated by a single event, common hysteria was frequently found to result from a number of *partial traumas* that formed "a *group* of provoking causes. These have only been able to exercise a traumatic effect by summation and they belong together in so far as they are in part components of a single story of suffering" (ibid.).

For a time Freud and Breuer considered the possibility that an experience may exercise a traumatic effect not through its content but by virtue of its occurring at a time of peculiar susceptibility to stimulation—for example, during the semihypnotic twilight of daydreaming, or autohypnosis, which precludes reaction to the event. Freud later (1923) rejected the "hypnoid state" as a causal agent in trauma and attributed pathogenicity only to *ideas* that are "in opposition to the predominant trend of the subject's mental life so that it provoked him into '*defence*'" (p. 237).

The early distinction between trauma per se and its pathological consequences led to a consideration of factors that might influence or determine the relation between the two. It was first proposed that traumas result in symptomatology when they cannot be sufficiently abreacted, usually because "the nature of the trauma excluded a reaction" (Breuer & Freud, p. 10). Here we find the earliest allusion to the issue of helplessness, which was later to occupy a central place in Freud's dual theory of anxiety. As is well known, early case studies indicated that trauma invariably involved a precocious seduction which produced no effect at the time but remained as a "memory trace" open to reactivation by the biological changes of puberty. These changes endowed the memories with a power they did not originally possess and caused them to operate as though they were contemporary events. Freud recognized, however, that postpubertal outbreaks of hysteria were not to be accounted for solely on the basis of biological changes; they were precipitated by postpubertal experiences and excitations that, by association, revived the memory traces of childhood traumas. In addition to content, or nature, Freud recognized the *quantitative* factor in trauma—the intensity of the stimulus, to which he assigned a *direct* effect on symptom formation. In later formulations he altered his views on the mechanism of symptom formation, but the quantitative factor never lost its importance as one of the determining elements in trauma.

Freud's gradual realization that the memories of childhood seduction reported by hysterics were frequently falsifications led to far-reaching advances in his views on the role of intrapsychic factors in neurosogenesis. These were discussed in detail in his paper on sexuality in the aetiology of the neuroses (1906). The traumatic memories, so called, were recognized as *fantasies* of seduction, elaborated in an attempt to ward off memories of the subject's own sexual activity, particularly infantile masturbation. Four modifications in his views followed. First, the external traumatic element gradually lost its importance and was replaced by *sexual activity,* either spontaneous or provoked, which then determined the course of sexual life after the advent of puberty. (Here Freud was apparently referring to the establishment of fixations and points of regression.) Second, the theory of the mechanism of hysterical symptoms was modified. "They were no longer to be regarded as direct derivatives of the repressed memories of childhood experiences; but between the symptoms and the childhood impressions there were inserted the patient's *phantasies* (or imaginary memories), mostly produced during the years of puberty, which on one side were built up out of and over the childhood memories and on the other side were transformed directly into symptoms" (1906, p. 274). Third, constitutional and hereditary factors were stressed in the causation of illness, replacing "accidental influences derived from experience" (p. 275). Fourth, the discovery that the childhood sexual history of people who remained well did not necessarily differ from that of neurotics led to the conclusion that "it was no longer a question of what sexual experiences a particular individual had had in his childhood, but rather of his reaction to those experiences— of whether he had reacted to them by 'repression' or not" (pp. 276–277).

Freud's work on the subject of trauma during the latter half of his career may be viewed as falling into two broad categories: the biological and the psychic. The first dealt with the stimulus barrier, while the latter was associated with the dual theory of anxiety.

The Stimulus Barrier

Trauma was defined in terms of the stimulus barrier in Freud's discussion of traumatic neurosis in the *Introductory Lectures* (1916–17): "We apply it [the term 'traumatic'] to an experience which within a short period of time presents the mind with an increase of stimulus too powerful to be dealt with or worked off in the normal way, and this must result in permanent disturbances of the manner in which energy operates" (p. 275). A few years later, in *Beyond the Pleasure Principle* (1920), he went on to deal with the causes and consequences of a breach in the barrier against stimuli. He recognized two causal factors that operate in complementary fashion: the strength or intensity of the stimulus with which the barrier is confronted, which can be measured only in relation to the strength of the barrier itself, which in turn is determined at least in part by constitutional factors, and the degree of preparedness of the barrier. Thus, breaches in the protective shield might be caused by "lack of any preparedness for anxiety, including lack of hypercathexis of the systems that would be the first to receive the stimulus" (p. 31). As a result of a breach in the protective shield, the mental apparatus is "flooded" and cannot master the stimulus in the usual way. Several consequences follow. First, the pleasure principle is, for the time being, put out of action. Second, a regression occurs in which primitive modes of functioning are resorted to in the attempt to master or bind the stimulus.

Though Freud's detailed consideration of the stimulus barrier was carried through in connection with traumatic war neuroses in which the failure of the protective shield was most dramatic, he made it clear that this concept applied equally to all pathological states and to normality as well.

Anxiety and Trauma

Freud's dual theory of anxiety, contained in *Inhibitions, Symptoms and Anxiety* (1926), carried important advances in his views of trauma. In this study he made the well-known distinction between *automatic anxiety* and *signal anxiety*. The former arises as a reaction to an experienced state of danger. Originally, as at birth, it is expedient, in that it provides for the initiation of appropriate cardiorespiratory activity. However, when it is produced later in life, it is inexpedient insofar as the reaction it initiates is inappropriate to the immediate danger. This reaction was designated as a "traumatic situation." *Signal anxiety*, on the other hand, is the response of the ego to the *threat* of danger, so that it can be avoided before it occurs. The threatening danger may be physical (external) if it is real or psychical (internal) if it is instinctual or a combination, in varying degrees, of both. Freud made it clear that the essence of danger is helplessness on the part of the ego in the face of an accumulation of excitation of either internal or external origin that cannot be dealt with.

In effect, signal anxiety has as its ultimate goal the protection against trauma. It is produced on the basis of the ego's comparison of its own strength with the magnitude of the danger that threatens. While this reconsideration of trauma and anxiety left the concept and definition of trauma essentially unchanged, a broader view was now taken of the metapsychology of trauma. In particular, two sets of determinants were emphasized: first, the strength of the ego as compared with the intensity of the stimulus; second, internal as compared to external sources of stimuli. The first set of determinants allowed for constitutional factors and to some extent for the role of past experience. The latter set allowed

for the role of fantasy as the psychic representation of the drives and the defenses.

In *Moses and Monotheism* (1939), published in the year of his death, Freud recapitulated his views concerning the characteristics and determinants of trauma on the one hand and the effects of trauma on the other. With regard to the determinants of trauma, he again emphasized the importance of the "complementary series"—the interaction between constitutional factors and experience. In this connection he noted that "it cannot be determined with certainty how long after birth this period of receptivity begins" (p. 74). Here, I believe, he implied that in accounting for trauma, it is extremely difficult to differentiate between the role of constitutional factors and that of very early life experiences. As for the effects of trauma, Freud divided them into *positive* and *negative*. The former are attempts to bring the trauma into operation once again, either to remember it or to make it real by repeating it in an analogous relationship with someone else. These were designated "fixations to the trauma" and "a compulsion to repeat." The negative effects have the opposite aim: nothing shall be remembered or repeated. These were defensive reactions and were expressed as "avoidances" or, if intensified, as inhibitions and phobias. These too were fixations, but with a contrary purpose. Alternatively, both the positive and the negative effects of trauma "may be taken up into what passes as a normal ego and, as permanent trends in it, may lend it unalterable character-traits" (p. 75).

The hypotheses formulated by Freud to account for the occurrence of, and consequences of, trauma have not been superseded or replaced. They have, however, been elaborated upon, and in the course of this process there has been a tendency to broaden the concept beyond Freud's definition. The elaborations have dealt primarily with the *preconditions of trauma* and the *effects of trauma*. The broadening tendency has led to the designation of "traumatic" to adverse pathological influences and conditions that do not include a manifest breakthrough of the stimulus barrier and an ensuring regressive state of helplessness. For the most part, these developments in the concept of trauma have stemmed from studies of the traumatic neuroses and from child analysis and developmental studies.

THE TRAUMATIC NEUROSES

Traumatic neuroses are neuroses (a) that are precipitated by a specific traumatic experience, and (b) whose content is centrally involved with the experience and its aftermath.

The traumatic neuroses of World War I lent supportive evidence to the concept of the stimulus barrier. At first glance, this evidence appeared to minimize the importance of internal variables such as predisposition, conscious and unconscious fantasies, and past experiences. But closer examination revealed that here too it was the individual's reaction to the event, rather than the event itself, that was crucial to the outcome. In his introduction to *Psycho-Analysis and the War Neuroses* (1919), Freud pointed out that the traumatic war neuroses and the transference neuroses of peace are essentially similar. In both instances the ego is afraid of being damaged, in the latter case by the libido, in the former by a danger that threatens from without. Beginning with a symposium at the Fifth International Psycho-Analytical Congress in 1918, at which papers were presented by Ferenczi, Abraham, and Simmel, and continuing through World War II, most psychoanalytic studies of the traumatic neuroses confirmed the overriding importance of predisposing factors. They also served to call attention to the importance of mastery. Freud, as well as many of his successors, saw the severe regression in trauma not simply as an overwhelming of the stimulus barrier but also as a psychic event that set in motion archaic pathological attempts to master what could not be mastered in the usual way.

The manifest features and characteristics of traumatic neuroses carry important implications for the concept of trauma in general. First, the outcome of trauma depends on the degree of success in mastering the traumatic stimulus. Second, if the abrupt overwhelming of the ego and the regression to archaic levels of functioning, as seen in the traumatic neuroses, are considered to be essential features of all traumatic events, then a clear-cut basis is established for differentiating between trauma on the one hand and all other detrimental psychic experiences on the other. Third, the primitive mechanisms that become operative in trauma are, in and of themselves, pathological. Whether or not pathology persists will depend on post-traumatic developments.

Studies of Holocaust victims have shed light on the effects of massive trauma and have confirmed the fact that while individuals differ in their degree of susceptibility to trauma, a limit exists beyond which even the most efficacious stimulus barrier will fail. Niederland (1968), among others, has described a constellation of symptoms often found in Holocaust victims, which he termed the "survivor syndrome." It is characterized by chronic depressive and anxiety reactions, insomnia, nightmares, personality changes (tendency to isolation, brooding, and alterations in personal identity), and somatization re-

actions including cardiovascular and gastrointestinal disturbances and headaches. On the basis of studies of Holocaust survivors in Israel, Klein (1974) has described the dynamics and mechanisms operative during and after prolonged, severe traumatization. While the trauma is occurring, there is fantasy formation based on past pleasurable experiences which are projected into the future, thereby maintaining hope. In the post-traumatic period, the affective components of the trauma are essentially denied, and instead there are oral demands, anxiety, and somatization reactions. With the beginning of adaptation to a new life, the deeper affective components are gradually worked through, following which there is depression, which leads to the gradual acceptance of the loss of love objects and a diminution of survivor guilt.

On the basis of army experiences during the Israeli wars of 1967 and 1975, Moses (1978) confirms that acute traumatic war neuroses evolve when existing patterns of dealing with stress prove ineffective and give way to regressive phenomena as well as ego constriction and impoverishment. He delineates two specific determinants of the ability to withstand battle trauma: self-esteem and a sense of belonging to a group and experiencing well-being in it (that is, good object relations).

Krystal (1978) has attributed the occurrence of acute trauma in the adult ("catastrophic trauma") to a *surrender* to inevitable danger, which initiates a progression from anxiety to a catatonoid state, aphanesis, and potentially to psychogenic death.

TRAUMA AND DEVELOPMENT

Psychoanalytic and developmental studies of children over the past three decades or so have broadened knowledge and understanding of trauma in several ways. On the descriptive level, they have provided detailed accounts of the context in which trauma occurs (Solnit & Kris, 1967). In addition, they have elucidated and specified the host of variables that constitute the preconditions for trauma, as well as those that determine its outcome. With regard to the latter, they have indicated that trauma may significantly affect the development of various ego functions, the superego, and object relations. They have of course confirmed that trauma is ubiquitous, and this has led to the necessity of distinguishing between significant and insignificant traumas.

Longitudinal developmental studies by analytically trained observers have left little doubt that acute disturbances in the earliest months of life may play an important role in determining the subsequent course of development—and this includes establishment of the preconditions for trauma. Boyer (1956) and numerous subsequent authors have suggested that before the infant can perceive stimuli, the mother serves as a supplementary barrier against both internal and external stimuli. Deficiencies in this maternal barrier result in ego weakness and in inadequate differentiation of ego and id. In addition, the child's own undeveloped stimulus barrier may be broken by maternal overstimulation or deprivation. Thus, maladaptation of the mother to the infant's anaclitic needs results in numerous breaches and impingements. By summation these may constitute a "nuclear cumulative trauma" that is later seen as a disturbed relation between mother and child and as a bias in ego and psychosexual development. On the theoretical level, it is questionable whether acute psychophysiological stress situations of early infancy should be regarded as traumas in the psychoanalytic sense of the term. A breach in an existing stimulus barrier followed by a feeling of helplessness on the part of the ego is a central feature of the psychoanalytic concept, while the earliest months of life are of their very nature pre–stimulus barrier and pre-ego. This theoretical issue does not, however, detract from the significance of very early events for the study of later trauma.

In this connection, recent studies have suggested that very early stimulation and experience may induce neurophysiological structuring (myelinization, arborization, and dentrification) that serves as an organic framework for later development. To the extent that these postulated neuronal trends (particularly those involved with the function of internalization) include negative dysphoric affects and experience, they constitute a primitive neurophysiological anlage for later traumatization.

Developmental and psychoanalytic studies have established a distinction between several different *types* of traumas. Some of these are essentially descriptive, whereas others are of etiological and dynamic significance.

Phase-specific trauma. As originally noted by Freud (1926), a correlation often exists between a traumatic stimulus of a particular kind and the libidinal phase in which it occurs. This "phase specificity" often determines not only whether a trauma will occur (as, for example, the experience of a castration threat during the phallic phase) but also the effect it will have on development. Greenacre (1950) has noted that the relation between the nature of the trauma and the timetable of libidinal development will determine whether the experience will tend to reinforce the libidinization of the current dominant phase or result in a regression to an earlier phase.

Retrospective trauma. Related to phase specificity, this category of trauma was elaborated by the research group that formulated the Hampstead Index. It refers to a perception of some particular situation that evokes the memory of an earlier experience, which, under present circumstances, becomes traumatic.

Screen trauma. Originally suggested by Glover (1929), this refers to memories of experiences that appear to have been traumatic but in fact cover other, usually earlier, traumatic experiences.

Partial trauma. Breuer and Freud (1893–95) noted that a number of experiences, none of which is itself traumatic, may exercise a traumatic effect by summation. A number of authors have extended this observation to include as trauma almost any unpleasant experience or state that carries an adverse psychological effect, either at the time of its occurrence or at some later time. The argument for this extension of the concept of trauma is essentially based on the fact that psychoanalytic observation of both children and adults frequently does not permit a distinction to be made between single dramatic occurrences on the one hand and a series of events or long-standing conditions on the other.

Strain trauma. The consideration noted immediately above led Ernst Kris (1956) to propose a differentiation between the effects of a single dramatic experience, which he called "shock trauma," and the effect of long-lasting situations that may cause traumatic effects by the accumulation of frustration tensions, which he called "strain trauma."

Deprivation trauma. Another extension of the concept of trauma has come from the well-known observations by Spitz (1945) of institutionalized children, as well as from contributions by Bowlby (1960), Racamier (1954), Rubinfine (1962), and others. These have established that a certain degree of external stimulation in general, and affective stimulation in particular, is necessary for id–ego differentiation, for normal drive maturation, and for the development of numerous ego functions, such as reality testing and the achievement of object constancy. The condition of marked paucity of external stimulation has been referred to as "deprivation trauma."

Anxiety trauma (traumatic anxiety). It has been suggested that signal anxiety, and particularly the intense anxiety associated with a situation that carries the threat of trauma, may itself constitute a trauma. In this connection it may be well to recall Freud's discussion of trauma and anxiety in *Inhibitions, Symptoms and Anxiety* (1926): "Anxiety is therefore on the one hand an expectation of trauma, and on the other a repetition of it in mitigated form" (p. 166). Thus, Freud's formulations cannot be reconciled with the idea that anxiety per se may constitute a trauma. Rather, anxiety serves to ward off trauma; the occurrence of trauma represents the failure of the anxiety signal to achieve its purpose.

Cumulative trauma. Masud Khan (1963) further extended the concept of trauma by maintaining that "cumulative trauma is the result of the breaches in the mother's role as a protective shield over the whole course of the child's development, from infancy to adolescence—that is to say, in all those areas of experience where the child continues to need the mother as an auxiliary ego to support his immature and unstable ego functions" (p. 290).

Among the important generalizations that have emerged from longitudinal developmental studies is that many of the factors that affect development adversely also increase the ego's vulnerability to trauma. These may be constitutional in origin; they may stem from deviant drive maturation involving strong fixations and regressions; or they may be connected with arrests or regressions in ego and superego development. Among the factors included here are weakness or impoverishment of various ego capacities, such as low frustration or drive tolerance, limitations in the range and flexibility of defenses, distortions in object relations, inadequate reality testing, and intolerance of superego demands. These deviations, and the conflicts to which they dispose, leave the ego without the energy needed to cope with and assimilate upsetting stimuli. This has been found to be particularly true when there is a correspondence between a given weakness or conflict on the one hand and the nature of the disturbing stimulus on the other.

Conversely, developmental studies have demonstrated that trauma may significantly affect subsequent development. Trauma may result not only in the fixation of defenses and in inhibitions but also in the disruption of ego capacities and in the narrowing of the range of techniques and patterns of behavior available for dealing with objects and with the environment. These findings have served to underscore the preconditions, or matrix, from which organized pathology emerges.

Anna Freud (1965) makes the following points regarding trauma. First, whether or not an event will be traumatic depends on innate libidinal and ego dispositions. Second, either excessive gratification or excessive frustration may constitute a trauma and result in fixation. Third, traumatic events should not be taken at face value but should be translated into their specific meaning for the child. Fourth, trauma

may result in regression of either the ego or the superego. Fifth, a relation may exist between certain kinds of trauma and the developmental phase attained; in particular, separation trauma occurs only before object constancy is achieved. Sixth, when separation trauma leads to ego regression, the regression is often permanent unless it is actively dealt with therapeutically.

CURRENT STATUS OF THE CONCEPT OF TRAUMA

Strictly considered, psychic trauma is a phenomenon, not a concept. It refers to the specific type of breakdown that occurs when, within a short period of time, the mind is presented with a quantity of stimulus too great to be dealt with or assimilated in the usual way. It represents the failure of the psychic apparatus to perform what may be considered its basic function—that of mediating between the organism and its needs, on the one hand, and the stimuli that constantly impinge on it, on the other. Of the two kinds of stimuli operative in trauma, the internal ones are instinctual in origin and usually involve a separation or loss. External stimuli vary considerably in nature and intensity, ranging from manifestly catastrophic or life-threatening situations to apparently inconsequential occurrences. In almost all traumatic events, both internal and external factors are present and together constitute a complementary series. The crucial variable is *intensity*—that is, whether the stimulus, or stimuli, are strong enough to pierce the stimulus barrier. The intensity of the stimulus, however, cannot be measured by any single criterion. Rather, its traumatic potential will depend on a number of factors, including constitutional predisposition, the state of the psychic apparatus, and the relatedness of the stimulus to prevailing drive-cathected wishes and conflicts.

The *preconditions of trauma* fall roughly into three categories: constitutional factors, the effect of past experience, and the psychic state prevailing at the time of perception of the traumatic stimulus. Constitutional factors include abnormally strong or deviant instinctual endowment on the one hand and innate ego weakness on the other. The latter may manifest as poor synthetic function, intolerance of or vulnerability to instinctual demands, or predisposition to anxiety.

Past experience serves to either compromise or strengthen those ego capacities called upon to deal with disturbing stimuli. Compromising factors include deleterious influences and conditions that contribute to the establishment of fixations and points of regression and to the accumulation of inner tensions and frustrations. The degree of inner conflict and the extent of regression are important, because both require the expenditure of ego energy, thereby making it unavailable for assimilating and binding stimuli. In addition, the overall balance between progressive and regressive developmental forces will affect predisposition to trauma by determining the degree of receptivity versus aversion to unfamiliar stimuli.

Disruptive or stressful events and experiences may serve to trigger subsequent trauma. The concepts of "partial trauma," "strain trauma," "cumulative trauma," and "retrospective trauma," as well as threats and fantasies, all describe specific preconditions for trauma proper. The degree of success achieved by the ego in coping with past experiences of these kinds will influence its vulnerability to later traumatization. Traumas that have not been mastered lead to massive repression, and this in turn predisposes to later trauma. Conversely, traumatic experiences that have been adequately mastered and assimilated serve as immunization against later trauma. However, since attempts at mastery rarely result in either complete success or total failure, it is difficult to predict which traumas will sensitize and which immunize, and to what extent and in what respects they may do either.

The more immediate predeterminants of trauma are comprised of the environmental and psychic setting in which the trauma occurs. Variables in this category that may play a specific or nonspecific role include recent environmental changes and stress, the presence of illness or fatigue, and the prevailing affective state. Of equal or greater importance is the nature and content of dominant memories, wishes, fantasies, and conflicts, and particularly their degree of correspondence to the perceived traumatic stimulus. Correspondence between these intrapsychic elements and the external stimulus may be fortuitous, or it may be due to manipulation of the environment in accordance with unconscious instinctual aims.

EFFECTS OF TRAUMA

The sudden inundation and overwhelming of the ego in trauma is usually followed immediately by a clearly discernible change in appearance and behavior, which indicates that a disruption of ego equilibrium has occurred. The ensuing *traumatic state* varies in intensity from one individual to another; it may last anywhere from a few minutes to days or weeks. Termination or reinstatement of ego activity may be abrupt or gradual. The acute traumatic state takes one of two forms: the traumatized individual may appear immobilized, frozen, and pale and may become extremely infantile and submissive in behavior; or else the trauma may be followed immediately by an emotional storm, accompanied by frenzied, undirected, disorganized behavior bordering on panic. Signs of autonomic dysfunction may serve to highlight either picture.

Dynamically, the experience of being traumatized confronts the ego with the task of belatedly mastering both the overwhelming stimulus and its immediate repercussions. One manifestation of the struggle for mastery is the post-traumatic anxiety dream, in which the trauma is reexperienced, either nakedly or in a disguised way, and psychically repeated in milder form. Another manifestation involves the reliving of the trauma in waking life, usually in play. Repetition, this time expectant and purposeful, serves to dissipate the energy of the stimulus by abreaction. Most frequently the repetition is not accurate but instead includes variations that favor assimilation. In the most common variation, the trauma that was experienced passively is recapitulated actively. In addition to abreaction, there is a turning of passivity into activity.

To the extent that these maneuvers succeed, the original overwhelming stimulus will be dissipated and gradually assimilated. To the extent that they fail, the traumatic experience will remain a dangerous, unassimilated, highly cathected memory, which the ego may deal with by recourse to pathological mechanisms. These include repression, denial, regression, and fixations to the trauma that are dominated by the repetition compulsion. Massive repression, when it is resorted to, is particularly important, because it predisposes to repeated traumatization in a specific way. In this connection, it has been stressed that no truly traumatic event is ever wholly assimilated, and that some degree of increased vulnerability invariably persists, if only to repetitions or near-repetitions of the original trauma.

The long-range outcome of trauma will hinge on vicissitudes in the balance between the pathological formations and the progressive forces, particularly those that involve the strengthening of ego capacities. Subsequent life experiences may of course shift the balance in either direction. Barring massive repression, continued growth and development will usually tend toward a gradual assimilation of the effects of trauma. In less favorable instances, the pathological formations persist and establish the basis for symptom formation, inhibitions, repeated traumatization, character disorders, and disturbances in behavior. When developmental forces do not succeed in overcoming the effects of trauma, the trauma in turn may affect the subsequent development of both the ego and the drives.

Clinical observations have indicated that adequate mastery of trauma may be followed by strengthening of the ego, improved adaptation, and accelerated development. Thus, with regard to the ego's attempts to deal with the effects of traumatic experiences, it may be said that "nothing succeeds like success"— and nothing fails like failure.

POST-CHILDHOOD TRAUMA

The past decade or so has seen increased interest in the post-childhood phases of life. This has come about primarily because of advances in our knowledge of the role of development, particularly the discovery that significant intrapsychic changes continue to occur throughout life. These include specific vulnerabilities to trauma.

Post-childhood trauma can be approached as a later edition of the childhood model, and the same metapsychological variations may be applied to both. More specifically, the nature and severity of adult trauma will be determined by the adult's vulnerability to regression. The outcome will be determined by those factors that influence the post-traumatic struggle for mastery. Adults are less vulnerable to trauma than children, because they have a longer path to regress before reaching a state of helplessness. They are less likely to suffer pathological aftereffects, because their more fully developed and differentiated ego has a better chance of mastering trauma.

In attempting to differentiate trauma on the basis of its occurrence during the various phases of the life cycle, the concept of phase specificity in the developmental, as opposed to the psychosexual sense, is particularly useful. The phase-specific developmental tasks associated with each period of the life cycle constitute the background or framework within which the challenge of trauma is imposed. As such, they will determine certain vulnerabilities and responses that are characteristic for each phase.

Trauma in latency, like trauma in pre-latency, is most commonly associated with the danger of separation from or loss of parents, and perhaps less frequently of body parts (castration). The relative paucity of inner resources and the instability of the psychic organization during the latency phase increase the potential for later pathological formations.

In adolescence, the psychic organism is still plastic and has not evolved into the more stable organization of the adult personality. While trauma will interfere with the developmental tasks of adolescence in a general way, two specific vulnerabilities should be noted. First, adolescents show marked oscillations between progressive and regressive movements. The regressive swings are frequently nondefensive and in the service of development. However, the defensive regression induced by trauma, *added* to (the normal) regressive developmental swings, will tend to overwhelm the progressive forces and make the regression permanent. Second, the heightened mobility of adolescence makes it likely that the traumatized adolescent will act out, instead of remembering and gradually mastering the trauma by reworking it intrapsychically. In addition, the acting out may become permanently integrated into his or her personality organization.

As for early adulthood, susceptibility to trauma is probably less than at any other stage of the life cycle. By the same token, it will be determined more heavily by past defect and weakness than at any other stage. One phase-specific source of vulnerability has to do with the fact that responsibility for family and parenting is greatest at this stage of life. The state of helplessness resulting from acute or massive trauma may therefore be particularly damaging to self-esteem and result in a regression to earlier phases in which self-esteem is not so crucial. When it occurs, the regression is toward dependency, often resulting in a role reversal between parent and child. Needless to say, preexisting dependence–independence conflicts constitute a specific vulnerability.

Trauma in the middle-aged and elderly must also be evaluated in the context of developmental challenges and pressures. During the second half of life, these include diminution of sexual potency and its impact on love relationships; the threat of displacement in work roles; anxieties in marital relationships due to the departure of children; awareness of aging, possible illness, and ensuing dependency; the inevitability of death and the realization that what can be achieved and enjoyed in life in now more limited. These (normal) pressures and challenges obviously constitute a specific vulnerability to trauma in this age-group, particularly when the traumatic stimulus or experience impinges on or reinforces them. The diminution of the ego's resilience and flexibility, as well as the weakening of its defense organization, which often occurs in this age-group, may effect the outcome of trauma by making the task of assimilation and mastery more difficult.

CURRENT ISSUES IN THE CONCEPT OF TRAUMA

Definition of trauma. Whether or not the word *trauma* should be restricted to events that involve a manifest breaking of the stimulus barrier and an ensuing state of helplessness remains a matter of opinion. The argument for broadening the definition rests essentially on two facts. First, clinical experience has often pointed to the difficulty of differentiating retrospectively between an acute disruptive event on the one hand and a series of events or a relatively chronic condition on the other. Second, it has not been demonstrated that any known psychic change or condition is *unique* or *specific* to *trauma* (excluding the traumatic event itself and, to some extent, the ensuing acute traumatic state). The argument for restricting the definition rests on the specific phenomenological and dynamic features of trauma. In trauma the ego is overwhelmed and put out of action, so that the organism is suddenly forced back to pre-ego mechanisms for dealing with the internal and external environment. This is in contrast to other experiences and conditions, which may compromise ego functions but do not render them inoperative. In my opinion, these differences should keep us from assuming a parallelism between trauma and adverse experiences in general. The proposal that we subdivide trauma into "acute" and "nonacute" types does not resolve the issue, if only because "nonacute trauma" is so nonspecific as to be useless.

Trauma and pathogenicity. While it is clear that the relation of trauma to pathology is not obligatory, observations indicate that trauma generates pathology in a number of specific ways. First, trauma, more than any other type of experience or influence, may result in circumscribed symptoms, inhibitions, traits, and fantasies that are highly detailed and specific in both content and form. Second, clinical observation suggests that the mechanisms available to the ego for belatedly mastering an overwhelming stimulus are particularly vulnerable to failure. While these mechanisms are not unique to the attempt to master trauma, they are associated with it with particular frequency.

To note several examples, the recapitulation of trauma may result not in abreaction and assimilation but in fixation to the trauma, dominated by the repetition compulsion. The massive repression that is sometimes resorted to in the attempt to overcome the effects of trauma almost invariably predisposes to repeated traumatization. The regression that often occurs in the wake of infantile trauma shows a marked tendency to persist. The experience of trauma may give rise to a need to avoid repetition of the trauma; but the required avoidance tends to become inappropriately broad and restrictive and, as such, pathological. Waelder (1967) referred to this phenomenon as "exaggerated defense." Even when traumas have lost their noxious valence, residues persist which require containment. In this connection, Blos (1968) has pointed out that stable character formation requires the automatization of this containment, which is achieved by the incorporation

of residual trauma into the character structure in an adaptive way. Failure results in character pathology. The need to deal with trauma after the fact often involves the elaboration of a rationalization or conscious explanation of the event. Such elaborations tend to persist as memory imprints after the traumatic occurrence and the affective response are forgotten. On the one hand, these imprints seem to aid in binding anxiety and in circumventing feelings of guilt. On the other, they interfere with reality testing by serving as organizers of future events which then appear to confirm the original explanation (Neubauer, 1967).

What these reactions to trauma have in common is not simply that all frequently fail in their defensive purposes but that *the reactions fail because they are belated*. It is this belated response, the need to deal with a *fait accompli*, that is so intimately related to trauma's pathogenic potential.

In regard to the outcome of trauma, I (1978) have suggested that this is often determined by the nature of the traumatic experience itself. Traumas that are truly fortuitous and do not involve the gratification of an unacceptable wish are usually not repressed but are dealt with by repetition either in dream or in waking life. The recapitulation in milder form, usually by turning passivity into activity, favors mastery. On the other hand, traumas that involve the gratification of an instinctual wish will more commonly be dealt with by repression, primarily because they include the element of guilt. Repression precludes recapitulation and abreaction and favors pathological formations.

Consider, if you will, two clinical examples. A five-year-old boy was returning home from kindergarten by himself when he was suddenly accosted by five considerably older "toughs" from an adjacent neighborhood. "Give us everything you've got, or we'll kill you," he was told. Paralyzed with fear, he was unable to comply with the command, whereupon one of the group went through his pockets and appropriated their contents. After a number of obscenities, threats, and punches, the group ran off, leaving the boy trembling in terror and deeply humiliated. It took several minutes before he was able to pick up a book he was carrying and resume his way home. In bed that night, plagued by feelings of terror, humiliation, and rage, the process of recapitulation and revision began. In the first version, he defied his attackers and with superhuman strength and courage defeated them all in one great battle. In a second, only slightly more realistic version, he challenged them to fight him one at a time and defeated each in turn. In the ensuing months, the memory of the trauma and its aftermath recurred with gradually diminishing frequency. Significantly, it was the unvarnished, accurate recall of the event and its affective horror that came spontaneously to mind; the revised versions that invariably followed were never elaborated independently. He never forgot the incident, but by early adulthood its affective components were no longer reexperienced, and it became simply a memory of childhood.

A married woman in her thirties entered analysis because of recurrent episodes of depression. She related that she had been an extremely affectionate little girl who loved to be held and cuddled. Her mother often teased her by calling her a "kissing bug." Shortly after the depressive episode that brought her into treatment subsided, she mentioned for the first time that she hated to travel, because it was all but impossible for her to defecate anywhere but at home, and that even there she could do so comfortably only if she was alone in the house with the bathroom door securely locked. She could say nothing further about this symptom except that it extended back to her childhood. Its genetic determinant remained obscure until the following memory emerged almost two years later. During a family visit, when she was about four years old, she had playfully sat on the lap of a young uncle she particularly liked. Her uncle, who was behind her, had slipped his hand inside her underpants and then insinuated his finger into her rectum. All she could add was that she was quite frightened, and that she was fairly certain that she didn't tell anyone what had happened.

Massive traumas constitute a separate category. Though usually dealt with by recapitulation, they most often prove pathogenic because of their intensity and duration. The repetitive reliving of them represents a continuing but vain attempt at mastery. The recapitulation persists because it fails, and instead of mastery and resolution, there is fixation to the trauma—that is, a traumatic neurosis.

Child sexual abuse, which may be considered a pediatric variant of massive trauma, has been the subject of increased attention and study during the past decade or so. Here, observation of abused children, as well as treatment of adolescents and adults who were abused in childhood, has indicated that the psychological damage resulting from abuse is not primarily due to the strength of the stimuli themselves. Rather, it is attributable to two factors: the failure of the young child's protective shield to assimilate and counteract the painful stimulus and the failure of the mother, or parent, to protect.

What distinguishes child sexual abuse from all other types of trauma is that the abuser is frequently the same person on whom the child depends for protection. In treatment, the abuse itself and the anger toward the abuser are usually recalled. What is more difficult to uncover, the perhaps more pathogenic, is the repressed hurt and rage toward the primary caretaker who failed to protect.

The symptomatic and developmental consequences of child abuse fall into two categories, which are not mutually exclusive. The child who was abused may be fearful, inhibited, and withdrawn or impulsive and uncontrollably aggressive. The former combination stems from the early feeling of helplessness and the expectation of disaster, which have not been mastered in any way. Developmentally, this results in deficits in self-esteem and basic trust, as well as a failure in the elaboration of a coherent sense of self. In the latter category, the feelings of anger and destructive rage erupt into actual behavior. In this connection, Steele (1986) has differentiated three forms of anger and aggression in children who were abused. One is an imitative, primitive identification with the maltreating caretakers, a simple identification with aggression itself. Second is anger that is felt as a "normal" biological fight response toward those who have attacked and hurt—either physically or by neglect. It is essentially a narcissistic injury to which the response is narcissistic rage. Third is the more familiar identification with the aggressor. This probably does not occur until well into the second year of life, and is regarded as a defense mechanism that requires a fairly well-developed ego.

Viewed in broader perspective, the significance of trauma lies in the fact that it is a prime manifestation of man's vulnerability to neurosis, and to psychic disturbance in general.

REFERENCES

Blos, P. (1968). Character formation in adolescence. *Psychoanal. Study Child,* 23:245–263.

Bowlby, J. (1960). Separation anxiety. *Int. J. Psychoanal.,* 41:89–113.

Boyer, L. B. (1956). On maternal overstimulation and ego defects. *Psychoanal. Study Child,* 11:236–256.

Breuer, J., & Freud, S. (1893–95). *Studies on Hysteria. SE,* 2.

Freud, A. (1965). *Normality and Pathology in Childhood.* New York: Int. Univ. Press.

Freud, S. (1906). My views on the part played by sexuality in the aetiology of the neuroses. *SE,* 7:271–279.

———. (1916–17). *Introductory Lectures on Psycho-Analysis. SE,* 15 & 16.

———. (1919). Introduction to "Psycho-Analysis and the War Neuroses." *SE*, 17:205–210.

———. (1920). *Beyond the Pleasure Principle. SE,* 18:3–64.

———. (1923). Two encyclopaedia articles. *SE,* 18:231–259.

———. (1926). *Inhibitions, Symptoms and Anxiety. SE,* 20:77–175.

———. (1939). *Moses and Monotheism. SE,* 23:3–137.

Furst, S. S. (1978). The stimulus barrier and the pathogenicity of trauma. *Int. J. Psychoanal.,* 59:345–352.

Glover, E. (1929). The screening function of traumatic memories. *Int. J. Psychoanal.,* 10:90–93.

Greenacre, P. (1950). The prepuberty trauma in girls. Rpt. in *Trauma, Growth, and Personality,* pp. 204–236. New York: Int. Univ. Press, 1952.

Khan, M. M. R. (1953). The concept of cumulative trauma. *Psychoanal. Study Child,* 18:286–306.

Klein, H. (1974). Delayed effects and after-effects of severe traumatization. *Israel Annals of Psychiat.,* 12:282–292.

Kris, E. (1956). The recovery of childhood memories in psychoanalysis. *Psychoanal. Study Child,* 11:54–88.

Krystal, H. (1978). Trauma and affects. *Psychoanal. Study Child,* 33:81–116.

Moses, R. (1978). Adult psychic trauma. *Int. J. Psychoanal.,* 59:353–363.

Neubauer, P. B. (1967). Trauma and psychopathology. In *Psychic Trauma,* ed. S. S. Furst, pp. 85–107. New York: Basic Books.

Niederland, W. (1968). Clinical observations on the "survivor syndrome." *Int. J. Psychoanal.,* 49:313–315.

Racamier, P. C. (1954). Study of early frustrations. *Rev. français Psychiat.,* 18:576–631. English abst. in *Amer. Rev. Psychoanal.,* 5 (1959): 92–96.

Rubinfine, D. (1962). Maternal stimulation, psychic structure and early object relations. *Psychoanal. Study Child,* 17:265–282.

Solnit, A. J., & Kris, M. (1967). Trauma and infantile experiences. In *Psychic Trauma,* ed. S. S. Furst, pp. 175–220. New York: Basic Books.

Spitz, R. A. (1945). Hospitalism. *Psychoanal. Study Child,* 1:53–72.

Steele, B. F. (1986). Child abuse. In *The Reconstruction of Trauma,* ed. A. Rothstein, pp. 59–72. Madison, Conn.: Int. Univ. Press.

Waelder, R. (1967). Trauma and the variety of extraordinary challenges. In *Psychic Trauma,* ed. S. S. Furst, pp. 221–234. New York: Basic Books.

Roberta K. Jaeger, M.D., and

Robert Michels, M.D.

24
───────

ADAPTATION

The term "adaptation" has been used in biology to designate the organism's capacity to cope with its environment and refers to both internal changes undergone by the organism (autoplastic) and alterations effected in the environment (alloplastic). Psychoanalysis views the mind as an aspect of the biological in man and provides a method by which the mind is apprehended and understood. Psychoanalysis thus preserves the original (that is, biological) meaning of adaptation, with special emphasis on the psychic life of the individual and on the important other people who largely constitute the environment.

Adaptation encompasses both the state of fitting together (adaptedness) and the process or processes that lead to that state. It thus has both static and dynamic meanings. Early psychoanalytic thought was greatly influenced by Darwinian evolutionary theory, and the proposition that mental capacities are adapted because of the same evolutionary processes that led to the adaptedness of physical capacities remains a central tenet of psychoanalytic theory. The ontogenesis of the individual (like the phylogenesis of the species) involves the maturation and repeated reworking of evolutionarily determined, preadapted potentialities as they interact with specific experiences during development to shape the evolving characteristics of the individual. For example, genetically determined sexual drives organize behaviors that are shaped and influenced by interaction with the environment, particularly the repeated experiences of gratification and frustration associated with intimate experiences involving other persons in the child's world. The patterns of adult sexual behavior that emerge from this process are adapted to cultural forms that reflect the world in which the child was reared, with its characteristic opportunities for sexual gratification and associated dangers. Psychoanalytic developmental theory is essentially the study of this process of ontogenetic adaptation.

One of the unique characteristics of the human is the flexibility of the innate biological potentiality that, together with an unusually prolonged stage of physical helplessness and social dependency, accounts for the great influence of experience and learning, rather than fixed genetic predisposition, in shaping the actuality of the individual. This results in the importance of environmental (learned) as well as constitutional determinants of behavior, with organismic factors determining general programs or goals of behavior rather than specific details. Psychoanalysis studies the unique ways in which each individual pursues these goals, as well as variations in early experience, the mental structures that stem from that experience and govern behavior, and the behaviors that result. For example, the need for social relationships and communal living is rooted in the biology of the species and the prolonged helplessness of the young, but the choice of companions, the structure of the family, the stability of relationships, the distribution of social roles, the links between affectionate, sexual, and dependent bonds, and the intrapsychic fantasies and meanings that develop in relation to these experiences and shape all subsequent behavior reflect psychological determinants operating within that biologically determined need.

Different orders of adaptation can be illustrated by focusing on progressively smaller structures. Let us consider language. The capacity for language is an important phylogenetic adaptation that enhances the ability of the species to cope with its environment, particularly the social environment so important in the lives of higher primates and man. This biological capacity, the neural substrate of language, is a product of evolutionary adaptation. Each member of the species develops this biological capacity in the course of individual ontogenesis through maturation and interaction with others in the social environment. This is both an adaptation to the contemporary social world of the child and a developmental adaptive process that leads to enhanced capacity in the adult. Finally, each specific language act can be viewed as an instance of an individual adapting to others and to the specific challenge of the immediate internal and external situation in a uniquely personalized fashion.

Although the concept of adaptation was first explicitly elaborated in psychoanalysis by Hartmann (1939), Freud had an implicit adaptational point of view. In 1924 he referred to autoplastic and alloplastic "changes" in a discussion of the distinction between neurosis and psychosis, in which he emphasized that normal behavior involves attempts at alteration of the real world (alloplastic change), while neurotic behavior involves a flight from that world, and psychotic behavior a disavowal and fantasized remodeling of it. Ferenczi had earlier used the terms "alloplastic" and "autoplastic" (1919), attributing them to Freud, but we have no record of Freud's earlier usage. Hartmann (1939) said that "Adaptation may come about by changes which the individual effects in his environment . . . as well as by appropriate changes in his psychophysical system. Here Freud's concepts of alloplastic and autoplastic change are apposite" (p. 26). He went on to state that a broad range of alloplastic adaptations is a unique characteristic of the human, and that there is also a third form of adaptation, the selection of a new environment, that combines aspects of both alloplastic and autoplastic change. Hartmann sums up his view of adaptation by saying: "We call a man well adapted if his productivity, his ability to enjoy life, and his mental equilibrium are undisturbed" (p. 23).

Hartmann anticipated contemporary philosophical discourse by denying the existence of a gap between the mind and the brain or body (Searle, 1984). As Hartmann said, "In our opinion the psychological is not an 'antithesis' to the biological, but rather an essential part of it." Instead of contrasting the psychological with the biological, Hartmann asked of the developmental process: "What part of it is congenital, what maturational, and what environmentally determined?" (p. 34). He firmly anchors psychoanalysis in biology. This relationship ensures that psychoanalytic inquiry continues to shed light on biological processes, just as early psychoanalysis explored the instinctual drives—a concept that bridges biology and psychology.

Hartmann describes two types of relationship between adaptation and developmental processes, depending on direction. "Progressive" adaptation coincides with development, whereas "regressive" adaptation, which may be quite successful, goes counter to development. The latter may provide only a temporary detour, as via fantasy, a concept elaborated by Kris (1934) as "regression in the service of the ego."

Hartmann (1939) elucidated another principle of significance for adaptation—change of function. Consideration of the adaptive significance of a specific behavior must differentiate between the current function of that behavior and its developmental or phylogenetic origins. It is common for the function of a behavior to change so as to serve an adaptive purpose which is quite different from, or even unrelated to, its original role. Evolutionary biologists have named this phenomenon, the recruitment of an existing structure for a new function, "exaptation," in contrast to adaptation. Hartmann, discussing it in terms of the development of the individual, refers to it as "change of function" and says: "A behavior-form which originated in a certain realm of life may, in the course of development, appear in an entirely different realm and role" (pp. 25–26).

The concept is particularly important in the psychoanalytic understanding of the relation of the drives and psychological conflicts that are so central to the mental life of the child and to the adult behaviors that have their origins in childhood. Much adult behavior, including both healthy and neurotic behavior, remains closely linked to its origins in childhood drives and is deeply embedded in psychic conflict. However, some psychological functions that "started in a situation of conflict may secondarily become part of the nonconflictual sphere"; and functions that originated in close relationship to instinctual drives may develop secondary autonomy relative to those drives (Hartmann, 1964, p. 123). This type of change of function often enhances the adaptive value of a behavior, but conflict and the drive determination of behavior are not necessarily maladaptive.

Change of function can, of course, also occur in the opposite direction, when a psychological function that was originally free of conflict becomes secondarily involved in psychic conflict, as in the neurotic impairment of basic cognitive or perceptual capacities. The first type of change is illustrated by the development of autonomous intellectual abilities stemming from defenses that controlled forbidden aggressive impulses, the second by hysterical symptoms in which primary capacities such as vision come to symbolize forbidden impulses and are impaired by the defenses against those impulses. Autonomous intellectual activity, neurotically derived, may serve adaptive purposes.

Adaptation is distinguished from other concepts that may subserve it. Hartmann (1958) coined the term "fitting together" to refer to the synthetic function of the ego and to the fit between mental structures—that is, the id, the ego, and the superego. His conceptualization of the mind involved states of equilibrium, both within and among the various mental structures and between them and the environment. In general, as Anna Freud (1965) pointed out, the better the fit between the agencies or structures, the better the adaptation, and the greater the freedom from illness.

Other psychoanalytic authors have employed terms that relate to "adaptation" but are not synonymous with it. Bowlby (1969) uses the term "modification" to refer to a change in the environment; but while this may contribute to adaptation, it is clearly a narrower concept. The same may be said of "adjustment," which includes only passive autoplastic change, for adaptation has both active and passive components. Hendrick's (1936) "instinct" for mastery, although congruent with an adaptational point of view, seems to stress the active components of adaptation by virtue of the word "instinct." Whether one speaks of "instinct" or "drive," the notion of "active" has been inherent historically.

Adaptation involves reality, and the individual's ability to perceive, evaluate, and influence reality has important implications for adaptation. The meaning of reality in psychoanalysis has evolved over time. Most modern psychoanalytic thinking emphasizes psychic reality, the inner mental representation or subjective reality that is shaped by drives, memories, and predispositions from within, as well as information from without. "Adaptation" is shorthand for "adaptation to the environment," and the reality referred to is usually external reality. The term "fitting together" is, in general, more ap-

propriate when speaking of psychic reality and adaptation.

Freud's original emphasis was on external reality (Breuer & Freud, 1893–95). In this early phase of analytic theorizing, a trauma from without—that is, based in external reality—was seen as setting neurotic conflict in motion. In 1911 Freud elaborated the concept of reality as it develops in the individual. A person's reality grows coincidentally with the development of the ego, and it was reality that was seen as preventing immediate satisfaction by prohibition of drive action. Simultaneously, secondary-process functioning comes to overlie and complement primary-process functioning. This more sophisticated, inhibited way of operating facilitates adaptation to reality and defers drive discharge. The demarcation between psychic and external reality is blurred insofar as the distinction is not addressed. In 1923, with the advent of the structural theory, the ego was envisioned as mediating between reality (environment) and the other psychic structures and thus emerged as the prime instrument of adaptation. External reality again became the focus of theory construction in 1926 with the formulation of the signal theory of anxiety. The adaptational viewpoint is inherent in *Symptoms, Inhibitions and Anxiety*. Symptomatic, maladaptive anxiety is distinguished from adaptive signal anxiety, which triggers coping or defensive responses to the danger situation. Adaptation is mediated by external action if the danger situation is real and internal action if the danger is based on a response triggered by an instinctual impulse. The affect of anxiety has also undergone a change of function, since it can be traced to the original response of the organism at birth, vital in activating the cardiorespiratory system. At that time it was obviously adaptive; when it emerges as a symptom rather than a signal, it has lost its adaptive value. On the other hand, since the essence of danger is helplessness in the face of overwhelming excitation of either internal or external origin, the transformation of this automatic anxiety into a signal controlled by the ego must be considered a new adaptive function.

Hartmann's view of the individual as born potentially adapted to the "average expected environment" because of ego apparatuses of primary autonomy is consistent with a view of the ego as *the* structure of adaptation. Waelder (1936) integrated prior notions of primary and secondary process with autoplastic and alloplastic adaptations. In this regard he saw man as the only creature doubly equipped with cognitive systems—the primary process for instituting autoplastic and the secondary process for instituting alloplastic adaptations, thereby placing man in a position uniquely suited to free him from the immediate compelling forces of the self and thus to overcome the adaptive obstacle inherent in the drives because of their untamability. By utilizing both emotional (intuitive primary-process) and logical reasoning (secondary-process) responses, man integrates self-interest and reality for optimal adaptation.

Although pleasure and reality are components of any adaptation, it should not be assumed that each contributes equally. Reality, and therefore the reality principle, has a special relationship to adaptation. By demonstrating that the reality principle is not on the same theoretical level as the pleasure principle and so cannot stand on equal footing, Hartmann (1939) elaborated the relationship. He described a broad reality in line with "biological adaptation" and a narrower one in line with certain ego functions. Thus the ego function of anticipation, so crucial for determining means and ends, is inherent in the notion of a reality principle and clearly subserves adaptation. The reality principle (in contrast to the pleasure principle) thus encompasses many functions which serve adaptive ends, which gives it a special connection to adaptation. In the adapting individual, reality thus both guides the vicissitudes of drives and affects the expression of the higher, more integrated, complex behaviors of the individual.

Adaptation concerns the relationship between the individual and his or her environment, and for psychoanalysis the most important aspect of the environment is psychosocial, the other significant figures in the individual's life. This has been amplified in the well-known work of Erikson (1961, 1962), and is easily demonstrable from the earliest stages of the infant's development in interaction with his or her primary caretakers, through the critical identifications and internalizations that lead to the formation of psychic structure, to the role of object relations throughout the life cycle. One corollary of the central role of the psychosocial environment is the extent to which the human environment adapts to the individual as the individual is adapting to it. This interactive adaptation is a key feature of modern theories of development, which emphasize how the infant shapes the mother's behavior as the mother is shaping the infant's and how pathology results from problems in this reciprocal process rather than from failures in one or the other of the participants (Shapiro & Stern, 1980).

Indeed, the prolonged period of helplessness and dependence in the development of man necessitates an adaptive viewpoint. This allows an understanding of human psychology to accommodate the enormous range of conditions to which a child may adapt with more or less success. For example, the abused child will cling and adapt to the abusive parent despite fear. On the other hand, the studies of wartime children by Anna Freud and Dorothy Burlingham (1943) showed their adaptation to dreadful realities with no fear or strong adverse reactions to bombings when in the company of mothers who did not show fear. In the first example, adaptation results in a pathological situation, although one may wonder whether a more optimal outcome is feasible. By contrast, Anna Freud and Dorothy Burlingham's work illustrates a nonpathological outcome coincident with adaptation. Both situations entail adaptation to an unusually harsh reality. The difference is attributable to the protective environment given to the immature psychic apparatus by the "good" mother in the second case, a factor conspicuously absent from the experience of the abused child. Child observation and developmental theory explicate the initial role of the mother as a stimulus barrier, a role that diminishes in importance with internalization and structuralization of the infant psychic organization. Maladaptation in the mother thus predisposes to maladaptation in the infant via the interaction of constitutional and environmental factors. This mutuality thus continuously brought about fits well with Loewald's (1971) model of mental activity. His metaphor of mind as organism is reminiscent of the sexual conjugation of paramecia, with the eventual emergence of two separate, somewhat changed individuals. This occurs originally between mother and infant and subsequently between the individual and any other important person—for example, the analyst.

Bowlby (1969), describing the achievement of developmental adaptation, speaks of the animal's need for a working model of its environment and also for one of its own skills and potentialities, both of which must be kept up-to-date. This assumes ongoing revision and awareness, either conscious or unconscious, of "me" and "not me." Such revision is made feasible by the development of reality testing, whereby the individual is able to remain in constant contact with the vicissitudes of his or her environment, even under conditions of stress that may result in temporary regression. Trauma, for example, produces such stress and regression, yet the incorporation of residual trauma in the formation of character, which occurs in late adolescence (Blos, 1968), results in increased freedom from the environment— the original source of the traumatic injury—and enhances adaptation by increasing the harmony with which the mind functions.

Blos views trauma as a universal in human development, which has the effect of upsetting homeostasis. If the residue of the trauma is assimilated through characterological stabilization (rendering it ego-syntonic), it no longer exacts a toll via ego inhibition, recurrent defensive intervention, and so forth. The creation of a more harmonious intrapsychic situation permits the individual to obtain more freedom to deal with reality. Once the trauma has become integrated into the ego, it ceases to alert the ego repetitiously via signal anxiety; the state of helplessness is thereby counteracted. Blos relates such adaptive incorporation of trauma to signal anxiety and character formation: "Character, then, is identical with patterned responses to signal anxiety or, more generally, with the conquest of residual trauma: not with its disappearance, nor its avoidance, but with its continuance within an adaptive formation" (p. 255). Character formation provides the internalization of a stable protective environment, thus increasing adaptive capacity—the ability to tangle with the environment.

A common misconception among both critics and advocates of psychoanalysis results from an overly simple exaggeration of the role of the environment in the causation of neurosis. This error is implicit when one "blames" the parents or supports an absurdly permissive attitude to child-rearing, which may masquerade as enlightened psychological understanding. Freud was careful to emphasize that the environment is etiological in producing neurosis only insofar as it increases *inner* conflict beyond the threshold for the individual. Constitutional and accidental factors may determine that threshold; but the environmental component of inner conflict is, perhaps, the most plastic. In any event, it is that aspect which furnishes access to change and hence is the focus of adaptive efforts. This is consistent with common sense, in that it is more external, more on the "boundary," which is the site of adaptation.

Psychoanalysis in its early years was not explicitly interested in the concept of adaptation. Its initial interest was in the motivational sources of behavior, drives, and unconscious forces, rather than in the effects of this behavior (at that time primarily symptoms) on the relationship between the individual and the external world. The term is not mentioned in the subject index of the *Standard Edition* of Freud's works, in Sterba's (1936) dictionary, or in *The Language of Psychoanalysis* by Laplanche and Pontalis (1974). However, it became a central concept with the shift from an exclusive focus on the motivational origins of behavior to the more balanced concerns of the structural theory—the ego as well as the id, the mental structures that mediate between drives and behavior, and the development of the concept of mechanisms of defense and their generalization to mechanisms of coping. Hartmann's seminal *Ego Psychology and the Problem of Adaptation* (1939) and his elaboration of its central ideas in subsequent papers (1964), including some written together with

Kris and Loewenstein (1964), were what gave status to the concept of (psychoanalytic) adaptation. The formulation of Rado's (1956) adaptational psychodynamics and Rapaport and Gill's (1959) points of view and assumptions of metapsychology placed the adaptive parallel with the dynamic, economic, structural, and genetic viewpoints, thereby establishing adaptation as a central concept in psychoanalysis, one that was always implicit but only now fully articulated.

In their survey of metapsychology, Rapaport and Gill (1959) discuss the question of whether the adaptive point of view is of the same level of abstraction as others or whether the propositions of psychoanalysis that are usually subsumed under the adaptive perspective can be derived without reference to environmental relations. They conclude that a system of metapsychology must include an adaptive point of view. But others have criticized this conclusion, arguing that the adaptive frame of reference is not on the same level as other frames (Schafer, 1970) and that it is not a psychoanalytic so much as a basic biological notion. Schafer's attempt to free psychoanalysis from biology goes counter to the assumptions of Hartmann and current philosophy and places adaptation outside the analyst's domain. Schafer opts for a more limited field of study. However, in defining one's field of interest at the microscopic level, one does not eliminate the fields brought into focus by less powerful lenses; one merely ceases to visualize them. Since there can be no individual without a human environment, some notion of adaptation is essential for any comprehensive conceptualization of the human mind, including the psychoanalytic one. Without this larger view, the most vital and interesting questions—indeed, areas to which psychoanalysis has already made contributions—become alien territory.

The fit between structures, from intrasystemic (for example, conflictual and nonconflictual spheres within the ego and various drives or motivational systems within the id) through intersystemic of increasing comprehensiveness (id–ego–superego, external world–ego), bears a complicated relation to the concepts of mental health and pathology. In general, the better the fit between structures, the greater the individual's ability to deal with the environment and the greater the contribution to successful adaptation. However, since conflict is a natural aspect of human development, we cannot consider pathological versus normal as coincidental with defense-born versus nondefense-born.

A defense may diminish anxiety secondary to unconscious conflict and aid adaptation, as in the case of sublimation and reaction formation in the course of normal character development. Furthermore, adaptation to reality may reduce tension between mental structures, as when the achievement of autonomy diminishes helplessness and so on. Even so, a successful defense may simultaneously be a failure in achievement. Similarly, a current maladaptation may be essential en route to a more inclusive, beneficial, subsequent adaptation. For example, denial of the seriousness of severe illness may interfere with proper treatment; on the other hand, some denial may be essential to the continuation of life and may correlate positively with prognosis. In extreme situations the relinquishment of an achievement may be required. Exercising autonomy in a concentration camp, for instance, might have led to immediate death. The spectrum of behaviors between total submission and total autonomy is wide indeed, and within it are various admixtures of dignity, compassion, and selfishness. Death is outside the realm of "adaptation" as viewed psychoanalytically, noble though it may sometimes be. This follows from the fact that the individual, not the species, is the subject of study in psychoanalysis; the individual is the unit from which all psychoanalytically-derived material issues.

Psychoanalysis began with the study of certain mental symptoms and the discovery that they had meaning and that the exploration of that meaning could influence their course. The symptoms were, of course, maladaptive, but adaptation was not a central concept. However, as this early focus broadened to include a wider range of behavior, healthy as well as pathological, the search for meanings led to a developmental psychology; and interest in the quality of relations with the environment and the development of patterns of coping both led to an interest in adaptation. This was inevitable if what had started as a method of treatment was to become a general psychology. The status of the concept of adaptation today is closely linked to the status of psychoanalysis as a general psychology. For those who believe that it is *a*—or even *the*—general psychology, adaptation is necessarily a central concept linking psychology to the rest of biology. For those who restrict their interest to a concern with meanings, the concept of adaptation is linked only to the history of psychoanalysis and to the scientific and biological roots of its earliest metaphors and interpretive systems.

REFERENCES

Blos, P. (1968). Character formation in adolescence. *Psychoanal. Study Child,* 23:245–263.

Bowlby, J. (1969). *Attachment and Loss.* New York: Basic Books.

Breuer, J., & Freud, S. (1893–95). *Studies on Hysteria. SE,* 2:3–331.

Erikson, E. H. (1961). *Insight and Responsibility.* New York: Norton.

———. (1962). Reality and actuality. *J. Amer. Psychoanal. Assn.,* 10:451–474.

Ferenczi, S. (1919). The phenomena of hysterical materialization. In *Further Contributions to the Theory and Technique of Psychoanalysis,* pp. 110–118. London: Hogarth Press, 1926.

Freud, A. (1965). *Normality and Pathology in Childhood.* New York: Int. Univ. Press.

Freud, A., & Burlingham, D. (1943). *War and Children.* New York: Medical War Books.

Freud, S. (1911). Formulations on the two principles of mental functioning. *SE,* 12:215–226.

———. (1923). *The Ego and the Id. SE,* 19:12–66.

———. (1924). The loss of reality in neurosis and psychosis. *SE,* 19:183–187.

———. (1926). *Inhibitions, Symptoms and Anxiety. SE,* 20:77–181.

Hartmann, H. (1939). *Ego Psychology and the Problem of Adaptation.* New York: Int. Univ. Press, 1958.

———. (1964). *Essays in Ego Psychology.* New York: Int. Univ. Press.

Hartmann, H., Kris, E., & Loewenstein, R. M. (1964). *Papers on Psychoanalytic Ego Psychology.* Psychological Issues, monograph 14. New York: Int. Univ. Press.

Hendrick, I. (1936). Ego development and certain character problems. *Psychoanal. Q.,* 5:320–346.

Kris, E. (1934). The psychology of caricature. Rpt. in *Psychoanalytic Explorations in Art,* pp. 173–188. New York: Int. Univ. Press, 1952.

Lampl-de Groot, J. (1966). Some thoughts on adaptation and conformism. In *Psychoanalysis—A General Psychology,* ed. R. M. Loewenstein, L. M. Newman, M. Schur, & A. J. Solnit, pp. 338–348. New York: Int. Univ. Press.

Laplanche, J., & Pontalis, J.-B. (1974). *The Language of Psychoanalysis.* New York: Norton.

Loewald, H. W. (1971). On motivation and instinct theory. *Psychoanal. Study Child,* 26:91–128.

Rado, S. (1956). *Psychoanalysis of Behavior.* New York: Grune & Stratton.

Rapaport, D., & Gill, M. M. (1959). The points of view and assumptions of metapsychology. Rpt. in *The Collected Papers of David Rapaport,* ed. M. M. Gill, pp. 795–811. New York: Basic Books, 1967.

Schafer, R. (1970). An overview of Heinz Hartmann's contributions to psychoanalysis. *Int. J. Psychoanal.,* 51:425–446.

Searle, J. (1984). *Minds, Brain and Science*. Cambridge, Mass.: Harvard Univ. Press.

Shapiro, T., & Stern, D. (1980). Psychoanalytic perspectives on the first year of life. In *The Course of Life*, ed. S. I. Greenspan & G. H. Pollock, vol. 1, pp. 113–128. Washington: National Institute of Mental Health.

Sterba, R. F. (1936). *Handwörterbuch der psychoanalyse*. Vienna: Internationaler Psychoanalytischer Verlag.

Waelder, R. (1936). The principle of multiple function. *Psychoanal. Q.*, 5:45–62.

PART V

INSTINCT THEORY,
SEXUALITY, AND
AFFECTS

Samuel Ritvo, M.D., and
Albert J. Solnit, M.D.

25

INSTINCT THEORY

INTRODUCTION AND DEFINITION

In attempting to understand normal human development and behavior as well as psychopathology, psychoanalysts, following Freud (1905, 1915), found it heuristically useful to assume that human beings function not only in response to the demands and conditions of their external environment but also in response to the demands and pressures of the inner environment, the body–mind interior. In this metaphorical way, psychoanalysts have called attention to the psychological and emotional impulses, tensions, or forces that characterize psychological aliveness, the psychic *tonus* that is associated with maturational and developmental change. Freud (1915) conceptualized these inner stimuli or activating tensions as the demand of the body on the mind for work and referred to them as instinctual drives.[1]

These psychic energies provide impetus, driving the mind to activity. The concept is a psychological one referring to psychic, not physiological, phenomena, though the psychic phenomena are an essential part of the total living organism and are thus biologically rooted, drawing on the tensions and energies of the living organism. As Anna Freud (1960) put it, "As analysts we do not deal with drive activity

1. English does not have a word that corresponds to the German *Trieb*. Strachey's choice of "instinct" was a very problematic one. See Waelder's (1960) discussion.

as such but with the mental representations of the drives" (p. 54).

The concept of instinctual drives in humans should be distinguished from the concept of instincts in lower animals, though they are related. In animals the concept of instinct refers to an innate capacity or necessity to respond to a set of specific external stimuli and internal needs in a programmed or patterned way. It should be noted, however, that modern biology is assigning an increasingly larger role to learning and experience in what was previously thought to be innate and patterned behavior in animals.

Instinctual drives in human beings are impelling forces of the internal state that eventuate in complex and varied behaviors. It is as though the body's metabolic activity, with its daily rhythms and epochal developmental changes, ebbing and flowing, is responded to by the mental apparatus as a leading organ of adaptation in terms of psychic tension and activity. This psychic tension arises from a constant internal stimulus from which there is no flight. It has an impelling motivational impact on the cognitive and affective mental states, which in turn have a determining influence on behavior. Thus, human drives refer to psychic phenomena, with mental representational characteristics that have a sustained influence on behavior. The drives are also responsive to maturational and developmental changes, the most dramatic being the increased urgency of libidinal wishes during puberty and at the time of menopause and the male climacteric.

Besides having a biological source of energy, instinctual drives were further elaborated by Freud (1915) as having an impetus, an aim, an object, and a source. The impetus is a quantitative feature which allows economic considerations; it represents the amount of force toward activity that the drive exerts.

The aim of an instinctual drive is always satisfaction, which may be immediate or deferred or a combination thereof. The aim may also be inhibited or deflected, resulting in partial or substitute satisfaction.

The object, the thing or person by means of which the drive achieves its aim, is the most variable feature of the instinctual drive. It may change repeatedly, or there may be an especially close attachment or fixation to an object. Focusing on the object of the drives has enabled psychoanalysts to appreciate the interdependence of the individual and his specific environment and to examine the typical reality situations which confront the person in the course of his or her development. Tracing the relationship between the child's needs and demands at various levels of development and his or her human environment has made possible the correlation of object formation and object relationships through successive stages of instinctual development.

The source of an instinctual drive is a stimulus arising from a somatic process. This is an assumption, since we actually know very little about the connection between actual somatic processes and psychological functions. A source may sometimes be inferred from an aim. This is most clearly seen in the development of leading erogenous zones from a predominance of orally associated and organized longings and behavior to those that are predominantly anally and later genitally associated and organized. Observations of how they are linked over the life cycle provide convincing evidence of the usefulness of the concept of psychic energy. This is further differentiated as sexual and aggressive forces striving for gratification. That is, aggression and libido are driving forces that motivate mental activity, which in turn influences human behavior.

This discussion of the concept of drives is limited to the way it is used in clinical psychoanalytic psychology. The concepts of "life" and "death instincts" are concepts of a different order (Freud, 1926, 1930), and the hypotheses concerning them must be proved or disproved biologically. They do not contribute greatly to our understanding of the specific functions of the drives (Hartmann, 1948).

FURTHER COMMENTS ON SOURCE, AIM, AND OBJECT

The sources of the drives are relevant because of their developmental aspects, as in the sequence of dominant but overlapping phases—oral, anal, phallic, and genital. Information about sources can help in classifying drive derivatives and in tracing their manifestations in the clinical phenomena observed in both adults and children. It should be kept in mind, however, that the drives are somatopsychic—that is, the source is somatic, but the effect is psychic.[2]

The great interest in the aims of the drives reflects the usefulness of this construct in the clinical psychoanalytic situation. The concept of instinctual drives makes it possible to follow the transformations of the aims in human beings and to recognize the readiness with which one aim can be substituted for another—for example, the child who, in the face of a conflict on the phallic-oedipal level, resorts regressively to an expression or discharge in an oral or anal mode. In the psychoanalytic situation the instinctual drive concept enables the analyst to comprehend and correlate the otherwise baffling situations presented by substitute and aim-inhibited expressions that convey an individual's needs, emotions, and ways of dealing with conflicts.

Psychoanalytic theory divides the instinctual drives into two groups of primal instincts, sexual and aggressive, rather than an indeterminate number of specific instincts. Though he made revisions in his drive theory over time, Freud always adhered to a dualistic theory, in keeping with the preeminent place of psychic conflict in psychoanalytic psychology.

Instinctual drives can be further characterized by the vicissitudes they undergo (Freud, 1915, p. 126):

1. Reversal into the opposite in which a passive experience is replaced by an active one; or, as observed in the psychoanalytic situation, the analysand experiences active or passive forms of gratification.

2. Object and subject may be interchanged, and

2. Brenner (1982, pp. 12–13) said: "Freud did not wish to rely on psychoanalytic data for the part of his . . . [instinct] theory that has to do with its source or origin since he believed that source to be a somatic one. Wholly reliable data on that source, he believed, could come only from other than analytic observations. They might come, for example, from the observation of sexual behavior, from a better knowledge of the nature and function of sex hormones, from comparative physiological and anatomical studies and the like."

the person may in fantasy participate in both roles—for example, in looking or in being looked at (scoptophilia-exhibitionism) or in hurting or in being hurt (sadism-masochism), demonstrating again the reversibility of the drive.

3. The instinctual drive may be turned against the self for defensive purposes, to prevent the discharge upon the love object, a basic mechanism in the formation of the superego; for example, self-criticism, inappropriate guilt, and self-destructive behavior reflect the turning of the drives against the self rather than the object.

4. The instinctual drive derivatives may be repressed and may require additional defensive efforts (that is, defense mechanisms) to support or elaborate the repression of the drives.

5. In sublimation, drive energies are transformed and discharged in mental activities that result in symbolic equivalents of the original instinctual drive impulses. The instinctual aim is inhibited and displaced onto an activity that may have a social or creative artistic value.

Thus defined, the concept of instinctual drive becomes a useful tool in the clinical psychoanalytic situation for the investigation and understanding of both psychopathology and normal and abnormal development. It is most fruitful when employed with the psychoanalytic method, because the conditions that invite and foster free association and transference enable the analyst and analysand to explore the preconscious and unconscious states. The instinctual drive derivatives, as well as the defenses and resistances they evoke, can be reliably and usefully inferred from their repeated and patterned appearances in those states. It is only with the psychoanalytic method that unconscious motivations can be optimally explored.[3]

REGULATION OF INSTINCTUAL DRIVES AND THEIR RELATION TO PSYCHIC STRUCTURE

An essential aspect of the theory of instinctual drives is their regulation and place in a systematic theory of mental functioning. According to the structural view of the organization and functioning of the mind, the instinctual drives operate largely unconsciously in the id and, if operating alone,

3. Psychoanalysts are eager to find other methods through which the validity and reliability of exploring the unconscious can be approached. So far, other approaches have been found so to distort what is being studied that a focus on unconscious motivation is impossible (see Kris, 1947).

would be regulated only by the pleasure principle, as their only aim is immediate satisfaction. But the drives also contribute impetus, motivation, and ideational content to the ego via the representations and derivatives of the drives that reach preconscious and conscious levels of awareness. When the derivatives of the drives reach these levels, they are subjected to the reality-testing and defensive functions of the ego, so that we can say that in the ego they are regulated by the reality principle.

Through its integrative and synthetic functions, the ego creates the substitute, compromise, or sublimated thought and behavior that on the one hand is appropriate and acceptable to the particular environment and on the other hand provides a degree of satisfaction of the needs and wishes arising from the unstable internal environment. When the ego is not able to achieve this task—for example, because of the intensity of the drive pressure, either directly from the id or by a reversal of the drive in the superego, or because of limitations in the defensive and adaptive capacities of the ego—signal anxiety may break out, and symptom formation ensue.

When the drive derivatives reach consciousness in the older child or adult, they have also been subjected to the superego, which is assumed to derive its force and peremptoriness from the drives. In this way the instinctual drives, by their vicissitudes of reversal, make a contribution to bringing conscience, moral standards, and cultural values to bear on thought and behavior.

SEXUAL AND AGGRESSIVE DRIVES

The value and power of the concept of instinctual drives are nowhere more apparent than in Freud's discovery (1905) of infantile sexuality, generally considered the keystone and most startling of his discoveries. Aggression, on the other hand, was considered one of the partial instincts of sexuality. Following this was a brief intermediary period in which Freud viewed aggression as part of the instinctual equipment of the ego, linked to self-preservation. In 1920 Freud opened up the study of aggression by treating it as an independent, inborn instinctual drive, the counterpart of sexuality.[4]

Subsequently, tracing the development of instinctual drives, both Hartmann (1964) and Jacobson (1964) made the assumption that initially the instinctual drives are undifferentiated and that only gradually do they develop into libido and aggression.

4. For a historical account of Freud's instinct theory, see Bibring's excellent overview (1941).

However, it is an error to view aggressive drives as having a symmetry with sexual drives and to try to match patterns and characteristics of sex and aggression. Symmetry is no guarantee of validation. Thus, Anna Freud (1971) stated that the analyst's conception of aggressive drives is frequently clouded by his or her concepts about sexual drives.

Aggressive and sexual drives differ in several ways. The periodicity, rhythm, buildup, and discharge characteristics are not the same. In aggression, neuromuscular and motoric characteristics and patterns are emphasized more than those characterized as sensuous or erotic. Motoric expressions relate more to representations reflecting characteristic neuromuscular functions than to erotic characteristics of engorgement or climactic discharge followed by satisfaction. Libido and aggression coexist, can almost never be viewed separately in the actual situation, and have broad areas of overlapping and converging functions. Or, as Anna Freud (1971) put it, "The bodily needs, in so far as they represent an instigation to mental activity, are called instincts or instinctual drives. As with libido, and many other psychic functions and structures, aggression, as an instinctual drive, can be inferred, but is not directly observable."

Hartmann and Loewenstein (1962) stated: "It is not unlikely that the direction-giving function of the superego works with a higher degree of neutralization of aggression than its enforcing function" (p. 71). Freud (1930) suggested that "when an instinctual trend undergoes repression, its libidinal elements are turned into symptoms, its aggressive components into a sense of guilt" (p. 139).

With the introduction of the concept of aggression, clinical studies went on to demonstrate the importance of unconscious guilt feelings, which in turn yielded an understanding of the formulation and dynamic functions of the superego (Freud, 1930). Clinical phenomena such as the negative therapeutic reaction and self-destructive tendencies became foci of psychoanalytic study as the fruitful relationship between instinctual drive theory and clinical observations became apparent.

The tendency to assume that aggression ultimately has a destructive aim, precipitating conflicts over loss and death wishes, must be balanced by findings that aggressive energies fuel psychic maturation and the defensive functions of the ego (Hartmann, 1948, 1955; Hartmann et al., 1949; Hartmann & Loewenstein, 1962) as well as by observations that aggressive discharge activities are frequently associated with recovery from maternal deprivation (Greenacre, 1960; Solnit, 1970, 1972).

Thus, the aims of aggression can be modified

through a simultaneous investment of the object with libido, which protects it from aggression, or by consideration and anticipation of danger to the individual if the aggressive act is carried out, or by conflict over moral values (Hartmann et al., 1949). The impact of aggression may be modified by displacement to other objects, by restriction of the aims of the aggressive impulses, by the sublimation of aggressive energy, or through the influences of fusion with libido. Sublimated or neutralized aggression can be integrated into the structure of the ego and the superego. In the ego it is available for the mastery and control of reality and for defensive purposes in intrapsychic conflict.

The theory of instinctual drives combined with the concept of maturation derived from psychoanalytic observation made possible a genetic–dynamic approach to psychosexual development, organized around leading erogenous and neuromuscular zones and their concomitant wishes, fantasies, and attendant behaviors. Originally these inferences were arrived at by reconstruction in the analyses of adults. Later, they were confirmed, extended, and modified by child analysis and direct observation of children.

DEVELOPMENTAL PERSPECTIVES

Human infants are relatively helpless and require an adult (parent) to feed, clothe, wash, soothe, and care for them. Adults also provide the regulatory care that helps children cope with, channel, and discharge their drive tensions. The soothing, stimulating, demanding parent does for the infant what the older child is able to regulate or repress for himself.

As the child matures and develops, he or she achieves an increasing capacity for self-regulatory control of these tensions or drives. The drives are modified and discharged in patterned ways, reflecting a compromise between the child's impulses and needs and demands for social or acceptable behavior by the parents and others. In the younger child, drive discharge almost always has a behavioral or motor component. In the older child, the discharge is increasingly expressed in affects and thought—that is, through trial actions of the mind.

The transformations of instinctual drives usually reflect the modifying, shaping imprint of the patterned ways in which the parents dealt with the child's urge for discharge, either by helping the child to express such drives, delay discharge, or utilize substitute gratifications—as in the case of the hungry, crying child who can be soothed temporarily by the mother's singing or by being provided with a favorite toy. Thus, the parents help the child postpone the gratifying discharge or provide alternative pathways for the child to achieve discharge of these drive tensions. The theory of instinctual drives gains explanatory value by positing the following:

1. There are patterns of instinctual drive tension that are relatively independent of environmental vicissitudes and that increase and decrease within the individual.

2. Such tension decrease is usually associated with pleasure or gratification, whereas tension increase is usually associated with unpleasure, frustration, and behavior that seeks discharge pathways.

3. Instinctual drive buildup and discharge patterns change gradually along predictable developmental lines. These patterns are associated with psychosexual and psychoaggressive characteristics reflecting maturational regularities and phase dominance.

The developmental progression from an infantile pattern of tension buildup/tension discharge to adolescent and adult patterns reflects the maturational aspect of instinctual drive and ego development.

Freud (1905) did not regard repression as wholly dependent on external social influences. He indicated that in the latency period internal dams against the instinctual drives emerge: "One gets an impression from civilized children that the construction of these dams is a product of education, and no doubt education has much to do with it. But in reality this development is organically determined and fixed by heredity, and it can occasionally occur without any help at all from education" (pp. 177–178). Thus, the "civilizing" of instinctual drive expression can be viewed as a consequence of maturation of the drives as well as the influence of ego and superego functions.

Although there are linkages between the somatic sources and the erogenous zones, this does not mean that libido arises from the mouth, anus, or genitals (Brenner, 1982, p. 14). However, these linkages reflect an orderly progression of psychosexual and psychoaggressive phase dominance.

What should be emphasized is that drive energy is a psychological, not a physiological, reference, in which mental activities are invested with libidinal and aggressive energies. In discussing the range of sexual maturational phenomena, Freud (1905) said:

The characteristics of infantile sexual life which we have hitherto emphasized are the facts that it is essentially autoerotic (i.e. that it finds its object in the infant's own body)[5] and that its individual component instincts are upon the whole disconnected and independent of one another in their

search for pleasure. The final outcome of sexual development lies in what is known as the normal sexual life of the adult, in which the pursuit of pleasure comes under the sway of the reproductive function and in which the component instincts, under the primacy of a single erotogenic zone, form a firm organization directed toward a sexual aim attached to some extraneous sexual object. [p. 197]

The psychoanalytic theory of instinctual drives supports clinical observations that each person is bisexual. Ordinarily, the male child has predominantly masculine psychological characteristics, harmonious with his biological equipment, whereas the female child has predominantly female characteristics, harmonious with her biological apparatus. An even more basic human polarity can be observed and is to some extent supported by the instinctual drive theory: namely, that all children and adults have opposite, or ambivalent, feelings and attitudes toward themselves and other persons who are important to them. What determines the preeminent valence of this feeling or affect is the degree to which affection, tenderness, and love prevail or are overwhelmed by angry reactions to frustration and deprivation (Stone, 1971).

All the psychosexual and psychoaggressive components of organized experience and attitudes coexist in a hierarchical organization. When we speak of oral, anal, and phallic phases, we are referring to the dominant, or major, ways in which these experiences and attitudes are organized along a developmental continuum. The orality patterns are organized for taking in or incorporating and fit the rhythm of nutrition and alimentation. Anality patterns emphasize functions of absorption, retention, and expulsion and have a more definite end point in terms of buildup and discharge of drive tensions. The phallic-genital phase, with its emphasis on penetrating and being penetrated, utilizes oral and anal fantasies and gratifications, as in foreplay, to move toward genitally organized fantasies and gratifications in its hierarchical assertion of adult sexuality.

Drive-tension discharge can be experienced passively or actively, which adds another dimension to our understanding of the flexibility of the instinctual drives. The child's ability to become active where, formerly, he was passive, as in motility, eating, and washing, is another continuum along which instinctual drives are observed.

As development progresses, the instinctual drives which threaten to tyrannize the young child's behavior gradually come under the domination of the ego's regulatory capacities. As this balance is estab-

5. For a later view, see Kris, 1951.

lished, the child becoming adult increasingly finds a more satisfying balance between adapting to the world into which he or she was born and changing that world so as to make it a more satisfactory one for him- or herself and for the children that may follow.

INSTINCTUAL DRIVES AND THE PSYCHOANALYTIC SITUATION

The concept of instinctual drive has a central role in the psychoanalytic situation and in psychoanalytic technique. Because of their constant demands, the drives and their derivatives continually press for representation and discharge. As the drives press for discharge, they simultaneously evoke the defensive, integrating, synthesizing, and reality-testing functions of the ego. The psychoanalyst, familiar with the nature and vicissitudes of the drives and their modes of seeking representation and discharge, has an indispensable aid in following the path of the wishes and fantasies instigated by the drives as they press from unconscious to preconscious and conscious representation. Listening to the ebb and flow of the analysand's associations, the analyst is able to note the points of interruption or shift in the line of thought that indicate a resistance that may be followed by the institution of a defense. The analyst may then be able to identify the wish or drive derivative that has activated the ego's response and so be in a position to frame and time interventions or interpretations that address the conflict from the standpoint of drive and defense.

All this is under the powerful sway of the transference, which is dynamically central in the psychoanalytic situation and the analysis. The transference, too, needs to be viewed in terms of the instinctual drives. In the regressive atmosphere of the psychoanalytic situation, with the patient turning to the analyst for help and with the suspension of active censorship in free association, the instinctual wishes and needs of the analysand, being more freely mobile, take the analyst as an object, directing the instinctual aims and the resistances and defenses against them at the analyst. This gives to long-standing neurotic conflicts an immediacy and direct relevance to current mental life, making it possible to bring them to consciousness. The ego can then bring its mature functioning to bear on resistances, defenses, and symptoms that were set in place at a time when the ego was immature or overwhelmed by a difficult or traumatic reality and by the internal stress from the instinctual drives.

SUMMARY

The concept of instinctual drives is central to psychoanalysis as a genetic–dynamic depth psychology. A translation of the German word *Trieb*, "instinctual drive" is to be distinguished from the concept of instinct as used in biology. Instinctual drive is a psychological concept referring to impelling, motivating forces arising from the body's metabolic activities, which appear in mental life in the form of their derivatives and transformations—wishes, fantasies, and behaviors. Thus, the daily and epochal changes, the ebbing and flowing of metabolic interactions with the mind, lead to the assumption of a psychic drive tension that has an impelling motivational impact on cognitive and affectual mental states. In turn, these have a significant and sustaining influence on behavior. The energy implicit in this motivating force is not physical but an operational concept that enables the psychoanalytic observer to follow the transformations of the drives in relation to their impetus, aim, object, and vicissitudes, linking and ordering an otherwise bewildering array of psychological phenomena.

In line with clinical observation, the instinctual drives are divided into two primal groups, sexual and aggressive. Historically, the concept of sexual drives was vital to the understanding of psychosexual development and its relation to neurosis and perversion. The introduction of the concept of aggression as an innate, independent drive led to new clinical insights, which underscored the importance of aggression in relation to unconscious guilt feelings and led to an understanding of the dynamic functions of the superego and the energy necessary for fueling maturation, development, and the defense mechanisms of the ego.

Nowhere is the concept of instinctual drive more useful than in the psychoanalytic situation itself, where it is indispensable to an understanding of transference and where the relationship between the drives, ever pressing for representation and discharge, and resistance and defense provide a reliable guide to the psychoanalyst in his or her interventions and interpretations.

REFERENCES

Bibring, E. (1941). The development and problems of the theory of instincts. *Int. J. Psychoanal.*, 22:102–131.

Brenner, C. (1982). *The Mind in Conflict.* New York: Int. Univ. Press.

Freud, A. (1960). Discussion of Dr. John Bowlby's paper [Grief and mourning in infancy and early childhood]. *Psychoanal. Study Child,* 15:53–62.

———. (1971). Remarks made at the Twenty-Seventh Congress of the International Psychoanalytical Association, Vienna.

———. (1972). Comments on aggression. *Int. J. Psychoanal.,* 53:163–172.

Freud, S. (1905). *Three Essays on the Theory of Sexuality. SE,* 7:125–243.

———. (1915). Instincts and their vicissitudes. *SE,* 14:111–140.

———. (1920). *Beyond the Pleasure Principle. SE,* 18:7–64.

———. (1926). *Inhibitions, Symptoms and Anxiety. SE,* 20:77–175.

———. (1930). *Civilization and Its Discontents. SE,* 21:59–145.

Greenacre, P. (1960). Regression and fixation. *J. Amer. Psychoanal. Assn.,* 8:703–723.

Hartmann, H. (1948). Comments on the psychoanalytic theory of instinctual drives. *Psychoanal. Q.,* 17:368–388.

———. (1955). Notes on the theory of sublimation. *Psychoanal. Study Child,* 10:9–30.

Hartmann, H., & Loewenstein, R. M. (1962). Notes on the superego. *Psychoanal. Study Child,* 17:42–81.

Hartmann, H., Kris, E., & Loewenstein, R. M. (1949). Notes on the theory of aggression. *Psychoanal. Study Child,* 3/4:9–36.

Jacobson, E. (1964). *The Self and the Object World.* New York: Int. Univ. Press.

Kris, E. (1947). The nature of psychoanalytic propositions and their validation. In *Freedom and Experience,* ed. S. Hook & M. R. Konwitz, pp. 239–259. Ithaca, N.Y.: Cornell Univ. Press.

———. (1951). Some comments and observations on early autoerotic activities. *Psychoanal. Study Child,* 6:95–116.

Solnit, A. J. (1970). A study of object loss in infancy. *Psychoanal. Study Child,* 25:257–272.

———. (1972). Aggression. *J. Amer. Psychoanal. Assn.,* 20:435–450.

Stone, L. (1971). Reflections on the psychoanalytic concept of aggression. *Psychoanal. Q.,* 40:195–244.

Waelder, R. (1960). *Basic Theory of Psychoanalysis.* New York: Int. Univ. Press.

George H. Wiedeman, M.D.

26
___

SEXUALITY

The psychoanalytic theory of sexuality is based on Freud's original discoveries, published in his epoch-making monograph *Three Essays on the Theory of Sexuality* (1905). It derives from (1) clinical observations of neurotic and sexually deviant patients; (2) Freud's self-analysis; (3) the discovery of repression and the dynamic effects of the unconscious; (4) the recognition of childhood sexuality and amnesia for the events of early childhood, including manifestations of sexuality; (5) Freud's thorough grounding in the scientific thought of his time, especially in neurophysiology; and (6) his encyclopedic knowledge of the humanities. Freud's original discoveries represented a scientific breakthrough in the exploration of sexuality. Until then, with few exceptions, this topic had been considered beyond the pale of serious scientific discourse. Psychoanalysis opened the way to subsequent observations and research on sexuality.

From an analytic point of view, sexuality is not only a sequence of behaviors and sensations leading to orgastic satisfaction of adults; a great many other manifestations of sensuality in children and adults are part of sexual life and development. Freud formulated a comprehensive theory of sexuality that represents a synthesis of psychological, physiological, and sociological factors relevant to the topic. In editions of the *Three Essays* following the first, he added new material and changed parts of the original text, taking into account new data as they be-

came available. Findings of the last decades must be integrated into psychoanalytic theory. Some of them were anticipated or implied in Freud's writings.

BIOLOGICAL ASPECTS OF SEXUALITY

In the *Three Essays* Freud (1905) expressed his intent to investigate sexuality independently of biology, even though biology lies on its borders, but he was unable to realize his intention to separate the psychological from the physiological aspects of sexuality. In his writings there are many references to somatic and physiological processes basic to sexuality, understood in the light of the research results that were available to him, many of which have been superseded by more recent discoveries. Freud was ahead of his time in some of his assumptions—for instance, when he made suggestions about "chemical substances," that is, hormones, that play an important part in sexuality.

A concept that Freud espoused strongly was the bisexuality of the human being. This term describes a constitutional predisposition that, interacting with the environment, leads to the presence of male and female somatic and masculine and feminine psychological attributes in the same individual. Bisexuality subsequently acquired several other meanings, the most important ones being the capacity of some persons to engage in sexual relations with members of the same and the opposite sex; the ability of both sexes to acquire masculine and feminine attributes through identification; the fact that in heterosexuals latent or unconscious and largely sublimated homosexual impulses are present and that, correspondingly, heterosexual tendencies exist in homosexuals, consciously and unconsciously (Freud, 1920). Until recently the biological substrate of bisexuality was hardly known. Our present state of knowledge is more advanced, even though future investigations are likely to establish new data on the physiological basis of sexuality and bisexuality.

The biological determination of sex originally depends on the presence of specific sex chromosomes in the fertilized ovum: XX in the female and XY in the male. For the first five weeks of gestation there is no differentiation of the embryo into male or female. In the sixth week of pregnancy the testes begin to develop in the XY embryo; by the eighth they begin to secrete testosterone. The primordial ovary forms later, during the twelfth week of gestation, in the XX embryo. Aside from producing testosterone, the fetal testes secrete a Mullerian duct-inhibiting substance that prevents the formation of a uterus, Fallopian tubes, and the upper part of a vagina. Testosterone transforms the Wolffian duct into the internal and external male reproductive organs. If the primordial gonads are experimentally removed in higher animals, the fetal hormonal link in the developmental chain is eliminated, and the embryo will differentiate as a female, regardless of chromosomal sex.

Occasionally, metabolic errors occur in XY fetuses, when either the production of testosterone does not take place or testosterone (androgen) insensitivity is already present during early gestation. In these instances the chromosomally male XY fetus will turn anatomically into a female. If the insensitivity to androgen is incomplete, the XY fetus may be born with ambiguous-looking genitals such that the phallus cannot be distinguished from a clitoris; other transitional hermaphroditic (intersex) anomalies may also be due to androgen insensitivity. Some abnormal chromosomal combinations (XXY, XO, and so on) show anatomical mixing of the two sexes along with other organic deformities and mental disorders. In the female fetus with the normal XX chromosomal combination but afflicted with the adrenogenital syndrome, abnormally functioning suprarenal glands produce excessive amounts of androgenic substances that lead to virilization of the female fetus, which may be born with an enlarged clitoris or even with a penis, although the internal genitals are normally female.

Once the primordial ovary or the testes are formed, the sex chromosomes have no influence on further sexual development. After the sixth week of gestation and throughout life the hormonal balance determines the somatic and physiological aspects of sexual dimorphism. In the adult, testosterone is considered to be the major biological stimulus of the sexual drive, influencing its intensity in both sexes. In men, deficiency of testosterone or administration of estrogen leads to decreased sexual drive and even impotence. In women, the cyclic hormonal changes that determine ovulation and the whole menstrual cycle are complex; there appears to be increased sexual drive around the time of ovulation, when the testosterone level is higher than at other times of the cycle.

Sexual dimorphism of the central nervous system is currently being investigated. The female cyclic versus the male noncyclic structural organization of the hypothalamus is an established fact (Money & Ehrhardt, 1972, pp. 57–64). The presence of groups of brain cell receptors for androgen, estrogen, and progestin makes it certain that male–female differences of the central nervous system are, to begin with, determined by the balance of the sex hormones (MacLusky & Naftolin, 1981). The correlation of hormonal changes during the menstrual cycle with changes in mood, fantasies, and overt behavior, as observed in analysis, has been described by Benedek (1963).

After birth, organic factors, which determine somatic dimorphism, remain active, but the closest human sociocultural and physical environment of the growing child, usually the family, becomes decisive in the evolution of sexual and gender identity, in object relationships and object choice, and in the cognitive and affective and other lines of development. There remains, of course, a constant interaction between biological and environmental factors. At times it is difficult to estimate with any degree of accuracy the contribution of the constitutional versus the environmental, but Freud's postulate that the two are complementary retains its validity. More recent data have clarified the fact that there is a sequence of basic factors that is essential to the development of somatic, psychological, and behavioral dimorphism through successive stages. First the chromosomal inheritance, then the hormonal balance, is the decisive somatic factor. The specifically human psychological dimensions of sexual dimorphism— gender identity, object choice, and so forth—are shaped primarily by the environment. The prerequisite for the establishment of adult genitality is the freedom from serious fixations and developmental arrests and a satisfactory resolution not only of oedipal but also of adolescent conflicts. This will be taken up in subsequent sections.

EARLY PSYCHOSEXUAL DEVELOPMENT

Human sexuality follows a maturational timetable that can be observed in every human being from infancy to adulthood. According to the genetic (or historical) point of view, developmental stages follow the epigenetic principle that biological and psychological growth advances according to a regularly observed ground plan (Erikson, 1959, pp. 52–59). Various erogenic (or erotogenic) zones have their time of ascendancy and dominance. They are centers of sensuous and pleasurable sensations that are prevalent during the different periods of psychosexual development. The earlier stages are succeeded by later ones, without, however, being deprived of their sensuous significance altogether. The transition from one stage to the next depends on the interplay of biological, maturational, and environmental factors; therefore, the ages at which changes from one stage to the next occur vary. Moreover, the stages are overlapping as well as sequential. From birth until about eighteen months the oral zone—lips, mouth, and tongue—is dominant. This is followed by the dominance of the anal zone—anus, rectum, and buttocks—from about eighteen months to three years of age. Evidence of the erogenous importance of the anal and urethral zones already appears prior to the age of eighteen months, however. Then, from between two and a half and three until five to six years the phallic zone—external genitals in both sexes—takes over as the leading erogenous zone.

As the sexual drive proceeds through the various stages of maturation and development, its gratification is at first largely autoerotic, achieved through stimulation of one's own body. During the oral phase, sensuous—in the broad sense, erotic or libidinal—gratification is at first associated with the fulfillment of nutritional needs through sucking, usually leading to relaxation and sleep. Aside from serving an indispensable physiological function, sucking, a pleasurable, rhythmically repeated activity, becomes erotically gratifying in the absence of food intake; stimulation of the mouth and the circum-oral area serves sensuous needs and reduces tension. The infant discovers the pleasures of sucking and mouthing his or her fingers, thumbs, toes, and a great many inanimate objects. As the oral period advances, oral-aggressive elements are added to the oral-erotic ones. This aggression may be turned against the self—that is, become autoaggression (A. Freud, 1951). Some of the most overt self-directed manifestations of aggression are rhythmic rocking and head banging during the second year of life. These mostly occur in response to frustration and impotent anger. If relations between a steady mothering person and the infant are minimal or nonexistent, as in many orphanages in the past, early genital play may be absent altogether. This is an indication of severe developmental arrest, with concomitant blocking of other developmental lines (Spitz & Wolff, 1949). Later on, oral fixations may lead to a variety of autoerotic and autoaggressive types of behavior, such as forced vomiting, rumination, nail biting, and thumb sucking (Millican et al., 1975), and may contribute to stammering. Along with the libidinal, other developmental lines—of object relations, gender identity, the ego, and the superego—proceed at the same time, influencing and being influenced by the evolution of sexuality.

As with the oral zone, the erogenic significance of the anal area is also connected with a vital physiological function—namely, elimination of the stool. The fecal column stimulates the erogenic mucous membrane of the bowel and is a "forerunner" of the penis during the anal period (Freud, 1918, p. 84). Withholding stools in defiance of the child-caring person demonstrates a clinging to anality; relinquishing the stool becomes a gift and sign of affection (Freud, 1917, p. 130). An unconscious equation of stool = penis = baby is established, and the giving up of feces becomes the prototype of castration (Freud, 1918, p. 84). This equation may remain an important element in the unconscious and may contribute to fantasies of anal birth and to the sexual desire for anal penetration. The assumption that the anus is a genital opening through which babies are born is based on the powerful anal sensations of the small child and the lack of a correct anatomical understanding and may persist in the unconscious alongside the correct anatomical knowledge of the older child or adult (Freud, 1908).

Urethral erotism, originally described by Abraham (1917), appears prior to the phallic-oedipal period. In the course of development, urethral erogeneity contributes to the formation of certain character traits, mainly ambition, competitiveness, and shame (Fenichel, 1945, p. 492). Urination may become connected with fantasies of active penetration and of damaging and destroying the object. It may become the equivalent of masturbation; wetting the bed in sleep or clothes during waking hours may become part of autoerotic gratifications (ibid., 1945, pp. 68–69). Passive "letting flow" can be a contributing factor to *ejaculatio praecox* in the adult man (Abraham, 1917). In some sexual perversions fantasies and practices of urinating at, or being urinated on, by sexual partners play an important role. This shows the persistence of urethral erotism.

Recent infant observation has demonstrated that anality is already evident between twelve and fifteen months. Urinary and phallic awareness usually follows anality by two to three months (Roiphe & Galenson, 1981, p. 232). Between the fifteenth and nineteenth months an "early genital phase" emerges as an "endogenous precipitate of anal and urethral awareness" (p. 272). Pleasurable urethral retention and letting go, analogous to manifestations of anal erotism, have been observed.

Testicles and the scrotal sac as important areas of sexual sensations were neglected until the 1960s in favor of an exclusive stress on the erotic significance of the penis (Bell, 1965). The contraction of the *tunica dartos* and cremaster muscles, leading to testicular retraction, represents a response to anxiety related to identification with the female and toilet training (Bell et al., 1971). Glenn (1971) discussed scrotal and testicular masturbation and their related fantasies.

Prior to the phallic-oedipal phase, awareness of the genitals and arousal occur in both sexes around the age of eighteen months. At the same time, anatomical differences are also discovered (Roiphe, 1968; Tyson, 1982; Galenson & Roiphe, 1976, 1980). The boy becomes aware of his penis even earlier, usually in the latter part of the first year. In the second year, with the increasing dominance of the anal zone and the gradual acquisition of bowel and bladder control, urethral erotism becomes manifest. During the "early genital phase" between fifteen and nineteen months of age, the girl shows a response to genital differences which leads to a transient sense of envy in relation to the boy's visible genitals and his ability to urinate standing up (Galenson & Roiphe, 1976).

When the child reaches the phallic-oedipal stage, the genitals become the focal point of sexual self-stimulation. Although the term "masturbation" is used at times in analytic literature in regard to infantile genital play, it is preferable to reserve it to the type of activity that results in sexual pleasure through volitional and rhythmic self-stimulation of the genitals (Marcus & Francis, 1975, p. 4). During the phallic-oedipal stage, object-related fantasies more and more generate and accompany sexual arousal and gratification.

When Freud published the *Three Essays on the Theory of Sexuality* (1905), he introduced the term "component or partial drives" (pp. 166–171); these are derived from the erogenic zones, including the oral, anal, urethral, and genital. But he also included the eyes and the skin musculature as erogenic areas related to the paired drives voyeurism-exhibitionism and sadism-masochism. In the adult, sexuality is organized under the dominance of genitality, while in childhood the component drives hold sway and are relatively independent of one another; the child is, as it were, "polymorphously perverse." Yet Freud differentiated the oral, anal, and genital drives as being under the "preponderating dominance of erotogenic zones" (pp. 191–192), whereas voyeurism-exhibitionism and sadism-masochism "from the very first involve other people" (p. 192). A comprehensive discussion of this difference between the theory of component drives and the theory of instinctual drives in general is contained in an article by Compton (1981). One should add that the oral, anal, urethral, and genital erogenous zones are correlated with specific psychosexual phases and successively achieve a degree of preeminence in the course of development. The same cannot be claimed for the eyes and the skin. These are perceptual modalities, like the auditory, olfactory, and gustatory ones. Experiences based on all the senses play an important role in sexual arousal and gratification. Regression to pre-oedipal sexuality is also frequently observed during latency and adolescence.

Before proceeding further, a brief comment is in order on the use of the terms "genital" and "pregenital," "phallic" and "pre-phallic." Originally Freud used the term "genital" to describe the dominant erogenic zone during the oedipal stage. To differentiate this early period from that of adult genitality, the term "phallic" was introduced. But the term "pre-phallic," to designate the pre-oedipal dominant erogenic zones, did not take hold, and "pregenital" is used to characterize what are actually pre-phallic stages of sexuality. More recently Roiphe and Galenson (1981, p. 274) have applied the term "early genital phase" to the period from sixteen until nineteen months of age.

Masturbatory patterns develop during the early genital phase. At this time girls appear more vulnerable to castration reactions than boys, who show exhibitionistic pride urinating standing up and tend to deny the observed anatomical differences between themselves and the girls. Paternal availability plays an important role in helping the boy establish a phallic body image in the second year of life.

Freud assumed that there was a "complete identity of the pre-Oedipus phase in boys and girls" (1931, p. 241). According to the classical analytic assumption, sexual identity or identification occurs as a consequence of the resolution of the oedipus complex. In another context Freud (1933) warned not to consider the development of femininity as determined by the woman's sexual function alone.

The introduction of the term "gender identity" into analytic thinking and literature in the 1960s contributed to a clearer understanding of the evolution of both masculinity and femininity. "Gender identity" was anticipated by Freud (1920) when he spoke of three sets of "characters" that determine psychosexual development: physical sexual characters, mental sexual characters, and kind of object choice. "Physical sexual characters" are reflected in the mind as the "body ego" (p. 170). Stoller (1968, p. 10) pointed out that "mental sexual characters" come closest to what at present would be termed "gender identity." Based on his extensive research, he formulated the concepts of gender identity, core gender identity, and gender role and brought them to the attention of the analytic community. The assumption that sexual identification or identity follows the resolution of the oedipus complex does not take into account the important contribution of pre-oedipal factors in the genesis of sexual identity, which, of course, also has anatomical and physiological roots. Freud referred to the latter as "physical sexual characters." Gender identity primarily has psychosocial connotations and is a bridge between the bio-psychological and the social. The adjectives referring to sex are "male" and "female"; those referring to gender are "masculine" and "feminine." The fundamental conviction, the core gender identity, "I am a boy" or "I am a girl," is firmly established by the age of three, at the beginning of the phallic phase. It remains almost unshakable throughout life (Stoller, 1968, p. 72).

The assignment or ascription of core gender identity by parents or other care-taking adults begins at birth and corresponds to the perceived anatomical structure of the child's genitals. The growing child is exposed to myriad verbal and nonverbal cues indicating what is male or female. Consciously and unconsciously, the adult's attitudinal, emotional, and physical approach to the child is different, depending on whether he or she is a boy or a girl. Gender identity, in its full complexity, evolves through all the developmental phases. The overt behavior in relation to others that expresses gender identity constitutes gender role. "Role," originally a sociological term, has been used to classify the social features of behavior, including those indicating gender. The sense of self and of gender identity and gender role presupposes the achievement of object constancy, the capacity for separate mental representation of self and objects. This takes place during the period of separation-individuation (Mahler, 1963). During the same period, self and object representations are formed. In addition, the child acquires role-relationship representations that express the interactions between himself and others through an "inner dialogue" (Sandler & Sandler, 1978). The child actually learns both sides of this dialogue and both gender roles, but, in line with the biological sex and

core gender identity, one or the other will be "brain-coded" as positive and fit to use, the other as negative and unfit to use (Money & Ehrhardt, 1972). Positive and negative coding is congruent with, but more circumscribed than, the analytic terms "cathexis" and "countercathexis."

It should be mentioned here that masculine and feminine aspects of gender identity and role also depend on the historical sociocultural environment. Gender identity is a postnatal development, independent of the chromosomal and anatomical sex (Money & Ehrhardt, 1972; Stoller, 1968). Exceptions have occasionally been reported, as when an XY boy with ambiguous genitals was brought up as a girl but rejected the ascription of feminine gender identity during adolescence under the influence of a "biological force," most likely due to the changed pubertal hormonal balance that impinges on the central nervous system (Stoller, 1968, pp. 65–66).

THE INFLUENCE OF OBJECTS AND STRUCTURAL DEVELOPMENT ON SEXUALITY

The biological basis of sexuality, the successive stages of psychosexual evolution, the formation of gender identity, and the psychic structural changes consequent to object relations combine to shape sexuality. Object relations and choice of sexual object undergo a developmental sequence that is parallel to, and determined by, the various other interacting developmental lines.

A favorable mother–child relationship is essential for the process of separation-individuation, the establishment of body boundaries, and a gender-appropriate body image. The presence of a strong father is important in helping the child to reduce the intensity of the symbiotic ties to the mother so as to progress toward individuation-separation and to master the rapprochement phase.

During the early phallic-oedipal phase, at about two and a half three years of age, the boy shows a prevalence of narcissistic elements, and the triadic oedipal situation is not yet fully evident. The boy is exhibitionistic and consolidates his body image (Tyson, 1982). He also shows breast envy and expresses wishes to possess and nurse a baby (pp. 65–66). The girl, during the early phallic-oedipal phase, shows "a second peak of the experience of envy" (Greenacre, 1953). Feminine core gender identity, however, has already been established prior to this time. The wish for a baby and preoccupation with sex differences exist simultaneously with penis envy. If there is no disturbance in the girl's prephallic object relationships and the parents encourage her femininity, she will be able to give up her phallic envy and establish an oedipal love relationship with her father. In classical analytic writings, penis envy was considered to be an essential factor in the formation of the girl's femininity. On the whole, the present analytic view is that penis envy cannot be considered the decisive element in the development of feminine gender identity, since that is already established prior to the phallic-oedipal stage (Blum, 1976, p. 186). It is worth mentioning here that boys experience envy of the father's big penis, comparing it to their own small one. Most analysts have encountered adult male patients whose preoccupation with the supposedly small size of their penises reflects these developmental vicissitudes.

During the pre-oedipal stages of development, the boy's and the girl's main love object is the mother. The girl subsequently shifts from her strong attachment to the mother to assume the oedipal loving relationship with the father, whereas the boy's attachment to his mother progresses from the pre-oedipal attachment to oedipal love. Concurrently, jealousy and even hostility develop in the relation to the parent of the same sex. These negative feelings coexist with attachment, affection, and dependence on the parent of the same sex and result in an ambivalence that is manifested in the feelings, fantasies, and behavior of the young child. The boy is confronted by an important task: namely, to reinforce his masculine gender identity and assume the male role. He therefore has to "disidentify" with the mother. The girl, however, has the task of shifting from her mother as the primary love object to a new one: namely, the father.

The term "phallic" refers to the heightened sexual response of the external genitalia in both sexes. Though the phallic phase precedes the oedipal, the designation "phallic-oedipal" is often used from an object relations perspective to indicate the marked shift in the relation to the parents and in the child's fantasy life. At first the boy does not realize that girls have external genitals that are different from his. When he discovers that they do not possess a penis, he often develops the fantasy that they will grow one later. Similar fantasies are encountered in girls as well, after they discover that they lack the boy's external genitals.

The boy also develops phallic wishes with some vague ideas of penetrating the mother. This is connected with strong phallic sensations. He also has hostile impulses and fantasies to rid himself of the father and, in line with the talionic principle, expects retribution from the father that would involve loss of the prized pleasure-giving organ; this is the main cause for castration anxiety. Castration threats are not usually expressed directly by parents but, rather, in symbolic and jocular form and by educational measures prohibiting exhibition of the penis and masturbation. Eventually the boy masters his castration anxiety by identifying with his father or a suitable substitute and idealizing him, thereby establishing the basic strictures of the superego: prohibition of both killing and incest.

Under the impact of her realization that she lacks a penis, the little girl develops fantasies that she has lost her penis, or that a penis may still grow, or that it is hidden somewhere inside her body. A narcissistic investment in an illusory penis may be so strong that the castration fear changes into fear of a destruction of the imagined internal organ (Jacobson, 1976, p. 528). Fantasies about an imaginary phallus have roots not only in the pre-phallic but also in later phases of development. Equating the whole body with the phallus may also fulfill the wish for a penis in an illusory fashion (Lewin, 1933). It is a post-phallic regression that leads to the genitalization of the whole body. Many males, on an unconscious level, have the conviction that the female possesses an internal phallus. If the male acquires the fantasy of equating his whole body with a phallus, it is sometimes due to strong feminine identification (Lewin, 1933, p. 37).

In the girl, hostile impulses toward the mother are enhanced during the oedipal period. The mother is blamed for the girl's lack of a penis. She also becomes the competitor for the affection of the father, from whom, the girl hopes, she will get a baby. The hostility toward the mother leads to guilt feelings. Eventually the girl's femininity is enhanced by identification with the mother.

According to Freud, the oedipus complex in the boy succumbs to destruction (*Untergang*) due to overwhelming castration fear. In the girl, Freud maintained that the oedipus complex "is not destroyed, but created, by the influence of castration" (Freud, 1931, p. 230)—that is, the perception that she lacks a penis. Eventually the wish for a penis is replaced by the wish for a baby (p. 128), and the oedipus complex is resolved, although more gradually than in the boy. Most analysts now believe that the oedipus complex in boys is not destroyed at the end of the oedipal phase but is resolved in the course of the subsequent stages of psychosexual development.

The child normally experiences attachment to and love for both parents. A prevalence of sexual feelings for the parent of the same sex, with jealousy toward the parent of the opposite sex, constitutes the "negative Oedipus complex" and reflects the original bisexuality of the child (Freud, 1923, p. 33). It may persist and contribute to sexual disturbances and homosexual object choice. An overly strong oedipal attachment to the parent of the opposite sex, a very strong positive oedipal complex, may lead to sexual inhibitions and potency disorders and may also contribute to homosexual object choice by extending the incest taboo to all those of the opposite sex. The outcome of the oedipal phase may be an "intermediate" resolution between the positive and negative complexes—that is, one or the other having greater weight and force. What is observed are series of resolutions of the oedipus complex (Freud, 1923, p. 34). The phallic-oedipal phase represents, as it were, a rehearsal for eventual adult genital primacy, early phallic dominance being limited by the physical and psychological immaturity of the small child.

The oedipal stage is followed by the latency period, a time of relative sexual quiescence, from about the age of five to six until twelve. Freud (1925) observed that latency was not absolute but that its degree depended on the sociocultural milieu of the growing child. Sexual latency may even be completely absent (Freud, 1916–17, p. 326). Socially sanctioned sexual activity during latency has been observed in some Stone Age tribal cultures that survived in isolated geographical locations till the twentieth century. The latency period is not a uniform state. Ego functions, interpersonal relations (object relations), sexuality, and other developmental lines evolve, interacting with one another.

Bornstein (1951) subdivided latency into two phases: early, from five to eight, and late, from eight to eleven. During the early period the danger of oedipal-incestuous strivings and fantasies is still great. It usually leads to anal-regressive manifestations in boys and reaction formations in girls. In the second phase, manifestations of anality are usually replaced by socially approved modes of behavior. Sexually segregated groups are formed. Late latency merges into preadolescence at ten to eleven years, when the initial pubertal changes occur. Puberty, the somatic and physiological progression from childhood to adulthood, occurs about one year earlier in girls than in boys. It is due to hormonal changes that lead to the growth of sexual organs, the establishment of secondary sexual characteristics, a bodily growth spurt, and the establishment of an adult physique.

Adolescence is the time of affective, cognitive, sexual, and psychosocial changes leading from childhood to adulthood. It may be limited to a brief rite of passage, as in early, "primitive" societies, or last several years, as in the industrialized societies of the present era, until the age of eighteen to nineteen years. During adolescence the dominance of the genital zone is ordinarily completed.

It is not possible to present the specific vicissitudes of psychosexual development during latency and adolescence in this chapter. During latency, modifications of the original pregenital and oedipal manifestations of sexuality take place. During adolescence, oedipal and pregenital impulses are awakened and mobilize various defenses and acting out. Derivatives of the oedipal complex profoundly influence the shape of adult sexuality in terms of aims, choice of objects, and functional sexual adequacy.

VARIATIONS OF PSYCHOSEXUAL DEVELOPMENT

Repression, reaction formation, and sublimation of early sexuality play a crucial role in the final shape of a person's sex life and character formation. Yet, oral, anal, and urethral erogeneity, subject to greater or lesser modifications in the course of development, remain of considerable erotic significance throughout life. This is expressed in the adult in sexual foreplay, fantasies, jokes, and so forth. The contribution of early sexuality to sexual inhibitions and deviations will be discussed next.

Vicissitudes of early development may lead to an uncertain sense of gender identity and to an inability to fulfill one's gender role. The persistence of strong erogeneity of the pregenital zones, the perseverance of primitive mechanisms, the inability to postpone gratification, and other features are frequently observed in persons whose sexuality is not organized under the dominance of genitality but retains and even emphasizes pregenital components.

Inhibitions and Sexual Dysfunction

Inhibited sexual desire, impotence, and anorgasmia are the most common manifestations of sexual dysfunction. Sexual inhibitions and fears may interfere with adequate sexual potency and response. In the male 10 to 15 percent of potency disorders are due to organic causes of various kinds—for example, diabetes mellitus, traumas affecting the spinal cord, and various neurological illnesses—but 80 to 90 percent are due to psychogenic factors (Kolodny et al., 1979, pp. 507–509). The absence of nocturnal penile erections during dream periods with rapid eye movements (REM) is strongly suggestive of organic pathology. The term "frigidity" in the female has now been replaced for the most part by the more specific term "orgasmic dysfunction" or "anorgasmia." Only 5 percent of women incapable of an orgasmic response have an organic impediment, 95 percent of anorgasmic women showing psychogenic causation (ibid., pp. 544–545).

These percentages indicate organic versus psychogenic causation among those who seek help for sexual problems. The overall distribution of impotence and anorgasmia among the general population is more difficult to ascertain. Men and women who manifest impotence and anorgasmia may be able to achieve orgasm with another partner or through masturbation induced by fantasies and physical stimulation. Masturbation, of course, is not limited to persons with sexual deviations and inhibitions. The age-old beliefs that masturbation causes all kinds of physical and mental disorders and that it is sinful and evidence of moral weakness have not prevented self-stimulation among the majority of children and adults. Spitz (1962) has shown that infants suffering from maternal deprivation do not engage in genital play. A recent estimate maintains that about 95 percent of men and 75 percent of women have at one time or another engaged in masturbation.

Inhibited sexual desire is observed in 35 percent of women and in 16 percent of all men (Kolodny et al., 1979, p. 564). A specific disturbance of sexual life has been described recently but hardly explored analytically: persons subjected to massive sexual traumas as children or as adults, such as incest or rape, may develop a phobic dread, with somatic manifestations of severe anxiety, at even the thought of sexual contact and may avoid any sexual activity. Yet, in some of them sexual arousal, erection, and orgasm may still be preserved (ibid., p. 557). This condition is analogous to traumatic neuroses of nonsexual origin.

Premature ejaculation (ejaculatio praecox) is a potency disturbance in the male characterized by ejaculation either before or shortly after penetration. Men afflicted with this disorder show performance anxiety, observe themselves, and usually assume that they will be disgraced in the eyes of the sexual partner. Shame and loss of self-esteem are then added to the underlying unconscious sources of anxiety and often lead to avoidance of sexual relations and the limiting of sexual activity to masturbation. Retarded ejaculation (ejaculatio retardata) is the converse of premature emissions: an erection can be maintained for a prolonged period during coitus without leading to ejaculation and orgasm. Coitus may then become painful for both partners, especially the woman.

Sexual gratification through coitus may be impossible if the woman is afflicted with dyspareunia or vaginismus. In dyspareunia, intromission of the penis and coital movements cause pain; in vaginismus, a functional spasm of the vaginal and associated pelvic muscles prevents penetration or makes it extremely difficult. Once organic causes for dyspareunia and vaginismus are excluded, these conditions fit dynamically and diagnostically into the group of conversion hysterias; so does the complete or partial anesthesia of the vaginal mucosa and sometimes even of the external genitals.

The original psychoanalytic conception of mature female orgasm postulated the transfer of erotic sensation from the clitoris to the vagina. Masters and Johnson (1966) found that there were common anatomical and physiological manifestations to all orgastic responses, independent of the area and means of stimulation. Any exciting sexual stimulation of the woman first leads to vaginal lubrication. Clitoral response follows, more rapidly if the clitoral body or the mons veneris area is stimulated directly than by stimulation of other erogenic zones—for example, the breasts—or by actual coital movements or by fantasies (pp. 48, 66). The clitoris serves "both as receptor and transformer of sensuous stimuli" (p. 45). From an anatomical and physiological point of view, clitoral and vaginal orgasm are not separate entities (p. 66). The fact that the clitoris is a true homologue of the penis cannot serve as proof of an "immature" clitoral feminine sexual response that is later replaced by a more "mature" vaginal orgastic response.

There are marked variations in the intensity and duration of orgasms (Glenn & Kaplan, 1968). Variations of the subjective "inner experience" depend on various factors: somatic, emotional, environmental, and so on (Heiman, 1968). It is the primacy and emotional investment in the coital experience with a partner that are the "sine qua non of a mature feminine attitude" (Moore, 1968, p. 582). Masters and Johnson (1966) subdivided the sexual act into four stages: excitement, plateau, orgasm, and resolution (see also Kolodny et al., 1979). From the analytic point of view, we are concerned primarily with the "inner experience" of sexual response, which depends on past developmental vicissitudes and on inner conflicts whose contents are largely unconscious.

Sexual Deviations

When Freud (1905) spoke of neuroses being the "negative" of perversions, he stressed the fact that in psychoneuroses the forbidden and defended instinctual impulses lead to the formation of symptoms, while in the sexual deviations at least one of the pregenital impulses is acted out with or without a partner. In this sense a sexual deviation becomes the "positive"—that is, manifest—expression of pre-genital sexuality. With deviant sexuality the adult can still achieve orgastic gratification, whereas the symptom with its "negative" aspect expresses a conflict between instinctual impulse and defense, resulting in a lack of pleasure. As a rule, repression is stronger in neuroses than in sexual deviations as far as the specific instinctual impulses are concerned, but the "positive" side of perversions does not free the sexually deviant person from neurotic symptoms or maladaptive behavior. Often the guilt and the conflicts associated with deviant forms of sexual activity cause considerable distress, especially loss of self-esteem, which is accentuated by social disapproval and legal prohibitions.

Undoubtedly, the deviation from heterosexual to homosexual object choice is the most important variant of sexuality in the human species.*

A total discrepancy between gender identity and anatomical sex results in transsexualism. Transsexuals have the firm conviction, cognitively and affectively, that they belong to the opposite sex; that their bodies, anatomically male or female, do not correspond to what they really are. They have the strongest desire to change from male to female or female to male. The ratio of male to female transsexuals is ten to one.

The population of transsexuals is by no means a homogenous one. One group shows relatively little impairment of ego functions, but there are others who show a primitive personality structure with various disorders. Stoller (1968, 1975) described one group of transsexuals whom he preferred to call "primary transsexuals" (Stoller and Herdt, 1982) and established specific developmental and psychodynamic constellations leading to such primary transsexuality. In the male transsexuals the family constellation shows an extreme closeness of the mother to one of her sons, with skin-to-skin contact up to the fourth or fifth year of life. The mother maximally avoids frustration as far as weaning, toilet training, and restriction of masturbation is concerned. She also tends to dress the boy in girls' clothes, turning him into the "mother's feminized phallus" (Stoller, 1968, p. 120). The father is usually either physically or "dynamically" absent. The deflection of the development of gender identity without other serious apparent disorders is under-

standable in terms of specific parent–child relations, including even the relationship of the transsexual boy's mother to her own parents. The resulting distortion of gender identity is sufficiently extreme not only to suspend castration anxiety but to make castration the goal of one's existence.

The female transsexuals also want to achieve a surgical transformation. The developmental factors are usually absence of the mother and an extremely close relation to the father from early infancy on.

In the diagnostic manual of the American Psychiatric Association, DSM-III (1979), the following sexual deviations were classified as "paraphilias": fetishism, transvestism, zoophilia, pedophilia, exhibitionism, voyeurism, sexual masochism, and sexual sadism. Prior to the publication of DSM-III, paraphilias were designated "sexual perversions," the term usually found in the analytic literature.

Attempts at a scientific, at least descriptive, classification of sexual aberration date back to the nineteenth century. Up to that time, rules concerning acceptable sexual behavior were part of established religious doctrines, and deviations were considered unspeakable crimes akin to heresies. Yet, introduction of a nomenclature did not eradicate the intolerance and contempt of the majority for the sexually deviant. Terms such as "variation," "deviation," "inversion," and, more recently, "paraphilia" did little to mitigate derogatory opinions and attitudes in relation to sexual deviance. What is considered a "normal" aspect of sexuality in one sociocultural environment may be a capital crime in another.

The types of sexuality now considered paraphilias exhibit characteristics that would hardly fall into the range of normality in any social setting. This, of course, does not gainsay the fact that most paraphiliacs are capable of functioning as full-fledged members of society. Yet, in sadomasochism, voyeurism-exhibitionism, pedophilia, and rare perversions, there are strong elements of aggression against the outside world and/or the self. In fetishism, transvestism, and zoophilia, the presence of a human partner can be dispensed with or at least minimized.

Relatively intact functioning of the ego in neuroses, character disorders, or psychoses may coexist with the paraphilias. In order to achieve sexual arousal and eventual orgasm, sexual deviants must reenact in fantasy and/or with a partner one or several components of childhood sexuality. By overemphasizing one component of pregenitality, they maintain the repression of the oedipus complex, castration fear, and guilt feelings that would block sexual pleasure and make orgasm impossible (Fenichel, 1945). Not infrequently, the perverse fantasy may

---

*Editor's note: Because of its importance and current controversy about psychoanalytic views concerning the subject, the editors decided to devote an entire chapter following this one to a full exploration of various aspects. Dr. Wiedeman's much abbreviated discussion of the subject has been omitted for that reason.

serve as the source of sexual arousal, leading to orgasm in the course of seemingly normal coitus with a partner.

Nearly all perversions are characterized by the presence of hostile, aggressive elements. Stoller (1975) maintained that the perversions constitute the "erotic form of hatred." In terms of the formulation based on the second theory of the sexual versus aggressive instinctual drives, one can observe that there is a prevalence or strong presence of aggressive instinctual derivatives and a weakening of the libidinal ones in perversions. This would especially apply to "cryptoperversions" (Stoller, 1975) such as rape, preference for prostitutes, Don Juanism, and nymphomania. Rape is often initiated by immature teenagers and men who feel compelled to prove their "masculinity." Social disorganization that stimulates and often legitimizes aggression, as during wars and political upheavals, contributes to the mass incidence of rape and other types of sadistic acts that the same persons would not have committed under conditions of societal control.

There is a dearth of clinical analytic observations on perversions (paraphilias) other than fetishism, transvestism, and sadomasochism. The aggressive, antisocial, and illegal aspects of perversions are not conducive to analytic treatment and investigation. Descriptions of paraphilias are available in a vast number of articles and books; but they are not illuminating in terms of the origin and etiology of these conditions, since psychodynamic data are absent, and the earliest recollections represent hardly more than screen memories.

After homosexuality, fetishism has been the sexual deviation most thoroughly investigated through analysis. It is nearly always males in whom it is encountered. The fetish is an inanimate object that is found necessary to achieve sexual arousal and orgasm, an object commonly associated with the female body. Women's undergarments, shoes, leather straps, and other articles of clothing are common fetishes. Some fetishes combine female and male attributes—for instance, a soft slipper with a hard, spiked heel. The fetish serves the double purpose of denying and affirming differences between the sexes (Greenacre, 1968). The human partner may be completely replaced by a fetish, and the contact with it, its specific texture, smell, and color are important. On the other hand, the fetish may become the indispensable preliminary to the sexual act with a partner. This applies to some hetero- and homosexual relations.

The basic psychodynamic facts on fetishism were presented by Freud (1927). He clearly recognized that the fetish represents an unconscious substitute for the woman's imaginary penis in the fetishist's mind. The boy assumes that both sexes have a phallus like he does, and he disavows that women do not possess this sensually gratifying and narcissistically invested organ. Full acknowledgment of the penislessness of women—originally of the mother—creates an overwhelming castration anxiety and inhibits sexual arousal and orgasm. The fetishist retains his belief in a female phallus yet at the same time gives it up. He knows the difference between the male and female sexual organs but must recreate a substitute for the fantasied female phallus to accord with his unconscious fantasy. Fetishism shows clearly the coexistence of two incompatible psychic trends, one that takes account of reality, another that disavows and denies reality: this is what Freud called a "psychical split" (1940, p. 202). The heterosexual fetishist is saved by the fetish from becoming an "absolute invert"—that is, exclusively homosexual—in whom castration fear precludes any sexual approach to the "castrated" woman (Freud, 1927). Fetishistic practices among homosexuals are frequently combined with sadomasochism, and leather plays an especially prominent role.

It is characteristic of the development of fetishism, as well as of transvestism, voyeurism, and exhibitionism, that early disturbances in the mother–infant relationship, impairment of object relations in general, and defective body and self images involving the genitals are crucially involved (Greenacre, 1968).

The transitional object (Winnicott, 1953) is almost ubiquitous in infancy but is ordinarily relinquished in childhood. The fetish, which resembles the transitional object in some formal aspects, becomes manifest in adulthood as a means of ensuring sexual functioning. Sexual fetishism, like other sexual deviations, is genetically related to early developmental stages (Greenacre, 1968). Almansi (1979) pointed out that fear of object loss in early life may lead to a hypercathexis and sexualization of the visual function and so constitute one of the elements in the psychogenesis of voyeurism.

Transvestism, the desire to wear, in part or totally, the clothes of the opposite sex—cross-dressing—presupposes a partial disorder of gender identity, but without the desire to change one's genitals to those of the opposite sex. Effeminate male homosexuals may also engage in cross-dressing. Cross-dressing may begin in childhood or in early adolescence (Jucovy, 1979). Transvestites may be heterosexual, homosexual, or asexual. Transvestism is an example of how developmental factors, impinging on the child from early infancy, assume a near complete dominance over somatic-constitutional givens.

Sadomasochism was discussed in Chapter 20 and will not be dealt with here.

SUMMARY

The most salient of the psychoanalytic discoveries and views on sexuality are as follows. Sexuality develops according to a timetable through various stages and in adulthood is organized under the dominance of genitality. This term, in its most basic sense, includes the capacity to engage in physical and affectionate relations with an adult partner. Elements of childhood sexuality become part of sexual foreplay and forepleasure, leading to genital orgastic fulfillment. If elements of childhood sexuality are enhanced through trauma or overgratification, fixations and developmental arrests occur, and the adult may be unable to reach genitality. Orgastic fulfillment is still striven for and is usually achieved, but it depends on pregenital modes, defenses against childhood traumas, and on fantasies whose origins in childhood either are obvious or can be understood through analysis. The most frequent deviation from the usual adult sexual pattern is homosexuality. What is considered normal versus abnormal sex depends on sociocultural factors. Yet in all societies, psychosexual development traverses the various stages, eventually leading to the capacity for genital union, procreation, and assumption of parental tasks. The most comprehensive view of sexuality is derived from the psychoanalytic discoveries initiated by Freud.

REFERENCES

Abraham, K. (1917). Ejaculatio praecox. Rpt. in Selected Papers of Karl Abraham, pp. 280–298. London: Hogarth Press, 1948.

Almansi, R. J. (1979). Scopophilia and object loss. Psychoanal. Q., 48:601–619.

American Psychiatric Association (1979). Diagnostic and Statistical Manual of Mental Disorders. Washington, D.C.

Bell, A. I. (1965). The significance of the scrotal sac and testicles for the prepuberty male. Psychoanal. Q., 34:182–206.

Bell, A. I., Stroebel, C. F., & Prior, D. D. (1971). Interdisciplinary study: scrotal sac and testes. Psychoanal. Q., 40:415–434.

Benedek, T. (1963). An investigation of the sexual cycle in women. Arch. Gen. Psychiat., 8:311–322.

Blum, H. P. (1976). Masochism, the ego ideal, and the psychology of women. J. Amer. Psychoanal. Assn., 76(suppl.):157–192.

Bornstein, B. (1951). On latency. Psychoanal. Study Child, 6:279–285.

Compton, A. (1981). On the psychoanalytic theory of instinctual drives: II. Psychoanal. Q., 50:210–212.

Erikson, E. H. (1959). Identity and the life cycle. Psychological Issues, Monograph 1. New York: Int. Univ. Press.

Fenichel, O. (1945). The Psychoanalytic Theory of Neurosis. New York: Norton.

Freud, A. (1951). Observations on child development. In Writings of Anna Freud, 4:143–162.

Freud, S. (1905). Three Essays on the Theory of Sexuality. SE, 7:130–243.

———. (1908). On the sexual theories of children. SE, 9:205–226.

———. (1910). Leonardo da Vinci and a Memory of His Childhood. SE, 11:59–137.

———. (1914). On narcissism. SE, 14:67–102.

———. (1916–17). Introductory Lectures on Psycho-Analysis. SE, 15 & 16.

———. (1917). On transformations of instinct as exemplified in anal erotism. SE, 17:125–133.

———. (1918). From the history of an infantile neurosis. SE, 17:3–123.

———. (1920). The psychogenesis of a case of homosexuality in a woman. SE, 18:145–172.

———. (1923). The Ego and the Id. SE, 19:3–66.

———. (1925). An Autobiographical Study. SE, 20:3–74.

———. (1927). Fetishism. SE, 21:149–157.

———. (1931). Female sexuality. SE, 21:225–243.

———. (1933). New Introductory Lectures on Psycho-Analysis. SE, 22:3–182.

———. (1940). An Outline of Psycho-Analysis. SE, 23:141–207.

Galenson, E., & Roiphe, H. (1976). Some suggested revisions concerning early female development. J. Amer. Psychoanal. Assn., 24(suppl.):29–57.

———. (1980). The preoedipal development of the boy. J. Amer. Psychoanal. Assn., 28:805–828.

Glenn, J. (1971). Testicular and scrotal masturbation. Int. J. Psychoanal., 50:353–362.

Glenn, J., & Kaplan, E. (1968). Types of orgasm in women. J. Amer. Psychoanal. Assn., 16:549–564.

Greenacre, P. (1953). Penis awe and its relation to penis envy. Rpt. in Emotional Growth, pp. 31–49. New York: Int. Univ. Press, 1981.

———. (1968). Perversions. Psychoanal. Study Child, 23:48–62.

———. (1969). The fetish and the transitional object. Psychoanal. Study Child, 24:144–164.

Heiman, M. (1968). Female sexuality. J. Amer. Psychoanal. Assn., 16:565–568.

Jacobson, E. (1976). Ways of female superego formation and the female castration conflict. *Psychoanal. Q.,* 45:525–538.

Jucovy, M. E. (1979). Transvestism. In *Sexuality,* ed. T. B. Karasu & C. W. Socarides, pp. 223–242. New York: Int. Univ. Press.

Kolodny, R. C., Masters, W. H., & Johnson, V. E. (1979). *Textbook of Sexual Medicine.* Boston: Little, Brown.

Lewin, B. D. (1933). The body as phallus. *Psychoanal. Q.,* 2:24–47.

MacLusky, N. J., & Naftolin, F. (1981). Sexual differentiation of the central nervous system. *Science,* 211:1294–1302.

Mahler, M. S. (1963). Certain aspects of the separation-individuation phase. *Psychoanal. Q.,* 32:1–141.

Marcus, I. M., & Francis, J. J., eds. (1975). Introduction. In *Masturbation from Infancy to Senescence,* pp. 1–8. New York: Int. Univ. Press.

Masters, W. H., & Johnson, V. E. (1966). *Human Sexual Response.* Boston: Little, Brown.

Millican, F., Lourie, R. S., & Dublin, C. C. (1975). Oral autoaggressive behavior and oral fixation. In Marcus & Francis, eds., 1975, pp. 145–160.

Money, J., & Ehrhardt, A. (1972). *Man and Woman, Boy and Girl.* Baltimore: Johns Hopkins Univ. Press.

Moore, B. E. (1968). Psychoanalytic reflections on the implications of recent physiological studies of female orgasm. *J. Amer. Psychoanal. Assn.,* 16:569–587.

Roiphe, H. (1968). On an early genital phase. *Psychoanal. Study Child,* 23:348–368.

Roiphe, H., & Galenson, E. (1981). *Infantile Origins of Sexual Identity.* New York: Int. Univ. Press.

Sandler, J., & Sandler, A.-M. (1978). On the development of object relationships and affects. *Int. J. Psychoanal.,* 59:285–296.

Socarides, C. W. (1978). *Homosexuality.* New York: Aronson.

Spitz, R. A. (1962). Autoerotism reconsidered. *Psychoanal. Study Child,* 22:402–425.

Spitz, R. A., & Wolff, K. M. (1949). Autoerotism. *Psychoanal. Study Child,* 3/4:85–120.

Stoller, R. (1968). *Sex and Gender.* New York: Science House.

———. (1975). *Perversion, the Erotic Form of Hatred.* New York: Pantheon Books.

Stoller, R., & Herdt, G. H. (1982). The development of masculinity. *J. Amer. Psychoanal. Assn.,* 30:29–60.

Tyson, P. (1982). A developmental line of gender identity, gender role, and choice of love object. *J. Amer. Psychoanal. Assn.,* 30:61–86.

Wiedeman, G. H. (1974). Homosexuality. *J. Amer. Psychoanal. Assn.,* 22:651–696.

Winnicott, D. W. (1953). Transitional objects and transitional phenomena. Rpt. in *Collected Papers,* pp. 229–242. New York: Basic Books, 1958.

Jon K. Meyer, M.D.

27

HOMOSEXUALITY

Homosexuality is a difficult subject because it has been so scrutinized, debated, and politicized. Views of homosexuality as an illness, a biological predisposition, a life-style, or a preference are distinguished by lack of consensus (Bell et al., 1981; Meyer, 1985). While such disagreements are by no means limited to our time or to psychoanalysis (Freud, 1905; Stoller et al., 1973; Wilson, 1990), analysis has been seen either as having special knowledge and empathy for homosexuals or as being baldly discriminatory, depending upon the vantage point of the one making the claim.

In recent decades, analysts have largely viewed homosexuality as born in conflict, pathological, and potentially but not easily curable. The question often seemed to be not whether homosexuality could or should be "cured" but the best way to attempt it (Wiedeman, 1962, 1974). But "questions of 'health' and 'illness' have become quite controversial of late" (Wyman, 1989, p. 629). Moreover, these controversies are by no means taking place in a vacuum. Scarcely a week goes by without some reassessment of the place of homosexuality in sports, the military, the professions, and the broader social scene.

A review of what psychoanalysis can and, perhaps, does know about homosexuality is unquestionably timely. In such a review, there is a responsibility for a balanced presentation, which respects the serious challenges to the analytic model but does not disregard fundamental and unique psychoanalytic contributions. The task is to scan the panorama of hypotheses for those that are substantiated by psychoanalytic observation, consistent with fundamental theory, and likely to be enduring.

THE CONTEXT OF THE CONTROVERSY

As noted, the topic of homosexuality is characterized more by controversy than by consensus. Although this has become acute recently, it is not new. The emphasis on sexuality and liberalism toward homosexuality and perversion in Freud's psychology were scandalous to *fin-de-siècle* society. Since sexuality was not only dealt with frankly but was also integral to theory, theoretical rifts (for example, between Freud, Jung, Adler, and Horney) often turned on differing interpretations of its role. Following World War II, psychoanalysis achieved the status of conventional wisdom. Accordingly, exuberant postwar work on sexuality was compared to a psychoanalytic standard that, as may have been appropriate to an expanding clinical discipline, emphasized the pathological. Since the various disciplines involved looked through dissimilar lenses, different observations were inevitable. In any event, categorical statements from all sides marked the deliberations among psychoanalysts, biologists, sociologists, and descriptive psychiatrists. For example, in 1948 Kinsey et al. questioned the pathogenicity of homosexuality. Bieber et al. (1962) took up Kinsey's challenge, responding that the essence of psychoanalytic theories was their assumption that "adult homosexuality is a psychopathological state" (p. 18).

Other analysts, however, cautioned that there were "well-integrated and productive," committed homosexuals who were capable of loving relationships and did not reveal the immature ego traits attributed to them (Panel, 1960, p. 556). It was suggested that the study of such men "might lead to a revision of our concepts of male homosexuality" (ibid.). Even though there were differences among psychoanalysts, Bell and Weinberg (1978) challenged the stereotype of the mentally ill homosexual. Although Stoller (1975a) noted that medicalization had helped destigmatize homosexuality by shifting it from the religious to the natural realm, Bell and Weinberg (1978) believed that heterosexual antipathy toward homosexuals had simply replaced condemnation of homosexual activity as sin with diagnosis as disease. They laid the responsibility squarely at the feet of psychoanalysis, the problematic medical model being "fostered in large part by Freud's view of psychosexual development" (p. 196). They outlined psychosexual development in dogmatic, pathocentric terms and saw psychoanalytic case histories as self-serving. In their view, these stereotypes were disconfirmed by the American Psychiatric Association's declassification of homosexuality as a mental disorder.

Recently, Isay (1989) and R. Friedman (1988) have also commented on the meaning of deleting homosexuality from the nomenclature. Isay saw psychoanalytic emphasis on pathogenic factors as a deleterious social influence, as underlined by "the effective testimony of gays on the social stigmatization of labeling homosexuality a disease" (1989, p. 14). In his view, diagnosis constricted opportunities for self-validation and expression, thereby engendering difficulties that were not psychopathological but reactions to a hostile milieu. For his part, Friedman took psychoanalysis to task for the "weak scientific support for psychoanalytic assumptions" as "illustrated by the recent history of the relationship between psychiatry and psychoanalysis with regard to homosexuality" (1988, p. 270). He saw psychoanalysts as properly held accountable for claims of pathology made from an "inadequate" data base, particularly by contrast with studies such as those by Saghir and Robins (1973) and Hooker (1957, 1972) (Friedman, 1988, p. 270). Similarly, Nadelson advised that homosexuality is not a disease or a mental illness, that psychoanalysis should not confuse dynamic understanding with diagnosis, and that psychoanalysts must be wary of generalizations, because

they see a small, select population (Panel, 1987, pp. 171–172).

In this context it was asked whether biology is not a more important etiological factor than is often assumed (Isay, 1989; R. Friedman, 1988), whether gender and sexual orientations may have conflictual origins but become adynamic and nonconflictual (R. Friedman, 1988), whether the concept of psychic determinism had outlived its usefulness (ibid.), and whether technical modifications might not be indicated in that pathology-oriented, or even dynamic, interpretations could be pernicious (Isay, 1989). Added to these alternative views were the more usual concerns about the utility of different models: object relations, deficit, pre-oedipal, structural, conflictual, or oedipal.

Although the major controversies have tended to focus on male homosexuality, the pre- and postwar women's movements also raised serious questions about psychoanalytic views of female sexuality and the status of female homosexuality (Young-Bruehl, 1990). For example, it was argued that the problematic treatment of female sexuality in early psychoanalytic theory meant that extending such theory to female homosexuality could only compound the problems (Panel, 1987). While Jones was among the first to comment on the "unduly phallo-centric view" of female development (1927, p. 459), more recently Chasseguet-Smirgel also spoke of the "misleading theoretical path which attempts to approach the problems of femininity through the study of male sexuality" (1970, p. 3). Despite attempts to rectify this situation, discussion of female homosexuality has been difficult because both the literature and the clinical experience are limited (Panel, 1962; Socarides, 1988).

In the eyes of some, psychoanalysis has gone from radical innovation to conservative bulwark in terms of its theoretical and clinical position regarding sexuality. Interestingly, psychoanalytic views vis-à-vis medicine were criticized as too liberal in Freud's day, as too identified more recently, and now as too conservative. Perhaps the issue is not so much the expectable divergence between psychoanalysis and other disciplines, due to different methodologies and data, but rather that psychoanalysis has continued to represent its unique observations, while extra-analytic trends in data selection and diagnosis have changed. Nonetheless, important tenets of psychoanalysis have been questioned, including the following: its view of the pathological status of homosexuality; its central, or basic, assumptions; its scientific status as compared with that of biology, sociology, and general psychiatry; the generalizability of its observations; the scope of dynamic understanding; the centrality of conflict and compromise formation; and whether technical revamping is indicated. These are no small questions in psychoanalytic epistemology, and each deserves a monograph of its own. Within the scope of this chapter, however, responses will have to be limited.

BASIC PSYCHOANALYTIC CONCEPTS

It is necessary to abstract basic psychoanalytic concepts, because questions around homosexuality go right to the fundamentals. My view of the fundamentals is similar to that of Guttman (1985), but I recognize that any outline involves selection and exclusion. I will focus on Freud's contributions, because his work, in large measure, began with the study of sexuality, and over a long career the refinement and comprehensiveness of his thought were remarkable.

Consideration of homosexuality was one aspect of a broader effort to understand sexuality, that most unruly of instincts (Freud, 1905), and its central role in the human psyche. Efforts to understand men and women whose eroticism drew them to the same sex began with the *Three Essays* (1905), which introduced the concepts of bisexual freedom to "range equally over male and female objects" (p. 145), infantile sexuality, initial maternal object attachments, the castration complex, the infantile core of adult sexuality, the ubiquity and importance of perverse sexuality, the quantitative rather than qualitative relationship between the deviant and the normal, and the reciprocal relationship between neurosis and deviation. Bisexuality was emphasized as the original condition, from which restrictions "in one direction or the other" (p. 146) led to heterosexuality or homosexuality.

The complemental series, or "etiological equation," suggested that constitution and experience were complementary (Freud, 1895, 1916–17). Freud thought it would be "one-sided" to attribute etiology to either heredity or experience and asserted that "A single pathogenic influence is scarcely ever sufficient; in the large majority of cases a *number* of aetiological factors are required, which support one another" (1906, p. 279). Though he acknowledged the importance of biology, he was reluctant to substitute biological problems for psychological ones, especially given the ample supply of the latter. Homosexuality had been explained as "a feminine brain in a masculine body," but in Freud's view there was "neither need nor justification for *replacing* the psychological problem by the anatomical one" (1905, p. 142; my emphasis).

The strength of psychoanalysis lay in its understanding of "accidental factors" (1905, p. 131), which were themselves complex and blurred the distinctions between illness and health. Freud observed that neurotic illnesses "cannot be sharply differentiated from health" (1906, p. 279) and that they were not to be "taken as proofs of general inferiority" (1910, p. 131). "We know too that we all produce such substitutive [neurotic] structures, and that it is only the number, intensity and distribution which justify . . . the practical concept of illness" (ibid.). Generally speaking, illness and health were regarded as differences of degree rather than distinctions in kind. The distinctions among various manifestations of motivated behavior were also blurred. Although differences among various forms of homosexuality were indisputable, "intermediate examples of every type" led to the conclusion that "we are dealing with a connected series" (1905, p. 138). This view unified the shadings of object choices, gender and sexual identity modifications, and perverse admixtures under the concept of homosexuality, rather than splintering them into multiple "homosexualities."

In a step that defined psychoanalysis not only as an environmental science but also as a science of the mind, Freud suggested that there were internal sexual factors in children, independent of external stimulation. (Even though he later qualified seduction's preemptive role, he never overlooked its importance in the life of children, particularly as regards the mother's seductive function as the stimulator of sexual life [Freud, 1931].) Once the role of internal processes was more fully appreciated, "'infantile sexual traumas' were . . . replaced by the 'infantilism of sexuality'" (1906, p. 275), and the way was opened for a more complete exploration of sexual development.

Over the years, a number of developmental dynamics were reported. Nevertheless, because compromise formations are mutable and are limited only by human inventiveness (Brenner, 1982), it is a practical—and mathematical—impossibility to specify every dynamism. Consequently, my review here is only illustrative, even if the examples it takes are well known, often cited, and demonstrate the vicissitudes of libidinal and aggressive drive derivatives. In 1910 Freud described a special attachment to the mother in the absence of the father, a degree of belief and interest in the mother's penis corresponding to that attachment and a proportional disappointment, disgust, and turning away from her with the fantasy of her castration. In this way, a homosexual man remains attached to a woman and, while appearing to be attracted only to men, "is in fact attracted by women in the same way as a normal man" (1910, p. 100). In discussing a case of female homosexuality, Freud (1920) emphasized the motivations of anger, hate, and revenge based upon disappointment in the positive oedipal rivalry with the mother. This disillusionment, however, was foreshadowed by an insufficiently maternal relationship because of the mother's narcissism and rejection. Jones (1927) suggested that the threatening element in female homosexuality was not merely castration but aphanisis. Regression in light of that threat promoted the crucial dynamics of intense oral eroticism and sadism. In 1922, Freud commented on similar aggressive derivatives in males—namely, jealousy and rivalry toward other men and boys leading to "an exceedingly hostile and aggressive attitude . . . which might sometimes reach the pitch of actual death-wishes" (p. 231). In a reaction formation, rivals might become lovers, while, with further altruistic revision, such dynamics might be linked with well-developed community and social interests.

In 1919 Freud integrated dynamic possibilities hierarchically under the male and female oedipus complexes, which signified not only the conflictual origins of homosexuality but also its place in the spectrum of normality. "The perversion is no longer an isolated fact in the child's sexual life, but falls into its place among the typical, not to say normal, processes of development. . . . It is brought into relation with the child's incestuous love-object, with its Oedipus complex" (p. 192).[1] The notion of the bipotentiality of the oedipus complex as "twofold, positive and negative" (1923, p. 33) was an extension of Freud's original idea of bisexuality. Repression of one or another component left the manifest "positive" or "inverted negative" constellation (pp. 33–34; see also Freud, 1924, 1925). Because of the impoundment of oedipal memories through repression, claims of congenital origins of homosexuality had only limited credibility (1919, p. 193). Whereas an "inverted" complex might serve as the basis of adult homosexuality, it might also remain unconscious in an otherwise unremarkable sexual life. Whatever the vicissitudes, "Analysis shows that in every case a homosexual object-tie was present and in most cases persisted in a *latent* condition" (1940, p. 155). Homosexuality was considered

a negative oedipal compromise formation, although the "negative" term had pejorative connotations not inherent in the idea.

As befitted the complexity of oedipal relationships, the pathways through it were complicated. The path for the male, however, seemed more straightforward: satisfaction of incestuous wishes conflicted with narcissistic investment in the penis, the latter usually taking precedence, and "object cathexes [were] . . . replaced by identifications" (1924, p. 176). On the other hand, female sexuality was a " 'dark continent' " (1926b, p. 212), and Groddeck (1923) noted that it was understandable why the boy took his mother as a love object but unclear how the girl became attached to the opposite sex. Much of the difficulty was related to an assumption that female development was a simple mirror of male development. It was soon realized, however, that the positive oedipus complex in the girl was brought about, rather than ended, by the fantasy of castration. Furthermore, the positive female oedipus complex had "a long prehistory" and was "in some respects a secondary formation" (1925, p. 251), since pre-oedipal attachments to mother were intense, active, and had the characteristics of a negative oedipus complex (1925, 1931). While this tie to mother might set the stage for homosexuality, Deutsch (1944) commented that the primary tie had to be strengthened by triangular disappointments, guilt, or need to make restitution, in order to create the clinical entity. Recognition of the active side of femininity in little girls and the nature of the identificatory processes with mother (Freud, 1931, p. 237) made it necessary to confront the importance of pre-oedipal development. In fact, there was a complementarity whereby the study of men led to recognition of the importance of the oedipus complex and that of women to recognition of the significance of the pre-oedipal period.

While the oedipus complex was seen as the focus of infantile sexual organization, it was soon incorporated within the broader structural model. For our purposes, an important aspect of a structural perspective is that it reminds us of sophisticated structuralizations and functions and the need to consider symptom formation in intricate and flexible ways (Freud, 1923, 1926a). For example, although the ego was described as "a precipitate of abandoned object-cathexes . . . contain[ing] the history of those object-choices," it also had capacities "which decide the extent to which a person's character fends off or accepts the influences of the history of his erotic object-choices" (123, p. 29). The ego concept was strengthened when Freud (1926a) suggested that it functioned to organize symptoms so that they represented important meanings. In 1931 Nunberg ob-

---

1. With regard to the term "perversion," often found objectionable, Freud initially distinguished between "inversion" of sexual object and "perversion" of sexual aim, but very shortly thereafter he referred to both more generically as perversions (1905, pp. 231ff.). This was not simply a matter of loose usage or a reversion to common parlance; it grew out of the idea that both were developmental inhibitions secondary to the effects of disposition, experience, and repression. By 1919, the distinction had been further obscured by the critical relationship of both to oedipal conflict.

served that the synthetic function of the ego integrated rather than simply added disparate elements of the personality. Such observations reemphasized the complex interdependence of fixation and regression in symptom formation (Freud, 1916–17, 1926a; A. Freud, 1965). In other words, what appeared to be developmental arrest or inhibition might be a combination of fixation and regression, representing a range of conflicts.

In 1920 Freud observed that a developmental sequence might appear inevitable retrospectively but be unpredictable prospectively. Limitations on the ability to predict symptom choice or clinical course were reflected in clinical experience and led to restraint in prognostications. The reversal of homosexuality was "never an easy matter," success depending upon "specially favourable circumstances" (p. 151). Even "success" allowed no more than access to the opposite sex through restoration of bisexual functions, providing a choice but by no means determining how it would be exercised.

In light of its views of development and pathogenesis, psychoanalysis was radical in its insistence on a dynamic understanding of homosexuality and its opposition to contemporary notions of degeneracy. It was "most decidedly opposed to . . . separating off homosexuals from the rest of mankind as a group of a special character" (1905, p. 145). The study of unconscious sexuality demonstrated that everyone was not only capable of homosexual object choice but had "in fact made one in their unconscious," a choice that played an important role in both health and illness. Furthermore, "the exclusive sexual interest felt by men for women is also a problem that needs elucidating and is not a self-evident fact" (p. 146). Some may consider these ideas unacceptably simple because they underestimate the differences between unconscious and manifest homosexuality, they link homosexual attachments to illness, and they compare heterosexuality and homosexuality. Nonetheless, the basic assumptions are that commonalities exist between different sexual orientations; that homosexual object choices are ubiquitous, even if they differ as regards access to consciousness and to the ego's executive apparatus; that unconscious data are relevant to explanatory hypotheses; and that heterosexuality also requires explanation.

The dualism of conflict and unity in mental function was a central theme in psychoanalytic observation and theory building (L. Friedman, 1977). Broadly speaking, the examination of homosexuality reflected two viewpoints that are analytically unremarkable but, to nonanalysts, often seen incompatible. On the one hand, Freud adamantly opposed

notions of degeneracy, observing that homosexuality was found in individuals who did not otherwise diverge from the norm and who in fact were of the highest intellect and culture (1905, pp. 138–139). This point was perhaps best reflected in his "letter to a grateful mother" (1951). On the other hand, he insisted on the significance of clinical findings of unconscious anxiety, conflict, and defensive struggles. These views are incompatible within a medical, disease model but are consistent within a paradigm in which unconscious motivation, anxiety, conflict, and defense are integral to the human condition.

CONTEMPORARY WORK

Contemporary analysts of different persuasions have built upon these foundations, although in general they have been less comprehensive and less liberal in their approach to homosexuality. For example, they have generally taken one side or the other in the normality–pathology dialectic. Among those who have written extensively on the subject are Lorand (1956), Bieber et al. (1962), Wiedeman (1962, 1974), Marmor (1965), Socarides (1968, 1978, 1988; Socarides & Volkan, eds., 1990), Stoller (1968, 1975a, 1975b), Ovesey (1969), Ostow, ed. (1974), Isay (1985, 1986, 1987, 1989), R. Friedman (1988), and Siegel (1988); (see also Panel, 1960, 1962, 1986). It is impossible to cover all this material in one chapter, so I have concentrated on representative authors with contrasting views.

Bieber and Socarides represent the pathocentric view. Bieber and his associates (1962) concluded that the *capacity* for homosexuality was part of the human condition but that the *tendency* to be heterosexual was the norm, modifiable only by pathology. Adult homosexuality was a character disorder caused by adverse family dynamics, designed to cope with profound fears of heterosexuality, and remediable in approximately one-quarter of cases. Sexual gratification was preserved by circumventing heterosexual fears and inhibitions through the pathological alternative of same-sex eroticism. The adaptation of homosexuality was "a tribute to man's biosocial resources in the face of thwarted heterosexual goal-achievement" (p. 303). For Socarides homosexuality was the pathological outcome of a skewed developmental process, and he included it among the perversions. Unlike Bieber, however, he emphasized pre-oedipal factors, commenting that homosexuality reflects an object relation rather than a structural conflict. The homosexual act alleviates anxiety, guilt, depression, and ego despair while strengthening object relations impaired by failure during separation-individuation (Panel, 1987, p. 173).

Isay and R. Friedman represent the normative viewpoint. In contrast to Bieber and Socarides, they questioned the conflictual origins and psychopathological status of homosexuality. Friedman (1988), like Socarides, emphasized pre-oedipal factors but in the service of a nonconflictual, nonpathological formulation. Unlike other authors, Friedman focused less on analytic data. In fact, Lewes (1990) refers to Friedman's originality in bringing nonanalytic research and theory to bear on analytic ideas. Isay (1989) emphasized a biological genesis of homosexuality, considering it "a nonpathological variant of human sexuality" (p. 15) that was "immutable from birth" (p. 21). He was not so much concerned with etiology as with changing analytic interventions. In his view, pathocentrism was not only erroneous, but, more important, it blinded the analyst to the injurious effects of such interpretations.

To consider these differences requires an organizing perspective, a role for which the complemental series model is suitable because it includes biology, environment, and dynamics. In addition, there are three classes of theory accounting for psychological phenomena, each representing one complemental series perspective. For example, in a not unrelated area, there are biological, environmental, and dynamic theories to account for the gender identity disorders (Meyer, 1982; Coates et al., 1991). The implications of biological, environmental, and dynamic views for treatment will also be reviewed.

BIOLOGICAL FACTORS

From beginning to end, Freud remained in the tradition of nineteenth-century natural science and repeatedly deferred to biology. He considered sexuality to lie "on the frontiers of biology" (1905, p. 133) and speculated that the ultimate understanding of homosexuality might lie with the biologists (1920, p. 171). Although he pleaded ignorance about what constituted "a feminine brain in a masculine body" and dismissed explanations based on "psychical hermaphroditism" (1905, pp. 141–142), he recognized that constitutional factors might give rise to congenital, as distinct from acquired, homosexuality (1920). The tension between biological and psychological explanations was reflected, however, in Freud's acknowledging biological contributions while insisting that the consequences of repression not be misinterpreted as evidence for congenital origins. More recently, others have struggled with this point. Thus Bieber et al. (1962, p. 173) and Socarides (1978, p. 404) expressed concern that invoking

constitutional factors might aid resistance by saying, in effect, "He was born that way." R. Friedman, by contrast, was of the opinion that biological factors were being underestimated (Panel, 1989a). I will briefly comment on the genetic and neurohormonal findings.

While higher concordances are found in homozygotic than dizygotic twins (although not at the 100 percent level reported in earlier studies), other postulates seem to rest on less firm ground. Hypotheses of "balanced superior heterozygote fitness" (in which heterozygosity for the "homosexual gene" might have survival and reproductive advantages analogous to sickle-cell trait) and favored kin selection (in which homosexual altruism toward kin conferred advantages on the bloodline) (R. Friedman, 1988) are plausible but unsubstantiated. They would not seem to compensate for homosexual reproductive disadvantages, leaving questions about the genetic hypothesis.

With regard to hormonal influences, it is important to distinguish organizing effects from activating/trophic effects. The initial efforts to find a hormonal basis for homosexuality examined activating/trophic functions. One hypothesis was that adult male homosexual behavior was related to abnormally low levels of circulating testosterone. However, Meyer-Bahlburg (1984) and R. Friedman (1988) have both commented that the search for postnatal hormonal influences was unproductive and the theory "by and large untenable" (Meyer-Bahlburg, 1984, p. 390). As a consequence, current work has focused on functional indicators of central nervous system organization by prenatal hormones. The experimental model derives from work with rodents in which sex-stereotypic aggressive, approach, and copulatory behaviors were permanently modified in a cross-sexual direction as a function of critically timed fetal or perinatal exposure to opposite sex hormones. This effect was produced in both male and female rats, without causing anomalies in internal or external genitalia. Adding strength to the model, subjecting pregnant rats to stress has recently been found to lower fetal testosterone temporarily (R. Friedman, 1988), suggesting that subtle effects on the pregnant mother may cause brain modifications in the fetus.

While the model is attractive, its extrapolations are based on assumptions that development of the rat and the human brain is comparable and that "homosexuality" in rat and human is homologous. While it seems likely that core mammalian development is consistent across species, the influence of these basic structures on behavior is not necessarily comparable. Because rat sexual behavior is "highly stereotyped and reflexive," whereas human behavior is "highly variable and to a considerable degree non-reflexive . . . the establishment of homologies even with respect to overt sexual behavior is very difficult" (Meyer-Bahlburg, 1984, p. 376). Meyer-Bahlburg further noted that "while research on rats can be heuristically useful, only human experimentation can establish whether or not . . . hormones have anything to do with sexual orientation in humans" (ibid.). Human and primate data are less available, more complex, and often contradictory.

One area in which rodent, primate, and human data are compatible is in the effects of prenatal hormones on "rough-and-tumble" play. These behaviors are dimorphic in the two sexes and are demonstrably influenced by prenatal androgenization. Females with congenital adrenal hyperplasia and consequent intrauterine exposure to androgens show increased levels of rough-and-tumble play. In adulthood there is a sexual predilection for other females, or both sexes, in about one-third of those studied (Ellis & Ames, 1987). The confounding body-image problem of varying degrees of genital masculinization, however, makes these women atypical relative to the usual homosexual female. With regard to males, various sources agree that pre-homosexual boys often engage less in, or are averse to, such play (Bieber et al., 1962; Bell et al., 1981; Green, 1987). R. Friedman (1988) postulated that errors in timing or levels of prenatal androgen would modify brain functioning so as to diminish rough play. Because timidity and aversion to roughness deviate from the male stereotype, the boy would then not be affirmed in a masculine role. Lack of affirmation would in turn affect masculine identification and predispose the boy to homosexuality. Related mechanisms could be postulated for girls exposed to androgen. In this model, variations in identity (for example, transsexual, feminine male homosexual, masculine male homosexual) and object choice (for example, obligatory homosexuality, bisexuality) would be a function of exposure to hormones.

In general, the confounding of biological, sociological, and psychological factors is the Gordian knot of hormonal research on gender and sexual identities. Meyer-Bahlburg warned that "None of the available studies permit us to fully exclude a confounding of the prenatal hormone factor with putative social factors" (1984, p. 386). In this light, Friedman was justified in his caution when he suggested that biological factors may exert an indirect influence on sexual orientation in some homosexual men. With our current knowledge, equal caution is indicated regarding homosexual women.

SOCIAL AND ENVIRONMENTAL FACTORS

In this section I will review studies of homosexual behavior and adjustment that utilize standardized interviews or tests. I consider these studies to be environmental, as distinct from experiential. Events are transformed into experience through internalization and unconscious transformation, and these studies either fail to consider unconscious intervening variables or include them in cursory fashion. For similar reasons, these reports are more informative about the expression or suppression of homosexuality than about its etiology and dynamics, although they have been extrapolated in those latter directions. But, while methodologically constrained, these studies do establish some boundaries for psychoanalytic formulations.

The postwar Kinsey studies of the American male and female (Kinsey, et al., 1948, 1953) have not been supplanted, although they have recently been challenged (Michael et al., 1994). Contemporaries saw the Kinsey results as showing surprisingly large proportions of men and women having homosexual experiences and/or commitments. For example, 37 percent of males had at least one overt, orgasmic homosexual experience between adolescence and old age. Four percent reported lifelong exclusive homosexuality. Over any given three-year period, 18 percent of males acknowledged at least as much homosexual as heterosexual behavior; 13 percent reported more homosexual than heterosexual; 10 percent said they were more or less exclusively homosexual; and 8 percent acknowledged being exclusively homosexual (1948, pp. 650–651). Acknowledged female homosexual activities were from one-third to one-half as frequent as male in any given category (1953, pp. 472–475). Despite the surprisingly high percentages, Kinsey thought that homosexual behavior would be even more prevalent if it were not culturally suppressed.

To Kinsey, such findings would be inexplicable were it not "that the capacity of an individual to respond erotically to any sort of stimulus, whether . . . provided by another person of the same or of the opposite sex, is basic in the species" (1948, p. 660), an idea not dissimilar to Freud's concept of bisexuality. Further extrapolation suggested that incidence, frequency, and intermixtures of sexual orientations made it difficult "to maintain . . . that psychosexual reactions between individuals of the same sex are rare and therefore abnormal or unnatural, or that they constitute within themselves evidence of neuroses or even psychoses" (1948, p. 659). However, Bieber et al. (1962) cautioned that the incidence or frequency of a condition bears no necessary relationship to its pathological status. One might also have reservations about whether multiple expressions of a condition constitute evidence of normalcy. In fact, a recent survey (Michael et al., 1994) found generally lower levels of homosexual attraction, sexual activity, and self-designation, lending credibility to some of the critiques of the Kinsey group's work.

Hooker (1957, 1965, 1972) compared responses of matched homosexual and heterosexual subjects on the Rorschach and Thematic Apperception tests. She found that in two-thirds of the sample, blind raters could not distinguish between homosexuals and nonhomosexuals. In that two-thirds, furthermore, homosexuals were often as well or better adjusted than matched heterosexuals.

Saghir and Robins (1973) used structured interviews to correlate childhood and adolescent characteristics, psychopathology, and social adjustment for male and female homosexuals. "What has come out . . . is a realization that homosexual men and women are not necessarily sick within . . . the definition of . . . pathology [as] interfering with health or with function" (p. 316). Later, a more ambitious attempt was made by Bell et al. to characterize male and female adjustment and to test etiological hypotheses. In 1978, they reported that their sample was at least as well adjusted as their heterosexual comparison group. In 1981, they attempted to tease out developmental pathways of sexual preference. They anticipated methodological objections but countered that their respondents were nonclinical and the data therefore less subject to a pathological bias, that they had avoided the problems of selective interpretation inherent in the examination of unconscious material, and that if "the differences between homosexual and heterosexual . . . development are . . . as great as psychoanalytic theory claims . . . it is hard to believe that such differences would not be reflected, at least to some extent, in what respondents report" (p. 4). They did not consider the possibilities that manifest data are also subject to interpretive bias, that childhood experience is reportable only in derivative form, and that, although the decision to undergo treatment indicates personal suffering, it is by no means simply correlated with social adjustment or accomplishment. With regard to developmental differences, the authors used statistical "path analysis" correlations that depend critically upon an adequate understanding of theory and the arrangement of variables in a theoretically predicted linear sequence. Since psychoanalytic theory does not lend itself to simple linear

sequences, the applicability of this method may be questioned.

They concluded that parental relationships and traits were insignificant in male homosexuality although perhaps of greater significance for females. In particular, relationships with mothers were noncontributory, while those with fathers were weakly contributory for both sexes. In their view, there was no evidence of Bieber's domineering mothers and weak fathers. Their strongest finding was that "Among both the women and men in our study, there is a powerful link between gender nonconformity and the development of homosexuality" (1981, p. 1988). Nonetheless, homosexuality was based on feelings and reactions "that cannot be traced back to a single social or psychological root" (p. 192).

In summary, studies over a number of years have attested to social adjustment in the majority of homosexuals, a finding which must be taken seriously. Although these studies favored nonconflictual models, methodological limitations weakened their conclusions regarding complex theories encompassing conflict and unconscious motivation.

DEVELOPMENTAL AND DYNAMIC FACTORS

On the basis of their study of experiential factors, Bieber and his associates saw homosexuality "as an outcome of exposure to highly pathologic parent–child relationships and early life situations" (1962, p. 173). Characteristic of these relationships were ties to "close-binding-intimate" mothers who were overinvolved and who overstimulated their sons while at the same time insisting that they conceal their sexuality by antisexual attitudes, prohibitions, and demasculinizing behavior. "Thus, the sons were caught in a double-bind: *maternal seductiveness— maternal sexual restrictions*" (p. 53). Relationships with fathers were also disturbed, traumatic withdrawal from their sons by "detached-hostile" fathers being the most common feature. The most frequent combination was a close-binding-intimate mother and a detached-indifferent father, the child being subject to a kind of double jeopardy. The children tended to seek reparative relationships with other males, establishing "the pathologic seeking of need fulfillment from men" (p. 114).

The oedipus complex played a critical role, with parental responses being crucial to the outcome (Bieber et al., 1962). Pre-homosexual boys were fearful of injury, withdrew from fights, and avoided usual boys' games. A significant number tended to be isolated or to play with girls. Such findings, later interpreted as compatible with neuroendocrine effects, were attributed by Bieber to parental influence. Close-binding mothers who were overly concerned about health and injury and restricted their sons' self-assertiveness acted synergistically with hostile, rejecting fathers who failed to provide adequate models or relationships with their sons. Echoing Freud's (1910) view that homosexual men remain unconsciously attracted to women, Bieber believed that because homosexuality was conditioned by heterosexual fears, "every homosexual is, in reality, a 'latent' heterosexual" (1962, p. 220).

Socarides (1978) classified homosexuality as oedipal, pre-oedipal, or schizo-homosexual along a gradient of object relations, drives, and ego functions. As his thought developed, he increasingly saw both male and female homosexuality as reflecting an object relations failure (Panel, 1987, p. 173). Although his schema included oedipal homosexuality, pre-oedipal issues were seen as "central to the homosexual's difficulties" because "the well-structured homosexual perversion does not arise from defending against oedipal conflict by a regression" (1978, p. 79). The usual male homosexual had a primary, dyadic pre-oedipal identification with his mother, any feminine attitude toward his father being merely a veneer. Separation anxiety, disturbance in ego boundaries and body image, oral-incorporative compulsions, acting-out character structures with poorly sublimated aggression, obligatory homosexual enactments, and an inadequate capacity to regulate self-esteem were the derivatives of this fixation (Socarides, 1978, 1988).

Siegel (1988) acknowledged indebtedness to Socarides in her understanding and treatment of homosexual women. While Siegel and her patients both began with the conviction that homosexuality was a "choice," she subsequently came to the conclusion that her patients had been driven to homosexuality by "developmental arrests that precluded heterosexual object choice" (p. xii). She emphasized pre-oedipal, object relations, and narcissistic mechanisms, believing that in her patients the "Oedipus complex remained vestigial at best" (p. 8). As evidence, she indicated that mother was retained as a love object and that there was no desire for father or a baby. Furthermore, she described her patients as lacking adequate internalized objects and internalized vaginal representations. She considered herself part of the "American . . . object relations school," taking literally the assumed correspondences between specific developmental phases and manifest adult pathology (p. 13). From a roughly compatible perspective, Dorpat (1988) averred that the conflicts of his female patients were exclusively pre-oedipal and manifested in selfobject transferences.

From a Kleinian standpoint, Quinodoz (1989) also emphasized the maternal attachments of female homosexuals, who, nonetheless, lacked satisfactory identities as either sex. Partners functioned as fetishes, not only representing the female phallus but also repairing faulty identities by aiding in the construction of "an omnipotent fantasy, imagining herself to be a man and/or woman" (p. 58). Partners were also employed as defenses against object-directed envy and destructiveness: possessing them reduced the need for envy, while preventing them from having husbands and children ameliorated the need for destructive attack. Although in 1970 McDougall commented on triangular factors and elements of regression in female homosexuality, she later (Panel, 1987) described it as a product of maternal dependency demands, with sexual partners being reparative, gratifying mother substitutes.

Although Socarides believed that homosexuality is essentially pre-oedipal, he emphasized the "Sachs mechanism," which explicitly depends upon oedipal developments (Compton, 1986). According to Sachs (1923), a gratifying fragment of infantile sexuality acceptable to the superego is the nucleus around which a deviation is organized. As the element selected for consciousness, it fosters the repression of the rest of infantile sexuality, the positive oedipus complex, and castration anxiety. Overall, despite the emphasis on pre-oedipal factors, when clinical material was presented, it seemed that object relations conflicts were enmeshed with oedipal, drive, and structural issues (Siegel, 1988; Socarides, 1978, 1988; Silverman, 1990).

R. Friedman (1988) also stressed pre-oedipal factors in the development of homosexuality, although from a different perspective and with different inferences. As Lewes, reviewing Friedman's book, put it: "By adopting Stoller's notion of core gender identity as having developed preoedipally, Friedman avoids invoking those oedipal and family dynamics that have traditionally been used to explain homosexuality" (1990, p. 305). Friedman acknowledged that adult male homosexuality often stemmed from modified childhood gender identity but did not consider the adult condition pathological. His thesis was that core gender identity, although perhaps initially sensitive to conflict, once formed, was no longer "subject to the vicissitudes of psychological conflict," that "conscious and unconscious fantasy is limited by CGI [core gender identity]" (1988, p. 232), and that core gender identity is "analogous to a cellular structure that has differentiated from a multipotential precursor" (p. 231). In perhaps his broadest statement, Friedman said: "In a sense, then, CGI may be thought of not simply as a psychological structure, but as a boundary of the entire mental life, including the unconscious" (p. 232).

Although to my knowledge no one else has so expanded the concept of gender identity, Friedman's ideas are similar to earlier postulates. At one time, male transsexualism was also considered to stem from a pure, nonconflictual, essentially healthy modification of core gender identity (Money & Gaskin, 1970–71; Stoller, 1975b). For example, Stoller considered the gender identity of certain male transsexuals "as an identity per se, not primarily as the surface manifestation of a never-ending unconscious struggle to preserve identity" (1975b, p. 2).[2] Transsexuals, like homosexuals in Freud's day (1905, p. 142), were often seen as psychological intersexes. While Friedman, Money, and Stoller elaborated their models exclusively for males, there was the possibility that such formulations might work better for females. Gender formation in females, who were considered not to have the male problem of disidentifying with mother (Greenson, 1968), has been viewed as a more stable function. "Primary femininity" (Stoller, 1976) seems to offer protection from gender disorder and homosexuality, in that both conditions are about one-third to one-half as frequent in women. On the other hand, just as simple comparisons between the male and female oedipus complex obscured female sexuality, analogous simplifications may distort female gender formation. For example, in Mahler's (1981) view, the girl's active sexual attachment to her mother and the required object shift may threaten gender identity. The girl must disidentify from part-object representations of her mother, which means going through "a tortuous and complicated splitting, repressive, and reintegrative process to attain and maintain her . . . gender identity" (p. 637). In this separation process, which may mean disavowing elements of gender identity, the girl does not have the boy's advantage of a father who is not only outside mother's orbit but also confirms gender identity.

In any event, the accumulated evidence has failed to support the postulate of nonconflictual gender modification in either sex (Meyer, 1982; Meyer & Dupkin, 1985; Coates et al., 1991). In fact, most inferences about nonconflictual gender modification were derived from adult histories that were questionable renditions of childhood (Meyer, 1980, 1982;

2. As a consequence of Robert Stoller's tragic and untimely death, we will never have the advantage of further development in his thinking. At least in informal conversations, however, he had moved away from his earlier ideas about nonconflictual modifications of gender.

Meyer & Dupkin, 1985; Ritvo, in Panel, 1989a). Since the early reports on children and adolescents (Green et al., 1972; Newman, 1970), few researchers or analysts have seen children with uncomplicated modifications of gender identity promising smooth transition to adult homosexuality. On the contrary, gender formation seems exquisitely sensitive to conflict and does not appear to impose limits on fantasy or become fixed in a manner analogous to cellular differentiation (Loeb & Shane, 1982; Meyer & Dupkin, 1985; Silverman, 1990; Westhead et al., 1990; Panel, 1991). This is not surprising considering that the dynamics related to male and female gender modifications are strong and highly conflictual attachments to the mother; absence of an effective involvement by the father; aggressivization of object ties, self representations, and body image; distortions in body-genital schematizations; early and severe castration anxieties; anxieties over loss; excessively harsh and severe superego precursors; and an ego that is weak in relation to internal and external stresses (Meyer, 1982; Panel, 1989a, 1991).

The postulate that gender identity becomes fixed and adynamic was one of the underpinnings of Friedman's nonconflictual model of homosexuality. A second foundation was a similar process envisioned for sexual identity. Most analysts would subscribe to some version of Socarides' (1988) observation that homosexuality has the dynamic characteristics of dreams, with manifest behavior bearing the same relation to unconscious meaning and motivation as the manifest dream to the latent content. Nevertheless, for Friedman, "the psychological mechanisms by which sexual fantasy is maintained after differentiation are not active. Once fantasies differentiate as exclusively homosexual, they persist as a consequence of now passive structuralization analogous to core gender identity differentiation" (1988, p. 247). Nadelson voiced similar ideas regarding female homosexuality. In her view, even if homosexual behavior had drive or defense origins (which she specified were pre-oedipal), it would become secondarily autonomous (Panel, 1987, p. 172). These assumptions were based on Hartmann's concept of secondary autonomy, an idea that may be problematic, since contemporary analysts in Hartmann's tradition are more likely to view such structures as compromise formations (Brenner, 1982; Wyman, 1989). In addition, it is hard to envision an adynamic sexual identity when the variables that modify development include seductiveness or threat on the part of either parent, excessively strong and conflicted sexual and aggressive drive derivatives, guilt over sexual and aggressive wishes, a strong and punitive superego, distortions in ego identifications and ego ideal, and the relative incapacity of the ego in the face of internal and external demands. It is interesting, however, that Bieber et al. (1962) had earlier put forward the obverse argument: that heterosexuals did not harbor repressed homosexual wishes because homosexuality was pathological and would not be found in the well-integrated personality.

Although the developmental perspective is common to these views, the envisioned processes are remarkably divergent. On the one hand are assumptions that conflict remains active and is stabilized only relatively by compromise formations. On the other, the continuing role of dynamics and compromises is relinquished in favor of perfect, nonconflictual fixations. In both, there is a dichotomous approach to pre-oedipal/gender identity and oedipal/sexual identity milestones that underestimates the interrelatedness of fixation, progression, and regression.

TREATMENT

Despite good reason for restraint, the therapeutic powers of analysis have not always been viewed modestly. In fact, the decades of the 1950s, 1960s, and 1970s were characterized not only by stress on pathology but also by therapeutic zeal. Descriptions of treatment reflected a view that homosexuality was not only curable but ought to be cured. In the pursuit of cure, parameters considered tolerable and/or necessary included suggestions that the patient seek out women (by analogy to phobias), intervention in the patient's career, advice on friendships, direction in social and cultural pursuits, and instruction in heterosexual relationships (Panel, 1960; Wiedeman, 1962, 1974). In the 1960 panel, it was suggested that the analyst undertaking treatment must have already decided that the patient was conflicted about his homosexuality and that a heterosexual solution was possible and would be attempted. Although some of the more extreme recommendations are no longer heard, parameters have not disappeared. Bieber et al. (1962) and Socarides (1968, 1978) employed some technical modifications, and variations of a different sort were suggested by Isay (1989).

In 1978, Socarides felt that "homosexuals could be treated most like phobics" (p. 403), with prohibition of homosexual activity (except when sexual release was necessary to modulate overwhelming aggression or anxiety) and encouragement of what might be considered counterphobic heterosexual activity. Furthermore, to foster solutions "outside the analyst's office," reduction in the depth and intensity of regression might be accomplished by manipulation of the regularity or frequency of sessions (p. 429). Mitchell (1981) criticized Bieber and Socarides, among others. In his view, they advocated a "directive-suggestive" approach (p. 68), based on the assumptions that homosexuality is invariably pathological, that heterosexuality is necessary for the patient's health and happiness, and that suggestion and manipulation outside the realm of clarification and interpretation were acceptable. He pointed out a countertransference conundrum in which it was assumed that homosexual males were defensively passive with regard to positive oedipal strivings without it being recognized that heterosexual activity at the behest of the analyst was a similar defensive compliance.

By 1988 Socarides had abandoned most forms of suggestion, although an atmosphere of confrontation remained. He spoke of meeting pre-oedipal conflicts "head on" and of acting to "eliminate" compensatory mechanisms and defenses (1988, p. 537). As he saw it, the necessary specific tasks were "decoding" the manifest behavior, elucidating the unconscious functions of the sexual acts, and "spoiling" the gratification (p. 543). By "spoiling" gratification, Socarides was at pains to clarify that he had in mind "uncovering conflict and comprehending the meaning of symbols" (p. 555), which, by making the eroticism less ego-syntonic, less functional, and less adequate as a defense, diminished its pleasurable qualities. An effort was made to "disclose and define to the patient the primary feminine identification with the mother that has led to the disturbance in his gender-defined self identity, the core of his disorder" (p. 544). Sexual enactments were interpreted in terms of their function to preserve identification with the mother—for example, the partner's penis as a representation of the mother's breast. Socarides noted that "it is not the fixated erotic experience per se . . . that is regressively reanimated . . . but rather it is the *early function* of the erotic experience that has been retained and regressively relied upon" (p. 522). Eroticization was understood as forestalling castration, separation, and fragmentation anxieties while maintaining self and object representations.

Socarides (1978, 1988) believed that oedipal homosexuality could be treated as a neurosis, because it was the product of a temporary regression. Despite his discussion of regressive reactivation of erotic functions, he considered true homosexuality a permanent fixation. In the case of true homosexuality, treatment must be supportive until psychoanalysis proper could begin. Analysis could, nevertheless, be successful except when faced with the most severe character deformations or ego fragmentations.

Once under way, prolonged treatment could be anticipated. He objected to assumptions that homosexuality was normal and should be treated as such. In his view, taking such a position "destroys therapeutic effectiveness and eliminates the possibility of the removal of symptomatology" (1988, p. 534), a point Siegel (1988) echoed for female homosexuality. In what may be the largest female series, Siegel analyzed twelve homosexual women, reporting eight in some detail. Despite her assessment of severe disturbances, over half her patients later became "fully heterosexual" (1988, p. xii). Quinodoz (1989) agreed with Socarides that the greater the ego strengths and the more nearly oedipal the conflicts, the more likely a positive outcome. However, he emphasized female homosexuality's frequently borderline nature and liability to psychosis, with associated defenses against both psychotic regression and oedipal progression. He reported difficulty in analyzing homosexual women because of their propensity for negative therapeutic reactions, a problem apparently not encountered by Siegel, a female herself. In that regard, female homosexuals may be like female transsexuals, who frequently have difficulty working with men.

A difference between the clinical reports of Socarides, Siegel, and Quinodoz and those of Isay is in the prominence given to aggression. In the former, aggression is a robust contributor to the clinical situation; whereas Isay's descriptions are primarily in libidinal terms, and, where mentioned, aggression is usually related to understandable frustrations or to those few patients whose homosexuality is considered defensive against oedipal rivalry.

Morgenthaler (1969) suggested that homosexual patients may attempt "to compel the analyst to adopt an intolerant attitude" (p. 109). Conversely, Isay (1989) emphasized the blindness of homophobic analysts to patients' needs. In Isay's view, the cure-minded analyst would find anti-homosexual material or compliant heterosexual wishes and fantasies so confirmatory of his or her preconceptions that transference meanings would be ignored. Particularly problematic were homophobic attitudes not overt and rationalized, as in some theories, but rather manifested unconsciously and subtly in the countertransference. Isay's responses to these difficulties included suggestions about theoretical orientation, technical approach, and selection of an analyst. In his view, not only were efforts to change sexual orientation "injurious" and "futile," but, more important, "perceiving sexuality as constitutional permits the therapist to understand and investigate the expression of a homosexual orientation with the same neutrality as he does heterosexuality" (1989, p. 21).

(In a similar use of the biological rationale, the report of hypothalamic differences between gay and straight men was treated by the media as a means of countering homophobia [Angier, 1991].)

While Isay avoided unequivocally endorsing "gay positive" or "gay affirmative" approaches, he felt such terms were useful to "stress the fact that traditional therapeutic approaches are 'gay negative'" (1989, p. 121). He believed that the guideline "must be the therapist's conviction that his patient's homosexuality is for him normal and natural." "Today, the therapists most inclined to feel this way will generally be homosexual themselves, although there is no guarantee that a gay therapist will not himself be encumbered by his own early conflicts and internalized homophobia" (p. 126). Isay accurately noted the transference and countertransference complications of homophobia but seemed to overlook a similar potential in homophilia.

It is assumed by various authors that the benefits of analysis should be made available to homosexual analysands, but there are marked differences as to whether the treatment should be seen as exclusively for the homosexual or for the homosexual *and* the homosexuality. There is therapeutic optimism but not the same insistence on change that characterized past decades. Clinical reports illustrate a diversity of phenomena beyond what might be suggested by more restrictive theoretical positions. One striking feature is the ubiquity of parameters. Modifications of technique and analytic set range from the obvious to the subtle and include direct interventions and manipulations, preconceptions about the pathology/normality spectrum, and distortions of neutrality.

DISCUSSION

Although dynamic understanding in psychoanalysis and diagnosis in psychiatry have sometimes been compared as if they were in the same domain, their bases and purposes differ. The goal in psychiatry is to label diseases or, if that ideal is unreachable, to define nonnormative and disadvantageous conditions (Spitzer, 1981). Because of linkages to the nonnormative and disadvantageous, diagnosis—in addition to its scientific claims—is a social act reflecting cultural values and stigmas, and diagnosis may itself contribute to stigma. For example, it is clear that assigning a label such as "lesbian" negatively modifies perceptions of sexually neutral characteristics (Snyder & Uranowitz, 1978). Perhaps it was appropriate therefore that the pre-1980 diagnostic considerations were, as chronicled by Bayer (1981) and Bayer and Spitzer (1982), responsive to efforts for social change. From these standpoints, when it was determined that homosexuality no longer qualified as a psychiatric diagnosis, many felt that a milestone had been passed in the effort to overcome unfair and unjust prejudice rationalized on the grounds of illness.[3] To the extent that declassification resulted in destigmatization, the change was in the psychoanalytic tradition of objecting to characterizations of flaw or taint.

By contrast to diagnosis, the analytic goal is to reveal the origins, nature, and outcome of dynamic processes, with no necessary assumption of cultural relevance, disease state, or inherent disadvantage. From the beginning, homosexuality was considered one of the developmental vicissitudes of the human race, in a tradition stressing that in sexuality normative and nonnormative were relative and that illness was merely a "practical" concept (Freud, 1910, p. 131). Furthermore, diagnostic issues are of limited moment, because sexual preference and activity outside the transference are matters of interest but not of vital concern. Stated another way, the patient's pre- and extra-analytic sexual behavior, so critical to formal diagnosis, is of much less significance analytically than the essential eroticism in the transference. In my view, the diagnostic issue is peripheral to psychoanalysis except insofar as it is paradigmatic of the split between those on the two sides of the pathology–normality dialectic.

It has been suggested that biological, sociological, and psychiatric data constitute a higher level of science which is ignored by psychoanalysis. Nevertheless, a fundamental position of psychoanalysis is embodied in the complemental series: that constitution, environment, and intrapsychic integration are complementary rather than exclusionary. The role of constitution is well established in our field (Ritvo et al., 1963; Silverman et al., 1975; Greenspan, 1989). While there are probably variables that predispose certain children to homosexuality, there is no evidence that such predispositions are necessary or sufficient (Silverman, 1990). Nevertheless, they cannot be dismissed as spurious. In acknowledging the contributions of biology, however, it should not be overlooked that the expression of endowment is conditioned by experience and shaped by elaborated meaning. The influence of the brain upon the mind is clear; the influence of the mind on the brain may be subtle but no less powerful (Kandel, 1979; Reiser, 1984; Meyer, 1988).

With regard to the potential contributions of epidemiological and descriptive models, there are what may be called "horizontal" and "vertical" realms of data. By horizontal is meant consciously available, broadly sampled interview data obtained from more or less large, representative samples; by vertical, indepth, anamnestic, transferential data obtained from small, more or less representative samples. The often cited studies by Kinsey et al. (1948, 1953) Hooker (1972), Saghir and Robins (1973), and Bell et al. (1981) are of reported conscious material and of limited samples of projections. Their deficiencies lie in the fact that, in the words of Freud, "the information received by our consciousness about our erotic life is especially liable to be incomplete, full of gaps, or falsified" (1920, p. 167). What is consciously remembered, deemed reportable, or briefly sampled is no more real or scientific than unconscious material. The latter is also real or scientific, but within other frames of reference and by other measures. Studies that exclude unconscious data or sample it in limited fashion are only minimally instructive within a psychoanalytic framework. The two classes of data are nevertheless complementary in setting limits on speculation. For example, if it were asserted that *every* homosexual is sufficiently dysfunctional to be readily identified as such or that homosexuality is *never* the product of a compromise formation against incestuous wishes and castration dangers, both claims would be demonstrably false.

A large number of psychogenetic factors have been cited in homosexuality, and no list can do them justice. Without any pretense at completeness, they have included seduction, distorted paternal and maternal relationships, narcissistic wounds, physical injury, the viewing of actual or inferred injury, illness, untimely or ill-prepared hospitalization, surgical or other procedures, separations, losses, heightened separation and/or castration anxieties, and schizophrenic, narcissistic, and borderline processes. Obviously, these possibilities are often interrelated. Among the various etiologies, Silverman (1990) referred to the generally acknowledged risk factors in boys whose feminine traits and lack of boyish interests required attention. While the elements of risk in girls have received less attention, the occurrence of extreme tomboyish behavior and the suppression of feminine interests are equivalent risk factors. Despite a long list of possible contributing factors, our capacity to predict a particular outcome or symptom choice is weak and calls for caution in saying that homosexuality is determined by specific conditions

---

3. Suppe (1984) argued that we were then left with the inconsistency of applying diagnoses to some paraphilias that, like homosexuality, are harmless, pleasurable, compatible with productive lives, only minimally responsive to intervention (which often comes only at the insistence of a third party), and may have biological as well as psychological correlates.

or dynamics. Silverman commented, "The complexity, variability, and length of the path leading to adult male homosexuality or bisexuality make it difficult to predict with certainty that any given child will . . . develop such an orientation" (1990, p. 177). Despite the lack of specificity, it seems likely that the great issues of development will be represented in any particular set of dynamics: that is, establishing and refining object ties and representations, channeling and sublimating the drives, creating serviceable psychic structures, and mastering the potential calamities of childhood (Brenner, 1982).

Recent theorizing about homosexuality has been characterized by attention to the pre-oedipal phase. Paradoxically, this pre-oedipal emphasis seems to imply less illness on the one hand—gender identity analogous to a differentiated "cellular" structure— and more illness on the other—dyadic object relations, ego deformations, narcissistic characters, and so forth. A related problem is the dichotomous view of pre-oedipal and oedipal phases implicit in much of the literature. Boesky (Panel, 1989b) objected to such dichotomies, noting that while pre-oedipal trauma does occur, affecting the developing ego, its effects do not persist in circumscribed, intact, or nonconflictual form in the adult. While pre-oedipal and oedipal periods are conceptually distinguishable, as are their gender and sexual identity components, in life they overlap and interact dynamically. Gender formation is a pre-oedipal development, with an important juncture at the rapprochement phase, but it is "not a simple dichotomous variable or a fixed normative endpoint in a linear developmental sequence" but rather a complex construction that "includes the possibility of retroactive transformations of previous meaning in the light of new libidinal and aggressive aims" (Ritvo, in Panel, 1989a, p. 801). Clearly, personality elements become consolidated during the pre-oedipal phase (Silverman et al., 1975; Silverman, 1980), but all evolving developmental currents converge around the oedipus complex and may contribute either to a normal oedipal consolidation and integration of sexuality or to an abnormal one with aberrant sexual development (P. Tyson, in Panel, 1989a). As a result of this convergence, oedipal sexual attractions, attachments, rivalries, jealousies, murderous wishes, and feelings of guilt contribute to both personality and pathology, even if in modified or incomplete form, and even in so-called pre-oedipal cases. Curtis suggested that "direct-line" theories ignoring "the complications of endopsychic transformations, elaborations, and distortions" (1983, p. 184) indicated a failure to appreciate Freud's reorientation from the environmental to the intrapsychic. Perhaps "direct-line," nonconflictual theories

of gender and sexual identity modifications are reflections of this problem.

While there is no question that some homosexuals have pre-oedipal elements in their character, in my experience there is insufficient reason to make that a distinguishing or defining characteristic. In development, the basic gender sense of maleness (boy) or femaleness (girl) is refined into masculinity (for example, tough boy) or femininity (for example, pretty girl) with further elaborations of sexual fantasies, personal eroticism, and object attractions (Panel, 1989a). These identities are not simply acquired; they are created and re-created. Where there are problems, suitable fixation points may become a focus for regressions which, as outlined by Sachs (1923), subserve complicated functions. Clinically, object relations difficulties, narcissistic problems, pre-oedipal anxieties, structural modifications, intersystemic conflicts, and oedipal anxieties are usually seen in combination.

Sexuality is a complex representation of formative experiences and is predictably a compromise formation of magnificent proportions. In supportive or manipulative therapies, the patient's homosexuality may be only peripheral to the work. It is inconceivable, however, that a patient could be analyzed without involving his or her homosexuality, even though an open mind is required as to whether the analysis will turn on the conflicts it entails. In the examination of such a central and sensitive subject as sexuality, the transference is often intense, as eroticism and aggression are externalized. The literature records many intentional and unintentional parameters in the treatment of homosexuality. Their general function may be to reduce transference intensity. They run the gamut from the restrictive and prohibitive to the endorsing and enabling: for example, from elements of therapeutic zeal (prejudgment of pathology, instructions, and "cure") to those of therapeutic agnosticism (prejudgment of normality, encouragement toward adjustment, and "noncure"). While variously rationalized, they certainly deviate from the neutrality that subserves transference analyzability.

For example, it has been suggested that a constitutional model is more neutral. There is no reason to assume, however, that a biological theory is more neutral per se than a conflict model (Stoller, 1973). If both heterosexuality and homosexuality were biological givens not subject to analysis, all manner of conflicted drive derivatives may be exempted from examination. It has also been suggested that, to avoid homophobia, an analyst with a normative view of homosexuality or a homosexual orientation should be found. If I understand correctly, the choice of an analyst on that basis would be, *prima facie,* adequate rationale, potentially creating another sanctuary for the resistance. Analysands, of course, have always exercised sex-related options in their choices of analysts. Selection by philosophical or sexual orientation is less significant than the elucidation of the reasons for that choice. In other words, for homosexual men and women to choose analysts committed to normalization is no problem, providing the choice and its rationale are subject to analysis. Similarly, the reasons for selecting an analyst with strong pathocentric views should be part of analytic inquiry. Neutrality denotes an alignment with the observing functions of the patient's ego while avoiding complicity with either gratifying (id) or criticizing (superego) operations. It seems equally nonneutral to normalize a sexual activity as to criticize it.

If the treatment of homosexuality is part of the psychoanalytic mainstream, then the work should be open and comfortable. While Mitchell (1981) has suggested that most analysts approach homosexual material as they would any other, I am not convinced that sexual variations are always welcomed in the transference. For that reason, there may be cause for redoubled effort in training analyses. There are no hard data, but some colleagues and candidates anecdotally report little or no experience with their own homoeroticism. Obviously, parallel concerns exist for gay candidates and their heteroeroticism. Since it is hard to imagine an analysand without same-sex and opposite-sex eroticism, absence of such material seems related to a combination of expectable resistance and problematic countertransference. Unfortunately, the effects of countertransference attitudes and enactments in training analyses are known to favor countertransference distortions in subsequent analyses (Baum, 1977; Shapiro, 1976; McLaughlin, 1981).

Whether homosexuality will change in the course of analysis depends upon its serviceability and stability, but prognostications are fundamentally conservative. Better integrated, more functional, and more pleasurable homosexuality may result from the analytic process, although heterosexual wishes and longings may remain. Conversely, homosexual activity may be reduced or abandoned in favor of heterosexuality, although homosexual fantasies may remain sweetly and powerfully erotic. Some may object that the retention of fantasies incongruent with sexual orientation indicates less than a successful analytic outcome. The criterion for success, however, is not extirpation of a particular eroticism. Given that psychoanalysis is the most powerful method available for the relief of neurotic suffering

and characterological impediments, it is nonetheless doubtful that massive, well-integrated constructions are ever completely removed.

A cultural sea change is under way, although to homosexual men and women it must seem glacially slow. The greatest obstacle to change is that many people feel threatened by homosexuality and tend to blame the homosexual for his or her eroticism. Although blame is clearly inappropriate and misplaced, psychoanalysis has sometimes been misunderstood as not only implying that the homosexual is "sick" but also as "blaming" him for his illness. Psychoanalysis, however, does not assign blame for any type of eroticism, even if it recognizes that we each have some responsibility for our erotic lives. From a psychoanalytic point of view, we are all more or less the architects of our own compromises, which may serve us more or less well. Although sometimes used synonymously in common language, in psychoanalysis *blame,* which implies fault, reproach, and culpability, and *responsibility,* which implies agency, authority, and capability, are very different concepts. The efforts of some analysts to minimize conflict and compromise formation, to simplify development, to emphasize biology, and to define behaviors descriptively or epidemiologically often seem to be based on a misunderstanding of those essential differences. Although some criticisms of psychoanalysis might be lessened by devaluing motivated psychic determinism, abandoning that concept would not actually serve anyone very well. The uniqueness and power of analytic understanding and treatment are based on the fact that we construct our own living compromise formations and have the potential for reconstructing them.

CONCLUSION

I have attempted to achieve a balance in what is a highly polarized area. While debate is testimony to the vitality of the field, it is important that in the clash of ideas we do not lose sight of a century's painstaking work.

The psychoanalytic tapestry is so rich that any particular emphasis flirts with reductionism. Nonetheless, I have chosen what I consider to be essential elements. Conceptualizations of homosexuality contribute to, and are informed by, general observations and principles. Unconscious or conscious experience with homosexuality is common to us all. The extent to which mental processes are subject to repression means that hypotheses that exclude unconscious data are incomplete. Whereas biological, environmental, and mental factors are recognized as complementary, psychoanalytic methodology has necessarily focused on the experiential and psychogenic, offering unparalleled information within those limits. Homosexuality is closely related to neuroses, to other deviations, and to normality, sharing with all its status as an outcome of the conflicts, repressions, and integrations of sexuality. The recognition of continuities between health and illness and among different clinical manifestations, not sample size, underlies the assumption that psychoanalytic findings are generalizable. Like other aspects of sexuality, homosexuality may be discussed from the perspectives both of creativity and normality and of limitations and illness.

The developmental model includes both pre-oedipal and oedipal factors, which are interrelated through structuralization, fixation, and regression. In view of the dynamic complexity and the capacity of the ego for transformation of experience, our ability to predict symptom choice is limited. Dynamics, while of unparalleled importance in an individual case, are generally illustrative rather than prescriptive. The serviceability of compromise formations, their kinship to normal processes, and accumulated clinical experience make psychoanalysis humble in its prognostications. In analyses unencumbered by parameters, the transference will vitalize pre-oedipal and oedipal dynamics and related modifications of gender and sexual identities. With the patient's recovery of his or her prehistory and motivations, unconscious compromises may become either conscious reaffirmations of homosexuality or new options.[4]

REFERENCES

Angier, N. (1991). The biology of what it means to be gay. *New York Times,* 1 Sept., sect. 4, pp. 1, 4.

Baum, O. (1977). Countertransference and the vicissitudes in an analyst's development. *Psychoanal. Rev.,* 64:539–550.

Bayer, R. (1981). *Homosexuality and American Psychiatry.* New York: Basic Books.

Bayer, R., & Spitzer, R. (1982). Edited correspondence on the status of homosexuality in the DSM-III. *J. Hist. Behav. Sci.,* 18:32–52.

Bell, A., & Weinberg, M. (1978). *The Homosexualities.* New York: Simon & Schuster.

Bell, A., Weinberg, M., & Hammersmith, S. (1981). *Sexual Preference.* Bloomington: Indiana Univ. Press.

Bieber, I., Dain, H., Dince, P., Drellich, M., Grand, H., Gundlach, R., Kremer, M., Rifkin, A., Wilbur, C., & Bieber, T. (1962). *Homosexuality.* New York: Basic Books.

Brenner, C. (1982). *The Mind in Conflict.* New York: Int. Univ. Press.

Chasseguet-Smirgel, J., ed. (1970). *Female Sexuality.* Ann Arbor: Univ. Michigan Press.

Coates, S., Friedman, R., & Wolfe, S. (1991). The etiology of boyhood gender identity disorder. *Psychoanal. Dialogues,* 1:481–523.

Compton, A. (1986). Neglected classics: Hans Sachs's "On the genesis of perversions." *Psychoanal. Q.,* 55:474–476, 489–492.

Curtis, H. (1983). Construction and reconstruction. *Psychoanal. Inq.,* 3:183–188.

Deutsch, H. (1944). *The Psychology of Women,* vol. 1. New York: Grune & Stratton.

Dorpat, T. (1988). Foreword to *Female Homosexuality,* by E. Siegel, pp. xv–xxiii. Hillsdale, N.J.: Analytic Press.

Ellis, L., & Ames, M. (1987). Neurohormonal functioning and sexual orientation. *Psychol. Bull.,* 101:233–258.

Freud, A. (1965). *Normality and Pathology in Childhood.* New York: Int. Univ. Press.

Freud, S. (1895). A reply to criticism of my paper on anxiety neurosis. *SE,* 3:119–139.

———. (1905). *Three Essays on the Theory of Sexuality. SE,* 7:123–243.

———. (1906). My views on the part played by sexuality in the aetiology of the neuroses. *SE,* 7:269–279.

———. (1910). *Leonardo da Vinci and a Memory of His Childhood. SE,* 11:57–137.

———. (1916–17). *Introductory Lectures on Psycho-Analysis,* Part III. *SE,* 16:243–476.

———. (1919). "A child is being beaten." *SE,* 17:175–204.

———. (1920). The psychogenesis of a case of homosexuality in a woman. *SE,* 18:145–172.

———. (1922). Some neurotic mechanisms in jealousy, paranoia and homosexuality. *SE,* 18:221–232.

———. (1923). *The Ego and the Id. SE,* 19:1–66.

———. (1924). The dissolution of the oedipus complex. *SE,* 19:171–179.

———. (1925). Some physical consequences of the anatomical distinction between the sexes. *SE,* 19:241–258.

———. (1926a). *Inhibitions, Symptoms and Anxiety. SE,* 20:75–175.

4. I wish to acknowledge my appreciation and gratitude to colleagues and friends at the Austen Riggs Center, Stockbridge, Mass., where I was Erik H. Erikson Scholar-in-Residence in 1991–92, for providing the structure, support, and kindness that made the work on this chapter possible.

———. (1926b). *The Question of Lay Analysis. SE,* 20:177–258.

———. (1931). Female sexuality. *SE,* 21:221–243.

———. (1940). *An Outline of Psycho-Analysis. SE,* 23:138–207.

———. (1951). A letter from Freud. *Amer. J. Psychiat.,* 107:786–787.

Friedman, L. (1977). Conflict and synthesis in Freud's theory of the mind. *Int. Rev. Psychoanal.,* 4:155–170.

Friedman, R. (1988). *Male Homosexuality.* New Haven: Yale Univ. Press.

Green, R. (1987). *The "Sissy Boy Syndrome" and the Development of Homosexuality.* New Haven: Yale Univ. Press.

Green, R., Newman, L., & Stoller, R. (1972). Treatment of boyhood "transsexualism." *Arch. Gen. Psychiat.,* 26:213–217.

Greenson, R. R. (1968). Dis-identifying from mother. *Int. J. Psychoanal.,* 49:370–374.

Greenspan, S. (1989). *The Development of the Ego.* Madison, Conn.: Int. Univ. Press.

Groddeck, G. (1923). *The Book of the It.* Rpt. New York: Int. Univ. Press, 1976.

Guttman, S. (1985). The psychoanalytic point of view. *Int. J. Psychoanal.,* 66:167–170.

Hooker, E. (1957). The adjustment of the male overt homosexual. *J. Proj. Tech.,* 21:18–31.

———. (1965). Male homosexuals and their "worlds." In Marmor, ed., pp. 83–107.

———. (1972). Homosexuality. In Final Report, NIMH Task Force on Homosexuality, pp. 11–21. Washington, D.C.: DHEW Publication No. (ADM) 76–357.

Isay, R. (1985). On the analytic therapy of homosexual men. *Psychoanal. Study Child,* 40:235–254.

———. (1986). The development of sexual identity in homosexual men. *Psychoanal. Study Child,* 41:467–489.

———. (1987). Fathers and their homosexually inclined sons in childhood. *Psychoanal. Study Child,* 42:275–294.

———. (1989). *Being Homosexual.* New York: Farrar, Straus & Giroux.

Jones, E. (1927). The early development of female sexuality. *Int. J. Psychoanal.,* 8:459–472.

Kandel, E. (1979). Psychotherapy and the single synapse. *New Eng. J. Med.,* 301:1028–1037.

Kinsey, A., Pomeroy, W., & Martin, C. (1948). *Sexual Behavior in the Human Male.* Philadelphia: Saunders.

Kinsey, A., Pomeroy, W., Martin, C., & Gebhard, P.

(1953). *Sexual Behavior in the Human Female.* Philadelphia: Saunders.

Lewes, K. (1990). Review of Friedman (1988). *Arch. Sex. Behav.,* 19:303–307.

Loeb, L., & Shane, M. (1982). The resolution of a transsexual wish in a five-year-old boy. *J. Amer. Psychoanal. Assn.,* 30:419–434.

Lorand, S., ed. (1956). *Perversions.* New York: Random House.

Mahler, M. S. (1981). Aggression in the service of separation-individuation. *Psychoanal. Q.,* 50:625–638.

Marmor, J., ed. (1965). *Sexual Inversion.* New York: Basic Books.

McDougall, J. (1970). Homosexuality in women. In Chasseguet-Smirgel, ed., pp. 171–212.

McLaughlin, J. (1981). Transference, psychic reality, and countertransference. *Psychoanal. Q.,* 50:639–664.

Meyer, J. (1980). Body ego, selfness, and gender sense. *Psychiat. Clin. North Amer.,* 3:21–36.

———. (1982). The theory of gender identity disorders. *J. Amer. Psychoanal. Assn.,* 30:381–418.

———. (1985). Ego-dystonic homosexuality. In *Comprehensive Textbook of Psychiatry,* ed. H. Kaplan & B. Sadock, vol. 1, pp. 1056–1065. Baltimore: Williams & Wilkins.

———. (1988). The concept of adult psychic structure. *J. Amer. Psychoanal. Assn.,* 36(suppl.):101–112.

Meyer, J., & Dupkin, C. (1985). Gender disturbance in children. *Bull. Menninger Clinic,* 49:236–269.

Meyer-Bahlburg, H. (1984). Psychoendocrine research on sexual orientation. In *Progress in Brain Research,* ed. G. DeVries et al., vol. 61, pp. 375–398. Amsterdam: Elsevier.

Michael, R., Gagnon, J., Lauman, E., & Kolata, G. (1994). *Sex in America.* Boston: Little, Brown.

Mitchell, S. (1981). The psychoanalytic treatment of homosexuality. *Int. Rev. Psychoanal.,* 8:63–80.

Money, J. (1970–71). Sex reassignment. *Int. J. Psychiat.,* 9:249–269.

Morgenthaler, F. (1969). Introduction to panel on disturbances of male and female identity as met with in psychoanalytic practice. *Int. J. Psychoanal.,* 50:109–112.

Newman, L. (1970). Transsexualism in adolescence. *Arch. Gen. Psychiat.,* 23:112–121.

Nunberg, H. (1931). The synthetic function of the ego. *Int. J. Psychoanal.,* 12:123–140.

Ostow, M., ed. (1974). *Sexual Deviation.* New York: Quadrangle.

Ovesey, L. (1969). *Homosexuality and Pseudohomosexuality.* New York: Science House.

Panel (1960). Theoretical and clinical aspects of

overt male homosexuality. C. Socarides, reporter. *J. Amer. Psychoanal. Assn.,* 8:552–566.

———. (1962). Theoretical and clinical aspects of overt female homosexuality. C. Socarides, reporter. *J. Amer. Psychoanal. Assn.,* 10:579–592.

———. (1986). Toward a further understanding of homosexual men. R. Friedman, reporter. *J. Amer. Psychoanal. Assn.,* 34:193–206.

———. (1987). Toward the further understanding of homosexual women. A. Wolfson, reporter. *J. Amer. Psychoanal. Assn.,* 35:165–173.

———. (1989a). Current concepts of the development of sexuality. S. A. Vogel, reporter. *J. Amer. Psychoanal. Assn.,* 37:787–802.

———. (1989b). Personal reflections on the role of sexuality in the etiology and treatment of the neuroses. S. Mayson, reporter. *J. Amer. Psychoanal. Assn.,* 37:803–812.

———. (1991). The etiology of boyhood gender identity disorder. P. Bernstein, reporter. Annual Meeting American Psychoanalytic Association, New Orleans.

Quinodoz, J.-M. (1989). Female homosexual patients in psychoanalysis. *Int. J. Psychoanal.,* 70: 55–63.

Reiser, M. (1984). *Mind, Brain, Body.* New York: Basic Books.

Ritvo, S., McCollom, A., Omwake, E., Provence, S., & Solnit, A. J. (1963). Some relations of constitution, environment, and personality as observed in a longitudinal study of child development. In *Modern Perspectives in Child Development,* ed. A. J. Solnit & S. Provence. New York: Int. Univ. Press.

Sachs, H. (1923). On the genesis of perversions. *Psychoanal. Q.,* 55(1986):477–488.

Saghir, M., & Robins, E. (1973). *Male and Female Homosexuality.* Baltimore: Williams & Wilkins.

Shapiro, D. (1976). The analyst's own analysis. *J. Amer. Psychoanal. Assn.,* 24:15–42.

Siegel, E. (1988). *Female Homosexuality.* Hillsdale, N.J.: Analytic Press.

Silverman, M. (1980). A fresh look at the case of Little Hans. In *Freud and His Patients,* ed. M. Kanzer & J. Glenn, vol. 2, pp. 93–120. New York: Aronson.

———. (1990). The prehomosexual boy in treatment. In Socarides & Volkan, eds., pp. 177–197.

Silverman, M., Rees, K., & Neubauer, P. B. (1975). On a central psychic constellation. *Psychoanal. Study Child,* 30:127–157.

Snyder, M. & Uranowitz, S. (1978). Reconstructing the past. *J. Pers. Soc. Psychol.,* 36:941–950.

Socarides, C. (1968). *The Overt Homosexual.* New York: Aronson.

———. (1978). *Homosexuality.* New York: Aronson.

———. (1988). *The Preoedipal Origin and Psychoanalytic Therapy of Sexual Perversions.* Madison, Conn.: Int. Univ. Press.

Socarides, C., & Volkan, V., eds. (1990). *The Homosexualities.* Madison, Conn.: Int. Univ. Press.

Spitzer, R. (1981). The diagnostic status of homosexuality in DSM-III. *Amer. J. Psychiat.,* 138: 210–215.

Stoller, R. (1968). *Sex and Gender,* vol. 1. New York: Science House.

———. (1973). Overview: the impact of new advances in sex research on psychoanalytic theory. *Amer. J. Psychiat.,* 130:241–251.

———. (1975a). *Perversion.* New York: Pantheon.

———. (1975b). *Sex and Gender,* vol. 2. New York: Aronson.

———. (1976). Primary femininity. *J. Amer. Psychoanal. Assn.,* 24(suppl.):59–78.

Stoller, R., Marmor, J., Bieber, I., Gold, R., Socarides, C., Green, R., & Spitzer, R. (1973). Symposium: should homosexuality be in the APA nomenclature? *Amer. J. Psychiat.,* 130:1207–1216.

Suppe, F. (1984). Classifying sexual disorders. *J. Homosex.,* 9(4):9–28.

Westhead, V., Olson, S., & Meyer, J. (1990). Gender identity disorders in adolescence. In *Atypical Adolescence and Sexuality,* ed. M. Sugar, pp. 87–107. New York: Norton.

Wiedeman, G. (1962). Survey of psychoanalytic literature on overt male homosexuality. *J. Amer. Psychoanal. Assn.,* 10:386–409.

———. (1974). Homosexuality, a survey. *J. Amer. Psychoanal. Assn.,* 22:651–696.

Wilson, E., Jr. (1990). Eros and sexuality in antiquity. *Psychoanal. Q.,* 59:75–101.

Wyman, H. (1989). Hartmann, health and homosexuality. *Psychoanal. Q.,* 58:612–639.

Young-Bruehl, E. (1990). *Freud on Women.* New York: Norton.

28

AGGRESSION: THEORIES REGARDING ITS NATURE AND ORIGINS

Aggression is a broad and inherently interdisciplinary topic. Many fields besides psychology, psychiatry, and psychoanalysis have contributed to our understanding of it. These include neurology and neurophysiology, genetics and evolutionary sciences, ethology, political science, sociology, anthropology, and other branches of the humanities. Clearly, it is not possible to review this vast literature here. Even to provide a truly comprehensive summary of just the psychoanalytic writings on the topic is difficult. The classical literature needs to be synthesized with the contemporary views. The differing viewpoints of drive theory, structural model, object relations approach, Kleinian formulation, developmental perspective, and self psychology need to be taken into account. Data gathered from varying sources—for example, logical and deductive theory building, reconstructions in psychoanalytic treatment of adults, analytically sophisticated observation of infants and children, analytic treatment of children, and the "applied" arena of psychopolitical studies—need to be pooled and brought together in some kind of conceptual harmony.

The task is perhaps not even possible within the confines of a single chapter, so my focus here will be quite restricted. I will not address the admittedly important areas of neurophysiological, biochemical, hereditary, and phylogenetic substrates of aggression; the neurotic, perverse, and characterological syndromes associated with sadomasochism, self-destructiveness, and violence; the impact of intense, unneutralized, overt aggression on the feasibility and technique of adult and child psychoanalysis; and the application of the psychoanalytic understanding of aggression to parent education for preventing the development of excessive hostility in children and to the study of law and justice and ethnic, racial, and international conflicts. Instead, I will concentrate on the various views of the nature and origins of human aggression as they have evolved through the history of psychoanalysis. I will begin with Freud's changing views on aggression. Then I will highlight the two major divergent post-Freudian trends—namely, the theoretical paths taken by Melanie Klein and Heinz Hartmann—in the study of aggression. Following this, I will summarize other significant contributions, including those of the British object relations school and self psychology. I will then address some contemporary reformulations and conclude by summarizing, synthesizing, and noting the newer vistas of theoretical concern and application. It seems best, however, to begin by defining our terms.

DEFINITION: ETYMOLOGY, MEANING, AND PSYCHOANALYTIC TERMINOLOGY

I view the phenomenon of aggression, and its psychological functions and representations, as the aggregate of diverse acts, having diverse origins, and bound together, sometimes loosely, by the nature of their impact on objects rather than by a demonstrably common and unitary drive. . . . This does not mean that certain elements of aggression do not have an instinctual origin or affiliation. [L. Stone, 1971, p. 195]

It is difficult to provide a straightforward psychoanalytic definition of the term "aggression" for many reasons. First, too many words (*aggression, aggressivity, aggressiveness, aggressive behavior, aggressive drive, aggressive instinct,* and so on) are used interchangeably in this realm. Second, the word *aggression* has come to stand for an enormous variety of phenomena and manifestations (L. Stone, 1971). It is an "unfortunate fact that we use the term 'aggression' when we also mean many other things" (Sandler, in Panel, 1972a, p. 13) and that aggression has become "an umbrella concept . . . [denoting] forms of energy, various types of drives, and a wide range of motivation and behavior" (Marcovitz, 1973, pp. 226–227). Third, confusion about what the term denotes also results from a tautological leap in psychoanalytic theorizing. To explain aggressive behavior, an underlying aggressive drive was postulated. Thus, a "descriptive concept was elevated into an explanatory one, and it was then assumed that the aggressive drive (i.e. the impetus to be aggressive) did not always result in aggressive behaviour" (Sandler, in Panel, 1972a, p. 14). No wonder that the denotative focus of aggression was lost. Finally, the rarity of linear correlations between drive, affect, fantasy, wish, defense, and behavior makes it puzzling as to which conceptual or phenomenological level is most suitable for the term "aggression." Is it better, for instance, to reserve it for the hypothesized instinctual drive and not use it in behavioral contexts or in the context of fantasy or affects?

In search of clarity, we turn to the literal meaning of the word *aggression*. Both the *Oxford English Dictionary* (1961, p. 182) and Webster's *New Universal Unabridged Dictionary* (1979, p. 36) emphasize the hostile, menacing meaning of the word. Yet, in citing its derivation from Latin and in discussing its verb form, *aggress,* both note two roots (*aggredi:* to attack, and *ad + gradi:* to step, to move towards). This expands the meaning of *aggression* to include not only hostile gestures but also active and assertive ones. Indeed, five out of six of the meanings given in the *Oxford Latin Dictionary* (1982, p. 84) for the root word *aggredior* refer to nonhostile, nondestructive actions.

The tension between an active-assertive and an attacking-destructive view of aggression is also evident in psychoanalytic glossaries (Eidelberg, 1968; Moore & Fine, eds., 1968, 1990; Rycroft, 1968; English & English, 1976). Some of these seem to have taken opposite sides in this dilemma. In a somewhat puzzling manner, Eidelberg (1968) states that aggression, "also referred to as an aggressive instinct-fusion, is a mixture of Eros and Thanatos, with Thanatos dominating" (p. 21). He does, however, make an interesting distinction between aggressive and sexual drives: aggressive pleasure is felt when the subject overcomes the resistance of the object, whereas sexual pleasure is felt by both the subject and the object and is achieved by the actions of both. Although tangential and idiosyncratic, Eidelberg's definition is a resolutely intrapsychic one. The American Psychoanalytic Association's first glossary (Moore & Fine, eds., 1968), on the other hand, declares bluntly that aggression means "attack or hostile action . . . [which] may take the form of physical assault as one extreme, or gentle, implicit verbal criticism as the other" (p. 18). This definition, making no mention of nondestructive aggression, equates aggression with hostility. While it goes on to mention an underlying aggressive instinctual drive, its emphasis is upon overt behavior. In contrast, Rycroft (1968) defines aggression as a "hypothetical force, instinct, or principle imagined to actuate a range of acts and feelings. It is frequently regarded as antithetical to sex or libido, in which case it is being used to refer to destructive drives. Even when being used as a synonym for destructiveness, controversy exists as to whether it is a primary drive, i.e., whether there is an aggressive, destructive instinct, or whether it is a reaction to frustration" (p. 4). Rycroft maintains an intrapsychic focus, hints at controversies, and, in regarding the traditional meaning of aggression to be "dynamism, self-assertiveness, expansiveness, [and] drive" (p. 5), firmly disengages aggression from inherent destructiveness. English and English (1976, p. 19) adopt an intermediate stance between Moore and Fine (1968) and Rycroft (1968). However, by portraying aggression as including hostile acts, behaviors consequent upon frustration, and manifestations of the will to power and of the hypothesized death instinct, these authors tend to become theoretically and phenomenologically overinclusive.

A more succinctly stated compromise position is that of the new glossary of the American Psychoanalytic Association (Moore & Fine, eds., 1990). Here, *aggression* is seen as referring to the "manifest strivings, either physical or verbal, to subjugate or prevail upon others" (p. 10). Various expressions of aggression are noted, as well as the fact that the term "aggression" is "sometimes broadened to include acts that seem to originate from initiative, ambition, or the just demand for rights. Such acts are sometimes designated *assertion* in order to indicate that they do not seem to arise from hostile motives" (p. 10). The definition goes on to discuss the aggressive drive underlying these manifestations. It notes the continuing debate as to whether the aggressive drive is innately destructive or becomes so as a result of frustration and conflict. It mentions that Freud's notion of the death instinct is not widely accepted by psychoanalysts, while acknowledging its assimilation into Kleinian theory. Further, the authors of the definition note that it is unclear whether aggression and libido are separate drive energies at birth or only gradually differentiate into separate strands. Finally, it touches upon the developmental vicissitudes of the aggressive drive, including its influence upon the structuralization of the superego.

This overview of the various definitions of aggression highlights certain dichotomies (Rangell, 1972, p. 5) that surface repeatedly in discussions of aggression: constructive versus destructive aggression, drive to mastery versus drive to destroy, innate versus reactive origin of destructiveness, and so on. These dichotomies have complex conceptual sources and historical origins.

ORIGIN: FREUD'S VIEWS ON AGGRESSION

I cannot bring myself to assume the existence of a special aggressive instinct alongside the familiar instincts of self-preservation and sex, and on an equal footing with them. [Freud, 1909, p. 140]

Starting from speculations on the beginning of life and from biological parallels, I drew the conclusion that, besides the instinct to preserve living substance and to join it into even larger units, there must exist another, contrary instinct seeking to dissolve those units and to bring them back to their primaeval, inorganic state. That is to say, as well as Eros there was an instinct of death. [Freud, 1930, pp. 118–119]

These statements portray the two nodal points in the evolution of Freud's thinking on aggression. The turning point in this long journey came in 1920, with the publication of *Beyond the Pleasure Principle*, thus somewhat late in the course of Freud's theory building. He himself acknowledged this by saying, "Why have we ourselves needed such a long time before we decided to recognize an aggressive instinct?" (Freud, 1933, p. 103). However, the time lag involved only metapsychological theorizing, not clinical observation (Laplanche & Pontalis, 1973). Freud had been keenly aware of aggression for a long time before he assimilated it into his theory. He had discerned the workings of aggression within

himself, shown in his early death wishes against his younger brother, his hostile oedipal feelings toward his father, and his need for an enemy in his life (Freud, 1900; Masson, 1985, p. 268; Gay, 1988, pp. 11, 396). Besides, he had noted the significance of aggression in clinical work. As early as 1896, he wrote of the "sexual aggression" (p. 165) passively suffered by hysterics and the "acts of aggression carried out with pleasure" (p. 168) by obsessional neurotics during their childhoods. The following year, in a letter to Fliess (Masson, 1985, p. 274), he showed his awareness of aggressiveness as a resistance to treatment. His earliest exposition of the oedipus complex, in *The Interpretation of Dreams*, contained a combination of libidinal and hostile trends and appeared under the heading "Dreams of the Death of Persons of whom the Dreamer is Fond" (1900, p. 248). Five years later, in his analysis of jokes, Freud noted how often these served the purpose of aggressiveness (1905b, p. 97). The same year, in reporting the Dora case, he underscored the ubiquity of the emergence of aggressiveness in psychoanalytic treatment (1905a, p. 117).

The publication of the *Three Essays on the Theory of Sexuality* in 1905 was an event of enormous import for the study of aggression. It was here that Freud began to develop his first instinct theory, though it was not until a few years later that he first explicitly referred to the "instincts of self-preservation and of sex" (1909, p. 140). In the *Three Essays*, however, he first focused attention on sadism and masochism, terms he acknowledged (1905c, p. 157) having borrowed from Krafft-Ebing. In tracing the roots of sadism, Freud observed:

The sexuality of most male human beings contains an element of *aggressiveness*—a desire to subjugate; the biological significance of it seems to lie in the need for overcoming the resistance of the sexual object by means other than the process of wooing. Thus sadism would correspond to an aggressive component of the sexual instinct which has become independent and exaggerated and, by displacement, has usurped the leading position. [1905c, pp. 157–158]

Sadism was a component of the sexual instinct and masochism was sadism turned around upon the subject's own self. Freud noted the "intimate connection between cruelty and the sexual instinct" (p. 159) and wondered if "this aggressive element of the sexual instinct is in reality a relic of cannibalistic desires—that is, it is a contribution derived from the apparatus for obtaining mastery, which is concerned with the satisfaction of the other and, ontogenetically, the older of the great instinctual needs" (ibid.).

The statement added a pre-oedipal substrate to sadism and hinted at connections between sadism and the striving for mastery. Both these themes gain strength through Freud's later statement that it "may be assumed that the impulse of cruelty arises from the instinct for mastery and appears at a period of sexual life at which the genitals have not yet taken over their later role" (sentence added in 1915 to 1905c, p. 193). Finally, not only did Freud correlate sadism, activity, instinct for mastery, and "the agency of the somatic musculature" (p. 198), he also spoke of masochism as a passive "instinct of cruelty" (p. 193). Thus, in 1905, Freud took three positions on aggression: that it is a component of sexual instinct; that it arises from an instinct for mastery (with the latter concept still waiting to be elevated to full instinct status); and that there might be an instinct of cruelty.

Four years later, however, he could not bring himself "to assume the existence of a special aggressive instinct" (1909, p. 140). To do so, he believed, would be to attribute to a single facet of the sexual instinct characteristics that were indispensable attributes of all instincts—namely, a source, aim, and object and a pressing quality and capacity to initiate action.

The criteria for an instinctual drive were made more specific and explicit in "Instincts and their vicissitudes" (1915). Freud held on to the dichotomy between sexual and ego instincts, once again assigning sadism to the sexual instinct. However, as Parens (1979) has argued, a tension similar to that in the *Three Essays* (1905c) between viewing aggression as a component of the sexual instinct and seeing it as a component of the ego instinct exists here as well. This is most evident in Freud's views on hate. First, he saw hate as resulting from transformed love (1915, p. 133), but then he concluded that "the true prototypes of the relation of hate are derived not from the sexual life, but from the ego's struggle to preserve and maintain itself" (p. 138). This dilemma regarding whether to place aggression under the sexual instincts or the ego instincts was automatically laid to rest with Freud's postulation of his second instinctual theory in 1920. Freud now subsumed the ego instincts under the sexual instinct and elevated aggression to an independent instinctual drive. In a "startling" (Jones, 1957, p. 266) theoretical move, he declared this aggressive drive to be the derivative of a death instinct, which, together with the sexual instinct, constituted the two main forces in the struggle of life.

Based upon observations of children turning passive traumatic experiences into play, certain analysands returning over and over again to painful past experiences, the behavior of those who must go through similar calamities repeatedly, and the painful preoccupations of war veterans, Freud suggested that there might be a wicked, self-destructive, "daemonic force" (1920, p. 35) at work in them. This force seemed to work in opposition to the pleasure principle. It is as though these individuals never comprehend the futility of their repetitions. Freud argued that this force was aligned with a fundamental attribute of mind which involved a search for reduction of all excitation to quiescence. At its deepest, this search for quiescence—the "Nirvana principle"[1] —was aimed at returning the living organism to its previous, inorganic state. He concluded that "*the aim of all life is death*" (p. 38) and thus gave voice to his celebrated concept of the death instinct.

The death instinct, at birth, is a threat to the self. Therefore, it is deflected outward by the influence of libido and ego, using the agency of somatic musculature. Freud termed this outwardly deflected component of the death instinct the "aggressive instinct" (*Aggressionstrieb*).[2] This conceptualization altered his earlier views of sadism and masochism. He now put forward the following proposal:

A portion of the death instinct is placed directly in the service of the sexual function, where it has an important part to play. This is sadism proper. Another portion does not share in this transposition outwards; it remains inside the organism and, with the help of accompanying sexual excitation . . . becomes libidinally bound there. It is in this portion that we have to recognize the original, erotogenic masochism. [1924b, pp. 163–164]

The earlier formulation in which sadism is primary and masochism secondary appears to be reversed here. The death instinct is, after all, at first self-directed, only later outer-directed. However,

---

1. Freud (1920, p. 56) acknowledged borrowing this expression from Barbara Low, a Sanskrit expert. The notion of "death instinct" thus, from the beginning, had an Eastern touch. Fechner, the renowned physiologist whose "constancy principle" led Freud to "Nirvana principle" was himself involved in Buddhism (Jones, 1957). And, Romain Rolland, from whom Freud (1930) obtained the semi-related concept of "oceanic feeling," was an avid reader and biographer of the nineteenth-century Indian mystics Ramakrishna and Vivekananda. It thus seems that the Indian mystic tradition was a background conceptual source for Freud's death instinct. This may have been part of why the concept appeared alien to Western minds.

2. The term, with differing emphasis, was introduced by Adler in 1908 (see Jones, 1957).

such thinking misses the point that neither the primary self-direction nor the primary outward direction of the death instinct are libidinally charged, a requirement for aggression to be either masochistic or sadistic. Indeed, Freud continued to imply (for example, 1930, p. 120) that there was both an inward and an outward discharge of aggression free of erotism.[3] Moreover, he retained the earlier formulation of masochism as self-directed sadism, merely renaming it "secondary masochism" (1924b, p. 164).

Over subsequent years, Freud became increasingly committed to his second dual instinct theory. In *The Ego and the Id*, he repeated this theory, adding that the death instinct operates silently (1923, p. 46). In *Civilization and Its Discontents*, he emphasized that "the inclination to aggression is an original, self-subsisting instinctual disposition in man, and . . . [the] aggressive instinct is the derivative and the main representative of the death instinct" (1930, p. 122). In polar opposition to his 1905 view that destructive aggression ("cruelty") may result from thwarting of the instinct for mastery, Freud now suggested that the "instinct of destruction, moderated and tamed, and, as it were, inhibited in its aim, must, when it is directed towards objects, provide the ego with the satisfaction of its vital needs and with control over nature" (1930, p. 121).

Thus we see Freud attempting to reconcile aggression with the instinct for mastery. In this connection, Parens's (1979, p. 54) observation that Freud often spoke of "an instinct of aggressiveness *and* destructiveness" and of "non-erotic aggressivity *and* destructiveness" (1930, pp. 119–120, my emphasis) is significant. Parens wonders if Freud was intending to distinguish destructive and nondestructive aggression. Perhaps. But even if this were true, the source of nondestructive aggression appears far from settled in Freud's writings. In 1905, the striving for mastery arose in its own right; in 1930, it resulted from inhibition of the aim of innate destructiveness.

In 1937 Freud again referred to the death instinct and related masochism, negative therapeutic reaction, and unconscious guilt to its derivative, the aggressive drive. Again, in passing, he seemed to distinguish "the instinct of aggression *or* of destruction according to its aims" (p. 243, my emphasis). Finally, in the *Outline*, he reiterated his formulation

of "two basic instincts" (1940, p. 148). The aim of one was to establish unities, that of the other to undermine connections and destroy things. Freud noted the lack of a term analogous to libido for the energy of the death instinct.[4] He also reiterated that when this instinct operates internally, it operates silently, coming to our notice only when it is diverted outward as an instinct of destruction. Freud emphasized that the two basic instincts, in spite of being opposed, frequently combined with each other. Indeed, this "concurrent and mutually opposing action of the two basic instincts gives rise to the whole variegation of the phenomena of life" (1940, p. 149).

DIVERGENCE: MELANIE KLEIN AND HEINZ HARTMANN AND THEIR RESPECTIVE FOLLOWERS

As far as a theory of drives is concerned, the analytic world has remained, since 1920, divided into two factions, with convictions ranging from complete or even extreme commitment to Freud's dualistic theory of drives to an equally complete rejection of the assumption of a death instinct with aggression as its representative. [A. Freud, 1972, p. 170]

The conceptual chasm between Freud's pre- and post-1920 views on aggression ultimately gave rise to a bifurcation of the Freudian theory of aggression. One group of analysts followed the death instinct route. The other chose to concentrate on the distinct nature of the aggressive drive, its modulation by the ego, and its role in psychic structure formation. Melanie Klein and Heinz Hartmann are representatives par excellence of these two lines of theoretical advance.

Klein became the most "uncompromising" (Gay, 1988, p. 402) exponent of the death instinct, the Freudian postulate that had been accepted by only a few early analysts (Ferenczi, 1929; Weiss, 1935; Menninger, 1938; and Eitingon, Federn, and Nunberg, according to Jones, 1957). In a series of striking, though controversial, contributions (1933, 1935, 1946, 1948, 1952), Klein elaborated a theory of neonatal instinctual life and its role in object relations during that period. Although Klein's wide-ranging views on instincts, internal objects, primitive ego defenses, and psychic structuralization and their subsequent extension by others (Heimann, 1952; Bion, 1956, 1959; Segal 1964; Rosenfeld,

---

3. Gaddini (1972) later noted that such outward discharge occurs through striated muscles, while the "discharge on the inside takes place through the smooth muscles of the vessels and mucous membranes" (p. 191). The significance of the latter for psychosomatic illness merits further exploration.

4. The terms "destrudo" and "mortudo" were suggested by Stekel and Weiss but never gained Freud's favor. The same is true of the term "Thanatos," coined by Stekel in 1909 and later used to denote the death instinct by Federn (see Jones, 1957, pp. 266–280).

1965; Grotstein, 1981) need not be summarized here, her particular emphasis on innate aggression is worth noting.

Klein saw the infant as threatened by destruction from within immediately following birth. Giving concreteness and specificity to Freud's (1920, 1930) notion of the death instinct being deflected outward, Klein proposed that such deflection results in the creation of an "all bad" external object. This, in turn, leads to persecutory anxieties. The primitive ego, which Klein saw as operant from birth, defends against these anxieties by splitting itself, introjecting the bad object and projecting a portion of the life instinct outward to create an "all good" object. Thus both life and death instincts are intimately linked with early object relations. The tendency to view objects as "all good" or "all bad," with the concomitant affects of greed and envy and defensive splitting of the ego, is characteristic of the earliest phase of life ("the paranoid position"). With increasing ego maturation, the inner origins of aggression are acknowledged, and projective mechanisms recede. The conviction of lack of inner aggression and guilt over it can no longer be maintained. Synthesis of good and bad part objects becomes possible, with a resultant deepening of object relations ("the depressive position"). Now the predominant ego anxiety is in the nature of ambivalence, guilt, and sadness, the defenses against which center around either hypomanic denial or gratitude and reparation.

Klein extended this scheme further, presenting a different view of the oedipus complex and superego structuralization. However, her views pose problems, by pushing the developmental timetable to earlier and earlier infancy, attributing an unrealistically elaborate fantasy life to the early ego (for a rebuttal of this particular criticism, see Hayman, 1989), positing a priori images of objects by viewing the first objects of the drives as extensions of the drives themselves, and ignoring the importance of the actual behavior of early caretakers in laying the foundations of the psychic structure. Yet, some of her concepts—such as the splitting defense, the gradual emergence of the capacity for ambivalence, mourning, and sadness, and the powerful role of constitutional givens (especially intense aggression) in severe psychopathology—have received increasingly serious attention.[5]

Heinz Hartmann, by contrast, has had a much more widespread influence on psychoanalytic theorizing, especially in the United States. While firmly adhering to a "primary aggressive propensity in

man," Hartmann discarded Freud's notion of a death instinct as a nonverifiable and clinically inapplicable "biological speculation" (Hartmann et al., 1949, p. 11). Highlighting differences between humans and animals, he proposed the term "instinctual drive" ("drive," for short) as preferable to "instinct" in the human context. Contrasting the aggressive drive with its libidinal counterpart, he noted that the two were alike in regard to *impetus* but differed in source, aim, and object. The source of libido, especially in its sequential relation to the erogenous zones, was clear. But the proposed relationship between aggression and musculature (Freud, 1915) explained discharge, not genesis. Moreover, both libidinal and aggressive tensions could be discharged by motor activity. The *source* of aggression, therefore, remained unclear. Sexual aims varied greatly, but the aim of aggression appeared "less diversified" (Hartmann et al., 1949, p. 18). Active aggression involved the "wish to harm, to master, or to destroy an object; passivity refers to the wish to be mastered, harmed, or destroyed" (p. 17). However, aggressive aims varied with the means of expression and the degree of instinctual discharge. With respect to the object, too, libido and aggression differed insofar as a full discharge of aggression endangered the object, whereas a full discharge of libido did not.

Hartmann delineated other important characteristics of aggression: namely, that aggressive discharge is less structured than libidinal discharge, which follows specific time curves; that aggressive and libidinal impulses might be more efficiently dealt with by different defenses; that aggressive and libidinal aims can both be inhibited by ego and superego dictates, but that aim inhibition of aggression also results from the object's investment with libido; that aggression, in a sublimated form, is more integrated into the ego and superego structure than libido, which, being capable of full discharge, is tied more closely to the object; that the discharge of aggressive tension, more than that of libidinal tension, depends on muscular activity; and that the aggressive drive, when neutralized, contributes to the self-preservation function. Hartmann also noted that four types of conflict lead to inhibition of the aim of aggression: instinctual conflict, conflict with reality, structural conflict involving the ego, and structural conflict involving the superego. In addition, there exist four processes that modify the impact of aggression: displacement, aim inhibition, fusion with libido, and sublimation. The last of these he saw as involving an energy change, the resultant neutralized aggressive energy fueling the ego's motor activity and the ego's and superego's countercathectic measures. Hart-

5. For recent assessments of Klein's contributions, see Kernberg, 1975b, 1980, and Greenberg & Mitchell, 1983.

mann thus added a third type to the two types of inward discharge of aggression (one silent and nonerotic, the other libidinized hence masochistic) already outlined by Freud. He stressed that the capacity to neutralize aggression is a criterion of the ego's strength and that the lack of such neutralization betrays a weak ego.

Regarding the origins of aggression, Hartmann (1939) began with the assumption of an undifferentiated phase of psychic structure during which both libido and aggression are centered in the self. Gradual localization of unpleasure outside the body invites the cathexis of its source with aggression. This protects the self and is pleasurable too, since it discharges aggressive tension. Such association of aggression with pleasure constitutes the basis of sadism, which, however, requires the additional element of libidinal pleasure in inflicting pain and humiliating someone. It can be viewed, therefore, only in the context of a well-developed object relation. Not all aggressive tendencies directed against objects are sadistic. Hartmann noted that while aggression was fueled by an inner driving force akin to libido, it could also be mobilized by deprivations and frustrations. What is found frustrating by the growing child, however, and the ways of expressing aggression over it vary according to the developmental phase (Freud, 1905c; Abraham, 1924). Characteristic ways include biting during the oral phase, spite and obstinacy during the anal phase, and hostile competitiveness with (and, by projection, fear of) the rival parent during the oedipal phase. During the second and third years of life, much transformation of aggression occurs, so equipping the ego with neutralized energy. In the oedipal phase, the aggression vested in the parents is internalized, with relatively less neutralization into the superego, which consequently retains an instinctual quality. The subsequent latency period is characterized by further neutralization of aggression and a widening of ego functions in the conflict-free sphere (Hartmann, 1939).

Hartmann's exposition of the genetic, dynamic, economic, and structural aspects of aggression became a touchstone for all later theoretical contributions to this topic. Waelder (1956), while accepting the proposition of an essential, or primary, destructiveness, drew attention to the adaptive aspects of aggression and to the relation between ego mastery and aggression. Hartmann's influence is also evident in Jacobson's (1964) theory of a primary undifferentiated phase, gradual drive differentiation, the role of aggression in demarcating real from wishful self presentations, and the importance of assimilating aggression to the deepening of object relations and the structuralization of the superego.

In 1971, a panel discussion focused on the role of aggression in adaptation. There, Hamburg (1973), representing an evolutionary approach, highlighted the "anlage of aggressive tendencies, transmitted genetically yet requiring environmental stimulation for full development" (p. 194). Marcovitz (1973) described the spectrum of aggression from curiosity, exploration, and self-assertion to dominance, exploitation, hostility, and hate. While he acknowledged its destructive aspects, he emphasized that without aggression there would be "no survival, no active drive toward learning, nor to the mastery of our own inner drives and of the challenges of the world around us" (p. 231). Nevertheless, he viewed aggression and libidinal gratification as inseparable in processes of adaptation. Joseph (1973), invoking Hendrick's (1942) "instinct of mastery," suggested that preoccupation with clinical problems precluded attention to the nonhostile aspects of aggression. He advocated a broadening of the definition of aggression to include all forceful behavior that involves approaching an object and saw the rooting reflex of the nursing infant as the prototype of aggression in the service of adaptation. Arlow (1973) noted that the innate aggressive propensity is modified by experience, especially by the earliest interactions of the individual with his or her environment. The macrocosm of society is established within the microcosm of the individual, and social structure, cultural history, and group values all play a significant role in the modulation of aggression and, in turn, adaptation. Psychoanalysis, however, permits the reconstruction of the omitted—that is, unconscious—motivations indispensable to the process of adaptation.

Papers presented at the Twenty-Seventh International Psycho-Analytical Congress in Vienna echoed the Klein–Hartmann divergence (see, for instance, the opposing positions of Gillespie [1971] and Rosenfeld [1971]). Hartmann's powerful influence was also amply evident (Heimann & Valenstein, 1972). Anna Freud (1972), for instance, concurred with him in rejecting the death instinct and in regard to the ambiguity of the source and changing aims of aggression. In contrast to Hartmann, however, she saw libidinal aims as more specific to the drive, while aggressive aims associated themselves with varying purposes. The two drives also differed in regard to their object. Libidinal development proceeded from a need-satisfying object to object constancy, but aggression did not take this step toward sustained commitment. A good lover is faithful, a good hater promiscuous; even the "fixed hate" (p. 165) of the paranoic is a vicissitude of the libido rather than of aggression.[6] At the same meeting, Sandler (in Panel, 1972a) attempted to clarify the dichotomy between the innate and the reactive origins of aggression. He proposed a "capacity to be aggressive" that exists alongside an instinctual drive and is mobilized by the ego to avoid unpleasure. Brenner (1971) emphasized that aggression and libido bear a similar relationship to the pleasure principle: their discharge causes pleasure, lack of discharge unpleasure. He noted that aggression has variable aims and that aggression and libido play comparable roles in psychic conflict. But it remained unclear whether aggression and sexuality differentiate gradually from a common matrix or are separate from birth on. In 1982, Brenner reiterated this stance, stressing that, once separated, both "libido and aggression are within the pleasure principle, not beyond it" (p. 39). He now sought to resolve the dilemma about the source of aggression by declaring that the drives have "no special, extracerebral source. Like all other psychic phenomena, they are an aspect of cerebral functioning" (ibid.).

Having reviewed the post-Hartmann contributions from within the ego psychology tradition, we can now go back full circle and add that, while Melanie Klein and Heinz Hartmann represented the two major theoretical trends after Freud, there was a third viewpoint as well.

DISSENT: BRITISH OBJECT RELATIONS THEORY AND SELF PSYCHOLOGY

[F]our theoretical shifts from classical psychoanalytic theory . . . were variously made by object relations theorists: the movement from a one-body to a multi-body psychology; the relegation of instinctual motivation from the center toward the periphery; the recognition of significant linkages other than the instinctual between the self and the object; and, the emphasis on the importance of self-development. [Bacal & Newman, 1990, p. 11]

Self-psychology has freed itself from the distorted view of psychological man espoused by traditional

6. Blum's (1981) concept of the "inconstant object" is a contemporary elaboration of this "fixed hate" theme. It refers to an ambivalently loved object which is felt as both persecutory and needed. It cannot be allowed to have a separate existence. The threat of betrayal by it must be tenaciously maintained. In a sense, such constant fear of persecution is the reciprocal of libidinal object constancy and a desperate effort to preserve an illusory constant object.

analysis . . . [which] had to carry the burden imposed on it by its need to make a bow to biology— via the quasi-biological conception of primary drives which are seen as being processed by a mental apparatus. [Kohut, 1982, p. 402]

While the Anna Freud–Melanie Klein controversy occupied center stage in British psychoanalysis, another scenario, involving the development of the object relations theory, quietly unfolded in the wings. Evolved by Suttie, Balint, Fairbairn, Winnicott, and Guntrip, this perspective either downplayed (Balint and Winnicott) or totally rejected (Suttie, Fairbairn, and Guntrip) the instinctual underpinnings of aggression. In this group of theorists, none is "more remarkable nor more unsung than Ian Suttie" (Bacal & Newman, 1990, p. 5). As early as 1924, he rejected instincts and declared human behavior to be basically motivated by a need for safety and companionship. Some years later, Suttie (1935) proposed that after an early phase of "infantile solipsism" (p. 29), the child undergoes a process of "psychic parturition" (p. 27) through which it becomes capable of independent existence. During this process, the need for the mother's love is intense, hence the vulnerability of separation anxiety. Anger or hate is "a development or intensification of separation-anxiety which in turn is roused by a threat against love. It is the maximal ultimate appeal in the child's power. . . . Its purpose is not death-seeking or death-dealing, but the preservation of the self from the isolation which is death, and the restoration of a love relationship" (p. 31).

Balint (1935) arrived at a similar conclusion regarding aggression. He too minimized the instinctual underpinnings of hate and aggression and located their origin in the absence of a gratifying relationship. However, it was Fairbairn (1943, 1944) who, out of this entire group, presented the most clearly spelled-out theory of psychic development and endopsychic structures. In sharp disagreement with Klein, who had paid only lip service to the environment, Fairbairn stressed the actual role of early caretakers in the child's personality formation. He proposed that an ego is present from birth on and that libido is not pleasure-seeking but object-seeking. It can attach itself to good as well as bad objects, and the latter investment explains aggression:

What Freud describes under the category of "death instincts" would thus appear to represent for the most part masochistic relationships with internalized bad objects. A sadistic relationship with a bad object which is internalized would also represent the appearance of a death instinct. As a matter of fact, such relationships are usually of a sa-domasochistic nature with a bias on the masochis-tic side of the scale; but in any case they are essentially libidinal manifestations. [Fairbairn, 1943, p. 79]

Winnicott also rejected the death instinct while re-taining the notion of innate aggression in the infant.[7] He seemed to think, however, that such "aggressive-ness is almost synonymous with activity" (1950, p. 204). Or, even more emphatically:

> Aggression is seen more as evidence of life. Un-der favourable conditions, fusion occurs between the erotic and the motility impulses, and then the term oral sadism becomes applicable, followed by all the developments of this theme. This is matched by the mother's wish to be imaginatively eaten. Failure of fusion, or loss of fusion that has been achieved, produces a potential element of pure destructiveness (i.e. without guilt-sense) in the individual. [1959, p. 127]

Winnicott saw even such destructiveness as devel-opmentally necessary, since its expression enables the child to discover that the mother can survive it. This facilitates his or her awareness (and later, ac-ceptance) of their separateness, making deeper rela-tions between them possible. Consequently, Win-nicott (1956) held that aggressive and outrageous behavior frequently implied the hope that someone would rectify the deficiencies of care experienced in childhood. Guntrip (1969), even more strongly, viewed conflicts over aggression (and sex) as up-ward defenses against a ruptured, tormented self. He asserted that the "frustration–aggression theory is the only one supported by clinical observation" (1971, p. 131). The notion that a powerful caldron of instincts governs human behavior is itself a de-fensive postulate, which protects us from viewing ourselves as fundamentally weak and vulnerable. Guntrip attributed self-destructiveness to a deep hatred of one's own vulnerability, which, in turn, resulted from anaclitic betrayals by others during in-fancy.

This bare-bones summary of the rich ideas of these innovative analysts does not do justice to them. Yet, the inclusion of this significant post-Freudian trend helps underscore the conceptual an-cestry of the contemporary self psychology view of aggression. The resemblance between Fairbairn's and Kohut's (1972, 1977) ideas, for instance, is

striking (Robbins, 1980; Akhtar, 1989; Bacal & Newman, 1990). Both regard a pristine, whole self to exist from the beginning, and both view its growth as depending more on satisfactory object relations than on libidinal gratification. Both view regression as a separate pathway, not a reversal of developmen-tal steps previously taken. Both discard the pleasure principle and instinctual drives, especially inborn ag-gression. Although Kohut recognizes an "elemental aggression" (1977, p. 120) which helps in the estab-lishment and maintenance of the self, he does not view it as a drive-related phenomenon. Moreover, he believes that such nondestructive aggressiveness "has a developmental line of its own—it does not develop out of primitive destructiveness" (p. 121). Destructive aggression, on the other hand, is a re-action to chronic and traumatic frustration of the phase-appropriate need for omnipotent control over the selfobjects of infancy and childhood.

While the resemblance between Fairbairn's and Kohut's views is clear, Fairbairn's influence on Kernberg's (1976, 1982, 1991a, 1991b) theory of aggression is less recognized. Fairbairn seems to have influenced both Kohut and Kernberg, albeit in different ways (Akhtar, 1989). Kohut elaborated on Fairbairn's "external" or environmental emphasis, Kernberg on Fairbairn's "internal" or structural fo-cus. Such influence of the British object relations theorists extends beyond Kohut and Kernberg, how-ever. Certain aspects of Parens's (1979, 1989a, 1989b) formulation of aggression, for instance, echo Winnicott's near equation of activity and aggression.

REFORMULATION: THE CONTRIBUTIONS OF HENRI PARENS AND OTTO KERNBERG

[T]he psychoanalytical study of child development would fill an urgent need, might usefully function as center of integration of various approaches and promises the only way to answer the questions with which we all are occupied, questions in which the problem of prevention is omnipresent. [Kris, 1950, p. 37]

With birth . . . pleasurable and unpleasurable sen-sations begin to be perceived and become attached to, though still confused with, beginning outside per-ceptions. Energic differentiation occurs; libidinal and aggressive cathectic gathering poles are formed around nuclei of as yet unorganized and discon-nected memory traces. [Jacobson, 1964, p. 52]

Responding to appeals by Hartmann (1950, 1958) and Kris (1950) and following their own intuition, a number of child analysts undertook observations of

---

7. Winnicott was the only one among these five theo-rists to have had extensive clinical experience with infants and children. This may partly explain his inability to reject innate aggression and its usefulness for development.

infants and young children in order to complement the reconstructive data of clinical psychoanalysis. Among the outstanding concepts that emerged from their work are the structuring of the libidinal object (Spitz, 1946, 1950, 1965), developmental lines (A. Freud, 1963), and separation-individuation theory (Mahler, 1965; Mahler & Furer, 1968; Mahler & McDevitt, 1968; Mahler et al., 1975). In the specific context of aggression, too, many of these investigators (for example, Solnit, 1966, 1972; Parens, 1973, 1979, 1980, 1984, 1989a, 1989b, 1991; McDevitt, 1983; Downey, 1984) made enormously significant contributions. The work of Parens especially offers a systematic reformulation of the concept of aggression.

In the course of his long-term, weekly observation of infants and young children, Parens noted that there is, practically from birth onward, "an inner-drivenness, a pressured internal thrust, to assert the infantile self upon the environment via sensorimotor functioning" (1989a, p. 112). Such activity put into question the classical assumption of aggression being inherently destructive, since this activity was in no way destructive. Instead, it served the purpose of "apprehending, assimilating and bringing the environment under control" (1979, p. 66). Parens wondered how to explain this activity. If it was an aspect of the primary ego autonomy, then what was its energy source? It could not be "deinstinctualized" ego energy, since that results from drive neutralization, and ego with the capacity to neutralize drives does not emerge until about six months of age (Hartmann, 1952; Schur, 1966; Spitz, 1965; Weil, 1976; Parens, 1979, 1989a; McDevitt, 1983). Yet, the activity was evident before that age. A second explanation was that the early ego possessed "noninstinctual energy" (Hartmann, 1939) of its own. But how is the "noninstinctual" energy different from the "deinstinctualized" energy? Do they mix or change into one another? Are they used for similar or different purposes? More significantly, how could such activity derive from noninstinctual energy when it had unmistakable instinctual qualities, such as inner drivenness and pressure?

Noting such discordance between the observable data and the classical theory of aggression, Parens undertook further longitudinal studies of children's manifestations of aggression. He detected four categories of aggressive behaviors: unpleasure-related destructive behaviors (for example, rage reaction of infancy), nonaffective destructive behaviors (akin to "prey aggression" in animals and represented by feeding activity[8]), nondestructive aggressive be-

haviors (for example, exploration, assertion), and pleasure-related destructive behaviors (for example, teasing, convincingly discernible only from the beginning of the second year of life).

Based upon these data, Parens proposed three fundamental trends of aggressive drive: nondestructive aggression, nonaffective destructiveness, and hostile destructiveness, each having a powerful heuristic value of its own. The first cast doubt on the death instinct theory of aggression and the continued assertion (for example, by Brenner, 1982) that, even without the death instinct, the primary aim of aggression is destruction, by showing that aggression "is not inherently only destructive" (Parens, 1989a, p. 115). The second disengaged destructiveness from hostility by demonstrating destructiveness for the purpose of alimentation and, therefore, self-preservation. The third had the most significant repercussions. While infantile rage reactions were its built-in prototype, hostile destructiveness emerged only gradually and in the context of greater ego maturity. Moreover, it required excessive unpleasure for its activation. Therefore, it should be avoidable by reducing excessive unpleasure, a deduction of enormous preventive potential (Parens et al., 1987).

Parens noted that many others (Storr, 1968; Kohut, 1977; Gunther, 1980; Rochlin, 1982; McDevitt, 1983) had also concluded that an innate motivational force of nondestructive aggression exists and that rage and hostility are not inborn but provoked experientially. He also emphasized that aggression is influenced by experience and maturation. Following the landmarks derived from Mahler's separation-individuation theory, Parens traced the epigenetic unfolding of aggression and elucidated the vicissitudes of hostile destructiveness during the oedipal phase, including their role in the structuralization of the superego.[9] Throughout his epigenetic model, Parens emphasized the reciprocal influence of the

---

8. Drawing a parallel with animal "prey aggression" and "rival aggression," Lantos (1958), too, distinguished be-

tween nonaffective and affect-laden aggression in man. While she viewed both as basically instinctual, she saw them as having different genetic origins and recommended that the former be simply labeled "activity."

9. With varying degrees of emphasis on its instinctual dimension, many other investigators have addressed the vicissitudes of aggression either throughout the life span (Erikson, 1950) or through the specific periods of infancy and early childhood (for example, Freud, 1924a; Jacobson, 1964; Mahler et al., 1975; A. Freud, 1972; Downey, 1984), adolescence (Blos, 1967), young adulthood (Escoll, 1991), middle age (Kernberg, 1980), and senescence (Erikson, 1950). For the period of early childhood, Downey's (1984) comments regarding the relationships between aggression and differentiation, aggression and transitional object formation, and aggression and visual modality are highly pertinent.

three trends of aggressive drive—nondestructive aggression, nonaffective destructiveness, and hostile destructiveness—upon each other.

By contrast, Kernberg (1976)—who has made profound contributions to the clinical aspects of severe character pathology associated with pronounced aggression (1984), sadomasochism (1991b), and hatred (1991a)—assigned the nondestructive and nonaffectively destructive aspects of aggression to the primary autonomous functions. His view of their energic source, though incompletely spelled out, appears to follow Hartmann's (1939, 1950), locating it in noninstinctual ego resources and in the energy resulting from drive neutralization. Kernberg (1982, 1991c) regarded only hostile destructiveness as relevant to the origin of aggression as a drive. Emphasizing the distinction between Freud's terms *Trieb* and *Instinkt* and echoing Hartmann et al. (1949), Kernberg (1982) reiterated that while instincts are discontinuous, rigid, innate predispositions, drives are relatively continuous motivational systems at the psychophysical interface. He therefore preferred the term "drive" in connection with (libido and) aggression. At this point, Kernberg parted company with Freud and Hartmann and proposed a considerably different formulation of drives (including, of course, the aggressive drive), which resulted in a "modification of the dual instinct theory" (1982, p. 915).

Kernberg collected the building blocks of his theory from the modern instinct theory in biology (Tinbergen, 1951; Lorenz, 1963; Wilson, 1975), Jacobson's (1971) psychoanalytic theory of affects, Mahler's (Mahler & Furer, 1968; Mahler et al., 1975) research on separation-individuation, and the empirical findings of Arnold (1970), Izard (1978), Knapp (1979), and Emde (1987). He suggested that affects constitute the earliest motivational system and are intimately involved in the fixation by memory of an internalized object relationship. Affects, emanating from "wired-in" instinctive components, are simply pleasurable or unpleasurable in the beginning. They link primitive object relations in two corresponding parallel series of gratifying and frustrating, or aversive, experiences. With ego growth and increasing sophistication of internalization processes, these pleasurable and unpleasurable affects are organized as love and hate. "Love and hate thus become stable intrapsychic structures, in genetic continuity through various developmental stages, and, by that very continuity, consolidate into libido and aggression. Libido and aggression, in turn, become hierarchically supraordinate motivational systems. . . . Affects, in short, are the building blocks or constituents of drives" (Kernberg, 1982, p. 908).

In Kernberg's view, aggression "as a drive results

from the integration of negative, or aversive affects" (1991c, p. 111). Like Hartmann, Kernberg holds a tight view of instinctual aggression; but, unlike Hartmann, he declares that drives are not external givens but evolve from affects. Like Klein, Kernberg emphasizes the role of instinctual aggression in the earliest internalizations; but, unlike Klein, he discards the death instinct. Like Fairbairn, Kernberg retains the importance of early object relations in the genesis of aggression; but, unlike Fairbairn, he regards the underpinnings of aggression as fundamentally instinctual in origin. Kernberg's theory, in essence, is a reconciliation of the Klein–Fairbairn schism under the influence of Hartmann's ego psychology. It therefore brings together the three major psychoanalytic trends in the study of aggression.

CODA: SYNTHESIS, REFLECTIONS, AND CONCLUSION

Those who reject the death drive are not aware that, when they do so without introducing another set of explanations for the phenomenon of death, they are simply scotomatizing the most relevant part of psychology, and then going on as if their theories still had some chance of being correct. [Eissler, 1971, p. 27]

A fire becomes, not less, but more truly a fire as it burns faster. It's the being consumed that pushes back the darkness, illumines whatever there is of good in our days and nights. If it weren't brief it wouldn't be precious. Let me say it flatly: We are lucky we die, and anyone who pushes away the awareness of death lives but half a life. [Wheelis, 1971, p. 68]

This survey of psychoanalytic theories concerning the nature and origins of aggression has highlighted the difficult questions in this area. For instance, is there an instinctual aggressive drive? Does it derive from the so-called death instinct? Or does it emanate from the integration of unpleasurable affects of early infantile life? Are libido and aggression of comparable metapsychological status? Does aggression serve adaptation? What is the relationship between self-preservation and aggression? Does the self-preservative capacity result from neutralized aggression? Or does a threat to self-preservation lead to the emergence of destructive aggression? Is aggression fundamentally destructive? Or are there nondestructive forms of aggression? Is aggression rendered constructive only by its fusion with libido? Or do the wholesome forms of aggression originate as such? Are cruelty, destructiveness, and sadomasochism inherent in human nature? Or are they consequences of frustrated libidinal aims, thwarted vigor, injured narcissism?

Attempts to answer these questions must, at the outset, tackle a more basic issue. This pertains to the very definition of aggression. The foregoing overview of the literature reveals that this fundamental question is far from settled. Clinical observations of aggressive behavioral equivalents are ubiquitous, and there seems to be a consensus that aggression manifests itself in myriad forms. Nevertheless, there is a dispute about what can be legitimately included under the rubric of aggression. It is here that the term seems to be employed in two different ways that may not be compatible. Some theorists restrict the definition of aggression to hostile destructiveness, while others extend it to include assertion and activity. Indeed, the term "aggression" has increasingly been used as if it accommodated both possibilities. But the practice does not justify the conclusion that such an accommodation has truly been achieved or is even possible. In fact, careful scrutiny reveals that the psychoanalytic discourse on aggression is riddled with tautological leaps, semantic overflow, and confusion between matters of fact and matters of definition. Circular reasoning also abounds, as when assertive, nondestructive behavior is called "aggressive" and is then advanced as proof that not all aggression is destructive in aim. The unfortunate use of the same language for empirical data and speculative theories adds to confusion in this area. My hope is that my discussion of aggression may provide greater clarification of the problems involved in the concept, if not the concept itself.

But, in a recapitulation aimed at raising further questions, I wish to note that five theoretical positions exist in this area. One extreme holds steadfastly to the death instinct theory (Freud, Ferenczi, Klein, Federn, Menninger, Eissler, and Rosenfeld) and posits aggression as a fundamentally destructive, outward deflection of such an instinctual substrate. The other extreme is represented by those theorists who have dissociated themselves from the instinctual basis of human motivation altogether (Suttie, Fairbairn, Guntrip, and Kohut). While their view allows for innate[10] assertiveness, which, under the influence of frustration, may turn into destructiveness, it definitely rules out innate destructiveness. Between these extremes lie three other views

which discard the death instinct while firmly adhering to the instinct theory and view aggression as one of the two basic instinctual drives. The first regards the aim of aggression as variable, though mainly involving destruction. It sees the infant's assertion, motility, and activity as emanating from a noninstinctual energy source to which neutralization of aggression may also add (A. Freud, Hartmann, Kris, Loewenstein, Waelder, and Brenner). The second position extends the scope of instinctual aggression to include infantile activity, assertion, and attempts at mastery. It considers both nondestructive and destructive aggression to be fueled from the same energy source. Moreover, it emphasizes that hostile destructiveness is only elicited by unpleasure (Winnicott and Parens). The third position excludes nondestructive activity from the concept of aggression and presents a concept of drive that is considerably different from the traditional view. It proposes that early pleasurable and unpleasurable affects (and their associated neonatal object relations) gradually consolidate into the libidinal and aggressive drives, which subsequently become supraordinate motivational systems (Kernberg).

The roots of all five positions can, in one way or another, be traced to Freud, a fact that attests to both the richness of Freud's ideas and the latitude in their interpretation. Such latitude of interpretation is a minor problem, however, compared to the definitional confusion that affects these theories. Moreover, the degree to which testable hypotheses can be derived from these viewpoints remains unclear. Finally, the fact that these theories have been derived from varying sources of data puts in question their comparability.

Finally, I would like to make some further remarks about two issues, one pertaining to the death instinct, the other to the relationship between assertion and aggression. My selection may seem arbitrary but is actually in keeping with the two key words—"origins" and "nature"—in the title of this chapter. The issue of the death instinct concerns origins; the assertion–aggression controversy, nature.

Klein's (1933, 1935, 1952) fierce allegiance to the death instinct, Eissler's (1971) loyal protest in favor of its retention, and Wheelis's (1971) poignant reminder of its experiential rumblings notwithstanding, most analysts have laid the postulate of a death instinct to rest. Yet, a close examination of psychoanalytic literature shows a recurring belief that there is, in man, a vague drivelike internal pull toward the loss of the boundaries, if not the existence, of the psychic self. Giving rise to such a belief are the merger fantasies, often associated with feeding and with sleep (Lewin, 1950), the deep-seated wish for

---

10. The distinction between "innate" and "instinctual" is significant here, since these theorists do not totally negate the former. In a different, broader context, this distinction is also exemplified in the various fundamental human motivational systems outlined by Lichtenberg (1989).

loss of human identity by "metamorphosis" (Lichtenstein, 1961), the everlasting wish for "the lost, original union with the mother" (Jacobson, 1964, p. 39), in the context of neonatal life "the drive to return to an earlier state where all was gratified automatically" (L. Stone, 1971, p. 236), man's eternal yearning to recapture the "coenesthetically remembered harmony of dual-unity stage" (Mahler, 1971, p. 186), "the search for oneness" (Kaplan, 1977), the neonates' "inborn and immediate wish to return to the intrauterine state" (Chasseguet-Smirgel, in Panel, 1991b, p. 751) and man's "nostalgia for primary narcissism" (Chasseguet-Smirgel, 1984, p. 29), the "someday" and "if only" fantasies (Akhtar, 1991), and an attempted reconciliation of "everything" and "nothing" fantasies that occurs "transiently in dreamless sleep and in the ecstasy of orgasm—but the promise of permanence can be realized only after our individual lives are over" (Shengold, 1991, · p. 7).

To be sure, these phenomena have their roots in diverse theoretical foundations, involve fantasy content not attributable to instinctual primitivity, and contain an unmistakable libidinal admixture with aggression. Yet, collectively, these notions do demand a reconceptualization of the death instinct idea. Such an examination might confirm the ubiquitous existence in man of a deep-seated wish for the loss of self boundaries, perhaps an echo of an early desire for (and memory of) fusion with the mother. It may be that this preverbal pull subsequently accrues fantasies from various levels of psychosexual development. Death too may enter this scenario, though not until long after infancy and childhood, perhaps not even until middle age. From then onward, the deep-seated desire for fusion with the mother might become intermingled with a longing for peace through death; a "death instinct" would thus have been set in motion. On the other hand, individuals who have been traumatized by early losses through death or themselves have faced early life-threatening crises might incorporate the notion of death into this substrate of fusion/oblivion-seeking much earlier. They might show evidence of possessing a "death instinct" even before middle age. Such a formulation of "death instinct" is clearly different from the one described earlier. In the context of this reconceptualization, the words *death* and *instinct* may both seem misplaced. Clearly, further thinking and more precise terminology are needed here.

Newer ways of thinking also seem needed in reference to healthy, nonconflictual activity and vigor and its relationship to aggression. Should it be called "nondestructive aggression" (Parens, 1979)? Or is it better simply to designate it "activity" (Lantos,

1958) and put it beyond the scope of studies of aggression? One plausible way out of this theoretical impasse has recently been suggested by Stechler (1987; Stechler & Halton, 1987; Lichtenberg, 1989). Stechler suggests that assertion derives from a universal exploratory tendency and aggression from a universal self-protective system. The latter reacts strongly and with dysphoric affects to threats from outside. If a child's assertions meet a punitive response from parents, the child reacts with dysphoria, which results in mutual contamination of assertion and aggression. When this is extensive, to all appearances an aggressive instinctual process has been set in motion. Lichtenberg (1989) voices a similar sentiment. He too regards assertion and aggression as being derived from separate and distinct bio-psychological origins. He concurs with Stechler that "the assertion system activates spontaneously in response to exploratory opportunities in the environment, whereas the aggression system is reactive to stimuli perceived as threatening or distress inducing" (p. 172). However, Lichtenberg favors "aversion" over "aggression" as the optimal designation for this latter system, because the innate response pattern comprising it is not only antagonism but also withdrawal. The important thing to note, however, is that both Stechler and Lichtenberg are seeking to retain the innate, "hard-wired" nature of assertion *and* aggression while conceptualizing their potentially dialectical ebb and flow within the modern systems theory context.

While further thought is needed to resolve this and other related questions—for example, the role of aggression in adaptation—efforts are already being directed to rendering the theoretical insights on aggression useful for day-to-day clinical work with difficult, sadomasochistic, perverse, suicidal, and borderline patients (Glick & Meyers, eds., 1988; Kernberg, 1975a, 1976, 1984; Kernberg et al., 1990; Rosenfeld, 1965; Volkan, 1976, 1987b). More significantly, the psychoanalytic understanding of aggression is beginning to yield guidelines for the prevention of excessive hostility and destructiveness. In this realm, the parent education strategies devised by Parens et al. (1987) are most promising. A related development concerns psychoanalytically-informed processes of negotiating for peace with antagonistic nations (Volkan, 1986, 1987a, 1988). While conceptual difficulties continue to exist, and unresolved questions still beckon from afar, the psychoanalytic study of aggression has clearly come a long way.[11]

11. My thanks go to Drs. Philip Escoll, George Klumpner, Selma Kramer, Henri Parens, and Sydney Pulver, M.D., for their helpful suggestions on earlier versions of this chapter.

REFERENCES

Abraham, K. (1924). A short study of the development of the libido. Rpt. in *Selected Papers of Karl Abraham,* pp. 418–501. New York: Basic Books, 1953.

Akhtar, S. (1989). Kohut and Kernberg. In *Self Psychology,* ed. D. W. Detrick & S. P. Detrick, pp. 329–362. Hillsdale, N.J.: Analytic Press.

———. (1991). Three fantasies related to unresolved separation-individuation. In *Beyond the Symbiotic Orbit,* ed. S. Akhtar & H. Parens., pp. 261–284. Hillsdale, N.J.: Analytic Press.

Arlow, J. A. (1973). Perspectives on aggression in human adaptation. *Psychoanal. Q.,* 42:178–184.

Arnold, M. B. (1970). Brain function in emotion. In *Physiological Correlates of Emotion,* ed. P. Black, pp. 261–285. New York: Academic Press.

Bacal, H. A., & Newman, K. M. (1990). *Theories of Object Relations.* New York: Columbia Univ. Press.

Balint, M. (1935). Critical notes on the pregenital organization of the libido. Rpt. in *Primary Love and Psycho-Analytic Technique,* pp. 37–58. London: Tavistock, 1965.

Bion, W. R. (1956). Development of schizophrenic thought. *Int. J. Psychoanal.,* 37:344–346.

———. (1959). Attacks on linking. *Int. J. Psychoanal.,* 40:308–315.

Blos, P. (1967). The second individuation process of adolescence. *Psychoanal. Study Child,* 22:162–186.

Blum, H. P. (1981). Object inconstancy and paranoid conspiracy. *J. Amer. Psychoanal. Assn.,* 29:789–813.

Brenner, C. (1971). The psychoanalytic concept of aggression. *Int. J. Psychoanal.,* 52:137–144.

———. (1982). *The Mind in Conflict.* New York: Int. Univ. Press.

Chasseguet-Smirgel, J. (1984). *Creativity and Perversion.* New York: Norton.

Downey, T. W. (1984). Within the pleasure principle. *Psychoanal. Study Child,* 39:101–136.

Eidelberg, L. (1968). "Aggression." In *Encyclopedia of Psychoanalysis,* pp. 21–22. New York: Free Press.

Eissler, K. R. (1971). Death drive, ambivalence, and narcissism. *Psychoanal. Study Child,* 26:25–78.

Emde, R. N. (1987). Constitutional aspects of the drives. Paper read at the meetings of the International Psychoanalytic Association, Montreal.

English, H. B., & English, A. C. (1976). *A Comprehensive Dictionary of Psychological and Psychoanalytic Terms.* New York: David McKay.

Erikson, E. H. (1950). *Childhood and Society.* New York: Norton.

———. (1982). *The Life Cycle Completed.* New York: Norton.

Escoll, P. (1991). Treatment implications of separation-individuation theory in the analysis of young adults. In *Beyond the Symbiotic Orbit,* ed. S. Akhtar & H. Parens, pp. 369–387. Hillsdale, N.J.: Analytic Press.

Fairbairn, R. (1943). The repression and the return of bad objects. Rpt. in *Psycho-Analytic Studies of the Personality,* pp. 59–81. London: Routledge & Kegan Paul, 1952.

———. (1944). Endopsychic structure considered in terms of object-relationships. Rpt. in *Psycho-Analytic Studies of the Personality,* pp. 82–132. London: Routledge & Kegan Paul, 1952.

Ferenczi, S. (1929). The unwelcome child and his death instinct. Rpt. in *Final Contributions to the Problems and Methods of Psycho-Analysis,* pp. 102–107. London: Hogarth Press, 1955.

Freud, A. (1963). The concept of developmental lines. *Psychoanal. Study Child,* 18:245–265.

———. (1972). Comments on aggression. *Int. J. Psychoanal.,* 53:163–171.

Freud, S. (1896). Specific aetiology of hysteria. *SE,* 3:163–168.

———. (1900). *The Interpretation of Dreams. SE,* 4 & 5.

———. (1905a). Fragment of an analysis of a case of hysteria. *SE,* 7:3–122.

———. (1905b). The purpose of jokes. *SE,* 8:90–116.

———. (1905c). *Three Essays on the Theory of Sexuality. SE,* 7:135–243.

———. (1909). Analysis of a phobia in a five-year-old boy. *SE,* 10:5–149.

———. (1915). Instincts and their vicissitudes. *SE,* 14:117–140.

———. (1920). *Beyond the Pleasure Principle. SE,* 18:7–64.

———. (1923). *The Ego and the Id. SE,* 19:12–68.

———. (1924a). The dissolution of the oedipus complex. *SE,* 19:173–182.

———. (1924b). The economic problem of masochism. *SE,* 19:157–170.

———. (1930). *Civilization and Its Discontents. SE,* 21:59–145.

———. (1933). *New Introductory Lectures on Psycho-Analysis. SE,* 22:3–182.

———. (1937). Analysis terminable and interminable. *SE,* 23:216–253.

———. (1940). *An Outline of Psycho-Analysis. SE,* 23:144–207.

Gaddini, E. (1972). Aggression and the pleasure principle. *Int. J. Psychoanal.,* 53:191–197.

Gay, P. (1988). *Freud: A Life for Our Time.* New York: Norton.

Gillespie, W. H. (1971). Aggression and instinct theory. *Int. J. Psychoanal.,* 52:155–160.

Glick, R. A., & Meyers, D. I., eds. (1988). *Masochism.* Hillsdale, N.J.: Analytic Press.

Greenberg, J. R., & Mitchell, S. A. (1983). *Object Relations in Psychoanalytic Theory.* Cambridge, Mass.: Harvard Univ. Press.

Grotstein, J. S. (1981). *Splitting and Projective Identification.* New York: Aronson.

Gunderson, J. (1985). *Borderline Personality Disorder.* Washington, D.C.: American Psychiatric Press.

Gunther, M. (1980). Aggression, self-psychology, and the concept of health. In *Advances in Self-Psychology,* ed. A. Goldberg, pp. 167–192. New York: Int. Univ. Press.

Guntrip, H. (1969). *Schizoid Phenomena, Object Relations, and the Self.* New York: Int. Univ. Press.

———. (1971). *Psychoanalytic Theory, Therapy, and the Self.* London: Hogarth Press.

Hamburg, D. A. (1973). An evolutionary and developmental approach to human aggressiveness. *Psychoanal. Q.,* 42:185–196.

Hamilton, J. W. (1966). Some dynamics of anti-Negro prejudice. *Psychoanal. Rev.,* 53:5–15.

Hartmann, H. (1939). *Ego Psychology and the Problem of Adaptation.* New York: Int. Univ. Press, 1958.

———. (1950). Comments on the psychoanalytic theory of the ego. In *Essays on Ego Psychology,* pp. 113–141. New York: Int. Univ. Press.

———. (1952). The mutual influence on the development of ego and id. In *Essays on Ego Psychology,* pp. 151–181. New York: Int. Univ. Press.

———. (1955). Notes on the theory of sublimation. In *Essays on Ego Psychology,* pp. 215–240. New York: Int. Univ. Press.

———. (1958). Discussion of Anna Freud's "Child Observation and Prediction of Development." *Psychoanal. Study Child,* 13:120–122.

Hartmann, H., Kris, E., & Lowenstein, R. M. (1949). Notes on the theory of aggression. *Psychoanal. Study Child,* 3/4:9–56.

Hayman, A. (1989). What do we mean by "phantasy?" *Int. J. Psychoanal.,* 70:105–114.

Heimann, P. (1952). Preliminary notes on some defence mechanisms in paranoid states. *Int. J. Psychoanal.,* 33:206–213.

Heimann, P., & Valenstein, A. F. (1972). The psycho-analytical concept of aggression. *Int. J. Psychoanal.,* 53:31–35.

Hendrick, I. (1942). Instinct and the ego during infancy. *Psychoanal. Q.,* 11:33–58.

Izard, C. (1978). On the ontogenesis of emotions and emotion–cognition relationships in infancy. In *The Development of Affect,* ed. M. Lewis & A. Rosenblum, pp. 389–413. New York: Plenum.

Jacobson, E. (1964). *The Self and the Object World.* New York: Int. Univ. Press.

———. (1971). *Depression.* New York: Int. Univ. Press.

Jones, E. (1957). *The Life and Work of Sigmund Freud,* vol. 3. New York: Basic Books.

Joseph, E. D. (1973). Aggression redefined. *Psychoanal. Q.,* 42:197–213.

Kaplan, L. (1977). *Oneness and Separateness.* New York: Simon & Schuster.

Kernberg, O. F. (1975a). *Borderline Conditions and Pathological Narcissism.* New York: Aronson.

———. (1975b). Melanie Klein. In *Comprehensive Textbook of Psychiatry,* ed. A. M. Freedman, H. I. Kaplan, & B. J. Sadock, vol. 1, pp. 641–650. Baltimore: Williams & Wilkins.

———. (1976). *Object Relations Theory and Clinical Psychoanalysis.* New York: Int. Univ. Press.

———. (1980). *Internal World and External Reality.* New York: Aronson.

———. (1982). Self, ego, affects, and drives. *J. Amer. Psychoanal. Assn.,* 30:893–918.

———. (1984). *Severe Personality Disorders.* New Haven: Yale Univ. Press.

———. (1991a). The psychopathology of hatred. *J. Amer. Psychoanal. Assn.,* 39(suppl.):209–238.

———. (1991b). Sadomasochism, sexual excitement, and perversion. *J. Amer. Psychoanal. Assn.,* 39:333–362.

———. (1991c). Some comments on early development. In *Beyond the Symbiotic Orbit,* ed. S. Akhtar & H. Parens, pp. 103–120. Hillsdale, N.J.: Analytic Press.

Kernberg, O. F., Selzer, M. A., Koenigsberg, H. W., Carr, A. C., & Appelbaum, A. H. (1990). *Psychodynamic Psychotherapy of Borderline Patients.* New York: Basic Books.

Klein, M. (1933). The early development of conscience in the child. In *Love, Guilt and Reparation and Other Works, 1921–1945,* pp. 248–257. New York: Free Press, 1975.

———. (1935). A contribution to the psychogenesis of manic-depressive states. In *Love, Guilt and Reparation and Other Works, 1921–1945,* pp. 262–289. New York: Free Press, 1975.

———. (1946). Notes on some schizoid mechanisms. In *Envy and Gratitude and Other Works 1946–1963,* pp. 1–24. New York: Free Press, 1975.

———. (1948). *Contributions to Psycho-Analysis (1921–1945)*. London: Hogarth Press.

———. (1952). The mutual influences in the development of ego and id. In *Envy and Gratitude and Other Works, 1946–1963*, pp. 57–60. New York: Free Press, 1975.

Knapp, P. H. (1979). Core processes in the organization of emotions. In *Affect: Psychoanalytic Theory and Practice*, ed. M. B. Cantor & M. L. Glucksman, pp. 51–70. New York: Wiley.

Kohut, H. (1972). Thoughts on narcissism and narcissistic rage. *Psychoanal. Study Child*, 27:360–400.

———. (1977). *The Restoration of the Self*. New York: Int. Univ. Press.

———. (1982). Introspection, empathy, and the semi-circle of mental health. *Int. J. Psychoanal.*, 63:395–407.

Kris, E. (1950). Notes on the development and on some current problems of psychoanalytic child psychology. *Psychoanal. Study Child*, 5:24–46.

Lantos, B. (1958). The two genetic derivations of aggression with reference to sublimation and neutralization. *Int. J. Psychoanal.*, 33:444–449.

Laplanche, J., & Pontalis, J.-B. (1973). *The Language of Psychoanalysis*. New York: Norton.

Lewin, B. D. (1950). *The Psychoanalysis of Elation*. New York: Norton.

Lichtenberg, J. D. (1989). *Psychoanalysis and Motivation*. Hillsdale, N.J.: Analytic Press.

Lichtenstein, H. (1961). Identity and sexuality. *J. Amer. Psychoanal. Assn.*, 9:179–260.

Lorenz, K. (1963). *On Aggression*. New York: Bantam Books.

Mahler, M. S. (1965). On the significance of the normal separation-individuation phase. In *Drives, Affects, Behavior*, ed. M. Schur, vol. 2, pp. 161–169. New York: Int. Univ. Press.

———. (1971). A study of the separation and individuation process and its possible application to borderline phenomena in the psychoanalytic situation. Rpt. in *The Selected Papers of Margaret S. Mahler*, vol. 2, pp. 169–187. New York: Aronson, 1979.

Mahler, M. S., & Furer, M. (1968). *On Human Symbiosis and the Vicissitudes of Individuation*. New York: Int. Univ. Press.

Mahler, M. S., & McDevitt, J. (1968). Observations on adaptation and defense *in statu nascendi*. *Psychoanal. Q.*, 37:1–21.

Mahler, M. S., Pine, F., & Bergman, A. (1975). *The Psychological Birth of the Human Infant*. New York: Basic Books.

Marcovitz, E. (1973). Aggression in human adaptation. *Psychoanal. Q.*, 42:226–233.

Masson, J. M. (1985). *The Complete Letters of Sigmund Freud to Wilhelm Fliess, 1887–1904*. Cambridge, Mass.: Harvard Univ. Press.

McDevitt, J. B. (1983). The emergence of hostile aggression and its defensive and adaptive modification during the separation-individuation process. *J. Amer. Psychoanal. Assn.*, 31(suppl.):273–300.

Menninger, K. A. (1938). *Man Against Himself*. New York: Harcourt, Brace.

Moore, B. E., & Fine, B. D., eds. (1968). *A Glossary of Psychoanalytic Terms and Concepts*. New York: American Psychoanalytic Association.

———. (1990). *Psychoanalytic Terms & Concepts*. New Haven: American Psychoanalytic Association and Yale Univ. Press.

Panel (1972a). Aggression. A. Lussier, reporter. *Int. J. Psychoanal.*, 53:13–19.

———. (1972b). Role of aggression in child analysis. E. Kestenberg, reporter. *Int. J. Psychoanal.*, 53:321–323.

———. (1990). Sadism and masochism in neurosis and symptom formation. F. M. Levin, reporter. *J. Amer. Psychoanal. Assn.*, 38:789–804.

———. (1991a). Sadism and masochism in character disorder and resistance. M. H. Sacks, reporter. *J. Amer. Psychoanal. Assn.*, 39:215–226.

———. (1991b). Sadomasochism in the perversions. S. Akhtar, reporter. *J. Amer. Psychoanal. Assn.*, 39:741–754.

Parens, H. (1973). Aggression. *J. Amer. Psychoanal. Assn.*, 21:34–60.

———. (1979). *The Development of Aggression in Early Childhood*. New York: Aronson.

———. (1980). An exploration of the relations of instinctual drives and the symbiosis-separation-individuation process. *J. Amer. Psychoanal. Assn.*, 28:89–114.

———. (1984). Toward a reformulation of the theory of aggression and its implications for primary prevention. In *Psychoanalysis: The Vital Issues*, ed. J. Gedo & G. H. Pollock, vol. 1, pp. 87–114. New York: Int. Univ. Press.

———. (1989a). Toward a reformulation of the psychoanalytic theory of aggression in early childhood. In *The Course of Life*, ed. S. I. Greenspan & G. H. Pollock, vol. 2, pp. 83–127. New York: Int. Univ. Press.

———. (1989b). Toward an epigenesis of aggression in early childhood. In *The Course of Life*, ed. S. I. Greenspan & G. H. Pollock, vol. 2, 129–161. New York: Int. Univ. Press.

———. (1991). Separation-individuation theory and the psychosexual theory. In *Beyond the Symbiotic*

Orbit, ed. S. Akhtar & H. Parens, pp. 3–34. Hillsdale, N.J.: Analytic Press.

Parens, H., Scattergood, E., Singeltary, W., & Duff, A. (1987). *Aggression in Our Children.* Northvale, N.J.: Aronson.

Rangell, L. (1972). Aggression, Oedipus and historical perspective. *Int. J. Psychoanal.,* 53:3–11.

Robbins, M. (1980). Current controversy in object relations theory as outgrowth of a schism between Klein and Fairbairn. *Int. J. Psychoanal.,* 61:477–492.

Rochlin, G. (1982). Aggression reconsidered. *Psychoanal. Inq.,* 2:121–132.

Rosenfeld, H. (1965). *Psychotic States.* New York: Int. Univ. Press.

———. (1971). Theory of life and death instincts. *Int. J. Psychoanal.,* 52:169–178.

Rycroft, C. (1968). *A Critical Dictionary of Psychoanalysis.* Rpt. London: Penguin Books, 1972.

Schur, M. (1966). *The Id and the Regulatory Principles of Mental Functioning.* New York: Int. Univ. Press.

Segal, H. (1964). *Introduction to the Work of Melanie Klein,* 2d ed. New York: Basic Books.

Shengold, L. (1991). *"Father, Don't You See I'm Burning?"* New Haven: Yale Univ. Press.

Solnit, A. J. (1966). Some adaptive functions of aggressive behavior. In *Psychoanalysis: A General Psychology,* ed. R. M. Loewenstein, L. M. Newman, M. Schur & A. J. Solnit, pp. 169–189. New York: Int. Univ. Press.

———. (1972). Aggression: a view of theory building in psychoanalysis. *J. Amer. Psychoanal. Assn.,* 20:435–450.

Spitz, R. A. (1946). Anaclitic depression. *Psychoanal. Study Child,* 2:313–342.

———. (1950). Anxiety in infancy. *Int. J. Psychoanal.,* 31:138–143.

———. (1965). *The First Year of Life.* New York: Int. Univ. Press.

Stechler, G. (1987). Clinical applications of a psychoanalytic systems model of assertion and aggression. *Psychoanal. Inq.,* 1:348–363.

Stechler, G., & Halton, A. (1987). The emergence of assertion and aggression during infancy. *J. Amer. Psychoanal. Assn.,* 35:821–838.

Stone, L. (1971). Reflections on the psychoanalytic concept of aggression. *Psychoanal. Q.,* 40:195–244.

Stone, M. H. (1980). *The Borderline Syndromes.* New York: McGraw-Hill.

———. (1989). Murder. *Psychiat. Clin. N. Amer.,* 12:643–652.

Storr, A. (1968). *Human Aggression.* New York: Atheneum.

Strenger, C. (1989). The classic and the romantic vision in psychoanalysis. *Int. J. Psychoanal.,* 70:593–610.

Suttie, I. (1924). Metapsychology and biology. *J. Neurol. Psychopathol.,* 5:61–70.

———. (1935). *The Origins of Love and Hate.* London: Kegan Paul, Trench, Trubner.

Tinbergen, N. (1951). An attempt at synthesis. In *The Study of Instinct,* pp. 101–127. New York: Oxford Univ. Press.

Volkan, V. D. (1976). *Primitive Internalized Object Relations.* New York: Int. Univ. Press.

———. (1986). The narcissism of minor differences in the psychological gap between opposing nations. *Psychoanal. Inq.,* 6:175–191.

———. (1987a). Psychological concepts useful in the building of political foundations between nations. *J. Amer. Psychoanal. Assn.,* 35:903–936.

———. (1987b). *Six Steps in the Treatment of Borderline Personality Organization.* Northvale, N.J.: Aronson.

———. (1988). *The Need to Have Enemies and Allies.* Northvale, N.J.: Aronson.

Waelder, R. (1956). Critical discussion of the concept of an instinct of destruction. *Bull. Phila. Assn. Psychoanal.,* 6:97–109.

Weil, A. (1976). The first year. In *The Process of Child Development,* ed. P. Neubauer, pp. 246–268. New York: Aronson.

Weiss, E. (1935). Todestrieb und Masochismus. *Imago,* 21:393–411.

Wheelis, A. (1971). The league of death. In *The Illusionless Man,* pp. 57–95. New York: Harper Colophon.

Wilson, E. O. (1975). *Sociobiology.* Cambridge, Mass.: Harvard Univ. Press.

Winnicott, D. W. (1950). Aggression in relation to emotional development. Rpt. in *Collected Papers,* pp. 204–218. New York: Basic Books, 1958.

———. (1956). The antisocial tendency. Rpt. in *Collected Papers,* pp. 306–316. New York: Basic Books, 1958.

———. (1959). Classification. Rpt. in *The Maturational Processes and the Facilitating Environment,* pp. 124–139. New York: Int. Univ. Press, 1965.

Leo Rangell, M.D.

29

AFFECTS

Affects are feelings. For practical purposes, the words *affects, feelings,* and *emotions* are interchangeable. Differentiation between these terms definitionally has been attempted from time to time but has not led to any satisfactory or generally accepted formulation.

AFFECTS IN PSYCHOANALYTIC THEORY

Affects have been a central focus of psychoanalytic theory as it has evolved from the beginning. Yet it has always been more possible and more satisfactory to conceptualize affects in their relationships to associated and interactive phenomena than to arrive at a theoretical understanding of the nature of affects themselves. Thus the derivation of affects from instincts, their relations to ego and superego, their associations with ideas, and their connections with somatic expression have all been incorporated into general and specific aspects of psychoanalytic theory. The understanding of their own central nature, however, has lagged behind and remains one of the most obscure areas, if not theoretical mysteries, of psychological, somatic, and psychosomatic theory.

Empirically, by serendipity or otherwise, the evolution of a psychoanalytic theory of affects has paralleled both the progress of general psychoanalytic theory and the ontogenetic development of the psychic apparatus. In the earliest phase of psychoanalytic theory, affects occupied a disproportionately large and central role, as the etiologic theory of strangulated affects held sway, and with it the theory of therapy by catharsis and abreaction. With the development of the theory of instincts and drives, affects came to occupy a secondary position alongside other instinctual derivatives, with the theory of therapy advancing to the analysis of conflict. With the ascendancy of the structural view, affects came to occupy a more limited and circumscribed place, resulting from an increasingly complex interaction between all three systems. Both affect theory and general psychoanalytic theory, moreover, are seen to parallel, in a remarkable way, the ontogenetic development of the psychic apparatus, from the original id dominance, through the gradually increasing role of the ego, to the contribution of the superego as well as of reality and the external worlds.

Rapaport (1953), presenting what has been considered the closest approximation to a definitive theory of affect, traced and documented the cumulative development of affect theory with the historical development of the general theory of psychoanalysis. Rapaport dated the first period of the theory of affects from the beginning 1890s to *The Interpretation of Dreams* in 1900. During this stage, when therapy was centered in catharsis and abreaction, Freud equated affect with a quantity of energy "like an electric charge over the memory traces of an idea." Drive, energy, and affect had not yet been effectively separated. Psychic tension of this still indeterminate nature was disposed of by action, affect, and binding through the work of thought.

The second period extended from 1900 to the publication of *The Ego and the Id* in 1923. During this time, in which Freud was developing his metapsychological framework, which approached psychological phenomena from multiple points of view, affects were looked upon as discharges into the interior from their origins in the unconscious. At this stage, according to Freud (1915b), "Affectivity manifests itself essentially in motor (secretory and vasomotor) discharge resulting in an (internal) alteration of the subject's own body without reference to the external world" (p. 179 n.).

Affect discharge, according to Rapaport, results in affect expression and affect felt, referring to the unconscious and conscious experiences of affects. The existence of innate discharge thresholds, which change in characteristics with developmental events, ushers in conflict, experientially and in theory. The dynamic, economic, and genetic metapsychological points of view are prominent in evolving theory during this phase.

Rapaport's third stage spanned the period from the introduction of the structural view (1923) and Freud's (1926) signal theory of anxiety to the present time. With an expanding and varied use of affect discharge channels, continuous ego development results in an increasingly complex hierarchy of drives, motivations, and affects, coordinated with secondary-process development and a constantly increasing neutralization of drives (Hartmann, 1939; Hartmann et al., 1946). The structural view, with its emphasis on the role of the ego, adds to the understanding of the developing affects throughout life. In mature adult life, continuous interaction between the three psychic structures produces changing tensions and discharges which combine and blend into an integrated whole. Affects proceed from being peremptory, explosive, and attacklike to becoming more and more controlled, modulated, and "tamed" (Fenichel, 1941; Kris, 1950). Along with the achievement of an effective anticipatory signal of anxiety, a rich and modulated affective life is associated with and equivalent to a strong ego.

Affects, ideas, and actions are derivative formations through which instincts are expressed and become known (Freud, 1900, 1915a; Nunberg, 1932; Brierley, 1937; Fenichel, 1945; Rapaport, 1951, 1953). Although affect is thus a derivative of instinct, it consists of more than its instinctual component. Just as external behavior is a composite of many preceding intrapsychic elements, consisting of compromises between instinctual drives, ego defenses, superego inputs, and other forms of ego

activity, which fuse the disparate elements into a cohesive whole, so are affects composed of ego and superego as well as instinctual components and external along with internal determinants.

The resulting affects are in constant contiguous relationships with other mental and also somatic elements. The overall phenomenon of subjective human experience, in which affect is embedded and of which it is a part, consists of feeling, an associated idea or set of ideas, and accompanying somatic changes. Although these three aspects of human experience are associated or even fused, they are not interchangeable and are definitionally separate. Affects and cognition are contiguous, connected, and reciprocal but not one. Every affect is associated with, but is not thereby the same as, the idea that evokes or accompanies it. Conversely, every idea evokes and is then associated with an accompanying affect, although in the case of some ideas or class of ideas the affect may be minimal to the point of virtual nonexistence. Just as idea and affect go together but are separate, so too for the affect and its accompanying somatic relationships. As the idea is not the affect, and vice versa, the physical experience is not the feeling, nor does the affect consist in the somatic phenomena that accompany it.

UNCONSCIOUS AFFECTS

A question of unique concern to psychoanalysis is whether affects or feelings can be unconscious as well as conscious. Freud was inconsistent on this point. While at one time he stated, "It is surely of the essence of an emotion that we should be aware of it, i.e. that it should become known to consciousness" (1915b, p. 177), in other contexts he spoke freely of affects being unconscious. He did so in the discussion of clinical cases, in theoretical remarks about anxiety and guilt, in referring to repressed affects in traumatic neurosis or psychoneurosis, and in describing repressed affects in the transference (Freud, 1937).

Analysts generally agree that unconscious affects are routine experience both in clinical work and in life and that affects can be as unconscious as ideation. With regard to the criterion of "subjective awareness" given in the definition of affects by Moore and Fine, eds. (1990), both "subjective" and "awareness" are to be acknowledged as, psychoanalytically, not synonymous with conscious. There can be, and routinely is, unconscious awareness of feelings as well as ideas. This quality of awareness, with and without consciousness, is included in subjectivity.

While recognizing Freud's dilemma with regard to this subject, many authors have concluded that affects can be unconscious and preconscious as well as conscious. For descriptions sharing varying degrees of emphasis and conviction, see Eissler, 1953; Jacobson, 1953a; Rapaport, 1953; Schafer, 1964; Lewin, 1965; Joffe & Sandler, 1968; Schur, in Panel, 1968; Pulver, 1971; Brenner, 1974; Loewald, in Panel, 1974; Rangell, in Panel 1974; and Sandler, 1983.

Another distinction relevant to unconscious affects, described by Freud and elaborated upon by Fenichel (1945) and Pulver (1974), is that affects in the unconscious can exist either as fully formed but repressed mental contents or as predispositions or potentials—that is, as having a more-than-usual readiness to be formed into and so operate as a particular affect. This distinction has a practical, clinical, as well as a theoretical, significance. The more structured and fully formed an affect is in the unconscious, the more it presses to be discharged, in either a direct or a derivative form, or the more it operates to instigate defenses to keep it repressed. A less-formed potential for affect is less pressing and has less need of defense or action or psychic definition. Eissler (1953) similarly stressed the clinical importance of distinguishing the different states and forms of the repressed impulses in the id and the affects in the ego. Of the same theoretical significance, Fenichel (1945) sees the hyperaffectivity that one encounters clinically or in life as a readiness for affective discharge.

PLEASURE AND UNPLEASURE

Approaching the subject from the standpoint of individual affects, we see that a major initial building block was set in place by Freud (1895c, 1900) early in the development of psychoanalytic theory, when he delineated the dichotomy of pleasure and unpleasure in psychic life. This polarity was described not only as an initial understanding of the nature of affects but as an enunciation of one of the basic regulatory principles of mental functioning. In accordance with this "pleasure–unpleasure principle," the human organism is motivated biologically or, as Freud came to enlarge it, bio-psychologically to seek pleasure and to avoid pain, unpleasure, or the traumatic state.

With reference to affects, the pleasure–unpleasure principle is a more accurate description of the two major divisions of affects than pleasure–pain, with which it is often loosely interchanged. Pain is generally conceived of as a somatic sensation, which, as it increases, can lead to the psychological feeling of

unpleasure or, more specifically, to the affect of anxiety. Diffuse unpleasure, which is undifferentiated in the earliest developmental periods, gradually becomes differentiated into more specific and delimited affective states, such as anxiety, depression, guilt, shame, and a variety of subtle combinations and derivatives of these.

Relating this first delineation of the pleasure–unpleasure principle to the economic point of view, Freud (1895c, 1900) first equated unpleasure with the buildup of psychic tension and pleasure with its discharge. With increasing experience, however, Freud (1905b) came to modify this oversimplified formulation, noting, for example, in regard to erotic tension, that high tensions of pleasurable affect can be enjoyable, while low tensions of painful feeling can be intolerable. In one of his last works, Freud (1940) concluded that qualitative considerations, as well as the rhythms of tension and discharge processes, need to be considered. Jacobson (1953a) elaborated on the influence of speed and rhythm on the pleasure–unpleasure qualities of feelings. Primitive affects are higher peaked and more sudden and explosive in their discharge processes. Low-speed discharge, Jacobson writes, can result in "pleasurable enduring feeling states," while combinations of high- and low-speed discharge processes may result in complex affect experiences as some of our most sublime pleasurable states.

THE AFFECT OF ANXIETY

A major affect delineated early and pursued intensively in Freud's emphasis on affective experience was anxiety. Freud (1926) considered anxiety to be not only "the nodal point of the neurosis" but a critical factor in normal behavior and psychic life in general. The conceptualization of this central affect by Freud underwent a developmental process that paralleled and was crucial to the development of general psychoanalytic theory. The course of the understanding of this affect may also be considered a model for the understanding of affects in general.

The specific and ubiquitous role of anxiety in both the causation and the resulting phenomenology of neurosis was recognized at once by Freud, although his views with regard to its origins and mode of operation underwent a metamorphosis during the course of his theory building. In his first references to its clinical role, beginning with the draft of a paper contained in a letter to Fliess in 1893, Freud saw anxiety as a physical sequel to abnormal sexuality, such as compulsive masturbation. In this type of psychopathology, which he called "neurasthenia," Freud saw neurosis as being first the physical, then the psychological aftereffects or accompaniments of this anxiety. In a later variation, Freud (1895b) detached from this group of sexually abnormal patients a separate group of cases characterized by too little rather than too much sexual discharge, as in incomplete or inhibited sexuality or *coitus interruptus*. On this early view, repression, which at that time meant inhibition, blocking, or defense in general, led to a state of being "dammed up," which then caused anxiety, which in turn resulted in the physical and derivative subjective psychological symptoms. The syndrome resulting was called by Freud "anxiety neurosis." Another name for these cases, which has come to have historical meaning, was "actual neurosis," in the sense that the anxiety by this conception was real, physical, and current—that is, an "actual" state, from which the clinical phenomenology resulting then became psychological in nature.

Another understanding of the affect of anxiety developed simultaneously from analyses of cases of hysteria and obsessional neurosis, which Freud (1894, 1895a, 1896, 1898, and so on) called "psychoneuroses," in contrast to anxiety or actual neuroses. A gradual evolution of psychoanalytic theory, shaped to explain continuing clinical observations, resulted in 1923 in a major revision of theory, culminating in a new theory of anxiety as its central pivot. Along with a change from a unitary to a dual instinct theory (Freud, 1920) and a tripartite division of the psychic apparatus into id, ego, and superego came the second, or signal, theory of anxiety (Freud, 1926). When instinctual discharge of sexual or aggressive drives is judged by the ego to constitute a danger, anxiety now ensues as a signal of this impending danger. The danger—for example, of loss of love, castration, or punishment by the superego—leads, among other possible outcomes, to the institution of defense. Anxiety is now the cause of repression, not its result, and is the cause of all neuroses, not just those labeled "anxiety neuroses."

Whereas analysts have universally accepted the signal theory of anxiety, there is a division of opinion regarding Freud's first theory. Although it was Freud himself who defined the new concept of anxiety, he hesitated to abandon his first theory and retained the two together in a way that is not clear. Most analysts—for example, Waelder (1960) and Brenner (1953)—think that Freud should have been willing to discard his first theory, and they have discarded it in their own formulations and understanding. Others—for example, Fenichel (1945), Blau (1952), and Rangell (1955, 1968)—see both mechanisms of anxiety operating together, but in all neuroses, not as separating one class of neurosis from another. In the unitary theory of anxiety I described,

the psychological and somatic aspects, focused on separately in Freud's two theories, exist together.

Traumatic states are part of every psychoneurosis, as pointed out by Fenichel (1945). The traumatic state, with its flooding by stimuli due to the breaching of the stimulus barrier, from within or without, is close to the condition described by Freud in anxiety neurosis as stemming from the damming up of instinctual pressure. In my view, following the institution of defenses brought about by anxiety signaling danger during the intrapsychic sequence leading to neurosis, continually pressing undischarged drives result in mounting instinctual tension, which constitutes a bio-psychological danger in itself. Underlying all psychological danger is fear of the traumatic state, which is the psycho-economic condition of unpleasure behind the original feeling of traumatic helplessness. The prototype of this state occurs at birth, which is the aspect of Rank's (1952) theory of the birth trauma that Freud accepted in his own studies of anxiety. Anxiety thus has a psychological origin—the fear of danger—which, following repression, leads to a somatic state—continuing instinctual pressure—which in turn leads once more to psychological as well as somatic danger. Psychosomatic and somatopsychic sequences thus affect and reinforce each other in circular fashion.

Attempts to understand anxiety both as an affect in itself and in relation to a variety of clinical phenomena have been numerous and persistent. Anxiety can serve as a model for the understanding of all other affects, and all are equally connected to these general theoretical concepts. Signal anxiety can be widened to the concept of signal affect (Schur, in Panel, 1968; Rangell, in Panel, 1974). When the ego permits a tentative instinctual discharge to test the reactions of the superego and the external world or engages in thought as experimental action (Freud, 1900, 1911a, 1933; Rapaport, 1950, 1951; Fenichel, 1945; Rangell, 1986), the result is an affective signal. While the anxiety signal occupies a special place in the subsequent formation of neurosis, the affective signal in everyday life can be one of pleasure (G. Klein, 1976) as well as unpleasure, of safety (Sandler, 1960) as well as of danger. Whereas the scanning for anxiety—that is, the presaging of danger—is a moment-by-moment ego function, the entire spectrum of unpleasurable affects can come into play, either in a general nonspecific way or with a specific, highly differentiated affect.

THE SIGNAL FUNCTION OF AFFECT

The signal function of affect, in addition to operating intrapsychically, leading toward either defense or action, is utilized externally as well, as a communicative signal in object relations. Affects come to have multiple functions (Rangell, in Panel, 1974): discharge in psycho-economic terms, expression in terms of the individual or self, and appeal as a signal in object relations. Affects as signals serve to alert both one's own ego internally and those to whom one relates externally. The role of affects in object relations, in their appeal or communication with external objects, has been stressed by many analysts, including Riviere (1936), Brierley (1937), Moore (in Panel, 1968), and Lofgren (in Panel, 1968), and by many observers of infants and children, such as Mahler (1963; Mahler et al., 1975), Emde (1983) describing the affective self, and Stern (1984) studying affect attunement, all following the pioneer work of Spitz (1965). Novey (1959) stresses the role of affects in communication via signaling on both an intrapsychic and an interpersonal level, just as Sandler and Rosenblatt (1962) pointed out the role of affects in the representational world. Modell (1971) goes further in stating that a complete, systematic theory of affects would have to be situated within the framework of object relations theory and group and individual psychology.

AFFECT DIFFERENTIATION

The quality and differentiation of specific affects, as well as the quantitative variations that are possible, span a spectrum which is typically human, and which, on the evolutionary scale, differentiates man from other animals. Just as Schur (1953, 1958) describes a spectrum of anxiety from explosive and uncontrolled to signal and thoughtlike, so with increasing development there is an increasing variety and hierarchy of experienced affects. Like all psychic elements, these undergo increasing maturation and differentiation during the course of the developmental process.

The nature of affects, in their structure and composition and in the characteristics of their expression, undergoes a developmental progression synchronous with the course of development generally. From the diffuse pleasure and unpleasure of early infancy, affects become less explosive and undifferentiated and more variegated, differentiated, modulated, and controlled. This is in keeping with Rapaport's (1953) description of an increasing hierarchy of motivational drives, resulting in an increasing modulation of affects from diffuse to subtle. While in earlier stages affects can be said to be more id-oriented, they gradually come more and more under ego control during ontogenetic development. Reider (in Panel, 1952), for example, sees rage as an early affect related to the id, specifically to the development of the expression of aggression; anxiety as coming later, with the specific achievement in ego development of the ability to anticipate; and guilt still later, after at least the beginnings of the formation of the superego. Similarly, Mittelmann (Panel, 1952) regards pleasure and rage as predominantly id affects, whereas anxiety and feelings of safety belong to the ego, and qualms of conscience and depression to the superego.

CLASSIFICATIONS OF AFFECTS

Classifications of affects have varied, and different authors have invoked different criteria. An early qualitative classification, beginning with Freud, was according to whether an affect falls on the pleasurable or unpleasurable side of the pleasure–unpleasure duality. Another is based on criteria of developmental progression and the relation of evolving affects to the maturing, developing psychic structures. One division is according to the relationship of affects to the two instinctual drives—namely love and hate—derived from the sexual and aggressive instincts respectively. Jacobson (1953a), basing her classification on the structural point of view, distinguishes affects deriving from intrasystemic tensions from those rooted in intersystemic conflicts. While analysts generally agree that the experience of affects resides in the ego, affects can originate from energic tensions anywhere within the psychic organization.

Affects have been divided into fixed and labile, simple and complex, single affects and those that are mixed or fused (Glover, 1939). There are positive and negative affects, primary and reactive affects, affects due to frustration and those resulting from gratification. Both Glover (1939) and Jones (1929) have described fear, guilt, and hate as primary derivatives of instinctual drives and other secondary affects as radiating from these. Affects due to the buildup of tension are separable from those brought about by the discharge of impulses (Freud, 1900; Brierley, 1937; Glover, 1939). The specific affective and somatic state of laughter (Freud, 1905a; Kris, 1939) is related to the suddenness of the release of built-up tension.

Greenacre (1959, 1960; and Panel, 1952) distinguishes two types of pleasure, active and passive, the pleasure of rest and that of activity. Pleasure, according to Greenacre, arises from explorations into "the not-so-familiar," although if this is too intense, anxiety or even trauma may result. Hendrick (1942) has described pleasure in mastery. This is consonant with ego pleasure, effectance pleasure, pleasure centering mainly in ego satisfaction, as described by C.

Bühler (1954), K. Bühler (1951), Harrison (1984), and others.

A special variety of affects studied has been the more chronic, long-lasting, and low-key condition of moods. Mahler et al. (1975), studying basic moods in relation to the separation-individuation process, referred to mood as "the habitual mode of response to inner and outer stimulations with positive or negative affects" (p. 213 n.). Along with "the taming of affects" (Fenichel, 1941; Kris, 1950) in later life, Jacobson (1957) and Weinshel (1970) have described moods as pervasive affects, diffusing discharge patterns throughout the ego. Moods thus show a relative degree of stability (Weinshel, 1970) and "may be indeed called a barometer of the ego state" (Jacobson, 1957, p. 75). Jacobson (1953a) described this process in terms of the control of energic discharge, resulting in the capacity to experience more modulated moods—that is, sustained low-level affects, chronic over time, in contrast to shorter-lasting, more circumscribed affects, up to uncontrolled and explosive affect discharges.

Jones (1929), studying the complex, reciprocal interrelationships between fear, guilt, and hate, describes the layering of affective states one upon the other. I have utilized the concept of agglutinated or conglomerate affective states, which present themselves clinically and then need to be destratified in the psychoanalytic process into their linear relationships (1978). Among specific affects that have been subjected to separate study, envy has been investigated by Melanie Klein (1957), who elaborated on its prominent role in psychic life. Riviere (1932) analyzed the affect of jealousy as combining grief, anger, and fear. Freud analyzed various more complex affects into their component backgrounds, including jealousy in relation to paranoia and homosexuality (Freud, 1922), guilt in the relation of the ego to the superego (Freud, 1920), and mourning and melancholia (Freud, 1917). Jacobson (1953b), Bibring (1953), Zetzel (1965), and others have studied depression, and Wurmser (1981) and Levin (1971) the affect of shame. Piers and Singer (1953) and Levin (1967) have distinguished between shame and guilt. Fenichel (1934) and Greenson (1953) have studied the state of boredom, Greenson (1962) the experience of enthusiasm, Arlow (1957) the feeling of smugness, and I (1954) have explored the affective state of poise. In each case, the authors traced the developmental histories of these affects and their typical associated ideational contents. In the case of poise, I traced the relationship of this state of affective balance to the somatic condition of stability or instability of the musculature and structures of the perioral or snout area, which I described as "the window to the emotions."

AFFECTS AS DEFENSE AND SYMPTOM

Brenner (1975) considers depressive affect on a par with anxiety as a coequal cause of defense. Guilt, shame, and all other affects, however, besides anxiety and depression, can similarly serve a signal function, and any affect of unpleasure can be a motive for defense (Rangell, 1978). While any affect of unpleasure can be a motive for defense, I believe (1978) that anxiety occupies a supraordinate position since, by contrast with any of the other affects, anxiety is never absent in the intrapsychic sequence of events prior to the institution of defensive activity. The common etiology for this anxiety concerns the possibility of the unpleasurable affect, whether depression, guilt, shame, or even anxiety itself getting out of control and leading to the traumatic state.

Affects, in addition to being motives for defense, can also themselves be defended against as derivatives of instinctual drives. They can serve as defenses as well as be defended against. Lewin (1950) has described the utilization of screen affects as a defense against other repressed elements, and Greenson (1954) has written about the defensive aspects of moods clinically and in life. Affects can also become ego-dystonic symptoms in their own right, coming about, like other symptoms, by compromise formations between the id and the ego. As symptom complexes they can be further repressed, so that a person may, for example, become aware only during analysis, following the undoing of defenses, of the existence of chronic depression or an anxiety state.

AFFECT, IDEATION, AND SOMATIC PHENOMENA

The most puzzling and elusive theoretical area in the psychoanalytic conceptualization of affect has to do with the relations between affect, ideation, and somatic phenomena. Affect, as pointed out by Schur (1969), is a response to cognition. Cognition, ideational or conceptual contents, may arise from outside or inside, from perception and experience of external events or from stimuli arising from either the psychic or the somatic interior. When affect is a response to an external event, perception and registration of the external condition first produce a cognitive response, which may be conscious or unconscious, which then results in the associated affect. Either the affect or the idea or both may be defended against, repressed, and rendered unconscious. And in either case, the repression may be primary or secondary—that is, simultaneous with perception and registration or as an "after-repression," whether after an instant of conscious recognition or after any length of time thereafter.

Brenner (1974), in what he terms a "unified theory of affects," includes ideation within the concept of affects. He classifies affects according to the ideational content associated with the sensation of pleasure or unpleasure. Affects consist of varying degrees of these sensations of pleasure and unpleasure and of fantasies, conscious or unconscious, that determine the differentiation of one affect from another. Thus, it is the concept of anticipated danger which makes for and characterizes the affect of anxiety, the idea of loss that determines depressive affect, and the sense of deserving punishment that makes for guilt.

Since Brenner includes in his definition only phenomena that can be observed during the psychoanalytic process, the somatic accompaniments of affect are omitted, whereas the accompanying ideation is considered part of the phenomenon. To most other theorists, however, both ideational and somatic phenomena are accompaniments of the affective experience but not definitionally part of affect itself. In keeping with the generally accepted formulation noted above—of Freud (1900, 1915a), Rapaport (1951, 1953), Fenichel (1945), and others—that thoughts, affects, and action are all separate derivatives of instincts, it would follow that however close all these are clinically, they are conceptually separate phenomena with their own boundaries, contents, and definitions. Ideation and affect, for example, are considered separate derivatives of instinctual drives as modified and influenced by ego and superego activity.

A differently oriented unification of affect theory is exemplified by the unitary theory of anxiety (Rangell, 1955, 1968), which, like other paradigms relating anxiety to affects in general, can also serve as a model for other affects. In this unification, which fuses together Freud's first and second theories of anxiety, it is the psychic and somatic aspects of anxiety formation that are integrated into a continuous sequential whole, phenomenologically, experientially, and theoretically.

There are no longer two separate theories of anxiety, but two—and actually more—factors that are part of and associated with the unfolding of all anxiety. On the other hand, feeling or affect is recognized as associated with, but nevertheless separable from, ideation. On the other hand, this formulation makes room for an association not only of affect and ideation but of both of these with their accompanying neurophysiological phenomena. While ideation accompanies and even determines the qualitative differences between specific affects, the cognitive accompaniment is no more the affect per se than is its somatic expression. Nevertheless, the inevitable association of the three allows for an operationally wider unification of affect, ideation, and somatic accompaniments.

Although affects, ideas, and related somatic phenomena typically occur together in the clinical situation, the need for separate conceptualization of each phenomenon is considered desirable and necessary by most analysts. Most authors consider the subject elusive, however, and even inconclusive. Noting Freud's separation of affects from ideas and perceptions, Loewald (in Panel, 1974) referred to this as an ineffable subject. He pointed out the unitary character of cognition and affect clinically, but also the fact that in other respects, by which he apparently meant theoretical considerations, they stand at opposite poles. Pulver (1971) sees complex clinical manifestations occurring but feels that a narrow definition of affect is necessary theoretically. For the broader context, Pulver prefers to use the term "affective phenomena." "Pure" affects, in the consideration of some, may be seen in epileptic rage or other ictal phenomena, in decerebrate or similar organic conditions, and perhaps in neonates or the earliest stages of infancy. That we do not see "pure" affects clinically, however, is no more reason for not considering them as a separate theoretical entity than is the case with instincts, which we also see only in derivative form and combined with other elements.

Following Rapaport's presentation of his most definitive paper, at the first panel on affects in 1952, Lewin, speaking from the floor, declared that we still do not have a psychoanalytic theory of affects. This opinion was repeated by the panel on "Affects and the psychoanalytic situation" held at the Thirtieth International Psychoanalytic Congress in Jerusalem in 1977. Brenner (in Panel, 1968) saw Rapaport's contribution as limited by his emphasis on theory while expressly avoiding references to subjective states. Sandler (1983) thought that Rapaport had failed to clarify the conceptual problems because of his adherence to a unitary theory of affect, which in Sandler's opinion encompassed "the physical, energic and experiential aspects within the same concept" (p. 82). Sandler, Pulver, and others wanted to reserve the term "affect" definitionally for the feeling state. "While physiological processes may be associated with feelings, it is important to distinguish between the two," Sandler (1983) states

(p. 88), making the same point about affects and somatic expression as others have made about affects and ideation.

Nevertheless, Greenacre (1960 and in Panel, 1952) stated that the deepest substrate of affect lies in physiological processes. Specific organ systems have different patterns of tension or relief pleasure, and out of this matrix are formed the complex affects of adult life. However, to satisfy the requirements for a theory of affect, one must face up to the difficulty of defining the nature of causation, the question of whether a physical or psychological or only a combined theory offers an "explanation" of any complex behavioral phenomenon.

The fact is that "explanation" in a total sense of the behavioral phenomenon of affect does not belong entirely within psychoanalysis. What Freud (1905b, 1911b, 1915a) said about instinct is also true of affect: that it is another phenomenon—feeling state or sensation?—belonging to the frontier between psyche and soma. Although the specific mechanisms, such as the psychophysiological synapses involved in the formation, evolution, and expression of affects, are not known or completely understood, the three closely associated phenomena, ideational, somatic, and affective, are linked together clinically and in theoretical contiguity. Interfaces between each respective pair unite the three in an integrated and harmonious experiential whole.

AFFECTS AND NEUROPHYSIOLOGY

We cannot straightforwardly equate the relationship between endorphins and impermeability to pain to a parallel relationship between any known chemical substance and susceptibility to or resistance against unpleasure. No comparable leap can be made from our understanding of the psychosomatic synapse in somatic pain to the same neurophysiological sequence in the production of affects. Knowledge of anxiolytic or antidepressant medication has not yet contributed definitively to an understanding of the psychology of anxiety states or the psychopathology of depression. Nor does our increasing knowledge of neurotransmitters or of the chemical agents operative across neural synapses aid us in understanding the psychodynamics of the production or maintenance of affective states.

Psychoanalysis has made an indispensable contribution to the understanding of affects, but there are other factors which lie outside its domain. For psychoanalysis provides data only on the psychological side of the psychosomatic and somatopsychic reciprocal arcs. Between perception, external or internal, and affect is a neurophysiological bridge which is the domain of somatic science to understand and expand. The role of neurophysiological processes in addition to psychological and metapsychological understanding has been stressed by Needles (1964), Moore (in Panel, 1974), and others.

Much remains to be discovered about neurophysiological differences in specific affective states. In his first theory of anxiety, Freud did not show, or know, how a state of increasing instinctual flooding led neurophysiologically to tension and stress and from these to the psychological experience of anxiety, even if he pointed in this direction. While the precise mechanism remains unknown, Greenacre (1941), among others who support this exploratory view of Freud's, cites the view of Cannon, which approaches the same phenomenon of dammed-up libido from a physiological angle. Describing how strong emotion and sympathetic and parasympathetic nervous system discharge energize each other reciprocally, Cannon writes: "Any high degree of excitement in the central nervous system—whether felt as anger, terror, pain, anxiety, joy, grief or deep disgust—etc." (cited by Greenacre, 1941, p. 36). The mechanism, however, remains unknown.

For a complete, integrated theory of affects, open-ended interfaces are necessary to bridge between contiguous areas of human functioning. This is consonant with the view expressed by Freud (1920), and held by many psychoanalysts and neurophysiologists since then. It is for this reason that one of the last panels on affects (1974) had the title "*Toward* a Theory of Affects" (my emphasis), and an article by a child analyst on the subject of affects (Emde, 1980) had the same word, *toward,* in its title. Psychoanalysis can provide only one strand in the necessary cooperative, multidisciplined approach.

REFERENCES

Arlow, J. A. (1957). On smugness. *Int. J. Psychoanal.,* 38:1–8.

Bibring, E. (1953). The mechanism of depression. In *Affective Disorders,* ed. P. Greenacre, pp. 13–48. New York: Int. Univ. Press.

Blau, A. (1952). In support of Freud's syndrome of "actual" anxiety neurosis. *Int. J. Psychoanal.,* 33:363–372.

Brenner, C. (1953). An addendum to Freud's theory of anxiety. *Int. J. Psychoanal.,* 34:18–24.

———. (1974). On the nature and development of affects. *Psychoanal. Q.,* 43:532–556.

———. (1975). Affects and psychic conflict. *Psychoanal. Q.,* 44:5–28.

Breuer, J., & Freud, S. (1893–95). *Studies on Hysteria. SE,* 2.

Brierley, M. (1937). Affects in theory and practice. Rpt. in *Trends in Psycho-Analysis*, ed. E. Jones, pp. 43–56. London: Hogarth Press, 1951.

Bühler, C. (1954). The reality principle. *Amer. J. Psychother.*, 8:626–647.

Bühler, K. (1951). On thought connections. In *Organization and Pathology of Thought*, ed. D. Rapaport, pp. 39–57. New York: Columbia Univ. Press.

Eissler, K. R. (1953). Notes upon the emotionality of a schizophrenic patient and its relation to problems of technique. *Psychoanal. Study Child*, 8:199–251.

Emde, R. N. (1980). Toward a psychoanalytic theory of affect. In *The Course of Life*, ed. S. I. Greenspan & G. H. Pollock, vol. 1, pp. 85–112. Washington, D.C.: U.S. Government Printing Office.

———. (1983). The prerepresentational self and its affective core. *Psychoanal. Study Child*, 38:165–192.

Fenichel, O. (1934). On the psychology of boredom. Rpt. in *Collected Papers of Otto Fenichel*, vol. 1 pp. 292–302. New York: Norton, 1953.

———. (1941). The ego and the affects. Rpt. in *Collected Papers of Otto Fenichel*, vol. 2, pp. 215–227. New York: Norton, 1954.

———. (1945). *The Psychoanalytic Theory of Neurosis*. New York: Norton.

Freud, S. (1894). The neuro-psychoses of defence. *SE*, 3:43–68.

———. (1895a). Obsessions and phobias. *SE*, 3:71–84.

———. (1895b). On the grounds for detaching a particular syndrome from neurasthenia under the description "anxiety neurosis." *SE*, 3:87–117.

———. (1895c). Project for a scientific psychology. Rpt. in *The Origins of Psychoanalysis*, pp. 347–445. New York: Basic Books, 1954.

———. (1896). The aetiology of hysteria. *SE*, 3:189–221.

———. (1898). Sexuality in the aetiology of the neuroses. *SE*, 3:261–285.

———. (1900). *The Interpretation of Dreams. SE*, 4 & 5.

———. (1905a). *Jokes and Their Relation to the Unconscious. SE*, 8.

———. (1905b). *Three Essays on the Theory of Sexuality. SE*, 7:125–243.

———. (1911a). Formulations on the two principles of mental functioning. *SE*, 12:213–226.

———. (1911b). Psycho-analytic notes on an autobiographical account of a case of paranoia (dementia paranoides). *SE*, 12:3–82.

———. (1915a). Instincts and their vicissitudes. *SE*, 14:109–140.

———. (1915b). The unconscious. *SE*, 14:159–215.

———. (1917). Mourning and melancholia. *SE*, 14:237–260.

———. (1920). *Beyond the Pleasure Principle. SE*, 18:3–64.

———. (1922). Some neurotic mechanisms in jealousy, paranoia and homosexuality. *SE*, 18:221–232.

———. (1923). *The Ego and the Id. SE*, 19:3–66.

———. (1926). *Inhibitions, Symptoms and Anxiety. SE*, 20:77–175.

———. (1933). *New Introductory Lectures on Psycho-Analysis. SE*, 22:3–182.

———. (1937). Constructions in analysis. *SE*, 255–269.

———. (1940). *An Outline of Psycho-Analysis. SE*, 23:141–207.

———. (1950). *The Origins of Psychoanalysis*. Rpt. New York: Basic Books, 1954.

Glover, E. (1939). The psychoanalysis of affects. Rpt. in *On the Early Development of Mind*, pp. 297–306. New York: Int. Univ. Press, 1956.

Greenacre, P. (1941). The predisposition to anxiety. Rpt. in *Trauma, Growth*, and *Personality*, pp. 27–82. New York: Norton, 1952.

———. (1959). Play in relation to creative imagination. Rpt. in *Emotional Growth*, vol. 2, pp. 555–574. New York: Int. Univ. Press, 1971.

———. (1960). Considerations regarding the parent–infant relationship. Rpt. in *Emotional Growth*, vol. 1., pp. 199–224. New York: Int. Univ. Press, 1971.

Greenson, R. R. (1953). On boredom. *J. Amer. Psychoanal. Assn.*, 1:7–21.

———. (1954). On moods and introjects. *Bull. Menninger Clinic*, 18:1–11.

———. (1962). On enthusiasm. *J. Amer. Psychoanal. Assn.*, 10:3–21.

Harrison, I. B. (1984). Function pleasure and Freudian theory. Unpublished manuscript.

Hartmann, H. (1939). *Ego Psychology and the Problem of Adaptation*. Rpt. New York: Int. Univ. Press, 1958.

Hartmann, H., Kris, E., & Loewenstein, R. M. (1946). Comments on the formation of psychic structure. *Psychoanal. Study Child*, 2:11–38.

Hendrick, I. (1942). Instinct and the ego during infancy. *Psychoanal. Q.*, 11:33–58.

Jacobson, E. (1953a). The affects and their pleasure–unpleasure qualities in relation to the psychic discharge processes. In *Drives, Affect, Behavior*, ed. R. M. Loewenstein, pp. 38–66. New York: Int. Univ. Press.

———. (1953b). Contribution to the metapsychology of cyclothymic depression. In *Affective Dis-*

orders, ed. P. Greenacre, pp. 49–83. New York: Int. Univ. Press.

———. (1957). On normal and pathological moods. *Psychoanal. Study Child,* 12:73–113.

Joffe, W. G., & Sandler, J. (1968). Comments on the psychoanalytic psychology of adaptation. *Int. J. Psychoanal.,* 49:445–454.

Jones, E. (1929). Fear, guilt and hate. Rpt. in *Papers on Psychoanalysis,* pp. 304–319. Baltimore: Williams & Wilkins, 1948.

Klein, G. S. (1976). *Psychoanalytic Theory.* New York: Int. Univ. Press.

Klein, M. (1957). *Envy and Gratitude.* New York: Basic Books.

Kris, E. (1939). Laughter as an expressive process. Rpt. in *Psychoanalytic Explorations in Art,* pp. 217–239. New York: Int. Univ. Press, 1952.

———. (1950). On preconscious mental processes. Rpt. in *Psychoanalytic Explorations in Art,* pp. 303–318. New York: Int. Univ. Press, 1952.

Levin, S. (1967). Some metapsychological considerations on the differentiation between shame and guilt. *Int. J. Psychoanal.,* 48:267–276.

———. (1971). The psycho-analysis of shame. *Int. J. Psychoanal.,* 52:355–362.

Lewin, B. D. (1950). *The Psychoanalysis of Elation.* New York: Norton.

———. (1965). Reflections on affect. In *Drives, Affects, Behavior,* ed. M. Schur, vol. 2, pp. 23–37. New York: Int. Univ. Press.

Mahler, M. S. (1963). Thoughts about development and individuation. *Psychoanal. Study Child,* 18:307–324.

Mahler, M. S., Pine, F., & Bergman, A. (1975). *The Psychological Birth of the Human Infant.* New York: Basic Books.

Modell, A. H. (1971). The origin of certain forms of pre-oedipal guilt and the implications for a psycho-analytic theory of affects. *Int. J. Psychoanal.,* 52:337–346.

Moore, B. E., & Fine, B. D., eds. (1990). *Psychoanalytic Terms and Concepts.* New Haven: Yale Univ. Press.

Needles, W. (1964). Comments on the pleasure–unpleasure experience. *J. Amer. Psychoanal. Assn.,* 12:300–314.

Novey, S. (1959). A clinical view of affect theory in psychoanalysis. *Int. J. Psychoanal.,* 40:94–104.

Nunberg, H. (1932). Quoted in Brierley, 1937, p. 45.

Panel (1952). The theory of affects. L. Rangell, reporter. *Bull. Amer. Psychoanal. Assn.,* 8:300–315.

———. (1968). Psychoanalytic theory of affects. L. B. Lofgren, reporter. *J. Amer. Psychoanal. Assn.,* 16:638–650.

———. (1974). Toward a theory of affects. P. Castelnuovo-Tedesco, reporter. *J. Amer. Psychoanal. Assn.,* 22:612–625.

———. (1977). Affects and the psychoanalytic situation. Thirtieth International Psychoanalytic Congress, Jerusalem.

Piers, G., & Singer, M. (1953). *Shame and Guilt.* Springfield, Ill.: Thomas.

Pulver, S. (1971). Can affects be unconscious? *Int. J. Psychoanal.,* 52:347–354.

———. (1974). Unconscious versus potential affects. *Psychoanal. Q.,* 43:77–84.

Rangell, L. (1954). The psychology of poise. *Int. J. Psychoanal.,* 35:313–332.

———. (1955). On the psychoanalytic theory of anxiety. *J. Amer. Psychoanal. Assn.,* 3:389–414.

———. (1968). A further attempt to resolve the "problem of anxiety." *J. Amer. Psychoanal. Assn.,* 16:371–404.

———. (1978). On understanding and treating anxiety and its derivatives. *Int. J. Psychoanal.,* 59:229–236.

———. (1986). The executive functions of the ego. *Psychoanal. Study Child,* 41:1–37.

Rank, O. (1952). *The Trauma of Birth.* New York: Brunner.

Rapaport, D. (1950). On the psycho-analytic theory of thinking. *Int. J. Psychoanal.,* 31:161–170.

———. (1953). On the psycho-analytic theory of affects. *Int. J. Psychoanal.,* 34:177–198.

Rapaport, D., ed. (1951). *Organization and Pathology of Thought.* New York: Columbia Univ. Press.

Riviere, J. (1932). Jealousy as a mechanism of defence. *Int. J. Psychoanal.,* 13:414–424.

———. (1936). The genesis of psychical conflict in early infancy. *Int. J. Psychoanal.,* 17:395–422.

Sandler, J. (1960). The background of safety. *Int. J. Psychoanal.,* 41:352–356.

———. (1983). On the psychoanalytic theory of affects. *Israel J. Psychiat. & Related Sciences,* 20:81–94.

Sandler, J., & Rosenblatt, B. (1962). The concept of the representational world. *Psychoanal. Study Child,* 17:128–145.

Schafer, R. (1964). The clinical analysis of affects. *J. Amer. Psychoanal. Assn.,* 12:275–299.

Schur, M. (1953). The ego in anxiety. In *Drives, Affects, Behavior,* ed. R. M. Loewenstein, pp. 67–103. New York: Int. Univ. Press.

———. (1958). The ego and the id in anxiety. *Psychoanal. Study Child,* 13:190–220.

———. (1969). Affects and cognition. *Int. J. Psychoanal.,* 50:647–653.

Spitz, R. A. (1965). *The First Year of Life*. New York: Int. Univ. Press.

Stern, D. N. (1984). Affect attunement. In *Frontiers of Infant Psychiatry,* ed. J. D. Call, E. Galenson & R. L. Tyson, pp. 3–14. New York: Basic Books.

Waelder, R. (1960). *Basic Theory of Neurosis*. New York: Schocken Books.

Weinshel, E. M. (1970). Some psycho-analytic considerations on moods. *Int. J. Psychoanal.,* 51:313–319.

Wurmser, L. (1981). *The Mask of Shame*. Baltimore: Johns Hopkins Univ. Press.

Zetzel, E. R. (1965). Depression and the incapacity to bear it. In *Drives, Affects, Behavior,* ed. M. Schur, vol. 2, pp. 243–274. New York: Int. Univ. Press.

PART VI

DEVELOPMENT, SELF, OBJECTS, AND IDENTIFICATION

Phyllis Tyson and
Robert L. Tyson, M.D.

30

DEVELOPMENT

DEFINITION AND KEY CONCEPTS

From the time Freud first pondered the ways in which childhood experience influences adult mental functioning, theories about how the mind evolves have been central in psychoanalytic thought. Freud's ideas were derived from genetic formulations—that is, from reconstructions of childhood based on adult memories. As psychoanalysis developed, theoreticians turned progressively more to child analysis and to the observation of infants and young children in order to understand the process of development as it was happening, supplementing the retrospective reconstruction of developmental experience. What follows is an attempt to convey our current understanding of the developmental process. We begin with a review of some basic concepts. We then give an account of the emergence of developmental theory and trace the evolution of central aspects of the personality over the course of the developmental process.

Psychoanalytic theory views development as an ongoing process, in which the psychic structures and functions determining the human personality gradually evolve from the personal experiences of a biologically maturing individual in interaction with important people in his or her environment (Settlage, 1980; Tyson & Tyson, 1990). To study the process of development, it is important to distinguish between the influence of innate givens and

that of personal experiences and then to understand the ways in which they interact in the formation of organized psychic structures.[1]

We are born with a distinctive set of competencies: capacities for cognition, perception, motility, and expression of affects, memory and linguistic abilities. Each of these matures according to a constitutionally determined schedule. We are also born with propensities for activity, for distinguishing between pleasure and unpleasure, for participating in human interactions, and for self-regulation. These biologically and genetically determined capacities, growth processes, and potentials are relatively independent of environmental influences. Although maturational processes generally unfold predictably and sequentially, it is often the case that environmental stimuli must activate the constitutionally determined schedule. Without such stimuli, delays and deviations may occur (Spitz, 1945, 1946a, 1946b; Provence & Lipton, 1962). Thus, in addition to the individual's innately determined developmental potential, affectively meaningful interactions with others have a crucial developmental impact. For example, such experiences form the basis of memory, and the individual constructs a sense of personal reality on the basis of this memory. In addition, memories of meaningful interactions and the exercise of

---

1. The term "structure" refers to stable systems with a slow rate of change (Rapaport & Gill, 1959).

innate capacities combine to form mental representations of the self, important objects, and the self in interaction with these objects. These mental representations provide the foundation for an underlying stable organization of hypothetical psychic structures, which then makes possible the emergence of psychological functioning, an ability that is not innate and not available at birth (Spitz, 1957).

At the same time, the difference between the developmental and functional levels of the child's mind and those of the mother generates a developmental potential. The mother's empathic, sensitive care-giving interacts and combines with the child's ongoing processes of internalization and identification, the processes through which the infant forms mental representations of him- or herself, of others, and of their interactions. The combination of caregiving with internalizing and identificatory processes, in the context of a developmental potential, brings the infant to successively more elaborate levels of psychic structure and organization (Loewald, 1960; Settlage, 1980). When mother–child interaction is too complicated, too simple, or otherwise inappropriate, deviations may occur. There is evidence to suggest that early environmental influences contribute to neural patterning: lack of sufficient interaction as in situations of neglect leads to mild mental retardation (Call, 1980); inappropriate, unpredictable, or too complicated interactions can give rise to a predisposition to anxiety, rage, or other disorganizing affects at times of distress. Such readily generated intense affects interfere with smooth self-regulation and so with handling of later experiences. Inasmuch as these patterns tend to be irreversible later, it can be said that interactions with the early environment may exert a constitutional influence (Greenacre, 1941, 1952; James, 1960; Weil, 1978).

Interactions with important others inevitably lead to dissonance, incompatibility, and conflict at times (Klein, 1976; Hartmann, 1939). However, the individual's efforts to resolve conflict have a developmental potential, because psychic functioning is elevated to successively higher levels as adaptive responses to cope with conflict are found. Hartmann (1939) particularly stressed the developmental potential of adaptation, pointing out that the child adapts to the environment in different ways, alloplastically and autoplastically (Freud, 1924b; Ferenczi, 1930).[2] *Alloplastic* means eliciting responses from the environment or relating to the environment

primarily according to inner needs and wishes. Alloplastic adaptation is crucial in earliest infancy when the infant must be capable of eliciting a response from the environment to ensure survival. While sometimes adaptive, continuing manipulation of the environment as the chief means of meeting inner needs or resolving conflict in later childhood or adult life suggests pathology. *Autoplastic* adaptation is the capacity to make compromises; that is, inner, or psychic, modifications are made in response to the perception of conflict. Such adaptation requires reality testing and is typical of both normal and neurotic functioning.

To understand development, we must consider the relationship between the innate and the experiential —that is, between intrinsic and extrinsic factors. Freud referred to the difficulty of estimating the relative influence of constitutional factors versus "accidental" events experienced in childhood. In what he called the "complemental series" he described the relationship between the two: "The constitutional factor must await experiences before it can make itself felt; the accidental factor must have a constitutional basis in order to come into operation" (Freud, 1905, pp. 239–240).

Erikson (1959), borrowing the concept of an epigenetic principle from biology, described the way in which necessary constituents of the developing personality must appear at the optimal times. Should a "part" be missing or fail to appear at the right time, development becomes distorted or pathological. The extent to which such developmental failures can be modified later by treatment designed to supply the missing "part" and thereby make up for earlier deficiencies remains questionable (R. L. Tyson, 1986).

Development is a spiraling process, with both forward and backward movement. Forward progression takes place when separately maturing capacities become linked and work in relation to one another. The result is higher-level functioning and greater organization and integration among psychic structures. Stress, conflict, danger, or frustration evoke modes of functioning more typical of earlier developmental phases. This is usually referred to as "regression," wherein the individual reverts, or retreats, to safer forms of satisfaction (drive regression), modes of relating (regression in object relations), sets of standards (superego regression), or ways of thinking (ego or cognitive regression). Anna Freud (1965) pointed out that episodes of regression are a normal, expectable part of development. If regression is "not blocked altogether by environmental disapproval and by internal repressions and restrictions" (p. 107), the slow method of trial and error, progression and temporary backsliding is conducive to healthy psychic growth. Early mastery may be suffi-

2. These adaptive principles are similar to Piaget's concepts of assimilation and accommodation, used in his description of cognitive development (Piaget & Inhelder, 1969).

cient for one stage yet insufficient to meet later internal and external demands; but, through regression in the service of progression, early conflicts, resolutions, and adaptations made on one level can be reworked and reintegrated at higher developmental levels. Developmental arrest, where progress appears to stop, on the other hand, implies failure in the developmental process. A developmental arrest may be confined to a limited area of development or affect several areas or be more global. However, the clinician often finds it difficult to distinguish between arrest or regression on the basis of behavioral manifestations alone, and developmental delay is seen more frequently than developmental arrest as such.

Not only is psychic structure formation dependent on repetitive, regressive, progressive, reorganizing, and continually transforming cyclical processes, but continuities are also apparent; for example, certain early established patterns of interpersonal relating (Emde, 1988) and modes of adaptation and functioning (Brody & Axelrad, 1970, 1978; Brody & Siegel, 1992) persist in later stages of development.

There are broad variations in the ways in which developmental progression contributes to the mature personality (Abrams, 1977). While sequential, progressive transformations are essential, so are the effects of past experiences on current mental functioning. Hence, the genetic point of view in psychoanalysis (Rapaport & Gill, 1959) takes a dual approach: the retrospective historical and the prospective developmental. The historical approach seeks to understand the linkage between past experience and current psychological phenomena. Psychoanalytic technique began with such reconstructive efforts when Freud recognized that childhood experiences were important determinants of adult neuroses (Breuer & Freud, 1893–95; Freud, 1905, 1923a, 1924a, 1926). The developmental approach, by contrast, attempts to understand psychological phenomena as they happen—that is, *in statu nascendi*. While the historical approach is at a disadvantage in being unable to recover the details of early experience as it actually happened, the developmental approach is limited by the fact that the psychological impact of experiences may not be apparent until a later date.

THEORETICAL FRAMEWORKS FOR CONCEPTUALIZING DEVELOPMENT

Psychosexual Development

Psychoanalytic developmental psychology has itself followed a developmental pathway. Freud (1905) conceptualized development in terms of the successive phases of sexuality, based on his observation

that sensual urges provide a motivation for psychic functioning, but that, over time, changes are evident in the bodily areas and organs through which sensual pleasures are sought.[3] These changes were epitomized in the oral, anal, and infantile (or childhood) genital phases of libidinal development.[4] Freud referred to the relatively quiescent time between age six or seven and puberty as the "latency phase," and the subordination of erotogenic zones to the genital zone in puberty he called "genital primacy." Although the sequencing of libidinal phases is biologically predetermined, these phases are not as distinct from one another as description suggests. Contemporary theory views each form, or mode, of libidinal pleasure, be it orality, anality, or genital pleasure, as a discrete subsystem with a unique developmental course, each with a time of relative ascendancy over other libidinal systems. Times when one form of pleasure appears to predominate over others may be viewed as a phase, in keeping with traditional theory, so long as we understand that each phase gradually blends into the next, while earlier-appearing elements in one or another subsystem "color" or influence the overall picture (Pine, 1985; Stern, 1985; Tyson & Tyson, 1990). Freud also observed that, as with adults disposed to sexual perversion, any bodily zone can serve as a potential source of pleasure for the child. This led him to characterize infantile sexuality as polymorphously perverse (Freud, 1905, p. 191).

In 1920, Freud expanded instinctual drive theory, and in what has become known as the dual drive theory, he postulated an aggressive drive alongside the sexual. This aggressive drive came to include not only acts with underlying aggressive and destructive motivations, accompanied by unpleasant affects such as anger and hostility, but also non-

3. Throughout his writing, Freud used the term "sexual" to refer to sensual pleasures derived from any area of the body; he used the term "libido" ("libidinal drive") to refer to the hypothesized energy underlying sexual or sensual pleasure, although in 1921 he stated that libido should be thought of more broadly as love, or a "love-force," of which sexuality is simply one manifestation.

4. In 1923, Freud made a crucial addition to his original description of infantile sexuality. He observed that, following the anal phase and before latency, there was a period at the height of which "interest in the genitals and in their activity acquires a dominating significance which falls little short of that reached in maturity" (1923b, p. 142). He originally called this the "infantile genital organization." Freud's understanding of this phase was limited to males, and so he came to refer to this as the phase of "phallic primacy" (p. 144). Since our present-day understanding of this phase includes a developmental line for both sexes, we feel it is more correct to use Freud's original term.

destructive forms of aggression such as those providing motivation for activity, mastery, and assertion.

With this revision, Freud's original, too simple view of early sexual phases was broadened, and notions of the object, the ego, and the roles of conflict and affect all come to be included with libidinal and aggressive drive components as integral aspects of psychosexual development.

Psychic Structure Formation

The advent of the structural hypothesis (Freud, 1923a) brought about a reorientation in developmental thinking. The drives were now seen to be functions of the id and, in Freud's view, were available at birth. While the psychosexual framework continued to be relevant, he paid more attention to the evolution of structures that oppose the drives. As early as 1911 he proposed that the search for safety and self-preservation leads to the replacement of the pleasure principle by the reality principle. Following his introduction of the structural hypothesis (1923a), Freud's concept of *das Ich* (translated as "ego" by Strachey) contained two meanings: that of an experiential self and that of a hypothetical psychic structure devoted to self-regulation. As a psychic structure, the ego was viewed as "a coherent organization of mental processes" consisting of all those functions that regulate the drives and adapt to reality (1923a, p. 17). Hartmann (1950, 1952) emphasized that, as a psychic structure, the ego functioned as the organizer, synthesizer, and regulator of the personality. In line with the structural hypothesis, Freud (1926) revised his theory of anxiety; he now saw affect as an ego function that signaled conflict and danger, rather than as something associated only with the drives. This signal function referred to a person's capacity to identify and acknowledge an affect like anxiety before it reaches overwhelming proportions. Thus, a conflict between an underlying drive and an opposing force can be identified, an accompanying danger situation and feared consequence can be imagined (fear of object loss, loss of the object's love, castration, or superego punishment), and the appropriate adaptive measures can be taken. Anna Freud (1936) described various means by which the ego responds to and wards off painful feelings and dangerous impulses, thereby elucidating the developmental unfolding of typical defense mechanisms.

Although Freud thought that the ego evolved as a consequence of conflict between the infant's drives and the demands of the external world, Hartmann (1939, 1952) disagreed; he asserted that certain ego functions were intrinsically available. He thought that "conflict-free" functions such as perception,

cognition, memory, speech, and motility had primary autonomy, in that they are neither created by nor appear as a result of conflict between instinctual wishes and the external world. In questioning the notion that the ego evolves from the id, Hartmann pointed out that neither the ego nor the id are functioning psychic structures at birth but that both are undifferentiated. The challenge then became one of discovering the steps by which each evolved. A plethora of ideas about development followed, and many ideas were put forth about the evolution of the id, the ego, and the superego.

Object Relations

Hartmann (1939; Hartmann et al., 1946) also pointed out that, in view of the infant's helplessness and total dependence on the parents during infancy and early childhood, the optimal unfolding of psychic structures depended on an "average expectable" environment, by which he meant adequate care-givers (adequate in both the physical and the emotional senses). Increasingly, developmental theory came to consider object relations. Though not stressed as such, relations with the object were always at least an implicit aspect of drive theory, the "libidinal object" being the vehicle through which drive gratification is sought and obtained. But Freud's emphasis was on the complexity of object relations during the infantile genital phase, wherein he elaborated the oedipus complex and underlined the role of conflict in the formation of an infantile neurosis, examining in particular the ways in which these conflicts contributed to superego formation. Hartmann's concept of the average expectable environment, by contrast, shifted the focus to the earliest object relations[5] and to the interactional nature of the developmental process. The interactions between the child's libidinal impulses, his or her early object relations, the building of self and object representations, and the emergence of more complex psychic structures were also studied. Jacobson (1954, 1964), for example, elucidated the contribution to superego development of early mental representations, distorted as they are by the infant's affective responses to the object.

Hartmann (1952, 1953, 1956) described two stages of object relations: the relation to the need-satisfying object and the achievement of object constancy—that is, "constant relations with the object independent of the state of the needs" (1953, p. 187). The concept of object constancy came to be associated with various developmental schemes

5. An area on which Melanie Klein had focused since the late 1920s, although her theories did not include structural theory as we know it.

(Fraiberg, 1969). Notable among them are the schemes of Spitz, Anna Freud, Piaget, and Mahler.

Spitz (1965) took the appearance of distinct reactions to strangers at about six to eight months of age as an indication of the achievement of the "stage of the libidinal object proper," when it is clear that the mother is preferred above all others.[6] In Anna Freud's view (in Panel, 1968), the presence of object constancy is indicated when the child's libidinal investment in the mother is preserved regardless of fluctuations in need satisfaction, at about the age of Spitz's libidinal object. Before this, the child is thought not to sustain a relationship with the object either in the absence of need or when gratification is not forthcoming. "Cognitive object constancy," as described by Piaget, refers to the persistence in memory of an integrated mental representation that can be evoked at will, a developmental achievement that appears somewhere between eighteen and twenty-four months. Mahler, by contrast, described libidinal object constancy as beginning only with some resolution of the ambivalence of the anal phase, between twenty-four and thirty-six months. In her view, libidinal object constancy first requires a stable mental representation of the mother in the cognitive sense. Following this, and related to the ideas of Jacobson (1954, 1964), there is a gradual integration of "good" and "bad" feelings about the object. The predominantly positive quality of the resulting maternal representation has the special function of producing in the child almost the same sense of security and comfort for a time as does the mother's actual presence. Mahler notes: "By object constancy we mean that the maternal image has become intrapsychically available to the child in the same way as the actual mother had been libidinally available—for sustenance, comfort, and love" (1968, p. 222).

Mahler and her colleagues (1975), in seeking further to understand the interrelationship between object relations and ego development, studied those processes entailed in the child acquiring a sense of the object and a sense of personal identity separate from the object. She delineated steps in what she called the "separation-individuation process," in which "separation" refers to the child gaining a capacity for independent functioning separate from the mother, and "individuation" to the process whereby the child distinguishes a sense of individual identity. The sequences of the separation-individuation process, with the subphases of differentiation, practicing, rapprochement, and "on the way to libidinal object constancy"—to some extent a lifelong process that may never be fully completed—provide a framework for understanding pre-oedipal object relations. Mahler also proposed "forerunners" of the separation-individuation process.

To emphasize the transition from the earliest stages to later ones in terms of object relations, she called the initial period the "normal autistic" phase and the second period the "normal symbiotic" phase. In so doing, she suggested that the infant's attention in the first few weeks of life is relatively inward-directed and that, following this, the infant experiences the mother and him- or herself as a "dual unity" (Mahler & Gosliner, 1955; Mahler, 1972a) with little affective differentiation between self and object. Although Mahler stressed that no pathological connotation was implied, by using labels associated with childhood pathological syndromes, she aroused not only misunderstanding but in some cases heated opposition. Therefore we (Tyson & Tyson, 1990) suggest the term "primary reciprocity" as best conveying the essentials of the first step in object relations, in which the infant is born innately prepared to participate in reciprocal interactions, and "beginnings of dialogue" to denote the second phase, so highlighting the reciprocal affective climate necessary for attachment.

Gender Development

Greater appreciation of the interrelatedness of psychosexuality, object relations, the sense of self, and ego and superego development, as well as the increase in understanding of genetic endowment and biological processes, has led to further insights in yet another area, that of gender identity. The notion of gender identity combines theories of sexual development, ego, superego, the sense of self, and object relations. Following Stoller, sexual development can be distinguished from gender. Sex is a biological designation, male or female. It is determined by the anatomical configuration of internal and external genital organs as well as a variety of physiological and biological forces. Sexual behavior, erotic life, sexuality, sensuality—all have bodily, biological, and physiological components. By contrast, gender is a psychological concept. Biological sex and a psychologically determined sense of gender identity are not necessarily directly related and are not necessarily identical. Gender identity combines and inte-

---

6. Spitz actually referred to "stranger anxiety," now more often called "stranger reactions," since there may be a wide range of reactions to strangers. In addition, Katan (1972) has called into question the concept of anxiety at this early stage, preferring to use the term "distress" because it implies the less well-developed capacity for memory, means–ends distinctions, and self-object differentiation appropriate at this stage of development.

grates a personal sense of self with biological sex; and a person's object relations and superego ideals, together with the impact of social and cultural influences, make important contributions. A wide variety of feelings, thoughts, fantasies, beliefs, and actions related to the sense of self and the self in interaction with others is associated in one way or another with gender.

Further distinctions can be made among gender identity, gender role identity, and sexual partner orientation. *Gender identity* refers to the broad mixture of masculinity and femininity that accrues as the sense of self develops. It is built on a variety of identifications made with each parent, and a wide variety of biological, psychological, social, and cultural factors make significant contributions (Stoller, 1968b, 1976). Gender identity begins with "core gender identity," the most primitive, nonconflictual, conscious and unconscious sense of belonging to one sex and not the other (Stoller, 1968a, 1968b, 1976). Around this central nexus, the varieties of masculine and feminine identifications that form the overall sense of gender identity gradually accrue. Roles taken, consciously or unconsciously, in sexual, social, and interpersonal interactions with others we refer to collectively as *gender role identity,* and they, too, are built on selective identifications with same- and opposite-sex parents throughout the course of development. *Sexual partner orientation* expresses one's preference regarding the sex of the sexual partner. Sexual partner orientation gives us no indication of gender identity. Although this preference has origins early in life with pre-oedipal and oedipal object relations, it may be neither firmly established nor a source of conflict until adolescence. Recently, theories about these separately evolving and intertwining developmental aspects of gender have been more fully elaborated and integrated (P. Tyson, 1982; Tyson & Tyson, 1990).

Freud did not have a theory about gender (Kleeman, 1976); his theories of masculinity and femininity were tied to sexual development and to what he understood about infantile masturbation. Although many disagreed with his views on femininity from the start, serious reassessment did not begin until the late 1960s. Theories about gender development have facilitated clarification and led to a major reformulation of female development. Although no single point of view able to command general acceptance has yet emerged, many useful ideas have been advanced. Theories of gender development have also made possible further refinement and extension of Freud's theory of male development. For example, it has always been said that female development is more difficult than male development because the

girl has to change objects in order to develop an oedipus complex. We now understand that the girl and the boy have different tasks and different developmental lines. The formation of gender identity is usually smoother for the girl because her primary identifications are made with a same-sex object, her mother, whereas a boy's development is complicated by his having to disidentify with his primary care-giver in order to form a confident sense of masculinity and evolve a male gender role.

A Framework for Viewing Development

It became increasingly evident that it was neither possible nor desirable to limit a psychoanalytic theory of development to the maturational sequences of the libidinal drive. Instead, a comprehensive framework was needed, one within which the complex network of human functioning could be considered. To this end, Anna Freud (1963, 1965) suggested that development be conceptualized as a series of predictable, interlocking, overlapping, and unfolding developmental lines. Believing that more was needed for assessment than isolated aspects of the child's personality, she emphasized the interaction between drive, ego, superego, and environmental influences. Her focus in formulating developmental lines was behavioral clusters (Neubauer, 1983), which represent a complex interlocking of psychic units reflecting structural components as well as adaptive, dynamic, and genetic influences. Examples of developmental lines were from dependency to emotional self-reliance and adult object relationships, from the body to the toy, and from play to work. Together, these lines were thought to provide an index to a child's emotional maturity, immaturity, normality or pathology, his or her developmental achievements or, on the other hand, failures. Not a metapsychological formulation, this concept is more like a map-making procedure which provides a framework within which developmental landmarks and externally observable behavior (for example, symptoms that may appear descriptively similar in different individuals) can be translated into internal implications. Viewing lines in relation to each other makes personality distortions and incongruities more readily apparent.

The concept of developmental lines has failed to realize its full potential, however, and few additional lines have been proposed. Nevertheless, Anna Freud's attention to the interaction among simultaneously emerging components of personality has led to a greater appreciation of the range of interacting factors that influence the developmental process. In an attempt to emphasize the interactive nature of development, we (Tyson & Tyson, 1990) have proposed the use of a systems perspective. From such a perspective, the developmental process can be conceptualized in terms of a variety of networking, branching, and interrelated systems. The developmental trajectory of each can be traced through the organization, transformation, and reorganization among its functions. In addition to the developmental trajectory of each system, we also recognize the emergence of an integrated organizational hierarchy among the systems, and relatively stable structural units can be identified according to the functions they perform. Consistent with the structural hypothesis, these can be conceptualized as id, ego, and superego, which maintain a dynamic equilibrium with each other and with the external world.

THE PROCESS OF DEVELOPMENT

We turn now to an outline of the developmental process as conceptualized in psychoanalysis. The traditional divisions are infancy (birth to three years),[7] early childhood (three to six years), latency (six to eleven or twelve years), adolescence, and adulthood. Within the first four of those divisions we consider in turn psychosexual development, object relations, gender, and psychic structure formation, so as to reflect the different points of view and at the same time demonstrate the ways in which they are interrelated in the "cascading" process of development (R. L. Tyson, 1986). Since there is as yet no generally accepted conceptualization of developmental processes in adulthood, we describe and discuss the currently more prominent notions in this area.

Infancy

PSYCHOSEXUAL DEVELOPMENT

Oral phase. Many researchers recognize that more goes on in the earliest weeks and months of life than simple drive gratification. This period has been named variously according to the particular investigator's theoretical orientation (for example, the oral phase, the undifferentiated phase of ego development, the "normal autistic" stage of object relations, the early portions of sensorimotor cognitive development). Hartmann (1939; 1950, p. 79) maintained that it was difficult to say what in a newborn's behavior could later be ascribed to ego functioning versus what could be considered as due to motiva-

7. Although in current usage, "infancy" is often considered to be from birth to three years, the more traditional psychoanalytic application of the term "infantile" refers to the first five years.

tional factors. Although the biological underpinnings of instinctual drives are present at birth, they take the form of pleasurable or unpleasurable, loving or hating, sexual or aggressive impulses only gradually and in the context of affective responses of important care-givers.

Feeding and sucking experiences provide the context for many of the earliest mother–infant interactions; the affective feedback established between mother and infant leads the infant to associate pleasure (or unpleasure) with these experiences. The stimulation of the oral mucous membrane associated with pleasurable feeding experiences in interaction with the mother has a soothing function apart from the mother. During sucking purely for pleasure, the child's attention is absorbed in rhythmical activity. This striving to obtain pleasure independently of nourishment led Freud to consider sucking as sexual (1933, p. 101).

Feeding is also the organizing activity around which perception and motor activities take place. The infant visually scans, focuses on the mother's face, and establishes eye contact, meanwhile rooting and sucking rhythmically. The infant's expanding ability to attend to outside stimuli during the state of "alert inactivity" (Wolff, 1959) decreases, however, when hunger remains unsatisfied and tolerance of frustration has been exceeded. Various reports of observations of early maturational variables such as those by Spitz (1945, 1946a, 1946b) and Dowling (1977) have documented the dual nature of the feeding situation crucial to normal development. That is, both the affective climate of an attentive, involved care-giver and oral sucking stimulation are necessary for optimal development; without one or the other, retardation in various systems becomes evident.

A new form of oral satisfaction emerges in the second six months, that of chewing and biting. The discomfort associated with the eruption of the first teeth is offset by the additional gratification obtained through biting. Abraham (1924) interpreted this behavior as aggressive, on the basis of reconstructions from analyses of adult patients whose aggressive tendencies were expressed in oral modes or employed oral symbolism. He assumed these to be direct carry-overs from infantile forms of oral gratification; hence the latter half of the first year came to be referred to as the "oral-sadistic" stage. Abraham's conclusion, however, is an example of a "genetic fallacy" (Hartmann, 1955, p. 221), in which adult behavior expressed in a particular mode is assumed to have originated in the phase of early childhood during which that mode first appears. But sadism not only implies pleasure in hurting; it also implies an intent to hurt, which in turn requires the capacity to fantasize the possibility of doing so; we know from developmental research that an infant of six to eight months does not have the cognitive capacity to construct such complex mental representations of his or her own self and of the object world, let alone to elaborate fantasies about intended action. Therefore, one is not justified in attributing such an intent to the infant at this early age, though a nursing mother bitten by a teething infant may well feel otherwise. Of course, later mother–child interactions may impart a sadistic meaning in the child's mind to biting activities (see Burgner & Kennedy, 1980).

Anal phase. Although pleasurable sensations are probably associated with the anal zone from soon after birth, in the second year, as greater sphincter control becomes possible, a prominent increase in anal erogeneity is evident. Gradually, the anal zone becomes the major focus of excitation. Now the toddler shows increasing interest in, and pleasurable attention to, the body functions and zones of defecation and urination and their products. Sensual pleasures associated with anal and urethral functioning can easily be observed as the toddler appears to find pleasure in touching, smelling, withholding, and expelling.

Disequilibrium and disharmony, a typical response to strongly divergent developmental trends, are also usual concomitants of the anal phase. Easily overwhelmed, overstimulated, or frustrated, the toddler gives vent to rage and other aspects of frustration. Under minimal stress he or she may easily become fretful, show anxious clinging and whining behavior, and throw temper tantrums. Differentiation between sexual and aggressive manifestations is discernible from the end of the first year when brief, directed expressions of anger appear as well as a more compelling and dominant urge toward mastery (Freud, 1905, p. 193; Hendrick, 1942); in the anal phase, more forceful manifestations of directed aggression appear along with other anal phase derivative behavior, such as growing possessiveness and acquisitiveness. Hostility may take various forms, from a mild degree of increased motor activity, to negativism and provocativeness, to focused angry attacks such as biting, hitting, scratching, or pushing others.

OBJECT RELATIONS

Primary reciprocity. During the first weeks, the infant's life is centered on the maintenance of biological homeostasis. Although most researchers agree that the infant is born preadapted to participate in re-

ciprocal interactions and that from the beginning of life he or she depends on, and actively responds to, appropriate sensorial and affective feedback, for the first month or so after birth the infant's behavior is predominantly affected by endogenously determined regulatory processes (Sander, 1962, 1964). During this period the principal task for mother and infant is to regulate and stabilize sleep–wake, day–night, and hunger–satiation cycles. In so doing, homeostatic equilibrium is established (Anders, 1982).

The beginnings of dialogue. A noticeable shift occurs in the infant's behavior around two months of age, in that he or she begins to actively anticipate and seek out reciprocal exchanges in emotion, vocalization, and various forms of playful interchange, collectively referred to as "dialogue" (Spitz, 1965). Mahler agreed with the general assumption that the important psychological achievement for the infant during this phase is to become firmly attached to the mother, who now becomes the most important love object; thus a sense of affective "oneness" is established. The smiling response specific to the mother (Spitz & Wolf, 1946) is an important indicator that this has been achieved. From this point on, the infant's activities, affects, and perceptions all appear to focus increasingly on the interpersonal interaction with the mother as the two engage actively in dialogue. This early dialogue provides a setting for the establishment of competence and reality-based self-esteem and for differentiating pleasure from unpleasure; the mutual holding, maintenance, and enrichment of the duality becomes, Call (1980, 1984) believes, the organizing principle for later forms of communication.

Separation-individuation. The process of separation and individuation begins in the differentiation subphase, the first of four such subphases. It starts around four to five months of age as the infant progressively shows greater interest in, and awareness of, the world beyond the mother–infant dialogue. He or she becomes more adept in hand, eye, and mouth coordination and begins to make the first moves away from the mother. Though the child pays increasing attention to the outside world as a source of pleasure and stimulation, his or her states of well-being or discomfort increasingly center on the presence or absence of the mother. The transitional object (Winnicott, 1953) appears as the infant "creates" an intermediate area of experience to accommodate his or her progressive self–object differentiation.

The practicing period is next. From about eight to ten months the infant shows an increasingly lively interest in testing and practicing emergent skills, in mastering motility, and in discovering the world about him or her. He or she moves away from and back to mother and becomes accustomed to the experience of physical separation and its psychological consequences. He "checks back," counting on the mother's emotional availability for approval and for what Furer (in Mahler, 1965) calls "emotional refueling."

The toddler appears to be exhilarated by his or her own capacities, shows an elated mood, and acts as though enamored with the world and with his or her own grandeur and omnipotence. A concomitant phenomenon with significance for internalization and structure formation is "low keyedness." At times during separation from the mother, the toddler shows diminished interest in the surroundings, becomes extra-sensitive to minor mishaps, and appears preoccupied. Mahler infers from this behavior that the infant very gradually becomes able to maintain a mental representation of the mother in her absence sufficient to sustain some degree of well-being rather than to require her constant presence (McDevitt, 1975).

With the onset of the rapprochement subphase, a new level of self-awareness follows the exhilaration of the practicing period, and the toddler now appears to have a distinct representation of him- or herself as a separate individual. Self-recognition, the use of personal pronouns, gestural directions to adults, and smiling associated with mastery upon achieving a goal are among the indicators of self-awareness and a personal identity (Lewis & Brooks-Gunn, 1979; Kagan, 1981; Emde, 1981).

Now the child negotiates the crucial final steps of "psychological birth" (Mahler et al., 1975). Self-awareness is accompanied by the painfully poignant realization of separateness, a disillusionment in omnipotence and grandeur, and the recognition that one's own and the object's wishes do not always coincide. These realizations usher in the rapprochement subphase; this is the time when the pleasures of the practicing period give way to increasing interpersonal conflict and to efforts to resolve such conflict, after which the child can continue a pleasurable reciprocity with the mother on a higher level (Mahler, 1972b). The characteristic acquisitiveness, envy, and negativism of the anal phase begin to appear, and the toddler is confronted with ambivalent feelings and incompatible aims. He or she wishes to be autonomous, to function independently, but also appears to seek closeness with the mother. Indeed, he or she oscillates between stubbornly asserting him- or herself against the wishes of the mother and cooperating with her, enjoying the familiar pleasure of "fitting together" (Sander, 1983). Mood swings and temper tantrums accompany the alternately rejecting and clinging behavior. Mahler inferred an increasing sense of psychological separateness, loneliness, and helplessness from the child's observable depressive moods, distress, and temper tantrums and from a now constant concern with mother's whereabouts.

To the extent to which the child resolves rapprochement conflict, he or she comes to have greater tolerance for ambivalence, and self and object representations come to have a predominantly positive quality. "Splitting of ambivalence" (displacing part of the ambivalence onto another object), internalization, and selective identification are among the methods used to resolve rapprochement conflicts. At times of crisis, when hostile feelings outweigh affectionate ones, however, the toddler's sense of safety is disrupted, and the mental representation of the mother becomes so buffeted by violent and angry feelings that the stability of the good feelings about the mother and the self is disrupted (McDevitt, 1975). Internalization is delayed, ego organizing functions are undermined, and libidinal object constancy is impaired or delayed.

The rapprochement subphase typically affects character style in one way or another, for we all retain some need for separateness, for closeness, for autonomy, and for dependency throughout life (Kramer & Akhtar, 1988). The way in which an individual manages these contradictory needs, as well as his or her capacity to maintain self-regulation in the face of anxiety or other intense emotion, will reflect the way in which rapprochement conflicts are resolved. If, rather than being overwhelmed, the toddler can tolerate upsurges of intense emotion when enraged at his or her frustrating mother and be helped to recognize his or her simultaneous loving feelings, he or she can then begin to integrate "good" and "bad" self and object images into stable representations. Internalization and identification then proceed smoothly, enhancing the independence of ego functioning.

According to Hartmann, "there is a long way from the object that exists only as long as it is need satisfying to that form of satisfactory object relations that includes object constancy" (1952, p. 163). The fourth subphase, called "on the way to libidinal object constancy," is never actually fully completed. As it begins, some resolution of, and greater tolerance for, ambivalence facilitates the stability of a maternal representation endowed primarily with loving feelings. Disappointment and rage are tempered and tolerated better, since the frustrating experiences with the mother can be counteracted with memories of her gratifying and loving behavior. If this more integrated view of the mother can hold together during times of affective storms, it begins to take on a new function: the images evoked by the mental representation of the mother take on a comforting function, and the child, through identification, is better able to comfort him- or herself (Furer, 1967). To the extent that the loving quality and sense of security and comfort associated with the mother can be felt during times of her absence, one may say that the child has reached a degree of stable and lasting libidinal object constancy. However, unlike earlier phases, the phase "on the way to object constancy" is open-ended (Mahler et al., 1975) because, developmentally speaking, no memory or mental representation can fully substitute for the reality of the love of the object.

The developmental significance of libidinal object constancy is not only that the child can integrate loving and affectionate, angry and hostile views of the object but also that the child can sustain a constant relationship with the mother. That is, in spite of frustration and disappointment, their basically loving relationship will endure. This affords a certain continuity of experience through the progressive and regressive fluctuations of subsequent developmental phases (Burgner & Edgcumbe, 1972). Now the child shifts from self-centered, demanding, clinging behaviors toward more mature object relationships characterized by affection, trust, and a regard for the interests and feelings of others.

Self constancy parallels object constancy. Increasing ego strength facilitates greater self-control accompanied by feelings of mastery and pride. Self-control elicits loving rather than angry responses from the object. Pride, together with loving responses from the object, helps the child to form and maintain a representation of him- or herself which, just as with the object representation, integrates different affectively toned "good" and "bad" self images. Self constancy implies that one's overall enduring self representation is one that is predominantly good and felt to be lovable and loving, and this view is sustained in spite of unpleasurable reflections about one's self.

Although this discussion has focused on the relationship with the primary care-giver, who is usually the mother, a similar process of building mental representations occurs with regard to the father, siblings, and other important objects. Early perceptual distinctions between the parents are evident, as is a discernible attachment to the father by at least eight months of age (Pedersen & Robson, 1969). Observational studies (Burlingham, 1973; Yogman, 1982) have substantiated the idea that there are definite differences in the ways in which fathers and mothers play with their infants, and with respect to this, Herzog (1980, 1982) has suggested that the father plays

an important role in developing the capacity to modulate aggressive manifestations. As development proceeds, the father and other objects play progressively greater roles. Mahler (1971; Mahler & Gosliner, 1955) and Abelin (1971) have described how the father, as a more neutral figure in the rapprochement struggle, may help the child break the symbiotic tie with the mother. He may also provide alternative means of self-esteem and safety. In addition, the boy increasingly looks to his father as a role model as he consolidates gender role identity, already having established "primary masculinity." The father's pride in his daughter's femininity can help reinforce the little girl's feminine identifications with her mother, identifications that may otherwise be undermined due to the rapprochement ambivalence felt toward the mother (Mahler, 1981; P. Tyson, 1986; Tyson & Tyson, 1990). The child's relationship with the father and the selective identifications made as a result help pave the way for later triadic object relations. Absence or loss of the father during early childhood may strain normal development in many areas of the emerging personality.

GENDER DEVELOPMENT

The formation of core gender identity starts with the sex hormones to which the fetus is exposed before birth and with the sex assignment made at birth. Parental handling and interactions with the child, based as they often are on the parents' attitudes toward the child's biological sex, make additional contributions. Core gender identity also accrues from the sense the infant makes of his or her own body. Perceptual, motor, and cognitive functioning facilitate the infant's building a body image through the integration of various oral, anal, urethral, and genital sensations that arise from intimate, affective interchanges with care-givers.

Many observers have noted that in the anal phase, alongside anal interests and a heightening of aggression, the toddler also demonstrates a heightened curiosity and interest in the genitals. Roiphe (1968; Roiphe & Galenson, 1981) thought that this genital interest and concern emerged with such regularity between the ages of fifteen and twenty-four months as to warrant the special designation "early genital phase." Genital self-stimulation usually increases, the toddler shows an emerging awareness of genital differences between the sexes, and varieties of affective reactions have been reported (Greenacre, 1953; Kleeman, 1976; Roiphe & Galenson, 1981). These affective reactions depend on a number of factors, but the reactions may then influence the relationships with care-givers and emerging feelings about the self. Girls seem especially prone to develop a "basic depressive mood" (Mahler, 1966) as well as intense penis envy, which may organize rapprochement conflicts and betray an underlying difficulty in the mother–child relationship (Grossman & Stewart, 1976). Boys may develop a castration fear, but in contrast to the later fear of punishment by the oedipal father, it is fear of the omnipotently viewed mother that causes anxiety in this early period. Then severe, pre-oedipal castration anxiety may undermine the boy's ability to establish a confident sense of masculinity and indicate pathology in the mother–child relationship (P. Tyson, 1989). The observations regarding genital awareness, albeit with accompanying potential vulnerabilities, lead us to conclude that as the sense of the self comes to be mentally represented, the self representation contains some notion of gender—thus, that core gender identity (Stoller, 1968b), while perhaps not solid, has been established.

PSYCHIC STRUCTURE FORMATION

Although this discussion will consider all psychic structures, the main focus will be on the ego and its synthesizing function. If we view the ego as a coherent organization of mental processes that functions to organize and regulate the personality, then understanding its development entails understanding the progressive integration and organization of its functions. It was to this integration that Spitz (1959) turned his attention. He observed that processes which initially emerged discretely came to be linked and to function in relation to one another and that at such times new behaviors and new affective expressions seemed to become available to the child. These affects and behaviors in turn facilitated changes in interpersonal interaction and fostered further development. Emphasizing this integration and organization among ego functions, Spitz suggested that development, rather than being continuous, was characterized by major shifts. Furthermore, he postulated that progressively complex stages of ego formation were signaled by the appearance of a new affective expression. Spitz limited his scheme to the first two years, but because our focus is on increasing organization within the ego system, it seemed to us to have an applicability beyond that. Indeed, our discussion of psychic structure formation will be in terms of Spitz's "organizers," and we will draw on our recently proposed extension of this scheme (P. Tyson, 1988; Tyson & Tyson, 1990).

The undifferentiated phase. From the point of view of psychic structures, the beginning of life is known as the "undifferentiated" phase (Hartmann et al., 1946) because of the absence of observable indications that the ego is functioning as a psychologically determined, inner regulating system or that the id is functioning to organize motivational systems. Proto-

types of affective expressions and cognitive, perceptual functions provide a state of "preadaptiveness" to the "average expectable environment" (Hartmann, 1939), with which the infant and mother establish an affective feedback system. There is good evidence to suggest that this affective feedback system provides the matrix from which all psychic systems emerge (Loewald, 1978; Gaensbauer, 1982). The neonate has a complicated organization of endogenously determined behaviors that function to maintain physiological homeostasis. But it is through the affective feedback system of mother–infant reciprocity that the physiologically based regulating system eventually becomes a psychological system that regulates behavior (Spitz, 1965; Sander, 1962; Weil, 1970). Organismic distress, diffuse tension states, and archaic excitations, whether due to a predisposition to anxiety (Greenacre, 1941), disturbance in physiological subsystems, disturbance in mother–infant synchrony (Sander, 1969; Sander et al., 1970), or delays in need satisfaction, may lead to a variety of defective ego functions and developmental interferences, should this delicate regulating function be overwhelmed (Weil, 1978).

The term "undifferentiated" has also been used to refer to the infant's presumed inability to distinguish between self and object. But there is much to suggest that the neonate is not undifferentiated in any simple sense (Call, 1964; Emde, 1981), and some researchers (for example, Stern, 1985) have criticized the concept of nondifferentiation, citing endogenously determined regulating behaviors and other evidence suggesting that infants are equipped from birth to make many subtle perceptual distinctions. From the psychoanalytic point of view, however, physiological regulation is not psychological regulation, and the capacity for self-regulation develops slowly over the first several years of life. Furthermore, the early ability to make perceptual distinctions among external stimuli is not the same thing as the gradual emergence of psychically available mental representations of self and object (Tyson & Tyson, 1990). Mahler and McDevitt (1982) infer from their observations of infant and toddler behavior that feelings about the self and feelings about the object as separate from the self only gradually become integrated with perceptual and cognitive awareness of the self and object to form psychically available mental representations.

The social smile. The first major developmental shift in ego organization occurs between two and three months of age. Spitz suggested that the emergence of a smile in response to external or social cues indicates this shift. (Earlier endogenous smiling is unrelated to social interaction.) The social smile denotes progress beyond inborn adaptations, and once it emerges, we see the infant become progressively more responsive to external stimuli. The mother quickly becomes the best elicitor of this smile, and it becomes an important part of the mother–child interaction.

Over the next months the infant shows evidence of developing rudimentary schemes of the outside world and of him- or herself. Kinesthetic and tactile sensations combine with visual and olfactory perceptions, motor activity, and recognition memory to enable the baby to draw together a cognitive schema of his or her body beyond the level of immediate sensory awareness (Hoffer, 1949, 1950; Greenacre, 1960), and a "primitive self-feeling" can be surmised (Mahler, 1968).

Eight-month distress.[8] A second major developmental step in ego organization can be inferred from the advent of a shift in behavior between seven and nine months. A greater range of affective expression becomes available, and discrete expressions of fear, surprise, joy, and anger are more easily observable as drive and affect differentiation progresses (Emde et al., 1976; Sroufe, 1977). Progress with regard to a wide range of ego functions such as memory, perception, thought processes (means–ends connections), locomotion, and judgment is observable, and the greater integration among these functions facilitates new pleasures in exploring as long as the infant's sense of safety (Sandler, 1960) is maintained. Mahler's use of the term "practicing" captures the essence of the infant's delight in perceiving and exploring a wider segment of the world. But the infant's response to a stranger or to novel stimuli shifts, often dramatically, at this time. Instead of pleasure and excited expectation, we observe noticeable hesitation and sometimes distress and avoidance. The mother's affective signal now becomes a key factor in the infant's adaptation. The infant "checks back" (Mahler et al., 1975) for a cue about safety in what has been called social referencing (see Emde, 1983), and the mother's response guides the infant's behavioral response. Pleasure in exploring the unfamiliar follows encouraging affective signals; distress, disorganization, and panic may result when mother is absent, unavailable, or unable to convey a sense of safety.

Although these emergent behaviors are in re-

sponse to the external world, later signal affects and defense mechanisms in response to internal danger are modeled on these early responses to external danger. Efficient response to danger, aided by the organizing auxiliary ego function of the mother, facilitates the structuralization of an ego capable of appropriate response to danger. When the object is unavailable (physically or emotionally) to provide an affective signal of safety, the affective distress caused by a strange person or situation may disrupt ego functioning. The mother's emotional availability therefore seems crucial to ego development in two ways: her reassuring affective signal is integral to the infant's push to explore and widen his or her intellectual horizons; and maternal intervention in response to disorganizing panic is crucial to the structuralization of the synthesizing, comforting, and defense functions of the ego. Without this timely intervention, affects later on may become sources of internal danger that undermine the ego's integrative and defensive functions, because the internalized regulatory mechanisms to cope effectively with disruptive affects have not been well developed.

The semantic "no." The third major shift in the ego's organizational complexity is marked by the emergence of speech at about fifteen to eighteen months. Because Spitz (1959) took the "no" gesture to indicate emerging speech as well as to be the earliest evidence of the infant's replacing action by communication, he labeled the "no" gesture the third psychic organizer, negativism being the emergent affect. Once usable language emerges, it fosters autonomy as well as increasingly complicated interactions with others. Speech organizes thought processes and mental operations, and wishes and needs can be more easily formulated and communicated. Spitz also understood the "no" to indicate identification with the aggressor and, as such, a defense mechanism in the proper sense of the word, as well as an early step in superego formation. Spitz thought that the semantic "no" and the ability to communicate also made a crucial contribution to furthering object relations.

Internalization of conflict—superego formation. During the anal rapprochement phase, increased ego complexity is marked by the following: advances in symbolization, which extend language capabilities and make fantasy possible; movement from developmental conflict to the beginnings of internalized conflict (Nagera, 1966); compliance and partial identification with the mother's wishes; emerging defenses of increasing complexity; and relinquishment or delay of a degree of drive gratification with evidence of early superego structuralization (Tyson

---

8. Spitz equated the infant's distress when confronted with a stranger with anxiety; however, it is now generally agreed that anxiety is a complex emotion requiring greater ego organization than is found in an eight-month-old (Katan, 1972).

& Tyson, 1984). Affects now become the complex structures that psychoanalytic theory generally takes them to be—that is, feelings with physiological components that are linked to thoughts, memories, wishes, and fantasies. For the first time we can posit anxiety in a true sense, as well as other complex affects such as depression and shame. The capacity for symbolization is basic to the emergence of complex affects. Symbolization makes language possible; once available, it quickly becomes a tool for thinking, organizing, reflecting, and mastery. Language furthers secondary-process organization, because it fosters causal thinking, categorization, and abstraction. Furthermore, language is an aid to impulse control and the modulation of affect (Katan, 1961). As Freud remarked, "The man who first flung a word of abuse at his enemy instead of a spear was the founder of civilization" (1893, p. 36).

Language and other forms of symbolism also become tools for the elaboration of an inner symbolic world, as inner speech expands play, fantasy, and dreams (Vigotsky, 1934; Roiphe & Galenson, 1981; Blum, 1978). Mental representations become more complex and are elaborated with the help of memory and fantasy. As development proceeds, many fantasies cease to be accessible to conscious awareness, although they continue to affect responses to reality (Arlow, 1969).

The new possibilities for self-reflection and for fantasies about the self increase the child's sense of individuality and further his or her wish for autonomy. They also contribute to the formation of ideal self and object representations and to early steps in superego development and help the child to consolidate his or her sense of a permanent and lasting object. As the child becomes more expert in the use of language, he or she increasingly distinguishes between inner wishes and fantasies and external reality and between his or her wishes and those of the ideally viewed mother, with all the consequences for conflict and ambivalence of the rapprochement phase.

With the ability to fantasize, the child can anticipate the consequences of his or her actions should he or she push for wish fulfillment. Because of the content of these fantasies, the child begins to experience inner conflict as well as anxiety that he or she may lose the object (mainly as a result of expressing anger), lose the object's love, or be punished for his or her actions or thoughts, as by castration in the case of the boy. For example, if the toddler vents his or her anger, the sense of "oneness" with the mother is disrupted, and the toddler may feel that he or she has actually lost the object or lost the object's love, thereby losing a necessary component of the ideal

sense of self (Joffe & Sandler, 1956); feelings of sadness, grief, or even depression may then follow (Mahler, 1966; Brenner, 1982). Typically, the anxiety derived from fantasying is externalized and displaced from the original object to another. This gives rise to behavior that, superficially, appears to be a conflict with the environment, often interpreted as "only" a transient manifestation of ordinary developmental stress. But, while the manifest behavior or symptom may be transient, the underlying conflict may persist and may compromise later development.

In the ordinary course of adaptation, defenses such as flight, denial, and reaction formation emerge (A. Freud, 1936) and assist the individual in coping with affects and libidinal impulses. As self-regulation and self-control become more possible, a new sense of mastery and pride in overcoming drive demands appears, which substitutes for immediate gratification. Aggression previously directed to the object may now be directed to the self when drive derivatives find expression, as when the child soils, wets, or becomes angry. The appearance of shame in response to inner stimuli comes to be a signal of intrapsychic conflict and of the structuralization of the inner voice of authority, an early step in superego formation. Although shame can be observed as early as fifteen months, at that time it is related to the mother's "shaming" the child. The response of shame to which we refer here is related to a shift in narcissistic valuation of the self consequent on the emerging superego.

Signal anxiety and libidinal object constancy. Although we speak of affects functioning as social signals from early on in life, it is a long way from proto-affects to affects functioning as signals to the ego in such a way that they instigate defenses and thereby restrict the affects to manageable proportions. The emergence of the signal function of anxiety and other affects reflects an advance in ego functioning which has developmental roots in the mother–child relationship of early infancy (Tolpin, 1971; Ritvo, 1981).

Structuralization and effective operation of the ego's signaling function begin with the mother's consistent response to the child's signals with soothing, organizing activities that reduce distress. At each developmental phase, the mother must adjust her response so as to guard against the infant becoming unduly distressed, while at the same time allowing sufficient challenge to encourage the tolerance of frustration and the development of self-coping mechanisms, thereby fostering internalization and independence. If she is successful, the attainment of a degree of libidinal object constancy will be accompanied by identifications with the competently consistent mother as well as by identifications with her soothing, regulating, and organizing functions. Adequate internalization of the mother's organizing functions while attaining a degree of emotional object and self constancy results in an ego organization capable of keeping instinctual tension within manageable limits (Hartmann, 1952, 1953), a capacity for affective control, and a capacity to limit anxiety to signal proportions as it becomes a trigger for defense mechanisms (P. Tyson, 1988; R. L. Tyson, 1991).

Early Childhood

PSYCHOSEXUAL DEVELOPMENT

The infantile genital organization. The final period of infantile sexuality is heralded by a concentration of pleasurable interest and excitement in the genitals. Genital excitation soon predominates over oral and anal pleasures, and the "component instincts" are superseded. Genital masturbation, with its associated fantasies, takes on a primary and dominant significance. Freud (1923b) noted that at the height of this phase, "interest in the genitals and in their activity acquires a dominating significance which falls little short of that reached in maturity" (p. 142).

Children of both sexes now become preoccupied with anatomical features and anatomical differences. In this phase the boy's interest turns to his genitals. He explores his testicles (Bell, 1961; Yasmajian, 1966, 1967) and experiences penile erections, which may give him a sensation of power and enhance his phallic exhibitionism. At the same time, awareness of father's much larger organ often leads the boy to penis preoccupation and envy and to wishes to possess an organ like that of his father. Given the sometimes overwhelming nature of penile sensations, as well as the bewilderment of detumescence, the little boy frequently becomes concerned about the potential loss of his precious organ, particularly if he feels guilty about the envy he harbors toward his father's penis. Earlier as well as current conflicts and anxieties may come to be organized around this castration complex.

On reaching this phase, girls also become genitally oriented, with an upsurge of erotic sensitivity. They localize the genital area and learn how to bring about sensual excitement and pleasurable erotic suffusion. Anatomical preoccupation may lead a girl to envy her mother's breasts and mature body, as well as her ability to have a baby. On the other hand, it may lead to penis envy; if already a developmental

motif, penis envy may now take on new meaning and reach new intensity, undermining the possibility of the girl finding a pleasurable sense of femininity.

During the early childhood period of genital dominance, gratification is gained primarily through genital masturbation, accompanied by increasingly elaborate sexual fantasies and wishes about both parents. These wishes and associated conflicts are elaborated in conscious and unconscious fantasy and form the basis of the positive and negative oedipus complexes, the emergence of which indicates progress in object relations development. Further elaborations in psychic structure formation take place with attempts to resolve oedipal conflicts.

OBJECT RELATIONS

Progress in drive development does not necessarily imply progress in object relations. Indeed, once the child reaches the phase of genital dominance, a distinction must be made between pre-oedipal dyadic and oedipal triadic levels of object relations, designated phallic-narcissistic and phallic-oedipal by Edgcumbe and Burgner (1975), who found divergence between the two levels in the nature of the child's wishes and fantasies directed toward objects.[9]

Infantile-genital narcissistic. In the early part of the infantile genital phase, object relations remain dyadic, and attention is focused on bodily and gender concerns. At this time the child typically seeks admiration from both parents for his or her physical prowess—"Look what I can do!" The narcissistic gratification resulting from the object's admiration helps the child to feel pride and confidence in his or her gender identity. Rivalry may be present with siblings or with one parent for the love and attention of the other. While competition is also common in a triadic situation, in this early phase the third person is viewed more as an intruder or disrupter of the wished-for narcissistic aggrandizement rather than as a libidinal rival. It is also important in this phase that a special bond is formed with the same-sex parent, who is now idealized. This idealization and the admiring, confirming response from that parent serve to further psychic structure organization and gender identity. Not only does the idealization form the basis of the ego ideal as the superego takes shape, but the idealized parent is also a model for gender role identifications.

9. The terms "phallic-narcissistic" and "phallic-oedipal" are well known. However, we feel that Freud's first term, "infantile genital," though more cumbersome, is more appropriate in light of present-day knowledge of gender development.

Oedipal object relations. Freud's understanding of the complex nature of object relations during what he called the oedipal phase remains one of his major contributions. The formation of an oedipus complex implies full triadic object relations and marks the highest level of development possible for the young child in terms of libidinal organization and object relations. From early on in life the infant has the capacity to relate to more than one object. (Abelin [1975] describes such triangular configurations.) However, "triadic object relations" refers to a situation in which wishes toward one object conflict with wishes toward another object—as, for example, when the child wishes to assume the role of one parent with regard to the other. The oedipus complex is characterized by wishes in the child's mind associated with and emerging from sexual, especially genital, excitation.

In the positive oedipus complex, sexual wishes are directed toward the parent of the opposite sex. The parent of the same sex is perceived as an omnipotent and feared rival, who magically knows or will know all the child's thoughts, such as the child's wish to be the preferred love object of the opposite-sex parent, as well as the wish to eliminate his or her chief competitor. The child comes to fear catastrophic retaliation from this parent for his or her fantasies, hopes, and wishes. However, the rivalry arouses enormous conflict because of the special bond the child also has with his or her rival; for the child loves, identifies with, and idealizes his or her rival. Fears of loss of the love of the admired oedipal rival press the child to find some resolution of his or her painfully conflicting wishes and feelings.

The negative oedipus complex (named in analogy to a photographic print, not to imply a value judgment) is just the opposite. Sexual wishes are directed toward the same-sex parent, and identifications are made with the opposite-sex parent, who is then viewed as the rival. Typically children oscillate between positive and negative oedipal wishes, but the positive position generally predominates.

Resolution of oedipal conflict involves coming to terms with the differences between the sexes and the differences between generations; further identifications are made with the parent of the same sex, and the child relinquishes hope of direct oedipal gratification. The child is helped in finding more suitable and realistic pathways for gratification by progressive ego and superego structuralization.

GENDER DEVELOPMENT

In the early part of the infantile genital phase the child's principal developmental tasks are to come to terms with the differences between the sexes and to consolidate a narcissistically valued intact sense of body-self and masculinity or femininity. Although a girl's penis envy or a boy's fear of castration may be ubiquitous during this phase, they undermine the child's pleasurable sense of femininity or masculinity. At this time the child usually begins to admire the same-sex parent; he or she wishes to be with him or her and to be like him or her in every way and seeks a special bond with that parent. If this parent can reciprocate and participate with the child in gender-specific activities, this parent can be idealized. By identifying with the ideal, the child is helped to establish more of a pleasurable sense of gender. Making gender role identifications is also an important aspect of the infantile genital phase. As the child comes to terms with his or her gender, he or she also typically wishes to identify with the idealized same-sex parent with regard to the role the ideal takes in interpersonal interactions. This involves leaving behind the role of baby and assuming a more mature role with mother and father. Indeed, oedipal progression depends on the boy or girl assuming (at least in fantasy) the role of one parent with regard to the other.

Sexual partner orientation now becomes a developmental issue for the first time, since the foundation for this choice is built on the child's oscillations between positive and negative oedipal wishes. However, conflicts over object choice do not usually cause undue anxiety at this early stage, and resolution is deferred until adolescence.

PSYCHIC STRUCTURE FORMATION

The oedipus complex, infantile neurosis, and guilt. Analytic experience has led to the conclusion that conflict is ubiquitous, that it is a part of the human condition. The possible variations of conflict during the oedipal phase are enormous; the child strives to satisfy libidinal and aggressive urges and at the same time to gain a measure of impulse control (Lustman, 1966), to meet the standards of his or her emergent superego, consolidate a narcissistically valued gender identity, maintain self-esteem in the face of disappointed wishes toward objects, and form triadic object relations. The appearance of oedipal conflict is not as important for psychic structure formation as the means by which the ego seeks to deal with it.

The oedipus complex generally constitutes the core conflict of infantile neurosis. Neurosis begins with internalization of interpersonal conflict, so that conflict is then among psychic agencies. Neurotic conflict leads to compromise formations whereby internal modifications are made in efforts to resolve conflict. The first steps in internalization of conflict are evident as early as the second half of the second year, as anxieties converge in the rapprochement period (Mahler, 1975). The phase-specific conflicts of the oedipus complex, combined with the demands of the emergent superego, increase the potential for neurotic conflict.

Infantile neurosis implies more than isolated internalized conflict, however; it implies a further step in psychic structuralization. Underlying this organization is the consolidation of the superego. Although evidence of superego functioning emerges earlier, it is not fully internalized, does not function to assert effective controls, and has an archaic, harsh, and punitive quality. In efforts to resolve painful oedipal conflicts, further identifications with parental moral codes and ethical standards are made. In the course of making these identifications, the various components of the superego become more integrated, and the superego becomes a more functional system. While early in life the superego is relatively easily projected and experienced as external, the structuralization and integration of the superego that accompanies infantile neurosis implies that internal disapproval takes over from the parents' actual disapproval and that internal approval supplements parental approval. Accordingly, conflict and turmoil, as well as sources of self-esteem, become internal and less easily influenced by the environment. Internal disapproval becomes a major source of danger; internal punishment is experienced as the painful affect of guilt. Guilt can thus be considered to be the sixth "psychic organizer," insofar as it signifies the structuralization of the superego and the integration of a psychic structure that responds to danger and conflict with internal modification. Since the conflicts, the sources of approval or disapproval, and the means for resolution are all now internal, the ego increasingly functions autonomously—that is, relatively independently of external support.

Eventually the wishes and conflicts of the oedipal phase succumb to repression. This frees the ego to deal more effectively with the expectations of a wider social world and the greater educational tasks encountered in latency.

Latency

Freud (1905) borrowed the term "period of sexual latency" from Wilhelm Fliess (p. 178, n. 1) to refer to a time of diminished sexual manifestations during the period from the sixth or seventh year of life until puberty. Freud viewed the complexities of this phase as a combination of biological processes, cultural and educational influences, and a reorganization of the ego's defensive structure partly influenced by superego development (1905, 1924a, 1926).

Several attempts have been made to divide latency into subphases. Alpert (1941) distinguished an "early phase," while Bornstein (1951) detailed an early and a late phase, taking into account the nature and role of the superego and defense mechanisms. Sarnoff (1976, p. 90) makes a tripartite division based on cognitive advances (see also Williams, 1972).

PSYCHOSEXUAL DEVELOPMENT

While Freud noted a diminution of observable sexual activity in latency, he recognized that the period was insufficiently understood. Thus, he wrote that the concept of sexual latency was "an educational ideal from which individual development usually diverges at some point and often to a considerable degree. From time to time a fragmentary manifestation of sexuality which has evaded sublimation may break through; or some sexual activity may persist through the whole duration of the latency period" (1905, p. 179).

The child undergoes a variety of developmental changes during these years. Though many observations indicate relative quiescence of erotic activity (Shapiro & Perry, 1976), both masturbatory activity and masturbation fantasies are present in the latency child almost universally from middle to late latency on into puberty (Clower, 1976). Fraiberg (1972) has pointed out that relief through masturbation may be very important for the psychic stability of the latency child. When masturbation fantasies and activities are forcibly suppressed, ego restrictions are likely; the child may then complain of excessive boredom and limit his or her freedom to play and to pursue other activities.

OBJECT RELATIONS

The diminution of drive pleasure combined with the strong prohibition of the superego and efficient defenses of the ego force the child's oedipal wishes into repression. Derivatives surface in family romance fantasies (Freud, 1908), but now a basically affectionate, reciprocal relationship with each parent is optimally established. Although object relations continue to be triadic, the child's partial abandonment of oedipal aims coincides with identifications with the same-sex parent that further consolidate gender identity and give access to an inner source of self-esteem as the child strives to become like his or her ideal.

Peer relationships become particularly important during the latency years. They offer displacements for the expression of oedipal wishes, and peer activities provide outlets for the expression of drive and superego themes in endless variations of "good" against "bad." Rules are particularly emphasized, and fairness is stressed. The newly consolidated, somewhat harsh superego often promotes defensive projection, leading children during this phase typically to blame others for their own wrongdoings.

The school setting is also an important part of object relations in latency. Teachers as well as peers become objects for oedipal displacement, and teachers are important alternative figures for identification.

GENDER DEVELOPMENT

Latency is a period for psychic integration and consolidation and so too for gender development. A sense of masculinity or femininity should now be in place, based on identifications with the ideal made during the early part of the infantile genital phase as well as on further identifications with the ideal made in attempts to resolve the oedipus complex. The wider social opportunities of the latency period help the child to integrate further a sense of gender as he or she finds opportunities to experience a variety of relationships with peers, with older children, and with adults other than parents, any of whom can provide models for further identifications. In this way, the wider social contacts help the child extend and elaborate the sense of gender.

Latency is also a time of practicing gender roles. Latency peer relationships are usually modeled on the idealized same-sex parent relationship established during the infantile-genital narcissistic phase. However, these now internalized role relationships can be elaborated by social and cultural influences, and a broader sense of gender role results.

PSYCHIC STRUCTURE FORMATION

The fate of masturbation and instinctual urges during latency is dependent on a number of factors in addition to diminished drive pressure. Among these are superego consolidation, increased ego complexity, and cognitive advances, as well as the expanding social world with its greater opportunities for displacement and sublimation. Consolidation of the superego is part of oedipal resolution; with an internalized set of morals and ideals, superego functions gradually take over from the parents and become the arbiters of feelings of guilt and self-esteem. Typically, superego demands are externalized and so are felt to originate in the external world. This externalization functions to defend against strict, rigid, uncompromising inner judgments and standards. But because internal judgments tend to be so harsh and uncompromising, external supports are required to control pressures both from drives and from superego directives. Although externalization is phase-appropriate, an important task of the ego during latency is to accommodate and become accustomed to the superego as an internal structure, as its functioning becomes increasingly autonomous.

A further important aspect of superego functioning now develops. The child begins to admit his or her own guilt and take responsibility for his or her actions. This begins with the child recognizing that not only do the parents enforce rules, but the parents also live by certain rules and moral and ethical codes. More than simply identifying with the parents' rules, which contributes to an internalized source of guilt when transgressions occur, the child now forms identifications with parents who also follow these rules and moral codes—that is, with parents who are responsible in their actions and accept responsibility for their actions. Now self-responsibility begins to substitute for parental responsibility.

As ego functions become less vulnerable to drive pressure and regression and the child becomes more adept at coping with guilt over sexual urges and masturbatory activities, he or she manifests a greater stability of mood and affect. Buxbaum (1980) commented that the consolidation of ego functions aids the inhibition and control of drives, while biologically determined drive diminution may facilitate the consolidation of ego functions: "It is not a question of priority, but a question of mutual influences" (p. 123).

A cognitive shift occurs at about age seven, when the child moves from the pre-operational egocentric way of thinking to the concrete operational mode (Piaget & Inhelder, 1969). Now thinking is not so dominated by personalization of perceptions and memories, and verbal expression is more separate from motor activity, by contrast with the younger child, who often uses the whole body to relate an event (Kris, 1939). With these achievements, the latency child is better able to view things from another's perspective (decentering) and to make more objective evaluations of others, an advance that contributes to more satisfactory relationships with peers, as well as to the ability to admit guilt and take responsibility for actions as the superego further consolidates.

Rational thinking and fantasy are increasingly kept separate as latency progresses, and fantasies become more restricted to "private" life. Masturbation fantasies may be defensively separated from the act and may themselves become an important pathway for gratification. In addition, family romance fantasies express oedipal wishes, and various monsters appear as symbolic superego figures in the child's play, fantasies, and dreams, the uncontrollable aspect of the monster being a reflection of the impulses being defended against.

Behavior becomes more consistent as habitual modes of reacting and relating are established in the form of enduring, if not necessarily endearing, character traits. These represent solutions to inner conflicts and, as such, remain fundamentally unaffected by environmental changes and manipulation. In this condition the child meets the biologically induced changes consequent on puberty and the emotional and psychological sequelae of adolescence.

Adolescence

The relative calm of latency is interrupted by the biological changes of puberty. Adolescence is the period of life devoted to the psychic reorganization required to accommodate this maturational change, and new steps are taken in all the developmental lines we have been following.

PSYCHOSEXUAL DEVELOPMENT

Biological sexual maturation brings about the intensification of genital sexual impulses. Sexual impulses related to the various erotogenic zones ordinarily become subordinate to the primacy of the genital zone (Freud, 1905), although derivatives of component instincts are also abundantly evident. Drive pressures lead to intensified masturbation impulses, elaboration of fantasies, and intensified conflicts (Laufer, 1968, 1976). In addition, from puberty on, the adolescent in reality is capable of heterosexual intercourse and procreation. This adds to the burden caused by increased drive pressure, and the actual presence of the objects of the individual's pre-oedipal and oedipal wishes may be a source of anxiety, taxing the ego's capacity for repression.

OBJECT RELATIONS

Vulnerability to regression to earlier modes of relating or of gratification arises when wishes and conflicts from previous phases reemerge. This is especially true for adolescents. Earlier dependency needs are revived, fears of loss of love resurface, resistance to dependency needs arises, and conflicts over independence return. Moreover, oedipal strivings, with conflicting wishes toward objects, also reappear. In other words, wishes and conflicts from all developmental phases resurface, and all must be reworked with the now better-equipped ego. Because of the phase-appropriate defense of externalization, these conflicts are felt by the adolescent not primarily as internal ones but as ongoing with the parent of the present, a circumstance that may make this period a volatile one for family relationships.

In order, ultimately, to find adequate substitutes

for primary objects in mature extra-familial relationships, the adolescent must "individuate" from infantile object ties. This involves not only becoming independent of the parents of the present but also becoming independent of automatic compliance with superego demands and disengaged from infantile, idealized representations of objects. Representations of the parents must be revised in accordance with a more mature view, so that selective adult identifications become possible. When this revision is incomplete, the parents of the present continue to be viewed as disappointing, and unrealistic hopes are transferred to extra-familial objects who, in turn, inevitably disappoint. Jacobson (1961) points out, however, that the degree of success achieved in the reorganization of object ties depends on the ability to retain some of the attachments and identifications of the past. Blos (1967) compares the "second individuation process of adolescence" to the pre-oedipal separation-individuation phases; he points out that the two periods have in common a heightened vulnerability of the personality organization and an urgency for changes in psychic structure in accordance with the forward maturational surge. Both are also times of vulnerable narcissistic balance, as the loosening of infantile object ties produces feelings of loneliness and isolation, which may be disruptive. Major difficulties arise when sweeping biological, cognitive, or social changes come before the ego and the superego are equipped to handle them and when the earlier reliance on parents to provide auxiliary ego functions is no longer possible.

GENDER DEVELOPMENT

The biological changes of puberty challenge the adolescent's sense of femininity or masculinity, his or her sense of gender role, and the previous position regarding choice of object. From the child's still immature body, the adolescent experiences a rapid maturation process; adjustments in the body-self and the body image must be made to accommodate these physical changes. In a relatively short time, these bodily changes bring into focus the increasingly obvious differences between female and male, child and adult. Often previous concerns relating to penis envy or fears of castration become manifest through preoccupation with the body as the adolescent tries to cope with the now sexually mature body and the discrepancies between the "ideal" body and the body the adolescent now has.

Gender role identity is also elaborated as part of the adolescent process. That is, pressures to find ways of interacting with potential lovers come with sexual maturity. In the early stages, the adolescent's style of interacting with the opposite sex may resemble a caricature of a feminine or masculine role, betraying underlying anxiety. However, the ultimate role the individual assumes in interacting with sexual objects begins to take shape in adolescence.

Establishing sexual partner orientation is primarily a task for adolescence. Although conflicts over object choice begin with the oedipus complex, in early childhood conflicting object-related wishes can exist side by side without leading to anxiety. But in adolescence the individual's sense of identity comes to be linked in some way or another with sexual preference, so that the resolution of conflicts over object choice becomes a major task. This is usually accomplished as part of the second individuation process as object-related conflicts associated with pre-oedipal and oedipal object relations are reworked. The outcome of this reworking is reflected in sexual partner orientation.

PSYCHIC STRUCTURE FORMATION

Adolescence brings a rapid increase in drive pressure and rapid physical, cognitive, and social changes. These rapid changes challenge the adolescent ego's defensive and integrating functions. The relative calm and harmony among psychic systems during latency are replaced by inevitable shifts, tensions, and imbalance, often manifest on the outside by unpredictable and uncontrollable mood swings. A major task for the adolescent is to regain a sense of psychic balance, so that a unique, individuated, and autonomous identity can emerge with an integrated, stabilized character structure. Paradoxically, it is only through drive, ego, and superego regression and psychic restructuring that this psychic balance can be found; hence, regression at this time is best viewed as chiefly in the service of normal developmental progression.

Imbalance and regression may first be seen in response to increased sexual pressures. Identifications must now be made with parents who are sexually active adults, yet oedipal incestuous wishes must remain repressed. To form these identifications, alterations must be made to ideals and moral codes. Because its beginnings lie in pre-oedipal and oedipal object relations, the superego must now undergo disorganization and reorganization (A. Freud, 1952). Modifications of the ego ideal accompany revisions in moral codes, and eventually the ego ideal comes to embody revised attitudes toward the parents and their sexuality and to the adolescent himself (Blos, 1968, 1972, 1976; Tyson & Tyson, 1984, 1990).

A shift in the relative power of the ego and the superego must also take place in order for the adolescent to become sexually active eventually. At the onset of latency, a strong superego is needed to support the relatively weak ego in the battle to control the drives. In adolescence the situation is reversed, for a degree of drive gratification is necessary to maintain psychic equilibrium; to permit this, the ego, rather than the superego, needs to be arbiter vis-à-vis the drives. Eventually the ego supports, supplants, and supplements superego functions so that a smooth collaboration between the two systems can emerge (Jacobson, 1961).

To cope with the challenges of adolescence and to support ego functioning, a number of defense mechanisms specific to adolescence typically develop (A. Freud, 1958). Attachments are made to persons outside the family, either older "leaders" or contemporaries. Such displacements (or object removal—Katan, 1951) enable the adolescent to focus on extra-familial, nonincestuous sources of gratification, to find acceptable substitutes for ideals and standards otherwise too closely linked to primary objects, but to allow the defenses against incestuous wishes to remain. Reversal of affect is another common defense; love is felt as hate, dependency wishes are turned into revolt, respect and admiration become contempt and derision. Although the adolescent may imagine him- or herself to be "free" with this defense, it belies his or her inability to detach him- or herself from infantile objects: "compulsive opposition to the parents proves as crippling in this respect as compulsive obedience" (A. Freud, 1958, p. 271). Frequently hostility is turned against the self; this may result in intense depression with suicidal wishes or impulses. Another pathological defense is withdrawal from the object world; pervasive ideas of grandeur, fantasies of saving the world, or hypochondriacal concerns then arise. Defenses against impulses are also common in adolescence. The "ascetic" adolescent wages "total war . . . against the pursuit of pleasure" (ibid., p. 276). Another defense against the impulses themselves is the uncompromising attitude of the adolescent who embraces certain ideas or principles and refuses to make concessions to practical and more reality-adapted attitudes.

The disruptive psychic realignment process of adolescence is accompanied by a shift in cognitive functioning; what Piaget and Inhelder (1969) called "formal operations," characterized by an advance in abstract thinking, now becomes possible. The middle to late adolescent comes to be preoccupied with formulating opinions, ideas, and ideals relevant to serious ethical, political, or social problems. Often, though not always, the fervor with which adolescents pursue ideals and ethical and philosophical problems has a defensive quality about it and may represent different sides of ongoing unconscious conflicts. The adaptive use of intellectual advances leads to the formation of what has been called a *Weltanschauung,* or a "view of the world" broader than one's own self or self interests. This widening of intellectual horizons may be accompanied by a flowering of intellectual and artistic creativity, facilitated by a seemingly phase-specific fluidity of interchange between primary and secondary processes (Noy, 1978).

A crucial task for the adolescent, which accompanies the psychic realignment process, is to forge a unique sense of personal identity, integrating various past and present aspects of the sense of self. Erikson (1956) saw self representations from earlier childhood, ideal self images, and images of the body-self as essential components of ego identity which are brought together by the ego's synthesizing function. This process neither begins nor ends with adolescence. It begins with self–object differentiation in infancy, and elements are added, altered, and superseded throughout life. What is unique about adolescent identity consolidation, however, is the extent to which both physical and cognitive maturational factors play a part, factors that must themselves be integrated with more or less realistic social, academic, and personal expectations and goals.

To the extent that a more stable integrated personal identity emerges and power shifts from superego to ego functioning, ego functioning serves to integrate and organize psychic life and dominate over instinctual and superego pressures. As a result, the individual experiences greater instinctual freedom, greater freedom of object choice and of thought, feeling, and action, and greater independence from external influences and from archaic id and superego pressures (Jacobson, 1961). To the extent that the ego gains autonomy and strength to maintain a stable and durable control system in accord with adult reality, these freedoms can be guaranteed.

Blos has studied how the adolescent constructs a unified adult character structure (1968, 1972, 1976). The topic is important, because psychic restructuring during adolescence makes it impossible to trace adult conflicts directly to childhood experiences; knowledge of the intervening latency and adolescent transformations is required, in accordance with the principle of multiple function (Waelder, 1936). With the formation of a mature character structure, reaction patterns become predictable, self-esteem regulation assumes a definite pattern, personal identity stabilizes, and affects normally fluctuate within a more tolerable range (Zetzel, 1964). The expression of deeply felt emotions between friends and lovers is linked with this more even-tempered condition. The emergence of mature love and the capacity for intimacy (Kernberg, 1974a, 1974b; Erikson, 1959) can be understood as affective indicators that character has been consolidated and that the adolescent has fulfilled the tasks of this phase of life.

Adulthood

A recent trend in psychoanalytic theory is to utilize earlier developmental principles in the study of later life; this has led to a profusion of ideas about what has been called "adult development." Concepts like epigenetic progression, regression, and psychic reorganization with biological change are now applied to the situation of adults. However, theories about adult development include social and cultural elements to a much greater extent than do psychoanalytic conceptualizations of the early years. Consequently, two major, as yet unanswered, questions pervade the recent profusion of ideas about the psychology of later life. First, is the formation of a new psychic structure a sine qua non for adult development, as it is earlier? Or is it sufficient that adaptational changes and elaboration of existing structure take place? Second, are biological changes in adulthood, including physiological and anatomical decline, necessarily linked to concomitant psychic changes in the same ways that maturational steps are linked to psychic structure formation in childhood and adolescence? Or is there a different relationship in the adult between somatic events and mental phenomena?

Jung was the first to assert that psychic development was ongoing, "from the cradle to the grave" (1933, p. 95). He proposed the post-adolescent personality stages of youth; midlife transition, from about thirty-five to forty years of age; and "the second half of life," a division that has been more or less taken up in subsequent formulations by others. Jung hinted that a successful transition in midlife required modifications in "our truths and ideals" (p. 108)—that is, in the superego constituents of introjects and ideals (though he disavowed the concept of the superego [p. 122], minimized the importance of psychosexual development, and held somatic factors to be unimportant). Psychosocial development after adolescence was cast by Erikson (1959) in a framework of sequential stages, with associated conflicts related to the attainment of capacities for intimacy, generativity, and ego integrity. He proposed a "generalization of sensual modes" for the psychosexual developmental line in old age (1982, p. 64) and asserted that throughout life the epigenetically unfolding stages of life remain "linked" in unspecified ways with somatic processes as well as with psychic and social forces. He saw ego integrity as at risk with advancing age, because of the loss of such links. Parenthood as a developmental phase (Benedek, 1959) and especially the experience of pregnancy by women (Bibring et al., 1961; Kestenberg, 1976) were suggested as phases closely connected with somatic or organic factors, experience of which was seen as specifically responsible for the appearance of new psychic structure, new components of the self representation, or new developmental steps in the adult.

In recent years many more researchers have explored the application of psychoanalytic developmental principles to life after adolescence. In general, these efforts have elaborated on Jung's original descriptions of adult stages or periods of enduring emotional and psychic change and described specific characteristics or tasks associated with each phase. These phases are seen as independent of biological events, although they are sometimes initiated by the perception of them, as, for example, the "average expectable," "normal," regressive or nonregressive reactions and adaptations to menopause or to the recognition of physical decline with advancing age (Gould, 1972; Vaillant, 1977; Levinson et al., 1978; Dewald, 1981; Jacques, 1981; Colarusso & Nemiroff, 1981).

In addition to the one used by Jung, other frameworks have been applied to the adult situation. Mahler's separation-individuation theory, for example, has been employed as a conceptual tool for understanding experience throughout life (Marcus, 1973; Sternschein, 1973; Winestine, 1973; Colarusso, 1990). A framework of transitional events, periods, and mechanisms has also been outlined (Connell & Furman, 1984).

One view of adult life focuses on the distinction between adaptation and development, the supposition being that adaptation as such does not always require new psychic structure. When structural change does appear as part of the lifelong developmental process, it is seen as a response to stimuli, disruptions, or challenges at various times and from various sources, including but not limited to maturational or biological ones (for example, Glenn, 1979; Settlage et al., 1988).

Another view of adult development equates adaptation with development (Colarusso & Nemiroff, 1981) and stresses that the magnitude of psychic changes in adulthood warrants the designation "development" (Colarusso, 1992, p. 118). According to this view, modification and evolution of psychic structures continues throughout life, but in later years, instead of being tied to maturational stages in the way it is earlier, it is defined by certain dynamic adult tasks that occur roughly within the chronological periods of early, middle, and late adulthood.

Both these latter viewpoints hold that conflicts and issues from earlier in life are relived, reworked, and transformed in succeeding periods of psychic reorganization (Rangell, 1963; Abrams, 1977). Because there is less of a link with biological factors, however, these processes appear to be highly variable in adults and are dependent on the continuing influence of unconscious conflicts and on the resources available to the individual from already existing psychic structure and functions.

To summarize, there is disagreement about whether the processes of adult life should be equated with the developmental processes of childhood and adolescence. The greater removal from biological factors makes it difficult at times to distinguish manifestations of a developmental process from learning, regression, identifications, disidentifications, or behavioral changes that come about as a consequence of adaptational pressures. It is well recognized, however, that psychic reorganization continues throughout adult life, such as the reevaluation and re-prioritizing of goals and standards in midlife, described by Jung and by others since. Some see these reevaluations as markers of stages or phases of adult development; others, for whom a maturational pull defines the developmental process, view them as necessary and inevitable adaptational changes.

REFERENCES

Abelin, E. L. (1971). The role of the father in the separation-individuation process. In *Separation-Individuation,* ed. J. McDevitt & C. Settlage, pp. 229–252. New York: Int. Univ. Press.

———. (1975). Some further observations and comments on the earliest role of the father. *Int. J. Psychoanal.,* 56:293–302.

Abraham, K. (1924). A short study of the development of the libido, viewed in the light of mental disorders. In *Selected Papers on Psycho-analysis,* pp. 418–501. New York: Basic Books, 1953.

Abrams, S. (1977). The genetic point of view. *J. Amer. Psychoanal. Assn.,* 25:417–426.

Alpert, A. (1941). The latency period. *Amer. J. Orthopsychiat.,* 11:126–132.

Anders, T. (1982). Biological rhythms in development. *Psychosom. Med.,* 44:61–72.

Arlow, J. A. (1969). Unconscious fantasy and disturbances of conscious experience. *Psychoanal. Q.,* 38:1–27.

Bell, A. (1961). Some observations on the role of the scrotal sac and the testicles. *J. Amer. Psychoanal. Assn.,* 9:261–286.

Benedek, T. (1959). Parenthood as a developmental phase. *J. Amer. Psychoanal. Assn.,* 7:389–417.

Bibring, G., Dwyer, T. F., Huntington, D. S., & Valenstein, A. F. (1961). A study of the psychological processes in pregnancy and the earliest mother–child relationship. *Psychoanal. Study Child*, 16:9–72.

Blos, P. (1967). The second individuation process of adolescence. *Psychoanal. Study Child*, 22:162–186.

———. (1968). Character formation in adolescence. *Psychoanal. Study Child*, 23:245–263.

———. (1972). The function of the ego ideal. *Psychoanal. Study Child*, 27:93–97.

———. (1976). The split parental image in adolescent social relations. *Psychoanal. Study Child*, 31:7–34.

Blum, H. P. (1978). Symbolic processes and symbol formation. *Int. J. Psychoanal.*, 59:455–471.

Bornstein, B. (1951). On latency. *Psychoanal. Study Child*, 5:279–286.

Brenner, C. (1982). *The Mind in Conflict*. New York: Int. Univ. Press.

Breuer, J., & Freud, S. (1893–95). *Studies on Hysteria. SE*, 2.

Brody, S., & Axelrad, S. (1970). *Anxiety and Ego Formation in Infancy*. New York: Int. Univ. Press.

———. (1978). *Mothers, Fathers, and Children*. New York: Int. Univ. Press.

Brody, S., & Siegel, M. G. (1992). *The Evolution of Character*. Madison, Conn.: Int. Univ. Press.

Burgner, M., & Edgcumbe, R. (1972). Some problems in the conceptualization of early object relationships: Part II. *Psychoanal. Study Child*, 27:315–333.

Burgner, M., & Kennedy, H. (1980). Different types of sadomasochistic behavior in children. *Dialogue*, 4:49–58.

Burlingham, D. (1973). The preoedipal infant–father relationship. *Psychoanal. Study Child*, 28:23–47.

Buxbaum, E. (1980). Between the Oedipus complex and adolescence. In *The Course of Life*, ed. S. I. Greenspan & G. H. Pollock, vol. 2: *Latency, Adolescence and Youth*, pp. 121–136. Washington, D.C.: DHHS Publication No. (ADM) 80-786.

Call, J. D. (1964). Newborn approach behavior and early ego development. *Int. J. Psychoanal.*, 45:286–294.

———. (1980). Attachment disorders in infancy. In *Comprehensive Textbook of Psychiatry*, 3d ed., ed. H. I. Kaplan, A. M. Freedman, & B. J. Sadock, vol. 3, pp. 2586–2597. Baltimore: Williams & Wilkins.

———. (1984). From early patterns of communication to the grammar of experience and syntax in infancy. In *Frontiers of Infant Psychiatry*, ed.

J. D. Call, E. Galenson & R. L. Tyson, vol. 2, pp. 15–29. New York: Basic Books.

Clower, V. L. (1976). Theoretical implications in current views of masturbation in latency girls. *J. Amer. Psychoanal. Assn.*, 24:109–126.

Colarusso, C. A. (1990). The third individuation. *Psychoanal. Study Child*, 45:170–194.

———. (1992). *Child and Adult Development*. New York: Plenum.

Colarusso, C. A., & Nemiroff, R. A. (1981). *Adult Development*. New York: Plenum.

Connell, J. P., & Furman, W. (1984). The study of transition. In *Continuities and Discontinuities in Development*, ed. R. N. Emde & R. J. Harmon, pp. 153–173. New York: Plenum.

Dewald, P. A. (1981). Adult phases of the life cycle. In *The Course of Life*, vol. 3: *Adulthood and the Aging Process*, ed. S. I. Greenspan & G. H. Pollock, pp. 35–53. Washington, D.C.: DHHS Publication No. (ADM) 80-786.

Dowling, S. (1977). Seven infants with esophageal atresia. *Psychoanal. Study Child*, 32:215–256.

Edgcumbe, R., & Burgner, M. (1975). The phallic narcissistic phase. *Psychoanal. Study Child*, 30:161–180.

Emde, R. N. (1981). Changing models of infancy and the nature of early development. *J. Amer. Psychoanal. Assn.*, 29:179–219.

———. (1983). The prerepresentational self and its affective core. *Psychoanal. Study Child*, 38:165–192.

———. (1988). Development terminable and interminable, I. *Int. J. Psychoanal.*, 69:283–296.

Emde, R. N., Gaensbauer, T., & Harmon, R. J. (1976). Emotional expression in infancy. Psychological Issues, monograph 37. New York: Int. Univ. Press.

Erikson, E. H. (1956). The concept of ego identity. *J. Amer. Psychoanal. Assn.*, 4:56–121.

———. (1959). *Identity and the Life Cycle*. Psychological Issues, monograph 1. New York: Int. Univ. Press.

———. (1982). *The Life Cycle Completed*. New York: Norton.

Ferenczi, S. (1930). Notes and fragments, II. In *Final Contributions to the Problems and Methods of Psycho-Analysis*, pp. 219–231. New York: Basic Books, 1952.

Fraiberg, S. (1969). Object constancy and mental representation. *Psychoanal. Study Child*, 24:9–47.

———. (1972). Some characteristics of genital arousal and discharge in latency girls. *Psychoanal. Study Child*, 27:439–475.

Freud, A. (1936). *The Ego and the Mechanisms of*

Defense. In *Writings of Anna Freud,* 2:3–179. Rev. ed. New York: Int. Univ. Press, 1966.

———. (1952). The mutual influences in the development of ego and id. In *Writings of Anna Freud,* 4:230–244. New York: Int. Univ. Press, 1968.

———. (1958). Adolescence. *Psychoanal. Study Child,* 13:255–278.

———. (1963). The concept of developmental lines. *Psychoanal. Study Child,* 18:245–265.

———. (1965). *Normality and Pathology in Childhood.* In *Writings of Anna Freud,* vol. 6:3–235. New York: Int. Univ. Press.

———. (1968). Panel discussion with J. Arlow (mod.), J. Lampl-de Groot, and D. Beres. *Int. J. Psychoanal.,* 49:506–512.

Freud, S. (1893). On the psychical mechanism of hysterical phenomena. *SE,* 3:25–39.

———. (1905). *Three Essays on the Theory of Sexuality. SE,* 7:125–243.

———. (1908). Character and anal erotism. *SE,* 9:169–175.

———. (1911). Formulations on the two principles of mental functioning. *SE,* 12:213–226.

———. (1920). *Beyond the Pleasure Principle. SE,* 18:7–64.

———. (1921). *Group Psychology and the Analysis of the Ego. SE,* 18:69–143.

———. (1923a). *The Ego and the Id. SE,* 19:3–66.

———. (1923b). The infantile genital organization. *SE,* 19:141–145.

———. (1924a). The dissolution of the oedipus complex. *SE,* 19:172–179.

———. (1924b). The loss of reality in neurosis and psychosis. *SE,* 19:183–187.

———. (1926). *Inhibitions, Symptoms and Anxiety. SE,* 20:77–175.

———. (1933). *New Introductory Lectures on Psycho-Analysis. SE,* 22:3–184.

Furer, M. (1967). Some developmental aspects of the superego. *Int. J. Psychoanal.,* 48:277–280.

Gaensbauer, T. J. (1982). The differentiation of discrete affects. *Psychoanal. Study Child,* 37:29–66.

Glenn, J. (1979). The developmental point of view in adult analysis. *J. Philadelphia Assn. Psychoanal.,* 6:21–38.

Gould, R. L. (1972). The phases of adult life. *Amer. J. Psychiat.,* 129:521–531.

Greenacre, P. (1941). The predisposition to anxiety. In *Trauma, Growth and Personality,* pp. 27–82. New York: Norton, 1952.

———. (1952). Pregenital patterning. *Int. J. Psychoanal.,* 33:410–415.

———. (1953). Penis awe and its relation to penis envy. In *Emotional Growth,* vol. 1, pp. 31–49. New York: Int. Univ. Press, 1971.

———. (1960). Considerations regarding the parent–infant relationship. In *Emotional Growth,* vol. 1, pp. 199–224. New York: Int. Univ. Press, 1971.

Grossman, W. I., & Stewart, W. (1976). Penis envy. *J. Amer. Psychoanal. Assn.,* 24(suppl.):193–212.

Hartmann, H. (1939). *Ego Psychology and the Problem of Adaptation.* New York: Int. Univ. Press, 1958.

———. (1950). Comments on the psychoanalytic theory of the ego. *Psychoanal. Study Child,* 5:74–96.

———. (1952). The mutual influences in the development of ego and id. In *Essays on Ego Psychology,* pp. 155–182. New York: Int. Univ. Press, 1964.

———. (1953). Contribution to the metapsychology of schizophrenia. In *Essays on Ego Psychology,* pp. 182–206. New York: Int. Univ. Press, 1964.

———. (1955). Notes on the theory of sublimation. In *Essays on Ego Psychology,* pp. 215–240. New York: Int. Univ. Press, 1964.

———. (1956). Notes on the reality principle. In *Essays on Ego Psychology,* pp. 241–267. New York: Int. Univ. Press, 1964.

Hartmann, H., Kris, E., & Loewenstein, R. (1946). Comments on the formation of psychic structure. *Psychoanal. Study Child,* 17:42–81.

Hendrick, I. (1942). Instinct and the ego during infancy. *Psychoanal. Q.,* 11:33–58.

Herzog, J. M. (1980). Sleep disturbance and father hunger in 18 to 28 month old boys. *Psychoanal. Study Child,* 35:219–233.

———. (1982). On father hunger. In *Father and Child,* ed. S. W. Cath, A. R. Gurwitt, & J. M. Ross, pp. 163–174. Boston: Little, Brown.

Hoffer, W. (1949). Mouth, hand and ego integration. *Psychoanal. Study Child,* 3/4:49–56.

———. (1950). The development of the body ego. *Psychoanal. Study Child,* 5:18–24.

Jacobson, E. (1954). The self and the object world. *Psychoanal. Study Child,* 9:75–127.

———. (1961). Adolescent moods and the remodeling of psychic structures in adolescence. *Psychoanal. Study Child,* 16:164–183.

———. (1964). *The Self and the Object World.* New York: Int. Univ. Press.

Jacques, E. (1981). The midlife crisis. In *The Course of Life,* vol. 3: *Adulthood and the Aging Process,* ed. S. I. Greenspan & G. H. Pollock, pp. 1–23. Washington, D.C.: DHHS Publication No. (ADM) 80-786.

James, M. (1960). Premature ego development. *Int. J. Psychoanal.,* 41:288–294.

Joffe, W. G., & Sandler, J. (1965). Notes on pain, depression and individuation. *Psychoanal. Study Child*, 20:394–424.

Jung, C. G. (1933). *Modern Man in Search of a Soul*. New York: Harcourt, Brace.

Kagan, J. (1981). *The Second Year—The Emergence of Self-Awareness*. Cambridge, Mass.: Harvard Univ. Press.

Katan, A. (1951). The role of "displacement" in agoraphobia. *Int. J. Psychoanal.*, 32:41–50.

———. (1961). Some thoughts about the role of verbalization in childhood. *Psychoanal. Study Child*, 16:184–188.

———. (1972). The infant's first reaction to strangers. *Int. J. Psychoanal.*, 53:501–503.

Kernberg, O. (1974a). Barriers to falling and remaining in love. *J. Amer. Psychoanal. Assn.*, 22:486–511.

———. (1974b). Mature love. *J. Amer. Psychoanal. Assn.*, 22:743–768.

Kestenberg, J. S. (1976). Regression and reintegration in pregnancy. *J. Amer. Psychoanal. Assn.*, 14:213–250.

Kleeman, J. A. (1976). Freud's views on early female sexuality in the light of direct child observation. *J. Amer. Psychoanal. Assn.*, 24(suppl.):3–27.

Klein, G. S. (1976). *Psychoanalytic Theory*. New York: Int. Univ. Press.

Kramer S., & Akhtar, S. (1988). The developmental context of internalized preoedipal object relations. *Psychoanal. Q.*, 57:547–576.

Kris, E. (1939). On inspiration. *Int. J. Psychoanal.*, 20:377–389.

Laufer, M. (1968). The body image, the function of masturbation, and adolescence. *Psychoanal. Study Child*, 23:114–136.

———. (1976). The past and the adolescent's sexual development. *Psychoanal. Study Child*, 36:181–192.

Levinson, D. J., Darrow, C. N., Klein, E. B., Levinson, M. H., & McKee, B., eds. (1978). *The Seasons of a Man's Life*. New York: Knopf.

Lewis, M., & Brooks-Gunn, J. (1979). *Social Cognition and the Acquisition of Self*. New York: Plenum.

Loewald, H. (1960). On the therapeutic action of psychoanalysis. *Int. J. Psychoanal.*, 41:16–33.

———. (1978). Instinct theory, object relations, and psychic structure formation. In *Papers on Psychoanalysis*, pp. 207–218. New Haven: Yale Univ. Press, 1980.

Lustman, S. L. (1966). Impulse control, structure, and the synthetic function. In *Psychoanalysis—A General Psychology*, ed. R. M. Loewenstein, L. M. Newman, M. Schur, & A. J. Solnit, pp. 190–221. New York: Int. Univ. Press.

Mahler, M. S. (1965). On the significance of the normal separation-individuation phase. In *Drives, Affects, Behavior*, vol. 2, ed. M. Schur, pp. 161–169. New York: Int. Univ. Press.

———. (1966). Notes on the development of basic moods. In *Selected Papers of Margaret Mahler*, pp. 59–75. New York: Aronson, 1979.

———. (1968). *On Human Symbiosis and the Vicissitudes of Individuation*, vol. 1: *Infantile Psychosis*. New York: Int. Univ. Press.

———. (1971). A study of the separation-individuation process and its possible application to borderline phenomena in the psychoanalytic situation. *Psychoanal. Study Child*, 26:403–424.

———. (1972a). On the first three subphases of the separation-individuation process. *Int. J. Psychoanal.*, 53:333–338.

———. (1972b). Rapprochement subphase of the separation-individuation process. *Psychoanal. Q.*, 41:487–506.

———. (1975). On the current status of the infantile neurosis. *J. Amer. Psychoanal. Assn.*, 23:327–333.

———. (1981). Aggression in the service of separation-individuation. *Psychoanal. Q.*, 50:625–638.

Mahler, M. S., & Gosliner, B. J. (1955). On symbiotic child psychosis. *Psychoanal. Study Child*, 10:195–212.

Mahler, M. S., & McDevitt, J. B. (1982). Thoughts on the emergence of the sense of self, with particular emphasis on the body self. *J. Amer. Psychoanal. Assn.*, 30:827–848.

Mahler, M. S., Pine, F., & Bergman, A. (1975). *The Psychological Birth of the Human Infant*. New York: Basic Books.

Marcus, I. M., reporter (1973). The experience of separation-individuation in infancy and its reverberations through the course of life: 2. Adolescence and maturity. *J. Amer. Psychoanal. Assn.*, 21:155–167.

McDevitt, J. B. (1975). Separation individuation and object constancy. *J. Amer. Psychoanal. Assn.*, 23:713–743.

Nagera, H. (1966). *Early Childhood Disturbances, the Infantile Neurosis, and the Adulthood Disturbances*. New York: Int. Univ. Press.

Neubauer, P. B. (1983). Anna Freud's legacy. *Psychoanal. Q.*, 52:507–513.

Noy, P. (1978). Insight and creativity. *J. Amer. Psychoanal. Assn.*, 26:717–748.

Pedersen, F. A., & Robson, K. S. (1969). Father participation in infancy. *Amer. J. Orthopsychiat.*, 39:466–472.

Piaget, J., & Inhelder, B. (1969). *The Psychology of the Child*. New York: Basic Books.

Pine, F. (1985). *Developmental Theory and Clinical Process.* New Haven: Yale Univ. Press.

Provence, S., & Lipton, R. C. (1962). *Infants in Institutions.* New York: Int. Univ. Press.

Rangell, L. (1963). Structural problems in intrapsychic conflict. *Psychoanal. Study Child,* 18:103–138.

Rapaport, D., & Gill, M. M. (1959). The points of view and assumptions of metapsychology. In *Collected Papers of David Rapaport,* ed. M. M. Gill, pp. 795–811. New York: Basic Books, 1967.

Ritvo, S. (1981). Anxiety, symptom formation and ego autonomy. *Psychoanal. Study Child,* 36:339–364.

Roiphe, H. (1968). On an early genital phase. *Psychoanal. Study Child,* 23:348–365.

Roiphe, H., & Galenson, E. (1981). *Infantile Origins of Sexual Identity.* New York: Int. Univ. Press.

Sander, L. W. (1962). Issues in early mother–child interaction. *J. Amer. Acad. Child Psychiat.,* 1:141–166.

———. (1964). Adaptive relationships in early mother–child interaction. *J. Amer. Acad. Child Psychiat.,* 3:231–264.

———. (1969). Regulation and organization in the early infant-caretaker system. In *Brain and Early Behavior,* ed. R. Robinson, pp. 311–332. London: Academic Press.

———. (1983). Polarity, paradox, and the organizing process in development. In *Frontiers of Infant Psychiatry,* ed. J. D. Call, E. Galenson, & R. L. Tyson, pp. 333–346. New York: Basic Books.

Sander, L. W., Stechler, G., Burns, P., & Julia, H. (1970). Early mother–infant interaction and 24-hour patterns of activity and sleep. *J. Amer. Acad. Child Psychiat.,* 9:103–123.

Sandler, J. (1960). The background of safety. *Int. J. Psychoanal.,* 41:352–356.

Sarnoff, C. (1976). *Latency.* New York: Aronson.

Settlage, C. F. (1980). The psychoanalytic theory and understanding of psychic development during the second and third years of life. In *The Course of Life,* vol. 1: *Infancy and Early Childhood,* ed. S. I. Greenspan & G. H. Pollock, pp. 523–539. Washington, D.C.: DHHS Publication No. (ADM) 80-786.

Settlage, C. F., Curtis, Z., Lozoff, M., Silberschatz, G., & Simburg, E. (1988). Conceptualizing adult development. *J. Amer. Psychoanal. Assn.,* 36:347–370.

Shapiro, T., & Perry, R. (1976). Latency revisited. *Psychoanal. Study Child,* 31:79–105.

Spitz, R. A. (1945). Hospitalism. *Psychoanal. Study Child,* 1:53–72.

———. (1946a). Anaclitic depression. *Psychoanal. Study Child,* 2:313–342.

———. (1946b). Hospitalism: a follow-up report. *Psychoanal. Study Child,* 2:113–117.

———. (1957). *No and Yes.* New York: Int. Univ. Press.

———. (1959). *A Genetic Field Theory of Ego Formation.* New York: Int. Univ. Press.

———. (1965). The evolution of dialogue. In *Drives, Affects, Behavior,* vol. 2, ed. M. Schur, pp. 170–190. New York: Int. Univ. Press.

Spitz, R. A., & Wolf, K. M. (1946). The smiling response. *Genetic Psychol. Mono.,* 34:57–125.

Sroufe, L. A. (1977). Wariness of strangers and the study of infant development. *Child Develpm.,* 48:731–746.

Stern, D. N. (1985). *The Interpersonal World of the Infant.* New York: Basic Books.

Sternschein, I., reporter (1973). The experience of separation-individuation in infancy and its reverberations through the course of life: 3. Maturity, senescence, and sociological implications. *J. Amer. Psychoanal. Assn.,* 21:633–645.

Stoller, R. J. (1968a). The sense of femaleness. *Psychoanal. Q.,* 37:42–55.

———. (1968b). *Sex and Gender.* New York: Science House.

———. (1976). Primary femininity. *J. Amer. Psychoanal. Assn.,* 24(suppl.):59–78.

Tolpin, M. (1971). On the beginnings of a cohesive self. *Psychoanal. Study Child,* 26:316–352.

Tyson, P. (1982). A developmental line of gender identity, gender role and choice of love object. *J. Amer. Psychoanal. Assn.,* 30:59–84.

———. (1986). Female psychological development. *Annu. Psychoanal.,* 14:357–373.

———. (1988). Psychic structure formation. *J. Amer. Psychoanal. Assn.,* 36(suppl.):73–98.

———. (1989). Infantile sexuality, gender identity, and obstacles to oedipal progression. *J. Amer. Psychoanal. Assn.,* 37:1051–1069.

Tyson, P., & Tyson, R. L. (1984). Narcissism and superego development. *J. Amer. Psychoanal. Assn.,* 32:75–98.

———. (1990). *Psychoanalytic Theories of Development.* New Haven: Yale Univ. Press.

Tyson, R. L. (1986). The roots of psychopathology and our theories of development. *J. Amer. Acad. Child Psychiat.,* 25:12–22.

———. (1991). Psychological conflict in childhood. In *Conflict and Compromise,* ed. S. Dowling, pp. 31–48. Madison, Conn.: Int. Univ. Press.

Vaillant, G. E. (1977). *Adaptation to Life.* Boston: Little, Brown.

Vigotsky, L. S. (1934). *Thought and Language.* Cambridge, Mass.: MIT Press, 1962.

Waelder, R. (1936). The principle of multiple function. *Psychoanal. Q.,* 5:45–62.

Weil, A. P. (1970). The basic core. *Psychoanal. Study Child,* 25:442–460.

———. (1978). Maturational variations and genetic-dynamic issues. *J. Amer. Psychoanal. Assn.,* 26: 461–491.

Williams, M. (1972). Problems of technique during latency. *Psychoanal. Study Child,* 27:598–617.

Winestine, M. E., reporter (1973). The experience of separation-individuation in infancy and its reverberations through the course of life: 1. Infancy and childhood. *J. Amer. Psychoanal. Assn.,* 21:135–154.

Winnicott, D. W. (1953). Transitional objects and transitional phenomena. *Int. J. Psychoanal.,* 34: 89–97.

Wolff, P. H. (1959). Observations on newborn infants. *Psychosom. Med.,* 21:110–118.

Yasmajian, R. V. (1966). The testes and body image formation in transvestitism. *J. Amer. Psychoanal. Assn.,* 14:304–312.

———. (1967). The influence of testicular sensory stimuli on the dream. *J. Amer. Psychoanal. Assn.,* 15:83–98.

Yogman, M. W. (1982). Observations on the father–infant relationship. In *Father and Child,* ed. S. H. Cath, Gurwitt, A., & J. M. Ross, pp. 101–122. Boston: Little, Brown.

Zetzel, E. R. (1964). The theory of therapy in relation to a developmental model of the psychic apparatus. *Bull. Philadelphia Assn. Psychoanal.,* 14:104–107.

31

SELF

Self is a necessary word, used every day, a noun related to the pronouns, employed most often as an adjective and as a prefix. It cannot be avoided in ordinary discourse, not even by psychoanalysts or philosophers. And in ordinary discourse it is readily understood. But there is no consensus among English-speaking psychoanalysts about whether it should be used as a technical, a theoretical, or an abstract word—or, if it is so used, how it can be defined in other than arbitrary ways.

Formal, "objective" concepts of self are problematic in the general sense because of the reflexive nature of the word: it is almost impossible to define as a noun except in terms of it*self*—tautologically. It has posed special problems for psychoanalysis and continues to do so. In this chapter I will survey these problems, but I cannot hope to solve them to general satisfaction.

Freud originally used several different words which, translated, mean approximately what we call the self in its everyday sense: an individual mind capable of conceiving its own operations either introspectively or inferentially. He also used various abstract terms for the underlying psychic structures and functions that might *account* for the self in experience and in action. To subsume the varying words, he eventually settled on *das Ich,* which in German can stand both for the first person pronoun and as an abstraction on higher levels. *Das Ich* is commonly and comfortably used in both senses; the German word *selbst,* by contrast, is ungainly and is not used very often in everyday discourse. In many other languages, single words can convey a range of meanings from the phenomenally obvious to the most abstract levels. The French for *das Ich* is *le moi;* in Spanish it is *el yo.* But in translation into English, it became not "the I" or "the me" but the *ego.*

The decision to translate the word as *ego* was a momentous one. *Ego* is not a common word in ordinary English. Except among analysts, it refers to vanity or narcissistic self-aggrandizement. The first person pronouns and, to a lesser extent, *self* are usual, ordinary words; but in English it seems strange to speak of "the I" or "the me." Hence, there is a tendency among English-speaking analysts to separate the terms: to limit the ego to abstract systemic or structural meanings and to use *self* and *self representation* in place of the phenomenal *Ich.* Going further, some analysts have extended the ordinary use of *self* to use of it also as a highly abstract noun, referring to something distinguishable from the abstract ego. Metapsychology, at least as put forward in English by these latter-day analysts, has acquired an embarrassment of riches: two abstract systemic concepts, a reasonably well-defined abstract ego, and an equally abstract—or even "superordinately" abstract—but poorly defined self.

The various points of view may be summarized thus:

A group of psychoanalysts, otherwise similar in

thought and practice, believe it is heuristically and logically valuable to separate *self* from *ego*. Clinical phenomena, they say, should be clearly distinguished from abstract theories; the ego is an abstraction referring to a set of psychic functions that cohere and (at least during periods of conflict with other systems) form a cohesive mental structure; the word *ego* implies systemic meanings. This group is not of one mind about the meaning of *self,* however. Although they all acknowledge its everyday experiential meanings, there is no consensus about whether it should have a place in psychoanalytic theory or, if used theoretically, how it should be defined.

A minority disagrees, claiming that *ego* should be used as Freud used *das Ich*. They believe that *das Ich* should have been translated as "the I" (a translocation of meaning somewhat easier to imagine than "the me"). *Ego* (or "the I") would then refer at one pole of meaning to an abstraction on a clinical level corresponding to *self* in its everyday sense and at the other pole of meaning to a coherent system of psychic functions. It would be an advantage, not a disadvantage, they say, to have a unitary term, *das Ich*. The reason why the functions defining the abstract ego cohere is the very fact that they have to do with the operations that people intuitively think of as referring to *self*. However, they recognize that longstanding customs do not change easily; analysts, like other people, will continue to use the words to which they are accustomed, and English-speaking analysts will use the separate words, *ego* and *self*. The aim of this minority group of analysts is merely to call attention to the heuristic advantage of regarding the phenomenal I as absolutely related to the abstract I.

More dissident psychoanalysts believe that *self* should not only be distinguished from *ego* but that on the highest levels of abstraction it can be *delineated* as separate from ego: it might be a fourth macrostructure of the mind, joining and relating to the id, the ego, and the superego. Alternatively, an abstract self might be on a still higher level, superordinate to ego, superego, and id.

I will not pursue semiotic and semantic issues further here, but will instead turn to the history of the uses of *ego* and *self* in psychoanalysis. I begin with Freud's explicit and implicit conceptions, then take up amendments proposed by Hartmann and others in the elaboration of ego psychology. From there, I will consider the positions outlined above and will then examine the arguments favoring and opposing each.

FREUD'S VIEWS

How perplexing Freud would have found it to learn that he had "neglected" the self (Levin, 1969) or that

he had "never developed an elaborate theory of the self" (Mitterauer & Pritz, 1978)! On the contrary, Freud spent his entire working life spawning more and more elegant theories about those meanings that in English subsume *self* or the first person pronouns. For most of the nineteenth century, psychology was psychology of the conscious. The self was what one privately thought it to be—on the conscious level. There were thinkers before Freud, of course, who thought of unconscious aspects of the mind (Ellenberger, 1970). Nietzsche, to take a late example, conceived a truly dynamic unconscious, although he had no way to validate his philosophical speculations. Freud, by contrast, was able to find validations. He patiently explored conflicts within the mind among forces and counterforces. On the one side was the self that could be experienced (at least potentially): what he variously called "will," "volition," "consciousness," and "das Ich" (early on he used quotation marks in an effort to avoid philosophical conundrums connected with German philosophical usage of *das Ich*). On the other side of such conflicts were the psychological influences variously referred to as "counterwill," "antithetical ideas," or "the unconscious." Thus, he constructed the first metapsychology (Brenner, 1980). His monumental, though premature, effort to construct a neuropsychology, the "Project for a scientific psychology" (1895), surely postulated a complex system to explain the self or ego. Why else would he call that system *das Ich?*

Although analysts have become accustomed to think of the system id–ego–superego as *the* structural theory, it was only Freud's last structural theory. He (and Anna Freud) saw the topographical system abstractly as well as phenomenologically and continued to use the earlier structural system side by side with the later system, bringing out one or the other depending upon the clinical context. It is unnecessary to trace here the development of Freud's topographical structural theory or the later disagreements with Freud about its continued value (see Arlow & Brenner, 1964; Gill, 1963). The point is that the Cs.–Pcs. system was an abstraction referring to the known self, while the Ucs., the dynamic unconscious—at least the part that was once conscious—referred to the unknown (but potentially partially knowable) self.

It is also unnecessary here to trace the development of the ego concept in Freud's work (see A. Freud, 1936, 1952; Hartmann, 1950, 1956; Laplanche & Pontalis, 1973). After developing the Cs.–Pcs. and Ucs. systems, Freud used *das Ich* casually, in an everyday sense. But when he turned away from the topographical systems (without, as mentioned above, abandoning them), he proposed elaborate abstract conceptions of the ego as a coherent organization (1923, 1926a). He continued thereafter to use ego-as-self and ego-as-system, relying on the context to make clear the level of abstraction. Some authors have suggested that Freud was not *aware* of the distinction.

What a poor opinion of Freud! He knew what he was doing. Referring to the ego, he said:

> We call this organization their '*Ich*'. . . . Now there is nothing new in this. Each one of us makes this assumption without being a philosopher, and some people even in spite of being philosophers. . . . You will probably protest at our having chosen simple pronouns . . . instead of giving them orotund Greek names. In psycho-analysis, however, we like to keep in contact with the popular mode of thinking and prefer to make its concepts scientifically serviceable rather than to reject them. [1926b, p. 195]

For all these firm words, Freud had agreed in 1919, for whatever reasons, to Strachey's translation of *das Ich* by the Latin "ego." Strachey (1961) admitted to difficulty with this translation, and sometimes he translated *das Ich* directly as "self." Presumably, Freud also agreed to the Latin "id" as the translation of *das Es*. "The It" would have been a much better choice. Recently, sharp criticisms have been made of these renderings, claiming that they do not do justice to Freud's full meanings of the terms and, in particular, disguise their affective meanings (Spruiell, 1981; Ornston, 1982; Bettelheim, 1983).

SEPARATE DEFINITIONS FOR SELF AND EGO

Hartmann in 1939, and later in collaboration with Kris and Loewenstein (1964), set out to systematize metapsychology as a general psychology. As one aspect of a life's work that was monumental in reach, Hartmann was interested in certain economic assumptions having to do with the more or less neutralized energic processes of the ego as an organization and those other, less neutralized energies having to do with narcissism. Following Loewenstein (1940), he pointed out that it was important to differentiate, as Freud had not, the concepts of ego, self, and person.

The matter of narcissism raises puzzles. Observably, a person can take himself as his own love object. This is normal during infancy and in altered forms is normal in later life. But some people continue to love themselves in primarily infantile ways, and all people do so some of the time. If this is true, however, an economic question is posed: how to distinguish those psychic energies that "power" the functions of the ego and that, by their nature, can

only be experienced indirectly, if at all, from those derivatives of libidinal investments of the self that *can* be experienced and thus clinically identified as narcissism. As Hartmann (1950) put it:

> [I]n using the term narcissism, two different sets of opposites often seem to be fused into one. The one refers to the self (one's own person) in contradistinction to the object, the second to the ego (as a psychic structure) in contradistinction to other substructures of personality. However, the opposite of object cathexis is not ego cathexis, but cathexis of one's own person, that is, self-cathexis; in speaking of self-cathexis we do not imply whether this cathexis is situated in the id, in the ego, or in the superego. This formulation takes into account that we actually do find "narcissism" in all three psychic systems; but in all these cases there is opposition to (and reciprocity with) object cathexis. It therefore will be clarifying if we define narcissism as the libidinal cathexis not of the ego but of the self. (It might also be useful to apply the term self-representation as opposed to object representation.) [Pp. 84–85]

Here, Hartmann identified *self* as "one's own person" and distinguished this self from its mental representations, just as external objects are distinguished from their representations. But in 1953, Hartmann spoke of "the cathexis of the self-image (a complex of representations)" (p. 185). The self would then be "a complex of representations," capable of being cathected with energy and thus, presumably, capable of operating as an intrapsychic agent. In 1955 he wrote: "If we accept it [this definition of narcissism as the cathexis of self], we may then speak of self-representation (in the case of libidinal cathexis: narcissism) in opposition to object representation" (p. 21).

He made similar statements again in 1956. Narcissism cannot be simply a matter of the ego, Hartmann averred, if the ego is viewed abstractly as a set of functions. It is a matter of the whole body and mind of the person—body, ego, id, and superego alike.

SOME CONSEQUENCES OF HARTMANN'S CONCEPTS

The influence of Hartmann and his colleagues on the development of ego psychology, especially in the United States, can hardly be overestimated. His work, together with Anna Freud's, allowed psychoanalysis to come closer to becoming a general psychology—or to becoming an important part of one. Without their efforts, it is hard to see what might have kept psychoanalysis from fragmenting into various irreconcilable forms of id psychology and object relations psychology. It is hard to see how mainstream psychoanalysis could have achieved sufficient coherence to allow it to take its place among related disciplines and gradually evolve and interact with them.

Nevertheless, new formulations may carry part-formulations that create unforeseen consequences. The separation of "self" from "ego" was such a part-formulation. In fact, Hartmann's formulations have given rise to fateful consequences when used by most subsequent writers concerned with self, not only those who adhere to the propositions of ego psychology developed after the 1940s but also others who, to varying degrees, have modified them. They influenced Edith Jacobson's (1964) work, which focused on the normal and pathological developmental distinctions between self and object representations and tended to treat psychic representations as small complex systems, quasi-autonomous agents of the mind (Schafer, 1968). Jacobson's ideas have influenced the object relations theories that have grown up, among them Kernberg's (1976). They have had a role in the overextensions by some writers of theories of separation-individuation (Mahler et al., 1975; Spruiell, 1979). They have also influenced the "self psychology" of Kohut (1977) and his followers, who rejected Hartmann's drive psychology on the one hand but temporarily elaborated his notions of narcissism and self on the other.

The temptation to go even further is manifest in proposals that the self should be considered as a fourth metapsychological macrostructure (Levin, 1969; Mitterauer & Pritz, 1978). The more extreme of these positions postulates a self that is a superordinate psychic organization, overarching the familiar ego, id, and superego (Gedo, 1979; Kernberg, 1982; Klein, 1976; Kohut, 1977, 1978).

A more interesting version, in my opinion, of the attempt to distinguish self from ego was advanced by Spiegel (1959), who carefully analyzed some of the semantic problems posed by the words *self, self representation,* and *self-awareness.* As Beres stressed later (1981), Spiegel began with the assumption that "self" is an abstraction to be distinguished from self-awareness. According to Spiegel, "Self-feeling is an ultimate, not further describable clinical fact, but the self is not a *clinical* fact in the same sense. . . . It is a conceptualization or a construct which we invoke to clarify clinical phenomena" (p. 87). It has value in both the study of the differentiation or lack thereof between the self and its objects and the study of alterations of self-awareness.

Along the same lines, developmental studies, such as those of Mahler and colleagues (Mahler et al., 1975; Mahler & McDevitt, 1982), have provided a framework for understanding more about the emergence of the self and its differentiation from objects. The concept of separation-individuation assumes that features of psychic functioning ordinarily related to the self constitute the framework and dimensions of self-fantasies. Spiegel (1959) emphasized the spatial and perceptual character of self language and its basis in fantasies about the body. Thus "self" is a "reference framework from which one has perspective" (Grossman, 1982, p. 928).

Grossman elaborated Spiegel's sophisticated line of thought. "Self" is fantasy, like a theory, a collection of conscious and unconscious fantasies. It is constructed like other fantasies but has a special importance in regulating behavior. Obviously, the stability of such fantasies, in interaction with fantasies of objects and their interdigitation with reliable representations of the external world, are of prime importance in adaptation. It is important to reiterate that *this* concept of self—that of Beres, Spiegel, and Grossman—is a clinical abstraction, like Freud's experienceable *das Ich;* it does not amount merely to self-awareness.

In summary, there is at least agreement among these later Freudian analysts that "self" refers to some intrapsychic pattern or structure, one that presumably becomes more unified and stable if the winds of development are favorable. These analysts assume that the various conscious and unconscious representations (including misrepresentations) of the self that are involved in sundry interactions with object representations are related. It is this relatedness and the putative synthesis that is supposed to occur—this psychical pattern in a slow rate of change—that is thought to constitute the identity of the person. For them, then, "self" becomes an abstraction for experiential and potentially experiential phenomena. Unfortunately, they do not make clear how this "pattern in a slow rate of change" is associated with their concepts of *ego* as system.

CRITICISMS OF HARTMANN'S CONCEPTS

The "clarifying distinction" leading to separate definitions of ego and self confused some analysts. While most mainstream analytic critics agree that, to be adequate, an economic drive theory must distinguish between erotic and aggressive cathexes of the ego-as-self and those presumably more neutralized energies powering the ego-as-system, there are three distinct sets of objections to Hartmann's reformulations.

First, there is no particular reason to assume that what we think of as psychic energies—for example, in the experience of some kind of self-love—and energies that cannot be experienced but have to be inferred abstractly—for example, those involved in internal conflicts—are of the same sort. "Psychic energy" is a metaphor, just as "physical energy" is.

Second, there are objections to the equation of narcissism with the libidinal cathexis of the self (Spruiell, 1975).

Third, there are objections to each of Hartmann's definitions of the word *self* (Laplanche & Pontalis, 1973; Spruiell, 1981).

These theoretical issues can only be summarized briefly here. At the present time, the specifics of a psychological economic theory can be postulated only with the aid of distant metaphors. Nor are models of hydrodynamic or electrical systems the only possible metaphors for mental quantities and the part they play in psychic dynamics. The demands of what is still hypothetical in psychic economics should not be allowed to become the basis of the whole of a theory.

Narcissism is still a bridge concept between what can be experienced and observed clinically and what can be thought of abstractly. Unfortunately, it has never been adequately integrated with the later theoretical concepts, of which "On narcissism" (Freud, 1914) was the harbinger. Freud wrote that paper before presenting his structural theory of id–ego–superego or his later dual instinctual drive theory. In fact, narcissism was originally contrasted with egoism, and this distinction reappeared even before 1920.[1]

Narcissism was indeed only introduced. The concept was applied to a normal developmental phase, a perversion, a type of object choice, the ego ideal, regulations of self-esteem, solely to omnipotence, or solely, as in Hartmann's formulations, to self-love. It would be more useful, and certainly less confusing, to think of all these as constituting related parts (Spruiell, 1975). But Hartmann's economic treatment of narcissism only in terms of self-love was a

1. Before the introduction of the concept of narcissism, Freud postulated a duality of psychic energies, libido (the sexual, species-preservative instincts) and ego instincts (the self-preservative instincts), which were manifested, Freud thought, by egoism. With the introduction of theories of narcissism, the ego also was presumed to be cathected by libido. For a period, the self-preservative instincts and egoism rarely appeared in the literature; it was not until the 1920s that Freud's last proposal of a duality of instincts appeared in the form of Eros and the death instinct. Nevertheless, Freud continued to refer to the older terms occasionally.

concretization, or at least a narrowing of the concept. He treated it as if it were self-evident and precise, easily transferable to the structural point of view. Yet, as an umbrella concept, it cannot account sufficiently for the myriad clinical phenomena dubbed "narcissistic," as Joffe and Sandler (1967) have documented clinically.

And what did Hartmann mean by the "self" when he spoke of it as being cathected by libido? As we have seen, he variously meant self representation, a collection of self representations, and a person as a whole. But if "self" means a person as a whole, then "self" is unnecessary except as an indicative pronoun; if "psychic apparatus," then it is simply a word for some individual mind in its totality. It is true that Freud occasionally (1915, p. 134; 1921, p. 130) used *Gesamt-Ich* to refer to "the ego as a whole," as distinct from the ego as one constituent of the system id–ego–superego. However, as Loewald (1973) remarks: "If self is something like Freud's *Gesamt-Ich* . . . , then, far from being a content or a structure within the mind, self would be the mind as cathected in its totality" (p. 450). But a totality cathecting a totality is problematic.

Did not Freud himself convince us of how powerful *im*personal aspects of mind are? Self-as-one's-whole-person (according to an outside observer) is an interpersonal, not an intrapsychic term.

Nor can a totality logically be equated with a *part* of the totality, a content, a psychic representation, or a collection of representations. The "representational world" as it is ordinarily conceived is no substitute for the structural, or systemic, point of view. The concept of mental representation varies, depending upon the metapsychological position taken (Friedman, 1980; J. Jacobson, 1983). A cogent paper by Boesky (1983) summarizes these variations and the unfortunate clinical consequences of thinking of representations as small systems of the mind. Such "systems" typically replace drive concepts. Self representations can no more *be* the self than objects can be the same as their representations. The postulated "representational world," which might better be called part of the internal world, is analogous to an intrapsychic map, as Hartmann pointed out in 1939 (p. 58). But the map is hardly the terrain.

Even the representation of wholeness is questionable. Although a person regularly perceives himself as an agent, he rarely experiences himself as a "whole." In states of altered consciousness, during orgasm or some forms of meditation, feelings of wholeness may be experienced—but, paradoxically, those are the very times when the delimitations and details of the self become blurred. It is a misunderstanding of the concept of psychic representation to equate self with its varying representations (Loewald, 1973).

Those who define the self as a the whole person are left with an interpersonal term with neither intrapsychic distinction nor theoretical place (Schafer, 1973). The question becomes: whole person according to whom? We cannot say, "according to the analysand," because one of the preoccupations of any analysis is to address the analysand's self-deceptions. We cannot say "according to the analyst," because the analyst has *immediate* knowledge only of his or her own self, however valuable that knowledge may be for empathic understanding.

Why then speak of "self" at all? Because we cannot help ourselves. Persons must identify themselves to each other and indicate who is being referred to and who is doing what and what we think we know about ourselves or other selves. But usually when an analyst is speaking to an analysand about the analysand's self, he or she means two things: first, the analyst is addressing the other's self-awareness, and second, *implying* that there is more to this "self" than the patient knows. At least in the analyst's own mind, the intention is to relate these experiences to a more complex set of guiding fantasies along with their nonexperiential operations, such as monitoring, stabilizing, resisting, compromising, acting upon, integrating, and so on. In other words, the analyst, though not necessarily the analysand, is thinking of what is signified by psychoanalytically useful abstractions. Beres, Spiegel, and Grossman would prefer to use the word *self* for the experiential aspects —that is, for a complex orienting *fantasy* of central importance. I would prefer to use it as a necessary, everyday word and then use the word *ego* to refer to *both* the phenomenal and the abstract ego, just as Freud preferred the range from the experiential to the nonexperiential that *das Ich* made possible.

Hartmann (1953) also mentioned "the cathexis of the self-image (a complex of representations)" (p. 185). Other analysts, such as Kernberg (1982), lump the various self representations together and call *that* self. Thus the self would be "embedded" as a "structure" in the ego. Presumably it is the ego-as-system, not the "structure," that would do the synthesizing, the lumping. No individual can *consciously* do it for him- or herself, of course; nor can it be done for him or her.

Finally, Hartmann, who argued persistently against tendencies to reify abstractions, spoke of our "finding narcissism in all systems." But how can narcissism, an abstraction, be "in" other abstractions? The difficulty with Hartmann's reformulation of ego and self is that it represents an overly systematized approach to what is, after all, a speculative mental economics. The result is a further detachment of the abstract concept of ego—the nonexperiential realm—from the experiential ego (Sandler & Joffe, 1969). Although Schafer (1973) (who would also refrain from using abstract conceptions of self) asserts that Hartmann did *not* use self and identity as metapsychological notions, it is impossible to agree with him. How can the "self," whether as "whole person" or as a representation, be cathected without assuming for it some sort of metapsychological status?

Hartmann sought to resolve a theoretical ambiguity concerning the ego. But the effort not only brought forth new problems, it weakened the original concept. As Laplanche and Pontalis (1973) put it:

> The attempt to identify and eliminate a supposed "terminological ambiguity" is . . . merely a way of avoiding a fundamental problem. . . . In our view this position builds upon a purely conceptual distinction, running ahead of a real solution to some essential problems. The danger . . . is that the real contribution of the Freudian usage may be lost. For Freud *exploits* traditional usages: he opposes organism to environment, subject to object, internal to external, and so on, while continuing to employ *"Ich"* at these different levels. What is more, he plays on the ambiguities thus created. . . . It is this complexity that is shunned by those who want a different word for every shade of meaning. [Pp. 131–132]

The ill-defined or undefinable self can become an empty abstraction: a signifier confused with an unknown and unknowable something that it is supposed to signify; an imaginary "structure" of the mind that is an object, a location, an agent, an originator of action—in short, a homunculus (Rangell, 1982). As for "self" as a theoretically highly abstract word, Glover (1966) called it "a journalistic term."

THE EGO AS BOTH PHENOMENOLOGICAL AND ABSTRACT CONCEPT

The arguments that follow do not dispute the assumptions about psychic function made by some of the contributors to the debate cited above, especially those of Spiegel (1959) and Grossman (1982). To repeat, the only disagreements have to do with whether there is heuristic value in separating "self" from "ego." Negative criticisms have been made of assumptions—mostly among ego psychologists in the United States—that distinctly separate the self from the ego. Positive arguments may be added for retaining Freud's dual meaning of *das Ich* (*whichever* word or words are used to translate it). However, it is unavoidable—and ironic—that these arguments are, and must be, cast in personal, subjective terms.

According to this view, the subjective quality of the word *self* cannot be eradicated. Therefore, the word can never be defined objectively. When I speak of self, I can speak with immediacy only of my own self. It is impossible to think of self without including its reflexive nature, the self experiencing itself. I can experience only *my* self directly, no other. But, sadly, the possibility of self-deception is always there. Even conscious experiences of the nature of my body are highly variable; the distortions of my body image are known to me through fantasy and dream; the distorted images of my body can be further inferred through my analysis (including my self-analysis). In more general terms, what I think is my reputation or value to others may be reasonably accurate or wildly out of keeping with the judgments of peers. More tellingly, my introspective judgments of what I *am* may be much less veridical—at least in some ways—than the analytic judgments of another person, especially if that person knows me well as an artist or a psychoanalyst might.

But even these more objective judgments have limitations. There is no way that another person can experience exactly what it is like to be me, no matter how much he or she is shown or told. Another person will come closest to knowing what I am "really" like if he or she knows a great deal about me and at the same time experiences that knowledge empathically—that is, is able to "put himself in my shoes" and imagine with feeling what it is like to be me. The other is assuming—with feeling—that my self has resemblances to his or her own self. Although we know that the capacity for empathy has always been essential for any successful psychoanalyst, empathy remains an insecure foundation on which to build knowledge. It is easy, even for the most experienced person, to *think* they are being empathetic when they are only deluding themselves in one way or another or confusing their own selves with the self of another.

I understand that there is more to my self than I can consciously know at any one time. Any individual who has worked productively in analysis has experienced the recovery from repression of aspects of his or her self that previously they would have stoutly denied. Inwardly, all of us know that there are things that can never be experienced directly but that in some sense *belong* to our selves and must, at least in some way, be connected with them. We know this because the evidence from within makes the inferences inescapable. Even what we call "id" and "superego" belong to the ego. Schilder (1950) discussed the extensions of the body image in the form of possessions. Outwardly, I know that I—my

"self"—can possess all sorts of things and may even come to believe in the possession of other people. William James (1890) included personal possessions in his very definition of self. Moreover, I may even confuse myself with my possessions. Going further, I may even confuse myself with other *people*. But if all goes reasonably well and I am able to mature to some extent, I may learn that although relations with other people make up part of myself, the people themselves do not. And I may learn that possessions may simultaneously belong to myself and to other people. I may learn to share without confusing who is who among the sharers. All that I have been saying is that my "self" consists of a series of more or less patterned and consistent fantasies and that these do not consist of what I think of as "me" alone, but "me" in relation to other parts of myself or other things or other people.

Now what an observer might call my "self" means what he or she *thinks* my self is or *assumes* my self is to me, consciously and unconsciously. Or the other's reference may be simply defining the location of an action, in the same way that locations of actions are defined by ordinary pronouns. Actually, what the observer means about this part of my mind is the part known subjectively and empathically by comparing it with his or her own self, and as objectively as possible by having made a series of more or less reliable observations as a natural scientist might. This is what it would be preferable to refer to, speaking on a theoretical level, as *ego* or my "I," provided these words imply both constructions derived closely from clinical events and more abstract inferences drawn from them and the collective experience of many analysts.

According to Freud's later theory, the only access to those parts of the mind designated id and superego is by way of the ego. When an observer sits back and thinks about me as an individual and does so in English, he or she is apt to call what is perceived an "ego," an ego that is capable of experiencing itself and that shows evidence at times of conflict and the existence of id and superego. If the observer thinks in German or French or Spanish, he or she will call the products of subjective and objective experiences and observations *das Ich, le moi,* and *el yo,* respectively. When an observer thinks about a person as a unique individual, he or she thinks about the ego's inner, experience-near relations with itself and other persons and its interactions with other aspects of the mind—the id, the superego, and representations of the world. When an analyst seeks to generalize about the egos of analysands and combines and compares his or her accumulated empirical observations with those of others—that is, when he or she moves from the individual to the group—he or she is using "ego" truly in its sense as an abstraction defined by its functions.

Clearly, Freud intended the words for the macro-structures of the structural theory to be derived from ordinary, everyday words which have the uncodified wisdom of the culture behind them. He could not have expressed himself more clearly than in the quotation (1926b) given earlier in the chapter. Thus the ego would be, as Freud said in 1933, "our very own 'I'" (p. 58, my translation). What we call the "id" would be the impersonal "It" within us—motivational forces that at unconstrained times can amount to the terrible. What we call the "superego" might be—although of course it won't be—the "over-I" or "beyond-me," the part of us that urges the subjection of certain personal interests to those of the collective. We can know intrapsychic life only in terms of what can be experienced, in terms of what is phenomenological. We can build theories of the deep structure of the mind, the nonexperiential, only by making valid inferences derived from the collective experiences of many analysts working over a long time in similar modes.

In summary, for Freud, *das Ich* meant—and from my point of view "ego" *ought* to mean—

a clinical construction closely related to what is thought to be the "self" of the subject, comprehended by the observer in analogy and/or in complementarity with his own self, and joined with that expanded, more "objective" knowledge of himself which might be termed personal *ego* knowledge (for examples, knowledge of his accustomed unconscious reactions and characterological propensities) usually acquired from his own personal analysis,

along with

the related, abstract, systemic meanings shared by other analysts operating according to the same fundamental scientific assumptions.

It is a virtue, not a vice, that both sets of meanings reside in the same word; the particular is thereby related to the general. As Laplanche and Pontalis (1973) said, the exploitation of this sort of ambiguity contained in one word amounts to embracing real complexity, by contrast with the spurious ease of simplicity and "neatness."

CRITICISMS OF THE UNITARY VIEW OF EGO

The criticisms of the unitary view just expressed fall into three categories: practice, the quest for objectivity, and the need for systematic economic concepts. Each area of criticism has its validity; at present, decisions can be based only upon what is most useful heuristically.

Just because Freud did not always distinguish between his meanings of *das Ich* as self or system does not mean that we should follow him, the argument goes. Unless a writer is extremely careful, it is easy to confuse his or her intentions: is what is referred to that which is phenomenologically observable in an individual or what can be inferred abstractly about minds in general? The practices developed on the basis of ego psychology have vastly improved the quality of analytic communication. True enough, one can never completely understand the self of another, but psychoanalysis has never pretended to be an exact science. It would be impractical to try to introduce new translations to replace "ego"; it would be clumsy and unworkable to expect authors always to write "phenomenal ego" when that is what they meant and "abstract ego" when they meant *that*. Better to leave existing semantic practices alone, the argument goes. "Self" is used so commonly in English that it retains great heuristic value even left undefined.

The second line of criticism focuses on the avowedly subjective nature of the arguments in favor of a unitary view of *das Ich*. Psychoanalysis has scientific difficulties enough, it is said, without dwelling on its inescapable subjectivity; such a focus could introduce the same ambiguities and uncertainties that reliance upon introspection alone entails. What is needed, the argument goes, is emphasis upon objective, empirical observations made by psychoanalysts. It goes without saying that there are problems as to the "purity" of these apperceptions, but better to focus on the positive nature of collective observations, with the built-in corrective tendencies implied, than to focus upon ephemeral and unanswerable questions having to do with what the "self" is, really.

Finally, the economic problem having to do with what energizes the "self" and what energizes the "ego" (as abstract system only) remains with us, even if Freud did not choose to deal with it. How can we develop psychoanalysis scientifically, this argument asks, without dealing with the internal inconsistencies in its fundamental economic theories?

THE SELF-AS-STRUCTURE IN INTERACTION WITH EGO AS STRUCTURE

A number of authors—for example, Levin (1969) and Mitterauer and Pritz (1978)—have urged the construction of an abstract self as a fourth (and hierarchically equal) macrostructure of the mind. As an equal of the ego, the self would "interact" with it, just as it would with the id and the superego. For a time, it seemed that Kohut might be coming to the same conclusion, but later he disavowed this particular suggestion (1979). Most critics have insisted that there are no clinical observations that can be brought forward to support such a reorganization of our structural abstractions and that the introduction of a fourth macrostructure would provide no heuristic advantages.

OTHER, SOMETIMES "SUPERORDINATE" VIEWS OF SELF

Actual or presumed defects in the Freudian explanations of certain clinical phenomena have always been occasions for theoretical alternatives. Sometimes, these interests have directly or indirectly stimulated modifications of mainstream thought. And sometimes, separate approaches have grown up around them. One that was popular for a time was Erikson's (1956, 1968, 1974) interest in "identity," a term that is usually, but not always, seen as synonymous with "self." The confusions that developed regarding the relationship of identity to ego (Glover, 1966) have now been subsumed by almost identical confusions about the relationship of self to ego. Abend (1974) has contributed a useful survey of the various ways the term has been used and the clinical confusions that can result. (See Chapter 35.)

As the popularity of "identity" waned, other developments, primarily of a cognitive stamp, waxed. Among them were the considerations of the "representational world" begun by Sandler and Rosenblatt (1962), attempts to develop various cognitive explanations to augment or replace standard metapsychology, a search for alternative explanations of the mental apparatus utilizing systems theory or computer science as models, and influences from those who see psychoanalysis as a hermeneutic activity opposed to empirical scientific work, rather than in consonance with it.

The popularity of two competing (but constantly changing) views of the self took center stage in the 1970s. Kernberg (1976, 1982), at first heavily influenced by Kleinian thought, addressed his theoretical speculations to problems of more disturbed patients, "borderline" and "narcissistic" personalities. Kohut (1971, 1977, 1978) was also interested in "narcissistic" personalities, but he defined them differently, on the basis of characteristic transference (or transference-like) reactions. The specific assumptions of the rival approaches will not be addressed here. (See, for examples, Calef & Weinshel, 1979, and Rangell, 1982, for critiques of Kernberg's system and Curtis, 1983, and Treurniet, 1983, for critiques of Kohut's and his followers' work.) Each resulted in a system which postulated a "superordinate self." Each also postulated an entity called the "grandiose self." But the two versions were defined so differently as to be unrelatable.

According to Kernberg (1974), the grandiose self represents a pathological condensation of three other inferred structures: the "real self," the "ideal self," and the "ideal object." Kohut (1977) says that the grandiose self is one pole of *the* "self" (deliberately left undefined). Kernberg (1982) urges two incompatible points about the relations between self and ego. On the one hand, he decries the division in translation of Freud's *das Ich* into "ego" and "self." On the other, he postulates a mature, overarching "superordinate self." He does not give his reasoning; nor is it self-evident. He states that the self "is an ego structure that originates from self-representations. . . . It is, in short, an ego function and structure that evolves gradually from the integration of its component self-representations into a supraordinate structure that incorporates other ego functions . . . and leads to the dual characteristics implied in Freud's *Ich*" (p. 905).

Kohut's early work referring to the self (summarized in 1971) was based on a modified economic theory (libido was seen in terms of two developing streams of motivational forces, one related to objects, the other to the individual's self-love and narcissistic idealizations of others). His later work (1977) postulates a separate line of development of a "bipolar self," which is completely independent of drives and their attendant intrapsychic conflicts. The resulting "self psychology," a version of object relations psychology, is discussed in Chapter 33 and will not be detailed here.

Essentially, the resulting theory postulates the development (and disorders of development) of a self that first relates to objects (as seen by an outside observer) although they might more accurately be termed "selfobjects" inasmuch as they exist in terms of the needs of the self from the inner viewpoint of the individual. If needs to be admired and loved ("mirrored") by the selfobject, usually (to the external observer) the parent, or to idealize selfobjects are not met, specific pathologies develop. These are to be distinguished from pathologies related to drives and conflicts. The resulting techniques of treatment depend on a vastly expanded concept of empathy.

It is to be noted that, although Ornstein (1981) implies that Kohut had a clear-cut conception of "self" from the beginning, Kohut himself publicly refrained from explicit definitions (Wolf, 1985). Kohut believed that a premature definition would inhibit and restrict further development of self-psychological concepts. As followers as well as non-followers of Kohut's thought acquire further experience, no doubt the clinical validity of the concepts will be determined, and almost certainly more explicit definitions of this meaning of self will be forthcoming. By contrast, evidence for or against Kernberg's theories, including his superordinate self, can hardly come from clinical evidence, inasmuch as they are made up of interlocking deductions. To date, most psychoanalysts have withheld judgment or have been openly dubious about the claims of either system (Curtis, 1983; Blum, 1982; Rangell, 1982; and Richards, 1982).

The same can be said of two other theories that postulate the centrality of the self, both from the standpoint of dissatisfactions with existing metapsychological formulations. George S. Klein (1976), in an effort to rid psychoanalysis of metapsychology altogether, proposed a "self-schema" capable of having both "human" and "systemic" attributes. However, as Richards (1982) points out, once the self-schema is defined as a psychic apparatus, something like a metapsychology becomes reinserted. John Gedo (1979) makes the epigenesis of a "self-organization" central. He focuses on a hierarchy of values and personal aims. The importance of biological motivations becomes integrated with goals and values. Technical recommendations based on this reorganization of theory await the test of time.

It may be that the tendency to reify and elevate self and identity to "superordinate" or "supraordinate" levels of abstraction is primarily a phenomenon of the English-speaking analytic world. But, as Glover (1966) suggested, the tendency began, at least, with Jung. Some analysts wish to locate some sort of "primal self" at the beginning, which might open up like a paper flower in a glass of water, or to discern overriding "identity themes," beginning with the earliest mother–infant relationship in which, it is thought, the mother's unconscious might serve as a sort of cast (Lichtenstein, 1963, 1965). There are universal wishes to discover "core" meanings of human life, both in its beginnings and in its ultimate purposes. There is nothing to criticize in such wishes or the theories derived from them, unless they invade the core propositions of psychoanalysis as a discipline.

CONCLUSIONS

The literature on the self is massive and confusing. Terms are not always concepts; sometimes they merely cover vacuums. A redundancy exists: "self," "identity," "identity themes" (along with mysterious hybrids: "ego identity" and "self identity"), variously refer to the individual, the mind (phenomenally or noumenally), or even something like a metaphysical fate, as in identity themes—enough to fill many volumes. Too often, attempts to clarify the Freudian system, or essentially replace it, extirpate its core, its basic concepts.

In this chapter I have taken up the beliefs of most mainstream analysts, in the United States at any rate, that "ego" should be defined only as an abstraction that includes a cohering set of psychic functions and that "self" is a different entity. An opposing argument among mainstream analysts (including myself) has it that the ego should be understood as a term exactly comparable to Freud's *das Ich,* a concept with a range of meanings, from constructs based on clinical observations to high levels of abstraction. Other propositions have been advanced by more dissident analysts: that "self" should be seen as a fourth macrostructure of the structural theory or that "self" should be seen as "superordinate" to the id–ego–superego system.

REFERENCES

Abend, S. (1974). Problems of identity. *Psychoanal. Q.,* 43:606–637.

Arlow, J. A., & Brenner, C. (1964). *Psychoanalytic Concepts and the Structural Theory.* New York: Int. Univ. Press.

Beres, D. (1981). Self, identity, and narcissism. *Psychoanal. Q.,* 50:515–534.

Bettelheim, B. (1983). *Freud and Man's Soul.* New York: Knopf.

Blum, H. P. (1982). Theories of self and psychoanalytic concepts. *J. Amer. Psychoanal. Assn.,* 30:959–978.

Boesky, D. (1983). The problem of mental representation in self and object theory. *Psychoanal. Q.,* 52:564–583.

Brenner, C. (1980). Metapsychology and psychoanalytic theory. *Psychoanal. Q.,* 49:189–214.

Calef, V., & Weinshel, E. M. (1979). The new psychoanalysis and psychoanalytic revisionism. *Psychoanal. Q.,* 48:470–491.

Curtis, H. (1983). Review of *The Search for the Self: Selected Writings of Heinz Kohut, 1958–1970. J. Amer. Psychoanal. Assn.,* 31:272–285.

Ellenberger, H. (1970). *The Discovery of the Unconscious.* New York: Basic Books.

Erikson, E. H. (1956). The problem of ego identity. *J. Amer. Psychoanal. Assn.,* 4:56–121.

———. (1968). *Identity.* London: Faber & Faber.

———. (1974). *Dimensions of a New Identity.* New York: Norton.

Freud, A. (1936). *The Ego and the Mechanisms of Defence*. New York: Int. Univ. Press.

——. (1952). The mutual influences in the development of ego and id. *Psychoanal. Study Child*, 7:42–50.

Freud, S. (1895). Project for a scientific psychology. *SE*, 1:295–397.

——. (1914). On narcissism. *SE*, 14:73–102.

——. (1915). Instincts and their vicissitudes. *SE*, 14:117–140.

——. (1921). *Group Psychology and the Analysis of the Ego. SE*, 18:69–143.

——. (1923). *The Ego and the Id. SE*, 19:12–66.

——. (1926a). *Inhibitions, Symptoms and Anxiety. SE*, 20:87–172.

——. (1926b). *The Question of Lay Analysis. SE*, 20:183–250.

——. (1933). *New Introductory Lectures on Psycho-Analysis. SE*, 22:5–182.

Friedman, L. (1980). The barren prospect of a representational world. *Psychoanal. Q.*, 49:215–233.

Gedo, J. (1979). *Beyond Interpretation*. New York: Int. Univ. Press.

Gill, M. M. (1963). *Topography and Systems in Psychoanalytic Theory*. New York: Int. Univ. Press.

Glover, E. (1966). Metapsychology or metaphysics. *Psychoanal. Q.*, 35:173–190.

Grossman, W. I. (1982). The self as fantasy. *J. Amer. Psychoanal. Assn.*, 30:919–938.

Hartmann, H. (1939). *Ego Psychology and the Problem of Adaptation*. New York: Int. Univ. Press, 1958.

——. (1950). Comments on the psychoanalytic theory of the ego. *Psychoanal. Study Child*, 5:74–96.

——. (1953). Contribution to the metapsychology of schizophrenia. *Psychoanal. Study Child*, 8:177–198.

——. (1955). Notes on the theory of sublimation. *Psychoanal. Study Child*, 10:9–29.

——. (1956). The development of the ego concept in Freud's work. *Int. J. Psychoanal.*, 37:425–438.

Hatmann, H., Kris, E., & Lowenstein, R. M. (1964). *Papers on Psychoanalytic Psychology*. Psychological Issues, monograph 14. New York: Int. Univ. Press.

Jacobson, E. (1964). *The Self and the Object World*. New York: Int. Univ. Press.

Jacobson, J. (1983). The structural theory and the representational world. *Psychoanal. Q.*, 52:543–563.

James, W. (1890). *The Principles of Psychology*. Chicago: W. Benton.

Joffe, W., & Sandler, J. (1967). Some conceptual problems involved in the consideration of disorders of narcissism. *J. Child Psychother.*, 2:56–66.

Kernberg, O. F. (1974). Barriers to falling and remaining in love. *J. Amer. Psychoanal. Assn.*, 22:486–511.

——. (1976). *Object Relations Theory and Clinical Psychoanalysis*. New York: Aronson.

——. (1982). Self, ego, affects and drives. *J. Amer. Psychoanal. Assn.*, 30:893–918.

Klein, G. S. (1976). *Psychoanalytic Theory*. New York: Int. Univ. Press.

Kohut, H. (1970). Moderator's opening and closing remarks to discussion of D. C. Levin's "The self." *Int. J. Psychoanal.*, 51:176–181.

——. (1971). *The Analysis of the Self*. New York: Int. Univ. Press.

——. (1977). *The Restoration of the Self*. New York: Int. Univ. Press.

——. (1978). *The Search for the Self*. Edited by P. Ornstein. New York: Int. Univ. Press.

——. (1979). The two analyses of Mr. Z. *Int. J. Psychoanal.*, 60:3–28.

Laplanche, J., & Pontalis, J.-B. (1973). *The Language of Psycho-Analysis*. New York: Norton.

Levin, D. (1969). The self. *Int. J. Psychoanal.*, 50:41–51.

Lichtenstein, H. (1963). The dilemma of human identity. *J. Amer. Psychoanal. Assn.*, 11:173–223.

——. (1965). Towards a metapsychological definition of the concept of self. *Int. J. Psychoanal.*, 46:117–128.

Loewald, H. W. (1971). On motivation and instinct theory. *Psychoanal. Study Child*, 26:91–128.

——. (1973). Review of *The Analysis of the Self*, by H. Kohut. *Psychoanal. Q.*, 42:441–451.

Loewenstein, R. M. (1940). The vital or somatic instincts. *Int. J. Psychoanal.*, 21:377–400.

Mahler, M. S., & McDevitt, J. (1982). Thoughts on the emergence of the sense of self, with particular emphasis on the body self. *J. Amer. Psychoanal. Assn.*, 30:827–848.

Mahler, M. S., Pine, F., & Bergman, A. (1975). *The Psychological Birth of the Human Infant*. New York: Basic Books.

Mitterauer, B., & Pritz, W. (1978). The concept of the self. *Int. Rev. Psychoanal.*, 5:179–188.

Ornstein, P. H. (1981). The bipolar self in the psychoanalytic treatment process. *J. Amer. Psychoanal. Assn.*, 29:353–376.

Ornston, D. (1982). Strachey's influence. *Int. J. Psychoanal.*, 63:409–426.

Rangell, L. (1982). The self in psychoanalytic theory. *J. Amer. Psychoanal. Assn.*, 30:863–892.

Richards, A. (1982). The superordinate self in psychoanalytic theory and in the self psychologies. *J. Amer. Psychoanal. Assn.,* 30:939–958.

Sandler, J., & Joffe, W. (1969). Towards a basic psychoanalytic model. *Int. J. Psychoanal.,* 50:79–90.

Sandler, J., & Rosenblatt, B. (1962). The concept of the representational world. *Psychoanal. Study Child,* 17:128–145.

Schafer, R. (1968). *Aspects of Internalization.* New York: Int. Univ. Press.

———. (1973). Concepts of self and identity and the experience of separation-individuation in adolescence. *Psychoanal. Q.,* 42:42–59.

Schilder, P. (1950). *The Image and Appearance of the Human Body.* New York: Int. Univ. Press.

Spiegel, L. A. (1959). The self, the sense of self, and perception. *Psychoanal. Study Child,* 14:81–109.

Spruiell, V. (1975). Three strands of narcissism. *Psychoanal. Q.,* 44:577–595.

———. (1979). Object relations theory. *J. Amer. Psychoanal. Assn.,* 27:387–398.

———. (1981). The self and the ego. *Psychoanal. Q.,* 50:319–344.

Strachey, J. (1961). Editor's Introduction. *SE,* 19:7–8.

Treurniet, N. (1983). Psychoanalysis and self psychology. *J. Amer. Psychoanal. Assn.,* 31:59–100.

Wolf, E. (1985). Personal communication.

32

OBJECTS AND OBJECT RELATIONSHIPS

The term "object" pervades psychoanalytic writing. Fundamentally, it means "someone else," by contrast with a subject, someone or something in the real or objective, as opposed to mental, world. Something "thrown before the senses" is the meaning of the Latin source word. The relativistic nature of the idea is apparent: there must be someone in order for there to be a someone else; there must be senses in order for something to be thrown before them and a mental world in order for something to be not of that world.

For psychoanalysis, the term "object" has additional, formal meanings. A useful, psychoanalytic definition is that of Brenner (1973, p. 98): "the term 'object' is used to designate persons or things of the external environment which are psychologically significant to one's psychic life, whether such things be animate or lifeless." Brenner's definition includes the ideas inherent in the generic usage. An object is to be distinguished from a subject; moreover, an object must be distinguished from its counterpart in the mind of the subject: *object* refers to an actual person or thing. The criteria for deciding whether someone or something is an object *for a particular person,* however, are psychological: the someone or something must be significant to the subject.

Brenner's definition leaves us with some problems. How does one operationalize "psychologically significant"? What is the relation between the other

person and whatever mental events or structures constitute "psychological significance?"

Brenner's definition and my endorsement of it are in some degree prescriptive for, rather than descriptive of, psychoanalytic usage. Freud, for example, did not consistently use *object* in this way. Sometimes in his work it clearly meant a real someone else, sometimes the mental counterpart of such a real someone else, sometimes an abstract construct in a theoretical context; but not infrequently it is impossible to decide. Usage by other analysts has also been variable. Some have argued that having a multiply ambiguous term is helpful, or even essential (see Chapter 31). I believe that such multiple usage causes confusion and fruitless dissent by masking just the problems we need to explore. In this chapter I will attempt to dissect, isolate, then relate meanings, so as to reduce ambiguity as far as possible.

Psychoanalysis is a theory of mind, and traditionally it seeks to explain human relationships on the basis of mental processes. The term "object" is central to such explanations. Human relationships, then, are the observational basis for theories that include the term "object." However, psychoanalysis also sees human relationships as formative of mind. Developmentally, for the child, relationships with parents and siblings are the nurture side of nature/nurture. Clinically, the relationship with the analyst is seen as necessary to produce mental change. Thus we explain relationships in terms of mind, and mind, partially, in terms of relationships, current and past. If mind is a function of brain, then mind as an expression of the biological nature of an individual is a straightforward idea. But mind as a function of nurture, of relationships, is more problematic. How does something that is outside an organism become an integral part of the mind of that organism? This is the fundamental problem of the object concept and of theories using that concept. More is involved, psychoanalysts believe, than is encompassed by traditional learning theories.

Object usually appears in psychoanalytic literature qualified by an adjective, such as "internal" or "external" or "real" or "fantasy," or as part of a compound term, such as "object relations" or "object representation." If it appears unqualified, the question "Object of what?" must be asked (Compton, 1986b). This question also helps to expose instances in which the word *object* is merely jargon; that is, it adds nothing to an everyday idea. An example is the common phrase "object relationship," which means nothing more than relationship.

Object relations, according to the viewpoint adopted here, designates the attitudes and behavior of someone toward his or her objects—that is, other people who are important to the subject (Brenner, 1973; Compton, 1987). This usage is not uniform in psychoanalytic writing either; for example, Moore has suggested (personal communication and Moore & Fine, eds., 1990, p. 129) that "object relationship" be used for interactions between a subject and another, actual person and "object relations" be reserved for psychological phenomena. Moore's usage is consistent with that of Kernberg (see Chapter 33). Another use of this term is in the common phrase "object relations theories," which will be discussed below.

Object representation is a term that always refers to psychological phenomena, but it is inherently an even more complex term, one that means, approximately, the mental counterpart of an object. Some analysts use it synonymously with "internal object" (see Moore & Fine, eds., 1990), but the bodies of literature that use the one term and the other are distinctly different, and so are the conceptual contexts —that is, the terms are parts of different and not necessarily compatible theories of mind. "Libidinal object" is often used as an equivalent to either one of these terms. Each of these concepts will be discussed in more detail below.

DEVELOPMENT OF THE OBJECT CONCEPT IN FREUD'S WORK

The term "object" entered Freud's writings in 1895 in its generic sense, as a way of indicating someone or something other than a subject. It first appeared in a diagram included in posthumously published private correspondence in the form "sexual object" located in the "external world" (1895a) and in a broader context in the "Project" (1895b). At that time Freud's orientation was more neurophysiological than psychological. Certain physical tensions such as hunger, thirst, or sexual excitation required what he called "specific actions" for their relief: because the sources of these excitations are within the subject organism, they cannot be left behind or otherwise avoided indefinitely, and an action specific to the anatomy of the excited organ is necessary. In the case of an infant, or in other situations of helplessness, there must be aid from someone else to relieve the stimulation or tension. The someone else performs the "specific action" for the infant; the pleasurable feelings which then arise as the tension is relieved or the need satisfied are associated with the percept of the someone else and, in Freud's neurological terms of that time, the neurones corresponding to that percept receive a permanent "cathexis" (1895b, pp. 318, 328–331). The "sexual object" corresponds to the "someone else," the percept of whom is retained as neuronal cathexis. This group of ideas contains the nucleus of the psychoanalytic object concept (Compton, 1986b).

As Freud's orientation became predominantly psychological, he nevertheless made clear that the theoretical mental apparatus that he then constructed was intended to be homologous with the underlying neural apparatus. The idea of the "wish"—a psychological construct—became central, but the essence of the theory of the "experience of satisfaction" remained. The associated percepts of the gratifying person were now seen to be stored as memory traces, or "mnemic images," and, at times of need, the thrust of the arising wish was to match a current percept with these memory traces. Freud called this the "theory of perceptual identity." The baby at the breast became a personification of these ideas in Freud's developing theories (1900, pp. 555–556, 602).

In 1905 Freud introduced the idea of instinctual drives to explain currents, such as wishes, in the mental apparatus. Sexuality, as an instinctual drive, was to be understood in terms of sexual aims and sexual objects—that is, drive objects. This idea, derived from the earlier theories concerning releasers of endogenous excitation, underwent steady, significant expansion over the next fifteen years, and "drive object" became the object concept characteristic of psychoanalysis (Compton, 1985b). It was not until 1915 that Freud presented a definition of "drive object," the only definition of "object" that appears in his work in any context:

The *object* of an instinctual drive is the thing in regard to which or through which the drive is able to achieve its aim. It is what is most variable about an instinctual drive and is not originally connected with it. . . . The object is not necessarily something extraneous; it may equally well be a part of the subject's own body. It may be changed any number of times. [Pp. 122–123]

Freud proposed that adult sexuality is the product of an organization of "component sexual drives," present from infancy and including oral, anal, phallic, sadistic/masochistic, and exhibitionistic/voyeuristic components. The component sexual drives were also characterized according to whether they were directed toward someone else or were not so directed; that is, as to whether they were object-directed or autoerotic. If the component sexual drive was object-directed, its object was called a "sexual object," a form of drive object. Directedness is one of the concepts derived from the idea of objects of drives. It may then be applied to other forms of psychological or personal expression.

Object choice, another term that Freud introduced in 1905, refers to the process whereby one renders someone else psychologically significant. It is important to distinguish between "sexual object," a drive concept, and "object choice." "Object choice" is also derived from the drive-object concept but is more complex than "directedness." While Freud's fundamental idea was that sexual drives are present from early infancy on, he was initially unsure as to whether object choice occurred before adolescence. It was not until 1923 that he said unequivocally that object choice occurs as early as the phallic-oedipal phase (1923b). At least one of the requirements for object choice is the confluence of sexual drives upon one and the same object. He proposed that the sexual drives follow, or "lean on," the ego (self-preservative) drives in locating an object, though this does not necessarily imply confluence.

Freud also recognized that the clinical phenomena related to object choice—loving and hating—cannot be subsumed under a theory of instinctual drives exclusively: loving and hating are *attitudes* that one person holds toward another, and explanation of personal attitudes requires constructs in addition to drive constructs (1915). He proposed several possible solutions to the problem of personal attitudes, the earliest of which was the theory of affectionate and sensual currents, separate in development, whose confluence upon the same object is also involved in object choice or, at least, in what he called "finding an object" in adolescence or adult life. "Object finding" is a third concept derived from the idea of drive objects: drive object plus personal attitudes

plus action are included. Freud said that the finding of an object in adult life is in fact a refinding of it: that is, a new person is chosen in adolescence or adult life partly on the basis of matching a model in memory from one's childhood, again meaning an object model from the oedipal phase. This idea is related to, but not the same as, the theory of perceptual identity.

The type of object choice that Freud postulated to result from the confluence of component sexual drives and ego drives, or the confluence of sexual and affectionate currents, came to be known as "anaclitic object choice" (*Anlehnungstypus:* leaning-on type), because of Freud's idea that the sexual drives "lean on" the ego drives. Freud later contrasted this type of object choice with what he called "narcissistic object choice." He approached the idea of narcissistic object choice somewhat differently from that of anaclitic object choice. The model for the object chosen was seen to be not the gratifying person of infancy but rather oneself. In these discussions Freud tended to replace the terms "sexual object" and "object choice" by "love object" and "object love." He also posed his explanations in terms of libido, the energy behind the sexual drives, rather than in terms of the sexual drives themselves (Compton, 1981).

Object choice was now said to involve a "libidinal cathexis" (investment) of the object; this applied to both types of object choice, though the nature of the libidinal cathexis was held to be different in each type. The term "libidinal object" has become common in psychoanalytic literature, tending to replace "drive object" as characterizing a psychoanalytic approach. The term, however, is particularly linked with Freud's ideas about narcissism and with that step in the evolution of his drive theory in which the distribution of libido was an especially prominent idea.

When Freud started investigating new clinical areas, his theoretical constructs underwent modification. This was true of his object concept, which was influenced by his study of homosexuality and paranoia from 1910 to 1915, resulting in the concepts of narcissism and narcissistic object choice, and then by his studies of depression, mania, and traumatic neuroses from 1915 on. Object loss and hostility became prominent concerns (as contrasted to object choice and love), and identification and related concepts became much more significant in Freud's explanatory models. With the increased prominence of the concept of identification, the object concept also assumed a larger role in psychoanalytic theory and eventually underwent some change as a consequence.

Identification refers to being or becoming like

someone else in one or more ways. The someone else functions as an object or model for the person who is doing the identifying. The object model in this sense is conceptually different from the mnemic-image model for choosing an object later in life. Freud's attention to identification led to theoretical concern with how the mental apparatus might be formed and with the significance of others, of objects, in the development of enduring—that is, structural—aspects of mind and of change (1921, 1923a). Freud connected identification especially, though not exclusively, with the loss of someone loved. In 1913 he had proposed that an unconscious cannibalistic fantasy was the instinctual drive basis of the process of identification. He also described identification as a kind of motivated thinking, a wishful putting oneself in the place of another, an unconscious imitation and assimilation.

Two of Freud's most significant collaborators, Ferenczi and Abraham, preferred different terms for discussing similar problems. Ferenczi introduced the term "introjection" in 1909 and subsequently used it as an all-purpose expression referring to essentially all modes of psychological relationship, but especially in contexts where Freud tended to say "identification." Abraham (1924) generally used the term "incorporation" in similar contexts, interchangeably with "introjection." Freud used "introjection" intermittently from 1915 onward, usually describing it as "Ferenczi's term," and generally when he was specifically referring to some process of modification of the ego. A fourth, related term, "internalization," was used by Freud with some frequency at the end of his work. These usages are important in subsequent developments in psychoanalytic theory, to which I shall return (Compton, 1985a).

Freud's most extensive discussions of identification were in 1917 and 1921, before he introduced the ego–id–superego model (1923a). In fact, modifications of the personality along the lines of being or becoming like someone else were significant considerations in the introduction of his new theory. Other people as models in one or more discrete to global respects came to be seen as factors in the formation of the superego particularly and of the structural ego as well. It was especially in relation to superego formation that Freud tended to use Ferenczi's term "introjection."

Another of the major sources of developments in the realm of the object concept was Freud's (1926) revision of his theory of anxiety. Prior to that time he had postulated that anxiety results from the transformation of repressed libido. In the revised theory he proposed that, at least after the period of early infantile helplessness, anxiety usually occurs as a signal of danger, in response to a developmentally determined—we might say, genetically encoded—sequence of danger situations: fear of loss of a loved object, fear of loss of an object's love, fear of castration, and fear of the superego or the powers of fate. This formulation heightened the importance of relationships and of the child's representations of objects in the psychoanalytic view of development in general (Compton, 1986a).

GENERAL POSITION OF THE "OBJECT" CONCEPT IN PSYCHOANALYTIC THEORY

I have indicated that the "object" concept is a device for explaining the relations between inside (the organism or the mind) and outside. The problems that arise in connection with "object" and related terms have to do with the conceptual difficulty still involved in this relation. One way to grasp this is via the question "How does anything which was not in or of the mind come to be in or of the mind?" This enables us to break down Freud's object concept into a series of component object concepts and see a little more clearly what is involved in the process.

The most basic of these object concepts is the object of a subject, a "phenomenal object." The initial mental step from the phenomenal, or real, object to a psychological concept is a percept, or "perceptual object." A retained percept is an "object memory," or memory trace, or mnemic image. In mental terms, the investment of such a memory trace or group of such traces by instinctual drives comes to signify a "drive object." A related but distinct theoretical object concept, based on the theory of what is invested, is the "libidinal object." Another idea of object was introduced by Freud in his 1915 discussion of loving and hating, one that I have called an "attitudinal object." An object memory trace may serve as a model for future object investments. An object percept or memory trace may also serve as a model for identification. The mechanisms by which identification occurs are obscure, but object as a model for identification is different from object as a model for a new object.

A group of mnemic images, organized in some cognitive way and through the investment of drives or libidinal cathexes may be designated as a "representational object" concept. The idea of object representation was not developed explicitly by Freud. In fact, neither the term "representation" nor the compound "object representation" appears in the English-language *Standard Edition* except in a very limited sense in Freud's writing on dreams.

Freud used the word *object*, usually unqualified, when referring, in relation to an explicit or implicit subject, to either an actual other person or thing or to the mental counterpart thereof. For clarity, "object representation" is here used to refer to accumulated mental images from a variety of experiences with another person which have been organized by both cognitive processes and drive investment. Freud also used the term "ego" in a variety of different senses without specifying its meaning. Hartmann (1950, 1964) and Jacobson (1964) introduced clarifications of these usages, which I follow. "Ego" refers to a structural mental system, one of the constructs of the ego–id–superego model of the mind, an organized group of functions usually found operating together in situations of mental conflict. "Self representation," analogous to object representation, refers to the unconscious, preconscious, and conscious mental representation of one's body and of one's mind; the cathexis of ego functions is to be distinguished from the cathexis of the self representation. "Self" is an auxiliary descriptive term, without formal meaning, used to refer to a person or subject as distinct from other persons or objects. (These clarifications are widely but not universally accepted. See Chapter 31. There are also questions about the concept of representation in a general sense, which will be considered below.)

These eight object concepts can be used to outline a hypothetical process showing how someone else becomes psychologically important to a subject, either as an event of adult life or as the result of a developmental sequence of emerging capacities. That "someone else" becomes an important factor in the mental life of a subject depends on ego functions such as memory and perception, as well as whatever other functions are involved in representing, self representing, and object representing, in change, and in identification. The ego–id–superego model has remained the dominant general theoretical scheme of psychoanalysis. "Reality" can be seen as a fourth major construct of this model. The other person or real or phenomenal object may then be viewed as a part of this (objective) reality. Adaptation may be viewed, biologically, as the process of the organism fitting in with reality or, psychologically, as the task of the ego, largely in establishing a fitting-in with another person or persons. The actual behavior of the other person is recognized as having considerable importance in the psychological functioning of the subject. This influence has been recognized and studied within a psychoanalytic framework chiefly for infancy and early childhood and to some degree for the clinical psychoanalytic situation itself, where transference phenomena are seen to depend partially on the actual behavior of the analyst.

Perception, while it does achieve an adult consensual norm, is never an exact replication in the mental realm of some objective stimulus of a sensory modality. Perception is an ego function which, while it may be relatively free of conflict in any given instance, is always influenced by past experience and present state of mind of the perceiving subject. An "object percept" is particularly susceptible to a variety of personal influences. "Perceptual object" is not identical with phenomenal object conceptually and is not an objective replication of that object.

Memory, also viewed as an ego function, refers to a complex group of processes, including registration, storage, recognition, and recall (Kris, 1956). Different capabilities are involved in recognizing a percept—by comparing it with a memory image—and in evoking an image in the absence of perceptual stimulation; the two kinds of memory entailed are known as "recognition memory" and "evocative memory" (Fraiberg, 1969). In relation to the object concept, it is important to distinguish between an "object image," which refers to experience or mental content—a "picture" of someone in one or more sensory modalities—and more complex and theoretical, nonexperiential constructs, such as "object representation." Differentiating this usage of object by the term "memory image" or "memorial object" does not really do justice to the complexity of the processes involved.

"Cathexis," the investment of a mental element by drive energy, is always understood to include both libido and aggression, terms that may indicate either the two general forms of instinctual drives or, more specifically, the psychic energy hypothesized to underlie them. The term "object cathexis" is, unfortunately, still used regularly to indicate some form of relationship with another person, whereas, properly, it means the investment of the mental presentation of another person with libidinal or aggressive drives or energy. "Libidinal object" is best understood to refer to both libidinal and aggressive cathexis of the mental presentation of some other person or thing and is usually intended to emphasize the importance of emotional, psychological significance as opposed to behavioral or interpersonal constructs. We assume that there is always a mixture of libidinal and aggressive cathexis. We infer that one or other type of drive may predominate from observations of the quality of the relationship and reports of the attitudes and feelings directed toward the other person.

Representation is a complex concept. Briefly, any "thing" that we see as an aspect of mental processes, we tend to see as "represented" mentally; "representation," then, is almost synonymous with "mental." Object representation is only a special instance of this. I have defined "object representation" as an amalgam of memory images of sensory or other experiential impressions of another person, organized by cognitive processes and drive investment. This definition, unfortunately, mixes quasi-experiential and theoretical terms and is therefore not altogether satisfactory, although I am not aware of any better definition. Object representation, nevertheless, is an important psychological factor in determining a person's relationship to someone else and, developmentally, is an important factor in the formation of mental structure itself. The concept implies some enduring aspect, in that the object representations formed in infancy serve as models throughout life. They also have some elasticity and capacity for change, and new object representations may be formed throughout life, albeit rooted in earlier images.

Much psychoanalytic work has sought to understand human development and behavior largely in terms of correlated self and object representations. In particular, the idea of psychic structure formation as a result of identification may be viewed in terms of interactions of object representations with the self representation in such a way that the self representation is modified (Jacobson, 1964). Object representation is a concept that has expanded considerably in recent years. I shall take up some of the controversial aspects of this expansion below.

OBJECT RELATIONS

Object relations refers to the behavior and attitudes of someone toward the persons or things in his or her environment that are psychologically important. This field of study represents an area of juncture between psychoanalytic psychology, which is a fundamentally mental—intrapsychic—theory and other views of human behavior that take a social or behavioristic stance in their conceptual formulations. It has proved difficult to keep both fields of observation, mental process and social interchange, simultaneously in view without loss of the distinction.

The psychoanalytic concepts that pertain to this area are object choice, object love, ambivalence, and object loss. Each of these concepts concerns human experience and behavior in relation to other persons but is also firmly anchored in ideas about the mental structures and processes that underlie such interchanges. All are partially in the realm of attitudinal object concepts, which have not been extensively developed as such in psychoanalysis. All may also be seen as intense emotional attitudes toward others which are relatively neglected in psychological systems other than psychoanalysis.

Ambivalence was used by Freud to indicate the simultaneous presence of loving and hating attitudes toward the same person. Before the concept of an aggressive drive was introduced, ambivalence had no firm theoretical basis. It was simply thought that ambivalence was a phase in development that was surpassed when a true object or genital relationship was established (Abraham, 1924). This is now thought to be an idealized view: all intense relationships are based upon both libidinal and aggressive cathexes of the representation of the object and are therefore in some degree ambivalent (Spitz, 1965).

Object choice continues to be discussed in two basic forms: "true" or "altruistic" or "anaclitic" versus "narcissistic." Some authors seem to believe that both these forms of object choice are pathological and that there is another form that is more mature or, at least, less pathological. I do not find such a category in Freud's work, and I have not discovered any theoretical justification for it in the work of others. It also seems to be true that love relationships include both concern for the other and his or her needs and a narcissistic or primarily self-satisfying element. Nevertheless, one or the other may predominate; there may be shifts in the relative proportions; and some people seem to be relatively incapable of the kind of love that fully recognizes the independent existence of the "other person."

Object love is rather loosely used and tends to be synonymous with "object choice," especially anaclitic object choice. The state of "being in love" and the factors involved in sustaining a love relationship, first explored by Freud (1921), have recently received more direct psychoanalytic attention (see Altman, 1977; Bak, 1973; Bergmann, 1980; Kernberg, 1976).

The area of object relations that has perhaps received the most attention since Freud is that of object loss. The effects on children of the loss of a parent or a sibling in the early years of life and the residual effects on adults of such losses have been studied through the direct observation of infants and children (A. Freud & Burlingham, 1945; Furman, 1974; Spitz, 1965; Pollock, 1961; and many others) and through the analyses of adults. In the latter, early object losses have been clearly demonstrated to have organizational effects on the personality (for example, Jacobson, 1965, 1971).

DEVELOPMENT AND OBJECTS

The classical, orienting schemes of development remain those of Freud: infantile sexual organizations and object-directedness. Freud's concept of infantile sexual organizations made use of two factors: the genetically encoded sequence of predominant body zones and the encoded sequence of predominant object-directed attitudes or modes. These are oral-cannibalistic, sadistic-anal, phallic-oedipal, latency, adolescent, and adult or genital organizations. He also proposed a sequence of object-directedness in the sense of the type of target for the drives or attitudes: autoerotic, narcissistic, object-directed homosexual, and object-directed heterosexual. This sequence takes its orientation from the type of object rather than the zone or attitude; temporal predominance or sequence for the types is not entirely clear, nor is there any specified relation between the drive organization and object-directedness sequences. Freud's scheme of danger situations, as mentioned above, was psychoenergic disequilibrium, loss of object, loss of object's love, castration, superego retribution, and retribution by the powers of fate. All these dangers except the first have an external referent (that is, an object) in the form of (a fantasy of) what someone else may do. Once again, the correlation of this scheme with the other two is not specified by Freud.

Psychoanalytic ideas about the development of the object concept require that we attend to the developmental scheme in itself (development of what?) and to the concepts that arise in the course of pursuing the scheme (object of what?). We can view this as an ontogenetic rendition of the question of how something not mental becomes mental.

The broadest, and perhaps the most useful, approach is that of Anna Freud (1965), which entails the concept of developmental lines. She says: "What we are looking for are the basic interventions between id and ego and their various developmental levels" (p. 63). The prototypic developmental line that she offers is that of object relations. I shall begin by looking at stages in the development of object relations, using the term "object relations" in the sense in which I have defined it, as referring to behavior and attitudes.

Although there is steadily mounting evidence of the active, interactional capacities of the neonate and young infant (for example, Emde et al., 1976), it continues to seem most expedient to conceptualize the initial relation of the infant and mother as essentially biological. The stage of need-satisfying relationship consists, then, of an earlier, biological need-satisfying phase and a subsequent psychological need-satisfying phase (Edgcumbe & Burgner, 1972). Need satisfaction is a part of all relationships; but a stage characterized by predominant or exclusive need satisfaction is nevertheless distinguishable. While psychological functioning may begin in the neonate at or shortly after birth, the beginning of

psychological *relationship* has to be placed somewhat later.

At about two months infants begin to smile in response to an approaching human face, at first if—and only if—they are hungry, but regularly in this way under such circumstances if that condition is met (Spitz, 1965). No other stimulus reliably gives rise to a smile. This phenomenon is known as "social smiling" and is taken as the first evidence of psychological relationship.

Obviously the development of the infant is a continuous process in most respects. There are also periods of qualitative change, such as the onset of social smiling, which are useful markers of developmental phases. A second such discontinuous phenomenon occurs at between six and eight months, the onset of "stranger anxiety." Prior to that time the baby, at about five months, seems to show a general increase in alertness and attention to what is, and who are, around him or her. But then comes a "sobering reaction" to the approach of an unfamiliar person. This is followed at about eight months by acute distress at the approach of a stranger, in marked contrast to smiling at the mother and, to a less pronounced extent, other family members. Another anxiety response of infancy, called "separation anxiety," manifested when the infant is in a need state and the mother cannot be located, also occurs; but it is distinctly different in the timing of its onset, peak intensity, relative unpredictability, and duration. Stranger anxiety as such usually lasts until age twenty-four to thirty-six months, and separation anxiety tends to peak at about that time (Emde et al., 1976).

The combination of stranger anxiety and special smiling at the mother is taken to mark the end of the need-satisfaction phase and the start of a stage of ambivalent relatedness. Locomotion also begins about this time, and the infant appears to be confidently exploring the environment and moving physically away from the mother. Accordingly, this developmental period has also been called the "separation-individuation phase" (Mahler et al., 1975), which lasts until anywhere from twenty-four to thirty-six months. In the middle of this time, at about eighteen months, during a subphase known as "rapprochement," the infant appears to lose confidence in being away from the mother but without losing the impetus to be away from her. A combination of insisting on her presence and physical contact, on the one hand, and pushing her away with unpleasant affective displays, on the other hand, results.

During this time the father, if available, can be observed to become of considerable importance to the infant. At thirty to thirty-six months, changes in the toddler's affects, which are by now verbalized as well as shown and enacted, indicate a transition to "the completely object-centered phallic oedipal phase" (A. Freud). "Oedipal" refers to a specific triangular configuration of object relations. Note that all the postulated stages of object relations have observable anchor points in behavior. In no instance is the designation of stage primarily theory-derived.

A period of increased anxiousness at about five years ushers in changes in the direction of being more subdued, less sexually oriented, more compliant, and more "educable." This is the latency phase, which persists until age ten to twelve, when preadolescent changes commence, followed by adolescence, during which the relationship to the parents is markedly altered and life tends to become organized around sexual/romantic/competitive interest in peers or reactions against such interests. Selection of some form of work or career direction and the establishment of a long-term sexual relationship with a partner are taken as marking the onset of adult life.

Before I try to explain the psychological bases of the developmental stages of object relations, it may be of help to show the relation of these stages to those proposed by Freud in the form of a table (see table 32.1).

Since a psychological relatedness does not exist at birth but comes into existence in the course of the first year of life and subsequently undergoes considerable development and change, both in the forms of relatedness and in the objects related to, we would like to know how this occurs. In attempting to furnish an explanation, psychoanalysis has taken on a task that other forms of psychology have generally avoided. Emotional factors are of paramount importance in relationships, yet cognitive—intellectual—capabilities cannot be overlooked. The dichotomy involved has been approached under a number of related but differing rubrics: emotional versus cognitive, drive and affect organization versus cognitive and perceptual organization, biological versus psychological, id versus ego. Perhaps the simplest way to state the problem is this: it is impossible for a child to have a love relationship with someone else until he "knows" that someone else exists, but the knowing in and of itself hardly constitutes a love relationship.

A significant influence on psychoanalytic views of the cognitive side of the development of object relations is the work of Jean Piaget on the development of intelligence in children. He addressed the questions of how and when a child develops the concept of another person who exists independently of the child's needs and perceptions. Piaget worked only with the child's behavior with inanimate objects, "things," not with other people, however, so his findings must be transposed with care to the study of the development of object relations in the psychoanalytic sense. Piaget found that only at five months does the child show unequivocal evidence of recognizing things he has seen before, an accomplishment ascribed by Piaget to a capacity he designated "recognition memory." Not until about eighteen months does the child persistently search for things out of his perceptual and motor field. Piaget called this the achievement of "object permanence," saying that the child had "constructed the object." This is evidence for the presence of a more advanced form of memory known as "evocative memory."

Piaget's ideas about constructing reality or constructing an object and about "object permanence" are important for psychoanalysis. According to the first of these ideas, it is necessary for any individual to create a mental category of objective reality: reality—and its most important aspect for children, other human beings—has to be constructed as part of the mind. "Permanence" is almost synonymous, for constituting objective reality is identical with recognizing the permanence of things. This has been recognized by Hartmann (1950) and Beres and Joseph (1970), among many others, and is contained in Frosch's concept of reality constancy (1966).

The most closely related psychoanalytic concept is that of object constancy. The time at which object constancy is achieved has been put at widely different ages by different authors—from six to twenty-four months or later—which many have found confusing. The discrepancy arises from differing definitions of the term "object constancy" (Fraiberg, 1969). A number of psychoanalytic authors begin by differentiating their object concept from that of academic psychology, to emphasize the psychoanalytic view of the importance of emotional factors. Spitz (1965) presented his carefully worked-out developmental scheme in terms of the development of the libidinal object (Mahler and A. Freud also used this term centrally). Spitz used the concept of "organizers" of mental life: sudden changes in important aspects of behavior that indicate the emergence of a new level of mental organization. The smiling response at two months and stranger anxiety at eight months are indications of such organizers. The first of Spitz's stages of the development of the libidinal object is the pre-objectal or objectless stage, a time without demonstrable psychological relationship, ending at about two months: the onset of the smiling response, or first organizer, marks the start of the second, pre-object phase, from two to eight months, in which the child distinguishes the human face

Table 32.1 Developmental Stages: Freud and Object Relations

Drive	Attitude	Organization	Directedness	Danger Situation	Object Choice	Object-Relatedness
oral	cannibalistic	oral-cannibalistic	autoerotic	energic disequilibrium	sexual object	need satisfaction, biological
			narcissistic	loss of object		need satisfaction, psychological
	sadistic		homosexual object-directed	loss of object's love		ambivalent object-relatedness
anal	retentive	sadistic-anal				
phallic	oedipal	phallic-oedipal	heterosexual object-directed	castration	object choice	object-centered
latency	educable			superego retribution		latent
adolescence	(complex)	genital			object finding	prelude struggle
adult					love relationship: maintain; lose	adult object relationship

from all other stimuli but does not distinguish one human face from another. The second organizer, stranger anxiety, marks the third stage, that of the "establishment of the libidinal object." The latter is not a stage so much as a developmental attainment, following which other people retain an individual identity in the mind of the child.

This is often called "libidinal object constancy." It indicates, according to the theory, that libidinal cathexis of some mental representation of the mother has taken place; this necessarily implies that the cognitive aspect of achieving representation has occurred. In fact, it entails several developmental achievements: the ability to perceive in a discriminatory way ("diacritic perceptual organization"), to retain some aspect of the perception, and to recognize it when it reappears (recognition memory). This much is thought to occur within the stage of need-satisfying object relationship: the object may be cathected and recognized when a need state exists, but the cathexis may be lost or removed when the need is satisfied or if frustration persists too long.

Remember that Piaget demonstrated that a child does not achieve thing permanence—that is, constitute the objective reality of something in the physical world—until about eighteen months. What relation might this have to "constituting the mother as an object"? It seems unlikely that a child could objectivate the mother on a qualitatively different timetable: a different object could not alter the structure of the cognitive act (Fraiberg, 1969). One could argue that, since people are more important to infants than things, the objectivation of the mother might well take temporal precedence over the objectivation of a physical item. But the reverse can also be asserted: that objectivation of an emotionally important person might be more difficult and take longer. Empirical and theoretical criteria for the attainment of object constancy have been stated, starting from differing orientations. One set of such criteria focuses on evidence that the child reliably recognizes the mother and differentiates her from all others. Another set requires evidence that the child can evoke the image of the absent mother—evocative memory, true representation in Piaget's framework—and settle on about eighteen months for the achievement of object constancy. A more stringent set of criteria is employed by Mahler et al. (1975): namely, the ability to evoke the image of the loving mother even when the real mother is absent or angry, and, by these criteria, the achievement of object constancy begins at about twenty-four months and is a more or less lifelong process.

Once again, the relationships between these developmental schemes, which pursue different aspects of development, may be made clearer in tabular form (see table 32.2).

Later, verbal developmental periods have been less controversial and also less well studied by direct observation to this point. Some of the findings of Piaget's psychology may well prove to be stimulating for the psychoanalytic study of these phases in the future.

There are a number of other aspects of development that are considered by psychoanalysis in terms of the object concept or concepts.

Identification with people who are psychologically important—becoming like someone in one or more respects—is important in psychological development. The process of constituting an object is sometimes viewed as a sort of reverse identification and called "self–object differentiation." Whether or not early infancy can be characterized as a time when the child "believes" he or she is fused with the mother, it seems likely that the process of identification is different at different developmental phases. Since identification depends on perception of attributes of an object model and registration and recall of those attributes, it follows that early identifications will be less discriminating or more global than later ones (Jacobson, 1964). Some special processes of identification are thought to be involved in the dissolution of the phallic-oedipal phase and the formation of the mental structure known as the superego. Identification may occur at any time of life. Self representation was described above as analogous to object representation. One way of describing identification in theoretical terms is to say that the self representation is modified according to the representation of an object model.

One further facet of the relation of people and things in psychoanalytic developmental psychology is what is called the "transitional object." This term was introduced by Winnicott (1953) for items, most often a blanket, to which children become closely attached and which they appear to use for comfort or soothing at such times as going to bed and entering new situations. Because such objects are often adopted before most analysts think the child has developed a true representational object capacity, the phenomenon has evoked considerable interest and is being actively studied. Winnicott's concept of transitional object has been widely utilized and apparently accepted, but it entails a number of difficult conceptual problems (Barkin, 1978). Some analysts see transitional object attachment as a normative developmental step, others as a step that may or may not occur and whose significance is unclear, and still others as always an indication of pathology.

Table 32.2 Comparative Developmental Parameters

Age (months)	Affect expression (Emde)	Mental operations (Piaget)	Perception & memory (Spitz)	Libidinal object (Spitz)	Separation-individuation (Mahler)	Object relations (A. Freud)	Sexual organizations (Freud)
0	quiescence, distress		coenesthetic perception	objectless	autistic	biological unity	autoerotism
1		reflex schemas					
2		new schemas				need satisfaction, psychological	oral-cannibalistic
3	social smiling	coordination	diacritic perception	preobject (1st organizer)	symbiotic		
4							
5		objects as extension of action or perception			(hatching)		
6			recognition memory		differentiation		
7					(locomotion)		
8	stranger anxiety	beginning objectivation		libidinal object (2nd organizer)		ambivalent object-relatedness	
9					practicing		
10							
11							
12	peak separation anxiety	solution by trial and error					
13							
14					rapprochement		
15							anal-sadistic
16							
17							
18		object permanence	evocative memory		rapprochement crisis		
19							
20							
21							
22							
23							
24					on the way to object constancy		

OBJECTS AND STRUCTURE

The ego, as a structural mental system, distinguished from the self and the self representation, is thought not to be present at birth but to form in the course of development. Since the functions that comprise the ego are largely those concerned with dealing with the real, or objective, world, many of the considerations mentioned under development of the object concept or cathexis also apply to development of the ego. The establishment of lasting object cathexis is thought to be a pivotal step in the formation of the ego as an organization of the autonomous (ego) functions operating prior to that time. Identifications are also of major significance in the development of ego functions.

The superego is that group of mental functions that has to do with conscience, morality, critical self-observation, self-punishment, and the holding up of ideals. Rudimentary functions of this kind exist prior to and during the phallic-oedipal phase. Prior to the age of five or six the child treats morality as a demand made by the environment; after that time, certain regulations are "internalized" (Hartmann & Loewenstein, 1962). Freud said that this occurs by "introjection" of the authority of the parents —that is, by identification with the conscience or superego of the parents. The superego, then, is the "heir of the oedipus complex," in that attitudes and cathexes that were outwardly directed once again become self-directed.

Once this structure has been formed, aspects of it may again be externalized. This also happens in other situations of mental conflict and is especially notable in adult analyses: the analyst becomes the representative of a superego prohibition or, for example, is assigned to one side of a conflict between active and passive sexual strivings (A. Freud, 1965).

ADDITIONAL ASPECTS OF THE OBJECT CONCEPT

Narcissism, in theoretical terms, is the cathexis of the self representation as opposed to the cathexis of object representations. Freud used the ambiguous term "ego" in this respect, as I have mentioned. Some analysts would prefer to say that the "self," rather than the self representation, is the object of cathexis. Besides the opposition of object and self representations in terms of the distribution of libidinal cathexes, narcissism is involved in the idealization of others and in the functioning of the superego.

Idealization of the love object—Freud initially called it "overvaluation"—is an aspect of the state of being in love. An infant is thought to experience a state that resembles a sense of omnipotent power

when some urgent need is met. When frustrations and a developing sense of reality interfere with this sense, rather than abandoning it altogether, the infant transfers the fantasied omnipotence to the parents, who are then described as "idealized objects" —or, more accurately, representations in a fantasy of omnipotent power that is highly invested emotionally. Other idealized aspects are also included: omniscience and "wonderfulness" in many senses. Being in love involves a revivification of these infantile fantasies, with a strong emphasis on the libidinal rather than the aggressive aspect.

The superego is another repository of infantile narcissism. Freud initially called this structure the "ego ideal or ideal ego"—implying an idea of what one might wish to be, in the senses of power or beauty or acclaim, rather than morality. This aspect of superego functioning is known as the holding up of ideals. These various relations between cathexes of object and self representations and between the ego and the superego are involved in the complex process of the maintenance or regulation of self-esteem.

Being in love is only one of many instances that I have passed over which involve the relation between infantile object choices and relationships with other persons in adult life. I shall now briefly consider three topics that are related to this issue.

Fixation may refer to an object or to a mode of gratification, or, combining the two, to a mode of relating characteristics of an earlier phase in the development of object relations. Brenner says, "We have good reason to believe . . . that no really strong libidinal cathexis is ever completely abandoned" (1973, p. 26). Kestenberg (1971) proposed that each step forward in sexual organization is accompanied by a sense of loss until a way is found to reestablish the essential feeling of gratification of the earlier mode and of the object of that mode. The fantasies of latency children and adolescents, especially what Freud called "family romance fantasies" (1909), seem to serve as bridging structures from earlier to later loves. When such processes do not occur to the usual extent, however they are explained, we speak of fixation. The flow of development (or libido) may also reverse direction, a process known as *regression*—a return in fantasy to an earlier mode of gratification or an earlier object.

These considerations bring up the problem of the relation of fantasy objects to real objects, especially in fantasies accompanying masturbation. The figures in conscious masturbation fantasies are in the category of mental images—that is, aspects of experiential mental content. They are usually composite disguises, derived from some aspect of current experience plus aspects of memory traces of experiences with prior love objects which are kept unconscious. These worked-over memory traces include aspects of the self representation as well as of layers of object representations, so that the masturbatory fantasy characteristically has the subject playing both male and female roles. While the specific properties of the amalgam may be different in fantasies that are not accompanied by sexual affect or a masturbatory action, the conscious mental images–fantasy objects are nevertheless derived from past experience.

Transference, from the standpoint of the object concept, is another instance in which representations of past love objects and past modes of gratification and traumatization are revivified and, combined with aspects of current experience, emerge as mental content. In this instance we are more concerned, at least initially, with transferred attitudes than with the underlying fantasies.

OBJECT RELATIONS THEORIES

I have defined object relations, following Brenner, as the attitudes and behavior of someone toward the people and things that are psychologically important to that person. In that sense the term "object relations" has little to do with what are called "object relations theories." An object relations theory is a system of psychological explanation characterized by a fundamental premise that the mind is essentially comprised of elements of some sort which are "taken in" from outside the subject organism. For the most part, the elements hypothetically taken in are aspects of functions of other persons. The taking-in process is usually designated by a single term, such as "incorporation" or "introjection" or "internalization," although these terms have not been defined within the framework of any object relations theory in any precise way. The resulting model of the mind necessarily explains mental functions in terms of relations between the various elements that have been taken in.

Object relations theories in the past have often been collectively designated as "the British school," because of their origin in England in the work of Melanie Klein, Fairbairn, Balint, and Winnicott. For some years, many analysts in South America have subscribed to object relations theories, and, more recently, these theories have found advocates in the United States. Kernberg is perhaps the most prominent American proponent of a recognized object relations theory, but Loewald, Meissner, Modell, and Schafer, among others, have also developed these ideas. According to the characterization that I have proposed, the theoretical statements of Kohut and

his followers in self psychology and those of J. Sandler also fall into the category of object relations theories.

The object concepts that comprise an important part of each of the object relations theories will be briefly discussed here; but the theories themselves will be taken up only to the extent necessary to see the context of the object concept.

Melanie Klein, whose ideas have antecedents in the work of Ferenczi and Abraham, was the first to develop an extensive object relations theory. She accepted Freud's proposals of fundamental life and death drives as matters of clinical observation. In her theory, "the ego," essentially an undefined term, is active at least from birth on, attempting to "deflect" the death instinct which threatens the organism. The ego adopts, or perhaps consists of, processes of projection, introjection, and splitting to achieve this deflection. From birth on, the ego carries out simultaneous acts of projection of libido and aggression and introjection of objects. (It is difficult to answer the question, object of what?) Object relations, then, according to this theory, exist from birth on. The results of these processes are, first, "introjects," or "internal objects." Then, because these processes occur over and over, the external objects into which aggression and libido have been projected are also introjected or reintrojected. Because of the mechanism of splitting, objects that are mostly libidinal and objects that are mostly aggressive arise, known as "good object," or "good breast," and "bad object," or "bad breast." There are, thus, in Klein's theory, shortly after birth, four objects: internal good and bad, external good and bad. All these fluctuate, and object relations exist between any combination, including between various internal objects. The objects are constructed, in this theoretical framework, by projection and introjection of libido, aggression, and the objects to which the instincts are attached, rather than through any cognitive process.

Once these internal objects have been established, theoretically in the manner just described, subsequent development is worked out in terms of relations between them, the ego, and the instincts. As Klein elaborated her theory, however, additional terms were required. On the basis of a comparison of paranoid-schizophrenic psychoses with manic-depressive psychoses in adults, Klein arrived at two developmental stages that, she proposed, normally occur in the first year of life and are never thereafter abandoned. She called them the "paranoid-schizoid position" and the "depressive position," distinguished on the basis of the type of anxiety the infant is postulated to feel and on the kind of "object" thought to be involved. "Part objects" are characteristic of the paranoid-schizoid position; examples include the good internalized breast, the bad devouring breast, and the penis of the father, to which good and bad qualities are also attributed. Attainment of the depressive position is concordant with a "relation to a whole object [so that] the mother and the father, and other members of the family are introjected as persons in good or bad aspects"—that is, as "whole objects," rather than part objects (Klein, 1952, 1959). Segal (1973), a follower of Klein, points out that Kleinian theory includes an additional category of objects known as "ideal objects," which enter into the interplay with all the other forms of internal and external objects.

Kleinian theory has been criticized on the grounds that it condenses most of development into the first year of life, neglects cognitive development almost entirely, proposes psychoses in infancy as part of normal development, and treats physical and mental processes as identical and in an ambiguously concrete way (see, for example, Arlow, 1980).

Fairbairn, who specifically called his work "an object relations theory of the personality" (1952), began as a follower of Klein but later diverged from her in many ways. From the start, he shared with her the idea that the "figures" that appear in dreams are "personifications" of mental structures. But when he found that the personifications were too complex and varied to be understood as id or ego or superego, he began to develop his own theory, based on the Kleinian idea of the early internalization of objects, which allowed for a multiplicity of mental structures that might be personified in a dream. While his terminology at times became exotic, he developed a set of propositions that were internally consistent though only questionably related to clinical evidence. He, like Klein, thought that an ego is present at birth, but he did away with the concepts of id and death instinct. The ego and, hence, drives were held to be object-seeking rather than pleasure-seeking. Internalization was seen as defensive, a process, and not just a fantasy, and the source of mental structure. Fairbairn proposed three internal objects, each of which carried with it a portion of the original ego, the object and ego portion forming the essential structural units of the mind. The conscious, or central, ego is associated with the main core of the internalized object, called the "ideal object." There are also two repressed internal objects: the "exciting, or libidinal object" and the "rejecting, or antilibidinal object" (earlier called the "internal saboteur"), each of which is associated with a corresponding repressed ego portion. Fairbairn distinguished between "natural objects" and "symbolic

objects" and used the term "part object" in a way quite similar to Klein.

Fairbairn's work has been criticized particularly on the grounds that the internal or internalized objects function within the theory as dynamic in and of themselves—that is, as suppliers of motivation.

Kernberg (1976, 1980) also presented his work under the designation of object relations theory and acknowledged his indebtedness to Klein and Fairbairn, among others. He attempted to combine an object relations theory, as explanatory of the earlier stages of development and more serious forms of psychopathology, with the ego–id–superego model, used to explain oedipal development and neurotic psychopathology. His fundamental concept was internalization, or introjection, and his fundamental building blocks of mind were units of internalized object relations, further specified as taking the form of a self image plus an object image linked by an affect. Drives arise secondarily from these units, in his view, as does all mental structure. Despite his efforts to link his work with ego psychology, Kernberg's object concept remained identical with that of Klein and Fairbairn and distinctly different from the various object concepts described earlier in this chapter.

Kohut, originator of the self psychology movement in the United States, said that the most crucial concept in his work was that of "selfobject" (1971, 1977) and that his concept of "transmuting internalization" correlated his theories of therapy and development. Kohut postulated an independent narcissistic libido, perhaps with several subtypes, at first in addition to Freud's libido concept, later instead of that concept. Selfobject was initially conceptualized within the framework of Freud's libido theory: selfobjects are "archaic objects cathected with narcissistic libido . . . still in intimate connection with the archaic self (i.e., objects which are not experienced as separate and independent of the self)" (1971, p. 3). Later (Kohut & Wolf, 1978), two kinds of selfobjects were postulated: "those who respond to and confirm the child's innate sense of vigor, greatness and perfection"—mirroring selfobjects— and "those to whom the child can look up and with whom he can merge as an image of calmness, infallibility and omnipotence"—the idealized parent imago (p. 414). (See also Ornstein, 1978, pp. 60–61.) The "self," Kohut's other major construct, is different from the concept of self representation and from that of self as defined earlier in this chapter; it remains to be clearly defined (although, again, see Kohut & Wolf, 1978). Kohut also used the term "imago" extensively, to indicate some mental object concept, but in an undefined way: how an image of an "object" comes into being as an imago is not specified. Withdrawal of cathexes of narcissistic libido from an imago because of a disappointment (due to empathic failure by the care-taking person) is followed by a process of internalization that involves "a depersonalizing of the introjected aspects of the image of the object . . . [so that] the internal structure now performs the functions which the object used to perform." This is what is called "transmuting internalization" (1971, pp. 49–51, 105–106).

From the standpoint of the object concept, Kohut's self psychology is clearly an object relations theory: mental structure is formed through the internalization of objects and the functions of objects. Kohut's theory has been criticized for its lack of definition of the central term "self" and for internal inconsistencies in general.

The last object relations theory that I will mention here is that of Sandler, who started with Freud's libidinal object concept, then introduced an intermediate-level theoretical construct that he called the "representational world" (Sandler & Rosenblatt, 1962). The construction of representations in the (mental) representational world, according to Sandler's theory, first of all makes perception possible and, later, is the basis of introjection when the superego is formed. He next tried to bridge the gap between psychoanalytic concepts of mental life and of actual behavior, by applying social theory to the latter (Sandler & Sandler, 1978), He then explained social role behavior as determined not by wishes and drives via interaction with psychological structures but rather by the interaction of self and object representations in the representational world. Sandler's effort to take constructs that apply to mental life from a theory of social behavior is criticized because it results in replacing mental constructs by a theory of social behavior.

SUMMARY

The pervasiveness of the concept "object" in psychoanalysis is illustrated by the scope of this chapter and the very wide range of observational and theoretical topics touched upon. The topic of almost every section is taken up from a different viewpoint in other chapters of this volume. Here I have considered one set of definitions of the fundamental terms in this area of conceptualization, traced the development of the object concept in Freud's work, attempted to locate the object concept in current psychoanalytic theory, then focused particularly on the place of the object concept in psychoanalytic understanding of human development, and ended with brief remarks on object relations theories.

REFERENCES

Abraham, K. (1924). A short study of the development of the libido. Rpt. in *Selected Papers of Karl Abraham,* pp. 418–502. New York: Basic Books, 1953.

Altman, L. (1977). Some vicissitudes of love. *J. Amer. Psychoanal. Assn.,* 25:35–52.

Arlow, J. A. (1969). Fantasy, memory and reality testing. *Psychoanal. Q.,* 38:28–51.

———. (1980). Object concept and object choice. *Psychoanal. Q.,* 49:109–133.

Bak, R. (1973). Being in love and object loss. *Int. J. Psychoanal.,* 54:1–8.

Barkin, L. (1978). The concept of the transitional object. In *Between Reality and Fantasy,* ed. S. A. Grolnick, L. Barkin & W. Muensterberger, pp. 513–536. New York: Aronson.

Beres, D., & Joseph, E. D. (1970). The concept of mental representation in psychoanalysis. *Int. J. Psychoanal.,* 51:1–9.

Bergmann, M. S. (1980). On the intrapsychic function of falling in love. *Psychoanal. Q.,* 49:56–77.

Brenner, C. (1973). *An Elementary Textbook of Psychoanalysis.* Rpt. New York: Anchor Books, 1974.

———. (1982). *The Mind in Conflict.* New York: Int. Univ. Press.

Compton, A. (1981). On the psychoanalytic theory of instinctual drives: II. *Psychoanal. Q.,* 50:219–237.

———. (1985a). The concept of identification in the work of Freud, Ferenczi, and Abraham. *Psychoanal. Q.,* 54:200–233.

———. (1985b). The development of the drive object concept in Freud's work, 1905–1915. *J. Amer. Psychoanal. Assn.,* 33:93–115.

———. (1986a). The beginnings of the object concept in psychoanalysis. In *Psychoanalysis: The Science of Mental Conflict,* ed. A. D. Richards & M. S. Willick, pp. 177–189. New York: Analytic Press.

———. (1986b). Freud: objects and structure, 1915–1938. *J. Amer. Psychoanal. Assn.,* 34:561–590.

———. (1987). Objects and attitudes. *J. Amer. Psychoanal. Assn.,* 35:609–628.

Edgcumbe, R., & Burgner, M. (1972). Some problems in the conceptualization of early object relationships: I. *Psychoanal. Study Child,* 27:283–314.

Emde, R. N., Gaensbauer, T. J., & Harmon, R. J. (1976). *Emotional Expression in Infancy.* Psychological Issues, monograph 37. New York: Int. Univ. Press.

Fairbairn, W. R. D. (1952). *Psycho-Analytic Studies*

of the Personality. London: Routledge & Kegan Paul.

———. (1963). Synopsis of an object relations theory of the personality. *Int. J. Psychoanal.,* 44:224–225.

Ferenczi, S. (1909). Introjection and transference. Rpt. in *Sex and Psychoanalysis,* pp. 30–79. New York: Dover Books, 1956.

Fraiberg, S. (1969). Libidinal object constancy and mental representation. *Psychoanal. Study Child,* 24:9–47.

Freud, A. (1965). *Normality and Pathology in Childhood.* New York: Int. Univ. Press.

Freud, A., and Burlingham, D. (1945). *Infants without Families.* New York: Int. Univ. Press.

Freud, S. (1895a). Draft G. Melancholia. *SE,* 1:200–206.

———. (1895b). Project for a scientific psychology. *SE,* 1:283–397.

———. (1900). *The Interpretation of Dreams. SE,* 4 & 5.

———. (1905). *Three Essays on the Theory of Sexuality. SE,* 7:125–243.

———. (1909). Family romances. *SE,* 9:235–241.

———. (1910). *Leonardo Da Vinci and a Memory of His Childhood. SE,* 11:63–137.

———. (1913). *Totem and Taboo, SE,* 13:1–161.

———. (1915). Instincts and their vicissitudes. *SE,* 14:111–140.

———. (1917). Mourning and melancholia. *SE,* 14:237–260.

———. (1921). *Group Psychology and the Analysis of the Ego. SE,* 18:67–143.

———. (1923a). *The Ego and the Id. SE,* 19:3–66.

———. (1923b). The infantile genital organization. *SE,* 19:141–145.

———. (1926). *Inhibitions, Symptoms and Anxiety. SE,* 20:77–175.

Frosch, J. (1966). A note on reality constancy. In *Psychoanalysis: A General Psychology,* ed. R. M. Loewenstein et al., pp. 349–376. New York: Int. Univ. Press.

Furman, E. (1974). *A Child's Parent Dies.* New Haven: Yale Univ. Press.

Hartmann, H. (1950). Comments on the psychoanalytic theory of the ego. In *Essays on Ego Psychology,* pp. 113–141. New York: Int. Univ. Press, 1964.

———. (1964). Introduction to *Essays on Ego Psychology,* pp. ix–xv. New York: Int. Univ. Press.

Hartmann, H., & Loewenstein, R. M. (1962). *Notes on the Superego. Psychological Issues,* monograph 14. New York: Int. Univ. Press.

Jacobson, E. (1964). *The Self and the Object World.* New York: Int. Univ. Press.

———. (1965). The return of the lost parent. In *Drives, Affects, Behavior,* ed. M. Schur, vol. 2, pp. 193–211. New York: Int. Univ. Press.

———. (1971). A special response to early object loss. In *Depression,* pp. 185–203. New York: Int. Univ. Press.

Kernberg, O. F. (1976). *Object Relations Theory and Clinical Psychoanalysis.* New York: Aronson.

———. (1980). *Internal World and External Reality.* New York: Aronson.

Kestenberg, J. S. (1971). From organ–object imagery to self and object representations. In *Separation-Individuation,* ed. J. B. McDevitt & C. F. Settlage, pp. 75–99. New York: Int. Univ. Press.

Klein, M. (1952). Some theoretical conclusions regarding the emotional life of the infant. In *Envy and Gratitude,* pp. 61–93. New York: Delacorte Press, 1975.

———. (1959). On the development of mental functioning. In *Envy and Gratitude,* pp. 236–246. New York: Delacorte Press, 1975.

Kohut, H. (1971). *The Analysis of the Self.* New York: Int. Univ. Press.

———. (1977). *The Restoration of the Self.* New York: Int. Univ. Press.

Kohut, H., & Wolf, E. S. (1978). The disorders of the self and their treatment. *Int. J. Psychoanal.,* 59:413–425.

Kris, E. (1956). The recovery of childhood memories in psychoanalysis. *Psychoanal. Study Child,* 11:54–88.

Mahler, M. S., Pine, F., & Bergman, A. (1975). *The Psychological Birth of the Human Infant.* New York: Basic Books.

Moore, B. E., & Fine, B. D., eds. (1990). *Psychoanalytic Terms and Concepts.* New Haven: Yale Univ. Press & American Psychoanalytic Association.

Ornstein, P. (1978). Introduction to *The Search for the Self,* vol. 1, pp. 1–106. New York: Int. Univ. Press.

Piaget, J. (1932). *The Language and Thought of the Child.* New York: Meridian Books, 1955.

———. (1936). *The Origins of Intelligence in Children.* New York: Int. Univ. Press.

Pollock, G. H. (1961). Mourning and adaptation. *Int. J. Psychoanal.,* 42:341–361.

Sandler, J., & Rosenblatt, B. (1962). The concept of the representational world. *Psychoanal. Study Child,* 17:285–296.

Sandler, J., & Sandler, A.-M. (1978). On the development of object relationships and affects. *Int. J. Psychoanal.,* 59:285–296.

Segal, H. (1973). *Introduction to the Work of Melanie Klein.* London: Hogarth Press.

Spitz, R. A. (1965). *The First Year of Life*. New York: Int. Univ. Press.

Wallerstein, R. S. (1973). Psychoanalytic perspectives on reality. Rpt. in *Psychotherapy and Psychoanalysis*, pp. 415–441. New York: Int. Univ. Press, 1975.

Winnicott, D. W. (1953). Transitional objects and transitional phenomena. *Int. J. Psychoanal.*, 34: 89–97.

33

PSYCHOANALYTIC OBJECT RELATIONS THEORIES

DEFINITIONS AND CONTROVERSIES: AN OVERVIEW

Psychoanalytic object relations theories constitute so broad a spectrum of approaches that it might be best to define them on the basis of what they include or exclude. The broadest definition might state that, by its very nature, psychoanalysis itself is an object relations theory: all psychoanalytic theorizing deals, after all, with the impact of early object relations on the genesis of unconscious conflict, the development of psychic structure, and the reactualization or enactment of past, pathogenic, internalized object relations in present transference developments in the psychoanalytic situation. But such a definition dissolves the specificity of the concept of object relations theory.

A second definition, the narrowest, would restrict object relations theory to the so-called British school, particularly the work of Melanie Klein (1946, 1948, 1957), Ronald Fairbairn (1954), and Donald Winnicott (1958, 1965, 1971). While historically appropriate, so restrictive a definition excludes the contributions from ego psychology by Erik Erikson (1959), Edith Jacobson (1964, 1971), Margaret Mahler and colleagues (Mahler & Furer, 1968; Mahler et al., 1975), Hans Loewald (1960, 1980), Joseph Sandler (1987), and myself (Kernberg, 1976, 1980, 1984), as well as the interpersonal approach of Harry Stack Sullivan (1953, 1962)

and Greenberg and Mitchell (1983) and Mitchell (1988).

A third definition of what constitutes object relations theory—my own—would include the British school *and* the ideas of the theoreticians just listed. Psychoanalytic object relations theories would then be defined as those that place the internalization, structuralization, and clinical reactivation (in the transference and countertransference) of the earliest dyadic object relations at the center of their motivational (genetic and developmental), structural, and clinical formulations. "Internalization of object relations" refers to the concept that, in all interactions of the infant and child with the significant parental figures, what the infant internalizes is not an image or representation of the other ("the object") but the relationship between the self and the other, in the form of a self image or self representation interacting with an object image or object representation. This internal structure replicates in the intrapsychic world both real and fantasied relationships with significant others. This third definition constitutes the frame for what follows.

Several major issues separate object relations theories, the most important of which is the extent to which a theory is perceived as harmonious with or in opposition to Freud's traditional drive theory (Freud, 1920, 1923, 1933); that is, whether object relations are seen as replacing drives as the motivational system for human behavior. From this perspective, Klein, Mahler, and Jacobson occupy one pole, in that they combine Freud's dual drive theory with an object relations approach. For Fairbairn and Sullivan, on the other hand, object relations themselves replace Freud's drives as the major motivational system. Contemporary interpersonal psychoanalysis as represented by Greenberg and Mitchell (1983) and Mitchell (1988), based on an integration of principally Fairbairnian (1954) and Sullivanian (1953, 1962) concepts, asserts the essential incompatibility between drive-based and object-relations-based models of psychic motivational systems. Winnicott (1958, 1965, 1971), Loewald (1960, 1980), and Sandler (1987), each for different reasons, maintain an intermediate posture; they perceive the affective frame of the infant–mother relationship as a crucial determinant in shaping the development of drives. While adhering to Freud's dual drive theory, I consider drives supraordinate motivational systems, with affects as their constituent components (Kernberg, 1976, 1984).

A related controversy has to do with the origin and role of aggression as a motivator of behavior. Those theoreticians who reject the idea of inborn drives (Sullivan) or equate libido with the search for object relations (Fairbairn) conceptualize aggression as secondary to the frustration of libidinal needs, particularly traumatic experiences in the early mother–infant dyad. Theoreticians who adhere to Freud's dual drive theory, by contrast, believe that aggression is inborn and plays an important part in shaping early interactions; this group includes Klein in particular and to some extent Winnicott, as well as the ego psychology object relations theoreticians. It should be noted, however, that although Fairbairn in theory rejects the idea of an inborn aggressive drive, in clinical practice he pays considerable attention to the structuralization of aggressively invested, internalized object relations and their interpretation in the transference.

Another area of controversy is the extent to which actual experiences with significant others in infancy and early childhood are seen as transformed by the combination of unconscious fantasy with the building of psychic structure that reflects intrapsychic conflicts. For the British school—in spite of the heavy emphasis of Winnicott and Fairbairn on the reality aspects of the early interactions between infant and mother—the effects of unconscious fantasy upon the development of psychic structures and the defensive reshaping of structuralized internalized object relationships result in a significant gap between actual early experience and unconsciously reactivated object relations in the transference, with Kleinians insisting on the fantastic nature of the in-

ternalized world of object relations. By contrast, for interpersonal psychoanalysts, particularly Sullivan (1953, 1962), Fromm-Reichmann (1950, 1959), and Guntrip (1961, 1968, 1971), early internalized object relations are maintained with relatively little structural change, so that transference developments tend to be interpreted as reflecting fairly closely actual, past, traumatic, internalized object relations. Along with Jacobson, Mahler, and Sandler, I take an intermediate position in this respect, with a particular emphasis on the characterological transformations and fixations of internalized object relations.

The various theories differ, too, in technique—that is, in the extent to which transference enactments are interpreted mostly in terms of the activation of the patient's intrapsychic conflicts versus whether transference and countertransference are seen as inextricably linked, the former being shaped in part by the latter and by the analyst's personality. This position views the patient–analyst dyad as a new, potentially growth-promoting experience which makes an important contribution to the resolution of the patient's unconscious conflicts.

Klein and her followers, as well as Jacobson, Mahler, and myself, are close to the classical technique that emphasizes the intrapsychic conflicts aspects of the transference, with a limited utilization of countertransference elements, although I focus more sharply than the others on countertransference, especially in my treatment of severe character pathology. Interpersonal psychoanalysis, as represented by Guntrip (1961, 1968), who was influenced by Fairbairn and Winnicott, and Greenberg and Mitchell (1983) and Mitchell (1988), places heavy emphasis on the mutual influence of transference and countertransference and the reality aspects of the therapeutic interactions derived from the analyst's personality.

Certain characteristics distinguish object relations theories in general from other approaches. My ego-psychological object relations theory differs from traditional ego psychology in its emphasis on the indissoluble integration of drives with object relations, in seeing each drive derivative as constituted by a self representation and a related object representation linked by an affect disposition. For Jacobson, Mahler, and myself, affects are not simply discharge manifestations of drives but sustained tension states that represent the drive derivative embedded in the relationship between self and object representation. By contrast, traditional ego psychology assumes a much looser relationship between drive derivatives and their investments in objects.

Also, ego-psychological object relations theory focuses strongly on the early, pre-oedipal stages of development, whereas traditional ego psychology stresses oedipal conflicts. In addition, whereas traditional ego psychology stresses the interplay of impulse and defense in terms of impersonal defense mechanisms directed against diffuse drive derivatives, ego-psychological object relations theory describes the impulse–defense equilibrium in terms of impulsively and defensively activated object relations in the transference (and countertransference) (Kernberg, 1987, 1988). Finally, ego-psychological object relations theory focuses on the structural characteristics of the early ego–id matrix before the consolidation of the tripartite structure, particularly in exploring severe psychopathologies; by contrast, traditional ego psychology tends to explore all psychopathology within the framework of the tripartite structure (Arlow & Brenner, 1964).

Interpersonal object relations theory has significant similarities to Kohut's (1971, 1972, 1977) self psychology. In fact, Fairbairn, Winnicott, Kohut, and Sullivan all stress the reality aspects of good versus bad mothering and the influence of satisfactory early relationships between the infant and the mother in setting up the structure of the normal self. A basic difference, however, between all object relations theories—including interpersonal psychoanalysis—and Kohut's self psychology is that Kohut's developmental model centers on the gradual consolidation of an archaic grandiose self in relationship to idealized "selfobjects," while all "bad" relationships are not conceptualized as internalized object relations; in Kohut's view, aggression is conceptualized as a disintegration product and not part of structured internalized object relations. By contrast with self psychology, object relations theories, even those that deny aggression as a drive (Fairbairn and Sullivan), stress the importance of the internalization of "bad" object relations—that is, aggressively invested, dissociated representations of self and objects. These differing formulations have significant impact on technique, particularly on the conceptualization and management of negative transference.

Finally, contrast may be made between object relations theories and French approaches, both Lacanian (Roudinesco, 1990) and mainstream psychoanalysis (Oliner, 1988). The latter has maintained close links with traditional psychoanalysis, including the British object relations theories. Insofar as Lacan (1966) conceptualizes the unconscious as a natural language and focuses on the cognitive aspects of unconscious development, he underemphasizes affect —a dominant element of object relations theories. At the same time, in postulating a very early oedipal structuralization of all infant–mother interactions, Lacan emphasizes archaic oedipal developments,

which implicitly links his formulations with those of Klein. French mainstream analysis also focuses on archaic aspects of oedipal developments, but it places a much more traditional emphasis on Freud's dual drive theory and on the affective nature of the early ego–id (Chasseguet-Smirgel, 1986). Insofar as neither mainstream nor Lacanian psychoanalysis spells out specific structural consequences of dyadic internalized object relations, however, neither one fits the definition that frames the field of object relations theory that I am proposing here.

Object relations theories have several additional characteristics in common. They all focus on the influence of the vicissitudes of early developmental stages in the formation of the psychic apparatus. They are all interested in normal and pathological development of the self and in identity formation; and they accept an internalized world of object relations as part of their conceptualization of the psychic apparatus. Insofar as they deal with the relationship between past and present intrapsychic and interpersonal object relations, they also provide links to family structure and group psychology. Their interest in the affective aspects of the relationship between self and object, between self representations and object representations, leads them to a particular concern with the origin and vicissitudes of early affects, which, in turn, provides a linkage between object relations theory, empirical research on affect development, and neurophysiology.

All object relations theories focus heavily on the enactment of internalized object relations in the transference and on the analysis of countertransference in the development of interpretive strategies. They are particularly concerned with severe psychopathologies, including those psychotic patients still approachable with psychoanalytic techniques, borderline conditions and severe narcissistic character pathology, and the perversions. Object relations theories explore primitive defensive operations and object relations both in cases of severe psychopathology and at points of severe regression with all patients.

REPRESENTATIVE OBJECT RELATIONS THEORIES

Melanie Klein

Klein's (1946, 1948) object relations theory fully incorporates Freud's dual drive theory, emphasizing particularly the importance of inborn aggression as a reflection of the death instinct. Both the death and the life instinct operate from birth on and influence the development of the earliest object relations; they determine the structure of early ego and early superego formation. Both the death and the life instinct find mental expression in the form of unconscious fantasy, the content of which represents the self and objects under the influence of primitive emotions reflecting the drives. Envy, greed, and, to some extent, jealousy later on are specific emotions derived from oral aggression. The life instinct, or libido, is expressed from birth on in pleasurable contacts with gratifying objects, primarily the good breast. These objects are invested with libido and are introjected as internal objects infused with emotions representing libido. The projection of the good inner object onto new objects is the basis of trust, of the wish to explore reality, and of learning and knowledge. Gratitude is the predominant emotion linked with the expression of libido.

The death instinct, active from birth on and expressed in primitive emotions, particularly envy, is projected outward in the form of fears of persecution and annihilation. All early experiences of tension and displeasure are expelled in an effort to preserve unsullied pleasure within the ego; these experiences are projected into what becomes persecutory objects. From the beginning of life, an ego is in operation, developing defenses against anxiety, processes of introjection and projection, and object relations and carrying out integration and synthesis. Anxiety constitutes the ego's response to the expression of the death instinct; it is reinforced by the separation caused by birth and by the frustration of oral needs.

Anxiety becomes fear of persecutory objects and later, through introjection of aggression in the form of internalized bad objects, the fear of being persecuted from within and without. Inner persecutors constitute the origin of primitive superego anxiety. The projection of inner tension states and of painful external stimuli constitutes the origin of paranoid fears; but the projection of pleasurable states, reflecting basically the life instinct, gives rise to basic trust. External stimuli invested with libido or aggression become primitive objects.

Objects are, at first, split-off or part objects and only later become total or whole objects; the tendency to perceive objects as either ideal (all good) or persecutory (all bad) is the consequence of the defense of splitting. The predominance of part object relationships in earliest life is a consequence of the maximal operation of splitting mechanisms at that time. Only later, when splitting mechanisms decrease, is a synthesis of good and bad aspects of objects possible; ambivalence toward whole objects can now be tolerated and acknowledged.

Klein described two basic constellations of defenses and object relations which constitute, from the first year of life on, ever-recurring polarities of human experience, being reenacted at all stages of psychosexual development. She called these the "paranoid-schizoid position" and the "depressive position." The paranoid-schizoid position is the earliest developmental stage; it culminates within the first half of the first year of life and is characterized by the predominance of splitting and other related mechanisms, by part object relations, and by paranoid fears about the preservation or survival of the ego. These paranoid fears stem from oral-sadistic and anal-sadistic impulses. Excessive persecutory fears can result in pathological strengthening and fixation at this first position, which underlies the development of schizophrenia and paranoid psychosis.

The principal defenses of the paranoid-schizoid position are splitting, idealization, denial of internal and external reality, stifling and artificiality of emotions, and projective identification. Projective identification, originally described by Klein, is of fundamental importance within this group of primitive defenses.

The depressive position dominates during the second half of the first year of life. Splitting processes begin to diminish, with a growing awareness that the good and bad external objects are really one and that mother as a whole object has good and bad parts. The infant's recognition of his or her own aggression toward the good object that has been perceived as bad reduces projection. By contrast with the persecutory fears characteristic of the paranoid-schizoid position, the predominant fear in the depressive position is no longer of external attack but of harming the good internal and external objects.

The basic fear concerning the survival of good internal and external objects constitutes depressive anxiety or guilt, the primary emotion of the depressive position. The preservation of good objects now becomes more important than the preservation of the ego. Internal bad objects that are no longer projected constitute the primary superego, which attacks the ego with guilt feelings. Within the superego, bad internal objects may contaminate good internal objects, which, because of their demanding or standard-setting nature, have also been internalized into the superego, bringing about cruel demands for perfection.

Under normal conditions, the following mechanisms characteristic of the depressive position permit the working through of that position: reparation —the origin, in Klein's thinking, of sublimation; an increase in reality testing; ambivalence—the capacity to become aware of and tolerate love and hate toward the same object, with love predominating over hate in emotional reactions to whole objects; and gratitude, which is reinforced by guilt. Normal mourning, for Klein, always implied guilt, reactivating the guilt of the depressive position; introjection not only of the lost external object but also of the internal good object that is felt to be threatened; and gratification at being alive, including the activation of manic triumph and secondary guilt over it.

Pathological developments of the depressive position are represented by the manic defenses, which include reactivation of idealization as a way of preserving the good internal and external objects in the face of ambivalence toward them, a sense of triumph over the lost object, and contempt. Another major pathological development of the depressive position is pathological mourning, characterized by the loss of the good external and internal objects caused by the fantasied destructive effects of the hatred directed toward them, failure of efforts at compensation by means of idealization, and a circular reaction of guilt, self-reproaches, and despair. Depressive psychosis constitutes the final outcome of pathological mourning, while hypomanic syndromes reflect the pathological predominance of the constellation of manic defenses. Such manic syndromes include, in addition to the manic defenses mentioned, identification with the superego, compulsive introjection, manic triumph, and extreme manic idealization.

Both the ego and the early superego are constituted, in Kleinian theory, of internalized object relations. All conflict-laden situations and developmental stages reactivate paranoid-schizoid and depressive object relations and defenses; the systematic analysis of these mechanisms in the transference is a central aspect of Kleinian technique (Segal, 1967).

Klein (1948) also proposed that the oedipus complex is activated toward the end of the first year of life. She believed that these early oedipal developments were secondary to the displacement from mother to father of the infant's paranoid-schizoid and depressive position. The transfer of oral dependency from mother to father dominates the early positive oedipus complex in girls and the early negative oedipus complex in boys, and the transfer of aggressive fears and fantasies from mother to father produces fantasies of dangerous sexual organs and destructive parental sexual relations. The projection of oral and anal-sadistic fantasies onto the genitals of both sexes colors early castration anxiety in both sexes. Oral envy of mother is the origin of penis envy in girls and oedipal jealousy and rivalry in both sexes. The transfer of good object relations to the oedipal object and to the fantasied sexual relations of the parents determines the capacity for normal oedipal identifications and development and the capacity for good sexual relations; the predominance

of aggressive infiltration of the fantastic views of the primal scene and of the relations with both parents results in severe oedipal inhibitions and conflicts.

Kleinian technique, in addition to focusing on the analysis of primitive object relations and defenses, strongly insists on the primacy of the analysis of the transference from very early on in the treatment and on the analysis in depth of transference developments to their dominant and, more often than not, primitive levels of anxiety. The early Kleinian tendency to interpret most transference reactions as reflecting the earliest developments in the first year of life, however, has gradually shifted in contemporary Kleinian technique toward an emphasis on the analysis of unconscious meanings in the "here and now" and a more gradual and cautious approach to genetic reconstructions. Segal (1981), Rosenfeld (1987), and Spillius and Feldman (1989) represent the mainstream Kleinian approach. Bion (1967, 1970) and Meltzer and colleagues (Meltzer, 1973; Meltzer et al., 1975; Meltzer & Williams, 1988) have developed particular extensions of Klein's approach that may be characterized as more radical transformations of classical psychoanalysis in the light of Kleinian developments.

Ronald Fairbairn

Fairbairn's (1954) object relations theory is closely related to Klein's. He proposed that an ego is present from birth, that libido is a function of the ego, and that there is no death instinct, aggression being in reaction to frustration or deprivation. For Fairbairn, the ego (and therefore libido) is fundamentally object-seeking, and libido is essentially reality-oriented in promoting the attachment of the infant to the earliest objects: first, the mother's breast, and later, the mother as a total person. The earliest and original form of anxiety, Fairbairn suggests, is separation anxiety, activated when frustrations—largely temporary separations from the mother—occur. These frustrations bring about the internalization of the object and also ambivalence toward it.

Fairbairn postulated that two aspects of the internalized object—its exciting and its frustrating aspects—are split off from the main core of the object and are repressed by the ego. There thus come to be two repressed internal objects: the exciting (or libidinal) and the rejecting (or antilibidinal) object. Both these internal objects carry with them into repression parts of the ego by which they are cathected, leaving the central ego unrepressed but acting as the agent of repression. In consequence, the original ego is split into three egos: a central (conscious) ego attached to an ideal object (ego ideal), a repressed libidinal ego attached to the exciting (or libidinal) object, and a repressed antilibidinal ego attached to the rejecting (or antilibidinal) object.

This tripartite structure differs from Freud's tripartite structure in that there is no id and all three structures are fundamentally ego structures. Fairbairn considers this splitting of the ego to be in the service of defense; the splitting of a fundamental core object that was libidinally invested, yet frustrating at the same time—a basic "schizoid" operation—leads to the repression of the frustrating aspect of the object as a bad internal object (the antilibidinal object) and of the exciting aspect of the object as the unavailable, repressed libidinal object.

In psychoanalytic treatment, the patient's initial relationship to the analyst as an ideal object reflects the activation of the central conscious ego as a defense against the repressed libidinal and antilibidinal internalized object relationships, which, however, gradually emerge in the transference. Fairbairn suggested that the exaggerated development of such an impoverished central ego as a product of excessive schizoid operations was characteristic of both schizoid and hysterical personalities.

Fairbairn believed that the infant's original fear was that his or her love for the mother would empty her out and destroy her, which led to the infant feeling futile and depleted. Fairbairn considered this fantasy an essential emotional experience of schizoid personalities, which imparted an aggressive quality to their dependent needs. Only later on, he suggested, was the frustration by the mother experienced as a consequence of the individual's own aggressive impulses, now projected onto the mother as a bad object and leading to the internalization of a bad internal object. Fairbairn saw these split-off internalized object relations not simply as fantasies but as endopsychic structures, the basic structures of the psychic apparatus.

For Fairbairn, the various erotogenic zones represented not the origin of libidinal stimuli but the channels available for expression of libidinal needs directed toward objects; he defined anal and phallic conflicts not in terms of libidinal stages but as particular "techniques" activated in a sequence of interactions and conflicts with parental objects.

Fairbairn saw the development of masochistic tendencies in the treatment as a basic manifestation in the transference of previously split-off, bad, internalized object relations; he considered interpreting such masochistic needs a key stage in resolving pathological schizoid states. He described the "masochistic defense" as a consequence of unconscious efforts to preserve the relationship with frustrating yet needed objects: the "absolution of blame" of the object on the part of the self transformed the uncon-

ditional badness of the object into a conditional one, and the experience of unconscious guilt expressed this effort to maintain a relationship with the frustrating object. He postulated that the psychoanalytic resolution of unconscious guilt feelings might bring about an intensification of the patient's resistances and of negative therapeutic reactions, because the patient would then be faced with coming to terms with his or her libidinal attachment to bad, ambivalently loved objects, a crucial aspect of internalized object relations.

Fairbairn retained a rather classical psychoanalytic technique throughout most of his professional life, adopting only minor modifications, late in his career, of the psychoanalytic setting to facilitate the patient's being able to see the analyst if he or she so desired. His principal followers include Sutherland (1989) and Guntrip (1961, 1968, 1971). The latter introduced significant changes into Fairbairn's approach, with an even more radical rejection of drive theory than in Fairbairn's original formulations.

Donald Winnicott

Winnicott's (1958, 1965, 1971) object relations theory is less systematized than the theories of Klein and Fairbairn. His writings have an evocative quality, which has had a profound influence on psychoanalytic theory and practice. But, although he maintained his allegiance to many of Freud's and Klein's formulations, there are potential contradictions between his ideas and some of theirs. While his approach is eminently compatible with that of Fairbairn, he did not fully work out these relationships; Guntrip attempted to achieve such an integration of Fairbairn's and Winnicott's thinking.

Winnicott's focus is the concept and origin of the self, the development of the infant's subjective sense of reality in the context of the relationship with the mother. Winnicott suggested that the infant's primary experience is an oscillation between integrated and unintegrated affective states and that the protective environment provided by the empathic presence of the "good enough mother" permits the infant to experience a nontraumatic gratification of his or her needs. This gratification gradually shapes a normal self experience through the repeated availability of the mother's gratifying presence in response to the activation of the infant's internal needs. The mother's capacity for appropriate physical handling of the infant's instinctive needs and her emotional "holding" of his affective needs—a capacity derived from the mother's "primary maternal preoccupation" during the final stage of pregnancy and the first few weeks or months of the infant's life—provide the infant with an appropriate object to foster the infant's fantasy of omnipotence that he or she is able to create the reality required for satisfaction. The infant's subjectively experienced initiative "impinges" on the "environment-mother," bringing about her empathic response and the gratification of his or her needs. The sense of omnipotence—the infant "creating" the needed object at the point of need—strengthens the early self experience and creates the basis for the later development of transitional objects and transitional experiences.

When the mother is not empathic to the infant's needs, fails to react to these needs, or reacts to them in a faulty way, the infant's experience is that of an external "impingement," which is traumatic. A basic defensive operation then occurs in the form of splitting between the infant's nascent, "true self"—which now withdraws into an internal world of fantasy—and an adaptive, "false self." The true self relates to an internal world of gratifying and frustrating object representations, roughly corresponding to Klein's internal world of object relations, while the false self deals with adaptation to external reality. Under excessively traumatic circumstances, with chronic failure in the mothering function, an exaggerated false self may lead to a chronic sense of inauthenticity and constitute the basis for severe psychopathology, including antisocial behavior. Cognitive functions may be recruited to rationalize the operation of the false self and to promote a defensive, intellectualized version of self and others that does not correspond to the authentic object-related needs of the true self.

Under optimal mothering conditions, the infant is able to adapt to a shared reality with the mother. The infant at first assumes this reality to be omnipotently created; gradually, when tolerance of unavoidable environmental frustration and failure increases, he or she creates what Winnicott calls a "transitional object," a concrete object that is the infant's "first possession"—that is, an object that is recognized as not part of the self and yet not part of external reality either. The transitional object fulfills the functions of a fantasied relationship that is unchallenged by mother and infant alike; it constitutes the origin of future "illusion." It is intermediate between illusion and reality and creates an intermediate "space" between internal reality and external reality that will evolve first into the illusional space of play and eventually into the creative areas of art, culture, and religion. The transitional object is "created" by the infant with the mother's tacit agreement during the second half of the first year of life. It gradually "dissolves" without any sense of loss or mourning during the second or third year of life. Winnicott posits a connection between normal development of transi-

tional objects and subsequent psychopathology of fetishism and fetishistic object relations.

The infant's relation with the transitional object replicates the relation with the mother both in reality and in his or her internal world. In expressing both libidinal and aggressive needs toward the transitional object and in that object's "survival," the infant is reassured that his or her aggression has not destroyed the object. Winnicott sees the origin of aggression in the child's initial "ruthlessness" in his or her treatment of the object, roughly corresponding to the time of Klein's paranoid-schizoid position. He modified Klein's transition from the paranoid-schizoid to the depressive position in his concept of the development of the "capacity for concern"—namely, the infant's gradual recognition that his or her ruthlessness corresponds to aggression directed to a bad object that is also a good object. The mother, at this stage, exercises her "holding function" in the sense of her symbolic "survival" following the onslaught of her infant's aggression. Winnicott describes the capacity of the infant both to "use" an object ruthlessly and to relate to it in dependent, lovingly gratifying ways; he describes the "capacity to be alone" as derived from the infant's capacity to be alone in the presence of the mother, assured of her potential availability, a capacity corresponding to Klein's concept of the consolidation of a good internal object and the related capacity for trust.

Winnicott considered patients who have achieved consolidation of a true self and development of a capacity for concern—the equivalent of Klein's consolidation of the depressive position—suitable for psychoanalysis. He considered those in whom a false self dominates and the normal trusting relationship to external objects has not become consolidated —particularly cases with severely schizoid pathology and antisocial behavior—as requiring modifications in analytic technique.

For these severely ill patients, Winnicott postulated that the analytic setting itself—its stability, reliability, and soothing quality—represents the "holding environment" that was prematurely disrupted and that the psychoanalyst must provide, by his or her own stability, reliability, and availability, the "environment mother" that the patient lacked in the past. Optimally, such a setting will permit the patient's benign regression to an early stage of nonintegration, which replicates the early nonintegrated state of the infant–mother relationship within which there was as yet no clear boundary between mother and infant. The analyst's tolerance and interpretation of the patient's need to regress, to be understood in regression, and, symbolically speaking, to be "held" by the analyst, may permit the reactivation of early traumatic circumstances, the undoing of the defensive withdrawal of the true self, and the beginning of the consolidation of object relations involving the true self and the early, gratifying and frustrating, maternal object.

As mentioned earlier, Winnicott significantly influenced, in addition to Guntrip, the mainstream of French psychoanalytic thinking, as well as ego-psychological object relations theories such as Modell's (1976) and interpersonal psychoanalysis as represented by Greenberg and Mitchell (1983) and Mitchell (1988). There are important potential correspondences between Winnicott's approach and Kohut's (1971, 1977) self psychology, but also very significant differences: Winnicott's conceptualization of a complex internal world includes aggressively determined, internalized object relations.

Harry Stack Sullivan

Sullivan (1953, 1962) was the chief proponent of interpersonal psychoanalysis. Just as Winnicott stated that "there is no such a thing as a baby," implying that the origin of psychological life resided in a mother–infant unit, so Sullivan took as the cornerstone of his approach the view that all psychological phenomena are interpersonal in origin and that psychic life starts out as the internalization of relations with significant others. Sullivan classified the essential human needs as "needs for satisfaction," corresponding to instinctively anchored biological needs, and "needs for security," implying the need for gratifying experiences with others, leading to a sense of an effective, safe self and a basic sense of goodness. Gratification of the needs for satisfaction increases security, brings about a sense of euphoria, and facilitates emotional growth. But undue frustrations of the needs for satisfaction affect the need for security as well; and undue frustration of the emotional need to relate to significant others—even in the face of the gratification of basic needs for satisfaction— determines the experience of anxiety and, if exaggerated, anxiety extended to a sense of personal "badness." Excessive anxiety is the fundamental cause of emotional illness, and the frustration of essential security needs is its origin.

For Sullivan, the development of a healthy sense of self depends on the "reflected appraisal by others"; acceptance by others creates a sense of a good self and promotes integration of the self in satisfying security needs. Sullivan described various stages in the capacity for appraisal of the interactions with others. The original, or "prototaxic," experiences are characteristic of the first month of life, before the capacity for differentiation of self from others develops; "parataxic" experience corresponds to the develop-

ment of distortions in early experiences with others, distortions that are reflected in the transference in psychotherapeutic treatment. The mature capacity for realistic assessment of one's relations with others is expressed in the "syntaxic" mode of experience.

These were essentially alternative ways of formulating Freud's primary and secondary processes, just as Sullivan's classification of needs for satisfaction and security replaced Freud's drive theory. Sullivan also proposed early defensive operations of "selective inattention"—roughly corresponding to Freud's preconscious—and "dissociation" as a more radical elimination of self-awareness—equivalent to Freud's mechanism of repression. Sullivan described three levels of development based on normal and conflictual early object relations. Gratifying internalized object relations lead to a sense of "euphoria" and inner goodness, which facilitates emotional growth and the deepening of both an external and an internalized world of object relations. This is the source of the "good me." Unsatisfactory relations with others, characterized by anxiety and frustrations of the need for security, give rise to a sense of a "bad me." The psychopathology of a dissociated "bad me" may lead, by projection, to paranoid developments. In intimate relationship to the "good me" and the "bad me," the individual develops "personifications" of significant others, particularly "good mother" and "bad mother"; here Sullivan described the intrapsychic structures common to all object relations theories. Extremely frustrating experiences leading to commensurate anxiety and profound personal disorganization are expressed in a sense of "not me," a primitive distortion and destruction of intrapsychic experience characteristic of psychosis. Sullivan described extreme conditions under which, by a process of "malevolent transformation," all object relations would be interpreted as essentially bad and dangerous, characteristic of paranoid psychoses.

Sullivan's approach to treatment focused on the need to reactivate in the transference the patient's dissociated "bad me" and "not me" experiences by providing an empathic, stable, sensitive interpersonal environment in which the patient gradually becomes able to tolerate the activation of dissociated parataxic relationships. For practical purposes, Sullivan focused on the understanding, ventilation, and interpretive resolution of negative transferences, assuming that such a resolution would unblock the patient's capacity for gratifying object relations, thereby facilitating the development of positive growth experiences in the psychotherapeutic relationship and the growth of a basic sense of goodness, a consolidation of the self, and emotional growth. Sullivan profoundly influenced Frieda Fromm-Reichmann (1950, 1959), Otto Will (1959), and Harold Searles (1965, 1986), who further developed Sullivan's approach to the psychoanalytic treatment of psychotic, particularly schizophrenic, patients. Searles, in developing a general theory of the treatment of patients with psychotic and borderline illness, integrated Kleinian concepts with his Sullivanian background, particularly those of Rosenfeld and Bion (both of whom worked with psychotic patients within a Kleinian frame of reference). Sullivan's approach, together with Fairbairn's, has profoundly influenced contemporary interpersonal psychoanalysis as represented by Greenberg and Mitchell (1983) and Mitchell (1988).

Edith Jacobson

Starting from an ego-psychological approach strongly influenced by Hartmann and colleagues (Hartmann et al., 1946; Hartmann & Loewenstein, 1962; Hartmann, 1964), Jacobson (1971) focused on affect development. She proposed that affects were not simply discharge processes but were the representations of drives intimately integrated with self and object representations from the earliest stages of development on. She evolved a conceptualization of how affects carry out fundamental intrapsychic regulatory functions by means of this investment of self and object representations. She also clarified the relationships between setting up affectively invested self and object representations, on the one hand, and the vicissitudes of ego and superego development, particularly their constituent constellations of self and object representations, on the other.

Jacobson integrated her findings in the treatment of patients with affective disorders and in adolescents with severe identity problems and narcissistic conflicts with Mahler and Furer's (1968) findings regarding autistic and symbiotic psychosis in childhood and separation-individuation. Mahler and Furer, in turn, had interpreted her findings in the light of Jacobson's (1964) earlier formulations.

Jacobson (1964) proposed that intrapsychic life starts out as a psychophysiological self within which ego and id are not differentiated. She suggested that the first intrapsychic structure was a fused, or undifferentiated, self-object representation, which gradually evolved under the impact of the relationship between mother and infant. This fused self-object representation (corresponding to Mahler's symbiotic stage of development) ends with the differentiation of the self representation from the object representation, which contributes to the capacity for differentiation of the self from the external world.

Jacobson saw the defensive re-fusion of self representation and object representation under severely traumatic circumstances as the origin of subsequent psychotic identifications characteristic of symbiotic psychosis in childhood and affective psychosis and schizophrenia in adulthood. She also described the defensive dissociation of fused or undifferentiated self-object representations invested with aggressive drive derivatives as the counterpart to the libidinally invested ones, so that, particularly under pathological circumstances, fused self-object representations of an "all good" and of an "all bad" nature coexisted while being mutually dissociated.

Gradually, during the stage of separation-individuation that dominates the second part of the first and second years of life, the differentiation of self and object representations in both the "good" and the "bad" segments of experience is achieved. This differentiation is followed, first, by the integration of the "good" and "bad" self representations and object representations and, later, by the development of ideal self representations and ideal object representations, which crystallize in order to restore a sense of an ideal relationship with the mother. It is the toned-down, ambivalent relation to the mother in reality that evokes the psychological need to re-create an ideal relationship in fantasy.

Efforts to deny and to devalue the bad aspects of self and of mother may lead to exaggerated fixation of dissociated "bad" self and object representations, which dominate the psychopathology of borderline conditions. Under optimal circumstances, by contrast, good and bad self representations become integrated into a consolidated concept of self, and good and bad representations of the mother, the father, and siblings evolve into integrated constellations of real and idealized objects and object relations, which become part of ego structures.

Jacobson postulated that the superego also evolves out of successive layers of internalized object relations: the first layer is represented by "bad" object representations and has a prohibitive, punishing quality, the second by ideal self and object representations that enact idealized superego demands. Again, under normal circumstances, the gradual integration of these bad and ideal layers of superego precursors leads to their being toned down and to the consequent internalization and integration of a third layer, consisting of the more realistic superego introjects of the oedipal period. The gradual individualization, depersonification, and abstraction of these three layers give rise to the healthy integrated superego of latency, puberty, and adolescence, when a partial reorganization brings about the transformation into the adult superego. Jacobson applied this model to the treatment of neurotic, borderline, and psychotically depressed patients.

It is tempting to trace parallels in Jacobson's, Mahler's, Klein's, and Fairbairn's theories. All of them focus on the vicissitudes of the internalization and gradual integration of self and object representations, on splitting or primitive dissociation and integration, and on the gradual building up of the overall psychic structures under the influence of the integration of early object relations.

Margaret Mahler

As a result of her observations of psychotic children with autistic and symbiotic psychoses and of mother–child relationships in the first few years of life, Mahler and colleagues (Mahler & Furer, 1968; Mahler et al., 1975) developed a theory of the psychostructural preconditions of autistic psychosis, symbiotic psychosis, normal and pathological separation-individuation, and the culmination of early development in object constancy and a consolidated tripartite structure.

Mahler hypothesized an earliest stage of development, the autistic phase, during the first month of life, predating the establishment of the symbiotic phase (which develops between the second and the sixth month). Toward the end of her life, however, on the basis of neonatal observations, she revised this idea, concluding that a normal autistic phase probably does not exist and that cases of autistic psychosis with strong psychological determinants are pathological developments.

The symbiotic phase of development (from two to six months) is characterized by cueing and matching between infant and mother wherein the infant experiences blissful states of merger with mother. The infant anticipates and initiates pleasurable responses in interacting with the mother and develops a sense of confidence and basic trust in the mother expressed in smiling and direct eye contact, which leads to the capacity of the infant to be alone as well as with the mother.

At that point—in the second half of the first year of life—the stage of separation-individuation sets in, to be completed toward the end of the third year. The first subphase of separation-individuation is "differentiation," or "hatching," which takes place between about the sixth and the tenth month and is characterized by an increase in the infant's scanning of the environment and checking back to mother for "visual refueling." The infant is now capable of being easily comforted by mother substitutes, while he or she also develops stranger anxiety, "custom inspection" in intensive visual interaction with mother's and others' faces, and a gradual ability to distinguish between what is animate and inanimate, good and bad.

The differentiation subphase is followed by "practicing," from roughly the eleventh to the sixteenth month, characterized by the mastery of upright locomotion, pleasure in exploring and in asserting "free will," the tendency to take the mother for granted except when prolonged separation leads to "low keyedness." Now the toddler develops a "love affair with the world," with a sense of omnipotence, an active, even aggressive autonomy, darting and running away from the mother but also wishing to share with her and to control her by means of "shadowing."

Practicing leads to the subphase of "rapprochement," between the eighteenth month and the end of the third year, when the toddler makes intense efforts to control the mother while clinging to her anxiously. This subphase culminates in what Mahler calls the "rapprochement crisis," characterized by an intensification of darting away alternating with temper tantrums. There is aggressive control of the mother and insistence on autonomy in response to her, with manifestations of sharp splitting characterized by idealizing clinging to the mother and aggressive separation from her. Pathology of the rapprochement crisis is marked by excessive separation anxiety, passivity or demandingness, depressive mood, pathological coercion and possessiveness of the mother, pathological envy, and temper tantrums and is related to severely disappointing, unavailable, or overintrusive mothers, to painful and sudden dissolutions of the child's fantasied omnipotence, and to traumatic circumstances causing excessive narcissistic frustration.

The next stage Mahler called "toward object constancy," a process that evolves over the fourth and fifth year of life, when the child develops an integrated sense of self, a differentiated relation with other adults and peers, an awareness in depth of the mother, and tolerance of ambivalence. During this phase, oedipal conflicts become clearly dominant.

Mahler's understanding of the underlying nature of internalized object relations, utilizing Jacobson's developmental model, implied dealing with mutually dissociated, or split-off, idealized and persecutory relationships within which self and object representations were fused, typically activated in the transference of psychotic patients. The psychoanalytic exploration of borderline conditions, by contrast, reflecting particularly the pathology of internalized object relations during the subphase of rapprochement, implied the analysis of mutually dissociated or split-off idealized and persecutory relationships within which the patient had achieved a clear capacity to differentiate between self and object representations in both segments. Harold Searles's (1965) description of stages in the psychoanalytic treatment of psychotic patients—namely, early, out-of-contact phase, intense symbiotic involvement, separation, and integration—also reflects a utilization of Mahler's concept of symbiotic psychosis and separation-individuation development. I utilized both Mahler's observations regarding pathological rapprochement crises and Jacobson's developmental schemas to provide a theoretical background for an approach to the psychoanalytic psychotherapy of borderline conditions.

Otto Kernberg

Like Jacobson and Mahler, I (1976, 1980, 1984, 1990) adhere to Freud's dual drive theory and consider drives indissolubly linked to object relations. I believe that libidinal and aggressive drive derivatives are invested in object relations from the very onset of the symbiotic phase described by Mahler. I propose that the ideational and affective representations of drives are originally undifferentiated from each other and that affect states representing the most primitive manifestations of drives are essential links of self and object representations from the very beginning (following Jacobson in this regard).

I postulate that affects constitute the primary motivational system and that, internalized or fixated as the very frame of internalized "good" and "bad" object relations, affects are gradually integrated into libidinal and aggressive drives to form hierarchically supraordinate motivational systems. In other words, primitive affects are the "building blocks" of the drives (Kernberg, 1990). I see unconscious intrapsychic conflicts as always between certain units of self and object representations under the impact of a particular drive derivative (clinically, a certain affect disposition reflecting the instinctual side of the conflict) and contradictory or opposing units of self and object representations and their respective affect dispositions reflecting the defensive structure. Unconscious intrapsychic conflicts are never simply between impulse and defense; rather, both impulse and defense find expression through certain internalized object relations.

In cases of severe psychopathology—in patients with borderline personality organization—splitting mechanisms stabilize such dynamic structures within an ego–id matrix and permit the contradictory aspects of these conflicts to remain—at least partially —conscious, in the form of primitive transferences.

By contrast, patients with neurotic personality organization present impulse–defense configurations that include specific unconscious wishes reflecting sexual and aggressive drive derivatives embedded in unconscious fantasies relating to the oedipal objects. Repressed unconscious wishes, however, always come in the form of corresponding units composed of self representation and object representation and an affect linking them (Kernberg, 1987, 1988).

Patients with neurotic personality organization present well-integrated superego, ego, and id structures; within the psychoanalytic situation, the analysis of resistances brings about the activation in the transference, first, of relatively global characteristics of these structures and, later, of the internalized object relations of which they are composed. The analysis of drive derivatives occurs in the context of the analysis of the relation of the patient's infantile self to significant parental objects as projected onto the analyst.

The borderline personality organization, by contrast, shows a predominance of pre-oedipal conflicts and psychic representations of pre-oedipal conflicts condensed with representations of the oedipal phase. Conflicts are not predominantly repressed and therefore unconsciously dynamic; rather, they are expressed in mutually dissociated ego states reflecting the defense of primitive dissociation or splitting. The activation of primitive object relations that predate the consolidation of ego, superego, and id is manifest in the transference as apparently chaotic affect states, which have to be analyzed in sequential steps as follows: first, the clarification of a dominant primitive object relation in the transference, with its corresponding self and object representation, and the dominant affect linking them; second, analysis of the alternative projection of self and object representation onto the therapist while the patient identifies with a reciprocal self or object representation of this object relationship, leading to the patient's gradual capacity to become aware of his or her identification with self and object in that relationship; and third, the interpretive integration of mutually split-off, idealized, and persecutory part object relations with the characteristics mentioned.

Such an analysis may gradually bring about a transformation of part object relations into total object relations and of primitive transferences (largely reflecting Mahler's stages of development that predate object constancy) into the advanced transferences of the oedipal phase. The analyst's exploration of the countertransference, including concordant and complementary identifications in it (Racker, 1957), facilitates transference analysis; and the analysis of primitive defensive operations, particularly splitting and projective identification, in the transference also contributes to strengthening the patient's ego.

I have also described (1976, 1984) the pathological condensation of idealized internalized object relations in the pathological grandiose self of narcissistic personalities and the gradual resolution of the pathological grandiose self in the transference as its component part object relationships are clarified and the corresponding dominant primitive defensive operations are interpreted.

Insofar as I have integrated findings regarding primitive defenses and object relations stemming from the Kleinian school and Fairbairn's and Sutherland's ideas about the essential dyadic structures involving self representation–object representation–affect with Jacobson's and Mahler's theoretical frames, my approach may be considered a major effort to integrate several object relations theories within an ego-psychological object relations theory model.

REFERENCES

Arlow, J. A., & Brenner, C. (1964). *Psychoanalytic Concepts and the Structural Theory*. New York: Int. Univ. Press.

Bion, W. R. (1967). *Second Thoughts*. New York: Basic Books.

———. (1970). *Attention and Interpretation*. London: Heinemann.

Chasseguet-Smirgel, J. (1986). *Sexuality and Mind*. New York: New York Univ. Press.

Erikson, E. H. (1959). *Identity and the Life Cycle*. Psychological Issues, monograph 1. New York: Int. Univ. Press.

Fairbairn, W. R. D. (1954). *An Object-Relations Theory of the Personality*. New York: Basic Books.

Freud, S. (1920). *Beyond the Pleasure Principle. SE*, 18:7–64.

———. (1923). *The Ego and the Id. SE*, 19:3–66.

———. (1933). *New Introductory Lectures on Psycho-Analysis. SE*, 22:3–184.

Fromm-Reichmann, F. (1950). *Principles of Intensive Psychotherapy*. Chicago: Univ. Chicago Press.

———. (1959). *Psychoanalysis and Psychotherapy*. Chicago: Univ. Chicago Press.

Greenberg, J. R., & Mitchell, S. A. (1983). *Object Relations in Psychoanalytic Theory*. Cambridge, Mass.: Harvard Univ. Press.

Guntrip, H. (1961). *Personality Structure and Human Interaction*. London: Hogarth Press.

———. (1968). *Schizoid Phenomena, Object Relations and the Self*. New York: Int. Univ. Press.

———. (1971). *Psychoanalytic Theory, Therapy, and the Self*. New York: Basic Books.

Hartmann, H. (1964). *Essays on Ego Psychology*. New York: Int. Univ. Press.

Hartmann, H., & Loewenstein, R. M. (1962). Notes on the superego. *Psychoanal. Study Child*, 17:42–81.

Hartmann, H., Kris, E., & Loewenstein, R. M. (1946). Comments on the formation of psychic structure. *Psychoanal. Study Child*, 2:11–38.

Jacobson, E. (1964). *The Self and the Object World*. New York: Int. Univ. Press.

———. (1971). *Depression*. New York: Int. Univ. Press.

Kernberg, O. F. (1976). *Object Relations Theory and Clinical Psychoanalysis*. New York: Aronson.

———. (1980). *Internal World and External Reality*. New York: Aronson.

———. (1984). *Severe Personality Disorders*. New Haven: Yale Univ. Press.

———. (1987). An ego-psychology object relations theory approach to the transference. *Psychoanal. Q.*,56:197–221.

———. (1988). Object relations theory in clinical practice. *Psychoanal. Q.*, 57:481–504.

———. (1990). New perspectives in psychoanalytic affect theory. In *Emotion: Theory, Research and Experience*, ed. R. Plutchik & H. Kellerman, pp. 115–130. New York: Academic Press.

Klein, M. (1946). Notes on some schizoid mechanisms. In *Development in Psycho-Analysis*, ed. J. Riviere, pp. 292–320. London: Hogarth Press.

———. (1948). *Contributions to Psycho-Analysis, 1921–1945*. London: Hogarth Press.

———. (1957). *Envy and Gratitude*. New York: Basic Books.

Kohut, H. (1971). *The Analysis of the Self*. New York: Int. Univ. Press.

———. (1972). Thoughts on narcissism and narcissistic rage. *Psychoanal. Study Child*, 27:360–400.

———. (1977). *The Restoration of the Self*. New York: Int. Univ. Press.

Lacan, J. (1966). *Ecrits*. Paris: Editions du Seuil.

Loewald, H. W. (1960). On the therapeutic action of psycho-analysis. *Int. J. Psychoanal.*, 58:463–472.

———. (1980). *Papers on Psychoanalysis*. New Haven: Yale Univ. Press.

Mahler, M. S., & Furer, M. (1968). *On Human Symbiosis and the Vicissitudes of Individuation*. New York: Int. Univ. Press.

Mahler, M. S., Pine, F., & Bergman, A. (1975). *The Psychological Birth of the Human Infant*. New York: Basic Books.

Meltzer, D. (1973). *Sexual States of Mind*. Strath Tay, Scotland: Clunie Press.

Meltzer, D., & Harris Williams, M. (1988). *The Apprehension of Beauty*. Strath Tay, Scotland: Clunie Press.

Meltzer, D., et al. (1975). *Explorations in Autism*. Aberdeen: Aberdeen Univ. Press.

Mitchell, S. A. (1988). *Relational Concepts in Psychoanalysis*. Cambridge, Mass.: Harvard Univ. Press.

Modell, A. H. (1976). "The holding environment" and the therapeutic action of psychoanalysis. *J. Amer. Psychoanal. Assn.*, 24:285–307.

Oliner, M. M. (1988). *Cultivating Freud's Garden in France*. Northvale, N.J.: Aronson.

Racker, H. (1957). The meanings and uses of countertransference. *Psychoanal. Q.*, 26:303–357.

Rosenfeld, H. (1987). *Impasse and Interpretation*. London: Tavistock Publications.

Roudinesco, E. (1990). *Jacques Lacan & Co*. Chicago: Univ. Chicago Press.

Sandler, J. (1987). *From Safety to Superego*. New York: Guilford Press.

Searles, H. (1965). *Collected Papers on Schizophrenia and Related Subjects*. New York: Int. Univ. Press.

———. (1986). *My Work with Borderline Patients*. Northvale, N.J.: Aronson.

Segal, H. (1967). Melanie Klein's techniques. In *Psychoanalytic Technique*, ed. B. B. Wolman, pp. 168–190. New York: Basic Books.

———. (1981). *The Work of Hanna Segal*. New York: Aronson.

Spillius, E. B., & Feldman, M. (1989). *Psychic Equilibrium and Psychic Change*. London: Tavistock/Routledge.

Sullivan, H. S. (1953). *The Interpersonal Theory of Psychiatry*. New York: Norton.

———. (1962). *Schizophrenia as a Human Process*. New York: Norton.

Sutherland, J. D. (1989). *Fairbairn's Journey into the Interior*. London: Free Association Books.

Will, O. A. (1959). Human relatedness and the schizophrenic reaction. *Psychiatry*, 22:205–223.

Winnicott, D. W. (1958). *Collected Papers*. New York: Basic Books.

———. (1965). *The Maturational Process and the Facilitating Environment*. New York: Int. Univ. Press.

———. (1971). *Playing and Reality*. New York: Basic Books.

Sander M. Abend, M.D., and

Michael S. Porder, M.D.

34

IDENTIFICATION

Identification is of central importance in the history of psychoanalysis and in the understanding of much of its theory, yet it remains a poorly defined and inadequately understood concept. The term is used to explain both symptom formation and the development of ego and superego structure, and thus of character and adaptation as well. It is also often specified as a defense mechanism and as an important component of how we normally learn. It is at times considered to be a consequence of object relationships, yet at other times an alternative to object relationships. Clarification of its meaning is even further complicated by the tendency that has become evident in recent years to use the same term to refer both to the process by which an identification is supposedly formed and to the product of that process itself.

A historical survey will demonstrate the increasing complexity and confusion that have characterized the employment of the term "identification." In summarizing this progressive development, we will also attempt to differentiate "identification" from such related terms as "imitation," "internalization," "incorporation," "introjection," and "projective identification," all of which are associated with it at one time or another in theoretical writings.

EARLY DEVELOPMENT OF THE CONCEPT

Freud's earliest clinical references to the idea of identification all seem to assume its commonsense meaning: a psychic connection based on a perceived or imagined quality of sameness. In *The Interpretation of Dreams* (1900) he repeated what he had written earlier in his letters to Fliess: namely, that one person could "identify" with another based on an unconscious libidinal wish to be in the place of the other person. Such wishes are conflictual and repressed. He named this phenomenon "hysterical identification" and distinguished it from what he called "hysterical imitation," in which the wishes involved are conscious.

In the "Fragment of an analysis of a case of hysteria" (1905), Freud explained a number of Dora's symptoms as due to hysterical identifications. For example, her abdominal pains and vaginal catarrh he ascribed to an identification with her mother, while her dyspnea he attributed to an identification with her father in the primal scene. While the motives for identification in this case stemmed primarily from erotic wish fulfillment, there are hints that guilt-induced self-punishment could also serve as a motive for identification, although Freud did not spell out this formulation specifically in that case study. Apparently, both the motives and the exact nature of the connections were unconscious until brought to light by the analytic work. In other work from the same period (1908, 1910), hysterical identification was also invoked to explain symptom formation.

As Freud began to develop his views on narcissism (1914), the term "identification" took on a new, more complex meaning. He postulated that there is a continuum for the distribution of libido, beginning with autoerotism and proceeding through stages of narcissism to true object love. It is important to keep in mind that at this stage in the evolution of Freud's developmental theory, there was no systematic concept of pre-oedipal object relations such as we have now, even though Freud had already published descriptions of the oral and anal phases of the libido as well as of anaclitic object ties. At this time he thought of true object cathexes as coming into existence only at the oedipal stage of development. These ideas apparently suggested to Freud that identifications formed during the earlier, narcissistic stage of development could be thought of as constituting an alternative to true object cathexes. Thus, he offered the formulation (1917) that when a highly ambivalent, libidinal object cathexis is withdrawn, as might happen after a severe disappointment, regression to such a narcissistic identification could follow.

This theory was based in part on the clinical observation that the self-accusations of melancholics were unconsciously deflected away from the memory of the lost, ambivalently loved object and instead redirected toward the sufferer's own self. In fact, the melancholic patient did not possess the traits of behavior that were being condemned, although they were clearly present in his or her unconscious impressions of the lost object. The conception thus arose that object relations that had been given up were somehow reinstated in the ego of the subject. In Freud's often-quoted phrase, "The shadow of the object falls upon the ego." He even went so far as to speculate that perhaps this was the only way that objects could be given up. Hence, the idea emerged that the ego is "a repository of abandoned object cathexes. Several fundamentally important ideas that have continued to influence psychoanalytic thinking about identification were thus introduced: that identification is related to object loss; that it alters the composition of the ego and thus provides a means for modifying its "structure"; and that this early form of identification may be connected with the process of "taking in" to the ego or self in some fashion, presumably by means of an oral incorporative fantasy.

Abraham (1924) synthesized these ideas further by developing a model of libidinal substages whose sequence he tied to the developmental framework of autoerotism, narcissism, and object cathexes that Freud had proposed. Abraham specified that the earliest model of taking in would be based on oral modes and that the oral imagery, so common in depressive illness, was specifically derived from unconscious cannibalistic and destructive fantasies. "Incorporation," a term that means literally taking into the body but is applied interchangeably as well to the fantasy of doing so, was consequently utilized in early descriptions of the most primitive forms of identification, such as those found in seriously depressed or psychotic patients. These identifications were said by Abraham to be orally destructive and "total" in character, whereas presumably more mature forms of incorporation or identification (the terms were not consistently distinguished from one another at that period in the evolution of psychoanalytic theory) were thought to be focused only on selected parts or qualities of the object; hence they were called "partial identifications" by Abraham. Since these, by definition, were not total and destructive in nature, they were thought to allow for the preservation of the object in fantasy. Therefore, "partial identifications" came to be understood as existing alongside the object relationship. They permitted the continuation of object relationships rather than completely replacing them. This formulation was soon questioned, however, because it led to unresolvable inconsistencies in theory (Fenichel, 1926). But it has not been discarded entirely. The terminology for different types of identification is further complicated by the fact that some analysts, such as Melanie Klein (1935) and her followers, thought of "part object" relationships as occurring earlier in development than "whole object" ones and hence as representing the most primitive form of object relationship. Nevertheless, for most analysts today, the term "total" identification is usually intended to connote an early, primitive, magical form of identification, less likely to be reflected in an actual modification of the individual's ego and generally assumed to be associated with the most severe forms of psychopathology.

Although Freud (1921) further elaborated his ideas about identification, he did not fundamentally alter his concept of the subject until the publication of his pivotal theoretical monograph *The Ego and the Id* in 1923. In this work, he was vitally interested in the means whereby instinctual restraints are made part of the growing child's own psychic apparatus— that is to say, are "internalized." How could one account for the surrendering of incestuous and parenticidal wishes during the resolution of the oedipus complex? Clearly, one could recognize that the child had taken over parental attitudes during this time or, in other words, had "identified" with parental moral standards and prohibitions. In this process, the object relations that have been surrendered—the intense, loving, possessive attachments to each parent —are replaced not by the setting up of obvious narcissistic identifications within the ego, as was postulated in the case of melancholic patients, but instead by the establishment of a new psychic structure, the superego. This "differentiated grade" within the ego was thought to consist of identifications with the parents of a new and different kind.

This formulation contained many inconsistencies, which were pointed out by Fenichel (1926), Rapaport (1957), and later Schafer (1968a). For example, Freud described these superego identifications as "first identifications," formed when the ego was weak; yet, at the same time, he referred to certain antecedent, primary, imitative identifications that also contribute to the composition of the superego. In addition, there was the idea, described above, that so-called narcissistic identifications are formed before the oedipal stage is even reached; therefore these must also precede the identifications thought to form the superego. Furthermore, Freud could not satisfactorily account for why the boy's erotic attachment to his mother was being replaced by a strengthened identification with his father! Subsequent years saw a gradual clarification of the complex nature of the oedipal stage of development, of the many factors that contribute to the formation of gender identity, and of what was long thought of as the "dissolution" of the oedipus complex. This evolutionary development in psychoanalytic theory helped to resolve certain of these troublesome paradoxes, but the theory of identification has nevertheless continued to be burdened by certain inconsistencies derived from the early formulations.

IDENTIFICATION AND ITS RELATION TO OTHER TYPES OF INTERNALIZATION

The Ego and the Id (1923) was also of landmark significance for the concept of identification, because it introduced the idea that identifications are crucial to the development of psychic structure as well as of symptom formation. Thus the groundwork was laid for heightened interest in studying identification as a psychic "process," rather than, as previously, concentrating on ascertaining the exact nature of the mental contents that constitute identifications. Terms such as "imitation," "internalization," "incorporation," and "introjection" are commonly used in efforts to describe different varieties of this postulated intrapsychic process. There is general agreement that the term "imitation" should be limited to that transient behavior based on a conscious wish to be like another which does not result in any permanent modification of the ego. "Internalization" is understood to refer to the general means whereby those regulatory functions that were formerly under the control of the external world are somehow taken into the psychic apparatus. However, in a broader sense, as emphasized by Hartmann (1939), "internalization" applies to the entire psychological eventuation by means of which objects, events—in fact, all aspects of the "real" world—come to be represented within the human mind by images of one kind or another. These images collectively constitute an internal psychic map of the actual world. Over the course of time, "internalization" has come to have a supraordinate relationship to the other terms we are considering; that is to say, "identification," "incorporation," "introjection," and the like are often thought of as varieties of internalization.

"Incorporation," as earlier noted, implies an unconscious fantasy of taking something into the body. While it is thought of as essentially an oral mode of functioning, the same term is also applied to fantasies that involve taking in by other means as well; anal, respiratory, visual, aural, and even tactile incorporation are all familiar clinically. The idea of incorporating qualities or aspects of others into the mind is an extension of these fantasies of physical incorporation; thus it was at first assumed that all identifications take place by means of some unconscious fantasy of incorporation. This was supported by the clinical finding that such fantasies of physical incorporation were often encountered in the clinical analysis of identifications. Nevertheless, it seems that a certain concretization based on the nature of these fantasies about physical processes had influenced psychological theory building itself. A sort of alimentary model of identification processes became standard, and emphasis on the relative degree of psychological assimilation of what was taken in seemed to become an important criterion for distinguishing different kinds of incorporation or identification from one another.

"Introjection" is a term designating a mental mechanism of taking in, the reciprocal of the long-familiar concept of projection. It often appears to be employed as a more abstract derivative of the earlier term "incorporation," though more emphasis tends to be placed on the consequent alteration in the composition of the self representations. For some theorists, the results of introjection, called "introjects," are distinguished from the products—that is, the particular mental contents—that result from identification. Although usage and attempts at definition and differentiation vary among analysts, the most common distinction between "introjection" and "identification" seems to rest on the degree to which the psychic contents in question appear to be assimilated or integrated into the subject's psychic apparatus. Thus, to give a simple clinical illustration, when a female patient reports that she feels her mother is a part of her, criticizing her constantly and making her uncomfortable when she deviates from demands she feels are being put on her, and that she does not experience these demands as completely her own, though she knows they are internal, most analysts would label this experienced presence an "introject." Except in the very sickest patients, there would be no hallucinating voice; yet the patient regards the "introject" as almost a foreign body within herself. On the other hand, another patient may recognize that she is very much like her mother in taste and dress or even that her mannerisms, some of her reactions to her children, or perhaps certain of her expressions of speech are almost identical with those of her mother. She may like or dislike any or all of these similarities, but she experiences them as her own. Most analysts would regard these as manifestations of "identifications."

Not all instances of either type are necessarily as much a part of consciousness as they are in these examples; nor are their relationships to the figures on whom they are based always as clear as to the individual in question. Still other varieties are more ambiguous in form and are difficult to classify as either introjects or identifications. The conception held by most analysts is that introjection is a more primitive, earlier form of psychic process, which is more likely to be seen in patients who display a greater degree of psychopathology. Most identifications, by contrast, are usually thought of as more fully and harmoniously absorbed into the psychic structure; they thus represent a later, more mature form of psychic process, more commonly encountered in healthier neurotic and normal individuals.

The special term "projective identification" has a different history from the concept of identification proper and those related concepts that are inevitably linked with it in clinical theory (see chapter 33). The term was introduced by Melanie Klein (1946), who postulated that during the so-called schizoid-paranoid and depressive positions in the first year of life, the infant projects outward, or into the breast, the bad impulses from inside, in order to protect the ego core from the death instinct. Then the infant fears retaliation from the now dangerous outside object, though he or she still retains some form of identity with it. This postulated mechanism, which is considered to be a primitive form of projection, she called "projective identification." The term is most commonly employed by psychoanalysts who are strongly influenced by Klein's theories generally; thus it appears especially frequently in the writings of many European and South American psycho-

analytic theorists.[1] Perhaps even more than the other terms mentioned, "projective identification" is employed and defined in different and therefore confusing ways by different authors. Kernberg (1975), is probably the best-known psychoanalyst in the United States to make use of the concept, but his ideas differ significantly from those of Klein (see chapter 33). He eliminates the emphasis on the death instinct and extends the time period in which projective identification is thought to occur normally in development through the second year of life. It should be noted that where the term is employed, it refers to hypothetical mental processes that are presumed to play a role in very early mental development. It is generally believed to be detectable in certain difficult-to-understand transference expressions encountered in clinical work, especially with more disturbed patients.

LATER CONTRIBUTIONS

Anna Freud's work, along with that of Fenichel (1936), Hartmann (1939), and other contemporaries, ushered in the era of ego psychology in psychoanalytic theory. Her monumental contribution to the refinement of psychoanalytic technique, *The Ego and the Mechanisms of Defense* (1936), presented the idea that identification could be thought of as a mental mechanism utilized for defensive purposes. One example of its defensive use is identification with the aggressor, a means of formulating certain clinical observations that were first expounded in this monograph. Although some theoreticians now regard the idea of defensive mechanisms as perhaps not the most satisfactory way to conceptualize defensive aspects of psychic activities (Schafer, 1968b; Brenner, 1976; Abend, 1981), the shorthand of the terminology is still widely used. "Identification with the aggressor," in particular, is a term frequently encountered in clinical writings and is unlikely to be misunderstood.

Rapaport took up the work of the ego psychologists and immersed himself in the conceptual problems inherent in the development of the mind. His most important paper relating to the topic of identification (1957) treats the subject at a considerable distance from clinical data. In keeping with his interest in the structuralization of the mind, he treats identifications and defenses in quasi-biological terms as a sort of compound concept. He sees them as fundamental aspects of the growing capacity to delay or alter the discharge of instinctual wishes and regards

1. See Etchegoyan, 1985, and Widlocher, 1985, for examples of its current utilization.

them as microstructures of the mind. A highly complex hierarchical organization of such microstructures contributes, according to Rapaport, to the differentiation of the mental apparatus into the major macrostructural entities of id, ego, and superego. Structures are, in his phraseology, "processes with a relatively slow rate of change." That is to say, he focuses on the evolution of fixed, more or less automatic aspects of the functioning of the mental apparatus, of a normal as well as a pathological nature. It is clear in this paper that he means the term "identification" to apply to much of the assimilated means of controlling instinctual discharge; this is so much a part of the characteristic operation of the individual's ego and superego systems that its relationship to the patient's past objects would never be recoverable in clinical material.

Jacobson (1964) believes that identification processes between mother and infant begin very early in life, gradually assuming more mature forms until the adult forms begin to predominate at around age three and a half. These processes continue to alter in form and content as maturation progresses, and, in turn, they contribute to that maturation. They constitute important components of the evolving ego and superego systems. In their earliest form, Jacobson calls them "affectomotor empathic" identifications, indicating the bonding between mother and infant. As awareness of separateness increases during the latter part of the first year and the second year of life, fantasies of fusion with the mother come into existence, aided by the relative fluidity of self–object boundaries and by the ease with which projective-introjective mechanisms are presumed to operate at that stage of life. She believes that these fantasies of fusion result in magical, total identifications of a kind she has observed in depressed and psychotic patients. She believes that these magical fusions are more akin to imitations than to true identifications; they do not result in true modifications of the ego.

However, she states that as early as the end of the first year, selective partial identifications begin to be made, often based on rivalry with siblings or with the father. Such partial identifications assume more prominence as the child matures, so that the child may actually become more like the object in some ways, though not in others. Thus, in sum, what she terms "psychotic identifications" are the result of wishful fantasies of merging with the object. They do not promote real ego growth, in contrast to those later identifications which are "selective and consistent," can be integrated into the ego, and thus may permanently alter the ego structure. These later identifications, she thinks, contribute to the development of enduring character traits, which are relatively stable, nonconflictual aspects of the composition of the ego.

One potential disadvantage of her schema is that the identifications tend to be regarded in a concrete fashion. It is as though they come to be thought of as building blocks, or literal components of psychic structure, rather than as dynamic contents of the mind. Thus, Jacobson treats "conflicting identifications" as if they are independent mental entities that can and do struggle against one another because of their intrinsically disparate natures and thereby somehow produce psychopathology. While this can be considered to be merely another example of psychoanalytic shorthand standing in for far more complicated ways of describing interrelated aspects of psychic conflict, it may have the unintended misleading effect of drawing analytic attention away from the task of unraveling the motivations and defenses involved in these complex, interwoven mental contents.

It should be emphasized that this caveat is directed against the possible misapplication of overly concretized interpretations of formulations about identification. This is a familiar problem which has plagued psychoanalytic theory in other contexts as well. There is obviously a widely accepted view that throughout psychological development, both in early childhood and much later, identifications with others who are envied, admired, loved, or feared form essential ingredients of the evolving character of every individual. Although the very word *structure* is prone to ambiguous usage, in that it is used at times in a nontechnical, commonsense way and at other times in a more technical sense to refer to relatively stable aspects of psychic functioning, analysts today would not expect to be misunderstood if they speak of identifications as components of psychic structure. Much learning, for example, is assumed to be facilitated by various wishes to identify with—that is to say, to become, or become like—other persons in the environment. Perhaps it is least likely to be misleading if one assumes that "identifications," when spoken of as components of psychic structure, are meant to refer to stable aspects of an individual's character, whose origins in wishful fantasies to be like someone else, even if they were conscious to begin with, have become more or less detached from such sources and have somehow gradually evolved into typical modes of psychological functioning.

Loewald (1973), like Jacobson, sees the development of more mature identifications as a gradual process. In his language, the less mature superego regulatory functions move away from the "ego core" and may be "externalized," much like a transitional object that has qualities of both self and nonself. Thus the tendency in sicker patients is to "reproject" or "externalize" their superego functions. By contrast, in healthier individuals, the superego regulatory mechanisms become part of the mature value systems of the ego.

Meissner (1970, 1971, 1972) also holds views that are compatible with the foregoing ideas, except that he prefers to call the more primitive, instinct-related mental products "introjects," reserving the term "identification" for the more integrated, adaptive, acquired ego activities that are essentially outside conflict. This distinction also utilizes a version of the concept of neutralized energies that contributes to the so-called higher-level adaptive processes of identification. All other internalizations he prefers to call "introjects." These include instances of identification with the aggressor, because, according to Meissner, this form of identification, as well as others like it, retain a closeness to instinctual drives, are involved in conflict, and may also be subjectively experienced as foreign to the self.

Schafer (1968a) also prefers to use the term "introject" to describe primitive forms of internalization. He characterizes such formations as "inner presences" or "primary process presences," which clinically are found to retain qualities of a two-person dialogue and thus may be described as not totally integrated or assimilated into the ego. It can be seen that there are congruences between Schafer's and Meissner's descriptions and understanding of introjects, Loewald's externalized or reprojected superego, Jacobson's psychotic identifications, and perhaps even the narcissistic identifications described by Freud (1917). Moreover, like the other authors cited, Schafer thinks of true identifications as better integrated into the individual's subjective self than the other structures, which he considers more primitive.

However, Schafer's (1968a) thoughtful exposition of the subject goes much further in delineating the theoretical issues associated with the identification concept. In particular, he is dissatisfied with explanations of identification and its correlates derived from ideas about the nature and distribution of psychic energy. Instead, he insists on the need to understand the motives for identification. His employment of the term "motive" is not strictly limited to describing wish fulfillment of various sorts; he uses the same word to describe such apparently purposive ego activities as defenses. He sees motivations derived from both libidinal and aggressive drives, which are pre-oedipal as well as oedipal in origin, as contributing to identifications. Schafer also notes

that even identifications that serve adaptive needs apparently far removed from the drives will reveal, if subjected to analytic scrutiny, that their underlying unconscious sources are the same fundamental erotic and aggressive wishes that motivate other identifications. As is apparent from these comments, he separates clinical discussions of identification from discussions more concerned with theoretical speculation about developmental processes, a position with which we are very much in accord.

RECENT PROPOSALS

Arlow, in a series of papers (1961, 1964, 1969, 1972), indicates the relationship between identification and unconscious fantasies in a variety of clinical situations. Brenner (1982) emphasizes the centrality of compromise formation as an organizing principle in both normal and pathological mental activities. The ideas of these authors, as well as those of Schafer (1968a), have influenced a group of analysts at the New York Psychoanalytic Institute, who collaborated in a study of the clinical manifestations of identifications. Having participated in this endeavor, we will briefly outline the conclusions reached, which attempt to clarify some of the confusing issues that still beset the theory of identifications.

It is proposed that identifications are best thought of as manifestations of unconscious fantasies of being or becoming like another individual. According to the principle of compromise formation, all such fantasies are a combination of drive derivatives, unpleasure, defenses, and superego influences. The analytic method, when applied to clinical examples of identification, can determine the unconscious motives for the identificatory fantasy.[2] Its drive components express various wishes for instinctual gratification, while the defenses may be said to have the reduction of unpleasure as their motive, and the superego contributions add expiatory, undoing, or punishment motives to the final result. Although all three varieties of motive were invariably present in each example studied, not all were equally important in the specific clinical situation in which an identification appeared; therefore, all may not be uncovered or interpreted in a given instance. The study also suggests that introjections and identifications are exactly the same with respect to these components, although their manifest form may differ because of variations in the quality of other ego func-

2. See Abend & Porder, 1986, for illustrative material.

SUMMARY

The view that prevails in the psychoanalytic literature is that there are varying developmental levels of internalization. This assumption rests on the phenomena of actual behavioral or structural change that accompany a given internalization and the degree of integration into the ego, as compared with a persistent subjective sense of strangeness or otherness of the quality in question. Were the conclusions of the study cited above to be widely adopted, this would have the effect of de-emphasizing the developmentally based distinctions among proposed varieties of internalization, thus ameliorating, if not eliminating altogether, one of the major areas of confusion for students of the theory of identification. Such unification and simplification are not likely to take place in the foreseeable future, however, because no consensus exists even among practitioners who share the same general viewpoint.

Perhaps because of the proliferation of psychoanalytic schools of thought using different conceptual frameworks, or perhaps because clinicians use the same terms differently or different terms to describe the same phenomena, the subject of identification remains a troublesome one for psychoanalysts and students of psychoanalysis. The term still refers to imagined mental processes as well as to mental contents. It is invoked to account for structuralization of the mind, to explain symptoms, to describe defenses, and to account for learning, therapeutic gains, and other changes in behavior. Its connection with object relationships is still confusing to many. Finally, its employment in diverse schemas by analysts with quite different beliefs regarding early mental development continues to handicap, rather than simplify, scientific communication.

REFERENCES

Abend, S. M. (1981). Psychic conflict and the concept of defense. *Psychoanal. Q.,* 50:67–76.

Abend, S. M., & Porder, M. S. (1986). Identification in the neuroses. *Int. J. Psychoanal.,* 67:201–208.

Abraham, K. (1924). A short study of the development of the libido, viewed in the light of mental disorders. Rpt. in *Selected Papers of Karl Abraham,* pp. 418–501. London: Hogarth Press, 1948.

Arlow, J. A. (1961). Ego psychology and the study of mythology. *J. Amer. Psychoanal. Assn.,* 9:371–393.

———. (1964). The Madonna's conception through the eyes. *Psychoanal. Study Soc.,* 3:13–25.

———. (1969). Unconscious fantasy and disturbances of conscious experience. *Psychoanal. Q.,* 38:1–27.

———. (1972). The only child. *Psychoanal. Q.,* 41:507–536.

Brenner, C. (1976). *Psychoanalytic Technique and Psychic Conflict.* New York: Int. Univ. Press.

———. (1982). *The Mind in Conflict.* New York: Int. Univ. Press.

Etchegoyan, R. H. (1985). Identification and its vicissitudes. *Int. J. Psychoanal.,* 66:3–18.

Fenichel, O. (1926). Identification. In *Collected Papers of Otto Fenichel,* vol. 1, pp. 97–112. New York: Norton, 1953.

———. (1936). *Problems of Psychoanalytic Technique.* New York: Psychoanalytic Quarterly.

Freud, A. (1936). *The Ego and the Mechanisms of Defense.* Rpt. New York: Int. Univ. Press, 1946.

Freud, S. (1900). *The Interpretation of Dreams. SE,* 4 & 5.

———. (1905). Fragment of an analysis of a case of hysteria. *SE,* 7:7–122.

———. (1908). Hysterical phantasies and their relation to bisexuality. *SE,* 9:159–166.

———. (1910). *Leonardo Da Vinci and a Memory of His Childhood. SE,* 11:63–137.

———. (1914). On narcissism. *SE,* 14:73–102.

———. (1917). Mourning and melancholia. *SE,* 14:243–258.

———. (1921). *Group Psychology and the Analysis of the Ego. SE,* 18:69–143.

———. (1923). *The Ego and the Id. SE,* 19:12–66.

Hartmann, H. (1939). *Ego Psychology and the Problem of Adaptation.* New York: Int. Univ. Press, 1958.

Jacobson, E. (1964). *The Self and the Object World.* New York: Int. Univ. Press.

Kernberg, O. F. (1975). *Borderline Conditions and Pathological Narcissism.* New York: Aronson.

Klein, M. (1935). A contribution to the psychogenesis of manic-depressive states. Rpt. in *Contributions to Psycho-Analysis.* London: Hogarth Press, 1948.

———. (1946). Some notes on schizoid mechanisms. *Int. J. Psychoanal.,* 27:99–110.

Loewald, H. W. (1973). On internalization. *Int. J. Psychoanal.,* 54:9–17.

Meissner, W. W. (1970). Notes on identification: I. *Psychoanal. Q.,* 39:513–589.

———. (1971). Notes on identification: II. *Psychoanal. Q.,* 40:227–302.

———. (1972). Notes on identification: III. *Psychoanal. Q.*, 41:224–260.

Rapaport, D. (1957). A theoretical analysis of the superego concept. Rpt. in *Collected Papers,* ed. M. M. Gill, pp. 685–709. New York: Basic Books, 1967.

Schafer, R. (1968a). *Aspects of Internalization.* New York: Int. Univ. Press.

———. (1968b). The mechanisms of defense. *Int. J. Psychoanal.*, 49:49–62.

Widlocher, D. (1985). The wish for identification and structural effects in the work of Freud. *Int. J. Psychoanal.*, 66:31–46.

Sander M. Abend, M.D.

35

IDENTITY

The term "identity" appears to have slipped into relative disuse in the past two decades, in part, perhaps, because of the concomitant rise in interest during this period in the concept of the self and the increased use of clinical terminology that reflects this change. It seems justifiable to add, however, that the fall from popularity of the identity concept is also, at least in part, a result of the failure of analysts to arrive at a clear, precise, generally accepted understanding of the meaning of the term. As a consequence of this difficulty, its clinical applications have remained to a considerable extent confusing and unsatisfactory for scientific purposes. Some analysts, like Kernberg (1967), find use for the concept in describing various manifestations of disorganization of the personality as "identity diffusion," a symptom that occurs in certain forms of severe pathology.

The very idea of identity seems to contain a certain degree of intrinsic ambiguity—witness its various meanings in standard English. It is derived from the Latin *idem,* meaning "the same"; but it is used both to describe a quality of sameness with something else and to imply an inner aspect of sameness over time. In the former sense it highlights a quality (or qualities) of the individual which is held in common with other individuals or groups, while in the latter it denotes in particular those special, unchanging features that enable a person to establish a unique, consistent sense of his or her own individu-

ality. Thus, depending on the situation, it may point either to likeness—that is to say, similarity—or to just the opposite—that is, those specific differences from others that serve to distinguish or "identify" one person as that person and no other.

Erikson (1956), who more than any other psychoanalytic author has addressed himself to the subject of identity, expresses this polarity most succinctly: "the term identity . . . connotes both a persistent sameness within oneself . . . and a persistent sharing of some kind of essential character with others" (p. 57). Although these qualities begin to be established early on in life, a final identity is not fixed until the close of adolescence. Erikson places considerable emphasis in this conception of identity on social roles, values, and ideals, though he does not limit his formulation to those alone. He also includes an external determinant of identity in the form of the responses of the surrounding society to the individual (recognition, expectations, and other feedback), which he believes contribute to self-definition and hence to identity formation. In part because his ideas rest so heavily on their social-descriptive aspects, other analysts have been dissatisfied with his formulations.

Some analysts have thought it more logical to approach the formation of identity as an aspect of early childhood development. Greenacre (1958) believes that the development of the body image becomes the core of identity formation. She stresses the effect of early tactile and visual perceptions on this process and observes that, although these begin to take place during the earlier oral and anal phases of development, they are especially significant in the phallic-oedipal period. Later modifications of identity in, and even after, adolescence do occur but are of lesser significance. Her view is that identity is a product of what Mahler (in Panel, 1958), who agrees with Greenacre's usage, termed the "separation-individuation processes" of early development and of the crystallization of the child's ideas about his or her own sexuality. These factors coalesce until, as Greenacre says, the child, "existing in a world of outer objects, knows he has thoughts and memory, appreciates relative size, but has knowledge of sexual differences, knows the names of his body parts and of himself. He is . . . aware of himself as a unit in a group" (pp. 625–626). She adds the observation that this core of identity formation is composed of wishful as well as realistic perceptions, memories, and ideas about oneself.

Jacobson (1964) attempted a further step toward rigorous theoretical clarification, putting emphasis on the establishment of self representations, mental contents she defines as "unconscious, preconscious, and conscious endopsychic representations of the bodily and mental self in the system ego" (p. 19). Early on, these are in tenuous relation to objective reality, but psychological maturation is accompanied by the formation of more and more realistic images of the self. In time, Jacobson says, "a concept of their sum total will simultaneously develop, i.e., an awareness of the self as a differentiated but organized entity which has continuity and direction." Her conclusion is that this awareness "will find an emotional expression in the experience of personal identity" (p. 23). She places herself closer to Greenacre and Mahler in understanding identity as the outgrowth in early childhood of the distinction of self from nonself but expresses some agreement with Erikson's ideas about identity formation as well, though she believes it too restrictive.

Eissler (in Panel, 1958) stresses the capacity to experience oneself as a continuum as the essential feature of identity. He believes that this is not firmly established until puberty. Lichtenstein (1961) proposes yet another view of identity, which he evolves partly on philosophical grounds. He suggests that man, unlike other creatures, seeks identity as a central theme of his entire life. This has its origin, according to him, in the earliest interactions with the mother, whose expectations and needs influence the child and to some degree affect all subsequent relationships. He assigns to this dyadic interpretation of identity a superordinate position in regulating human

activity. Although his ideas have not found wide acceptance among other analysts, they serve to further illustrate the broad range of interpretations and attempted definitions of identity that has plagued theoreticians and clinicians alike.

Some twenty years ago, I undertook an extensive review of the subject (Abend, 1974), in which I favored, on the grounds of promoting better conceptual clarity and clinical utility, a more restrictive usage of the term "identity," one suggested by Erikson (1956) and later elaborated by Blos (1962). I continue to prefer to think of identity as a consequence of the characteristic consolidations of young adulthood and to use the concept of problems of identity as referring to clinical manifestations of difficulties surrounding those consolidations. I believe that the processes in early childhood development that lead a young child to an awareness of his or her personal identity—that is, of knowledge of him- or herself as distinct from others—are best thought of as the evolution of a psychological self. According to my redefinition, the term "identity" should be reserved for the "loosely organized set of conscious and preconscious self-representations that serve to define the individual in a variety of social contexts. Included in its composition we would expect to find ideas regarding specific professional, social, and sexual roles and preferences, aspects of the person's political and religious ideology and other unique values, and his more important personal interests and avocations" (p. 620).

In attempting to apply these redrawn distinctions to clinical material, I also enlarged upon an observation of Spiegel's (1959) to underline the fact that patients' thoughts and feelings about their identities, as reported in psychoanalytic sessions, should not necessarily be assumed to refer to what analysts themselves understand by the term. Identity, like the self, is an abstraction which has no concrete existence in the mind. Patients cannot actually be aware of these entities any more than they can perceive their egos or their superegos as such, although they may describe psychological phenomena that analysts find it convenient to formulate by employing those abstract concepts. To call attention to this important clinical fact, I suggest that all subjective data obtained from patients that express ideas about their identities, or selves, be referred to by the terms "sense of identity" or "sense of self." Analytic material of that kind, it should be remembered, can only be understood accurately, as is generally true of other productions of patients, with the aid of free association to establish its true psychological meaning.

To illustrate, it would be correct for analysts to refer to patients who display disturbances in the assumption of comfortable and stable social, sexual, and professional roles as having identity problems. Impostors and "as if" characters represent severe instances of identity disturbance so defined; but there exist many milder variations as well. However, patients who complain of being uncertain of their identity or of who they are or how they fit in with others may not necessarily display these characteristics. Analysis of their comments often reveals that they are merely giving expression at the manifest level to underlying unconscious fantasies of weakness, smallness, sexual aberration, and so forth which bear no literal relation to those features of self-definition and social adjustment subsumed under the concept of identity.

In my clinical examples, of both patients with true identity problems and those whose difficulties were expressed as a subjectively disturbed sense of identity, the most important causative factors were often unconscious conflicts involving aspects of sexual identity. This is in accord with long-standing psychoanalytic recognition of the enormous significance in both normal and pathological development of those conscious and unconscious ideas about genital anatomy and sexual functioning that contribute to a person's sexual identity. While this general observation is as old as psychoanalysis itself, researchers in recent years have attempted to further refine our understanding of certain aspects of the development of sexual identity through studies of people with serious physical sexual anomalies and those with gross manifest disturbances of sexual identity. In these sophisticated developmental studies child observation facilities have been utilized as well.

Among psychoanalysts, Stoller (1968) has made the most extensive use of the first kind of data, while Galenson and Roiphe (1981) have contributed important findings regarding sexual development on the basis of their studies of the behavior of toddlers in a research nursery setting. Stoller uses the term "core gender identity" to refer to the formation of an unalterable (pre)conscious sense of one's own gender, which he notes is established in normal persons by the time of the phallic stage. This remains unchanged throughout life, even though what he calls "gender identity" in the larger sense, which corresponds to what is usually referred to by others as "sexual identity," influenced as it is by other psychological forces including unconscious conflicts, is constantly being developed and modified. He suggests that the core gender identity is the result of three components: (1) the anatomy of the external genitalia, through its appearance, its impact on both the child's and the parents' thoughts about the child's gender, and by means of the physical sensa-

tions these organs produce; (2) learned awareness of gender derived from parent–child interactions which influence ideas, expectations, and experiences; and (3) a postulated—but so far impossible to demonstrate—biological factor of a hormonal or neural nature.

Galenson and Roiphe (1981) have described what they term an "early genital phase," which normally occurs between fifteen and twenty-four months in children of both sexes. Their material documents the presence of reactions in all children which indicates an earlier, more important discovery of genital differences than psychoanalytic theory had previously assumed to be the case. Typical reactions are characteristically different in little boys and little girls. These researchers concluded that the latter part of the second year of life is a critical period in the development of sexual identity, because it contributes to the shaping of the oedipal constellation which follows shortly thereafter. These findings are in accord with the empirical observations of Stoller (1968) and of Money and Ehrhardt (1972), who agree that core gender identity is established by the end of the second year of life.

In psychoanalytic clinical presentations, a common but conceptually misleading kind of terminology is often employed that disregards core gender identity altogether. Patients are spoken of as having a masculine or a feminine identification or identity, or it is stated that some material derives from such identifications or identities. In such loose usage, the idea of a sexual identity seems to be employed almost interchangeably with the term "sexual identification." In either case, this usage implies the existence of a coherent, concrete element of the personality constituting a unitary structure of one or the other—that is, masculine or feminine—kind. But clinical observations show, to the contrary, that manifestations of identifications with the opposite sex or the same sex are neither simple nor unitary; and the same may be said of their underlying determinants. Various derivatives of these complexities have been observed and reported by many analysts, beginning with Freud. The contrasexual identifications, which are the ones usually emphasized in clinical discussions, are in fact seen to be a set of fantasies, derived from different sources, involving multiple and complex motivations.

REFERENCES

Abend, S. M. (1974). Problems of identity. *Psychoanal. Q.*, 43:606–637.

Blos, P. (1962). *On Adolescence*. New York: Free Press of Glencoe.

Erikson, E. H. (1956). The problem of ego identity. *J. Amer. Psychoanal. Assn.,* 4:56–121.

Galenson, E., & Roiphe, H. (1981). *Infantile Origins of Sexual Identity.* New York: Int. Univ. Press.

Greenacre, P. (1958). Early physical determinants in the development of the sense of identity. *J. Amer. Psychoanal. Assn.,* 6:612–627.

Jacobson, E. (1964). *The Self and the Object World.* New York: Int. Univ. Press.

Kernberg, O. F. (1967). Borderline personality organization. *J. Amer. Psychoanal. Assn.,* 15:641–685.

Lichtenstein, H. (1961). Identity and sexuality. *J. Amer. Psychoanal. Assn.,* 9:179–260.

Money, J., & Ehrhardt, A. A. (1972). *Man and Woman, Boy and Girl.* Baltimore: Johns Hopkins Univ. Press.

Panel (1958). Problems of identity. David L. Rubinfine, reporter. *J. Amer. Psychoanal. Assn.,* 6:131–142.

Spiegel, L. A. (1959). The self, the sense of self, and perception. *Psychoanal. Study Child,* 14:81–109.

Stoller, R. J. (1968). *Sex and Gender.* New York: Science House.

PART VII

CONFLICT, DEFENSE, STRUCTURAL THEORY, AND METAPSYCHOLOGY

David Beres, M.D.

36

CONFLICT

Conflict, which implies opposition, is intrinsic to life and ubiquitous in human psychic activity. It takes many forms, which may be categorized in one or two groups. The first, directly observable, includes conflict between the individual and the forces of nature, between the individual and society, between the individual and the group, and between one individual and another. The second group is intrapsychic, inferred from data obtained by the psychoanalytic method; it includes, on the one hand, conflict between wishes, impulses, feelings, and thoughts and, on the other hand, the prohibitions, inhibitions, and ideals that comprise the human psyche. Behind the observable, external conflicts of the first group there are always unconscious elements of the second group, analogous to the distinction between manifest and latent dream content. Obversely, intrapsychic conflicts are manifested in observable phenomena such as symptoms, actions, and thoughts.

Conflict may be resolved, or it may lead to pathology. With resolution, there may follow growth, development, and sublimation. Psychoanalysis since its earliest days has dealt with conflict, both implicitly and explicitly, as a central facet of human psychic activity, whether normal or pathological.

Behind the slow mutual effort of psychoanalyst and analysand in the clinical situation is the ever-present question: "What is the conflict?" The patient presents him or herself with a symptom such as a phobia, an organic malfunction, difficulties in relation to persons, mood disturbances, anxieties, depression, disturbances of self-esteem, or sexual disturbances. He or she may or may not verbalize a sense of conflict. In any case, a conscious statement of a conflict by the patient must, like the manifest content of a dream, be subjected to psychoanalytic scrutiny to reveal the unconscious latent conflict. Attention must be directed to the latter as well as to the former.

Clinical evidence for the existence of conflict appears first of all in the complaints with which the patient presents him- or herself. The evidence is strengthened by affect disturbances, especially anxiety and depression; by exaggerated characterological manifestations—ambivalence, doubting, and indecision; and by parapraxes and dream content. Freud noted that inhibition in a dream represents conflict, what he called a "conflict of will" (1900, p. 246).

The assumed absence of conflict in perversion, character disorder, narcissism, and self-pathology must be seriously questioned. Here too, only psychoanalytic investigation can decide.

In his earliest writings Freud (Breuer & Freud, 1893–95, pp. 268ff.) described conflict as the opposition between ideas, wishes, and emotions, on the one hand, and the conscious dictates of morality, on the other. Later he recognized that conflict could be totally unconscious, and on this basis he formulated the concept of conflict among what he termed "different substructures of the psychic system." These substructures are the components of the structural theory of psychic function—id, ego, and superego.

An instinctual drive, libidinal or aggressive, expressed as a wish, an impulse, or a fantasy, seeks gratification. The ego function of impulse control may allow gratification. In that case the result is "pleasure," discharge of the impulse in an act of love or hate, as the impulse dictates. But this function of impulse control may instead either consciously or unconsciously signal a danger situation and prevent gratification of the impulse. Instead of pleasure, the individual experiences "unpleasure," manifested in one or another affective state—anxiety, guilt, or depression.

In 1926, in *Inhibitions, Symptoms and Anxiety,* Freud listed a hierarchy of danger situations that elicit unpleasure. For the infant, the danger is loss of a loved object. When self and nonself, along with object constancy, become defined, the danger is loss of love. With further development, the danger is injury or mutilation, manifested in fantasies of castration. With internalization of moral precepts, the danger is superego disapproval, what Freud called "social anxiety." This progression does not mean that the early danger situations disappear as the later ones appear. As the progression develops, there is persistence of the early danger situations with intermixture and overlap. To his early emphasis on sexuality as the basis of conflict, Freud later added conflicts based on aggression.

The person may be consciously aware of the danger situation, or the response may be unconscious. In either case it is based on earlier experiences of a traumatic nature. In the infant the experience is actual and immediate. The infant has not yet developed the ego function of anxiety, and the response is an organismic state of unpleasure, often with somatic accompaniments.

One cannot speak of conflict in the structural sense in an infant whose psyche has not yet differentiated the substructures of id, ego, and superego. The current danger situation in the individual who has differentiated these substructures is a new edition of the infantile danger based on its unconscious reactivation.

Conflict is a complex phenomenon which evades facile generalization. The usual formulation of conflict as between id and ego calls for further definition. Recognition of a danger situation involves a number of ego functions, especially memory and judgment, though these may be based on unconscious psychic activity. This recognition is accompanied by an unpleasurable affective response and ideational content, also possibly based on uncon-

scious psychic activity. Ego defenses are mobilized to eliminate or minimize the unpleasurable affect and to prevent discharge of the drive derivative that brought on the danger situation. At which point shall we speak of conflict?

Is it enough to say that conflict is between the id drive derivative and ego defense? Basically this is true, since the ego is conceptualized as mediating by its functions between the id, the superego, and external reality; and it is useful, speaking metaphorically, to designate conflict as opposition between id and ego. But the situation is actually more complicated. The danger situation cannot be separated from the accompanying affect, and the affective response of unpleasure, whether anxiety or depression, evokes the defenses. Although the conflict is described as between impulses and defenses, between id and ego, it is necessary to note that since affect is involved, there is also the effort to diminish or eliminate the affective state of unpleasure, either anxiety or depression. Hence, although the ego defenses are not in conflict with the affective state, without the latter there would be no conflict. In various publications Charles Brenner (1975, 1976, 1982) has discussed the interaction in conflict of drive derivatives, affect, ideation, and defense.

In 1911 Karl Abraham wrote: "We fear a coming evil; we grieve over one that has occurred" (p. 137). Thus, depressive affect, as well as anxiety, may signal conflict, a distinction recently emphasized by Brenner (1982).

Conflict is not only between id and ego. It may also be between ego and superego or between ego and the external world.[1] The role of the superego in conflict adds to its complexity. The superego introduces guilt, with subsequent depressive affect and the need for punishment. Although depression, according to Abraham and Brenner, follows a past occurrence, loss, or trauma, there is still impending danger of further punishment and loss with the additional affect of anxiety.

Conflict between ego and superego derives from the danger situation of superego disapproval. The sense of self, a complex of ego functions, seeks approval and love, at first from external sources, the

---

1. It must be emphasized that these are metaphorical statements. Id, ego, and superego are abstract terms, and it is inaccurate to postulate conflict between abstractions. Conflict is between the *functions* subsumed under these abstract terms. It is precisely the clinical observation of the grouping of functions in conflict and adaptation that supports the heuristic value of the structural theory. Awareness of the metaphorical use of the terms id, ego, and superego avoids the danger of reification.

parents, and later, with internalization, from the superego. In this conflict ego is on one side, superego on the other. The accompanying affects in this conflict are guilt and depression, which serve as the signals to evoke ego defenses. Ego–superego conflict cannot appear before there is internalization of the moral attitudes, ideals, and prohibitions that comprise superego functions. Before this occurs in the child (and also in some adults), the conflict is between the child's wish to gratify his or her impulses and the danger of losing parental (in the adult, social) approval. The gradual internalization of parental and social standards may be spoken of as a superego precursor.

Conflict, whether between id and ego or between ego and superego, is followed by an attempt at compromise, bringing in the synthetic function of the ego and resulting in what is called "compromise formation." The compromise formation may result in a symptom, a character change, or adaptation. If the signal function fails to mobilize adequate defense and compromise formation, the situation deteriorates into an overwhelmingly disruptive experience—panic in the case of anxiety, despair and even suicide in the case of depression.

I

Conflict takes on wider significance in relation to society, whether it be the society of the family or the society of the group. Such conflict expresses itself in the distinction between the pleasure principle and the reality principle (Freud, 1911).

Ego functions serve to gratify certain id impulses as well as to inhibit others. The determining factor is the surrounding reality, which includes the ethical demands of the family and society. The id impulse may not in itself be inherently dangerous; it becomes so because of external counterpressures which are later internalized as the superego.

According to the pleasure principle, the child seeks gratification of his or her drives but soon learns that he or she must, to a greater or lesser degree, conform to the demands of external reality—that is, conform to what Freud called the "reality principle." It follows that conflict from this point of view is between the search for pleasure and the restrictions of reality and that it is therefore unavoidable and ubiquitous in both normal and pathological states. As Freud (1930) made clear, it is the price man must pay to maintain civilization.

There is evidence that conflict in early life has an essential role in character development and in the development of ego and superego functions. The early experiences and conflicts in the mother–child relationship and the father–child relationship are the foundation for the later coping mechanisms and defenses of the individual. A familiar psychoanalytic observation is that the defensive maneuvers of the adult may be similar to those used in early life, which appear again in transference resistance in the psychoanalytic situation.

Conflict may result in one of the following conditions:

1. Any action to gratify an id impulse requires the services of some ego functions. If the impulse would result in a danger situation, the inhibition of these ego functions helps to avoid the danger and the conflict. This response is especially evident in the inhibition of sexual functions.

2. The defenses may not be adequate to eliminate the danger and the unpleasure. The defenses distort and disguise the impulse, which nevertheless achieves discharge and partial gratification in disguised and distorted form. This compromise, if not disabling, may be adaptive in relation to the social functioning of the individual; it may reduce the acute danger situation and unpleasure but result in a disturbed body function or disturbed thought process—that is, a symptom. In the latter instance a new conflict ensues: on one side the self-dystonic symptom, on the other the ego defenses.

3. The most satisfactory outcome of a current conflict is, of course, a "normal" resolution with elimination of unpleasure and continued adequate functioning, especially in the area of the conflict. Freud (1937) raised the question: "Is it possible by means of analytic therapy to dispose of a conflict between an instinct and the ego, or of a pathogenic instinctual demand upon the ego, permanently and definitely?" (p. 224). In his answer he emphasized the limits of psychoanalytic therapy. He called upon the "Witch Metapsychology" and offered the theory of the "taming of the instincts" along with the "alteration of the ego" as factors promoting coping. The relation between the "strength of the instinct" and the "strength of the ego" determines the outcome of a conflict, whether pathology or resolution.

We are dealing here with unquantifiable elements. It is well established that the intensity of instinctual drives, as clinically observed, varies at different periods of development—puberty, adolescence, parenthood, and menopause, for example. In normal development the ego functions mature and increase their efficacy and adaptive capacities.

An important element in the response to conflict, in addition to defense, is the role of other ego functions. The response is markedly affected by the specific ego functions available to the individual to cope with the danger situation and the accompanying affective state. The sense of reality and the testing of reality are especially important in this regard. A child with an as yet undeveloped reality function will respond to a danger situation far differently from how he or she will respond later when the capacity to evaluate situations more realistically has developed. Other ego functions are also involved, including thought, judgment, memory, and the synthetic function. The defenses also pass through a developmental and maturational process, as does the capacity of the ego to regulate and control instinctual drive impulses. In each instance it is the development and maturation of the specific functions that are crucial.

II

In this section I shall take up briefly some specific problems.

Conflict and creativity. Conflict and neurosis are not synonymous. As we saw in the preceding section, neurosis is only one of several possible outcomes of the psyche's effort to resolve or modify conflict. This applies to all aspects of human activity, including social relations, work, and artistic and scientific creativity.

Many psychoanalytic writings and literary articles attribute the artist's creativity to neurosis. Artists are no more immune to conflict and pathology than are other humans; indeed, much pathology is evident in the life of artists. Conflict may motivate the artist in his work, but the creative act stems not from whatever pathology may exist but from the artist's talent and from those ego functions that are not impaired by his or her pathology. What the artist contributes is a distinctive response to conflict related to his or her greater sensitivity to unconscious forces than others.

External and inner conflict. The relation of external conflict to inner psychic conflict is one of mutual interaction. Phenomenologically, the external conflict may be one in which the individual is faced with the need to choose between alternatives or deal with external danger. Behind the external conflict, however, is a deeper, unconscious conflict, activated by the external situation. Under analytic scrutiny, the unconscious conflict is usually found to be rooted in infantile fantasies. The external situation gets woven into the fabric of the unconscious fantasy, resulting in an intermixture of intrapsychic conflict and external conflict. It is not uncommon, particularly in today's turbulent world, for profound intrapsychic conflicts to find external expression in dedication to some social movement. The existence of the intra-

psychic conflict does not, of course, determine the value or lack of value of the social movement. There is a difference between a struggle for human rights and terrorism, though both may have a similar base in intrapsychic conflict.

The distinction between "realistic" and "neurotic" conflict is more a semantic than a significant issue. Most obvious is the use of the term "realistic conflict" to refer to a conscious conflict relating to an external occurrence. But even in these instances the ever-present unconscious element compromises the designation "realistic."

The label "neurotic conflict" may be applied to the secondary conflict surrounding symptomatic neurosis. This conflict may involve the unpleasure of the symptoms of the neurosis. The neurosis is a compromise formation, whereas the source of the original conflict persists and requires further adaptive resolution. In addition, the neurosis may involve impairment of ego functions, which in turn evokes conflict. The secondary conflict surrounding the neurosis may be with fantasied objects or with real objects to which fantasied roles are assigned. The latter type is especially evident in oedipal fantasies.

Pre-oedipal and oedipal conflict. A frequent clinical distinction is that between pre-oedipal and oedipal conflicts. It is well established that the clinical manifestations of conflict differ at different phases of development. It is also well established clinically that the oral and anal wishes of early childhood may persist into adulthood and influence the manifestations of the oedipal conflict. But the appearance of pre-oedipal elements in an adult conflict does not always point to a pre-oedipal conflict. It may indeed be so in cases of fixation and regression. But in other cases it may be the expression of oedipal conflict in pre-oedipal terms.

Pre-oedipal conflicts center around danger situations relating to loss of the love object and loss of love. Separation-individuation and ambivalence are prominent elements of infantile conflicts. The child's struggle is between the urge to separate from the symbiotic mother and the desire for reunion, the latter with the danger of engulfment.

Ambivalence evokes a conflict surrounding the person with whom the child, and later the adult, is in close relationship. The ambivalence stems from the mixed libidinal and aggressive drive impulses directed toward the same object and the danger in unconscious fantasy of losing or destroying the object if the aggressive impulses are given full expression. The preservation of the object becomes an important consideration in a clinical understanding of object relationships and symptomatic difficulties.

As the child's sexuality develops, there appears

the typical, and in our culture ubiquitous, conflict involving the child's relationship to the father and the mother, the oedipal conflict. This conflict is in most instances the core conflict in psychoneurosis and carries with it the fantasy of injury and mutilation, through castration.

Conflict and psychosis. The presence of conflict in psychosis has been recognized since the early days of psychoanalysis, although the theoretical basis has not as yet been fully established. In 1896 Freud designated paranoia "a psychosis of defence" that "proceeds from the repression of disturbing memories" (p. 174). Later, following the structural formulation of the psyche, he proposed that psychosis is the result of a conflict between "the ego and the external world" (1924, p. 149), with manifestations resulting from defensive withdrawal from the distressing reality.

More recently, Arlow and Brenner (1969) emphasized the role of conflict in psychosis, manifest in the interaction of drive impulse and ego defense. I agree with them that the concepts which Freud applied so fruitfully to the neuroses can also be applied with great advantage to the psychoses, where they provide a more useful frame of reference than the earlier concepts of decathexis, hypercathexis, and recathexis.

The psychotic patient is subject to the same instinctual drives as the neurotic or normal person. The differences lie in the intensity of the drives, both libidinal and aggressive, and in the capacity of the ego to control or modify them. These are matters that require further exploration.

The role of deviant ego function in psychosis (and in severe character disorders and narcissistic disorders) is clinically observable; but the extent to which this is due to developmental factors (either congenital or the result of early trauma) versus defensive regression must be carefully evaluated in each patient. A further question, difficult to answer at this stage of our knowledge, is what determines both the developmental defects and the tendency to regression in coping with conflict.

Where regression is a predominant defense, ego functions suffer marked distortion. This is especially evident in the case of the reality function, which Freud (1924) considered an inherent element in psychosis. The distorted reality function in psychosis, however, is a result of the conflict, not its source, and involves other components of this function—adaptation to reality, testing of reality, and the sense of reality (see also Beres, 1956).

Compromise formation between drive and defense is less successful in psychotic conflict than in psychoneurosis, and may even be ineffective, as measured by the adaptive capacities of the patient. The

outcome of compromise in psychoneurosis is a symptom or an inhibition of function; in psychosis it may be hallucination or delusion, which defends against the return to consciousness of the repressed ideas, memories, or fantasies. These may appear in changed form as uncontrolled overt acts of a sexual or aggressive nature.

Phenomenological and structural aspects of conflict. Consideration of the concept of conflict differs according to whether it is approached from a phenomenological or a structural viewpoint. Neither approach excludes the other.

Typical examples of the phenomenological approach to conflict relate to the conflict between passivity and activity and that between dependence and independence. The child is from the moment of birth in relationship to another person, the mother. The helplessness of the neonate, the utter dependence on the mother, gradually gives way to increasing separation, individuation, and independence. One cannot speak of a conflict in the early stages of this process. Until the child has developed the capacity to distinguish between self and nonself, and so for object constancy, there may be distress and unpleasure, but not intrapsychic conflict.

The adult patient may also present phenomenological aspects of conflicts between passivity and activity or between dependence and independence. But the adult brings to these conflicts a more or less developed psychic structure, a complex of psychic functions, not the unstructured chaos of the infant mind. The adult's instinctual drive impulses are expressed as wishes and unconscious fantasies of infantile bliss. The dangers, conscious or unconscious, are loss of the object and loss of love. Ego defenses are mobilized, and superego functions introduce ideal demands and the danger of punishment for failing to live up to these demands.

Therefore, what appears phenomenologically in the adult as a conflict between passivity and activity or between dependence and independence is found on psychoanalytic scrutiny to be a conflict between id drive derivatives and ego defenses or between superego demands and ego defenses. Both the phenomenological and psychoanalytic approaches are necessary to gain a comprehensive picture.

In every conflict there is the ever-present object: the person, real or fantasied. This involves the concept of object relations. It does not mean, as some authors have argued, that there is a separate object relations theory in opposition to the structural theory. Object relations and structural concepts are both part of psychoanalytic psychology. To separate them is to create a false dichotomy.

Manifestations of conflict. Various factors influence

the manifestation of conflict, including the developmental level of the individual, the nature of the psychopathology, and the cultural surroundings.

The progression of human development from infancy to death gives rise to a series of inevitable crises and conflicts that vary from one phase of development to another. The toddler faces the conflict of separation; the six-year old, the developed oedipal conflict; the puberty child, the conflict around masturbation; the adolescent, the conflict of impending adulthood, of love and professional choice; the young adult, marriage and parenthood; the older adult, the loss of youth; the aged, the fear of death. In each instance there remains the analytic task of determining the unconscious factors and fantasies underlying the overt manifestations, the relation of the current conflict to infantile residua, and the role of id, ego, and superego functions.

Conflict is present in every pathological state, whether psychoneurotic, psychotic, character disorder, or self disorder. The patient with character disorder or self disorder may deny an inner conflict and assume that his or her conflict is only with others, with society, with the "establishment." But on analytic scrutiny, an intrapsychic conflict will always be revealed. The basic danger situations described by Freud operate in every case, though to varying degree in each individual. The different ego defenses, the different state of development of the ego and superego functions, the intensity of the drive impulses, all combine to influence the overt clinical picture.

The influence of cultural factors on the nature of conflict in the individual is most significant in conflicts involving superego functions. Parental attitudes reflecting the social surrounding will determine ethical standards, the goals of education, the basis of self-esteem, and the limits of aggression and will thus determine the area of conflict.

Intrasystemic and intersystemic conflict. The distinction between intrasystemic and intersystemic conflict (Hartmann, 1951) is based on the structural theory of psychic function. Intersystemic conflict, as has been discussed, is defined as between id and ego or ego and superego. These are abstract concepts which serve to codify in theory the clinical manifestations of conflict.

Intrasystemic conflict is most evident in conflict between opposing instinctual drives, between hostile and loving impulses in ambivalence, between retention and elimination in the child in anal conflict. Different ego interests may be in conflict with each other. Similarly, the moral superego structures may make contradictory demands.

A striking example of intrasystemic conflict is the phenomenon of fetishism, which Freud (1927) described as a "splitting of the ego." This entails a partial distortion of the reality function, with part of external perception being disavowed and two contradictory attitudes existing side by side. This is evident in the fetishist who, with the help of the fetish, disavows the absence of a penis in the female at the same time that he is consciously aware of the actuality.

Another example of intrasystemic conflict is in cases of contradictory identifications, as with the two parents, one of whom is seen as "good," the other as "bad." To accept identity with the "good" parent may mean to give up valued qualities of the "bad" parent. Where this would result in gender confusion, severe conflict may ensue, involving the wish to assume a sexual role opposite to the actual sex and the defense opposing this wish.

Conflict-free results and autonomy of function. Heinz Hartmann, in *Ego Psychology and the Problem of Adaptation* (1939), introduced the concept of a conflict-free ego sphere, an indication of the increasing influence of psychoanalysis on general psychology as well as of the interrelationship of these two disciplines. Hartmann noted that the concept of a conflict-free ego sphere refers to processes, not to a "province of the mind" (p. 9). He said: "Not every adaptation to the environment, or every learning and maturation process, is a conflict" (p. 8). He referred to the development "*outside of conflict* of perception, intention, object comprehension, thinking, language, recall-phenomena" (p. 8), as well as to motor development. These are the "autonomous" functions of the ego, which may, however, subsequently be involved in conflict. Conversely, ego functions that develop out of conflict may subsequently achieve autonomy (that is, secondary autonomy).

Autonomy is relevant to specific ego functions, not to ego as a global structure. To speak of "ego autonomy" is to reify an abstraction. Hartmann defined autonomy as "stability of . . . ego function, or, more precisely, its resistivity to regression and instinctualization" (1955, p. 229).

Ego functions do not operate in isolation. They are subject to the influence of drives, the superego, and the outer world. Where these influences create conflict, the autonomy of the ego function is disturbed, and the free activity of autonomy is lost. In an earlier paper (1971) I wrote: "Autonomy of ego function implies freedom—freedom from the disturbing influence of conflict, and freedom to operate with appropriate efficiency according to the role of the specific function in the psyche's organization and in relation to id, superego, and the external world" (p. 11).

The human psyche is a unit, capable of adaptation to the inner forces of the instinctual drives and to the demands of the external environment. For this it requires the activity of functions subsumed in psychoanalytic theory under the concepts of ego and superego. The development and maturation of these functions are the result of the interaction between conflict and conflict-free processes under the influence of the synthetic function of the ego.

Vulnerability to conflict. Are some patients particularly vulnerable to conflict? Freud believed that such a tendency to conflict exists, attributing it to the intervention of "an element of free aggressiveness." Clinical observation supports this hypothesis. In patients fixated at early levels of drive function with unresolved aggressive impulses, unconscious guilt and rage reactions will more readily be subject to conflict.

Another factor that increases the tendency to conflict is immaturity of ego and superego, especially in relation to others. Dependence on the external object, whether parent or parent-surrogate, and minimal internalization of superego function subject the individual to frustration when needs are not gratified, with subsequent aggressive responses and conflict.

Multiple factors in conflict resolution. The child's experience in coping with the unavoidable conflicts to which he or she is exposed in the course of maturing will influence the development of defense patterns, ideals or moral attitudes, and ego and superego functions.

Recent emphasis on narcissistic disorders has led to a debate between "self psychology" and "structural (i.e., ego.) psychology" (Kohut 1971, 1977). The basic issue of difference is the clinical approach of the two psychologies. The self psychologist claims the priority and dominance of the self analysis; the ego psychologist works with the analysand's productions whether these apply to structural or self matters.

Kohut maintains that sexual fantasies (and presumably neurotic conflicts) are secondary results of the "discharge of intense narcissistic tensions" (1971, p. 72). He postulates that the underlying structural conflict, especially the oedipal conflict, becomes evident and is to be analyzed only in the terminal phase of the self analysis.

"Self" and "ego" are both abstract terms. Psychic activity can only be observed by its functions of which the "sense of self" is basic to what are called "disorders of the self" and to narcissism (Beres, 1981). This function is subject to conflict and to malfunction. The conflict may lead to compromise formation and, as the symptom is a compromise in a structural conflict, so it may be considered that narcissistic disorders are compromise formations of conflicts in the sense of self.

Conflict, ego synthetic function, and compromise formation. Every patient who seeks out an analyst is a person in conflict. The conflict may be between wishes and inner prohibitions or between wishes and social demands; or it may be in the area of self-esteem, in the image the person has of him- or herself. In every instance it may be either a conscious or an unconscious conflict.

Two factors coexist in every case of psychopathology, in the child as in the adult—intrapsychic conflict and developmental deviation. Both demand scrutiny, though one or the other may predominate.

Conflict and narcissism. I have noted Freud's caution regarding the limits of psychoanalytic therapy as a means of permanently disposing of a conflict. Resolution of a conflict implies at best that the conflict no longer interferes with appropriate functioning and that unpleasurable affects are reduced or eliminated. This may be accomplished through the individual's own capacities or, as in the case of psychoanalytic therapy, through insight into, and understanding of, the unconscious factors involved.

I recognize the happy circumstance that many persons overcome their infantile conflicts as they mature and come closer to a "normal" life. With or without therapy, some individuals learn renunciation, compromise, or adaptation. Some are fortunate enough to be able to sublimate conflict and create art or science.

Conflict is not pathological. Without conflict there would be no need for sublimation and no art and no science. Without conflict the individual would remain permanently a child.

Adaptation does not necessarily mean acceptance of the established order. Over the centuries, men and women who have refused to surrender in their conflict against tyranny, oppression, and injustice have made possible the progression, however limping and halting, of society toward justice and freedom.

Every overt action or thought is influenced by unconscious factors, some rooted in conflict, others conflict-free. The conflictual elements will have been subjected to compromise formation with either resolution or neurotic symptomatology. In the latter instance, the compromise may result in actions that have sublimatory value in work or social relations. Even the compromise of a conflict not fully resolved may result in a contribution to society; this should be judged and valued accordingly, without regard to the unconscious elements that influenced it.

Conflict remains a potent element in psychoanalytic theory and practice. The capacity of the ego to synthesize, to effect a compromise formation that leads the psyche from conflict to adaptation, sublimation, and growth, is the significant factor in the resolution of conflict, the aim of psychoanalytic therapy.

REFERENCES

Abraham, K. (1911). Notes on the psycho-analytical investigation and treatment of manic-depressive insanity and allied conditions. Rpt. in *Selected Papers on Psycho-Analysis*, pp. 137–156. London: Hogarth Press, 1948.

Arlow, J. A., & Brenner, C. (1969). The psychopathology of the psychoses. *Int. J. Psychoanal.*, 50:5–14.

Beres, D. (1956). Ego deviation and the concept of schizophrenia. *Psychoanal. Study Child*, 11:164–235.

———. (1971). Ego autonomy and ego pathology. *Psychoanal. Study Child*, 26:3–23.

———. (1981). Self, identity, and narcissism. *Psychoanal. Q.*, 50:515–534.

Brenner, C. (1975). Affects and psychic conflict. *Psychoanal. Q.*, 44:5–28.

———. (1976). *Psychoanalytic Technique and Psychic Conflict*. New York: Int. Univ. Press.

———. (1982). *The Mind in Conflict*. New York: Int. Univ. Press.

Breuer, J., & Freud, S. (1893–95). *Studies on Hysteria. SE*, 2.

Freud, S. (1896). Further remarks on the neuro-psychoses of defence. *SE*, 3:159–185.

———. (1900). *The Interpretation of Dreams. SE*, 4 & 5.

———. (1911). Formulations on the two principles of mental functioning. *SE*, 12:218–226.

———. (1924). Neurosis and psychosis. *SE*, 19:149–153.

———. (1926). *Inhibitions, Symptoms and Anxiety. SE*, 20:87–174.

———. (1927). Fetishism. *SE*, 21:149–157.

———. (1930). *Civilization and Its Discontents. SE*, 21:59–145.

———. (1937). Analysis terminable and interminable. *SE*, 23:200–253.

Hartmann, H. (1939). *Ego Psychology and the Problem of Adaptation*. New York: Int. Univ. Press, 1958.

———. (1951). Technical implications of ego psychology. Rpt. in *Essays on Ego Psychology*, pp. 142–154. New York: Int. Univ. Press, 1964.

———. (1955). Notes on the theory of sublimation. Rpt. in *Essays on Ego Psychology*, pp. 215–240. New York: Int. Univ. Press, 1964.

Kohut, H. (1971). *The Analysis of the Self*. New York: Int. Univ. Press.

———. (1977). *The Restoration of the Self*. New York: Int. Univ. Press.

Martin S. Willick, M.D.

37

DEFENSE

The concept of defense has been a cornerstone of psychoanalytic theory since the inception of Freud's investigations. Today, no discussion of theoretical, developmental, or clinical issues can reasonably take place without consideration of the concept of defense. As basic and fundamental as it is, however, it has been altered, revised, and refined as clinical experience has sharpened the psychoanalyst's awareness of the complexities of psychological development and psychic conflict.

Defenses are unconscious mental processes instituted by the ego to ward off painful affects such as anxiety and depression. They arise out of intrapsychic conflict, but they may be part of normal adaptation and character development or involved in pathological symptoms and character traits. Defenses may be utilized quite early in life in a normal and adaptive way; but if they persist unchanged as development proceeds, they may become part of pathological compromise formation.

A HISTORY OF THE CONCEPT OF DEFENSE

A brief historical survey of the evolution of the psychoanalytic concept of defense can serve both to clarify its meaning and to explicate some of the controversy regarding its usage. Freud first introduced the term in "The neuro-psychoses of defence" (1894). In this paper, which foreshadowed the structural theory, he wrote that in order to ward off

unacceptable ideas or feelings that would cause "distressing affect," a person unconsciously resorts to certain mental processes that oppose these ideas or feelings and render them less disturbing. These mental processes, which take place outside the person's awareness, he called "defenses." This was one of Freud's earliest statements about conflict within the mind, wherein one part has wishes or feelings that another part finds objectionable, opposing their continued presence in consciousness. In opposing them, the part of the mind later known as the ego institutes defenses against the awareness of these unacceptable thoughts or feelings.

Freud went even further in that early paper when he noted that certain symptoms or certain types of illness were characterized by the use of a particular kind of defense. In hysteria, he wrote, the energy associated with the unacceptable idea, feeling, or impulse was converted into a bodily sensation or movement, and the defensive process was called "conversion." In obsessional neurosis, on the other hand, the defense was displacement, whereby the affect or emotion associated with the unacceptable idea was displaced onto another, seemingly unrelated idea. In the psychotic state he called "hallucinatory confusion," the objectionable idea was denied, and often external reality was denied as well. Shortly thereafter, in "Further remarks on the neuro-psychoses of defence" (1896), Freud pointed out that in paranoia, the defense used was projection, whereby the objectionable impulse was attributed to someone or something outside the person's own self. By 1896, therefore, Freud had already propounded his view that the choice of neurosis was closely associated with the prominent defense used in the conflict situation.

While Freud continued to write about these particular kinds of defenses and to define others, such as reaction formation, undoing, and isolation, his interest soon shifted to the defense of repression, which came to occupy the central place in his theories of neurosogenesis. During his earlier work, as a matter of fact, he frequently used the term "repression" in place of, or interchangeably with, "defense." Freud conceived of repression as the major defensive process whereby ideas were kept out of consciousness by a considerable expenditure of energy he called "countercathexis." This energy from the ego was necessary, he thought, to counter the pressure or energy associated with unconscious ideas or impulses pressing for discharge.

The introduction of the structural theory in *The Ego and the Id* (1923) and the revision of the theory of anxiety in *Inhibitions, Symptoms and Anxiety* (1926) constituted a major advance in Freud's conceptualizations and in psychoanalytic theory. Previously, anxiety was considered to be the result of repression. Now, repression was seen to be initiated by anxiety rather than causing it. It was made clear that all defenses are unconscious mental processes and that repression was only one of many defenses, although it maintained its position as the most prominent one, often operating along with other defenses.

The concept of defense could now be accurately assigned its place within the new structural model. The "unacceptable ideas" that Freud had written about early in his work were the mental representatives of the two basic drives, libido and aggression. These drives or instincts—*Trieb* is Freud's term—which constantly press for discharge in behavior and thought, comprised that structure of the mind that Freud called the id. The derivatives of the drives, those ideas and wishes through which the drives found expression, were warded off or defended against by the various defenses. The defenses were functions of the ego, that structure of the mind which mediated between the drives and the external world. At times, the ego would allow id impulses and their mental representations and derivatives to find suitable expression and gratification; at other times, when it judged that their emergence would lead to some danger to itself, it would oppose them, the entire process most often taking place unconsciously.

The dangers that aroused the ego's defensive op-

erations were enumerated by Freud. They were loss of the object, loss of love of the object, fear of castration, and condemnation by one's own conscience. Instinctual expression, then, could give rise to dangers not only from the external world, which for a small child is most often the parents; but as development proceeds, danger could come from an internalized agency called the superego, which could punish the ego for permitting instinctual gratification. Here, then, Freud established a developmental sequence with specific anxieties for specific phases of development.

"Defense" now came to be a general term for describing the way the ego protected itself against the dangers or calamities that Freud had enumerated. He also wrote about "signal anxiety," small amounts of anxiety that unconsciously set in motion defensive operations in anticipation of the feared danger situation.

In 1936, Anna Freud published *The Ego and the Mechanisms of Defense*. She elaborated upon, refined, and clarified the concept of defense, in relation not only to the theory of psychic conflict but also to the technique of psychoanalysis. She emphasized that defenses were unconscious processes that had to be understood as well as analyzed. In therapy, it was not merely a matter of showing a patient what his or her defenses were, whereupon the unconscious wishes would emerge; painstaking effort had to be exerted to induce the patient to become consciously aware of the defenses that he or she utilized. In addition, analyst and patient must explore the historical development of the use of these particular defenses. She noted that symptoms were compromise formations, in which the part played by the ego was "the unvarying use of a special method of defense, when confronted with a particular instinctual demand" (p. 34).

She constructed a list of these "special methods of defense," which by now were called "defense mechanisms." They were repression, regression, reaction formation, displacement, projection, isolation, undoing, denial, turning against the self, and reversal. She added the mechanisms of identification with the aggressor and altruistic surrender. She also observed that there were defenses against affects as well as against perceptions of reality that produced painful affects. For the latter, she described the defenses of denial in fantasy or by word or act.

Another important aspect of the concept of defense was introduced by Wilhelm Reich (1949). He stressed that an individual's defensive operations become embedded in his or her personality or character and that these traits of character must be analyzed along with the content of the person's associations, memories, feelings, and dreams. He stressed that these traits become so fixed and rigid that they function like a "character armor," which is very difficult to alter or to analyze. Reich also pointed out that these same traits of character functioned as powerful resistances to change and to analytic treatment.

The work of Melanie Klein and the British school of psychoanalysis emphasized defenses that were thought by them to be utilized in the infant's first year of life. Klein (1946), working with children and disturbed adults, noted defensive operations, from which she reconstructed the presence of these early modes of defensive organization. She described the defenses of splitting of the object and the impulses, splitting of the ego, idealization, denial of inner and outer reality, the stifling of emotions, projection, introjection, omnipotence, and projective identification. Klein also stressed that some of these defenses, such as projection and introjection, were, at the same time, the early mental processes whereby the structure of the ego is developed and differentiation takes place.

THE MECHANISMS OF DEFENSE

Before continuing with the history of the development of the concept of defense, it would be helpful to define the various defense mechanisms used by the ego. But first I would like to emphasize again that defenses are normal operations used to protect the ego from unpleasurable affects. They usually do not operate singly but rather in association with other defenses. They are unconscious mental processes which are a component of psychic conflict and compromise formation, and they have dynamic and developmental aspects. While most defenses are used by everyone, in certain states and illnesses one or two defenses are used so prominently and persistently that the defenses almost define the state or illness. They play a role in symptom formation, character development, and all aspects of mental life. We consider defenses to be pathological only when they are utilized so rigidly and persistently that they become the most prominent feature of the structure of the pathological symptom, character trait, or personality organization. I shall return to these issues when I resume my historical survey.

But next I will list the various defense mechanisms. I will adopt an alphabetical ordering, since it is not really possible to list them either in order of importance or according to some developmental, chronological classification.

Denial. This defense mechanism has many meanings. The term is most properly used to indicate that a person does not take in, acknowledge, or believe some aspect of reality. It is a mechanism regularly used by children to ward off feelings of helplessness or inadequacy by fantasizing or acting as if they were strong and powerful. For example, a young boy who is especially concerned with his vulnerability may put on a Superman costume and for a period of time really believe he is indestructible. Or a young child who has looked forward to a special outing may look outside at the rain and insist that it is not raining.

The term is used loosely, unfortunately, to designate any warding off of emotion or a patient's resistance to interpretation of his or her feelings; but it is better reserved for the blocking out of external reality. For example, a woman was brought to the hospital two days after her husband died of a coronary during their twenty-fifth wedding anniversary party. She was agitated and confused and believed her husband was alive and was being kept from seeing her. Denial of a real event or perception is, of course, indicative of faulty reality testing, so denial, in severe form, is seen in psychotic reactions. But milder forms of denial of reality exist in normal as well as neurotic people, such as the patient who walked past her analyst in a store, looked at his face, and did not see him. The term is also used to designate the warding off of painful affects, such as the manic patient's warding off of depressive feelings or the dying patient who denies the facts of his illness.

Displacement. In this defense mechanism, ideas and feelings that a person may have toward an important object or thing are repressed and then experienced in relation to another animate or inanimate object which represents the former. For example, a son may repress hatred of his father but be angry and defiant toward another authority figure in his life, or, while masturbating, he may be completely unaware of sexual feelings toward his mother while thinking about his aunt or a female high school teacher.

Displacement is seen most commonly in phobias, such as Freud's famous case of Little Hans, who displaced his fear of his father onto horses. But it also plays a role in many symptoms and normal attitudes. Displacement is also commonly found to be present in the manifest content of dreams.

Identification. This uses the fantasy of being like another person or adopts behavior and character traits derived from another person. Some aspects of identification are part of normal development, whereas some are more clearly reactions to unacceptable wishes or feelings. For example, a little boy who feels painfully small and weak may copy his father's behavior in order to feel big and strong. In a particular form of identification known as "identification with the aggressor," a person attempts to avoid a passive, frightened state by becoming like the person who frightened him. Thus, a girl may angrily scold her younger sister in exactly the same way in which her mother has just scolded her. It is important to bear in mind that these behaviors are not consciously determined. It is also not unusual in the course of analytic work to find that an important aspect of a patient's attitude or behavior toward the analyst is derived from an unconscious identification with a parent who behaved in an aggressive way toward the patient in childhood. A patient who was brutally scornful toward her analyst for many months gradually realized that she had suffered from the same treatment at the hands of her father.

Intellectualization. This is a process which psychologically binds the instinctual drives in intellectual activities, especially as a measure of control. It is exemplified by typical adolescent preoccupations with philosophy and religion to ward off the tumultuous sexual and aggressive feelings of that period. Not infrequently, intellectualization is used during the course of psychoanalytic treatment as a resistance against achieving emotional insight. It operates along with the defense of isolation.

Isolation. This mechanism, which is the one most used by obsessive-compulsive personalities, consists of the separation of ideas from the emotions that usually accompany them. For example, a person may have the thought that his father will die, yet he experiences no emotion along with the thought; or a patient may tell his analyst that he has angry thoughts about him, but he does not feel angry. If isolation is severe, it can result in a general blunting of emotion. Sometimes a person's thoughts seem unbidden, alien, or unconnected; hence anxiety and guilt are diminished even though the thoughts are conscious. "Isolation" also refers to dissociating related thoughts from one another so that their connection is not grasped.

Projection. In this process an unacceptable feeling, impulse, or idea is attributed to another person or thing. The person who is projecting has no awareness that the impulse or idea is his own. While projection is a ubiquitous and at times normal mental process, it is frequently predominant in sicker individuals, so is often accompanied by a diminution in reality testing. It is the major defense of paranoid patients, who frequently repress their own hateful thoughts and attribute these thoughts to a person or a group that they feel will harm them. However, all kinds of impulses can be projected, such as love, greed, envy, and sexual desire. Superego attitudes

can also be projected, as in the case where a patient believes that her analyst disapproves of some thought or behavior, while it is actually her own conscience that disapproves. In this case the patient, through projection, avoids the distressing feeling of guilt.

Projective identification. There is not much consensus about this mechanism as yet. Melanie Klein, writing about the paranoid-schizoid position during the first six months of life, described a defense wherein parts of the self and of internal objects are split off and projected into the external object, which then becomes controlled by and identified with the projected parts. Kernberg (1967) regarded projective identification as a primitive form of projection in which the person who projects an impulse, usually an aggressive one, onto another person not only fears attack but also has a certain degree of empathy for the attacker because of a loosening of ego boundaries.

Rationalization. In this defense a more logical, reasoned explanation for behavior, thoughts, or feelings is given by a person in order to conceal unconscious meanings or motives that would arouse anxiety or guilt in that person. The person who is rationalizing is usually unaware of these repressed meanings or motives.

Reaction formation. This is a mechanism whereby an attitude is repressed and kept unconscious and is replaced in consciousness or behavior by its opposite. For example, hateful thoughts and feelings are repressed, and the individual is aware only of loving ones. Or sloppiness and pleasure in a mess are replaced by excessive neatness and cleanliness, stubbornness by compliance, selfishness by altruism. Many reaction formations get to be so rigid and global that they become an intrinsic part of a person's character. Such major reaction formations are sometimes considered to be discrete defense mechanisms themselves. Altruism and asceticism are representative of the latter.

Reaction formation is particularly prominent in obsessive-compulsive neurosis, although it plays a role in everyone's life. One may also see the sudden emergence of reaction formations in very sick patients, such as the schizophrenic who becomes an ascetic in order to control impulses he believes are too pleasure-seeking.

Regression. This complex behavior pattern or psychic phenomenon is a fundamental characteristic of mental life. When the term is used to designate a defensive process, it can refer to drive, ego, or superego functioning. In the first of these, it refers to a return to the wishes and aims of the earlier oral and anal phases, in an effort to avoid the anxieties of the phallic phase. Thus, a woman might express intense longings to sit in her male analyst's lap and be taken care of, while her unconscious wishes for intercourse with him and a baby are repressed. An example of the regression of ego functioning for the purpose of defense would be a five-year-old boy who reverts to sucking his thumb and wanting a bottle when his sister is born. It is clear that there is instinctual regression in this situation as well, with phallic, oedipal wishes and aggression being warded off.

Repression. This is the commonest and most prominent defensive operation used in mental life, and it frequently operates in conjunction with other defenses. It occupies a singular place in the history of psychoanalytic concepts. It refers to the barring from consciousness of ideas, feelings, thoughts, fan-.tasies, and memories. It is assumed that this is an active process requiring a considerable expenditure of psychic energy which is attributed to the ego and is called "countercathexis."

Ideas, fantasies, and memories associated with the instinctual drives are constantly pressing for discharge and entry into consciousness, where they can lead to action and gratification. The defense of repression keeps these thoughts in the unconscious part of the mind. But various repressed ideas, fantasies, and memories may overcome what is keeping them repressed and become conscious in dreams, slips of the tongue, daydreams, and symptoms.

Although repression can take place at any time during life, it regularly occurs with respect to memories of childhood. The repression of memories from this period is known as infantile amnesia. In adult life, repression is particularly apparent in amnesias, fugue states, and in patients who tend to have symptoms and character traits associated with hysteria. However, repression is used as a defense by all people, whether they are normal or fit into some diagnostic category of pathology.

Reversal. This defense, as well as turning against the self, was considered by Freud to come into play quite early in life. It refers mainly to turning love into hate and hate into love for defensive purposes. A man in analysis who was frightened of his unconscious longing to love and be loved by his analyst was constantly angry and scornful of him. In this case, reversal into its opposite is similar to reaction formation. Reversal is also a very common mechanism in dreams.

Splitting. This term was originally used by Freud to describe the contrasting attitudes of the fetishist,

who is both consciously aware of the anatomy of the female genital and denies that a woman does not have a penis by his symbolic use of the fetish. It is also used to designate the defensive displacement of transference feelings toward the analyst onto another person, as in "splitting of the transference."

Melanie Klein wrote about splitting as a very early defense mechanism utilized by an infant to deal with what she regarded as the death instinct. Kernberg (1967) clarified the contemporary use of the concept, defining it as a primitive defense, seen most often in borderline patients, that keeps separate the good and bad self and object representations. Thus, one person is seen as all good, while another is all bad; or one experiences oneself as all bad, while the other is seen as all good. The defense is used to protect the object or the self against aggressive impulses. Kernberg also used the term to describe the defensive maintenance of contradictory ego states and attitudes within an individual without the emotional awareness or conviction of the contradiction.

Sublimation. Although the term was originally used to designate a defense mechanism, sublimation is now considered to be a normal aspect of ego functioning and ego maturation. As a defense, it refers to the transformation of an activity gratifying an infantile drive derivative into a more socially acceptable and creative activity. For example, a child who is particularly gratified by smearing and playing with feces may replace this pleasure by enjoyment of painting and sculpting as an adult.

Turning against the self. This was one of the first defense mechanisms discussed by Freud, who considered it to be a very early defensive process. It is actually quite a complex operation, in which the object of a drive, usually aggression, is changed from another person to the self. It is therefore seen frequently in depression and masochism. In these conditions, the ego defends itself against the fear of its aggression; the person's conscience also plays a role in turning the aggression away from the object toward the self.

Undoing. This defense mechanism is utilized in obsessive acts. It comprises the second stage of a two-stage act which undoes or denies the sexual or aggressive wish expressed in the first stage. It is not uncommon for obsessional people to imagine that their car has run over someone if they hear a noise. They will return to check and retrace the same route, thereby undoing the death wishes expressed in their initial fantasy. A patient had to repetitively turn off a water faucet after he always allowed it to drip. He had to undo his first wish to soil and wet.

FURTHER CONSIDERATIONS OF THE CONCEPT OF DEFENSE

As has been mentioned, the publication of Anna Freud's book (1936) led to a reconsideration of the concept of defense and an important revision in technique. Psychoanalysts now paid as much attention to a patient's unconscious defense mechanisms as to the unconscious wishes that led to their being invoked. As Anna Freud said, analysts must now stand equidistant from the id, the ego, and the superego, meaning that elements from each of these structures must be analyzed. An important component of the ego functions were the defenses, which had a unique, individual development of their own in each patient. According to Waelder (Panel, 1967), whereas Freud's *Inhibitions, Symptoms and Anxiety* (1926) required analysts to ask what it is that the patient is afraid of, Anna Freud's book elaborated this question into the more complex one: "When the patient is afraid, how does he behave?"

I now turn to some dissatisfactions that arose concerning the idea of discrete defense mechanisms. Anna Freud was aware that the defense mechanisms rarely operate singly but occur together, with repression frequently among them. The result is that some defenses are quite complex, while others appear to have a simpler structure. In addition, when analysts describe a defense or report on an analytic session in which a particular defense mechanism was employed, there is not always agreement about its definition. For example, reversal into its opposite may be more appropriately termed reaction formation when hateful feelings are repressed and only loving ones are present. To make matters more complicated, a given behavior or psychological state can serve defensive purposes and provide instinctual gratification at one and the same time.

Let us take a not uncommon example from analytic practice. A young woman is frightened of her increasingly loving feelings toward her male analyst which are also a revival of her oedipal attachment to her father. She unconsciously fears that her feelings of love will make her vulnerable to rejection and punishment. In the face of these anxieties, she unconsciously mobilizes defensive operations. She represses her feelings of love and so has little or no awareness of them. At the same time, she displaces these loving feelings onto an older man she has recently met. In addition to using the defenses of repression and displacement, she is also gratifying certain unconscious wishes. She is gratifying her loving feelings in the relationship with the older man. She is also gratifying her hostility, in that she feels little love for her analyst but hopes to make

him feel rejected and jealous. In this regard, she may be utilizing another defense—namely, identification with the aggressor—insofar as she is doing to the analyst what her father did to her when he went to bed each night with her mother. One can readily see that this defense also expresses her hostility.

Therefore, a person's actual behavior or psychological attitude, when it is the outcome of a "defense mechanism," most often turns out to be a quite complicated structure involving drive derivatives or wishes, fears aroused by them, defenses against these fears, as well as superego components. Considerations such as these led Brenner (1982) to propose that "there are no special mechanisms of defense. Whatever ensues in mental life which results in a diminution of anxiety or depressive affect— ideally in their disappearance—belongs under the heading of defense" (p. 72). Because any and all ego activities can be, and are, used for defensive purposes, as well as for instinctual gratification, Brenner maintains that it is an error to speak of special defense mechanisms. "It is the function served by what one does that determines whether it is properly called defense" (p. 79, emphasis omitted).

While Brenner's view is in accord with what we observe clinically, it seems desirable to continue to use the term "defense mechanism" to define a particular ego function when it is used for defensive purposes. For example, when a patient says, after reporting a dream, "That woman was *not* my mother," we agree that the defense of negation is being used. While it is true that this particular function of the ego involving perception and memory can be defined only by its usage—in this case, to deny that it was the mother—there is reason to retain the term, provided Brenner's more inclusive observations are kept in mind. It is also important to note that what originated as a simple list of defensive operations has proved to be a complex interaction between drive, defense, reality, and superego pressures, even if the list is likely to remain with us because of common usage and familiarity.

Anna Freud herself returned to the investigation of defensive operations in *Normality and Pathology in Childhood* (1965). To assess clinically whether defenses are normal or pathological, she asked analysts to consider the following:

whether defense is employed specifically against *individual drives* . . . or, more generally, against drive activity and instinctual pleasure as such;

whether defenses are *age adequate,* too primitive, or too precocious;

whether defense is *balanced,* i.e., whether the ego has at its disposal the use of many of the important mechanisms or is restricted to the excessive use of single ones;

whether defense is *effective,* especially in its dealing with anxiety;

whether it results in equilibrium or disequilibrium, lability, mobility, or deadlock within the structure;

whether and how far the child's defense against the drive is dependent on the object world or independent of it. [Pp. 142–143]

One can readily see that Anna Freud has considerably broadened and refined her discussion of the complex nature of defensive processes and their place in normal and pathological functioning. Some of her reconsiderations received considerable impetus from the publication of Heinz Hartmann's *Ego Psychology and the Problem of Adaptation* (1939). In this work, Hartmann drew attention to, and emphasized the role of, defensive operations in normal adaptations in the face of external as well as internal threats to the functioning of the ego.

There have been a number of panels of the American Psychoanalytic Association as well as a recent supplement to the association's journal (1983) devoted to a reassessment of the concept of defense. Two of the panels (1967, 1970) were concerned with changes in the defensive operations brought about by psychoanalytic treatment and the technique of analysis with regard to defenses. In 1967, most discussants agreed that analysis brings about a modification in the use of defensive operations rather than their disappearance. During the course of treatment there are modifications in the patient's awareness and expression of the drives, in the ego's modulation of drive expression, in awareness of the use of defensive operations in the face of fears of drive discharge, and in the understanding of the role of the superego in the conflict situation. In short, there are many changes on many different levels, and change in the defensive organization cannot be evaluated separately from the other changes that take place.

The issue of psychoanalytic technique also came under scrutiny in the 1967 panel. It was noted that with the increasing emphasis on ego psychology, many analysts were being taught to interpret to the patient the defenses he or she uses before interpreting the wishes being defended against by these defenses. Most of the panelists on that occasion agreed that this was too blanket a statement. What seems to be most common in clinical practice is that defenses and what is being defended against are interpreted together, although this is not always possible. To complicate matters further, as has been said already,

defenses themselves contain wishful elements and fantasy content.

The topic of resistance was also taken up by the panel. Greenson (in Panel, 1967) defined resistance as "all those forces within the patient which oppose the procedures and processes of analysis, i.e., which hinder the patient's free association, which interfere with the patient's attempts to remember and to gain and assimilate insight, which operate against the patient's reasonable ego and his wish to change" (p. 153). At the same time, as Anna Freud had already stressed, the analysis of these resistances yields important information about the patient's habitual mode of defense and, at times, information about the origin and development of these particular kinds of defenses. Therefore, attention to and analysis of resistance occupy a central place in the technique of analysis.

THE DEVELOPMENT OF DEFENSES AND THE CONCEPT OF PRIMITIVE DEFENSES

Since defenses are functions of the ego, they must take part in the general growth and maturation of the ego. They change over time and have a development of their own. Certain functions of an infant's ego may be considered to be precursors of defenses. Freud often used a model of fight or flight to describe an organism's response to danger. Early reactions of flight can be considered to be precursors of later defenses. For example, infants frequently react to pain or excessive stimuli by a general physical withdrawal or turning away. Such reactions may be precursors of the defense of denial. It is important to note, however, that a precursor is not the same as the later defense and that even early manifestations of a particular defense are different from later ones because of the maturation of the ego.

Another interesting aspect of the development of defensive operations concerns the question raised by Anna Freud (1936) as to the possibility of developing a chronological classification of defenses. She hoped that we would come to understand which defenses were employed very early in life and which were utilized later, when further ego development had taken place. She was following a suggestion made by Freud (1926) that "It may well be that before its sharp cleavage into an ego and an id, and before the formation of a super-ego, the mental apparatus makes use of different methods of defence from those which it employs after it has reached these stages of organization" (p. 164). Anna Freud wrote that "possibly each defense mechanism is first evolved in order to master some specific instinctual urge and so is associated with a particular phase of infantile development" (p. 51). She went on to say that repression and sublimation could not be employed until relatively late in development, whereas regression, reversal, and turning against the self were probably among the earliest defense mechanisms used by the ego. However, she noted that the chronology of psychic processes was still one of the most obscure fields of analytic theory.

Despite this note of caution, a number of analysts have tried to classify defensive processes in terms of order of appearance. The earlier defenses are frequently called "primitive," or "lower-level," defenses, whereas the later ones are known as "higher-level" defenses. It is important to bear in mind, however, that it is not easy to know what mental processes are going on in an infant, let alone what defensive processes are taking place. Defenses are not observable behaviors (although certain inferences about them can be drawn from behavior) but unconscious mental processes.

Nevertheless, inference drawn from child observation studies and analyses of children have led to certain tentative conclusions. In general, defenses such as splitting, projective identification, denial, projection, introjection, turning against the self, and reversal are considered to be the earliest defenses used by the child. By contrast, repression, reaction formation, displacement, undoing, isolation, sublimation, and intellectualization are thought to come into prominence only later in the child's development.

The term "primitive defenses" is also used to describe the defenses used by psychotic and borderline patients and patients undergoing severe regression. As a corollary, the terms "higher-level" or "more mature" are used to designate the defenses utilized by normal individuals or patients with neurotic conflicts who are generally considered to be functioning with a greater degree of ego integration and organization. It is often said that sicker patients retain the primitive defenses of early childhood because of fixations or developmental failures and that they are therefore unable to utilize the higher-level defenses that require a more mature level of ego organization. Another explanation of the appearance of these primitive defenses in more disturbed individuals would be that they reappear along with other signs of severe regression of the ego.

Just as it does not seem possible to devise a chronological classification of defenses, so it appears that the division of defenses into primitive and higher-level and its correlation with degree of psychopathology may not be accurate. What is "primitive" is not the defense that is employed but the integrity of the ego involved in conflict. The sicker a patient is, the more we see poor ego integration, poor ego organization, and the breakdown of a number of ego functions. The defensive process called into service in such patients appears primitive primarily because of the poor ego organization.

In keeping with our view of the complexity of defensive operations, we must evaluate the entire situation in which a defense is employed. Let us take a not uncommon clinical example. A physician was dying of cancer, and his legs were swollen with edema. When a close friend of his entered his hospital room, he exclaimed, "Look, I'm finally getting better. Look at the weight I've put on in my legs!" Using a term like "denial" to describe this defense is accurate according to our terminology, whereas calling it a primitive defense and relating it to very early mental functioning is quite misleading. To evaluate the clinical picture, we must define the kind and degree of denial, the persistence of its use, its function in the life of the particular individual, its dynamic meaning, and the relative integrity of other ego functions, which may very well be intact.

We should also bear in mind that borderline and psychotic patients use defenses like repression, reaction formation, displacement, and isolation; in short, even severely regressed patients can use so-called higher-level defenses. Correspondingly, normal individuals and neurotics use the supposedly primitive defenses of denial, projection, and splitting. The idea that there are specific primitive defense mechanisms and specific higher-level defenses does not seem to be in accord with clinical phenomena. These phenomena are better understood by examining the degree of ego regression, the intactness of ego functions, the quality of object relations, and quantitative factors involved in intrapsychic conflict.

SUMMARY

We have seen that any behavior, attitude, or mental process can be used as a defense; hence the list of defense mechanisms that I have drawn up could be added to, refined, and elaborated upon. Indeed, some other terms that have been used to describe defenses are "abstinence," "avoidance," "amnesia," "acting out," "counterphobic behavior," "dissociation," "dedifferentiation," "internalization," "introjection," "inhibition," "renunciation," and "warding off."

In summary, then, defenses are unconscious mental activities of the ego that serve to protect the ego from unpleasurable affects such as anxiety and depressive affect. The ways in which any individual protects him- or herself from unpleasure are still being studied. They may have a certain consistency within each individual or may vary a great deal.

They may be used too persistently or too rigidly; on the other hand, there may be a relative lack of necessary defensive operations. The task of psychoanalysis is to show each patient why, when, and how he or she uses defensive maneuvers to avoid the typical dangers of intrapsychic life and to gain some understanding of the unique development of defensive processes in that particular individual. It is fair to say that without the concept of defense, psychoanalysis would not be a theory of human conflict. Therefore, the concept of defense will continue to occupy a central role in psychoanalytic theory and practice.

REFERENCES

Brenner, C. (1982). *The Mind in Conflict*. New York: Int. Univ. Press.

Freud, A. (1936). *The Ego and the Mechanisms of Defense*. Rpt. New York: Int. Univ. Press, 1966.

———. (1965). *Normality and Pathology in Childhood*. New York: Int. Univ. Press.

Freud, S. (1894). The neuro-psychoses of defence. *SE*, 3:43–68.

———. (1896). Further remarks on the neuro-psychoses of defence. *SE*, 3:159–185.

———. (1923). *The Ego and the Id. SE*, 19:3–66.

———. (1926). *Inhibitions, Symptoms and Anxiety. SE*, 20:77–175.

Hartmann, H. (1939). *Ego Psychology and the Problem of Adaptation*. New York: Int. Univ. Press, 1958.

Klein, M. (1946). Some notes on schizoid mechanisms. *Int. J. Psychoanal.*, 27:99–110.

Kernberg, O. F. (1967). Borderline personality organization. *J. Amer. Psychoanal. Assn.*, 15:641–685.

Panel (1967). Defense organization of the ego and psychoanalytic technique. E. Pumpian-Mindlin, reporter. *J. Amer. Psychoanal. Assn.*, 15:150–165.

———. (1970). The fate of defenses in the psychoanalytic process. J. Krent, reporter. *J. Amer. Psychoanal. Assn.*, 18: 177–194.

Reich, W. (1949). *Character Analysis*. New York: Orgone Institute Press.

38

STRUCTURAL THEORY

Psychoanalytic models of the mind are developed to provide the most advantageous way of accounting for clinically observed phenomena. Freud's two major models are commonly referred to as the topographic and structural models, though they represent groups of related ideas that Freud never systematically differentiated. The earlier topographic model was superseded when clinical observations forced Freud to conclude that unconscious intrapsychic conflict could be better understood by a metaphorical division of the mind into three major functional systems: the id, the ego, and the superego. At first he called these functional organizations "agencies," but they are now more often referred to as "structures." Generally, the term "structure" is understood to be a metaphor (without neuro-anatomic coordinates) that connotes the functional stability, organizational aspects, and interrelatedness of the id, the ego, and the superego).[1]

Structural theory was introduced with Freud's tripartite model of the mind in 1923. It has undergone significant development since then and has gained wide acceptance. Though there are other models that could be called structural, in the main this chapter

will define and discuss modern structural theory as based on the tripartite model, since that is the most generally accepted understanding of the term. It will also deal with the reasons why this structural theory is especially suited to accounting for the phenomena of normal and pathological conflict, despite certain criticisms of the theory, which will be mentioned.

First, however, it will be useful to distinguish between four terms: "tripartite model," "structural theory," "ego psychology," and metapsychology. The first three terms are roughly synonymous and have been used almost interchangeably in the literature, but there are reasons for noting differences in their connotation at this time. The difference between "tripartite model" and "structural theory" is essentially attributable to theoretical refinement and progress between early and later forms of the theory, for there are important differences between Freud's original tripartite model (often called the "structural hypothesis") and modern structural theory as it has gradually evolved. These will be indicated later in the chapter. The term "ego psychology" is used less commonly now than it was in the 1950s. It is a metonymic condensation utilizing a *pars pro toto* term and therefore obscures the interrelatedness of the three major structures and the significance of the id and the superego in structural theory.

The frequent equating of metapsychology with structural theory is more misleading, however, be-

---

1. However, the term "psychic structure" has been used differently by various authors (see Rapaport, ed., 1951; Rapaport, 1957, 1960; Loewald, 1962a; Beres, 1965; Holt, 1962, 1967; Nagera, 1967; Guttman, 1973; Schwartz, 1981; Levey, 1984–85; Boesky, 1988).

cause the distinction is one of frames of reference. Before 1923 Freud used the term "metapsychology" to indicate the dynamic, economic, and topographic dimensions of his theoretical framework. In a widely quoted definition of metapsychology Rapaport and Gill (1959) added a genetic and adaptive dimension to Freud's original list, and others have regarded the tripartite model as contributing still another, or structural, dimension; but the frames of reference are different. In the formation of the major psychic structures a developmental dimension is inherent in their differentiation and in the vicissitudes of their interaction. Therefore the structural theory does include a genetic element, and dynamic, topographic, and economic aspects are involved as well. But the five dimensions of Rapaport and Gill constitute highly diverse assumptions derived from widely varying premises, and their definition of metapsychology rests centrally on problematic views of Freud regarding psychic energy (Boesky, 1988).

Gradually, several other definitions of metapsychology have evolved, and there is no single definition that would be acceptable to all psychoanalysts today (Brenner, 1980). (See, however, Moore & Fine, eds., 1990, for an attempt.) Arlow (1975, 1984) assumed that structural theory is supraordinate to the various points of view, or dimensions, of metapsychology, but there is disagreement as to whether metapsychology should be understood to subsume structural theory, be equated with it, or be distinguished from it. The latter choice is the premise of this chapter. As used here, the term "metapsychology" will refer only to concepts and propositions that are beyond what can be derived, confirmed, or disconfirmed by data gathered in the psychoanalytic situation (Arlow, 1975)—that is, concepts on a higher abstract level, far removed from the clinical data.

PRE-STRUCTURAL THEORY: THE TOPOGRAPHIC MODEL

Precursors of Freud's structural views have been noted in ever earlier phases of his writings by various authors, and the topographic model has been designated by some as the first structural model; but there are fundamental differences between the topographic and tripartite theoretical models. Detailed descriptions of the topographic model are available in chapter 7 of Freud's *Interpretation of Dreams* (1900) and in summary form in, for example, Arlow & Brenner, 1964. What follows here will be very condensed for reasons of space.

The topographic model was developed as a general theory of the mind. It expressed Freud's discovery that neurotic symptoms, parapraxes, jokes, and dreams all had a similar underlying "form." The topographic model divided the mind (psychic apparatus) into three systems, defined by their relation or accessibility to consciousness and also by their utilization of "bound" versus "mobile" psychic energy. Mobile energy was rapidly "discharged" by the primary process, the manner of functioning characteristic of the system Ucs. Observable data related to the primary process in particular included the phenomena of condensation and displacement evident in dreams, neurotic symptoms, parapraxes, and jokes and also discernible in folklore, creative art, legends, and mythology. The system Ucs. represented mental elements that were accessible to consciousness only with difficulty or not at all. The system Pcs. "contained" mental elements that were readily accessible to consciousness. This was the province of the secondary process, which was defined by a slower discharge of "bound" energy, resulting in turn in a higher "cathectic level" in the system Pcs. The system Cs. (or Pcpt.-Cs.) included whatever was conscious at a given moment. The higher energy potential of the system Pcs. was a developmental achievement that provided the Pcs. with inhibitory capacities. As we shall see later, these energy concepts were carried over into the later structural theory, with confusing consequences.

Libido was the metaphoric psychic energy that arose in the somatic sources of the sexual drives and accounted for the subjective *vis a tergo* quality and the theoretically postulated "force" of the drives. These views were essential to Freud's definitions of the regulatory principles, and he maintained that all pathological mental phenomena could be accounted for in terms of the libido theory (Freud, 1905; 1923, p. 44). Freud persisted in his theoretical commitment to the libido theory until the end of his life.

Following Freud's series of papers on metapsychology (1914, 1915a, 1915b, 1915c) were three further works foreshadowing the 1923 book that introduced the structural theory. These were "A metapsychological supplement to the theory of dreams" (1917a), "Mourning and melancholia" (1917b), and *Group Psychology and the Analysis of the Ego* (1921). These indicated that reality testing was a function of the ego and that identification was an important aspect of ego development and developed more fully the concept of the ego ideal[2] first proposed in his paper "On narcissism" (1914) (as sum-

2. Many analysts have followed Hartmann, Kris, and Loewenstein in replacing the ego ideal with the idealizing and self-critical functions of the superego—for example, Lampl-de Groot, 1964.

marized by Brenner, 1982b). The reasons that led Freud to postulate a second theory of the mind will be discussed at some length in the section comparing the topographic and tripartite models.

THE TRIPARTITE MODEL

In 1923 Freud proposed a tripartite division of the mind on the basis of which mental functions were generally allied with one another but in mental conflict were opposed. The first agency was the id, which represented the drives. The second was the ego, which opposed the drives but could also act as the executant of the drives. The ego mediated between the drives and the external world. Just as the ego emerged from the id, so too the superego (the third agency) became differentiated from the ego and was responsible for the moral and idealizing functions.

The Id

The functions of the id center around the basic needs of humankind that compel gratification, in particular the pressures resulting from the sexual and aggressive drives. These drives were thought to be always fused to some extent, though in widely varying proportions. Hence, insofar as the drive component was concerned, most clinically observed phenomena were understood to constitute mixtures of sexual and aggressive drives. The concepts of fusion and defusion of the drives were very important to Freud in his 1923 formulation of the structural theory, because of his continuing theoretical commitment to the libido theory, but they are not widely accepted now.

If the drives did not evoke unpleasure, they could be gratified with the assistance of the ego either in reality or in fantasy. If the wishes evoked by the drives caused too much unpleasure, they were warded off by certain functions of the ego in accordance with the pleasure principle—that is, the tendency of the mind to seek pleasure and avoid unpleasure. Freud (1926) therefore concluded that it was anxiety that was responsible for the appearance of conflict between id and ego in every child's development. Anxiety was thus viewed as having profound significance as a developmental pressure toward structural differentiation.

Whereas the system Ucs. was governed by the primary process in the topographic model, it was now the id that functioned in accordance with the primary process. The primary process still had two dimensions. The clinical coordinate comprised all the observable data manifesting condensation and displacement, while the more abstract coordinate

consisted of a group of energic concepts including the cathectic level, the mode of energy (mobile or bound), and the speed of discharge (rapid or delayed). Here, then, was yet another way in which Freud carried forward metapsychological energy concepts into his new structural theory. Just as in his earlier topographic view each of the systems was defined by its economic or energic dimension, so too in the structural theory of 1923 the id and the ego (and less precisely the superego) were to be distinguished by their energic investments.

The Ego

Freud (1923) defined the ego as a "coherent organization of mental processes" that included reality testing, control of partial processes, perception, motility, memory, thinking, language, and adaptation to reality. The means that the ego employed against the id were the defenses. The ego was also the "seat of the affects." (Freud had no intention of compiling a "list" of all ego functions, since this would have entailed an unachievable mapping of the human mind.) Structural theory calls attention explicitly to the developmental relatedness and continuities between ego functions in childhood and those in later life. The ego was said to mediate between the id and the outer world. It functioned in accordance with the reality principle and the secondary process. We have already considered the linkages between the primary process, the id, and the system Ucs. and between the secondary process, the system Pcs., and the ego in Freud's writings. While it is true that he made those strict and schematic divisions in some of his writings, Freud cautioned against such a simplistic dichotomy of the primary and secondary processes as early as 1895. At that time he said (in regard to an earlier and different ego): "consciousness does not cling to the ego but can become an addition to any psi processes. It warns us, too, against possibly identifying primary processes with unconscious ones. *Here are two invaluable hints for the future!*" (p. 340).

The Superego

The superego was defined by Freud as the group of psychic functions having to do with ideal aspirations, moral commands, and prohibitions. Both reward and punishment resulted from its functioning. Dealing with moral issues, the superego was roughly synonymous with conscience, except for the fact that its functioning was to a very significant extent unconscious. Freud's view of the formation of the superego derived from his observations of the inevitable developmental conflict experienced by children in the oedipal phase. The incestuous and parenticidal wishes of the oedipal child evoke enormous conflict because of the attendant anxieties of object loss, loss of the object's love, and fear of castration. The child therefore, to a considerable extent, relinquishes these dangerous wishes and identifies with the moral standards of the parents. Thus the superego was said by Freud to be formed via identification. This identification then strengthened the oedipal child's defenses against frightening wishes. This formulation illustrates the previously mentioned integral importance of the developmental point of view within the structural theory. It also highlights the effect of early conflicts on later ego and superego functions in a manner far deeper and more useful clinically than the prior conceptions of libidinal fixation and regression in the narrower sense of those terms within the topographic model.

COMPARISON OF THE TOPOGRAPHIC AND TRIPARTITE MODELS

The monograph by Arlow and Brenner (1964) remains the definitive comparison of the topographic and tripartite structural theories. These authors show that although there are similarities between the two models, the differences are more important. The two models share the principle of psychic determinism, the existence of important unconscious mental processes, the economic assumptions of mobile versus bound mental energy, and the developmental tendency toward delayed discharge of mental energy with consequent increase in the efficiency of mental functioning. Both theories emphasize conflict and regression, and mental agencies play a role in both. Each also includes the concepts of overdetermination and compromise formation.

But there are also significant incompatibilities. In the topographic model, defense was considered synonymous with repression, and repression produced anxiety. In the structural model (after Freud, 1926) this view was exactly reversed, and anxiety evoked defense. Furthermore, anxiety was linked to object relations from earliest infancy; anxiety evoked defenses of which repression was only one; and the central significance of early developmental factors became far more important than they had been in the topographic model. Although both models derived psychic energy from the drives, the structural theory gave a better account of self-directed aggression. The topographic view of the mental apparatus as a reflex arc confuses our view of regression, *especially* in dreams. Compromise formation is also better described in the structural theory.

Arlow and Brenner systematically demonstrated the advantages of the structural theory. Clinically, it accounts better for the phenomena of intrapsychic conflict, because it divides the mind more accurately in accordance with the data—for example, unconscious fantasies: first, because the inhibitory or anti-drive processes in the mind (ego functions) are unconscious, as well as the drive-related ones; and second, because important elements of the superego are unconscious as well. Freud was correct to say that the antithesis of conscious versus unconscious had not withstood the test of time. Finally, the modern view of the treatment tasks of both patient and analyst is far better described in structural than topographic terms (see also Arlow, 1975).

As Brenner (1982a) points out, the 1926 revision of the theory of anxiety truly marks the beginning of modern psychoanalysis. That is because it radically altered our concept of the treatment task from the uncovering of repressed memories to the investigation of the interaction of drives, defenses, and superego, together with a careful analysis of the motivation for the defenses and the nature of the dangers that burden the defensive capacities of the ego. In the structural model, we are seeking to make the patient conscious not only of the drive-determined aspects of his or her conflicts but of their defensive and superego aspects as well. That is how we help the patient to strengthen the integrative, organizing, and controlling functions of the ego. In that way we enhance the possibility of drive gratification without symptom formation.

POST-FREUDIAN CONTRIBUTIONS TO STRUCTURAL THEORY

The period immediately following Freud's introduction of the tripartite model and continuing into the present has seen the gradual evolution of a modern structural theory based on the contributions of many analysts. Their work has further elucidated the interrelated nature of the development and functioning of the major structures. In addition, they have put the aggressive drive on an equal footing with the libidinal, demonstrated that conflict can be normal as well as pathological, described the relation of affects to conflict, specified the nature of defenses and compromise formations, and refined structural theory so as to better account for object relationships and adaptation to the environment.

Nunberg (1930) gave explicit attention to the unifying and binding functions of the ego. Since these reconcile the conflicting elements in the drives, bring them into harmony with the requirements of reality, and strike a balance between the claims of the superego and reality on the one hand and the id on the other, Nunberg subsumed them under the term "synthetic function" of the ego. Waelder (1930) articulated the integrative core of the structural hypothesis in his polyphonic formulation of the "principle of multiple function." Viewed in this context, any psychic act must be considered an ego-coordinated compromise between the id, ego, and superego and the repetition compulsion. Thus, whereas Nunberg stressed the synthetic, unifying tendency of the ego, Waelder emphasized its innate problem-solving character (Brenner, 1982a).

Anna Freud (1936) helped clarify the defensive functions of the ego by describing a group of processes she called "defense mechanisms"; these are means whereby the ego avoids or minimizes unpleasure arising from drive wishes. In this classic contribution she enhanced modern psychoanalytic technique significantly by advising the analyst to adopt an equidistant posture vis-à-vis each of the three major agencies of the mind, a strategy that generations of analysts have found advantageous in understanding resistance and transference and making technical interventions. Together with her coworkers, thirty years later, Anna Freud (1965) made another important application of the structural theory to psychoanalytic nosology with the introduction of the developmental profile.

Hartmann (1939, 1964) and Hartmann, Kris, and Loewenstein (1946, 1949) made additions to Freud's structural theory that are of major importance. Hartmann's contributions in particular epitomized the movement known as "ego psychology," which reached its peak in the 1950s. Hartmann viewed the ego as a substructure of personality defined by its functions, as distinct from the experiential aspects of the person. He warned that one could never speak accurately of "the ego" holistically, but only of characteristics of one or other of its functions. Nevertheless, he documented the significance of the ego (through its collective functioning) for the centralization of functional control and showed it to be the basis for man's evolutionary independence from the immediate impact of stimuli. Unlike Freud, who saw the ego as developing out of the id, Hartmann postulated an undifferentiated id–ego anlage during the earliest phase of infancy. He showed that, through a "change of function," what started in a situation of conflict between drives and defenses may become secondarily part of a "nonconflictual sphere" (1939). Such functions he called examples of "secondary autonomy," positing that the resistance of those functions to reinstinctualization represented an index of ego strength. "Primary autonomy" referred to the drive-independent origin of certain apparatuses of the ego such as motility and the perceptual modalities. (For a criticism of Hartmann's view of primary autonomy, see Glover, 1961.)

Hartmann followed Freud in his systematic emphasis on the developmental aspects of the structural theory. Together with Kris and Loewenstein (1946) he distinguished differentiation (specialization) from integration (the emergence of a new function out of previously incoherent functions). Differentiation and integration were the broad basis for structuralization: the gradual developmental differentiation of the three major systems. These authors also distinguished maturation-growth processes that were relatively independent of environmental interactions from developmental processes in which environmental influence was highly important (p. 18). For example, superego formation is relatively more independent of maturation processes than is ego development. This view foreshadows a later conclusion by Arlow (1982) that although from a developmental standpoint the superego is the functional center via internalization for the transition from outer to inner conflict, its development continues long after the oedipal phase.

Continuing with Hartmann's ideas, to retain love the child must control his or her instincts. This means that id–ego differentiation becomes more complete as the child grows (structuralization). So the defenses directed against the child's drives develop, enhance, and maintain structural differentiation (Hartmann et al., 1946, p. 28). The earliest stages of ego development could thus be described from several angles: as a process of differentiation leading to a more complete demarcation of id and ego, of self and outer reality; and as a process leading from the pleasure ego to the reality ego, to the development of the reality principle, to progress from early narcissism to object relationships, to the traversing of the cardinal danger situations, and to the emergence of the secondary process.

But, they stressed, it is important always to observe the interrelatedness of these processes during the course of development. Hartmann, for example, used his concept of change of function to elucidate the "genetic fallacy" that simplistically attributes complex later functioning (for example, surgical skill) to a drive component (such as the "anal drive") from early childhood. He favored the notion of intrasystemic conflict (as distinguished from intersystemic conflict) to account for opposing tendencies of the ego, which could oppose the drives but also help toward their gratification, could be realistic but also rationalize, and so on (Hartmann, 1964, pp. 113–141). (For a further discussion of the problematic concept of intrasystemic conflict, see Rangell [1963a, 1963b].) Hartmann's position was that the id, ego, and superego were never conceived of as independent parts of the personality that invariably opposed each other, but as three centers of psychic functioning that could be characterized according to their interrelatedness. Under specific conditions, each of the centers might expand or recede under the influence of the other two systems.

Earlier, Fenichel (1941, 1945) had made noteworthy applications of structural theory to aspects of technique and psychodynamics. In 1951 Hartmann returned to this subject, specifying the therapeutic advantages of the structural theory in his essay "Technical implications of ego psychology." It was possible now, he said, for the analyst to deal with the patient's total personality and not merely with the opposition of drives and defenses. The most incisive change introduced by the structural model was to add to the prior stratified view of accessibility to consciousness the picture of the mind as an integrated organic whole, subdivisible into centers of mental functioning. This made it possible to better understand unexpected consequences of interpretation, both adverse and positive. Thus Hartmann (1951) wrote of the "multiple appeal" of certain interpretations that, as a consequence of the dynamic imbalance evoked by them, could set in motion processes far beyond the "local" reactions in a stimulated "area." Going beyond a dynamic view, the structural view comprehensively examined the interrelatedness of functional centers. Dynamic shifts are never isolated; they can be viewed meaningfully only in a "field."

Hartmann, Kris, and Loewenstein (1949) also showed that the gratification of aggressive wishes is fully equivalent to libidinal gratification. This placed the aggressive drives on an equal footing with the sexual drives with respect to their importance in causing neurotic symptoms. (This conclusion contrasts with Freud's emphasis on the libidinal and Melanie Klein's emphasis on the aggressive drive.)

Throughout his writings Hartmann stressed that conflict could be normal as well as pathological, that the etiology of health would shed light on the etiology of neurosis, and that Freud was right to hope that psychoanalysis would ultimately become a general psychology (for example, Hartmann, 1952, p. 11). For this last to happen, however, the consequences of utilizing data gathered outside the psychoanalytic treatment situation would have to be clarified; the extrapolation of data from the direct observation of children is an example, and applied psychoanalysis presents similar methodological problems.

In his essay "The mutual influences in the development of ego and id" (1952), Hartmann explained the basic significance of what he called the "body ego" in accounting for the development of the ego. Using the apt phrase "the genetic turn," he gave extensive consideration to Freud's discovery of the decisive relevance of early life for subsequent health or neurosis. He repeatedly and explicitly stressed the crucial significance of object relations, the child's interaction with his or her parents, the reality factor, and what Kris called the "new consideration for the environment." In so doing, he increased our understanding of the special object-related emphasis of Freud's 1926 introduction of the cardinal dangers of object loss, loss of the object's love, castration, and punishment by the superego. Contrary to the assertion that structural theory is a "closed system" (a psychic apparatus reacting only to stimuli), it is still insufficiently understood that structural theory has always included its own object relations theory as one of its central premises.

For some years now, Hartmann's contributions to structural theory have fallen by the wayside, and there has been a tendency to dismiss him for oversystematizing. But, as outlined here, his contributions were major and will probably be found to have enduring value, even if criticisms of his views about psychic energy are valid. On this point, he followed Freud, hinging his definitions of id, ego, and superego not only on their functions but also on the nature and amount of energy invested in them. He also used problematic energy concepts in his views of neutralization, sublimation, and reinstinctualization (Boesky, 1986).

A series of important contributions to structural theory by Brenner culminated in his book *The Mind in Conflict* (1982a). In this work he argued that clinical data, as well as data from other sources, support the view that the unpleasure associated with drive wishes is of two sorts: anxiety and depressive affect. Depressive affect is just as important as anxiety in arousing conflict, and each sort of unpleasure plays a substantial role in every major conflict originating in early childhood and persisting throughout life. He also revised the concept of defense by noting that any aspect of ego functioning can be used for defensive purposes, thus questioning whether there are specific ego functions used only for defense (the so-called defense mechanisms). Suggesting that superego formation and functioning are considerably more complex than previously thought, he postulated that libidinal wishes (not aggression alone) play a significant role. He also proposed that the concept of compromise formation be expanded to include normal consequences of conflict as well as pathological ones. As an example, he postulated that the superego does not only cause conflict; it is also a normal *consequence* of psychic conflict and is *itself* a compromise formation.

Brenner defined conflict as existing between drive derivatives, anxiety and/or depressive affect, and defense (but he would include reality and superego considerations as components as well). This definition is much closer to the level of clinical observation than the definitions of Freud and Waelder, who viewed conflict more abstractly as between id, ego, and superego. Brenner here usefully distinguishes between a drive derivative and a drive. A drive derivative is a wish for gratification that can be inferred via the psychoanalytic method; it is unique and personal. The concept of the drives, by contrast, is a generalization about drive derivatives based on many individual observations and inferences and applies to all persons (Brenner, 1982a, p. 25). Brenner sees his view of compromise formation as differing from Waelder's concept of multiple function because of differences in how they conceive of the role of the ego in mediating conflict. Waelder regarded problem solving as an inherent tendency of the ego and thought that the ego dealt with the problems presented by the id, superego, reality, and the repetition compulsion in its eightfold dual interactions with those four coordinates somewhat as a pre-programmed computer might. Brenner, by contrast, viewing the situation experientially rather than in terms of problem solving, believed that the interaction of id, ego, and superego is evoked by conflict under the influence of the pleasure principle. A third difference is important: Brenner's definition of compromise formation has no necessary link to the confusing concept of repetition compulsion.

ISSUES WITHIN STRUCTURAL THEORY

Criticism of structural theory ranges from selective questions within an overall framework of acceptance to global dismissal. A host of widely diverse criticisms will be discussed later. At this point, however, it will be useful to present important questions about certain aspects of structural theory. As mentioned already, psychic energy, a concept that is as integral to Freud's tripartite structural model as it was to his topographic model, is increasingly regarded as anachronistic and clinically irrelevant. This topic, questions about the nature of the id, and the place of object relations within the context of structural theory have been selected for consideration.

Questions about the Economic Point of View
In a panel discussion some years ago (1963b) it was recalled that Freud had attributed at least three characteristics to psychic energy: quantity, direction, and displaceability. These subsequently became the elements of what later would be described as the economic and dynamic aspects of metapsychology. These attributes of psychic energy are directly linked to Freud's earliest views of the affects, first stated in

"The neuro-psychoses of defence" (1894): "in mental functions something is to be distinguished—a quota of affect or sum of excitation—which possesses all the characteristics of a quantity (though we have no means of measuring it), which is capable of increase, diminution, displacement and discharge, and which is spread over the memory-traces of ideas somewhat as an electric charge is spread over the surface of a body" (p. 60).

Though Freud refined his views about affects extensively, he never changed his basic ideas about psychic energy carried over from this early hypothesis about affects. In his early writings he made it clear that he considered his distinction between free and bound energy to be his deepest insight into the nature of "nervous energy." His views of energy discharge were the basis for his definitions of the regulatory principles. He never relinquished his belief in the "actual neuroses," which he thought were caused by accumulations of libido without psychological motivation. One of the strongest arguments against the usefulness of the concept of psychic energy is visible here. If psychic energy as postulated by Freud can exist in a "mindless" state—that is, unlinked to ideation—then we have no methodology within the constraints of the clinical psychoanalytic situation to either prove or disprove its existence. Freud also placed himself in an untenable position with his adherence to the notion of the so-called actual neuroses, which he saw as nervous conditions exclusively due to quantitatively pathological accumulations of libido caused by unhealthy sexual practices. Actual neuroses of this type are not accepted by most modern analysts. By definition, they were due to contemporary ("aktual") accumulations of libido and were not influenced by ideation, conflict, or motivation. Our methodology for validation is not applicable to mental phenomena that are nonideational.

As we have already seen, Freud considered his libido theory indispensable to his metapsychology. It is not surprising, then, that he carried these confusing metapsychological views of energy forward into his new structural theory. He not only defined the three systems in terms of their energic potentials; he also viewed the very process of structure formation in energic terms. In *The Ego and the Id* (1923) Freud linked the transformation of mobile into bound energy with the realm of object relations in his statement that the desexualization of the oedipus complex was achieved via an identification that substituted for a drive gratification (see the discussion of Moore's comments in the next section). This desexualization was said to produce defusion of the sexual and aggressive drives. Modell (Panel, 1963b) showed that Freud also used energy concepts in his view of the regulatory principles as a property of the entire psychic apparatus.

Criticisms of the concept of psychic energy, libido theory, drives, and the economic dimension of metapsychology reached a climax in the years toward the end of the careers of Hartmann, Kris, and Loewenstein (Apfelbaum, 1965; Applegarth, 1971, 1977; Rosenblatt & Thikstun, 1970, 1977). The advantages and disadvantages of energy concepts were considered by Wallerstein (1977) and by Gill (1977). Horowitz (1977) offered a defense of the quantitative approach.

Questions about the Id

Schur (1966) noted that in his writings Freud sometimes seemed to reduce the id to a purely energic concept. Quite aside from questions about psychic energy itself, Schur saw such a view as logically untenable when it came to trying to account for the clinical phenomena of conflict. In intersystemic conflict (between id, ego, and superego) it would posit an opposition between motivations and nonideational psychic energy—a confusion in frames of reference. Another ambiguity pointed out by Schur (1966, pp. 61–62) was that on the one hand Freud assumed that the id was present neonatally and was immutable, while on the other he postulated maturational (phases of sexual development) and developmental changes (addition of "the repressed"). Schur also argued against reducing the id to an energy concept on the grounds that the id followed the laws of the primary process and must therefore be viewed as organized. Here, however, he failed to note the distinction made by Beres (Panel, 1963a) between early ego activities and id functions (see below). This is especially evident in his linking the emergence of the "structured" id to the appearance of the first wish (pp. 68–69). Although wishes would have to entail ego activity, Schur designated them as functional units of the id. Observation can give evidence only of very early wishes that themselves may be compromise formations or early wishes opposed by some form of inhibitory influence. Schur's "structured" id therefore confuses id and early ego functions and is as unsatisfactory as the purely energic id he correctly criticizes. But his views of the regulatory principles deserve a more detailed consideration than is possible here. (For another view of Schur's monograph, see Loewald, 1966.)

The instinctual drives constitute another focus of confusion and controversy in relation to the id. Freud's (1920) final dual instinct theory opposed Eros and Thanatos and entailed biological correlates that radically transcended the psychoanalytic frame of reference. Most analysts today reject Freud's concept of the death instinct, but the majority accept the aggressive and sexual drives as roughly equal in importance clinically and theoretically. Though the id is commonly thought to be the province of the drives, Beres (Panel, 1963a) warned against the fallacy of assigning contents to the id as though it had spatial reference. He also excluded wishes from id functions, since wishes are structurally altered expressions of the drives. Wishes are usually compromise formations in which some derivative of a drive is combined with contributions from the ego and the superego. In the same panel Moore defined the id as an abstraction referring to the expression of drive representations that are manifestations of undifferentiated or unneutralized energies relatively unmodified by realistic self or object interests. The structural theory, in Moore's view, occurred as a refinement of Freud's theoretical explanations of the transformation of the instincts as influenced by objects and the needs of the self.

Object Relations and Structural Theory

In contrast to certain object relations theorists who view structural theory as outmoded are five major figures whose considerations of object relations have been within the context of structural theory.

Edith Jacobson (1964) systematically elaborated Hartmann's distinction between the ego and self representations. Utilizing the developmental point of view, she traced the complex building of self and object representations to the foundation of identifications and the wish for reunion with the mother. Her work was founded on extensive clinical experience with depression, psychoses, and narcissistic disturbances.

In numerous papers over a span of many years Loewald (1960, 1962a, 1962b, 1970, 1971, 1983) has especially stressed the advantages of the structural model over the topographic model in providing a far more accurate and deeper view of the role of the drives. In the topographic model the drives were viewed as impinging from without on a psychic apparatus that did not want to be disturbed, whereas in the organismic structural model the drives assumed a place as forces within the mind. Loewald claimed that the person as an experiencing human being was not accounted for in many metapsychological treatises on impersonal forces, and he showed how, from the outset, those inchoate forces become personalized as motivation via object ties (1960, 1971).

But Loewald has also taken exception to the views of other structural theorists (1966). Perhaps what most separates him from others is his view of the role of the drives in the earliest phases of development. He stressed the primary significance of the object during infancy as an organizing influence on the drives and believed that Freud and others erroneously stressed the reverse. There is a consistency in his extension of these views to his explanation of how psychoanalytic treatment cures (1960, 1970) and to sublimation (1983). The complexity of the relations between drives and objects in the course of psychic development is the basis for one of the disagreements between advocates of structural theory and object relations theorists of various persuasions.

The contributions of Mahler (1972; Mahler et al., 1975) epitomize the significance of the developmental point of view in structural theory. Her meticulous observations confirmed the earlier prediction of Kris about the ultimate importance of longitudinal observations of children. She has added to our understanding of the fundamental significance of object relations in the processes of structural differentiation.

Sandler and Rosenblatt (1962) regarded the construction of the representational world (consisting of the person's integrated self and object representations) as a product of ego functions. The representational world, they believed, offers a set of indications that guide the ego to adaptive or defensive activities. In their opinion representational concepts also offer a better account of narcissism and developmental issues related to the superego. In a later work Sandler and Sandler (1978) proposed a modification of our view of the development of drives and affects by paying more attention to environmental interaction with the primary object. In this respect the Sandlers' views resemble Loewald's.

Kernberg (1975, 1976) extended Jacobson's views of self and object representations in a systematic investigation of the implication of object relations theory for psychoanalytic nosology, character development, and the formation of psychic structure and made technical proposals that are a logical outgrowth of his views.

The views of Jacobson, Kernberg, Sandler, and Loewald are similar in at least two respects: these authors were convinced both of the clinical insufficiency of prior structural concepts and of the advantages of greater attention to developmental interactions between the very young child and the mother. For an introduction to the disagreements about the meaning and value of the "representational" point of view, see Friedman, 1980; J. Jacobson, 1983; Boesky, 1983; and Rothstein, 1983.

CRITICISMS OF STRUCTURAL THEORY

The premise that psychoanalysis is a natural science has been challenged. Those who contend that psychoanalysis is not a science reject structural theory because it is intended to be scientific. Thus, Schafer (1976, 1983) believes that psychoanalysis should focus on issues of meaning rather than transmuting meaning into abstract causal hypotheses regarding functions and energies. Closely related are the objections of those who view structural theory as impersonal and so contributing to the loss of what is unique, personal, and human in the psychoanalytic task. They regard structural theory as irrelevant, because they say it is too far removed from the realities of clinically observable data. Schafer proposed action language as an alternative to structural theory, because he thought it was closer to clinical experience; but it seems to require an almost behavioristic posture for the analyst. Wiedeman (1972) among others cited the advantages of systems theory over structural theory.

Sandler (1974) agreed with those who saw structural theory as too removed from clinical data. In his view, it did not account for unconscious peremptory urges not exclusively instinctual, which must be regarded as a function of various aspects of the psychic apparatus. He offered the example of the adult patient who uses impelling, unconscious childhood defensive maneuvers "automatically." He believed that advocates of structural theory neglected Freud's "second censor" between the systems Pcs. and Cs., as well as the importance of intrasystemic conflict with the ego. He proposed reconceptualizing our view of conflict so as to bring out the contrast between "peremptory urges" and inhibiting tendencies.

In relation to Sandler's views, it is necessary to distinguish "peremptory urges" from certain contiguous concepts—the repetition compulsion and compromise formations, for example. Waelder (1930, p. 48) noted that the ego is subject to the repetition compulsion and uses behaviors imposed on it by the disposition to repeat in order to overcome the menacing drives and the demands of the superego. It is of course correct that certain urges that are experienced as peremptory are not exclusively instinctual; but that is true of any compromise formation, and Sandler's peremptory urges seem to be examples of compromise formations. Similarly, some of what we often call the id in the sense of drive-propelled automatisms is actually itself the result of compromise. A clinical example would be irresistible and repetitious self-damaging forms of "acting out." In this context Arlow (1975) observed: "Clinically, it can be demonstrated that many functions of the ego are characterized by a driving, impulsive quality, ordinarily identified with the *modus operandi* of the id" (p. 516; see also Arlow & Brenner, 1964). Superego manifestations are also compromise formations and may be similarly impelling. Hence, actual clinical phenomena entail complex interactions of groups of compromise formations. Viewing such interactions as occurring between compromise formations often represents a more advantageous theoretical level of abstraction because it is closer to observable data than are id, ego, and superego interactions.

While Sandler is correct in saying that "structural hierarchies" do not account for such a fundamental polarity as activity versus passivity, neither does the concept of intrasystemic conflict that he and Hartmann defended. Hartmann (Panel, 1963c) gave as examples of intrasystemic conflict the facts that the ego could achieve insight but also "resisted" and that the id could express passive as well as active drive urges. I would suggest, however, that what appears from the point of view only of the ego (an abstraction at the highest level) to be intrasystemic conflict can be seen from a level much closer to clinical observation to be the participation of two different groups of ego functions in two different compromise formations—one resulting in resistance, the other in a therapeutic alliance. The alliance itself, however, is by no means devoid of conflict and compromise (see Brenner, 1979); important aspects of it may also function as resistance. A clinical example is the ingratiating, intellectualized attempts of certain patients to "cooperate" with the analyst. The conflict between active and passive wishes can also be seen as conflicting compromise formations rather than intrasystemic conflict. There are a vast number of commonly observed clinical situations that seem to be intrasystemic when viewed only from the angle of "interests." One example is the fact that while early conflict solutions survive as appealing repetitions, they can themselves engender conflict with the occurrence of a new reality. The principal objection to the topographic model, it will be recalled, was the misleading assignment of both sides of conflict within the same system (both drives and defenses were in the system Ucs.). The notion of intrasystemic conflict reintroduces the same dilemma, in that both sides of a conflict are again postulated as being in the same system. What appear to be intrasystemic conflicts within the ego or the id are actually motivational conflicts, the resultant of highly complex compromise formations.

In recent years a small group of analysts has criticized the structural theory in more global terms. These authors have questioned certain fundamental assumptions. George Klein (1973, 1976) and Roy Schafer (1976), for instance, have questioned the relevance of the structural theory to an understanding of conflict, Kohut (1977, 1979) the premise that conflict is fundamental to an understanding of mental suffering. In each instance the authors have proposed alternative models or frames of reference that

are discontinuous with, or impossible to articulate coherently within, structural theory. One point of agreement, however, is their contention that structural theory fails to account for the motivation of a person because of its distance from clinical data and its dessicated abstractions, which depend too heavily on an outmoded scientific model committed to anachronistic energy concepts. Gill (1977) expressed a rather common criticism of metapsychology as a description of man discharging quantities of blind energy, in contrast to the view of G. Klein and others that man is a creature of intentions who strives after meaningful goals. Here, as elsewhere in discussions critical of structural theory, there seems to be an erroneous equation of metapsychology with structural theory. G. Klein (1976, p. 171) asserted that an integrating center beyond the ego was theoretically necessary. But his proposals for substituting abstract "schemata" for id, ego, and superego do not appear either clinically more advantageous or theoretically less abstract than structural theory. Actually, the differences between the views of G. Klein, Kohut, and Schafer are far more important than their areas of agreement. Readers unfamiliar with these issues can find basic sources in the following references: G. Klein, 1973, 1976; Kohut, 1971, 1977, 1979; Gill, 1977; Schafer, 1976, 1983.

Kohut and his followers contend that important forms of psychopathology are due to deficits in the formation of psychic structure rather than conflicts after structure formation. They believe that the earlier in life these deficits occur, the less useful structural theory is, because in their view the pathology precedes structure formation developmentally; therapeutic interventions must therefore be oriented to dyadic rather than triadic conflicts. By contrast, I believe such views to be incorrect, because structural differentiation, conflict, and developmental processes take place simultaneously rather than sequentially (A. Freud, 1974). Numerous critiques of Kohut's views are now available (for example, Loewald, 1973; Stein, 1979; Boesky, 1991).

THE EVOLUTION OF THE TRIPARTITE MODEL INTO MODERN STRUCTURAL THEORY

It will help to clarify modern structural theory if we briefly recapitulate the steps in the gradual evolution of Freud's 1923 tripartite model into its current form. Freud himself contributed the first alteration in 1926 with his revision of his theories of affect and defense and his discussion of the cardinal danger situations. Subsequently, Nunberg, Waelder, Anna Freud, and Fenichel refined structural theory with more complex views of the ego, its interactions with the id and the superego, and the nature of its defensive processes. Hartmann, with Kris and Loewenstein, delineated the complexity of the developmental and functional interrelatedness of the three structures and explicated more fully the ego as the seat of central organization and control. Arlow documented the anachronistic persistence of certain topographical notions in misunderstandings of structural theory and extensively illustrated the advantages of structural theory in the formation and validation of interpretations (1979) and in accounting for unconscious fantasy. Brenner introduced fundamental changes in the structural theory of affects, defense, and the formation of the superego; he also redefined the relation between the id and drive derivatives, as well as the components of conflict and compromise formation.

These developments demonstrate that there are significant theoretical and technical differences between the 1923 tripartite model and modern structural theory. The magnitude and scope of the changes that have taken place can only be outlined here schematically. Beginning with the sexual and self-preservative instincts, we have moved to the sexual and aggressive drives, from the original equation of defense and repression to the use of any mental function in the service of defense, from the view of repression as causing anxiety to exactly the reverse, from postulating only anxiety as the source of conflict to the dual equivalence of anxiety and depressive affect, and from the view of the superego as formed primarily by introjection and identification to the superego itself consisting of a complex group of compromise formations. The continuities between the earlier and current versions must be kept clearly in mind, but it is important to recognize the differences in evaluating the validity of criticisms of structural theory, which must be addressed to particular aspects at varying stages in the development of the theory. For these reasons, it is seriously misleading to continue to use the term "ego psychology" to refer to modern structural theory.

CONCLUSION

Psychoanalytic theory, like the theory of other sciences, should be as close to the level of observation as is compatible with the need to achieve useful generalizations. There is no ego or id in the real world or "in" any person's mind. These are merely theoretical abstractions ("scaffoldings," to use Freud's apt metaphor) that are useful for designating types of mental functioning that result from innate biological potentials as influenced by interactions and identifications with objects. Even theoretically, there are no "pure" id, ego, or superego agencies that "exist"

or interact with each other, just as Truth cannot interact with Beauty because these too are abstractions. Nevertheless, the inferred abstractions have proved to be highly useful in practice and theory. Criticisms of the theory as overly abstract and clinically irrelevant are more valid in regard to the energic postulates of the 1923 tripartite model than to modern structural theory.

From its inception, structural theory has been integrally related to clinically observable phenomena. Freud (1937), for example, chose to frame his definitive discussion of resistance in structural terms. Anna Freud's developmental profile demonstrates the advantages of structural theory as a framework for psychoanalytic nosology. The theory is supported by compelling clinical observations gathered by psychoanalysts over a span of some seventy years; moreover, important beneficial changes in their patients are regarded as structural in nature. It has contributed to the concepts of psychoanalysis as the science of the mind in conflict and psychoanalysis as a general psychology because of the ubiquity of conflict in health and in mental illness. There is no other model that has met with as much acceptance or has demonstrated so many clinical advantages. For all that, it is an imperfect and continuously evolving theory with obvious gaps. Having clarified the irrelevance of consciousness to conflict and pathogenesis, we have yet to account for the place of consciousness in numerous aspects of mental life, especially in relation to insight and therapeutic change. We have only begun to refine our understanding of the internalization of experience. Major trends in its evolution in the past twenty years have been increasing dissatisfaction with earlier energy concepts; increased understanding of affects, defenses, the components of conflict, and narcissistic phenomena; and a move away from the closed-system view of the psychic apparatus as well as of the psychoanalytic treatment situation. The future, it is hoped, will bring further refinements.

REFERENCES

Apfelbaum, B. (1965). Ego psychology, psychic energy, and the hazards of quantitative explanation in psychoanalytic theory. *Int. J. Psychoanal.*, 46:168–182.

Applegarth, A. (1971). Comments on aspects of the theory of psychic energy. *J. Amer. Psychoanal. Assn.*, 19:379–416.

———. (1977). Psychic energy reconsidered. *J. Amer. Psychoanal. Assn.*, 25:599–602.

Arlow, J. A. (1975). The structural hypothesis. *Psychoanal. Q.*, 44:509–525.

———. (1979). The genesis of interpretation. *J. Amer. Psychoanal. Assn.*, 27(suppl.):193–206.

———. (1982). Problems of the superego concept. *Psychoanal. Study Child*, 37:229–244.

———. (1984). The psychoanalytic process in regard to the development of transference and interpretation. In *Psychoanalysis: The Vital Issues*, ed. G. H. Pollock & J. Gedo, vol. 2, pp. 21–44. New York: Int. Univ. Press.

Arlow, J. A., & Brenner, C. (1964). *Psychoanalytic Concepts and the Structural Theory*. New York: Int. Univ. Press.

Beres, D. (1965). Structure and function in psychoanalysis. *Int. J. Psychoanal.*, 46:53–63.

Boesky, D. (1983). The problem of mental representation in self and object theory. *Psychoanal. Q.*, 52:564–583.

———. (1986). Questions about sublimation. In *Essays in Honor of Charles Brenner*, ed. A. Richards & M. Willick, pp. 153–176. Hillsdale, N.J.: Analytic Press.

———. (1988). The concept of psychic structure. *J. Amer. Psychoanal. Assn.*, 36(suppl):113–136.

———. (1991). The authors respond. In *Conflict and Compromise*, ed. S. Dowling, pp. 173–189. Madison, Conn.: Int. Univ. Press.

Brenner, C. (1973). *An Elementary Textbook of Psychoanalysis*. 2d ed. New York: Int. Univ. Press.

———. (1976). *Psychoanalytic Technique and Psychic Conflict*. New York: Int. Univ. Press.

———. (1979). Working alliance, therapeutic alliance, and transference. *J. Amer. Psychoanal. Assn.*, 27(suppl.):137–158.

———. (1980). Metapsychology and psychoanalytic theory. *Psychoanal. Q.*, 49:189–214.

———. (1982a). *The Mind in Conflict*. New York: Int. Univ. Press.

———. (1982b). Unpublished MS.

Fenichel, O. (1941). *Problems of Psychoanalytic Technique*. Albany, N.Y.: Psychoanalytic Quarterly, Inc.

———. (1945). *The Psychoanalytic Theory of Neurosis*. New York: Norton.

Freud, A. (1936). *The Ego and the Mechanisms of Defense*. New York: Int. Univ. Press, 1966.

———. (1974). A psychoanalytic view of developmental psychopathology. In *Writings of Anna Freud*, 8:57–74. New York: Int. Univ. Press, 1981.

Freud, A., Nagera, H., & Freud, W. E. (1965). Metapsychologic assessment of the adult personality. *Psychoanal. Study Child*, 20:9–41.

Freud, S. (1894). The neuro-psychoses of defence. *SE*, 3:43–68.

———. (1895). Project for a scientific psychology. *SE*, 1:283–347.

———. (1900). *The Interpretation of Dreams. SE*, 4 & 5.

———. (1905). *Three Essays on the Theory of Sexuality. SE*, 7:125–243.

———. (1914). On narcissism. *SE*, 14:67–102.

———. (1915a). Instincts and their vicissitudes. *SE*, 14:111–140.

———. (1915b). Repression. *SE*, 14:141–158.

———. (1915c). The unconscious. *SE*, 14:159–215.

———. (1917a). A metapsychological supplement to the theory of dreams. *SE*, 14:217–235.

———. (1917b). Mourning and melancholia. *SE*, 14:237–260.

———. (1920). Beyond the Pleasure Principle. SE, 18:3–64.

———. (1921). *Group Psychology and the Analysis of the Ego. SE*, 18:67–143.

———. (1923). *The Ego and the Id. SE*, 19:3–66.

———. (1926). *Inhibitions, Symptoms and Anxiety. SE*, 20:77–175.

———. (1937). Analysis terminable and interminable. *SE*, 23:209–253.

Friedman, L. (1980). The barren prospect of a representational world. *Psychoanal. Q.*, 49:215–233.

Gill, M. M. (1977). Psychic energy reconsidered. *J. Amer. Psychoanal. Assn.*, 25:581–598.

Glover, E. (1961). Some recent trends in psychoanalytic theory. *Psychoanal. Q.*, 30:86–107.

Guttman, S. (1973). Psychoanalysis and Science. In *The Annual of Psychoanalysis*, pp. 73–81. New York: Quadrangle.

Hartmann, H. (1939). *Ego Psychology and the Problem of Adaptation*. New York: Int. Univ. Press, 1958.

———. (1950). Comments on the psychoanalytic theory of the ego. In *Essays on Ego Psychology*, pp. 113–141. New York: Int. Univ. Press, 1964.

———. (1951). Technical implications of ego psychology. *Psychoanal. Q.*, 20:31–43.

———. (1952). The mutual influences in the development of the ego and id. *Psychoanal. Study Child*, 7:9–30.

———. (1955). Notes on the theory of sublimation. *Psychoanal. Study Child*, 10:9–29.

———. (1956). The development of the ego concept in Freud's work. *Int. J. Psychoanal.*, 37:425–438.

———. (1964). *Essays on Ego Psychology*. New York: Int. Univ. Press.

Hartmann, H., Kris, E., & Loewenstein, R. M. (1946). Comments on the formation of psychic structure. *Psychoanal. Study Child*, 2:11–38.

506 Dale Boesky

———. (1949). Notes on the theory of aggression. *Psychoanal. Study Child*, 3/4:9–36.

Holt, R. R. (1962). A critical examination of Freud's concept of bound vs. free cathexis. *J. Amer. Psychoanal. Assn.*, 10:475–525.

———. (1967). The development of the primary process. In *Motives and Thought*, ed. R. R. Holt, pp. 344–383. Psychological Issues, monograph 18/19. New York: Int. Univ. Press.

Horowitz, M. (1977). The quantitative line of approach in psychoanalysis. *J. Amer. Psychoanal. Assn.*, 25:559–580.

Jacobson, E. (1964). *The Self and the Object World*. New York: Int. Univ. Press.

Jacobson, J. (1983). The structural theory and the representational world. *Psychoanal. Q.*, 52:514–563.

Kernberg, O. F. (1975). *Borderline Conditions and Pathological Narcissism*. New York: Aronson.

———. (1976). *Object Relations Theory and Clinical Psychoanalysis*. New York: Aronson.

Klein, G. S. (1973). Two theories or one? *Bull. Menninger Clinic*, 37:102–132.

———. (1976). *Psychoanalytic Theory*. New York: Int. Univ. Press.

Kohut, H. (1971). *The Analysis of the Self*. New York: Int. Univ. Press.

———. (1977). *The Restoration of the Self*. New York: Int. Univ. Press.

———. (1979). The two analyses of Mr. Z. *Int. J. Psychoanal.* 60:2–27.

Kris, E. (1950). Notes on the development and on some current problems of psychoanalytic psychology. *Psychoanal. Study Child*, 5:24–46.

Lampl-de Groot, J. (1964). Remarks on genesis, structuralization, and functioning of the mind. *Psychoanal. Study Child*, 19:48–57.

Levey, M. (1984–85). The concept of structure in psychoanalysis. In *The Annual of Psychoanalysis*, pp. 137–153. New York: Quadrangle.

Loewald, H. W. (1960). On the therapeutic action of psychoanalysis. *Int. J. Psychoanal.*, 41:16–33.

———. (1962a). Superego and time. In *Papers on Psychoanalysis*, pp. 43–52. New Haven: Yale Univ. Press, 1980.

———. (1962b). The superego and the ego ideal. *Int. J. Psychoanal.*, 43:264–268.

———. (1966). Book review and discussion. In *Papers on Psychoanalysis*, pp. 53–68. New Haven: Yale Univ. Press, 1980.

———. (1970). Psychoanalytic theory and the psychoanalytic process. In *Papers on Psychoanalysis*, pp. 277–301. New Haven: Yale Univ. Press, 1980.

———. (1971). On motivation and instinct theory. *Psychoanal. Study Child*, 26:91–128.

———. (1973). Review of *The Analysis of the Self* by H. Kohut. *Psychoanal. Q.*, 42:441–451.

———. (1983). Sublimation. Freud Lecture, New York Psychoanalytic Society. D. Berger, reporter. *Psychoanal. Q.*, 52:319–321.

Mahler, M. S. (1972). On the three subphases of the separation-individuation process. *Int. J. Psychoanal.*, 53:333–338.

Mahler, M. S., Pine, F., & Bergman, A. (1975). *The Psychological Birth of the Human Infant*. New York: Basic Books.

Moore, B. E., & Fine, B. D., eds. (1990). *Psychoanalytic Terms and Concepts*. New Haven: Yale Univ. Press.

Nagera, H. (1967). The concept of structure and structuralization. *Psychoanal. Study Child*, 22:77–102.

Nunberg, H. (1930). The synthetic function of the ego. *Int. J. Psychoanal.*, 12:123–140.

Panel (1958). The psychoanalytic theory of thinking. J. A. Arlow, reporter. *J. Amer. Psychoanal. Assn.*, 6:143–153.

———. (1963a). The concept of the id. E. Marcovitz, reporter. *J. Amer. Psychoanal. Assn.*, 11:151–160.

———. (1963b). The concept of psychic energy. A. H. Modell, reporter. *J. Amer. Psychoanal. Assn.*, 11:605–618.

———. (1963c). The significance of intrapsychic conflict. J. Nemiah, reporter. *J. Amer. Psychoanal. Assn.*, 11:619–627.

Rangell, L. (1963a). The scope of intrapsychic conflict. *Psychoanal. Study Child*, 18:75–102.

———. (1963b). Structural problems in intrapsychic conflict. *Psychoanal. Study Child*, 18:103–138.

Rapaport, D. (1957). Cognitive structures. In *Contemporary Approaches to Cognition*, ed. J. Bruner et al., pp. 157–200. Cambridge, Mass.: Harvard Univ. Press.

———. (1960). *The Structure of Psychoanalytic Theory*. Psychological Issues, monograph 6. New York: Int. Univ. Press.

Rapaport, D., ed. (1951). *The Organization and Pathology of Thought*. New York: Columbia Univ. Press.

Rapaport, D., & Gill, M. M. (1959). The points of view and assumptions of metapsychology. *Int. J. Psychoanal.*, 40:153–162.

Rosenblatt, A., & Thikstun, J. (1970). A study of the concept of psychic energy. *Int. J. Psychoanal.*, 51:265–278.

———. (1977). Energy, information, and motivation. *J. Amer. Psychoanal. Assn.*, 25:537–558.

Rothstein, A. (1980). Toward a critique of the psychology of the self. *Psychoanal. Q.*, 49:423–455.

———. (1983). *The Structural Hypothesis*. New York: Int. Univ. Press.

Sandler, J. (1960). The background of safety. *Int. J. Psychoanal.*, 41:352–356.

———. (1974). Psychological conflict and the structural model. *Int. J. Psychoanal.*, 55:53–62.

Sandler, J., & Rosenblatt, B. (1962). The concept of the representational world. *Psychoanal. Study Child*, 17:128–145.

Sandler, J., & Sandler, A.-M. (1978). On the development of object relationships and affects. *Int. J. Psychoanal.*, 59:285–296.

Schafer, R. (1976). *A New Language for Psychoanalysis*. New Haven: Yale Univ. Press.

———. (1983). *The Analytic Attitude*. New York: Basic Books.

Schur, M. (1966). *The Id and the Regulatory Principles of Mental Functioning*. New York: Int. Univ. Press.

Schwartz, F. (1981). Psychic structure. *Int. J. Psychoanal.*, 62:61–72.

Stein, M. (1979). Review of *The Restoration of the Self* by H. Kohut. *J. Amer. Psychoanal. Assn.*, 27:665–680.

Sterba, R. (1934). The fate of the ego in analytic therapy. *Int. J. Psychoanal.*, 15:117–126.

Strachey, J. (1934). The nature of the therapeutic action of psycho-analysis. *Int. J. Psychoanal.*, 15:126–159.

Waelder, R. (1930). The principle of multiple function. *Psychoanal. Q.*, 5(1936):45–62.

Wallerstein, R. (1977). Psychic energy reconsidered. *J. Amer. Psychoanal. Assn.*, 25:529–536.

Wiedeman, G. (1972). Comments on the structural theory of personality. *Int. J. Psychoanal.*, 53:307–314.

Alvin Frank, M.D.

39

METAPSYCHOLOGY

"Metapsychology" refers to the collection of theoretical postulates underlying and explaining the less abstract, more experientially based theories of psychoanalysis. It provides their logic and basic elements. Freud called it the "theoretical assumptions on which a psycho-analytic system could be founded" (1917, p. 222). It is considered "the highest level of abstraction in the continuum from clinical observation to psychoanalytic theory" (Moore & Fine, eds., 1990, p. 119). In an exposition of sequential levels of conceptualization in psychoanalytic thinking, Waelder proposed the following in order of increasing abstraction:

At the level of observation is included that which the analyst actually hears, sees, and infers as potentially directly observable.

At the level of clinical interpretation are interconnections and relationships between observed data and other observations and inferences.

At the level of clinical generalizations, broader statements can be made from constellations of data and interpretations pertaining to particular subjects, e.g., demographic groups, specific symptoms or illnesses, environmental impacts, and so forth.

At the level of clinical theory are posited theoretical constructs implicit in, relevant to, or deriving from the above.

More abstract still is the level of metapsychology. [1962, pp. 251-252]

Freud himself was an inveterate and enthusiastic theorizer and systematizer. Any of his works, regardless of its particular emphasis and level of presentation, was apt to be interrupted by a metapsychological question or citation. Particularly important contributions are chapter 7 of *The Interpretation of Dreams* (1900), the explicitly titled and incomplete "Papers on metapsychology" (1915a, 1915b, 1915c), *Beyond the Pleasure Principle* (1920), the addenda to *Inhibitions, Symptoms and Anxiety* (1926), and "Analysis terminable and interminable" (1937). His two series of *Introductory Lectures* (1916–17, 1933) included serious efforts at metapsychological articulation and integration.

The most serious formal metapsychological exposition after Freud's was that of Rapaport and Gill (1959), who attempted to present the essence of psychoanalytic metapsychology in one definitive work. Because of its uniqueness and a significant degree of success, it is still regarded by many analysts and theoreticians as the authoritative analytic metatheoretical statement.

Because of the similarity in terminology and because of its epistemological context, metapsychology is sometimes confused with "metaphysics." The similarity is coincidental and homophonic rather than substantive. Freud originally coined the term to designate a view beyond conscious experience— literally, "beyond psychology" as the word *psychology* was at that time applied and understood. In uncritical parlance the term "metapsychological" is also used to embrace the theoretical systems that it subsumes. Any theoretical examination or discourse is sometimes imprecisely designated "metapsychological." In this chapter I will, to the best of my ability, employ the term in the more limited and carefully defined sense of Moore and Fine, eds. (1990), Waelder (1962), and Rapaport and Gill (1959).

Prior to the last decade, metapsychological study, discourse, and debate was regarded as critical to psychoanalytic scholarship. Since that time, it has seemed to lose relevance, and theoretical presentations have more often followed more focused and reified modes. Yet the metapsychology of Freud and his first generation of followers is of extraordinary historical value and provides a logic with which to compare later contributions.

Metapsychology is conventionally presented in terms of a series of five viewpoints, or frames of reference. They are designated dynamic, economic, structural (originally termed "topographic"), genetic, and adaptive. The dynamic postulates the dimension of directed psychological "forces," and the economic that of undirected psychological energy within the mental apparatus. The structural viewpoint provides for the representability of recurring and enduring psychological phenomena. The genetic provides a temporal dimension to psychological phenomena, and the adaptive argues for the inclusion of interpersonal, societal, and, in a broad sense, environmental phenomena relevant to, and as interacting with, influencing, and being influenced by, the postulated singular mind.

In addition, certain psychoanalytic metatheoretical assumptions are so pervasive as to be treated implicitly within the viewpoints rather than being specifically discussed and are therefore apt to be overlooked. Before I turn to a detailed consideration of the viewpoints, I shall review these common assumptions, since they provide a vantage point from which to consider the former.

THE PERVASIVE ASSUMPTIONS OF METAPSYCHOLOGY

1. Metapsychology provides the underpinnings for a theory of mind (sometimes termed the "mental apparatus") rather than of neurology of neurophysiology. However, it is a theory of mind as a biopsychological entity. This theory views man as contending with his inner, evolved, animal origins in the context of the necessity to perceive and respond to inner and outer environments by virtue of endowed capacities. Biology and psychology are viewed

within this conceptual scheme as employing different and singular modes of investigation and discourse. While some degree or form of relationship between mind and brain is assumed, biological laws cannot be applied to psychological phenomena, or vice versa. Whether the nature of the relationship is characterizable is unknown; but the ultimate determination and specification of the relationship do not affect this assumption. Freud was particularly prone periodically to express a hope that biology would some day provide ultimate answers, and at times his theoretical speculations crossed over into biology. These occasional excursions do not play a significant part in current metatheoretical thinking, however.

2. The essence of psychoanalytic metapsychology is the application of abstract assumptions to subjective experience and phenomena as reported and observed. The translation is from the subjective to the explicitly objective.

3. Psychic phenomena are considered to be determined, rather than random, events. The determination employs a sequential logic; phenomena are explained on the basis of an assumed progression from stimulus or stimuli, cause, or reason, through a resulting mechanism or process, to a result or outcome. Although the origins of the causal elements are unknown, and perhaps unknowable, hypothetical entities corresponding to the five metapsychological viewpoints are invoked as the most reasonable tools for organizing systematic consideration of the less abstract psychological constructs. This kind of sequential reasoning prejudices the theoretician against teleologic reasoning, which may nevertheless be quite defensible and even indicated clinically.

4. It is postulated that the operations of these variables are lawful, rather than chance. The ultimate origin of the relevant laws is also currently unknown, and perhaps unknowable, if frequently the subject of speculation. Operative laws include the possibility that a multiplicity of causes may interact to produce a given result. There are a variety of laws explaining the way in which the various elements interact to produce a result. In addition, the impact of a given cause is not limited to a single result. Psychological phenomena are characterized in terms of both their nature (the qualitative) and their magnitude (the quantitative). Generally, Freud considered quantitative factors more basic, critical, influential, and ultimate than qualitative ones.

5. The laws and phenomena described are inherently impersonal. Such personal considerations as intention and motive are assumed only at lower levels of abstraction.

6. It is considered reasonable within this system

that there are multiple laws pertaining to comparable operations, which might act independently or in some sort of interrelated fashion. Vicissitudes of a given element or construction may or may not involve the application of one or several laws, depending on other variables.

7. The subject matter can be of greater or lesser magnitude or complexity. Elemental units may or may not be treated in a way identical to multiple or complex constructions. Provisions exist for both. Multiple or complex constructions are considered to have the potential for characteristics other than those provided through the additive effects of their elements.

8. It is assumed that these general laws and principles, ultimately derived from observations of distinctive individuals, can be reapplied to the conceptualization and explanation of unique, specific phenomena. The possibilities of generalization are complementary to assumptions of inherent individual uniqueness. This individuality is held to be explicable on the basis of both intrinsic (relating to endowment) and extrinsic (such as experiential) factors and their interactions and reciprocities.

THE POINTS OF VIEW OF METAPSYCHOLOGY

In the exposition of the pervasive assumptions, it was possible to be reasonably consistent in presenting them in a manner more or less appropriate to their level of abstraction. In what follows, even the attempt at rigor is problematic, particularly with regard to the economic and structural viewpoints. Traditionally, it has often been left to the individual to infer metatheoretical propositions from the models that serve as metapsychological theoretical subsystems. Given the historical, semantic, and heuristic significance and relevance of this time-honored procedure, it is followed here.

The first three metapsychological designations were Freud's. He believed that with the presentation of "a psychical process in its dynamic, topographical and economic aspects, we should speak of it as a *metapsychological* presentation" (1915b, p. 181). The adaptive and genetic viewpoints were implicit in Freud and in the writings of other theoreticians, particularly Hartmann, Kris, Loewenstein, and Erikson. Rapaport and Gill first explicitly applied the characterization of viewpoints to them. A model or models exist consisting of the application of each or several principles in such a way as to constitute a corresponding theoretical system or systems.[1]

1. Gedo and Goldberg (1973) have comprehensively reviewed the applications of models "to make easier the understanding of complex, abstract theoretical propositions

The Dynamic Viewpoint

This was the first viewpoint explicitly proposed by Freud. He used it to distinguish the dynamic (rather than merely descriptive) nature of unconsciousness. The dynamic conception of mental phenomena was presented as the consideration of the play of forces in the mind which worked together or against each other. Such propositions include a source, a direction, a magnitude, and an implicit or explicit object. These are models of energy with direction, comparable in some ways to vectors. Dynamic models presuppose a variety of sources. Sometimes it is suggested that they are ultimately biological or biologically derived, through such theoretical organizational entities as the system unconscious or the id. At other times, the source is another sort of psychological "structural" configuration, such as ego instincts, ego defenses, self interests, or preconscious repressive forces. In the structural formulations the origin of the energy of the dynamism is often a source of conjecture, debate, or confusion.

The dynamic viewpoint provides for the possibility of such things as conflict or impulsion. Conflicts are often categorized in terms of the parameters of the models of the involved dynamisms:

"Instinctual conflicts" refers to conflicts between incompatible drives. For example, conflicts may exist between loving and hateful, active and passive, masculine and feminine forces at a given time.

"Environmental conflicts" occur as the result of the governing mental agencies' collaboration with drive forces that conflict with external realities. For example, sexual or aggressive dynamisms may oppose either the world's lack of tolerance or the restrictions imposed by specific individuals.

A "structural conflict" may occur when drive forces face opposition from internal agencies. For example, aggressive or sexual dynamisms may arouse the forces of conscience as represented in the mind. Such intersystemic conflicts also include the possibility of tensions between two such

---

through the use of more easily encompassable pictorial or verbal analogies." I follow them in Suzanne Langer's (1962) characterization: "A model always illustrates a principle of construction or operation, it is a symbolic projection of its object which need not resemble it in appearance at all but must permit one to match the factors of the model with respective factors of the object, according to some convention. The convention governs the selectiveness of the model; to all items in the selected class the model is equally true, to the limit of its accuracy, that is, to the limit of the formal simplification imposed by the symbolic translation" (p. 59).

mental agencies as the ego and the superego, for example, when the functions of adaptation and morality are at odds. Intrasystemic conflicts involve the disparate aims of contending interests within the same mental agency. For example, ego interests that are self-directed, such as egoism, may be at odds with the ego's defensive functions, which guard against inner anxiety or shamefulness.

A variety of possible outcomes to conflict include the qualification that the end product may not be the simple resultant of the impacts of the forces involved. A dynamism, when completely thwarted by another, may be inhibited (one variety of "repressed") or diverted to other than its original object. Several dynamisms may combine to produce a given result. One may overwhelm another in such a way as to give it direct expression. This last circumstance explains, at an observable level, not only explicit, intended behavior but the phenomenon known as "parapraxis." Here, a previously thwarted impulsive force manifests itself through a mistake, a slip of the tongue, forgetting, and so forth. Another very common, observable outcome of contentions between two hypothesized opposing forces is a compromise allowing each a degree of success. This sort of compromise formation allows an understanding of certain symptomatology.

The Economic Viewpoint

The economic viewpoint provides for excitation and discharge of energy. The original model of energy was termed "libidinal." It was considered to lack any inherent qualities or characteristics. Investment of psychic organizations with libido was said to involve "cathexis"; loss of libidinal investment was termed "decathexis." Energy could be "bound"— that is, undergo a transformation leading to relative stability and thus a higher threshold for discharge. It followed laws termed in their first formulations "primary" and "secondary" processes. The originally occurring primary process was characterized by easy mobility, low discharge thresholds, ease of displacement (movement from one structural organization to another), and condensation (combination of energies). The subsequent secondary process had the opposite characteristics —namely, stability, with associated delayed, controlled discharge and high thresholds through binding. The appellations of these laws were extended to psychological systems whose characteristics corresponded to these energic processes. It was assumed that there was generally, for a given psychological entity at any given time, a finite amount of energy available for employment and investment. Quantities of energy were critical.

For an organization to be viable, a certain amount of energy must be invested in it.

The energies were initially thought to follow a relatively simple law of compelled discharge, variously termed the "pleasure–unpleasure principle" or the "Nirvana" principle. Discharge was postulated as corresponding to experiential pleasure. Accumulations of energy were thought to correspond to experiences of unpleasantness or inner tension. It was held that the inherent tendency was for discharge of energy and reduction to a state of zero or minimal excitation. Discharged energies could be employed in, and corresponded to, various behavioral phenomena, including thought, action, or affective expression.

In a later reformation, Freud postulated two, opposed classes of energy: libido and aggressive energy. Libidinal energy corresponded roughly to constructive, life-engendering aims, aggressive energy to destructive, life-threatening aims. Psychic organizations and representations could be invested with varying proportions of the two energies, corresponding with various theoretical and corresponding clinical phenomena. Aggressive and libidinal energies were proposed as existing from the first within the psychic organization. Aggressive energy abiding there from the beginning constitutes erotogenic masochism. It could also be discharged through muscular activity, diverted outward through the influence of libido. It could then be considered the destructive instinct, the will to mastery, the will to power, or sadism proper. The process whereby antithetical energies were combined was referred to as "fusion" or "amalgamation." It was thought that each energy could lose its inherent characteristics. Aggressive energy could be deaggressivized, libidinal energies delibinidinzed, or desexualized; and generically, energy could be neutralized. These processes could also be reversed, so that energies could regain their inherent characteristics.

Hartmann proposed that the two forms of energy are at times used in specialized ways or have particular operational characteristics. For example, he suggested that defenses and resistances most often implicate aggressive energy; similarly, drives striving for discharge were fueled by libidinal energy. Freud described individual variations in energy investment both quantitatively and qualitatively. First, the absolute amount of energy and the relative proportions of the two kinds varied as a result of both intrinsic and extrinsic factors. Second, certain characteristics of the energies, involving their more or less stable investment characteristics, were labeled metaphorically as "adhesiveness" versus "mobility" or "plasticity."

Further, Freud later regarded the Nirvana principle as a manifestation of the aims of aggressive energy, an ambiguous semiphilosophical concept he termed the "death instinct." He now believed that the pleasure principle was related to the impact of the libido. The modification of the pleasure principle through influences from the environment he termed the "reality principle." The exposition of these principles did not imply a supersession of one by the other; Freud explicitly stated that they coexisted. He also suggested that the Nirvana and pleasure principles might ultimately be replaced by a qualitative factor, perhaps some rhythm of energy accumulation and discharge, rather than its absolute quantity.

Freud considered the origin of the energies to be ultimately biological. At times he characterized them as on the borderline between biology and psychology, but most usually as psychological representations of biological stimuli. Much of the time these connections were ambiguous. Within the individual, he believed that these energies followed a sequential, anatomically determined pattern of development. This sequence consists of the well-known oral, anal, phallic, and genital erogenous zones and periods. The deployment of libidinal energy in objects also followed a sequence. It began with a narcissistic phase, in which no distinction is made between one's own psychological self and that of other individuals. This led to an anaclitic phase, in which the relationship with others is determined by need, tensions, and satisfactions. Then follows the phase of object constancy, in which others exist, have significance, and evoke a response in terms of their own inherent nature and actions. Aggressive energies, in a later formulation in the period of ego psychology, were considered to be incompletely integrated with libidinal development during the oral, anal, and phallic phases. Object constancy required the integration of discharge of both drives.

The quantity of energy is the critical factor in the economic viewpoint and models. An overabundance of energy relative to the psychic organizations' capacities for accumulation and discharge is hypothesized as producing a traumatic state, a profound overstimulation of the mental apparatus. Freud theorized that the biological counterpart could be the overstimulation of the experience of birth. A relative lack of energy is implicated, by contrast, in states of apathy and some depressions. Disproportionate accumulations of energy in representations of a person's own self coincide with narcissistic phenomena, whereas a disproportionate investment of energy in the representations of others is compatible with selflessness and altruism. In view of the fixed amount of energy hypothesized as available at any specific time, there was believed to be a reciprocal

relationship between narcissistic and object investment. This was sometimes characterized as the "U-tube phenomenon." The quantity of energy available within a given person's psychic systems fluctuated over the life cycle, the biological phenomena of puberty supplementing, the menopause and aging depleting, the psychic energies available. The environment was also considered to be potentially stimulating or unexciting.

The economic viewpoint as elaborated by Freud and later by the ego psychologists (for example, Hartmann, 1964; Rapaport, 1967) represents the most controversial and ill-defined metapsychological system. An influential group of psychoanalytic theoreticians favor its elimination. They object to it on the basis of its biologism, as well as the many conflicts and discrepancies that exist between its assumptions and reasonable inferences from the observed data. However, it is difficult to conceive of a meaningful and adequate theoretical system that would not provide for the considerations represented by the economic viewpoint. The criticisms can be usefully employed toward a revision of the model of energy subsumed by the economic viewpoint. I believe that a reasonable statement at this time, consistent with the thinking of most of those who share this view, would include the following.

The economic viewpoint as involving excitation, discharge, and particularly quantities of energy is still a useful working assumption, despite the fact that the ultimate origin of the energies characterized is unknown. It is inescapable that these energies, although inherently related to biological vicissitudes, are more distant from these vicissitudes than was previously hypothesized. In all probability, either excesses or depletion of energy can be implicated in symptomatology and phenomenology. However, a caveat to the effect that such assumptions must also include consideration of the concurrent status of structural entities is imperative. For example, the hypothesized traumatic state, when excitement quantitatively exceeds the capacity of the mental apparatus, is a result of the relative strength of each variable, rather than the absolute amount of excitation per se. The observable swings in energic phenomenology in puberty may be viewed as a result of energic upsurges in a setting of structural weakness, the latter due to a variety of dramatic developmental stresses and challenges.

It is still consistent with lower-level theories and data to conceive of a dual instinct theory, involving at least two qualitatively different forms of energy. Their characterization as aggressive and libidinal continues to be useful. It is consistent with the needs within the theoretical-metatheoretical system to consider both as existing within the mental apparatus from its observable beginnings. The absolute quantity and relative proportion of each are still considered to be related to both intrinsic and extrinsic factors. There is presumed to be some relationship between psychological phenomena such as psychopathology and the proportion and quantity of each energy. Such vicissitudes and idioms as cathexis, binding, fusion, deaggressivization, and delibidinalization or neutralization are considered reasonable. It is assumed, as before, that these processes can be reversed. The formulations characterized as the primary and secondary processes are still considered to be useful and valid. Whether the particular energies are used in specialized ways is a moot point. The question of which energies are responsible for the functioning of structural entities such as the ego or the self is considered to be a red herring, largely related to the inherent limitations of each model. There is considerable agreement, however, that energies so used, whatever their origin, are relatively neutralized.

There is little support for the so-called Nirvana, pleasure, reality, or rhythm principles as characterizing energic phenomena as explicated by Freud. It is generally agreed that the metatheoretical model should be flexible enough to provide for the observation that at times increases of inner energic tension can be either pleasurable or unpleasurable. The same is true of depletion of intrapsychic energies. There is more emphasis on applying these possibilities to specific situations and relating them to other dimensions and variables than insistence on them as inviolable dogma. For example, increases in tension may initially and observably lead to pleasure. If the tension is too prolonged or too great, however, they may paradoxically be associated with discomfort and unpleasure. Examples of these phenomena are foreplay versus sexual consummation or many situations of anticipation and satisfaction. Hence it is mandated that the metatheoretical system should at least not contradict such lower-level observations.

The question of a finite amount of energy at any given time is considered ambiguous. Clinical observations indicate great variations on the basis of other phenomenology. For example, profound conflict may involve the appearance of an absolute depletion of energy, when in fact vast quantities of energy are being expended against each other. Similarly, the effective employment of energy through, and as a result of, structuralization obscures issues of absolute quantity. Observed phenomena involving relationships between energy and structure generally occur in situations in which definitive determinations of

relative quantities are impossible. The metatheoretical system is considered to be responsible for consideration of these variables. A reciprocity between self and object investment in a way consistent with the model of the U-tube phenomenon is not considered tenable.

The implication of the specific natures of energies is also considered a moot point. Certainly, the singular, unwavering characterization of each energy as either life-engendering or death- and destruction-seeking has been muted. The patterns of development of both self- and object-related energies described above are still considered valid. The metatheory is held responsible for providing grounds for many previously unappreciated complexities in the genesis and evolution of the individual which have emerged as the result of continuing observations and deductions.

The Structural Metapsychological Viewpoint and Models of the Mind

The structural viewpoint characterizes and considers the representations and organization of recurring and enduring psychological phenomena. Rapaport and Gill (1959) described it as consisting of *"propositions concerning the abiding psychological configurations (structures) involved in the phenomenon. . . . Structures are configurations of a slow rate of change"* (pp. 802–803). Provision is made for structures of varying complexity. Elemental units may or may not be treated in the same way as multiple or complex constructions. An example of the model of a prototypical elemental structure is that of the memory trace, the representation of an impression of a given event. It may be of greater or lesser content, complexity, or meaning. It can then be organized in a variety of ways and serve a variety of functions. Thus the representation of an interaction with a parent may be organized in terms of a particular aspect or comprehensive representation of the parent, of one's self as subjectively experienced, of interactions of particular sorts such as those involving impulse discharge or inhibition, a statement or representation of the world generally as expanded from the parents as the center of the child's world, and so forth. It may then serve, among other things, as part of a system of representation of others, self representations, or conscience. It may be integrated into personality, capacities, behavioral modes, and environmental expectations.

Structure originates and evolves in consequence of both intrinsic and extrinsic factors. The relation of the time of its origin, the psychological birth of the individual, to his or her biological birth is a matter of speculation. There are provisions for considering structure(s) both as relatively permanent, once established, and discontinuously or continuously evolving. Earlier structures may be integrated, superseded, destroyed, or endure independently or latently with the introduction of their successors.

As the organizations of elemental units achieve their greatest complexity, they are termed "systems." At some point, systems within a given framework of organization may be described in terms of their own inherent characteristics and their interactions with each other. There are a number of reifications of such systems that constitute models, as defined earlier. In my discussion of the structural viewpoint I shall present the essence of some significant and illustrative psychoanalytic structure models of the mind. To be considered are the classical topographic and tripartite models of Freud, as well as several later ones which I designate as the "superordinate ego of ego psychology," the "incorporative and projective self," the "pathological unintegrated component subselves," and the "deficiency-prone bipolar self."

At times in psychoanalytic theorizing, a given model has been mistakenly construed to constitute the whole of the structural point of view. Not only does this represent an epistemologic error; it presupposes an ideal of exclusivity, an expectation that in fact has never been met. For example, the original topographic model has never been completely superseded by the tripartite model that Freud designed as its successor. New models are designed to address specific, previously ignored issues and phenomena, to correct limitations and defects inherent in their predecessors, and to account for new data. They are often characterized as paradigmatic by their proponents.

Topographic model. Freud's original structural model was termed "topographic." It was made explicit in *The Interpretation of Dreams,* used almost exclusively until 1912, and continued to have preeminent status until 1923. Fairly close to experiential data, it was intended to conceptualize the phenomenology of consciousness and unconsciousness as relevant to a variety of psychological experiences. It was comprised of three formations: the unconscious (Ucs.), the preconscious (Pcs.), and the conscious. The Ucs. was filled with primitive content (including memories), was primitively organized, and followed illogical laws of functioning (termed the "primary process"). It was believed to resemble the psychic organization characteristic of the infant and very young child. Some estimate of its characteristics could be formed by studying such phenomena as dreams, wit, and the symptomatology of neuroses and psychoses. With the development of

logical, realistic mentation ("secondary process"), which Freud saw as associated with the development of verbal symbols, the infantile wishful impulses and memories were set apart by the development of the preconscious system. The separation was achieved by virtue of a postulated "repression barrier" of opposed energies which separated the two systems. The energies of the original wishful impulses and memories were believed to be diverted and redirected by the Pcs. against their original source.

The Pcs. was also the repository of acquired standards and prohibitions. Freud considered it as a reasonably uniform structure; later it was conceived as involving a gradation of complexity, organization, and contents. Its contents were originally conceived to be uniformly accessible; but later formulations considered a spectrum of availability.

Consciousness was the result of the operations of the third system, Cs., termed the "sense organ of consciousness." Unlike the other two systems, no memories could be recorded in Cs., whose quality was fleeting and depended upon the investing of a special energy, "attention cathexis," in the contents of the Pcs. Unconscious material was not directly available via this mechanism; it could only be translated through Pcs. representations.

The advantages of the topographic model in considering the levels and vicissitudes of conscious accessibility of mental contents have resulted in its continuing usage, despite its proclaimed supersession by other constructs.

Tripartite model. The tripartite model was proposed by Freud in 1923 to explain a variety of data which analysts then addressed. In part, this was because of their expanding clinical scope and ambitiousness, but it was also the result of the recognized limitations and contradictions of the earlier model. In particular, it was intended to treat issues of conflict and its outcome; conscience and ideals and their relevance, vicissitudes, and influences; and the interrelationships of psychopathology, personality, and the process of clinical psychoanalysis. It was originally designed to be integrated with important topographic features, although, paradoxically, it was explicitly designed to supersede that model.

The id is the continuously fueled source of primitive energies. It is unorganized and strives only for satisfaction. It comprises most of the psychological phenomenology resulting from the instinctual endowment of the person. Its laws are those of the earlier Ucs. Logic is irrelevant. There is no recognition of time, and there are no judgments. It is dominated by the laws of the quantitative economic factors. Ideation is irrelevant in its functioning. The nature of its representations and organization is ambiguous. The id is entirely unconscious and can be perceived only through its influences on the other two systems (also called "agencies"), the ego and the superego.

The ego is the executive agency of the mind. It reconciles the demands, pressures, forces, and constraints of the id, external reality, and its own ideal and moral aspects, the superego. It is derived from the id through the perceptions of inner (originally bodily) and external states and realities. It is the seat of consciousness, the organ of perception and memory, the controller of motility and action. The economic pleasure principle of the id is superseded here by the reality principle. Energies are derived from the id in various ways. In part the ego is sharply separated from the id by the repression barrier; in part they meet in an ill-defined merger, a portion of which is constituted by defenses other than repression. As implied, portions of the ego are phenomenologically preconscious, other portions unconscious.

The superego is a portion of the ego, the ego's ideal, and is the ideal and moral agency (that is, conscience) of the mental apparatus. It is the product of the destruction of the oedipus complex in the middle of the first decade of life, formed through the massive incorporation of parental representations and the energies with which the parents were invested, with emphasis on the aggressive. Relevant to the superego are those representations that represent ideals, control, and prohibition. Hence, discrepancies between the superego and the ego dynamisms are responsible for corresponding subjective phenomena of guilt and shame. The superego is partly conscious and partly unconscious. In development there is an intimate relationship between the drives and the parents who thwart their expression. These restraints are now constituted in the superego. The interpersonal constellation is replicated in the intimate relationship between the superego and the aggressive drive, to the detriment of the moral agency's capacity to respond to external reality.

Many analysts consider the superego to consist of two relatively distinct portions, different but interrelated functional organizations. The first, concerned with the establishment and propagation of standards and ideals, is often presumed to be more closely related to the earlier identifications with the parents before the oedipus conflict and more intimately involved in fluctuations of self-esteem. Hence, it is considered to represent the superego's narcissistic origins and facets of experience. It is considered to be primarily associated with the phenomenology of humiliation and shame. The second, the superego proper, is often assumed to be more directly related

to the prohibitions associated with the parental representations of the oedipus complex. It is hence considered to be more intimately associated with guilt per se.

The tripartite model is thus seen to be more distant from clinical data and more abstractly based than the preceding topographical model. With the formulation of the tripartite model, the goal of psychoanalysis became to strengthen the ego, a relatively stable and permanent mental organization, rather than simply to lift repressions. With this model, psychoanalysis could now approach problems of personality as related to symptomatology.

Superordinate ego model. Given this emphasis on the ego as the agency of change, it is not surprising that a later group of analysts, led particularly by Anna Freud, Hartmann, Kris, Loewenstein, Rapaport, and Erikson, would make it the object of their attention and study. The aims and ambitions of the innovators were to create a general psychology that would supersede the more limited conflict psychology of the earlier models; be able to integrate observations and data from other fields of endeavor (particularly child observation) and consider in detail the role of the ego in adaptation both as related and unrelated to libidinal or aggressive drives or conflicts; and lead a better understanding of its workings as the critical organization in treatment. This model, although using the concept of ego from the tripartite model, employed it at a level of abstraction considerably more distant from observable data than its predecessor. They treated the tripartite model as if it were observable data rather than a theoretical model and started the process of abstraction anew. The result was thus an abstraction of an abstraction.

The superordinate ego model postulated the existence of capacities with adaptive value unrelated to drive or conflictual vicissitudes, which developed at a unique, inherent rate. Similarly, the ego itself was thought to have a degree of adaptive autonomy. Proposals regarding the origins, development, maldevelopment, and impact of these variables were made. From this vantage point, the ego itself was considered to consist of a number of organizations, each with coordinating and organizing capacities. Conflicts within the ego, as well as between the ego and the other agencies or external realities, were recognized, characterized, and dissected. The vicissitudes of each of the energies within the ego, including the implications for its particular organizations and suborganizations, could be considered in detail. A degree of specialization was attributed to each of the energies, in terms of both functions and propensity for particular pathological constellations.

Energy could be neutralized, lose much of its original nature, and hence become available for use at the behest of the ego. Other configurations could also undergo "estrangement" from drive origins. These ideas were subsequently applied to a limited consideration of defects within the ego and consequent pathology related to deficiency rather than excess, frustration, or conflict.

Whereas the ego of the tripartite model was explicitly a product and an agent of conflict, the ego in this model had so-called autonomous functions, relatively removed from conflict in origin, evolution, and operation. Such functions were intrinsic, although hardly immune to drive and conflictual disruption. Some functions, conceived in conflict, could attain autonomy through a change of function.

The ego psychologists were in the forefront of psychoanalysis for over three decades, beginning in the late 1930s. But the relatively abstract level of theorization in this model was considered impractical, fanciful, and clinically irrelevant by many analysts. In addition, to a greater degree than with previous models, the model itself was treated as if it were observational data, and formulations became increasingly more abstract based on the model's inferred qualities.

Introjective-projective model. Another model, which gained importance from the late 1920s on could be characterized as the introjective-projective or incorporating-extruding self. The self here refers to the psychological organization or suborganizations of a person, presumably at a relatively low level of abstraction close to observational data. Some of the formulations, however, seem considerably more abstract, despite their direct application to clinical material. This is a model first employed extensively by Melanie Klein and later by some of the analysts labeled object relations theorists, such as Jacobson and Kernberg. Here noxious pathological structures are considered as originally derived from particular early periods of development. They are then treated in terms of the possibilities of their relationship to the self or selves. Early drives or ideas as perceived in others are incorporated into one's own psychological gestalt, projected into others from one's inner self, or undergo a potentially very complex variety of such vicissitudes. The psychological structures are often primitive in their inherent nature as well as in the individual's life experience. For example, Klein postulated that in the oral-sadistic phase of very early childhood the child's attack on the mother's breast leads to its representation in the child's

psyche as both destroyed and destructive. A contrasting loving and loved breast is also represented. Wishes directed toward the self, the mother, and later the father involve fantasies of their bodily contents. The interaction of these fantasies and the child's intense desires and affects gives rise to a whole menage of elements, whose representations within the child create a variety of psychological configurations. The splitting of representations of the nature of one's self or others into good and bad, sustaining and destructive, loved and hated, and the introjection or projection of these constellations create a number of clinical pathological possibilities. These fantastic products can impinge on and interfere with the perception of, and interaction with, people in one's life, as well as one's self, in various deleterious ways.

The idiom of these formulations is often graphic and biological; the models appeal to their innovators as explaining in a convincing way the enduring pathology that is a consequence of perceived and experienced childhood relationships recorded as representations of the involved subjects, impulses and drives, ideas, and objects. This is a model designed to characterize both the subject's inner experience and his or her experience of the world. Both the constituted phenomena and the defensive efforts needed to maintain the individual in the face of intense pathological disruptions are held responsible for illness and maladaptations. Many of the originators of these formulations were interested in their usefulness in explaining severe mental disorders, including marked narcissistic character pathology and symptomatology, schizoid and borderline personalities and phenomena, and the psychoses.

Pathological unintegrated component subselves model. This is the work of a number of theorists, including some members of the British school of object relations, who advance a more socially derived structural model. The malignant interpersonal experiences of childhood are here presumed to result in various primitive self nuclei, which, because of their pathological nature, cannot become part of a single, cohesive, integrated, superordinate self organization. For example, Winnicott postulates a "false self," mandated by insensitive maternal reactions to, and expectations of, the child. It persists as a dominant entity throughout life, preempting the "true" or "real self." Fairbairn's childhood constructs, the pleasure-seeking "libidinal self" and the prohibitive "antilibidinal self," endure to the detriment of the adult "ideal" or "central" self. These formulations are also designed to provide understanding of, and a therapeutic rationale for the treatment of, severely disturbed patients.

Deficiency-prone bipolar self model. This is derived from the work of Heinz Kohut (1977). This self, also a superordinate structure, is defined as the core or bedrock of the personality. The two poles represent early individual strivings and ambitions on the one hand and social ideas and standards within the individual on the other. A tension between the two activates basic talents and skills. Critical for the development of an intact self is the interaction of the child with selfobjects, persons in the environment who perform a function within the child's psychological structure. An optimum presence of selfobject empathy leads to structuralization of the self. The selfobjects, usually the parents but invariably those in parenting roles, provide both a reflection of the child's basic worth and examples that can be idealized as healthy standards. Deficiencies in the self, the result of chronic attitudes inconsistent with healthy parenting functions, are considered as basic to psychological disorder. The existence of tripartite structures is acknowledged, but their functioning is dependent on the foundation of a more or less stable and cohesive self. Acknowledged conflicts involving such structural entities are relatively minimal, atraumatic, and nonpathogenic unless there is an underlying disorder (that is, defect) of the self. Libido is conceived of almost metaphorically as investing the self with positive qualities; aggression is merely secondary to a disruption of the cohesiveness of the self. Basic faults in the self lead to severe psychopathology, including psychosis and borderline states. Less severe disorders involve the narcissistic behavior and symptomatic disorders.

The formulation of these ideas, apparently intended to be relatively close to observational data, was originally part of an attempt to understand narcissistic disorders. It was subsequently expanded into a much more ambitious general theory of personality and illness. Treatment was now designed to provide structure-building "transmuting internalizations." Thus, defective and absent structure, the result of the failure of the selfobjects during the formative years, was provided anew. In the most severe disorders the possible influences of predisposing failures of endowment were also acknowledged.

The self psychologists thus attempted to introduce an organizational entity consistent with an inherently motivated personality constellation deterred in its healthy strivings only by disruptions of continuity or fragmentations that invoke a variety of responses designed to restore the intactness of the self organization. Psychopathology was seen not only as a consequence of the defects themselves but as the result of attempts to compensate for defects or restore the intactness of the self. Kohut speculated that self pathology was a product of our times. By contrast with the overpopulated, overstimulating milieu of Freud's Vienna, the understimulating, lonely, impersonal environment of contemporary life was prone to give rise to disorders of the self rather than classic psychopathology.

Self psychology is notable for its distance from the vision of man struggling with his innate, inescapable biological endowment. Subjectivity is given unique credence. Others are held primarily responsible for the subjects' disorders. It is also noteworthy for its pervasive emphasis on deficiency as pathogenic and on the possibility of acquiring in adulthood, through analysis, precisely what one has missed in childhood.

It was clear that, in time, constructs of the British object relations theorists and Kohut would mandate sweeping changes in metapsychology. Ultimately it was to be modified to provide assumptions more suited to a central focus on man as a social being. In this version, interpersonal needs are considered to be primary, and drives merely representations of affects secondary to the inherently striving personality and its pathology.

The Genetic Point of View

The genetic viewpoint provides a temporal dimension to psychological phenomena. It includes provision for the characterization and distinction of such phenomena over time and for laws explaining their mutuality, reciprocity, and other influences from the standpoint of both progression and regression. It includes perspectives and vantage points of past, present, and future. It is understood here that "psychological phenomena" include any of the dimensions characterized as points of view and that one can apply this definition of these assumptions to the vicissitudes of energy, force (dynamisms), structure, and adaptation.

The characterization "genetic" is meant to convey a sense of both origins and evolution and reflects an emphasis on progression. Rapaport and Gill (1959), who gave it its first explicit exposition, defined it as demanding *"that the psychoanalytic explanation of any psychological phenomenon include propositions concerning its psychological origin and development"* (p. 804). Accordingly, it is presumed that psychological phenomena do have a point of origin, which may or may not coincide with birth, and a discernible evolution rather than springing into the world in definitive form at some particular time. Innate constitutional givens are assumed, which may impart qualities, either enduring or evolving or both, and may or may not interact with chance environmental factors. Ideal sequential progression—that is, a flawless evolution—is contrasted with more common, problematic progression with deficits (absences of evolution), fixations (discrete failures of evolution and retention of earlier forms), or deviant anormative developments. As implied, normative sequences are proposed. The present, unfolding endowment in the evolving psychological configurations or entities interacts with the assumably predictable environment to constitute models of evolution. There is latitude for the impact of chance factors as definable single or multiple or continuing influences over time. The impact of any element may be time-specific or time-dependent. For example, a particular, ostensibly provocative event may lead to specific consequences at some times, nonspecific consequences at some other times, and no consequences at still other times. Earlier forms and way stations may or may not endure, be invokable, or exert a continuing influence with the passage of time. Deficits and anormative developments continue to represent not only determinative influences but potential vulnerabilities. Whether or not a particular outcome ensues is related not only to inherent patterns but also to both predictable and chance vicissitudes. Time itself is a critical variable here.

Briefly stated, there is an inherent, progressing, intrinsic ground plan. It is influenced by extrinsic factors. The product of this interaction can be projected normatively. However, as the result of variation in either intrinsic or extrinsic factors, an anormative evolution and outcome may ensue.

Application of the genetic point of view is held to be valid in regard to phenomena of greater or lesser complexity and of simpler or more complex organization. The interrelationships between environmental and innate constitutional or maturational phenomena are considered to be relevant to the genetic point of view as long as the elements and final products of observation and deduction are of psychological modes. Conceptualizations regarding these interrelationships can be integrated into this frame of reference.

The recognition of regression as a temporal phenomenon in psychoanalysis actually antedated recognition of progression. As early as 1893 Breuer and Freud concluded that hysterics suffer mainly from reminiscences (p. 7)—that is, a return to the memories of the past responsible for their hysterical symptomatology. In chapter 7 of *The Interpretation of Dreams* (1900), Freud both proposed developmental schema and described three possible forms of regression. Two were time-related. What he then called "temporal regression" was a return to older psychic structures, particularly infantile memories.

By contrast, "formal regression" involved the substitution of primitive modes of expression and representation for adult modes.

Central to any consideration of regression is the tenet that the present can stimulate a return to the past in a variety of ways. Current experience may touch on specific significant memories and related phenomenology in such a way as to invoke particular reactions appropriate to the nature of the stimulus. For example, contemporary aggressive impulses may stimulate and reactivate past reactions of fear of retaliation and injury. Adult erotic attractions may reawaken childhood sexual prohibitions. On the other hand, the current situation may overload the mental apparatuses' capacities in such a way as to lead to a nonspecific regression to more primitive ideation, organization, motivations, or coping mechanisms. For example, aggressive or erotic wishes may provoke a defensive return to passive postures consistent with early childhood dependency modes. Nonspecific regressions are usually to points of fixation.

Certain physiological states—for example, sleep or illness—can in the natural course of events stimulate such regressions, both specific and nonspecific. For example, the events of a given day may activate specific memories and situations from the past. The process of sleep regularly facilitates a nonspecific reactivation of earlier states. Given these facilitating mechanisms, the result may be a dream combining current impressions, past states and motivations, and a primitive regressive model of expression and experience.

Perceptions, memories, and the organization of past events and gestalts are influenced by current events. Current needs, conflicts, life situations, and stresses may evoke particular memories and memory organizations appropriate to the peculiar nature of the stress or memory organizations characteristic of the nonspecific psychological regression provoked by a particular stress.

The Adaptive Viewpoint

The adaptive point of view allows for consideration of the interrelationships between the individual psychological entity and the environment. There is provision for reciprocal influences and impacts, with resulting changes in the individual (autoplastic), the environment (alloplastic), or both. The environment is variously considered to include particular and significant others or small groups of others such as parents, sibling(s), and family. Here a distinction must be made between these others and their intrapsychic representations, their structural counterparts. The environment further includes extended social groups such as classes and society, as well as individuals with implied status in those groups such as their leaders and followers; social institutions relevant to the extended groups such as laws, mores, and culture; and even the natural (nonhuman) world and phenomena.

The environment may be construed as relatively predictable and as existing in assumable, normative ways. For example, various theories cite an "average expectable environment" or a "good enough mother." On the other hand, isolated, unusual, particular, or unpredictable environmental circumstances are also considered. The impact of the environment may be focused and time-limited, as in stress trauma, or chronic and less specific, as in strain trauma. It may be considered in relation to specific individual propensities or nonspecifically. It may result in such diverse phenomena as stress, excitation, deprivation, permission, satisfaction, frustration, compulsion, stimulation, weakening or strengthening of intrapsychic capacities, stimulation of maturation or regression, and so forth. As implied, the result may be judged to be beneficial or deleterious or both simultaneously. The criteria for such evaluations may vary with the context and perspective. The result may be considered as the product of the environmental impact per se or attributable solely to the individual's propensities or both.

At the opposite end of the spectrum, individual (albeit sometimes ubiquitous) propensities and conflicts may manifest themselves in institutions in the environment. The perception of, and reaction to, the environment is only ideally free of idiosyncratic individual propensities and influences. Nevertheless, there is provision for consideration of such ideal models in their own right and in terms of their relationships with other facets of the individual or the entity as a whole. Individual characteristics, either idiosyncratically or environmentally determined, may influence the state of adaptation to the environment—that is, the resultant relationship of individual, social group, society, and world. The patterns and vicissitudes of the evolution of these different facets in the individual as affecting the reciprocal interaction with the environment can be characterized, and these formulations are considered psychoanalytic. Environmental phenomenology is considered within the purview of psychoanalytic theorizing when originating in, influencing, or impacting upon the individual. Similarly, psychoanalytic theorizing can be applied to these areas, and their influence on the individual can be conceptualized in psychoanalytic terms and elaborated into concepts.

DISCUSSION

Metapsychology has been, almost from its origins, controversial within psychoanalysis. Most psychoanalysts are clinicians rather than theoreticians; the distance between the couch and theory, let alone between one theory and another, at times seems intolerably great. The uniquely psychoanalytic propositions of metapsychology stand outside conventional accepted "scientific" thought, and the differences are accentuated by Freud's nineteenth-century jargon and organization. With scientific, technical, or methodological advances in the world of scientific and humanistic thought, there are often proposals from some analysts who want to reshape psychoanalytic theoretical propositions to suit these ideas. Information theory, computer theory, systems theory, and linguistics are examples of transiently popular candidates for provision of the logic, terminology, models, or mechanisms to reformulate psychoanalytic epistemology.

The most common antimetapsychological indictments can be roughly categorized as follows. First, it is argued that metapsychology is a historical anomaly, a vestige of interrelated chance occurrences, such as the fact that Freud was a physician who thought and theorized using natural science and physicalistic models and idioms, conceived of psychopathology as illness, and purportedly applied neurological models to what was actually humanistic data and phenomena.

It is also argued that metapsychology is no more than a sophisticated system of archaic, concretistic, infantile logic and fantasies. Another objection is that metapsychology lends itself to misuse in the form of pseudoexplanations, reifications, personifications, or jargon. Another contention is that metapsychology is irrelevant to, and incompatible with, clinical psychoanalysis, because it substitutes impersonal and mechanistic contexts for phenomena that can be understood only humanistically. Finally, there is the undeniable contention that the theoretical systems of metapsychology prejudice the very activity of clinical observations.

On several occasions, including his last book, Freud referred to his theorizations as a kind of conceptual scaffolding. He emphasized the necessity and desirability of revisions, which observations and deductions over time must inevitably mandate. Whether Freud's metapsychology will continue in its present form constitutes no argument; either it will go on changing in response to an evolving science, or it will fall by the wayside in favor of a more appropriate epistemological organization. But any investigative and therapeutic endeavor such as psychoanalysis must inevitably give rise to theorization based on certain assumptions. One is only deluding oneself if one requires that the propositions involved be independent of metatheoretical assumption. This belief, while calculated to instill a certainty that error is avoided, can only compound error by refusing to understand how understanding is shaped.

SUMMARY

Rapaport and Gill (1959) refer to metapsychology as "that *minimal* set of assumptions on which the psychoanalytic theory rests" (p. 796). If one takes this definition literally, its essence can be elaborated in a few sentences. Metapsychology, the more or less organized underlying assumptions of the theories of psychoanalysis, employs a lawful, sequential logic. Psychological theories are considered and formulated in the contexts of force, excitation, time, organization, and adaptation. These dimensions are considered as interrelated. The ultimate origin of the laws is currently held to be unknown and perhaps unknowable. They include the possibility of a multiplicity of causes either converging or diverging. The laws and dimensions are inherently impersonal; personal considerations are appropriate only at a level of abstraction close to observational data and theorization.

The different variables also lend themselves to the formulation of models, reifications of theoretical principles in such a way as to facilitate study and understanding. While these models are inherently competitive, they are not necessarily exclusive.

Some theoreticians advocate a primarily social, interpersonal orientation as one of these tenets. However, fundamental to these assumptions for most analysts is the idea of man as endowed, driving, driven, and striving in a world of neither his design nor his choosing. To dismiss a priori the struggle with one's inescapable inner nature is thought to ignore observations not only from the consulting room, but from everyday life, our times, and history.

REFERENCES

Breuer, Josef, & Freud, Sigmund (1983–95). *Studies on Hysteria. SE,* 2.

Frank, A. (1979). Two theories or one? Or none? *J. Amer. Psychoanal. Assn.,* 27:169–207.

Freud, S. (1900). *The Interpretation of Dreams. SE,* 4 & 5.

———. (1915a). Instincts and their vicissitudes. *SE,* 14:117–140.

———. (1915b). Repression. *SE,* 14:143–158.

———. (1915c). The unconscious. *SE,* 14:161–204.

———. (1916–17). *Introductory Lectures on Psycho-Analysis. SE,* 15 & 16.

———. (1917). A metapsychological supplement to the theory of dreams. *SE,* 14:222–235.

———. (1920). *Beyond the Pleasure Principle. SE,* 18:3–64.

———. (1923). *The Ego and the Id. SE,* 19:3–66.

———. (1926). *Inhibitions, Symptoms and Anxiety. SE,* 20:77–175.

———. (1933). *New Introductory Lectures on Psycho-Analysis. SE,* 22:3–182.

———. (1937). Analysis terminable and interminable. *SE,* 23:209–253.

Gedo, J., & Goldberg, A. (1973). *Models of the Mind.* Chicago: Univ. Chicago Press.

Greenberg, J., & Mitchell, S. (1983). *Object Relations in Psychoanalytic Theory.* Cambridge, Mass.: Harvard Univ. Press.

Hartmann, H. (1964). *Essays on Ego Psychology.* New York: Int. Univ. Press.

Kernberg, O. F. (1980). *Internal World and External Reality.* New York: Aronson.

Kohut, H. (1977). *The Restoration of the Self.* New York: Int. Univ. Press.

Langer, S. (1962). *Philosophy in a New Key.* 2d ed. New York: Mentor Books.

Moore, B. E., & Fine, B. D., eds. (1990). *Psychoanalytic Terms and Concepts.* New Haven: American Psychoanalytic Association & Yale Univ. Press.

Rapaport, D. (1967). *The Collected Papers of David Rapaport,* ed. M. M. Gill. New York: Basic Books.

Rapaport, D., & Gill, M. M. (1959). The points of view and assumptions of metapsychology. Rpt. in Rapaport, 1967, pp. 795–811.

Segal, H. (1973). *Introduction to the Work of Melanie Klein.* New York: Basic Books.

Waelder, R. (1962). Psychoanalysis, scientific method and philosophy. Rpt. in *Psychoanalysis: Observation, Theory, and Application,* pp. 248–274. New York: Int. Univ. Press, 1976.

PART VIII

PSYCHOANALYTIC EDUCATION AND RESEARCH

40

EDUCATION
AND TRAINING IN
PSYCHOANALYSIS

Freud's definition of psychoanalysis (1923) also serves to introduce the methods and goals of psychoanalytic education in institutes accredited by the Board on Professional Standards of the American Psychoanalytic Association.[1] Psychoanalysis is "a procedure for the investigation of mental processes, especially unconscious phenomena; a method of treatment based upon this procedure, and a set of observations and facts gathered in this way which gives rise to a cohesive body of theory regarding human behavior."[2]

THE TRIPARTITE STRUCTURE OF PSYCHOANALYTIC EDUCATION

Education in psychoanalysis has traditionally taken a tripartite form, corresponding to the dimensions of Freud's definition. All candidates whose educational goal is the attainment of competence to conduct a psychoanalysis undergo a full personal psychoanalysis, treat several patients in psychoanalysis under supervision, and attend an organized curriculum

1. The procedures and principles described in this chapter are derived from my knowledge of the American Psychoanalytic Association and refer only to institutes accredited by that association.
2. From Standards for Training in Psychoanalysis, American Psychoanalytic Association, edition of 1984.

of seminars on the theory and clinical practice of psychoanalysis. All three are regarded as essential to a good education in psychoanalysis. Further, institutes plan their programs so that candidates experience all three concurrently.

When students work with patients under supervision while studying and discussing clinical and theoretical issues in seminars and undergoing personal analysis, they are constantly compelled to examine and challenge previous assumptions about themselves. Such stimulation of unconscious personal factors affecting their lives and work with patients thereby enhances their increasing self-awareness as it emerges in the personal (training) psychoanalysis. These experiences of insight into their own unconscious mental lives in turn make it possible for student analysts to develop a more profound understanding of patients' inner lives and the rationales for psychoanalytic techniques for uncovering them, relatively freer of inhibitions, distortions, and psychological "blind spots" due to warded-off unresolved conflicts. The institute's structure facilitates this constructive pressure toward self-scrutiny and self-knowledge in all three parts of the tripartite process of psychoanalytic education.

Many analysts consider the personal psychoanalysis the most vital requirement for becoming a psychoanalyst. It is in the personal analysis that the beginning psychoanalyst experiences, with conviction, with empathic as well as intellectual understanding, the multiplicity of psychic phenomena that he or she will need to elicit and observe in others. Only as an analysand in the immediacy of the analytic situation does one come to understand what unconscious resistance really means. Similarly, one needs to know subjectively, before one can really know and meaningfully interpret in one's psychoanalytic patients, such manifestations of the unconscious mind as characterological defenses, repressed childhood memories, the unfolding of the developmental phases of childhood, the relationship between particular forms of psychopathology and the interplay between actual childhood experience and phase-specific unconscious fantasy, the powerful universal reality of transference, the way free association "feels" when it happens and when it does not, what it means to experience the full force of the termination of an analysis and a final separation in the analyst–analysand relationship, and how and with what emotions one evaluates what has been accomplished and what remains to be done, either in further self-analytic work or in a future analysis. It is in the personal analysis during training that one learns first about the impact in oneself of *being* a psychoanalyst, how patients affect the analyst's emotional life, and, in turn, how this affects analytic technique, and how an individual patient's ways of relating to the analyst, especially the patient's transferences, can affect the analyst's ways of relating to the patient, especially the analyst's countertransferences.

Because the so-called training analysis is considered so important in the educational process, the Board on Professional Standards must approve institutes' nominees for the position of training analyst. In addition, the qualifications of all those who are designated "supervising analyst" are presented for review by the Board. Institutes implement the Board's requirements for such appointments through careful evaluation procedures, in order to ensure that prospective training and/or supervising analysts are individuals of high personal and professional standing among their colleagues who have had both extensive and intensive experience as clinical analysts and as scholars and teachers of psychoanalysis. Most institutes review actual clinical work of potential nominees in order to ensure that its quality and range are such that he or she is fully qualified for the essential training tasks of analyzing and supervising those who will become analysts themselves.

The second leg of the tripartite journey of analytic education is the experience of conducting analyses of at least three patients under the supervision of experienced supervising analysts. In order to ensure that candidates have achieved an acceptable degree of competence to select appropriate patients and to conduct the analyses of both men and women independently, institutes usually offer seminars on the selection of patients for analysis. Candidates are expected to work with nonpsychotic patients of both sexes and to have supervision in all phases of at least one analysis, including the phase of termination. Both in the training analysis of candidates and in supervised analyses, patients are seen preferably five times a week, four times a week being the minimal acceptable frequency. Candidates are expected to be able to conceptualize their clinical work in writing and to demonstrate, in periodic written reports, such things as their understanding of their patients' psychodynamics, including the formulation of major conflicts and defenses and their own rationale for handling this material; the genesis of current conflicts, symptoms, and character pathology; the development, vicissitudes, and analysis of transference manifestations, and, when evident, the transference neurosis; their reflections on difficulties of working with the patient, including problems arising from countertransference and from inexperience; and, especially toward the end of the analysis, a retrospective overview of the process and the course of the treatment. The writing of reports is considered an important educational experience, one that introduces the candidate to the scholarly sharing with others of observations and questions in the interests of expanding theoretical and clinical knowledge.

The third dimension of psychoanalytic education is an organized curriculum of seminars which usually continues for about four years. Most curricula include readings in all the basic psychoanalytic literature—from the early writings of Sigmund Freud through contemporary analytic writings. Many institutes have groupings of courses arranged in hierarchical or spiral sequences, proceeding, for example, from earlier to later concepts organized historically or from simple to more complex approaches, often correlated with the stage of the candidates' clinical experience. In addition, a sequence of seminars may use the clinical experiences of teachers or students as the basis for examining clinical and theoretical assumptions underlying the analyst's formulations and interventions.

Among the groupings of courses, typical sequences include theoretical concepts; the interpretation of dreams, including the study of Freud's classic work of 1900, and the clinical uses of dreams in analysis; courses in development, including psychosexual phases, object relations, character formation, and phase-specific psychic structural organization; clinical and theoretical understanding of unconscious conflict, compromise formation, and typical unconscious fantasies. Usually these issues are considered from infancy on, and courses work their way through the periods of childhood, latency, adolescence, and adult life, including the years of maturity and aging. Courses in psychopathology comprise another typical sequence; sometimes these are organized developmentally, and usually they are grouped according to severity, with an emphasis on how the nature and degree of pathology affect psychoanalytic treatment. Clinical courses instruct candidates in the details of clinical theory and the technique of psychoanalysis. Clinical seminars often take the form of continuous case seminars in which candidates present material to instructors and other candidates, re-creating periods of analyses they are conducting through discussions of the details of individual sessions. Courses organized and taught by child and adolescent analysts include the study of early development, the systematic or experimental observation of children and adolescents, the techniques of analysis applicable at different ages, comparisons between the analysis of children, adolescents, and adult patients, and clinical presentations of continuous material from the analysis of a child or an adolescent. Many institutes offer courses on research in psychoanalysis, on the application of analytic concepts to the arts and humanities, and on comparative approaches to psychoanalytic theory and technique of schools of psychoanalytic thought other than traditional Freudian ones.

The curriculum is meant to interdigitate with the candidate's experience of conducting psychoanalyses under supervision. In fact, theoretical or conceptual material is often taught at the beginning and then repeated at later points when clinical analytic experience allows understanding and questioning at more profound levels than was possible earlier in the training period.

In most institutes, each part of the program is evaluated regularly. Curricula are studied and revised as students and teachers make critical comments and suggestions. Feedback to and from candidates about every aspect of the educational experience keeps the program dynamic and attuned to the needs, backgrounds, and special problems of candidates. These approaches allow candidates to participate actively in their own education, including their rates of progression. Psychoanalytic education, like psychoanalytic treatment, must be individualized within certain parameters, and institutes today are increasingly attentive to the special qualities of the individuals they are educating to become analysts.

Some of the individual issues that may be considered in planning the overall educational program include, for example, different needs and problems of women candidates, many of whom are becoming analysts in the very years that they have children and

young families. The educational backgrounds of candidates today vary considerably. Candidates come into analytic institutes at widely different ages, bringing quite divergent experience. Some are medically trained and just beginning residency programs in psychiatry, while others have completed such programs and may have worked for some years as psychotherapists. Some residency programs have psychodynamic emphases; others are primarily biologically oriented. Other candidates may have doctorates in psychology, mental health, or social work, with educational and professional achievement equivalent to that of physicians. A few individuals in these fields who do not have the formal degree requirements or clinical experience but have other exceptional qualifications are screened by a national committee before being granted a waiver of such requirements. These may be persons with backgrounds in the arts, the humanities, or the nonclinical sciences. This group may require special work arranged by the institute to prepare them to be responsible as clinicians conducting analytic treatment of patients. It has been noted that some candidates from nonmedical psychological disciplines have far greater intellectual knowledge of psychoanalysis than some of their classmates who are recent graduates of medical school.

While this varied background provides a diversity of viewpoints that can be enriching to psychoanalysis, it also makes it obligatory that education and training be highly personalized. Aside from their differing backgrounds, great individual variations of other sorts are considered by the education committees or equivalent responsible bodies in institutes. Candidates are carefully evaluated, usually twice a year, for special interventions, for decisions about progression in the sequences of seminars, for approval to take on analytic patients, or for other relevant issues affecting their progress. While most training analysts in institutes do not give any reports on the training analysis (a subject today of perhaps diminishing discussion and controversy around the country), institutes do pay close attention to evaluations by seminar instructors, supervisors, and others. They attempt to establish an optimal pace of progress toward graduation of students who must not only master a body of knowledge but must also acquire competence to conduct a complex treatment modality. Furthermore, it is widely known that the acquisition of this knowledge and skill depends on and uses the student's largely unconscious psychological life. Becoming an analyst requires both inner and outer exploration of the self and others. How it is learned, how smooth or bumpy the journey, how long it takes, how complete it can be during the phase of candidacy—all these dimensions vary from individual to individual, include many questions that are only partially answerable, and depend on factors only partly within view of the educational organization.

Since the education of an analyst is so individualized and since each candidate requires the close attention and work of many others, only a few candidates can be fully trained at any time. This is true even in fairly large institutes with many faculty members and training and supervising analysts.

REQUIREMENTS FOR ADMISSION TO PSYCHOANALYTIC INSTITUTES

Basic requirements are defined in the bylaws of the American Psychoanalytic Association. Under these regulations, until relatively recently, the basic educational prerequisites were graduation from an approved medical school and matriculation in a residency training program in psychiatry in an approved psychiatric facility. Interested individuals usually applied any time after graduation from medical school, but institutes have, on occasion, accepted applications made before graduation. By the time of graduation from a psychoanalytic institute, it is expected that the individual will have completed the psychiatric residency program.

The previous, exclusively medical prerequisites for training in psychoanalysis within the American Psychoanalytic Association have a complex historical background which is beyond the scope of this chapter. Suffice it to say that from the beginning many American institutes had on their faculties distinguished lay analysts who had been trained in Europe. In the late 1950s special provision was made for the training of nonmedical candidates with special interests and qualifications in research. These were individuals who had achieved recognition within their own professions for their work as scholars, researchers, and teachers in fields allied with psychoanalysis. They were expected to have the personal qualities required of all analytic candidates and to supply data that would demonstrate to a committee of the Board on Professional Standards (the Committee on Research and Special Training, or CORST) that a training in clinical psychoanalysis would enable them to contribute substantially to work in their own fields. If the institute, after *its* evaluation, approved them for training, it submitted an application to CORST for *its* review. If CORST approved, it presented the institute's request for a waiver of the medical-psychiatric requirements to the Board for its approval. With such approval, the institute could offer clinical education in psychoanalysis equivalent in all respects to that offered to medical candidates. While there are still such "research candidates" in training, this program is to be seen in the light of more recent developments, which allow clinical psychoanalytic education to be offered to individuals from educational and professional backgrounds overlapping those in the CORST group.

In 1975 the first of a series of committees was appointed to explore the feasibility and then the desirability of accepting carefully selected nonmedical applicants who wished to become practicing clinicians. These committees studied the personal qualities such individuals should possess; the nature of the educational and professional experiences that would be the best preparation for analytic training; the implications for the organizations and the profession of psychoanalysis of such a change; and, after the approval in principle of the idea of accepting graduates of doctoral programs in psychology and mental health, the means to evaluate such applicants. Since 1986 a national Committee on Nonmedical Clinical Training (CNMCT) has reviewed applications by the local institutes, and waivers have been granted by the Board on Professional Standards permitting them to accept applicants found to be qualified. This demonstrated the feasibility and desirability of expanding the range of educational backgrounds making for eligibility, and after several years of working with CNMCT, it was judged that institutes no longer needed review by the Board in most instances. Finally, bylaw amendments authorizing a change in admission requirements were approved by a vote of the members of the Association in 1991. Persons with a doctorate in psychology, mental health, and social work are now fully eligible for psychoanalytic training and membership in the American Psychoanalytic Association on the same basis as psychiatrists. Review of such applications by a national committee and waivers are no longer necessary. For nonmedical applicants judged by institutes to be well qualified although they lack certain of the formal requirements stated in the bylaws, CNMCT will continue to give assistance to the institutes as they prepare to apply for a waiver.

Finally, a number of institutes, though not all, accept individuals in programs of nonclinical education in psychoanalysis. Candidates include scholars in various disciplines such as biology, early childhood development, and education; religion, art history, and theater; writers and teachers of the arts, sciences, or humanities; researchers in allied fields; and others whose work may be enriched by such an education but who do not need the direct experience of clinical work for their primary professional purposes. People who have completed such programs have contributed substantially to the scientific and intellectual lives of their institutes and societies, their professions, and the American Psychoanalytic Association (see Chapter 43).

Recently, the Association adopted a formal category of affiliation called Academic Associate for those who have completed nonclinical programs and whose institutes apply on their behalf for this designation.

MEMBERSHIP IN THE AMERICAN PSYCHOANALYTIC ASSOCIATION, CERTIFICATION, AND ACCREDITATION OF INSTITUTES

Prerequisites and standards for membership in the American Psychoanalytic Association have traditionally depended on psychoanalytic educational achievements. Since 1948 the Committee on Membership, a committee of the Board on Professional Standards, has been charged with responsibility to oversee, review, and occasionally suggest modifications of standards for membership. Those deemed eligible for election to membership are presented to the Executive Council for its approval. Until 1977, the Committee on Membership reviewed the educational credentials of those applying for active membership; and for many years, written summaries of clinical analytic work needed to be presented. In 1977, the Association accepted the establishment of explicit certification procedures based on those followed by the Committee on Membership, and a Committee on Certification was formed to carry out this review of the clinical analytic competence of graduates of institutes. Those certified could then apply for active membership if they wished; as before, the Executive Council approved such applications. The procedures used by the Committee on Certification have been continuously studied and refined; at present they emphasize competence in current work, rather than in supervised work done before graduation. They often include interviews with applicants, to help the Committee obtain a clearer sense of their abilities and understanding.

In the meantime, other categories of membership were established. Candidates who have been approved by their institutes to begin treating patients under supervision were, and still are, eligible for affiliate membership. Associate membership was available upon graduation from full clinical programs at approved institutes for a period of three years while the graduate prepared for certification. Later this type of membership was continued beyond three years for an unlimited period for those who had not achieved certification but who applied for the category of extended associate membership.

At the December 1991 meeting of the Association a proposal to amend the bylaws in order to establish a single category of membership for all graduates of accredited institutes received overwhelming endorsement by the Board on Professional Standards and the Executive Council. This amendment, approved in 1992, ensures eligibility for active membership in the American Psychoanalytic Association upon graduation from an accredited institute for all graduates. Associate and extended associate membership categories have been eliminated. At the same time current certification requirements for participation on the Board on Professional Standards and Executive Council have been maintained. Only members who are certified may become Fellows of the Board or members of the committees of the Board and vote on bylaw amendments. All officers and training and supervising analysts are certified.

Active membership in the national organization is an important step in the development of a sense of analytic identity, facilitating participation in Association activities concerning national issues that vitally affect the professional, scientific, and educational dimensions of psychoanalysis. Graduation attests to the fact that an individual has had a sound education in an institute accredited by the American Psychoanalytic Association and has met the requirements for graduation set by the local institute. It is now regarded as sufficient qualification for active membership in the Association. Certification, on the other hand, consists of a thorough review of an individual's competence to conduct psychoanalytic treatment by a nationally constituted body of peers from outside the applicant's own institute. In this way, evaluations are less likely to be influenced by personal relationships or conflicts of interest that may occur when the candidate is evaluated by his or her local colleagues. In virtually all professions, certification is thought to represent a higher degree of competency and is accorded greater prestige than simple membership. In general, those responsible for educational programs in institutes are certified, and as noted above, certification is a requirement for the most responsible positions in the American Psychoanalytic Association.

The most important committee involved in assessing educational programs is the Committee on Institutes (COI). Composed of about twenty experienced members of different institutes, this committee maintains ongoing relations with every approved institute. Through liaison committees, workshops, discussion groups, and other means of maintaining communication, the Committee keeps in touch with the interests, ideas, and problems of each institute.

A Committee on New Training Facilities works closely with newly developing groups, from study groups of a few individuals to provisional institutes that function virtually autonomously, as they progress toward full accreditation by the Board.

Once every seven or eight years, a subcommittee of the COI (with the addition of a member of the Committee on Child and Adolescent Analysis) makes a site visit of several days to an institute. During these days the site visit subcommittee observes every important educational and administrative function of the institute. It audits classes, attends supervisory sessions, and monitors meetings of all major committees. Site visitors meet with faculty members and candidates and work with those who have primary responsibility for the program. They prepare a written report on the visit, which is often revised in response to the institute's comments about preliminary drafts. The aim of this collaboration is to develop an accurate, unbiased, clear, informative, and useful report. This report and other feedback from follow-up discussions, usually held at meetings of the American Psychoanalytic Association, are generally considered very carefully within the institute, which often works to improve aspects of the program based on these observations and the institute's own concurrent self-observation. Where indicated, the COI may offer varying kinds and de-

grees of assistance to an institute, from additional ongoing discussions of issues, to special brief site visits, to participating for a time with the institute in carrying out certain functions needing special attention. The Committee on Institutes is, in effect, the body that serves to re-accredit institutes, and its approval means that the institute continues to meet the minimal standards of the Board on Professional Standards and offers psychoanalytic education of high quality.

Throughout the country it is recognized that accredited institutes of the American Psychoanalytic Association strive steadily and devotedly in all the ways referred to in this chapter to meet standards of psychoanalytic education which serve the public responsibly and the discipline of psychoanalysis creditably.

REFERENCE

Freud, S. (1900). *The Interpretation of Dreams. SE,* 4 & 5.

41

PSYCHOANALYSIS AND RESEARCH

The relation between psychoanalysis and research has several aspects: psychoanalysis is a *method* of research; it is a *theory* that has stimulated research; and psychoanalysis—the clinical process—has itself been the *object* of numerous research studies.[1] Each of these aspects comprises a crucial phase of psychoanalytic research. Each aspect incorporates different investigative paradigms, different research methodologies, and different kinds of data. Not surprisingly, given the range of these differences, the psychoanalytic literature has seen a good deal of debate concerning the nature and definition of psychoanalytic research. For example, some analysts have asserted that every clinical psychoanalysis constitutes a piece of psychoanalytic research. Indeed, some have suggested that the data obtained in the psychoanalytic situation are such that only clinical case studies (the time-honored method of psychoanalytic reporting) can do justice to the richness and complexity of psychoanalytic data. Other investigators have proposed that, while the usefulness of the clinical situation for generating psychoanalytic hypotheses is unparalleled, the clinical situation itself is not, and can never be, subject to the kinds of controlled study necessary to constitute formal research (Hook, ed., 1959; Eysenck, 1963; Fisher & Greenberg, 1977; Holt, 1978; Chassan, 1979; Grünbaum, 1984). Finally, many authors have stressed the need for controlled experimental study of psychoanalytic phenomena which draw on clinical case studies but also utilize investigative methods developed by other sciences (Pumpian-Mindlin, ed., 1952; Bellak, 1961; Engel, 1968b; Wallerstein & Sampson, 1971; Luborsky & Spence, 1978; Grünbaum, 1982; Silverman et al., 1982; Edelson, 1986, 1988; Jones & Windholz, 1990).

These views are not as contradictory as they appear, since different investigative paradigms are in fact appropriate to the different varieties of psychoanalytic research which I listed earlier. In fact, psychoanalytic research has traditionally incorporated three major investigative models: naturalistic, experimental, and quasi-experimental, each being of varying relevance to different kinds of psychoanalytic research. In this chapter I will briefly describe research falling into all three categories of investigation, but I will emphasize what I take to be the *basic* research of psychoanalysis: research yielded by use of the psychoanalytic method itself.

NATURALISTIC RESEARCH

Naturalistic observation outside the consulting room has constituted a steady undercurrent in psycho-

---

1. In this chapter I will use the term "research" to refer to empirical research; other chapters of this book address theoretical research issues; e.g., the status of psychoanalysis as theory, the usefulness of metapsychology, the relevance of brain research to psychoanalysis, and so on.

analytic research. The preeminent example is child observation. Freud's early observations of children at play have been succeeded by increasingly sophisticated child observation settings in which myriad aspects of child development have been studied (A. Freud, 1939–45; Sears, 1943; Benjamin, 1961; Spitz, 1965; Wolff, 1966; Escalona, 1968; Bowlby, 1969; Mahler et al., 1975; Ainsworth et al., 1978; Frailberg, 1980; Roiphe & Galenson, 1981; Bretherton & Waters, eds., 1985; Stern, 1985; Zeanah et al., 1989). Through these studies, much has been discovered about the young child's mental organization. A few major examples of such research include Escalona's studies of adaptation patterns among infants, Bowlby's observations concerning attachment and the capacity for mourning in the very young child, Benjamin's work on the development of anxiety, Mahler's identification of phases in the process of·infantile separation from the mother, Roiphe and Galenson's elaboration of sexual identity formation in the second year of life, and the work of Anders and Stern regarding the importance of the overall environmental context as opposed to singular traumatic events for infant development (Zeanah et al., 1989). The findings of child observation studies have significantly influenced child-rearing practices, social policy, and educational methods. For example, huge changes in adoption and hospital procedures resulted from Spitz's observations of children in a foundling home and a penal institution's nursery. Care of handicapped children, as well as methods in child guidance and nursery school settings, have been much affected by the findings of Anna Freud and her co-workers. Early intervention in disturbed mother–infant interaction is an outgrowth of research conducted by many: studies by Spitz and Fraiberg have been centrally important.

Naturalistic investigation has also been important in the application of psychoanalytic theory to related fields of study. For example, in the area of psychosomatics, Engel's classic investigations relied on open-ended interviews and long-term naturalistic observation of patients, as well as data gained from actual psychoanalyses. Their studies led Engel and his co-workers to conclude that psychosomatic factors are involved in the genesis of many if not all organic diseases; in addition, Engel (1968a) pointed to certain psychological mechanisms which appear related to the activation of particular bodily systems. As the field of psychoneuroimmunology is increasingly emphasized in the study of disease, it seems likely that studies in the tradition of Engel's will gain increasing importance in the investigation of mind–body interaction.

The naturalistic field studies of cultural anthropology have also been heavily influenced by psychoanalytic thinking. Such studies, following in the psychoanalytically sophisticated tradition of Róheim, have dominated culture-and-personality research: Mead's Balinese and New Guinea studies (Mead, 1930; Mead & Bateson, 1942), Devereux's work on the Mohave (1939), Whiting's investigation of the Kwoma (1941), Parsons's observations of southern Italian families (1964), and the Le Vines's (1966) studies of the Gusii are among the most significant. (See La Barre, 1958, and Rabow, 1983a, for more extensive review.) In these and other areas of applied psychoanalysis, psychoanalytic theory has played an important role in the development of hypotheses as well as in the interpretation of observations.[2]

FORMAL EXPERIMENTAL RESEARCH

Formal experimental research has also advanced psychoanalytic understanding. Carefully controlled experimental studies of attention, perception, memory, learning, dreaming, sensory deprivation, and hypnotic states have made use of tests and laboratory techniques developed outside of psychoanalysis and have significantly widened the scope of psychoanalytic knowledge. Among the most impressive and most psychoanalytically sophisticated of this research have been studies conducted by Fisher and Paul (1959), Gardner et al. (1959), Gil and Brenman (1959), Paul (1959), Dement and Fisher (1960), Schwartz and Rouse (1961), Goldberger and Holt (1961), Klein (1970), Spence and Gordon (1973), Foulkes (1978), and Silverman et al. (1982)—a list that is representative but by no means complete. Interestingly, there was a real burst of optimism concerning the integration of psychoanalysis with certain branches of academic psychology during the 1950s, probably due in large part to the influence of David Rapaport. Since that time interest appears to have waned, although there have been several attempts since then to summarize and evaluate experimental investigations of psychoanalytic concepts (Fisher & Greenberg, 1977; Kline, 1982; Masling, ed., 1983).

Gardner et al. (1959) demonstrated the importance, under a variety of conditions, of individual consistencies in the use of certain dimensions of cognitive control. They showed that these controls—

---

2. For a review of research in other areas of applied psychoanalysis (political science, history, philosophy, linguistics, economics, social psychology, and sociology), see Rabow, 1983a, 1983b. For a fuller discussion of applied psychoanalysis, see Chapter 43.

or cognitive styles—constitute essential aspects of ego organization, adaptation to reality, and choice of defense. Paul's (1959) studies of memory examined how people learn and remember verbal material that is extended, connected, and meaningful (as opposed to lists of unrelated words or nonsense syllables). Paul attempted to understand the processes involved in terms of Hartmann's (1964) concept of the ego apparatus.

The results of Dement and Fisher's (1960) experiments concerning the great increase in time devoted to dreaming following dream deprivation suggested a quantitative dream need as well as an actual dream deficit that accrues when total dream time per night does not approximate the established baseline average for an individual. Schwartz and Rouse (1961) conducted experiments concerning the ways in which mental representations are associated and factors affecting the distribution of attention among those mental representations. Goldberger and Holt (1961) examined how perceptual structures are disturbed under conditions of sensory deprivation, the ready loss of perceptual constancy under these conditions, and the correlation between reactions to sensory deprivation and ways in which different individuals handle primary-process manifestations. Klein (1970) investigated many aspects of how cognition is motivated and the active interplay between motives and the conditions that permit effective perceiving.

Gill and Brenman's (1959) studies of hypnosis, incorporating both clinical and experimental data, led them to define the hypnotic state in terms of the mobilization of particular regressive transferences as well as in terms of certain ego alterations; their investigations explored aspects of hypnotizability, physiologic correlates, clinical applications, and the relation of hypnosis to allied ego states. Fisher and Paul (1959) studied effects of subliminal visual stimulation on dreams and images and elaborated conditions that facilitate subliminal visual registration and the impact of such registration on a variety of ego functions. Spence and Gordon (1973) examined the effects of subliminal stimulation on the expression of drive derivatives. Finally, Silverman et al. (1982) demonstrated that subliminal presentation of "psychodynamically relevant stimuli" permits experimental study of unconscious processes, particularly in relation to activation of psychopathological responses.

Experimental research with nonhuman primates has also contributed to psychoanalytic thinking and offered evidence bearing on psychoanalytic hypotheses. For example, Harlow and Mears's (1979) lifetime of experimentation with rhesus monkeys provided insight into a wide range of human experience, from the nature of anaclitic depression and maternal comfort (his famous experiments with cloth versus wire mother surrogates) to the development of curiosity.

In general, experimental research has been most productive when it has commenced where naturalistic observation leaves off, since it is not the job of the experimentalist to confirm the existence of data reported by the naturalist observer. Thus the most useful (but rather rare) experimental research in psychoanalysis has been designed by those who have been sophisticated regarding the psychoanalytic observations that nature itself permits, both in and out the consulting the room. Some authors have put this point of view even more strongly, stating that, despite the *potential* relevance of experimental research to psychoanalysis, the majority of experiments designed to test psychoanalytic propositions prove meaningless, precisely because the experimenters have been naïve and ill-educated regarding the nature of psychoanalytic observation and theory (Kubie, 1952; Rapaport, 1959; Bachrach et al., 1991).

QUASI-EXPERIMENTAL RESEARCH: PSYCHOANALYSIS AS A RESEARCH METHOD

Finally, the heart of psychoanalytic research undertakes to study the singular data obtained in the psychoanalytic situation itself. This is the basic research of psychoanalysis, since the analytic situation provides the only conditions under which the central phenomena of psychoanalytic theory emerge in a systematically observable way.

The process of psychoanalysis remains unparalleled as a method whereby the workings of the human mind may be observed, a method in which human subjectivity comes under scientific scrutiny. Use of the psychoanalytic method has led to the observation of certain facts about people, and those observations have provided the basis for the development of psychoanalytic theory. Aspects of psychoanalytic theory vary in their distance from direct observation. But Freud was emphatic that the whole body of psychoanalytic theory is a superstructure which must be altered as the evidence requires. *Observations* constitute the foundation of psychoanalysis. The theory that describes and seeks to explain those observations can be replaced, even discarded, without damaging the essential structure of psychoanalysis (Freud, 1914, p. 77).

This statement of psychoanalytic methodology is a very important one; in fact, it is this statement which renders psychoanalysis a true research method.

Its implementation may be difficult, but the principle of noncircularity which such a statement asserts is as relevant to psychoanalysis as it is to any investigative method employed in any science. If a theory itself derives from certain observations, it cannot dictate that those same observations *must* occur, meanwhile claiming the observations as verifications of the theory.

Use of the psychoanalytic method yields quasi-experimental research, as described by Wallerstein (1964):

> the psychoanalytic situation . . . fulfills essentially the requirements of a quasi-experimental research model. . . . [It] is a relatively stabilized, recurring, experimental situation in which the experimenter (the analyst) introduces independent variables (interpretations and other specifiable interventions) and can then predict and ascertain their impact on all the dependent variables within the situation, in which after all he has the fullest conditions of access to the subjective data that enter consciousness . . . ever devised. [p. 681]

While many of the external variables that affect the psychoanalytic situation remain uncontrolled, an *approximate* constancy of the *essential* aspects of the psychoanalytic environment can be maintained.

Because there has been much controversy over how and to what extent the psychoanalytic situation fills the criterion of noncircularity described above, it is worth spelling out the premises on which the psychoanalytic situation is based, as opposed to the postulates that it seeks to verify. In my view, this controversy remains a lively and very important one, both within the field of psychoanalysis and in dialogues between psychoanalytic investigators and those from other fields.

The psychoanalytic method, like every method of research, relies on certain givens which render observation possible. Those givens—as opposed to the general body of psychoanalytic theory—are not treated as revisable on the basis of each psychoanalytic investigation. They are two. The first is an underlying, assumed postulate regarding the nature of what is under investigation: *the assumption of psychic determinism.* Psychic events observed in the psychoanalytic situation are assumed to be lawfully and meaningfully related to each other. Second, the psychoanalytic method depends upon consistent use of a particular observational instrument: *free association* and its corollary, *interpretation of resistance* (or the lessening of obstacles to the patient's free associations by the analyst). These are the givens. They do not concern the content of the patient's associations. The job of the analyst as psychoanalytic

investigator (and, incidentally, as clinician) is to facilitate the patient's ability to free-associate, not to suggest the contents of the patient's associations. The patient provides the content, and theories regarding content may be hypothesized and tested as each patient reveals further content. Free association and interpretation of resistance constitute *actual observational tools* insofar as they make possible the emergence and systematic observation of phenomena that do not emerge and are not systematically observable without their use. Freud, for the first time in the history of science, elaborated the principles that underlie the capacity of the mind to associate ideas with each other and with feelings into tools for systematic observation (Bernfeld, 1941). He thereby made it possible for psychoanalysis to organize around a particular observational technique, just as every field of science has tended to crystallize around observational techniques uniquely appropriate to itself (Kubie, 1956).

The fact that analysts are human and, as participant-observers, influence the field of their observations and are themselves influenced in their observations by theories concerning what they believe should be observable does not alter the principles of psychoanalytic investigation that I have described. It is increasingly recognized that such "interferences" affect observation in every branch of science. Even more important, the fact that the nature of psychoanalytic data is subjective and is influenced by the relationship between patient and analyst does not alter the character of the investigative model I have put forth.

Indeed, it was precisely the subjective and interpersonal nature of psychoanalytic data that led to the development of psychoanalysis as a method for investigating the mind. In attending to the patient's associations and in helping the patient overcome resistances, the analyst has the opportunity to experience and observe the transferences that are inevitably produced by the analytic relationship, as does the patient. Bit by bit, they obtain knowledge of the patient's unconscious mental functioning that is not accessible to observation in any other way. It is in this sense that the techniques of free association and interpretation of resistance constitute unique observational instruments which produce the basic data of psychoanalytic research and render psychoanalysis a research method. Since these data are not obtainable in any full way by other methods, investigators who attempt to test psychoanalytic propositions must be sophisticated regarding the use of the psychoanalytic microscope, the distinctive observational instruments that allow psychoanalytic observation—a sophistication that requires extensive training and experience in the actual clinical situation, both as patient and as analyst.

The question of testing psychoanalytic propositions leads one to consider that psychoanalysis is not only a *method* of research; it is also the *object* of research. Systematic research which takes the psychoanalytic process as its object raises some enormously complex questions regarding research methodology. Yet it is crucial, not so much to obtain simple confirmation or refutation of psychoanalytic theory, but to refine, modify, and advance the development of psychoanalysis in all its functions: as a clinical method, as a method of research, and as a general psychological theory. Without adequate research, incompatible and even incorrect ideas tend to be retained with little modification.

The difficulties of conducting research on the psychoanalytic process have been enumerated repeatedly. First, because psychoanalysis is a method of treatment, manipulation of the psychoanalytic situation itself is generally not possible. While *post facto* manipulation of clinical data makes systemic study feasible, many problems remain. Briefly, they include difficulties of recording and organizing the data (for example, the data are not public, are overwhelming in mass and complexity, are not quantifiable in the ordinary sense, are subjective, and so on); difficulties regarding sampling, replicability, and control or manipulation of variables; difficulties resulting from the multi-determined and over-determined nature of psychoanalytic phenomena; difficulties in making exact observations and in obtaining consensus regarding the nature of the observations; and difficulties in making precise links between psychoanalytic concepts and their empirical referents. Perhaps most difficult of all is to distinguish observation from inference, given the complexity of the phenomena under study and the attribution of unconscious meaning to what is directly observed. Because of these problems, psychoanalytic prediction, postdiction, outcome studies, and validation of hypotheses are exceedingly complicated undertakings.

Nonetheless, beginnings have been made. A number of researchers have thoughtfully addressed various of these problems (see Escalona, 1952; Rapaport, 1959; Bellak, 1961; Engel, 1968b; Wallerstein & Sampson, 1971; Luborsky & Spence, 1978; Edelson, 1988; Jones & Windholz, 1990; Bachrach et al., 1991). A few research projects have implemented solutions to these problems and have, like the Menninger Research Project, set about making *explicit* those judgments and predictions that are *implicit* in clinical work, thus developing testable hypotheses of the working propositions of the psychoanalytic theo-

ry of therapy (Bellak & Smith, 1956; Knapp, 1963; Luborsky & Auerbach, 1969; Kernberg et al., 1972; Dahl, 1974, 1983; Gill & Hoffman, 1982; Weiss et al., 1986). Bellak and Smith as well as Knapp conducted prediction studies in which independent judges studied recorded analytic material from several patients and made short-term predictions concerning changes in the patient. Luborsky and Auerbach developed a way of systematically collecting and reliably analyzing conditions that lead to the appearance of symptoms during analytic sessions (for example, momentary forgetting, stomach pain, and migraine headaches). Their symptom–context method can be applied to less clearly symptomatic behaviors as well, such as changes in states of consciousness, the appearance of dreams, blank states, and so on.

Bachrach et al. (1991) have formulated criteria for evaluating research on psychoanalytic outcomes.

1. It must be demonstrated that the treatment being evaluated is taking place.

2. The treatment studied must be being conducted by practitioners of sufficient knowledge, skill, and experience in accord with accepted standards of practice.

3. Treatments can be meaningfully evaluated only in relation to clinical conditions to which they are applicable.

4. The patient must be a suitable candidate for the treatment.

5. Germane variables must be adequately specified conceptually, operationally, and reliably and must be studied systematically.

They extensively reviewed the formal research literature pertinent to psychoanalytic outcome and found

> the research yield consistent with the accumulated body of clinically derived psychoanalytic knowledge, e.g., patients suitable for psychoanalysis derive substantial therapeutic benefit; analyzability and therapeutic benefit are relatively separate dimensions and their extent is relatively unpredictable from the perspectives of initial evaluation among seemingly suitable cases. The studies all contain clinical and methodological limitations which are not more substantial than in other forms of psychotherapy research, but they have not substantially advanced psychoanalytic knowledge." [Bachrach et al., 1991]

Psychoanalytic outcome research is still in its infancy.

Several long-term studies of the psychoanalytic process stand out as particularly significant to the field. The Menninger Project, the largest and longest research study of clinical psychoanalysis, was formally initiated in 1954. Forty-two adult patients who had been diagnosed as suffering from neurotic, borderline, latent psychotic, or characterological disturbances were the subjects of the study; they were in treatments ranging from supportive psychotherapy to psychoanalysis. The data included material from initial stages of treatment, termination, and follow-up two years after the end of treatment. The data were analyzed by a number of methods, and the findings were integrated by Kernberg et al. in 1972. A few of the major findings were as follows. Patients with high initial ego strength are likely to do well in any treatment modality, but psychoanalysis brings about the highest degree of improvement. Patients with low ego strength ("borderline personality organization") benefit most from a specific kind of blending of expressive and supportive techniques which consistently focuses on transference phenomena. Initial motivation for change and psychological-mindedness do not have major prognostic significance.

Gill and Hoffman (1982) compared the effects of transference interpretations judged to be correctly made with the effects of not making such interpretations during various phases of analysis; they concluded that the transference tends to be underinterpreted by many analysts. Finally, Weiss et al. (1986) developed a model of the psychoanalytic process that permits them successfully to predict for a given patient the effects of different kinds of interpretations made by the analyst. Their model includes systematic and case-specific predictions that address short-term effects within analytic hours as well as long-term behavioral and attitudinal changes in the patient.

In addition to these studies of the psychoanalytic process itself, a number of other studies have focused on topics such as the qualities of patients deemed suitable for analysis, personality qualities of psychoanalysts, outcomes of second analyses, predictors of good psychoanalytic outcome, and so on. Luborsky and Spence (1978) and Bachrach et al. (1991) have published review articles that carefully describe many of these studies.

So far, those who have conducted formal research on the psychoanalytic process have agreed about several things. First, such research is possible, despite its great complexity. Second, it requires extensive clarification of terminology, conceptualization, and inference process within the field of psychoanalysis. And third, the very complexity of the phenomena under study dictates that single lines of investigation will rarely be particularly informative

but that converging lines of evidence may start to capture the richness of psychoanalytic events in the context of a systematizing effort.

REFERENCES

Ainsworth, M., Blehar, M., Waters, E., & Wall, S. (1978). *Patterns of Attachment*. Hillsdale, N.J.: Erlbaum.

Bachrach, H. R., Galatzer-Levy, R., Skolnikoff, A., & Waldron, S. (1991). On the efficacy of psychoanalysis. *J. Amer. Psychoanal. Assn.*, 39:871–916.

Bellak, L. (1961). Research in psychoanalysis. *Psychoanal. Q.*, 30(4):519–548.

Bellak, L., & Smith, M. B. (1956). An experimental exploration of the psychoanalytic process. *Psychoanal. Q.*, 25:385–414.

Benjamin, J. D. (1961). Some developmental observations relating to the theory of anxiety. *J. Amer. Psychoanal. Assn.*, 9:652–668.

Bernfeld, S. (1941). The facts of observation in psychoanalysis. *J. Psychol.*, 12:289–305.

Bowlby, J. (1969). *Attachment and Loss*. 2 vols. New York: Basic Books.

Bretherton, I., & Waters, E., eds. (1985). Growing points in attachment theory and research. *SRCD Monographs*, 49/6, serial no. 209.

Chassan, J. B. (1979). *Research Design in Clinical Psychology and Psychiatry*. New York: Irvington.

Dahl, H. (1974). The measurement of meaning in psychoanalysis by computer analysis of verbal contexts. *J. Amer. Psychoanal. Assn.*, 22:37–57.

———. (1983). On the definition and measurement of wishes. In *Empirical Studies of Psychoanalytical Theories*, ed. J. Masling, pp. 39–67. Hillsdale, N.J.: Erlbaum.

Dement, W. C., & Fisher, C. (1960). Studies in dream deprivation and satiation (abst.). *Psychoanal. Q.*, 29:671.

Devereux, G. (1939). The social and cultural implications of incest among the Mohave Indians. *Psychoanal. Q.*, 8:510–533.

Dollard, J. (1937). *Caste and Class in a Southern Town*. New York: Doubleday.

Edelson, M. (1986). Causal explanations in science and psychoanalysis. *Psychoanal. Contemp. Thought*, 41:89–128.

———. (1988). *Psychoanalysis: A Theory in Crisis*. Chicago: Univ. Chicago Press.

Engel, G. L. (1968a). The psychoanalytic approach to psychosomatic medicine. In *Modern Psychoanalysis*, ed. J. Marmor. New York: Basic Books.

———. (1968b). Some obstacles to the development of research in psychoanalysis. (With discussions and closing comments by David Beres,

Mark Kanzer, Robert S. Wallerstein, and Elizabeth R. Zetzel.) *J. Amer. Psychoanal. Assn.,* 16:195–229.

Escalona, S. (1952). Problems in psychoanalytic research. *Int. J. Psychoanal.,* 33:11–21.

———. (1968). *The Roots of Individuality.* Chicago: Aldine Publishing.

Eysenck, H. (1963). *Uses and Abuses of Psychology.* Baltimore: Penguin.

Fisher, C., & Paul, I. H. (1959). The effect of subliminal visual stimulation on images and dreams. *J. Amer. Psychoanal. Assn.,* 7:35–83.

Fisher, S., & Greenberg, R. (1977). *The Scientific Credibility of Freud's Theories and Therapy.* New York: Basic Books.

Foulkes, D. (1978). *A Grammar of Dreams.* New York: Basic Books.

Fraiberg, S. (1980). *Clinical Studies in Infant Mental Health.* New York: Basic Books.

Frèud, A. (1939–45). Infants without Families. In *Writings of Anna Freud,* vol. 3. New York: Int. Univ. Press.

Freud, S. (1914). On narcissism. *SE,* 14:67–102.

Gardner, R., Holzman, P., Klein, G., Linton, H., & Spence, D. (1959). *Cognitive Control.* Psychological Issues, monograph 4. New York: Int. Univ. Press.

Gill, M. M., & Brenman, M. (1959). *Hypnosis and Related States.* New York: Int. Univ. Press.

Gill, M. M., & Hoffman, I. (1982). A method for studying the analysis of aspects of the patient's experience of the relationship in psychoanalysis and psychotherapy. *J. Amer. Psychoanal. Assn.,* 30:137–166.

Goldberger, L., & Holt, R. R. (1961). Experimental interference with reality contact (perceptual isolation). In *Sensory Deprivation and Isolation,* ed. P. Soloman et al., pp. 130–142. Cambridge, Mass: Harvard Univ. Press.

Grünbaum, A. (1982). Psychoanalytic theory tested "on the Couch"? *Psychoanal. & Contemp. Thought,* 5:155–256, 311–438.

———. (1984). *The Foundations of Psychoanalysis.* Berkeley, Calif.: Univ. California Press.

Harlow, H., & Mears, C. (1979). *The Human Model.* New York: Wiley.

Hartmann, H. (1964). *Essays in Ego Psychology.* New York: Int. Univ. Press.

Holt, R. (1978). Ideological and thematic conflicts in the structure of Freud's thought. In *The Human Mind Revisited,* ed. Sydney Smith, 51–98. New York: Int. Univ. Press.

Hook, S., ed. (1959). *Psychoanalysis, Scientific Method and Philosophy.* New York: New York Univ. Press.

Jones, E., & Windholz, M. (1990). The psychoanalytic case study. *J. Amer. Psychoanal. Assn.,* 38:985–1015.

Kernberg, O., Burstein, E., Coyne, L., Appelbaum, A., Horwitz, L., & Voth, H. (1972). Psychotherapy and psychoanalysis. *Bull. Menninger Clinic,* 36:1–275.

Klein, G. (1970). *Perception, Motives and Personality.* New York: Knopf.

Kline, P. (1982). *Fact and Fantasy in Freudian Theory.* 2d ed. London & New York: Methuen.

Knapp, P. H. (1963). Short-term psychoanalytic and psychosomatic predictions. *J. Amer. Psychoanal. Assn.,* 11:245–280.

Kubie, L. S. (1952). Problems and techniques of psychoanalytic validation and progress. In *Psychoanalysis as Science,* ed. E. Pumpian-Mindlin, pp. 74–89. Stanford Univ. Press.

———. (1956). The use of psychoanalysis as a research tool. *Psychiat. Res. Reports,* 6:112–136.

La Barre, W. (1958). The influence of Freud on anthropology. *Amer. Imago,* 15:275–328.

Le Vine, R. A., & Le Vine, B. (1966). *Nyansongo, a Gusii Community in Kenya.* New York: Wiley.

Luborsky, L., & Auerbach, A. H. (1969). The symptom–context method. *J. Amer. Psychoanal. Assn.,* 17:68–99.

Luborsky, L., & Spence, D. (1978). Quantitative research on psychoanalytic therapy. In *Handbook of Psychotherapy and Behavior Change,* 2d ed., ed. S. Garfield & A. Bergin. New York: Wiley.

Mahler, M. S., Pine, F., & Bergman, A. (1975). *The Psychological Birth of the Human Infant.* New York: Basic Books.

Masling, J., ed. (1983). *Empirical Studies of Psychoanalytic Theories,* vol. 1. Hillsboro, N.J.: Erlbaum.

Mead, M. (1930). *Growing up in New Guinea.* New York: William Morrow.

Mead, M., & Bateson, G. (1942). *Balinese character.* N.Y. Acad. Sci., special publication 2.

Parsons, A. (1964). Is the oedipus complex universal? *Psychoanal. Study Soc.,* 3:278–328.

Paul, I. H. (1959). *Studies in Remembering.* Psychological Issues, monograph 2. New York: Int. Univ. Press.

Pumpian-Mindlin, E., ed. (1952). *Psychoanalysis as Science.* Stanford: Stanford Univ. Press.

Rabow, J. (1983a). Psychoanalysis and social science. *J. Psychohist.,* 12(1).

———. (1983b). Psychoanalysis and sociology. *Annu. Rev. Sociol.,* 9:555–578.

Rapaport, D. (1959). *The Structure of Psychoanalytic Theory.* Psychological Issues, monograph 10. New York: Int. Univ. Press, 1960.

Roiphe, H., & Galenson, E. (1981). *Infantile Origins of Sexual Identity*. New York: Int. Univ. Press.

Schwartz, F., & Rouse, R. (1961). *The Activation and Recovery of Associations*. Psychological Issues, monograph 9. New York: Int. Univ. Press.

Sears, R. R. (1943). *Survey of Objective Studies of Psychoanalytic Concepts*. New York: Social Science Research Council.

Silverman, L., Lachmann, F., & Milich, R. (1982). *The Search for Oneness*. New York: Int. Univ. Press.

Slater, P. (1966). *Microcosm: Structural, Psychological and Religious Evolution in Groups*. New York: Wiley.

Spence, D., & Gordon, C. (1973). *Activation and Assessment of an Early Oral Study*. Psychological Issues, monograph 30. New York: Int. Univ. Press.

Spitz, R. A. (1965). *The First Year of Life*. New York: Int. Univ. Press.

Stern, D. (1985). *The Interpersonal World of the Infant*. New York: Basic Books.

Wallerstein, R. (1964). The role of prediction in theory building in psychoanalysis. *J. Amer. Psychoanal. Assn.*, 12:675–691.

Wallerstein, R., & Sampson, H. (1971). Issues in research in the psychoanalytic process. *Int. J. Psychoanal.*, 52:11–50.

Weiss, J., Sampson, H., et al. (1986). *The Therapeutic Process*. New York: Guilford Press.

Whiting, J. M. (1941). *Becoming a Kwoma*. New Haven: Yale Univ. Press.

Wolff, P. H. (1966). *The Causes, Controls, and Organization of Behavior in the Neonate*. Psychological Issues, monograph 17. New York: Int. Univ. Press.

Zeanah, C. H., Anders, T., Seifer, R., & Stern, D. (1989). Implications of research on infant development for psychodynamic theory and practice. *J. Amer. Acad. Child Adolesc. Psychiat.*, 28:657–668.

42

PSYCHOANALYSIS AND THE BRAIN

We are living during a worldwide scientific revolution in which knowledge of the brain and behavior is expanding dramatically, leading to a convergence of psychological and neuroscientific viewpoints.[1] In Edinburgh, Trevarthen has illuminated the micro-orchestration of mother–infant communication, while in the United States Demos, Stern, Basch, Lichtenberg, and others have clarified details of infant development, which make it apparent that we begin our lives with many surprising abilities that facilitate bonding. The newer work on infant development can be seen as properly following upon the pioneering child research of Anna Freud, Melanie Klein, D. W. Winnicott, René Spitz, and others.

MacLean has created a triune brain theory from which Antrobus, Baer, Moore, and others have derived many significant insights. In fact, it was MacLean who coined the term "limbic system" and along with Papez mapped out the anatomical details we now take for granted, as if its role in affect had always been understood. Today MacLean continues his research in Washington on such subjects as the relationship between speech, language, bonding, and the programming of the thalamostriate division of the limbic system.

1. Exact references are omitted, especially at the beginning of this chapter, in order to avoid interrupting the flow of the opening discussion. However, full references for the names mentioned can be found at the end of the text.

In Edmonton, Flor-Henry (1985) has explored various correlations between psychopathological states and right–left brain EEG asymmetries, while Lassen, in Copenhagen, and Ingvar, in Lund, have exploited an extraordinary brain-scanning technology that allows visualization and quantification of regional differences in cerebral blood flow in "real time." These pioneers have provided some of the first maps of the brain in the psychophysiological realm (in parallel with other special noninvasive techniques for brain mapping such as magnetic resonance imaging, CAT scanning, BEAM, and positron emission tomography). The specific advantage of brain-mapping work, especially prominent in the research of Roland and Friberg, collaborators of Lassen and Ingvar, is that it provides opportunities to test out hypotheses about brain and behavior. Drugs and their receptor sites can be spatially localized by such means, and changes in neurochemical and physiological parameters can now be observed and compared before and after various treatments.

Crow, in London, and Reynolds, in Nottingham, have elucidated the pathophysiology of "positive" and "negative" symptoms in schizophrenia, especially with regard to functions of the left temporal pole and the frontal cortex. In the United States, Andreason et al. (1994), using magnetic resonance imaging (MRI), have found abnormalities in the thalamus that theoretically could explain the symptoms. In Oslo, Retterstøl has patiently conducted 30-

(plus)-year follow-up studies on some paranoid classes of schizophrenia, while in Tokyo, Saitoh et al. have extended Crow's work with detailed electrophysiological studies of variables of attention in conditions of severe ego disturbance, and Kim et al. (1994) and Itoh have greatly expanded our knowledge of the cerebellum's contribution to learning (paving the way, for example, for research on cerebellar problems in another condition entailing a severe ego deficit, infantile autism). Itoh's work builds dramatically on his earlier studies with Sir John Eccles and Szentágothai (1967), the result being that neurotic and psychotic illnesses are now more clearly definable in terms of basic brain mechanisms of neural control.

In the United States, neurologically informed psychoanalysts such as Reiser at Yale, Basch and Gedo in Chicago, Schwartz in Washington, D.C., Sashin in Boston, Moore in Atlanta, and Hadley in Wisconsin, to name just a few, have sought to establish further clinical correlations between mind and brain, working toward a unified theory of brain and behavior. Such a theory would be the psychological equivalent of what in theoretical physics is called by Hawking, only half jokingly, the "Theory of Everything."

In addition, a large number of basic brain scientists, including Kandel, Chugani, Phelps, Geschwind, Galaburda, Kent, Kety, Lashley, MacLean, Merzenich, Pribram, Sperry, and others too numerous to name, have made invaluable contributions to our basic scientific understanding of such phenomena as learning, memory, and brain plasticity. In fact, it is virtually impossible briefly to summarize any area of interdisciplinary brain research without leaving out significant, or even critical, research. For this reason I can provide only a highly selective vignette, or sample, of the rapidly expanding domain of both brain and psychoanalytic investigation, choosing necessarily from what lies close to my own interest and knowledge. It is my hope, however, that my examples will not be found to be too far removed from what is important and representative within the larger field.

Despite much progress, we should not be congratulating ourselves on how much we know, since many significant questions regarding the integration of mind and brain remain unanswered for a number of reasons. First is the awesome complexity of the brain itself, the investigation of which is probably the most difficult task mankind has ever undertaken. Real understanding of the brain will take our best efforts for generations to come. A second reason relates to long-standing philosophical and religious debates that depreciate man's striving toward such

an integrated understanding. Most notable has been the debate between dualism/vitalism (as represented by the line of thought extending from Plato through St. Augustine, Descartes, Leibnitz, Spinoza, Eccles, and Popper) and modern materialism (as represented by Hippocrates, Galen, Aristotle, Democritus, Pelagius, Hobbes, Armstrong, and Freud). This debate hinges upon whether all aspects of mental life are capable of being understood in terms of fundamental brain mechanisms. Although this seems to me to be a correct assertion, the position I hold is the more pragmatic one that at least *some* psychological aspects of behavior and *some* findings in brain chemistry, anatomy, and physiology may now be successfully related to each other.

A third reason for the difficulty in performing interdisciplinary studies of mind/brain is the fact that our medical education system tends to produce two somewhat exclusive categories of specialists: neuroscientists relatively uninterested in the humanistic or psychological and psychiatrists or psychoanalysts relatively uninterested in things neurological. Those who have taken an interest in both perspectives have risked rejection by both groups.

Yet psychiatry and psychoanalysis have benefited greatly from research on mind/brain correlations, so it would seem vital that these continue. Later I will try to convince the reader of this point by presenting some of the ideas of Gedo, Lichtenberg, and Sameroff, who have incorporated updated, neuroscientific knowledge (in the form of multiple, complex "functional-motivational systems") into their revised, psychoanalytic models.

In *The Mapping of Mind: The Intersection of Psychoanalysis and Neuroscience* (1991), I delineate in some detail the rapidly evolving field of mind/brain studies. However, in a brief chapter such as this I have fewer options: I can concentrate on an overview, or I can pay attention to a small area of the larger field. I have decided on the latter.

During the last few decades we have witnessed an explosion of knowledge in the area of neurotransmitters and research on neuroglia. We have progressed from Schildkraut and Kety's catecholamine hypothesis to much more complex theories describing the expanding number and spatial distribution of the hundreds of psychoactive substances produced in the body (not merely in the brain). Several examples stand out as exemplifying the enormous complexity of this one branch of research: the multiplicity of brain peptides localized in the hypothalamus (as reported, for example, by Makara et al., 1980); the similar diversity of neurotransmitters in the basal ganglia, especially the striatum, as reported by Graybiel (1984) and Iverson (1984). (These two structures of the brain constitute critical control mechanisms with an inner organization that boggles the mind, in some cases seeming to reduplicate much of the complexity of the entire rest of the brain in microcosm!) As Yamawaki et al. (1994) have summarized, current work on depression no longer focuses upon monoamines, but rather on serotonin (5-HT) and 5-HT2 receptors; while dopamine has proved decisive in the area of psychosis research.

Depression, ego disturbances, and disorders of movement represent related phenomena often encountered in clinical psychiatric and psychoanalytic practice.

Flor-Henry (1985), as noted above, has creatively, but carefully, described the relationship between some exhibitionistic psychopathology and disturbances of EEG hemispheric asymmetry, attempting to elucidate the basic pathophysiology involved. M. Harrow (1994) has created a model of schizophrenia that integrates the biological and the psychological, noting an imbalance between frontal and limbic areas of the brain, possibly relating to synaptic density. He assumes that high stress causes heightened cognitive arousal during the acute phase of the disorder. The result is an intermingling of personal concerns and wishes into conscious thinking and a selective disorder in monitoring one's own ideas. The latter is probably secondary to an impairment in the effective use of long-term stored memory as to what is socially and contextually appropriate. And T. J. Crow (1982, 1986a, 1986b, 1986c) has provided evidence that the illness we call schizophrenia represents in all likelihood several different illnesses, at least one of which (in right-handers) is probably a retroviral disease contracted in utero as a result of the mother's having influenza during the second trimester of gestation. Finally, molecular biologists have even begun to locate and reproduce the genes that lead to such disorders. Genes causing a significant number of illnesses have now been located, including several genes that might be causative of manic-depressive illness (so-called bipolar depression). We have clearly come far since the days of Abraham's and Freud's original biological and psychodynamic speculations about such illnesses as manic depression and dementia praecox. But we should not derogate the hypotheses they generated, since it was their insightfulness that opened the way to further research. Recall that it was Freud himself who speculated (on clinical, psychological grounds) about the probable existence of sexual hormones, before they were generally discovered! Psychoanalysis has always had a place in the neuroscientific revolution.

Infantile autism, obsessive-compulsive disorder, and panic disorder, to mention additional clinical examples, represent further areas in which considerable interdisciplinary research has occurred in the past decade. When I entered medical school, these topics were barely on the agenda; at the present time, specific medications have been introduced in the United States which help the latter two conditions, and several drugs have been tested for the first condition in Japan and elsewhere. In addition, the attention drawn to such brain structures as the cerebellum (by many workers in the psychiatric field, including myself) has resulted in more careful investigation of the role of cerebellar pathology in learning disabilities, including its newly appreciated role in the psychopathology of infantile autism. This does not entirely replace the pioneering insights of psychoanalytic observers such as Bruno Bettelheim, Winnicott, Bowlby, Spitz, Provence, Modell, Kohut, and others regarding the importance for recovery of a loving, nurturing, human environment, but it certainly allows for a fuller consideration of how environmental and experiential factors might interact.

Another prominent area of research concerns anxiety, which includes such topics as post-traumatic stress syndrome and panic attack syndrome. Following Freud's work on war neuroses during World War I and Grinker and Spiegel's work in World War II, a younger generation has expanded knowledge of these disorders from the Vietnam experience as well as from man's increasingly traumatic life-style. For example, research on panic attack syndrome includes studies (at Washington University Medical School in St. Louis) that show abnormal metabolic activity in the right parahippocampal gyrus, possibly reduced or altered by the drugs now preferred for treating this condition.

A second example of modern research on a variety of what Freud called the "traumatic neuroses" (as opposed to the so-called narcissistic neuroses) concerns obsessive-compulsive illness. Baxter (1990) has suggested the possibility that this illness may be related to alterations in the striatum that prevent the normal (caudate-based) inhibition of motor, affective, or cognitive patterns, which then become repetitive (that is, "obsessive" or "compulsive," depending upon which area of the caudate or lenticular nucleus is affected). Clearly, there is much current interest in the basal ganglia (cf. Graybiel et al., 1994), and there is much to learn and appreciate about those brain areas that eliminate irrelevant information, inhibit repetitive cycles, or gate (control the flow of) sensory input. In this regard we can expect a concentration on prefrontal, cerebellar, and basal ganglia mechanisms in the future, since these three areas are critical for neural control. They are also visualizable by the latest non-invasive scanning technology.

Neuropsychoimmunology is another novel area that barely existed a few decades ago but that now makes its own unique contribution to mind/brain integration. We have long appreciated that feelings influence the course of physical illness. Long ago Cannon described "voodoo death," and we have the example of couples who have lived together for years not infrequently dying within a short interval of each other (and the same is known to occur with animals living together in zoos). Now, thanks to experts who combine knowledge of immunology and neuroscience, we are in a better position to appreciate more exactly how the brain affects the course of certain physical illnesses, altering vulnerabilities to infectious disease, cancers, and so forth. We can also better appreciate how the immune system feeds information into the brain itself, functioning as a kind of "radar" regarding bodily events outside the central nervous system. Cells of the immune system are also capable of producing neurotransmitters, which may be released into the peripheral blood. In this research domain K. Biziere (1994) has written eloquently as follows: "We are more aware of research on how the C.N.S. affects the immune system (I.S.), but significant research is currently afoot to study . . . neuropsychiatric disorders which may result from normal or abnormal immune responses . . . leading to excessive concentrations of certain cytokines within the C.N.S." Cytokines are produced by, and released from, immune cells but pass through the blood–brain barrier.

Clearly, this discussion could be extended by a very considerable length were one to attempt any systematic overview of the many research areas covered under the general rubric of mind/brain correlations. At this point, I would prefer to focus instead upon details of particular areas of major psychoanalytic interest. Those curious about details of the broader subject may wish to consult my recent book (1991) or the excellent works of Reiser (1984), Schwartz (1985), and Flor-Henry (1983a, 1983b, 1985).

FREUD'S "PROJECT FOR A SCIENTIFIC PSYCHOLOGY"

Although Freud never published his "Project" (1895), there can be little doubt that this "psychology for neurologists" represent a Rosetta stone for understanding Freud's theoretical writings, particularly, for example, chapter 7 of *The Interpretation of Dreams* (1900). As Strachey (1950) describes, Freud was not afraid of integrating mind and brain:

Freud's attempted approach seventy years ago to a description of mental phenomena in physiological terms might well seem to bear a resemblance to certain modern approaches to the same problem. It has been suggested . . . that the human nervous system may be regarded in its workings as similar to or even identical with an electronic computer—both of them machines for the reception, storage, processing and output of information. It has been plausibly pointed out that in the complexities of the "neuronal" events described here by Freud, and the principles governing them, we may see more than a hint or two at the hypotheses of information theory and cybernetics in their application to the nervous system. To take a few instances of this similarity of approach, we may note first Freud's insistence on the prime necessity for providing the machine with a "memory"; again, there is his system of "contact-barriers" [a description of the neurone hypothesis, which Freud anticipated before other neurologists gained fame through its discovery and description], which enables the machine to make a suitable "choice," based on the memory of previous events, between alternative lines of response to an external stimulus; and, once more, there is, in Freud's account of the mechanism of perception, the introduction of the fundamental notion of feed-back as a means of correcting errors in the machine's own dealings with the environment. [Pp. 292–293]

Strachey refers to Pribram's (1962) detailed elaboration of Freud's "Project," and reference should also be made to Pribram and Gill's book on the subject (1976).

By all accounts, Freud invented an early version of the idea of a cybernetic or information-processing system, just as he discovered the "neurone hypothesis" in this early manuscript (Basch, 1975). We may consider some of the reasons why Freud failed to understand defense against perceptions. Freud began with the belief that "in order to prevent the generation of excessive anxiety one must be able to defend oneself not only against unmanageable aspects of instinctual stimulation, but also against re-experiencing or recalling potentially traumatic perceptions from the external world" (Basch, 1983, 125). He understood that repression could protect against instinctual derivatives (endogenous stimuli) but felt that perceptual activity and consciousness constituted a single system which did not allow the possibility of external perceptions, with their strong or significant sensory quality, being defended against. This was his (erroneous) conclusion both in the "Project" and in his letter no. 39 to Wilhelm Fliess. In 1911, as Basch notes (ibid.), Freud again recognized this gap when he said, "a system living according to the pleasure principle must have devices to enable it to withdraw from the stimuli of reality" (1911, p. 220). Basch traces Freud's movement toward solving this problem to his paper "The loss of reality in neurosis and psychosis" (1924a), in which Freud speculates that whatever the mechanism is that protects us from reality perceptions, it functions like repression and must involve "a withdrawal of the cathexis sent out by the ego" (p. 153). Freud concludes that in neurosis "a piece of reality is avoided by a sort of flight, whereas in psychosis it is remodelled" (1924b, p. 185).

Basch (1983) makes the same point: "It has been established in the field of perceptual psychology that contrary to Freud's hypothesis Pcpt = Cs, perception and consciousness are neither identical nor simultaneous. Perception precedes consciousness by a measurable amount of time and given the complexity of the neuronal network [of the brain], there is ample opportunity to evaluate the significance of that percept and judge its suitability for consciousness" (p. 149). Basch underscores this point when he notes that "the data-processing capacity of the brain has now been established to be in the neighborhood of ten trillion bits or decisions per second [and therefore most brain activity is part of the dynamic unconscious], while approximately only ten bits of information per second can be admitted to conscious awareness" (p. 149). To put this differently, the answer long sought by Freud as to how we defend against perceptions is as follows: we retain in memory perceptions per se, but defend against these by lending them various levels of personal significance ranging from "highly significant" to "essentially inconsequential." Such a disavowal of meaning is an extremely important psychological defense mechanism, originally described by Freud (but nearly lost in translation). The rediscovery and clarification of this defense we owe especially to Basch (1983).

PSYCHOANALYSIS AND THE TWO CEREBRAL HEMISPHERES

The rediscovery of the psychological defense of disavowal (the downplaying of the personal meaning of a recognized, accurately perceived event, accessible to conscious and preconscious memory) and its distinction from denial (in which a piece of reality is nonexistent to the ego, substantially perceptually distorted, and/or not accessible to memory at all)[2] represent an important clinical contribution to psychoanalysis. In addition, this work contributed to an interest in discovering possible connections between such phenomena as psychological "defenses" on the one hand and neurophysiological mechanisms on the other. One way to explore such terrain has been to start with what is known about the differing roles of the two cerebral hemispheres. For those interested in pursuing this area in more detail, the subject of brain asymmetry has been reviewed in general (Springer & Deutsch, 1981; Levy, 1974; Meyersberg & Post, 1979; Flor-Henry, 1983a, 1983b, 1985) as well as with regard to psychoanalysis (Galin, 1974; Levin & Vuckovich, 1983).

The two hemispheres essentially constitute two brains and are capable of sharing or sequestering their internally or externally generated experiences. Sperry (1974) has pointed out, however, that they share one "consciousness." Cortical morphological differences between the hemispheres have been observed before birth. Handedness is essentially a reflection of "brainedness" (Annett, 1985), and the archeological record suggests that it goes back millions of years. According to Levy (1974), approximately 89 percent of the population is genotypically right-handed, and most (99.67 percent) of this group is left-hemispheric-dominant for language. Of the 16 percent of phenotypic sinistrals, 56 percent have left-language dominance and 44 percent right-language dominance. Females show less cerebral dominance than males; that is, their brains are more symmetrical regarding the parsing of various functions. These asymmetries have profound implications for the nature of human experience, as well as for the responsiveness and recovery rates to brain injuries. For example, aphasia, which was studied by Freud (1891a, 1891b) extensively, hits males more devastatingly than females, and the male degree and rate of recovery from aphasia are much lower than for females. Clearly, there are critical differences between the brains of men and women, a point rarely entertained in developing a psychology that would apply to both.

It will help to review briefly some of the differences between the hemispheres. The following comments apply to a right-handed individual who is left-brain-dominant for language. The right hemisphere is a leading part of the brain's systems concerned

2. Denial is also referred to as a "repudiation" of reality, which means that the experiencing subject regards some detail of reality as essentially nonexisting or totally absent. This is significantly different, however, from two other defenses: disavowal and isolation of affect (see Basch, 1983).

with intuition and the formation of gestalts, the processing of tactile input, visuomotor and spatial skills, facial expression, the prosody (metrical composition) of language, time synthesis, and tonal reproduction and recognition, exclusive of musical scores (note that the musical quality of speech is extremely important, since without this we find it extremely difficult to encode or decode the emotional meaning of speech).

Thus, although the left brain is usually described as dominant with regard to language, this so-called "dominance" is really an oversimplification. The right brain also makes a major contribution to language, especially as regards word fluency, prosody (the musical quality of speech), and verbal memory (Tucker et al., 1977). Moreover, although the left hemisphere contains Broca's and Wernicke's areas, which control systems for the transformation of thoughts into formal spoken language (Broca's), as well as the encoding and decoding of ideas into language (Wernicke's), the right hemisphere contains areas that are the counterparts to these two left-sided language areas (Kandel, 1983). These right-sided areas (located in analogous positions to Broca's and Wernicke's areas on the left) are apparently what we use to create the affective components of language rather than our language's formal syntactical and phonologial structures.

The left hemisphere is primarily associated with serial experience, with logic and reasoning, and with most of the learning that we associate with school. Such information has been called "explicit" or "declarative" knowledge by research psychologists, indicating that it is retrievable by direct, language-based questioning. This is in contrast to "implicit" or "procedural" knowledge, which is characteristic of some of the brain's other memory systems—for example, the vestibulocerebellar system. In this system information is stored as a motor memory and is most easily retrieved through "priming"—that is, by action modes or sensory stimulation. It may help to note here that when we identify enactments and reliving in an analysis, we are able to see that they provide the necessary "priming" for the recovery of some of the early (preverbal) events in the patient's life, though they are not exclusively limited to that period.

Thus, it follows that some significant, and probably early, experience is captured in a form that will not be tapped by our analysands unless the proper sensory stimulus is provided within the analysis. From this perspective, one could make an argument that the analyst who is somewhat more willing to talk (say at those times when the analysand is trying to recall something that is just out of reach and be-

comes silent for some extended period of time because his or her recall efforts are failing, and he or she needs help) may stimulate components of the analysand's missing memory through spontaneous comments, by means of the evocative effect of the tone of the analyst's voice, visual imagery, and so forth (see Levin, 1990, for a detailed discussion of the complicated aspects of such interventions; see also Gedo, 1978, for further examples and theoretical commentary on this point).

When Freud (1891a) wrote extensively on aphasia as a cerebral disconnection syndrome, he was in effect not only advancing a novel refutation of the narrow, anatomical localization models of cerebral function of his day but establishing a perspective that could serve multiple purposes. Freud's approach would now be called a general systems perspective, in which "a mental phenomenon corresponds to each part of the chain [of events], or to several parts. The psychic is, therefore, a process parallel to the physiological, a 'dependent concomitant'" (1891a, p. 55). Freud was to apply this same perspective repeatedly, elaborating upon what he felt to be the elements of a system subserving multiple mental faculties. He thus attempted to describe their system relationships. Employing this systems perspective, one might consider a somewhat novel explanation of "conflict" as that state in which the system relationship of the two hemispheres becomes disturbed.[3] This includes most importantly the possibility of functional interhemispheric blocks between the hemispheres. That is, if the hemispheres are capable of sharing information with each other or with other areas (such as the prefrontal cortex), then they are also capable of blocking out such connectedness. A brief description of the possible manifestations of interhemispheric blocking follows, along with a discussion of its mechanisms (Levin & Vuckovich, 1983; see also Levin, 1991). In brief, the position generally taken is that the "willful" control of the flow of information within the brain occurs by some unknown process akin to the manner in which regional cerebral blood

3. Here I am referring to a novel explanation of psychological defense. I had previously considered this a novel *definition* of defense, but Burness Moore has correctly pointed out that "explanation" is more accurate than "definition." I am referring to types of conflict in which the basic mechanism is a communication block between the two cerebral hemispheres. However, I do not claim that there might not be other explanations for conflict at a basic science level. Moreover, all conflict is not alleged to be the result of interhemispheric blockage, although some conflicting tendencies may well represent exactly this phenomenon.

flow increases in association with spontaneous thinking (Roland & Friberg, 1985).

If one imagines an isolated left hemisphere (isolated in the sense of being without input from the right hemisphere—that is, without emotionally weighted information clarifying the degree and quality of the personal meaning[s] of an "event"), then one is left with only the detailed perceptions of the experience in memory, with much less "color" (in the sense of emotional coloring). It might, for example, make it harder or even impossible to understand the significance of the event, just as it is difficult to establish the meaning of a message communicated, say, in the emotionless computer voice used by the telephone company. Such "black and white" pictures, or words without emotional coloring, illustrate the internal state corresponding to the psychological defense of "disavowal." In contrast to this, one can imagine an isolated right hemisphere. One would then have the presence of some significant quantum of affect; but without specific memories of an "event" to go along with the affect, the affective state itself might be unintelligible. This would coincide with what is usually termed "repression." It was thinking along such lines that, in part, originally gave rise to the idea that interhemispheric communication blocks might provide a fundamental explanation for these psychological defenses at a basic science level (Levin & Vuckovich, 1983, pp. 179–186; Levin, 1991; Galin, 1974).

Some may believe that this hypothesis regarding a possible correspondence or even an isomorphism between repression/disavowal and left/right or right/left interhemispheric blocks is either wrong or of little clinical relevance to psychoanalysis; however, the following considerations and examples may help persuade the reader not to discard the hypothesis immediately, especially since it also has the advantage of being testable experimentally.

If the two cerebral hemispheres are functionally differentiated as described above (with the right brain particularly oriented toward affect, prosody, and facial expression, the left toward formal logic, rules, and syntactical language), then there is the possibility that during psychoanalytic work the analyst may facilitate a bridging between the analysand's hemispheres, by being sensitive to the "language" of each hemispheric input independently (see Levin, 1980). The analyst might help with the visualization of "color" intensity, by overcoming disavowed affect, and also potentially help as well with the retrieval of forgotten (repressed) perceptual details, to which specific affect attaches. In this manner, isolated information in part of the nervous system would become input for the rest of the brain,

and the overall system would be functionally enlarged. From this perspective, one aspect of the integrative function that we know to be an attribute of the analytic process would become understandable in terms of known brain functions and known psychological variables (such as disavowed states and repressions). Some clinical case material may help to explain further the relevance of such research to psychoanalysis.

The first comes from Galin (1974), who reports on the following case from Sperry's split-brain research. The experimental subject described here has had her corpus callosum severed for the experimental treatment of epilepsy: "One film segment [of Sperry's research] shows a female patient being tested with a tachistoscope. . . . In the series of neutral geometrical figures being presented at random to the right and left [visual] fields, a nude pinup was included and flashed to the right (nonverbal) hemisphere. The girl blushes and giggles. [The experimenter] asks 'What did you see?' She answers 'Nothing, just a flash of light,' and giggles again, covering her mouth with her hand. 'Why are you laughing then?' [asks the experimenter], and she laughs again and says 'Oh doctor Sperry, you have some machine'" (p. 573). As Galin points out, if you did not know that this patient had a commisurotomy of her corpus callosum, you might interpret her behavior as demonstrating a number of perceptual defenses in order to avoid what appear to be embarrassing sexual feelings. Actually, though, her right hemisphere is reacting to something her left hemisphere has no knowledge of because of an anatomical disconnection.

Another example (without anatomical complications) will point out the phenomena under discussion even more clearly and help make still more credible the physiological/psychological correlations being asserted here. This second example is taken from the analysis of a patient who began to talk in a detached, disavowed manner.

[While she talked] her analyst's attention wandered to the patient's left hand, which was shifting periodically into a "gun" gesture [completely] out of her awareness. When this gesture was called to the patient's attention, she responded by remembering that she had read in graduate school about right–left brain studies, including Ferenczi's observation that the left side of the body (i.e., the right hemisphere) appears more in touch with the unconscious. (The patient did not [at this time] know of the analyst's interest in the subject of right–left brain studies.) She simultaneously became aware of and experienced significant anger toward the analyst, which during the session she gradually was able to relate with increasing certainty to the analyst's upcoming vacation. Finally, at the end of the hour, she began to recall some specific memories of being taken advantage of sexually by certain parental substitutes in childhood [i.e., during the absence of her parents]. [Levin & Vuckovich, 1987, p. 185]

It is apparent that this second example is not unusual in psychoanalysis; in fact, the reader may wonder why such a mundane example is presented here. However, if we consider the unique perspective being presented within this discussion of research on left–right brain, we can see that by interfering with disavowal (that is, by pointing out to the patient the gun gesture, which she was unaware of), the analyst created a sequence of developments in which repression was unmasked or undone. But if these two defenses (disavowal and repression) go together more often than can be by chance, it becomes important to consider the possibility that they may represent communication blocks between the two cerebral hemispheres, in exactly opposite directions. If this is correct, then the mechanism relating to the kind of (standard) psychoanalytic intervention noted in the second case would be as follows. First, the analyst becomes aware of the patient's disavowed state by finding his own interest drifting; but, unlike the patient, he does not dismiss her hand gesture as meaningless. Next, the analyst points out what the patient's left hand is portraying gesturally. Then the patient becomes aware of her own disavowed affect of anger or rage. Finally, this affect leads her to memories of some personally significant but disavowed "event" (in "episodic" memory) and associated repressed details (in "semantic" memory [see Basch, 1983]), which *together* allow for the integration of affect and cognition around the traumatic, developmental experience with parental substitutes. From the patient's perspective, this is like finding a hidden "gravestone" (that is, something "disavowed"), which now points to something deeply "buried" (namely, the "repressed").

As a sidelight, it is probably of no small significance that the two hemispheres come together (in terms of the first major wave of myelinization of the corpus callosum) during the oedipal period (around three and a half). This suggests that one reason for the importance of oedipal-level anxiety, in addition to the well-known psychoanalytic reasons, is that during this period the child is experiencing a critical developmental shift in psychological defensive strategy: he or she is passing from a time when "events" and wishes are nontraumatic, by virtue of the fact

that the hemispheres are functionally isolated anatomically, to a period when such a functional separation can occur only as a result of some internal decision making within the brain. Put somewhat differently, one of the tasks of the oedipal child is to deal with the affects generated by the observations and correlations that he or she is increasingly capable of making. Before this age, it seems likely that the child is relatively protected by the anatomical isolation of the hemispheres as well as by hemispheric immaturity itself. Afterward, defensive needs may require a reinstitution of the interhemispheric disconnection. This would have to be initiated by some internal decision-making process within the brain and have a physiological basis, resulting in a regressive isolation of the hemispheres; it would mark the beginning of the psychological phenomena we call repression and disavowal, and infantile amnesia would also be one of its manifestations. It should be obvious that such defensive disconnection need not be total, since a quantitative shift in threshold might make a significant qualitative difference, starting around the age of three and a half, when the two hemispheres become able to share information with each other, with the prefrontal cortex, and with other areas. Clearly, this is not intended to be an all-encompassing explanation of such defensive phenomena; there are undoubtedly other—perhaps many—neurophysiological mechanisms by which the same defense may be accomplished.

Two further notes. First, the analyst seems to be in a favored position to recognize when the analysand is unaware of either a critical affect (right hemisphere input), a critical memory (left hemisphere input), or a correlation between the two. Secondly, it is possible that what is described clinically as functioning in primarily a "hysterical" mode (favoring repression) or an "obsessive" mode (favoring disavowal) could possibly reflect a fundamental human tendency to isolate the hemispheres on a physiological basis for the purpose of psychological defense or adaptation (Levin & Vuckovich, 1983; Levin, 1991).

BRAIN PLASTICITY, LEARNING, AND PSYCHOANALYSIS

I will now review aspects of the brain's plasticity, or capacity to alter its way of functioning to adapt to needs. It is by means of integration of all of the different subsystems of the brain at various levels of organization that learning and "therapeutic" process occur. In other words, if one assumes that emotional growth involves learning, then our wish to expand our understanding of how psychoanalysis works (that is, to facilitate learning in the psychoanalytic setting) depends upon our understanding the basis of learning. (For details, see Albus, 1971, 1981; Alkon, 1985; Levin, 1990; Levin & Vuckovich, 1987; Rosenzweig & Bennett, eds., 1976; Thompson, 1986, 1987; Young, 1978; Lynch et al., eds., 1984.) In what follows I review some of what is known about brain plasticity and its relevance to psychoanalysis.

Four adult mechanisms for learning are known: development of new neuronal branches and synapses, use of reverberating circuits, use-dependent modification of existing circuits, and the alteration of pre- and post-synaptic processes (Alkon, 1985, p. 1037). All organizational levels within the nervous system are capable of change in response to experience and thus contribute to the learning process. At the beginning of life, "the embryonic and newborn brain extends many more neural processes than will ultimately be employed by the adult organism. Subsequently, inappropriate neural connections will be pruned away by the death of nerve cells" (Snyder, 1984, p. 1255). This constitutes one major means of early brain synaptic organization and reorganization. Of course, optimal experience with caretakers is a critical factor in establishing optimal synaptic organization. Recent experiments also confirm that in all likelihood no new neurons appear during our lifetime (Rakik, 1985). This is not true of the avian brain, however (Nottebohm, 1985), opening the intriguing possibility that in the future man may learn how to unlock the human potential for neuronogenesis.

A distinction can be made between plastic change and learning. In a sense, any change in the tendency to respond can be seen as a simple form of learning; however, in lower animals this is usually referred to as "sensitization" rather than "discriminative" (that is, specific) learning (see Young, 1978, p. 83). Thus, although all patterned change in behavior represents learning, all learning does not involve complex, discriminative ability.

Psychoanalysts were sufficiently interested in the neurophysiological basis of memory to invite Kandel (1983) to report on his findings at a plenary session of the American Psychoanalytic Association. He showed that at the microbiological level, short-term memory (much better understood than long-term) can be correlated with a neurochemical cascade involving known neuroactive substances. For example, in serotonergic neurons there is a sequential transformation of intraneuronal adenosine triphosphate (ATP) into pyrophosphate and $3'5'$-AMP (the so-called second messenger). These products

cause the activation of ionic channels for calcium at the synaptic membrane level, and an alteration of the operator gene ensues that causes previously "unexpressed" genetic material in the nucleus of the nerve cell to express itself. In this manner the neuron may respond to environmental factors by producing different neurotransmitters, and thus participate in different chemical pathways.

Equally exciting, at the level of the somatomotor strip (the so-called cortical homunculus or map) Merzenich et al. (1984) have correlated learning with significant cortical cellular changes. They have shown, for example, that with the increased use of a finger (in monkeys and presumably also in man) the cortical homunculus changes, with the area (representing the involved finger) growing in size. Also, in amputation experiments, when a finger is removed, the cortical cells learn about the change, and the cortical map changes so that the area of cortex previously representing the amputated finger now represents the fingers on either side of the lost digit. There can be no question but that learning is also associated with changes at the cortical level and relates to the plastic manner in which cortical cells represent a given motor (or sensory) field.

From the standpoint of learning theory, human development represents the acquisition of skills (autonomous ego functions) based upon various inborn biological potentials (that is, upon the genetic blueprint) the release of which is significantly affected by experience. Human objects are thus required for optimal development.[4] Most interestingly, the genetic blueprint is decisive not only for its specification of *what* is to be learned but also for *how* this learning is to be accomplished (M. Stern, 1988). For example, analytic work with individuals who suffer from learning disabilities has made it clear that we are not all born with the same internal programs for learning. In fact, some people appear to be substantially unprepared for learning within various realms.

In examining the subject of cerebral asymmetry, we discovered that some internal decision making is required in order to coordinate the hemispheres dur-

---

4. A fascinating aspect of brain research deals with the narrower question of exactly how it is that environment and genetic loading interact. The key is appreciating the role of voluntary action. Any voluntary action always simultaneously serves as a test of one's hypothesis about (a particular aspect of) the world (Jeannerod, 1985; see also Levin, 1994a) and therefore leads ultimately to the defining and refinding of internal self-in-the-world models. Also, some maps of the world are literally etched into the brain, as can be seen from the work of Merzenich et al. (1984).

ing the performance of any particular task. Specifically, it is helpful to match a given problem with the learning subsystem of the brain most adapted to this kind of problem. In a paper on brain plasticity, I and Vuckovich (1987) explored how such internal, automatic decision making might occur. In particular, we make the case that the cerebellum, through the corticovestibulocerebellar subsystem, would seem to be a major candidate for coordinating such pattern matching within the brain. In a nutshell we are asserting that the cerebellum handles thoughts the same way it handles movement. Itoh, whose work was cited at the beginning of this chapter, provides extensive details as to how this might be accomplished, and the interested reader is invited to study Itoh's thoughtful contributions to learning theory (as well as Levin, 1991). Lest anyone doubt the significance of the cerebellum to ego development (Frick, 1982) and learning (Itoh, 1986), it is now known that infantile autism is most probably a specific consequence of cerebellar malfunction (Hadley, 1989).

Brain scientists (see especially Galaburda et al., 1978; Geschwind & Galaburda, 1985), social workers (Palombo, 1985), psychologists, and educators have long been interested in the important subject of learning disability. It becomes increasingly important that psychoanalysts also be aware and knowledgeable in this area, especially since without the proper knowledge they may end up making such errors as misidentifying learning disability phenomena as "sadomasochistic." The point is that all hurtful, self-damaging, self-defeating behavior is not intended to be so at an unconscious level; some individuals fail because they do not know how to do something. The school-age group with significant learning disability probably makes up at least 10 percent of the child population, and this may not be different at the university level. In my opinion, a similar percentage of adult psychiatric patients are also learning-disabled, and most of this group suffers as well from not ever having had testing, a proper diagnosis, or remediation.

One additional problem deserves a brief comment. Since learning disability is defined operationally as the inability to achieve satisfactorily in spite of normal intelligence, the diagnosis of learning disability itself depends upon the precise assessment of intelligence. But if one is not familiar with learning disabilities testing, then it is easy to underestimate a person's intelligence (since the tester will not conduct the test in ways that allow for the patient's intelligence to be expressed) and so underestimate the extent of a learning disability.

Space does not permit an in-depth discussion of psychoanalysis and learning disability, but it is my opinion that special care is required so as not to fall into the trap of misdiagnosing problems, misinterpreting motives, or improperly estimating a patient's abilities. Palombo (1985, 1987) should be consulted for his thoughtful discussion of the clinical issues involved in psychodynamic work with this neurocognitively disturbed population.

At this point a final comment upon the vestibulocerebellar system seems in order. This system has been described in detail (Levin & Vuckovich, 1987), especially with regard to its role in learning. What is also usually considered under the rubric of brain plasticity is the capacity to acquire sensorimotor schema, and although those interested in learning have not always taken much notice of this phase of learning (with the prominent exception of Piaget, who started from this perspective), it seems that over recent decades the role of motor learning has become an important topic within the psychology of learning in general. It now seems probable that learning about oneself, others, and the (inanimate) world occurs first on the basis of vestibular and proprioceptive input, recorded by the vestibulocerebellar system (Chugani & Phelps, 1986). This fact is important for psychoanalysis because it means that our core sense of self is a reflection of a known system of the brain. Consequently, our ability to modify this core will hinge upon our developing a refined knowledge about this system (Levin, 1988b).

SOME FINAL COMMENTS ON THE EVOLUTION OF PSYCHOANALYTIC THEORY

Successful neuropsychoanalytic bridging should assist the search for better psychoanalytic models, just as psychoanalytic perspectives have intelligently guided neuroscientific research from the beginning. One such interdisciplinary model is the Gedo and Goldberg (1973) hierarchical, developmental model, as modified most recently by Gedo (1989; see also Levin, 1989; Lichtenberg, 1989a, 1989b). This model is unique in a number of respects that are germane to the present discussion. First, it takes into account the prime data of clinical psychoanalysis upon which all other major, psychoanalytic models are based; thus, it is overarching. Second, it makes the time or developmental dimension explicit and is therefore easier to apply clinically to both the shifting motivational-structural axis of a life course (see below) and the regressive and progressive moves within a treatment. Third, it is consistent with the intense work in the field of infant observation studies, as summarized by Lichtenberg (1983, 1989a, 1989b), D. Stern (1985), Demos (1985), and others. Fourth, it is internally consistent.

Gedo's model is closely related to the ideas of Lichtenberg, who stated recently that "psychoanalytic theory is not at its core so much a theory of structure as it is a theory of structural motivation" (1989b, p. 57). After the fashion of Levey (1984–85), Gedo (1989), and Sameroff (1983), Lichtenberg describes how the meaning of psychic structure changes throughout development, identifying the following "functional-motivational systems" or goals which can serve sequentially as axes around which structural developments can be organized: "(1) the need to fulfill physiological needs; (2) the need for attachment and affiliation; (3) the need for assertion and exploration; (4) the need to react aversively through antagonism and/or withdrawal; (5) the need for sensual and sexual pleasure" (1989b, p. 60). By acknowledging such multiple motivational goals that extend beyond dual instinct theory and ego psychology, these psychoanalytic innovations are changing psychoanalytic theory in a fundamental way.

To elaborate, the formal linkage of Gedo and Goldberg's (1973) model to Freud's reflex arc, structural, and topographic models is dispensed with in Gedo's current hierarchical model because of the incompatible assumptions among the different traditional models. What Gedo (Wilson & Gedo, 1993) retains is the developmental sequence that takes into account the multiple motivations described by Lichtenberg. These specific motivations correspond roughly to Gedo's stages of self-definition, self-organization, and self-regulation. Moreover, Gedo (and Lichtenberg as well) retains the current psychoanalytic tripartite oedipal phase model of Freud, which appears in the hierarchical model as the stage involving the renunciation of incompatible wishes that threaten adaptive equilibrium.

What is interesting here is the general agreement that the meaning of "structure" changes throughout development (Sameroff, 1983; Levey, 1984–85; Lichtenberg, 1989b; Gedo, 1989). In other words, during each stage (mode) of development, the central organizing principle is seen to change: from regulating stimulus input, which is crucial at the beginning of life, to organizing around real objects with the goal of forming a nuclear self, to a stage wherein the functions provided by self-objects facilitate the further crystallization of a cohesive personhood, to a phase governed by ego, superego, and id regulation, to a conflict-free sphere in which a hierarchy of goals and values is further arranged, appropriate to the subject's needs at a given time. But what determines this changing fulcrum of development?

This question, a pivotal one for psychoanalysis, is answered by Gedo and Levin as follows: the genetic blueprint itself determines the timetable for changing motivational structure. Consider, for example, what is known about the genetic control system for biological development. Our DNA contains a small number of closely associated genes (the homeobox) which have been conserved over a large number of species, the purpose of which is to control development—that is, the order in which the rest of the genes will be activated in the developmental sequence and presumably during the lifetime of an individual (see Levin, 1989). What changes between species is not the overall sequence (for example, making a body axis, then adding limbs to it, and so on) but the details regarding what body plan is to be used, which limb types, and so forth. In the case of insects, wings are included in the step of forming limb buds upon an already established anterior–posterior body axis; in our own instance, the addition of human limbs occurs as the corresponding step. It follows that, for human psychological development as well, the sequence of appearance of motivational-functional systems conforms to a fixed, species-specific plan. What psychoanalysis is urgently in need of is a map of the neurological, developmental sequence.

Some may argue that by including such factors as genetics and biological motivations Gedo, Lichtenberg, Sameroff, and others are generating models that are not truly psychoanalytic. But this would apply to Freud himself, since he too was struggling with the problem posed by the complexity of multiple, motivational systems. For example, in his paper "On narcissism" (1914) Freud postulated narcissistic motives, which challenged the then psychoanalytic establishment with developmental ideas that were inconsistent with his own libido theory. He did the same thing again in *Totem and Taboo* (1913) when he considered the role of magical thinking in narcissistic development, and, within the Vienna Psychoanalytic Society, when he observed that a case of Federn's did not represent a neurotic fixation (that is, something to be seen within the model of drives and defenses) but rather represented "infantile" arrest in development (Nunberg & Federn, eds., 1975, pp. 145–146). Clearly, at this time in his theoretical thinking, Freud was aware of multiple, "functional-motivational systems." If he did not integrate his new insights into his theory of the time, we can sympathize, since he was then experiencing the need to defend psychoanalysis (in the form of libido theory) from attacks by Adler, Jung, and others.

Furthermore, theory innovators such as Gedo, Sameroff, and Lichtenberg are also following the lead of Anna Freud, Hartmann, and Rapaport. Anna

Freud's concept of multiple lines of development is itself a precursor to a general systems theory perspective; it remains a very short step to the idea of multiple motivational goals at different phases of the life cycle (see Gedo, 1989; Levin, 1989). Moreover, Hartmann's view of the evolution of the self involved an adaptive process of "autonomous ego development," by which he meant that the multiple motivational systems of brain biology needed to be integrated into our field. And Gedo quotes Rapaport as himself following a Piagetian schema in which, epistomologically, "the possibility of knowing is rooted in the organic adaptation from this basic root, a hierarchical series of thought-organizations [which] arises, in the course of maturation and development, culminating in reality-adequate thinking" (Gedo, 1986, p. 65). It is my belief that such "thought-organizations" are economically expressed by the theoretical revisions of Gedo, Sameroff, and Lichtenberg. Such revisions follow the best psychoanalytic traditions in attempting to develop models that encompass our ever expanding knowledge of mind and brain.[5]

SUMMARY AND CONCLUSIONS

Psychoanalysis is changing so as to take into account the explosion of knowledge within neuroscience. The increasing knowledge of the brain is leading to a convergence of all the fields that study human behavior and experience, and some overarching, general theories that begin to approximate a general psychology are emerging. I have discussed the importance of this revolution for psychoanalysis in particular.

I have used the work of Basch on the important subject of psychological defenses, as a point of departure for a more detailed examination of some basic brain mechanisms that may underlie defense. In the process I have stressed the importance of distinguishing between such overlapping defenses as disavowal, denial, and isolation of affect. I have also considered the important role of interhemispheric information transfer in psychoanalytic interpretations and the possible role of brain asymmetry and information blocks in the specific psychological defenses mentioned. Finally I commented on the importance of brain plasticity and the possible regulating, integrating role of the cerebellum and corticovestibulo-cerebellar system in bridging the hemispheres. All

these subject areas have a relationship to the phenomenon of learning, a central issue in all brain-related sciences and a subject of seminal importance to psychoanalysis.

Examples were given to suggest the utility and aptness of these interdisciplinary perspectives, particularly the phenomenon of priming of so-called procedural memories. Such priming may be initiated in analysis by enactments and reliving, thereby aiding the rediscovery of early memories. The special case of learning disabilities was also presented as a reminder of the complications that accrue when our diagnostic knowledge is limited. Our patients rely upon us to be exquisitely careful about how we understand and interpret the maturation of their behavior.[6]

Finally, the discussion has touched upon some of the theoretical revision within psychoanalysis which is itself based upon the convergence of psychoanalytic and neuroscientific discoveries. My hope is that the kind of neuroscientific knowledge presented in this chapter will be integrated with the best psychoanalytic research, so that psychoanalysis may continue to be a major contributor to the brain-related sciences, and vice versa.

REFERENCES

Albus, S. (1971). A theory of cerebellar function. *Math. Bioscience,* 10:25–61.

———. (1981). *Brain, Behavior and Robotics.* Peterborough, N.H.: BYTE Books/McGraw-Hill.

Alkon, D. L. (1985). Calcium-mediated reduction of ionic currents. *Science,* 30:1037–1045.

Andreasen, N. C., Arndt, S., Swayze II, V., Cizadlo, T., Flaum, M., O'Leary, D., Ehrhardt, J. C., & Yuh, W. T. C. (1994). Thalamic abnormalities in schizophrenia visualized through magnetic resonance image averaging. *Science,* 266:294–298.

Annett, M. (1985). *Left, Right Hand and Brain.* Hillsdale, N.J.: Erlbaum.

Baer, D. M. (1989). Neurobiological aspects of anger/rage. Paper read at the American Psychoanalytic Association.

Basch, M. F. (1975). Perception, consciousness, and Freud's "Project." *Annu. Psychoanal.,* 3:3–20.

——— (1983). The perception of reality and the

5. Those interested in a more complete discussion of these models of Gedo et al. will appreciate Wilson & Gedo, 1993, which gives a synopsis of their background, implications, and application.

6. The reader is also referred to other advances which are beyond the scope of this brief summary chapter, such as Levin & Kent, 1995; Levin, 1994a, 1994b. These take up in considerable detail specific mind–brain integrations regarding such matters as the relationship between free association and learning and the role of transference in expanding databases of mind and brain.

disavowal of meaning. *Annu. Psychoanal.*, 11: 125–153.

Baxter, L. R. (1990). Brain imaging as a tool in establishing a theory of brain pathology in obsessive compulsive disorder. *J. Clin. Psychiat.* 51:22–25.

Biziere, K. (1994). Modulation of immune response by the C.N.S. Paper read to the International Symposium on Mind–Body Problems, Osaka, Japan.

Chugani, H. I., & Phelps, M. E. (1986). Maturational changes in cerebral function in infants determined by FDG positron emission tomography. *Science*, 231:840–843.

Crow, T. J. (1982). The biology of schizophrenia. *Experientia*, 38:1275–1282.

———. (1986a). The continuum of psychosis and its implication for the structure of the gene. *Brit. J. Psychiat.*, 149:419–429.

———. (1986b). Left-brain, retrotransposons, and schizophrenia. *Brit. Med. J.*, 293:3–4.

———. (1986c). Secular changes in affective disorder and variations in the psychosis gene. *Arch. Gen. Psychiat.*, 1012–1014.

Demos, E. V. (1985). The revolution in infancy research. Paper read to the American Society of Adolescence, Dallas, Texas.

Eccles, J., Szentágothai, J., & Itoh, M. (1967). *The Neural Machine.* New York: Springer.

Flor-Henry, P. (1983a). *The Cerebral Basis of Psychopathology.* Littleton, Mass.: Wright-PSG.

———. (1983b). Neuropsychological studies in patients with psychiatric disorders. In *Neuropsychology of Human Emotion*, ed. K. M. Hilman & P. Satz, pp. 193–220. New York: Guilford Press.

———. (1985). Psychiatric aspects of cerebral lateralization. *Psychiat. Ann.*, 15:429–434.

Freud, A. (1965). *Normality and Pathology of Childhood.* New York: Int. Univ. Press.

Freud, S. (1891a). *On Aphasia.* New York: Int. Univ. Press, 1953.

———. (1891b). On the interpretation of aphasias. *SE*, 3:240–241.

———. (1895). Project for a scientific psychology. *SE*, 1:203–392.

———. (1900). *The Interpretation of Dreams. SE*, 4 & 5.

———. (1911). Formulations on the two principles of mental functioning. *SE*, 12:213–226.

———. (1913). *Totem and Taboo. SE*, 13:1–161.

———. (1914). On narcissism. *SE*, 14:73–102.

———. (1924a). Neurosis and psychosis. *SE*, 19: 149–156.

———. (1924b). The loss of reality in neurosis and psychosis. *SE*, 19:183–190.

Friberg, L., & Roland, P. E. (1987). Functional activation and inhibition of regional cerebral blood flow and metabolism. In *Basic Mechanisms of Headache,* ed. J. Olesen & L. Edvinsson, pp. 2–30. Amsterdam: Elsevier.

Frick, R. B. (1982). The ego and the vestibulocerebellar system. *Psychoanal. Q.*, 51(1):95–122.

Galaburda, A. M., LeMay, M., Kemper, T. L., & Geschwind, N. (1978). Right–left asymmetries in the brain. *Science*, 199:852–856.

Galin, D. (1974). Implications for psychiatry of left-right cerebral specialization. *Arch. Gen. Psychiat.*, 31:572–583.

Gazzaniga, M. (1970). *The Dissected Brain.* New York: Appleton-Century-Crofts.

Gedo, J. (1978). The analyst's affectivity and the management of transference. Paper read at the Chicago Psychoanalytic Society.

———. (1979). *Beyond Interpretation.* New York: Int. Univ. Press.

———. (1984). *Psychoanalysis and Its Discontents.* New York: Guilford Press.

———. (1986). *Conceptual Issues in Psychoanalysis.* Hillsdale, N.J.: Analytic Press.

———. (1989). Psychoanalytic theory and Occam's razor. Paper read at the Chicago Psychoanalytic Society.

Gedo, J., & Goldberg, A. (1973). *Models of the Mind.* Chicago: Univ. Chicago Press.

Geschwind, N., & Galaburda, A. M. (1985). Cerebral lateralization: III. *Arch. Neurol.*, 42:634–654.

Graybiel, A. M. (1984). Neurochemically specified subsystems in the basal ganglia. In *Functions of the Basal Ganglia*, ed. D. Evered & M. O. O'Connor, pp. 114–149. London: Pitman Press.

Graybiel, A. M., Aosaki, T., Flaherty, A. W., & Kimura, M. (1994). The basal ganglia and adaptive motor control. *Science*, 265:1826–1831.

Hadley, J. L. (1985). Attention, affect and attachment. *Psychoanal. & Contemp. Thought*, 8: 529–550.

———. (1987). Discussion of "Psychological development and the changing organization of the brain," by Fred M. Levin. Chicago Institute for Psychoanalysis.

———. (1989). Personal communication.

Harrow, M. (1994). What factors are involved in the vulnerability of schizophrenics to delusions and thought disorder? Paper presented to the International Symposium on Mind–Body Problems, Osaka, Japan.

Hawking, S. W. (1988). *A Brief History of Time.* New York: Bantam Books.

Ingvar, D. H. (1979). Brain activation patterns revealed by measurements of regional cerebral blood flow. In *Progress in Clinical Neurophysiol-*

ogy, ed. J. E. Desmedt, vol. 6, pp. 200–215. London: S. Karger.

Itoh, M. (1981). *Blueprints of the Brain.* Tokyo: Shizen.

———. (1982). Questions in modeling the cerebellum. *J. Theor. Biol.,* 99:81–86.

———. (1984). Cerebellar plasticity and motor learning. *Exp. Brain Res.,* 9:165–169.

———. (1985). Synaptic plasticity in the cerebellar cortex that may underlie the vestibulo-ocular adaption. In *Adaptive Mechanisms in Gaze Control,* ed. A. Berthoz & M. Jones, pp. 213–221. Amsterdam: Elsevier.

———. (1986). *The Cerebellum and Neural Control.* New York: Raven Press.

Iverson, S. D. (1984). Behavioral effects of manipulation of basal ganglia neurotransmitters. In *Functions of the Basal Ganglia,* ed. D. Evered & M. O. O'Connor, pp. 183–200. London: Pitman Press.

Jeannerod, M. (1985). *The Brain Machine.* Cambridge, Mass.: Harvard Univ. Press.

Kandel, E. (1976). *The Cellular Basis of Behavior.* New York: Freeman.

———. (1983). From metapsychology to molecular biology. *Amer. J. Psychiat.,* 140:1277–1293.

Kandel, E., & Spencer, W. A. (1968). Cellular neurophysiological approaches to the study of learning. *Physiol. Rev.,* 48:65–135.

Kent, E. (1981). *The Brains of Men and Machines.* Peterborough, N.H.: BYTE/McGraw-Hill.

Kety, S. (1982). The evolution of concepts of memory. In *The Neural Basis of Behavior,* ed. A. L. Beckman, pp. 95–101. Jamaica, N.Y.: Spectrum Publishers.

Kim, S.-G., Uğurbil, K., & Strick, P. L. (1994). Activation of a cerebellar output nucleus during cognitive processing. *Science,* 265:949–951.

Lashley, K. S. (1950). In search of the engram. *Symposium Soc. Exp. Biol.,* 4:454–482.

Lassen, N. A. (1987). Cerebral blood flow measured by Xenon-133. *Nucl. Med. Comm.,* 8:535–548.

———. (1994). Where do thoughts occur? Paper presented to the International Symposium on Mind–Body Problems. Osaka, Japan.

Lassen, N. A., & Ingvar, D. H. (1961). The blood flow of the cerebral cortex determined by radioactive krypton-85. *Experientia,* 17:42–43.

Lassen, N. A., Ingvar, D. H., & Skinhoj, E. (1978). Brain function and blood flow. *Sci. Amer.,* 23:62–71.

Levey, M. (1984–85). The concept of structure in psychoanalysis. *Annu. Psychoanal.,* 12/13:137–154.

Levin, F. M. (1980). Metaphor, affect, and arousal. *Annu. Psychoanal.,* 8:321–348.

———. (1988a). Introduction to *Repetition and Trauma,* ed. L. S. Stern, pp. 3–38. Hillsdale, N.J.: Analytic Press.

———. (1988b). Psychological development and the changing organization of the brain. Paper read at the American Psychoanalytic Association.

———. (1989). Discussion of "Psychoanalytic theory and Occam's razor," by J. Gedo, paper read at the Chicago Psychoanalytic Society.

———. (1991). *The Mapping of Mind.* Hillsdale, N.J.: Analytic Press.

———. (1994a). The relationship between Freud's free-associative method, learning, and the self-induced priming of memory. Paper read to the Houston Psychoanalytic Society, Houston, Texas.

———. (1994b). Notes, Oct. 26–27, Psyche '94, the International Symposium on Mind–Body Problems, Osaka, Japan. *Psychoanal. Q.,* 64:429–432.

Levin, F. M., & Kent, Ernest W. (1995). Psychoanalysis and Knowledge, II. *Annu. Psychoanal.* (In press).

Levin, F. M., & Vuckovich, D. M. (1983). Psychoanalysis and the two cerebral hemispheres. *Annu. Psychoanal.,* 11:171–199.

———. (1987). Brain plasticity, learning, and psychoanalysis. *Annu. Psychoanal.,* 15:19–96.

Levy, J. (1974). Psychobiological implications of bilateral symmetry. In *Hemispheric Functions in the Human Brain,* ed. S. Dimond & G. Beaumont, pp. 121–183. New York: Halsted Press.

Lewy, A. J., Jack, R. L., & Singer, C. M. (1985). Treating phase typed chronobiological sleep and mood disorders with appropriately timed bright artificial light. *Psychopharmacol. Bull.,* 21:368–372.

Lichtenberg, J. D. (1983). *Psychoanalysis and Infant Research.* Hillsdale, N.J.: Analytic Press.

———. (1989a). *A Psychoanalytic Theory of Motivation.* Hillsdale, N.J.: Analytic Press.

———. (1989b). A theory of motivational-functional systems as psychic structure. *J. Amer. Psychoanal. Assn.,* 3:57–72.

Lynch, G., McGough, J. L., & Weinberger, N. M., eds. (1984). *Neurobiology of Learning and Memory.* New York: Guilford Press.

MacLean, P. (1985). Stepwise brain evolution with respect to socialization and speech. Paper read at the American Academy of Adolescence, Dallas, Texas.

Makara, G. B., Palkovits, M., & Szentágothai, J. (1980). The endocrine hypothalamus and the hormonal response to stress. In *Selye's Guide to*

Stress Research, ed. H. Selye, pp. 280–337. New York: Van Nostrand Reinhold.

Merzenich, M. M., Randall, J. N., Stryker, M. P., Cynander, M. S., Schoppmann, A., & Zook, J. M. (1984). Somatosensory cortical maps change following digit amputation in adult monkeys. *J. Comp. Neurol.,* 224:591–605.

Meyersberg, H. A., & Post, R. M. (1979). A holistic developmental view of neural and psychological processes. *Brit. J. Psychiat.,* 135:139–155.

Moore, B. E. (1988). On affects. In *Fantasy, Myth, and Reality,* ed. H. Blum, Y. Kramer, A. D. Richards & A. Richards, pp. 401–419. New York: Int. Univ. Press.

Moore, B. E., & Fine, B. D. eds. (1990). *Psychoanalytic Terms and Concepts.* New Haven: Yale Univ. Press.

Nottebohm, F. (1985). Neuronal replacement in adulthood. *Ann. N.Y. Acad. Sci.,* 457:143–162.

Nunberg, H., & Federn, E. eds. (1975). *Minutes of the Vienna Psychoanalytic Society,* vol. 4. New York: Int. Univ. Press.

Palombo, J. (1985). The treatment of borderline neurocognitively impaired children. *Clin. Soc. Wk. J.,* 13:117–128.

———. (1987). Selfobject transferences in the treatment of borderline neurocognitively impaired children. *Child & Adolesc. Soc. Wk. J.,* 1:18–33.

Pribram, K. H. (1962). The neuropsychology of Sigmund Freud. In *Experimental Foundations of Clinical Psychology,* ed. A. J. Bachrach, pp. 442–468. New York: Basic Books.

Pribram, K. H., & Gill, M. M. (1976). *Freud's "Project" Reassessed.* New York: Basic Books.

Provence, S., & Lipton, R. (1962). *Infants in Institutions.* New York: Int. Univ. Press.

Rakik, P. (1985). Limits of neurogenesis. *Science,* 227:1054–1056.

Reiser, M. F. (1984). *Mind, Brain, Body.* New York: Basic Books.

Retterstøl, N. (1983). Course of paranoid psychosis in relation to diagnostic group. *Psychiat. Clin.,* 16:198–206.

———. (1985). The course of paranoid psychoses in relation to diagnostic grouping. In *Psychiatry,* ed. P. Pichot, P. Berner, R. Wolf, & K. Thau, pp. 551–556. New York: Plenum.

Reynolds, G. P. (1987). Dopamine receptor asymmetry in schizophrenia. *Lancet,* 25 Apr., p. 979.

Roland, P. E., & Friberg, L. (1985). Localization of cortical areas activated by thinking *J. Neurophysiol.,* 53:1219–1243.

Rozenzweig, M. R., & Bennett, E. L., eds. (1976). *Neural Mechanisms of Learning and Memory.* Cambridge, Mass.: MIT Press.

Saitoh, O., Niwa, S., Hiramtsu, K., Kameyama, T., Rymer, K., & Itoh, K. (1984a). Abnormalities in late positive components of event-related potentials may reflect a genetic predisposition to schizophrenia. *Biol. Psychiat.,* 19:293–303.

———. (1984b). P-300 in siblings of schizophrenic probands. In *Advances in Biological Psychiatry,* ed. J. Mendelwicz & H. M. van Praag, pp. 46–59. New York: Karger.

Sameroff, A. (1983). Developmental systems. In *Handbook of Child Psychology,* ed. P. Mussen, pp. 237–294. New York: Wiley.

Sashin, J. T. (1985). Affect tolerance. *J. Sociol. Biol. Structure,* 8:175–202.

Schwartz, A. (1987a). Drives, affects, behavior, and learning. *J. Amer. Psychoanal. Assn.,* 35:467–506.

———. (1987b). Reification revisited. Manuscript copy.

Snyder, S. H. (1984). Neurosciences. *Science,* 225:1255–1257.

Sperry, R. W. (1968). Hemisphere disconnection and unity in conscious awareness. *Amer. Psychol.,* 23:723–733.

Spitz, R. A. (1945). Hospitalism. *Psychoanal. Study Child,* 1:53–74.

———. (1965). *The First Year of Life.* New York: Int. Univ. Press.

Springer, S. P., & Deutsch, G. (1981). *Left Brain, Right Brain.* San Francisco: Freeman.

Stern, D. (1985). *The Interpersonal World of the Infant.* New York: Basic Books.

Stern, M. (1988). *Repetition and Trauma,* ed. L. B. Stern. Hillsdale, N.J.: Analytic Press.

Strachey, J. (1950). Editor's Introduction to Freud's Project. *SE,* 1:292–293.

Thompson, R. F. (1986). The neurobiology of learning and memory. *Science,* 233:941–947.

———. (1987). Activity-dependence of network properties. In *The Neural and Molecular Basis of Learning,* ed. J.-P. Changeux & M. Konishi, pp. 473–550. Chichester, N.Y.: Wiley.

Trevarthen, C. (1984). Hemispheric specialization. In *Handbook of Physiology,* ed. S. R. Gieger et al., vol. 2, pp. 1129–1190. Washington, D.C.: American Physiological Society.

———. (1985). Facial expressions of emotion in mother–infant interaction. *Hum. Neurobiol.,* 9:21–32.

Tucker, D. M., Watson, R. T., & Heilman, K. M. (1977). Discrimination and evocation of affec-

tively intoned speech in patients with right pari-
etal disease. *Neurology,* 27:947–950.

Wilson, A., & Gedo, J. (1993). *Hierarchical Concepts in Psychoanalysis.* New York: Guilford
Press.

Yamawaki, S., Uchitomi, Y., Kugaya, A., Hayashi,
T., Okamoto, Y., Takebayashi, M., Motohashi, N.,
& Yamawaki, S. (1994). Depressive symptoms
induced by IFN therapy. Paper read to the Inter-
national Symposium on Mind–Body Problems,
Osaka, Japan.

Young, J. Z. (1978). *Programs of the Brain.* New
York: Oxford Univ. Press.

43

APPLIED
PSYCHOANALYSIS

Applied psychoanalysis utilizes knowledge gained from clinical observations to shed light upon human nature, history, culture, and society outside of any clinical setting. Although by its nature it is deprived of the advantages of a clinical setting, it can use a portion of the technique of clinical psychoanalysis in the investigation of extra-clinical subjects. The analytic scholar, critic, or social scientist may employ both evenly suspended attention and the awareness of normally unconscious memories and fantasies aroused in him- or herself (Freud, 1912) in order to begin to identify and understand the indications of the psychic unconscious in the subject being researched. Also, as in clinical psychoanalysis, the investigator's awareness of countertransference allows him or her to sort out and subtract what is subjective from what is objective in his or her perceptions and investigations (Devereux, 1967; Hanly, 1991).

Applied psychoanalysis is a historical discipline which, on the basis of various kinds of evidence, seeks to reconstruct the psychological factors at work in the lives of individuals and peoples, past and present, that have contributed to their scientific, cultural, technological, political, social, military, or artistic achievements and failures. But clinical psychoanalysis too is a historical discipline insofar as it seeks to reconstruct the patient's past in order that he or she may remember rather than repeat it. The most important differences between applied psychoanalysis and clinical psychoanalysis are the absence

of free associations, transference, and the analytic process (Eissler, 1965, p. 165). Outside the clinical setting one is limited to interviews in the case of field work in the social sciences and, in the humanities, to the letters, documents, records, works of art, literature, philosophy, and so forth of otherwise unavailable persons (Hanly, 1991).

This comparative description of applied psychoanalysis needs to be supported by a denotative definition of the range and variety of studies in the field. A connotative definition—that is, one that would generalize the findings of applied psychoanalysis—is an impossible task at the present time because of the diversity of fields in the humanities and social sciences to which psychoanalysis has been applied. The best that can be attained is a mixed definition that is connotative within fields of application and denotative across fields. Even connotative definitions within a single field as rich and diverse as, for example, psychoanalysis and literature are of necessity inadequate. For the present, one can only construct signposts to serve as a guide to the field in terms of major issues and problems.

It is not easy to summarize Freud's contributions to applied psychoanalysis, let alone construct satisfactory generalizations to cover the hundreds of studies that have followed; but a classification of Freud's works can provide general headings to divide this vast country into more manageable provinces.

PSYCHOANALYSIS, RELIGION, AND PHILOSOPHY

Freud contributed four studies (1907b, 1927, 1930, 1939) to the fields of religion and philosophy, as well as brief articles and comments scattered throughout his work.

In his analysis of religious beliefs, Freud outlined the extent to which such beliefs owe their origin to the need to deny the elements of irremediable disappointment and helplessness in the human condition. Psychoanalysis does not try to prove that religious beliefs are false; it has shown that they are illusions. From the fact that an idea has a subjective origin as a wish fulfillment, it does not follow that there can be no object corresponding to that idea in reality. But psychoanalysis has established, by means of its analysis of religious belief, that any such correspondence must be based on the facts of nature, not on the innateness of the idea of God or religious or mystical experiences or morality. Freud (1927) points out that all the efforts by philosophers to demonstrate the existence of God by rational arguments have ended in failure. Further studies are needed of the cultural and historical variations of the objects and aims of religious belief and the varieties of religious experience. Meissner (1986), Leavy (1988), and Rizzuto (1979). by contrast with Freud, have sought to find an authentic place for religion in life and in psychoanalysis.

Psychoanalytic findings have a number of implications for problems in philosophy as well. Psychoanalytic observations offer empirical evidence against (1) traditional (Descartes, 1641; Locke, 1690) as well as contemporary (Sartre, 1943; Merleau-Ponty, 1945) theories of mind that treat consciousness as a defining characteristic of what is mental; (2) traditional (Descartes, 1641; Kant, 1785) as well as contemporary (Sartre, 1943; Campbell, 1951) theories of motivation that postulate an uncaused act of will or spontaneity of consciousness as the source of human actions; (3) traditional (Plato; Descartes, 1641; Kant, 1781; Hegel, 1807) or contemporary (Merleau-Ponty, 1945; Heidegger, 1927; Jaspers, 1949) epistemological theories that postulate either ideas or organizing principles innate to the mind as the foundations of knowledge; and (4) traditional (Plato; Aquinas, 1266–72; Kant, 1785) ethical theories that treat moral laws as eternal, universal laws of mind or nature. Stated positively, psychoanalytic findings imply (1) that any satisfactory philosophical theory of mind cannot equate what is conscious and preconscious with what is mental; (2) that all human behavior is subject to the law of causality; (3) that the mind depends for its knowledge of reality on sense perceptions; and (4) that moral values have a historical (developmental) origin for both societies and individuals.

These implications of psychoanalysis for philosophy indicate directions for new studies; relatively little work in ontology, epistemology, and ethics has been done in this area. Hartmann (1950), for example (perhaps as a result of his lack of familiarity with technical philosophical problems, methods, and propositions), does not consider the bearing of psychoanalysis on a broad range of philosophical questions, even though he presents a perceptive examination of the impact of analysis upon the consciences and conduct of analyzed persons. The work of Lazerowitz (1955, 1964, 1968), who by combining linguistic and logical analysis with psychoanalysis has constructed a new understanding of philosophy and its problems, is little known by psychoanalysts.

Representative studies in the application of psychoanalysis to philosophy may be grouped into four broad categories: the study of the thinker thinking (genetic influences upon system building), by Feuer (1963, 1970), Scharfstein and Ostow (1952), Wisdom (1945, 1953), and myself (Hanly, 1970); the study of the psychological significance of philosophical texts, by Kligerman (1957), Lowenberg (1953), and myself (Hanly, 1977); the study of the general relationship between psychoanalysis and philosophy and of the psychological sources of philosophical thinking, by Feuer (1959) and Scharfstein and Ostow (1970); and the study of the implications of psychoanalytic findings for philosophical problems, by Feuer (1955), Hospers (1952), and myself (Hanly, 1979).

This brief elucidation of the application of psychoanalysis to philosophy allows us to identify a type of application that is more strictly logical and theoretical in nature. In addition to researching the psychogenesis of systems of philosophical ideas in the lives of philosophers, one can work out the logical bearing of psychoanalytic findings on questions in philosophy. In ethics, for example, psychoanalytic findings can illuminate the controversy between systems that treat pleasure and those that treat duty as the greatest good; in the philosophy of mind, psychoanalysis can bring some crucial facts to bear upon the free will controversy. This type of application does not labor under the special problems involved in constructing genetic interpretations. It is a method that can be usefully employed in examining any theory, philosophical or otherwise, as long as that theory concerns some aspect of human nature; hence it also links psychoanalysis to political theory, anthropology, sociology, general psychology, and the theory of literary criticism.

Such studies parallel the efforts of post-Darwinian thinkers to work out the implications of evolutionary theory for philosophy, theology, the humanities, and the social sciences. Just as in the case of evolutionary theories, philosophers such as Bergson (1911) and Teilhard de Chardin (1971) first tried to soften the impact of Darwin's findings by clinging to a teleological view of nature that was no longer tenable, so certain thinkers even within psychoanalysis wish to cling to the veridicality of introspection, freedom of the will, and religion, despite the doubt that psychoanalytic discoveries have cast upon them.

It is nevertheless worth noting that the relationship between psychoanalysis and disciplines in the humanities and social sciences is reciprocal rather than unilateral. Just as psychoanalysts can "psychoanalyze" philosophy, so philosophers can "philosophize" psychoanalysis. Sociologists can use psychoanalysis, but they can also theorize about psychoanalysis and study the impact upon society of its clinical and other applications. Psychoanalysis can be used to study literature, but scholars may also study texts of Freud *as* literature.

The hermeneutic philosophers Ricoeur (1970) and Habermas (1971) in incorporating psychoanalysis into their philosophies abandoned certain of Freud's basic tenets, among them psychic determinism. Grünbaum (1984) has used the philosophy of science to repudiate the hermeneutic philosophizing of psychoanalysis and to attack psychoanalysis for its failure to measure up to the inductive standards of empirical science, while Mackay (1989) has used notions of explanation and empirical knowledge drawn from the philosophy of science to demonstrate the scientific nature of Freud's explanatory constructs and their epistemological and ontological basis.

Lazerowitz (1968) is outstanding among philosophers (although he is not unique) in his synthesis of psychoanalysis and Wittgenstein's (1918, 1953) philosophical linguistic analysis to construct a critique of philosophical theorizing and an implicit defense of empirical knowledge. By means of his Wittgensteinian analysis of many philosophical assertions, Lazerowitz seeks to show that they fail to make descriptive sense; by means of his Freudian analysis, he seeks to show that they have affective meanings that express unconscious fantasies about life and reality. Lazerowitz is somewhat unusual among philosophers in his preference, as he attempts to illuminate philosophic questions, for using psychoanalytic findings and theories as he finds them rather than reworking psychoanalysis to make it more congenial to certain idealistic philosophical assumptions.

PSYCHOANALYSIS, LITERATURE, AND THE ARTS

Freud's love of literature, sculpture, and painting yielded studies of literature (1907a, 1913a, 1916), biographical sketches of Leonardo da Vinci (1910b) and Dostoevsky (1928) and a study of aesthetics (1908). In general, the contributions of psychoanalysis to the study of literature fall into five main categories: content, form, creativity, the biography of the writer or artist, and the theory of criticism and aesthetics.

Psychoanalytic interpretations of the content of literature (symbolism, metaphor, simile, character, theme, plot, and so on) run the risk of the intentional fallacy: that is, of constructing the meaning of the work not from the work itself but from the presumed intention of the writer. Literary works may be treated as self-sufficient structures of meaning for the purposes of psychoanalytic interpretation, however; an excellent example of such a procedure is Freud's *Gradiva* piece (1907a); another is Jones's (1949) study of *Hamlet,* which, drawing upon Freud's comments (1900), relies for its interpretation upon the content of the play itself rather than upon a study of Shakespeare's life.

All the same, the intentional fallacy is not so fallacious as some scholars and literary critics would claim it to be. Once the importance of unconscious intentions (inspiration) in creativity is recognized, it is possible to understand how a writer may comprehend neither where his or her ideas come from nor the meaning of his or her work; the writer is conscious neither of some of his or her ideas (fantasies) nor of their influence upon the writing. However, when a psychoanalytic interpretation of a text is made in order to construct a psychoanalytic biographical sketch of its author, the likeness has no more reliability than the evidence in the text for the interpretation from which it was drawn. The further interpretive use of the sketch can be justified only by increasing its reliability. In turn, its reliability can be increased only by either the corroborating historical evidence of letters, diaries, autobiographies, contemporary reports, and so on or by textual evidence above and beyond that on which the biographical sketch was based originally.

There is a certain facile liberalism shared by some academics, intellectuals, and analysts which substitutes "tolerance for other points of view" for scientific and scholarly rigor and the search for truth. This attitude of "tolerance" allows for a psychoanalytic interpretation of art or a Marxist or an existentialist one, without taking any interpretation seriously. But every sound interpretation must have a solid basis in objective evidence: seeing something from a psychoanalytic point of view is not enough. The seeing must make sense of something in the object—the work of art, biography, social or cultural institution, or whatever. The evidence must be in the "text"—that is, in the object—and available for anyone to see.

It is precisely their attention to detail that justifies psychoanalytic interpretations such as the Freud–Jones interpretation of the repressed oedipal rivalry in *Hamlet,* which is supported by so many details in the play and is further corroborated, it seems to me, by Hamlet's finally killing Claudius not so much to revenge his father's murder as in revenge for his mother's death. Hamlet remains to the end in thrall to his ambivalence. Hamlet's unconscious ambivalence decides his fate, just as the gods decided the fate of Oedipus.

Psychoanalytic studies commit the intentional fallacy when they derive the meaning of a poem, novel, or play primarily or solely from hypotheses concerning the unconscious fantasies, memories, and thoughts that are assumed to have contributed to its creation. Freud, in his study of Leonardo da Vinci (1910b), comes close to committing this fallacy in his argument that the Mona Lisa is an embodiment of the childhood memories of the painter's mother, whereas the *Gradiva* (1907a) study is based entirely on textual evidence. Freud concedes that Leonardo was influenced by his model for the Mona Lisa but insists that the Gioconda evoked memories of his mother's loving smile. It is the reactivation of maternal memories that accounts for the ubiquitous presence of the same smile in the countenances of both female and male figures in his last great paintings. It is this ubiquity of a certain secretive form of womanly tenderness, seductiveness, and pleasure that provides evidence for the interpretation and also suggests Leonardo's sublimated homosexuality.

The psychoanalytic interpretation of a work, however much it may be assisted by knowledge of the psychology of the artist, must be substantiated by the work itself. Even the oedipal theme, which, in its variations, is at the core of many great works of literature, finds its way into them via plot, character, symbol, and so forth, without recourse to the consciousness of the artists who create the works. These "formal" and thematic elements of the play or novel evoke in the audience or reader an unconscious sense of the oedipal drama, giving rise in consciousness to powerful affective responses. Psychoanalytic interpretation, in applied as in clinical work, requires that what is unconscious be rendered conscious. Thus, in applied psychoanalysis one seeks to construct interpretations of meanings that ordinarily re-

main unconscious or preconscious but are substantiated by thematic and formal elements in the work itself that are conscious. In making such interpretations, however, one must be sensitive as well to the conscious elements of design and observation, which are also an integral part of the work of creation. Great literature is a synthesis of the known, the partly known, and the unknown in the artist and in the art through which he or she holds up to nature a mirror of reflections and disguises.

Applied psychoanalytic studies of artists, while they may facilitate the interpretation of various works, more frequently seek to shed light on developing motives, relationships, and life experiences that, in combination with innate talents, lead an individual into an adult life of artistic creativity of a particular form and with particular thematic interests. Bonaparte (1949), Eissler (1961, 1963), and many others have constructed this kind of biography, which, as Greenacre (1963) has shown, can be extended to the study of scientific creativity as well.

Freud (1908) believed the special gift of the artist or creative writer to be an unanalyzable ego endowment. He also suggested that our pleasure in "form" allows us to tolerate, vicariously, in either the real theater or the theater of the mind, the pleasure of instinctual gratifications otherwise forbidden. With further developments in the understanding of the organization of ego functions and the ego defenses and their modes of operation, it has become possible to comprehend something of the psychogenesis of artistic and literary form. This field of inquiry, however, remains relatively little explored. Read (1951), Waelder (1965), Kris (1952), and Devereux (1970), for example, have ventured into it. One aspect of the genius of creative writers and artists is the ability to substitute an aesthetic order (which permits the expression of the psychic unconscious, even if disguised) for a moral order that either prohibits such expression altogether or compromises it with anxiety. In this respect psychoanalysis has preserved and deepened with new insights a tradition in aesthetics originating in Aristotle's *Poetics* and continuing in Schiller (1795).

Psychoanalysis is also in a position to make useful contributions to the understanding of the relationships between content and form—a subject of central importance to art and literary criticism. Psychoanalysis offers the idea that successful integration of content and form in art is the outcome of the creative resolution of conflict between the instinctual unconscious and the defenses of the ego. For example, in Cézanne's painting one discovers in the geometric forms that emerge from his landscapes his efforts "to join the erring hands of nature." The danger of Mother Nature's provocatively errant hands is overcome by the "uncovering" in nature of geometric lawfulness. The result is an impression of vibrant, colorful serenity.

A novelist like Dostoevsky portrays characters who would be unbelievable and horrifying as real persons, but who are not only believable but interesting and even sympathetic within the aesthetically ordered world of the novel. Within the aesthetic order provided by form, the imagination of the writer can create characters who acquire psychic reality for us even though they do what most real people would only dream of doing. It is probably to the taming of narcissism historically (through the transformation of magical rites into religious pageantry and ritual and finally into theater, literature, and the arts) that we can attribute the capacity of civilized people to enjoy aesthetic experience. From the ancient Greeks (Aristotle) to the present, individuals have been able to find catharsis, psychic enrichment, and harmony in the controlled narcissistic regression that enables them to enter into the worlds of literature, theater, and the arts. These curious links between dream, psychosis, daydream, artistic creativity, and aesthetic experience, the investigation of which Freud began, have opened a large field for applied psychoanalysis (see especially Kris, 1952).

Having thus pointed to the importance of ego psychology for applied psychoanalysis. it is also worth reminding ourselves of the unique creative power of primary-process thought activity. Although it is the ego that acquires and develops linguistic and other expressive skills, and although it is the ego that works an integration of content and form that allows art to hold a mirror up to nature, the primary-process thought activities have a synthetic, creative power of their own; the ego processes by themselves cannot achieve this synthesis. Any dreamer is able to invent an imaginary world populated by persons performing actions in places unknown to, and unrecognized by, the dreamer him- or herself. Great art acquires an essential part of its verisimilitude as well as its mysteriousness, its intriguing ambiguity, its symbolic depth, and parts of its formal structure (metaphor, simile, symbol, allegory) not only from the ego and the unconscious within the ego but from the instinctual unconscious as well. Applied psychoanalysis need not abandon old insights in its pursuit of new ones. Some representative studies which interpret literature and art from the vantage point of the creativity of primary-process thought activity are

Calef, 1969; Lesser, 1956; Schier, 1950; Schneider, 1954; Wangh, 1950; and Weiss, 1953.

PSYCHOANALYSIS AND THE SOCIAL SCIENCES

Freud contributed seminal works to the application of psychoanalysis to the social sciences: to anthropology (1913b), to sociology and politics (1921), to history (1930), and to the study of culture (1930).

The problem of values and ideology cannot be disregarded in this field. Marcuse (1955) has attempted an integration of psychoanalysis and Marxism by relating repression in the individual to surplus repression and alienation in the society. Freud (1930) was interested in the Soviet social experiment and sympathized with the communist objective of a more equitable distribution of economic and social goods; but he rejected Marxist utopianism on the grounds that social conflict would not be eradicated even if an adequate supply of goods and services could be equitably distributed to all. Psychoanalysis has no alternative but to safeguard its own discoveries of the contributions made to social conflict by the psychosexual development of individuals; it is thus obliged, on scientific grounds, to question utopianism of the right, left, and center, and to insist upon a realistic understanding of social problems and potential solutions insofar as they have significant psychological factors.

Studies in this area fall into two broad categories: those that elaborate the interconnections between the social sciences and psychoanalysis and those that limit themselves to specific problems. The same division occurs with respect to literature, in the distinction between psychoanalytic studies of literary theory (for example, Trilling, 1945; Kris, 1952, 1953) and psychoanalytic studies of individual works (for example, Beres, 1951; Leites, 1947). Among those that elaborate interrelations between psychoanalysis and another discipline there are the following: in political theory, Lasswell, 1930; in sociology, Parsons, 1950, and Hartmann, 1950; in anthropology, Roheim, 1947, 1950b, and Devereux, 1972; and in history, Langer, 1958, and Gay, 1985. These studies tend to be methodological, focusing on epistemological issues in structural and causal interrelationships between processes studied by psychoanalysis and processes studied by the related discipline.

Everywhere in applied psychoanalysis is the problem of combining expertise in two different, technically demanding fields. One obvious solution is for the researcher to be trained in both fields: Roheim and Devereux, for example, are each expert in both psychoanalysis and anthropology. But dual training is not necessarily the solution, as the example of Kardiner (1939) demonstrates (see Fenichel, 1944). Although trained in psychoanalysis, Kardiner waters it down in applying it to anthropology; by contrast, Lasswell (1930) without any analytic training, applies psychoanalysis to politics with rigor and real understanding. By its very nature, applied psychoanalysis is interdisciplinary, and the most knowledgeable and gifted analysts may make errors because of insufficient familiarity with the field of application. Some of the least satisfactory writings of some of the best psychoanalysts (for example, Abraham) have been their papers in applied psychoanalysis. To solve the problem, either psychoanalysts should become scholars in an applied field, or scholars should become psychoanalysts, or scholars and analysts should work collaboratively. Each of these solutions has its difficulties, but they represent the best charts available for steering a course, as recommended by Freud, between the Scylla of attributing too much to the unconscious and the Charybdis of attributing too little to it.

Fine studies of the second type—that is, studies that limit themselves to specific problems—are greater in number, in part, not doubt, because smaller-scale interpretive studies do not require a command of the entire field of application. In the field of politics one may cite as examples Adorno, 1950; Feuer, 1969; Leites, 1953; and Rangell, 1980; in history, Arlow, 1951; Eissler, 1965; Erikson, 1958; Flugel, 1920; Fornari, 1966; George & George, 1956; and Sachs, 1933; in anthropology, Roheim, 1950b, and Devereux, 1969; in sociology, Calef, 1950; Fenichel, 1946; and Roheim, 1950a).

The social sciences present at least one special problem and challenge for applied psychoanalysis. The empirical social sciences depend upon data collected in the field, and the integrity of fieldwork is threatened by four kinds of methodological and epistemic disturbances: (1) in the observer, of his or her own observing capacity; (2) in the observer's observing capacity, caused by the subject studied; (3) in the subjects, caused by the observer; and (4) intrinsic to the communicative capacities of the respondents.

These are problems of objectivity with which clinical psychoanalysis constantly struggles. The study of transference and countertransference can form the basis of a contribution by psychoanalysis to the methodology of the social sciences, as Devereux (1967) has demonstrated. Substantively, the psychoanalytically trained observer should be able to detect in behavior, customs, and social and institutional arrangements the signs that reveal the influence of unconscious motives, whether of the ego or the id. The classical controversy in cultural anthropology concerning the universality of the oedipus complex is a test case for a broad range of methodological and substantive issues in this field of applied psychoanalysis.

PSYCHOANALYSIS AND LANGUAGE

Freud (1910a) drew our attention to a correspondence between the replacement of an image by its opposite in the dream work and the use in language (particularly in ancient Egyptian) of a single word to designate contrary states of things, objects, or relations. He speculated that this phenomenon, as well as others, such as phonetic reversal to form new words, derived from the earliest efforts of children and of our ancient ancestors to make sense of their worlds and to communicate it to others. He saw these rudimentary forms of prelinguistic thought involved in the transition to language as remaining active in primary-process thought activity. He also thought that the removal of repressions depends on being able to give verbal expression to unconscious memories and fantasies. Language, in the topographical model, is both a function of secondary process and the therapeutic instrument for the work of resolving psychic conflict.

Such sparse, yet suggestive statements about language in Freud's writings have been joined with linguistics, semiotics, and the philosophies of Hegel and Heidegger in the work of Lacan (1956, 1966), who reflected on the way languages work and examined symptom formation as language, on the assumption that the unconscious is structured like a language. He explored the role of language in psychological development and in the analytic process and attempted to lay foundations for the psychoanalysis of language. Derrida (1967, 1980) pursued a similar integration of psychoanalysis and language, taking texts of Freud and Lacan as his point of departure. The study of Freud's texts as literature —for example, Freud's use of rhetorical devices— can also be combined with close textual exegesis, without the special assumptions adopted by Lacan and Derrida (see Mahony, 1982, 1987; Marcus, 1984).

The philosophy of language can be applied to the language and concepts of psychoanalytic theory as well. Drawing on the British school of ordinary language philosophy (Ryle, 1949), itself inspired by Wittgenstein (1918, 1953), Schafer (1976, 1978) has sought to replace the metapsychological language of psychoanalytic theory with an "action language" that he finds to be closer to people, patients, and the analytic process. He approaches psychoanalytic theory and the basic concepts of analytic understanding through the philosophy of language. This direction is the reciprocal of Lacan's project of a psychoanalysis of language. Schafer's work, however, retains intact all Freud's basic psychological discoveries, whereas Lacan has altered them, despite his declared commitment to a return to the Freud texts.

THE FUNDAMENTAL PROBLEM OF APPLIED PSYCHOANALYSIS

The fundamental problem of applied psychoanalysis is that there is no analysand to respond with free associations to the analyst's interpretations and reconstructions. One of Freud's most boldly controversial studies of religion (1939) illustrates the problem. The logical structure of Freud's argument can be broken down into the following series of hypotheses: (1) the laws of mental functioning are essentially invariant, historically and culturally; (2) the laws of dream formation are also the laws of myth formation; (3) when a woman takes an infant out of water in a dream, the woman is the mother of the child; (4) when in the legend of Moses an Egyptian princess takes the infant from the river, she is to be identified as the mother of the baby, who must therefore be an Egyptian; (5) the ancient Hebrews who created the legend had a motive for repressing their knowledge of Moses' identity as an Egyptian, and hence this truth could find expression only in symbolic form.

The problem with Freud's argument is that the mental processes of the ancient Hebrews who created the legend are available to us only through the legend itself and through other similar historical evidence. The interpretation must be derived deductively—which is to say, indirectly. It cannot be confirmed empirically except insofar as the first three steps can be corroborated by contemporary clinical investigations.

Although applied psychoanalysis is limited to speculations and, at best, probable knowledge, there is a procedure by which the probability of applied interpretations may be increased, its success depending upon the richness of the material available. This procedure consists of deriving from a construction a description of some other aspect of the subject that would exist if the construction were true. Freud's (1910b) study of Leonardo is a good illustration.

Freud, on the basis of biographical evidence and Leonardo's screen memory from childhood (the so-called vulture fantasy), put forward the hypothesis of a childhood that caused Leonardo to become a sublimated homosexual. Given this hypothesis, evidence of ambiguity of sexual identity should exist in Leonardo's paintings. We can all see (as many art historians have) that the intriguing, sexually evocative smile of the Mona Lisa is also found on the soft and youthful John the Baptist. This dramatic bisexuality in Leonardo's great late paintings supports Freud's interpretation. The ability to develop such tests in applied psychoanalysis depends of course upon the richness and the reliability of the extant evidence, because this must substitute, so far as substitution is possible, for the free associations of an analysand.

THE CONTRIBUTION OF APPLIED PSYCHOANALYSIS TO THE DEVELOPMENT OF PSYCHOANALYSIS

Applied psychoanalysis, in addition to its contribution to scholarship and theorizing in the fields of application, also contributes to the development of core psychoanalytic knowledge in at least two ways. It contributes to the development of psychoanalysis as a general psychology. Freud (1901, 1905) initiated such researches, and they have been much developed since. Applied psychoanalysis constitutes an important aspect of the bridge that links the psychology of the neurosis to a general psychology of human nature. It is by means of applied psychoanalytic studies that we are able to reveal the universality of psychic conflict and its derivatives in all aspects of human existence.

Applied psychoanalysis has also made important contributions to clinical psychoanalysis. Freud's (1911) study of Schreber is essentially an applied psychoanalytic work. Freud's discovery of the oedipus complex no doubt owed something to his reading of Oedipus Rex and Hamlet. Calef and Weinshel (1981) have usefully exploited the concept of "gaslighting," drawn from a classic film, to clarify certain aspects of introjection and its influence on transference and countertransference. Proust's literary genius enabled him to use his personal experience of homosexuality (Painter, 1989) to brilliantly evoke a sadomasochistic homosexual encounter. Shengold (1988) has used applied psychoanalytic interpretations of Proust's descriptions to explore aspects of the psychology of anality. Despite its methodological limitations, applied psychoanalysis can repay in these ways its debt to clinical psychoanalysis.

REFERENCES

Adorno, T. W. (1950). *The Authoritarian Personality*. New York: Harper.

Aquinas, T. (1266–72). *Introduction to St. Thomas Aquinas,* ed. A. C. Pegis. New York: Random House, 1948.

Arlow, J. A. (1951). The consecration of the prophet. *Psychoanal. Q.,* 20:374–397.

Beres, D. (1951). A dream, a vision and a poem. *Int. J. Psychoanal.,* 32:97–116.

———. (1959). The contribution of psychoanalysis to the biography of the artist. *Int. J. Psychoanal.,* 40:26–37.

Bergson, H. (1911). *Creative Evolution*. London: Macmillan.

Bonaparte, M. (1949). *The Life and Works of Edgar Allen Poe*. Rpt. New York: Humanities Press, 1971.

Calef, V. (1950). Justice and the arbitrator. *Amer. Imago,* 7:259–277.

———. (1969). Lady Macbeth and infanticide. *J. Amer. Psychoanal. Assn.,* 17:528–48.

Calef, V., & Weinshel, E. (1981). Some clinical considerations of introjection. *Psychoanal. Q.,* 50:44–66.

Campbell, C. A. (1951). Is "free will" a pseudo-problem? *Mind,* 50:446–465.

Derrida, J. (1967). Freud and the scene of writing. In *Writing and Difference,* pp. 196–231. Chicago: Univ. Chicago Press, 1985.

———. (1980). *The Post Card*. Chicago: Univ. Chicago Press, 1987.

Descartes, R. (1641). Meditations on first philosophy. In *The Philosophical Works of Descartes*. New York: Omer Publications, 1955.

Devereux, G. (1967). *From Anxiety to Method in the Behavioral Sciences*. Paris: Mouton.

———. (1969). *Reality and Dream*. New York: New York Univ. Press.

———. (1970). The structure of tragedy and the structure of psyche in Aristotle's *Poetics*. In *Psychoanalysis and Philosophy,* ed. C. Hanly & M. Lazerowitz, pp. 46–75. New York: Int. Univ. Press.

———. (1972). *Ethnopsychanalyse complementariste*. Paris: Flammarion.

Eissler, K. R. (1961). *Leonardo da Vinci*. New York: Int. Univ. Press.

———. (1963). *Goethe*. 2 vols. Detroit: Wayne State Univ. Press.

———. (1965). *Medical Orthodoxy and the Future of Psychoanalysis*. New York: Int. Univ. Press.

Erikson, E. H. (1958). *Young Man Luther*. New York: Norton.

Fenichel, O. (1944). Remarks on Fromm's *Escape from Freedom*. In *The Collected Papers of Otto Fenichel,* ed. H. Fenichel & D. Rapaport, vol. 2, pp. 260–277. New York: Norton, 1954.

———. (1946). Elements of a psychoanalytic theory of anti-Semitism. In *The Collected Papers of Otto Fenichel,* ed. H. Fenichel & D. Rapaport, vol. 2, pp. 335–348. New York: Norton, 1954.

Feuer, L. (1955). *Psychoanalysis and Ethics*. Springfield, Ill.: Thomas.

———. (1959). The bearing of psychoanalysis upon philosophy. *Philos. & Phenomenol. Research,* 19:323–340.

———. (1963). Anxiety and philosophy. *Amer. Imago,* 20:411–449.

———. (1969). *The Conflict of Generations*. London: Heinemann.

———. (1970). Unconscious sources of Kant's philosophy. In *Psychoanalysis and Philosophy,* ed. C. Hanly & M. Lazerowitz, pp. 76–125. New York: Int. Univ. Press.

Flugel, J. C. (1920). On the character and married life of Henry VIII. *Int. J. Psychoanal.,* 1:24–55.

Fornari, F. (1966). *The Psychoanalysis of War*. New York: Anchor Books, 1974.

Freud, S. (1900). *The Interpretation of Dreams. SE,* 4 & 5.

———. (1901). *The Psychopathology of Everyday Life. SE,* 6:1–279.

———. (1905). *Jokes and Their Relation to the Unconscious. SE,* 8:9–236.

———. (1907a). Delusions and dreams in Jensen's *Gradiva. SE,* 9:7–95.

———. (1907b). Obsessive actions and religious practices. *SE,* 9:117–127.

———. (1908). Creative writers and day-dreaming. *SE,* 9:143–153.

———. (1910a). The antithetical meaning of primal words. *SE.* 11:155–161.

———. (1910b). *Leonardo Da Vinci and a Memory of His Childhood. SE,* 11:59–137.

———. (1911). Psycho-analytic notes on an autobiographical account of a case of paranoia (dementia paranoides). *SE,* 12:12–82.

———. (1912). Recommendations to physicians practising psycho-analysis. *SE,* 12:111–120.

———. (1913a). The theme of the three caskets. *SE,* 12:291–301.

———. (1913b). *Totem and Taboo. SE,* 13:1–162.

———. (1916). Some character-types met with in psycho-analytic work. *SE,* 14:311–333.

———. (1921). *Group Psychology and the Analysis of the Ego. SE*, 18:67–143.

———. (1927). *The Future of an Illusion. SE*, 21:3–56.

———. (1928). Dostoevsky and parricide. *SE*, 21:175–196.

———. (1930). *Civilization and Its Discontents, SE*, 21:64–145.

———. (1939). *Moses and Monotheism. SE*, 23:7–137.

Gay, P. (1985). *Freud for Historians*. Oxford: Oxford Univ. Press.

George, A. L., & George, J. R. (1956). *Woodrow Wilson and Colonel House*. New York: John Day.

Greenacre, P. (1963). *The Quest for the Father*. New York: Int. Univ. Press.

Grünbaum, A. (1984). *The Foundations of Psychoanalysis*. Berkeley: Univ. Calif. Press.

Habermas, J. (1971). *Knowledge and Human Interests*. Boston: Beacon Press.

Hanly, C. (1970). On being and dreaming. In *Psychoanalysis and Philosophy*, ed. C. Hanly & M. Lazerowitz, pp. 155–187. New York: Int. Univ. Press.

———. (1977). An unconscious irony in Plato's *Republic. Psychoanal. Q.*, 46:116–147.

———. (1979). *Existentialism and Psychoanalysis*. New York: Int. Univ. Press.

———. (1991). *The Problem of Truth in Applied Psychoanalysis*. New York: Guilford Press.

Hartmann, H. (1950). The application of psychoanalytic concepts to social science. *Psychoanal. Q.*, 19:385–392.

Hegel, G. W. F. (1807). *The Phenomenology of Mind*. London: S. Sonnenschien, 1910.

Heidegger, M. (1927). *Being and Time*. London: SCM Press, 1962.

Hospers, J. (1952). Free will and psychoanalysis. In *Readings in Ethical Theory*, ed. W. Sellars & J. Hospers, pp. 560–575. New York: Appleton-Century-Crofts.

Jaspers, K. (1949). *The Perennial Scope of Philosophy*. New York: Philosophical Library.

Jones, E. (1949). *Hamlet and Oedipus*. New York: Norton, 1976.

Kant, I. (1781). *Critique of Pure Reason*. London: Macmillan, 1950.

———. (1785). *Groundwork of the Metaphysic of Morals*. London: Hutchinson, 1947.

Kardiner, A. (1939). *The Individual and His Society*. New York: Columbia Univ. Press.

Kligerman, C. (1957). A psychoanalytic study of the confessions of St. Augustine. *J. Amer. Psychoanal. Assn.*, 5:469–484.

Kris, E. (1952). *Psychoanalytic Explorations in Art*. New York: Int. Univ. Press.

———. (1953). Psychoanalysis and the study of creative imagination. In *The Selected Papers of Ernst Kris*, pp. 473–493. New Haven: Yale Univ. Press, 1975.

Lacan, J. (1956). *Speech and Language in Psychoanalysis*. Baltimore: Johns Hopkins Univ. Press, 1981.

———. (1966). *Ecrits*. London: Tavistock, 1977.

Langer, W. L. (1958). The next assignment. *Amer. Hist. Rev.*, 63:283–304.

Lasswell, H. (1930). *Psychopathology and Politics*. Chicago: Univ. Chicago Press.

Lazerowitz, M. (1955). *The Structure of Metaphysics*. London: Routledge & Kegan Paul.

———. (1964). *Studies in Metaphilosophy*. London: Routledge & Kegan Paul.

———. (1968). *Philosophy and Illusion*. London: George Allen & Unwin.

Leavy, S. A. (1988). *In the Image of God: A Psychoanalyst's View*. New Haven: Yale Univ. Press.

Leites, N. (1947). Trends in affectlessness. *Amer. Imago*, 4:89–112.

———. (1953). *A Study of Bolshevism*. Glencoe, Ill.: Free Press.

Lesser, S. (1956). *Fiction and the Unconscious*. Boston: Beacon Press.

Locke, J. (1690). *An Essay Concerning Human Understanding*. In *Locke's Philosophical Works*, vol. 1. London: George Bell, 1898.

Lowenberg, R. D. (1953). From Immanuel Kant's self-analysis. *Amer. Imago*, 10:307–321.

Mackay, N. (1989). *Motivation and Explanation*. Madison, Conn.: Int. Univ. Press.

Mahony, P. (1982). *Freud as Writer*. New York: Int. Univ. Press.

———. (1987). *Psychoanalysis and Discourse*. London: Tavistock.

Marcus, S. (1984). *Freud and the Culture of Psychoanalysis*. Boston: George Allen & Unwin.

Marcuse, H. (1955). *Eros and Civilization*. Boston: Beacon Press, 1966.

Meissner, W. W. (1986). *Psychoanalysis and Religious Experience*. New Haven: Yale Univ. Press.

Merleau-Ponty, M. (1945). *Phenomenology of Perception*. London: Routledge & Kegan Paul, 1962.

Painter, G. D. (1989). *Marcel Proust*. Harmondsworth: Penguin, 1990.

Parsons, T. (1950). Psychoanalysis and the social structure. *Psychoanal. Q.*, 19:371–384.

Plato. *Republic*. New York: Liberal Arts Press, 1948.

Rangell, L. (1980). *The Mind of Watergate*. New York: Norton.

Read, N. (1951). Psychoanalysis and the problem of aesthetic value. *Int. J. Psychoanal.*, 32:73–82.

Ricoeur, P. (1970). *Freud and Philosophy*. New Haven: Yale Univ. Press.

Rizzuto, A.-M. (1979). *The Birth of the Living God: A Psychoanalytic Study*. Chicago: Univ. Chicago Press.

Roheim, G., ed. (1947). *Psychoanalysis and the Social Sciences*. New York: Int. Univ. Press.

———. (1950a). The oedipus complex, magic and culture. *Psychoanal. & Soc. Sci.*, 2:173–228.

———. (1950b). *Psychoanalysis and Anthropology*. New York: Int. Univ. Press.

Ryle, G. (1949). *The Concept of Mind*. London: Hutchinson's Univ. Library.

Sachs, H. (1933). The delay of the machine age. *Psychoanal. Q.*, 2:404–424.

Sartre, J.-P. (1943). *Being and Nothingness*. New York: Philosophical Library, 1956.

Schafer, R. (1976). *A New Language for Psychoanalysis*. New Haven: Yale Univ. Press.

———. (1978). *Language and Insight*. New Haven: Yale Univ. Press.

Scharfstein, B.-A. (1970). The need to philosophize. In *Psychoanalysis and Philosophy*, ed. C. Hanly & M. Lazerowitz, pp. 258–279. New York: Int. Univ. Press.

Scharfstein, B.-A., & Ostow, M. (1952). The unconscious sources of Spinoza's philosophy. *Amer. Imago*, 9:221–237.

Schier, J. (1950). The blazing sun. *Amer. Imago*, 7:143–162.

Schiller, J. C. F. von (1795). *On the Aesthetic Education of Man in a Series of Letters*. New Haven: Yale Univ. Press, 1954.

Schneider, D. E. (1954). *The Psychoanalyst and the Artist*. New York: Int. Univ. Press.

Shengold, L. (1988). *Halo in the Sky*. New York: Guilford Press.

Teilhard de Chardin, P. (1971). *Christianity and Evolution*. London: Collins.

Trilling, L. (1945). *The Liberal Imagination*. New York: Viking Press, 1947.

Waelder, R. (1965). *Psychoanalytic Avenues to Art*. New York: Int. Univ. Press.

Wangh, M. (1950). The tragedy of Iago. *Psychoanal. Q.*, 19:202–212.

Weiss, J. (1953). Cézanne's technique and scopophilia. *Psychoanal. Q.*, 22:413–418.

Wisdom, J. O. (1945). The unconscious origins of Schopenhauer's philosophy. *Int. J. Psychoanal.*, 26:44–52.

———. (1953). *The Unconscious Origins of Berkeley's Philosophy*. London: Hogarth Press.

Wittgenstein, L. (1918). *Tractatus Logico-Philosophicus*. London: Routledge & Kegan Paul.

———. (1953). *Philosophical Investigations*. Oxford: Blackwell.

INDEX

Ablon, S. L., 174

Abreaction, 49, 89

Abstinence, 14, 15–16, 99, 105, 107, 111, 115, 121. *See also* Neutrality

Abuse. *See* Trauma

Acquired characteristics, heritability of, 272, 275–76

Acting out: acting in, 135; analyst's role, 138–39; analyzability and, 139–40; as communication, 131, 135, 137, 138, 140, 142; contributing factors, 139–40; defensive, 138, 139; definition of, 130, 131, 134–39, 141, 187; management, 140; as pathology, 136–38, 139–40, 141, 313; positive or useful, 138, 140, 141; as repetition, 135–38, 139, 140, 142, 313; as resistance, 130–31, 135, 137, 140; transference and, 112, 112n, 135–38, 139, 140, 141, 142

Action: absence from psychoanalysis, 130; adaptive, 133, 142; aggression and, 372; by analyst, 138–39; definition, 131, 131n, 132, 133, 141; in development, 132–33, 313; and the ego, 132, 413; enactment, 87, 91–92, 121, 126, 127, 138–39, 142; neurotic, 187; nonverbal communication, 135, 160; normal behavior, 131–33, 141–42; pathological, 133–34, 136–37, 139–40, 141, 142; symptomatic, 133–34, 138, 142, 187; theories of, 131–33; thought and, 131–32, 211, 330. *See also* Acting out

Actual neurosis, 221, 222, 384, 500

Adaptation: action, 133, 142; aggression, 370, 376; alloplastic and autoplastic, 318, 319–20, 518; to average expectable environment, 213, 398, 405, 519; to character, 201, 203, 204–05, 314, 319–20; compromise formations, 199; conflict, 483; constitutional or innate factors, 272, 285, 321, 519; defenses, 193, 321–22, 407; definitions of, 317–18, 319, 415; development and, 318–19,

320, 396, 396n, 415; drives and, 318–19, 327; by the ego, 213, 319–20, 327; fantasies, 156; identification, 156, 205, 468; individual variability in, 519; language as, 318; mastery, 370; metapsychology, 518–19; narcissism, 198, 232, 241; and the pleasure principle, 320; primary-process, 319–20; in psychoanalytic theory, 317–22, 518–19; to reality, 296, 298, 300, 319–20, 322; reality testing and, 298, 320, 396; secondary-process, 213, 319–20; social, 213, 518–19; somatization, 223; symbolism as, 153; to trauma, 320–21, 519

Adolescence: action in, 133, 313; affects, 33, 413; character formation, 202, 414; defenses, 413–14; identity and self, 413–14, 471, 472; object relations, 412, 413, 440, 458; psychic structures, 412, 413–14; sexuality, 33–34, 35, 256, 340, 412–13; trauma in, 313

Adolescent psychoanalysis: difficulties, 33–35, 38, 41; techniques, 26, 34–35; transference in, 34. *See also* Child psychoanalysis

Affective disorders, 458

Affects: in adolescence, 33, 413; character and, 202, 203; conflict, 477, 478; defense and, 386, 486, 487, 490; definition and classification of, 381–82, 385–86, 387–88, 407, 451, 500; denial of, 487; development of, 382, 385, 396, 407, 411, 413, 443, 458, 460; drives and, 385, 451, 460; and the ego, 382, 384, 385, 398, 496; as energy, 381–82, 383, 385; and the id, 385; in infancy, 37; as instincts, 374, 375, 382, 385, 386, 387; interpretation, 20; memory and, 374; moods, 386 (*see also* Character); neurophysiology, 190, 225–26, 387–88, 542, 543; in object relations, 385, 443, 451, 452, 458, 460; and the pleasure principle, 383, 385; repression of, 386–87; signal, 384–85; somatization and, 221, 222, 225–26, 387; strangulated, 381; and symptom formation, 188,

John Dewey Library
Johnson State College
Johnson, Vermont 05656